Get Ahead of the Curve

For Parkin, Powell and Matthews, Sixth Edition

Great news!
MyEconLab can help you improve your marks!

With your purchase of a copy of this textbook, you received a Student Access Kit for **MyEconLab** for Parkin, Powell and Matthews, Sixth Edition. Your Student Access Kit looks like this:

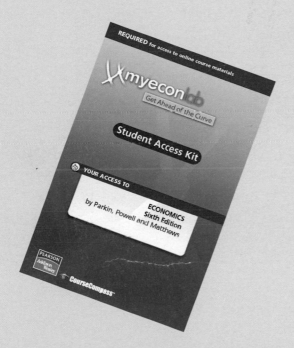

DON'T THROW IT AWAY!

What is **MyEconLab** and how will it help you? **MyEconLab** is an online learning environment for Economics. *Online Practice Tests* measure your progress and generate a personalized *Study Plan* to show you where to focus your study. *Exercises*

and *tutorials* give you ample opportunity to practice and improve. An advanced *graphing tool* helps you understand how the concepts, numbers and graphs are connected. Each exercise links to the appropriate page in your e-text, which includes animated graphs with audio and an interactive glossary.

In addition **MyEconLab** includes valuable features that further your understanding of how economics impacts on your life. **MyEconLab** also provides resources for extra help when you need it.

◆ *Economics in the News* – news links updated weekly during the academic year
◆ *Online Office Hours* – extra help from the authors via email
◆ *Research Navigator* – a one-stop resource for college research assignments

To activate your prepaid subscription:

1. Locate the **MyEconLab** Student Access Kit that came bundled with your textbook.
2. Ask your lecturer for your **MyEconLab** course ID.*
3. Go to www.myeconlab.com/europarkin. Follow the instructions on the screen and use the access code in your **MyEconLab** Student Access Kit to register as a new user.

* If your lecturer does not provide you with a course ID, you can still access some of the online resources list above. Go to www.myeconlab.com/europarkin to register.

To change the way students see the world – that has been our aim throughout the six editions of this book.

The cover depicts a landscape viewed through a geometric icon.

The landscape is the economic world. And the icon represents the clarity that economic science brings to our view and understanding of the economic world.

When we view the landscape without the economic lens, we see questions but not answers. The lens provides answers by enabling us to focus on the unseen structures that shape our world. It is a tool that enables us to see the invisible.

This book equips students with the economic lens, shows them how to use it, and enables them to gain their own informed and structured view of the economic world.

SIXTH EDITION

ECONOMICS

PARKIN POWELL MATTHEWS

PEARSON

Addison
Wesley

Harlow, England • London • New York • Boston • San Francisco • Toronto
Sydney • Tokyo • Singapore • Hong Kong • Seoul • Taipei • New Delhi
Cape Town • Madrid • Mexico City • Amsterdam • Munich • Paris • Milan

Pearson Education Limited
Edinburgh Gate
Harlow
Essex CM20 2JE
England

and Associated Companies throughout the world

Visit us on the World Wide Web at:
www.pearsoned.co.uk

Original edition entitled *Economics* published by Addison-Wesley Publishing
Company, Inc.
A Pearson Education company

This edition published by Pearson Education Limited 2005
© Pearson Education Limited 2000, 2003, 2005
Authorised for sale only in Europe, the Middle East and Africa

ISBN 10: 0-321-31264-3
ISBN 13: 978-0-321-31264-8

British Library Cataloguing-in-Publication Data
A catalogue record for this book is available from the British Library

Library of Congress Cataloging-in-Publication Data
Parkin, Michael, 1939-
    Economics / Michael Parkin, Melanie Powell, and Kent Matthews.— 6th ed.
        p. cm.
    Includes index.
    ISBN 0-321-31264-3 (pbk.)
        1. Economics. I. Powell, Melanie. II. Matthews, Kent. III. Title.

    HB171.5.P313 2005b
    330—dc22

                                                                2004062675

10 9 8 7 6 5 4 3
10 09 08 07 06 05

Typeset in 9/12.5pt Stone Serif by 35
Printed and bound by Mateu-Cromo Artes Graficas, Madrid, Spain

The publisher's policy is to use paper manufactured from sustainable forests.

About the Authors

Michael Parkin received his training as an economist at the Universities of Leicester and Essex in England. Currently in the Department of Economics at the University of Western Ontario, Canada, Professor Parkin has held faculty appointments at the University of Manchester, the University of Essex, Brown University and Bond University. He is a past president of the Canadian Economics Association and has served on the editorial boards of the *American Economic Review* and the *Journal of Monetary Economics* and as managing editor of the *Canadian Journal of Economics*. Professor Parkin's research on macroeconomics, monetary economics and international economics has resulted in over 160 publications in journals and edited volumes, including the *American Economic Review*, the *Journal of Political Economy*, the *Review of Economic Studies*, the *Journal of Monetary Economics* and the *Journal of Money, Credit and Banking*. He became most visible to the public with his work on inflation that discredited the use of wage and price controls. Michael Parkin also spearheaded the movement towards European monetary union. Professor Parkin is an experienced and dedicated teacher of introductory economics.

Melanie Powell took her first degree at Kingston University and her MSc in economics at Birkbeck College, London University. She has been a research fellow in health economics at York University, a principal lecturer in economics at Leeds Metropolitan University, and the director of economic studies and part-time MBAs at the Leeds University Business School. She is now a Reader at Derby University Business School. Her main interests as a microeconomist are in applied welfare economics, and she has many publications in the area of health economics and decision making. Her current research uses the experimental techniques of psychology applied to economic decision making.

Kent Matthews received his training as an economist at the London School of Economics, Birkbeck College University of London and the University of Liverpool. He is currently the Sir Julian Hodge Professor of Banking and Finance and Head of Economics at the Cardiff Business School. He has held research appointments at the London School of Economics, the National Institute of Economic and Social Research, the Bank of England and Lombard Street Research Ltd and faculty positions at the Universities of Liverpool, Western Ontario, Leuven, Liverpool John Moores and Humbolt Berlin. He is the author (co-author) of 6 books and over 50 articles in scholarly journals and edited volumes.

To Our Students

Brief Contents

Guided Tour

Learning Objectives

Each chapter begins with a list of **learning objectives**, which enables students to see exactly where the chapter is going and to set their goals before they begin the chapter. We link these goals directly to the chapter's major headings.

Chapter Opener

Each chapter opens with a brief student-friendly **vignette**, accompanied by an attractive, attention-grabbing image. The vignette and image raise questions that both motivate the student and focus the chapter. We carry this story into the main body of the chapter, and relate it to the chapter-ending *Reading Between the Lines* or *Business Case Study* feature for a cohesive learning experience.

CDs to Burn!

Why do some prices like those of CDs and mobile phones slide, while others like the prices of houses rocket, and yet others like the price of bananas follow a roller-coaster ride? Find out in this chapter. And put what you learn to work explaining why the price of electricity rocketed in France and Germany in 2003 in *Reading Between the Lines* at the end of the chapter.

Review Quiz

A **review quiz** at the end of most major sections enables students to determine whether a topic needs further study before moving on. These quizzes tie directly to the chapter's learning objectives.

Review Quiz

1 What are the two key factors that generate economic growth?
2 How does economic growth influence the production possibilities frontier?
3 What is the opportunity cost of economic growth?
4 Why has Hong Kong experienced faster economic growth than the European Union has?

Key Terms

Highlighted **key terms** within the text simplify the student's task of learning the vocabulary of economics. Each highlighted term appears in an end-of-chapter list and in an end-of-book glossary, with page numbers, are emboldened in the index, and can also be found online in the Web glossary and Flash Card features.

We're now going to study the effects of a price ceiling in the housing market. A **price ceiling** is a regulation that makes it illegal to charge a price higher than a specified level. When a price ceiling i[...] rents in housing markets, it is called a [...] How does a rent ceiling affect the way [...] market works?

Price ceiling A regulation that makes it illegal to charge a price higher than a specified level. (p. 119)

Price discrimination The practice of selling different units of a good or service for different prices or of charging one customer different prices for different quantities bought. (p. 253)

Price effect The effect of a change in the price on the quantity of a good consumed, other things remaining the same. (p. 167)

Key Terms

Black market, 120
Minimum wage, 123
Price ceiling, 119
Price floor, 123
Price support, 132
Production quota, 132
Rent ceiling, 119
Search activity, 119
Subsidy, 131
Tax incidence, 125

Diagrams to Show Economic Action

The goal of the **diagrams** is to show 'where the economic action is'. Graphical analysis is the most powerful tool available for teaching and learning economics. We have developed the diagrams with the study and review needs of the student in mind, and feature:

◆ Original curves consistently shown in blue
◆ Shifted curves, equilibrium points and other important features highlighted in red
◆ Colour-blended arrows to suggest movement
◆ Graphs paired with data tables
◆ Diagrams labelled with boxed notes
◆ Extended captions that make each diagram and its caption a self-contained object for study and review.

Boxes

A new feature to this edition are **boxes**, which explore for the student the application of theory in the real world. Often accompanied by tables and figures comprising of real data, the boxes help contextualise the issue at hand for the student, whilst also encouraging them to apply their knowledge to the economic world around them.

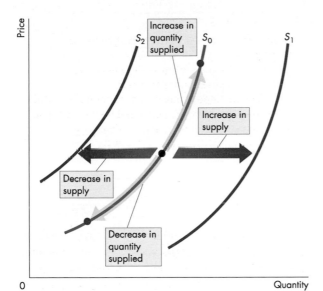

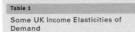

Box 4.3
Real-world Income Elasticities of Demand

Table 1 shows some estimates of the income elasticities of demand in the United Kingdom. Basic food items such as fresh meat are income inelastic, while luxury goods such as wines and spirits are income elastic. Some goods such as tobacco and bread have income elasticities that are negative, so they are defined as inferior goods. However, their elasticity values are very close to zero.

The demand for food is income inelastic – elasticity less than 1. But income elasticity varies with income. The figure shows the effect of the *level* of income on the income elasticity of demand for food in 10 countries. In a country with low incomes, such as Tanzania, the income inelasticity of demand for food is around 0.75, while in the high-income countries of Europe and North America, the income elasticity of demand for food is much lower. These numbers tell us that a 10 per cent increase in income leads to a 7.5 per cent increase in the demand for food of in India, a 3 per cent increase in France, and a less than 2 per cent increase in the United States.

Table 1
Some UK Income Elasticities of Demand

Good or service	Elasticity
Normal elastic demand	
Wine	2.6
Services	1.8
Spirits	1.7
Durable goods	1.5
Normal inelastic demand	
Fruit juice	0.9
Beer	0.6
Green vegetables	0.1
Fresh meat	0.0
Cereals	0.0
Inferior	
Tobacco	−0.1
Bread	−0.3

Sources: Ministry of Agriculture, Food and Fisheries, *Household Food Consumption and Expenditure*, 1992, London, HMSO. C. Godfrey, Modelling Demand. In *Preventing Alcohol and Tobacco Problems*, Vol. 1, (A. Maynard and P. Tether, eds), Avebury, 1990. J. Muellbauer 'Testing the Barten Model of Household Composition Effects and the Cost of Children', *Economic Journal*, (September 1977).

Figure 1
Income Elasticities in 10 Countries

As income increases, the income elasticity of demand for food decreases. Low-income consumers spend a larger percentage of any increase in income on food than do high-income consumers.

Source: Henri Theil, Ching-Fan Chung and James L. Seale Jr, *Advances in Econometrics*, Supplement 1, International Evidence on Consumption Patterns Greenwich, Connecticut, JAI Press Inc. 1989.

Reading Between the Lines and Business Case Studies

In *Reading Between the Lines* and *Business Case Studies*, which appear at the end of each chapter, we show the student how to apply the tools they have just learned by analyzing an article from a newspaper or news Web site. The Sixth Edition features 28 new items and 5 classics from the previous edition. Critical Thinking questions about the article appear with the end-of-chapter questions and problems.

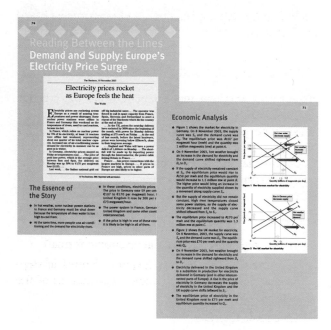

End-of-Chapter Study Material

Each chapter closes with a concise **summary** organized by major topics, lists of **key terms** (all with page references), **problems**, **critical thinking** questions, and **web exercises.**

The end-of-chapter problems are organized in pairs. The solution to the odd-numbered problem in each pair may be found at MyEconLab; the parallel even-numbered problem is left for students to solve on their own. This arrangement offers help to students and flexibility to lecturers who want to assign problems for credit.

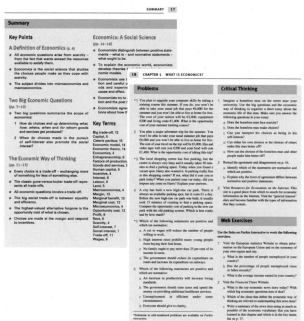

Study Guide

The Sixth Edition Study Guide by Melanie Powell and Derek Fry is carefully coordinated with the text, MyEconLab, and the Test Banks. Each chapter of the Study Guide contains:

◆ Key concepts
◆ Helpful hints
◆ True/false/uncertain questions that ask students to explain their answers
◆ Multiple-choice questions
◆ Short-answer questions
◆ Common questions or misconceptions that the student explains as if he or she were the lecturer

Each part allows students to test their cumulative understanding with sample midterm tests.

Guided Tour – MyEconLab

Packaged with every new book, MyEconLab puts students in control of their own learning through a suite of study and practice tools tied to the online, interactive version of the textbook and other media tools. At the core of MyEconLab are the following features:

◆ Practice tests
◆ Personalized study plan
◆ Additional practice exercises
◆ Tutorial instruction
◆ Powerful graphing tool

Practice Tests

Practice tests for each section of the textbook enable students to test their understanding and identify the areas in which they need to do further work. Lecturers can customize the practice tests or leave students to use the two pre-built tests.

Personalized Study Plan

Based on a student's performance on a practice test, a personal study plan is generated that shows where further study needs to focus. This study plan consists of a series of additional practice exercises.

Additional Practice Exercises

Generated by the student's own performance on a practice test, additional practice exercises are keyed to the textbook and provide extensive practice and link students to the e-text with animated graphs and to other tutorial instruction resources.

Tutorial Instruction

Launched from the additional practice exercises, tutorial instruction is provided in the form of solutions to problems, step-by-step explanations, and other media-based explanations.

Powerful Graphing Tool

A powerful graphing tool integrated into the practice tests and additional practice exercises lets students manipulate graphs so that they get a better feel for how the concepts, numbers and graphs are connected. Questions that use the graphing tool (like all the other questions) can be submitted and marked.

Additional MyEconLab Tools

1. E-text (the entire textbook in electronic format)
2. Animated figures (all the textbook figures in step-by-step animations with audio explanations of the action)
3. Electronic tutorials
4. Glossary – key terms from the textbook
5. Glossary Flashcards
6. Office Hours
7. Weekly *Economics in the News* updates and archives
8. Links to the most useful economic data and information sources on the Internet.

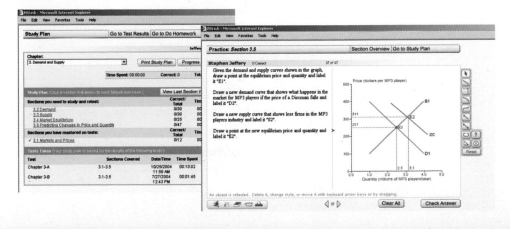

Preface

This book presents economics as a serious, lively, and evolving science. Its goal is to open students' eyes to the "economic way of thinking" and to help them gain insights into how the economy works and how it might be made to work better.

We provide a thorough and complete coverage of the subject, using a straightforward, precise, and clear writing style.

We are conscious that many students find economics hard, so we place the student at centre stage and write for the student. We use language that doesn't intimidate and that allows the student to concentrate on the substance.

We open each chapter with a clear statement of learning objectives, a brief student-friendly vignette and an illustration to grab attention. We illustrate principles with examples that are selected to hold the student's interest and to make the subject lively. And we put principles to work by using them to illuminate current real-world problems and issues.

We present some new ideas, such as dynamic comparative advantage, game theory, the modern theory of the firm, public choice theory, rational expectations, new growth theory, and real business cycle theory. But we explain these topics with familiar core ideas and tools.

Today's introductory economics course springs from today's issues – the information revolution and the new economy, the expansion of global trade and investment, the economic shockwaves after 9/11, global terrorism and corporate scandals. But the principles that we use to understand these issues remain the core principles of our science.

Governments and international agencies place continued emphasis on long-term fundamentals as they seek to promote economic growth. This book reflects this emphasis.

To help promote a rich, active learning experience, we have developed a comprehensive online learning environment featuring a dynamic e-book, interactive tutorials and quizzes, weekly news updates, and more.

The Sixth Edition Revision

ECONOMICS, Sixth Edition, retains all of the improvements achieved in its predecessor with its thorough and detailed presentation of modern economics, emphasis on real-world examples and critical thinking skills, diagrams renowned for pedagogy and precision and path-breaking technology.

New to this edition are:

◆ A thoroughly revised introductory chapter

◆ Revised and updated microeconomics content

◆ Revised and updated macroeconomics content

◆ MyEconLab

Revised Introductory Chapter

Chapter 1 has been thoroughly revised to place greater emphasis on the role of incentives in influencing people's choices and on the central question: Can choices made in the pursuit of self-interest also serve the social interest? This question is introduced through ten pressing issues in today's world that are explored further at various later points in the text. A description of the factors of production and their incomes has been moved from Chapter 2 into this chapter Also we have restored this chapter's appendix on graphs in economics.

Revised and Updated Microeconomics Content

In addition to thorough and extensive updating, the microeconomics chapters feature the following eight major revisions:

1. The Economic Problem (Chapter 2): An improved discussion of efficiency; a better paced explanation of comparative advantage and the gains from specialization and exchange.

2. Markets in Action (Chapter 6): An expanded section on taxes that consolidates material distributed across two chapters in the previous edition and that emphasizes the fact that elasticities of demand and supply, not governments, allocate the burden of a tax; an improved section on intervention in markets for farm products and the EU Common Agricultural Policy.

3. Organizing Production (Chapter 9): An expanded explanation of the consequences of asymmetric information for the principal–agent problem.

4. Output and Costs (Chapter 10): A new appendix on isoquants and isocost lines and the derivation of the least-cost factor inputs.

5. Monopolistic Competition and Oligopoly (Chapter 13): An amplified explanation of the effects of advertising on price and output in monopolistic competition and the roles of signalling and brand names; an expanded explanation of natural barriers that lead to oligopoly and an improved discussion of oligopoly games and how game theory illuminates the question of when and whether the pursuit of self-interest leads to outcomes that are in the social interest.

6. Government Regulation and Competition Policy (Chapter 14): Repositioned after the chapters on monopoly and oligopoly; a general introduction to the public choice approach; new material on price cap regulation.

7. Public Goods and Common Resources (Chapter 16): New section on the problem of the commons with special emphasis on overfishing and rainforest depletion.

8. Economic Inequality and Redistribution (Chapter 18): Improved description of inequality and explanation of the Gini coefficient; new material on the sources of inequality including a discussion of the sources of increased inequality in recent years.

Revised and Updated Macroeconomics Content

In addition to thorough and extensive updating, including the major revision of the UK National Accounts of 2004, the macroeconomics chapters feature the following nine major revisions:

1. A First Look at Macroeconomics (Chapter 19): This revised chapter overviews the macroeconomic landscape, previews the issues, and shows a productivity growth slowdown matters vastly more than a recession by contrasting the magnitudes of the Lucas wedge and the Okun gap in the United Kingdom.

2. Measuring GDP and Economic Growth (Chapter 20): Thoroughly revised chapter that provides a sharper focus on the definition and measurement of GDP along with a carefully paced explanation of the new chained-volume measure and its method of calculation.

3. Monitoring Cycles, Jobs and Inflation (Chapter 21): This chapter now includes two new sections: one on the identification of cycles (including growth cycles)

and another on the Retail Prices Index and the Consumer Prices Index.

4. Aggregate Supply and Aggregate Demand (Chapter 22): This chapter includes a new section that defines and explains the Keynesian, classical, and monetarist schools of macroeconomic thought.

5. At Full Employment: The Classical Model (Chapter 23) and Expenditure Multipliers: The Keynesian Model (Chapter 24). These two chapters now lay the foundation for going forward to study fluctuations and growth. Chapter 23 has a new introductory section on the classical model and a simplified explanation of the determinants of potential GDP. Dynamic aspects of the classical model are placed at the end of the chapter. (The chapter may be delayed to the position it occupied in the previous edition if preferred.)

6. Fiscal Policy (Chapter 25): This chapter includes an expanded coverage of supply-side effects of tax wedges on potential GDP.

7. Money (Chapters 26 and 27): These chapters have been reorganized and revised in several important ways. Chapter 26 now goes from defining money to explaining how banks create it, what determines the demand for it, and how money market equilibrium determines the interest rate. The quantity theory of money has been moved to the inflation chapter (Chapter 29). Chapter 27 explains how the Bank of England (and central banks in general) influence the monetary base and money supply and explains why central banks today target the interest rate rather than the quantity of money.

8. Economic Growth (Chapter 30): Revised explanation of classical, neoclassical, and new growth theory using the more standard productivity curve approach.

9. Macroeconomic Policy Challenges (Chapter 32): Another major reworking of the instruments, goals, and intermediate targets of monetary policy, and an in-depth exploration of alternative rules for avoiding inflation and achieving sustainable long-term growth including the Taylor rule and the conduct of monetary policy by the ECB as well as Bank of England.

MyEconLab

MyEconLab is a turnkey, online solution for your economics course. Featuring a new and powerful graphing engine and testing bank, students are able to self-test and generate a study plan, and lecturers are able to assign homework and capture their students' performance in a grade book. With a tight, everything-in-one-place organization around the new testing tool, questions include fill-in-the-blank, true/false, multiple-choice, numerical, and complete-the-graph. Because questions are generated algorithmically, there are up to 40,000 questions per chapter!

Previous users of *Economics In Action* and the Web site will find MyEconLab an exciting and powerful resource. Practice tests for each section of the textbook enable students to test their ability and identify the areas in which they need further work. Based on a student's performance on a practice test, a personalized study plan shows where further study needs to focus. Once students have received their study plan, additional practice exercises, keyed to the textbook, provide extensive practice and link directly to the e-text, with animated graphs and audio and other resources.

Users of MyEconLab will revel in the powerful graphing tool integrated into both the practice tests and practice exercises. This tool enables students to manipulate graphs and see how the concepts, numbers, and graphs are connected. A new, powerful feature is that questions using the graphing tool (like all other questions) can be submitted and marked.

For review and self-assessment, MyEconLab provides tutorials launched directly from the practice exercises. Using the tutorial instruction, students can see a demonstration of step-by-step solutions to practice problems, or they can participate in guided, step-by-step tutorials that promote self-discovery.

For the Lecturer

This book enables you to achieve three objectives in your principles course:

◆ Focus on the economic way of thinking.

◆ Explain the issues and problems of our time.

◆ Choose your own course structure.

Focus on the Economic Way of Thinking

You know how hard it is to encourage a student to think like an economist. But that is your goal. Consistent with this goal, the text focuses on and repeatedly uses the central ideas: choice; tradeoff; opportunity cost; the margin; incentives; the gains from voluntary exchange; the forces of demand, supply, and equilibrium; the pursuit of economic rent; the tension between self-interest and the social interest, and the scope and limitations of government actions.

Explain the Issues and Problems of Our Time

Students must *use* the central ideas and tools if they are to begin to *understand* them. There is no better way to motivate students than by using the tools of economics to explain the issues that confront today's world. Issues such as globalization and the emergence of China as a major economic force; the new economy with new near-monopolies such as eBay and the widening income gap between rich and poor; the post 9/11 economy and the reallocation of resources towards counter-terrorism and the defence that it entails; corporate scandals and the principal–agent problems and incentives faced by corporate managers; HIV/AIDS and the enormous cost of drugs for treating it; the disappearing tropical rain forests and the challenge that this problem of the commons creates; the challenge of managing the world's water resources; the persistent unemployment.

Choose Your Own Course Structure

You want to teach your own course. We have organized this book to enable you to do so. We demonstrate the book's flexibility in the flexibility chart and alternative sequences table that appear on pp. xviii–xxi. You can use this book to teach a traditional course that blends theory and policy or a current policy issues course. Your micro course can emphasize theory or policy. You can structure your macro course to emphasize long-term growth and supply-side fundamentals. Or you can follow a traditional macro sequence and emphasize short-term fluctuations. The choices are yours.

Lecturer's Manual

Melanie Powell, working with Derek Fry, has created a Lecturer's Manual. Each chapter contains an outline, what's new in the Sixth Edition, teaching suggestions, a look at where we have been and where we are going, the PowerPoint slides, a description of the electronic supplements, additional discussion questions, answers to the Review Quizzes, solutions to end-of-chapter problems, additional problems, and solutions to the additional problems. The chapter outline and teaching suggestions sections are keyed to the PowerPoint lecture notes.

Test Banks

Two Test Banks with 5,000 questions, provide multiple-choice, true-false, numerical, short-answer, problems and essay questions. Mark Rush of the University of Florida reviewed and edited all existing questions to ensure their clarity and consistency with the Sixth Edition. These Test Banks are available electronically on a Lecturer's CD-ROM and in the lecturers' resources section of MyEconLab.

PowerPoint Resources

Robin Bade and Michael Parkin have developed a Microsoft PowerPoint lecture presentation for each chapter that includes all the figures from the text, animated graphs, and brief speaking notes. The slide outlines are based on the chapter outlines in the Lecturer's Manual, and the speaking notes are based on the Lecturer's Manual teaching suggestions. The presentations can be used electronically in the classroom or can be printed to create hard-copy transparency masters.

Lecturer's CD-ROM with Computerized Test Banks

This CD-ROM contains Computerized Test Bank files, Test Bank and Lecturer's Manual files in Microsoft Word, and PowerPoint files. Both test banks are available in Test Generator Software (TestGen with QuizMaster). Fully networkable, it is available for

Windows and Macintosh. TestGen's graphical interface enables lecturers to view, edit, and add questions; transfer questions to tests; and print different forms of tests. Tests can be formatted with varying fonts and styles, margins, and headers and footers, as in any word-processing document. Search and sort features let the lecturer quickly locate questions and arrange them in a preferred order. QuizMaster, working with your university's computer network, automatically marks the exams, stores the results on disk, and allows the lecturer to view or print a variety of reports.

MyEconLab

The Web site that accompanies *Economics*, Sixth Edition breaks new ground by providing a structured environment in which students can practice what they learn and test their understanding and then pursue a study plan that is generated from their performance on practice tests. MyEconLab provides rich content resources keyed to the electronic textbook as well as flexible tools that enable lecturers to easily and effectively customize online course materials to suit their needs.

Lecturers can create and assign tests, quizzes, or homework assignments that incorporate graphing questions. MyEconLab saves lecturers time by automatically marking all questions and tracking results in an online marks book. The complete Test Bank is also preloaded into MyEconLab, giving lecturers ample material from which they can create assignments.

Once registered for MyEconLab, lecturers have access to downloadable supplements such as the Lecturer's Manual, PowerPoint lecture notes, and Test Banks. Lecturers also have access to a "Consult the Author" feature that allows them to ask questions of and make suggestions to authors via e-mail and receive a response within 24 hours.

For more information about MyEconLab, or to request an Instructor Access Code, visit http://www.myeconlab.com/europarkin.

Acknowledgements

We extend our gratitude and thanks to the many people who have contributed to this new edition of our text and to all those who made such important contributions to the previous editions on which this one is based. So many people have provided help and encouragement either directly or indirectly that it is impossible to name them all.

We particularly thank our colleagues, present and past, who have helped to shape our understanding of economics and who have provided help in the creation of this new edition. We thank our reviewers who have read and commented on our work and provided countless good ideas that we have eagerly accepted. We also thank our families for their input and patience.

We particularly acknowledge and express our deep gratitude to Robin Bade whose innovative work on the most recent Canadian edition has been invaluable to us. We also thank Robin for her meticulous reading of this edition and for the uncountable, some detailed and some major, improvements she has brought to it.

We thank Richard Parkin for his work of the graphics, both in the text and on our Web site.

We thank Derek Fry for his work (with Melanie) on the Study Guide and Lecturer's Manual.

We could not have produced this book without the help the people for whom it is written, our students. We thank the several thousand students we have been privileged to teach over many years. Their comments on previous editions (and on our teaching) whether in complaint or praise have been invaluable.

Last, we thank the many outstanding editors, media specialists, and others at Pearson Education who contributed to the concerted publishing effort that brought this edition to completion. They are Editorial Director, Sadie McClelland; Senior Acquisitions Editor, Paula Harris; Development Editor, David Cox; Pre-Press Manager, Bridget Allen; Senior Editor, Karen Mclaren; Senior Project Controller, Angela Hawksbee; Design Manager, Kevin Ancient; Electronic Projects Editor, Melanie Beard; Content Systems Manager, Stephen Jeffery; Head of Marketing, Clare Sismey, and Marketing Manager, Jo Barber. Michelle Neil, Executive Media Producer, managed the development of MyEconLab.

As always, the proof of the pudding is in the eating! The value of this book will be decided by its users and whether you are a student or a teacher, we encourage you to send us your comments and suggestions.

Michael Parkin,
University of Western Ontario,
michael.parkin@uwo.ca

Melanie Powell
University of Derby,
m.j.powell@derby.ac.uk

Kent Matthews,
Cardiff University,
MatthewsK@Cardiff.ac.uk

Flexibility Chart

Core

1 What is Economics?

2 The Economic Problem

3 Demand and Supply

4 Elasticity

5 Efficiency and Equity

A chapter that provides a non-technical explanation of efficiency and equity that unifies the micro material and permits early coverage of policy issues in Chapters 14–16.

10 Output and Costs

11 Perfect Competition

12 Monopoly

13 Monopolistic Competition and Oligopoly

17 Demand and Supply in Factor Markets

Policy

6 Markets in Action

A chapter that gives extensive applications of demand and supply

14 Government Regulation and Competition Policy

Introduces the public choice theory of government and sets the scene for the following policy chapters. The first part of this chapter along with Chapters 15 and 16 can be covered any time after Chapter 5.

Optional

1 Appendix: Graphs in Economics

Useful for students with a fear of graphs.

1 Mathematical Note: Equations to Straight Lines

3 Mathematical Note: Demand, Supply and Equilibrium

7 Utility and Demand

This chapter may be covered before demand in Chapter 3.

8 Possibilities, Preferences and Choices

An unusual full chapter on indifference curves ensures that if you want to cover this material, you can do so with confidence. (Other texts condense this topic to render it indigestable.)

9 Organizing Production

This chapter may be skipped or assigned as reading.

10 Appendix: Producing at Least Cost

17 Appendix: Market Power in the Labour Market

Three Alternative Sequences for Microeconomics

Traditional Theory and Policy

1 What is Economics?

2 The Economic Problem

3 Demand and Supply

4 Elasticity

5 Efficiency and Equity

6 Markets in Action

7 Utility and Demand

8 Possibilities, Preferences and Choices

9 Organizing Production

10 Output and Costs

11 Perfect Competition

12 Monopoly

13 Monopolistic Competition and Oligopoly

14 Government Regulation and Competition Policy

15 Externalities

16 Public Goods and Common Resources

17 Demand and Supply in Factor Markets

18 Economic Inequality and Redistribution

Microeconomics with a Business Emphasis

1 What is Economics?

2 The Economic Problem

3 Demand and Supply

4 Elasticity

5 Efficiency and Equity

6 Markets in Action

9 Organizing Production

10 Output and Costs

11 Perfect Competition

12 Monopoly

13 Monopolistic Competition and Oligopoly

14 Government Regulation and Competition Policy

15 Externalities

17 Demand and Supply in Factor Markets

Microeconomics with a Policy Emphasis

1 What is Economics?

2 The Economic Problem

3 Demand and Supply

4 Elasticity

5 Efficiency and Equity

6 Markets in Action

7 Utility and Demand

9 Organizing Production

10 Output and Costs

11 Perfect Competition

12 Monopoly

14 Government Regulation and Competition Policy

15 Externalities

16 Public Goods and Common Resources

17 Demand and Supply in Factor Markets

18 Economic Inequality and Redistribution

Four Alternative Sequences for Macroeconomics

Contents

Credits

Chapter 1: Carphone Warehouse (p. 3); cartoon (p. 4), © 1985 The New Yorker Collection from cartoonbank.com. All Rights Reserved; weather map (p. 14), PA WeatherCentre Ltd.

Chapter 2: Eurotunnel (p. 31).

Part 2: produce in Paris (p. 51), © Paul Almasy/Corbis.

Chapter 3: CD manufacture (p. 53), © The Steve Bicknell Style Library/Alamy.

Chapter 4: counter bar with different juices (p. 77), © Imagebroker/Alamy.

Chapter 5: friendly produce man (p. 97), © Jules Perrier/Corbis; cartoon (p. 105), © 1985 The New Yorker Collection from cartoonbank.com. All Rights Reserved.

Chapter 6: London Belsize Park estate agents boards (p. 117), © Jeremy Hoare/Alamy.

Chapter 7: water running from faucet (p. 141), © Royalty-Free/Corbis; diamonds on black velvet (p. 141), © Rick Gayle/Corbis.

Chapter 8: young woman in supermarket reading food labels (p. 159), © David Stewart/Getty Images; cartoon (p. 166), © 1998 The New Yorker Collection from cartoonbank.com. All Rights Reserved.

Part 3: workers assemble engines at General Motors plant in Baltimore, Maryland (p. 177), © Jim Pickerell/Alamy.

Chapter 9: SAP AG (p. 179); cartoon (p. 186), © David Austin, *Financial Times*; Box 9.1 table and figure from *Observatory of European SMEs 2002/No 2: SMEs in Europe*, http://europa.eu.int/comm/enterprise/enterprise_policy/analysis/doc/smes_observatory_2002_report2_en.pdf, reprinted with permission from the European Communities.

Chapter 10: sea of cars (p. 201), © Terry W. Eggers/Corbis.

Chapter 11: woman looking at a shop window full of electrical consumer goods on sale (p. 227), © Leslie Garland Picture Library/Alamy.

Chapter 12: Google (p. 251); cartoon (p. 264) from *Voodoo Economics*, © Chronicle Books, San Francisco (Hamilton, W., 1992).

Chapter 13: London Tesco Extra supermarket entrance (p. 273), © Justin Kase/Alamy.

Part 4: Prime Minister Tony Blair during Prime Minister's Questions at the House of Commons, London (p. 305), © PA Photos.

Chapter 14: train and railway tracks Madrid, Spain (p. 307), © Jon Arnold Images/Alamy; Box 14.1 table from 'Privatization and business restructuring: change and continuity in the privatized industries', *The Review of Policy Issues*, 1(2), reprinted with permission of the author (Parker, D., 1994); Box 14.4 table from *Global Competitiveness Report*, reprinted with permission from the World Economic Forum; Business Case Study figure from 'Hain plays national champion', *The Guardian*, 11th May (Gow, D. & Milner, M., 2001), © The Guardian.

Chapter 15: air pollution (p. 329), © Gary Parker/Science Photo Library.

Chapter 16: the European Parliament in Strasbourg (p. 347), © Durand Patrick/Corbis Sygma.

Chapter 17: David Beckham of Real Madrid (p. 365), © Popperfoto/Alamy; Business Case Study table reprinted with permission from Towers Perrin.

Chapter 18: J.K. Rowling (p. 395), © Rune Hellestad/Corbis; Box 18.2 figure from *Key facts and figures about the European Union*, http://www.europa.eu.int/comm/publications/booklets/eu_glance/44/en-1.pdf, reprinted with permission from the European Communities; Policy Case Study figure from 'Expenditure on healthcare in the UK: a review of the issues', *Fiscal Studies*, 22(2), p. 15, reprinted with permission from the Institute of Fiscal Studies (Propper, C., 2001).

Chapter 19: the family barbecue (p. 417), © Lambert/Getty Images; family with piano and sheet music (p. 417), © Hulton-Deutsch Collection/Corbis.

Chapter 20: businessman looking at computer monitors (p. 437), © Kelvin Murray/Getty Images.

Chapter 21: an unemployed ex-coal miner in the job centre (p. 457), © Philip Wolmuth/Panos Pictures; Table 21.1 reprinted with permission from the Economic Cycle Research Institute (ECRI), New York, www.businesscycle.com.

Chapter 22: surfer on a wave (p. 479), © Royalty-Free/Corbis; cartoon (p. 495), © 1991 The New Yorker Collection from cartoonbank.com. All Rights Reserved.

Chapter 23: rolling ship in rough seas (p. 503), © Robert Harding Picture Library Ltd/Alamy.

Chapter 24: Luciano Pavarotti in concert (p. 525), © European Press Agency/PA Photos.

Part 6: the Bank of England (p. 553), © Angelo Hornak/Corbis.

Chapter 25: Britain's Chancellor of the Exchequer, Gordon Brown (p. 555), © Kirsty Wigglesworth/PA Photos.

Chapter 26: Euro notes and coins (p. 581), © Image Source/Alamy.

Chapter 27: a huge Euro sign beside the headquarters of the European Central Bank in Frankfurt (p. 603), © Kai Pfaffenbach/Reuters/Corbis.

Chapter 28: The Beatles (p. 625), © Norman Parkinson Limited/Fiona Cowan/Corbis.

Chapter 29: banknotes of Europe on fire (p. 653), © pintailpictures/Alamy.

Chapter 30: Oriental Pearl Tower (p. 679), © Wolfgang Kaehler/Corbis.

Chapter 31: David Hutton with line of hungry men (p. 701), © Bettmann/Corbis.

Part 7: container ship moored in harbour (p. 747), © Henry Beeker/Alamy.

Chapter 33: passenger jet in flight over clouds (p. 749), © Lester Lefkowitz/Getty Images; Figure 33.5 from *Agricultural Policies in OECD Countries: At a Glance*, 2004, reprinted with permission from OECD.

Chapter 34: multi currency die (p. 771), © Matthias Kulka/Corbis; Box 34.1 figure from 'An estimate of the effect of common currencies on trade and income', *The Quarterly Journal of Economics*, 117(2), May, pp. 437–466 (Frankel, J. & Rose, A., 2002) © 2002 by the President and Fellows of Harvard College and the Massachusetts Institute of Technology.

We are grateful to the following for permission to reproduce copyright material:

Office for National Statistics for Box 6.1 table, Box 9.2 figure, Box 14.3 table, Box 17.1 figure, Figure 18.1, Figure 18.2, Figure 18.3, Figure 18.4, Figure 18.5, Figure 18.6, Box 18.1 figure, Box 18.3 figure, Figure 19.8, Figure 19.10, Table 20.1, Table 20.2, Figure 21.2, Figure 21.3, Figure 21.4, Figure 21.8, Figure 21.9, Figure 21.10, Figure 21.12, Figure 21.13, Figure 22.14, Box 24.1 figure, Table 25.1, Figure 25.1, Figure 25.2, Figure 25.3, Figure 25.4, Figure 25.7, Box 29.1 figure, Table 34.1, Figure 34.1, Table 34.2 and Figure 34.2, Crown copyright material is reproduced with the permission of the Controller of Her Majesty's Stationery Office and the Queen's Printer for Scotland.

The Business Publishing Ltd for extracts from the articles 'Le sandwich is upper crust as French say adieu to long lunch' by Pierre Tran published in *The Business* 2 November 2003, 'Ireland plans to stick a tax on chewing gum' by Neil Thapar published in *The Business* 3 November 2003, and 'Electricity prices rocket as Europe feels the heat' by Tim Webb published in *The Business* 10 November 2003; Guardian Newspapers Limited for an extract from the article 'EC launches airline ticket price enquiry' by Andrew Osborn published in *The Guardian* 20 December 2003 © The Guardian 2003; Times Newspapers Limited for extracts from the articles 'Coffee bean and gone' by George Pendle published in *The Times* 2 March 2001 © Times Newspapers Limited 2001, 'EU sugar subsidies reward rich, says Oxfam' by Carl Mortishead published in *The Times* 14 April 2004 and 'Economy gives signs of robust condition' by Gary Duncan published in *The Times* 1 July 2004 © Times Newspapers Limited 2004; The Eco-nomist Newspaper Limited for extracts from the articles 'How good is Google?' published in *The Economist* 30 October 2002 © The Economist Newspaper Limited, London 2002, and 'Boom, bust and hubris' published in *The Economist* 29 July 2004 © The Economist Newspaper Limited, London 2004; The Telegraph Group Limited for an extract from the article 'Dramatic rise of the 'flexible friend'' by Richard Alleyne published on www.telegraph.co.uk 30 July 2004 © The Telegraph Group Ltd (2004); and Financial Gazette for an extract from the article 'Zimbabwe's inflation slows down' by Charles Rukuni published in *Financial Gazette* 22 July 2004.

We are grateful to the Financial Times Limited for permission to reprint the following material:

French health move: tobacconists fuming after new rise in cigarette tax, © *Financial Times*, 6 January 2004; High oil prices hitting world recovery, © *Financial Times*, 4 May 2004; VAT scam leaves £23 bn hole in UK's import figures, © *Financial Times*, 10 July 2003; Buoyant jobs market boosts case for rate rise, © *Financial Times*, 17 June 2004; Workers from New EU states sets to ease staff shortages, © *Financial Times*, 30 July 2004; Heavy household debt 'a threat to growth', © *Financial Times*, 2 July 2004; Austrian tax cuts worry the Germans as jobs disappear, © *Financial Times*, 24 June 2004; Easy does it on rate rises, says ECB, © *Financial Times*, 27 July 2004; ECB urges eurozone structural overhaul, © *Financial Times*, 9 July 2004; South Korean consumer confidence plummets, © *Financial Times*, 6 August 2004; Hot money swells China's currency reserves, © *Financial Times*, 15 April 2004.

In some instances we have been unable to trace the owners of copyright material and we would appreciate any information that would enable us to do so.

Part 1
The Scope of Economics

Talking with Bengt Holmstrom

Bengt Holmstrom is Paul A. Samuelson Professor of Economics in the department of economics and the Sloan School of Management at MIT. Born in 1949 in Helsinki, Finland, he studied mathematics and operations research at the University of Helsinki as an undergraduate and then worked as an operations researcher before going to Stanford University as an economics graduate student. Professor Holmstrom's research on the way firms use contracts and incentives has provided a major advance in our understanding of the mechanisms that operate inside firms. Beyond his academic research, Professor Holmstrom is a consultant to a number of major corporations including Nokia, the leading supplier of mobile phones, of which he is also a director.

Michael Parkin talked with Bengt Holmstrom about his work and the progress that economists have made in understanding firms and the way they operate.

How did you get interested in the economics of the firm?

I was interested in the firm as an undergraduate and I went from my undergraduate degree to work as an operations research analyst at a large firm in Finland. I worked with a group who were building and trying to implement a very large corporate planning model.

I didn't build the model but I was the person that was supposed to make it work. As I was trying to do that, it didn't take me long to realize the need to get back to the data and to avoid people playing games with the data. My interest in incentives was entirely driven by this experience.

You changed the way economists think about the firm by describing it as an incentive system. What do you mean?

When people talk about incentives, they tend to think about some explicit rewards system like a salesperson's commission or a stock option for an executive or something like that.

The key insight has been to understand that incentives are influenced in an enormous number of ways, indirectly and implicitly. Constraints are one of the very important pieces of the incentives system. For instance, such things as bureaucratic rules are an important piece of the overall picture. There are many different ways of getting people to do what you think they should be doing.

It might be that the best incentive is to pay no incentive! Incentives can be terribly damaging if they are poorly designed.

The firm is an incentive system is an expression of the fact that you need to think about *all* the possible ways in which you can influence people's actions and then how you orchestrate the instruments that are available. These instruments include promotion incentives, rewards, or just praise. The narrow view that it's just a matter of paying a bonus or something like that is very misguided.

Can you give an example?

I think there are lots. There's a big debate right now about airport security that's a wonderful illustration of the insight that the firm is an incentive system and an illustration of the possibility of having incentives that are too strong in the wrong place. One view is that profit-making companies that run the airport security checking are too oriented towards profit and too little oriented towards quality, because the quality checks come so infrequently. The standard argument is that if they make a mistake they must pay for it, so they have a strong incentive to deliver high quality work. But if accidents happen extremely frequently, that sort of feedback mechanism is just too weak. I'm not saying that it is the right step, but it is a logical reason for moving in the direction of taking away profit-making incentives from airport security checking.

The very existence of the firm comes from the fact that it is there to remove and restructure incorrect incentives – excessively high-powered incentives that come from the market – and to get people to cooperate. In the market, it is hard to cooperate because everyone is working for his or her own benefit, which works very well if there are a lot of alternatives. But when there are a small number of traders, or where quality is hard to assess, bringing the activity inside the firm is very natural.

One firm, Enron, was big news during 2002. What does economics tell us about what went wrong at Enron?

I think Enron, like most of these disaster cases, teaches that misplaced incentives lead to potentially big mistakes. It's almost tautological to say that if wrong-doing was done, it was done because the incentives weren't aligned right. Now, how much of it was a design flaw and how much was just a flaw of the overall system is harder to judge. There were certainly regulatory problems – energy production regulations had changed, the energy market had been opened up and arbitrage opportunities created. Some of the activities of

Enron that sought to profit from this new regulatory environment were entirely legal.

Then there was financial innovation. It's an old, old idea that it would be nice to remove debts from the balance sheet of a firm to make it look better to investors. And apparently new financial instruments had been created to make off-balance sheet operations possible. Some of them were clearly questionable and perhaps some of them illegal.

But the other problem – and this is a system problem, not just an Enron problem – is that when things are going well and everybody believes that the world is moving forward, it's very hard to question something. You go further and further out on a limb, and then the limb breaks and you learn that that was too much.

Is it important for an academic economist to have professional interests in the "real world"?

I think everybody's different. For me it has been important because I got interested in incentives through non-academic work. That's where I started and I was just lucky that incentives happened to be a very topical issue when I entered the field.

I don't think one could, in any sense, say that everybody must have real-world experience. You have to find your own sources of stimulation and what makes you curious and what makes you interested. For some people that's just being exceedingly theoretical and not thinking about much else. Some are very talented that way; other people desperately need some connection with the real world. For me that has been very valuable.

Do you think that economics is good subject in which to specialize?

There are many reasons to like economics. It goes well beyond the sort of boring notion of economics being about numbers. It is about social systems and deals with incredibly important questions for society at large. It is about poverty and wealth, about the success in the West and economic disasters in Africa and other places. As an economist, you can have a really big impact if you understand these systems. It's a great social subject in general. It connects to history and other fascinating topics. For me it has been incredibly inspiring.

◆ ◆ ◆ ◆ ◆ ◆ ◆ ◆ ◆

Chapter 1

What is Economics?

After studying this chapter you will be able to:

◆ Define economics and distinguish between microeconomics and macroeconomics

◆ Explain the big questions of economics

◆ Explain the key ideas that define the economic way of thinking

◆ Describe how economists go about their work as social scientists

Choice, Change, Opportunity and Challenge

You are studying economics, the science of choice, at a time of enormous change, opportunity and challenge. Mobile phones, iTunes and other new technologies are making our lives easier and more fun. Global terrorism and other new challenges are making our lives more difficult. How will the choices we make respond to the changing opportunities and challenges we face? What are the principles that guide our choices? Find out in this chapter.

A Definition of Economics

All economic questions arise because we want more than we can get. We want a peaceful and secure world. We want clean air and rivers. We want long and healthy lives. We want good schools and universities. We want space and comfort in our homes. We want a huge range of sports and recreational gear from running shoes to motor bikes. We want the time to enjoy sports and games, reading books and magazines, seeing films, listening to music, travelling and so on.

What each one of us can get is limited by time, by the income we earn and by the prices we must pay. Everyone ends up with some unsatisfied wants. As a society, what we can get is limited by our productive resources. These resources include the gifts of nature, human labour and ingenuity, and tools and equipment that we have produced.

Our inability to satisfy all our wants is called **scarcity**. The poor and the rich alike face scarcity. A child in Tanzania is hungry and thirsty because her parents can't afford food and the well in her village is dirty and almost empty. The scarcity that she faces is clear and disturbing. But even David Beckham, a millionaire, faces scarcity. He wants to spend the weekend playing football *and* filming an advert, but he can't do both. We face scarcity as a society. We want to provide better health care *and* better education *and* a cleaner environment and so on. Scarcity is everywhere. Even parrots face scarcity!

Faced with scarcity, we must *choose* among the available alternatives. The child in Tanzania must *choose* between dirty water and scraps of bread. David Beckham must *choose* the football *or* the filming. As a society, we must *choose* among healthcare, education and the environment.

The choices that we make depend on the incentives that we face. An **incentive** is a reward that encourages or a penalty that discourages an action. If heavy rain fills the well, the child in Tanzania has an *incentive* to choose more water. If the fee for filming is £1 million, David Beckham has an incentive to skip the football and make the advert. If computer prices tumble, we have an *incentive* as a society to connect more schools to the Internet.

Economics is the social science that studies the *choices* that individuals, businesses, governments and entire societies make as they cope with *scarcity* and the *incentives* that influence and reconcile those choices. The subject divides into two main parts

◆ Microeconomics

◆ Macroeconomics

Microeconomics

Microeconomics is the study of the choices that individuals and businesses make, the way these choices interact in markets and the influence of governments. Some examples of microeconomic questions are: Why are people buying more mobile phones? How would a tax on downloading music affect the sales of CDs?

Macroeconomics

Macroeconomics is the study of the performance of the national economy and the global economy. Some examples of macroeconomic questions are: Why did production and jobs shrink in 2001? Why has Japan's economy stagnated? Can the Bank of England bring prosperity by keeping interest rates low?

Not only do I want a cracker—we all want a cracker!

Review Quiz

1   Find stories in today's newspaper to illustrate the definition of economics with examples of scarcity, incentives and choices in the United Kingdom and around the world.
2   Find stories in today's newspaper that illustrate the distinction between microeconomics and macroeconomics.

Two Big Economic Questions

Two big questions summarize the scope of economics:

◆ How do the choices that people make end up determining what, how, when, where and for whom goods and services get produced?

◆ When do choices made in the pursuit of self-interest also promote the social interest?

What, How, When, Where and For Whom?

Goods and services are the objects that people value and produce to satisfy wants. Goods are physical objects such as golf balls. Services are actions performed such as cutting hair and filling teeth.

What?

We produce a dazzling array of goods that range from food and houses to sports clothing and equipment. And we produce a wide variety of services that range from dental care to cosmetic surgery.

What we produce changes over time. Every year, changes in technology allow us to build better equipped homes, more interesting and useful sporting equipment and deliver a more pleasant experience in the dentist's chair. And technological advance makes us incredibly more productive at producing food and manufactures.

By far the largest part of what people in the rich industrial countries produce today are services such as retail and wholesale services, health services and education. Goods are a small and decreasing part of what we produce.

What determines whether we build better homes or develop better sporting facilities; produce more food or more retail services? How do these choices change over time? And how are they affected by the ongoing changes in technology that make an ever-wider array of goods and services available to us?

Economics helps us to answer questions like these about *what* we produce.

How?

Think about how furniture is made. You can go to IKEA and buy a factory-made kitchen that you assemble yourself, or you can go to a local carpenter who will design and make solid wood kitchen units to your personal specification. Look around you and you will see many examples of the same job being done in different ways. In some shops checkout staff key in prices, in others they use a laser scanner. One farmer might keep track of livestock feeding schedules using paper and pencil records, while another uses a personal computer.

Goods and services are produced by using productive resources that economists call **factors of production**. Factors of production are grouped into four categories:

◆ Land

◆ Labour

◆ Capital

◆ Entrepreneurship

Land

The "gifts of nature" that we use to produce goods and services are called **land**. In economics, land is what in everyday language we call *natural resources*. It includes land in the everyday sense together with metal ores, oil, gas and coal, water and air. Our land surface and water resources are renewable and some of our mineral resources can be recycled. But the resources that we use to create energy are non-renewable – they can be used only once.

Labour

The work time and work effort that people devote to producing goods and services is called **labour**. Labour includes the physical and the mental efforts of all the people who work on farms and construction sites and in factories, shops and offices. The *quality* of labour depends on **human capital**, which is the knowledge and skill that people obtain from education, on-the-job training and work experience. You are building your own human capital today as you work on your economics course, and your human capital will continue to grow as you become better at your job.

Capital

The tools, instruments, machines, buildings and other constructions that businesses now use to produce goods and services are called **capital**. In everyday language, we talk about money, shares and bonds as being capital. These items are financial capital. They play an important role in enabling people to lend to businesses and provide businesses with financial resources, but they are not used to produce goods and services. Because they are not productive resources, they are not capital.

Entrepreneurship

The human resource that organizes labour, land and capital is called **entrepreneurship**. Entrepreneurs come up with new ideas about what and how to produce, make business decisions and bear the risks that arise from these decisions.

How do the quantities of factors of production that get used to produce the many different goods and services get determined? Why do we use machines in some cases and people in others? Does mechanization and technological change destroy more jobs than it creates? Does introducing new technology make us better or worse off?

Economics helps us to answer questions like these about *how* things are made.

When?

Sometimes, production slackens off and even shrinks in what is called a *recession*. At other times, production expands rapidly. We call these ebbs and flows of production the *business cycle*. When production falls, jobs are lost and unemployment climbs; when production rises, jobs are created and unemployment falls.

During the 1990s, production decreased in Central and Eastern Europe as these countries changed the way they organized their economies.

What makes production rise and fall? Can government action prevent production from falling?

Economics helps us to answer questions like these about *when* goods and services are produced.

Where?

The Kellogg Company, of Battle Creek, Michigan, makes breakfast cereals in 20 countries and sells them in 160. In today's global economy, people who are separated by thousands of miles, cooperate to produce many goods and services.

Why is there a strong concentration of telecommunications industries in Finland? Why are financial services concentrated in Frankfurt and London?

Economics helps us to answer questions like these about *where* goods and services are produced.

For Whom?

Who gets the goods and services that are produced depends on the incomes that people earn. A large income enables a person to buy large quantities of goods and services. A small income leaves a person with few options and small quantities of goods and services. People earn their incomes by selling the services of the factors of production they own:

1 Land earns **rent**.

2 Labour earns **wages**.

3 Capital earns **interest**.

4 Entrepreneurship earns **profit**.

Labour earns about 70 per cent of total income and this percentage has been remarkably constant. But income is shared very unequally among individuals. J.K. Rowling earns more than £20 million a year from her Harry Potter series and its spin-offs, while a petrol station attendant earns only about £5 an hour.

Some differences in income are persistent. On average, men earn more than women and whites earn more than ethnic minorities. Europeans earn more on average than Asians who in turn earn more than Africans. A typical annual income in the poorest counties of the world is just a few hundred pounds, less than the equivalent of a typical weekly wage in the richest countries of the world.

Education has a big impact on income. In Table 1.1 you can see how gaining a UK university degree and school-level qualifications add to income. Each level of qualification raises average income.

Why is the distribution of income so unequal? Why do women and minorities earn less than white males? Why do Europeans earn more than Africans? Why do university graduates earn more than people with only a few O Levels?

Economics helps us to answer questions like these about *for whom* goods and services are produced.

Let's now examine the second big question. It is a harder question both to appreciate and answer.

Table 1.1

Rate of Return from Education

	Degree	A Level	5+ O Levels
	(per cent per year)		
Men	17.5	13.0	21.0
Women	35.0	11.0	26.0

The rate of return from education measures the average increase in earnings that results from education.

Source: Blundell, R. *et al.* (1999) "Human Capital Investment: the returns from education and training to the individual, the firm and the economy", *Fiscal Studies*, 20.

When is the Pursuit of Self-interest in the Social Interest?

Every day, you and 300 million other Europeans, along with 6.1 billion people in the rest of the world, make economic choices that result in "What", "How", "Where", "When" and "For Whom" goods and services get produced.

Are the goods and services produced, and the quantities in which they are produced, the right ones? Do the factors of production employed get used in the best possible way? Do the goods and services that we produce go to the people who benefit most from them?

Self-interest

You know that your own choices are the best ones for you – or at least you think they're the best at the time that you make them. You use your time and other resources in the way that makes most sense to you. But you don't think much about how your choices affect other people. You order a home delivery pizza because you're hungry. You don't order it thinking that the delivery person or the cook needs an income. You make choices that are in your **self-interest** – choices that you think are best for you.

When you act on your choices, you come into contact with thousands of others who produce and deliver the things that you decide to buy or who buy the things that you sell. These people have made their own choices – what to produce and how to produce it, who to hire or who to work for and so on. Like you, everyone else makes choices that they think are best for them. When the pizza delivery person shows up at your home, he's not doing you a favour.

Social Interest

Could it be possible that when each one of us makes choices that are in our own best interest, it turns out that these choices are also the best for society as a whole? Choices that are the best for society as a whole are said to be in the **social interest**.

Economists have been trying to find the answer to this question since 1776, the year of American independence and the year in which Adam Smith's monumental book, *The Nature and the Causes of the Wealth of Nations*, was published. The question is a hard one to answer but a lot of progress has been made. Much of your economics course helps you to learn what we know about this question. To help you start thinking about the question, we're going to illustrate it with ten topics that generate heated discussion in today's world. You're already at least a little bit familiar with each one of them. They are:

◆ Privatization

◆ Globalization

◆ The new economy

◆ The economic response to 9–11

◆ Corporate scandals

◆ HIV/AIDS

◆ Disappearing tropical rainforests

◆ Water shortages

◆ Unemployment

◆ Deficits and debts

Privatization

9 November, 1989 is a date that will long be recalled in the world's economic history books. On that day the Berlin Wall tumbled and with its destruction, two Germanys embarked on a path towards unity.

West Germany was a nation designed on the model of the rest of Western Europe. In these nations, people own property and operate businesses. Privately owned businesses produce goods and services and trade them freely with their customers in shops and markets. All this economic activity is conducted by people who pursue their own self-interest.

East Germany was a nation designed on the model of the Soviet Union – a communist state. In such a state, people are not free to operate businesses and trade freely with each other. The government owns the factories, shops and offices, and it decides what to produce, how to produce it and for whom to produce. Economic life is managed in detail by a government central economic planning agency, and each individual follows instructions. The entire economy is operated like one giant company.

The Soviet Union collapsed soon after the fall of the Berlin Wall and splintered into a number of independent states, each of which embarked on a process of privatization. China, another communist state, began to encourage private enterprise and to move away from its sole reliance on public ownership and central economic planning during the 1980s.

Today, only Cuba remains a communist state, and even there, communism is beginning to crack and privatization is beginning to creep in.

Do publicly owned businesses coordinated by the central planning system of communism serve the social interest better than private businesses that trade freely in markets like they do in Europe? Or is it possible that our economic system serves the social interest more effectively?

Globalization

Whenever world leaders hold summit meetings, anti-globalization protests accompany them. Globalization – the expansion of international trade and investment – has been going on for centuries, but during the 1990s, advances in microchip, satellite and fibre-optic technologies brought a dramatic fall in the cost of communication and accelerated the process. A phone call or even a video conference with people who live 10,000 miles apart has become an everyday and easily affordable event. Every day, 20,000 people travel by air between Europe and America and another 20,000 between America and East Asia.

The result of this explosion of communication is a globalization of production decisions. When Nike decides to increase the production of sports shoes, people who live in China, Indonesia or Malaysia get more work. As more and more people use credit cards, people in Barbados get hired to key in the data from sales slips. When Sony wants to create a new game for PlayStation 2, or when Steven Spielberg wants a movie animation sequence, programmers in India or New Zealand write the code. And when China Airlines wants some new airplanes, it is most likely that Europeans who work for Airbus or Americans who work for Boeing will build them.

As part of the process of globalization, Europe produces more services and fewer manufactured goods. And China and the small economies in East Asia produce an expanding volume of manufactures.

The economies of Asia are also growing more rapidly than are those of Europe and the United States. China is already the world's second largest economy in terms of production and, on current trends, by 2013 it will be the world's largest economy. This rapid economic expansion in Asia will bring further changes to the global economy as the wealthier Chinese and other Asians begin to travel and buy more of the goods and services that are produced in Europe and other parts of the world. Globalization will proceed at an accelerated pace.

But globalization is leaving some behind. The nations of Africa and parts of South America are not sharing in the prosperity that globalization is bringing to other parts of the world.

Is globalization a good thing? Who does it benefit? Globalization is pretty clearly in the interest of the owners of multinational companies that profit by producing in low-cost regions and selling in high-price regions. But is globalization in your interest and the interest of the young worker in Malaysia who sews your new running shoes? Is it in the social interest?

The New Economy

The 1980s and 1990s were years of extraordinary economic change that have been called the *Information Revolution*. Economic revolutions don't happen very often. The previous one, the *Industrial Revolution*, occurred between 1760 and 1830 and saw the transformation from rural farm life to urban industrial life for most people. The revolution before that, the *Agrarian Revolution*, occurred around 12,000 years ago and saw the transformation from a life of hunting and gathering to a life of settled farming.

Placing the events of the last 20 years of the twentieth century on the status of those two previous revolutions might be a stretch. But the changes that occurred during those years were incredible. And they were based on one major technology – the microprocessor or computer chip. Gordon Moore of Intel predicted that the number of transistors that could be placed on one integrated chip would double every 18 months (Moore's Law). This prediction turned out to be remarkably accurate. In 1980, a PC chip had 60,000 transistors. By 2000, chips with more than 40 million transistors were in machines like the laptop you may use.

The spin-offs from faster and cheaper computing were widespread. Telecommunications became much faster and cheaper, music and movie recording become more realistic and cheaper, millions of routine tasks that previously required human decision and action were automated. You encounter these automated tasks everyday when you check out at the supermarket, call directory assistance, or call a government department or large business.

All the new products and processes and the low-cost computing power that made them possible were produced by people who made choices in the pursuit of self-interest. They did not result from any grand design or government economic plan.

When Gordon Moore set up Intel and started making chips, no one had told him to do so and he wasn't thinking how much easier it would be for you to turn in your essay on time if you had a faster PC. When Bill Gates dropped out of Harvard to set up Microsoft, he wasn't trying to create the best operating system and improve people's computing experience. These and the thousands of other entrepreneurs were in hot pursuit of the big payoff that many of them achieved. Yet their actions did make everyone else better off. They did advance the social interest.

But could more have been done? Were resources used in the best possible way during the information revolution? Did Intel make the best possible chips and sell them in the right quantities for the right prices? Or was the quality of chips too low and the price too high? And what about Microsoft? Did Bill Gates have to be paid $30 billion to produce the successive generations of Windows and Word? Were these programs developed in the social interest?

The Economic Response to 9–11

The awful events of 11 September, 2001 (commonly called 9–11) created economic shockwaves that will last for some years and changed "What", "How", "Where", "When" and "For Whom" goods and services get produced.

The biggest changes in production occurred in travel, accommodation and security. Much business travel was replaced by teleconferencing. Much holiday travel left the air and went onto the motorways and highways. Foreign trips were cut back. Airlines lost business and cut back on their own orders for new airplanes. Banks that had lent money to airlines wrote off millions of euros in losses.

Sales of recreational vehicles increased. And airports, although operating at lower capacity, beefed up their security services. Tens of thousands of new security agents were hired and state-of-the-art scanners were installed.

Thousands of people made choices in pursuit of their self-interest that led to these changes in production. But were these changes also in the social interest?

Corporate Scandals

In 2000, the names Enron and WorldCom meant corporate integrity and spectacular success. But today, they are tainted with scandal.

Founded in 1985, Enron expanded to become America's seventh largest business by 2001. But its expansion was built on an elaborate web of lies, deceit and fraud. In October 2001, after revelations by one of its former executives, Enron's directors acknowledged that by inflating reported income and by hiding debts, they had made the company appear to be worth considerably more than it was actually worth. Investigators uncovered fraud that made millions of dollars for the company's executives but that wiped out its shareholders' wealth.

Scott Sullivan, a highly respected financial officer, joined WorldCom in 1992 and helped turn it into one of the world's telecommunications giants. In his last year with the company, Sullivan's salary was $700,000 and his bonus (in stock options) $10 million. But just ten years after joining the company, Sullivan was fired and arrested for allegedly falsifying the company's accounts, inflating its book profits by almost $4 billion and inflating his own bonus in the process. Shortly after these events, WorldCom filed for bankruptcy protection in the largest bankruptcy filing in US history, laid off 17,000 workers and wiped out its stockholders' wealth.

These cases illustrate the fact that sometimes, in the pursuit of self-interest, people break the law. Such behaviour is not in the social interest. Indeed, the law was established precisely to limit such behaviour.

But some corporate behaviour is legal yet regarded by some as inappropriate. For example, many people think that top executive salaries are out of control. In some cases, executives who have received huge incomes have brought ruin to the companies that they manage.

The people who hired the executives acted in their own self-interest and appointed the best people they could find. The executives acted in their own self-interest. But what became of the self-interest of the shareholders and the customers of these companies. Didn't they suffer? Aren't these glaring examples of conflict between self-interest and the social interest?

HIV/AIDS

The World Health Organization and the United Nations estimate that 42 million people were suffering from HIV/AIDS in 2002. During that year, 3 million died from the disease and there were 5 million new cases. Most of the HIV/AIDS cases – 30 million of them in 2002 – are in Africa, where incomes average around £3 a day. The most effective available treatment for HIV/AIDS is an antiretroviral drug made by the large multinational drug companies. The cost of this treatment is around £1,200 a year – more than the £3 a day the average person earns.

Developing new drugs is a high-cost and high-risk activity. And if the activity were not in the self-interest of the drug companies, they would stop the effort. But once developed, the cost of producing a drug is just a few pence a dose. Would it be in the social interest for drugs to be made available at the low cost of producing them?

Disappearing Tropical Rainforests

Tropical rainforests in South America, Africa and Asia support the lives of 30 million species of plants, animals and insects – approaching 50 per cent of all species on the planet. These rainforests provides us with the ingredients for many goods including soaps, mouth washes, shampoos, food preservatives, rubber, nuts and fruits. The Amazon rainforest alone converts about 1 trillion pounds of carbon dioxide into oxygen each year.

Yet tropical rainforests cover less than two per cent of the Earth's surface and are heading for extinction. Logging, cattle ranching, mining, oil extraction, hydroelectric dams and subsistence farming are destroying the equivalent of two football fields every second. At the current rate of destruction, most tropical rainforest ecosystems will be gone by 2030.

Each one of us makes economic choices that are in our self-interest to consume products, some of which are destroying this natural resource. Are our choices damaging the social interest? And if they are, what can be done to change the incentives we face and change our behaviour?

Water Shortages

The world is awash with water – it is our most abundant resource. But 97 per cent of it is seawater. Another 2 per cent is frozen in glaciers and ice. The 1 per cent of the earth's water that is available for human consumption would be sufficient if only it were in the right places. Finland, Canada and a few other places have more water than they can use, but Australia, Africa and California (and many other places) could use much more water than they can get.

Some people pay less for water than others. Californian farmers, for example, pay less than Californian households. Some of the highest prices for water are faced by people in the poorest countries who must either buy water from a water-dealer's truck or carry water in buckets over many miles.

In the United Kingdom, water is provided by private water companies. In the United States, public enterprises deliver the water.

In India and Bangladesh, plenty of rain falls, but it falls during a short wet season and the rest of the year is dry. Dams could help, but not enough have been built in those countries.

Are national and global water resources being managed properly? Are the decisions that we each make in our self-interest to use, conserve and transport water also in the social interest?

Unemployment

During the 1930s, in a period called the *Great Depression*, more than 20 per cent of the workforce was unemployed. Even today, approaching 40 per cent of teenagers are unemployed in many countries. Why can't everyone who wants a job find one? If economic choices arise from scarcity, how can resources be left unused?

People get jobs because other people think they can earn a profit by hiring them. And people accept a job when they think the pay and other conditions are good enough. So the number of people with jobs is determined by the self-interest of employers and workers. But is the number of jobs also in the social interest?

Deficits and Debts

Every year since 1992, Americans have bought goods and services from the rest of the world in excess of what foreigners bought from them to the tune of $4 trillion or 40 per cent of a year's production in the United States. To pay for these goods and services, Americans are borrowing from the rest of us.

These enormous deficits and the debts they create cannot persist indefinitely and will somehow have to be repaid. Are the choices that Americans are making to buy from and sell to the rest of the world in the social interest?

We've just looked at ten topics that illustrate the big question: Do choices made in the pursuit of self-interest also promote the social interest?

You'll discover, as you work through this book, that much of what we do in the pursuit of our self-interest does indeed further the social interest. But there are areas in which social interest and self-interest come into conflict. You'll discover the principles that help economists to figure out when the social interest is being served, when it is not and what might be done when it is not.

Review Quiz

1 Give some examples, different from those in the chapter, to illustrate what, how, where, when and for whom goods and services get produced.
2 Think of some examples of goods that you think have high or low value. Explain why you care about how, where and when these goods get produced and who gets them.
3 Use headlines from the recent news to illustrate the potential for conflict between self-interest and the social interest.

The Economic Way of Thinking

The definition of economics and the questions that you've just reviewed tell you about the scope of economics. But they don't tell you how economists think about these questions and go about seeking answers to them.

You're now going to begin to see how economists approach economic questions. In this section, we'll look at the ideas that define the *economic way of thinking*. This way of thinking needs practice, but it is powerful and as you become more familiar with it, you'll begin to see the world around you with a new and sharp focus.

Choices and Trade-offs

Because we face scarcity, we must make choices. And when we make a choice, we select from the available alternatives. For example, you can spend the weekend studying for your next economics test or having fun with your friends, but you can't do both of these activities at the same time. You must choose how much time to devote to each. Whatever choice you make, you could have chosen something else instead.

You can think about your choice as a trade-off. A **trade-off** is an exchange – giving up one thing to get something else. When you choose how to spend your weekend, you face a trade-off between studying and going out with your friends.

Guns versus Butter

The classic trade-off is between "guns" and "butter" that stand for any pair of goods. They might actually be guns and butter. Or they might be broader categories such as defence goods and food. Or they might be any pair of specific goods or services such as orange juice and bottled water, footballs and cricket balls, schools and hospitals, haircuts and career advice.

Regardless of the specific objects that guns and butter represent, the guns-versus-butter trade-off captures a hard fact of life: If we want more of one thing, we must trade something else in exchange for it.

The idea of a trade-off is central to the whole of economics. We'll look at some examples, beginning with three of the big questions: what, how and for whom? We can view each of these questions about the goods and services that get produced in terms of trade-offs.

What, How and For Whom Trade-offs

Each of the questions what, how and for whom goods and services are produced involves a trade-off that is similar to that between guns and butter.

"What" Trade-offs

What goods and services get produced depends on choices made by each one of us, by our government and by the businesses that produce the things we buy.

Each of these choices involves a trade-off. Each one of us faces a trade-off when we choose how to spend our income. You go to the pictures this week, but you forgo a few cups of coffee to buy the ticket. You trade off coffee for seeing a film.

The government faces a trade-off when it chooses how to spend our taxes. Parliament votes for more defence goods but cuts back on student grants – Parliament trades off education for defence. Businesses face a trade-off when they decide what to produce. Gillette hires David Beckham and allocates resources to designing and marketing a new vibrating shaver but cuts back on its development of a new toothbrush. Gillette trades off toothbrushes for shavers.

"How" Trade-offs

How goods and services get produced depends on choices made by the businesses that produce the things we buy. These choices involve a trade-off. For example, Blockbuster opens a new video store with automated vending machines and closes an older store with traditional manual service. Blockbuster trades off labour for capital.

"For Whom" Trade-offs

For whom goods and services are produced depends on the distribution of buying power. Buying power can be redistributed – transferred from one person to another – in three ways: by voluntary payments, by theft, or through taxes and benefits organized by government. Each of these forms of redistribution brings a trade-off.

For example, we face a trade-off when we choose how much to contribute to an Oxfam appeal. You donate £5 and cut your spending. You trade off your own spending for a small increase in economic equality.

We make choices that influence redistribution by

theft when we vote to make theft illegal and devote resources to law enforcement. We trade off goods and services for an increase in the security of our property.

We also vote for taxes and welfare arrangements that redistribute buying power from the rich to the poor. Government redistribution confronts society with what has been called the **big trade-off** – the trade-off between equality and efficiency. Taxing the rich and making transfers to the poor bring greater economic equality. But taxing productive activities such as running a business, working hard, and saving and investing in capital discourages these activities. So taxing productive activities means producing less. A more equal distribution means there is less to share.

You can think of the big trade-off as being the problem of how to share a pie that everyone contributes to baking. If each person receives a share of the pie that reflects the size of her or his effort, everyone will work hard and the pie will be as large as possible. But if the pie is shared equally, regardless of contribution, some talented bakers will slacken off and the pie will shrink. The big trade-off is one between the size of the pie and how equally it is shared. We trade off some production for increased equality.

Choices Bring Change

What, how and for whom goods and services are produced changes over time. And choices bring change. The quantity and range of goods and services available today in Europe is much greater than that in Africa. And the economic condition of Europeans today is much better than it was a generation ago. But the quality of economic life (and its rate of improvement) doesn't depend purely on nature and on luck. It depends on many of the choices made by each one of us, by governments and by businesses. And these choices involve trade-offs.

One choice is that of how much of our income to consume and how much to save. Our saving can be channelled through the financial system to finance businesses and to pay for new capital that increases production. The more we save and invest, the more goods and services we'll be able to produce in the future. When you decide to save an extra £1,000 and forgo a holiday in Spain, you trade off the holiday for a higher future income. If everyone saves an extra £1,000 and businesses invest in more equipment that increases production, the average consumption per person rises. As a society, we trade off current consumption for economic growth and higher future consumption.

A second choice is how much effort to devote to education and training. By becoming better educated and more highly skilled, we become more productive and are able to produce more goods and services. When you decide to remain in university for another two years to complete a post-graduate degree and forgo a huge chunk of leisure time, you trade off leisure today for a higher future income. If everyone becomes better educated, production increases and income per person rises. As a society, we trade off current consumption and leisure time for economic growth and higher future consumption.

A third choice, usually made by businesses, is how much effort to devote to research and the development of new products and production methods. Airbus can divert production engineers into research on a new aircraft or leave them producing existing types of aircraft. More research brings greater production in the future but means smaller current production – a trade-off of current production for greater future production.

Seeing choices as trade-offs emphasizes the idea that to get something, we must give up something.

Opportunity Cost

The highest-valued alternative that we give up to get something is the **opportunity cost** of the activity chosen. "There's no such thing as a free lunch" is not just a clever one-liner. It expresses the central idea of economics: that every choice involves a cost.

You can drop out of university, or you can keep studying. If you drop out and take a job at McDonald's, you earn enough to buy some CDs, go to the pictures and spend lots of free time with your friends. If you remain in university, you can't afford these things. You will be able to buy these things when you graduate, and that is one of the payoffs from being in university. But for now, when you've bought your books, you have nothing left for CDs and the cinema. And doing homework leaves little time to spend with your friends. The opportunity cost of being in university is the highest-valued alternative that you would have done if you dropped out.

All the what, how and for whom trade-offs that we've just considered involve opportunity cost. The opportunity cost of some guns is the butter forgone; the opportunity cost of a cinema ticket is the number of cups of coffee forgone. And the choices that bring change also involve opportunity cost. The opportunity cost of more goods and services in the future is less consumption today.

Choosing at the Margin

You can allocate the next hour between studying and e-mailing your friends. But the choice is not all or nothing. You must decide how many minutes to allocate to each activity. To make this decision, you compare the benefit of a little bit more study time with its cost – you make your choice at the **margin**.

The benefit that arises from an increase in an activity is called **marginal benefit**. For example, suppose that you're spending four nights a week studying and your average mark is 60 per cent. You decide that you want a higher mark and decide to study an extra night each week. Your mark now rises to 70 per cent. The marginal benefit from studying for one additional night a week is the 10 point increase in your mark. It is *not* the 70 per cent. The reason is that you already have the benefit from studying for four nights a week, so we don't count this benefit as resulting from the decision you are now making.

The cost of an increase in an activity is called **marginal cost**. For you, the marginal cost of increasing your study time by one night a week is the cost of the additional night not spent with your friends (if that is your best alternative use of the time). It does not include the cost of the four nights you are already studying.

To make your decision, you compare the marginal benefit from an extra night of study with its marginal cost. If the marginal benefit exceeds the marginal cost, you study the extra night. If the marginal cost exceeds the marginal benefit, you do not study the extra night.

By evaluating marginal benefits and marginal costs and choosing only those actions that bring greater benefit than cost, we use our scarce resources in the way that makes us as well off as possible.

Responding to Incentives

Our choices respond to incentives. A change in marginal cost or a change in marginal benefit changes the incentives that we face and leads us to change our choice.

For example, suppose your economics lecturer gives you some homework and tells you that all the questions will be on the next exam. The marginal benefit from working these questions is large, so you diligently work them all. In contrast, suppose that your maths lecturer sets some homework and tells you that none of the questions will be on the next exam. The marginal benefit from working these questions is lower, so you skip some of them.

A central idea of economics is that we can predict how choices will change by looking at changes in incentives. More of an activity is undertaken when its marginal cost falls or its marginal benefit rises; less of an activity is undertaken when its marginal cost rises or its marginal benefit falls.

Incentives are also the key to reconciling self-interest and the social interest. When our choices are *not* in the social interest, it is because we face the wrong incentives. One of the challenges for economists is to discover the incentive systems that result in self-interested choices leading to the social interest.

Human Nature, Incentives and Institutions

Economists take human nature as given and view people as acting in their self-interest. All people – consumers, producers, politicians and civil servants – pursue their self-interest.

Self-interested actions are not necessarily *selfish* actions. You might decide to use your resources in ways that bring pleasure to others as well as to yourself. But a self-interested act gets the most value for *you* based on *your* view about value.

If human nature is given and if people act in their self-interest, how can we take care of the social interest? Economists answer this question by emphasizing the crucial role that institutions play in influencing the incentives that people face as they pursue their self-interest.

Private property protected by a system of laws and markets that enable voluntary exchange are the fundamental institutions. You will learn as you progress with your study of economics that where these institutions exist, self-interest can indeed promote the social interest.

Review Quiz

1 Provide three everyday examples of a trade-off and describe the opportunity cost involved in each.
2 Provide three everyday examples to illustrate what we mean by choosing at the margin.
3 What are the marginal benefits and marginal costs that you've encountered in the choices you've made today?
4 How do economists predict changes in choices?
5 What do economists say about the role of institutions in promoting the social interest?

Economics: A Social Science

Economics is a social science and like all scientists, economists distinguish two types of statement:

1 What *is*

2 What *ought to be*

Statements about what *is* are called *positive* statements and they might be right or wrong. We test a positive statement by checking it against the facts. When a chemist does an experiment in her laboratory, she is testing a positive statement.

Statements about what *ought to be* are called *normative* statements and they cannot be tested. When the European Parliament debates a motion, it is ultimately deciding what ought to be and making a normative statement.

To see the distinction between positive and normative statements, consider the following statements about health care. "Universal health care will cut the amount of work time lost to illness" is a positive statement. "Every European should have equal access to health care" is a normative statement.

The task of economic science is to discover positive statements that are consistent with what we observe in the economic world. This task breaks into three steps:

◆ Observation and measurement

◆ Model building

◆ Testing models

Observation and Measurement

Economists observe and measure data on such things as the quantities of natural and human resources, wages and work hours, the prices and quantities of the goods and services, taxes and government spending, and the items bought from and sold to other countries.

Model Building

The second step towards understanding how the economic world works is to build a model. An **economic model** is a description of some aspect of the economic world that includes only those features of the world that are needed for the purpose at hand. A model is simpler than the reality it represents. What a model includes and what it leaves out result from assumptions about what is essential and what are inessential details.

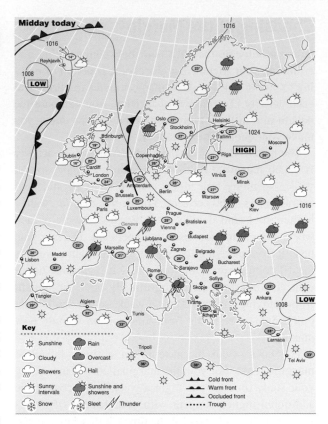

Map supplied by PA WeatherCentre Ltd

You can see how ignoring details is useful – even essential – to our understanding by thinking about a model that you see every day: the TV weather map. The weather map is a model that helps to predict the temperature, wind speed and direction, and rainfall over the next few days. The weather map shows lines called isobars – lines of equal barometric pressure. It doesn't show the motorways because we assume that the pattern of air pressure, not the location of the motorways, determines the weather.

An economic model is similar to a weather map. For example, an economic model of a mobile phone network will include items such as the cost of using a mobile phone but it will ignore such details as the tunes people use for ring tones.

Testing Models

The third step is testing the model. A model's predictions may correspond, or be in conflict, with the facts. By comparing the model's predictions with the facts, we are able to test a model and develop an economic theory. An **economic theory** is a generalization that summarizes what we think we understand about the economic choices that people make and the performance of industries and entire economies. It is a bridge between an economic model and the real economy.

The process of building and testing models creates theories. For example, meteorologists have a theory that if the isobars form a particular pattern (a model), then it will rain (reality). They have developed this theory by repeated observation and testing of models.

Economics is a young science. It was born in 1776 with the publication of Adam Smith's *Wealth of Nations*. Since then, economists have discovered some useful theories. But in many areas, economists are still looking for answers. Let's look at some of the obstacles to progress in economics.

Obstacles and Pitfalls in Economics

Economic experiments are difficult to perform and economic behaviour has many simultaneous causes. For these two reasons, it is difficult to unscramble cause and effect in economics.

Unscrambling Cause and Effect

By changing one factor at a time and holding all the other relevant factors constant, we isolate the factor of interest and investigate its effects in the clearest possible way. This logical device, which all scientists use to identify cause and effect, is called *ceteris paribus*. **Ceteris paribus** is a Latin term that means "other things being equal" or "if all other relevant things remain the same". Ensuring that other things are equal is crucial in many activities, including athletic events, and all successful attempts to make scientific progress use this device.

Economic models (like the models in all other sciences) enable the influence of one factor at a time to be isolated in the imaginary world of the model. When we use a model, we are able to imagine what would happen if only one factor changed. But *ceteris paribus* can be a problem in economics when we try to test a model.

Laboratory scientists, such as chemists and physicists, perform experiments by actually holding all the relevant factors constant except for the one under investigation. In the non-experimental sciences such as economics (and astronomy), we usually observe the outcomes of the simultaneous operation of many factors. Consequently, it is hard to sort out the effects of each individual factor and to compare the effects with what a model predicts. To cope with this problem, economists take three complementary approaches.

First, they look for pairs of events in which other things are equal (or similar). Data from different European countries might be used, for example, to study the effects of unemployment benefits on the unemployment rate. Second, economists use statistical tools called econometrics. Third, they perform experiments. This relatively new experimental approach puts real subjects in a decision-making situation and varies their incentives to discover how they respond to one factor at a time.

Economists try to avoid fallacies – errors of reasoning that lead to a wrong conclusion. Two fallacies are common, and you need to be on your guard to avoid them. They are the:

◆ Fallacy of composition
◆ *Post hoc* fallacy

Fallacy of Composition

The fallacy of composition is the (false) statement that what is true of the parts is true of the whole or that what is true of the whole is true of the parts. Think of the statement, "Stand up at the football match to get a better view." If one person stands and the rest remain seated, the statement is true. If everyone stands, the statement is false. What is true for a part isn't true for the whole.

For an economic example, suppose a business fires some workers to cut costs and improve its profits. If all businesses take similar actions, people have less to spend, businesses sell less and profits don't improve.

Post Hoc Fallacy

Another Latin phrase – *post hoc ergo propter hoc* – means "after this, therefore because of this". The *post hoc* fallacy is the error of reasoning that a first event causes a second event because the first occurred before the second. Suppose you are a visitor from a far-off world. You observe lots of people shopping in early December and then you see them opening gifts and partying on Christmas Day. Does the shopping cause Christmas? you wonder. After a deeper study, you discover that Christmas causes the shopping. A later event causes an earlier event.

Unravelling cause and effect is difficult in economics. And just looking at the timing of events often doesn't help. For example, does a stock market boom cause the economy to expand or does the anticipation of an expanding economy cause the stock market to boom? To disentangle cause and effect, economists use economic models and data and, to the extent that they can, perform experiments.

Economics is a challenging science and economists often disagree on issues of theory and on whether the evidence supports or contradicts theory. But the difficulty of getting answers in economics does not mean economists disagree on everything. Disagreement and debate are part of the way in which science develops new answers to current problems and is the sign of a healthy science!

Agreement and Disagreement

Economists have a reputation for not agreeing. Perhaps you've heard the joke: "If you laid all the economists in the world end to end, they still wouldn't reach agreement." But actually, while economists like to argue about theory, there is a remarkable amount of agreement. Here is a sample of the degree of consensus[1] on a range of issues.

Seventy per cent of economists agree that:

Rent ceilings cut the availability of housing.

Import restrictions have larger costs than benefits.

Wage and price controls do not help slow inflation.

Wage contracts are not a primary cause of unemployment.

Sixty per cent of economists agree that:

Monopoly power of big oil companies was not the cause of a rise in the price of petrol during the Kuwait crisis.

Curtailing the power of environmental agencies would not make the economy more efficient.

If the budget is to be balanced, it should be balanced over a business cycle, not every year.

But economists are divided on these issues:

Anti-monopoly laws should be enforced more vigorously to curtail monopoly power.

Effluent taxes are better than pollution limits.

The government should try to make the distribution of income more equal.

Review these statements carefully. Notice that economists are willing to offer their opinions on normative issues as well as their professional views on positive questions.

Disagreements on positive issues arise when the available evidence is insufficient for a clear conclusion

to be reached. Because it is difficult to conduct experiments in economics, it is often not possible to generate sufficient evidence to achieve a consensus.

Disagreements on normative issues arise from differences in values or priorities. It is hardly surprising that economists disagree so much on normative issues as they are just a reflection of similar disagreements amongst society in general. (Think about how much physicists, chemists and biologists disagree on issues such as global warming.)

One of the benefits of studying economics is that it helps you to analyze economic and business issues in a more rigorous way. For example, now that you are aware of the difference between positive and normative statements and the problems of the fallacy of composition and the *post hoc* fallacy, you will be on the lookout to identify these problems in other people's arguments. When you read newspaper articles, be on the lookout for normative propositions dressed up as positive propositions. Ask yourself if the writer has fallen into a fallacy trap when he or she draws conclusions from evidence. If you can identify these problems, you will know that the conclusions drawn are less reliable than they first appeared. Alternatively, if the writer has been careful to consider these problems, you may be more inclined to accept his or her conclusions.

Review Quiz

1 What is the distinction between a positive statement and a normative statement? Provide an example (different from those in the chapter) of each type of statement.
2 What is a model? Think of a model that you might use (probably without thinking of it as a model) in your everyday life?
3 What is a theory? What is wrong with the statement 'It might work in theory but it doesn't work in practice'? (Hint: Think about what a theory is and how it is used.)
4 What is the *ceteris paribus* assumption and how is it used?
5 Provide some everyday examples of the fallacy of composition and the *post hoc* fallacy.

Economics makes extensive use of graphs, as you will quickly discover. If you are comfortable with graphs, jump right into Chapter 2. But if you find graphs hard to work with, spend a bit of time becoming familiar with the basics of making and using graphs in the appendix to this chapter that begins on p. 19.

---

[1] These views of economists are taken from Richard M. Alston, J.R. Kearl and Michael B. Vaughan, "Is There a Consensus Among Economists?" *American Economic Review*, May 1992, 82, 203–209.

Summary

Key Points

A Definition of Economics (p. 4)

◆ All economic questions arise from scarcity – from the fact that wants exceed the resources available to satisfy them.

◆ Economics is the social science that studies the choices people make as they cope with scarcity.

◆ The subject divides into microeconomics and macroeconomics.

Two Big Economic Questions
(pp. 5–10)

◆ Two big questions summarize the scope of economics:

1 How do choices end up determining *what*, *how*, *where*, *when* and *for whom* goods and services get produced?

2 When do choices made in the pursuit of *self-interest* also promote the *social interest*?

The Economic Way of Thinking
(pp. 11–13)

◆ Every choice is a trade-off – exchanging more of something for less of something else.

◆ The classic guns-versus-butter trade-off represents all trade-offs.

◆ All economic questions involve a trade-off.

◆ The big social trade-off is between equality and efficiency.

◆ The highest-valued alternative forgone is the opportunity cost of what is chosen.

◆ Choices are made at the margin and respond to incentives.

Economics: A Social Science
(pp. 14–16)

◆ Economists distinguish between positive statements – what is – and normative statements – what ought to be.

◆ To explain the economic world, economists develop theories by building and testing economic models.

◆ Economists use the *ceteris paribus* assumption and careful observation, statistical methods and experiments to try to disentangle cause and effect.

◆ Economists try to avoid the fallacy of composition and the *post hoc* fallacy.

◆ Economists agree on a wide range of questions about how the economy works.

Key Terms

Big trade-off, 12
Capital, 5
Ceteris paribus, 15
Economic model, 14
Economic theory, 14
Economics, 4
Entrepreneurship, 6
Factors of production, 5
Goods and services, 5
Human capital, 5
Incentive, 4
Interest, 6
Labour, 5
Land, 5
Macroeconomics, 4
Margin, 13
Marginal benefit, 13
Marginal cost, 13
Microeconomics, 4
Opportunity cost, 12
Profit, 6
Rent, 6
Scarcity, 4
Self-interest, 7
Social interest, 7
Trade-off, 11
Wages, 6

Problems

*1 You plan to upgrade your computer skills by taking a training course this summer. If you do, you won't be able to take your usual job that pays €6,000 for the summer and you won't be able to live at home for free. The cost of your tuition will be €2,000, equipment €200 and living costs €1,400. What is the opportunity cost of your summer training course?

2 You plan a major adventure trip for the summer. You won't be able to take your usual summer job that pays €6,000 and you won't be able to live at home for free. The cost of your travel on the trip will be €3,000, film and video tape will cost you €200 and your food will cost €1,400. What is the opportunity cost of taking this trip?

*3 The local shopping centre has free parking, but the centre is always very busy and it usually takes 30 minutes to find a parking space. Today when you found a vacant spot, Harry also wanted it. Is parking really free at this shopping centre? If not, what did it cost you to park today? When you parked your car today, did you impose any costs on Harry? Explain your answers.

4 A city has built a new high-rise car park. There is always an available parking spot, but it costs €1 a day. Before the new high-rise car park was built, it usually took 15 minutes of cruising to find a parking space. Compare the opportunity cost of parking in the new car park with the old parking system. Which is less costly and by how much?

*5 Which of the following statements are positive and which are normative:

a A cut in wages will reduce the number of people willing to work.

b High interest rates prohibit many young people from buying their first home.

c No family ought to pay more than 25 per cent of its income in taxes.

d The government should reduce its expenditure on roads and increase its expenditure on railways.

6 Which of the following statements are positive and which are normative:

a An increase in productivity will increase living standards.

b The government should raise taxes and spend the money on providing additional healthcare services.

c Unemployment is efficient under some circumstances.

d Everyone should give to charity.

---

*Solutions to odd-numbered problems are available on Parkin Interactive.

Critical Thinking

1 Imagine a homeless man on the street near your university. Use the big questions and the economic way of thinking to organize a short essay about the economic life of this man. Make sure you answer the following questions in your essay:

a Does the homeless man face scarcity?

b Does the homeless man make choices?

c Can you interpret his choices as being in his self-interest?

d Can either his own choices or the choices of others make this man better off?

e How can the choices of the homeless man and other people make him better off?

2 Reread the agreement and disagreement on p. 16.

a Identify which of the statements are normative and which are positive.

b Explain why the level of agreement differs between normative and positive statements.

3 Visit *Resources for Economists on the Internet*. This site is a good place from which to search for economic information on the Internet. Visit the "general interest" sites and become familiar with the types of information that they contain.

Web Exercises

Use the links on *Parkin Interactive* to work the following exercises.

1 Visit the European statistics Website to obtain information on the European Union and on the economy of your own region and city.

a What is the number of people unemployed in your country?

b Has the percentage of people unemployed risen or fallen recently?

c What is the average income earned in your country?

2 Visit the *Financial Times* Website.

a What is the top economic news story today? With which big economic questions does it deal?

b Which of the ideas that define the economic way of thinking are relevant to understanding this news item?

c Write a summary of the news item using as much as possible of the economic vocabulary that you have learned in this chapter and which is in the key terms list on p. 17.

CHAPTER 1 APPENDIX
Graphs in Economics

After studying this appendix, you will be able to:

◆ Make and interpret a time-series graph, a cross-section graph, and a scatter diagram

◆ Distinguish between linear and non-linear relationships and between relationships that have a maximum and a minimum

◆ Define and calculate the slope of a line

◆ Graph relationships among more than two variables

Graphing Data

A graph represents a quantity as a distance. Figure A1.1 shows two examples. A distance on the horizontal line represents temperature. A movement from left to right shows an increase in temperature. The point marked 0 represents zero degrees. To the right of 0, the temperature is positive. To the left of 0, the temperature is negative. A distance on the vertical line represents height. The point marked 0 represents sea level. Points above 0 represent metres above sea level. Points below 0 (indicated by a minus sign) represent metres below sea level.

By setting two scales perpendicular to each other, as in Figure A1.1, we can visualize the relationship between two variables. The scale lines are called *axes*. The vertical line is the *y*-axis, and the horizontal line is the *x*-axis. Each axis has a zero point, which is shared by the two axes. This common zero point is called the *origin*.

To show something in a two-variable graph, we need two pieces of information: the value of the *x* variable and the value of the *y* variable. For example, off the coast of Norway on a winter's day, the temperature is 0 degrees – the value of *x*. A fishing boat is located 0 metres above sea level – the value of *y*. This information appears at the origin at point *A* in Figure A1.1. In the heated cabin of the boat, the temperature is a comfortable 24 degrees. Point *B* represents this information. The same 24 degrees in the cabin of an airliner 9,000 metres above sea level is at point *C*.

Figure A1.1

Making a Graph

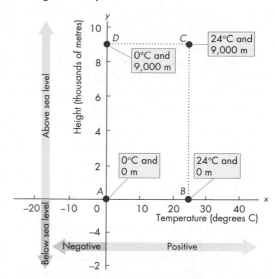

Graphs have axes that measure quantities as distances. Here, the horizontal axis (*x*-axis) measures temperature, and the vertical axis (*y*-axis) measures height. Point *A* represents a fishing boat at sea level (0 on the *y*-axis) on a day when the temperature is 0°C. Point *B* represents inside the cabin of the boat at a temperature of 24°C. Point *C* represents inside the cabin of an airliner 9,000 metres above sea level at a temperature of 24°C. Point *D* represents an ice cube in an airplane 9,000 metres above sea level.

Finally, the temperature of the ice cube in the drink of the airline passenger is shown by the point marked *D*. This point represents 9,000 metres above sea level at a temperature of 0 degrees.

We can draw two lines, called *coordinates*, from point *C*. One, called the *y*-coordinate, runs from *C* to the horizontal axis. Its length is the same as the value marked off on the *y*-axis. The other, called the *x*-coordinate, runs from *C* to the vertical axis. Its length is the same as the value marked off on the *x*-axis. We describe a point in a graph by the values of its *x*-coordinate and its *y*-coordinate.

Graphs like that in Figure A1.1 can show any type of quantitative data on two variables. Economists use three types of graphs based on the principles in Figure A1.1 to reveal and describe the relationships among variables. They are:

◆ Time-series graphs

◆ Cross-section graphs

◆ Scatter diagrams

Time-series Graphs

A **time-series graph** measures time (for example, months or years) on the *x*-axis and variables in which we are interested on the *y*-axis. Figure A1.2 is an example of a time-series graph.

In Figure A1.2, we measure time in years running from 1972 to 2002. We measure the price of coffee (the variable that we are interested in) on the *y*-axis.

The point of a time-series graph is to enable us to visualize how a variable has changed over time and how its value in one period relates to its value in another period.

A time-series graph conveys an enormous amount of information quickly and easily, as this example illustrates. It shows:

1   The *level* of the price of coffee – when it is *high* and *low*. When the line is a long way from the *x*-axis, the price is high, as it was, for example, in 1977. When the line is close to the *x*-axis, the price is low, as it was, for example, in 1992.

2   How the price *changes* – whether it *rises* or *falls*. When the line slopes upward, as in 1976, the price is rising. When the line slopes downward, as in 1987, the price is falling.

3   The *speed* with which the price changes – whether it rises or falls *quickly* or *slowly*. If the line is very steep, then the price rises or falls quickly. If the line is not steep, the price rises or falls slowly. For example, the price rose quickly in 1976 and slowly in 1985. The price fell quickly in 1987 and slowly in 1991.

A time-series graph also reveals whether there is a trend. A **trend** is a general tendency for a variable to move in one direction. A trend might be upward or downward. In Figure A1.2, you can barely see a trend in the price of coffee. There is a very slight upward trend. That is, although the price rose and fell, the general tendency was for it to rise very slightly – the price had a slight upward trend.

A time-series graph also helps us to detect cycles in variables. In Figure A1.2, you can see some clear cycles in the price of coffee. The price rises and falls in a series of cycles with peaks in 1977, 1986 and 1997 – almost exactly ten-year intervals. The cycles have troughs in 1981 and 1998, again, almost a ten-year interval.

Finally, a time-series graph lets us compare the variable in different periods quickly. Figure A1.2 shows that the average price was higher in the 1970s than in the 1990s. When we graph data at monthly intervals, we discover seasonal variations.

Figure A1.2

A Time-series Graph

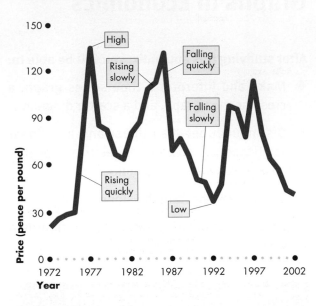

A time-series graph plots the level of a variable on the *y*-axis against time (day, week, month or year) on the *x*-axis. This graph shows the price of coffee (in pence per pound) each year from 1972 to 2002. It shows us when the price of coffee was *high* and when it was *low*, when the price *increased* and when it *decreased*, and when it changed *quickly* and when it changed *slowly*.

You can see that a time-series graph conveys a wealth of information. And it does so in much less space than we have used to describe only some of its features. But you do have to "read" the graph to obtain all this information.

Cross-section Graphs

A **cross-section graph** shows the values of an economic variable for different groups in a population at a point in time. Figure A1.3 shows an example. This graph is called a *bar chart*.

The bar chart in Figure A1.3 shows the percentage of young males who participate in various sporting activities. This figure enables you to compare the popularity of different activities. And you can do so much more quickly and clearly than by looking at a list of numbers. For example, you can quickly see that football is twice as popular as tennis or cricket and that very few young males do aerobics.

Figure A1.3

A Cross-Section Graph

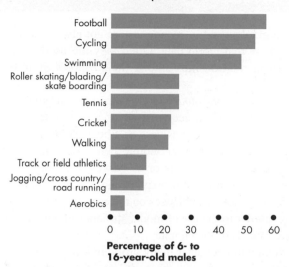

Percentage of 6- to 16-year-old males

A cross-section graph shows the level of a variable across the members of a population. This bar chart shows the percentage of young males who participate in various sporting activities.

Scatter Diagrams

A **scatter diagram** plots the value of one variable against the value of another variable. Such a graph reveals whether a relationship exists between two variables and describes their relationship. Figure A1.4(a) shows the relationship between consumption expenditure and income. Each dot shows expenditure per person and income per person in a given year from 1992 to 2003. The dots are "scattered" within the graph. The dot labelled A tells us that in 1997, income per person was £9,670 and consumption expenditure per person was £9,000. The dots in this graph form a pattern, which reveals that as income increases, expenditure increases.

Figure A1.4(b) shows the relationship between the number of international phone calls and the price of a call. This graph shows that as the price per minute falls, the number of calls increases.

Figure A1.4(c) shows a scatter diagram of inflation and unemployment in the United Kingdom. Here, the dots show no clear relationship between these two variables. The dots reveal that there is no simple relationship between these two variables.

Figure A1.4

Scatter Diagrams

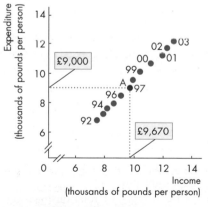

(a) Expenditure and income

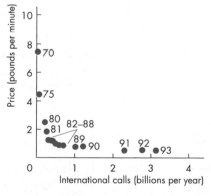

(b) International phone calls and prices

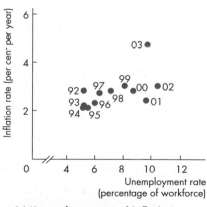

(c) Unemployment and inflation

A scatter diagram reveals the relationship between two variables. Part (a) shows the relationship between expenditure and income. Each point shows the values of the two variables in a specific year. For example, point A shows that in 1997, average income was £9,670 and average expenditure was £9,000. The dots form a pattern that shows that as income increases, expenditure increases.

Part (b) shows the relationship between the price of an international phone call and the number of calls made. This graph shows that as the price of a phone call falls, the number of calls made increases. Part (c) shows a scatter diagram of the inflation rate and unemployment rate in the United Kingdom. This graph shows that inflation and unemployment are not closely related.

Breaks in the Axes

Figure A1.4(a) and Figure A1.4(c) have breaks in their axes, as shown by the small gaps. The breaks indicate that there are jumps from the origin, 0, to the first values recorded.

In Figure A1.4(a), the breaks are used because the lowest values exceed £6,000. With no breaks in the axes, there would be a lot of empty space, all the points would be crowded into the top right corner and it would be hard to see the relationship between these two variables. By breaking the axes, we bring the relationship into view.

Putting a break in the axes is like using a zoom lens to bring the relationship into the centre of the graph and magnify it so that it fills the graph.

Misleading Graphs

Breaks can be used to highlight a relationship. But they can also be used to mislead – to make a graph that lies. The most common way of making a graph lie is to use axis breaks and either to stretch or compress a scale. For example, suppose that in Figure A1.4(a), the *y*-axis that measures expenditure ran from zero to £45,000 while the *x*-axis was the same as the one shown. The graph would now create the impression that despite a huge increase in income, expenditure had barely changed.

To avoid being misled, it is a good idea to get into the habit of looking closely at the values and the labels on the axes of a graph before you start trying to interpret it.

Correlation and Causation

A scatter diagram that shows a clear relationship between two variables, such as Figure A1.4(a) or Figure A1.4(b), tells us that the two variables have a high correlation. When a high correlation is present, we can predict the value of one variable from the value of the other variable. But correlation does not imply causation.

Sometimes a high correlation is a coincidence, but sometimes it does arise from a causal relationship. It is likely, for example, that rising income causes rising expenditure (Figure A1.4a) and that the falling price of a phone call causes more calls to be made (Figure A1.4b).

You've now seen how we can use graphs in economics to show economic data and to reveal relationships between variables. Next, we'll learn how economists use graphs to construct and display economic models.

Graphs Used in Economic Models

The graphs used in economics are not always designed to show real-world data. Often they are used to show general relationships among the variables in an economic model.

An *economic model* is a stripped down, simplified description of an economy or of a component of an economy such as a business or a household. It consists of statements about economic behaviour that can be expressed as equations or as curves in a graph. Economists use models to explore the effects of different policies or other influences on the economy in ways that are similar to the use of model airplanes in wind tunnels and models of the climate.

You will encounter many different kinds of graphs in economic models, but there are some repeating patterns. Once you've learned to recognize these patterns, you will instantly understand the meaning of a graph. Here, we'll look at the different types of curves that are used in economic models, and we'll see some everyday examples of each type of curve. The patterns to look for in graphs are the four cases in which:

◆ Variables that move in the same direction

◆ Variables that move in opposite directions

◆ Variables that have a maximum or a minimum

◆ Variables that are unrelated

Variables That Move in the Same Direction

A relationship in which two variables move in the same direction is called a **positive relationship** or a **direct relationship**. Figure A1.5 shows some examples of positive relationships. Notice that the line that shows such a relationship slopes upward.

Figure A1.5 shows three types of relationships, one that has a straight line and two that have curved lines. But all the lines in these three graphs are called curves. Any line on a graph – no matter whether it is straight or curved – is called a *curve*.

A relationship shown by a straight line is called a **linear relationship**. Figure A1.5(a) shows a linear relationship between the number of miles travelled in 5 hours and speed. For example, point *A* shows that

Figure A1.5

Positive (Direct) Relationships

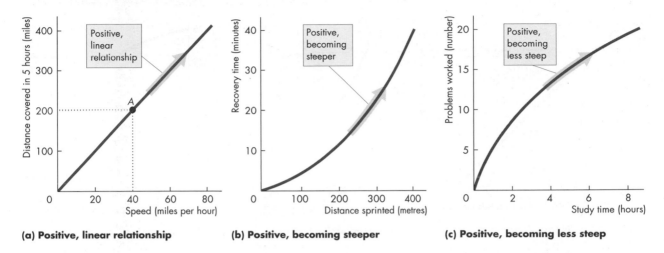

(a) Positive, linear relationship   **(b) Positive, becoming steeper**   **(c) Positive, becoming less steep**

Each part of this figure shows a positive (direct) relationship between two variables. That is, as the value of the variable measured on the *x*-axis increases, so does the value of the variable measured on the *y*-axis. Part (a) shows a linear relationship – as the two variables increase together, we move along a straight line.

Part (b) shows a positive relationship such that as the two variables increase together, we move along a curve that becomes steeper. Part (c) shows a positive relationship such that as the two variables increase together, we move along a curve that becomes less steep.

we will travel 200 miles in 5 hours if our speed is 40 miles an hour. If we double our speed to 80 miles an hour, we will travel 400 miles in 5 hours.

Figure A1.5(b) shows the relationship between distance sprinted and recovery time (the time it takes the heart rate to return to its normal resting rate). This relationship is an upward-sloping one that starts out quite flat but then becomes steeper as we move along the curve away from the origin. The reason this curve slopes upward and becomes steeper is because the additional recovery time needed from sprinting an additional 100 metres increases. It takes less than 5 minutes to recover from the first 100 metres but more than 10 minutes to recover from the third 100 metres.

Figure A1.5(c) shows the relationship between the number of problems worked by a student and the amount of study time. This relationship is an upward-sloping one that starts out quite steep and becomes flatter as we move away from the origin. Study time becomes less productive as you increase the hours spent studying and become more tired.

Variables That Move in Opposite Directions

A relationship between variables that move in opposite directions is called a **negative relationship** or an **inverse relationship**. Figure A1.6 shows some examples. Figure A1.6(a) shows the relationship between the number of hours available for playing squash and for playing tennis when the total is 5 hours. One extra hour spent playing tennis means one hour less playing squash and vice versa. This relationship is negative and linear.

Figure A1.6(b) shows the relationship between the cost per mile travelled and the length of a journey. The longer the journey, the lower is the cost per mile. But as the journey length increases, the cost per mile decreases, and the fall in the cost is smaller, the longer the journey. This feature of the relationship is shown by the fact that the curve slopes downward, starting out steep at a short journey length and then becoming flatter as the journey length increases. This relationship arises because some of the costs are fixed.

Figure A1.6

Negative (Inverse) Relationships

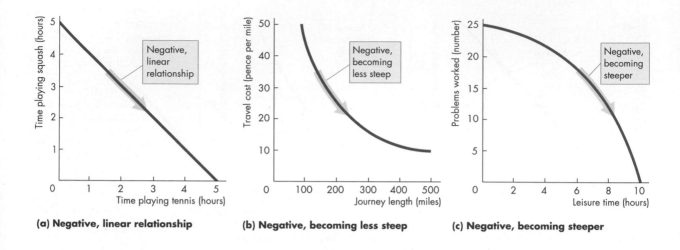

(a) Negative, linear relationship   **(b) Negative, becoming less steep**   **(c) Negative, becoming steeper**

Each part of this figure shows a negative (inverse) relationship between two variables. That is, as the value of the variable measured on the *x*-axis increases and the value of the variable measured on the *y*-axis decreases. Part (a) shows a linear relationship. The total time spent playing tennis and squash is 5 hours. As the time spent playing tennis increases, the time spent playing squash decreases and we move along a straight line. Part (b) shows a negative relationship such that as the journey length increases, the curve becomes less steep. Part (c) shows a negative relationship such that as leisure time increases, the curve becomes steeper.

Figure A1.6(c) shows the relationship between the amount of leisure time and the number of problems worked by a student. Increasing leisure time produces an increasingly large reduction in the number of problems worked. This relationship is a negative one that starts out with a gentle slope at a small number of leisure hours and becomes steeper as the number of leisure hours increases. This relationship is a different view of the idea shown in Figure A1.5(c).

Variables That Have a Maximum or a Minimum

Many relationships in economic models have a maximum or a minimum. For example, firms try to make the largest possible profit and to produce at the lowest possible cost. Figure A1.7 shows relationships that have a maximum or a minimum.

Figure A1.7(a) shows the relationship between rainfall and wheat yield. When there is no rainfall, wheat will not grow, so the yield is zero. As the rainfall increases up to 10 days a month, the wheat yield increases. With 10 rainy days each month, the wheat yield reaches its maximum at 40 tonnes per hectare (point *A*). Rain in excess of 10 days a month starts to lower the yield of wheat. If every day is rainy, the wheat suffers from a lack of sunshine and the yield decreases to zero. This relationship is one that starts out sloping upward, reaches a maximum, and then slopes downward.

Figure A1.7(b) shows the reverse case – a relationship that begins sloping downward, falls to a minimum, and then slopes upward. Most economic costs are like this relationship. An example is the relationship between the travel cost per mile and speed for a car trip. At low speeds, the car is creeping in a traffic snarl-up. The number of miles per gallon is low, so the cost per mile is high. At high speeds, the car is travelling faster than its efficient speed, using a large quantity of petrol, and again the number of miles per gallon is low and the cost per mile is high. At a speed of 55 miles an hour, the cost per mile is at its minimum (point *B*). This relationship is one that starts out sloping downward, reaches a minimum, and then slopes upward.

Figure A1.7

Maximum and Minimum Points

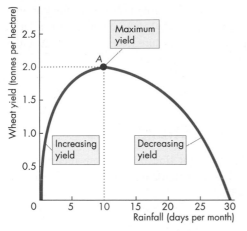

(a) Relationship with a maximum

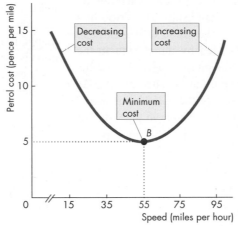

(b) Relationship with a minimum

Part (a) shows a relationship that has a maximum point, *A*. The curve slopes upward as it rises to its maximum point, is flat at its maximum, and then slopes downward. Part (b) shows a relationship with a minimum point, *B*. The curve slopes downward as it falls to its minimum, is flat at its minimum, and then slopes upward.

Variables That Are Unrelated

There are many situations in which no matter what happens to the value of one variable, the other variable remains constant. Sometimes we want to show the independence between two variables in a graph, and Figure A1.8 shows two ways of achieving this.

In describing the graphs in Figures A1.5 to Figure A1.7, we have talked about curves that slope upward or slope downward and curves that become steeper and less steep. Let's spend a little time discussing exactly what we mean by slope and how we measure the slope of a curve.

Figure A1.8

Variables That Are Unrelated

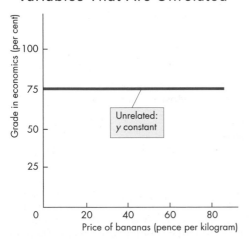

(a) Unrelated: *y* constant

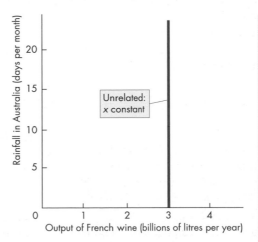

(b) Unrelated: *x* constant

This figure shows how we can graph two variables that are unrelated. In part (a), a student's grade in economics is plotted at 75 per cent on the *y*-axis regardless of the price of bananas on the *x*-axis. The curve is horizontal. In part (b), the output of the vineyards of France on the *x*-axis does not vary with the rainfall in Australia on the *y*-axis. The curve is vertical.

The Slope of a Relationship

We can measure the influence of one variable on another by the slope of the relationship. The **slope** of a relationship is the change in the value of the variable measured on the y-axis divided by the change in the value of the variable measured on the x-axis. We use the Greek letter Δ (*delta*) to represent "change in." So Δy means the change in the value of the variable measured on the y-axis, and Δx means the change in the value of the variable measured on the x-axis. The slope of the relationship is:

$$\frac{\Delta y}{\Delta x}$$

If a large change in the variable measured on the y-axis (Δy) is associated with a small change in the variable measured on the x-axis (Δx), the slope is large and the curve is steep. If a small change in the variable measured on the y-axis (Δy) is associated with a large change in the variable measured on the x-axis (Δx), the slope is small and the curve is flat.

We can make the idea of slope sharper by doing some calculations.

The Slope of a Straight Line

The slope of a straight line is the same regardless of where on the line you calculate it. The slope of a straight line is constant.

Figure A1.9

The Slope of a Straight Line

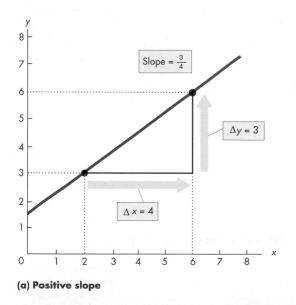

(a) Positive slope

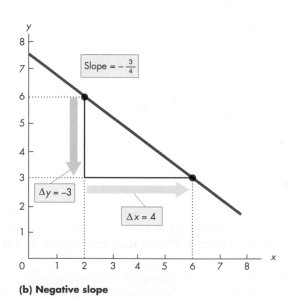

(b) Negative slope

To calculate the slope of a straight line, we divide the change in the value of the variable measured on the y-axis (Δy) by the change in the value of the variable measured on the x-axis (Δx), as we move along the curve. Part (a) shows the calculation of a positive slope. When x increases from 2 to 6, Δx equals 4. That change in x brings about an increase in y from 3 to 6, so Δy equals 3. The slope ($\Delta y/\Delta x$) equals 3/4. Part (b) shows the calculation of a negative slope. When x increases from 2 to 6, Δx equals 4. That increase in x brings about a decrease in y from 6 to 3, so Δy equals –3. The slope ($\Delta y/\Delta x$) equals –3/4.

Let's calculate the slopes of the lines in Figure A1.9. In part (a), when x increases from 2 to 6, y increases from 3 to 6. The change in x is +4: that is, Δx is 4. The change in y is +3: that is, Δy is 3. The slope of that line is:

$$\frac{\Delta y}{\Delta x} = \frac{3}{4}$$

In part (b), when x increases from 2 to 6, y decreases from 6 to 3. The change in y is *minus* 3: that is, Δy is –3. The change in x is *plus* 4: that is, Δx is 4. The slope of the curve is:

$$\frac{\Delta y}{\Delta x} = \frac{-3}{4}$$

Notice that the two slopes have the same magnitude (3/4), but the slope of the line in part (a) is positive (3/4), while the slope in part (b) is negative (–3/4). The slope of a positive relationship is positive; the slope of a negative relationship is negative.

The Slope of a Curved Line

The slope of a curved line is trickier. The slope of a curved line is not constant. Its slope depends on where on the line we calculate it. There are two ways to calculate the slope of a curved line: You can calculate the slope at a point, or you can calculate the slope across an arc of the curve. Let's look at the two alternatives.

Slope at a Point

To calculate the slope at a point on a curve, you need to construct a straight line that has the same slope as the curve at the point in question. Figure A1.10 shows how this is done. Suppose you want to calculate the slope of the curve at point A. Place a ruler on the graph so that it touches point A and no other point on the curve, then draw a straight line along the edge of the ruler. The straight red line is this line, and it is the *tangent* to the curve at point A. If the ruler touches the curve only at point A, then the slope of the curve at point A must be the same as the slope of the edge of the ruler. If the curve and the ruler do not have the same slope, the line along the edge of the ruler will cut the curve instead of just touching it.

Now that you have found a straight line with the same slope as the curve at point A, you can calculate the slope of the curve at point A by calculating the slope of the straight line. Along the straight line, as x increases from

Figure A1.10

Slope at a Point

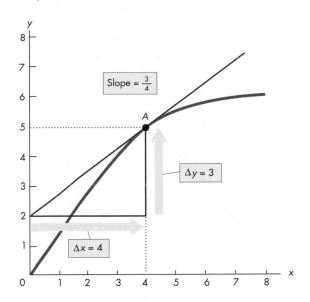

To calculate the slope of the curve at point A, draw the red line that just touches the curve at A – the tangent. The slope of this straight line is calculated by dividing the change in y by the change in x along the line. When x increases from 0 to 4, Δx equals 4. That change in x is associated with an increase in y from 2 to 5, so Δy equals 3. The slope of the red line is 3/4. So the slope of the curve at point A is 3/4.

0 to 4 ($\Delta x = 4$) y increases from 2 to 5 ($\Delta y = 3$). The slope of the line is:

$$\frac{\Delta y}{\Delta x} = \frac{3}{4}$$

So the slope of the curve at point A is 3/4.

Slope Across an Arc

An arc of a curve is a piece of a curve. In Figure A1.11, you are looking at the same curve as in Figure A1.10. But instead of calculating the slope at point A, we are going to calculate the slope across the arc from B to C. You can see that the slope is greater at B than at C. When we calculate the slope across an arc, we are calculating the average slope between two points. As we move along the arc from B to C, x increases from 3 to 5 and y increases from 4 to 5.5. The change in x is 2 ($\Delta x = 2$), and the change in y is 1.5 ($\Delta y = 1.5$).

Figure A1.11

Slope Across an Arc

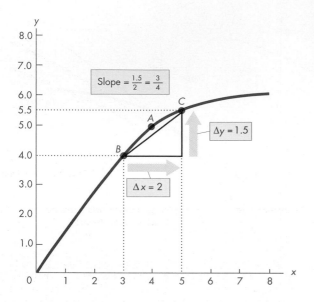

To calculate the average slope of the curve along the arc *BC*, draw a straight line from point *B* to point *C*. The slope of the line *BC* is calculated by dividing the change in *y* by the change in *x*. In moving from *B* to *C*, Δ*x* equals 2 and Δ*y* equals 1.5. The slope of the line *BC* is 1.5 divided by 2, or 3/4. So the slope of the curve across the arc *BC* is 3/4.

The slope of the line is:

$$\frac{\Delta y}{\Delta x} = \frac{1.5}{2} = \frac{3}{4}$$

So the slope of the curve across the arc *BC* is 3/4.

This calculation gives us the slope of the curve between points *B* and *C*. The actual slope calculated is the slope of the straight line from *B* to *C*. This slope approximates the average slope of the curve along the arc *BC*. In this particular example, the slope across the arc *BC* is identical to the slope of the curve at point *A*. But the calculation of the slope of a curve does not always work out so neatly. You might have some fun constructing some more examples and some counter examples.

You now know how to make and interpret a graph. But so far, we've limited our attention to graphs of two variables. We're now going to learn how to graph more than two variables.

Graphing Relationships Among More Than Two Variables

We have seen that we can graph the relationship between two variables as a point formed by the *x*- and *y*-coordinates in a two-dimensional graph. You may be thinking that although a two-dimensional graph is informative, most of the things in which you are likely to be interested involve relationships among many variables, not just two. For example, the amount of ice cream consumed depends on the price of ice cream and the temperature. If ice cream is expensive and the temperature is low, people eat a lot less ice cream than when ice cream is inexpensive and the temperature is high. For any given price of ice cream, the quantity consumed varies with the temperature; and for any given temperature, the quantity of ice cream consumed varies with its price.

Figure A1.12 shows a relationship among three variables. The table shows the number of litres of ice cream consumed each day at various temperatures and ice cream prices. How can we graph these numbers?

To graph a relationship that involves more than two variables, we use the *ceteris paribus* assumption.

Ceteris Paribus

We noted in the chapter (see p. 15) that every laboratory experiment is an attempt to create *ceteris paribus* and isolate the relationship of interest. We use the same method to make a graph when more than two variables are involved.

Figure A1.12(a) shows an example. There, you can see what happens to the quantity of ice cream consumed as the price of ice cream varies when the temperature is held constant. The line labelled 20°C shows the relationship between ice cream consumption and the price of ice cream if the temperature remains at 20°C. The numbers used to plot that line are those in the third column of the table in Figure A1.12. For example, if the temperature is 20°C, 10 litres are consumed when the price is 30 pence a scoop and 52 litres are consumed when the price is 10 pence a scoop. The curve labelled 25°C shows consumption as the price varies if the temperature remains at 25°C.

We can also show the relationship between ice cream consumption and temperature when the price of ice cream remains constant, as shown in Figure A1.12(b). The curve labelled 30 pence shows how the consumption of ice cream varies with the temperature

Figure A1.12

Graphing a Relationship Among Three Variables

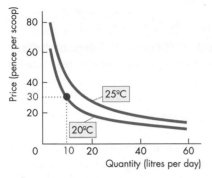

(a) Price and consumption at a given temperature

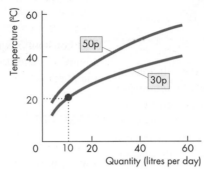

(b) Temperature and consumption at a given price

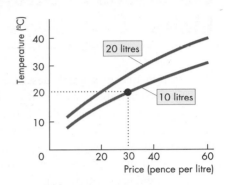

(c) Temperature and price at a given consumption

Price (pence per scoop)	Ice cream consumption (litres per day)			
	5°C	10°C	20°C	25°C
10	2	10	52	91
20	1	3	18	32
30	0	2	**10**	17
40	0	1	6	10
50	0	1	5	8
60	0	1	4	6

The quantity of ice cream consumed depends on its price and the temperature. The table gives some hypothetical numbers that tell us how many litres of ice cream are consumed each day at different prices and different temperatures. For example, if the price is 30 pence a scoop and the temperature is 20°C, 10 litres of ice cream are consumed. This set of values is highlighted in the table and each part of the figure.

To graph a relationship among three variables, the value of one variable is held constant. Part (a) shows the relationship between price and consumption when temperature is held constant. One curve holds temperature at 20°C and the other at 25°C. Part (b) shows the relationship between temperature and consumption when price is held constant. One curve holds the price at 30 pence a scoop and the other at 50 pence a scoop. Part (c) shows the relationship between temperature and price when consumption is held constant. One curve holds consumption at 10 litres and the other at 20 litres.

when ice cream costs 30 pence a scoop. On that curve, 10 litres are consumed when the temperature is 20°C. A second curve shows the relationship when ice cream costs 50 pence a scoop.

Figure A1.12(c) shows the combinations of temperature and price that result in a constant consumption of ice cream. One curve shows the combination that results in 10 litres a day being consumed, and the other shows the combination that result in 20 litres a day being consumed. A high price and a high temperature lead to the same consumption as a lower price and a lower temperature. For example, 10 litres of ice cream are consumed at 20°C and 30 pence a scoop, at 25°C and 40 pence a scoop, and at 10°C and 10 pence a scoop.

You can think of the curve in the graph as shifting when one of the factors on which its position depends changes. A change in temperature shifts the curve in part (a); a change in price shifts the curve in part (b); and a change in the quantity consumed shifts the curve in part (c). You will encounter graphs like the ones in Figure A1.15 at several points in your study of economics.

With what you have learned about graphs, you can move forward with your study of economics. There are no graphs in this book that are more complicated than those that have been explained in this appendix. Use this appendix as a refresher if you find that you're having difficulty interpreting or making a graph.

Mathematical Note
Equations to Straight Lines

If a straight line in a graph describes the relationship between two variables, we call it a *linear relationship*. Figure 1 shows the linear relationship between Cathy's expenditure and income. Cathy spends £100 a week (by borrowing or spending her past savings) when income is zero. And out of each pound earned, Cathy spends 50 pence (and saves 50 pence).

All linear relationships are described by the same general equation. We call the quantity that is measured on the horizontal (or *x*-axis) *x* and we call the quantity that is measured on the vertical (or *y*-axis) *y*. In the case of Figure 1, *x* is income and *y* is expenditure.

A Linear Equation

The equation that describes a linear relationship between *x* and *y* is:

$$y = a + bx$$

In this equation, *a* and *b* are fixed numbers and they are called constants. The values of *x* and *y* vary so these numbers are called variables. Because the equation describes a straight line, it is called a *linear equation*.

The equation tells us that when the value of *x* is zero, the value of *y* is *a*. We call the constant *a* the *y-axis*

intercept. The reason is that on the graph the straight line hits the *y*-axis at a value equal to *a*.

The constant *b* tells us by how much *y* changes (Δy) as *x* changes (Δx). That is:

$$\Delta y = b\Delta x$$

The constant *b* equals $\Delta y/\Delta x$ and is the slope of the line. Figure 1 illustrates the *y*-axis intercept and the slope of the line.

Positive Relationships

Figure 1 shows a positive relationship – the two variables *x* and *y* move in the same direction. All positive relationships have a slope that is positive. In the equation to the line, the constant *b* is positive. In this example, the *y*-axis intercept, *a*, is 100. The slope *b* equals $\Delta y/\Delta x$, which is 100/200 or 0.5. The equation to the line is:

$$y = 100 + 0.5x$$

Negative Relationships

Figure 2 shows a negative relationship – the variables *x* and *y* move in the opposite direction. All negative relationships have a slope that is negative. In the equation to the line, the constant *b* is negative. In the example in Figure 2, the *y*-axis intercept, *a*, is 30. The slope, *b*, equals $\Delta y/\Delta x$, which is –20/2 or –10. The equation to the line is:

$$y = 30 + (-10)x$$

or

$$y = 30 - 10x$$

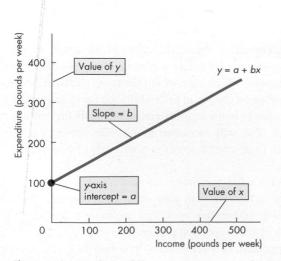

Figure 1 Linear relationship

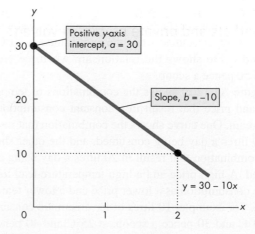

Figure 2 Negative relationship

Chapter 2

The Economic Problem

After studying this chapter you will be able to:

◆ Define the production possibilities frontier and calculate opportunity cost

◆ Distinguish between production possibilities and preferences and describe an efficient allocation of resources

◆ Explain how current production choices expand future production possibilities

◆ Explain how specialization and trade expand our production possibilities

◆ Describe alternative methods for coordinating choices and allocating resources

Good, Better, Best

What places limits on our ability to produce the things we want? How can we expand our capacity to produce? How do we benefit by trading with others? Does everyone gain in a market exchange, or does only the seller gain? Why have markets and private property evolved?

Production Possibilities and Opportunity Cost

Every working day, in mines and factories, shops and offices, on farms and construction sites, 150 million European workers produce a vast variety of goods and services valued at €50 billion. But the quantities of goods and services that we can produce are limited by both our available resources and by technology. And if we want to increase our production of one good, we must decrease our production of something else – we face trade-offs.

You are going to learn about the production possibilities frontier, which describes the limit to what we can produce and provides a neat way of thinking about and illustrating the idea of a trade-off.

The **production possibilities frontier** (*PPF*) is the boundary between those combinations of goods and services that can be produced and those that cannot. To illustrate the *PPF*, we focus on two goods at a time and hold the quantities produced of all the other goods and services constant. That is, we look at a *model* economy in which everything remains the same (*ceteris paribus*) except for the production of the two goods we are considering.

Let's look at the production possibilities frontier for CDs and pizza, which stand for *any* pair of goods or services.

Production Possibilities Frontier

The *production possibilities frontier* for CDs and pizza shows the limits to the production of these two goods, given the total resources available to produce them. Figure 2.1 shows this production possibilities frontier. The table lists some combinations of the quantities of pizzas and CDs that can be produced in a month given the resources available. The figure graphs these combinations. The *x*-axis shows the quantity of pizzas produced, and the *y*-axis shows the quantity of CDs produced.

The *PPF* illustrates *scarcity* because we cannot attain the points outside the frontier. They are points that describe wants that can't be satisfied. We can produce at all the points *inside* the *PPF* and *on* the *PPF*. They are attainable points. Suppose that in a typical month, we produce 4 million pizzas and 5 million CDs. Figure 2.1 shows this combination as point *E* and as possibility *E* in the table. The figure also shows other production possibilities.

Figure 2.1

The Production Possibilities Frontier

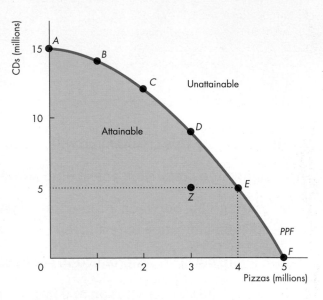

Possibility	Pizzas (millions)		CDs (millions)
A	0	and	15
B	1	and	14
C	2	and	12
D	3	and	9
E	4	and	5
F	5	and	0

The table lists six points on the production possibilities frontier for CDs and pizza. Row *A* tells us that if we produce no pizza, the maximum quantity of CDs we can produce is 15 million. Points *A*, *B*, *C*, *D*, *E* and *F* in the figure represent the rows of the table. The line passing through these points is the production possibilities frontier (*PPF*).

The *PPF* separates the attainable from the unattainable. Production is possible at any point *inside* the orange area or *on* the frontier. Points outside the frontier are unattainable. Points inside the frontier such as point *Z* are inefficient because resources are either wasted or misallocated. At such points, it is possible to use the available resources to produce more of either or both goods.

For example, we might stop producing pizza and move all the people who produce it into producing CDs. Point *A* in the figure and possibility *A* in the table show this case. The quantity of CDs produced increases to 15 million, and pizza production dries up. Alternatively, we might close the CD factories and switch all the resources into producing pizza. In this situation, we produce 5 million pizzas. Point *F* in the figure and possibility *F* in the table show this case.

Production Efficiency

We achieve **production efficiency** if we cannot produce more of one good without producing less of some other good. When production is efficient, we are at a point *on* the *PPF*. If we are at a point *inside* the *PPF*, such as point *Z*, production is *inefficient* because we have some *unused* resources or we have some *misallocated* resources or both.

Resources are unused when they are idle but could be working. For example, we might leave some of the factories idle or some workers unemployed.

Resources are *misallocated* when they are assigned to tasks for which they are not the best match. For example, we might assign skilled pizza makers to work in a CD factory and skilled CD makers to work in a pizza shop. We could get more pizza *and* more CDs from these same workers if we reassigned them to the tasks that more closely match their skills.

If we produce at a point inside the *PPF* such as *Z*, we can use our resources more efficiently to produce more pizzas, more CDs, or more of *both* pizzas and CDs. But if we produce at a point *on* the *PPF*, we are using our resources efficiently and we can produce more of one good only if we produce less of the other. That is, along the *PPF*, we face a *trade-off*.

Trade-off Along the *PPF*

Every choice *along* the *PPF* involves a *trade-off* – we must give up something to get something else. On the *PPF* in Figure 2.1, we must give up some CDs to get more pizza or give up some pizza to get more CDs.

Trade-offs arise in every imaginable real-world situation, and you reviewed several of them in Chapter 1. At any given point in time, we have a fixed amount of labour, land, capital, and entrepreneurship. By using our available technologies, we can employ these resources to produce goods and services. But we are limited in what we can produce. This limit defines a boundary between what we can attain and what we cannot attain.

This boundary is the real-world's production possibilities frontier, and it defines the trade-offs that we must make. On our real-world *PPF*, we can produce more of any one good or service only if we produce less of some other goods or services.

When doctors say that we must spend more on AIDS and cancer research, they are suggesting a trade-off: more medical research for less of some other things. When Tony Blair says that he wants to spend more on education and healthcare, he is suggesting a trade-off: more education and healthcare for less defence expenditure or less private spending (because of higher taxes). When an environmental group argues for less logging in tropical rainforests, it is suggesting a trade-off: greater conservation of endangered wildlife for less hardwood. When your parents say that you should study more, they are suggesting a trade-off: more study time for less leisure or sleep.

All trade-offs involve a cost – an opportunity cost.

Opportunity Cost

The *opportunity cost* of an action is the highest-valued alternative forgone. The *PPF* helps us to make the concept of opportunity cost precise and enables us to calculate it. Along the *PPF*, there are only two goods, so there is only one alternative forgone: some quantity of the other good. Given our current resources and technology, we can produce more pizzas only if we produce fewer CDs. The opportunity cost of producing an additional pizza is the number of CDs we *must* forgo. Similarly, the opportunity cost of producing an additional CD is the quantity of pizzas we *must* forgo.

For example, at point *C* in Figure 2.1, we produce fewer pizzas and more CDs than at point *D*. If we choose point *D* over point *C*, the additional 1 million pizzas *cost* 3 million CDs. One pizza costs 3 CDs.

We can also work out the opportunity cost of choosing point *C* over point *D* in Figure 2.1. If we move from point *D* to point *C*, the quantity of CDs produced increases by 3 million and the quantity of pizzas produced decreases by 1 million. So if we choose point *C* over point *D*, the additional 3 million CDs *cost* 1 million pizzas. So 1 CD costs 1/3 of a pizza.

Opportunity Cost is a Ratio

Opportunity cost is a ratio. It is the decrease in the quantity produced of one good divided by the increase in the quantity produced of another good as we move along the production possibilities frontier.

Because opportunity cost is a ratio, the opportunity cost of producing an additional CD is equal to the *inverse* of the opportunity cost of producing an additional pizza. Check this proposition by returning to the calculations we've just worked through. When we move along the *PPF* from C to D, the opportunity cost of a pizza is 3 CDs. The inverse of 3 is 1/3, so if we decrease the production of pizza and increase the production of CDs by moving from D to C, the opportunity cost of a CD must be 1/3 of a pizza. You can check that this number is correct. If we move from D to C, we produce 3 million more CDs and 1 million fewer pizzas. Because 3 million CDs cost 1 million pizzas, the opportunity cost of 1 CD is 1/3 of a pizza.

Increasing Opportunity Cost

The opportunity cost of a pizza increases as the quantity of pizzas produced increases. Also, the opportunity cost of a CD increases as the quantity of CDs produced increases. This phenomenon of increasing opportunity cost is reflected in the shape of the *PPF* – it is bowed outward.

When a large quantity of CDs and a small quantity of pizzas are produced – between points A and B in Figure 2.1 – the frontier has a gentle slope. A given increase in the quantity of pizzas *costs* a small decrease in the quantity of CDs, so the opportunity cost of a pizza is a small quantity of CDs.

When a large quantity of pizzas and a small quantity of CDs are produced – between points E and F in Figure 2.1 – the frontier is steep. A given increase in the quantity of pizzas *costs* a large decrease in the quantity of CDs, so the opportunity cost of a pizza is a large quantity of CDs.

The *PPF* is bowed outward because resources are not all equally productive in all activities. People with several years of experience working for Philips are good at producing CDs but not very good at making pizzas. So if we move some of these people from Philips to Domino's, we get a small increase in the quantity of pizzas but a large decrease in the quantity of CDs. Similarly, people who have spent years working at Domino's are good at producing pizzas, but they have no idea how to produce CDs. So if we move some of these people from Domino's to Philips, we get a small increase in the quantity of CDs but a large decrease in the quantity of pizzas. The more of either good we try to produce, the less productive are the additional resources we use to produce that good and the larger is the opportunity cost of a unit of that good.

Increasing Opportunity Costs are Everywhere

Just about every activity that you can think of is one with an increasing opportunity cost. We allocate the most skilful farmers and the most fertile land to the production of food. And we allocate the best doctors and the least fertile land to the production of healthcare services. If we shift fertile land and tractors away from farming to hospitals and ambulances and ask farmers to become hospital porters, the production of food drops drastically and the increase in the production of healthcare services is small. The opportunity cost of a unit of healthcare services rises. Similarly, if we shift our resources away from healthcare towards farming, we must use more doctors and nurses as farmers and more hospitals as hydroponic tomato factories. The decrease in the production of health-care services is large, but the increase in food production is small. The opportunity cost of a unit of food rises. This example is extreme and unlikely, but these same considerations apply to most pairs of goods.

There may be some rare situations in which opportunity cost is constant. Switching resources from bottling ketchup to bottling mayonnaise is a possible example. But in general, when resources are reallocated, they must be assigned to tasks for which they are an increasingly poor match. Increasing opportunity costs are a general fact of life.

Review Quiz

1 How does the production possibilities frontier illustrate scarcity?
2 How does the production possibilities frontier illustrate production efficiency?
3 How does the production possibilities frontier show that every choice involves a trade-off?
4 How does the production possibilities frontier illustrate opportunity cost?
5 Why is opportunity cost a ratio?
6 Why does the PPF for most goods bow outward, so that opportunity cost of a good increases as the quantity produced increases?

We've seen that what we can produce is limited by the production possibilities frontier. We've also seen that production on the *PPF* is efficient. But we can produce many different quantities on the *PPF*. How do we choose among them? How do we know which point on the *PPF* is the best one?

Using Resources Efficiently

You've seen that points inside the *PPF* waste resources or leave them unused and are inefficient. You've also seen that points *on* the *PPF* are efficient – we can't produce more of one good unless we forgo some units of another good. But there are many such points on the *PPF*. Each point on the *PPF* achieves production efficiency. What quantities of CDs and pizzas best serve the social interest?

This question is an example of real-world questions of enormous consequence such as: How much should we spend on treating AIDS and how much on cancer research? Should we expand education and healthcare programmes or cut taxes? Should we spend more on the preservation of rainforests and the conservation of endangered wildlife?

To answer these questions, we must find a way of measuring and comparing costs and benefits.

The *PPF* and Marginal Cost

The limits to production, which are summarized by the *PPF*, determine the marginal cost of each good or service. **Marginal cost** is the opportunity cost of producing *one more unit*. We can calculate marginal cost in a way that is similar to the way we calculate opportunity cost. *Marginal cost* is the opportunity cost of *one* additional pizza – the quantity of CDs that *must* be given up to get one more pizza – as we move along the *PPF*.

Figure 2.2 illustrates the marginal cost of pizza. If pizza production increases from zero to 1 million – a move from *A* to *B* – the quantity of CDs decreases from 15 million to 14 million. So the opportunity cost of a pizza is 1 CD.

If pizza production increases from 1 million to 2 million – a move from *B* to *C* – the quantity of CDs decreases by 2 million. So the opportunity cost of a pizza is 2 CDs.

You can repeat this calculation for an increase in pizza production from 2 million to 3 million, from 3 million to 4 million, and finally from 4 million to 5 million. Figure 2.2 shows the opportunity costs as a series of steps. Each additional pizza costs more CDs than the preceding pizza.

We've just calculated the opportunity cost of a pizza and generated the steps in Figure 2.2(a). The opportunity cost of a pizza is also the *marginal cost* of producing a pizza. In Figure 2.2(b), the line labelled *MC* shows the marginal cost.

Figure 2.2

The *PPF* and Marginal Cost

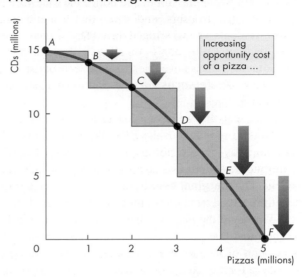

(a) *PPF* and opportunity cost

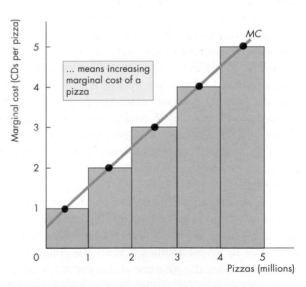

(b) Marginal cost

Opportunity cost is measured along the *PPF* in part (a). If the production of pizzas increases from zero to 1 million, the opportunity cost of a pizza is 1 CD. If the production of pizza increases from 1 million to 2 million, the opportunity cost of a pizza is 2 CDs. The opportunity cost of a pizza increases as the production of pizza increases. Part (b) shows the marginal cost of a pizza as the *MC* curve.

Preferences and Marginal Benefit

Look around your classroom and notice the wide variety of shirts, caps, trousers, and shoes that you and your fellow students are wearing today. Why is there such a huge variety? Why don't you all wear the same styles and colours? The answer lies in what economists call preferences. **Preferences** are a description of a person's likes and dislikes.

You've seen that we have a concrete way of describing the limits to production: the *PPF*. We need a similarly concrete way of describing preferences. To describe preferences, economists use the concept of marginal benefit. The **marginal benefit** of a good or service is the benefit received from consuming one more unit of it.

We measure the marginal benefit of a good or service by the most that people are *willing to pay* for an additional unit of it. The idea is that you are not willing to pay more for a good than it is worth to you. But you are willing to pay an amount up to what it is worth. So the willingness to pay for something measures its marginal benefit.

Economists use the marginal benefit curve to illustrate preferences. The **marginal benefit curve** shows the relationship between the marginal benefit of a good and the quantity of that good consumed. It is a general principle that the more we have of any good or service, the smaller is its marginal benefit and the less we are willing to pay for an additional unit of it. This tendency is so widespread and strong that we call it a principle – the *principle of decreasing marginal benefit*.

The basic reason why the marginal benefit of a good or service decreases as we consume more of it is that we like variety. The more we consume of any one good or service, the more we can see other things that we would like better.

Think about your willingness to pay for pizza (or any other item). If pizza is hard to come by and you can buy only a few slices a year, you might be willing to pay a high price to get an additional slice. But if pizza is all you've eaten for the past few days, you are willing to pay almost nothing for another slice.

In everyday life, we think of what we pay for goods and services as the money that we give up – pounds or euros. But you've learned to think about cost as other goods or services forgone, not a money cost. So you can think about willingness to pay in the same terms. The price you are willing to pay for something is the quantity of other goods and services that you are willing to forgo. Let's continue with the example of CDs and pizzas and illustrate preferences this way.

Figure 2.3

Preferences and the Marginal Benefit Curve

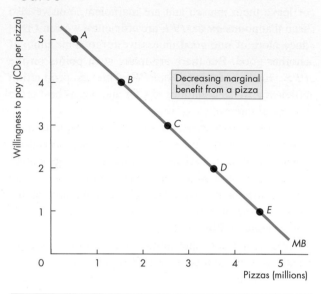

Possibility	Pizzas (millions)	Willingness to pay (CDs per pizza)
A	0.5	5
B	1.5	4
C	2.5	3
D	3.5	2
E	4.5	1

The smaller the quantity of pizzas produced, the more CDs people are willing to give up for an additional pizza. If pizza production is 0.5 million, people are willing to pay 5 CDs per pizza. But if pizza production is 4.5 milllion, people are willing to pay only 1 CD per pizza. Willingness to pay measures marginal benefit. And decreasing marginal benefit is a universal feature of people's preferences.

Figure 2.3 illustrates preferences as the willingness to pay for pizza in terms of CDs. In row *A*, pizza production is 0.5 million, and at that quantity, people are willing to pay 5 CDs per pizza. As the quantity of pizza produced increases, the amount that people are willing to pay for it falls. When pizza production is 4.5 million, people are willing to pay only 1 CD per pizza.

Let's now use the concepts of marginal cost and marginal benefit to describe the efficient quantity of pizzas to produce.

Efficient Use of Resources

When we cannot produce more of any one good without giving up some other good, we have achieved *production efficiency*, and we're producing at a point on the *PPF*. When we cannot produce more of any good without giving up some other good that we *value more highly*, we have achieved **allocative efficiency** and we are producing at the point on the *PPF* that we prefer above all other points.

Suppose in Figure 2.4, we produce 1.5 million pizzas. The marginal cost of a pizza is 2 CDs and the marginal benefit from a pizza is 4 CDs. Because someone values an additional pizza more highly than it costs to produce, we can get more value from our resources by moving some of them out of producing CDs and into producing pizzas.

Now suppose we produce 3.5 million pizzas. The marginal cost of a pizza is now 4 CDs, but the marginal benefit from a pizza is only 2 CDs. Because the additional pizza costs more to produce than anyone thinks it is worth, we can get more value from our resources by moving some of them away from producing pizzas and into producing CDs.

But suppose we produce 2.5 million pizzas. Marginal cost and marginal benefit are now equal at 3 CDs. This allocation of resources between pizzas and CDs is efficient. If more pizzas are produced, the forgone CDs are worth more than the additional pizzas.

If fewer pizzas are produced, the forgone pizzas are worth more than the additional CDs.

Review Quiz

1 What is marginal cost? How is it measured?
2 What is marginal benefit? How is it measured?
3 How does the marginal benefit from a good change as the quantity produced of that good increases?
4 What is production efficiency and how does it relate to the production possibilities frontier?
5 What is allocative efficiency and what conditions must be satisfied to achieve it?
6 Explain the distinction between production efficiency and allocative efficiency.

You now understand the limits to production and the conditions under which resources are used efficiently. Your next task is to study the expansion of production possibilities.

Figure 2.4

Efficient Use of Resources

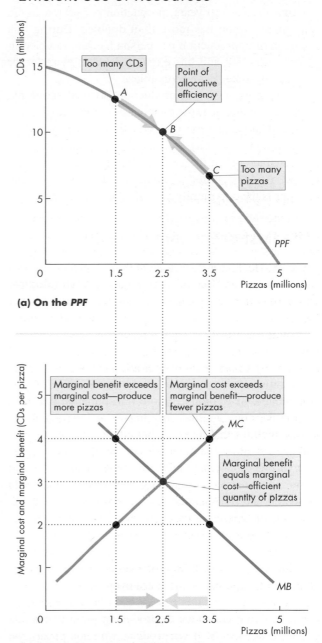

(a) On the PPF

(b) Marginal benefit equals marginal cost

The greater the quantity of pizzas produced, the smaller is the marginal benefit (*MB*) from pizza – the fewer CDs people are willing to give up to get an additional pizza. But the greater the quantity of pizzas produced, the greater is the marginal cost (*MC*) of pizza – the more CDs people must give up to get an additional pizza. When marginal benefit equals marginal cost, resources are being used efficiently.

Economic Growth

During the past 30 years, production per person in the European Union has more than doubled. During this same period, production per person has also doubled in North America and has expanded by an even larger amount in some Asian economies.

Such an expansion of production is called **economic growth**. Economic growth increases our *standard of living*. But the expansion of production possibilities does not overcome scarcity and avoid opportunity cost. We face a trade-off in the choices that make our economy grow. And the faster we make production grow, the greater is the opportunity cost of economic growth.

The Cost of Economic Growth

Two key factors influence economic growth: technological change and capital accumulation. **Technological change** is the development of new goods and of better ways of producing goods and services. **Capital accumulation** is the growth of capital resources, which includes *human capital*.

As a consequence of technological change and capital accumulation, we have an enormous quantity of cars that enable us to produce more transportation than was available when we had only horses and carriages; we have satellites that make global communications possible on a scale that is much larger than that produced by the earlier cable technology. But new technologies and new capital have an opportunity cost. To use resources in research and development and to produce new capital, we must decrease our production of consumption goods and services. Let's look at this opportunity cost.

Instead of studying the *PPF* of pizzas and CDs, we'll hold the quantity of CDs produced constant and examine the *PPF* for pizzas and pizza ovens.

Figure 2.5 shows this *PPF* as the blue curve *ABC*. If we devote no resources to producing pizza ovens, we produce at point *A*. If we produce 3 million pizzas, we can produce 6 pizza ovens at point *B*. If we produce no pizza, we can produce 10 ovens at point *C*.

The amount by which our production possibilities expand depends on the resources we devote to technological change and capital accumulation. If we devote no resources to this activity (point *A*), our *PPF* remains at *ABC* – the blue curve in Figure 2.5. If we cut the current production of pizza and produce 6 ovens (point *B*), then in the future, we'll have more capital and our *PPF* will rotate outward to the position shown by the red

Figure 2.5

Economic Growth

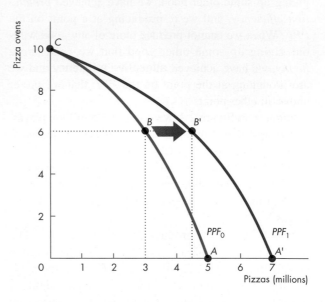

PPF_0 shows the limits to the production of pizza and pizza ovens, with the production of all other goods and services remaining the same. If we devote no resources to producing pizza ovens and produce 5 million pizzas, we remain at point *A*. But if we decrease pizza production to 3 million and produce 6 ovens, at point *B*, our production possibilities expand. After one period, the *PPF* rotates outward to PPF_1 and we can produce at point *B'*, a point outside the original *PPF*. We can rotate the *PPF* outward, but we cannot avoid opportunity cost. The opportunity cost of producing more pizzas in the future is fewer pizzas today.

curve. The fewer resources we devote to producing pizza and the more resources we devote to producing ovens, the greater is the expansion of our production possibilities.

Economic growth is not free. To make it happen, we devote resources to producing new ovens and less to producing pizza. In Figure 2.5, we move from *A* to *B*. There is no free lunch. The opportunity cost of more pizzas in the future is fewer pizzas today. Also, economic growth is no magic formula for abolishing scarcity. On the new production possibilities frontier, we continue to face a trade-off and opportunity cost.

The ideas about economic growth that we have explored in the setting of the pizza industry also apply to nations as you can see in the following box.

Box 2.1
Economic Growth in the European Union and Hong Kong

If a country devotes all its resources to producing consumption goods and none to research and capital accumulation, its production possibilities in the future will be the same as they are today. To expand our production possibilities in the future, we must devote fewer resources to producing consumption goods and some resources to accumulating capital and developing technologies so that we can produce more consumption goods in the future. The decrease in today's consumption is the opportunity cost of an increase in future consumption.

The experiences of the European Union and some East Asian economies such as Hong Kong make a striking example of the effects of our choices on the rate of economic growth. In 1970, the production possibilities per person in the European Union were much larger than those in Hong Kong. The member states of the European Union devoted one-fifth of their resources to accumulating capital and the other four-fifths to consumption. In 1970, the European Union was at point *A* on its *PPF* in Figure 1. Hong Kong devoted one-third of its resources to accumulating capital and two-thirds to consumption. In 1970, Hong Kong was at point *A* on its *PPF*.

Since 1970, both countries have experienced economic growth, but growth in Hong Kong has been more rapid than that in the European Union. Because Hong Kong devoted a bigger fraction of its resources to accumulating capital, its production possibilities have expanded more quickly.

By 2004, the production possibilities per person in Hong Kong had reached a similar level to those in the European Union. If Hong Kong continues to devote more resources to accumulating capital than we do (at point *B* on its 2004 *PPF*), it will continue to grow more rapidly. But if Hong Kong increases consumption and decreases capital accumulation (moving to

point *C* on its 2004 *PPF*), then its economic growth rate will slow.

The European Union is typical of the rich industrial countries, which include the United States, Canada and Japan. Hong Kong is typical of the fast-growing Asian economies, which include Taiwan, Thailand, South Korea and China. Growth in these countries slowed during the Asia crisis of 1998 but quickly rebounded. Production possibilities expand in these countries by between 5 and almost 10 per cent a year. If these high growth rates are maintained, these other Asian countries will eventually close the gap on the European Union as Hong Kong has done.

Figure 1

Economic Growth in the European Union and Hong Kong

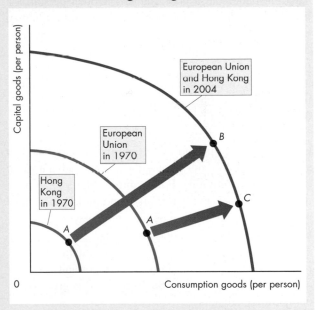

Review Quiz

1 What are the two key factors that generate economic growth?
2 How does economic growth influence the production possibilities frontier?
3 What is the opportunity cost of economic growth?
4 Why has Hong Kong experienced faster economic growth than the European Union has?

Next, we're going to study another way in which we expand our production possibilities – the amazing fact that *both* buyers and sellers gain from specialization and trade.

Gains from Trade

People can produce for themselves all the goods that that they consume, or they can concentrate on producing one good (or perhaps a few goods) and then trade with others – exchange some of their own goods for those of others. Concentrating on the production of only one good or a few goods is called *specialization*.

We are going to discover how people gain by specializing in the production of the good in which they have a *comparative advantage* and trading with each other.

Comparative Advantage

A person has a **comparative advantage** in an activity if that person can perform the activity at a lower opportunity cost than anyone else. Differences in opportunity costs arise from differences in individual abilities and from differences in the characteristics of other resources.

No one excels at everything. One person is an outstanding batter but a poor catcher; another person is a brilliant lawyer but a poor teacher. In almost all human endeavours, what one person does easily, someone else finds difficult. The same applies to land and capital. One plot of land is fertile but has no mineral deposits; another plot of land has outstanding views but is infertile. One machine has great precision but is difficult to operate; another is fast but often breaks down.

Although no one excels at everything, some people excel and can outperform others in many activities. But such a person does not have a *comparative* advantage in each of those activities. For example, Maria Sharapova is a faster runner and better all-round athlete than most people. But she is an even better tennis player. Her *comparative* advantage is in playing tennis.

Because people's abilities and the quality of their resources differ, they have different opportunity costs of producing various goods. Such differences give rise to comparative advantage.

Let's explore the idea of comparative advantage by looking at two CD factories: one operated by Ace and the other by Galaxy. You will see how two producers can exploit comparative advantage to increase their total output. With specialization and exchange, we can produce and consume far greater quantities of goods and services than we would if we tried to produce for ourselves everything that we consume.

Production Without Trade

To simplify the story quite a lot, suppose that CDs have just two components: a disc and a plastic case. Ace and Galaxy each have a production line for discs and a production line for cases and each firm produces all its own discs and cases. Total production from each factory is 3,000 CDs (6,000 CDs in total) an hour.

Table 2.1 shows the production possibilities for each factory. Let's look carefully at the numbers.

Ace's Factory

Ace produces 3,000 discs and 3,000 cases: its possibility *B* in Table 2.1. But Ace can produce different quantities. If Ace uses all its resources to make discs, it can produce 12,000 discs an hour – possibility *E*. And if it uses all its resources to make cases, it can produce 4,000 cases an hour – possibility *A*. To produce more cases, Ace must decrease its production of discs. For each case produced, it must decrease its production of discs by 3. So

Ace's opportunity cost of producing 1 case is 3 discs.

Similarly, if Ace wants to increase its production of discs, it must decrease it production of cases. And for each 3,000 discs produced, it must decrease its production of cases by 1,000. So

Ace's opportunity cost of producing 1 disc is 1/3 of a case.

Table 2.1

Production Possibilities in Two Factories

	Ace			Galaxy	
	Discs	Cases		Discs	Cases
Possibility	(thousands per hour)		Possibility	(thousands per hour)	
A	0	4	E'	0	12
B	3	3	D'	1	9
C	6	2	C'	2	6
D	9	1	B'	3	3
E	12	0	A'	4	0

Ace and Galaxy can produce discs and cases. The numbers show their production possibilities. If Ace produces possibility *B*, it can produce 3,000 cases and 3,000 discs an hour. If Galaxy produces possibility *B'*, it can produce 3,000 cases and 3,000 discs an hour.

Galaxy's Factory

Galaxy produces 3,000 discs and 3,000 cases: its possibility *B'* in Table 2.1. But Galaxy's factory has machines that are custom made for case production, so they are more suitable for producing cases than discs. And Galaxy's workers are more skilled in making cases.

These differences between the two factories mean that Galaxy's production possibilities are different from Ace's. If Galaxy uses all its resources to make discs, it can produce 4,000 an hour – possibility *A'*. If it uses all its resources to make cases, it can produce 12,000 an hour – possibility *E'*.

To produce more discs, Galaxy must decrease its production of cases. For each 1,000 additional discs produced, it must decrease its production of cases by 3,000. So

Galaxy's opportunity cost of producing 1 disc is 3 cases.

Similarly, if Galaxy wants to increase its production of cases, it must decrease its production of discs. For each 3,000 additional cases produced, it must decrease its production of discs by 1,000. So

Galaxy's opportunity cost of producing 1 case is 1/3 of a disc.

Differences in Opportunity Cost

Which of the two producers has a comparative advantage in producing discs and which in producing cases? Recall that comparative advantage arises from differences in opportunity cost. Which of the two producers has the lower opportunity cost of discs and which has the lower opportunity cost of cases?

You can see that Galaxy has a lower opportunity cost of producing cases. Galaxy's opportunity cost of a case is 1/3 of a disc, whereas Ace's is 3 discs. So Galaxy has a comparative advantage at producing cases.

You can also see that Ace has a lower opportunity cost of producing discs. Ace's opportunity cost of a disc is 1/3 of a case, whereas Galaxy's is 3 cases. So Ace has a comparative advantage at producing discs.

Because Galaxy has a comparative advantage in producing cases and Ace has a comparative advantage in producing discs, both Ace and Galaxy can gain from specialization and trade with each other.

Figure 2.6 shows Ace's and Galaxy's production possibilities frontiers and summarizes the above discussion.

Figure 2.6

Comparative Advantage

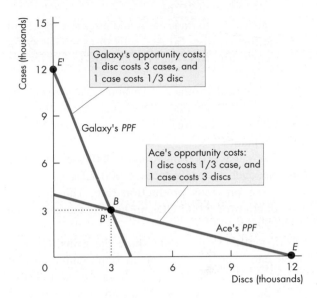

Along Ace's *PPF*, the opportunity cost of 1 disc is 1/3 of a case and the opportunity cost of 1 case is 3 discs. Along Galaxy's *PPF*, the opportunity cost of 1 disc is 3 cases. Ace and Galaxy produce 3,000 cases and 3,000 discs an hour. Galaxy's opportunity cost of cases is less than Ace's, so Galaxy has a comparative advantage in cases. Ace's opportunity cost of discs is less than Galaxy's, so Ace has a comparative advantage in discs.

Achieving the Gains from Trade

If Ace, which has a comparative advantage in producing discs, puts all its resources into that activity, it can produce 12,000 discs an hour – point *E* on its *PPF*. If Galaxy, which has a comparative advantage in producing cases, puts all its resources into that activity, it can produce 12,000 cases an hour – point *E'* on its *PPF*.

By specializing, Ace and Galaxy together can produce 12,000 cases and 12,000 discs an hour, double the total production they can achieve without specialization.

By specialization and trade, Ace and Galaxy can get *outside* their individual production possibilities frontiers. To achieve the gains from specialization, Ace and Galaxy must trade with each other.

Table 2.2 and Figure 2.7 show how Ace and Galaxy gain from trade. They make the following deal: Ace agrees to increase its production of discs from 3,000 an hour to 12,000 an hour – a move along its *PPF* from point *B* to point *E* in Figure 2.7(a). Galaxy agrees to increase its production of cases from 3,000 an hour to 12,000 an hour – a move along its *PPF* from point *B'* to point *E'* in Figure 2.7(b).

They also agree to trade cases and discs at a "price" of one case for one disc. So Ace sells discs to Galaxy for one case per disc, and Galaxy sells cases to Ace for one disc per case.

With this deal in place, Ace and Galaxy exchange along the red "Trade line". They exchange 6,000 cases and 6,000 discs, and Ace moves to point *F* and Galaxy moves to point *F'*.

Each now has 6,000 discs and 6,000 cases, or 6,000 CDs. So each now produces 6,000 CDs an hour – double the previous production rate. This increase in production of 6,000 CDs an hour is the gain from specialization and trade.

Both parties to the trade share the gains. Galaxy, which can produce discs at an opportunity cost of 3 cases per disc, can buy discs from Ace at a cost of 1 case per disc. Ace, which can produce cases at an opportunity cost of 3 discs per case, can buy cases from Galaxy at a cost of 1 disc per case.

Table 2.2

Achieving the Gains from Specialization

	Ace			Galaxy	
	Discs	Cases		Discs	Cases
Possibility	(thousands per hour)		Possibility	(thousands per hour)	
A	0	4	*E'*	0	12
B	3	3	*D'*	1	9
C	6	2	*C'*	2	6
D	9	1	*B'*	3	3
E	12	0	*A'*	4	0

Ace and Galaxy can produce discs and cases. The numbers in the table show their production possibilities. For Ace, the opportunity cost of 1 disc is 1/3 of a case and the opportunity cost of 1 case is 3 discs. If Ace produces on row *B*, it can produce 3,000 cases and 3,000 discs an hour. For Galaxy, the opportunity cost of 1 disc is 3 cases and the opportunity cost of 1 case is 1/3 of a disc. If Galaxy produces on row *B'*, it can produce 3,000 cases and 3,000 discs an hour.

Figure 2.7

The Gains from Trade

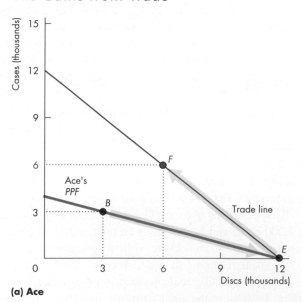

(a) Ace

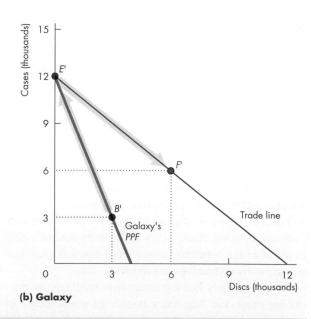

(b) Galaxy

Ace and Galaxy initially produce at points *B* and *B'* on their respective *PPF*s. Ace has a comparative advantage in discs, and Galaxy has a comparative advantage in cases. If Ace specializes in discs, it produces at point *E* on its *PPF*. If Galaxy specializes in cases, it produces at point *E'* on its *PPF*. They exchange cases for discs along the red "Trade line".

Galaxy buys discs from Ace for less than its opportunity cost of producing them, and Ace buys cases from Galaxy for less than its opportunity cost of producing them. Ace goes to point *F* and Galaxy goes to point *F'* – points outside their individual *PPF*s – where each produces 6,000 CDs an hour. Ace and Galaxy increase production with no change in resources.

For Galaxy, the cost of a disc falls from 3 cases to 1 case. So it gets its discs more cheaply than it can produce them itself. For Ace, the cost of a case falls from 3 discs to 1 disc. So it gets its cases more cheaply than it can produce them itself. Because both Ace and Galaxy obtain the items they buy from the other at a lower cost than that at which they can produce the items themselves, they both gain from specialization and trade.

Gains from Trade in the Global Economy

The gains that we achieve from international trade are also similar to those achieved by Ace and Galaxy. When Europeans buy T-shirts from China and when China buys Airbus airplanes, both the Chinese and Europeans gain. Europeans get shirts at a lower cost than that at which firms in Europe can produce them, and the Chinese get their planes at a lower cost than that at which Chinese firms can produce them.

Ace and Galaxy are equally productive. Ace can produce the same quantities of discs as Galaxy can produce cases. But this equal productivity is not the source of the gains from specialization and trade. The gains arise from *comparative* advantage and would be available even if one of the trading partners was much more productive than the other. To see that the gains arise from comparative advantage, let's look again at Ace and Galaxy but with Galaxy being much more productive than before.

Absolute Advantage

A person has an **absolute advantage** if that person can produce more goods with a given amount of resources than another person can. Absolute advantage arises from differences in productivity. A person who has better technology, more capital, or is more skilled than another person has an absolute advantage. Absolute advantage also applies to firms and to nations.

The gains from trade arise from *comparative* advantage, so people can gain from trade in the presence of *absolute* advantage. To see how, suppose that Galaxy invents and patents a new production process that makes it *four* times as productive as it was before in the production of both cases and discs. With its new technology, Galaxy can produce 48,000 cases an hour (4 times the original 12,000) if it puts all its resources into making

cases. Alternatively, it can produce 12,000 discs (4 times the original 3,000) if it puts all its resources into making discs. Galaxy now has an absolute advantage.

But Galaxy's *opportunity cost* of 1 disc is still 3 cases. And this opportunity cost is higher than Ace's. So Galaxy can still get discs at a lower cost by exchanging cases for discs with Ace.

In this example, Galaxy will no longer produce only cases – it will produce some discs as well. But Ace will fully specialize in producing discs.

The key point to recognize is that even though someone (or some nation) has an absolute advantage, this fact does not destroy comparative advantage.

Dynamic Comparative Advantage

At any given point in time, the resources and technologies available determine the comparative advantages that individuals and nations have. But just by repeatedly producing a particular good or service, people become more productive in that activity, a phenomenon called **learning-by-doing**. Learning-by-doing is the basis of *dynamic* comparative advantage.

Dynamic comparative advantage is a comparative advantage that a person (or a business or a country) possesses as a result of having specialized in a particular activity and, as a result of learning-by-doing, having become the producer with the lowest opportunity cost.

Hong Kong and Singapore are examples of countries that have pursued dynamic comparative advantage vigorously. They have developed industries such as biotechnology in which initially they did not have a comparative advantage but, through learning-by-doing, became low opportunity cost producers in those industries.

Review Quiz

1　What gives a person, a business or a country a comparative advantage?
2　Is production still efficient when people specialize?
3　Why do people specialize and trade?
4　What are the gains from specialization and trade?
5　What is the source of the gains from trade?
6　Distinguish between comparative advantage and absolute advantage.
7　How does dynamic comparative advantage arise?

Coordinating Choices and Allocating Resources

You've seen how people can gain by specializing at producing those goods and services in which they have a comparative advantage and trading with each other. But for 6 billion individuals to specialize and produce millions of different goods and services, choices must be coordinated. And the millions of goods and services that they produce must be allocated to the people who will use and consume them.

Many possible methods are available for coordinating choices and allocating resources and they can be placed into three broad groups:

◆ Commands
◆ Rules and conventions
◆ Markets

Commands

Commands or orders can coordinate choices and allocate resources. These commands might be backed up by force or some form of voluntary agreement such as the majority rule or an employment agreement.

When a command system is used to coordinate an entire economy and allocate almost all of the economy's resources, the economic system is a **planned economy**. Before the collapse of the Soviet Union in the early 1990s, Russia and several other Eastern European and Asian countries were planned economies. And before the 1980s, China was a planned economy. Today, only North Korea and Cuba are planned economies.

Experience with planned economies is generally unfavourable. Such an economy can work when there is a clear national objective such as winning a war. But in normal times, a planning system is too bureaucratic to do an efficient job.

Command systems play an important role in smaller organizations than entire nations. They are used in businesses or what economists call firms. A **firm** is an economic unit that employs factors of production and organizes them to produce and sell goods and services. Tesco and Virgin Atlantic are examples of firms.

A firm uses a command system when a manager gives an instruction to a worker and then monitors that worker's performance. Commands in firms coordinate a huge amount of economic activity. The mobile phone maker Nokia, for example, coordinates the production of the many components that go into a mobile phone and coordinates the marketing and distribution of its products.

But a firm can get too big. It can become too costly to keep track of all the information that a firm needs to coordinate its activities. For this reason, all firms specialize and trade with each other – like Ace and Galaxy do in the example you've just studied.

For example, Britain's largest retailer, Tesco, could produce all the things that it sells in its stores. And it could produce all the raw materials that are used to produce the things that it sells. But if Tesco did behave in this way, it would not remain Britain's largest retailer for very long. It would not be exploiting its comparative advantage and would be producing many items that it could buy at a lower cost from other firms.

Rules and Conventions

Rules and conventions are used to coordinate choices and allocate resources. Some examples are: winner takes all contests; first-come-first-served; equal shares for all; and women and children first.

For example, we use contests to get the best performance out of professional athletes, tennis players and golfers. And we use equal shares in allocating votes for publicly provided resources and in allocating access to necessities such as basic health services.

Like commands, rules and conventions cannot bear the entire burden of ensuring that our choices get coordinated and resources get used efficiently.

The most widely used method is the third: markets.

Markets

In ordinary speech, the word *market* means a place where people buy and sell goods such as fish, meat, fruits, and vegetables. In economics, a *market* has a more general meaning. A **market** is any arrangement that enables buyers and sellers to get information and to do business with each other. An example is the global market in oil. This market is not a place. It is a network of oil producers, users, wholesalers, brokers and others who buy and sell oil.

Markets have evolved because they coordinate choices. In organized markets, enterprising individuals and firms, each pursuing their own self-interest, profit from buying or selling the items in which they specialize. But markets can work only when property rights exist.

Figure 2.8

Circular Flows in the Market Economy

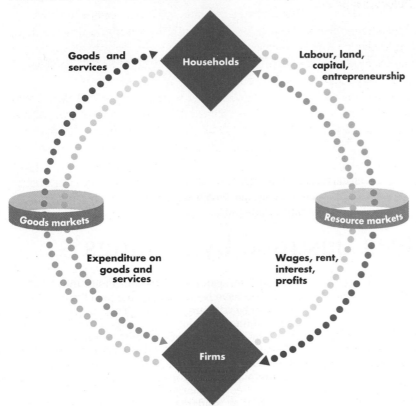

Households and firms make economic choices. Households choose the quantities of labour, land, capital, and entrepreneurship to sell or rent to firms in exchange for wages, rent, interest, and profit. Households also choose how to spend their incomes on the various types of goods and services available. Firms choose the quantities of factors of production to hire and the quantities of the various goods and services to produce. Goods markets and factor markets coordinate these choices of households and firms. Factors of production and goods flow clockwise (red), and money payments flow counter clockwise (green).

Property rights are social arrangements that govern the ownership, use and disposal of resources, goods, and services. Property rights extend to *real property* (land, buildings and durable goods such as plant and equipment) *financial property* (shares, bonds and money in the bank) and *intellectual property* (books, music, computer programs and inventions).

Circular Flows Through Markets

Figure 2.8 shows the flows that result from the choices that households and firms make and its note describes these flows.

How Markets Coordinate Choices

Markets coordinate individual decisions through price adjustments. Suppose there is a shortage of fresh-baked bread. A rise in the price of fresh-baked bread encourages bakers to produce more and encourages some consumers to switch from fresh-baked bread to packaged bread. The shortage disappears and the choices of sellers and buyers are coordinated.

Similarly, if there is a surplus of fresh-baked bread, a fall in its price encourages bakers to produce less and encourages some consumers to switch from packaged bread to fresh-baked bread. The surplus disappears and the choices of sellers and buyers are coordinated.

Review Quiz

1 Why are social arrangements such as markets and property rights necessary?
2 What are the main functions of markets?

Your next task is to learn more about how markets work. But first, you can put what you've learned in this chapter to work in *Reading Between the Lines* on pp. 46–47, which explores the opportunity cost of the choices facing school leavers.

Reading Between the Lines

Opportunity Cost: A Student's Choice

By Justin Parkinson BBC NEWS:
http://news.bbc.co.uk/go/pr/fr/-/1/hi/education/3046985.stm
Published: 2003/05/21 13:20:12 GMT

Tuition fees 'justified by earnings'

Plans to allow prestigious universities to charge up to £3,000 a year for courses are justified by their students' higher future earnings, a study suggests.

Graduates from the Russell Group[1] – which represents 19 of the UK's leading universities – can expect to make between £9,000 and £22,000 more over a lifetime than their counterparts from newer institutions, researchers at the London School of Economics (LSE) found. The government is planning to allow higher fees to be charged for some courses from 2006 . . .

Higher education minister Margaret Hodge said, "By asking everyone to pay the same tuition fee regardless of the university they go to, we have been implying the benefits of every university are the same. They are not. By enabling universities to charge differential fees, we are… recognising difference, diversity and the premium that some universities can give you over others. This is an economic justification for allowing some universities to charge more than others. If potential students thought and acted rationally, then they would be willing to invest more in universities that offered them a better return on their investment."

The earnings of groups of graduates from 1985, 1990 and 1995 were evaluated for the study. They had all previously achieved similar results at A-level and had come from similar social backgrounds. Researchers found those who had attended a Russell Group institution could expect to earn 6% more than graduates of newer universities. If the difference in fees was decided by labour market values, prestigious universities could charge up to £7,250 a year more, they added. . . .

[1] The English universities in the Russell Group are Birmingham, Bristol, Cambridge, Imperial College, Kings College London, Leeds, Liverpool, London School of Economics, Manchester, Newcastle, Nottingham, Oxford, Sheffield, Southampton, University College London and Warwick. The other members are Cardiff, Edinburgh and Glasgow.

The Essence of the Story

◆ Universities in the Russell Group want to charge tuition fees that exceed the new £3,000 limit.

◆ The higher education minister says that if students behave rationally, they will be willing to pay more for an education in a university that generates a higher return from that education.

◆ Universities in the Russell Group say that their graduates earn 6 per cent more than graduates of new universities and this greater rate of return justifies a higher tuition fee.

Economic Analysis

◆ The opportunity cost of a university education is consumption goods and services forgone.

◆ The return to a university education is an increase in lifetime production possibilities that increases future consumption.

◆ Figure 1 shows the rate of return on a university education – the increase in salary generated by university education minus the cost of a university education, expressed as a percentage of the cost. A university education generates a higher rate of return than other types of investment.

◆ Figure 2 illustrates the limits to a school leaver's choices. If the student decides not to attend university, her consumption is limited by the blue *PPF*. She consumes no educational goods and services and is at point *A*.

◆ Working full time, the school leaver has an income of £14,000 a year and remains on the blue *PPF*.

◆ By attending university, the student incurs an opportunity cost. She moves from point *A* to point *B* along her *PPF*, forgoes £7,000 of current consumption and consumes £10,000 of educational goods and services.

◆ As a graduate of a new university, she can earn £19,000 working full time, so her production possibilities expand to the purple *PPF* in Figure 2. She consumes at point *C*.

◆ As a graduate of a university in the Russell Group, she can earn £25,000 working full time, so her production possibilities expand to the red *PPF* in Figure 2. She consumes at point *D*.

◆ A school leaver might be willing to pay a higher tuition fee to get to the red *PPF* in Figure 2. In this case, she would forgo more than £7,000 of current consumption and move to a point on the blue *PPF* to the left of *B*.

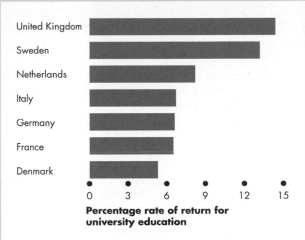

Figure 1   Returns from university education

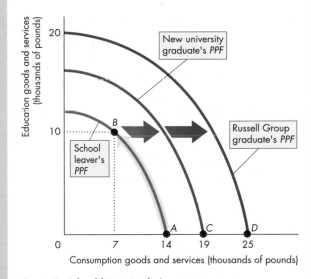

Figure 2   School leaver's choices

Summary

Key Points

Production Possibilities and Opportunity Cost (pp. 32–34)

- The production possibilities frontier, *PPF*, is the boundary between attainable and unattainable production.

- Production efficiency occurs at points on the *PPF*.

- Along the *PPF*, the opportunity cost of producing more of one good is the amount of the other good that must be given up.

- The opportunity cost of all goods increases as production of the good increases.

Using Resources Efficiently (pp. 35–37)

- The marginal cost of a good is the opportunity cost of producing one more unit.

- The marginal benefit from a good is the maximum amount of another good that a person is willing to forgo to obtain more of the first good.

- The marginal benefit of a good decreases as the amount of the good available increases.

- Resources are used efficiently when the marginal cost of each good is equal to its marginal benefit.

Economic Growth (pp. 38–39)

- Economic growth, which is the expansion of production possibilities, results from capital accumulation and technological change.

- The opportunity cost of economic growth is forgone current consumption.

Gains from Trade (pp. 40–43)

- A person has a comparative advantage in producing a good if that person can produce the good at a lower opportunity cost than everyone else.

- People gain by specializing in the activity in which they have a comparative advantage and trading.

- Dynamic comparative advantage arises from learning-by-doing.

Coordinating Choices and Allocating Resources (pp. 44–45)

- Choices are coordinated and resources are allocated by commands, by rules and conventions, and by markets.

- Using commands, firms coordinate a large amount of economic activity, but there is a limit to the efficient size of a firm.

- Markets coordinate the economic choices of people and firms.

- Markets can work efficiently only when property rights exist.

Key Figures

Key Terms

Problems

*Solutions to odd-numbered problems are available on *Parkin Interactive*.

*1 Use the graph below to calculate Peter's opportunity cost of an hour of tennis when he increases the time he plays tennis from:

a 4 to 6 hours a week.

b 6 to 8 hours a week.

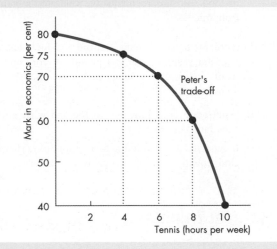

2 Use the graph to calculate Mary's opportunity cost of an hour of skating when she increases her time spent skating from:

a 2 to 4 hours a week.

b 4 to 6 hours a week.

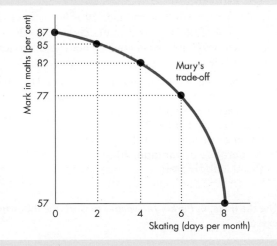

*3 In problem 1, describe the relationship between the time Peter spends playing tennis and the opportunity cost of an hour of tennis.

4 In problem 2, describe the relationship between the time Mary spends skating and the opportunity cost of an hour of skating.

*5 Peter, in problem 1, has the marginal benefit curve shown in the graph at the top of the next column:

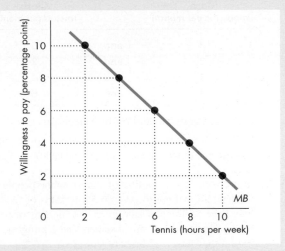

a If Peter is efficient, what his mark?

b Why would Peter be worse off getting a higher mark?

6 Mary, in problem 2, has the following marginal benefit curve:

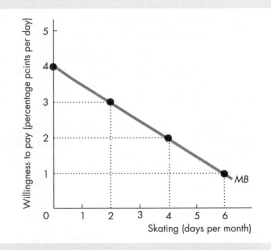

a If Mary is efficient, how much does she skate?

b Why would Mary be worse off if she spent more time skating?

*7 Leisureland's production possibilities in 2004 are:

Food (kilograms per month)		Sunscreen (litres per month)
300	and	0
200	and	50
100	and	100
0	and	150

a Draw a graph of Leisureland's production possibilities frontier in 2004.

b What are Leisureland's opportunity costs of producing food and sunscreen at each output in the table?

8 Jane's Island's production possibilities are:

Corn (kilograms per month)		Cloth (metres per month)
3	and	0
2	and	2
1	and	4
0	and	6

a Draw a graph of the *PPF* on Jane's Island.

b What are Jane's opportunity costs of producing corn and cloth at each output in the table?

*9 In problem 7, to get a litre of sunscreen the people of Sunland are willing to give up 5 kilograms of food if they have 25 litres of sunscreen, 2 kilograms of food if they have 75 litres of sunscreen, and 1 kilogram of food if they have 125 litres of sunscreen.

a Draw a graph of Sunland's marginal benefit from sunscreen.

b What is the efficient quantity of sunscreen?

10 In problem 8, to get a metre of cloth Jane is willing to give up 1.5 kilograms of corn if she has 2 metres of cloth, 1 kilogram of corn if she has 4 metres of cloth, and 0.5 kilograms of corn is she has 6 metres of cloth.

a Draw a graph of Jane's marginal benefit from cloth.

b What is Jane's efficient quantity of cloth?

*11 Busyland's production possibilities are:

Food (kilograms per month)		Sunscreen (litres per month)
150	and	0
100	and	100
50	and	200
0	and	300

Calculate Busyland's opportunity costs of food and sunscreen at each output in the table.

12 Joe's Island's production possibilities are:

Corn (kilograms per month)		Cloth (metres per month)
6	and	0
4	and	1
2	and	2
0	and	3

Calculate Joe's opportunity costs of producing corn and cloth at each output in the table.

*13 In problems 7 and 11, Leisureland and Busyland each produce and consume 100 pounds of food and 100 gallons of sunscreen per month, and they do not trade. Now the countries begin to trade with each other.

a What good does Leisureland sell to Busyland and what good does it buy from Busyland?

b If Leisureland and Busyland divide the total output of food and sunscreen equally, what are the gains from trade?

14 In problems 8 and 12, Jane's Island and Joe's Island each produce and consume 4 pounds of corn and 2 yards of cloth and they do not trade. Now the islands begin to trade.

a What good does Jane sell to Joe and what good does Jane buy from Joe?

b If Jane and Joe divide the total output of corn and cloth equally, what are the gains from trade?

Critical Thinking

1 Study *Reading Between the Lines* news article about student choices on pp. 46–47 and answer the following questions:

a Why is the *PPF* for education goods and services and consumption goods and services bowed outward?

b At what point on the blue *PPF* in Figure 1 on p. 47, is the combination of education goods and services and consumption goods and services efficient?

c Students are facing rising tuition fees. Does this make the opportunity cost of education increase, decrease, or remain unchanged?

Web Exercise

Use the links on *Parkin Interactive* to work the following exercise.

1 Read about the costs to working mothers and the female poverty trap and then answer the following questions:

a Why have the opportunity costs to working mothers fallen over time,

b Why are the opportunity costs lower for highly educated women?

Part 2
How Markets Work

The Amazing Market

The four chapters that you will study in this part explain how markets work. A market is an amazing instrument. It enables people who have never met and who know nothing about each other to interact and do business. It also enables us to allocate our scarce resources to the uses that we value most highly.

You will begin in Chapter 3 by learning about the laws of demand and supply. You will discover the forces that make prices adjust to coordinate buying plans and selling plans. In Chapter 4, you will learn how to calculate, interpret and use the concept of elasticity to predict how prices and quantities respond to the forces that operate in markets to change demand and supply. In Chapter 5, you will discover the conditions under which a competitive market sends resources to their most highly valued uses. And finally, in Chapter 6, you will learn what happens when governments intervene in markets to fix minimum or maximum prices, impose taxes or quotas, or make some goods illegal.

All businesses operate in markets and success in business requires a thorough understanding of market forces.

Chapter 3

Demand and Supply

After studying this chapter you will be able to:

◆ Describe a competitive market and think about a price as an opportunity cost

◆ Explain the main influences on demand

◆ Explain the main influences on supply

◆ Explain how demand and supply determine prices and quantities bought and sold

◆ Use demand and supply to make predictions about changes in prices and quantities

CDs to Burn!

Why do some prices like those of CDs and mobile phones slide, while others like the prices of houses rocket, and yet others like the price of bananas follow a roller-coaster ride? Find out in this chapter. And put what you learn to work explaining why the price of electricity rocketed in France and Germany in 2003 in *Reading Between the Lines* at the end of the chapter.

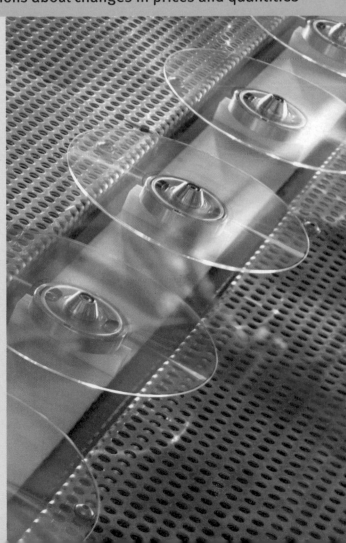

Price and Opportunity Cost

When you need a new pair of running shoes, want a sandwich or a bottle of water, decide to upgrade your CD player, or need to go home for the holidays, you must find a place where people sell those items or offer those services. The place in which you find them is a *market*. You learned in Chapter 2 (p. 44) that a market is any arrangement that enables buyers and sellers to get information and to do business with each other.

A market has two sides: buyers and sellers. There are markets for *goods* such as apples and hiking boots, for *services* such as haircuts and tennis lessons, for *resources* such as computer programmers and earth-movers, and for other manufactured *inputs* such as memory chips and car parts. There are also markets for money such as the euro and the dollar and for financial securities such as BP shares. Only our imagination limits what can be traded in markets.

Some markets are physical places where buyers and sellers meet and where an auctioneer or a broker helps to determine the prices. Examples of this type of market are the London Stock Exchange and the Billingsgate Fish Market.

Some markets are groups of people spread around the world who never meet and know little about each other but are connected through the Internet or by telephone and fax. Examples are the e-commerce markets and currency markets.

But most markets are unorganized collections of buyers and sellers. You do most of your trading in this type of market. An example is the market for football boots. The buyers in this multi-million pound a year market are the several million people who play football (or who want to make an exotic fashion statement).

The sellers are the tens of thousands of retail sports equipment and footwear stores. Each buyer can visit several different stores, and each seller knows that the buyer has a choice of stores.

A Competitive Market

Markets vary in the intensity of competition that buyers and sellers face. In this chapter, we're going to study a **competitive market** – a market that has many buyers and many sellers, so no single buyer or seller can influence the price.

Producers offer items for sale only if the price is high enough to cover their opportunity cost. And consumers respond to changing opportunity cost by seeking cheaper alternatives to expensive items.

We are going to study the way people respond to *prices* and the forces that determine prices. But to pursue these tasks, we need to understand the relationship between a price and an opportunity cost.

Money Price and Relative Price

In everyday life, the *price* of an object is the number of pounds or euros that must be given up in exchange for it. Economists refer to this price as the **money price**.

The *opportunity cost* of an action is the highest valued alternative forgone. If, when you buy a coffee, the highest-valued thing you forgo is some chewing gum, then the opportunity cost of the coffee is the *quantity* of gum forgone. We can calculate the quantity of gum forgone from the money prices of coffee and gum.

If the money price of coffee is £1 a cup and the money price of gum is 50 pence a pack, then the opportunity cost of one cup of coffee is two packs of gum. To calculate this opportunity cost, we divide the price of a cup of coffee by the price of a pack of gum and find the *ratio* of one price to the other. The ratio of one price to another is called a **relative price**, and a *relative price is an opportunity cost*.

We can express the relative price of coffee in terms of gum or any other good. The normal way of expressing a relative price is in terms of a "basket" of all goods and services. To calculate this relative price, we divide the money price of a good by the money price of a "basket" of all goods (called a *price index*). The resulting relative price tells us the opportunity cost of the good in terms of how much of the "basket" we must give up to buy it.

The theory of demand and supply that we are about to study determines *relative prices*, and the word "price" means *relative* price. When we predict that a price will fall, we do not mean that its *money* price will fall – although it might. We mean that its *relative* price will fall. That is, its price will fall *relative* to the average price of other goods and services.

Review Quiz

1   What is the distinction between a money price and a relative price?
2   Explain why a relative price is an opportunity cost.
3   Think of examples of goods whose money price and relative price have risen and have fallen.

Let's begin our study of demand and supply, starting with demand.

Demand

If you demand something, then you

1 Want it,

2 Can afford it, and

3 Plan to buy it.

Wants are the unlimited desires or wishes that people have for goods and services. How many times have you thought that you would like something "if only you could afford it" or "if it weren't so expensive"? Scarcity guarantees that many – perhaps most – of our wants will never be satisfied. Demand reflects a decision about which wants to satisfy.

The **quantity demanded** of a good or service is the amount that consumers plan to buy during a given time period at a particular price. The quantity demanded is not necessarily the same as the quantity actually bought. Sometimes the quantity demanded exceeds the amount of goods available, so the quantity bought is less than the quantity demanded.

The quantity demanded is measured as an amount per unit of time. For example, suppose that you buy one cup of coffee a day. The quantity of coffee that you demand can be expressed as 1 cup per day, 7 cups per week, or 365 cups per year.

Many factors influence buying plans and one of them is price. We look first at the relationship between the quantity demanded of a good and its price. To study this relationship, we keep all other influences on buying plans the same and we ask: How, other things remaining the same, does the quantity demanded of a good change as its price changes?

The law of demand provides the answer.

The Law of Demand

The **law of demand** states:

> **Other things remaining the same, the higher the price of a good, the smaller is the quantity demanded; and the lower the price of a good, the greater is the quantity demanded.**

Why does a higher price reduce the quantity demanded? For two reasons:

◆ Substitution effect

◆ Income effect

Substitution Effect

When the price of a good rises, other things remaining the same, its *relative* price – its opportunity cost – rises. Although each good is unique, it has *substitutes* – other goods that can be used in its place. As the opportunity cost of a good rises, people buy less of that good and more of its substitutes.

Income Effect

When the price of a good rises and other influences on buying plans remain unchanged, the price rises *relative* to incomes. Faced with a higher price and unchanged income, people cannot afford to buy all the things they previously bought. They must decrease the quantities demanded of at least some goods and services, and normally, the good whose price has increased will be one of the goods that people buy less of.

To see the substitution effect and the income effect at work, think about the effects of a change in the price of a recordable compact disc – a CD-R. Several different goods are substitutes for a CD-R. For example, a tape and pre-recorded CD provide services similar to those of a CD-R.

Suppose that a CD-R initially sells for £3 and then its price falls to £1.50. People now substitute CD-Rs for audiotapes and pre-recorded CDs – the substitution effect. And with a budget that now has some slack from the lower price of a CD-R, people buy more CD-Rs – the income effect. The quantity of CD-Rs demanded increases for these two reasons.

Now suppose that a CD-R initially sells for £3 and then the price doubles to £6. People now substitute pre-recorded CDs and audiotapes for CD-Rs – the substitution effect. Faced with a tighter budget, people buy fewer CD-Rs – the income effect. The quantity of CD-Rs demanded decreases for these two reasons.

Demand Curve and Demand Schedule

You are now about to study one of the two most used curves in economics: the demand curve. And you are going to encounter one of the most critical distinctions: the distinction between *demand* and *quantity demanded*.

The term **demand** refers to the entire relationship between the price of the good and the quantity demanded of the good. Demand is illustrated by the demand curve and the demand schedule. The term *quantity demanded* refers to a point on a demand curve – the quantity demanded at a particular price.

Figure 3.1 shows the demand curve for CD-Rs. A **demand curve** shows the relationship between the quantity demanded of a good and its price when all other influences on consumers' planned purchases remain the same.

The table in Figure 3.1 is the *demand schedule*, which lists the quantities demanded at each price when all the other influences on consumers' planned purchases remain the same. For example, if the price of a CD-R is 50 pence, the quantity demanded is 9 million a week. If the price is £2.50, the quantity demanded is 2 million a week. The other rows of the table show the quantities demanded at prices of £1.00, £1.50 and £2.00.

We graph the demand schedule as a demand curve with the quantity demanded of CD-Rs on the *x*-axis and the price of a CD-R on the *y*-axis. The points on the demand curve labelled *A* through *E* correspond to the rows of the demand schedule. For example, point *A* on the graph shows a quantity demanded of 9 million discs a week at a price of 50 pence a disc.

Willingness and Ability to Pay

We can also view a demand curve as a willingness-and-ability-to-pay curve. And the willingness and ability to pay is a measure of *marginal benefit*.

If a small quantity is available, the highest price that someone is willing and able to pay for one more unit is high. As the quantity available increases, the marginal benefit falls and the highest price that someone is willing and able to pay falls along the demand curve.

In Figure 3.1, if only 2 million discs are available each week, the highest price that someone is willing to pay for the 2 millionth disc is £2.50. But if 9 million discs are available each week, someone is willing to pay 50 pence for the last disc bought.

A Change in Demand

When any factor that influences buying plans other than the price of the good changes, there is a **change in demand**. Figure 3.2 illustrates an increase in demand. When demand increases, the demand curve shifts rightward and the quantity demanded is greater at each and every price. For example, at a price of £2.50, on the original (blue) demand curve, the quantity demanded is 2 million discs a week. On the new (red) demand curve, the quantity demanded is 6 million discs a week. Look closely at the numbers in the table in Figure 3.2 and check that the quantity demanded is greater at each price.

Figure 3.1

The Demand Curve

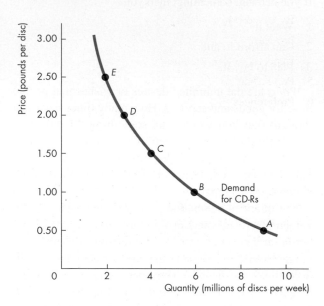

	Price (pounds per disc)	Quantity demanded (millions of discs per week)
A	0.50	9
B	1.00	6
C	1.50	4
D	2.00	3
E	2.50	2

The table shows a demand schedule for CD-Rs. At a price of 50 pence a disc, 9 million a week are demanded; at a price of £1.50 a disc, 4 million a week are demanded. The demand curve shows the relationship between quantity demanded and price, everything else remaining the same. The demand curve slopes downward: As price decreases, the quantity demanded increases.

The demand curve can be read in two ways. For a given price, the demand curve tells us the quantity that people plan to buy. For example, at a price of £1.50 a disc, the quantity demanded is 4 million discs a week. For a given quantity, the demand curve tells us the maximum price that consumers are willing and able to pay for the last disc available. For example, the maximum price that consumers will pay for the 6 millionth disc is £1.00.

Six main factors bring changes in demand. They are changes in:

1 The prices of related goods
2 Expected future prices
3 Income
4 Expected future income
5 Population
6 Preferences

1 Prices of Related Goods

The quantity of a good that consumers plan to buy depends on the prices of its substitutes. A **substitute** is a good that can be used in place of another good. A bus ride is a substitute for a train ride and a pre-recorded CD is a substitute for a CD-R. If the price of a pre-recorded CD rises, people buy fewer CDs and more CD-Rs. The demand for CD-Rs increases.

The quantity of a good that people plan to buy also depends on the prices of its complements. A **complement** is a good that is used in conjunction with another good. Fish and chips are complements and so are CD-Rs and CD burners. If the price of a CD burner falls, people buy more CD burners *and more* CD-Rs. A fall in the price of a CD burner increases the demand for CD-Rs in Figure 3.2.

2 Expected Future Prices

If the price of a good is expected to rise in the future and if the good can be stored, the opportunity cost of obtaining the good for future use is lower today than it will be when the price has increased. So people retime their purchases – they substitute over time. They buy more of the good now before its price is expected to rise (and less later), so the demand for the good increases.

For example, suppose that Spain is hit by a frost that damages the season's orange crop. You expect the price of orange juice to rise in the future. So you fill your freezer with enough frozen juice to get you through the next six months. Your current demand for frozen orange juice has increased, and your future demand has decreased.

Similarly, if the price of a good is expected to fall in the future, the opportunity cost of buying the good today is high relative to what it is expected to be in the future. So again, people retime their purchases. They buy less of the good now before its price falls, so the

Figure 3.2

An Increase in Demand

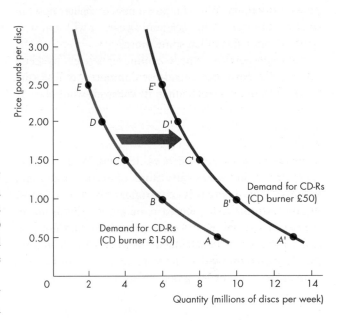

Original demand schedule (CD burner £150)			New demand schedule (CD burner £50)		
	Price (pounds per disc)	Quantity demanded (millions of discs per week)		Price (pounds per disc)	Quantity demanded (millions of discs per week)
A	0.50	9	A'	0.50	13
B	1.00	6	B'	1.00	10
C	1.50	4	C'	1.50	8
D	2.00	3	D'	2.00	7
E	2.50	2	E'	2.50	6

A change in any influence on buyers' plans other than the price of the good itself results in a new demand schedule and a shift of the demand curve. A change in the price of a CD burner changes the demand for CD-Rs.

At a price of £1.50 a disc, 4 million discs a week are demanded when a CD burner costs £150 (row *C* of the table) and 8 million CD-Rs a week are demanded when a CD burner costs £50. A *fall* in the price of a CD burner *increases* the demand for CD-Rs. The demand curve shifts *rightward*, as shown by the shift arrow and the resulting red curve.

demand for the good decreases today and increases in the future.

Computer prices are constantly falling, and this fact poses a dilemma. Will you buy a new computer now, in time for the start of the academic year, or will you wait until the price has fallen some more?

Because people expect computer prices to keep falling, the current demand for computers is less (the future demand is greater) than it otherwise would be.

3 Income

Consumers' income influences demand. When income increases, consumers buy more of most goods, and when income decreases, consumers buy less of most goods. Although an increase in income leads to an increase in the demand for *most* goods, it does not lead to an increase in the demand for *all* goods. A **normal good** is one for which demand increases as income increases. An **inferior good** is one for which demand decreases as income increases. Long-distance transport has examples of both normal goods and inferior goods. As incomes increase, the demand for air travel (a normal good) increases and the demand for long-distance bus trips (an inferior good) decreases.

4 Expected future income

When expected future income increases, demand might increase. For example, a sales person gets the news that she will receive a big bonus at the end of the year, so she decides to buy a new car right now.

5 Population

Demand also depends on the size and the age structure of the population. The larger the population, the greater is the demand for all goods and services; the smaller the population, the smaller is the demand for all goods and services.

For example, the demand for parking spaces or cinema seats or CD-Rs or just about anything that you can imagine is much greater in London than it is in Lands End.

Also, the larger the proportion of the population in a given age group, the greater is the demand for the goods and services used by that age group. For example, the number of older people is increasing relative to the number of babies. As a result, the demand for walking frames and nursing home services is increasing at a faster pace than that at which the demand for prams and nappies is increasing.

Table 3.1

The Demand for CD-Rs

The Law of Demand

The quantity of CD-Rs demanded

Decreases if:	Increases if:
◆ The price of a CD-R rises	◆ The price of a CD-R falls

Changes in Demand

The demand for CD-Rs

Decreases if:	Increases if:
◆ The price of a substitute falls	◆ The price of a substitute rises
◆ The price of a complement rises	◆ The price of a complement falls
◆ The price of a CD-R is expected to fall in the future	◆ The price of a CD-R is expected to rise in the future
◆ Income falls*	◆ Income rises*
◆ Expected future income falls	◆ Expected future income rises
◆ The population decreases	◆ The population increases

*A CD-R is a normal good.

6 Preferences

Demand depends on preferences. *Preferences* are an individual's attitudes towards goods and services. For example, a rock music fanatic has a much greater preference for CD-Rs than does a tone-deaf technophobe. As a consequence, even if they have the same incomes, their demands for CD-Rs will be very different.

Table 3.1 summarizes the influences on demand and the direction of those influences.

A Change in the Quantity Demanded versus a Change in Demand

Changes in the factors that influence buyers' plans cause either a change in the quantity demanded or a change in demand. Equivalently, they cause either a movement along the demand curve or a shift of the demand curve. The distinction between a change in the quantity demanded and a change in demand is the same as that between a movement along the demand curve and a shift of the demand curve.

A point on the demand curve shows the quantity demanded at a given price. So a movement along the demand curve shows a **change in the quantity demanded**. The entire demand curve shows demand. So a shift of the demand curve shows a *change in demand*. Figure 3.3 illustrates and summarizes these distinctions.

Movement Along the Demand Curve

If the price of a good changes but everything else remains the same, there is a movement along the demand curve. Because the demand curve slopes downward, a fall in the price of a good increases the quantity demanded of it and a rise in the price of the good decreases the quantity demanded of it – the law of demand.

In Figure 3.3, if the price of a good falls when everything else remains the same, the quantity demanded of that good increases and there is a movement down the demand curve D_0. If the price rises when everything else remains the same, the quantity demanded of that good decreases and there is a movement up the demand curve D_0.

A Shift of the Demand Curve

If the price of a good remains constant but some other influence on buyers' plans changes, there is a change in demand for that good. We illustrate a change in demand as a shift of the demand curve. For example, if the price of a CD burner falls, consumers buy more CD-Rs regardless of the price of a CD-R. That is what a rightward shift of the demand curve shows – more CD-Rs are bought at each and every price.

In Figure 3.3, when any influence on buyers' planned purchases changes, other than the price of the good, there is a *change in demand* and the demand curve shifts. Demand *increases* and the demand curve *shifts rightward* (to the red demand curve D_1) if the price of a substitute rises, the price of a complement falls, the expected future price of the good rises, income increases (for a normal good), expected future income increases, or the population increases.

Demand *decreases* and the demand curve *shifts leftward* (to the red demand curve D_2) if the price of a substitute falls, the price of a complement rises, the expected future price of the good falls, income decreases (for a normal good), expected future income decreases, or the population decreases. (For an inferior good, the effects of changes in income are in the direction opposite to those described above.)

Figure 3.3

A Change in the Quantity Demanded versus a Change in Demand

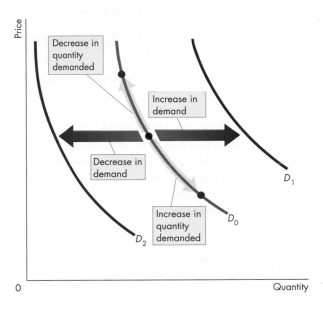

When the price of the good changes, there is a movement along the demand curve and *a change in the quantity demanded,* shown by the blue arrows on demand curve D_0.

When any other influence on buyers' plans changes, there is a shift of the demand curve and a *change in demand*. An increase in demand shifts the demand curve rightward (from D_0 to D_1). A decrease in demand shifts the demand curve leftward (from D_0 to D_2).

Review Quiz

1   Define the quantity demanded of a good or service.
2   What is the law of demand and how do we illustrate it?
3   If a fixed amount of a good is available, what does the demand curve tell us about the price that consumers are willing to pay for that fixed quantity?
4   List all the influences on buying plans that change demand and for each influence say whether it increases or decreases demand.
5   What happens to the quantity of Palm Pilots demanded and the demand for Palm Pilots if the price of a Palm Pilot falls and all other influences on buying plans remain the same?

Supply

If a firm supplies a good or a service, the firm

1 Has the resources and technology to produce it,

2 Can profit from producing it, and

3 Plans to produce it and sell it.

A supply is more than just having the *resources* and the *technology* to produce something. *Resources and technology* are the constraints that limit what is possible.

Many useful things can be produced, but they are not produced because it is profitable to do so. (No one produces electric bed-making machines, for example!) Supply reflects a decision about which technologically feasible items to produce.

The **quantity supplied** of a good or service is the amount that producers plan to sell during a given time period at a particular price. The quantity supplied is not necessarily the same amount as the quantity actually sold. Sometimes the quantity supplied is greater than the quantity demanded, so the quantity bought is less than the quantity supplied.

Like the quantity demanded, the quantity supplied is measured as an amount per unit of time. For example, suppose that Ford produces 1,000 cars a day. The quantity of cars supplied by Ford can be expressed as 1,000 a day, 7,000 a week, or 365,000 a year. Without the time dimension, we cannot tell whether a particular number is large or small.

Many factors influence selling plans and again, one of them is price. We look first at the relationship between the quantity supplied of a good and its price. And again, as we did when we studied demand, to isolate this relationship, we keep all other influences on selling plans the same and we ask: How, other things remaining the same, does the quantity supplied of a good change as its price changes?

The law of supply provides the answer.

The Law of Supply

The **law of supply** states:

> **Other things remaining the same, the higher the price of a good, the greater is the quantity supplied; and the lower the price of a good, the smaller is the quantity supplied.**

Why does a higher price increase the quantity supplied? It is because *marginal cost increases*. As the quantity produced of any good increases, the marginal cost of producing the good increases. (You can refresh your memory of increasing marginal cost in Chapter 2, p. 35.)

It is never worth producing a good if the price received for it does not at least cover the marginal cost of producing it. So when the price of a good rises, other things remaining the same, producers are willing to incur a higher marginal cost and increase production. The higher price brings forth an increase in the quantity supplied.

Let's now illustrate the law of supply with a supply curve and a supply schedule.

Supply Curve and Supply Schedule

You are now going to study the second of the two most used curves in economics: the supply curve. And you're going to learn about the critical distinction between *supply* and *quantity supplied*.

The term **supply** refers to the entire relationship between the quantity supplied and the price of a good. Supply is illustrated by the supply curve and the supply schedule. The term *quantity supplied* refers to a point on a supply curve – the quantity supplied at a particular price.

Figure 3.4 shows the supply curve of CD-Rs. A **supply curve** shows the relationship between the quantity supplied of a good and its price when all other influences on producers' planned sales remain the same. The supply curve is a graph of a supply schedule.

The table in Figure 3.4 sets out the supply schedule for CD-Rs. A *supply schedule* lists the quantities supplied at each price when all the other influences on producers' planned sales remain the same. For example, if the price of a CD-R is 50 pence, the quantity supplied is zero – in row A of the table. If the price of a disc is £1.00, the quantity supplied is 3 million discs a week – in row B. The other rows of the table show the quantities supplied at prices of £1.50, £2.00, and £2.50.

To make a supply curve, we graph the quantity supplied on the x-axis and the price on the y-axis, just as in the case of the demand curve. The points on the supply curve labelled A through E correspond to the rows of the supply schedule. For example, point A on the graph shows a quantity supplied of zero at a price of 50 pence a disc.

Figure 3.4

The Supply Curve

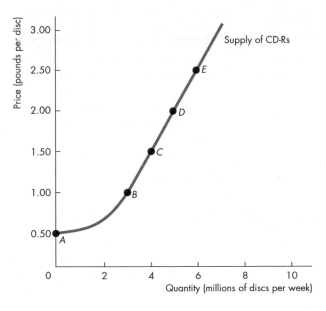

	Price (pounds per disc)	Quantity supplied (millions of discs per week)
A	0.50	0
B	1.00	3
C	1.50	4
D	2.00	5
E	2.50	6

The table shows the supply schedule of CD-Rs. For example, at a price of £1.00, 3 million discs a week are supplied; at a price of £2.50, 6 million discs a week are supplied. The supply curve shows the relationship between the quantity supplied and price, everything else remaining the same. The supply curve usually slopes upward: As the price of a good increases, so does the quantity supplied.

A supply curve can be read in two ways. For a given price, it tells us the quantity that producers plan to sell at that price. And for a given quantity, it tells us the minimum price that producers are willing to accept for that quantity.

Minimum Supply Price

The supply curve, like the demand curve, has two interpretations. It is the minimum-supply-price curve. It tells us the lowest price at which someone is willing to sell another unit.

If a small quantity is produced, the lowest price at which someone is willing to sell one more unit is low. But if a large quantity is produced, the lowest price at which someone is willing to sell one more unit is high.

In Figure 3.4, if 6 million discs a week are produced, the lowest price that a producer is willing to accept for the 6 millionth disc is £2.50. But if only 4 million discs are produced each week, a producer is willing to accept £1.50 for the 4 millionth disc.

A Change in Supply

When any factor that influences selling plans other than the price of the good changes, there is a **change in supply**. Five main factors bring changes in supply. They are changes in:

1   The prices of factors of production
2   The prices of related goods produced
3   Expected future prices
4   The number of suppliers
5   Technology

1 Prices of Factors of Production

To see why prices of factors of production influence supply, think about the supply curve as a minimum-supply-price curve. If a costs of production rise, the lowest price a producer is willing to accept rises, so supply decreases. For example, during 2001, the price of jet fuel increased and the supply of air transport decreased. A rise in the wages of disc producers decreases the supply of CD-Rs.

2 Prices of Related Goods Produced

The prices of related goods and services that firms produce influence supply. For example, if the price of a pre-recorded CD rises, the supply of CD-Rs decreases. CD-Rs and pre-recorded CDs are *substitutes in production* – goods that can be produced by using the same resources. If the price of beef rises, the supply of leather increases. Beef and leather are *complements in production* – goods that must be produced together.

3 Expected Future Prices

If the price of a good is expected to rise, the return from selling the good in the future is higher than it is today. So supply decreases today and increases in the future.

4 The Number of Suppliers

The larger the number of firms that produce a good, the greater is the supply of the good. And as firms enter an industry, the supply in that industry increases. As firms leave an industry, the supply in that industry decreases.

5 Technology

The term "technology" is used broadly to mean the way that factors of production are used to produce a good. Technology changes both positively and negatively. A positive technology change occurs when a new method is discovered that lowers the cost of producing a good. An example is new methods used in the factories that make CDs. A negative technology change occurs when an event such as extreme weather or natural disaster increases the cost of producing a good. A positive technology change increases supply, and a negative technology change decreases supply.

Figure 3.5 illustrates an increase in supply. When supply increases, the supply curve shifts rightward and the quantity supplied is larger at each and every price.

For example, at a price of £1.00, on the original (blue) supply curve, the quantity supplied is 3 million discs a week. On the new (red) supply curve, the quantity supplied is 6 million discs a week. Look closely at the numbers in the table in Figure 3.5 and check that the quantity supplied is larger at each price.

Table 3.2 summarizes the influences on supply and the directions of those influences.

A Change in the Quantity Supplied versus a Change in Supply

Changes in the factors that influence producers' planned sales cause either a change in the quantity supplied or a change in supply. Equivalently, they cause either a movement along the supply curve or a shift of the supply curve.

A point on the supply curve shows the quantity supplied at a given price. A movement along the supply curve shows a **change in the quantity supplied**. The entire supply curve shows supply. A shift of the supply curve shows a *change in supply*.

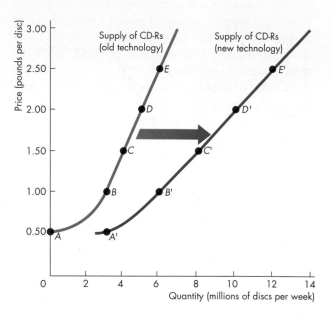

Figure 3.5

An Increase in Supply

Original supply schedule Original technology			New supply schedule New technology		
	Price (pounds per disc)	Quantity supplied (millions of discs per week)		Price (pounds per disc)	Quantity supplied (millions of discs per week)
A	0.50	0	A'	0.50	3
B	1.00	3	B'	1.00	6
C	1.50	4	C'	1.50	8
D	2.00	5	D'	2.00	10
E	2.50	6	E'	2.50	12

A change in any influence on sellers' plans other than the price of the good itself results in a new supply schedule and a shift of the supply curve. For example, if CD producers invent a new, cost-saving technology, the supply of CD-Rs changes.

At a price of £1.50 a disc, 4 million discs a week are supplied when producers use the old technology (row C of the table) and 8 million discs a week are supplied when producers use the new technology. An advance in technology *increases* the supply of CD-Rs. The supply curve shifts *rightward*, as shown by the shift arrow and the resulting red curve.

Figure 3.6 illustrates and summarizes these distinctions. If the price of a good falls and everything else remains the same, the quantity supplied of that good decreases and there is a movement down the supply curve S_0. If the price of a good rises and everything else remains the same, the quantity supplied increases and there is a movement up the supply curve S_0. When any other influence on selling plans changes, the supply curve shifts and there is a *change in supply*. If the supply curve is S_0 and if production costs fall, supply increases and the supply curve shifts to the red supply curve S_1. If production costs rise, supply decreases and the supply curve shifts to the red supply curve S_2.

Table 3.2

The Supply of CD-Rs

The Law of Supply

The quantity of CD-Rs supplied

Decreases if:	*Increases if:*
◆ The price of a CD-R falls	◆ The price of a CD-R rises

Changes in Supply

The supply of CD-Rs

Decreases if:	*Increases if:*
◆ The price of factor of production used to produce CD-Rs rises	◆ The price of factor of production used to produce CD-Rs falls
◆ The price of a substitute in production rises	◆ The price of a substitute in production falls
◆ The price of a complement in production falls	◆ The price of a complement in production rises
◆ The price of a CD-R is expected to rise in the future	◆ The price of a CD-R is expected to fall in the future
◆ The number of CD-R producers decreases	◆ The number of CD-R producers increases
	◆ A more efficient technology for producing CD-Rs is used

*A CD-R is a normal good.

Figure 3.6

A Change in the Quantity Supplied versus a Change in Supply

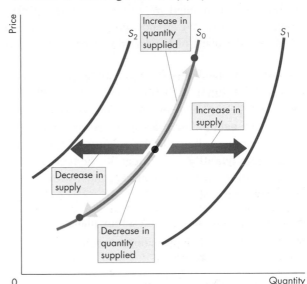

When the price of the good changes, there is a movement along the supply curve and *a change in the quantity supplied,* shown by the blue arrows on supply curve S_0.

When any other influence on selling plans changes, there is a shift of the supply curve and a *change in supply*. An increase in supply shifts the supply curve rightward (from S_0 to S_1), and a decrease in supply shifts the supply curve leftward (from S_0 to S_2).

Review Quiz

1. Define the quantity supplied of a good or service.
2. What is the law of supply and how do we illustrate it?
3. What does the supply curve tell us about the price at which firms will supply a given quantity of a good?
4. List all the influences on selling plans, and for each influence say whether it changes supply.
5. What happens to the quantity of Palm Pilots supplied and the supply of Palm Pilots if the price of a Palm Pilot falls?

Your next task is to use what you've learned about demand and supply and understand how prices and quantities are determined.

Market Equilibrium

We have seen that when the price of a good rises, the quantity demanded *decreases* and the quantity supplied *increases*. We are now going to see how prices coordinate the plans of buyers and sellers and achieve equilibrium.

Equilibrium is a situation in which opposing forces balance each other. Equilibrium in a market occurs when the price balances the plans of buyers and sellers. The **equilibrium price** is the price at which the quantity demanded equals the quantity supplied. The **equilibrium quantity** is the quantity bought and sold at the equilibrium price. A market moves towards its equilibrium because:

◆ Price regulates buying and selling plans.

◆ Price adjusts when plans don't match.

Price as a Regulator

The price of a good regulates the quantities demanded and supplied. If the price is too high, the quantity supplied exceeds the quantity demanded. If the price is too low, the quantity demanded exceeds the quantity supplied. There is one price at which the quantity demanded equals the quantity supplied. Let's work out what that price is.

Figure 3.7 shows the market for CD-Rs. The table shows the demand schedule (from Figure 3.1) and the supply schedule (from Figure 3.4). If the price of a disc is 50 pence, the quantity demanded is 9 million discs a week, but no discs are supplied. There is a shortage of 9 million discs a week. This shortage is shown in the final column of the table. At a price of £1.00 a disc, there is still a shortage, but only of 3 million discs a week. If the price of a disc is £2.50, the quantity supplied is 6 million discs a week, but the quantity demanded is only 2 million. There is a surplus of 4 million discs a week. The one price at which there is neither a shortage nor a surplus is £1.50 a disc. At that price, the quantity demanded equals the quantity supplied: 4 million discs a week. The equilibrium price is £1.50 a disc, and the equilibrium quantity is 4 million discs a week.

Figure 3.7 shows that the demand curve and the supply curve intersect at the equilibrium price of £1.50 a disc. At each price *above* £1.50 a disc, there is a surplus. For example, at £2.00 a disc, the surplus is 2 million discs a week, as shown by the blue arrow.

Figure 3.7

Equilibrium

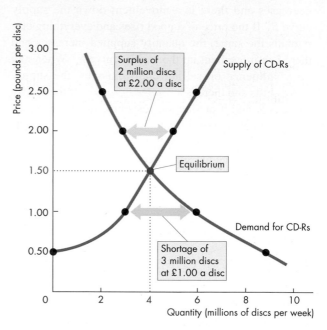

Price (pounds per disc)	Quantity demanded	Quantity supplied	Shortage (−) or surplus (+)
	(millions of discs per week)		
0.50	9	0	−9
1.00	6	3	−3
1.50	**4**	**4**	**0**
2.00	3	5	+2
2.50	2	6	+4

The table lists the quantities demanded and quantities supplied as well as the shortage or surplus of discs at each price. If the price is £1.00 a disc, 6 million discs a week are demanded and 3 million are supplied. There is a shortage of 3 million discs a week, and the price rises.

If the price is £2.00 a disc, 3 million discs a week are demanded and 5 million are supplied. There is a surplus of 2 million discs a week, and the price falls.

If the price is £1.50 a disc, 4 million discs a week are demanded and 4 million are supplied. There is neither a shortage nor a surplus. Neither buyers nor sellers have any incentive to change the price. The price at which the quantity demanded equals the quantity supplied is the equilibrium price.

At each price *below* £1.50 a disc, there is a shortage of discs. For example, at £1.00 a disc, the shortage is 3 million discs a week, as shown by the red arrow.

Price Adjustments

You've seen that if the price is below equilibrium, there is a shortage and that if the price is above equilibrium, there is a surplus. But can we count on the price to change and eliminate a shortage or surplus? We can, because such price changes are beneficial to both buyers and sellers. Let's see why the price changes when there is a shortage or a surplus.

A Shortage Forces the Price Up

Suppose the price of a CD-R is £1. Consumers plan to buy 6 million discs a week, and producers plan to sell 3 million discs a week. Consumers can't force producers to sell more than they plan, so the quantity that is actually offered for sale is 3 million discs a week. In this situation, powerful forces operate to increase the price and move it towards the equilibrium price. Some producers, noticing lines of unsatisfied consumers, raise the price. Some producers increase their output. As producers push the price up, the price rises towards its equilibrium. The rising price reduces the shortage because it decreases the quantity demanded and increases the quantity supplied. When the price has increased to the point at which there is no longer a shortage, the forces moving the price stop operating and the price comes to rest at its equilibrium.

A Surplus Forces the Price Down

Suppose the price of a CD-R is £2. Producers plan to sell 5 million discs a week, and consumers plan to buy 3 million discs a week. Producers cannot force consumers to buy more than they plan, so the quantity that is actually bought is 3 million discs a week. In this situation, powerful forces operate to lower the price and move it towards the equilibrium price. Some producers, unable to sell the quantities of discs they planned to sell, cut their prices. In addition, some producers scale back production. As producers cut the price, the price falls towards its equilibrium. The falling price decreases the surplus because it increases the quantity demanded and decreases the quantity supplied. When the price has fallen to the point at which there is no longer a surplus, the forces moving the price stop operating and the price comes to rest at its equilibrium.

The Best Deal Available for Buyers and Sellers

When the price is below equilibrium, it is forced up towards the equilibrium. Why don't buyers resist the increase and refuse to buy at the higher price? Because they value the good more highly than the current price and they cannot satisfy all their demands at the current price. In some markets – for example, the auction markets that operate on eBay – the buyers might even be the ones who force the price up by offering to pay higher prices.

When the price is above equilibrium, it is bid down towards the equilibrium. Why don't sellers resist this decrease and refuse to sell at the lower price? Because their minimum supply price is below the current price and they cannot sell all they would like to at the current price. Normally, it is the sellers who force the price down by offering lower prices to gain market share from their competitors.

At the price at which the quantity demanded equals the quantity supplied neither buyers nor sellers can do business at a better price. Buyers pay the highest price they are willing to pay for the last unit bought, and sellers receive the lowest price at which they are willing to supply the last unit sold.

When people freely make offers to buy and sell and when buyers try to buy at the lowest possible price and sellers try to sell at the highest possible price, the price at which trade takes place is the equilibrium price – the price at which the quantity demanded equals the quantity supplied. The price coordinates the plans of buyers and sellers, and no one has an incentive to change it.

Review Quiz

1. What is the equilibrium price of a good or service?
2. Over what range of prices does a shortage arise?
3. Over what range of prices does a surplus arise?
4. What happens to the price when there is a shortage?
5. What happens to the price when there is a surplus?
6. Why is the price at which the quantity demanded equals the quantity supplied the equilibrium price?
7. Why is the equilibrium price the best deal available for both buyers and sellers?

Predicting Changes in Price and Quantity

The demand and supply theory that we have just studied provides us with a powerful way of analyzing influences on prices and the quantities bought and sold. According to the theory, a change in price stems from a change in demand, a change in supply, or a change in both demand and supply. Let's look first at the effects of a change in demand.

A Change in Demand

What happens to the price and quantity of CD-Rs if the demand for CD-Rs increases? We can answer this question with a specific example. Between 1998 and 2001, the price of a CD burner fell from £150 to £50. Because the CD burner and CD-R discs are complements, the demand for discs increased, as is shown in the table in Figure 3.8. The original demand schedule and the new one are set out in the first three columns of the table. The table also shows the supply schedule for CD-Rs.

When demand increases, there is a shortage at the original equilibrium price of £1.50 a disc. To eliminate the shortage, the price must rise. The price that makes the quantity demanded and quantity supplied equal again is £2.50 a disc. At this price, 6 million discs are bought and sold each week. When demand increases, both the price and the quantity increase.

Figure 3.8 shows these changes. The figure shows the original demand for and supply of CD-Rs. The original equilibrium price is £1.50 a disc, and the quantity is 4 million discs a week. When demand increases, the demand curve shifts rightward. The equilibrium price rises to £2.50 a disc, and the quantity supplied increases to 6 million discs a week, as highlighted in the figure. There is an *increase in the quantity supplied* but *no change in supply* – a movement along, but no shift of, the supply curve.

To see the effect of a decrease in demand, start at a price of £2.50 a disc with 6 million discs a week, and then work out what happens if demand decreases to its original level. Such a decrease in demand might arise from a fall in the price of an MP3 player (a substitute for CD-R technology).

The decrease in demand shifts the demand curve leftward. The equilibrium price falls to £1.50 a disc, and the equilibrium quantity decreases to 4 million discs a week.

Figure 3.8

The Effects of a Change in Demand

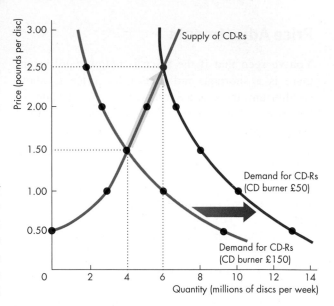

Price (pounds per disc)	Quantity demanded (millions of discs per week)		Quantity supplied (millions of discs per week)
	CD burner £150	CD burner £50	
0.50	9	13	0
1.00	6	10	3
1.50	**4**	8	**4**
2.00	3	7	5
2.50	2	**6**	**6**

With the price of a CD burner at £150, the demand for CD-Rs is the blue demand curve. The equilibrium price is £1.50 a disc, and the equilibrium quantity is 4 million discs a week. When the price of a CD burner falls from £150 to £50, the demand for CD-Rs increases and the demand curve shifts rightward to become the red curve.

At £1.50 a disc, there is now a shortage of 4 million discs a week. The price of a disc rises to a new equilibrium of £2.50. As the price rises to £2.50, the quantity supplied increases – shown by the blue arrow on the supply curve – to the new equilibrium quantity of 6 million discs a week. Following an increase in demand, the quantity supplied increases but supply does not change – the supply curve does not shift.

We can now make our first two predictions:

1 **When demand increases, both the price and the quantity increase.**

2 **When demand decreases, both the price and the quantity decrease.**

A Change in Supply

When Verbatim and other producers introduce new cost-saving technologies in their CD-R production plants, the supply of CD-Rs increases. The table in Figure 3.9 shows the new supply schedule (the same as that in Figure 3.5). What are the new equilibrium price and quantity? The answer is highlighted in the table: the price falls to £1.00 a disc, and the quantity increases to 6 million a week. You can see why by looking at the quantities demanded and supplied at the original price of £1.50 a disc. The quantity supplied at that price is 8 million discs a week, and there is a surplus of discs. The price falls. Only when the price is £1.00 a disc does the quantity supplied equal the quantity demanded.

Figure 3.9 illustrates the effect of an increase in supply. It shows the demand curve for CD-Rs and the original and new supply curves. The initial equilibrium price is £1.50 a disc, and the quantity is 4 million discs a week. When the supply increases, the supply curve shifts rightward. The equilibrium price falls to £1.00 a disc, and the quantity demanded increases to 6 million discs a week, highlighted in the figure. There is an *increase in the quantity demanded* but *no change in demand* – a movement along, but no shift of, the demand curve.

We can reverse this change in supply. If we start out at a price of £1.00 a disc with 6 million discs a week being bought and sold, we can work out what happens if supply decreases to its original level. Such a decrease in supply might arise from an increase in the cost of labour or raw materials. The decrease in supply shifts the supply curve leftward. The equilibrium price rises to £1.50 a disc, and the equilibrium quantity decreases to 4 million discs a week.

We can now make two more predictions:

1 **When supply increases, the quantity increases and the price falls.**

2 **When supply decreases, the quantity decreases and the price rises.**

Figure 3.9

The Effects of a Change in Supply

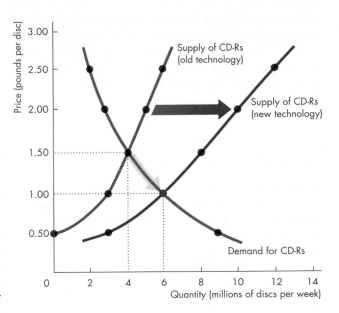

Price (pounds per disc)	Quantity demanded (millions of discs per week)	Quantity supplied (millions of discs per week)	
		Old technology	New technology
0.50	9	0	3
1.00	**6**	3	**6**
1.50	**4**	**4**	8
2.00	3	5	10
2.50	2	6	12

With the old technology, the supply of CD-Rs is shown by the blue supply curve. The equilibrium price is £1.50 a disc, and the equilibrium quantity is 4 million discs a week. When the new technology is adopted, the supply of CD-Rs increases and the supply curve shifts rightward to become the red curve.

At £1.50 a disc, there is now a surplus of 4 million discs a week. The price of a CD-R falls to a new equilibrium of £1.00 a disc. As the price falls to £1.00, the quantity demanded increases – shown by the blue arrow on the demand curve – to the new equilibrium quantity of 6 million discs a week. Following an increase in supply, the quantity demanded increases but demand does not change – the demand curve does not shift.

A Change in Both Demand and Supply

You can now predict the effects of a change in either demand or supply on the price and the quantity but what happens if *both* demand and supply change together? To answer this question, we look first at the case in which demand and supply move in the same direction and then we look at the case in which they move in opposite directions.

Demand and Supply Change in the Same Direction

We've seen that an increase in the demand for CD-Rs raises its price and increases the quantity bought and sold. And we've seen that an increase in the supply of CD-Rs lowers its price and increases the quantity bought and sold. Let's now examine what happens when both of these changes occur together.

The table in Figure 3.10 brings together the numbers that describe the original quantities demanded and supplied and the new quantities demanded and supplied after the fall in the price of the CD burner and the improved CD-R production technology. These same numbers are illustrated in the graph. The original (blue) demand and supply curves intersect at a price of £1.50 a disc and a quantity of 4 million discs a week. The new (red) supply and demand curves also intersect at a price of £1.50 a disc but at a quantity of 8 million discs a week.

An increase in either demand or supply increases the quantity. So when both demand and supply increase, so does the equilibrium quantity. An increase in demand raises the price, and an increase in supply lowers the price, so we can't say whether the price will rise or fall when demand and supply increase together. In this example, the price does not change. But notice that if demand increases by slightly more than the amount shown in the figure, the equilibrium price will rise. And if supply increases by slightly more than the amount shown in the figure, the equilibrium price will fall.

We can now make two more predictions:

1 When *both* demand and supply increase, the quantity increases and the price might increase, decrease, or remain the same.

2 When *both* demand and supply decrease, the quantity decreases and the price might increase, decrease, or remain the same.

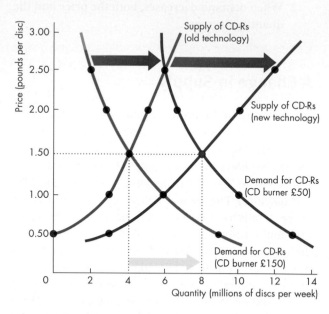

Figure 3.10

The Effects of an Increase in Both Demand and Supply

	Original quantities (millions of discs per week)		**New quantities** (millions of discs per week)	
Price (pounds per disc)	**Quantity demanded** (CD burner £150)	**Quantity supplied** (old technology)	**Quantity demanded** (CD burner £50)	**Quantity supplied** (new technology)
0.50	9	0	13	3
1.00	6	3	10	6
1.50	**4**	**4**	**8**	**8**
2.00	3	5	7	10
2.50	2	6	6	12

When the price of a CD burner is £150 and firms use the old technology to produce discs, the price of a disc is £1.50 and the quantity is 4 million discs a week.

A fall in the price of the CD burner increases the demand for CD-Rs and improved technology increases the supply of CD-Rs. The new supply curve intersects the new demand curve at £1.50 a disc, the same price as before, but the equilibrium quantity increases to 8 million discs a week. These increases in demand and supply increase the quantity but leave the price unchanged.

Demand and Supply Change in Opposite Directions

Suppose that demand and supply change together in *opposite* directions. A new technology increases the supply of CD-Rs. But now the price of an MP3 download rises. An MP3 download is a *complement* of a CD-R. With more costly MP3 downloads, some people switch from buying CD-Rs to buying pre-recorded CDs. The demand for CD-Rs decreases.

The table in Figure 3.11 describes the original and new demand and supply schedules and the original (blue) and new (red) demand and supply curves. The original equilibrium price is £2.50 a disc, and the quantity is 6 million discs a week. The new supply and demand curves intersect at a price of £1.00 a disc and at the original quantity of 6 million discs a week.

A decrease in demand or an increase in supply lowers the price. So when a decrease in demand and an increase in supply occur together, the price falls.

A decrease in demand decreases the quantity, and an increase in supply increases the quantity, so we can't say for sure which way the quantity will change when demand decreases and supply increases at the same time. In this example, the quantity doesn't change. But notice that if demand had decreased by slightly more than is shown in the figure, the quantity would have decreased. And if supply had increased by slightly more than is shown in the figure, the quantity would have increased.

We can make two more predictions:

1 **When demand decreases and supply increases, the price falls and the quantity might increase, decrease, or remain the same.**

2 **When demand increases and supply decreases, the price rises and the quantity might increase, decrease, or remain the same.**

Review Quiz

1   What is the effect on the price of a CD-R and the quantity of CD-Rs if (a) the price of a PC falls or (b) the price of an MP3 download rises or (c) more firms produce CD-Rs or (d) CD-R producers' wages rise or (e) any two of these events occur together? (Draw the diagrams!)

To complete your study of demand and supply, take a look at *Reading Between the Lines* on pp. 70–71, which looks at the rocketing price of electricity in 2003.

Figure 3.11

The Effects of a Decrease in Demand and an Increase in Supply

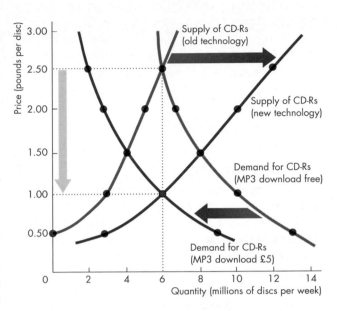

	Original quantities (millions of discs per week)		New quantities (millions of discs per week)	
Price (pounds per disc)	Quantity demanded (MP3 download free)	Quantity supplied (old technology)	Quantity demanded (MP3 download £5)	Quantity supplied (new technology)
0.50	13	0	9	3
1.00	**10**	**3**	**6**	**6**
1.50	8	4	4	8
2.00	7	5	3	10
2.50	**6**	**6**	**2**	**12**

When MP3 downloads are free and firms use the old technology to produce discs, the price of a CD-R is £2.50 and the quantity is 6 million discs a week.

A rise in the price of an MP3 download decreases the demand for CD-Rs and improved technology increases the supply of CD-Rs. The new equilibrium price is £1.00 a disc, a lower price, but in this case the quantity remains constant at 6 million discs a week. This decrease in demand and increase in supply lower the price but leave the quantity unchanged.

Reading Between the Lines

Demand and Supply: Europe's Electricity Price Surge

The Business, 10 November 2003

Electricity prices rocket as Europe feels the heat

Tim Webb

Electricity prices are rocketing across Europe as a result of soaring temperatures and power shortages. Some nuclear power stations were offline in France and Germany this weekend as the temperatures of rivers, used to cool reactors, became too hot.

In France, which relies on nuclear power for 75% of its electricity, at least 14 reactors were offline last weekend, representing about one quarter of its total nuclear capacity. Increased use of air-conditioning means demand for electricity in summer can be as great as in winter.

In Germany, electricity prices surged on Friday as temperatures rose. . . . The price of peak time power, which is the average price between 8am and 8pm, for delivery on Monday was up 59% to €170 per megawatt hour (£119). . . .

Last week, . . . the Italian national grid cut off big industrial users . . . The operator was forced to call in spare capacity from France, Spain, Slovenia and Switzerland to avert a repeat of the blackouts which hit the country at the end of June.

. . . In the UK, prices for next-day delivery have rocketed by 300% since the beginning of the month, with power for Monday delivery trading at £73 mw/h on Friday . . . At the end of last month, before the latest heatwave, prices were hovering below £20mw/h, close to their long-term average.

. . . England and Wales will have a power deficit of 1,440mw on Monday. . . . The shortfall will be made up by importing power through the Interconnector, the power cable linking Britain to France. . . .

France . . . has power connections with the largest markets in Europe. . . . If prices in France are high, prices in other parts of Europe are also likely to be higher.

The Essence of the Story

◆ In hot weather, some nuclear power stations in France and Germany must be shut down because the temperature of river water is too high to cool them.

◆ At the same time, more people use air conditioning and the demand for electricity rises.

◆ In these conditions, electricity prices surge. The price in Germany rose 59 per cent from €107 to €170 per megawatt hour. In the United Kingdom it rose by 300 per cent to £73 megawatt/hour.

◆ The power system in France, Germany, the United Kingdom and some other countries is interconnected.

◆ If the price is high in one of these countries, it is likely to be high in all of them.

Economic Analysis

◆ Figure 1 shows the market for electricity in Germany. On 8 November 2003, the supply curve was S_0 and the demand curve was D_0. The equilibrium price was €107 per megawatt hour (mwh) and the quantity was 1 million megawatts (mw) at point A.

◆ On 9 November 2003, hot weather brought an increase in the demand for electricity and the demand curve shifted rightward from D_0 to D_1.

◆ If the supply of electricity remained constant at S_0, the equilibrium price would rise to €150 per mwh and the equilibrium quantity would increase to 1.5 million mw at point B. The higher price would bring an increase in the quantity of electricity supplied shown by a movement along supply curve S_0.

◆ But the supply of electricity did not remain constant. High river temperatures closed some power stations, so the supply of electricity decreased and the supply curve shifted leftward from S_0 to S_1.

◆ The equilibrium price increased to €170 per mwh and the equilibrium quantity was 1.3 million mw at point C.

◆ Figure 2 shows the UK market for electricity. On 8 November, 2003, the supply curve was S_0 and the demand curve was D_0. The equilibrium price was £70 per mwh and the quantity was Q_0.

◆ On 9 November 2003, hot weather brought an increase in the demand for electricity and the demand curve shifted rightward from D_0 to D_1.

◆ Electricity delivered in the United Kingdom is a *substitute in production* for electricity delivered in Germany (and in other interconnected parts of Europe). A rise in the price of electricity in Germany decreases the supply of electricity in the United Kingdom and the UK supply curve shifts leftward to S_1.

◆ The equilibrium price of electricity in the United Kingdom rose to £73 per mwh and equilibrium quantity increased to Q_1.

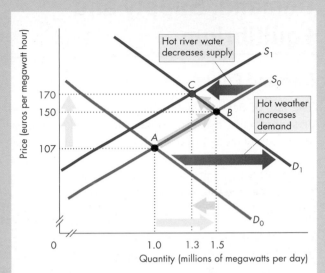

Figure 1 The German market for electricity

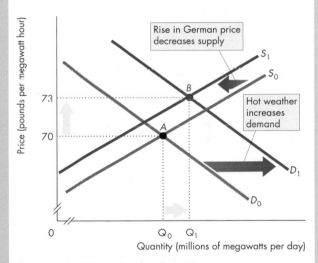

Figure 2 The UK market for electricity

Mathematical Note
Demand, Supply and Equilibrium

Demand Curve

The law of demand states that as the price of a good or service falls, the quantity demanded of it increases. We illustrate the law of demand by setting out a demand schedule, drawing a graph of the demand curve, or writing down an equation. When the demand curve is a straight line, the following linear equation describes it:

$$P = a - bQ_D$$

where P is the price and Q_D is the quantity demanded. The a and b are positive constants.

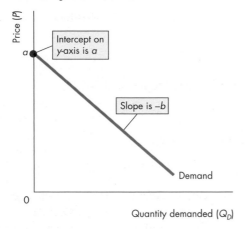

The demand equation tells us three things:

1 The price at which no one is willing to buy the good (Q_D is zero). That is, if the price is a, then the quantity demanded is zero. You can see the price a on the graph. It is the price at which the demand curve hits the y-axis – what we call the demand curve's "intercept on the y-axis".

2 As the price falls, the quantity demanded increases. If Q_D is a positive number, then the price P must be less than a. And as Q_D gets larger, the price P becomes smaller. That is, as the quantity increases, the maximum price that buyers are willing to pay for the good falls.

3 The constant b tells us how fast the maximum price that someone is willing to pay for the good falls as the quantity increases. That is, the constant b tells us about the steepness of the demand curve. The equation tells us that the slope of the demand curve is $-b$.

Supply Curve

The law of supply states that as the price of a good or service rises, the quantity supplied of it increases. We illustrate the law of supply by setting out a supply schedule, drawing a graph of the supply curve, or writing down an equation. When the supply curve is a straight line, the following linear equation describes it:

$$P = c + dQ_S$$

where P is the price and Q_S the quantity supplied. The c and d are positive constants.

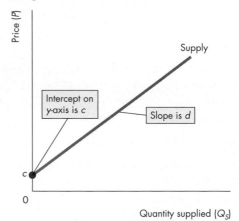

The supply equation tells us three things:

1 The price at which no one is willing to sell the good (Q_S is zero). If the price is c, then the quantity supplied is zero. You can see the price c on the graph. It is the price at which the supply curve hits the y-axis – what we call the supply curve's "intercept on the y-axis".

2 As the price rises, the quantity supplied increases. If Q_S is a positive number, then the price P must be greater than c. And as Q_S increases, the price P gets larger. That is, as the quantity increases, the minimum price that sellers are willing to accept rises.

3 The constant d tells us how fast the minimum price at which someone is willing to sell the good rises as the quantity increases. That is, the constant d tells us about the steepness of the supply curve. The equation tells us that the slope of the supply curve is d.

Market Equilibrium

Demand and supply determine market equilibrium. Figure 3 shows the equilibrium price (P^*) and equilibrium quantity (Q^*) at the intersection of the demand curve and the supply curve.

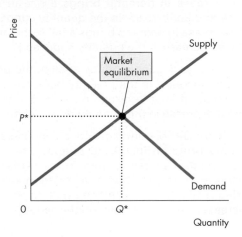

We can use the equations to find the equilibrium price and equilibrium quantity. The price of a good will adjust until the quantity demanded equals the quantity supplied. That is:

$$Q_D = Q_S$$

So at the equilibrium price (P^*) and equilibrium quantity (Q^*):

$$Q_D = Q_S = Q^*$$

To find the equilibrium price and equilibrium quantity: first substitute Q^* for Q_D in the demand equation and Q^* for Q_S in the supply equation. Then the price is the equilibrium price (P^*), which gives:

$$P^* = a - bQ^*$$

$$P^* = c + dQ^*$$

Notice that:

$$a - bQ^* = c + dQ^*$$

Now solve for Q^*:

$$a - c = bQ^* + dQ^*$$

$$a - c = (b + d)Q^*$$

$$Q^* = \frac{a - c}{b + d}$$

To find the equilibrium price (P^*) substitute for Q^* in either the demand equation or the supply equation.

Using the demand equation:

$$P^* = a - b\left(\frac{a - c}{b + d}\right)$$

$$P^* = \frac{a(b + d) - b(a - c)}{b + d}$$

$$P^* = \frac{ad + bc}{b + d}$$

Alternatively, using the supply equation:

$$P^* = c + d\left(\frac{a - c}{b + d}\right)$$

$$P^* = \frac{c(b + d) + d(a - c)}{b + d}$$

$$P^* = \frac{ad + bc}{b + d}$$

An Example

The demand for ice cream is:

$$P = 400 - 2Q_D$$

The supply of ice cream is:

$$P = 100 + 1Q_S$$

The price of an ice cream is expressed in pence and the quantities are expressed in ice creams per day.

To find the equilibrium price (P^*) and equilibrium quantity (Q^*), substitute Q^* for Q_D and Q_S and substitute P^* for P.

That is:

$$P^* = 400 - 2Q^*$$

$$P^* = 100 + 1Q^*$$

Now solve for Q^*:

$$400 - 2Q^* = 100 + 1Q^*$$

$$300 = 3Q^*$$

$$Q^* = 100$$

And:

$$P^* = 400 - 2(100) = 200$$

The equilibrium price is £2 an ice cream, and the equilibrium quantity is 100 ice creams per day.

Summary

Key Points

Price and Opportunity Cost (p. 54)

◆ A competitive market is one that has so many buyers and sellers that no one can influence the price.

◆ Opportunity cost is a relative price.

◆ Demand and supply determine relative prices.

Demand (pp. 55–59)

◆ Demand is the relationship between the quantity demanded of a good and its price when all other influences on buying plans remain the same.

◆ The higher the price of a good, other things remaining the same, the smaller is the quantity demanded – the law of demand.

◆ Demand depends on the prices of substitutes and complements, expected future prices, income, expected future income, population, and preferences.

Supply (pp. 60–63)

◆ Supply is the relationship between the quantity supplied of a good and its price when all other influences on selling plans remain the same.

◆ The higher the price of a good, other things remaining the same, the greater is the quantity supplied – the law of supply.

◆ Supply depends on the prices of resources used to produce a good, the prices of related goods produced, expected future prices, the number of suppliers, and technology.

Market Equilibrium (pp. 64–65)

◆ At the equilibrium price, the quantity demanded equals the quantity supplied.

◆ At prices above equilibrium, there is a surplus and the price falls.

◆ At prices below equilibrium, there is a shortage and the price rises.

Predicting Changes in Price and Quantity (pp. 66–69)

◆ An increase in demand brings a rise in the price and an increase in the quantity supplied. (A decrease in demand brings a fall in the price and a decrease in the quantity supplied.)

◆ An increase in supply brings a fall in the price and an increase in the quantity demanded. (A decrease in supply brings a rise in the price and a decrease in the quantity demanded.)

◆ An increase in demand and an increase in supply bring an increased quantity, but the price might rise, fall, or remain the same. An increase in demand and a decrease in supply bring a higher price, but the quantity might increase, decrease, or remain the same.

Key Figures

Key Terms

Problems

*1 What is the effect on the price of an audiotape and the quantity of audiotapes sold if:

  a The price of a CD rises?

  b The price of a Walkman rises?

  c The supply of CD players increases?

  d Consumers' incomes increase?

  e Workers who make audiotapes get a pay rise?

  f The price of a Walkman rises at the same time as the workers who make audiotapes get a pay rise?

2 What is the effect on the price of a DVD player and the quantity of DVD players sold if:

  a The price of a DVD rises?

  b The price of a DVD falls?

  c The supply of DVD players increases?

  d Consumers' incomes decrease?

  e The wage rate of workers who produce DVD players increases?

  f The wage rate of workers who produce DVD players rises and at the same time the price of a DVD falls?

*3 Suppose that the following events occur one at a time:

  (i) The price of crude oil rises.

  (ii) The price of a car rises.

  (iii) All speed limits on highways are abolished.

  (iv) Robot technology cuts car production costs.

  Which of these events will increase or decrease (state which):

  a The demand for petrol?

  b The supply of petrol?

  c The quantity of petrol demanded?

  d The quantity of petrol supplied?

4 Suppose that the following events occur one at a time:

  (i) The price of airfares halve.

  (ii) The price of beef falls.

  (iii) A cheap, strong cloth, a close substitute for leather, is invented.

  (iv) A new high-speed technology for cutting leather is invented.

  Which of these events will increase or decrease (state which):

  a The demand for leather bags?

  b The supply of leather bags?

  c The quantity of leather bags demanded?

  d The quantity of leather bags supplied?

*5 The figure illustrates the market for pizza.

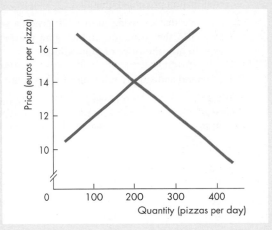

  a Label the curves in the figure.

  b What are the equilibrium price of a pizza and the equilibrium quantity of pizza?

6 The figure illustrates the market for fish.

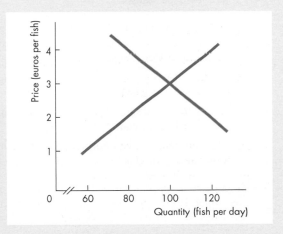

  a Label the curves in the figure.

  b What are the equilibrium price of fish and the equilibrium quantity of fish?

*7 The table sets out the demand and supply schedules for chewing gum.

Price (pence per packet)	Quantity demanded	Quantity supplied
	(millions of packets a week)	
20	180	60
30	160	80
40	140	100
50	120	120
60	100	140
70	80	160
80	60	180

a Draw a graph of the gum market and mark in the equilibrium price and quantity.

b Suppose that chewing gum is 70 pence a packet. Describe the situation in the gum market and explain how the price of gum adjusts.

8   The demand and supply schedules for crisps are

Price (pence per bag)	Quantity demanded	Quantity supplied
	(millions of bags per week)	
50	160	130
60	150	140
70	140	150
80	130	160
90	120	170
100	110	180

a Draw a graph of the crisps market and mark in the equilibrium price and quantity.

b Suppose that crisps are 60 pence a bag. Describe the situation in the market for crisps and explain how the price adjusts.

*9   In problem 7, suppose that a fire destroys some gum-producing factories and the supply of gum decreases by 40 million packs a week.

a Has there been a shift of or a movement along the supply curve of gum?

b Has there been a shift of or a movement along the demand curve for gum?

c What are the new equilibrium price and equilibrium quantity of gum?

10 In problem 8, suppose a new dip comes onto the market, which is very popular and the demand for crisps increases by 30 million bags per week.

a Has there been a shift of or a movement along the supply curve of crisps?

b Has there been a shift of or a movement along the demand curve for crisps?

c What are the new equilibrium price and equilibrium quantity of crisps?

*11 In problem 9, suppose an increase in the teenage population increases the demand for gum by 40 million packs per week at the same time as the fire occurs. What are the new equilibrium price and quantity of gum?

12 In problem 10, suppose that a virus destroys several potato farms with the result that the supply of crisps decreases by 40 million bags a week at the same time as the dip comes onto the market. What are the new equilibrium price and quantity of crisps?

Critical Thinking

1   Study *Reading Between the Lines*, pp. 70–71 and then:

a Explain why the Italian national grid cut off the electricity supply to big industrial users in November 2003.

b Explain the impact of this move on the market for electricity in Italy.

c Draw demand and supply curves to illustrate the impact of the heat wave on the price and quantity of electricity in Italy in November 2003.

Web Exercises

Use the links at *Parkin Interactive* to work the following exercises.

1   Obtain data on the prices and quantities of wheat.

a Make a figure similar to Figure 3.7 on p. 64 to illustrate the market for wheat in 2001 and 2002.

b Show the changes in demand and supply and the changes in the quantity demanded and the quantity supplied that are consistent with the price and quantity data.

2   Obtain data on the price of oil.

a Describe how the price of oil has changed over the past five years.

b Draw a demand-supply graph to explain what happens to the price when there is an increase or a decrease in supply and no change in demand.

c What do you predict would happen to the price of oil if a new drilling technology permitted deeper ocean sources to be used?

d What do you predict would happen to the price of oil if a clean and safe nuclear technology were developed?

e What do you predict would happen to the price of oil if cars were powered by batteries instead of by internal combustion engines?

3   Read the *Economics in History* on Discovering the Laws of Demand and Supply and then:

a Explain why there was so much interest in trying to understand the principles of demand and supply during the period of the Industrial Revolution.

b Explain why Alfred Marshall is considered to be the 'father' of modern economics.

Chapter 4

Elasticity

After studying this chapter you will be able to:

◆ Define, calculate and explain the factors that influence the price elasticity of demand

◆ Define, calculate and explain the factors that influence the cross elasticity of demand and the income elasticity of demand

◆ Define, calculate and explain the factors that influence the elasticity of supply

Squeezing Out Revenue

A new juice bar opens and offers low-price smoothies that attract lots of customers. But is that a smart decision? Could the firm generate more revenue with higher prices and fewer customers? If a cafe opens next door, by how much will the price of a smoothie have to fall to avoid losing customers to the new rival? This chapter introduces tools that help to answer questions like these. And *Reading Between the Lines* at the end of the chapter shows you how the French government is using these same tools to combat cigarette smoking.

Price Elasticity of Demand

Andy operates a juice bar. He knows that if the supply of smoothies increases the price of a smoothie will fall. But will the price fall by a large amount and the quantity increase by a little? Or will the price barely fall and the quantity increase by a large amount? To answer this question, Andy needs to know how the quantity demanded responds to a change in price.

Figure 4.1 shows two possible scenarios in Andy's local smoothie market. Figure 4.1(a) shows one scenario, and Figure 4.1(b) shows the other.

In both cases, supply is initially S_0. In part (a), the demand for smoothies is shown by the demand curve D_A. In part (b), the demand for smoothies is shown by the demand curve D_B. Initially, in both cases, the price is £3 a smoothie and the quantity of smoothie produced and consumed is 10 smoothies an hour.

Now three new juice bars open and the supply of smoothies increases. The supply curve shifts rightward to S_1. In case (a), the price falls by £2 to £1 a smoothie, and the quantity increases by only 5 to 15 smoothies an hour. In contrast, in case (b), the price falls by only £1 to £2 a smoothie and the quantity doubles to 20 smoothies an hour.

The different outcomes arise from differing degrees of responsiveness of the quantity demanded to a change in price. But what do we mean by responsiveness? One answer is slope. The slope of demand curve D_A is steeper than the slope of demand curve D_B.

In this example, we can compare the slopes of the two demand curves. But we can't always do so. The reason is that the slope of a demand curve depends on the units in which we measure the price and quantity. And we often must compare the demand curves for different goods and services that are measured in unrelated units. For example, a juice bar operator might want to compare the demand for smoothies with the demand for sandwiches. Which quantity demanded is more responsive to a price change?

This question can't be answered by comparing the slopes of two demand curves. The units of measurement of smoothies and sandwiches are unrelated. But the question *can* be answered with a measure of responsiveness that is independent of units of measurement. Elasticity is such a measure.

The **price elasticity of demand** is a units-free measure of the responsiveness of the quantity demanded of a good to a change in its price, when all other influences on buyers' plans remain the same.

Figure 4.1

How a Change in Supply Changes Price and Quantity

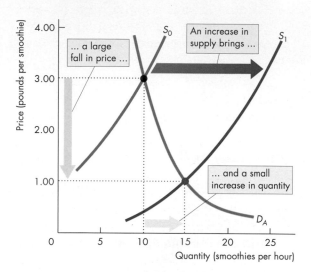

(a) Large price change and small quantity change

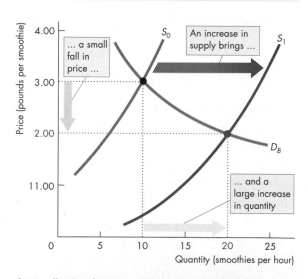

(b) Small price change and large quantity change

Initially, the price is £3 a smoothie and the quantity sold is 10 smoothies an hour. Then supply increases from S_0 to S_1. In part (a), the price falls by £2 to £1 a smoothie, and the quantity increases by 5 to 15 smoothies an hour.

In part (b), the price falls by only £1 to £2 a smoothie, and the quantity increases by 10 to 20 smoothies an hour. The price change is smaller and the quantity change is larger in case (b) than in case (a). The quantity demanded is more responsive to price in case (b) than in case (a).

Calculating Price Elasticity of Demand

We calculate the price elasticity of demand with the same data that we use to construct a demand curve – data on the quantity demanded at different prices when all other influences on buying plans remain the same. We use these numbers in the formula:

$$\text{Price elasticity of demand} = \frac{\text{Percentage change in quantity demanded}}{\text{Percentage change in price}}$$

Let's calculate the elasticity of demand for smoothies using the demand curve in Figure 4.2. This figure zooms in on the demand curve for smoothies and shows how the quantity demanded responds to a small change in price. Initially, the price is £3.10 a smoothie and 9 smoothies an hour are sold – the original point in the figure. The price then falls to £2.90 a smoothie, and the quantity demanded increases to 11 smoothies an hour – the new point in the figure. When the price falls by 20 pence a smoothie, the quantity demanded increases by 2 smoothies an hour.

To calculate the price elasticity of demand, we express the changes in price and quantity as percentages of the *average price* and *average quantity*. By using the average price and average quantity, we calculate the elasticity at a point on the demand curve midway between the original point and the new point.

The original price is £3.10 and the new price is £2.90, so the average price is £3. The 20 pence price decrease is 6.67 per cent of the average price. That is:

$$\Delta P/P_{AVE} = (£0.20/£3.00) \times 100 = 6.67\%$$

The original quantity demanded is 9 smoothies and the new quantity demanded is 11 smoothies, so the average quantity demanded is 10 smoothies. The increase in the quantity demanded of 2 smoothies is 20 per cent of the average quantity. That is:

$$\Delta Q/Q_{AVE} = (2/10) \times 100 = 20\%$$

So the price elasticity of demand, which is the percentage change in the quantity demanded (20 per cent) divided by the percentage change in price (6.67 per cent) is 3. That is:

$$\text{Price elasticity of demand} = \frac{\%\Delta Q}{\%\Delta P}$$
$$= \frac{20\%}{6.67\%}$$
$$= 3$$

Figure 4.2

Calculating the Elasticity of Demand

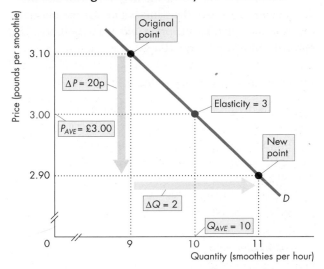

The elasticity of demand is calculated by using the formula:*

$$\text{Price elasticity of demand} = \frac{\text{Percentage change in quantity demanded}}{\text{Percentage change in price}}$$

$$= \frac{\%\Delta Q}{\%\Delta P}$$

$$= \frac{\Delta Q/Q_{AVE}}{\Delta P/P_{AVE}}$$

$$= \frac{2/10}{0.20/3.00}$$

$$= 3$$

(handwritten:) 20/30 = 66.67%
2.5/8.75 = 2.9%
200%
0.22%

This calculation measures the elasticity at an average price of £3.00 a smoothie and an average quantity of 10 smoothies an hour.

* In the formula, the Greek letter delta (Δ) stands for "change in" and %Δ stands for "percentage change in".

Average Price and Quantity

We use the *average* price and *average* quantity because it gives the most precise measurement of elasticity – midway between the original and new point. If the price falls from £3.10 to £2.90, the 20 pence price change is 6.45 per cent of £3.10. The 2 smoothies change in quantity is 22.2 per cent of 9 smoothies, the original quantity. So if we use these numbers, the price elasticity of demand is 22.2 divided by 6.45, which equals 3.44. If the price *rises* from £2.90 to £3.10, the 20 pence price change is 6.9 per cent of £2.90. The 2 smoothies change in quantity is 18.2 per cent of 11 smoothies, the original quantity. If we use these numbers, the price elasticity of demand is 18.2 divided by 6.9, which equals 2.64.

By using percentages of the *average* price and *average* quantity, we get the same value for the elasticity regardless of whether the price falls from £3.10 to £2.90 or rises from £2.90 to £3.10.

Percentages and Proportions

When we divide the percentage change in quantity by the percentage change in price, the 100s cancel. A percentage change is a *proportionate* change multiplied by 100. The proportionate change in price is $\Delta P/P_{AVE}$, and the proportionate change in quantity demanded is $\Delta Q/Q_{AVE}$. So if we divide $\Delta Q/Q_{AVE}$ by $\Delta P/P_{AVE}$, we get the same answer as we get by using percentage changes.

A Units-free Measure

Elasticity is a *units-free measure* because the percentage change in each variable is independent of the units in which the variable is measured. And the ratio of the two percentages is a number without units.

Minus Sign and Elasticity

When the price of a good *rises*, the quantity demanded *decreases* along the demand curve. Because a *positive* change in price brings a *negative* change in the quantity demanded, the price elasticity of demand is a negative

number. But it is the magnitude, or *absolute value*, of the price elasticity of demand that tells us how responsive – how elastic – demand is. To compare price elasticities of demand, we use the magnitude of the elasticity and ignore the minus sign.

Inelastic and Elastic Demand

Figure 4.3 shows three demand curves that cover the entire range of possible elasticities of demand. In Figure 4.3(a), the quantity demanded is constant regardless of the price. If the quantity demanded remains constant when the price changes, then the price elasticity of demand is zero and the good is said to have a **perfectly inelastic demand**. One good that has a very low price elasticity of demand (perhaps zero over some price range) is insulin. Insulin is of such importance to some diabetics that if the price rises or falls, they do not change the quantity they buy.

If the percentage change in the quantity demanded equals the percentage change in price, then the price elasticity equals 1 and the good is said to have a **unit elastic demand**. The demand in Figure 4.3(b) is an example of unit elastic demand.

Between the cases shown in Figure 4.3(a) and Figure 4.3(b) is the general case in which the percentage change in the quantity demanded is less than the percentage change in price. In this case, the price elasticity of demand is between zero and 1 and the

Figure 4.3

Inelastic and Elastic Demand

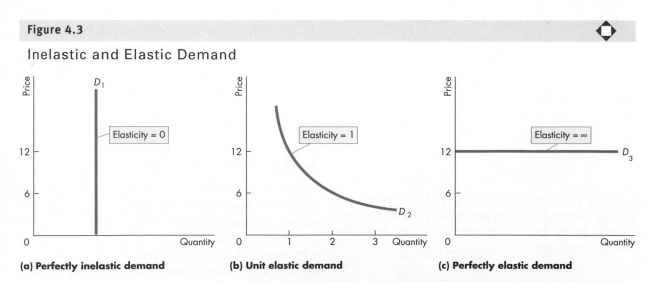

(a) Perfectly inelastic demand   **(b) Unit elastic demand**   **(c) Perfectly elastic demand**

Each demand illustrated here has a constant elasticity. The demand curve in part (a) illustrates the demand for a good that has a zero elasticity of demand. The demand curve in part (b) illustrates the demand for a good with a unit elasticity of demand. And the demand curve in part (c) illustrates the demand for a good with an infinite elasticity of demand.

good is said to have an **inelastic demand**. Food and housing are examples of goods with inelastic demand.

If the quantity demanded changes by an infinitely large percentage in response to a tiny price change, then the price elasticity of demand is infinity and the good is said to have a **perfectly elastic demand**. Figure 4.3(c) shows a perfectly elastic demand. An example of a good that has a very high elasticity of demand (almost infinite) is a salad from two campus machines located side by side. If the two machines offer the same salads for the same price, some people buy from one machine and some from the other. But if one machine's price is higher than the other's, by even a small amount, no one will buy from the machine with the higher price. Salads from the two machines are perfect substitutes.

Between the cases in Figure 4.3(b) and Figure 4.3(c) is the general case in which the percentage change in the quantity demanded exceeds the percentage change in price. In this case, the price elasticity of demand is greater than 1 and the good is said to have an **elastic demand**. Cars and furniture are examples of goods that have elastic demand.

Elasticity Along a Linear Demand Curve

Elasticity and slope are not the same, but they are related. To understand how they are related, let's look at elasticity along a straight-line demand curve – a demand curve that has a constant slope.

Figure 4.4 illustrates the calculation of elasticity along a straight-line demand curve. First, suppose the price falls from £5 to £3 a smoothie. The quantity demanded increases from zero to 10 smoothies an hour. The average price is £4 a smoothie, and the average quantity is 5 smoothies. So:

$$\text{Price elasticity of demand} = \frac{\Delta Q/Q_{AVE}}{\Delta P/P_{AVE}}$$

$$= \frac{10/5}{2/4}$$

$$= 4$$

That is, the price elasticity of demand at an average price of £4 a smoothie is 4.

Next, suppose that the price falls from £3 to £2 a smoothie. The quantity demanded increases from 10 to 15 smoothies an hour. The average price is now £2.50 a smoothie, and the average quantity is 12.5 smoothies an hour.

So:

$$\text{Price elasticity of demand} = \frac{5/12.5}{1/2.5}$$

$$= 1$$

That is, the price elasticity of demand at an average price of £2.50 a smoothie is 1.

Finally, suppose that the price falls from £2 to zero. The quantity demanded increases from 15 to 25 smoothies an hour. The average price is now £1 and the average quantity is 20 smoothies an hour. So:

$$\text{Price elasticity of demand} = \frac{10/20}{2/1}$$

$$= 1/4$$

That is, the price elasticity of demand at an average price of £1 a smoothie is 1/4.

You've now seen how elasticity changes along a straight-line demand curve. At the mid-point of the curve, demand is unit elastic. At prices above the mid-point, demand is elastic. At prices below the mid-point, demand is inelastic.

Figure 4.4

Elasticity Along a Linear Demand Curve

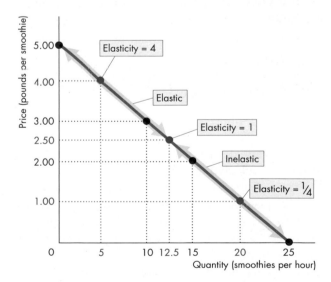

On a linear demand curve, elasticity decreases as the price falls and the quantity demanded increases. Demand is unit elastic at the mid-point of the demand curve (elasticity is 1). At prices above the mid-point, demand is elastic; at prices below the mid-point, demand is inelastic.

Total Revenue and Elasticity

The **total revenue** from the sale of a good equals the price of the good multiplied by the quantity sold. When a price changes, total revenue might or might not change. And a rise in price does not always increase total revenue.

The change in total revenue depends on the elasticity of demand in the following way:

1   If demand is elastic, a 1 per cent price cut increases the quantity sold by more than 1 per cent and total revenue increases.

2   If demand is inelastic, a 1 per cent price cut increases the quantity sold by less than 1 per cent and total revenue decreases.

3   If demand is unit elastic, a 1 per cent price cut increases the quantity sold by 1 per cent and so total revenue does not change.

Figure 4.5 shows how we can use this relationship between elasticity and total revenue to estimate elasticity using the total revenue test. The **total revenue test** is a method of estimating the price elasticity of demand by observing the change in total revenue that results from a change in the price, when all other influences on the quantity sold remain the same.

1   If a price cut increases total revenue, demand is elastic.

2   If a price cut decreases total revenue, demand is inelastic.

3   If a price cut leaves total revenue unchanged, demand is unit elastic.

In Figure 4.5(a), over the price range from £5 to £2.50, demand is elastic. Over the price range from £2.50 to zero, demand is inelastic. At a price of £2.50, demand is unit elastic.

Figure 4.5(b) shows total revenue. At a price of £5, the quantity sold is zero (part a), so total revenue is zero (part b). At a price of zero, the quantity demanded is 25 smoothies an hour and total revenue is again zero.

A price cut in the elastic range brings an increase in total revenue – the percentage increase in the quantity demanded is greater than the percentage decrease in price.

A price cut in the inelastic range brings a decrease in total revenue – the percentage increase in the quantity demanded is less than the percentage decrease in price. At unit elasticity, total revenue is at a maximum.

Figure 4.5

Elasticity and Total Revenue

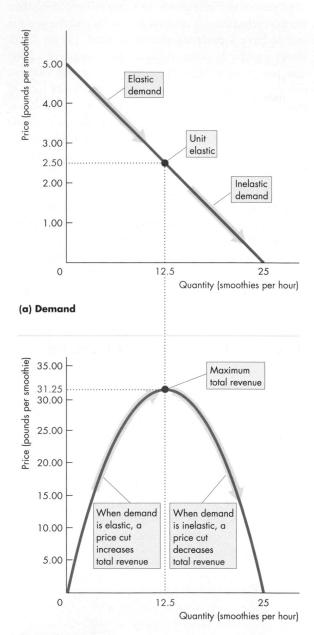

(a) Demand

(b) Total revenue

When demand is elastic, in the price range from £5 to £2.50, a decrease in price in part (a) brings an increase in total revenue in part (b). When demand is inelastic, in the price range from £2.50 to zero, a decrease in price in part (a) brings a decrease in total revenue in part (b). When demand is unit elastic, at a price of £2.50 in part (a), total revenue is at a maximum in part (b).

Your Expenditure and Your Elasticity

When a price changes, the change in your expenditure on the good depends on *your* elasticity of demand.

1 If your demand is elastic, a 1 per cent price cut increases the quantity you buy by more than 1 per cent and your expenditure on the item increases.

2 If your demand is inelastic, a 1 per cent price cut increases the quantity you buy by less than 1 per cent and your expenditure on the item decreases.

3 If your demand is unit elastic, a 1 per cent price cut increases the quantity you buy by 1 per cent and your expenditure on the item does not change.

So if you spend more on an item when its price falls, your demand for that item is elastic; if you spend the same amount, your demand is unit elastic; and if you spend less, your demand is inelastic.

The Factors That Influence the Elasticity of Demand

What makes the demand for some goods elastic and the demand for others inelastic? The magnitude of the elasticity of demand depends on:

◆ The closeness of substitutes

◆ The proportion of income spent on the good

◆ The time elapsed since a price change

Closeness of Substitutes

The closer the substitutes for a good or service, the more elastic is the demand for it. For example, oil from which we make petrol has substitutes but none that are currently very close (imagine a steam-driven, coal-fuelled car). So the demand for oil is inelastic. Plastics are close substitutes for metals, so the demand for metals is elastic.

The degree of substitutability between two goods also depends on how narrowly (or broadly) we define them. For example, the elasticity of demand for meat is low, but the elasticity of demand for beef or pork is high. The elasticity of demand for personal computers is low, but the elasticity of demand for a Gateway, Dell, or IBM computer is high.

In everyday language we call some goods, such as food and housing, *necessities* and other goods, such as exotic vacations, *luxuries*. A necessity is a good that has poor substitutes and that is crucial for our well-being. So generally, a necessity has an inelastic demand.

In the table in Box 4.1, food and oil might be classified as necessities.

A luxury is a good that usually has many substitutes, one of which is not buying it. So a luxury generally has an elastic demand. In the table in Box 4.1, furniture and motor vehicles might be classified as luxuries.

Box 4.1
Some Real World Price Elasticities of Demand

The table below shows some estimates of price elasticities of demand in the United Kingdom. These values range from 1.4 for fresh meat, the most elastic in the table, to zero for bread, the least elastic in the table.

You can see that the items with an elastic demand include luxuries (wine and spirits) while items with an inelastic demand include necessities (bread and green vegetables). You can also see that luxuries that are habit forming (tobacco and beer) also have an inelastic demand.

Services, with unit elasticity, is such a broad category that it almost certainly hides wide variations in elasticity across the different services.

Table 1

UK Price Elasticities of Demand

Good or service	Elasticity
Elastic demand	
Fresh meat	1.4
Spirits	1.3
Wine	1.2
Unit elasticity	
Services	1.0
Cereals	1.0
Inelastic demand	
Durable goods	0.9
Fruit juice	0.8
Green vegetables	0.6
Tobacco	0.5
Beer	0.5
Bread	0.0

Sources: Ministry of Agriculture, Food and Fisheries, *Household Food Consumption and Expenditure*, 1992, London, HMSO. C. Godfrey, 'Modelling Demand', *Preventing Alcohol and Tobacco Problems*, Vol. 1, (A. Maynard and P. Tether, eds), Avebury, 1990. J. Muellbauer, 'Testing the Barten Model of Household Composition Effects and the Cost of Children', *Economic Journal*, (September 1977).

Proportion of Income Spent on the Good

Other things remaining the same, the greater the proportion of income spent on a good, the more elastic is the demand for it.

Think about your own elasticity of demand for toothpaste and housing. If the price of toothpaste doubles, you consume almost as much as before. Your demand for toothpaste is inelastic. If flat rents double, you shriek and look for more students to share accommodation with you. Your demand for housing is more elastic than your demand for toothpaste. Why the difference? Housing takes a large proportion of your budget, and toothpaste takes only a tiny proportion. You don't like either price increase, but you hardly notice the higher price of toothpaste, while the higher rent puts your budget under severe strain.

Time Elapsed Since Price Change

The longer the time that has elapsed since a price change, the more elastic is demand. When the price of oil increased by 400 per cent during the 1970s, people barely changed the quantity of oil and petrol they bought. But gradually, as more efficient auto and airplane engines were developed, the quantity used decreased. The demand for oil has become more elastic as more time has elapsed since the huge price hike. Similarly, when the price of a PC fell, the quantity of PCs demanded increased only slightly at first. But as more people have become better informed about the variety of ways of using a PC, the quantity of PCs bought has increased sharply. The demand for PCs has become more elastic.

Review Quiz

1   Why do we need a units-free measure of the responsiveness of the quantity demanded of a good or service to a change in its price?
2   Can you define and calculate the price elasticity of demand?
3   Why, when we calculate the price elasticity of demand, do we express the change in price as a percentage of the *average* price and the change in quantity as a percentage of the *average* quantity?
4   What is the total revenue test and why does it work?
5   What are the main influences on the elasticity of demand that make the demand for some goods elastic and the demand for other goods inelastic?
6   Why is the demand for a luxury generally more elastic than the demand for a necessity?

Box 4.2
Price Elasticity of Demand for Food

You can see the proportion of income spent on food and the price elasticity of demand for food in 10 countries in the figure below. In general, the larger the proportion of income spent on food, the more price elastic is the demand for food. In a very poor country like Tanzania, where 62 per cent of income is spent on food, the price elasticity of demand for food is 0.77. In contrast, in Germany where 15 per cent of income is spent on food, the elasticity of demand for food is just 0.23. These figures make sense. In a country that spends a large proportion of its income on food, an increase in the price of food forces people to make a bigger adjustment to the quantity of food they buy than in a country in which only a small proportion of income is spent on food.

Figure 1

The Price Elasticity of Demand for Food in Ten Countries

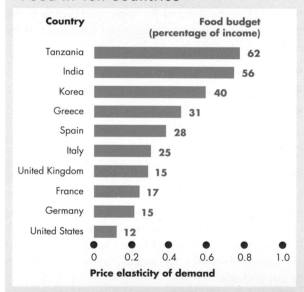

As income increases and the proportion of income spent on food decreases, the demand for food becomes less elastic.

Source: Henri Theil, Ching-Fan Chung and James L. Seale Jr, *Advances in Econometrics, Supplement 1, International Evidence on Consumption Patterns.* Greenwich, Connecticut, JAI Press Inc. 1989.

You've now completed your study of the *price* elasticity of demand. Two other elasticity concepts tell us about the effects of other influences on demand. Let's look at these other elasticities of demand.

More Elasticities of Demand

Back at the juice bar, Andy is trying to work out how a cut in the price of soft drinks at the cafe next door will affect the demand for his smoothies. He knows that smoothies and soft drinks are substitutes. And he knows that when the price of a substitute for smoothie falls, the demand for smoothies will decrease. But by how much? He also knows that smoothies and salads are complements. And he knows that if the price of a complement of smoothies falls, the demand for smoothies will increases. So he wonders whether he might keep his customers by cutting the price he charges for salads. But again, by how much?

To answer these questions, Andy needs to calculate some cross elasticities of demand. Let's examine this elasticity measure.

Cross Elasticity of Demand

We measure the influence of a change in the price of a substitute or complement by using the concept of the cross elasticity of demand. The **cross elasticity of demand** is a measure of the responsiveness of the demand for a good to a change in the price of a substitute or complement, other things remaining the same. We calculate the *cross elasticity of demand* by using the formula:

$$\text{Cross elasticity of demand} = \frac{\text{Percentage change in quantity demanded}}{\text{Percentage change in price of substitute or complement}}$$

The cross elasticity of demand can be positive or negative. It is *positive* for a *substitute* and *negative* for a *complement*.

Substitutes

Suppose that the price of smoothie is constant and 11 smoothies an hour are sold. Then the price of a soft drink falls from 50p to 30p. No other influence on buying plans changes and the quantity of smoothies sold decreases to 9 an hour.

The change in the quantity demanded is −2 smoothies – the new quantity, 9 smoothies, minus the original quantity, 11 smoothies. The average quantity is 10 smoothies. So the quantity of smoothies demanded changes by −20 per cent. That is:

$$\Delta Q / Q_{AVE} = (-2/10) \times 100 = -20\%$$

The change in the price of a soft drink, a substitute for smoothie, is −20p – the new price, 30p, minus the original price, 50p. The average price is 40p a soft drink. So the price of a soft drink falls by 50 per cent (−50). That is:

$$\Delta P / P_{AVE} = (-20/40) \times 100 = -50\%$$

So the cross elasticity of demand for smoothies with respect to the price of a soft drink is:

$$\frac{-20\%}{-50\%} = 0.4$$

Figure 4.6 illustrates the cross elasticity of demand. Smoothies and soft drinks are substitutes. Because they are substitutes, when the price of a soft drink *falls*, the demand for smoothies *decreases*. The demand curve for smoothie shifts leftward from D_0 to D_1.

Because a *fall* in the price of a soft drink brings a *decrease* in the demand for smoothies, the cross elasticity of demand for smoothies with respect to the price of a soft drink is *positive*. Both the price and the quantity change in the same direction.

Figure 4.6

Cross Elasticity of Demand

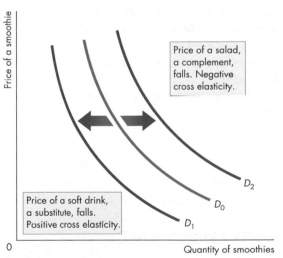

A soft drink is a substitute for a smoothie. When the price of a soft drink falls, the demand for smoothies decreases and the demand curve for smoothie shifts leftward from D_0 to D_1. The cross elasticity of the demand is positive.

A salad is a complement of a smoothie. When the price of a salad falls, the demand for smoothies increases and the demand curve for smoothies shifts rightward from D_0 to D_2. The cross elasticity of the demand is negative.

Complements

Now suppose that the price of smoothie is constant and 9 smoothies an hour are sold. Then the price of a salad falls from £2.50 to £1.50. No other influence on buying plans changes and the quantity of smoothies sold increases to 11 an hour.

The change in the quantity demanded is the opposite of what we've just calculated: The quantity of smoothies demanded increases by 20 per cent (+20).

The change in the price of a salad, a complement of smoothie, is the same as the percentage change in the price of a soft drink that we've just calculated: The price of a salad rises by 50 per cent (+50). So the cross elasticity of demand for smoothies with respect to the price of a salad is:

$$\frac{+20\%}{-50\%} = -0.4$$

Because smoothies and salads are complements, when the price of a salad *falls*, the demand for smoothies *increases*. The demand curve for smoothie shifts rightward from D_0 to D_2. Because a *fall* in the price of a salad brings an *increase* in the demand for smoothies, the cross elasticity of demand for smoothies with respect to the price of a salad is *negative*. The price and quantity change in *opposite* directions.

The magnitude of the cross elasticity of demand determines how far the demand curve shifts. The larger the cross elasticity (absolute value), the greater is the change in demand and the larger is the shift in the demand curve.

If two items are very close substitutes, such as two brands of spring water, the cross elasticity is large. If two items are close complements, such as fish and chips, the cross elasticity is large.

If two items are somewhat unrelated to each other, such as a newspaper and a smoothie, the cross elasticity is small – perhaps even zero.

Income Elasticity of Demand

The economy is expanding and people are enjoying rising incomes. This prosperity is bringing an increase in the demand for most types of goods and services. But by how much will the demand for smoothies increase? The answer depends on the **income elasticity of demand**, which is a measure of the responsiveness of the demand for a good or service to a change in income, other things remaining the same.

The income elasticity of demand is calculated by using the formula:

$$\text{Income elasticity of demand} = \frac{\text{Percentage change in quantity demanded}}{\text{Percentage change in income}}$$

Income elasticities of demand can be positive or negative and fall into three interesting ranges:

◆ Greater than 1 (*normal* good, income elastic)
◆ Positive and less than 1 (*normal* good, income inelastic)
◆ Negative (*inferior* good)

Income Elastic Demand

Suppose that the price of smoothie is constant and 9 smoothies an hour are sold. Then incomes rise from £475 to £525 a week. No other influence on buying plans changes and the quantity of smoothies sold increases to 11 an hour.

The change in the quantity demanded is 2 smoothies. The average quantity is 10 smoothies, so the quantity demanded increases by 20 per cent. The change in income is £50 and the average income is £500, so incomes increase by 10 per cent. The income elasticity of demand for smoothies is:

$$\frac{20\%}{10\%} = 2$$

As income increases, the quantity of smoothies demanded increases faster than income. The demand for smoothies is income elastic. Other goods in this category include ocean cruises, international travel, jewellery and works of art.

Income Inelastic Demand

If the percentage increase in the quantity demanded is less than the percentage increase in income, the income elasticity of demand is positive and less than 1. In this case, the quantity demanded increases as income increases, but income increases faster than the quantity demanded. The demand for the good is income inelastic. Goods in this category include food, clothing, newspapers, and magazines.

Inferior Goods

If the quantity demanded of a good decreases when income increases, the income elasticity of demand is negative. Goods in this category include small motorcycles, potatoes, and rice. Low-income consumers buy most of these goods.

Box 4.3
Real-world Income Elasticities of Demand

Table 1 shows some estimates of the income elasticities of demand in the United Kingdom. Basic food items such as fresh meat are income inelastic, while luxury goods such as wines and spirits are income elastic. Some goods such as tobacco and bread have income elasticities that are negative, so they are defined as inferior goods. However, their elasticity values are very close to zero.

The demand for food is income inelastic – elasticity less than 1. But income elasticity varies with income. The figure shows the effect of the *level* of income on the income elasticity of demand for food in 10 countries. In a country with low incomes, such as Tanzania, the income inelasticity of demand for food is around 0.75, while in the high-income countries of Europe and North America, the income elasticity of demand for food is much lower. These numbers tell us that a 10 per cent increase in income leads to a 7.5 per cent increase in the demand for food of in India, a 3 per cent increase in France, and a less than 2 per cent increase in the United States.

Table 1

Some UK Income Elasticities of Demand

Good or service	Elasticity
Normal elastic demand	
Wine	2.6
Services	1.8
Spirits	1.7
Durable goods	1.5
Normal inelastic demand	
Fruit juice	0.9
Beer	0.6
Green vegetables	0.1
Fresh meat	0.0
Cereals	0.0
Inferior	
Tobacco	−0.1
Bread	−0.3

Sources: Ministry of Agriculture, Food and Fisheries, *Household Food Consumption and Expenditure*, 1992, London, HMSO. C. Godfrey, Modelling Demand. In *Preventing Alcohol and Tobacco Problems*, Vol. 1, (A. Maynard and P. Tether, eds), Avebury, 1990. J. Muellbauer 'Testing the Barten Model of Household Composition Effects and the Cost of Children', *Economic Journal*, (September 1977).

Figure 1

Income Elasticities in 10 Countries

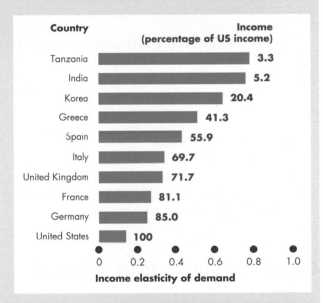

As income increases, the income elasticity of demand for food decreases. Low-income consumers spend a larger percentage of any increase in income on food than do high-income consumers.

Source: Henri Theil, Ching-Fan Chung and James L. Seale Jr, *Advances in Econometrics, Supplement 1, International Evidence on Consumption Patterns*. Greenwich, Connecticut, JAI Press Inc. 1989.

Review Quiz

1 What does the cross elasticity of demand measure?
2 What does the sign (positive versus negative) of the cross elasticity of demand tell us about the relationship between two goods?
3 What does the income elasticity of demand measure?
4 What does the sign (positive versus negative) of the income elasticity of demand tell us about a good?
5 Why does the level of income influence the magnitude of the income elasticity of demand?

You've now completed your study of the *price* elasticity of demand, the *cross elasticity* of demand and the *income elasticity* of demand.

We're now going to look at the other side of a market and examine the elasticity of supply.

Elasticity of Supply

When demand increases, the equilibrium price rises and the equilibrium quantity increases. But does the price rise by a large amount and the quantity increase by a little? Or does the price barely rise and the quantity increase by a large amount?

The answer depends on the responsiveness of the quantity supplied to a change in price. You can see why by studying Figure 4.7, which shows two possible scenarios in a local smoothie market. Figure 4.7(a) shows one scenario, and Figure 4.7(b) shows the other.

In both cases, demand is initially D_0. In part (a), the supply of smoothie is shown by the supply curve S_A. In part (b), the supply of smoothie is shown by the supply curve S_B. Initially, in both cases, the price is £3 a smoothie and the quantity produced and consumed is 10 smoothies an hour.

Now increases in incomes and population increase the demand for smoothies. The demand curve shifts rightward to D_1. In case (a), the price rises by £2 to £5 a smoothie and the quantity increases by only 5 to 15 an hour. In contrast, in case (b), the price rises by only 20p to £3.20 a smoothie and the quantity increases by 10 to 20 smoothies an hour.

The different outcomes arise from differing degrees of responsiveness of the quantity supplied to a change in price. We measure the degree of responsiveness by using the concept of the elasticity of supply.

Calculating the Elasticity of Supply

The **elasticity of supply** measures the responsiveness of the quantity supplied to a change in the price of a good when all other influences on selling plans remain the same. It is calculated by using the formula:

$$\text{Price elasticity of supply} = \frac{\text{Percentage change in quantity supplied}}{\text{Percentage change in price}}$$

We use the same method that you learned when you studied the elasticity of demand. (Refer back to p. 79 to check this method.) Let's calculate the elasticity of supply along the supply curves in Figure 4.7.

In Figure 4.7(a), when the price rises from £3 to £5, the price rise is £2 and the average price is £4, so price rises by 50 per cent of the average price.

Figure 4.7

How a Change in Demand Changes Price and Quantity

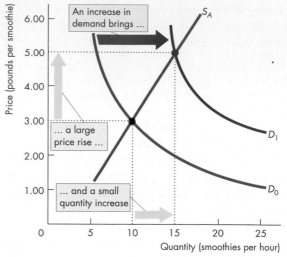

(a) Large price change and small quantity change

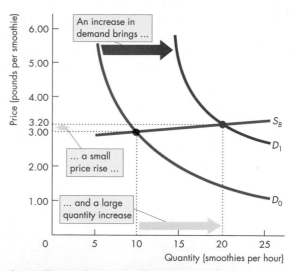

(b) Small price change and large quantity change

Initially, the price is £3 a smoothie and the quantity sold is 10 smoothies an hour. Then increases in incomes and population increase the demand for smoothies. The demand curve shifts rightward to D_1. In part (a) the price rises by £2 to £5 a smoothie, and the quantity increases by 5 to 14 smoothies an hour. In part (b), the price rises by only 25p to £3.25 a smoothie and the quantity increases by 10 to 20 smoothies an hour. The price change is smaller and the quantity change is larger in case (b) than in case (a). The quantity supplied is more responsive to price in case (b) than in case (a).

The quantity increases from 10 to 15 smoothies an hour, so the increase is 5 smoothies, the average quantity is 12.5 smoothies an hour, and the quantity increases by 40 per cent.

The elasticity of supply is equal to 40 per cent divided by 50 per cent, which equals 0.8.

In Figure 4.7(b), when the price rises from £3 to £3.20, the price rise is 20p and the average price is £3.10, so the price rises by 6.45 per cent of the average price. The quantity increases from 10 to 20 smoothies an hour, so the increase is 10 smoothies, the average quantity is 15 smoothies, and the quantity increases by 66.67 per cent. The elasticity of supply equals 66.67 per cent divided by 6.45 per cent, which equals 10.34.

Figure 4.8 shows the range of elasticities of supply. If the quantity supplied is fixed regardless of the price, the supply curve is vertical and the elasticity of supply is zero. Supply is perfectly inelastic. This case is shown in Figure 4.8(a). A special intermediate case is when the percentage change in price equals the percentage change in quantity. Supply is then unit elastic. This case is shown in Figure 4.8(b). No matter how steep the supply curve is, if it is linear and passes through the origin, supply is unit elastic. If there is a price at which sellers are willing to offer any quantity for sale, the supply curve is horizontal and the elasticity of supply is infinite. Supply is perfectly elastic. This case is shown in Figure 4.8(c).

The Factors That Influence the Elasticity of Supply

The magnitude of the elasticity of supply depends on:

◆ Resource substitution possibilities
◆ Time frame for the supply decision

Resource Substitution Possibilities

Some goods and services can be produced only by using unique or rare productive resources. These items have a low, even perhaps a zero, elasticity of supply. Other goods and services can be produced by using commonly available resources that could be allocated to a wide variety of alternative tasks. Such items have a high elasticity of supply.

A Van Gogh painting is an example of a good with a vertical supply curve and a zero elasticity of supply. At the other extreme, wheat can be grown on land that is almost equally good for growing corn. So it is just as easy to grow wheat as corn, and the opportunity cost of wheat in terms of forgone corn is almost constant. As a result, the supply curve of wheat is almost horizontal and its elasticity of supply is very large. Similarly, when a good is produced in many different countries (for example, wheat, sugar and beef), the supply of the good is highly elastic.

Figure 4.8

Inelastic and Elastic Supply

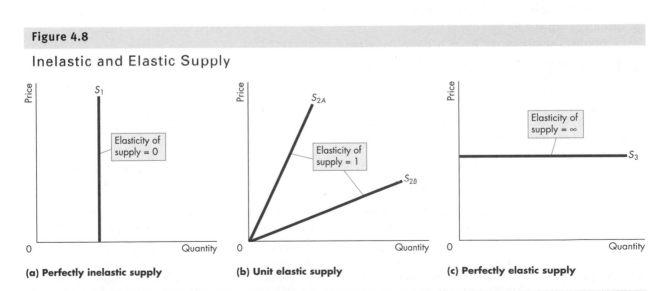

(a) Perfectly inelastic supply   **(b) Unit elastic supply**   **(c) Perfectly elastic supply**

Each supply illustrated here has a constant elasticity. The supply curve in part (a) illustrates the supply of a good that has a zero elasticity of supply. The supply curve in part (b) illustrates the supply of a good with a unit elasticity of supply. All linear supply curves that pass through the origin illustrate supplies that are unit elastic. The supply curve in part (c) illustrates the supply of a good with an infinite elasticity of supply.

The supply of most goods and services lies between these two extremes. The quantity produced can be increased but only by incurring a higher cost. If a higher price is offered, the quantity supplied increases. Such goods and services have an elasticity of supply between zero and infinity.

Time Frame for Supply Decisions

To study the influence of the length of time elapsed since a price change we distinguish three time frames of supply:

1 Momentary supply

2 Long-run supply

3 Short-run supply

When the price of a good rises or falls, the *momentary supply curve* shows the response of the quantity supplied immediately following a price change.

Some goods, such as fruits and vegetables, have a perfectly inelastic momentary supply – a vertical supply curve. The quantities supplied depend on crop planting decisions made earlier. In the case of oranges, for example, planting decisions have to be made many years in advance of the crop being available.

The momentary supply curve is vertical because, on a given day, no matter what the price of oranges, producers cannot change their output. They have picked, packed and shipped their crop to market, and the quantity available for that day is fixed.

In contrast, some goods have a perfectly elastic momentary supply. Long-distance phone calls are an example. When many people simultaneously make a call, there is a big surge in the demand for telephone cables, computer switching and satellite time, and the quantity bought increases. But the price remains constant. Long-distance carriers monitor fluctuations in demand and reroute calls to ensure that the quantity supplied equals the quantity demanded without changing the price.

The *long-run supply curve* shows the response of the quantity supplied to a change in price after all the technologically possible ways of adjusting supply have been exploited. In the case of oranges, the long run is the time it takes new plantings to grow to full maturity – about 15 years. In some cases, the long-run adjustment occurs only after a completely new production plant has been built and workers have been trained to operate it – typically a process that might take several years.

The *short-run supply curve* shows how the quantity supplied responds to a price change when only *some* of the technologically possible adjustments to production have been made. The short-run response to a price change is a sequence of adjustments. The first adjustment that is usually made is in the amount of labour employed. To increase output in the short run, firms work their labour force overtime and perhaps hire additional workers. To decrease their output in the short run, firms either lay off workers or reduce their hours of work. With the passage of time, firms can make additional adjustments, perhaps training additional workers or buying additional tools and other equipment.

The short-run supply curve slopes upward because producers can take actions quite quickly to change the quantity supplied in response to a price change. For example, if the price of oranges falls, growers can stop picking and leave oranges to rot on the trees. Or if the price rises, they can use more fertilizer and improved irrigation to increase the yields of their existing trees. In the long run, they can plant more trees and increase the quantity supplied even more in response to a given price rise.

Review Quiz

1 Why do we need to measure the responsiveness of the quantity supplied of a good or service to a change in its price?

2 Can you define and calculate the elasticity of supply?

3 What are the main influences on the elasticity of supply that make the supply of some goods elastic and the supply of other goods inelastic?

4 Can you provide examples of goods or services whose elasticities of supply are (a) zero, (b) greater than zero but less than infinity and (c), infinity?

5 How does the time frame over which a supply decision is made influence the elasticity of supply?

You have now learned about the elasticities of demand and supply. Table 4.1 summarizes all the elasticities that you've met in this chapter.

In the next chapter, we study the efficiency of competitive markets. But before leaving elasticity, *Reading Between the Lines* on pp. 92–93 puts the elasticity of demand to work looking at the effects of a rise in a tax on the price, quantity, and tax revenue raised.

Table 4.1

A Compact Glossary of Elasticities of Demand

A relationship is described as	When its magnitude is	Which means that
Price Elasticity of Demand		
Perfectly elastic or infinitely elastic	Infinity	The smallest possible increase in price causes an infinitely elastic large decrease in the quantity demanded*
Elastic	Less than infinity but greater than 1	The percentage decrease in the quantity demanded exceeds the percentage increase in price
Unit elastic	1	The percentage decrease in the quantity demanded equals the percentage increase in price
Inelastic	Greater than zero but less than 1	The percentage decrease in the quantity demanded is less than the percentage increase in price
Perfectly inelastic or completely inelastic	Zero	The quantity demanded is the same at all prices
Cross Elasticity of Demand		
Perfect substitutes	Infinity	The smallest possible increase in the price of one good causes an infinitely large increase in the quantity demanded of the other good
Substitutes	Positive, less than infinity	If the price of one good increases the quantity demanded of the other good also increases
Independent	Zero	The quantity demanded of one good remains constant regardless of the price of the other good
Complements	Less than zero	The quantity demanded of one good decreases when the price of the other good increases
Income Elasticity of Demand		
Income elastic (normal good)	Greater than 1	The percentage increase in the quantity demanded is greater than the percentage increase in income
Income inelastic (normal good)	Less than 1 but greater than zero	The percentage increase in the quantity demanded is less than the percentage increase in income
Negative income elastic (inferior good)	Less than zero	When income increases, quantity demanded decreases
Price Elasticity of Supply		
Perfectly elastic	Infinity	The smallest possible increase in price causes an infinitely large increase in the quantity supplied
Elastic	Less than infinity but greater than 1	The percentage increase in the quantity supplied exceeds the percentage increase in the price
Inelastic	Greater than zero but less than 1	The percentage increase in the quantity supplied is less than the percentage increase in the price
Perfectly inelastic	Zero	The quantity supplied is the same at all prices

* In each description, the directions of change may be reversed. For example, in this case: the smallest possible *decrease* in the price causes an infinitely large *increase* in the quantity demanded.

Reading Between the Lines

Elasticity: French Taxes Cut Smoking

The Financial Times, 6 January, 2004

French health move: Tobacconists fuming after new rise in cigarette tax

Jo Johnson

Yesterday, . . . the (French) government braved the wrath of tobacconists with the third tax increase in 12 months . . . Mr Jacques Chirac . . . has every chance of being able to fulfil his pledge to cut smoking by 30 per cent among young people and by 20 per cent among adults within five years.

To the delight of campaigners, cigarette sales in France are estimated to have fallen by 12–13% in 2003, following a 3.5 per cent fall in 2002. The cumulative impact of tax rises – 8.6 per cent in 2002, 11 per cent in January 2003, 20 per cent in October and now yesterday's 8–10 per cent – is starting to bite. Studies consistently show that taxation and pregnancy are the two most effective ways of stopping smoking.

'It is unprecedented', says Gerard Dubois, chairman of the French Alliance Versus Tobacco, an umbrella organisation for 29 anti-smoking groups, 'Calls to quit-smoking helplines have risen seven-fold in the past year.' He says sales of nicotine gum and patches, made by pharmaceutical giants such as GSK and Pfizer, have increased 89 per cent in the year to September, while turnover of Zyban, an anti-depressant taken by many people giving up smoking, is up 20 per cent.

Campaigners regret, however, that the government is not pressing its advantage further. The political clout of France's 32,000 tobacconists, furious that French cigarettes are now the most expensive in the EU after those sold in the UK, has prompted Jean-Pierre Raffarin, prime minister, to promise a four year freeze on duties. This is expected to apply from this year. . . .

Yesterday's 8–10 per cent increase in cigarette taxes means that the average pack of 20 costs around €5 ($3.50) compared with just €2.50 in neighbouring Spain and €2.90 in Luxembourg . . .

The Essence of the Story

◆ The French government has raised taxes on cigarettes 4 times in the past 2 years as part of a health policy to cut smoking.

◆ It is estimated that sales of cigarettes in France fell 3.5 per cent in 2002 and 12 to 13 per cent in 2003.

◆ Cigarette taxes in France were increased by 8.6 per cent in 2002, 31 per cent overall in 2003, and 8 to 10 per cent in January 2004.

◆ Higher taxes on cigarettes help stop people smoking.

◆ French cigarettes at €5 a pack are now among the most expensive in the European Union.

Economic Analysis

◆ The price elasticity of demand equals the percentage change in the quantity demanded divided by the percentage change in price, using the *average* quantity and *average* price.

◆ The news article does not give details of all the price and quantity changes in France at the time but these can be found in other sources as detailed in Table 1.

◆ Table 1 shows cigarette tax and the price and quantity of cigarettes bought in France in 2002 and 2003.

◆ Table 1 also shows the changes in price and quantity and the average price and quantity as well as the calculation of the price elasticity of demand for cigarettes in France.

◆ Based on these numbers, as the tax and price of cigarettes increased, the quantity of cigarettes bought decreased, and the elasticity of demand for cigarettes in France is 0.3.

◆ Figure 1 illustrates the calculation of the price elasticity of demand for cigarettes in France in 2002–2003.

◆ The price increased from €3.46 to €3.89 per pack, an increase of €0.43. The average price was €3.68.

◆ The quantity of cigarettes demanded decreased from 180 billion packs to 173.7 billion packs, a decrease of 6.3 billion packs. The average quantity was 176.9 billion packs.

◆ Price elasticity of demand $= \dfrac{6.3/176.9}{0.43/3.68} = 0.3$.

◆ Because the demand for cigarettes is inelastic, a large price rise is needed to achieve only a modest decrease in the quantity of cigarettes smoked.

Table 1

Cigarette Tax, Price and Quantity in France

Year	Tax (percentage of price)	Price (euros per pack)	Quantity (billions of packs)
2002	72.5	3.46	180.0
2003	76.0	3.89	173.7
Changes	–	+0.43	–6.3
Averages	–	3.68	176.9

Source: Tobacco Manufacturers Association and Eurostat.

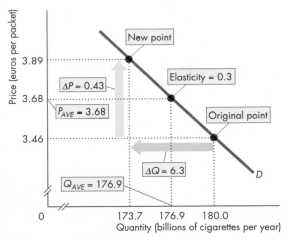

Figure 1 Price elasticity of demand

Summary

Key Points

Price Elasticity of Demand (pp. 78–84)

◆ Elasticity is a measure of the responsiveness of the quantity demanded of a good to a change in its price.

◆ Price elasticity of demand equals the percentage change in the quantity demanded divided by the percentage change in price.

◆ The larger the magnitude of the price elasticity of demand, the greater is the responsiveness of the quantity demanded to a given change in price.

◆ Price elasticity of demand depends on how easily one good serves as a substitute for another, the proportion of income spent on the good and the length of time elapsed since the price change.

◆ If demand is elastic, a decrease in price leads to an increase in total revenue. If demand is unit elastic, a decrease in price leaves total revenue unchanged. And if demand is inelastic, a decrease in price leads to a decrease in total revenue.

More Elasticities of Demand

(pp. 85–87)

◆ Cross elasticity of demand measures the responsiveness of demand for one good to a change in the price of a substitute or a complement.

◆ The cross elasticity of demand with respect to the price of a substitute is positive. The cross elasticity of demand with respect to the price of a complement is negative.

◆ Income elasticity of demand measures the responsiveness of demand to a change in income. For a normal good, the income elasticity of demand is positive. For an inferior good, the income elasticity of demand is negative.

◆ When the income elasticity of demand is greater than 1, the percentage of income spent on the good increases as income increases.

◆ When the income elasticity of demand is less than 1 but greater than zero, the percentage of income spent on the good decreases as income increases.

Elasticity of Supply (pp. 88–91)

◆ Elasticity of supply measures the responsiveness of the quantity supplied of a good to a change in its price.

◆ The elasticity of supply is usually positive and ranges between zero (vertical supply curve) and infinity (horizontal supply curve).

◆ Supply decisions have three time frames: momentary, long run and short run.

◆ Momentary supply refers to the response of sellers to a price change at the instant that the price changes.

◆ Long-run supply refers to the response of sellers to a price change when all the technologically feasible adjustments in production have been made.

◆ Short-run supply refers to the response of sellers to a price change after some of the technologically feasible adjustments in production have been made.

Key Figures and Table

Key Terms

Problems

*1 Rain spoils the strawberry crop. As a result, the price rises from £2 to £3 a box and the quantity demanded decreases from 1,000 to 600 boxes a week. Over this price range,
  a What is the price elasticity of demand?
  b Describe the demand for strawberries.

2 Good weather brings a bumper tomato crop. The price falls from £7 to £5 a load, and the quantity demanded increases from 300 to 500 loads a day. Over this price range,
  a What is the price elasticity of demand?
  b Describe the demand for tomatoes.

*3 The figure shows the demand for DVD rentals.

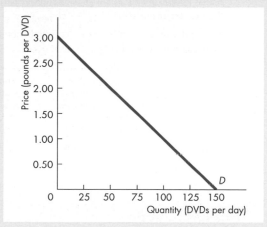

  a Calculate the elasticity of demand for a rise in rental price from £3 to £5.
  b At what price is the elasticity of demand equal to 1?

4 The figure shows the demand for pens.

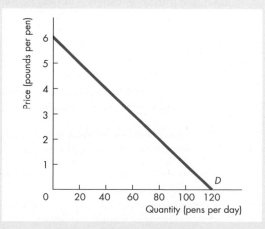

  a Calculate the elasticity of demand for a rise in price from £6 to £10.
  b At what prices is the elasticity of demand equal to 1, greater than 1, and less than 1?

*5 If the quantity of dental services demanded increases by 10 per cent when the price of dental services falls by 10 per cent, is the demand for dental service inelastic, elastic, or unit elastic?

6 If the quantity of haircuts demanded decreases by 10 per cent when the price of a haircut rises by 5 per cent, is the demand for haircuts elastic, inelastic, or unit elastic? Explain your answer.

*7 The demand schedule for computer chips is

Price (euros per chip)	Quantity demanded (millions of chips per year)
200	50
250	45
300	40
350	35
400	30
450	25
500	20

  a What happens to total revenue if the price falls from €400 to €350 a chip?
  b What happens to total revenue if the price falls from €350 to €300 a chip?
  c At what price is total revenue at a maximum? Use the total revenue test to answer this question.
  d At an average price of €350, is the demand for chips elastic or inelastic? Use the total revenue test to answer this question.

8 The demand schedule for sugar is

Price (euros per pound)	Quantity demanded (millions of pounds per year)
5	35
10	30
15	25
20	20
25	15
30	10
35	5

  a What happens to total revenue if the price of sugar rises from €5 to €15 per pound?
  b What happens to total revenue if the price rises from €15 to €25 per pound?
  c At what price is total revenue at a maximum? Use the total revenue test to answer this question.
  d At an average price of €20 a pound, is the demand for sugar elastic or inelastic? Use the total revenue test to answer this question.

*9 In problem 7, at €250 a chip, is the demand for chips elastic or inelastic? Use the total revenue test to answer this question.

10 In problem 8, at €10 a pound, is the demand for sugar elastic or inelastic? Use the total revenue test to answer this question.

*11 If a 12 per cent rise in the price of an orange smoothie decreases the quantity of orange smoothies demanded by 22 per cent and increases the quantity of apple smoothies demanded by 14 per cent, calculate the cross elasticity of demand between orange smoothies and apple smoothies.

12 If a 5 per cent fall in the price of chicken decreases the quantity of beef demanded by 20 per cent and increases the quantity of chicken demanded by 15 per cent, calculate the cross elasticity of demand between chicken and beef.

*13 Alex's income has increased from £3,000 to £5,000. Alex increased his consumption of bagels from 4 to 8 a month and decreased his consumption of doughnuts from 12 to 6 a month. Calculate Alex's income elasticity of demand for (a) bagels and (b) doughnuts.

14 Judy's income has increased from £13,000 to £17,000. Judy increased her demand for concert tickets by 15 per cent and decreased her demand for bus rides by 10 per cent. Calculate Judy's income elasticity of demand for (a) concert tickets and (b) bus rides.

*15 The table gives the supply schedule for long-distance phone calls.

Price (cents per minute)	Quantity supplied (millions of minutes per day)
10	200
20	400
30	600
40	800
50	900

Calculate the elasticity of supply when

a The price falls from 40 cents to 30 cents a minute.

b The average price is 20 cents a minute.

16 The table gives the supply schedule for jeans.

Price (dollars per pair)	Quantity supplied (millions of pairs per year)
120	2,400
125	2,800
130	3,200
135	3,600

Calculate the elasticity of supply when

a The price rises from £125 to £135 a pair.

b The average price is £125 a pair.

Critical Thinking

1 Read the news article in *Reading Between the Lines* on p. 92 about the French cigarette taxes and then:

a Using the numbers in the table below, calculate the price elasticity of demand for cigarettes in France for the years 2003 to 2004. Use the method shown on p. 79.

b Explain what your calculated value for price elasticity from part a above means.

c Do you think the revenue collected from the tobacco tax in France during 2004 will rise or fall compared to 2003? Explain your answer.

d What will happen to French cigarette tax revenue if many people go to Spain or Luxembourg to buy their cigarettes in 2004?

e Why did tobacconists in France complain about the increase in cigarette tax?

Year	Tax (percentage of price)	Price (euros per pack)	Quantity (billions of packs)
2003	76.0	3.89	173.7
2004	79.0	5.00	155.5

Web Exercises

Use the links on *Parkin Interactive* to work the following exercises.

1 Obtain information on the price of petrol during the recent past and then:

a Use demand, supply and elasticity to explain the recent changes in the price of petrol.

b Find the latest price of crude oil.

c Use demand, supply and elasticity to explain the recent changes in the price of crude oil.

2 Use the information you obtained in web exercise 1 and find the information you need to answer:

a What are the costs that make up the total cost of a gallon of petrol?

b If the price of crude oil falls by 10 per cent, by what percentage would you expect the price of petrol to change, other things remaining the same?

c In light of your answer to part (b), which elasticity of demand is greater: for crude oil or for petrol.

Chapter 5

Efficiency and Equity

After studying this chapter you will be able to:

◆ Define efficiency

◆ Distinguish between value and price and define consumer surplus

◆ Distinguish between cost and price and define producer surplus

◆ Explain the conditions under which markets move resources to their highest-valued uses and the sources of inefficiency in our economy

◆ Explain the main ideas about fairness and evaluate claims that markets result in unfair outcomes

More for Less

We try to use our time and spend our incomes in ways that get the most out of our limited resources. Producers strive to cut costs and make the largest possible profit. With everyone pursuing self-interest, what happens to the social interest? Do markets deliver an outcome that is best for everyone? And why, in the market for air travel, do customers end up paying different prices for the same trip? Find some answers in this chapter and in *Reading Between the Lines* at the end of the chapter.

Efficiency and Social Interest

When does the pursuit of self-interest also serve the social interest? Economists have thought hard about this question and have most to say about one aspect of the "social interest", allocative efficiency.

Allocative efficiency (defined in Chapter 2, p. 37) occurs when it is not possible to produce more of one good without giving up the production of some other good that is valued more highly. Achieving allocative efficiency also means that it is not possible to make someone better off without making someone else worse off. Allocative efficiency does not depend on the distribution of economic benefit. In principle, we can all agree that one situation, *A*, is efficient and another situation, *B*, is inefficient. Efficiency is not a cold, mechanical concept. It is a concept based on value, and value is based on people's feelings. For example, if people value a nuclear-free environment more highly than they value cheap electric power, it is efficient to use higher-cost, non-nuclear technologies to produce electricity.

Let's review the idea of allocative efficiency by returning to the example of Chapter 2 and thinking about the efficient quantity of pizzas. To produce more pizzas, we must give up some other goods and services. For example, we might give up some sandwiches. So to produce more pizzas, we forgo sandwiches. If we have fewer pizzas, we can have more sandwiches. What is the efficient quantity of pizzas to produce? The answer depends on marginal benefit and marginal cost.

Marginal Benefit

If we consume one more pizza, we receive a marginal benefit. **Marginal benefit** is the benefit that a person receives from consuming one more unit of a good or service. The marginal benefit from a good or service is measured as the maximum amount that a person is willing to pay for one more unit of it. So the marginal benefit from a pizza is the maximum amount of other goods and services that people are willing to give up to get one more pizza. The marginal benefit from pizza decreases as the quantity of pizzas consumed increases – the principle of *decreasing marginal benefit*.

We can express the marginal benefit from a pizza as the number of sandwiches that people are willing to forgo to get one more pizza. But we can also express marginal benefit as the pound value of other goods and services that people are willing to forgo. Figure 5.1 shows the marginal benefit from pizza expressed in this way. As the quantity of pizza increases, the value of other items that people are willing to forgo to get one more pizza decreases.

Marginal Cost

If we produce one more pizza, we incur a marginal cost. **Marginal cost** is the opportunity cost of producing *one more unit* of a good or service. The marginal cost of a good or service is measured as the value of the best alternative forgone. So the marginal cost of a pizza is the value of the best alternative forgone to get one more pizza. The marginal cost of a pizza increases as the quantity of pizza produced increases – the principle of *increasing marginal cost*.

We can express marginal cost as the number of sandwiches we must forgo to produce one more pizza. But we can also express marginal cost as the pound value of other goods and services we must forgo.

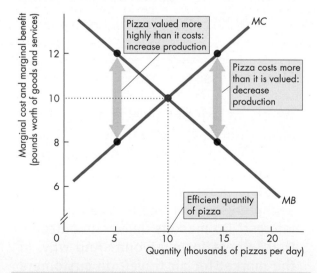

Figure 5.1

The Efficient Quantity of Pizza

The marginal benefit curve (*MB*) shows what people *are willing to* forgo to get one more pizza. The marginal cost curve (*MC*) shows what people *must* forgo to get one more pizza. If fewer than 10,000 pizzas a day are produced, marginal benefit exceeds marginal cost. Greater value can be obtained by producing more pizzas. If more than 10,000 pizzas a day are produced, marginal cost exceeds marginal benefit. Greater value can be obtained by producing fewer pizzas. If 10,000 pizzas a day are produced, marginal benefit equals marginal cost and the efficient quantity of pizza is available.

Figure 5.1 shows the marginal cost of pizza expressed in this way. As the quantity of pizza produced increases, the value of other items we must forgo to produce yet one more pizza increases.

Efficiency and Inefficiency

To determine the efficient quantity of pizza, we compare the marginal cost of a pizza with the marginal benefit of a pizza. There are three possible cases:

◆ Marginal benefit exceeds marginal cost
◆ Marginal cost exceeds marginal benefit
◆ Marginal benefit equals marginal cost

Marginal Benefit Exceeds Marginal Cost

Suppose the quantity of pizzas produced is 5,000 a day. Figure 5.1 shows that at this quantity, the marginal benefit of a pizza is £12. That is, when the quantity of pizzas available is 5,000 a day, people are willing to pay £12 for the 5,000th pizza.

Figure 5.1 also shows that the marginal cost of the 5,000th pizza is £8. That is, to produce one more pizza, the value of other goods and services that we must forgo is £8. If pizza production increases from 4,999 to 5,000, the value of the additional pizza is £12 and its marginal cost is £8. If this pizza is produced, the value of the pizza produced exceeds the value of the goods and services we must forgo by £8. Resources will be used more efficiently – they will create more value – if we produce an extra pizza and fewer other goods and services. This same reasoning applies all the way up to the 9,999th pizza. Only when we get to the 10,000th pizza does marginal benefit not exceed marginal cost.

Marginal Cost Exceeds Marginal Benefit

Suppose the quantity of pizzas produced is 15,000 a day. Figure 5.1 shows that at this quantity, the marginal benefit of a pizza is £8. That is, when the quantity of pizzas available is 15,000 a day, people are willing to pay £8 for the 15,000th pizza.

Figure 5.1 also shows that the marginal cost of the 15,000th pizza is £12. That is, to produce one more pizza, the value of the other goods and services that we must forgo is £12.

If pizza production decreases from 15,000 to 14,999, the value of the one pizza forgone is £8 and its marginal cost is £12. So if this pizza is not produced, the value of the other goods and services produced exceeds the value

of the pizza forgone by £8. Resources will be used more efficiently – they will create more value – if we produce one fewer pizza and more other goods and services. This same reasoning applies all the way down to the 10,001st pizza. Only when we get to the 10,000th pizza does marginal cost not exceed marginal benefit.

Marginal Benefit Equals Marginal Cost

Suppose the quantity of pizzas produced is 10,000 a day. Figure 5.1 shows that at this quantity, the marginal benefit of a pizza is £10. That is, when the quantity of pizzas available is 10,000 a day, people are willing to pay £10 for the 10,000th pizza.

Figure 5.1 also shows that the marginal cost of the 10,000th pizza is £10. That is, to produce one more pizza, the value of other goods and services that we must forgo is £10.

In this situation, we cannot increase the value of the goods and services produced by either increasing or decreasing the quantity of pizza. If we increase the quantity of pizza, the 10,001st pizza costs more to produce than it is worth. And if we decrease the quantity of pizza produced, the 9,999th pizza is worth more than it costs to produce. So when marginal benefit equals marginal cost, resource use is efficient.

Review Quiz

1   If the marginal benefit of a pizza exceeds the marginal cost of a pizza are we producing too much pizza and too little of other goods and services, or are we producing too little pizza and too much of other goods and services?
2   If the marginal cost of a pizza exceeds the marginal benefit of a pizza are we producing too much pizza and too little of other goods and services, or are we producing too little pizza and too much of other goods and services?
3   What is the relationship between the marginal benefit of a pizza and the marginal cost of a pizza when we are producing the efficient quantity of pizza?

Does a competitive market in pizza produce the efficient quantity of pizza? Let's begin to answer this question.

Value, Price and Consumer Surplus

To investigate whether a competitive market is efficient, we need to learn about the connection between demand and marginal benefit and the connection between supply and marginal cost.

Value, Willingness to Pay and Demand

In everyday life we talk about "getting value for money." When we use this expression we are distinguishing between *value* and *price*. Value is what we get and the price is what we pay.

The **value** of one more unit of a good or service is its *marginal benefit*. Marginal benefit can be expressed as the maximum price that people are *willing to pay* for another unit of the good or service. The willingness to pay for a good or service determines the demand for it.

In Figure 5.2(a) the demand curve shows the quantity demanded at each price. For example, when the price of

a pizza is £10, the quantity demanded is 10,000 pizzas a day. In Figure 5.2(b), the demand curve shows the maximum price that people are willing to pay when there is a given quantity. For example, when 10,000 pizzas a day are available, the most that people are willing to pay for a pizza is £10. This second interpretation of the demand curve means that the marginal benefit from the 10,000th pizza is £10.

When we draw a demand curve, we use a *relative price*, not a *money* price. A relative price is expressed in euro units, but it measures the number of pounds worth of other goods and services forgone to obtain one more unit of the good in question (see Chapter 3, p. 54). So a demand curve tells us the quantity of other goods and services that people are willing forgo to get an additional unit of a good. But this is what a marginal benefit curve tells us too. So:

A demand curve is a marginal benefit curve.

We don't always have to pay the maximum price that we are willing to pay. When we buy something, we often get a bargain. Let's see how.

Figure 5.2

Demand, Willingness to Pay and Marginal Benefit

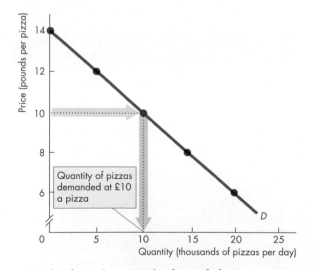

(a) Price determines quantity demanded

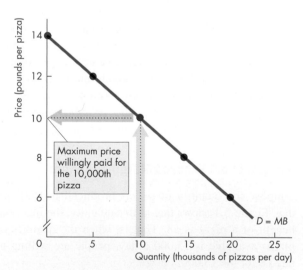

(b) Quantity determines willingness to pay

The demand curve for pizza, *D*, shows the quantity of pizza demanded at each price, other things remaining the same. The demand curve also shows the maximum price that consumers are willing to pay for the last pizza if a given quantity of pizza is available. In part (a) at a price of £10, the quantity demanded is 10,000 pizzas a day.

In part (b), if 10,000 pizzas a day are available, the maximum price that consumers are willing to pay for the 10,000th pizza is £10. So the demand curve is also the marginal benefit curve.

Consumer Surplus

When people buy something for less than it is worth to them, they receive a consumer surplus. A **consumer surplus** is the value of a good minus the price paid for it, summed over the quantity bought.

To understand consumer surplus, let's look at Lisa's demand for pizza in Figure 5.3. Lisa likes pizza, but the marginal benefit she gets from it decreases quickly as her consumption increases.

To keep things simple, suppose Lisa can buy pizza by the slice. If a pizza costs £1.40 a slice, Lisa spends her fast-food budget on items that she values more highly than pizza. At £1.20 a slice, she buys 10 slices a week. At £1 a slice, she buys 20 slices a week; at 80 pence a slice, she buys 30 slices a week; and at 60 pence a slice, she eats nothing but pizza and buys 40 slices a week.

Lisa's demand curve for pizza in Figure 5.3 is also her *willingness-to-pay* or marginal benefit curve. It tells us that if Lisa can have only 10 slices a week, she is willing to pay £1.20 for the 10th slice. Her marginal benefit from the 10th slice is £1.20. If she can have 20 slices a week, she is willing to pay £1 for the 20th slice. Her marginal benefit from the 20th slice is £1.

Figure 5.3 also shows Lisa's consumer surplus from pizza when the price is £1 a slice. At this price, she buys 20 slices a week. The most that Lisa is willing to pay for the 20th slice is £1, so its marginal benefit equals the price she pays for it.

But Lisa is willing to pay almost £1.40 for the first slice. So the marginal benefit from this slice is close to 40 pence more than she pays for it. So on her first slice of pizza, she receives a *consumer surplus* of almost 40 pence. At a quantity of 10 slices of pizza a week, Lisa's marginal benefit is £1.20 a slice. So on the 10th slice, she receives a consumer surplus of 20 pence.

To calculate Lisa's consumer surplus, we find the consumer surplus on each slice she buys and add them together. This sum is the area of the green triangle – the area below the demand curve and above the market price line. This area is equal to the base of the triangle (20 slices a week) multiplied by the height of the triangle (40 pence a slice) divided by 2, which is £4.

The area of the blue rectangle in Figure 5.3 shows what Lisa pays for pizza, which is £20. This area is equal to 20 slices a week multiplied by £1 a slice.

All goods and services are like the pizza example you've just studied. Because of decreasing marginal benefit, people receive more benefit from their consumption than the amount they pay.

Figure 5.3

A Consumer's Demand and Consumer Surplus

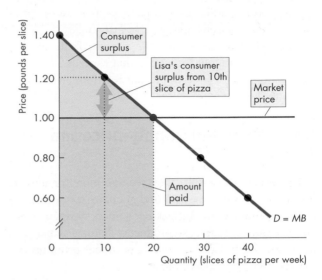

Lisa's demand curve for pizza tells us that at £1.40 a slice, she does not buy pizza. At £1.20 a slice, she buys 10 slices a week; at £1 a slice, she buys 20 slices a week. Lisa's demand curve is also her marginal benefit curve, so her demand curve also tells us that she is willing to pay £1.20 for the 10th slice and £1 for the 20th slice. She actually pays £1 a slice – the market price – and buys 20 slices a week. She spends £20 a week on pizza – the area of the blue rectangle. Lisa's consumer surplus from pizza is £4 – the area of the green triangle.

Review Quiz

1   Explain how to measure the value or marginal benefit from a good or service.
2   Explain the relationship between marginal benefit and the demand curve.
3   What is consumer surplus and how is it measured?

You've seen how we distinguish between value – marginal benefit – and price. And you've seen that buyers receive a consumer surplus because marginal benefit exceeds price. Next, we're going to study the connection between supply and marginal cost and learn about producer surplus.

Cost, Price and Producer Surplus

What you are going to learn about cost, price and producer surplus parallels the related ideas of value, price and consumer surplus that you've just studied.

Firms are in business to make a profit. To do so, they must sell their output for a price that exceeds the cost of production. Let's investigate the relationship between cost and price in more detail.

Cost, Minimum Supply-price and Supply

When firms earn profit, they receive more (or at least receive no less) for the sale of a good or service than the cost of producing it. Just as consumers distinguish between *value* and *price*, so producers distinguish between *cost* and *price*. Cost is what a producer gives up and price is what a producer receives.

The cost of producing one more unit of a good or service is its *marginal cost*. The marginal cost is the minimum price that producers must receive to induce them to produce another unit of the good or service. This minimum acceptable price determines the quantity supplied.

In Figure 5.4(a), the supply curve shows the quantity supplied at each price. For example, when the price of a pizza is £10, the quantity supplied is 10,000 pizzas a day. In Figure 5.7(b), the supply curve shows the minimum price which producers must be offered to produce a given quantity of pizza. For example, the minimum price which producers must be offered to get them to produce 10,000 pizzas a day is £10 a pizza. This second view of the supply curve means that the marginal cost of the 10,000th pizza is £10. The supply curve S is also the marginal cost curve, MC.

Because the price is a relative price, a supply curve tells us the quantity of other goods and services that firms *must forgo* to produce one more unit of the good. But a marginal cost curve also tells us the quantity of

Figure 5.4

Supply, Minimum Supply-price and Producer Surplus

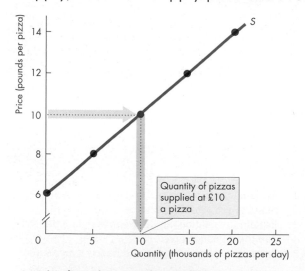

(a) Price determines quantity supplied

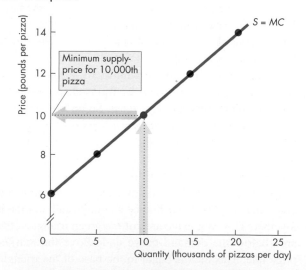

(b) Quantity determines minimum supply-price

The supply curve of pizza, S, shows the quantity of pizza supplied at each price, other things remaining the same. The supply curve of pizza also shows the minimum price that producers must be offered for the last pizza to produce a given quantity. Part (a) shows that at a price of £10, the quantity supplied is 10,000 pizzas a day.

Part (b) shows that to get firms to produce 10,000 pizzas a day, the minimum price that producers must be offered for the 10,000th pizza is £10. So the supply curve is also the marginal cost curve.

other goods and services that firms must forgo to get one more unit of the good. So:

A supply curve is a marginal cost curve.

If the price producers receive exceeds the cost they incur, they earn a producer surplus. This producer surplus is analogous to consumer surplus.

Producer Surplus

When the price exceeds marginal cost, the firm obtains a producer surplus. A **producer surplus** is the price of a good minus the opportunity cost of producing it, summed over the quantity sold. To understand producer surplus, let's look at Mario's supply of pizza in Figure 5.5.

Mario can produce pizza or bake bread that people like a lot. The more pizza he bakes, the less bread he can bake. His opportunity cost of pizza is the value of the bread he must forgo. This opportunity cost increases as Mario increases his production of pizza. If a pizza sells for only £6, Mario produces no pizzas. He uses his kitchen to bake bread. Pizza just isn't worth producing. But at £8 a pizza, Mario produces 50 pizzas a day, and at £10 a pizza, he produces 100 pizzas a day.

Mario's supply curve of pizza is also his *minimum supply price* curve. It tells us that if Mario can sell only one pizza a day, the minimum that he must be paid for it is £6. If he can sell 50 pizzas a day, the minimum that he must be paid for the 50th pizza is £8, and so on.

Figure 5.5 also shows Mario's producer surplus. If the price of a pizza is £10 Mario plans to sell 100 pizzas a day. The minimum that he must be paid for the 100th pizza is £10. So its opportunity cost is exactly the price he receives for it. But his opportunity cost of the first pizza is only £6. So this first pizza costs £4 less to produce than he receives for it. Mario receives a *producer surplus* from his first pizza of £4. He receives a slightly smaller producer surplus on the second pizza, less on the third, and so on until he receives no producer surplus on the 100th pizza.

Figure 5.5 shows Mario's producer surplus as the blue triangle formed by the area above the supply curve and below the price line. This area is equal to the base of the triangle (100 pizzas a day) multiplied by the height (£4 a pizza) divided by 2, which equals £200 a day. Figure 5.5 also shows Mario's opportunity costs of production as the red area below the supply curve, which is £800 a day.

Figure 5.5

A Producer's Supply and Producer Surplus

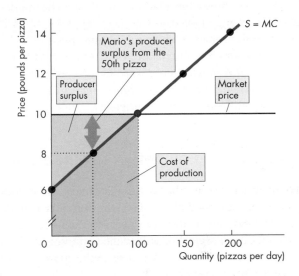

Mario's supply curve of pizza tells us that at a price of £6, Mario plans to sell no pizzas. At a price of £8, he plans to sell 50 pizzas a day; and at a price of £10, he plans to sell 100 pizzas a day. Mario's supply curve also tells us that the minimum he must be offered is £8 for the 50th pizza a day and £10 for the 100th pizza a day.

If the market price is £10 a pizza, he sells 100 pizzas a day and receives £1,000. The red area shows Mario's cost of producing pizza, which is £800 a day, and the blue area shows his producer surplus, which is £200 a day.

Review Quiz

1   Explain the relationship between the marginal cost or opportunity cost of producing a good or service and the minimum supply price – the minimum price that producers must be offered.
2   Explain the relationship between marginal cost and the supply curve.
3   What is producer surplus? How do we measure it?

Consumer surplus and producer surplus can be used to measure the efficiency of a market. Let's see how we can use these concepts to study the efficiency of a competitive market.

Is the Competitive Market Efficient?

Figure 5.6 shows the market for pizza. The market forces that you studied in Chapter 3 (pp. 64–65) will pull the pizza market to its equilibrium price of £15 a pizza and equilibrium quantity of 10,000 pizzas a day. Buyers enjoy a consumer surplus (green area) and sellers enjoy a producer surplus (blue area). But is this competitive equilibrium efficient?

Efficiency of Competitive Equilibrium

The demand curve tells us the marginal benefit from pizza. If the only people who benefit from pizza are the people who buy it, then the demand curve for pizza measures the marginal benefit to the entire society from pizza. We call the marginal benefit to the entire society, marginal social benefit, *MSB*. In this case, the demand curve *D* is also the *MSB* curve.

You've also seen that the supply curve tells us the marginal cost of pizza. If the only people who bear the cost of pizza are the people who produce it, then the supply curve of pizza measures the marginal cost to the entire society of pizza. We call the marginal cost to the entire society, marginal *social* cost, *MSC*.

In this case, the supply curve *S* is also the *MSC* curve. So where the demand curve and the supply curve intersect in part (a), marginal social benefit equals marginal social cost in part (b). This condition delivers an efficient use of resources for the entire society. If production is less than 10,000 pizzas a day, the marginal pizza is valued more highly than its opportunity cost. If production exceeds 10,000 pizzas a day, the marginal pizza costs more to produce than the value that consumers place on it. Only when 10,000 pizzas a day are produced is the marginal pizza worth exactly what it costs.

The competitive market pushes the quantity of pizza produced to its efficient level of 10,000 a day. If production is less than 10,000 pizzas a day, a shortage raises the price, which increases production. If production exceeds 10,000 pizzas a day, a surplus lowers the price, which decreases production. So, a competitive pizza market is efficient.

Notice that when the efficient quantity is produced, the sum of consumer surplus and producer surplus is maximized. Buyers and sellers acting in their self-interest end up promoting the social interest.

Figure 5.6

An Efficient Market for Pizza

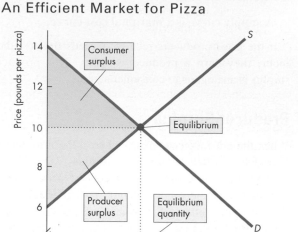

(a) Equilibrium and surpluses

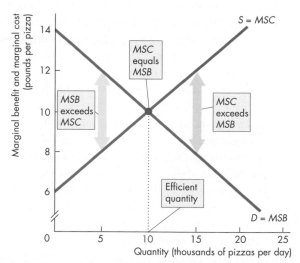

(b) Efficiency and marginal benefit and marginal cost

Competitive equilibrium in part (a) occurs when the quantity demanded equals the quantity supplied. Consumer surplus is the area under the demand curve and above the price – the green triangle. Producer surplus is the area above the supply curve and below the price – the blue triangle.

Resources are used efficiently in part (b) when marginal social benefit, *MSB*, equals marginal social cost, *MSC*. The efficient quantity in part (b) is the same as the equilibrium quantity in part (a). The competitive pizza market produces the efficient quantity of pizza. At the competitive equilibrium, the sum of the consumer surplus and the producer surplus is maximized.

The Invisible Hand

Writing in his book, *The Wealth of Nations*, in 1776, Adam Smith was the first to suggest that competitive markets send resources to the uses in which they have the highest value.

Smith wrote: "It is not from the benevolence of the butcher, the brewer, or the baker that we expect our dinner, but from their regard to their own interest." He believed that each participant in a market is "led by an invisible hand to promote an end [the efficient use of resources] which was no part of his intention".

You can see the invisible hand at work in the cartoon. The cold drinks vendor has both cold drinks and shade. He has an opportunity cost of each and a minimum supply price of each. The reader on the park bench has a marginal benefit from a cold drink and from shade. You can see that the marginal benefit from shade exceeds the price, but the price of a cold drink exceeds its marginal benefit. The transaction that occurs creates producer surplus and consumer surplus. The vendor obtains a producer surplus from selling the shade for more than its opportunity cost, and the reader obtains a consumer surplus from buying the shade for less than its marginal benefit. In the third frame of the cartoon, both the consumer and the producer are better off than they were in the first frame. The umbrella has moved to its highest-valued use.

The Invisible Hand at Work Today

The invisible hand relentlessly performs the activities illustrated in the cartoon to achieve the outcome shown in Figure 5.6. And rarely has the market been working as hard as it is today. Think about some of the changes taking place in our economy that the market is guiding towards an efficient use of resources.

New technologies have cut the cost of producing computers. As these advances have occurred, supply has increased and the price has fallen. Lower prices have encouraged an increase in the quantity of computers demanded of this now less costly tool. The marginal benefit from computers is brought to equality with their marginal cost.

An early frost cuts the supply of grapes. With fewer grapes available, the marginal benefit from grapes increases. A shortage of grapes raises their price, so the market allocates the smaller quantity available to the people who value them most highly.

Market forces persistently bring marginal cost and marginal benefit to equality and maximize the sum of consumer surplus and producer surplus.

Obstacles to Efficiency

Although markets generally do a good job at sending resources to where they are most highly valued, they do not always get it right. Sometimes, markets produce too much of a good or service, and sometimes they produce too little. The most significant obstacles to achieving an efficient allocation of resources in a market economy are:

◆ Price ceilings and price floors

◆ Taxes, subsidies and quotas

◆ Monopoly

◆ External costs and external benefits

◆ Public goods and common resources

Price Ceilings and Price Floors

A *price ceiling* is a regulation that makes it illegal to charge a price higher than a specified level. An example is a price ceiling on housing rents, which some local and regional authorities impose. A *price floor* is a regulation that makes it illegal to pay a price below a specified level. An example is the minimum wage. The presence of a price ceiling or a price floor blocks the market forces and might result in a quantity produced that differs from the efficient quantity. (We study price ceiling and price floors in Chapter 6.)

Taxes, Subsidies and Quotas

Taxes increase the prices paid by buyers and lower the prices received by sellers. Taxes decrease the quantity produced. All kinds of goods are taxed, but the highest taxes are on petrol, alcohol and tobacco.

Subsidies, which are payments by the government to producers, decrease the prices paid by buyers and increase the prices received by sellers. Subsidies increase the quantity produced.

Quotas, which are limits to the quantity that a firm is permitted to produce, restrict output below the efficient quantity. Farms are sometimes subject to quotas. (We study quotas in Chapter 6.)

Monopoly

A *monopoly* is a firm that has sole control of a market. For example, Microsoft has a near monopoly on operating systems for personal computers. Although a monopoly can earn large profit, it prevents the market from achieving an efficient use of resources. The goal of a monopoly is to maximize profit. To achieve this goal, it produces less than the efficient quantity and raises its price. (We study monopoly in Chapter 12.)

External Costs and External Benefits

An *external cost* is a cost borne not by the producer but borne by other people. When an electric power utility burns coal to generate electricity, it produces acid rain that damages vegetation and crops. The utility does not consider the cost of pollution when it decides the quantity of electric power to supply. Its supply is based on its own production costs, not on the costs that it inflicts on others. As a result, the utility produces more power than the efficient quantity.

An *external benefit* is a benefit that accrues to people other than the buyer of a good. When an old building is restored, lots of people get pleasure from seeing it. But the building's owner only thinks about her marginal benefit when she decides whether to do the restoration. So the demand for restoring buildings does not include all the benefits that accrue. In this case, the quantity falls short of the efficient quantity. (We study external costs and external benefits in Chapter 15.)

Public Goods and Common Resources

A *public good* is a good or service that is consumed simultaneously by everyone, even if they don't pay for it. Examples are national defence and the enforcement of law and order. Competitive markets would produce too small a quantity of public goods because of a *free-rider problem* – it is not in each person's interest to buy her or his share of a public good. So a competitive market produces less than the efficient quantity.

Common resources are resources that no one owns and that everyone can use. Examples are the fish in the ocean and city parks. A competitive market generally leads to the overuse of such resource (We study public goods and common resources in Chapter 16.)

The obstacles to efficiency that we've just reviewed result in two possible outcomes:

◆ Underproduction
◆ Overproduction

Underproduction

Suppose that one firm owned all the pizza outlets in a city and that it produces only 5,000 pizzas a day. Figure 5.7(a) shows that at this quantity, consumers are willing to pay £12 for the marginal pizza – marginal benefit is £12. The marginal cost of a pizza is only £10. So people are willing to pay more for a pizza than what producers must be offered.

The sum of consumer surplus and producer surplus is decreased by the amount of the grey triangle in Figure 5.7(a). This triangle is called deadweight loss. **Deadweight loss** is the decrease in consumer surplus and producer surplus that results from producing an inefficient quantity of the good.

The 5,000th pizza brings a benefit of £12 and costs only £8 to produce. If we don't produce this pizza, we are wasting £4. Similar reasoning applies all the way up to the 9,999th pizza. By producing more pizza and less of other goods and services, we get more value from our resources.

The deadweight loss is borne by the entire society. It is not a loss for the consumers and a gain for the producer. It is a *social* loss.

Figure 5.7

Underproduction and Overproduction

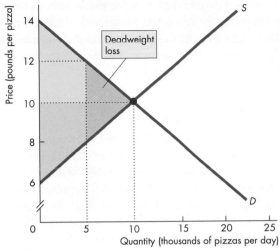

(a) Underproduction

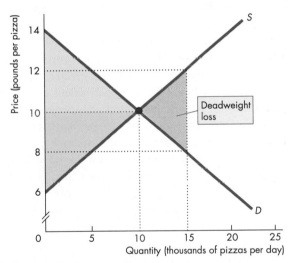

(b) Overproduction

If pizza production is cut to only 5,000 a day, a deadweight loss (the grey triangle) arises in part (a). Consumer surplus and producer surplus (the green and blue areas) are reduced. At 5,000 pizzas, the benefit of one more pizza exceeds its cost. The same is true for all levels of production up to 10,000 pizzas a day.

If production increases to 15,000 pizzas a day, a deadweight loss arises in part (b). At 15,000 pizzas a day, the cost of the 15,000th pizza exceeds its benefit. The cost of each pizza above 10,000 exceeds its benefit. Consumer surplus plus producer surplus equals the sum of the green and blue areas minus the deadweight loss triangle.

Overproduction

Suppose the pizza lobby gets the government to pay the pizza producers a fat subsidy and that production increases to 15,000 a day. Figure 5.7(b) shows that at this quantity, consumers are willing to pay only £8 for the marginal pizza but the opportunity cost of this pizza is £12. It now costs more to produce the marginal pizza than consumers are willing to pay for it. The gap gets smaller as production approaches 10,000 pizzas a day, but it is present at all quantities greater than 10,000 a day.

The deadweight loss from overproduction is shown by the grey triangle in Figure 5.7(b). The sum of consumer surplus and producer surplus is smaller than its maximum by the amount of deadweight loss. The 15,000th pizza brings a benefit of only £8 but costs £12 to produce. If we produce this pizza, we are wasting £4. Similar reasoning applies all the way down to the 10,001st pizza. By producing less pizza and more of other goods and services, we get more value from our resources.

Review Quiz

1   Do competitive markets use resources efficiently? Explain why or why not.
2   Do markets with a price ceiling or price floor, taxes, subsidies or quotas, monopoly, external costs or external benefits, or public goods or common resources result in the quantity produced being the efficient quantity?
3   What is deadweight loss and under what conditions does it occur?
4   Does a deadweight loss occur in a competitive market when the quantity produced equals the competitive equilibrium quantity and the resource allocation is efficient?

You now know the conditions under which the resource allocation is efficient. You've seen how a competitive market can be efficient and you've seen some impediments to efficiency.

But is an efficient allocation of resources fair? Does the competitive market provide people with fair incomes for their work? And do people always pay a fair price for the things they buy? Don't we need the government to step into some competitive markets to prevent the price from rising too high or falling too low? We'll now study these questions.

Is the Competitive Market Fair?

When a natural disaster strikes, such as a severe winter storm or a major flood, the prices of many essential items jump. The reason the prices jump is that some people have a greater demand and greater willingness to pay when the items are in limited supply. So the higher prices achieve an efficient allocation of scarce resources. News reports of these price hikes almost never talk about efficiency. Instead, they talk about **equity** or fairness. The claim often made is that it is unfair for profit-seeking dealers to cheat the victims of natural disaster.

Similarly, when low-skilled people work for a wage that is below what most would regard as a "living wage", the media and politicians talk of employers taking unfair advantage of their workers.

How do we decide whether something is fair or unfair? You know when *you* think something is unfair. But how do you know? What are the *principles* of fairness?

Philosophers have tried for centuries to answer this question. Economists have offered their answers too. But before we look at the proposed answers, you should know that there is no universally agreed upon answer.

Economists agree about efficiency. That is, they agree that it makes sense to make the economic pie as large as possible and to bake it at the lowest possible cost. But they do not agree about equity. That is, they do not agree about what are fair shares of the economic pie for all the people who make it. The reason is that ideas about fairness are not exclusively economic ideas. They touch on politics, ethics and religion. Nevertheless, economists have thought about these issues and have a contribution to make. So let's examine the views of economists on this topic.

To think about fairness, think of economic life as a game – a serious game. All ideas about fairness can be divided into two broad groups. They are:

◆ It's not fair if the *result* isn't fair
◆ It's not fair if the *rules* aren't fair

It's not Fair if the *Result* isn't Fair

The earliest efforts to establish a principle of fairness were based on the view that the result is what matters. The general idea was that it is unfair if people's incomes are too unequal. It is unfair that bank presidents earn millions of pounds a year while bank tellers earn only thousands of pounds a year. It is unfair that a shop owner enjoys a large profit and her customers pay higher prices in the aftermath of a flood.

There was a lot of excitement during the nineteenth century when economists thought they had made the incredible discovery that efficiency requires equality of incomes. To make the economic pie as large as possible, it must be cut into equal pieces, one for each person. This idea turns out to be wrong, but there is a lesson in the reason that it is wrong. So this nineteenth century idea is worth a closer look.

Utilitarianism

The nineteenth century idea that only equality brings efficiency is called *utilitarianism*. **Utilitarianism** is a principle that states that we should strive to achieve "the greatest happiness for the greatest number". The people who developed this idea were known as utilitarians. They included some famous thinkers, such as Jeremy Bentham and John Stuart Mill.

Utilitarianism argues that to achieve "the greatest happiness for the greatest number", income must be transferred from the rich to the poor up to the point of complete equality – to the point that there are no rich and no poor.

They reasoned in the following way: first, everyone has the same basic wants and are similar in their capacity to enjoy life. Second, the greater a person's income, the smaller is the marginal benefit of a pound. The millionth pound spent by a rich person brings a smaller marginal benefit to that person than the marginal benefit of the thousandth pound spent by a poorer person. So by transferring a pound from the millionaire to the poorer person, more is gained than is lost and the two people added together are better off.

Figure 5.8 illustrates this utilitarian idea. Tom and Jerry have the same marginal benefit curve, *MB*. (Marginal benefit is measured on the same scale of 1 to 3 for both Tom and Jerry.) Tom is at point *A*. He earns £5,000 a year, and his marginal benefit of a pound is 3. Jerry is at point *B*. He earns £45,000 a year, and his marginal benefit of a pound is 1. If a pound is transferred from Jerry to Tom, Jerry loses 1 unit of marginal benefit and Tom gains 3 units. So together, Tom and Jerry are better off. They are sharing the economic pie more efficiently. If a second pound is transferred, the same thing happens: Tom gains more than Jerry loses. And the same is true for every pound transferred until they both reach point C. At point C, Tom and Jerry have £25,000 each, and each has a marginal benefit of 2 units. Now they are sharing the economic pie in the most efficient way. It is bringing the greatest attainable happiness to Tom and Jerry

Figure 5.8

Utilitarian Fairness

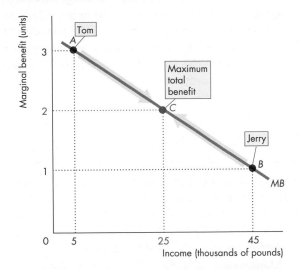

Tom earns £5,000 and has 3 units of marginal benefit at point A. Jerry earns £45,000 and has 1 unit of marginal benefit at point B. If income is transferred from Jerry to Tom, Jerry's loss is less than Tom's gain. Only when each of them has £25,000 and 2 units of marginal benefit (at point C) can the sum of their total benefit increase no further.

The Big Trade-off

One big problem with the utilitarian ideal of complete equality is that it ignores the costs of making income transfers. The economist, Arthur Okun, in his book *Equality and Efficiency: The Big Tradeoff*, described the process of redistributing income as like trying to transfer water from one barrel to another with a leaky bucket. The more we try to increase equity by redistributing income, the more we reduce efficiency. Recognizing the cost of making income transfers leads to what is called the **big trade-off** – a trade-off between efficiency and fairness.

The big trade-off is based on the following facts. Income can be transferred from people with high incomes to people with low incomes only by taxing the high incomes. Taxing people's income from employment makes them work less. It results in the quantity of labour being less than the efficient quantity. Taxing people's income from capital makes them save less. It results in the quantity of capital being less than the efficient quantity. With smaller quantities of both labour and capital, the quantity of goods and services produced is less than the efficient quantity. The economic pie shrinks.

The trade-off is between the size of the economy and the degree of equality with which its produce is shared. The greater the amount of income redistribution through income taxes, the greater the inefficiency – the smaller is the economic pie.

A second source of inefficiency arises because a pound taken from a rich person does not end up as a pound in the hands of a poorer person. Some of it is spent on administration of the tax and transfer system. The cost of tax-collection agency, the Inland Revenue, and the welfare administering agency, the Department of Work and Pensions, must be paid with some of the taxes collected. Also, taxpayers hire accountants, auditors and lawyers to help ensure that they pay the correct amount of taxes. These activities use skilled labour and capital resources that could otherwise be used to produce goods and services that people value.

You can see that when all these costs are taken into account, taking a pound from a rich person does not give a pound to a poor person. It is even possible that with high taxes, those with low incomes end up being worse off. Suppose, for example, that highly taxed entrepreneurs decide to work less hard and shut down some of their businesses. Low-income workers get fired and must seek other, perhaps even lower-paid, work.

Because of the big trade-off, those who say that fairness is equality propose a modified version of utilitarianism.

Make the Poorest as Well Off as Possible

A Harvard philosopher, John Rawls, proposed a modified version of utilitarianism in a classic book entitled *A Theory of Justice*, published in 1971. Rawls says that, taking all the costs of income transfers into account, the fair distribution of the economic pie is the one that makes the poorest person as well off as possible. The incomes of rich people should be taxed and, after paying the costs of administering the tax and transfer system, what is left should be transferred to the poor. But the taxes must not be so high that they make the economic pie shrink to the point that the poorest person ends up with a smaller piece. A bigger share of a smaller pie can be less than a smaller share of a bigger pie. The goal is to make the piece enjoyed by the poorest person as big as possible. Most likely this piece will not be an equal share.

The "fair results" idea requires a change in the results after the game is over. Some economists say these changes are themselves unfair and propose a different way of thinking about fairness.

It's not Fair if the *Rules* aren't Fair

The idea that it's not fair if the rules aren't fair is based on a fundamental principle that seems to be hard-wired into the human brain. It is the **symmetry principle**. The symmetry principle is the requirement that people in similar situations be treated similarly. It is the moral principle that lies at the centre of all the big religions. It says, in some form or other, "behave towards others in the way you expect them to behave towards you".

In economic life, this principle translates into *equality of opportunity*. But equality of opportunity to do what? This question is answered by the late Harvard philosopher, Robert Nozick, in a book entitled *Anarchy, State, and Utopia*, published in 1974.

Nozick argues that the idea of fairness as an outcome or result cannot work and that fairness must be based on the fairness of the rules. He suggests that fairness obeys two rules. They are:

1 The state must enforce laws that establish and protect private property.

2 Private property may be transferred from one person to another only by voluntary exchange.

The first rule says that everything that is valuable must be owned by individuals and that the state must ensure that theft is prevented. The second rule says that the only legitimate way a person can acquire property is to buy it in exchange for something else that the person owns. If these rules, which are fair rules, are followed, then the economic pie is shared, provided that the pie is baked by people, each on of whom voluntarily provides services in exchange for a share of the pie offered in compensation.

These rules satisfy the symmetry principle. And if these rules are not followed, the symmetry principle is broken. You can see these facts by imagining a world in which the laws are not followed.

First, suppose that some resources or goods are not owned. They are common property. Then everyone is free to participate in a grab to use these resources or goods. The strongest will prevail. But when the strongest prevails, the strongest effectively *owns* the resources or goods in question and prevents others from enjoying them.

Second, suppose that we do not insist on voluntary exchange for transferring ownership of resources from one person to another. The alternative is *involuntary* transfer. In simple language, the alternative is theft.

Both of these situations violate the symmetry principle. Only the strong get to acquire what they want.

The weak end up with only the resources and goods that the strong don't want.

In contrast, if the two rules of fairness are followed, everyone, strong and weak, is treated in a similar way. Everyone is free to use their resources and human skills to create things that are valued by themselves and others and to exchange the fruits of their efforts with each other. This is the only set of arrangements that obeys the symmetry principle.

Fairness and Efficiency

If private property rights are enforced and if voluntary exchange takes place in a competitive market, resources will be allocated efficiently if there are no:

1 Price ceilings and price floors.

2 Taxes, subsidies and quotas.

3 Monopolies.

4 External costs and external benefits.

5 Public goods and common resources.

And according to the Nozick rules, the resulting distribution of income and wealth will be fair. Let's study a concrete example to examine the claim that if resources are allocated efficiently, they are also allocated fairly.

A Price Hike in a Natural Disaster

A severe winter storm has frozen the pipes that deliver drinking water to a city. With no thaw in sight, the price of bottled water jumps from £1 a bottle to £8 a bottle in the 30 or so shops that have water for sale.

First, let's agree that the water is being used *efficiently*. There is a fixed amount of bottled water in the city, and given the quantity available, some people are willing to pay £8 to get a bottle. The water goes to the people who value it most highly. Consumer surplus and producer surplus are maximized.

So the water resources are being used efficiently. But are they being used fairly? Shouldn't people who can't afford to pay £8 a bottle get some of the available water for a lower price that they can afford? Isn't the fair solution for the shops to sell water for a lower price that people can afford? Or perhaps it might be fairer if the government bought the water and then made it available to people through a government store at a "reasonable" price. Let's think about these alternative solutions to the water problem of this city. Should water somehow be made available at a more reasonable price?

Shop Offers Water for £5

Suppose that Kris, a shop owner, offers water at £5 a bottle. Who will buy it? There are two types of buyers. Harry is an example of one type. He values water at £8 – is willing to pay £8 a bottle. Recall that given the quantity of water available, the equilibrium price is £8 a bottle. If Harry buys the water, he consumes it. Harry ends up with a consumer surplus of £3 on the bottle, and Kris receives £3 less of producer surplus.

David is an example of the second type of buyer. David would not pay £8 for a bottle. In fact, he wouldn't even pay £5 to consume a bottle of water.

But he buys a bottle for £5. Why? Because he plans to sell the water to someone who is willing to pay £8 to consume it. When David buys the water, Kris again receives a producer surplus of £3 *less* than she would receive if she charged the going market price. David now becomes a water dealer. He sells the water for the going price of £8 and earns a producer surplus of £3.

So by being public-spirited and offering water for less than the market price, Kris ends up £3 a bottle worse off and the buyers end up £3 a bottle better off. The same people consume the water in both situations. They are the people who value the water at £8 a bottle. But the distribution of consumer surplus and producer surplus is different in the two cases. When Kris offers the water for £5 a bottle, she ends up with a smaller producer surplus and Harry and David end up with a larger consumer surplus and producer surplus.

So which is the fair arrangement? The one that favours Kris or the one that favours Harry and David? The fair rules view is that both arrangements are fair. Kris voluntarily sells the water for £5 so, in effect, she is helping the community to cope with its water problem. It is fair that she should help, but the choice is hers. She owns the water. It is not fair that she should be compelled to help.

Government Buys Water

Now suppose instead that the government buys all the water. The going price is £8 a bottle, so that's what the government pays. Now the government offers the water for sale for £1 a bottle, its "normal" price.

The quantity of water supplied is exactly the same as before. But now, at £1 a bottle, the quantity demanded is much larger than the quantity supplied. There is a shortage of water.

Because there is a large water shortage, the government decides to ration the amount that anyone may buy. Everyone is allocated one bottle. So everyone lines up to collect his or her bottle. Two of these people are Harry and David. Harry, you'll recall, is willing to pay £8 a bottle. David is willing to pay less than £5. But they both get a bargain. Harry drinks his £1 bottle and enjoys a £7 consumer surplus. What does David do? Does he drink his bottle? He does not. He sells it to another person who values the water at £8. And he enjoys a £7 producer surplus from his temporary water-trading business.

So the people who value the water most highly consume it. But the consumer and producer surpluses are distributed in a different way from what the free market would have delivered. Again the question arises, which arrangement is fair?

The main difference between the government scheme and Kris's private charitable contributions lies in the fact that to buy the water for £8 and sell it for £1, the government must tax someone £7 for each bottle sold. So whether this arrangement is fair depends on whether the taxes are fair.

Taxes are an involuntary transfer of private property so, according to the fair rules view, taxes are unfair. But most economists, and most people, think that there is such a thing as a fair tax. So it seems that the fair rules view needs to be weakened a bit. Agreeing that there is such a thing as a fair tax is the easy part. Deciding what is a fair tax brings endless disagreement and debate.

Review Quiz

1. What are the two big approaches to fairness?
2. Explain the utilitarian idea of fairness and what is wrong with it.
3. Explain the big trade-off and the idea of fairness developed to deal with it.
4. What is the main idea of fairness based on fair rules? Explain your answer.

You've now studied the two biggest issues that run right through the whole of economics: efficiency and equity, or fairness. In the next chapter, we study some sources of inefficiency and unfairness. And at many points throughout this book – and in your life – you will return to and use the ideas about efficiency and fairness that you've learned in this chapter. *Reading Between the Lines* on pp. 112–113 looks at fairness and efficiency in the EU market for airline tickets.

Reading Between the Lines

Inefficiency: European Airline Ticket Pricing

The Guardian, 20 December 2003

EC launches airline ticket price inquiry

Andrew Osborn

The European Commission launched a surprise investigation into air ticket prices yesterday, asking British Airways, British Midland and Virgin Atlantic whether they unfairly vary their ticket prices from one European country to another.

Responding to hundreds of complaints, Brussels said it suspected that airlines are charging customers wildly different prices for identical flights, depending upon where the ticket is bought.

The services of the Commission have written to 18 European airlines asking each of them whether it charges different prices for the same ticket depending on the country of residence. . . . Such a pricing policy, the Commission suggested, may be in breach of the EU's internal market rules.

The Commission . . . claimed that price differences were sometimes as much as 300%.

Other airlines it contacted included Air France, Aer Lingus, Alitalia, Lufthansa, KLM, Finnair, Olympic Airlines, Iberia and SAS. . . .

Low fair airlines such as Ryannair were not implicated. The 18 airlines have until the end of February to explain their pricing policies. . . . The Commission claimed that the pricing problems appeared to be particularly acute for internet purchases where firms use a customer's postal or credit card address to determine country of residence . . .

Air France defended its pricing policy. "There is a cost linked to providing a passenger in a foreign city with a ticket," said a spokesman.

SAS added that airlines had the right to tailor their prices to different countries. "We have different prices depending on where you buy. It's correct to set the price according to the market situation in each country."

The Essence of the Story

◆ European airlines are charging different prices for the same flights, depending upon where the ticket is bought.

◆ The European Commission believes that this pricing policy might be unfair. It is investigating the pricing policy of 18 major European airlines.

◆ The price for the same ticket can vary by as much as 300 per cent.

◆ The airlines say the price differences reflect real costs and market differences.

Economic Analysis

◆ The European Commission would like airline tickets to be sold in competitive markets.

◆ Figure 1 illustrates a competitive market for flights from London to Paris.

◆ The demand curve, D, is also the marginal benefit curve MB. This curve tells us the value to consumers of one more trip.

◆ The supply curve, S, is also the marginal cost curve, MC. This curve tells us the cost of transporting an additional passenger from London to Paris.

◆ In a competitive market, equilibrium occurs at point A, the intersection of the demand curve and the supply curve.

◆ The equilibrium price is £50 and the number of passengers is Q_A per week. Production is efficient because marginal benefit equals marginal cost and the sum of the consumer surplus (green area) and producer surplus (blue area) is maximized.

◆ The European Commission suspects that the market for flights from London to Paris is not efficient because some passengers are charged a lot more than £50 for the trip.

◆ If the average price is £75, then Figure 2 shows that the number of passengers is Q_B.

◆ At point B, the market is inefficient because marginal benefit exceeds marginal cost and a deadweight loss (grey area) arises.

◆ At point B, producer surplus is greater than at point A and consumer surplus is smaller. But deadweight loss decreases the sum of the consumer surplus and producer surplus.

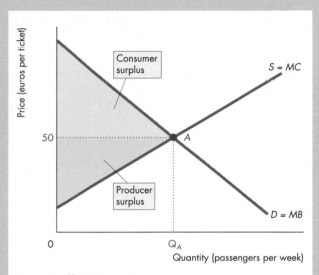

Figure 1 Efficient quantity

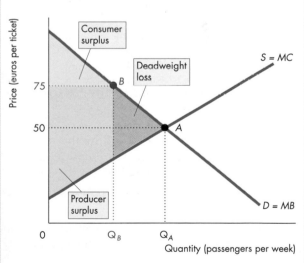

Figure 2 Inefficient quantity

Summary

Key Points

Efficiency and Social Interest
(pp. 98–99)

◆ The marginal benefit received from a good or service – the benefit of consuming one additional unit – is the *value* of the good or service to its consumers.

◆ The marginal cost of a good or service – the cost of producing one additional unit – is the *opportunity cost* of one more unit to its producers.

◆ Resources allocation is efficient when marginal benefit equals marginal cost.

Value, Price and Consumer Surplus
(pp. 100–101)

◆ Marginal benefit is measured by the maximum price that consumers are willing to pay for a good or service, which is also demand.

◆ Value is what people are *willing to* pay; price is what people *must* pay.

◆ Consumer surplus equals value minus price, summed over the quantity consumed.

Cost, Price and Producer Surplus
(pp. 102–103)

◆ Marginal cost is measured by the minimum price producers must be offered to increase production by one unit, which is also supply.

◆ Opportunity cost is what producers pay; price is what producers receive.

◆ Producer surplus equals price minus opportunity cost, summed over the quantity produced.

Is the Competitive Market Efficient?
(pp. 104–107)

◆ In a competitive equilibrium, marginal benefit equals marginal cost and resource allocation is efficient.

◆ Monopoly restricts production and creates deadweight loss.

◆ A competitive market provides too small a quantity of public goods because of the free-rider problem.

◆ A competitive market provides too large a quantity of goods and services that have external costs and too small a quantity of goods and services that have external benefits.

Is the Competitive Market Fair?
(pp. 108–111)

◆ Ideas about fairness divide into two groups: those based on the notion that the *results* are not fair, and those based on the notion that the *rules* are not fair.

◆ Fair results ideas require income transfers from the rich to the poor.

◆ Fair rules ideas require property rights and voluntary exchange.

Key Figures

Key Terms

Problems

*Solutions to odd-numbered problems are available on *Parkin Interactive*.

*1 The figure shows the demand for and supply of floppy discs.

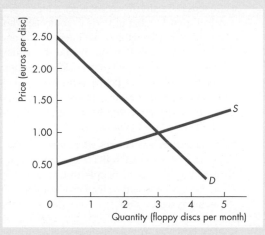

a What are the equilibrium price and equilibrium quantity of floppy discs?

b Calculate the amount that consumers paid for floppy discs.

c What is the consumer surplus?

d What is the producer surplus?

e Calculate the cost of producing the floppy discs.

f What is the efficient quantity of floppy disks?

2 The figure shows the market for CDs.

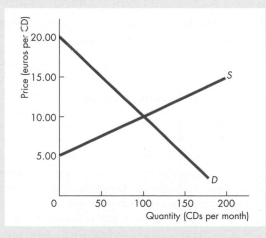

a What are the equilibrium price and equilibrium quantity of CDs?

b Calculate the amount that consumers paid for CDs.

c What is the consumer surplus?

d What is the producer surplus?

e Calculate the cost of producing the CDs.

f What is the efficient quantity of CDs?

*3 The table gives the demand and supply schedules for sandwiches.

Price	Quantity demanded	Quantity supplied
(pounds per sandwich)	(sandwiches per hour)	
0	400	0
1	350	50
2	300	100
3	250	150
4	200	200
5	150	250
6	100	300
7	50	350
8	0	400

a What is the maximum price that consumers are willing to pay for the 250th sandwich?

b What is the minimum price that producers are willing to accept for the 250th sandwich?

c Are 250 sandwiches a day less than or greater than the efficient quantity?

d If the sandwich market is efficient, what is the consumer surplus? (Draw the graph.)

e If the sandwich market is efficient, what is the producer surplus? (Draw the graph.)

f If sandwich makers produce 250 a day, what is the deadweight loss? (Draw the graph.)

4 The table gives the demand and supply schedules for sunscreen.

Price	Quantity demanded	Quantity supplied
(pounds per bottle)	(bottles per day)	
0	900	0
1	800	100
2	700	200
3	600	300
4	500	400
5	400	500
6	300	600
7	200	700
8	100	800
9	0	900

a What is the maximum price that consumers are willing to pay for the 300th bottle?

b What is the minimum price that producers are willing to accept for the 300th bottle?

c Are 300 bottles a day less than or greater than the efficient quantity? (Draw the graph.)

d If the market for sunscreen is efficient, what is the consumer surplus? (Draw the graph.)

e If the market for sunscreen is efficient, what is the producer surplus? (Draw the graph.)

f If sunscreen bottlers produce 300 bottles a day, what is the deadweight loss?

*5 The table gives the demand and supply schedules for train travel for Ben, Beth and Bill.

Price (pence per passenger mile)	Quantity demanded (passenger miles)		
	Ben	**Beth**	**Bill**
5	550	350	70
10	500	300	60
20	450	250	50
30	400	200	40
40	350	150	30
50	300	100	20
60	250	50	10
70	200	0	0

a If the price of train travel is 40 pence a passenger mile, what is the consumer surplus of each traveller?

b If the price of train travel is 40 pence a passenger mile, which traveller has the largest consumer surplus? Explain why.

c If the price of train travel rises to 50 pence a passenger mile, what is the change in consumer surplus of each traveller?

6 The table gives the demand and supply schedules for airline travel for Ann, Arthur and Abby.

Price (pounds per passenger mile)	Quantity demanded (passenger miles)		
	Ann	**Arthur**	**Abby**
3.75	550	700	350
5.00	500	600	300
6.25	450	500	250
7.50	400	400	200
8.75	350	300	150
10.00	300	200	100
11.25	250	100	50
12.50	200	0	0

a If the price is £10 a passenger mile, what is the consumer surplus of each traveller?

b If the price is £10 a passenger mile, which traveller has the largest consumer surplus? Explain why.

c If the price falls to £7.50 a passenger mile, what is the change in consumer surplus of each traveller?

Critical Thinking

1 Study Reading *Between the Lines* on pp. 112–113 and then answer the following questions:

a Suppose British Airways charges a higher price for a trip from London to Paris to someone who buys the ticket in Denmark than it does to someone who buys the ticket in London. Would this policy lead to underproduction or overproduction of trips from London to Paris for people who buy the ticket in Denmark? Use the concepts of marginal benefit, marginal cost, price, consumer surplus and producer surplus to explain your answer.

b If the airlines are correct when they say that their pricing system just reflects differences in costs of selling tickets to people in different regional markets, what would be the impact of removing the pricing system?

2 Explain how you would calculate your consumer surplus on an item that you buy regularly.

3 Write a short description of how you would determine whether the allocation of your time between studying different subjects is efficient. In what units would you measure marginal benefit and marginal cost? Use the concepts of marginal benefit, marginal cost, price, consumer surplus and producer surplus in your answer.

Web Exercise

Use the links on *Parkin Interactive* to work the following exercise.

1 In 2001, the European Commission investigated why the prices of DVDs in the European Union were higher than those in the United States. The price differential was maintained because regional tagging of DVDs made the US DVDs unreadable on European players. Consider the impact of regional tagging and then answer the following questions:

a Does regional tagging lead to underproduction or overproduction of DVDs? Use the concepts of marginal benefit, marginal cost, price, consumer surplus and producer surplus to explain why.

b As DVD rewriting technology becomes cheaper, more pirate copies will be made and they will sell at very low prices. How will piracy change consumer surplus and producer surplus of legitimate EU DVD producers? Will the DVD market be more efficient? Explain your answer.

c If EU producers are correct when they say that the tagging system raises their cost above those of US producers, what will be the impact of removing regional tagging on the producer surplus in Europe?

Chapter 6

Markets in Action

After studying this chapter you will be able to:

◆ Explain how housing markets work and how price ceilings create housing shortages and inefficiency

◆ Explain how labour markets work and how minimum wage laws create unemployment and inefficiency

◆ Explain the effects of a tax

◆ Explain why farm prices and revenues fluctuate and how subsidies, production quotas and price supports influence farm production, costs and prices

◆ Explain how markets for illegal goods work

Turbulent Times

With rocketing property prices, it costs a pretty packet to rent a flat in one of Britain's cities! Should the government put a cap on the rents that landlords can charge? Or what about increasing the minimum wage for which someone can be employed? Find out in this chapter. Also learn how the EU Common Agricultural Policy works, what it costs the EU taxpayer, why it needs to be reformed and why reform is not easy to achieve.

Housing Markets and Rent Ceilings

In January 1995, in the Gelderland province of the Netherlands, floods wrecked hundreds of homes causing more than €450 million worth of damage. How did the region cope with such a vast reduction in the supply of housing? This extreme decrease in supply provides a valuable look at how a housing market works.

The Market Before and After the Flood

Figure 6.1 shows the market for housing in the Gelderland. The demand curve for housing is *D*. There is a short-run supply curve, labelled *SS*, and the long-run supply curve, labelled *LS*.

The short-run supply curve shows how the quantity of housing supplied varies as the price (rent) varies, while the number of houses and flats remains constant. The short-run supply response arises from the intensity with which existing buildings are used. The quantity of housing supplied increases if families rent out rooms that they previously used themselves, and it decreases if families use rooms they previously rented to others.

The long-run supply curve shows how the quantity of housing supplied responds to a change in the price after enough time has elapsed for new houses and flats to be built or for existing one to be destroyed. In Figure 6.1, we assume that the long-run supply curve is *perfectly elastic*. This assumption is reasonable if the marginal cost of building is much the same regardless of whether there are 5,000 or 15,000 flats and houses in existence.

The equilibrium price (rent) and quantity are determined at the point of intersection of the *short-run* supply curve and the demand curve. Before the flood, the equilibrium rent is €1,000 a month and the quantity is 10,000 units of housing.

After the flood, the supply of housing decreases and the short-run supply curve shifts leftward to *SS_A* in Figure 6.1(a). If people use the housing with the same intensity as before the flood and if the rent remains at €1,000 a month, only 4,400 housing units are available. But at €1,000 a month, there is a shortage of housing. So the rent does not remain at €1,000 a month. With only 4,400 housing units available, the maximum rent that someone is willing to pay for the last available unit is €1,200 a month. So the rent rises until the shortage is eliminated. In Figure 6.1(a), the rent rises to €1,100 a month.

Figure 6.1

The Gelderland Housing Market in 1995

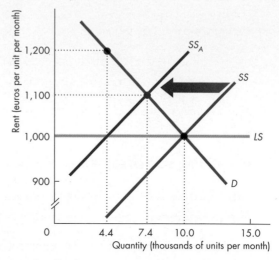

(a) After flood

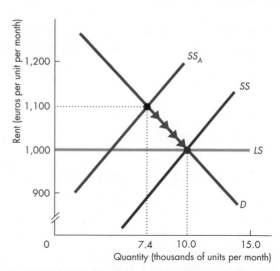

(b) Long-run adjustment

Before the flood, the housing market is in equilibrium with 10,000 housing units being rented each month at €1,000 a month in part (a). After the flood, the short-run supply curve shifts from *SS* to *SS_A*. The rent rises to €1,100 a month, and the quantity of housing falls to 7,400 units.

With the rent at €1,100 a month, it is profitable to renovate or rebuild flats and houses. With renovation and rebuilding, the short-run supply curve gradually shifts rightward in part (b). The rent gradually falls to €1,000 a month and the quantity of housing gradually increases to 10,000 units.

Long-run Adjustments

The response we've just seen takes place in the short run. What happens in the long run? With sufficient time for renovation and building, supply increases. The long-run supply curve tells us that in the long run, housing will be supplied at a rent of €1,000 a month. Because the rent of €1,100 a month exceeds the long-run supply price of €1,000 a month, there will be a building boom.

As time passes, more housing is renovated or rebuilt; the short-run supply of housing increases and the short-run supply curve gradually shifts rightward.

Figure 6.1(b) illustrates the long-run adjustment. As more housing is built, the short-run supply curve shifts rightward and intersects the demand curve at lower rents and higher quantities. The market equilibrium follows the arrows down the demand curve. The building boom ends when there is no further profit in renovating or building housing units. The process ends when the rent is back at €1,000 a month and 10,000 units of housing are available.

We've just seen how a housing market responds to a decrease in supply. And we've seen that a key part of the adjustment process is a rise in the rent. Suppose the government passes a law to stop the rent from rising. What happens then?

A Regulated Housing Market

We're now going to study the effects of a price ceiling in the housing market. A **price ceiling** is a regulation that makes it illegal to charge a price higher than a specified level. When a price ceiling is applied to rents in housing markets, it is called a **rent ceiling**. How does a rent ceiling affect the way the housing market works?

The effect of a price (rent) ceiling depends on whether it is imposed at a level that is above or below the equilibrium price (rent). A price ceiling set *above* the equilibrium price has no effect because market forces are not constrained by the price ceiling. The force of the law and the market forces are not in conflict.

But a price ceiling set *below* the equilibrium price has powerful effects because it prevents the price from regulating the quantities demanded and supplied. The force of the law and the market forces are in conflict, and one (or both) of these forces must yield to some degree.

What would have happened after the flood if a rent ceiling of €1,000 a month had been imposed? Figure 6.2

Figure 6.2

A Rent Ceiling

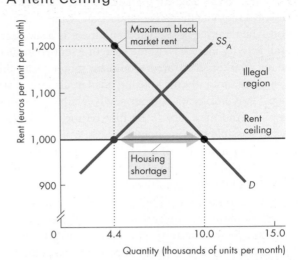

A rent above €1,000 a month is illegal (in the grey-shaded illegal region). At a rent of €1,000 a month, the quantity of housing supplied after the flood would have been stuck at 4,400 units. Someone would have been willingly to pay €1,200 a month for the 4,400th unit. Frustrated renters spend time searching for housing and frustrated renters and landlords make deals in a black market.

shows that a rent ceiling that exceeds €1,000 a month is in the grey-shaded illegal region of the figure. At a rent of €1,000 a month, the quantity of housing supplied is 4,400 units and the quantity demanded is 10,000 units. So there is a shortage of 5,600 units – the quantity demanded exceeds the quantity supplied by 5,600 units.

But the story does not end here. Somehow 4,400 units of available housing have to be allocated among the people who demand 10,000 units. How is the allocation achieved? When a rent ceiling creates a housing shortage, two developments occur. They are:

◆ Search activity

◆ Black markets

Search Activity

The time spent looking for someone with whom to do business is called **search activity**. We spend some time in search activity almost every time we buy something. You want the latest hot CD, and you know four shops that stock it. But which shop has the best deal? You need to spend a few minutes on the telephone finding out. In some markets, we spend a lot of time searching. An example is the used car market. People spend a lot of time checking out alternative dealers and cars.

But when a price is regulated and there is a shortage, search activity increases. In the case of a rent-controlled housing market, frustrated would-be renters scan the newspapers, not only for housing ads but also for death notices! Any information about newly available housing is useful. And they race to be first on the scene when news of possible housing breaks.

The *opportunity cost* of a good is equal not only to its price but also to the value of the time spent searching the good. So the opportunity cost of housing is equal to the rent (a regulated price) plus the time and other resources spent searching for the restricted quantity available. Search activity is costly. It uses time and other resources, such as telephones, cars, and petrol that could have been used in other productive ways. A rent ceiling controls the rent portion of the cost of housing, but it does not control the opportunity cost, which might even be *higher* than the rent would be if the market were unregulated.

Black Markets

A **black market** is an illegal market in which the price exceeds the legally imposed price ceiling. Black markets occur in rent-controlled housing markets. They also occur in the market for tickets to big sporting events and rock concerts, where "scalpers" operate.

When rent ceilings are in force, frustrated renters and landlords constantly seek ways of increasing rents. One common way is for a new tenant to pay a high price for worthless fittings, such as charging €2,000 for threadbare curtains. Another is for the tenant to pay an exorbitant price for new locks and keys called "key money." The level of a black market rent depends on how tightly the rent ceiling is enforced. With loose enforcement, the black market rent is close to the unregulated rent. But with strict enforcement, the black market rent is equal to the maximum price that renters are willing to pay for the available housing.

With strict enforcement of the rent ceiling in the Gelderland example shown in Figure. 6.2, the quantity of housing available remains at 4,400 units. A small number of people offer housing for rent at €1,200 a month – the highest rent that someone is willing to pay – and the government detects and punishes some of these black market traders.

Inefficiency of Rent Ceilings

In an unregulated market, the market determines the rent at which the quantity demanded equals the quantity supplied. In this situation, scarce housing resources are allocated efficiently. *Marginal benefit* equals *marginal cost* (see Chapter 5, p. 99).

Figure 6.3 shows the inefficiency of a rent ceiling. If the rent is fixed at €1,000 a month, 4,400 units are supplied. Marginal benefit is €1,200 a month. The blue triangle above the supply curve and below the rent ceiling line shows producer surplus. Because the quantity of housing is less than the competitive quantity, there is a deadweight loss, shown by the grey triangle. This loss is borne by the consumers who can't find housing and by producers who can't supply housing at the new lower price. Consumers who do find housing at the controlled rent gain. If no one incurs search cost, consumer surplus is shown by the sum of the green triangle and the red rectangle. But search costs might eat up part of the consumer surplus, possibly as much as the entire amount that consumers are willing to pay for the available housing, (the red rectangle).

Are Rent Ceilings Fair?

Do rent ceilings achieve a fairer allocation of scarce housing? Chapter 5 (pp. 108–111) explores the complex ideas about fairness. According to the *fair rules* view, anything that blocks voluntary exchange is unfair, so rent ceilings are unfair. But according to the *fair result* view, a fair outcome is one that benefits the less well off. So according to this view, the fairest outcome is the one that allocates scarce housing to the poorest. To see whether rent ceilings help to achieve a fairer outcome in this sense, we need to consider how the market allocates scarce housing resources in the face of a rent ceiling.

Blocking rent adjustments doesn't eliminate scarcity. Rather, because it decreases the quantity of housing available, it creates an even bigger challenge for the housing market. So somehow the market must ration a smaller quantity of housing and allocate that housing among the people who demand it. When the rent is not permitted to allocate scarce housing, what other mechanisms are available?

Some possible mechanisms are a lottery, a waiting list (a queue) and discrimination. Each of these has problems of both fairness and efficiency.

Figure 6.3

The Inefficiency of a Rent Ceiling

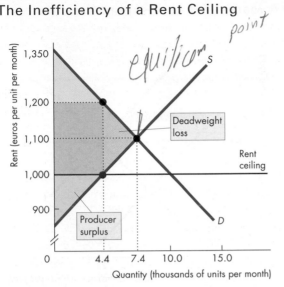

A rent ceiling of €1,000 a month decreases the quantity of housing supplied to 4,400 units. Producer surplus shrinks to the blue triangle and a deadweight loss (the grey triangle) arises. If people use no resources in search activity, consumer surplus is the green triangle plus the red rectangle. But if people use resources in search activity equal to the amount they are willing to pay for available housing (red rectangle), the consumer surplus shrinks to the green triangle.

Review Quiz

1   How does a decrease in the supply of housing change equilibrium rents in the short run?
2   What are the effects of a rise in rent? Who gets to consume the scarce resources?
3   What are the long-run effects of higher rents following a decrease in the supply of housing?
4   What is a rent ceiling and what are the effects of a rent ceiling set above the equilibrium rent?
5   What is a rent ceiling and what are the effects of a rent ceiling set below the equilibrium rent?
6   How do scarce housing resources get allocated when a rent ceiling is in place? Is the allocation fair? Explain.

You now know how a price ceiling works. Next, we'll learn about the effects of a price floor by studying minimum wages in the labour market.

The Labour Market and Minimum Wage

For each one of us, the labour market is the market that influences the jobs we get and the wages we earn. In the labour market, employers are on the demand side and workers are on the supply side. Firms decide how much labour to demand, and the lower the wage rate, the greater is the quantity of labour demanded. Households decide how much labour to supply, and the higher the wage rate, the greater is the quantity of labour supplied. The wage rate adjusts to make the quantity of labour demanded equal to the quantity supplied.

Equilibrium wage rates give some people high incomes but leave many more people with low incomes. And the labour market is constantly hit by shocks that often hit the lowest paid the hardest. The most pervasive of these shocks is the arrival of new labour-saving technologies that decrease the demand for low-skilled workers and lower their wage rates.

During the 1980s and 1990s, for example, the demand for telephone operators and television repair technicians decreased. Throughout the past 200 years, the demand for low-skilled farm labourers has steadily decreased.

How does the labour market cope with this continuous decrease in the demand for low-skilled labour? Doesn't it mean that the wage rate of low-skilled workers is constantly falling?

To answer these questions, we must study the market for low-skilled labour in both the short run and the long run.

A Market for Low-skilled Labour

In the short run, there are a given number of people who have a given skill, training, and experience. Short-run supply of labour describes how the number of hours of labour supplied by this given number of people changes as the wage rate changes. To get them to work more hours, they must be offered a higher wage rate.

In the long run, people acquire new skills and find new types of jobs. The number of people in the low-skilled labour market depends on the wage rate in this market compared with other opportunities. If the wage rate of low-skilled labour is high enough, people will enter this market. If the wage rate is too low, people will leave it. Some will seek training to enter higher-skilled labour markets, and others will stop working. The long-run supply of labour is the relationship between the quantity of labour supplied and the wage rate after enough time has passed for people to enter or leave the low-skilled labour market. If people can freely enter and leave the low-skilled labour market, the long-run supply of labour is *perfectly elastic*.

Figure 6.4 represents the market for unskilled labour in France. Other things remaining the same, the lower the wage rate, the greater is the quantity of labour demanded by firms. The demand curve for labour, *D* in part (a), shows this relationship between the wage rate and the quantity of labour demanded. Other things remaining the same, the higher the wage rate, the greater is the quantity of labour supplied by households. But the longer the period of adjustment, the greater is the *elasticity of supply* of labour. The short-run supply curve is *SS* and the long-run supply curve is *LS*. In the figure, the *LS* curve is assumed to be perfectly elastic. This market is in equilibrium at a wage rate of €6 an hour and 22 million hours of labour employed.

What happens if a labour-saving invention decreases the demand for low-skilled labour? Figure 6.4(a) shows the short-run effects of such a change. Before the new technology is introduced, the demand curve is the curve labelled *D*. After the introduction of the new technology, the demand curve shifts leftward to D_A. The wage rate falls to €5 an hour, and the quantity of labour employed decreases to 21 million hours. But this short-run effect on the wage rate and employment is not the end of the story.

People who are now earning only €5 an hour look around for other opportunities. They see many other jobs (in markets for other types of skills) that pay more than €5 an hour. One by one, workers decide to take a college course or take a job that pays less but offers on-the-job training. As a result, the short-run supply curve begins to shift leftward.

Figure 6.4(b) shows the long-run adjustment. As the short-run supply curve shifts leftward, it intersects the demand curve D_A at higher wage rates and lower levels of employment. The process ends when workers have no incentive to leave the low-skilled labour market and the short-run supply curve has shifted all the way to SS_A. At this point, the wage rate has returned to €6 an hour, and employment has decreased to 20 million hours a year.

Sometimes, the adjustment process is rapid. At other times, it is slow and the wage rate remains low for a long period. To boost the incomes of the lowest-paid workers, governments intervene in the labour market and set a minimum wage that employers are required to pay. Let's look at the effects of the minimum wage.

Figure 6.4

A Market for Low-skilled Labour

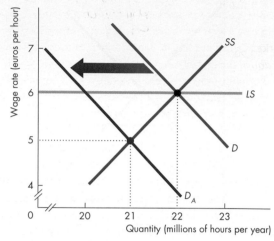

(a) After invention

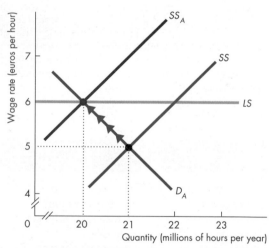

(b) Long-run adjustment

Part (a) shows the immediate effect of a labour-saving invention on the market for low-skilled labour. Initially, the wage rate is €6 an hour and 22 million are employed. A labour-saving invention shifts the demand curve from *D* to D_A. The wage rate falls to €5 an hour and employment decreases to 21 million hours a year.

With a lower wage rate, some workers leave this market and the short-run supply curve starts to shift gradually leftward to SS_A in part (b). The wage rate gradually increases, and the employment level decreases. In the long-run, the wage rate returns to €6 an hour and employment decreases to 20 million hours a year.

A Minimum Wage

A **price floor** is a regulation that makes it illegal to trade at a price lower than a specified level. When a price floor is applied to labour markets, it is called a **minimum wage**. If a minimum wage is set *below* the equilibrium wage, the minimum wage has no effect. The minimum wage and market forces are not in conflict. If a minimum wage is set *above* the equilibrium wage, the minimum wage is in conflict with market forces and does have some effects on the labour market. Let's study these effects by returning to the market for low-skilled labour.

Suppose that with an equilibrium wage rate of €5 an hour in Figure 6.4(a), the government imposes a minimum wage of €6 an hour. Figure 6.5 shows the minimum wage as the horizontal red line labelled "Minimum wage". A wage below this level is illegal, in the grey-shaded illegal region. At the minimum wage rate, 20 million hours of labour are demanded (point *A*) and 22 million hours of labour are supplied (point *B*), so 2 million hours of available labour are unemployed.

With only 20 million hours demanded, some workers are willing to supply that 20 millionth hour for €4. Frustrated unemployed workers spend time and other resources searching for hard-to-find jobs.

Inefficiency and the Minimum Wage

In an unregulated labour market, everyone who is willing to work for the going wage rate gets a job. And the market allocates the economy's scarce labour resources to the jobs in which they are valued most highly.

The minimum wage frustrates the market mechanism and results in unemployment – wasted labour resources – and an inefficient amount of job search.

Figure 6.6 illustrates the inefficiency of the minimum wage. There is a deadweight loss because at the quantity of labour employed, 20 million hours, the value to the firm of the marginal worker exceeds that wage rate for which that person is willing to work.

But the total loss exceeds the deadweight loss. At the equilibrium level of employment, unemployed people have a big incentive to spend time and effort looking for work. The red rectangle shows the potential loss from this extra job search. This loss arises because someone who finds a job earns €6 an hour (from the demand curve) but would have been willing to work for €4 an hour (from the supply curve). So everyone who is unemployed has an incentive to search hard and use resources that are worth the €2-an-hour surplus to find a job.

Figure 6.5 ◆

The Minimum Wage and Unemployment

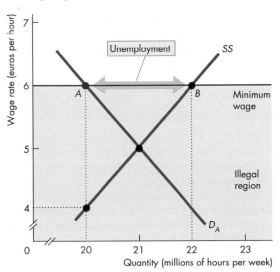

A wage rate of €5 an hour is illegal (in the grey shaded illegal region). At a minimum wage of €6 an hour, 20 million hours are hired but 22 million hours are available. Unemployment *AB* of 2 million hours a year is created.

Figure 6.6 ◆

The Inefficiency of a Minimum Wage

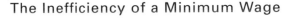
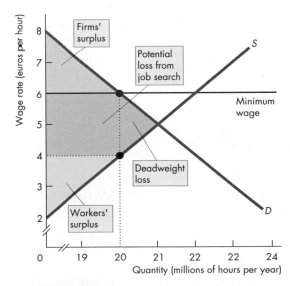

A minimum wage shrinks the firms' surplus (blue) and workers' surplus (green) and creates a deadweight loss (grey). If people use resources in job search equal to the amount they are able to gain by finding a job, the red rectangle is also lost.

Box 6.1
The Minimum Wage in Action

The minimum wage is a hot topic in Europe today. Currently, nine member states of the European Union (Belgium, France, Greece, Ireland, Luxembourg, the Netherlands, Portugal, Spain and the United Kingdom) have a national minimum wage. In three countries (Greece, Portugal and Spain), the minimum wage is around €500 a month. In the other six countries, the minimum wage exceeds €1,000 a month and in Luxembourg and the Netherlands, it exceeds €1,200 a month. In all these countries, the minimum wage is adjusted upward at regular intervals.

Denmark, Germany and Italy have no national minimum wage, but each major industry group has a minimum wage rate.

The UK Minimum Wage

Minimum wage law was introduced in the United Kingdom in April 1999. Table 1 sets out the UK minimum wage rates.

Table 1

UK Minimum Wage Rates

Year	Wage rate (pounds per hour) 18 to 21 years	21 years and over
1999	3.00	3.60
2003	3.80	4.50
2004	4.10	4.85

Source: Office for National Statistics, 2004.

A Single Market or Many Markets?

Some economists believe the European labour market is a single integrated market and that within this market, competition will create an increasingly low-wage workforce.

These economists say that firms will move to low-wage countries and governments will compete for new firms by trimming welfare and training costs. Some of these economists advocate an EU-wide minimum wage to try to prevent downward pressure on wage rates.

Almost all of the discussion of the minimum wage in Europe centres on equity considerations. The assumption is that it simply not fair that people should work for wage rates below some minimum. There is little discussion of the employment consequences of the minimum wage. Virtually no consideration is given to the fact that businesses today operate in a global market, not a regional market.

But some economists believe that with an EU-wide minimum wage, low-paid workers would gain higher wages only at the cost of fewer jobs and longer spells of unemployment.

Unemployment and the Minimum Wage

You've seen from the analysis of the minimum wage that it is predicted to create unemployment. This prediction is surprisingly hard to test. Most of the research that has been designed to find the relationship between the minimum wage and unemployment has been done in the United States, where a minimum wage law has been in place since 1938.

The consensus estimate is that in the United States, a 10 per cent increase in the minimum wage decreases teenage employment by between 1 and 3 per cent.

While this effect is small, it is significant because the minimum wage swings between about 35 per cent and 50 per cent of the average wage.

Whether these US findings apply in Europe we can only speculate. But it would be very surprising if the European labour market behaved much differently from its US counterpart.

The major lesson from the real-world experience in low-wage labour markets is that the solution to low pay is human capital accumulation.

Review Quiz

1   How does a decrease in the demand for low-skilled labour change the wage rate in the short run?
2   What are the long-run effects of a lower wage rate for low-skilled labour?
3   What is a minimum wage? What are the effects of a minimum wage set below the equilibrium wage?
4   What are the effects of a minimum wage that is set above the equilibrium wage?

Next we're going to study a more widespread government action in markets: taxes. We'll see how taxes change prices and quantities. You will discover the surprising fact that while the government can impose a tax, it can't decide who will pay the tax! And you will see that a tax creates a deadweight loss.

Taxes

Everything you earn and almost everything you buy is taxed. Income taxes and social security contributions are deducted from your earnings and sales taxes are added to the bill when you buy something. Employers also pay a social security contribution for their workers, and producers of tobacco products, alcoholic drinks, and petrol pay a tax every time they sell something.

Who *really* pays these taxes? Because the income tax and social security tax are deducted from your pay, and the sales tax is added to the prices that you pay, isn't it obvious that *you* pay these taxes? And isn't it equally obvious that your employer pays the employer's contribution to the social security tax and that tobacco producers pay the tax on cigarettes?

You're going to discover that it isn't obvious who *really* pays a tax and that lawmakers don't make that decision. We begin with a definition of tax incidence.

Tax Incidence

Tax incidence is the division of the burden of a tax between the buyer and the seller. When the government imposes a tax on the sale of a good*, the price paid by the buyer might rise by the full amount of the tax, by a lesser amount, or not at all. If the price paid by the buyer rises by the full amount of the tax, then the burden of the tax falls entirely on the buyer – the buyer pays the tax. If the price paid by the buyer rises by a lesser amount than the tax, then the burden of the tax falls partly on the buyer and partly on the seller. And if the price paid by the buyer doesn't change at all, then the burden of the tax falls entirely on the seller.

Tax incidence does not depend on the tax law. The law might impose a tax on sellers or on buyers, but the outcome is the same in either case. To see why, let's look at the tax on cigarettes.

A Tax on Sellers

During 2003, the government of France increased the tax on the sale of cigarettes three times. We'll assume that the percentage tax increase over the year is equivalent to €1.50 a pack. To work out the effects

of this tax on the sellers of cigarettes, we begin by examining the effects on demand and supply in the market for cigarettes.

In Figure 6.7, the demand curve is D, and the supply curve is S. With no tax, the equilibrium price is €3 per pack and 350 million packs a year are bought and sold. A tax on sellers is like an increase in cost, so it decreases supply. To determine the position of the new supply curve, we add the tax to the minimum price that sellers are willing to accept for each quantity sold. You can see that without the tax, sellers are willing to offer 350 million packs a year for €3 a pack. So with a €1.50 tax, they will offer 350 million packs a year only if the price is €4.50 a pack. The supply curve shifts to the red curve labelled $S + tax\ on\ sellers$.

Equilibrium occurs where the new supply curve intersects the demand curve at 325 million packs a year. The price paid by buyers rises by €1 to €4 a pack. And the price received by sellers falls by 50 cents to €2.50 a pack. So buyers pay €1 of the tax and sellers pay the other 50 cents.

Figure 6.7

A Tax on Sellers

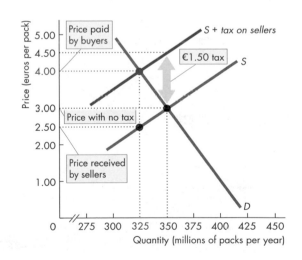

With no tax, 350 million packs a year are bought and sold at €3 a pack. A tax on sellers of €1.50 a pack shifts the supply curve leftward to $S + tax\ on\ sellers$. The equilibrium quantity decreases to 325 million packs a year, the price paid by buyers rises to €4 a pack, and the price received by sellers falls to €2.50 a pack. The tax raises the price paid by buyers by less than the tax and lowers the price received by sellers, so buyers and sellers share the burden of the tax.

---

*These propositions also apply to services and factors of production (land, labour and capital).

A Tax on Buyers

Suppose that instead of taxing sellers, the French government taxes cigarette buyers €1.50 a pack. A tax on buyers lowers the amount they are willing to pay the seller, so it decreases demand and shifts the demand curve leftward. To determine the position of this new demand curve, we subtract the tax from the maximum price that buyers are willing to pay for each quantity bought.

You can see in Figure 6.8 that without the tax, buyers are willing to buy 350 million packs a year for €3 a pack. So with a €1.50 tax, they will buy 350 packs a year only if the price including the tax is €3 a pack, which means that they're willing to pay the seller only €1.50 a pack. The demand curve shifts to become the red curve labelled *D – tax on buyers*.

Equilibrium occurs where the new demand curve intersects the supply curve at a quantity of 325 million packs a year. The price received by sellers is €2.50 a pack, and the price paid by buyers is €4 a pack.

Figure 6.8

A Tax on Buyers

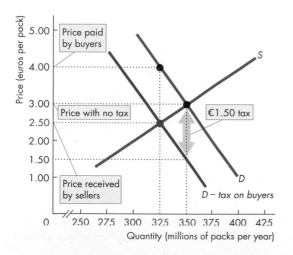

With no tax, 350 million packs a year are bought and sold at €3 a pack. A tax on buyers of €1.50 a pack shifts the demand curve leftward to *D – tax on buyers*. The equilibrium quantity decreases to 325 million packs a year, the price paid by buyers rises to €4 a pack and the price received by sellers falls to €2.50 a pack. The tax raises the price paid by buyers by less than the tax and lowers the price received by sellers, so buyers and sellers share the burden of the tax.

Equivalence of Tax on Buyers and Sellers

You can see that the tax on buyers in Figure 6.8 has the same effects as the tax on sellers in Figure 6.7. The quantity decreases to 325 million packs a year, the price paid by buyers rises to €4 a pack and the price received by sellers falls to €2.50 a pack. Buyers pay €1 of the €1.50 tax. Sellers pay the other 50 cents of the tax.

Can We Share the Burden Equally?

Suppose that the government wants the burden of the cigarette tax to fall equally on buyers and sellers and declares that a 75 cents tax be imposed on each. Is the burden of the tax then shared equally?

You can see that it is not. The tax is still €1.50 a pack. You've seen that the tax has the same effect regardless of whether it is imposed on sellers or buyers. So imposing half the tax on one and half on the other is like an average of the two cases you've examined. In this case, the demand curve shifts downward by 75 cents and the supply curve shifts upward by 75 cents. The equilibrium quantity is still 325 million packs. Buyers pay €4 a pack, of which 75 cents is tax. Sellers receive €2.50 a pack (€3.25 from buyers minus the 75 cents tax).

The key point is that when a transaction is taxed, there are two prices: the price paid by buyers, which includes the tax; and the price received by sellers, which excludes the tax. Buyers respond only to the price that includes the tax because that is the price they pay. Sellers respond only to the price that excludes the tax because that is the price they receive. A tax is like a wedge between the buying price and the selling price. It is the size of the wedge, not the side of the market – demand side or supply side – on which the tax is imposed that determines the effects of the tax.

Payroll Taxes

In some countries, governments impose a payroll tax and share the tax equally between both employers (buyers) and workers (sellers). But the principles you've just learned apply to this tax too. The market for labour, not the government, decides how the burden of a payroll tax is divided by firms and workers.

In the cigarette tax examples, the buyers end up bearing twice the burden of the tax borne by sellers. In general, the division of the burden of a tax between buyers and sellers depends on the elasticities of demand and supply, as you will now see.

Tax Division and Elasticity of Demand

The division of the total tax between buyers and sellers depends partly on the elasticity of demand. There are two extreme cases:

◆ Perfectly inelastic demand – buyers pay

◆ Perfectly elastic demand – sellers pay

Perfectly Inelastic Demand

Figure 6.9(a) shows the UK market for insulin. Demand is perfectly inelastic at 100,000 bottles a day, regardless of the price, as shown by the vertical curve *D*. That is, a diabetic would sacrifice all other goods and services rather than not consume the insulin bottle that provides good health. The supply curve of insulin is S. With no tax, the price is £2 a bottle and the quantity is 100,000 bottles a day.

If insulin is taxed at 20 pence a bottle, we must add the tax to the minimum price at which drug companies are willing to sell insulin. The result is the new supply curve *S + tax*. The price rises to £2.20 a bottle, but the quantity does not change. Buyers pay the entire sales tax of 20 pence a bottle.

Perfectly Elastic Demand

Figure 6.9(b) illustrates the UK market for pink marker pens. Demand is perfectly elastic at 50 pence a pen, as shown by the horizontal curve *D*. If pink markers are less expensive than the other pens, everyone uses pink. If pink pens are more expensive than the others, no one uses pink. The supply curve is *S*. With no tax, the price of a pink marker is 50 pence and the quantity is 4,000 a week.

If a tax of 10 pence is imposed on pink marker pens but not on other colours, we add the tax to the minimum price at which sellers are willing to offer pink pens for sale. The new supply curve is *S + tax*. The price remains at 50 pence a pen and the quantity decreases to 1,000 a week. The tax leaves the price paid by buyers unchanged but lowers the amount received by sellers by the full amount of the tax. Sellers pay the entire tax on a pink pen.

We've seen that when demand is perfectly inelastic, buyers pay the entire tax and when demand is perfectly elastic, sellers pay the entire tax. In the usual case, demand is neither perfectly inelastic nor perfectly elastic and the tax is split between buyers and sellers. The division depends on the elasticity of demand. The more inelastic the demand, the larger is the amount of the tax paid by buyers.

Figure 6.9

Tax and the Elasticity of Demand

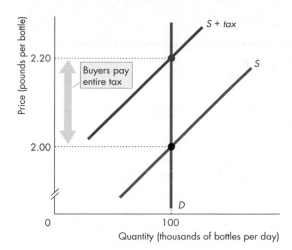

(a) Inelastic demand

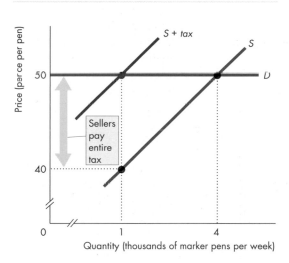

(b) Elastic demand

Part (a) shows the market for insulin, where demand is perfectly inelastic. With no tax, the price is £2 a bottle and the quantity is 100,000 bottles a day. A sales tax of 20 pence a bottle shifts the supply curve to *S + tax*. The price rises to £2.20 a bottle, but the quantity bought does not change. Buyers pay the entire tax.

Part (b) shows the market for pink pens. The demand for pink pens is perfectly elastic. With no tax, the price of a pen is 50 pence and the quantity is 4,000 pens a week. A sales tax of 10 pence a pink pen shifts the supply curve to *S + tax*. The price remains at 50 pence a pen, and the quantity of pink pens sold decreases to 1,000 a week. The sellers pay the entire tax.

Tax Division and Elasticity of Supply

The division of the tax between buyers and sellers depends, in part, on the elasticity of supply. There are two extreme cases:

◆ Perfectly inelastic supply – sellers pay
◆ Perfectly elastic supply – buyers pay

Perfectly Inelastic Supply

Figure 6.10(a) shows the market for water from a UK mineral spring which flows at a constant rate that can't be controlled. The quantity supplied is 100,000 bottles a week, as shown by the supply curve *S*. The demand curve for the water from this spring is *D*. With no tax, the price is 50 pence a bottle and the 100,000 bottles that flow from the spring are bought.

Suppose this spring water is taxed at 5 pence a bottle. The supply curve does not change because the spring owners still produce 100,000 bottles a week even though the price has fallen. But buyers are willing to buy the 100,000 bottles only if the price is 50 pence a bottle. So the price remains at 50 pence a bottle. The tax reduces the price received by sellers to 45 pence a bottle and sellers pay the entire tax.

Perfectly Elastic Supply

Figure 6.10(b) illustrates the market for sand from which computer-chip makers extract silicon. The supply of this sand is perfectly elastic at 10 pence a kilogram. The supply curve is *S*. The demand curve for sand is *D*. With no tax, the price is 10 pence a kilogram and 5,000 kilograms a week are bought.

If sand is taxed at 1 penny a kilogram, we add the tax to the minimum supply-price. Sellers are now willing to offer any quantity at 11 pence a kilogram along the curve *S + tax*. The price rises to 11 pence a kilogram and 3,000 kilograms a week are bought. The price paid by buyers has increased by the full amount of the tax. Buyers pay the entire tax.

We've seen that when supply is perfectly inelastic, sellers pay the entire tax and when supply is perfectly elastic, buyers pay the entire tax. In the usual case, supply is neither perfectly inelastic nor perfectly elastic and the tax is split between sellers and buyers. But how the tax is split depends on the elasticity of supply. The more elastic the supply, the larger is the amount of the tax paid by buyers.

Figure 6.10

Tax and the Elasticity of Supply

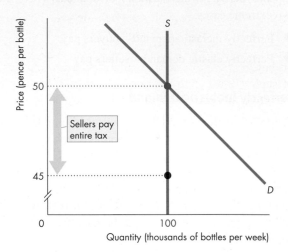

(a) Inelastic supply

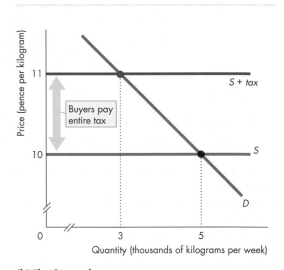

(b) Elastic supply

Part (a) shows the market for water from a mineral spring. Supply is perfectly inelastic. With no tax, the price is 50 pence a bottle. With a tax of 5 pence a bottle, the price remains at 50 pence a bottle. The number of bottles bought remains the same, but the price received by sellers decreases to 45 pence a bottle. Sellers pay the entire tax.

Part (b) shows the market for sand. Supply is perfectly elastic. With no tax, the price is 10 pence a kilogram. A tax of 1 penny a kilogram increases the minimum supply-price to 11 pence a kilogram. The supply curve shifts to *S + tax*. The price increases to 11 pence a kilogram. Buyers pay the entire tax.

Taxes in Practice

Supply and demand are rarely perfectly elastic or perfectly inelastic. But some items tend towards one of the extremes. For example, alcohol, tobacco and petrol have low elasticities of demand and high elasticities of supply. So the burden of these taxes falls more heavily on buyers than on sellers. Labour has a low elasticity of supply and a high elasticity of demand. So despite the government's desire to split the social security contribution equally between workers and employers, the burden of this tax falls mainly on workers.

The most heavily taxed items are those that have either a low elasticity of demand or a low elasticity of supply. For these items, the equilibrium quantity doesn't decrease much when a tax is imposed. So the government collects a large tax revenue and the deadweight loss from the tax is small.

It is unusual to tax an item heavily if neither its demand nor its supply is inelastic. With an elastic supply *and* demand, a tax brings a large decrease in the equilibrium quantity and a small tax revenue.

Taxes and Efficiency

We've seen that a tax can place a wedge between the price buyers pay and the price sellers receive. The price buyers pay is also the buyers' willingness to pay or marginal benefit. The price sellers receive is also the sellers' minimum supply price, which equals marginal cost.

So because a tax puts a wedge between the buyers' price and the sellers' price, it also puts a wedge between marginal benefit and marginal cost and creates inefficiency. With a higher buyers' price and a lower sellers' price, the tax decreases the quantity produced and consumed and a deadweight loss arises. Figure 6.11 shows the inefficiency of a tax. With a tax, both consumer surplus and producer surplus shrink. Part of each surplus goes to the government in tax revenue the purple area in the figure. And part of each surplus becomes a deadweight loss – the grey area.

In the extreme cases of perfectly inelastic demand and perfectly inelastic supply, the tax does not change the quantity bought and sold and there is no deadweight loss. The more inelastic is either demand or supply, the smaller is the decrease in quantity and the smaller is the deadweight loss.

In a market in which there is overproduction, a tax can help to achieve a more efficient use of resources. We will examine this case in Chapter 15 where we study externalities.

Figure 6.11

Taxes and Efficiency

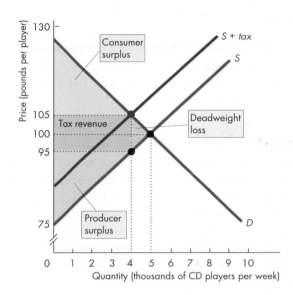

With no tax on CD players, 5,000 a week are bought and sold at £100 each. With a tax of £10 a CD player, the buyers' price rises to £105 a player, the sellers' price falls to £95 a player, and the quantity decreases to 4,000 CD players a week.

With the tax, consumer surplus shrinks to the green area and the producer surplus shrinks to the blue area. Part of the loss of consumer surplus and producer surplus goes to the government as tax revenue, which is shown as the purple area. A deadweight loss arises, which is shown by the grey area.

Review Quiz

1   How does the elasticity of demand influence the effect of a tax on the price paid by buyers, the price received by sellers, the quantity, the tax revenue and the deadweight loss?
2   How does the elasticity of supply influence the effect of a tax on the price paid by buyers, the price received by sellers, the quantity, the tax revenue and the deadweight loss?
3   Why does a tax create a deadweight loss?

Next, we look at agricultural markets and see how governments intervene in these markets to try to stabilize and boost farm revenues.

Intervening in Agricultural Markets

Farmers' lives are filled with uncertainty, fluctuating output, and fluctuating prices and revenues. Can governments help farmers by intervening in the markets for farm products? In this section, we examine agricultural markets and see how the weather and government policies influence them.

Harvest Fluctuations

Figure 6.12 shows the market for wheat. The demand curve for wheat is D. Once farmers have harvested their crop, they have no control over the quantity supplied and supply is inelastic along a *momentary supply curve*. With a normal harvest, the momentary supply curve is MS_0, the price is €160 a tonne, the quantity produced is 4 million tonnes and farm revenue is €640 million.

Poor Harvest

In Figure 6.12(a), a poor harvest decreases the quantity produced to 3 million tonnes. The momentary supply curve shifts leftward to MS_1, the price rises to €40 a tonne, and farm revenue increases to €720 million. A *decrease* in supply brings a rise in price and an *increase* in farm revenue.

Bumper Harvest

In Figure 6.12(b), a bumper harvest increases the quantity produced to 5 million tonnes. The momentary supply curve shifts rightward to MS_2, the price falls to €80 a tonne and farm revenue decreases to €400 million. An *increase* in supply brings a fall in price and a *decrease* in farm revenue.

Elasticity of Demand

Farm revenue and the quantity produced move in opposite directions because the demand for wheat is *inelastic*. The percentage change in price exceeds the change in the quantity demanded. In Figure 6.12(a), the increase in revenue from the higher price (€240 million the light blue area) exceeds the decrease in revenue from the smaller quantity (€160 million the red area). In Figure 6.12(b), the decrease in revenue from the lower price (€320 million the red area) exceeds the increase in revenue from the increase in the quantity sold (€80 billion the light blue area).

Figure 6.12

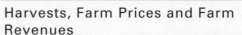

Harvests, Farm Prices and Farm Revenues

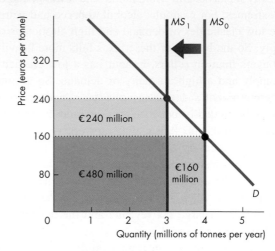

(a) Poor harvest: revenue increases

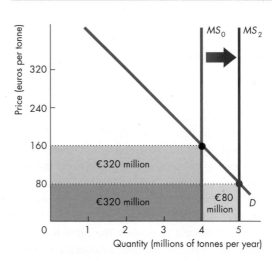

(b) Bumper harvest: revenue decreases

The demand curve for wheat is D. In normal times, the supply curve is MS_0, and 4 million tonnes are sold for €160 a tonne. In part (a), a poor growing season decreases supply, shifting the supply curve to MS_1. The price increases to €240 a tonne and farm revenue *increases* from €640 million to €720 million – the increase in revenue from the higher price (light blue area) exceeds the decrease in revenue from the smaller quantity (red area). In part (b), a bumper harvest increases supply, shifting the supply curve to MS_2. The price decreases to €80 a tonne and farm revenue *decreases* to €400 million – the decrease in revenue from the lower price (red area) exceeds the increase in revenue from the increase in the quantity sold (light blue area).

If demand is *elastic*, farm revenue and the quantity produced fluctuate in the same direction. Bumper harvests increase revenue and poor harvests decrease it. But the demand for most agricultural products is inelastic, so the case we've studied is the relevant one.

Avoiding a Fallacy of Composition

Although *total* farm revenue increases when there is a poor harvest, the revenue of those *individual* farmers whose entire crop is wiped out decreases. Those whose crop is unaffected gain. So a poor harvest is not good news for all farmers.

Government Intervention

Because the markets for farm products often confront farmers with low incomes, government intervention occurs in these markets. Three methods of intervention are used in markets for farm products, often in combination. They are:

◆ Subsidies
◆ Production quotas
◆ Price supports

Subsidies

The producers of peanuts, sugar beet, milk, wheat and many other farm products receive subsidies. A **subsidy** is a payment made by the government to a producer. To discover the effects of a subsidy, we'll look at a market for peanuts. Figure 6.13 shows this market. The demand for peanuts is D and the supply of peanuts is S. With no subsidy, equilibrium occurs at a price of €40 a tonne and a quantity of 40 million tonnes of peanuts per year.

Suppose that the government introduces a subsidy on peanuts of €20 a tonne. A subsidy is like a negative tax. You've seen earlier in this chapter that a tax is equivalent to an increase in cost. A subsidy is equivalent to a decrease in cost. And a decrease in cost brings an increase in supply.

To determine the position of the new supply curve, we subtract the subsidy from farmers' minimum supply-price. Without a subsidy, farmers are willing to offer 40 million tonnes a year for €40 a tonne. So with a subsidy of €20 a tonne, they will offer 40 million tonnes a year if the price is as low as €20 a tonne. The supply curve shifts to the red curve labelled $S - subsidy$.

Figure 6.13

A Subsidy Increases Production

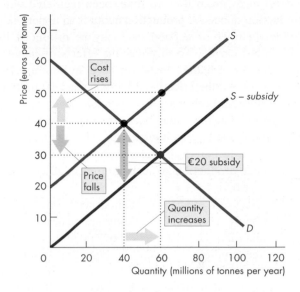

With no subsidy, 40 million tonnes a year are produced at €40 a tonne. A subsidy of €20 a tonne shifts the supply curve rightward to $S - subsidy$. The equilibrium quantity increases to 60 million tonnes a year, the price falls to €30 a tonne, and the price plus subsidy received by farmers rises to €50 a tonne. In the new equilibrium, marginal cost (on the blue supply curve) exceeds marginal benefit (on the demand curve) and a deadweight loss arises from overproduction.

Equilibrium occurs where the new supply curve intersects the demand curve at 60 million tonnes a year. The price falls by €10 to €30 a tonne. But the price plus subsidy received by farmers rises by €10 to €50 a tonne.

Because the supply curve is the marginal cost curve, and the demand curve is the marginal benefit curve, a subsidy raises marginal cost above marginal benefit and creates a deadweight loss from overproduction.

Subsidies spill over to the rest of the world. Because they lower the price, subsidized farmers offer some of their output for sale on the world market, which lowers the price in the rest of the world. Faced with lower prices, farmers in other countries decrease production and receive smaller revenues.

Farm subsidies are a major obstacle to achieving an efficient use of resources in the global markets for farm products and are a source of tension between Europe, the United States and poorer developing nations.

Production Quotas

The markets for sugar beet, milk and cotton, (among others) have, from time to time, been regulated with production quotas. A **production quota** is an upper limit to the quantity of a good that may be produced in a specified period. To discover the effects of quotas, we'll look at a market for sugar beets in Figure 6.14. With no quota, the price is €30 a tonne and 60 million tonnes of sugar beets per year are produced.

Suppose that the sugar beet growers want to limit total production to get a higher price. They persuade the government to introduce a production quota that limits sugar beet production to a maximum of 40 million tonnes a year.

The effect of a production quota depends on whether it is set below or above the equilibrium quantity. If the government introduced a quota above 60 million tonnes a year, the equilibrium quantity in Figure 6.14, nothing would change because sugar beet growers are already producing less than the quota. But a quota of 40 million tonnes is less than the equilibrium quantity. Figure 6.14 shows the effects of this quota.

To implement the quota, each grower is assigned a production limit and the total of the production limits equals 40 million tonnes. Production that in total exceeds 40 million tonnes is illegal, so we've shaded the illegal region with the quantity above the quota. Growers are no longer permitted to produce the equilibrium quantity because it is in the illegal region. As in the case of price ceilings and price floors, market forces and political forces are in conflict.

When the government sets a production quota, it does not regulate the price. Market forces determine it. In the example in Figure 6.14, with production limited to 40 million tonnes a year, the market price rises to €50 a tonne.

The quota not only raises the price but also *lowers* the marginal cost of producing the quota because the sugar beet growers slide down their supply (and marginal cost) curves.

A production quota is inefficient because it results in underproduction. At the quota quantity, marginal benefit is equal to the market price and marginal cost is less than the market price, so marginal benefit exceeds marginal cost.

Because of these effects of a quota, such arrangements are often popular with producers and in some cases, producers, not governments, attempt to implement them. But it is hard for quotas to work when they are voluntary. The reason is that each producer has an

Figure 6.14

A Quota Limits Production

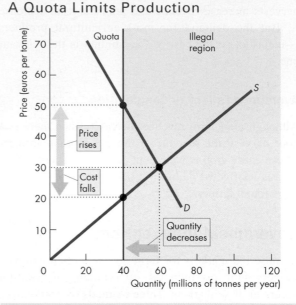

With no quota, 60 million tonnes a year are produced at €30 a tonne. A quota of 40 million tonnes a year restricts total production to that amount. The equilibrium quantity decreases to 40 million tonnes a year, the price rises to €40 a tonne, and the farmers' marginal cost falls to €20 a tonne. In the new equilibrium, marginal cost (on the supply curve) is less than marginal benefit (on the demand curve) and a deadweight loss arises from underproduction.

incentive to cheat and produce a little bit more than the allotted quota. You can see why by comparing the market price and marginal cost. If one producer could get away with a tiny increase in production, her or his profit would increase. But if all producers cheat by producing more than the quota, the market moves back towards the unregulated equilibrium and the gain for producers disappears.

Price Supports

A **price support** is the government guaranteed minimum price of a good. A price support in an agricultural market operates in a similar way to a *price floor* in other markets. It creates a surplus. But there is a crucial difference between a price floor and a price support. With a price support, the government buys the surplus and ends up with unwanted inventories.

Figure 6.15 shows how a price support works in the market for wheat. The competitive equilibrium price of wheat is €130 a tonne, and 4 million tonnes are

Figure 6.15

A Price Support

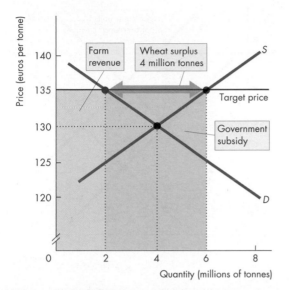

With no price support, 4 million tonnes are produced at €130 a tonne. A price support of €135 a tonne raises the price to €135 a tonne, decreases the quantity sold to 2 million tonnes, and increases the quantity produced to 6 million tonnes. The price support creates a surplus of 4 million tonnes. To maintain the price support, the government buys the surplus for €540 million a year. If the government does not buy the surplus, the price returns to €130 a tonne.

produced and bought. If the government sets a price support of €135 a tonne, then the price increases to €135 a tonne and the quantity demanded decreases to 2 million tonnes.

The quantity supplied increases to 6 million tonnes. Farmers produce a surplus of 4 million tonnes. This method of stabilizing farm revenue would fail without a method of taking up the surplus produced. If farmers are left to find a market for their surplus, then the price will fall below the price support to the competitive price of €130 a tonne.

If, on the other hand, the government buys the surplus at the support price, then the price will remain at the price support. If the government systematically buys more than it sells, it will end up with a large inventory or stockpile.

Such has been the outcome in the European Union (see Box 6.2), which has mountains of butter and lakes of wine! The cost of buying and storing the inventory falls on taxpayers and the winners from a price support are large, efficient farms.

Box 6.2
The EU Common Agricultural Policy

The EU Common Agricultural Policy (CAP) is the world's most extensive farm support programme. The CAP was set up in 1957 to make sure the bad experiences of wartime shortages and low farm incomes would not be repeated.

The centrepiece of the programme is a price support system that works in a similar way to the one described in Figure 6.15. (A complicating factor arises from EU imports from the rest of the world, but the basic story is the same.)

If the CAP target price is consistently higher than the world price, the European Union will always buy more agricultural produce than it sells. Such a policy creates surpluses in the form of mountains of grain, beef and butter. Payments for buying and storing the EU surpluses take 50 per cent of the EU budget!

Table 1 shows the rising cost of these payments.

Table 1

The Cost of the CAP Price Supports

Year	Price support costs (millions of euros)
1980	11.3
1990	26.5
2000	40.5
2002	44.3

Source: Eurostat, 2004.

Review Quiz

1 How do poor harvests and bumper harvests influence farm prices and farm revenues?
2 Explain how a subsidy influences farm prices and output. How does a subsidy affect farm revenues?
3 Explain how a production quota influences farm prices and output. How does a production quota affect farm revenues?
4 Explain how a price support influences farm prices and output. How does a price support affect farm revenues?

Governments intervene in some markets by making it illegal to trade in a good. Let's now see how these markets work.

Markets for Illegal Goods

The markets for many goods and services are regulated, and buying and selling some goods is illegal. The best known examples of illegal goods are drugs, such as cannabis, Ecstasy, cocaine and heroin.

Despite the fact that these drugs are illegal, trade in them is a multi-billion pound global business. This trade can be understood by using the same economic model and principles that explain trade in legal goods.

To study the market for illegal goods, it is first necessary to examine how the market in these items would work if they were not illegal goods. We will then have a benchmark of prices and quantities that we can compare with those that would prevail when trade in the items is illegal. We will also see how legalizing and taxing a currently illegal good might limit the consumption of such a good.

A Free Market for Drugs

Figure 6.10 shows a market for a drug. The demand curve, D, shows that, other things remaining the same, the lower the price of the drug, the larger is the quantity demanded. The supply curve, S, shows that other things remaining the same, the lower the price of the drug, the smaller is the quantity supplied. If drugs are not illegal, the quantity bought and sold would be Q_C and the price would be P_C.

A Market for Illegal Drugs

When a good is illegal, the cost of trading in the good increases. By how much the cost increases and on whom the cost falls depend on the penalties for breaking the law and the effectiveness with which the law is enforced. The larger the penalties and the more effective the policing, the higher are the costs of trading the drug. Penalties might be imposed on sellers, buyers, or both.

Penalties on Sellers

If selling drugs is illegal, sellers will face fines and prison sentences if their activities are detected. Penalties for selling illegal drugs are part of the cost of supplying those drugs. These penalties lead to a decrease in supply and shift the supply curve of the drug leftward. To determine the new supply curve, we add the cost of breaking the law to the minimum price that drug dealers are willing to accept. In Figure 6.16, the cost of breaking the law by selling drugs (*CBL*) is added to the minimum

Figure 6.16

A Market for an Illegal Good

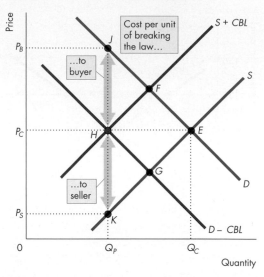

The demand curve for drugs is *D* and the supply curve is *S*. If drugs are not illegal, the quantity bought and sold is Q_C at a price of P_C at point *E*. If selling drugs is illegal, the cost of breaking the law by selling drugs (*CBL*) is added to the minimum supply-price and supply decreases to $S + CBL$. The market moves to point *F*. If buying drugs is illegal, the cost of breaking the law is subtracted from the maximum price that buyers are willing to pay, and demand decreases to $D - CBL$. The market moves to point *G*. With both buying and selling illegal, the supply curve and the demand curve shift and the market moves to point *H*. The market price remains at P_C, but the market price plus the penalty for buying rises to P_B (point *J*) and the market price minus the penalty for sellers falls to P_S (point *K*).

price that dealers will accept and the supply curve shifts leftward to $S + CBL$. If penalties are imposed only on sellers, the market moves from point *E* to point *F*. The price rises and the quantity bought decreases.

Penalties on Buyers

If buying drugs is illegal, buyers face fines and prison sentences if their activities are detected. Penalties for buying the illegal drugs fall on buyers and the cost of breaking the law must be subtracted from the value of the good to determine the maximum price that buyers are willing to pay. Demand decreases and the demand curve shifts leftward. In Figure 6.10, the demand curve shifts to $D - CBL$. If penalties are imposed only on buyers, the market moves from point *E* to point *G*. The market price falls and the quantity bought decreases.

Penalties on Both Sellers and Buyers

If penalties are imposed on sellers *and* buyers, both supply and demand decrease. In Figure 6.16, the costs of breaking the law are the same for both buyers and sellers, so the demand and supply curves shift leftward by the same amounts. The market moves to point H. The market price remains at the competitive market price, but the quantity bought decreases to Q_P. The buyer pays P_C plus the cost of breaking the law, which is P_B. And the seller receives P_C minus the cost of breaking the law, which is P_S.

The larger the penalty and the greater the degree of law enforcement, the larger is the decrease in demand and/or supply and the greater is the shift of the demand and/or supply curve. If the penalties are heavier on sellers, the supply curve shifts further than the demand curve and the market price rises above P_C. If the penalties are heavier on buyers, the demand curve shifts further than the supply curve and the price falls below P_C. In many European countries, the penalties on sellers of illegal drugs are larger than those on buyers. As a result, the decrease in supply is much larger than the decrease in demand. The quantity of drugs traded decreases and the price is higher than in a free market.

With high enough penalties and effective law enforcement, it is possible to decrease demand and/or supply so that the quantity bought is zero. But in reality, such an outcome is unusual. The key reason is the high cost of law enforcement and insufficient resources for the police to achieve effective enforcement. Because of this situation, some people suggest that drugs (and other illegal goods) should be legalized and sold openly but should also be taxed at a high rate in the same way that legal drugs such as alcohol are taxed. How would such an arrangement work?

Legalizing and Taxing Drugs

From your study of the effects of taxes, it is easy to see that the quantity of drugs bought could be decreased if drugs were legalized and taxed. A sufficiently high tax could be imposed to decrease supply, raise the price and achieve the same decrease in the quantity bought as with a prohibition on drugs. The government would collect a large tax revenue. Such a debate in the United Kingdom concerning cannabis led the government to reduce penalties on the illegal trade in 2003 but not to legalize the trade. We'll look at some of the issues that influenced this decision now.

Illegal Trading to Evade the Tax

It is likely that an extremely high tax rate would be needed to cut the quantity of drugs bought to the level prevailing with a prohibition. It is also likely that many drug dealers and consumers would try to cover up their activities to evade the tax. If they did act in this way, they would face the cost of breaking the law – the tax law. If the penalty for tax law violation is as severe and as effectively policed as drug-dealing laws, the analysis we've already conducted applies also to this case. The quantity of drugs bought would depend on the penalties for law breaking and on the way in which the penalties are assigned to buyers and sellers.

Taxes versus Prohibition: Some Pros and Cons

Which is more effective: prohibition or taxes? In favour of taxes and against prohibition is the fact that the tax revenue can be used to make law enforcement more effective. It can also be used to run a more effective education campaign against illegal drug use. In favour of prohibition and against taxes is the fact that prohibition sends a signal that might influence preferences, decreasing the demand for illegal drugs. Also, some people intensely dislike the idea of the government profiting from trade in harmful substances.

Review Quiz

1 How does imposing a penalty on buying a drug influence demand and the quantity consumed?
2 How does imposing the penalty on selling a drug influence supply and the quantity consumed?
3 Is there an economic case for legalizing drugs?
4 Is there any case for legalizing drugs?

You now know how to use the demand and supply model to study government interventions in markets. You've seen how price ceilings, minimum wages, taxes, subsidies, quotas and price supports, create inefficient resource use. You've also seen how in a market for an illegal good, the quantity can be decreased by imposing penalties or by legalizing and taxing the good.

Before you leave this topic, take a look at *Reading Between the Lines* on pp. 136–137 and see why some economists think the CAP needs radical reform and why reform is hard to achieve.

Reading Between the Lines
Price Supports:
EU CAP Reforms

BBC, 22 January 2003 http://news.bbc.co.uk/1/hi/world/europe/2685065.stm
Published: Wednesday, 22 January, 2003, 18:46 GMT

Europe unveils farm reform plans

The European Commission has unveiled plans to reform the system of paying subsidies to farmers, despite strong opposition from France and other nations.

Agriculture Commissioner Franz Fischler is trying to revolutionise the subsidies system – axing the traditional link between subsidies and the level of food production.

Instead, farmers would receive a single payment which would be reduced over time. . . .

Under the plans, bigger farms would fare worse than smaller ones – meaning the plans face strong opposition in countries with larger farms, including the UK . . . .

The Common Agricultural Policy (CAP), seen for years as a sacred cow, costs around half the EU's budget of 95 billion euros.

But Mr Fischler says its existence in its old form could no longer be justified . . . .

The traditional linking of subsidy and output led to Europe's notorious wine lakes and butter mountains, as farmers were led down the path of mass production regardless of whether there was a market.

But supporters said it played an essential role in keeping the farming sector afloat, and warned that abandoning farmers to market forces would send many into freefall.

Mr Fischler insisted that farmers would be among those to benefit from scrapping the link – and denied claims that farmers suffer or would be paid to produce nothing.

The Essence of the Story

◆ In January 2003, the EC proposed reforms to the Common Agricultural Policy.

◆ The link between subsidies and production would be cut.

◆ Farmers will receive direct payments that are independent of production.

◆ Guaranteed minimum farm prices have led to massive surpluses and a programme that consumes a half of the EU budget.

Economic Analysis

◆ Figure 1 shows the EU price support system for beef in 2003 – the data for the figure are from EU sources.

◆ Figure 1 shows the EU demand curve for beef, D_{03}, and the EU supply curve for beef, S_{03}.

◆ With no intervention, the price would be €3,250 per tonne and the quantity produced would be 6.6 million tonnes.

◆ The European Union sets the target price at €3,750 per tonne. At this price, the quantity of beef supplied increases to 7 million tonnes.

◆ At the target price, quantity demanded decreases to 6.3 million tonnes and a beef surplus of 0.7 million tonnes is created.

◆ The European Union buys the surplus at €3,750 a tonne, paying out €2.65 billion to beef farmers (the red area). Farm revenues are €26 billion (blue plus red areas).

◆ Figure 2 shows the impact of cutting the target price to €3.40 a tonne by 2005 as part of the reforms, assuming demand and supply of beef stays the same.

◆ The beef surplus is reduced and the subsidy to beef farmers falls to €1.02 billion.

◆ Figure 2 shows farm revenues also fall. But proposed direct payments to farmers will partly compensate for the loss of revenue without increasing the quantity supplied.

◆ You can see that removing the link between production and the subsidy paid improves the efficiency of the EU beef market.

◆ You can also see why reform is hard to achieve: farmers have a lot to lose from reform and will organize to oppose it.

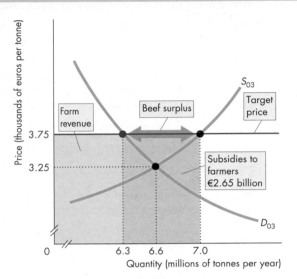

Figure 1 EU beef market in 2003

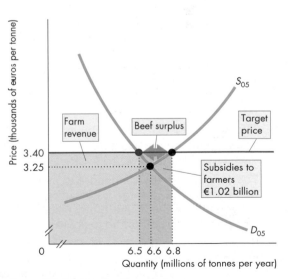

Figure 2 Reforming beef market

Summary

Key Points

Housing Markets and Rent Ceilings (pp. 118–121)

◆ A decrease in the supply of housing raises rents.

◆ Higher rents stimulate building and in the long run, the quantity of housing increases and rents fall.

◆ If a rent ceiling is set below the equilibrium rent it creates a housing shortage, wasteful search and a black market.

The Labour Market and Minimum Wage (pp. 121–124)

◆ A decrease in the demand for low-skilled labour lowers the wage and reduces employment.

◆ The lower wage rate encourages people with low skill to acquire more skill, which decreases the supply of low-skill labour and, in the long run, raises their wage rate.

◆ A minimum wage set above the equilibrium wage rate creates unemployment and increases the amount of time spent searching for a job.

◆ A minimum wages hits low-skilled young people hardest.

Taxes (pp. 125–129)

◆ A tax raises price but usually by less than the tax.

◆ The shares of tax paid by buyers and sellers depend on the elasticity of demand and the elasticity of supply.

◆ The less elastic the demand and more elastic the supply, the greater is the price increase, the smaller is the quantity decrease, and the larger is the portion of the tax paid by buyers.

◆ If demand is perfectly elastic or supply is perfectly inelastic, sellers pay the entire tax. And if demand is perfectly inelastic or supply is perfectly elastic, buyers pay the entire tax.

Intervening in Agricultural Markets (pp. 130–133)

◆ Farm revenues fluctuate because supply fluctuates. Because the demand for most farm products is inelastic, a decrease in supply increases farm revenue while an increase in supply decreases farm revenue.

◆ A subsidy is like a negative tax. It lowers the price and leads to inefficient overproduction.

◆ A quota leads to inefficient underproduction, which raises price.

◆ A price support leads to inefficient over-production.

◆ The Common Agricultural Policy uses costly price supports.

Markets for Illegal Goods (pp. 134–135)

◆ Penalties on sellers of an illegal good increase the cost of selling the good and decrease its supply. Penalties on buyers decrease their willingness to pay and decrease demand for the good.

◆ The higher the penalties and the more effective the law enforcement, the smaller is the quantity bought.

◆ A tax that is set at a sufficiently high rate will decrease the quantity of a drug consumed, but there will be a tendency for the tax to be evaded.

Key Figures

Key Terms

Problems

*1 The figure below shows the demand for and supply of rental housing in Village:

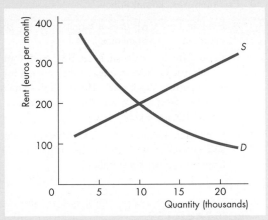

a What is the equilibrium rent and equilibrium quantity of rented housing?

If a rent ceiling is set at €150 a month, what is:

b The quantity of housing rented?

c The shortage of housing?

d The maximum price that someone is willing to pay for the last unit of housing available?

2 The figure below shows the demand for and supply of rental housing in Township:

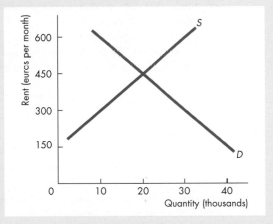

a What is the equilibrium rent and equilibrium quantity of rented housing?

If a rent ceiling is set at €300 a month, what is:

b The quantity of housing rented?

c The shortage of housing?

d The maximum price that someone is willing to pay for the last unit available?

---

*Solutions to odd-numbered problems are available on *Parkin Interactive*.

*3 The table gives the demand for and supply of teenage labour in a UK town.

Wage rate (pounds per hour)	Quantity demanded	Quantity supplied
	(hours per month)	
2	3,000	1,000
3	2,500	1,500
4	2,000	2,000
5	1,500	2,500
6	1,000	3,000

a What are the equilibrium wage rate and level of employment?

b What is the quantity of unemployment?

c If a minimum wage of £3 an hour is set for teenagers, how many hours do they work?

d If a minimum wage of £3 an hour is set for teenagers, how many hours of their labour are unemployed?

e If a minimum wage is set at £5 an hour for teenagers, how many hours of their labour are employed and unemployed?

f If a minimum wage is set at £5 an hour and demand increases by 500 hours a month, what is the wage rate paid to teenagers and how many hours of their labour are unemployed?

4 The table gives the demand for and supply of secondary school leavers in a UK town.

Wage rate (pounds per hour)	Quantity demanded	Quantity supplied
	(hours per month)	
6	9,000	4,000
7	8,000	5,000
8	7,000	6,000
9	6,000	7,000
10	5,000	8,000

a What are the equilibrium wage rate and level of employment?

b What is the level of unemployment?

c If a minimum wage is set at £7 an hour, how many hours do secondary school leavers work?

d If a minimum wage is set at £7 an hour, how many hours of labour are unemployed?

e If a minimum wage is set at £9 an hour, how many hours of their labour are employed and unemployed?

f If the minimum wage is £9 an hour and demand increases by 500 hours a month, what is the wage rate paid to secondary school leavers and how many hours of their labour are unemployed?

*5 The table gives the demand and supply schedules for chocolate brownies in the United Kingdom.

Price (pence per brownie)	Quantity demanded	Quantity supplied
	(millions per day)	
50	5	3
60	4	4
70	3	5
80	2	6
90	1	7

a If brownies are not taxed, what is the price of a brownie and how many are consumed?

b If brownies are taxed at 20 pence each, what is the price and how many brownies are consumed? Who pays the tax?

6 The table gives the demand and supply schedules for coffee in a UK town.

Price (pounds per cup)	Quantity demanded	Quantity supplied
	(cups per hour)	
1.50	90	30
1.75	70	40
2.00	50	50
2.25	30	60
2.75	10	70

a If there is no tax on coffee, what is the price and how much coffee is consumed?

b If a tax of 75 pence a cup is introduced, what is the price, how much coffee is consumed and who pays the tax?

*7 The demand and supply schedules for rice are

Price (pounds per box)	Quantity demanded	Quantity supplied
	(packets per week)	
1.00	3,500	500
1.10	3,250	1,000
1.20	3,000	1,500
1.30	2,750	2,000
1.40	2,500	2,500
1.50	2,250	3,000
1.60	2,000	3,500

If the government introduces a subsidy on rice of 30 pence a packet, what are the price of rice, the marginal cost of producing rice, and the quantity produced?

8 In problem 7, if instead of a subsidy, the government sets a quota of 2,000 packets a week, what now are your answers?

Critical Thinking

1 Read the article in *Reading Between the Lines* on pp. 136–137 about the proposed reforms to the EU Common Agricultural Policy:

a Explain how CAP uses a target price for beef to maintain EU farm incomes.

b Food safety scares such as BSE and foot and mouth disease have decreased the demand for beef at the current target price. How will this change in demand affect farm revenues and government subsidies? Illustrate your answer.

c Explain how cutting the link between production and subsidies will affect the efficiency of the Common Agricultural Policy?

Web Exercises

Use the links on *Parkin Interactive* to get information to work the following exercises.

1 Read the Web page on the Irish tax on carrier bags:

a Why does the Irish government tax carrier bags?

b Carrier bags appeared to be a free good to supermarket shoppers before the tax. Do you think they are produced at zero cost?

c If carrier bags are not produced at zero cost, do you think that the market underproduces or overproduces carrier bags when they appear free to customers? Explain your answer.

d How do you think the tax on carriers bags will influence efficiency in the market for carrier bags?

2 Read the Web page on the CAP and the beef market.

a Explain how CAP uses a target price for beef to maintain farm incomes.

b Explain why a EU import tariff on beef is needed.

c Show on a graph the effect of an import tariff on beef.

d Draw a graph that illustrates the impact on beef surpluses of a fall in the demand for beef as a result of the BSE crisis between 1998 and 2000.

e Would you expect the import tariff to rise or fall when the demand for beef falls?

3 Obtain information about cigarette smuggling in the European Union.

a Why are cigarettes smuggled in the European Union?

b Who are the gainers and the losers?

c What are the measures being used to stop cigarette smuggling?

d How would you improve on current policy?

Chapter 7

Utility and Demand

After studying this chapter you will be able to:

◆ Explain the connection between individual demand and market demand

◆ Describe preferences using the concept of utility and distinguish between total utility and marginal utility

◆ Explain the marginal utility theory of consumer choice

◆ Use the marginal utility theory to predict the effects of changing prices and incomes

◆ Explain the paradox of value

Water, Water, Everywhere

It is obvious that the benefits of water vastly outweigh the benefits of diamonds. Why then is water so cheap while diamonds are so expensive? Find out in this chapter. Also, find out in *Reading Between the Lines* at the end of the chapter how people are making choices when they are confronted with new alternatives as juice and soup bars spring up in our towns.

Individual Demand and Market Demand

In the earlier chapters, we've used *market* demand curves. We can derive a market demand curve from *individual* demand curves. Let's see how.

The relationship between the total quantity demanded of a good or service and its price is called **market demand**. And the relationship between the quantity demanded of a good or service by an individual and its price is called *individual demand*. The market demand is the sum of all the individual demands.

Figure 7.1 illustrates the relationship between individual demands and market demand. In this example, Lisa and John are the only people. The market demand is the total demand of Lisa and John.

At £3 a cinema ticket, Lisa demands 5 films a month

and John demands 2 films, so that the total quantity demanded in the market is 7 films a month. Figure 7.1 illustrates the relationship between the individual demand curves and the market demand curve. Lisa's and John's demand curves for films are shown in parts (a) and (b). The market demand curve is shown in part (c). When the price is £3 a ticket, the quantities demanded by Lisa and John sum horizontally to give the total quantity demanded in the market.

The market demand curve is the horizontal sum of the individual demand curves and is formed by adding the quantities demanded by each individual at each price.

We're going to investigate what shapes market demand by looking at what shapes individual demand. We do this by studying how an individual makes consumption choices.

Figure 7.1

Individual Demand and Market Demand Curves

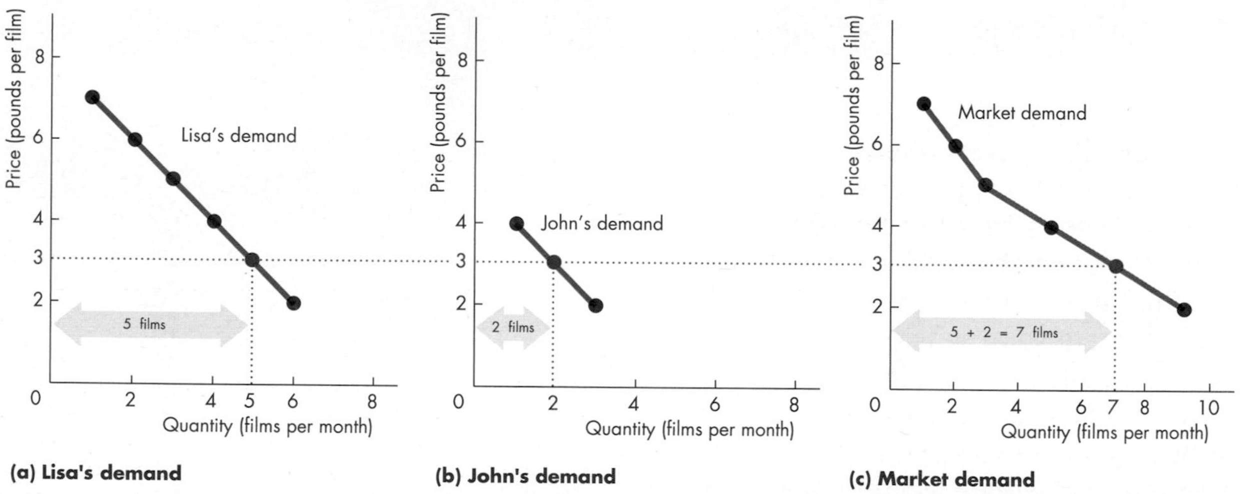

(a) Lisa's demand **(b) John's demand** **(c) Market demand**

Price (pounds per ticket)	Quantity of films demanded		
	Lisa	John	Market
7	1	0	1
6	2	0	2
5	3	0	3
4	4	1	5
3	5	2	7
2	6	3	9

The table and the graph illustrate how the quantity of films demanded varies as the price of a cinema ticket varies.

In the table, the market demand is the sum of the individual demands. For example, at a price of £3 a cinema ticket, Lisa demands 5 films and John demands 2 films, so the total quantity demanded in the market is 7 films.

In the graph, the market demand curve is the horizontal sum of the individual demand curves. So when the price is £3, the market demand curve shows the quantity demanded is 7 films, the sum of the quantities demanded by Lisa and John.

Consumption Choices

An individual's consumption choices are determined by many factors and we can model the impact of these factors using two new concepts:

◆ Consumption possibilities
◆ Preferences

Consumption Possibilities

An individual's consumption choices are constrained by the individual's income and by the prices of goods and services. The individual has a given amount of income to spend and cannot influence the prices of the goods and services that he or she buys.

An individual's *budget line* describes the limits to her or his consumption choices. Let's consider Lisa. Lisa has an income of £30 a month and she plans to buy only two goods: cinema films and cola. The price of a cinema ticket is £6; the price of cola is £3 a six-pack. If Lisa spends all her income, she will reach the limits to her consumption of cinema films and cola.

Figure 7.2 illustrates Lisa's possible consumption of films and cola. Rows *A* through *F* in the table show six possible ways of allocating £30 to these two goods. For example, Lisa can see 2 films for £12 and buy 6 six-packs of cola for £18 (row *C*). Points *A* through *F* in the graph illustrate the possibilities presented in the table. The line passing through these points is Lisa's budget line.

Lisa's budget line is a constraint on her choices. It marks the boundary between what she can afford and what she cannot afford. She can afford all the points on the line and inside it. She cannot afford points outside the line. Lisa's consumption possibilities depend on the price of a cinema ticket, the price of cola, and her income. Her consumption possibilities change when the price of a cinema ticket, the price of a six-pack of cola or her income changes.

Preferences

How does Lisa divide her £30 between these two goods? The answer depends on her likes and dislikes – her *preferences*. Economists use the concept of utility to describe preferences. The benefit or satisfaction that a person gets from the consumption of a good or service is called **utility**. Let's now see how we can use the concept of utility to describe preferences.

Figure 7.2

Consumption Possibilities

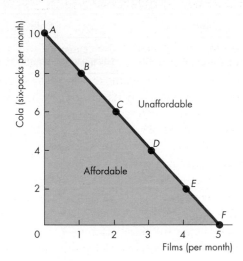

Possibility	Films Quantity (number)	Films Expenditure (pounds)	Cola Quantity (six-packs)	Cola Expenditure (pounds)
A	0	0	10	30
B	1	6	8	24
C	2	12	6	18
D	3	18	4	12
E	4	24	2	6
F	5	30	0	0

Rows *A* to *F* in the table show six possible ways of allocating £30 to films and cola. For example, Lisa can see 2 cinema films and buy 6 six-packs of cola (row *C*). The combination in each row costs £30. These possibilities are points *A* to *F* in the graph. The line through those points is a boundary between what Lisa can afford and what she cannot afford. Her choices must lie along the line *AF* or inside the orange area.

Total Utility

Total utility is the total benefit or satisfaction that a person gets from the consumption of goods and services. Total utility depends on the level of consumption – more consumption generally gives more total utility. The units of utility are arbitrary. Suppose we tell Lisa that we want to measure her utility. We're going to call the utility from no consumption zero. And

Table 7.1

Lisa's Total Utility from Films and Cola

Films		Cola	
Quantity (number per month)	Total utility	Quantity (six packs per month)	Total utility
0	0	0	0
1	50	1	75
2	88	2	117
3	121	3	153
4	150	4	181
5	175	5	206
6	196	6	225
7	214	7	243
8	229	8	260
9	241	9	276
10	250	10	291
11	256	11	305
12	259	12	318
13	261	13	330
14	262	14	341

we are going to call the utility she gets from 1 film a month 50 units. We then ask her to tell us, on the same scale, how much she would like 2, 3 and more films up to 14 a month. We also ask her to tell us, on the same scale, how much she would like 1 six-pack of cola a month, 2 six-packs and more up to 14 six-packs a month. Table 7.1 shows Lisa's answers.

Marginal Utility

Marginal utility is the change in total utility that results from a one-unit increase in the quantity of a good consumed. When the number of films Lisa sees increases from 4 to 5 a month, her total utility from films increases from 150 units to 175 units. So for Lisa, the marginal utility of seeing a fifth film each month is 25 units. The table in Figure 7.3 shows the calculation of Lisa's marginal utility from films. Notice that marginal utility appears midway between the quantities of films. It does so because it is the change in number of films seen from 4 to 5 that produces the marginal utility of 25 units. The table displays calculations of marginal utility for each number of films seen from 1 to 5.

Figure 7.3(a) illustrates the total utility that Lisa gets from seeing films. The more films Lisa sees in a month, the more total utility she gets. Figure 7.3(b) illustrates her marginal utility. This graph tells us that as Lisa sees more films a month, the marginal utility that she gets from films decreases. For example, her marginal utility decreases from 50 units for the first film to 38 units for the second film and to 33 units for the third. We call this decrease in marginal utility as the quantity of the good consumed increases the principle of **diminishing marginal utility**.

Marginal utility is positive but diminishes as consumption of the good increases. Why does marginal utility have these two features? In Lisa's case, she likes films and the more she sees the better. That's why marginal utility is positive. The benefit that Lisa gets from the last film seen is its marginal utility. To see why marginal utility diminishes, think about the following two situations: In one, you've been studying every night for 15 nights in a row and you've been just too busy finishing assignments to see a film. A friend comes by and persuades you to see a new film. The utility you get from that film is the marginal utility from seeing one film in a month. In the second situation, you've been on a cinema binge for the past 15 nights, and you have not even seen an assignment or test. You are happy enough to go to see one more film, but the thrill that you get out of that 16th film in 16 days is not very large. It is the marginal utility of the 16th film in a month.

Temperature: An Analogy

Utility is similar to temperature. Both are abstract concepts and both have units of measurement that are arbitrary. You know when you feel hot and you know when you feel cold. But you can't *observe* temperature. You can observe water turning to steam if it is hot enough or turning to ice if it is cold enough. And you can construct an instrument – a thermometer – that can help you to predict when such changes will occur. We call the scale on the thermometer *temperature* and we call the units of temperature *degrees*. But these degree units are arbitrary. For example, we can accurately predict that when a Celsius thermometer shows a temperature of 0, water will turn to ice. This same event occurs when a Fahrenheit thermometer shows a temperature of 32. So the units of measurement of temperature don't matter.

The concept of utility helps us make predictions about consumption choices in much the same way that the

Figure 7.3

Total Utility and Marginal Utility

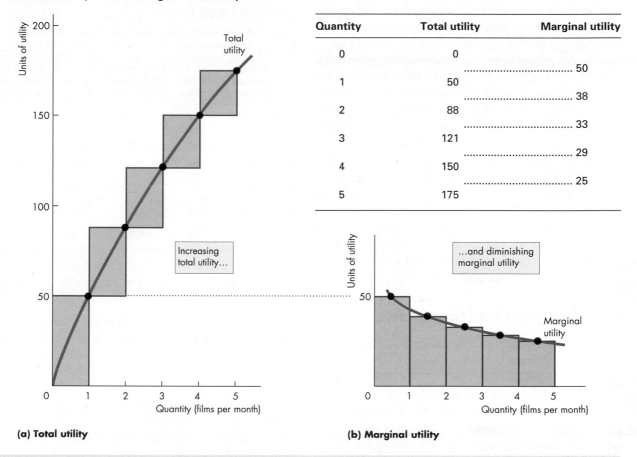

Quantity	Total utility	Marginal utility
0	0	
		50
1	50	
		38
2	88	
		33
3	121	
		29
4	150	
		25
5	175	

(a) Total utility

(b) Marginal utility

The table shows that as Lisa sees more films, the total utility she derives from films increases. The table also shows her marginal utility – the change in total utility resulting from the last film seen. Marginal utility declines as Lisa sees more films. The figure graphs Lisa's total utility and marginal utility from films. Part (a) shows her total utility. It also shows as a bar the extra utility she gains from each additional film she sees – her marginal utility. Part (b) shows how Lisa's marginal utility from films diminishes by placing the bars shown in part (a) side by side as a series of declining steps.

concept of temperature helps us make predictions about physical phenomena.

Admittedly, marginal utility theory does not enable us to predict how buying plans change with the same precision that a thermometer enables us to predict when water will turn to ice or steam. But the theory gives us important insights into buying plans and has some powerful implications, as you're about to discover. It helps us to understand why people buy more of a good or service when its price falls, why people buy more of most goods when incomes increase and it resolves the paradox of value.

Review Quiz

1. Explain how a consumer's income and the prices of goods limit consumption possibilities.
2. What is utility and how do we use the concept of utility to describe a consumer's preferences?
3. What is the distinction between total utility and marginal utility?
4. What is the key assumption about marginal utility?

Maximizing Utility

An individual's income and the prices of goods and services limit the individual's choices, and the individual's preferences determine the utility that he or she can obtain from each consumption possibility. The key assumption of marginal utility theory is that the individual chooses the consumption possibility that maximizes total utility. This assumption of utility maximization is a way of expressing the fundamental economic problem: scarcity. People's wants exceed the resources available to satisfy these wants, so they must make hard choices. In making choices, they try to get the maximum attainable benefit – that is, they try to maximize total utility.

Let's see how Lisa allocates her £30 a month between films and cola to maximize her total utility. We'll continue to assume that the price of a cinema ticket is £6 and the price of cola is £3 a six-pack.

The Utility-maximizing Choice

The most direct way of calculating how Lisa spends her income to maximize her total utility is by making a table like Table 7.2. The rows of this table show the same affordable combinations of films and cola that lie along Lisa's budget line in Figure 7.2. The table records three things: first, the number of films seen and the total utility derived from them (the left side of the table); second, the number of six-packs consumed and the total utility derived from them (the right side of the table); and third, the total utility derived from both films and cola (the centre column).

The first row of Table 7.2 records the situation when Lisa sees no films and buys 10 six-packs of cola. In this case, she gets no utility from films and 291 units of total utility from cola. Her total utility from films and cola (the centre column) is 291 units. The rest of the table is constructed in the same way.

The consumption of cola and films that maximizes Lisa's total utility is highlighted in the table. When Lisa sees 2 films and drinks 6 six-packs, she gets 313 units of total utility. This is the best Lisa can do given that she has only £30 to spend and given the prices of cinema tickets and six-packs of cola. If she buys 8 six-packs of cola, she can see only 1 film. Lisa gets 310 units of total utility, which is 3 less than the maximum attainable. If she sees 3 films and she can drink only 4 six-packs of cola. Lisa gets 302 units

Table 7.2

Lisa's Utility-maximizing Combinations of Films and Cola

	Films			Cola	
	Quantity (number per month)	Total utility	Total utility from films and cola	Total utility	Quantity (six-packs per month)
A	0	0	291	291	10
B	1	50	310	260	8
C	2	88	313	225	6
D	3	121	302	181	4
E	4	150	267	117	2
F	5	175	175	0	0

of total utility, which is 11 less than the maximum attainable.

We've just described a consumer equilibrium. A **consumer equilibrium** is a situation in which a consumer has allocated all his or her available income in the way that, given the prices of goods and services, maximizes his or her total utility. Lisa's consumer equilibrium is 2 films and 6 six-packs.

In finding Lisa's consumer equilibrium, we measured her *total* utility from all the affordable combinations of films and cola. But there is a better way of determining her consumer equilibrium. It uses the idea that you first met in Chapter 1. Let's look at this alternative.

Equalizing Marginal Utility per Pound Spent

A consumer's total utility is maximized by following the rule:

Spend all the available income and equalize the marginal utility per pound spent on all goods.

The **marginal utility per pound spent** is the marginal utility from a good divided by the price of the good. For example, Lisa's marginal utility from seeing the first film, MU_F, is 50 units of utility. The price of a cinema ticket, P_F, is £6, which means that the marginal utility per pound spent on 1 film a month, MU_F/P_F, is 50 units divided by £6, or 8.33 units of utility per pound.

You can see why following this rule maximizes total utility by thinking about a situation in which Lisa has spent all her income but the marginal utilities per pound are not equal. Suppose that Lisa's marginal utility per pound spent on cola, MU_C/P_C, exceeds that on films. By spending a pound more on cola and a pound less on films, her total utility from cola rises and her total utility from films falls. But her utility gain from cola exceeds her utility loss from films, so her total utility increases. Because she's consuming more cola, her marginal utility from cola has fallen. And because she sees fewer films, her marginal utility from films has risen. Lisa keeps increasing her consumption of cola and decreasing her consumption of films until the two marginal utilities per pound spent are equal, or when:

$$\frac{MU_F}{P_F} = \frac{MU_C}{P_C}$$

Table 7.3 sets out Lisa's marginal utilities per pound spent on each good. Each row exhausts Lisa's income of £30. In row B, Lisa's marginal utility from films is 50 units (use Table 7.1 to calculate the marginal utilities). Because the price of a ticket is £6, Lisa's marginal utility is 8.33. Marginal utility per pound spent on each good, like marginal utility itself, decreases as more of the good is consumed.

Lisa maximizes her total utility when the marginal utility per pound spent on films is equal to the marginal utility per pound spent on cola – possibility C in Table 7.3: Lisa sees 2 films and drinks 6 six-packs a month.

Figure 7.4 shows why the rule "equalize marginal utility per pound spent on all goods" works. Suppose that instead of seeing 2 films and drinking 6 six-packs (possibility C), Lisa sees 1 film and drinks 8 six-packs (possibility B). She then gets 8.33 units of utility from the last pound spent on films and 5.67 units from the last pound spent on cola. Lisa can increase her total utility by buying less cola and seeing more films. If she sees one additional film and spends less on cola, her total utility from films increases by 8.33 units and her total utility from cola decreases by 5.67 units. Her total utility increases by 2.66 units per pound as shown by the blue area.

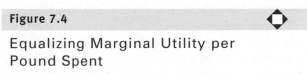

Figure 7.4

Equalizing Marginal Utility per Pound Spent

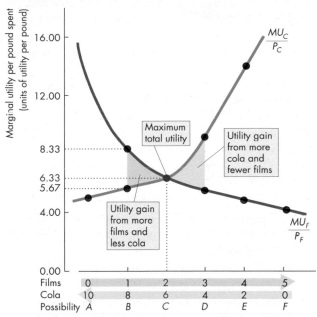

If Lisa sees 1 film and consumes 8 six-packs of cola (possibility B) she gets 8.33 units of utility from the last pound spent on films and 5.67 units of utility from the last pound spent on cola. She can get more total utility by seeing 1 more film.

If she consumes 4 six-packs and sees 3 films (possibility D), she gets 5.50 units of utility from the last pound spent on films and 9.33 units of utility from the last pound spent on cola. She can get more total utility by seeing 1 fewer film a month. When Lisa's marginal utility per pound spent on films equals her marginal utility per pound spent on cola, her total utility is maximized.

Table 7.3

Equalizing Marginal Utilities per Pound Spent

	Films (£6 per ticket)			Cola (£3 per six-pack)		
	Quantity	Marginal utility	Marginal utility per pound spent	Six-packs	Marginal utility	Marginal utility per pound spent
A	0	0		10	15	5.00
B	1	50	8.33	8	17	5.67
C	**2**	**38**	**6.33**	**6**	**19**	**6.33**
D	3	33	5.50	4	28	9.33
E	4	29	4.83	2	42	14.00
F	5	25	4.17	0	0	

Alternatively, suppose that Lisa sees 3 films and drinks 4 six-packs (possibility *D*). Now her marginal utility per pound spent on films (5.50) is less than her marginal utility per pound spent on cola (9.33). Lisa can now increase her total utility by seeing one less film and spending more cola, as the green area shows.

The Power of Marginal Analysis

The method we've just used to find Lisa's utility-maximizing choice of films and cola is an example of the power of marginal analysis. By comparing the marginal gain from having more of one good with the marginal loss from having less of another good, Lisa is able to ensure that she gets the maximum attainable utility.

The rule to follow is simple: if the marginal utility per pound spent on films exceeds the marginal utility per pound spent on cola, see more films and drink less cola; if the marginal utility per pound spent on cola exceeds the marginal utility per pound spent on films, drink more cola and see fewer films.

More generally, if the marginal gain from an action exceeds the marginal loss, take the action. You will meet this principle time and again in your study of economics. And you will find yourself using it when you make your own economic choices, especially when you must make a big decision.

Units of Utility

In maximizing total utility by making the marginal utilities per pound spent equal for both goods, the units in which utility is measured do not matter. Any arbitrary units will work. It is in this respect that utility is like temperature. Predictions about the freezing point of water don't depend on the temperature scale; and predictions about an individual's consumption choice don't depend on the units of utility.

Review Quiz

1 What is Lisa's goal when choosing the quantities of films she sees or cola she drinks?
2 What are the two conditions that are met if a consumer like Lisa is maximizing utility?
3 Explain why equalizing the marginal utilities of all good does *not* maximize utility.
4 Explain why equalizing the marginal utility per pound spent on each good *does* maximize utility.

Predictions of Marginal Utility Theory

We're now going to use marginal utility theory to make some predictions. In Chapter 3, we assumed that a fall in the price of a good, other things remaining the same, brings an increase in the quantity demanded of that good – the law of demand. We also assumed that a fall in the price of a substitute decreases demand and a rise in income increases demand for a normal good. We're now going to see that these assumptions are predictions of marginal utility theory.

A Fall in the Price of a Ticket

A fall in the price of a cinema ticket, other things remaining the same, changes the quantity of films demanded and brings a movement along the demand curve for films. We've already found one point on Lisa's demand curve for films: when the price of a ticket is £6, Lisa sees 2 films a month. Figure 7.4 shows this point on Lisa's demand curve for films.

To find another point on her demand curve for films, we need to work out what Lisa buys when the price of a ticket changes. Suppose that the price of a ticket falls from £6 to £3 and nothing else changes.

To work out the effect of this change in price of a cinema ticket on Lisa's buying plans, we must first determine the combinations of films and cola that she can afford at the new prices. Then we calculate the new marginal utilities per pound spent. Finally, we determine the combination that makes the marginal utilities per pound spent on films and cola equal.

The rows of Table 7.4 show the combinations of films and cola that exhaust Lisa's £30 of income when the price of a cinema ticket is $3 and the price of a six-pack is £3. Lisa's preferences do not change when prices change, so her marginal utility schedule remains the same as that in Table 7.3. Divide her marginal utility from films by £3 to get the marginal utility per pound spent on films.

Lisa now sees 5 films and drinks 5 six-packs. She *substitutes* films for cola. Figure 7.4 shows both these effects. In part (a), we've found another point on Lisa's demand curve for films. We've discovered that her demand curve obeys the law of demand. In part (b), we see that a fall in the price of a ticket decreases the demand for cola. The demand curve for cola shifts leftward. For Lisa, cola and films are substitutes.

Table 7.4

How a Change in Price of a Cinema Ticket Affects Lisa's Choices

Films (£3 per ticket)		Cola (£3 per six-pack)	
Quantity	Marginal utility per pound spent	Six-packs	Marginal utility per pound spent
0		10	5.00
1	16.67	9	5.33
2	12.67	8	5.67
3	11.00	7	6.00
4	9.67	6	6.33
5	8.33	5	8.33
6	7.00	4	9.33
7	6.00	3	12.00
8	5.00	2	14.00
9	4.00	1	25.00
10	3.00	0	

A Rise in the Price of Cola

In Figure 7.5(b), we know only one point on Lisa's demand curve for cola when the price of a cinema ticket is £3. To find Lisa's demand curve for cola, we must see how she responds to a change in the price of cola. Suppose that the price of cola rises from £3 to £6 a six-pack. The rows of Table 7.5 show the combinations of films and cola that exactly exhaust her £30 of income when the price of a cinema ticket is £3 and the price of a six-pack is £6. Again, Lisa's preferences don't change when the price changes. Divide Lisa's marginal utility from cola by £6 to get her marginal utility per pound spent on cola.

Lisa now drinks 2 six-packs a month and sees 6 films a month. Lisa *substitutes* films for cola.

Figure 7.6 illustrates both these effects. In part (a), we've found another point on Lisa's demand curve for cola. And we've confirmed that this demand curve obeys the law of demand.

In part (b), we see that Lisa increases the number of films she sees when the price of cola rises and the price

Figure 7.5	

A Fall in the Price of a Cinema Ticket

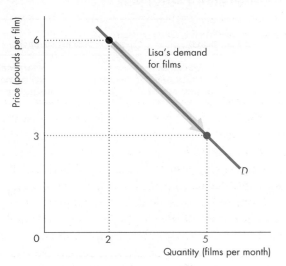

(a) Demand for films

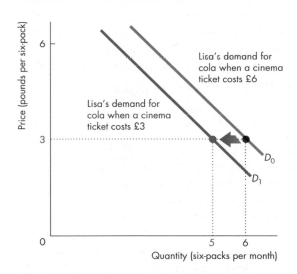

(b) Demand for cola

When the price of a cinema ticket falls and the price of cola remains the same, the quantity of films demanded by Lisa increases. In part (a), Lisa moves along her demand curve for films. Also when the price of a cinema ticket falls, Lisa's demand for cola decreases. In part (b), her demand curve for cola shifts leftward from D_0 to D_1.

of a cinema ticket remains constant. The demand curve for films shifts rightward. For Lisa, films and cola are substitutes.

Table 7.5

How a Change in the Price of Cola Affects Lisa's Choices

Films (£3 per ticket)		Cola (£6 per six-pack)	
Quantity	Marginal utility per pound spent	Six-packs	Marginal utility per pound spent
0		5	4.17
2	12.67	4	4.67
4	9.67	3	6.00
6	**7.00**	**2**	**7.00**
8	5.00	1	12.50
10	3.00	0	

Marginal utility theory predicts these two results:

1 When the price of a good rises, the quantity demanded of that good decreases.

2 If the price of one good rises, the demand for another good that can serve as a substitute increases.

These predictions of marginal utility theory sound familiar because they correspond to the assumptions that we made about demand in Chapter 3. There, we assumed that the demand curve for a good slopes downward and that a rise in the price of a substitute of a good increases the demand for the good.

We have now seen that marginal utility theory predicts how the quantities of goods and services that people demand respond to price changes. The theory enables us to derive an individual's demand curve and predict how the demand curve for one good shifts when the price of another good changes.

Marginal utility theory also helps us to understand one further thing about demand – how it changes when income changes. Let's study the effects of a change in income on demand.

Figure 7.6

A Rise in the Price of Cola

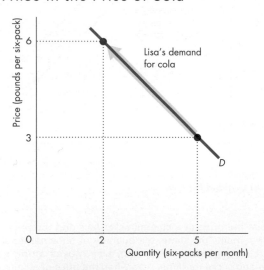

(a) Demand for cola

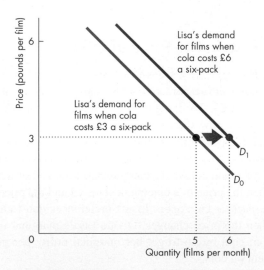

(b) Demand for films

When the price of cola rises and the price of a cinema ticket remains the same, the quantity of cola demanded by Lisa decreases. In part (a), Lisa moves along her demand curve for cola.

Also, when the price of cola rises, Lisa's demand for films increases.
In part (b), her demand curve for films shifts rightward from D_0 to D_1.

A Rise in Income

Let's suppose that Lisa's income increases to £42 a month and that that the price of a cinema ticket is £3 and the price of cola is £3. We saw in Table 7.4 that with these prices and with an income of £30 a month, Lisa sees 5 films and drinks 5 six-packs a month. We want to compare this choice of films and cola with Lisa's choice when her income is £42. Table 7.6 shows the calculations needed to make the comparison. With £42, Lisa can see 14 films a month and drink no cola or buy 14 six-packs a month and see no films or choose any combination of the two goods in the rows of the table. We calculate the marginal utility per pound spent in exactly the same way as we did before and find the quantities at which the marginal utility per pound spent on films equals the marginal utility per pound spent on cola. With an income of £42, the marginal utility per pound spent on each good is equal when Lisa sees 7 films and drinks 7 six-packs of cola a month.

By comparing this situation with that in Table 7.4, we see that with an additional £12 a month, Lisa drinks 2 more six-packs and sees 2 more films. This response arises from Lisa's preferences, as described by her marginal utilities. Different preferences produce different quantitative responses. With a larger income, the consumer buys more of a *normal* good and less of an *inferior* good. For Lisa, cola and films are normal goods. When her income increases, Lisa buys more of both goods.

You have now completed your study of marginal utility theory of an individual's consumption choices. Table 7.7 summarizes the key assumptions, implications and predictions of the theory.

Table 7.6

Lisa's Choices with an Income of £42 a Month

Films (£3 per ticket)		Cola (£3 per six-pack)	
Quantity	Marginal utility per pound spent	Six-packs	Marginal utility per pound spent
0		14	3.67
1	16.67	13	4.00
2	12.67	12	4.33
3	11.00	11	4.67
4	9.67	10	5.00
5	8.33	9	5.33
6	7.00	8	5.67
7	6.00	7	6.00
8	5.00	6	6.33
9	4.00	5	8.33
10	3.00	4	9.33
11	2.00	3	12.00
12	1.00	2	14.00
13	0.67	1	25.00
14	0.33	0	

Table 7.7

Marginal Utility Theory

Assumptions

◆ A consumer derives utility from the goods consumed.

◆ Each additional unit of consumption yields additional utility; marginal utility is positive.

◆ As the quantity of a good consumed increases, marginal utility decreases.

◆ A consumer's aim is to maximize total utility.

Implication

Utility is maximized when all the available income is spent and when the marginal utility per pound spent is equal for all goods.

Predictions

◆ Other things remaining the same, the higher the price of a good, the lower is the quantity bought (the law of demand).

◆ The higher the price of a good, the greater is the quantity bought of substitutes for that good.

◆ The larger the consumer's income, the greater is the quantity demanded of normal goods.

Marginal Utility and Elasticity

Why is the demand for some things price elastic while the demand for others is price inelastic? The main answer in Chapter 4 is that a good with close substitutes has an elastic demand and a good with poor substitutes has an inelastic demand. This answer is correct. But you can now provide a deeper answer based on marginal utility theory.

You've seen that for any pair of goods, X and Y, the consumer maximizes utility when:

$$\frac{MU_X}{P_X} = \frac{MU_Y}{P_Y}$$

(MU is marginal utility, P is price, and the subscripts X and Y denote the two goods.)

When P_X falls, the consumer buys more X to drive down MU_X and maintain the above equality. So the percentage change in MU_X equals the percentage change in P_X. If the demand for X is elastic, the percentage increase in the quantity of X demanded exceeds the percentage decrease in P_X. Consequently, if as the quantity of X consumed increases, the percentage decrease in MU_X is less than the percentage increase in the quantity of X, the demand for X is elastic.

By the same reasoning, if as the quantity of X consumed increases, the percentage decrease in MU_X exceeds the percentage increase in the quantity of X, the demand for X is inelastic.

Review Quiz

1   When the price of a good falls and the prices of other goods remain the same, what happens to the consumption of the good whose price has fallen and to the consumption of other goods?
2   Elaborate your answer to question 1. For which good does demand change and for which good does the quantity demanded change?
3   If all goods are normal goods, how does an increase in a consumer's income change the quantity of each good bought?

Marginal utility theory explains *all* choices, including how we allocate our time between work and leisure. This choice is one of the themes in Economics in History on *Parkin Interactive*.

We're going to end this chapter by returning to the concept of efficiency and the distinction between price and value.

Efficiency, Price and Value

Marginal utility theory helps us to deepen our understanding of the concept of efficiency and also helps us to see more clearly the distinction between value and price. Let's see how.

Consumer Efficiency and Marginal Benefit

When Lisa allocates her limited budget to maximize utility, she is using her resources efficiently. Any other allocation of her budget would waste some resources.

But when Lisa has allocated her limited budget to maximize utility, she is *on* her demand curve for each good. A demand curve is a description of the quantity demanded at each price when utility is maximized. When we studied efficiency in Chapter 5, we learned that value equals marginal benefit and that a demand curve is also a willingness-to-pay curve. It tells us a consumer's *marginal benefit* – the benefit from consuming an additional unit of a good. You can now give the idea of marginal benefit a deeper meaning:

> **Marginal benefit is the maximum price that a consumer is willing to pay for an extra unit of a good or service when utility is maximized.**

The Paradox of Value

For centuries, philosophers have been puzzled by a paradox that we raised at the start of this chapter. Water, which is essential to life itself, costs little, but diamonds, which are useless in comparison to water, are expensive. Why? Adam Smith tried to solve this paradox. But not until the theory of marginal utility had been developed could anyone give a satisfactory answer.

You can solve this puzzle by distinguishing between *total* utility and *marginal* utility. The total utility that we get from water is enormous. But remember, the more we consume of something, the smaller is its marginal utility. We use so much water that its marginal utility – the benefit we get from one more glass of water – diminishes to a small value. Diamonds, on the other hand, have a small total utility relative to water, but because we buy few diamonds, they have a high marginal utility. When a consumer has maximized her total utility, she has allocated her budget in the way that makes the marginal utility per pound spent equal

Figure 7.7

◆

The Paradox of Value

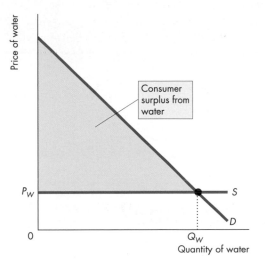

(a) Water

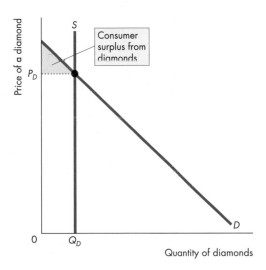

(b) Diamonds

Part (a) shows the demand for water, D, and the supply of water, S. The supply is assumed to be perfectly elastic at the price P_W. At this price, the quantity of water consumed is Q_W and the consumer surplus from water is the large green triangle. Part (b) shows the demand for diamonds, D, and the supply of diamonds, S. The supply is assumed to be perfectly inelastic at the quantity Q_D. At this quantity, the price of a diamond is P_D and the consumer surplus from diamonds is the small green triangle. Water is valuable – has a large consumer surplus – but is cheap. Diamonds are less valuable than water – have a smaller consumer surplus – but are expensive.

for all goods. That is, the marginal utility from a good divided by the price of the good is equal for all goods.

This equality of marginal utilities per pound spent holds true for diamonds and water: diamonds have a high price and a high marginal utility; water has a low price and a low marginal utility. When the high marginal utility of diamonds is divided by the high price of diamonds, the result is a number that equals the low marginal utility of water divided by the low price of water. The marginal utility per pound spent is the same for diamonds as for water.

Another way to think about the paradox of value uses *consumer surplus*. Figure 7.7 explains the paradox of value by using this idea. The supply of water in part (a) is perfectly elastic at price P_W, so the quantity of water consumed is Q_W and the consumer surplus from water is the large green area. The supply of diamonds in part (b) is perfectly inelastic at the quantity Q_D, so the price of a diamond is P_D and the consumer surplus from diamonds is the small green area. Water is cheap but brings a large consumer surplus, while diamonds are expensive but bring a small consumer surplus.

Review Quiz

1 Can you explain why, along a demand curve, consumer choices are efficient?
2 Can you explain the paradox of value?
3 Is the marginal utility from water or from diamonds greater? Is the total utility from water or from diamonds greater? Is the consumer surplus from water or from diamonds greater?

You have now completed your study of the marginal utility theory. And you've seen how the theory can be used to explain our real-world consumption choices. You can see the theory in action once again in *Reading Between the Lines* on pp. 154–155, where it is used to interpret what is happening in the high street as soup bars give coffee bars a run for their money.

The next chapter presents an alternative theory of consumer behaviour. To help you see the connection between the two theories of consumer behaviour, we'll continue with the same example. We'll meet Lisa again and discover another way of understanding how she gets the most out of her £30 a month.

Reading Between the Lines
Utility Theory: Coffee Has-been?

The Times, 2 March 2001

Coffee been and gone?

George Pendle

Is the sweet success of the coffee shop craze beginning to turn a little bitter? Double tall, half-and-half skinny decafs just don't seem to offer the same pizzazz anymore. At least that is the message in a report by Mintel, which found that one in four people feel the drinks served in coffee shops are too expensive . . .

The branded coffee shop was a defining product of the 1990s . . . A recent study by property consultant Healey and Baker found that the British now spend more time in coffee bars than the Italians and the French . . . A report by Allegra says that the number of branded coffee shops in the UK is forecast to grow from 850 to 1,700 by 2004.

The supposed public dissatisfaction with coffee bars has not yet affected sales, although there is growing competition in the shape of juice and soup bars. Companies such as Soup and New Covent Garden Soup Company are starting to make their presence felt, although there has yet to be a chain with a comparably strong brand presence.

Lorrie Morgan, director of marketing at Costa Coffee, is not worried by the Mintel report: 'If only 15 per cent of adults used branded coffee shops in the last 12 months there is still so much room to grow.' . . . As for the high prices for a latte, especially with the recent slump in coffee bean prices, this is put down to increasing rent and wage costs. '£1.70 to treat yourself for five or ten minutes isn't all that much. That's not to say it's cheap, nor that we want to keep our prices up forever, but 74 per cent of people disagree that it is expensive.'

The Essence of the Story

◆ The British craze for the coffee shop may be ending.

◆ One in four people surveyed thought that drinks in coffee shops were too expensive.

◆ Consumers can now choose between coffee shops and the new range of juice and soup bars opening in many towns.

◆ Although the price of coffee beans has fallen, the price of a coffee in a coffee shop is still about £1.70.

◆ Despite the fact that some coffee drinkers are switching to alternatives, the high price has not cut coffee-shop sales or the potential for growth.

Economic Analysis

◆ British consumers love the coffee shop, but they also like the new soup bars. Lisa is a typical consumer with £17.00 a week to spend on coffee or soup at lunchtimes.

◆ If there is no soup bar in town and a coffee costs £1.70 per cup, Lisa could buy 10 cappuccinos a week. But if a soup bar opens, Lisa faces a new choice.

◆ Each row of the table shows the combinations of coffee and soup that Lisa can buy with £17.00 if the price of a cappuccino is £1.70 and the price of a pot of fresh soup is £3.40.

◆ The table also shows Lisa's marginal utility of soup and coffee. The first pot of soup gives her more additional utility than the first two cappuccinos, but soup is more expensive than coffee.

◆ To maximize her utility, Lisa compares the marginal utility per pound spent on coffee to the marginal utility per pound spent on soup when making a choice of what to drink at lunchtime.

◆ Figure 1 shows that Lisa maximizes her utility by choosing 4 cappuccinos and 3 pots of soup a week, at possibility C.

◆ If Lisa drinks 8 cups of coffee and 1 pot of soup a week, possibility E in Figure 1, she can gain more utility by having fewer cups of coffee and more soup. If Lisa is at possibility B, she can gain more utility by increasing coffee consumption and cutting soup consumption.

◆ Figure 2 shows Lisa's demand curve for cappuccinos, D_0, before the soup bar opens. The price of a cappuccino does not change when the soup bar opens, but Lisa plans to buy fewer cappuccinos. Her demand curve for cappuccinos shifts leftward to D_1.

◆ Sales of coffee bar drinks will still grow as along as the increase in demand from new customers outstrips the decrease in demand from existing customers like Lisa.

Table 1
Lisa's Choice

	Soup (£3.40 per pot)			Cappuccino coffee (£1.70 per cup)		
	Quantity (pots)	Marginal utility	Marginal utility per pound	Quantity (cups)	Marginal utility	Marginal utility per pound
A	5	35	14	0	–	–
B	4	50	20	2	56	33
C	3	65	26	4	44	26
D	2	80	32	6	41	24
E	1	100	40	8	35	21
F	0	–	–	10	30	18

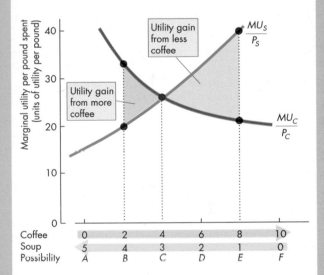

Figure 1 Maximizing utility

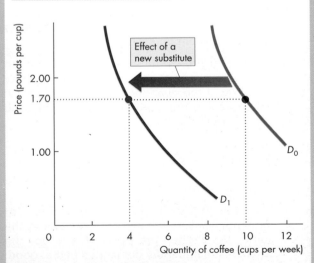

Figure 2 Lisa's demand for coffee

Summary

Key Points

Individual Demand and Market Demand (p. 142)

◆ Individual demand is the relationship between the price of a good and the quantity demanded by a single individual.

◆ Market demand is found by summing horizontally all the individual demand curves.

Consumption Choices (pp. 143–145)

◆ Individual's choices are determined by consumption possibilities and preferences.

◆ A consumer's consumption possibilities are constrained by his or her income and the prices of goods and services. Some combinations of goods and services are affordable, and some are not affordable.

◆ A consumer's preferences can be described by marginal utility.

◆ The key assumption of the marginal utility theory is that the marginal utility of a good decreases as consumption of it increases.

◆ Marginal utility theory assumes that people buy the affordable combination of goods and services that maximizes their total utility.

Maximizing Utility (pp. 146–148)

◆ Total utility is maximized when all the available income is spent and when the marginal utility per pound spent on each good is equal.

◆ If the marginal utility per pound spent on good A exceeds that on good B, total utility increases if the quantity purchased of good A increases and the quantity purchased of good B decreases.

Predictions of Marginal Utility Theory (pp. 148–152)

◆ Marginal utility theory predicts the law of demand. That is, other things remaining the same, the higher the price of a good, the smaller is the quantity demanded of that good.

◆ Marginal utility theory also predicts that other things remaining the same, the larger the consumer's income, the larger is the quantity demanded of a normal good.

Efficiency, Price and Value (pp. 152–153)

◆ When a consumer maximizes utility, he or she uses resources efficiently.

◆ Marginal utility theory resolves the paradox of value.

◆ When we talk about value, we are thinking about *total* utility or consumer surplus. But price is related to *marginal* utility.

◆ Water, which we consume in large amounts, has a high total utility and a large consumer surplus, but the price of water is low and the marginal utility from water is low.

◆ Diamonds, which we consume in small amounts, has a low total utility and a small consumer surplus, but the price of a diamond is high and marginal utility from diamonds is high.

Key Figures and Table

Key Terms

Problems

*Solutions to odd-numbered problems are available on *Parkin Interactive*.

*1 Judy's and Dan's demand schedules for cola are:

Price (cents per carton)	Quantity demanded by Judy (cartons per week)	Quantity demanded by Dan (cartons per week)
10	12	6
30	9	5
50	6	4
70	3	3
90	1	2

If Judy and Dan are the only two individuals, what is the market demand for cola?

2 Lee's and Lou's demand schedules for CDs are:

Price (euros per CD)	Quantity demanded by Lee (CDs per year)	Quantity demanded by Lou (CDs per year)
6	12	10
8	9	8
10	6	6
12	3	4
14	0	2

If Lee and Lou are the only two individuals, what is the market demand for CDs?

*3 Jason enjoys rock CDs and spy novels and spends €60 a month on them. The following table shows the utility he gets from each good:

Quantity per month	Utility from rock CDs	Utility from spy novels
1	60	20
2	110	38
3	150	53
4	180	64
5	200	70
6	206	75

a Draw graphs showing Jason's utility from rock CDs and from spy novels.

b Compare the two utility graphs. Can you say anything about Jason's preferences?

c Draw graphs that show Jason's marginal utility from rock CDs and from spy novels.

d What do the two marginal utility graphs tell you about Jason's preferences?

e If rock CDs and spy novels both cost €10 each, how does Jason spend the €60?

4 Mary enjoys classical CDs and travel books and spends €75 a month on them. The following table shows the utility she gets from each good:

Quantity per month	Utility from classical CDs	Utility from travel books
1	90	120
2	110	136
3	126	148
4	138	152
5	146	154

a Draw graphs showing Mary's utility from classical CDs and from travel books.

b Compare the two utility graphs. Can you say anything about Mary's preferences?

c Draw graphs that show Mary's marginal utility from classical CDs and from travel books.

d What do the two marginal utility graphs tell you about Mary's preferences?

e If a classical CD and a travel book cost €15 each, how does Mary spend the €75 a month?

*5 Max enjoys windsurfing and snorkelling. He obtains the following utility from each of these sports:

Hours per day	Utility from windsurfing	Utility from snorkelling
1	120	40
2	220	76
3	300	106
4	360	128
5	400	140
6	412	150
7	422	158

Max has €35 to spend and he can spend as much time as he likes on his leisure pursuits. Windsurfing equipment rents for €10 an hour, and snorkelling equipment rents for €5 an hour.

a Draw a graph that shows Max's budget line.

b How long does he spend windsurfing and how long does he spend snorkelling?

6 Pete enjoys rock concerts and the opera. The table shows the utility he gets from each activity:

Concerts per month	Utility from rock concerts	Utility from operas
1	120	200
2	100	160
3	80	120
4	60	80
5	40	40
6	20	0

Pete has €200 a month to spend on concerts. A rock concert ticket is €20, and an opera ticket is €40. How many rock concerts and how many operas does Pete attend?

*7 In problem 5, Max's sister gives him €20 to spend on his leisure pursuits, so he now has €55.

a Draw a graph that shows Max's consumption possibilities.

b How many hours does Max choose to windsurf and how many hours does he choose to snorkel now that he has €55 to spend?

8 In problem 6, Pete's uncle gives him €60 to spend on concert tickets, so he now has €260.

a Draw a graph that shows Pete's consumption possibilities.

b How many rock concerts and how many operas does he now attend?

*9 In problem 7, if the rent on windsurfing equipment decreases to €5 an hour, how many hours does Max now windsurf and how many hours does he snorkel?

10 In problem 6, if the price of a opera ticket decreases to €20, how many rock concerts and operas will Pete attend?

*11 Max takes a Club Med vacation, the cost of which includes unlimited sports activities. There is no extra charge for equipment. If Max windsurfs and snorkels for 6 hours a day, how many hours does he windsurf and how many hours does he snorkel?

12 Pete, in problem 6, wins a lottery and has more than enough money to satisfy his desires for rock concerts and opera. He decides that he would like to attend a total of 7 concerts each month. How many rock concerts and how many operas does he now attend?

Critical Thinking

1 Read the article in *Reading Between the Lines* on pp. 154–155 and then:

a Draw a graph of Lisa's budget line given that her income rinks is £17.00, and a cappuccino costs £1.70 and soup costs £3.40 a pot.

b Draw Lisa's marginal utility curves for both soup and cappuccino coffee from the table. In what ways are the two marginal utility curves different? Is the demand for soup or cappuccino likely to be more elastic?

c Use a graph to show the impact on the demand for coffee and the demand for soup of a fall in price of coffee to £1.13 a cup. Explain how the relationship between utility and price has changed for coffee.

d Use a graph to show the impact on the demand for coffee and the demand for soup of a fall in the price of soup when the price of coffee is £1.70 a cup. Explain how the relationship between utility and price has changed for soup.

e If the new soup and juice bars are attracting customers away from coffee bars, what do you think will happen to the price of coffee? Explain your answer.

2 In recent years, bottled water, fruit drinks and sports drinks have become very popular. Use the marginal utility theory to explain the rise in popularity of these "new age" drinks.

3 Why do you think the percentage of income spent on food has decreased while the percentage of income spent on cars has increased during the past 50 years? Use the marginal utility theory to explain these trends.

4 Smoking is banned on all airline flights. Use marginal utility theory to explain how the ban:

a Effects the utility of smokers.

b Influences the decisions of smokers.

c Effects the utility of non-smokers.

d Influences the decisions of non-smokers.

Web Exercise

Use the links on *Parkin Interactive* to work the following exercise.

1 Read what Henry Schimberg, CEO of Coca-Cola Enterprises, says about the market for bottled water. Use the marginal utility theory to explain and interpret his remarks.

Chapter 8

Possibilities, Preferences and Choices

After studying this chapter you will be able to:

◆ Describe a household's budget line and show how it changes when a price or income changes

◆ Make a map of preferences by using indifference curves and explain the principle of diminishing marginal rate of substitution

◆ Predict the effects of changes in prices and income on consumption choices

◆ Predict the effect of changes of wage rates on work–leisure choices

Menus of Choice

We spend a lot of our time making choices. We choose how to spend our income. And when we've decided to spend some of it on ice cream, we sometimes take an incredible amount of time to ponder the flavour to go for. Our choices are not static: they change over time. What determines our choices and what makes our choices change? How do we choose the best affordable use of our limited income and time? Find out in this chapter.

Consumption Possibilities

Consumption choices are limited by income and by prices. A household has a given amount of income to spend and cannot influence the prices of the goods and services it buys. It takes prices as given. A household's **budget line** describes the limits to a household's consumption choices. Let's look at Lisa's[1] budget line.

The Budget Line

Lisa is the only person in her household and she has an income of £30 a month to spend. She consumes two goods – cinema films and cola. Cinema tickets cost £6 each; cola costs £3 for a six-pack. If Lisa spends all of her income, she will reach the limit of her consumption of films and cola.

Figure 8.1 shows the affordable ways for Lisa to consume films and cola. Each row shows an affordable way to consume films and cola that just uses up Lisa's monthly income of £30. The numbers in the table define Lisa's household consumption possibilities. We can graph these consumption possibilities as points A to F in Figure 8.1.

Divisible and Indivisible Goods

Some goods – called divisible goods – can be bought in any quantity desired. Examples are petrol and electricity. We can best understand the model of household choice we're about to study if we assume that all goods and services are divisible. For example, Lisa can consume half a film a month *on average* by seeing one film every two months. When we think of goods as being divisible, the consumption possibilities are not just the points A to F shown in Figure 8.1, but these points plus all the intermediate points that form the line running from A to F. Such a line is a budget line.

Lisa's budget line is a constraint on her choices. She can afford all the points on the line and inside it. She cannot afford points outside the line. The constraint on her consumption depends on prices and her income, and the constraint changes when prices or her income change. Let's see how by studying an equation that describes her consumption possibilities.

---

[1] If you have read the preceding chapter on marginal utility theory, you have already met Lisa. This tale of her thirst for cola and zeal for films will sound familiar to you – up to a point. But in this chapter we're going to use a different method for representing preferences – one that does not require us to resort to the idea of utility.

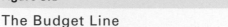

Figure 8.1

The Budget Line

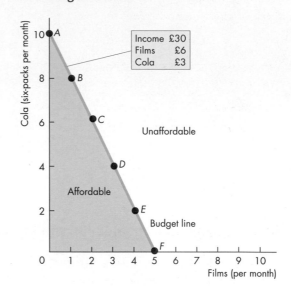

Consumption possibility	Films (per month)	Cola (six-packs per month)
A	0	10
B	1	8
C	2	6
D	3	4
E	4	2
F	5	0

Lisa's budget line shows the boundary between what she can and cannot afford. Each row of the table lists Lisa's affordable combinations of films and cola when her income is £30, the price of cola is £3 a six-pack, and the price of a cinema ticket is £6. For example, row A tells us that Lisa exhausts her £30 income when she buys 10 six-packs and sees no films.

The figure graphs Lisa's budget line. Points A to F on the graph represent the rows of the table. For divisible goods, the budget line is the continuous line AF. To calculate the equation for Lisa's budget line, start from the fact that expenditure equals income. That is:

$$(£3 \times Q_C + £6 \times Q_F) = £30$$

Divide by £3 to obtain:

$$Q_C + 2Q_F = 10$$

Subtract $2Q_F$ from both sides to obtain:

$$Q_C = 10 - 2Q_F$$

The Budget Equation

We can describe the budget line by using a *budget equation*. The budget equation starts with the fact that:

$$\text{Expenditure} = \text{Income}$$

Expenditure is equal to the sum of the price of each good multiplied by the quantity bought. For Lisa:

Expenditure = (Price of cola × Quantity of cola)

+ (Price of a cinema ticket × Quantity of films)

Call the price of cola P_C, the quantity of cola Q_C, the price of a cinema ticket P_F, the quantity of films Q_F, and income Y. We can write Lisa's budget equation as:

$$P_C Q_C + P_F Q_F = Y$$

Using the prices Lisa faces, £3 for a six-pack and £6 for a cinema ticket, and Lisa's income, £30, we get:

$$\text{£3}Q_C + \text{£6}Q_F = \text{£30}$$

Lisa can choose any quantities of cola (Q_C) and films (Q_F) that satisfy this equation. To find the relationship between these quantities, divide both sides of the equation by the price of cola (P_C) to get:

$$Q_C + \frac{P_F}{P_C} \times Q_F = \frac{Y}{P_C}$$

Now subtract the term $P_F/P_C \times Q_F$ from both sides of this equation to give:

$$Q_C = \frac{Y}{P_C} - \frac{P_F}{P_C} \times Q_F$$

For Lisa, income (Y) is £30, the price of a cinema ticket (P_F) is £6 and the price of a six-pack (P_C) is £3. So Lisa must choose the quantities of films and cola to satisfy the equation:

$$Q_C = \frac{\text{£30}}{\text{£3}} - \frac{\text{£6}}{\text{£3}} \times Q_F$$

$$Q_C = 10 - 2 \times Q_F$$

To interpret the equation, look at the budget line in Figure 8.1 and check that the equation delivers that budget line. First set Q_F equal to zero. The budget equation tells us that Q_C, the quantity of cola, is Y/P_C, which is 10 six-packs. This combination of Q_F and Q_C is the one shown in row A of the table in Figure 8.1. Next, set Q_F equal to 5. Q_C is now equal to zero (row F of the table). Check that you can derive the other rows.

The budget equation contains two variables chosen by the household (Q_F and Q_C) and two variables (Y/P_C and P_F/P_C) that the household takes as given. Let's look more closely at these variables.

Real Income

A household's **real income** is its income expressed as the quantity of goods that it can afford to buy. Lisa's real income in terms of cola is Y/P_C. This quantity is the maximum number of six-packs that Lisa can buy. It is equal to her money income divided by the price of cola. Lisa's income is £30 and the price of cola is £3 a six-pack, so her real income is 10 six-packs of cola. In Figure 8.1, real income is the point at which the budget line intersects the y-axis.

Relative Price

A **relative price** is the price of one good divided by the price of another good. In Lisa's budget equation, the variable (P_F/P_C) is the relative price of a film in terms of cola. For Lisa, P_F is £6 a film and P_C is £3 a six-pack, so P_F/P_C is equal to 2 six-packs per film. That is, to see one more film, Lisa must give up 2 six-packs.

You've just calculated Lisa's opportunity cost of a film. Recall that the opportunity cost of an action is the best alternative forgone. For Lisa to see 1 more film a month, she must forgo 2 six-packs. You've also calculated Lisa's opportunity cost of cola. For Lisa to buy 2 more six-packs a month, she must give up seeing 1 film. So her opportunity cost of 2 six-packs is 1 film.

The relative price of a film in terms of cola is the magnitude of the slope of Lisa's budget line. To calculate the slope of the budget line, recall the formula (see the Chapter 1 Appendix): slope equals the change in the variable measured on the y-axis divided by the change in the variable measured on the x-axis as we move along the line. In Lisa's case (Figure 8.1), the variable measured on the y-axis is the quantity of cola and the variable measured on the x-axis is the quantity of films. Along Lisa's budget line, as cola decreases from 10 to 0 six-packs, films increase from 0 to 5. So the slope of the budget line is 10 six-packs divided by 5 films, or 2 six-packs per film. The magnitude of this slope is exactly the same as the relative price we've just calculated. It is also the opportunity cost of a film.

A Change in Prices

When prices change, so does the budget line. The lower the price of the good measured on the horizontal axis, other things remaining the same, the flatter is the

Figure 8.2

Changes in Prices and Income

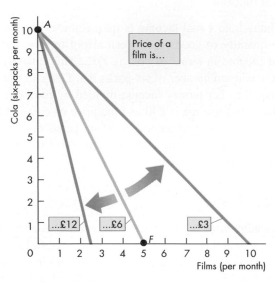

(a) A change in price

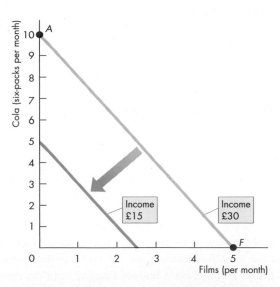

(b) A change in income

In part (a), the price of a cinema ticket changes. A fall in the price from £6 to £3 rotates the budget line outward and makes it flatter. A rise in the price from £6 to £12 rotates the budget line inward and makes it steeper.

In part (b), income falls from £30 to £15 while prices remain constant. The budget line shifts leftward but its slope does not change.

budget line. For example, if the price of a cinema ticket falls to £3, real income in terms of cola does not change but the relative price of seeing a film falls. The budget line rotates outward and becomes flatter as shown in Figure 8.2(a). The higher the price of the good measured on the horizontal axis, other things remaining the same, the steeper is the budget line. For example, if the price of a cinema ticket rises to £12, the relative price of seeing a film increases. The budget line rotates inward and becomes steeper as shown in Figure 8.2(a).

A Change in Income

A change in *money* income changes real income but does not change relative prices. The budget line shifts, but its slope does not change. The bigger a household's money income, the bigger is real income and the further to the right is the budget line. The smaller a household's money income, the smaller is real income and the further to the left is the budget line. Figure 8.2(b) shows the effect of a change in income on Lisa's budget line. The initial budget line when Lisa's income is £30 is the same one that we began with in Figure 8.1. The new budget line shows how much Lisa can consume if her income falls to £15 a month. The two budget lines have the same slope – are parallel – because the relative price is the same in both cases. The new budget line is closer to the origin than the initial one because Lisa's real income has decreased.

Review Quiz

1 What does Lisa's budget line show?
2 What is (a) Lisa's real income in terms of cinema films and (b) Lisa's opportunity cost of cola?
3 If a European household has an income of €40 and consumes only bus rides at €4 each and magazines at €2 each, what is the equation that describes the household's budget line?
4 If the price of one good changes, what happens to the relative price and to the slope of the household's budget line?
5 If a household's money income changes, but prices don't change, what happens to the household's real income and its budget line?

We've studied the limits to which a household's consumption can go. Let's now see how we can describe the household's preferences.

Preferences and Indifference Curves

Preferences are your likes and dislikes. You can actually make a map of a person's preferences. A preference map is based on the intuitively appealing assumption that people can sort all the possible combinations of goods they might consume into three groups: preferred, not preferred and indifferent. To make this idea more concrete, we asked Lisa to rank various combinations of films and cola.

Figure 8.3(a) shows part of Lisa's answer. She tells us that she currently sees 2 films and consumes 6 six-packs a month at point *C* in Figure 8.3. She then lists all the combinations of films and cola that she thinks is just as good as her current consumption. When we plot these combinations of films and cola, we get the green curve shown in Figure 8.3(a). This curve is the key element in a map of preferences and is called an indifference curve.

An **indifference curve** is a line that shows combinations of goods among which a consumer is *indifferent*. The indifference curve in Figure 8.3(a) tells us that Lisa is just as happy to consume 2 films and 6 six-packs a month at point *C* as to consume the combination of films and cola at point *G* or at any other point along the curve.

Lisa also says she prefers any of the combinations of films and cola above the indifference curve in Figure 8.3(a) – the yellow area – to any combination on the indifference curve. And she prefers any combination on the indifference curve to any combination in the grey area below the indifference curve.

The indifference curve in Figure 8.3(a) is just one of a whole family of such curves. This indifference curve appears again in Figure 8.3(b). It is labelled I_1 and it passes through points *C* and *G*. The curves labelled I_0 and I_2 are two other indifference curves. Lisa prefers any point on indifference curve I_2 to any point on indifference curve I_1 and she prefers any point on I_1 to any point on I_0. We refer to I_2 as being a higher indifference curve than I_1 and I_1 as being higher than I_0. And because Lisa prefers I_2 to I_1 and I_1 to I_0, these indifference curves do not intersect.

A preference map is a series of indifference curves that look like contour lines on a map. Like looking at a map, we can draw some conclusions about the terrain. Similarly, by looking at the shape of the indifference curves, we can draw conclusions about a person's preferences.

Let's see how to "read" a preference map.

Figure 8.3

A Preference Map

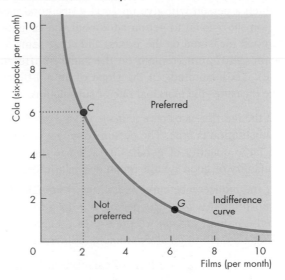

(a) An indifference curve

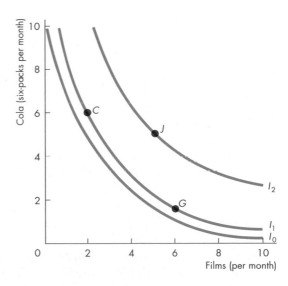

(b) Lisa's preference map

In part (a), Lisa consumes 6 six-packs of cola and 2 films a month at point *C*. She is indifferent between all the points on the green indifference curve such as *C* and *G*. She prefers any point above the indifference curve (yellow area) to any point on it, and she prefers any point on the indifference curve to any point below it (grey area). A preference map is a number of indifference curves. Part (b) shows three – I_0, I_1, and I_2 – that are part of Lisa's preference map. She prefers point *J* to point *C* or *G*, so she prefers any point on I_2 to any point on I_1.

Marginal Rate of Substitution

The **marginal rate of substitution** (or *MRS*) is the rate at which a person will give up good *y* (the good measured on the *y*-axis) to get an additional unit of good *x* (the good measured on the *x*-axis) and at the same time remain indifferent (remain on the same indifference curve). The magnitude of the slope of an indifference curve measures the marginal rate of substitution.

1 If the indifference curve is *steep*, the marginal rate of substitution is *high*. The person is willing to give up a large quantity of good *y* in exchange for a small quantity of good *x* while remaining indifferent

2 If the indifference curve is *flat*, the marginal rate of substitution is *low*. The person is willing to give up only a small amount of good *y* in exchange for a large amount of good *x* to remain indifferent

Figure 8.4 shows you how to calculate the marginal rate of substitution. Suppose that Lisa drinks 6 six-packs and watches 2 films at point *C* on indifference curve I_1. To measure her marginal rate of substitution, we measure the absolute magnitude of the slope of the indifference curve at point *C*. To measure this magnitude, place a straight line against, or tangent to, the indifference curve at point *C*. Along that line, as the quantity of cola decreases by 10 six-packs, the number of films increases by 5 – 2 six-packs per film. So at point *C*, Lisa is willing to give up cola for films at the rate of 2 six-packs per film – a marginal rate of substitution of 2.

Now, suppose that Lisa sees 6 films and drinks 1.5 six-packs at point *G* in Figure 8.4. Her marginal rate of substitution is now measured by the magnitude of the slope of the indifference curve at point *G*. That slope is the same as the slope of the tangent to the indifference curve at point *G*. Here, as cola consumption increases by 4.5 six-packs, film consumption decreases by 9 – an average of $^1/_2$ six-packs per film. So at point *G*, Lisa is willing to give up cola for films at the rate of $^1/_2$ six-packs per film – a marginal rate of substitution of $^1/_2$.

As Lisa sees more films and drinks less cola, her marginal rate of substitution diminishes. Diminishing marginal rate of substitution is the key assumption of consumer theory. The assumption of **diminishing marginal rate of substitution** is a general tendency for the marginal rate of substitution to diminish as the consumer moves along an indifference curve, increasing consumption of the good on the *x*-axis and decreasing consumption of the good on the *y*-axis.

Figure 8.4

The Marginal Rate of Substitution

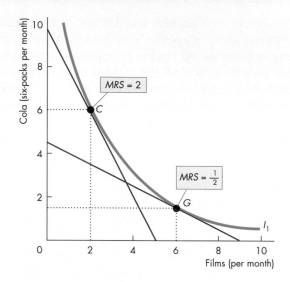

The magnitude of the slope of an indifference curve is called the marginal rate of substitution (*MRS*). The red line at point *C* tells us that Lisa is willing to give up 10 six-packs to see 5 films. Her marginal rate of substitution at point *C* is 10 divided by 5, which equals 2. The red line at point *G* tells us that Lisa is willing to give up 4.5 six-packs to see 9 films. Her marginal rate of substitution at point *G* is 4.5 divided by 9, which equals 1/2.

Your Own Diminishing Marginal Rate of Substitution

Think about your own diminishing marginal rate of substitution. Suppose that in one month you drink 10 six-packs of cola and see no films. You would probably be happy to give up lots of cans of cola just to see one film. But now suppose that in a month, you see 6 films and drink only 1 six-pack of cola. Most likely, you will probably not now be willing to give up a few cans of cola to see an extra film. As a general rule, the greater the number of films you see, the smaller is the quantity of cola you will give up to see an extra film.

The shape of the indifference curves incorporates the principle of the diminishing marginal rate of substitution because the curves are bowed towards the origin. The tightness of the bend of an indifference curve tells us how willing a person is to substitute one good for another while remaining indifferent. The examples that follow will make this point clear.

Degree of Substitutability

Most of us would not regard films and cola as being close substitutes for each other. Substitutes are goods that can be used in place of each other. But to some degree, we are willing to substitute between these two goods. No matter how enthusiastic you are for cola, there is surely some increase in the number of films you can see that will compensate you for being deprived of a can of cola. Similarly, no matter how addicted you are to films, surely some number of cans of cola will compensate you for being deprived of seeing one film. A person's indifference curves for films and cola might look something like those shown in Figure 8.5(a).

Close Substitutes

Some goods substitute so easily for each other that most of us do not even notice which we are consuming. The different brands of personal computers are an example. As long as it runs "Intel inside" and runs Windows, most of us don't care whether our PC is a

Dell, a Compaq, an Elonex or any of a dozen other brands. The same holds true for marker pens. Most of us don't care whether we use a marker pen from the university bookshop or the local supermarket. When two goods are perfect substitutes, their indifference curves are straight lines that slope downward, as Figure 8.5(b) illustrates. The marginal rate of substitution between perfect substitutes is constant.

Complements

Some goods cannot substitute for each other at all. Instead, they are complements. The complements in Figure 8.5(c) are left and right running shoes. Indifference curves of perfect complements are L-shaped. For most of us, one left running shoe and one right running shoe are as good as one left running shoe and two right ones. Having two of each is preferred to having one of each, but two of one and one of the other is no better than one of each.

The extreme cases of perfect substitutes and perfect complements shown here don't often happen in reality. But they do illustrate that the shape of the indifference

Figure 8.5

The Degree of Substitutability

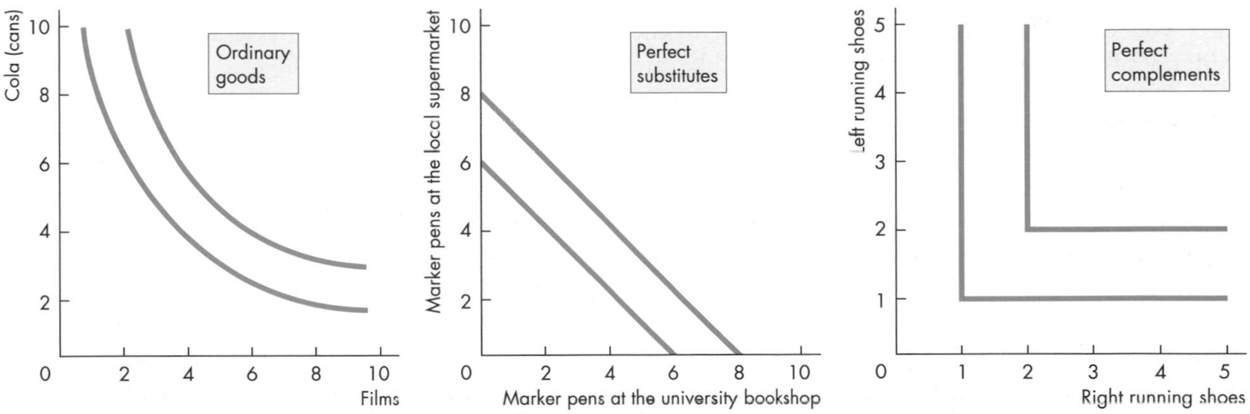

(a) Ordinary goods   **(b) Perfect substitutes**   **(c) Perfect complements**

The shape of the indifference curves reveals the degree of substitutability between two goods. Part (a) shows the indifference curves for two ordinary goods: films and cola. To consume less cola and remain indifferent, one must see more films. The number of films that compensates for a reduction in cola increases as less cola is consumed.

Part (b) shows the indifference curves for two perfect substitutes. For the consumer to remain indifferent, one fewer marker pen from the local supermarket must be replaced by one extra marker pen from the university bookshop. Part (c) shows two perfect complements – goods that cannot be substituted for each other at all. Two left running shoes with one right running shoe is no better than one of each. But having two of each is preferred to having one of each.

*"With the pork I'd recommend
an Alsation white or a coke."*

curve shows the degree of substitutability between two goods. The more perfectly substitutable the two goods, the more nearly are their indifference curves straight lines and the less quickly does the marginal rate of substitution diminish. Poor substitutes for each other have tightly curved indifference curves, approaching the shape of those shown in Figure 8.5(c).

As you can see in the cartoon, according to the waiter's preferences, Alsatian white and Coke are perfect substitutes and each is a complement of pork. We hope the customers agree with him.

The two components of the model of household choice are now in place: the budget line and the preference map. We will use these components to work out the consumer's choice.

Predicting Consumer Behaviour

We are now going to develop a model to predict the quantities of films and cola that Lisa *chooses* to buy. Figure 8.6 shows Lisa's budget line from Figure 8.1 and her indifference curves from Figure 8.3(b). We assume that Lisa consumes at her best affordable point, which is 2 films and 6 six-packs of cola – point *C*. Here Lisa:

1   Is on her budget line.
2   Is on the highest attainable indifference curve.
3   Has a marginal rate of substitution between films and cola equal to the relative price of films and cola.

For every point inside the budget line, such as point *I* in Figure 8.6, there are points on the budget line that Lisa prefers. For example, she prefers all the points on

Figure 8.6

The Best Affordable Point

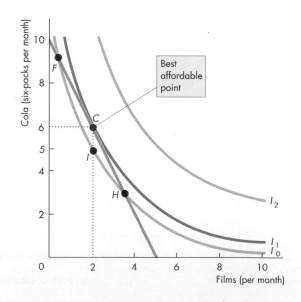

Lisa's best affordable point is *C*. At that point, she is on her budget line and also on the highest attainable indifference curve. At a point such as *H*, Lisa is willing to give up more films in exchange for cola than she has to. She can move to point *I*, which is just as good as point *H* and have some unspent income. She can spend that income and move to *C*, a point that she prefers to point *I*.

the budget line between *F* and *H* to point *I*. So she chooses a point on the budget line.

Every point on the budget line lies on an indifference curve. For example, point *H* lies on the indifference curve I_0. At point *H* in Figure 8.6, Lisa's marginal rate of substitution is less than the relative price. Lisa is willing to give up more films in exchange for cola than the budget line says she must give up. So Lisa moves along her budget line towards point *C*. As Lisa moves, she passes through a number of indifference curves (not shown in the figure) located between I_0 and I_1. All of these indifference curves are higher than I_0 and therefore Lisa prefers any point on them to point *H*. But when Lisa gets to point *C*, she is on the highest attainable indifference curve. If she keeps moving along the budget line, she starts to encounter indifference curves that are lower than I_1. So Lisa chooses point *C*.

At the best affordable point, the marginal rate of substitution (the magnitude of the slope of the indifference curve) equals the relative price (the magnitude of the slope of the budget line). That is, at the best affordable point, the budget line is tangential to the indifference curve.

You can now use this model of household choice to predict the effects on consumption of changes in prices and income. We'll begin by studying the effects of a price change.

A Change in Price

The effect of a change in price on the quantity of a good consumed is called the **price effect**. We will use Figure 8.7(a) to work out the price effect of a fall in the price of a cinema ticket. We start with tickets costing £6 each, cola costing £3 a six-pack, and with Lisa's income at £30 a month. In this situation, she consumes at point *C*, where her budget line is tangent to her highest attainable indifference curve, I_1. She consumes 6 six-packs and 2 films a month.

Now suppose that the price of a cinema ticket falls to £3. With a lower price of a ticket, the budget line rotates outward and becomes flatter. (Check back with Figure 8.2(a) for a reminder on how a price change affects the budget line.) The new budget line is the darker orange line in Figure 8.7(a). Lisa's best affordable point is *J*, where she sees 5 films and consumes 5 six-packs of cola. She cuts her cola consumption from 6 to 5 six-packs, and increases the number of films she sees from 2 to 5 a month. Lisa substitutes films for cola when the price of a cinema ticket falls and the price of cola and her income remain constant.

Figure 8.7

Price Effect and Demand Curve

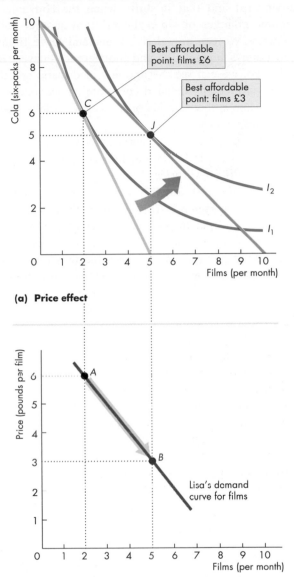

(a) Price effect

(b) Demand curve

Initially, Lisa consumes at point *C* in part (a). If the price of a cinema ticket falls from £6 to £3, she consumes at point *J*. The increase in films from 2 to 5 per month and the decrease in cola from 6 to 5 six-packs is the price effect. When the price of a cinema ticket falls, Lisa sees more films. She also consumes less cola.

Part (b) shows Lisa's demand curve for films. When the price of a ticket is £6, she sees 2 a month, at point *A*. When the price of a ticket falls to £3, she sees 5 a month, at point *B*. Lisa's demand curve traces out her best affordable quantity of films as the price of a cinema ticket varies.

The Demand Curve

In Chapter 3, we asserted that the demand curve slopes downward and that it shifts when the consumer's income changes or when the price of another good changes. We can now derive a demand curve from a consumer's budget line and indifference curves. By doing so, we can see that the law of demand and the downward-sloping demand curve are consequences of the consumer choosing his or her best affordable combination of goods.

To derive Lisa's demand curve for films, we lower the price of a cinema ticket and find her best affordable point at different prices, holding all other things constant. We just did this for two ticket prices in Figure 8.7(a). Figure 8.7(b) highlights these two prices and two points that lie on Lisa's demand curve for films. When the price of a cinema ticket is £6, Lisa sees 2 films a month at point A. When the price falls to £3, she increases the number of films she sees to 5 films a month at point B. The demand curve is made up of these two points plus all the other points of Lisa's best affordable consumption of films at each ticket price – more than £6, between £6 and £3, and less than £3 – given the price of cola and Lisa's income. As you can see, Lisa's demand curve for films slopes downward – the lower the price of a cinema ticket, the more films she watches each month. This is the law of demand.

Next, let's examine how Lisa adjusts her consumption when her income changes.

A Change in Income

The effect of a change in income on consumption is called the **income effect**. Figure 8.8(a) shows the income effect when Lisa's income falls. With an income of £30, the price of a cinema ticket £3 and the price of cola £3 a six-pack, she consumes at point J – 5 films and 5 six-packs. If her income falls to £21, she consumes at point K – 4 films and 3 six-packs. So when Lisa's income falls, she consumes less of both goods. Films and cola are normal goods.

The Demand Curve and the Income Effect

A change in income leads to a shift in the demand curve, as shown in Figure 8.8(b). With an income of £30, Lisa's demand curve is D_0, the same as in Figure 8.7. But when her income falls to £21, she plans to see fewer films at each price, so her demand curve shifts leftward to D_1.

Figure 8.8

Income Effect and Change in Demand

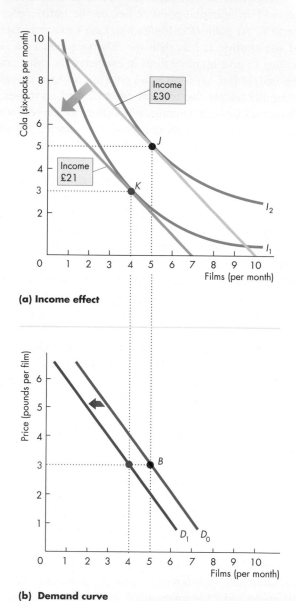

(a) Income effect

(b) Demand curve

When Lisa's income is £30, she consumes at point J in part (a) and her demand for films is D_0 in part (b). A change in income shifts the budget line, changes the best affordable point and shifts the demand curve.

In part (a), when Lisa's income decreases from £30 to £21, she consumes at point K. Lisa sees fewer films and consumes less cola. In part (b), when Lisa's income decreases to £21, her demand curve for films shifts leftward to D_1. Lisa's demand for films decreases because she now sees fewer films at each price.

Substitution Effect and Income Effect

For a normal good, a fall in price *always* increases the quantity bought. We can prove this assertion by dividing the price effect into two parts:

◆ The substitution effect
◆ The income effect

Figure 8.9(a) shows the price effect and Figure 8.9(b) divides the price effect into its two parts.

Substitution Effect

The **substitution effect** is the effect of a change in price on the quantities bought when the consumer (hypothetically) remains indifferent between the original and the new combinations of goods consumed. To work out Lisa's substitution effect, when the price of a cinema ticket falls, we cut her income by enough to leave her on the same indifference curve as before.

When the price of a ticket falls from £6 to £3, let's suppose (hypothetically) that we cut Lisa's income to £21. What's special about £21? It is the income that is just enough, at the new ticket price, to keep Lisa's best affordable point on the same indifference curve as her original consumption point C. Now Lisa's budget line is the light orange line in Figure 8.9(b). With the lower ticket price and less income, Lisa's best affordable point is K on indifference curve I_1. The move from C to K is the substitution effect of the price change. The substitution effect of the fall in the ticket price is an increase in the consumption of films from 2 to 4. The direction of the substitution effect never varies: when the relative price of a good falls, the consumer substitutes more of that good for the other good.

Income Effect

To calculate the substitution effect, we gave Lisa a £9 pay cut. Now let's give Lisa her £9 back. The £9 increase in income shifts Lisa's budget line outward, as shown in Figure 8.9(b). The slope of the budget line does not change because both prices remain constant. This change in Lisa's budget line is similar to the one illustrated in Figure 8.8. As Lisa's budget line shifts outward, her best affordable point becomes J on indifference curve I_2 in Figure 8.9(b). The move from K to J is the income effect of the price change: as Lisa's income increases, she increases her consumption of films. For Lisa, films are a normal good. For a normal good, the income effect reinforces the substitution effect.

Figure 8.9

Substitution Effect and Income Effect

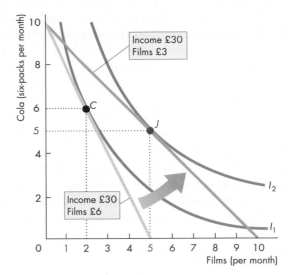

(a) Price effect

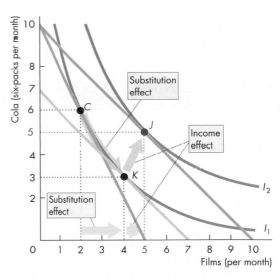

(b) Substitution effect and income effect

The price effect in part (a) can be separated into a substitution effect and an income effect in part (b). To isolate the substitution effect, we confront Lisa with the new price but keep her on her original indifference curve, I_1. The substitution effect is the move from C to K. To isolate the income effect, we confront Lisa with the new price of films but increase her income so that she can move from the original indifference curve, I_1, to the new one, I_2. The income effect is the move from K to J.

Inferior Goods

The example that we have just studied is that of a change in the price of a normal good. The effect of a change in the price of an inferior good is different. Recall that an inferior good is one whose consumption decreases as income increases. For an inferior good, the income effect is negative. Thus for an inferior good a lower price does not always lead to an increase in the quantity demanded. The lower price has a substitution effect that increases the quantity demanded. But the lower price also has a negative income effect, which reduces the demand for the inferior good. Thus the negative income effect offsets the substitution effect to some degree. If the negative income effect exceeded the positive substitution effect, the demand curve would slope upward. The substitution effect usually dominates – confirming the law of demand.

Back to the Facts

We have used the indifference curve to explain how consumer spending has changed over the years. Spending patterns are determined by best affordable choices and these choices change over time as incomes and prices change.

Review Quiz

1   When a consumer chooses the combination of goods and services to buy, what is she or he trying to achieve?
2   Using the terms "budget line", "marginal rate of substitution" and "relative price", explain the conditions required for the consumer to find the best affordable combination of goods and services to buy.
3   If the price of a normal good falls, what happens to the quantity demanded of that good?
4   If the consumer's income falls, what happens to the demand for a normal good?
5   Into what two effects can we divide the effect of a price change?
6   For a normal good, does the income effect reinforce the substitution effect or does it partly offset the substitution?

The model of household choice can explain many other household choices. Let's look at one of them: the choice between work and leisure.

Work–Leisure Choices

Households make many choices other than those about how to spend their income on the various goods and services available. We can use the model of consumer choice to explain a wide range of other household choices such as how much labour to supply and how much time to spend on leisure rather than work.

Labour Supply

Every week, we allocate hours between working – called *labour* – and all other activities – called *leisure*. We can use the theory of household choice to show how we allocate our time between labour and leisure.

The more hours we spend on leisure, the smaller is our income. The relationship between leisure and income is described by an *income–time budget line*. The orange lines in Figure 8.10(a) show Lisa's income–time budget lines. If Lisa devotes the entire week to leisure – 168 hours – she has no income and is at point Z. By supplying labour in exchange for a wage, she can convert hours into income along the time–budget line.

The slope of the time–budget line is determined by the hourly wage rate. If the wage rate is £2 an hour, Lisa faces the flattest budget line. If she worked for 68 hours a week, she would make an income of £136 a week. If the wage rate is £4 an hour, she faces the middle budget line. If the wage rate is £6 an hour, she faces the steepest budget line.

Lisa buys leisure by not supplying labour and by forgoing income. The opportunity cost of an hour of leisure is the hourly wage rate forgone.

Figure 8.10(a) also shows Lisa's indifference curves for income and leisure. Lisa chooses her best attainable point. This choice of income and time allocation is just like her choice of films and cola. She gets onto the highest possible indifference curve by making her marginal rate of substitution between income and leisure equal to her wage rate. Lisa's choice depends on the wage rate she can earn. At a wage rate of £2 an hour, Lisa chooses point A and works 20 hours a week (168 – 148) for an income of £40 a week. At a wage rate of £4 an hour, she chooses point B and works 35 hours a week (168 – 133) for an income of £140 a week. At a wage rate of £6 an hour, she chooses point C and works 30 hours a week (168 – 138) for an income of £180 a week.

Figure 8.10

The Supply of Labour

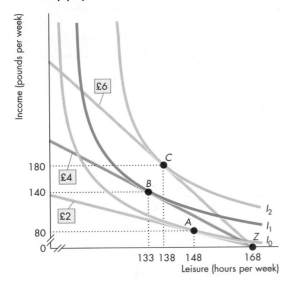

(a) Time allocation decision

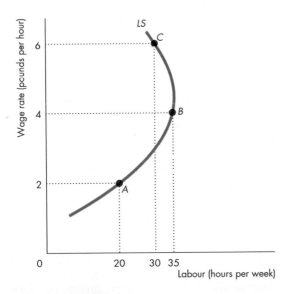

(b) Labour supply curve

In part (a), at a wage rate of £2 an hour, Lisa takes 148 hours of leisure and works 20 hours a week at point *A*. If the wage rate increases from £2 to £4 an hour, she decreases her leisure to 133 hours and increases her work to 35 hours a week at point *B*. But if the wage rate increases from £4 to £6 an hour, Lisa *increases* her leisure to 138 hours and *decreases* her work to 30 hours a week at point *C*. Part (b) shows Lisa's labour supply curve. Points *A*, *B* and *C* on the supply curve correspond to Lisa's choices on her income–time budget line in part (a).

The Labour Supply Curve

Figure 8.10(b) shows Lisa's labour supply curve. This curve shows that as the wage rate increases from £2 an hour to £4 an hour, Lisa increases the quantity of labour supplied from 20 hours a week to 35 hours a week. But when the wage rate increases to £6 an hour, she decreases her quantity of labour supplied to 30 hours a week.

Lisa's supply of labour is similar to that for the economy as a whole. As wage rates have increased. At first, this pattern seems puzzling. We've seen that the hourly wage rate is the opportunity cost of leisure. So a higher wage rate means a higher opportunity cost of leisure. This fact on its own leads to a decrease in leisure and an increase in work hours. But instead, we've cut our work hours. Why? Because our incomes have increased. As the real wage rate increases, real incomes increase, so people demand more of all normal goods. Leisure is a normal good, so as incomes increase, people demand more leisure.

The higher wage rate has both a *substitution effect* and an *income effect*. The higher wage rate increases the opportunity cost of leisure and so leads to a substitution effect away from leisure. The higher wage rate increases income and so leads to an income effect towards more leisure.

This theory of household choice can explain why the average working week has fallen steadily from 70 hours a week in the nineteenth century to 35 hours a week today. Although people substitute work for leisure as wage rates increase, they also use their higher incomes to consume more leisure. The theory can also explain why more women now have jobs in the labour market. Increasing wage rates and improvements in their job opportunities have led to a substitution effect away from working at home and towards working in the labour market.

Review Quiz

1   What is the opportunity cost of leisure?
2   Why might a rise in the wage rate lead to an increase in leisure and a decrease in work hours?

You have now completed your study of consumer choice. But before moving on to the next topic, spend a bit of time with *Reading Between the Lines* on pp. 172–173 and see how we can use indifference curves to explain how you choose your lunch.

Reading Between the Lines

Indifference Curves: Gourmet sandwiches or American hamburgers?

The Business, 2 November 2003

Le sandwich is upper crust as French say adieu to long lunch

Pierre Tran

John Montague, the fourth Earl of Sandwich, invented the sandwich but it has taken the French genius for food to raise this English invention to new levels of refinement and profit.

Fifteen years ago, the French spent an average 75 minutes at a leisurely sit-down lunch with a carafe of wine. Now executives and staff are abandoning restaurants for sandwiches, eaten hurriedly in a shop or at their office desks, British or American style.

Sandwiches are more popular because the French want to spend less time on midday meals. These days their lunch breaks are likely to last no more than 25 minutes. They use the time gained to work, shop, go to the gym or get home earlier.

This being France, the country's sandwich is more than limp cheese or boring ham slices between bread. Gastronomic legitimacy has been conferred on the snack by a

Michelin-garlanded chef, Alain Ducasses. . . . Their gourmet fare sells at an eye-watering €7 ($4.80) to €10 each.

Cheaper sandwich shops are also booming. The market for French-style fillings in long split loaves or baguettes grew yearly by between 8% and 12% over the past five years, outstripping 1.85% growth in the classic restaurant sector . . .

Enthusiasm for sandwiches has hit the French hamburger market, which has shrunk to two big players: McDonald's and Quick. For every burger sold, seven French-style sandwiches are bought. 'The French are bored with hamburgers, which tend to be driven by one product – burger and fries', Boutboul says (*a restaurant consultant*). McDonald's has fought back with a more varied menu but this lacked credibility, he said. . . . Burger King withdrew from France some years ago.

© The Business, 2003. Reprinted with permission.

The Essence of the Story

◆ The working French want to spend less time over lunch—just 25 minutes compared to 75 minutes 15 years ago.

◆ The traditional British sandwich is becoming the most popular fast food for a quick lunch in France.

◆ A top of the range gourmet sandwich in France might cost between €7 and €10.

◆ French enthusiasm for the sandwich as their favourite fast food has led to a fall in the demand for American hamburgers.

Economic Analysis

◆ Lisa is a business student taking a year's work placement in Paris. She only has half an hour for lunch and so has to choose between fast foods.

◆ Figure 1 shows Lisa's indifference curves, I_0, I_1 and I_2 for best gourmet French sandwiches and cheaper hamburgers.

◆ The magnitude of the slope of an indifference curve is the marginal rate of substitution (*MRS*). The *MRS* tells how many units of gourmet sandwiches Lisa is willing to give up to gain one more hamburger while remaining on the same indifference curve.

◆ If Lisa consumes on indifference curve I_0, at point *A*, she is willing to give up one gourmet sandwich to get one extra hamburger—the move from *A* to *B*.

◆ On indifference curve I_2, at point *C*, she is willing to give up less than one gourmet sandwich to get one extra hamburger—the move from *C* to *D*.

◆ Figure 2 shows Lisa's choices for fast-food lunches each week.

◆ When Lisa was a student, the highest indifference curve she could reach was I_0. Her best affordable point was 4 hamburgers and no gourmet sandwiches a week.

◆ With her new job, the highest indifference curve Lisa can reach is I_2. Her best affordable point is now 2 hamburgers and 3 gourmet sandwiches each week.

◆ French consumers, like Lisa, prefer gourmet sandwiches to hamburgers. By not eating in restaurants, their incomes have risen like Lisa's, and they are buying more gourmet sandwiches and fewer hamburgers.

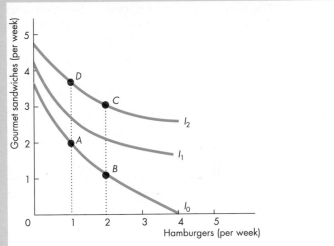

Figure 1 Preferences for fast food lunches

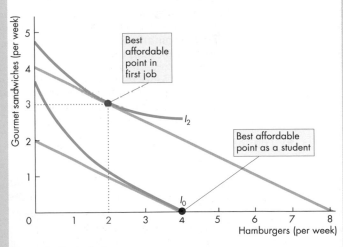

Figure 2 Lisa's choices

Summary

Key Points

Consumption Possibilities
(pp. 160–162)

◆ The budget line is the boundary between what a household can and cannot afford given its income and the prices of goods.

◆ The point at which the budget line intersects the y-axis is the household's real income in terms of the good measured on that axis.

◆ The magnitude of the slope of the budget line is the relative price of the good measured on the x-axis in terms of the good measured on the y-axis.

◆ A change in price changes the slope of the budget line. A change in income shifts the budget line but does not change its slope.

Preferences and Indifference Curves (pp. 163–166)

◆ A consumer's preferences can be represented by indifference curves. An indifference curve joins all the combinations of goods between which the consumer is indifferent.

◆ A consumer prefers any point above an indifference curve to any point on it and any point on an indifference curve to any point below it. Indifference curves bow towards the origin.

◆ The magnitude of the slope of an indifference curve is called the marginal rate of substitution.

◆ The marginal rate of substitution diminishes as consumption of the good measured on the y-axis decreases and consumption of the good measured on the x-axis increases.

Predicting Consumer Behaviour
(pp. 166–170)

◆ A household consumes at its best affordable point. This point is on the budget line and on the highest attainable indifference curve and has a marginal rate of substitution equal to the relative price.

◆ The price effect can be divided into a substitution effect and an income effect.

◆ The substitution effect is the effect of a change in price on consumption when the consumer (hypothetically) remains indifferent between the original situation and the new situation.

◆ The substitution always results in an increase in consumption of the good whose relative price has decreased.

◆ The income effect is the effect of change in income on consumption.

◆ For a normal good, the income effect reinforces the substitution effect. For an inferior good, the income effect offsets the substitution effect.

Work–Leisure Choices
(pp. 170–171)

◆ The indifference curve model of household choice enables us to understand how a household allocates its time between leisure and work.

◆ Work hours have decreased and leisure hours have increased because the income effect on the demand for leisure has been greater than the substitution effect.

Key Figures

Key Terms

Problems

*1 Sara has an income of €12 a week. Popcorn costs €3 a bag, and cola costs €3 a can.

   a What is Sara's real income in terms of cola?

   b What is her real income in terms of popcorn?

   c What is the relative price of cola in terms of popcorn?

   d What is the opportunity cost of a can of cola?

   e Calculate the equation for Sara's budget line (placing bags of popcorn on the left side).

   f Draw a graph of Sara's budget line with cola on the x-axis.

   g In part (f), what is the slope of Sara's budget line? What does it represent?

2 Marc has an income of €20 per week. CDs cost €10 each and beer costs €5 a can.

   a What is Marc's real income in terms of beer?

   b What is his real income in terms of CDs?

   c What is the relative price of beer in terms of CDs?

   d What is the opportunity cost of a can of beer?

   e Calculate the equation for Marc's budget line (placing cans of beer on the left side).

   f Draw a graph of Marc's budget line with CDs on the x-axis.

   g In part (f), what is the slope of Marc's budget line? What does it represent?

*3 Sara's income and the prices she faces are the same as in problem 1. The figure illustrates Sara's preferences.

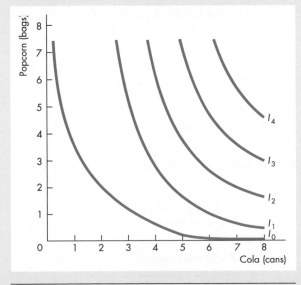

   a What are the quantities of popcorn and cola that Sara buys?

   b What is Sara's marginal rate of substitution of popcorn for cola at the point at which she consumes?

4 Marc's income and the prices he faces are the same as in problem 2. The figure illustrates his preferences.

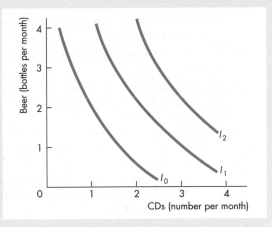

   a What are the quantities of beer and CDs that Marc buys?

   b What is Marc's marginal rate of substitution of CDs for beer at the point at which he consumes?

*5 Now suppose that in the situation described in problem 3, the price of cola falls to €1.50 per can but the price of popcorn and Sara's income remain constant.

   a Find the new quantities of cola and popcorn that Sara buys.

   b Find two points on Sara's demand curve for cola.

   c Find the substitution effect of the price change.

   d Find the income effect of the price change.

   e Is cola a normal good or an inferior good for Sara?

   f Is popcorn a normal good or an inferior good for Sara?

6 Now suppose that in problem 4, the price of a CD falls to €5 and the price of beer and Marc's income remain constant.

   a Find the new quantities of beer and CDs that Marc buys.

   b Find two points on Marc's demand curve for CDs.

   c Find the substitution effect of the price change.

   d Find the income effect of the price change.

   e Are CDs a normal good or an inferior good for Marc?

   f Is beer a normal good or an inferior good for Marc?

*Solutions to odd-numbered problems are available on Parkin *Interactive.*

*7 Pam buys slices of cake and books. The price of cake is €1 a slice and the price of a book is €2. Each month, Pam spends all of her income and buys 30 slices of cake and 5 books. Next month, the price of cake will fall to 50 cents a slice and the price of a book will rise to €5. Assume that Pam's preference map is similar to that in Figure. 8.5(a). Use a graph to answer the following questions.

   a Will Pam be able to buy 30 slices of cake and 5 books next month?

   b Will Pam want to buy 30 slices of cake and 5 books?

   c Which situation does Pam prefer: cake at €1 a slice and books at €2 each, or cake at 50 cents a slice and books at €3 each?

   d If Pam changes the quantities that she buys next month, which good will she buy more of and which will she buy less of?

   e When the prices change next month, will there be both an income effect and a substitution effect at work or just one of them?

8 Yangjie buys smoothies and sushi. The price of a smoothie is €5, and the price of sushi is €1 a piece. Each month, Yangjie spends all of her income and buys 10 smoothies and 20 pieces of sushi. Next month, the price of a smoothie will fall to €3 and the price of sushi will rise to €2 a piece. Assume that Yangjie's preference map is similar to that in Figure 8.5(a). Use a graph to answer the following questions.

   a Will Yangjie be able to buy 10 smoothies and 20 pieces of sushi next month?

   b Will Yangjie want to buy 10 smoothies and 20 pieces of sushi? Explain your answer.

   c Which situation does Yangjie prefer: smoothies at €5 each and sushi at €1 a piece or smoothies at €3 each and sushi at €2 a piece?

   d If Yangjie changes the quantities that she buys next month, which good will she buy more of and which will she buy less of?

   e When the prices change next month, will there be both an income effect and a substitution effect at work or just one of them? Explain.

*9 Yangjie can earn €15 an hour and she chooses to work for 40 hours a week. Then Yangjie's wage rate increases to €25 an hour. If Yangjie now chooses to work for more than 40 hours a week, describe her indifference curves and explain her choice in terms of the income effect and the substitution effect.

10 If when Yangjie's wage rate increases to €25 an hour. she chooses to work for fewer than 40 hours a week, describe her indifference curves and explain her choice in terms of the income effect and the substitution effect.

Critical Thinking

1 Read the article in *Reading Between the Lines* on pp. 172–173 and then answer the following questions:

   a Suppose that the price of a gourmet sandwich halved while Lisa is still a student.

      i What would happen to the slope of her budget line?

      ii Would Lisa buy more or fewer gourmet sandwiches? Use an indifference curve drawing to explain your answer.

   b Lisa gets her first job. Suppose she finds gourmet sandwiches a bit boring and now prefers hamburgers.

      i How does the shape of her indifference curves between gourmet sandwiches and hamburgers change?

      ii Use a graph to explain whether she will buy more or less gourmet sandwiches if the price of a gourmet sandwich does not change.

      iii Will gourmet sandwiches be a luxury good or an inferior good for Lisa now?

2 VAT is a tax on most goods and services in Europe. Until recently, there was no VAT on newspapers and magazines in the United Kingdom. The European Union has made the United Kingdom impose VAT on newspapers and magazines. When this change occurred:

   a What happened to the relative price of magazines and coffee?

   b What happened to the budget line showing the quantities of magazines and coffee you can buy?

   c How would your purchases of magazines and coffee change?

   d Why would the European Union want to impose the tax on all goods and services and not allow some to be free of tax?

Web Exercise

Use the link on *Parkin Interactive* to work the following exercise.

1 Read the Economics in History feature called Understanding Human Behaviour, then answer the following questions:

   a What is the role of technology in explaining women's increased participation in the workforce over the past 100 years? Use a graph to illustrate your answer.

   b On the basis of your experience and study of economics, do you think that family decisions are in any part economic decisions? Explain.

Part 3
Firms and Markets

Understanding Firms and Markets

Our economy is constantly changing. Every year, new goods appear and old ones disappear. New firms are born and old ones die. This process of change is initiated and managed by firms operating in markets.

When a new product is invented, just one or two firms sell it initially. For example, when the personal computer first became available, there was an Apple and an IBM. The IBM-PC had just one operating system, DOS, made by Microsoft. One firm, Intel, made the chip that ran the IBM-PC. These are examples of *monopoly* that you will meet in Chapter 12.

But not all industries with just one producer are monopolies. In many cases, the firm that is first to produce a new good faces severe competition from new rivals. As demand increases to make space for more than one firm, an industry becomes increasingly competitive. Even with just two rivals, the industry changes its face in a dramatic way. *Duopoly* – two firms competing – illustrates this dramatic change. The two firms must pay close attention to each other's production and prices and must predict the effects of their own actions on the actions of the other firm. As the number of rivals grows, the industry becomes an *oligopoly*, a market in which a small number of firms devise strategies and pay close attention to the strategies of their competitors.

With the continued arrival of new firms in an industry, the market eventually becomes competitive. Competition might be limited because each firm produces its own special version or brand of a good. This case is called *monopolistic competition* because it has elements of both monopoly and competition. Chapter 13 explores the behaviour of firms in monopolistic competition and oligopoly.

When competition is extreme, a case that we call *perfect competition*, the market changes again, and in a dramatic way. Now the firm is unable to influence the price at which it sells its output. Chapter 11 explains this case.

Often, an industry that is competitive becomes less so as bigger and more successful firms swallow up the smaller firms, either by driving them out of business or by acquiring their assets. Through this process, an industry might return to oligopoly or even monopoly. You can see such a movement in the car making, banking and textbook publishing industries today.

By studying firms and markets, we gain a deeper understanding of the forces that allocate scarce resources and begin to see the anatomy of the invisible hand.

We begin, in Chapters 9 and 10, by describing the problems that all firms share and learn about the structure of a firm's costs.

Chapter 9

Organizing Production

After studying this chapter you will be able to:

◆ Explain what a firm is and describe the economic problems that *all* firms face

◆ Distinguish between technological efficiency and economic efficiency

◆ Define the principal–agent problem and describe how different types of business organizations cope with this problem

◆ Describe and distinguish between the different markets in which firms operate

◆ Explain why firms coordinate some economic activities and markets coordinate others

Spinning a Web

When Tim Berners-Lee invented the World Wide Web in 1990, he paved the way for the creation of thousands of profitable businesses. One of these is SAP, Europe's biggest software producer. How does SAP and the other 20 million firms that operate in Europe make business decisions? How do businesses operate efficiently? Why do firms produce some things but outsource others? Find out in this chapter.

The Firm and its Economic Problem

The 20 million firms in the European Union differ in their size and in the scope of what they do. But they all perform the same basic economic functions. Each **firm** is an institution that hires productive resources and organizes those resources to produce and sell goods and services.

Our goal is to predict firm behaviour. To do so, we need to know a firm's goals and the constraints it faces. We begin with the goals.

The Firm's Goal

Most firms make statements about their goals in their annual reports and accounts. If you read these reports you will see that some firms talk about making a quality product, others about business growth, market share, or job satisfaction for their workforce. All of these goals are pursued, but they are not the fundamental goal. They are means to that goal.

A firm's fundamental goal is to maximize profit. A firm that does not aim for maximum profit will eventually go out of business or be bought by firms that do aim to maximize profit.

What is the profit that a firm seeks to maximize? To answer this question, let's look at an example of a small airport restaurant called Bites run by its owner.

Measuring a Firm's Profit

Bites is a successful restaurant business. The restaurant earns a revenue of €400,000 a year. Its expenses are €80,000 a year for foods, €20,000 for energy, water and other utilities bills, €120,000 for labour, and €10,000 in interest on a bank loan. With receipts of €400,000 and expenses of €230,000, Bites annual surplus is €170,000.

Bites' accountant lowers this number by €20,000, to cover the depreciation (fall in value) of the firm's buildings and equipment during the year. (Accountants use EU rules based on standards established by the accounting profession to calculate the depreciation.) So the accountant reports that Bites' profit is €150,000 a year.

The accountant measures cost and profit to ensure that the firm pays the correct amount of income tax and to show the bank how its loan has been used. But we want to predict the decisions that a firm makes. These decisions respond to *opportunity cost* and *economic profit*.

Opportunity Cost

The opportunity cost of any action is the highest-valued alternative forgone. The action that you choose not to do – the highest-valued alternative forgone – is the cost of the action that you choose to do. For a firm, the opportunity cost of production is the value of the firm's best alternative use of its resources.

Opportunity cost is a real alternative forgone. But so that we can compare the cost of one action with that of another action, we express opportunity cost in money units. A firm's opportunity costs are:

◆ Explicit costs
◆ Implicit costs

Explicit Costs

Explicit costs are paid in money. The amount paid for a resource that could have been spent on something else, so it is the opportunity cost of using the resource. For Bites, its expenditures on foods, utilities, wages and bank interest are explicit costs.

Implicit Costs

A firm incurs implicit costs when it forgoes an alternative action but does not make a payment. A firm incurs implicit costs when it:

1 Uses its own capital.

2 Uses its owner's time or financial resources.

The cost of using its own capital is an implicit cost – and an opportunity cost – because the firm could rent the capital to another firm. The rental income forgone is the firm's opportunity cost of using its own capital. This opportunity cost is called the **implicit rental rate** of capital.

People rent houses, apartments, cars, telephones and videotapes. Firms rent photocopiers, earth-moving equipment, satellite-launching services and so on. If a firm rents capital, it incurs an *explicit* cost. If a firm buys the capital it uses, it incurs an *implicit* cost. The implicit rental rate of capital is made up of:

1 Economic depreciation.

2 Interest forgone.

Economic depreciation is change in the *market* value of capital over a given period. It is calculated as the market price of the capital at the beginning of the period minus its market price at the end of the period. For example, suppose that the owner of Bites could have sold the restaurant buildings and equipment on 31 December 2003, for €400,000. If she can sell the same capital on 31 December 2004, for €375,000, the economic depreciation during 2004 is €25,000 – the fall in the market value of the equipment. This €25,000 is an implicit cost of using the capital during 2004.

The funds used to buy capital could have been used for some other purpose. And in their next best use, they would have yielded a return – an interest income. This *interest forgone* is part of the opportunity cost of using the capital. For example, the owner could have bought government bonds instead of a restaurant. The interest forgone on the government bonds is an implicit cost of operating a restaurant.

Cost of Owner's Resources

A firm's owner often supplies *entrepreneurial ability* – the productive resource that organizes the business, makes business decisions, innovates, and bears the risk of running the business. The return to entrepreneurship is profit and the *average* return for supplying entrepreneurial ability is called **normal profit**. Normal profit is part of a firm's opportunity cost because it represents the cost of a forgone alternative – running another firm. If normal profit in the small restaurant business is €50,000 a year, this amount must be added to the firm's costs to determine its opportunity cost.

The owner of a firm can also supply labour (in addition to entrepreneurship). The return to labour is a wage. And the opportunity cost of the owner's time spent working for the firm is the wage income forgone by not working in the best alternative job. Suppose that the owner could have earned €40,000 a year working for someone else. By working in the restaurant business and forgoing this income, the owner incurs an opportunity cost of €40,000 a year.

Economic Profit

What is the bottom line – the profit or loss of the firm? A firm's **economic profit** is equal to its total revenue minus its opportunity cost. The firm's opportunity cost is the sum of its explicit costs and implicit costs. And the implicit costs, remember, include *normal profit*. The

return to entrepreneurial ability is greater than normal in a firm that makes a positive economic profit. And the return to entrepreneurial ability is less than normal in a firm that makes a negative economic profit – a firm that incurs an economic loss.

Economic Accounting: A Summary

Table 9.1 summarizes the economic accounting concepts using our example business, Bites. The business earns €400,000 in total revenue and its opportunity cost (explicit costs plus its implicit costs) is €365,000. So its economic profit is €35,000.

To achieve the objective of maximum economic profit, all businesses must make five basic decisions:

1 What goods and services to produce and in what quantities.

2 What techniques of production to use – how to produce.

3 How to organize and compensate its managers and workers.

4 How to market and price its products.

5 What to produce itself and what to buy from other firms.

In all these decisions, a firm's actions are limited by the constraints that it faces. We look at these constraints next.

Table 9.1

Economic Accounting

Item		Amount (euros)
Total revenue		**400,000**
Opportunity costs		
Foods	80,000	
Utilities	20,000	
Wages paid	120,000	
Bank interest paid	10,000	
Total explicit costs		**230,000**
Owner's wages forgone	40,000	
Owner's interest forgone	20,000	
Economic depreciation	25,000	
Normal profit	50,000	
Total implicit costs		**135,000**
Total cost		**365,000**
Economic profit		**35,000**

The Firm's Constraints

Three features of a firm's environment limit the maximum profit it can make. They are:

◆ Technology constraints
◆ Information constraints
◆ Market constraints

Technology Constraints

Economists define technology broadly. A **technology** is any method of producing a good or service. Technology includes the detailed designs of machines. It also includes the layout of the workplace and the organization of the firm. For example, the shopping centre is a technology for producing retail services. It is a different technology from catalogue shopping, which in turn is different from the high street stores.

It might seem surprising that a firm's profits are limited by technology. Every year we learn about the latest technological advances that will revolutionize future production and consumption. Technology is advancing, but to produce more output and gain more revenue with current technology, a firm must hire more resources and incur greater costs. At any point in time, the increase in profit that the firm can achieve is limited by the technology currently available. For example, using its current plant and workforce, BMW can produce some maximum number of cars per day. To produce more cars per day, BMW must hire more resources, which increases BMW's costs and limits the increase in profit that BMW can make by selling the additional cars.

Information Constraints

A business manager can never possess all the information needed to make decisions. Businesses lack information about the present and the future – uncertainty. For example, suppose you plan to buy a new computer for your business. When should you buy it? The answer depends on how the price is going to change in the future. Where should you buy it? The answer depends on the prices at many different suppliers. To get the best deal, you must compare the quality and price in all the different shops. The opportunity cost of actually getting all this information and making all these comparisons will exceed the cost of the computer!

Similarly, a firm is constrained by limited information about the quality and effort of its workforce, the current and future plans of its customers and the plans of its competitors. Workers may slacken off when managers believe they are working hard. Customers may switch to competing suppliers. Firms must face competition from new firms and the new products and services they offer.

Firms try to create incentive systems for workers to ensure they work hard even when no one is monitoring their efforts. Firms also spend billions every year on market research and product development. But none of these efforts and expenditures eliminates the problems of incomplete information and uncertainty. Again, the cost of coping with limited information and uncertainty itself limits profit.

Market Constraints

What each firm can sell and the price it can obtain is constrained by the willingness of customers to pay and by the prices and marketing efforts of other firms. Similarly, the resources that each firm can buy and the prices it must pay are limited by the willingness of people to work for and invest in the firm. Firms spend billions every year marketing and selling their products. Some of the most creative minds strive to find the right message that will produce a knockout television advertisement. Market constraints and the expenditures firms make to overcome them limit the profit a firm can make.

Review Quiz

1 Why is profit maximisation the ultimate goal of all firms?
2 Why do accountants and economists calculate a firm's cost and profit in different ways?
3 What are the items that make opportunity cost different from the accountants' measure of cost?
4 Why is normal profit an opportunity cost?
5 What are the constraints that each firm faces? Explain how each constraint limits the profit that a firm can make.

In the rest of this chapter and in Chapters 10 to 13, we study the decisions that firms make. You will learn how to predict a firm's behaviour as the response to the constraints that it faces and to changes in those constraints. We begin by taking a closer look at the technology constraints that firms face.

Technological and Economic Efficiency

Microsoft workers possess a large amount of human capital. But the firm uses a small amount of physical capital. In contrast, an oil extraction company employs a huge amount of drilling equipment (physical capital) and relatively little labour. Why? The answer lies in the concept of efficiency. There are two concepts of production efficiency: technological efficiency and economic efficiency. **Technological efficiency** occurs when the firm produces a given output by using the least amount of inputs. **Economic efficiency** occurs when the firm produces a given output at least cost. Let's explore the two concepts of efficiency by studying an example.

Suppose that there are four alternative techniques for making TV sets:

A *Robot production.* One person monitors the entire computer-driven process.

B *Production line.* Workers specialize in a small part of the job as the emerging TV set passes them on a production line.

C *Bench production.* Workers specialize in a small part of the job but walk from bench to bench to perform their tasks.

D *Hand-tool production.* A single worker uses a few hand tools to make a TV set.

Table 9.2 sets out the amounts of labour and capital required by each of these four methods to make 10 TV sets a day. Which of these methods are technologically efficient?

Technological Efficiency

Recall that technological efficiency occurs when the firm produces a given output by using the least inputs. Table 9.2 shows that method A uses the most capital but the least labour. Method D uses the most labour but the least capital. Methods B and C use less capital but more labour than method A and less labour but more capital than method D. Compare methods B and C. Method C requires 100 workers and 10 units of capital to produce 10 TV sets. Those same 10 TV sets can be produced by method B with 10 workers and the same 10 units of capital. Because method C uses the same amount of capital and more labour than method B, each of the other three methods is techno-logically efficient.

Table 9.2

Four Ways of Making 10 TV Sets a Day

| | Quantities of inputs | |
Method	Labour	Capital
A Robot production	1	1,000
B Production line	10	10
C Bench production	100	10
D Hand-tool production	1,000	1

Economic Efficiency

Recall that economic efficiency occurs when the firm produces a given output at least cost. Suppose that labour costs £75 per person-day and that capital costs £250 per machine-day. Table 9.3 calculates the costs of using the different methods. By inspecting the table, you can see that method B has the lowest cost. Although method A uses less labour, it uses too much expensive capital. And although method D uses less capital, it uses too much expensive labour.

Method C, which is technologically inefficient, is also economically inefficient. It uses the same amount of capital as method B but 10 times as much labour, so it costs more. A technologically inefficient method is never economically efficient.

Although method B is the economically efficient method in this example, method A or D could be economically efficient with different input prices.

First, suppose that labour costs £150 a person-day and capital costs only £1 a machine-day. Table 9.4(a) now shows the costs of making a TV set. In this case, method A is economically efficient. Capital is now so cheap relative to labour that the method that uses the most capital is the economically efficient method.

Table 9.3

The Costs of Making 10 TV Sets a Day

Method	Labour cost (£75 per day)		Capital cost (£250 per day)		Total cost cost	Cost per TV set
A	£75	+	£250,000	=	£250,075	£25,007.50
B	**750**	+	**2,500**	=	**3,250**	**325.00**
C	7,500	+	2,500	=	10,000	1,000.00
D	75,000	+	250	=	75,250	7,525.00

Table 9.4

Costs of Three Ways of Making 10 TV Sets a Day

(a) High labour costs

Method	Labour cost (£150 per day)		Capital cost (£1 per day)		Total cost	Cost per TV set
A	£150	+	£1,000	=	£1,150	£115.00
B	1,500	+	10	=	1,510	151.00
D	150,000	+	1	=	150,001	15,000.10

(b) High capital costs

Method	Labour cost (£1 per day)	Capital cost (£1,000 per day)		Total cost	Cost per TV set
A	£1	+ £1,000,000	=	£1,000,001	£100,000.10
B	10	+ 10,000	=	10,010	1,001.00
D	1,000	+ 1,000	=	2,000	200.00

Second, suppose that labour costs only £1 a person-day while capital costs £1,000 a machine-day. Table 9.4(b) shows the costs in this case. Method D, which uses a lot of labour and little capital, is now the least-cost method and economically efficient method.

So technological efficiency depends only on what is feasible; economic efficiency depends on the relative costs of resources. The economically efficient method is the one that uses the smaller amount of a more expensive resource and a larger amount of a less expensive resource. If a firm is not economically efficient, it will have relatively high costs and low profit and will eventually go out of business.

Review Quiz

1 Define technological efficiency. Is a firm technologically efficient if it uses the latest technology? Why?
2 Define economic efficiency. Is a firm economically inefficient if it can cut costs by producing less? Why?
3 Explain the key distinction between technological efficiency and economic efficiency.
4 Why do some firms use lots of capital and not much labour, while others use not much capital and lots of labour?

Next we will study the impact of information constraints and the diversity of organizational structures they generate.

Information and Organizations

Each firm organizes the production of goods and services by combining and coordinating the productive resources it hires. But there is variety across firms in how they organize production. Firms use a mixture of two systems:

◆ Command systems
◆ Incentive systems

Command Systems

A **command system** is a method of organizing production that uses a managerial hierarchy. Commands pass downward through the managerial hierarchy and information passes upward. Managers spend most of their time collecting and processing information about the performance of the people under their control and making decisions about commands to issue and how best to get those commands implemented.

The military uses the purest form of command system. Command systems in firms are not as rigid as they are in the military. But they share some similar features. A chief executive officer (CEO) sits at the top of a firm's command system. Senior executives who report to and receive commands from the CEO specialize in managing production, marketing, finance, personnel and perhaps other aspects of the firm's operations. Beneath these senior managers might be several tiers of middle management ranks that stretch downward to the managers that supervise the day-to-day operations of the business. Beneath these managers are the people who operate the firm's machines and who make and sell goods and services.

Small-scale firms have one or two layers of managers while large-scale firms have several layers. As production processes have become ever more complex, management ranks have swollen. Today, more people have management jobs than ever before. But the information revolution of the 1990s slowed the growth of management and, in some industries, it decreased the number of layers of managers and brought a shake-out of middle managers.

Managers make enormous efforts to be well informed in order to make good decisions and issue commands that end up using resources efficiently. But managers always have incomplete information about what is happening in the divisions of the firm for which they are responsible. It is for this reason that firms use incentive systems as well as command systems to organize production.

Incentive Systems

An **incentive system** is a method of organizing production that uses a market-like mechanism inside the firm. Instead of issuing commands, senior managers create compensation schemes that will induce workers to perform in ways that maximize the firm's profit.

Selling organizations use incentive systems most extensively. Sales representatives who spend most of their working time alone and unsupervised are induced to work hard by being paid a small salary and a large performance-related bonus.

But incentive systems operate at all levels in a firm. A CEO's compensation plan includes a share in the firm's profit, and factory floor workers sometimes receive compensation based on the quantity they produce.

Mixed Systems

Firms will use both commands and incentives in a mixed system if it will help to maximize profit. They use commands when it is easy to monitor performance or when a small deviation from an ideal performance is very costly. They use incentives when monitoring performance is either not possible or too costly to be worth doing.

For example, it is easy and not very costly to monitor the performance of workers on a production line. If one person works too slowly, the entire line slows. So a production line is organized with a command system. In contrast, it is very costly for shareholders to judge whether their CEO is worth a million pound annual bonus. If the bonus is not paid, the CEO has less incentive to act in the shareholders' interest. Incentives and the contracts that create them are an attempt to cope with a general problem called the principal–agent problem.

The Principal–Agent Problem

The **principal–agent problem** is the problem of devising compensation rules that induce an *agent* to act in the best interest of a *principal*. For example, the shareholders of the HSBC are *principals* and the bank's senior managers are *agents*. The shareholders (the principals) must induce the senior managers (agents) to act in the shareholders' best interest.

Similarly, senior managers (principals) must induce middle managers (agents) to work efficiently. There is a chain of principal–agent relationships throughout most firms.

Agents, whether they are managers or workers, pursue their own goals and often impose costs on a principal. For example, the goal of a shareholder of the HSBC Bank (a principal) is to maximize the bank's profit. But the bank's profit depends on the actions of its managers (agents) who have their own goals. Senior managers may want to expand the size of their workforce to gain status and respect when this technology is not efficient. So the bank must constantly strive to find ways of improving performance and increasing profits.

Asymmetric Information

An important source of the principal–agent problem is asymmetric information. **Asymmetric information** occurs when valuable information is available to one person but is too costly for anyone else to obtain. When one person has more information than others, they can use this to their own advantage.

Asymmetric information creates two special problems for business managers:

◆ Moral hazard
◆ Adverse selection

Moral hazard

Moral hazard exists when one of the parties to an agreement has an incentive after the agreement is made to act in a way that brings him or herself benefit at the expense of the other party. Moral hazard arises because it is too costly for the injured party to monitor the advantaged party. A good example is the problem of paying sales staff a fixed wage. Once paid, the sales staff face a moral hazard. They have an incentive to put in no further effort to sell more goods, lowering the employer's profit.

Adverse Selection

Adverse selection is the tendency for people to enter into agreements in which their personal information can be used to their own advantage over less informed parties. Using the same example as for moral hazard, a firm that offers sales staff a fixed wage will attract lazy sales staff. Motivated sales staff will prefer to work for someone who pays by results. The fixed wage adversely selects sales staff who know they are poorly motivated and reduces the employer's profits.

Coping with the Principal–Agent Problem

Issuing commands does not address the principal–agent problem. In most firms, the shareholders can't monitor the managers and often the managers can't monitor workers. Each principal must create incentives that induce each agent to work in the interests of the principal, reducing moral hazard and adverse selection. Three ways of attempting to cope with the principal–agent problem are:

◆ Ownership
◆ Incentive pay
◆ Long-term contracts

Ownership

By assigning to a manager or worker ownership (or part-ownership) of a business, the principal can sometimes induce a job performance that increases a firm's profits. Share-ownership schemes for senior managers are quite common and firms increasing award bonuses in the form of company shares. Share-ownership schemes for workers are becoming more common as more employees are already investing independently in shares.

The cartoon illustrates how the principal–agent problem is addressed by share ownership. The employee is happy to own shares when the company is doing well because owners benefit from dividends and an increasing share price. This reduces the moral hazard if the returns on shares rise with employee effort. But if the employee is not working in the interests of shareholders, the employee is the first to know because of asymmetric information. Share ownership can reduce adverse selection as more motivated staff will have an incentive to join firms who offer share ownership as part of reward packages.

Incentive Pay

Incentive pay schemes – pay related to performance – are very common. They are based on a variety of performance criteria such as profits, production or sales targets. Promoting an employee for good performance is another example of an incentive pay scheme. Like share ownership, performance-related pay reduces moral hazard and adverse selection problems.

Long-term Contracts

Long-term contracts tie the long-term fortunes of managers and workers (agents) to the success of the principal(s) – the owner(s) of the firm. For example, a multi-year employment contract for a CEO encourages that person to take a long-term view and devise strategies that achieve maximum profit over a sustained period.

FUNNY MONEY   BY   Austin

AS AN EMPLOYEE I'M HAPPY TO BE GIVEN SHARES..   .. BUT AS A SHAREHOLDER..   .. I WOULDN'T EMPLOY A LAYABOUT LIKE ME.

Risk and the Principal–Agent Problem

Share ownership, incentive pay and long-term contracts are three incentive schemes that firms can use to raise efficiency Part of the reason why incentive schemes raise efficiency is explained by the difference between principals and agents in their attitude to risk. Risk arises when we have to make decisions when the outcome of our decisions is uncertain. **Risk** is a situation in which more than one outcome can occur and the probability (or likelihood) of the outcomes can be estimated. For example, the probability that you will win the UK lottery jackpot next week is about 1 in 14 million.

Risk aversion measures the different value people place on the opportunity cost of risk. There is an enormous difference between Richard Branson, who favours more risky ventures for his Virgin empire, and high street bank managers, who favour more safe investments. Bank managers are more risk averse than Richard Branson

To see how we can measure risk aversion let's look at an example. Suppose you have to choose between two summer jobs. A supermarket job pays £5,000 for certain. The other is a sales job with performance-related pay. If your sales are below target you get £3,000 and if your sales are above target you get £9,000. You think there is a 50 per cent chance you will achieve above target sales and a 50 per cent chance you will not. So on average, the sales job will pay £6,000, £1,000 more than the supermarket job. When asked which you prefer, you say that one is as good as the other. This implies the additional £1,000 earned on average from the sales job is just enough to compensate you for taking the risk that you might not meet the target. You are risk averse because you require compensation for taking a risk and you value the opportunity cost of taking this risk at £1,000.

In general, shareholders (principals) are less risk averse than employees (agents). Shareholders can spread the risk of poor performance by agents by holding shares in many firms. Employees are more risk averse about low future income as they rely on one income only. In an uncertain environment with poor information, incentive schemes raise profitability but expose more risk averse employees to greater variability in their future income. After all, employees may work harder because of the incentive but then find profits do not rise because of factors outside their control. The incentive scheme will be efficient if it balances the cost of exposing more risk averse employees (agents) to higher risk against the benefit of reducing risk for the less risk averse shareholder (principals).

Incentive schemes give rise to different types of business organization. For example, a firm comprising just one person will not face the problems of asymmetric information with employees or the shareholder monitoring problems. The principal–agent problem seems to be mainly a problem of larger firms. So why isn't all production organized by small firms? The answer lies in the balance of benefits of size against the costs of coping with the principal–agent problem. So let's look at these now.

Types of Business Organization

The three main types of business organization are:

◆ Proprietorship
◆ Partnership
◆ Company

Proprietorship

A *proprietorship* is a firm with a single owner – a proprietor – who has unlimited liability. *Unlimited liability* is the legal responsibility for all the debts of a firm up to an amount equal to the entire wealth of the owner. If a sole proprietorship cannot pay its debts, those to whom the firm owes money can claim the personal property of the owner. The proprietor makes management decisions, receives the firm's profits and is responsible for its losses. Profits are taxed at the same rate as other sources of the proprietor's income.

Partnership

A *partnership* is a firm with two or more owners who have unlimited liability. Partners must agree on an appropriate management structure and on how to divide the firm's profits among themselves. The profits of a partnership are taxed as the personal income of the owners. But each partner is legally liable for all the debts of the partnership (limited only by the wealth of an individual partner). Liability for the full debts of the partnership is called *joint unlimited liability*.

Company

A *company* is a firm owned by one or more limited liability shareholders. *Limited liability* means that the owners have legal liability only for the value of their initial investment. This limitation of liability means that if the company becomes bankrupt, its owners are not required to use their personal wealth to pay the company's debts.

Company profits are taxed independently of shareholders' incomes. Because shareholders pay taxes on the income they receive as dividends on shares, corporate profits are taxed twice. The shareholders also pay capital gains tax on the profit they earn by selling a share for a higher price than they paid for it.

Company shares generate capital gains when a company retains some of its profit and reinvests it in profitable activities. So even retained earnings are taxed twice because the capital gains they generate are taxed.

Pros and Cons of Different Types of Firms

So why are there so many different types of business organization? Why are firms structured in different ways? The different types of business organization that you have looked at arise as different ways of trying to

cope with the principal–agent problem. Each type of business has advantages in particular situations. Because of its special advantages, each type continues to exist. Each type also has its disadvantages, which explains why it has not driven out the other two types.

Table 9.5 sets out the pros and cons of the different types of firms.

For example, making decisions in partnerships is relatively easy but production can be high cost. By contrast, companies can produce at low cost but decision making can be difficult because of their size and complexity. Because of the balance of advantages and disadvantages, each type continues to exist throughout Europe and the rest of the world. Companies dominate where they are the most profitable. This is usually when a large amount of capital is required. Proprietorships and partnerships dominate when they are most profitable, usually where flexibility in decision making is critical.

Partnerships are small-scale firms while companies are large-scale firms that employ many people. You can now examine the relationship between size and profitability by reading the Box 9.1: European Firms in Action.

Table 9.5

The Pros and Cons of Different Types of Firms

Type of firm	Pros	Cons
Proprietorship	◆ Easy to set up ◆ Simple decision making ◆ Profits taxed only once as owner's income	◆ Bad decisions not checked by need for consensus ◆ Owner's entire wealth at risk ◆ Firm dies with owner ◆ Capital is expensive ◆ Labour is expensive
Partnership	◆ Easy to set up ◆ Diversified decision making ◆ Can survive withdrawal of partner ◆ Profits taxed only once as owners' incomes	◆ Achieving consensus may be slow and expensive ◆ Owners' entire wealth at risk ◆ Withdrawal of a partner may create capital shortage ◆ Capital is expensive
Company	◆ Owners have limited liability ◆ Large-scale, low-cost capital available ◆ Professional management not restricted by ability of owners ◆ Perpetual life ◆ Long-term labour contracts cut labour costs	◆ Complex management structure can make decisions slow and expensive ◆ Profits taxed twice as company profit and as shareholders' income

Box 9.1
European Firms in Action

The Importance of Very Small Firms

There are approximately 3 million firms in the United Kingdom and more than 90 per cent of them are very small businesses, which employ fewer than 10 workers. Small firms comprise a similarly high percentage of firms in most EU countries.

Table 1 shows the relative importance of firms of different sizes in 20 countries in Europe (EU15 plus Iceland, Liechtenstein, Norway and Switzerland). Very small firms (those with fewer than 10 employees) comprise 93 per cent of all firms and they employ 34 per cent of all workers. At the other size extreme, large firms (those with more than 250 employees) comprise only 0.2 per cent of all firms. But because these firms are large, they account for a similar amount of total employment as the very small firms.

Table 1

The Size Structure of European Firms

Number of employees	Size	Percentage of all firms	Percentage of firms' employment
<10	Micro	93.0	34
10 < 50	Small	6.0	19
50 < 250	Medium	0.8	13
250	Large	0.2	34

Source: Europa.eu.int/comm/enterprise/enterprise_policy/ analysis/doc/smes_observatory_2002_report2_en.pdf.

Firm Size and Profitability

Figure 1 shows the relationship between the profitability of firms and firm size in the same 20 countries in Europe (EU 15 plus Iceland, Liechtenstein, Norway and Switzerland). Profitability is the company's gross operating surplus expressed as a percentage of the value of its production.

The average profit rate across all firms is 39 per cent. Large and medium firms have profit rates that exceed the average, and small and micro sized firms have profit rates below the average. The advantages of large scale in dealing with the principal–agent problem may exceed the benefits of small size in Europe's competitive economies.

Figure 1

Profitability of European Firms by Size

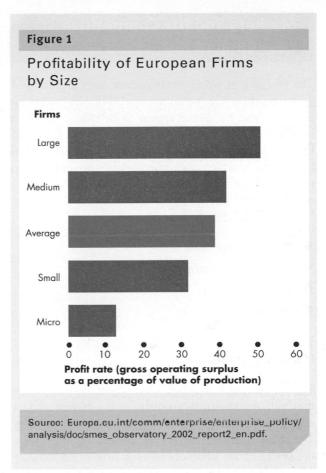

Source: Europa.eu.int/comm/enterprise/enterprise_policy/ analysis/doc/smes_observatory_2002_report2_en.pdf.

Review Quiz

1 Explain the distinction between a command system and an incentive system in business organizations.
2 What is the principal–agent problem and what are the ways in which firms try to cope with it?
3 What are the three types of firm? Explain their advantages and disadvantages.
4 Why do all three types of firm survive and in which sectors is each type most prominent?

You've now seen how technological constraints influence a firm's use of capital and labour and how information constraints influence the organization of firms. We'll look at market constraints next to see how they influence the environment in which firms compete.

Markets and the Competitive Environment

The markets in which firms operate vary a great deal. Some markets are highly competitive and profits are hard to come by. Some appear to be almost free from competition and firms in these markets earn large profits. Some markets are dominated by fierce advertising campaigns in which each firm seeks to persuade buyers that it has the best products. Some markets display a war-like character.

Economists identify four market types:

◆ Perfect competition
◆ Monopolistic competition
◆ Oligopoly
◆ Monopoly

Perfect Competition

Perfect competition arises when there are many firms that sell an identical product, many buyers and no restrictions on the entry of new firms into the industry. The many firms and buyers are all well informed about the prices of the products of each firm in the industry. The worldwide markets for corn, rice, and other grain crops are examples of perfect competition.

Monopolistic Competition

Monopolistic competition is a market structure in which a large number of firms compete by making similar but slightly different products. Making a product slightly different from the product of a competing firm is called **product differentiation**.

Production differentiation gives a monopolistically competitive firm an element of monopoly power. The firm is the sole producer of the particular version of the good in question. For example, in the market for running shoes, Nike, Reebok, Fila, and Asics all make their own version of the perfect shoe. Each of these firms is the sole producer of a particular brand and so has a monopoly on that particular brand of shoe.

Differentiated products need not be different products. What matters is that consumers perceive the products to be different. For example, different brands of ibuprofen tablets are chemically identical and differ only in their packaging.

Oligopoly

Oligopoly is a market structure in which a small number of firms compete. Computer software, aeroplane manufacture, and international air transportation are examples of oligopolistic industries. Oligopolies might produce almost identical products, such as the colas produced by Coca-Cola and Pepsi Co. Or they might produce differentiated products such as the Volkswagen Golf and the Peugeot 205.

Monopoly

Monopoly arises when there is one firm which produces a good or service for which no close substitute exists and in which the firm is protected from competition by a barrier preventing the entry of new firms. In some places, the phone, gas, electricity and water suppliers are local monopolies – monopolies restricted to a given location. Microsoft, the software developer that created Windows, the operating system used by PCs, is an example of a global monopoly.

Perfect competition is the most extreme form of competition. Monopoly is the most extreme absence of competition. The other two market types fall between these extremes.

Many factors must be taken into account to determine which market structure describes a particular real-world market. One of these factors is the extent to which the market is dominated by a small number of firms. To measure this feature of markets, economists use indexes called measures of concentration. Let's look at these measures.

Measures of Concentration

To measure concentration in a market, we survey the firms and determine the size of each firm. We then calculate the percentage of the market accounted for by the largest firms in that market. Two decisions must be made to measure concentration: the indicator of firm size and the number of firms to include in the group of largest firms.

The most common measure of concentration uses total revenue and puts five firms in the group of largest firms. The result is the **five-firm concentration ratio**, which is the percentage of total revenue (or the value of sales) in an industry accounted for by the five firms with the largest value of sales. The range of the concentration ratio is from almost zero for perfect competition to 100 for monopoly.

Table 9.6

Concentration Ratio Calculations

Shoemakers		Egg farmers	
Firm	**Sales (millions of pounds)**	**Firm**	**Sales (millions of pounds)**
Lace-up plc	250	Bills's	0.9
Finefoot plc	200	Sue's	0.7
Easyfit plc	180	Jane's	0.5
Comfy plc	120	Tom's	0.4
Loafers plc	70	Jill's	0.2
Top 5 sales	820	Top 5 sales	2.8
Other 10 firms	190	Other 1,000 firms	349.2
Industry sales	1,010	Industry sales	352.0

Five-firm concentration ratios:

Shoemakers: $\dfrac{820}{1,010} = 81\%$ Egg farmers: $\dfrac{2.80}{352} = 0.8\%$

Table 9.6 shows two hypothetical calculations of the five-firm concentration ratio, one for shoe manufacturing and one for egg farming. In this example, there are 15 firms in the shoe manufacturing industry. The largest five have 81 per cent of the sales, so the five-firm concentration ratio for that industry is 81 per cent. In the egg industry, with 1,005 firms, the top five firms account for only 0.8 per cent of total industry sales. In this case, the five-firm concentration ratio is 0.8 per cent.

The five-firm concentration ratio helps us measure the degree of competitiveness of a market. A low concentration ratio indicates a high degree of competition, and a high concentration ratio indicates an absence of competition. In the extreme case of monopoly, the concentration ratio is 100 per cent because the largest (and only) firm makes the entire industry sales. Between these extremes, the five-firm concentration ratio is regarded as being a useful indicator of the likelihood of collusion among firms in an oligopoly. If the concentration ratio exceeds 60 per cent, it is likely that firms have a high degree of market power and may collude and behave like a monopoly.

If the concentration ratio is less than 40 per cent, the industry is regarded as competitive. A concentration ratio between 40 and 60 per cent indicates that the market structure is oligopoly.

Limitations of Concentration Measures

Concentration ratios are useful, but they have some limitations. They must be supplemented by other information to determine the market structure of an industry and the degree of market power of firms in that industry. The three key problems are:

◆ The geographical scope of the market

◆ Barriers to entry and firm turnover

◆ Market and industry correspondence

Geographical Scope of Market

Concentration ratio data are based on a national view of the market. Many goods are sold on a national market, but some are sold on a regional market and some on a global one. The brewing industry is a good example of one in which the local market is more relevant than the national market. So although the national concentration ratio for brewers is in the middle range, there is a high degree of concentration in the brewing industry in most regions. The car industry is an example of one for which there is a global market. So although the largest five car producers in the United Kingdom account for 80 per cent of all cars sold by UK producers, they account for a smaller percentage of the total UK car market, which includes imports. In the global market for cars, UK producers account for an even smaller percentage of total sales.

Barriers to Entry and Firm Turnover

Measures of concentration do not indicate the severity of any barriers to entry in a market. Some industries, for example, are highly concentrated but their markets have virtually free entry and a high turnover of firms. A good example is the market for local restaurants. Many small towns have few restaurants, but there are few restrictions on entering the restaurant industry. So firms enter and exit with great regularity.

Even if the turnover of new firms in a market is limited, an industry might be competitive because of *potential entry* – because a few firms in the market face competition from many firms that can easily enter the market and will do so it economic profits are available.

Market and Industry Correspondence

The classifications used to calculate concentration ratios allocate every firm in the economy to a particular industry. But markets for particular goods do not usually correspond to these industries.

Markets are often narrower than industries. For example, the basic industrial chemicals industry, which has a medium concentration ratio, operates in many separate markets for individual products (for instance tobacco and cement), each one of which has few substitutes. So this industry, which looks relatively competitive, operates in some monopolistic markets.

Another problem arises from the fact that firms make many products. For example, the tobacco firms also operate in the food and insurance industries. The privatized water companies operate hotels and printing works. The value of sales for each firm can overestimate their contribution to the industry to which they have been assigned.

If concentration ratios are combined with information about the geographical scope, barriers to entry and the extent to which large, multi-product firms straddle a variety of markets, they can provide a basis for classifying industries. The less concentrated an industry and the lower its barriers to entry, the more closely it approximates the perfect competition case. The more concentrated an industry and the higher the barriers to entry, the more it approximates the monopoly case.

Table 9.7 summarizes the characteristics of different market structures and their concentration ratios.

Market Structures in Europe

The majority of markets for goods and services in Europe are highly competitive and only a few markets are monopolies. For example, more than 70 per cent by value of goods and services bought and sold in the United Kingdom are traded in highly competitive markets. Where monopoly does arise, it is usually in the public services although with privatization, public services have become more competitive.

But market power can still be strong in markets when privatization attracts few new entrants such as in the telecommunications industry. Less than 6 per cent of goods and services traded in the UK markets are essentially uncompetitive. Oligopoly is more common in manufacturing than in the services sector, but more than 55 per cent of UK manufacturing industries have a concentration ratio of less than 40 per cent.

The overall level of concentration in an economy can be measured by the proportion of total output accounted for by the largest 100 firms. The UK aggregate concentration ratio in manufacturing increased in the post-war period, indicating an increase in market power, but it levelled off in the 1970s and 1980s and has fallen in recent years. The increase in concentration resulted from several waves of merger activity and the growth of transnational companies serving new global markets. But given the growth in world trade and advances in telecommunications and low-cost transport, many UK firms operate in global markets, which are highly competitive.

Table 9.7

Market Structure

Characteristics	Perfect competition	Monopolistic competition	Oligopoly	Monopoly
Number of firms in industry	Many	Many	Few	One
Product	Identical	Differentiated	Either identical or differentiated	No close substitutes
Barriers to entry	None	None	Moderate	High
Firm's control over price	None	Some	Considerable	Considerable or regulated
Concentration ratio	0	Low	High	100
Examples	Agricultural products	Cosmetics, bread, clothing	Washing powders, cereals	Local water utility, postal letter service

Box 9.2
UK Concentration Ratios in Action

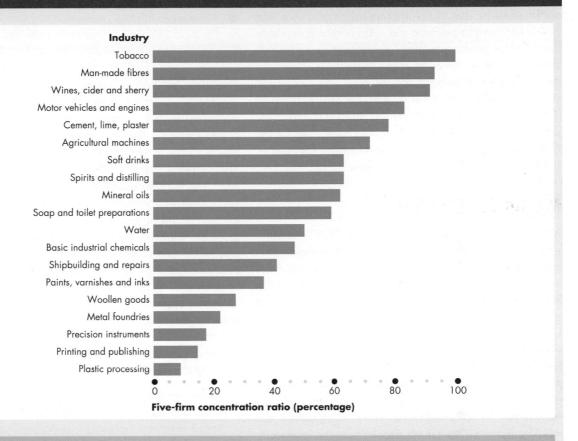

Industry

Source: Central Statistical Office, *Report of the Census of Production, Business Monitor*, London, HMSO, 2000.

Concentration in the UK Economy

Concentration ratios for the United Kingdom are derived from the Census of Production. This census is undertaken by the UK government and provides information on the sales, employment and structure of every manufacturing firm in the United Kingdom.

Figure 1 shows the five-firm concentration ratio for a selection of industries. Low concentration ratios are found in plastics, printing, metal foundries and wool, all of which are competitive industries. High concentration ratios are found in tobacco, man-made fibres, wines and ciders, and motor vehicles, all of which have a high degree of market power. Intermediate concentration ratios are found in mineral oils, water supply and basic chemicals, all of which have a limited degree of market power.

Review Quiz

1   What are the four market types? Explain the distinguishing characteristics of each.
2   Describe and explain the main measures of market concentration.
3   Under what conditions do measures of concentration give a good indication of the degree of competition in the market?
4   Is our economy competitive? Is it becoming more competitive or less competitive?

You now know the variety of market types and the way we classify firms and industries into the different market types. Our final question in this chapter is what determines the items that firms decide to buy from other firms rather than produce for themselves?

Firms and Markets

At the beginning of this chapter, we defined a firm as an institution that hires factors of production and organizes them to produce and sell goods and services. To organize production, firms coordinate the economic decisions and activities of many individuals. But firms are not the only coordinators of economic decisions. As we learned in Chapter 3, markets also coordinate decisions. By adjusting prices, markets make the decisions of buyers and sellers consistent – make the quantities demanded equal to the quantities supplied of the many different goods and services.

Market Coordination

Markets can coordinate production. For example, markets might coordinate the production of a rock concert. A promoter hires a stadium, some stage equipment, audio and video recording engineers and technicians, some rock groups, a superstar, a publicity agent and a ticket agent – all market transactions – and sells tickets to thousands of rock fans, audio rights to a recording company and video and broadcasting rights to a television network – another set of market transactions. If rock concerts were produced like cornflakes, the firm producing them would own all the capital used (stadiums, stage, sound and video equipment) and would employ all the labour needed (singers, engineers, sales persons and so on).

What determines whether a firm or markets coordinate a particular set of activities? Why is the production of cornflakes coordinated by a firm and the production of a rock concert coordinated by markets? The answer is cost. Taking account of the opportunity cost of time as well as the costs of the other inputs, people use the method that costs least. In other words, they use the economically efficient method.

Firms coordinate economic activity when they can perform a task more efficiently than markets. In such a situation, it is profitable to set up a firm. If markets can perform a task more efficiently than a firm, people will use markets and any attempt to set up a firm to replace such market coordination will be doomed to failure.

Why Firms?

There are four key reasons why, in many instances, firms are more efficient than markets as coordinators of economic activity. Firms achieve:

◆ Lower transactions costs
◆ Economies of scale
◆ Economies of scope
◆ Economies of team production

Transactions Costs

The idea that firms exist because there are activities in which they are more efficient than markets was first suggested by a University of Chicago economist and Nobel Laureate, Ronald Coase.[1] Coase focused on the firm's ability to reduce or eliminate transactions costs. **Transactions costs** are the costs arising from finding someone with whom to do business, of reaching an agreement about the price and other aspects of the exchange, and of ensuring that the terms of the agreement are fulfilled. *Market* transactions require buyers and sellers to get together and to negotiate the terms and conditions of their trading. Sometimes lawyers have to be hired to draw up contracts. A broken contract leads to still more expenses. A *firm* can lower such transactions costs by reducing the number of individual transactions undertaken.

Consider, for example, two ways of getting your creaking car fixed:

1 *Firm coordination*. You take the car to the garage. Parts and tools as well as the mechanic's time are coordinated by the garage owner and your car gets fixed. You pay one bill for the entire job.

2 *Market coordination*. You hire a mechanic who diagnoses the problems and makes a list of the parts and tools needed to fix them. You buy the parts from the local breaker's yard and rent the tools from ABC Rentals. You hire the mechanic again to fix the problems. You return the tools and pay your bills – wages to the mechanic, rental to ABC and the cost of the parts used to the breaker.

You will choose the method on the basis of the opportunity cost of your own time as well as the costs of the other inputs that you'd have to buy. You will use the economically efficient method or least cost method.

Although the firm has to undertake several transactions to do the job, it can spread the cost across many customers. So there is a huge reduction in the number of individual transactions that take place if people get their cars fixed at the garage rather than going through a sequence of market transactions.

[1] Ronald H. Coase 'The Nature of the Firm', *Economica* (November 1937) pp. 386–405.

Economies of Scale

When the cost of producing a unit of a good falls as its output rate increases, **economies of scale** exist. Many industries experience economies of scale; car manufacturing is an example. One firm can produce 4 million cars a year at a lower cost per car than 200 firms each producing 20,000 cars a year. Economies of scale arise from specialization and the division of labour that can be reaped more effectively by firm coordination rather than market coordination.

Economies of Scope

A firm experiences **economies of scope** when it uses its specialized and often expensive resources to produce a range of goods and services. For example, SAP hires specialist programmers, designers, marketing experts and sales representatives and uses their skills across an enormous range of e-business systems and other products that meet the specialized needs of a wide variety of software users. As a result, SAP coordinates the resources that produce e-business solutions and other business software at a lower cost than the cost of producing each one of these products in a large number of small specialist firms.

Economies of Team Production

A production process in which a group of individuals each specializes in mutually supportive tasks is *team production*. Sport provides the best example of team activity. Some team members specialize in striking and some in defending, some in speed and some in strength. The production of goods and services offers many examples of team activity. For example, production lines in car plants and TV manufacturing plants work most efficiently when individual activity is organized in teams, each specializing in a small task. You can also think of an entire firm as being a team. The team has buyers of raw materials and other inputs, production workers and sales persons. There are even specialists within these various groups. Each individual member of the team specializes, but the value of the output of the team and the profit that it earns depend on the coordinated activities of all the team's members. The idea that firms arise as a consequence of the economies of team production was first suggested by Armen Alchian and Harold Demsetz of the University of California at Los Angeles.[2]

---

[2] Armen Alchian and Harold Demsetz, 'Production, Information Costs, and Economic Organization', *American Economic Review* (December 1972) 57, 5, pp. 777–795.

Because firms can economize on transactions costs, reap economies of scale and scope, and organize efficient team production, it is firms rather than markets that coordinate most of our economic activity. Reductions in transactions costs explain why Ford, which started hand-building cars in the early 1900s, developed into a company with functional divisions based on production line technology in the 1940s. But there are limits to the economic efficiency of firms. If a firm becomes too big or too diversified in the things that it seeks to do, the cost of management and monitoring per unit of output begins to rise and, at some point, the market becomes more efficient at coordinating the use of resources. This explains why Ford restructured into a global transnational company, effectively creating a set of smaller, more independent national companies. It also explains why companies, such as Hanson Trust, target segments of large, ailing transnational companies to run as separate, more profitable companies.

Sometimes firms enter into long-term alliances with each other that cut out market transactions and make it difficult to see where one firm ends and another begins. For example, when Rover became part of BMW, it had a long-term relationship with Honda as a supplier of gearboxes. Long-term alliances are also common between supermarkets and manufacturers. Famous cereal manufacturers produce supermarket own-label brands as well as their own more established brands.

Review Quiz

1 Describe the main ways in which economic activity can be coordinated.
2 What determines whether a firm or markets coordinate production?
3 What are the main reasons why firms can often coordinate production at lower cost than markets?

In this chapter you have begun your study of firms and markets. You have discovered that profit maximization is the main goal of firms, but that a firm's ability to maximize profit is constrained by its technology constraints, information constraints and market constraints. You can read about how Europe's biggest software company, SAP, dealt with its technology constraints in the *Business Case Study* on pp. 196–197.

In the next chapter, you will learn about the relationship between cost and output at different levels of output. These cost–output relationships are common to all types of firm in all types of markets.

Business Case Study
Constraints on Profit

Europe's biggest software company: SAP

The Company

SAP, a German company, is Europe's software giant. It became a public traded company in 1988 and now employs over 30,000 people in more than 50 countries. It runs 36,000 installations of its software serving 10 million users in 21,000 organizations across 120 countries. Its customers include other corporate giants such as Sony and Microsoft.

The Products

SAP specializes in writing and installing business software, particularly collaborative e-business systems for firms in all types of industries and markets. These Enterprise Resource Planning systems help companies to run their back-office functions such as distribution, accounting and manufacturing. SAP began to grow in the late 1990s with its provision of millennium bug products and services.

Competition and Market Constraints

SAP's main rivals are US companies like Oracle, Siebel Systems and PeopleSoft. The market for the services of these companies was severely cut in 2001 with the economic slowdown in the United States and limited growth potential in computer hardware. But SAP's sales and profits have rocketed since 1999 whilst competitors recorded losses. First quarter figures for 2004 are similar, with a 23 per cent rise in profits.

Information Constraints

SAP was founded in 1972 by five former IBM systems engineers. As it has grown, SAP has adopted a standard corporate structure. Its CEO is Mr Henning Kagermann, but three of its original founders still control 40 per cent of the shares.

Technology Constraints

In the late 1990s, SAP realized that its profit was limited by traditional software delivery systems. In 1999, the company launched a new Enterprise Resource Planning website called mySAP.com. The site supports all types of business software and allows employees, customers and business partners to work together more efficiently, by increasing information flows, raising supply chain efficiency and improving customer-to-business relationships.

SAP is now developing Internet partnerships with related organizations. In June 2001, SAP linked up with IBM and Compaq to gain access to new customers like Shell Oil. In 2003, SAP established links with Dell computers and in 2004, SAP began negotiations with Microsoft in a bid to oust Oracle from its rank as second largest software supplier. Microsoft even considered a bid for SAP.

Economic Analysis

◆ SAP is in business to maximize profit. It faces all the economic problems described in this chapter.

◆ SAP operates in a global oligopoly market where a few large firms compete worldwide for customers and where products and technologies change quickly. Its profits are constrained by technology, information and market constraints.

◆ Tables 1 and 2 compare SAP's performance relative to its main competitor. SAP expanded employment between 1999 and 2002, whereas Oracle cut employment.

◆ In 1999, SAP lagged behind Oracle which had begun to develop Internet services. SAP was constrained by its existing technology. SAP responded by launching its own Internet services in 1999 to raise efficiency by capturing economies of scale and scope.

◆ Business software is provided at lowest cost if software firms can specialize. SAP's Internet strategy helped it to specialize in software management, cutting transactions costs and capturing economies of team production. Tables 1 and 2 shows the dramatic rise in SAP's profits compared to Oracle's profit fall.

◆ Software company sales are constrained by market conditions and the slowdown in the US economy in 2001 decreased demand for software. Tables 1 and 2 show how Oracle's sales fell whilst SAP's sales rocketed.

◆ The figure shows the share of ownership by founder managers in 2000 for SAP and Oracle. The original founders have maintained greater control in SAP than in Oracle. This may have helped to reduce principal–agent problems for senior management in SAP, cutting costs and raising profit.

Table 1

SAP's Position

	1999/00	2002/03
Employment	24,480	30,251
(1-year growth)	13%	3.0%
Profit ($million)	596	1,354
(1-year growth)	2%	53.5%
Sales ($million)	5,881	8,831.3
(1-year growth)	14%	13.4%

Table 2

Oracle's Position

	1999/00	2002/03
Employment	42,927	40,650
(1-year growth)	4%	−3.2%
Profit ($million)	2,561	2,301
(1-year growth)	59%	3.7%
Sales ($million)	10,860	9,475
(1-year growth)	7%	−2%

Source: http://cobrands.hoovers.com/

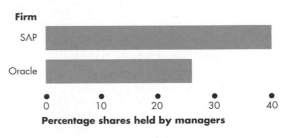

Figure 1 Share of ownership by founder members

Summary

Key Points

The Firm and its Economic Problem (pp. 180–182)

- Firms hire and organize factors of production to produce and sell goods and services.

- Firms seek to maximize economic profit (total revenue minus opportunity cost).

- Technology, information and markets limit the firm's profit.

Technological and Economic Efficiency (pp. 183–184)

- A method of production is technologically efficient when it is not possible to increase output without using more inputs.

- A method of production is economically efficient when the cost of producing a given output is as low as possible.

Information and Organizations (pp. 184–189)

- Firms use a combination of command systems and incentive systems to organize production.

- Faced with incomplete information and uncertainty, firms induce managers and workers to perform in ways that are consistent with the firm's goals.

- Proprietorships, partnerships and companies use ownership, incentives and long-term contracts to cope with the principal–agent problem.

Markets and the Competitive Environment (pp. 190–193)

- Perfect competition occurs when there are many buyers and sellers of an identical product and when firms can easily enter the market.

- Monopolistic competition occurs when a large number of firms compete with each other by making slightly different products.

- Oligopoly occurs when a small number of producers compete with each other.

- Monopoly occurs when one firm produces a good or services for which there is no close substitutes and the firm is protected by a barrier that prevents the entry of competitors.

- Concentration ratios measure the degree of competition in markets.

Firms and Markets (pp. 194–195)

- Firms coordinate economic activities when they can perform a task more efficiently – at lower cost – than markets can.

- Firms economize on transactions costs and achieve the benefits of economies of scale, economies of scope and of team production.

Key Tables

Key Terms

Problems

cost €1,000, the pocket calculator costs €10, and the pencil and paper cost €1.

a Which, if any, of the methods is technologically efficient?

b Which method is economically efficient if the wage rate is

  i €5 an hour?

  ii €50 an hour?

  iii €500 an hour?

4 Sue can do her accounting assignment using a personal computer (PC); a pocket calculator; a pocket calculator and a pencil and paper; or a pencil and paper. With a PC, Sue completes the job in half an hour; with a pocket calculator, it takes 4 hours; with a pocket calculator, pencil and paper, it takes 5 hours; and with a pencil and paper, it takes 14 hours. The PC and its software cost €2,000, the pocket calculator costs €15, and the pencil and paper cost €3.

a Which, if any, of the methods is technologically efficient?

b Which method is economically efficient if Sue's wage rate is

  i €10 an hour?

  ii €20 an hour?

  iii €50 an hour?

*5 Alternative ways of laundering 100 shirts are:

Method	Labour (hours)	Capital (machines)
A	1	10
B	5	8
C	20	4
D	50	1

a Which methods are technologically efficient?

b Which method is economically efficient if the hourly wage rate and the implicit rental rate of capital are:

  i Wage rate €1, rental rate €100?

  ii Wage rate €5, rental rate €50?

  iii Wage rate €50, rental rate €5?

6 Alternative ways of making 100 shirts a day are:

Method	Labour (hours)	Capital (machines)
A	10	50
B	20	40
C	50	20
D	100	10

*1 One year ago, Jack and Jill set up a vinegar bottling firm (called JJVB). Use the following information to calculate JJVB's explicit costs and implicit costs during its first year of operation:

a Jack and Jill put €50,000 of their own money into the firm.

b They bought equipment for €30,000.

c They hired one employee to help them for an annual wage of €20,000.

d Jack gave up his previous job, at which he earned €30,000, and spent all his time working for JJVB.

e Jill kept her old job, which paid €30 an hour, but gave up 10 hours of leisure each week (for 50 weeks) to work for JJVB.

f JJVB bought €10,000 of goods and services from other firms.

g The market value of the equipment at the end of the year was €28,000.

2 One year ago, Ms Moffat and Mr Spieder opened a cheese firm (called MSCF). Use the following information to calculate MSCF's explicit costs and implicit costs during its first year of operation:

a Moffat and Spieder put €70,000 of their own money into the firm.

b They bought equipment for €40,000.

c They hired one employee to help them for an annual wage of €18,000.

d Moffat gave up her previous job, at which she earned €22,000, and spent all her time working for MSCF.

e Spieder kept his old job, which paid €20 an hour, but gave up 20 hours of leisure each week (for 50 weeks) to work for MSCF.

f MSCF bought €5,000 of goods from other firms.

g The market value of the equipment at the end of the year was €37,000.

*3 Four methods of completing a tax return are: a personal computer (PC), a pocket calculator, a pocket calculator with pencil and paper, a pencil and paper. With a PC, the job takes an hour; with a pocket calculator, it takes 12 hours; with a pocket calculator and pencil and paper, it takes 12 hours; and with a pencil and paper, it takes 16 hours. The PC and its software

*Solutions to odd-numbered problems are available on *Parkin Interactive*.

a Which methods are technologically efficient?

b Which method is economically efficient if the hourly wage rate and rental rate are:

   i   Wage rate €1, rental rate €100?

   ii   Wage rate €5, rental rate €50?

   iii Wage rate €50, rental rate €5?

*7 Sales of the firms in the tattoo industry are:

Firm	Sales (euros)
Bright Spots	450
Freckles	325
Love Galore	250
Native Birds	200
Tiny Tattoo	200
Other 15 firms	800

a Calculate the five-firm concentration ratio.

b What is the structure of the tattoo industry?

8 Sales of the firms in the pet food industry are:

Firm	Sales (thousands of euros)
Small Collar Co.	50
Big Collar Co.	50
Shiny Coat Co.	75
Friendly Pet Co.	60
Nature's Way Co.	65
Other 7 firms	350

a Calculate the five-firm concentration ratio.

b What is the structure of the industry?

Critical Thinking

1 Study the *Business Case Study* about the European software company, SAP, on pp. 196–197 and then:

a Describe the economic problem that SAP faced in the late 1990s.

b Use the links on *Parkin Interactive* to find information about SAP's main competitors. What are their economic problems?

c Use the links on *Parkin Interactive* to find information about SAP's performance in the third quarter of 2001. Why is SAP suggesting that it must cut labour costs in the United States? What does it hope to achieve by doing this?

d Compare and contrast how SAP achieves technological efficiency and economic efficiency.

e SAP and its competitors provide software services which help other companies to reduce their costs and become more efficient. Why might the demand for SAP's services buck the trend when the economy slows down?

2 By 2004, three of the 100 UK companies with the fastest growth had created share-option schemes to make employees part-owners of the business. These companies were Vivid Imaginations, LGC and RFIB Group. Their annual profits increased by 51, 46 and 40 per cent respectively.

a What internal problems might have led these firms to encourage employees to be part owners?

b How can such schemes affect the growth rate of profits?

Web Exercises

Use the links on *Parkin Interactive* to work the following exercises.

1 Obtain information about the car industry.

a What are the main economic problems faced by car producers?

b Why are car producers merging?

2 Obtain information about the steel industry.

a What are the main economic problems faced by steel producers?

b Is the number of steel producers likely to increase or decrease during the next few years? Why?

Chapter 10

Output and Costs

After studying this chapter you will be able to:

◆ Distinguish between the short run and the long run

◆ Explain the relationship between a firm's output and its costs in the short run

◆ Derive and explain a firm's short-run cost curves

◆ Explain the relationship between a firm's output and costs in the long run

Survival of the Fittest

What does a firm have to do to be a survivor? Does size guarantee survival? Why do some very small firms survive? Why do some firms, such as Powergen, operate flat out with no spare capacity while others such as car makers have plenty of slack and wish they could sell more?

Time Frames for Decisions

People who operate firms make many decisions. All of these decisions are aimed at one overriding objective: maximum attainable profit. But the decisions are not all equally critical. Some of the decisions are big ones. Once made, they are costly (or impossible) to reverse. If such a decision turns out to be incorrect, it might lead to the failure of the firm. Some of the decisions are small ones. They are easily changed. If one of these decisions turns out to be incorrect, the firm can change its actions and survive.

The biggest decision that any firm makes is what industry to enter. For most entrepreneurs, their background knowledge and interests drive this decision. But the decision also depends on profit prospects. No one sets up a firm without believing it will be profitable. And profit depends on total revenue and opportunity cost (see Chapter 9, pp. 180–181).

The firm that we'll study has already chosen the industry in which to operate. It has also chosen its most effective method of organization. But it has not decided the quantity to produce, the quantities of resources to hire, or the price at which to sell its output.

Decisions about the quantity to produce and the price to charge depend on the type of market in which the firm operates. Perfect competition, monopolistic competition, oligopoly and monopoly all confront the firm with their own special problems.

But decisions about how to produce a given output do not depend on the type of market in which the firm operates. These decisions are similar for *all* types of firms in *all* types of markets.

The actions that a firm can take to influence the relationship between output and cost depend on how soon the firm wants to act. A firm that plans to change its output rate tomorrow has fewer options than one that plans to change its output rate six months from now.

To study the relationship between a firm's output decision and its costs, we distinguish two decision time frames:

◆ The short run
◆ The long run

The Short Run

The **short run** is a time frame in which the quantities of some resources are fixed. For most firms, the fixed resources are the firm's technology, buildings and capital. The management organization is also fixed in the short run. We call the collection of fixed resources the firm's *plant*. So in the short run, a firm's plant is fixed.

For our firm, Neat Knits, the fixed plant is its factory building and its knitting machines. For an electric power utility, the fixed plant is its buildings, generators, computers and control systems. For an airport, the fixed plant is the runways, terminal buildings and traffic control facilities.

To increase output in the short run, a firm must increase the quantity of variable inputs it uses. Labour is usually the variable input. So to produce more output, the owner of Neat Knits, Sam, must hire more labour and operate its knitting machines for more hours per day. Similarly, an electric power utility must hire more labour and operate its generators for more hours per day. An airport must hire more labour and operate its runways, terminals and traffic control facilities for more hours per day.

Short-run decisions are easily reversed. The firm can increase or decrease output in the short run by increasing or decreasing the labour hours it hires.

The Long Run

The **long run** is a time frame in which the quantities of *all* resources can be varied. That is, the long run is a period in which the firm can change its *plant*.

To increase output in the long run, a firm is able to choose whether to change its plant as well as whether to increase the quantity of labour it hires. The owner of Neat Knits can decide whether to install some additional knitting machines, use a new type of machine, reorganize its management or hire more labour. An electric power utility can decide whether to install more generators. And an airport can decide whether to build more runways, terminals and traffic-control facilities.

Long-run decisions are *not* easily reversed. Once a plant decision is made, the firm must live with it for some time. To emphasize this fact, we call the *past* cost of buying a plant that has no resale value a **sunk cost**. A sunk cost is irrelevant to the firm's decisions. The only costs that influence its decisions are the short-run cost of changing its labour inputs and the long-run cost of changing its plant.

We're going to study costs in the short run and the long run. We begin with the short run and describe the technology constraint the firm faces.

Short-run Technology Constraint

To increase output in the short run, a firm must increase the quantity of labour employed. We describe the relationship between output and the quantity of labour employed by using three related concepts:

1 Total product
2 Marginal product
3 Average product

These product concepts can be illustrated either by product schedules or by product curves. We'll look first at the product schedules.

Product Schedules

Table 10.1 shows some data that describe Neat Knits' total product, marginal product and average product.

Table 10.1

Total Product, Marginal Product and Average Product

	Labour (workers per day)	Total product (jumpers per day)	Marginal product (jumpers per worker)	Average product (jumpers per worker)
A	0	0		
			 4	
B	1	4		4.00
			 6	
C	2	10		5.00
			 3	
D	3	13		4.33
			 2	
E	4	15		3.75
			 1	
F	5	16		3.20

Total product is the total amount produced. Marginal product is the change in total product resulting from a one-unit increase in labour. For example, when labour increases from 2 to 3 workers a day (row *C* to row *D*), total product increases from 10 to 13 jumpers a day. (Marginal product is shown between the rows because it is the result of a change in the quantity of labour.) The marginal product of going from 2 to 3 workers is 3 jumpers. Average product of an input is total product divided by the quantity of an input employed. For example, 3 workers produce 13 jumpers a day, so the average product of 3 workers is 4.33 jumpers per worker.

The numbers tell us how Neat Knits' production changes as more workers are employed, for a fixed level of plant and machines. They also tell us about the productivity of Neat Knits' labour force.

Look first at the columns headed "Labour" and "Total product". **Total product** is the maximum output that a given quantity of labour can produce. The table shows how total product increases as Neat Knits employs more labour. For example, when Sam employs 1 worker, total product is 4 jumpers a day and when he employs 2 workers, total product is 10 jumpers a day. Each increase in employment brings an increase in total product.

Marginal product tells us how much total product increases when employment increases by one unit. The **marginal product** of labour is the change in total product resulting from a one-unit increase in the quantity of labour employed. It is calculated by dividing the change in total product by the change in labour. For example, when the quantity of labour increases from 2 to 3 workers, total product increases from 10 to 13 jumpers. The change in total product – 3 jumpers – is divided by the change in labour – 1 worker – so the marginal product of the third worker is 3 jumpers.

The average product shows how productive workers are on the average. The **average product** of labour is equal to total product divided by the quantity of labour employed. For example, in Table 10.1, 3 workers can knit 13 jumpers a day, so the average product of labour is 13 divided by 3, which is 4.33 jumpers per worker.

If you look closely at the numbers in Table 10.1, you can see some patterns. For example, as employment increases, marginal product at first increases and then begins to decrease. For example, marginal product increases from 4 jumpers a day for the first worker to 6 jumpers a day for the second worker and then decreases to 3 jumpers a day for the third worker. Average product also at first increases and then decreases. The relationships between these concepts of product and the number of workers employed can be seen more clearly by looking at the product curves.

Product Curves

The product curves are graphs of the relationships between employment and the three product concepts you've just studied. They show how total product, marginal product and average product change as employment changes. They also show the relationships among the three concepts. Let's look at the product curves.

Total Product Curve

Figure 10.1 shows Neat Knits' total product curve, *TP*. As employment increases, so does the number of jumpers knitted. Points *A* to *F* on the curve correspond to the same rows in Table 10.1.

The total product curve is similar to the *production possibilities frontier* (explained in Chapter 2, p. 32). It separates the attainable output levels from those that are unattainable. All the points that lie above the curve are unattainable. Points that lie below the curve, in the orange area, are attainable. But they are inefficient – they use more labour than is necessary to produce a given output. Only the points *on* the total product curve are technologically efficient.

Look carefully at the shape of the total product curve. As employment increases from zero to 1 worker per day, the curve becomes steeper. Then, as employment continues to increase to 3, 4, and 5 workers per day, the curve becomes less steep. The steeper the slope of the total product curve, the greater is marginal product, as you are about to see.

Figure 10.1

Total Product Curve

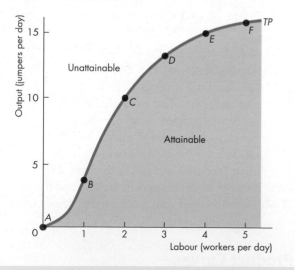

The total product curve (*TP*), based on the data in Table 10.1, shows how many jumpers Neat Knits can produce when it uses 1 knitting machine and different amounts of labour. For example, using 1 knitting machine, 2 workers can produce 10 jumpers a day (row *C*). Points *A* to *F* on the curve correspond to the rows of Table 10.1. The total product curve separates the attainable output from the unattainable output.

Marginal Product Curve

Figure 10.2 shows Neat Knits' marginal product of labour with 1 machine. Part (a) reproduces the total product curve from Figure 10.1. Part (b) shows the marginal product curve, *MP*.

In part (a), the heights of the orange bars illustrate the marginal product of labour. Marginal product is also measured by the slope of the total product curve. Recall that the slope of a curve is the change in the value of the variable measured on the *y*-axis – output – divided by the change in the variable measured on the *x*-axis – labour input – as we move along the curve. A 1-unit increase in labour input, from 2 to 3 workers, increases output from 10 to 13 jumpers, so the slope from point *C* to point *D* is 3, the same as the marginal product that we've just calculated.

We've calculated the marginal product of labour for a series of unit increases in the amount of labour. But labour is divisible into smaller units than one person. It is divisible into hours and even minutes. By varying the amount of labour in the smallest imaginable units, we can draw the marginal product curve shown in Figure 10.2(b). The *height* of this curve measures the *slope* of the total product curve at a point. The total product curve in part (a) shows that an increase in employment from 2 to 3 workers increases output from 10 to 13 jumpers (an increase of 3). The increase in output of 3 jumpers appears on the vertical axis of part (b) as the marginal product of going from 2 to 3 workers. We plot that marginal product at the mid-point between 2 and 3 workers. Notice that marginal product shown in Figure 10.2(b) reaches a peak at 1 unit of labour and at that point marginal product is more than 6. The peak occurs at 1 unit of labour because the total product curve is steepest at 1 unit of labour.

The total, marginal and average product curves are different for different firms and different types of goods. BMW's product curves are different from those of your local supermarket, which in turn are different from those of Sam's jumper factory. But the shapes of the product curves are similar, because almost every production process incorporates two features:

◆ Increasing marginal returns initially
◆ Diminishing marginal returns eventually

Increasing Marginal Returns

Increasing marginal returns occur when the marginal product of an additional worker exceeds the marginal product of the previous worker. Increasing marginal returns

Figure 10.2

Marginal Product

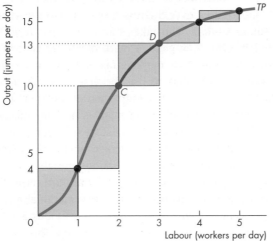

(a) Total product

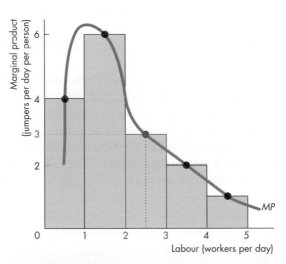

(b) Marginal product

Marginal product is illustrated in both parts of the figure by the orange bars. The height of each bar indicates the size of the marginal product. For example, when labour increases from 2 to 3, marginal product is the orange bar whose height is 3 jumpers. (Marginal product is shown midway between the labour inputs to emphasize that it is the result of *changing* inputs – moving from one level to the next.) The steeper the slope of the total product curve (*TP*) in part (a), the larger is marginal product (*MP*) in part (b). Marginal product increases to a maximum (when 1 worker is employed in this example) and then declines – diminishing marginal product.

arise from increased specialization and division of labour in the production process. For example, if Sam employs just one worker at Neat Knits, that person has to learn all the different aspects of jumper production: running the knitting machines, fixing breakdowns, packaging and mailing jumpers and buying and checking the type and colour of the wool. All of these tasks have to be done by that one person.

If Sam employs a second person, the two workers can specialize in different parts of the production process. As a result, two workers produce more than twice as much as one. The marginal product of the second worker is greater than the marginal product of the first worker. Marginal returns are increasing.

Diminishing Marginal Returns

Most product processes experience increasing marginal returns initially. But all production processes eventually reach a point of diminishing marginal returns. **Diminishing marginal returns** occur when the marginal product of an additional worker is less than the marginal product of the previous worker.

Diminishing marginal returns arise from the fact that more and more workers are using the same machinery in the same plant. As more workers are added, there is less and less for the additional workers to do that is productive. For example, if Sam employs a third worker, output increases but not by as much as it did when he added the second worker. In this case, after two workers are employed, all the gains from specialization and the division of labour have been exhausted. By employing a third worker, the factory produces more jumpers, but the equipment is being operated closer to its limits. There are even times when the third worker has nothing to do because the plant is running without the need for further attention. Adding yet more and more workers continues to increase output but by successively smaller amounts. Marginal returns are diminishing. This phenomenon is such a pervasive one that it is called 'the law of diminishing returns'. The **law of diminishing returns** states that:

> **As a firm uses more of a variable input, with a given quantity of fixed inputs, the marginal product of the variable input eventually diminishes.**

You will be using the concept of diminishing marginal returns again when you study a firm's costs. But before we do that, let's look at the average product of labour and the average product curve.

Average Product Curve

Figure 10.3 illustrates Neat Knits' average product of labour, *AP*, and the relationship between the average and marginal product. Points *B* to *F* on the average product curve are plotted from the same rows in Table 10.1. Average product increases from 1 to 2 workers (its maximum value is at point *C*) but then decreases as yet more workers are employed. Average product is largest when average product and marginal product are equal, and the marginal product curve cuts the average product curve at the point of maximum average product. For employment levels at which the marginal product exceeds average product, average product is increasing. For employment levels at which marginal product is less than average product, average product is decreasing.

The relationship between the average and marginal product curves is a general feature of the relationship between the average and marginal values of any variable. Let's look at a familiar example.

Figure 10.3

Average Product

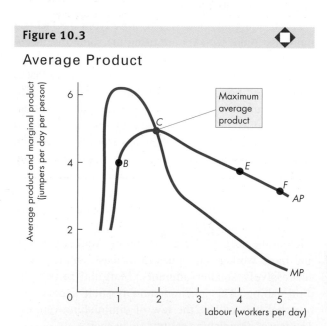

The figure shows the average product of labour, *AP*, and the marginal product of labour, *MP*, and the relationship between the shapes of the two curves. With 1 worker per day, marginal product exceeds average product, so average product is increasing. With 2 workers per day, marginal product equals average product, so average product is at its maximum. With more than 2 workers per day, marginal product is less than average product, so average product is decreasing.

Marginal Marks and Average Marks

Another relationship between an average and a marginal variable is that between Sam's average mark and his marginal marks over 5 terms. (Sam is also a part-time business student who takes one course per term.) In the first term, Sam gains a mark of 50 per cent in his statistics exam. This mark is his marginal mark. It is also his average mark as it is the first exam taken. Sam takes French in the second term and gets 60 per cent in the exam. The French exam mark is now his marginal mark, but his average mark rises to 55 per cent, the average of 50 and 60. His average mark rises because his marginal mark is greater than his previous average mark – it pulls his average up. In the third term, Sam takes economics, his best subject. His marginal mark is 70 per cent, which is higher than his previous average. His marginal mark pulls his average up, this time to 60 per cent, the average of 50, 60 and 70. In the fourth term, Sam takes accounting. Unfortunately, he achieves only 60 per cent in the exam. This time, his marginal mark is equal to his previous average – so his average does not change. In the fifth term, Sam takes management but achieves only 50 per cent in the exam. This time his marginal mark is below his previous average and it drags his average down to 58 per cent: the average of 50, 60, 70, 60 and 50 per cent.

This example of an everyday relationship between marginal and average values agrees with the relationship between marginal and average product that we have just discovered. Sam's average mark increases when the mark on the last course taken, the marginal mark, exceeds his previous average. The average mark falls when the mark on the marginal course is below his previous average. His average mark is constant (it neither increases nor decreases) when the mark for the marginal course equals his previous average.

Review Quiz

1   Explain how the marginal product of labour and the average product of labour change as the quantity of labour employed increases.
2   Why does marginal product eventually diminish?
3   Explain how average product changes when marginal product exceeds average product and when average product exceeds marginal product.

Why should Sam care about Neat Knits' product curves? He cares because they influence costs. Let's look at Neat Knits' costs.

Short-run Cost

To produce more output in the short run, a firm must employ more labour, which means it must increase its costs. We describe the relationship between output and costs by using three concepts:

◆ Total cost
◆ Marginal cost
◆ Average cost

Total Cost

A firm's **total cost** (*TC*) is the cost of *all* the factors of production it uses. We divide total cost into two categories: total fixed cost and total variable cost.

Total fixed cost (*TFC*) is the cost of the firm's fixed inputs. For Sam, total fixed cost includes the cost of renting knitting machines and normal profit, which is the opportunity cost of his entrepreneurship (see Chapter 9 p. 181). The quantities of a fixed input don't change as output changes, so total fixed costs is the same at all levels of output.

Total variable cost (*TVC*) is the cost of the firm's variable inputs. For Sam, labour is the variable input, so this component of costs is his wage bill. Total variable cost changes as total product changes.

Total cost is the sum of total fixed costs and total variable cost. That is:

$$TC = TFC + TVC$$

The table in Figure 10.4 shows Neat Knits' total costs. With one knitting machine that Neat Knits rents for £25 per day, *TFC* is £25 a day. To produce jumpers, Neat Knits hires labour, which costs £25 per day. *TVC* is the number of workers multiplied by £25. For example, to produce 13 jumpers a day, Neat Knits hires 3 workers and its *TVC* is £75. *TC* is the sum of *TFC* and *TVC*, so to produce 13 jumpers a day, Neat Knits' total cost, *TC*, is £100. Check the calculation in each row of the table.

Figure 10.4 shows Neat Knits' total cost curves, which graph total cost against total product. The green total fixed cost curve (*TFC*) is horizontal because total fixed cost does not change when output changes. It is constant at £25. The purple total variable cost (*TVC*) and the blue total cost (*TC*) curve both slope upward because total variable cost increases as output increases. The arrows highlight total fixed cost as the vertical distance between the *TVC* and *TC* curves.

Figure 10.4

Short-run Total Cost

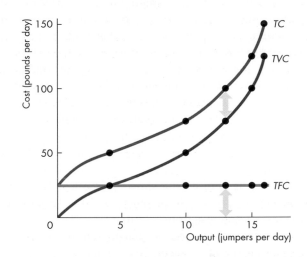

Labour (workers per day)	Output (jumpers per day)	Total fixed cost (*TFC*)	Total variable cost (*TVC*)	Total cost (*TC*)
			(pounds per day)	
0	0	25	0	25
1	4	25	25	25
2	10	25	50	75
3	13	25	75	100
4	15	25	100	125
5	16	25	125	150

Sam rents a knitting machine for £25 a day. This amount is Neat Knits' total fixed cost. Sam hires workers at a wage rate of £25 a day, and this cost is Neat Knits' total variable cost. For example, if Sam employs 3 workers, its total variable cost is (3 × £25), which equals £75.

Total cost is the sum of total fixed cost and total variable cost. For example, when Sam employs 3 workers, its total cost is £100 – total fixed cost of £25 plus total variable cost of £75.

The graph shows Neat Knits' total cost curves. Total fixed cost (*TFC*) is constant – it graphs as a horizontal line – and total variable cost (*TVC*) increases as output increases. Total cost (*TC*) also increases as output increases. The vertical distance between the total cost curve and the total variable cost curve is total fixed cost, as illustrated by the two arrows.

Marginal Cost

In Figure 10.4, total variable cost and total cost increase at a decreasing rate at small outputs and begin to increase at an increasing rate as output increases. To understand these patterns in the changes in total cost, we need to use the concept of *marginal cost*.

A firm's **marginal cost** is the change in total cost resulting from a one-unit increase in output. Marginal cost (MC) is calculated as the change in total cost (ΔTC) divided by the change in output (ΔQ). That is:

$$MC = \frac{\Delta TC}{\Delta Q}$$

The table in Figure 10.5 shows this calculation. For example, an increase in output from 10 to 13 jumpers increases total cost from £75 to £100. The change in output is 3 jumpers, and the change in total cost is £25. The marginal cost of one of those 3 jumpers is (£25 ÷ 3), which equals £8.33.

Figure 10.5 graphs the marginal cost as the red marginal cost curve, MC. This curve is U-shaped because, when Sam hires a second worker, marginal cost decreases, but when he hires a third, a fourth and a fifth worker, marginal cost successively increases.

Marginal cost decreases at low outputs because of economies from greater specialization. It eventually increases because of *the law of diminishing returns*. The law of diminishing returns means that each additional worker produces a successively smaller addition to output. So to get an additional unit of output, ever more workers are required. Because more workers are required to produce one additional unit of output, the cost of the additional output – marginal cost – must eventually increase.

Marginal cost tells us how total cost changes as output changes. The final cost concept tells us what it costs, on the average, to produce a unit of output. Let's now look at Neat Knits' average costs.

Average Cost

Average cost is the cost per unit of output. There are three average costs:

1　Average fixed cost

2　Average variable cost

3　Average total cost

Average fixed cost (AFC) is total fixed cost per unit of output. **Average variable cost** (AVC) is total variable cost per unit of output. **Average total cost** (ATC) is total cost per unit of output. The average cost concepts are calculated from the total cost concepts as follows:

$$TC = TFC + TVC$$

Divide each total cost term by the quantity produced, Q, to give:

$$\frac{TC}{Q} = \frac{TFC}{Q} + \frac{TVC}{Q}$$

or:

$$ATC = AFC + AVC$$

The table in Figure 10.5 shows the calculation of average total costs. For example, when output is 10 jumpers, average fixed cost is (£25 ÷ 10), which equals £2.50, average variable cost is (£50 ÷ 10), which equals £5.00, and average total cost is (£75 ÷ 10), which equals £7.50. Note average total cost is equal to average fixed cost (£2.50) plus average variable cost (£5.00).

Figure 10.5 shows the average cost curves. The green average fixed cost curve (AFC) slopes downward. As output increases, the same constant fixed cost is spread over a larger output. The blue average total cost curve (ATC) and the purple average variable cost curve (AVC) are U-shaped. The vertical distance between the average total cost and average variable cost curves is equal to average fixed cost – as indicated by the arrows. That distance shrinks as output increases because average fixed cost declines with increasing output.

The red marginal cost curve (MC) intersects the average variable cost curve and the average total cost curve at their minimum point. That is, when marginal cost is less than average cost, average cost is decreasing, and when marginal cost exceeds average cost, average cost is increasing. This relationship holds for both the ATC and the AVC curves and is another example of the relationship you saw in Figure 10.3 between average product and marginal product and in Sam's exam marks.

Why the Average Total Cost Curve is U-shaped

Average total cost, ATC, is the sum of average fixed cost, AFC, and average variable cost, AVC. So the shape of the ATC curve combines the shapes of the AFC and AVC curves. The U-shape of the average total

Figure 10.5

Marginal Cost and Average Costs

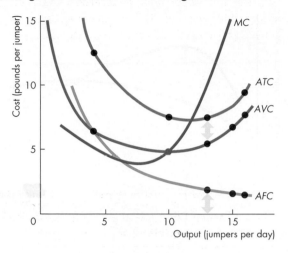

Marginal cost is calculated as the change in total cost divided by the change in output. When output increases from 4 to 10, an increase of 6, total cost increases by £25 and marginal cost is £25 ÷ 6, which equals £4.17. Each average cost concept is calculated by dividing the related total cost by output. When 10 jumpers are produced, AFC is £2.50 (£25 ÷ 10), AVC is £5 (£50 ÷ 10), and ATC is £7.50 (£75 ÷ 10).

The graph shows the marginal cost curve and the average cost curves. The marginal cost curve (MC) is U-shaped and intersects the average variable cost curve and the average total cost curve at their minimum points. Average fixed cost (AFC) decreases as output increases. The average total cost curve (ATC) and average variable cost curve (AVC) are U-shaped. The vertical distance between these two curves is equal to average fixed cost, as illustrated by the two arrows.

Labour (workers per day)	Output (jumpers per day)	Total fixed cost (TFC)	Total variable cost (TVC)	Total cost (TC)	Marginal cost (MC)	Average fixed cost (AFC)	Average variable cost (AVC)	Average total cost (ATC)
		(pounds per day)				(pounds per jumper)		
0	0	25		25				
					.... 6.25			
1	4	25	25	50		6.25	6.25	12.50
					.... 4.17			
2	10	25	50	75		2.50	5.00	7.50
					.... 8.33			
3	13	25	75	100		1.92	5.77	7.69
					.... 12.50			
4	15	25	100	125		1.67	6.00	8.33
					.... 25.00			
5	16	25	125	150		1.56	7.81	9.38

cost curve arises from the influence of two opposing forces:

1 Spreading fixed cost over a larger output

2 Eventually diminishing returns

When output increases, the firm spreads its fixed costs over a larger output and its average fixed cost decreases – its average fixed cost curve slopes downward.

Diminishing returns means that as output increases, ever-larger amounts of labour are needed to produce an additional unit of output. So average variable cost even-tually increases and the firm's AVC curve eventually slopes upward.

The shape of the average total cost curve combines these two effects. Initially, as output increases, both average fixed cost and average variable cost decrease, so average total cost decreases and the ATC curve slopes downward. But as output increases further and diminishing returns set in, average variable cost begins to increase. Eventually, average variable cost increases more quickly than average fixed cost decreases, so average total cost increases and the ATC curve slopes upward.

Cost Curves and Product Curves

The technology that a firm uses determines its costs. Figure 10.6 shows the links between the firm's technology constraint (its product curves) and its cost curves. The upper part of the figure shows the average product curve and the marginal product curve – like those in Figure 10.3. The lower part of the figure shows the average variable cost curve and the marginal cost curve – like those in Figure 10.5.

The figure highlights the links between technology and costs. As labour increases initially, marginal product and average product rise and marginal cost and average variable cost fall. Then, at the point of maximum marginal product, marginal cost is a minimum. As labour increases further, marginal product diminishes and marginal cost increases. But average product continues to rise and average variable cost continues to fall. Then at the point of maximum average product, average variable cost is a minimum. As labour increases further, average product diminishes and average variable cost increases.

Shifts in the Cost Curves

The position of a firm's short-run cost curves depends on two factors:

◆ Technology
◆ Prices of factors of production

Technology

A technological change that increases productivity shifts the total product curve upward. It also shifts the marginal product curve and the average product curve upward. With better technology, the same inputs can produce more output, and so technological change lowers cost and shifts the cost curves downward.

For example, advances in robotic production techniques have increased productivity in the car industry. As a result, the product curves of BMW, Renault and Volvo have shifted upward and their cost curves have shifted downward. But the relationships between their product curves and cost curves have not changed. The curves are still linked in the way shown in Figure 10.6.

Often, a technological advance results in a firm using more capital (a fixed input) and less labour (a variable input). For example, today the telephone companies use computers to provide directory assistance in place of the

Figure 10.6

Product Curves and Cost Curves

A firm's marginal product curve is linked to its marginal cost curve. If marginal product rises, marginal cost falls. If marginal product is a maximum, marginal cost is a minimum. If marginal product diminishes, marginal cost rises.

A firm's average product curve is linked to its average variable cost curve. If average product rises, average variable cost falls. If average product is a maximum, average variable cost is a minimum. If average product diminishes, average variable cost rises.

Table 10.2

A Compact Glossary of Costs

Term	Symbol	Definition	Equation
Fixed cost		Cost that is independent of the output level; cost of a fixed input	
Variable cost		Cost that varies with the output level; cost of a variable input	
Total fixed cost	*TFC*	Cost of the fixed inputs (equals their number times their unit price)	
Total variable cost	*TVC*	Cost of the variable inputs (equals their number times their unit price)	
Total cost	*TC*	Cost of all inputs	$TC = TFC + TVC$
Total product (output)	*TP*	Total quantity produced (Q)	
Marginal cost	*MC*	Change in total cost resulting from a one-unit increase in total product	$MC = \Delta TC \div \Delta Q$
Average fixed cost	*AFC*	Total fixed cost per unit of output	$AFC = TFC \div Q$
Average variable cost	*AVC*	Total variable cost per unit of output	$AVC = TVC \div Q$
Average total cost	*ATC*	Total cost per unit of output	$ATC = AFC + AVC$

human operators they used in the 1980s. When such a technological change occurs, total cost decreases, but fixed costs increase and variable costs decrease. This change in the mix of fixed cost and variable cost means that at low output levels, average total cost might increase, while at high output levels, average total cost decreases.

Prices of Factors of Production

An increase in factor prices increases costs and shifts the cost curves. But the way the curves shift depends on which factor prices change. A change in rent or some other component of *fixed* cost shifts the fixed cost curves (*TFC* and *AFC*) and the total cost curve (*TC*) upward, but leaves the variable cost curves (*AVC* and *TVC*) and the marginal cost curve (*MC*) unchanged. A change in wages or some other component of *variable* cost shifts the variable curves (*TVC* and *AVC*), the total cost curve (*TC*) and the marginal cost curve (*MC*) upward, but leaves the fixed cost curves (*AFC* and *TFC*) unchanged.

You have now completed your study of short run costs. All the concepts that you've met are summarized in a compact glossary in Table 10.2.

Review Quiz

1 Describe the relationship between a firm's short-run cost curves.
2 How does marginal cost change as output increases (a) initially, and (b) eventually?
3 What does the law of diminishing returns imply for the shape of the marginal cost curve?
4 What is the shape of the average total cost curve and why?
5 What are the shapes of the average variable cost curve and average total cost curve and why?

Long-run Cost

In the short run, a firm can vary the quantity of labour but the quantity of capital is fixed. So the firm has variable costs of labour and fixed costs of capital. In the long run, the firm can vary both the quantity of labour and the quantity of capital. So in the long run, all the firm's costs are variable. We are now going to study the firm's costs in the long run, when all costs are variable costs and when the quantity of labour and capital vary.

The behaviour of long-run costs depends on the firm's production function. The *production function* is the relationship between the maximum output attainable and the quantities of both labour and capital.

The Production Function

Table 10.3 shows Neat Knits' production function. The table lists the total product for four different quantities of capital. The quantity of capital is defined as the plant size. Plant 1 represents a factory with 1 knitting machine, the short-run example we studied before. The other three plants have 2, 3 and 4 machines. If Sam doubles the plant size to 2 knitting machines, the various amounts of output that labour can produce are shown in the third column of the table. The other two columns show the outputs of yet larger plants. Each column in the table could be graphed as a total product curve for each plant size.

Diminishing Returns

Diminishing returns occur in all four plants as the labour input increases. You can check that fact by doing similar calculations for the larger plants to those you've already done for a plant with one machine. Regardless of the plant size, as the labour input increases, its marginal product (eventually) decreases.

Diminishing Marginal Product of Capital

Just as we can calculate the marginal product of labour for each plant size, we can also calculate the marginal product of capital for each quantity of labour. The *marginal product of capital* is the change in total product divided by the change in capital employed when the amount of labour employed is constant. It is the change in output resulting from a one-unit increase in the quantity of capital employed.

Table 10.3

The Production Function

Labour (workers per day)	Output (jumpers per day)			
	Plant 1	Plant 2	Plant 3	Plant 4
1	4	10	13	15
2	10	15	18	21
3	13	18	22	24
4	15	20	24	26
5	16	21	25	27
Knitting machines (number)	1	2	3	4

The table shows the short-run total product data for four plant sizes with different numbers of machines. The bigger the plant, the larger is the total product for any given amount of labour employed. But for a given plant size, the marginal product of labour diminishes. For a given quantity of labour, the marginal product of capital diminishes.

For example, if Neat Knits employs 3 workers and increases the number of machines from 1 to 2, output increases from 13 to 18 jumpers a day. The marginal product of capital is 5 jumpers a day. The marginal product of capital diminishes. If with 3 workers, Neat Knits increases the number of machines from 2 to 3, output increases from 18 to 22 jumpers a day. The marginal product of the third machine is 4 jumpers a day, down from 5 jumpers a day for the second machine.

We can now see what the production function implies for long-run costs.

Short-run Cost and Long-run Cost

Continue to assume that labour costs £25 per worker per day and capital costs £25 per machine per day. Using these input prices and the data in Table 10.3, we can calculate and graph the average total cost curves for factories with different plant sizes. We've already studied the costs of a factory with 1 machine in Figures 10.5 and 10.6. The average total cost curve for that case is shown in Figure 10.7 at ATC_1. Figure 10.7 also shows the average total cost curve for a factory with 2 machines, ATC_2, with 3 machines, ATC_3, and with 4 machines, ATC_4.

Figure 10.7

Short-run Costs of Four Different Plants

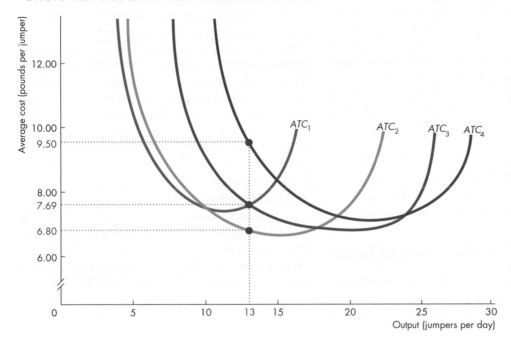

The figure shows short-run average total cost curves for four different quantities of capital. Neat Knits can produce 13 jumpers a day with 1 knitting machine on ATC_1, or with 3 knitting machines on ATC_3 for an average cost of £7.69 per jumper. It can produce the same number of jumpers by using 2 knitting machines on ATC_2 for £6.80 per jumper or with 4 machines on ATC_4 for £9.50 per jumper. If Neat Knits produces 13 jumpers a day, the least-cost method of production – the long-run method – is with 2 machines on ATC_2.

You can see, in Figure 10.7, that plant size has a big effect on the firm's average total cost. Two things stand out.

1 Each short-run average total cost curve is U-shaped.

2 For each short-run average total cost curve, the larger the plant, the greater is the output at which average total cost is a minimum.

Each short-run average total cost curve is U-shaped because, as the quantity of labour increases, its marginal product at first increases and then diminishes. These patterns in the marginal product of labour, which we examined in some detail for the plant with 1 knitting machine on pp. 204–205, occur at all plant sizes.

The minimum average total cost for a larger plant occurs at a greater output than it does for a smaller plant because the larger plant has a higher fixed cost and therefore, for any given output level, a higher average fixed cost.

Which one of the short-run average cost curves Neat Knits operates on depends on its plant size. In the long run, plant size is determined by the owner, Sam. His choice of plant size depends on the output he plans to produce. The reason is that the average total cost of producing a given output depends on the plant size.

To see why, suppose that Sam plans to produce 13 jumpers a day. With 1 machine, the average total cost curve is ATC_1 (in Figure 10.7) and the average total cost of 13 jumpers a day is £7.69 per jumper. With 2 machines, on ATC_2, average total cost is £6.80 per jumper. With 3 machines on ATC_3, average total cost is £7.69 per jumper, the same as with 1 machine. Finally, with 4 machines, on ATC_4, average total cost is £9.50 per jumper.

The economically efficient plant size for producing a given output is the one that has the lowest average total cost. For Neat Knits, the economically efficient plant to use to produce 13 jumpers a day is the one with 2 machines.

In the long run, Neat Knits chooses the plant size that minimizes average total cost. When a firm is producing a given output at the least possible cost, it is operating on its long-run average cost curve.

The **long-run average cost curve** is the relationship between the lowest attainable average total cost and output when both the plant size and labour are varied. The long-run average cost curve is a planning curve. It tells the firm the plant size and the quantity of labour to use at each output to minimize cost. Once the plant size is chosen, the firm operates on the short-run cost curves that apply to that plant size.

The Long-run Average Cost Curve

Figure 10.8 shows Neat Knits' long-run average cost curve, *LRAC*. This **long-run average cost** curve is derived from the short-run average total cost curves in Figure 10.7. For output up to 10 jumpers a day, the average total cost is lowest on ATC_1. For output rates between 10 and 18 jumpers a day, average total cost is lowest on ATC_2. For output rates between 18 and 24 jumpers a day, average total cost is lowest on ATC_3. For output rates in excess of 24 jumpers a day, average total cost is lowest on ATC_4.

In Figure 10.8, the segment of each *ATC* curve for which that plant has the lowest average total cost is shown as dark blue. The scallop-shaped curve made up of these segments is the long-run average cost curve.

Economies and Diseconomies of Scale

Economies of scale are features of a firm's technology that lead to falling long-run average cost as output increases. When economies of scale are present, the *LRAC* curve slopes downward. The *LRAC* in Figure 10.8 shows that Neat Knits experiences economies of scale for outputs up to 15 jumpers per day.

With given input prices, economies of scale occur when the percentage increase in output exceeds the percentage increase in inputs. If economies of scale are present, when a firm doubles all inputs, its output will more than double, and so average costs fall.

The main source of economies of scale are the specialization of labour and capital. For example, if BMW produces only 100 cars a week, each worker and each machine must be capable of performing many different tasks. But if it produces 10,000 cars a week, each worker and each piece of equipment can be highly specialized. Workers specialize in a small number of tasks at which they become highly proficient. Capital can also be specialized and more productive.

Constant returns to scale are features of a firm's technology that lead to constant long-run average costs as output increases. With constant returns, the *LRAC* is horizontal.

With given input prices, constant returns to scale occur if the percentage increase in output equals the percentage increase in inputs. If constant returns are present, when a firm doubles its inputs, its output will double and so its average total cost remains the same. For example, BMW can double its production of its 5-series by doubling its production facility for those cars.

Figure 10.8

The Long-run Average Cost Curve

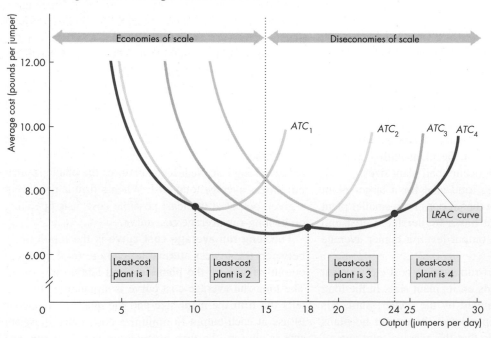

In the long run, Neat Knits can vary both capital and labour inputs. The long-run average cost curve traces the lowest attainable average total cost of production. Neat Knits produces on its long-run average cost curve if it uses 1 machine to produce up to 10 jumpers a day, 2 machines to produce between 10 and 18 jumpers a day, 3 machines to produce between 18 and 24 jumpers a day, and 4 machines to produce more than 24 jumpers a day. Within these ranges, Neat Knits varies its output by varying its labour input.

BMW can build an identical production line and hire an identical number of workers. With the two identical production lines, BMW produces exactly twice as many cars.

Diseconomies of scale are features of a firm's technology that lead to rising long-run average costs as output increases. When diseconomies of scale are present, the *LRAC* curve slopes upward. In Figure 10.8, Neat Knits experiences diseconomies of scale at outputs greater than 15 jumpers.

With given input prices, diseconomies of scale occur if the percentage increase in output is less than the percentage increase in inputs. If diseconomies of scale are present, a firm doubles all its inputs and its output less than doubles, so its average total cost increases.

Decreasing returns to scale occur in all production processes at some output rate, but may not appear until a very large output rate is achieved. The most common source of decreasing returns to scale is the increasingly complex management and organizational structure required to control a large international firm. The larger the organization, the larger are the number of layers in the management pyramid and the greater are the costs of monitoring and maintaining control of the production and marketing process.

Minimum Efficient Scale

A firm experiences economies of scale up to some output level. Beyond that level, it moves into constant returns to scale or diseconomies of scale. A firm's **minimum efficient scale** is the smallest quantity of output at which long-run average cost reaches its lowest level. The minimum efficient scale plays a role in determining market structure, as you will learn in the next three chapters. The minimum efficient scale also helps to answer some questions about real businesses.

Economies of Scale at Neat Knits

Neat Knits' production technology, shown in Table 10.3, illustrates economies of scale and diseconomies of scale. If Sam decides to double the labour and capital input from 1 of each to 2 of each, output more than doubles, rising from 4 jumpers to 15 jumpers per day. Neat Knits is experiencing economies of scale and the long-run average cost decreases. But if Sam decides to increase inputs from 2 workers and 2 machines to 3 of each, inputs increase by 50 per cent but output increases by less than 50 per cent, rising from 15 jumpers to 22 jumpers per day. Now Neat Knits experiences

diseconomies of scale and its long-run average costs increase. Neat Knits experiences a minimum efficient scale at 15 jumpers per day.

Generating Electric Power and Producing Cars

At the beginning of this chapter, we noted that producers of electric power such as Powergen often operate flat out. On the coldest days, the firm doesn't have enough production equipment on hand to meet demand and has to buy power from other producers. You can now see why this occurs and why Powergen doesn't build a bigger plant. Powergen uses the plant size that minimizes average total cost for the level of output on a typical day. It produces above minimum efficient scale and experience diseconomies of scale. That is, Powergen has short-run average total cost curves like ATC_3 in Figure 10.8. If Powergen had a larger plant, its average total cost of producing its normal output would be higher than necessary.

We also noted at the beginning of the chapter that most car makers can produce far more cars than they can sell. Why do car makers have expensive equipment lying around that isn't fully used? You can now answer this question. Car producers experience economies of scale. The minimum cost of production occurs on a short-run average total cost curve that looks like ATC_1 in Figure 10.8.

Review Quiz

1. What does a firm's production function show and how is it related to a total product curve?
2. Does the law of diminishing returns apply to capital as well as labour? Explain.
3. What does a firm's long-run average cost curve show? How is it related to the firm's short-run average cost curve?
4. What are economies and diseconomies of scale? How do they arise? What do they imply for the shape of the long-run average cost curve?
5. How is a firm's minimum efficient scale determined?

You have now studied how a firm's costs vary as it changes its inputs and output. The appendix presents an alternative analysis of costs. Our next task is to study how firms determine the quantity to produce, the price to charge and the profits they make. The *Business Case Study* applies what you have learned about a firm's cost curves. It looks at the product and costs of European airlines.

Business Case Study
Short-run and Long-run Costs

The Airline Consolidation Crisis

The Industry before 2000

The European airline industry in 2000 had too many firms for them all to operate profitably. The industry had more than 40 national airlines. Of these, 15 were major international carriers and some were airlines that specialized in European routes.

Between 1995 and 2000, the number of passengers carried by Europe's airline industry increased by 5 per cent annually.

Despite this rising output, airlines' profit margins were slim and rarely exceeded 3 per cent[1] (a lower return than that earned on money in the bank!).

Even Europe's large airlines were small by world standards. The 7 largest European airlines carried only 47 per cent of passenger traffic compared with the 7 largest US airlines, which carried more than 80 per cent of US passenger traffic.[2]

European Airlines in Crisis

Airline	Staff cuts in 2000	Employees in 2000	Capacity/ operating cuts in 2001	Passengers in 2000 (millions)	Wage cuts in 2001
Aer Lingus	2,500	6,600	25%	7	
Alitalia	2,500	23,500		25	
British Airways	7,000	56,000	10%	48	✓15%
Iberia	3,000	29,000	11%	30	✓10%
KLM	2,500	33,700	15%	16	✓
Lufthansa		69,500	3 routes	40	
Sabena		11,000	Insolvency	11	
SAS	9,000	30,000	(shut down)		
Swiss Air	2,600	71,000	(shut down)		

Source: Airline web pages and BBC (19 October 2001), Round-up: Aviation in crisis.

The Crisis

The events of 11 September 2001, decreased the demand for international and European air travel by 30 per cent within a week.

Faced with this large decrease in demand, several European airlines announced they were insolvent. Most airlines announced massive cuts in staff and many announced wage freezes, wage cuts and cuts in services. The table summarizes these responses. Airline share prices plunged and airlines failed to pay dividends. Losses of up to £7 billion worldwide were reported.

Strategies for Survival

Rigas Dognais, former chairman and CEO of Olympic Airways, said European airlines must consolidate through cross-border mergers and acquisitions to survive.[3] KLM reported a €133 million loss in 2002, but Air France reported a €111 million profit. By September 2003, Air France agreed a merger with KLM, with an estimated cut in costs of up to €495 million a year.[4] Alitalia is keen to join the merged group but is currently state owned and in severe financial difficulties. British Airways tried and failed to merge with KLM. Instead, in 2003, British Airways introduced its 'Future Size and Shape' strategy to cut routes, staff and capital, shaving £800 million from its £7 billion annual costs by 2004.

[1] *Financial Times* (9 October 2001), Brussels unwilling to offer airlines aid.
[2] *Financial Times* (15 October 2001), R. Doganis, Opinion: Saving Europe's airlines.

[3] Ibid.
[4] BBC (30 September 2003). Does KLM–Air France Make Sense? and European Airlines Join Forces.

Economic Analysis

◆ Figure 1 shows the total product curves for Air France and KLM passenger services before and after their merger.

◆ In 2000, the airlines operated on TP_0. Air France employed 65,000 people and carried 41 million passengers a year and KLM employed 34,000 people and carried 23 million passengers a year.

◆ The merged Air France–KLM operates on the total product curve TP_1 in Figure 1. The merged airline can produce the combined output of 64 million passengers a year with fewer employees than the combined pre-merger workforces.

◆ Figure 2 shows the effect of the merger on average total cost. Air France and KLM operate on ATC_0 before the merger.

◆ The merged airline operates on the average total cost curve ATC_1.

◆ The merger increases total fixed cost, so for low passenger numbers, ATC_1 is higher than ATC_0. But the greater productivity of the merged airline lowers average total cost for outputs in the range that the airline experiences.

◆ By looking at the ATC curves, you can see why responding to the crisis of 2001 needed more than short-run cuts in staff numbers. A decrease in employment and output might end up increasing average total cost as an airline slides leftward along its ATC curve.

◆ Either a cut in wages (and other costs) or an increase in output per unit of labour is needed to bring the airlines back to profitability.

◆ BA's strategy of cutting wages and shedding unprofitable routes and planes is an attempt to achieve greater output per unit of labour.

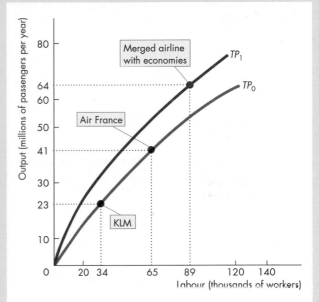

Figure 1 Total product

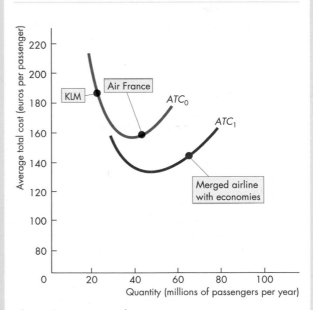

Figure 2 Average total cost

Summary

Key Points

Time Frames for Decisions (p. 202)

◆ In the short run, the quantity of one input in production is fixed and the quantities of another can be varied.

◆ In the long run, the quantities of all inputs can be varied.

Short-run Technology Constraint (pp. 203–207)

◆ A total product curve shows how much output a firm can produce using a given quantity of capital and different quantities of labour.

◆ Initially, marginal product increases as the quantity of labour increases. But eventually, marginal product diminishes – the law of diminishing marginal returns.

◆ Average product increases initially and eventually diminishes.

Short-run Cost (pp. 207–211)

◆ As output increases, total fixed cost is constant, and total variable cost and total cost increase.

◆ As output increases, average variable cost, average total cost and marginal cost decrease at small outputs and increase at large outputs. These costs curves are U-shaped.

Long-run Cost (pp. 212–215)

◆ Long-run cost is the cost of production when all inputs – labour as well as plant and equipment – have been adjusted to their economically efficient levels.

◆ There is a set of short-run cost curves for each different plant size. There is one least-cost plant for each output. The larger the output, the larger is the plant that will minimize average total cost.

◆ The long-run average cost curve traces the relationship between the lowest attainable average total cost and output when both capital and labour inputs can be varied.

◆ With economies of scale, the long-run average cost curve slopes downward. With diseconomies of scale, the long-run average cost curve slopes upward.

Key Figures and Table

Key Terms

Problems

*1 Rubber Dinghies' total product schedule is:

Labour (workers per week)	Output (rubber boats per week)
1	1
2	3
3	6
4	10
5	15
6	21
7	26
8	30
9	33
10	35

a Draw the total product curve.

b Calculate the average product of labour and draw the average product curve.

c Calculate the marginal product of labour and draw the marginal product curve.

d What is the relationship between average product and marginal product when Rubber Dinghies produces (i) fewer than 30 boats a week and (ii) more than 30 boats a week?

2 Charlie's Chocolates' total product schedule is:

Labour (workers per day)	Output (boxes per day)
1	12
2	24
3	48
4	84
5	132
6	192
7	240
8	276
9	300
10	312

a Draw the total product curve.

b Calculate the average product of labour and draw the average product curve.

c Calculate the marginal product of labour and draw the marginal product curve.

d What is the relationship between the average product and marginal product when Charlie's Chocolates produces (i) less than 276 boxes a day and (ii) more than 276 boxes a day?

---

*Solutions to odd-numbered problems are available on *Parkin Interactive*.

*3 In problem 1, the price of labour is €400 a week and total fixed cost is €1,000 a week.

a Calculate total cost, total variable cost and total fixed cost for each output and draw the short-run total cost curves.

b Calculate average total cost, average fixed cost, average variable cost and marginal cost at each output and draw the short-run average and marginal cost curves.

4 In problem 2, the price of labour is €50 per day and total fixed costs are €50 per day.

a Calculate total cost, total variable cost and total fixed costs for each level of output and draw the short-run total cost curves.

b Calculate average total cost, average fixed cost, average variable cost and marginal cost at each level of output and draw the short-run average and marginal cost curves.

*5 In problem 3, suppose that Rubber Dinghies' total fixed cost increases to €1,100 a week. Explain what changes occur to the short-run average and marginal cost curves.

6 In problem 4, suppose that the price of labour increases to €70 per day. Explain what changes occur to the short-run average and marginal cost curves.

*7 In problem 3, Rubber Dinghies buys a second plant and now the total product of each quantity of labour doubles. The total fixed cost of operating each plant is €1,000 a week. The wage rate is €400 a week.

a Set out the average total cost schedule when Rubber Dinghies operates two plants.

b Draw the long-run average cost curve.

c Over what output range is it efficient to operate one plant and two plants?

8 In problem 4, Charlie's Chocolates buys a second plant and now the total product of each quantity of labour doubles. The total fixed cost of operating each plant is €50 a day. The wage rate is €50 a day.

a Set out the average total cost curve when Charlie's operates two plants.

b Draw the long-run average cost curve.

c Over what output range is it efficient to operate one plant and two plants?

*9 In problem 3, suppose that Rubber Dinghies' total fixed cost decreases to €800 a week. Explain what changes occur to the short-run average and marginal cost curves.

10 In problem 4, suppose that the price of labour decreases to €40 per day. Explain what changes occur to the short-run average and marginal cost curves.

*11 The table shows the production function of Bonnie's Balloon Rides.

Labour (workers per day)	Output (rides per day)			
	Plant 1	Plant 2	Plant 3	Plant 4
1	4	10	13	15
2	10	15	18	21
3	13	18	22	24
4	15	20	24	26
5	16	21	25	27
Balloons (number)	1	2	3	4

Bonnie pays €500 a day for each balloon she rents and €250 a day for each balloon operator she hires.

a Find and graph the average total cost curve for each plant size.

b Draw Bonnie's long-run average cost curve.

c What is Bonnie's minimum efficient scale?

d Explain how Bonnie uses her long-run average cost curve to decide how many balloons to rent.

12 The table shows the production function of Cathy's Cakes.

Labour (workers per day)	Output (cakes per day)			
	Plant 1	Plant 2	Plant 3	Plant 4
1	20	40	55	65
2	40	60	75	85
3	65	75	90	100
4	65	85	100	110
Ovens (number)	1	2	3	4

Cathy pays €100 a day for each oven she rents and €50 a day for each kitchen worker she hires.

a Find and graph the average total cost curve for each plant size.

b Draw Cathy's long-run average cost curve.

c Over what output range does Cathy experience economies of scale?

d Explain how Cathy uses her long-run average cost curve to decide how many ovens to rent.

Critical Thinking

1 Read the *Business Case Study* on pp. 216–217 about the problems of the European airlines and use the links on *Parkin Interactive* to read the original articles.

a What is the main difference between the structure of the US airlines and the European airlines?

b Why did the European airlines find it difficult to maintain profits when demand decreased?

c If an airline like Sabena is insolvent, why might it be the target for a takeover by another airline?

d Why have so few European airlines agreed to mergers or takeovers?

e What would be the effect of mergers in the European airline industry?

f Why does Robert Ayling, former BA CEO, say that the European airlines need a much more flexible method of providing aeroplanes?

g Why do some industry experts think that the proposed KLM–Air France merger might fail to reap economies of scale?

2 A telecommunication company is considering replacing human telephone operators with computers. Create your own example and graph:

a The average cost curves and the marginal cost curve when the firm uses human operators.

b The average cost curves and the marginal cost curve when the firm uses computers.

Web Exercises

Use the links on *Parkin Interactive* to work the following exercise.

1 Read about teleworking and then:

a What is the short-run impact of introducing teleworking on company costs?

b Why does teleworking involve investing in new technology?

c What is the long-run impact of introducing teleworking on company costs?

d What do you think are the advantages and disadvantages for employees of teleworking?

e Why did companies think that employees would take more time off when teleworking?

f Why might employees tend to work harder as a result of teleworking from home as opposed to working from an office or depot?

CHAPTER 10 APPENDIX
Producing at Least Cost

After studying this appendix, you will be able to:

◆ Make an isoquant map and explain the law of diminishing marginal rate of substitution

◆ Explain an isocost line and how a change in factor price shifts it

◆ Calculate the least-cost technique of production

Isoquants and Factor Substitution

A firm's long-run production function describes all the technically feasible combinations of labour and capital that can produce given output levels. Whatever goods it produces, a firm can choose between labour-intensive or capital-intensive production techniques. To move from one technique to another, a firm must change the combination of labour and capital it uses – a change called factor substitution.

In this appendix, you are going to use a new model to find the best combination of factors.

Figure A10.1 shows Neat Knits' production function. The figure shows that in the long run, Neat Knits can use three different combinations of labour and capital to produce 15 jumpers a day, and two different combinations to produce 10 and 21 jumpers a day. So to maximize profit, Neat Knits uses the least-cost combination of labour and capital that minimizes its total cost.

An Isoquant Map

An **isoquant** is a curve that shows the different combinations of labour and capital required to produce a given quantity of output. The word isoquant means "equal quantity". There is an isoquant for each output level. A series of isoquants is called an **isoquant map**. Figure A10.2 shows an isoquant map for Neat Knits with three isoquants: one for 10 jumpers a day, one for 15 jumpers a day and one for 21 jumpers a day. Each isoquant shown is based on the production function in Figure A10.1.

Figure A10.1

Neat Knits' Production Function

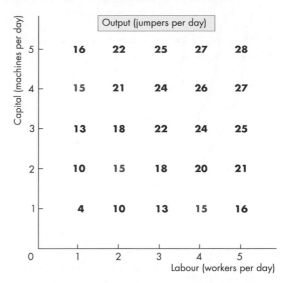

The figure shows how many jumpers can be produced each day using different combinations of labour and capital. For example, Neat Knits can produce 15 jumpers a day using 1 worker and 4 machines, or 2 workers and 2 machines, or 4 workers and 1 machine.

Although all goods and services can be produced using a variety of alternative production techniques, the ease with which labour and capital can be substituted for each other varies from industry to industry. The production function reflects the ease of factor substitution and can be used to calculate the degree of substitutability between factors. This calculation involves the marginal rate of substitution of labour for capital. The **marginal rate of substitution of labour for capital** is the increase in labour needed per unit decrease in capital to allow output to remain constant. Let's look at this in more detail.

The Marginal Rate of Substitution

The marginal rate of substitution is the magnitude of the slope of an isoquant. Figure A10.3 shows the isoquant for 13 jumpers a day. Pick any point on this isoquant and imagine decreasing capital by the smallest conceivable amount and increasing labour by the amount necessary to keep output constant at 13 jumpers. As we decrease the quantity of capital and increase the quantity of labour to keep output constant at 13 jumpers a day, we travel down along the isoquant.

Figure A10.2

An Isoquant Map

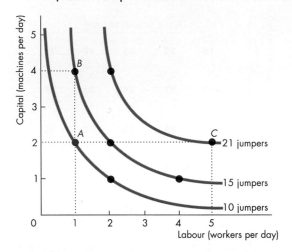

The figure shows an isoquant map for just three isoquants for Neat Knits. The isoquants correspond to the production function for 10, 15 and 21 jumpers a day. If Neat Knits uses 2 machines and 1 worker (at point *A*), it produces 10 jumpers a day. If it uses 4 machines and 1 worker (point *B*), it produces 15 jumpers a day. If it uses 2 machines and 5 workers (point *C*), it produces 21 jumpers a day.

Figure A10.3

The Marginal Rate of Substitution

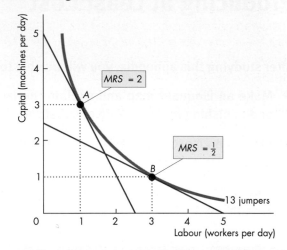

The marginal rate of substitution is measured by the absolute magnitude of the slope of the isoquant. For example, use the red line that is tangential to the isoquant at point *A*. Calculate the slope of that line to find the slope of the isoquant at point *A*. The magnitude of the slope at point *A* is 2, so the marginal rate of substitution of labour for capital is 2. The marginal rate of substitution at point *B* is found from the slope of the red line at point *B*. The slope is 1/2, so the marginal rate of substitution of labour for capital at point *B* is 1/2.

In Figure A10.3, the marginal rate of substitution at point *A* is the absolute magnitude of the slope of the straight red line that is tangent to the isoquant at point *A*. The slope of the isoquant at point *A* equals the slope of the line. To calculate the slope, move along the red line from 5 knitting machines and no workers to 2.5 workers and no knitting machines. Capital decreases by 5 knitting machines and labour increases by 2.5 workers. The magnitude of the slope is 5 divided by 2.5, which equals 2. So when using technique *A* to produce 13 jumpers a day, the marginal rate of substitution of labour for capital is 2.

The marginal rate of substitution at point *B* is the absolute magnitude of the slope of the straight red line that is tangent to the isoquant at point *B*. Along this red line, if capital decreases by 2.5 knitting machines, labour increases by 5 workers. The magnitude of the slope is 2.5 knitting machines divided by 5, which equals 1/2. So when using technique *B* to produce 13 jumpers a day, the marginal rate of substitution of labour for capital is 1/2.

The marginal rates of substitution we have just calculated obey the **law of diminishing marginal rate of substitution** which states that:

The marginal rate of substitution of labour for capital diminishes as the amount of labour increases and the amount of capital decreases.

The law of diminishing marginal rate of substitution determines the shape of the isoquant. When the capital factor is large and the labour factor is small, the isoquant is steep and the marginal rate of substitution of labour for capital is large. As the capital factor decreases and the labour factor increases, the isoquant becomes flatter and the marginal rate of substitution of labour for capital diminishes. Isoquants bow towards the origin.

You are going to use an isoquant map to work out a firm's least-cost technique of production, but first we must add the firm's costs to the model.

Isocost Lines

An **isocost line** shows the combinations of labour and capital that can be bought for a given total cost. Suppose Neat Knits' total cost is £100 per day. Knitting-machine operators are hired for £25 a day and knitting machines are rented for £25 a day. Figure A10.4 shows five possible combinations of labour and capital (*A*, *B*, *C*, *D* and *E*) that Neat Knits can employ for £100. Point *B*, for example, shows that Neat Knits can use 3 machines (costing £75) and 1 worker (costing £25). If neat Knits can employ workers and machines for fractions of a day, then any combination along the line *AE* will cost Neat Knits £100 a day. This line is Neat Knits' isocost line for a total cost of £100.

The Isocost Equation

An isocost equation describes an isocost line. The variables that affect a firm's total cost (*TC*) are the price of labour (P_L), the price of capital (P_K), the quantity of labour (*L*) and the quantity of capital (*K*).

The cost of the labour is ($P_L \times L$). The cost of capital is ($P_K \times K$). And total cost is the sum of these two costs.

Equation 1 shows a firm's total cost:

$$P_L L + P_K K = TC \qquad (1)$$

Equation 2 shows the total cost for Neat Knits using the numbers in the example that we're using. The wage rate is £25 a day and the capital rental rate is also £25 a day. So Neat Knits' total cost is:

$$£25L + £25K = £100 \qquad (2)$$

To calculate the isocost equation, divide the firm's total cost by the price of capital and then subtract (P_L/P_K)L from both sides of the resulting equation. Equation 3 is the isocost equation:

$$K = \frac{TC}{P_K} - \frac{P_L}{P_K} \times L \qquad (3)$$

Equation 3 tells us how the firm can vary the quantity of capital as it varies the quantity of labour, holding total cost constant. Equation 4 is Neat Knits' isocost equation:

$$K = 4 - L \qquad (4)$$

Equation 4 corresponds to the isocost line in Figure A10.4.

Figure A10.4

Neat Knits' Factor Possibilities

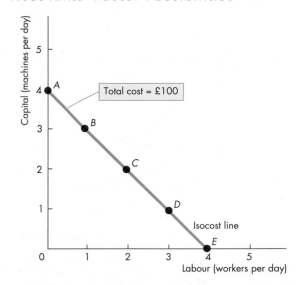

If labour and capital each cost £25 per unit a day, for a total cost of £100, Neat Knits can employ the combinations of labour and capital shown by points *A* to *E*. The line through these points is an isocost line. It shows all possible combinations of labour and capital that Neat Knits can hire for a total cost of £100 when labour and capital cost £25 per unit a day.

The Isocost Map

An **isocost map** is a series of isocost lines, each one of which represents a different total cost but for given prices of labour and capital.

The larger the total cost, the greater are the quantities of labour and capital that can be employed. Figure A10.5 shows an isocost map. The middle isocost is the one you've seen before for a total cost of £100, when labour and capital cost £25 a day each. The other two isocost lines are for a total cost of £125 and £75, holding constant the factor prices at £25 each. The larger the total cost, the further out is the isocost line from the origin.

The Effect of Factor Prices

The magnitude of the slope of the isocost lines shown in Figure A10.5 is 1. The slope tells us that 1 unit of labour costs 1 unit of capital. To decrease its capital by 1 unit and keep its total cost at £100 a day, Neat Knits must increase the quantity of labour by 1 unit.

Figure A10.5

An Isocost Map

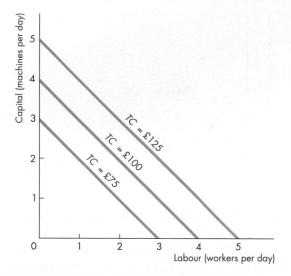

There is an isocost line for each level of total cost. This isocost map shows three isocost lines, one for a total cost of £75, one for £100 and one for £125. For each isocost line here, the price of labour and capital is £25 each. The slope of any isocost line is determined by the relative price of the two factors. The larger the total cost, the farther is the isocost line from the origin.

Figure A10.6

Factor Prices and the Isocost Line

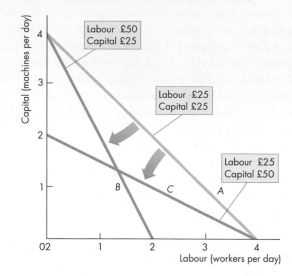

The slope of the isocost line depends on the relative factor prices. Three cases are shown (each for a total cost of £100 a day). If both labour and capital have a price of £25 a day, the isocost line is line *A*. If the price of labour rises to £50 but the price of capital remains at £25, the isocost line becomes steeper and is line *B*. If the price of capital rises to £50 and the price of labour remains at £25, the isocost line becomes flatter and is line *C*.

If factor prices change, the slope of the isocost line changes. You can see the effect of factor prices on the slope of the isocost line by recalling the isocost equation:

$$K = \frac{TC}{P_K} - \frac{P_L}{P_K} \times L \qquad (3)$$

If the wage rate rises to £50 a day and the rental rate of a machine remains at £25 a day, then 1 unit of labour costs 2 units of capital. The relative price of labour to capital becomes £50/£25 which is 2. The isocost line becomes the steeper line *B* in Figure A10.5.

If the capital rental rate rises to £50 a day and the wage rate remains at £25 a day, then 1 unit of capital costs 2 units of labour. The relative price of labour to capital becomes £25/£50 which is 0.5. The isocost line becomes the less steep line *C* in Figure A10.5.

The higher the relative price of labour, the steeper is the isocost line. The magnitude of the slope of the isocost line measures the relative price of labour in terms of capital – the price of labour divided by the price of capital.

The Least-cost Technique

The **least-cost technique** is the combination of labour and capital that minimizes the total cost of producing a given level of output.

Suppose Neat Knits wants to produce 15 jumpers a day, given that capital and labour cost £25 a day. What is the least-cost technique that Neat Knits can use? Figure A10.7 shows the isoquant for an output of 15 jumpers and two isocost lines, each drawn for a situation where labour and capital cost £25 each. One isocost is for a total cost of £125 and the other for £100.

At point *A* in Figure A10.7, Neat Knits can produce 15 jumpers using 1 worker and 4 machines. With this technique, the total cost is £125. Point *C*, which uses 4 workers and 1 machine, is another technique that the firm can use to produce 15 jumpers for the same cost of £125. At point *B*, Neat Knits uses 2 machines and 2 workers to produce 15 jumpers, but the cost is £100. So

Figure A10.7

The Least-Cost Technique of Production

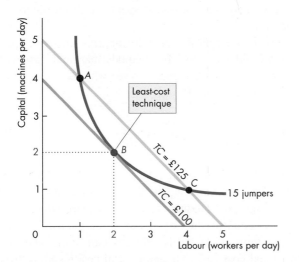

An output of 15 jumpers can be produced using 4 machines and 1 worker at point *A*, or using 1 machine and 4 workers at point *C*. Both techniques lies on the isocost line where total cost is £125. An output of 15 jumpers can also be produced using 2 machines and 2 workers at point *B*. Point *B* is the least-cost technique of producing 15 jumpers as this lies on the lowest isocost line where total cost is £100. At point *B*, the isoquant for 15 jumpers is tangential to the isocost line for £100. The slope of the isoquant (the marginal rate of substitution) and the slope of the isocost line (the relative price of the factors) are the same.

point *B* is the least-cost technique or the economically efficient technique for producing 15 jumpers, when machines and workers cost £25 a day each.

Figure A10.7 shows that there is only one way for Neat Knits to produce 15 jumpers for £100, but several ways to produce 15 jumpers for more than £100. Techniques shown by points *A*, *B* and *C* are just examples. The points between *A*, *B* and *C* are also possible ways of producing 15 jumpers for a cost above £100 but less than £125. Isocost lines exist between those shown which cut the isoquant for 15 jumpers at points between *A*, *B* and *C*. Neat Knits could also produce 15 jumpers for a cost higher than £125 by moving to a point on the isoquant that cuts an isocost line higher than those shown.

The only technique that is least cost is at point *B* in Figure A10.7. Neat Knits cannot produce 15 jumpers for less than £100. If an isocost line existed below a total

cost of £100, it would not touch the isoquant for 15 jumpers. This is because when machines and workers cost £25 per day each, any amount less than £100 will not buy the factors needed to produce 15 jumpers.

Marginal Rate of Substitution and Marginal Products

The marginal rate of substitution and the marginal products are linked by an interesting formula:

The marginal rate of substitution of labour for capital equals the marginal product of labour divided by the marginal product of capital.

A few steps of reasoning are needed to establish this proposition.

First, we know that output changes when a firm changes the amounts of labour and capital employed. The change in output that results from a change in one of the factors is determined by the marginal product of the factor. So:

$$\text{Change in output} = (MP_L \times \Delta L) + (MP_K \times \Delta K) \quad (4)$$

Equation 4 shows a change in output equals the marginal product of labour, MP_L, multiplied by the change in labour, ΔL, plus the marginal product of capital, MP_K, multiplied by the change in capital, ΔK.

Suppose that Neat Knits wants to change its labour and capital factors but remain on its isoquant producing the same number of jumpers. To stay on the same isoquant, the change in output must be zero. We can make the change in output zero in equation (4) to give equation (5):

$$MP_L \times \Delta L = MP_K \times \Delta K \quad (5)$$

To stay on an isoquant when labour increases, capital must decrease. That is, when labour increases by ΔL, capital must decrease by:

$$MP_L \times \Delta L = MP_K \times -\Delta K \quad (6)$$

Equation 6 states that the marginal product of labour multiplied by the increase in labour equals the marginal product of capital multiplied by the decrease in capital. Dividing both sides of equation 6 by the increase in labour, ΔL, and then dividing both sides by the marginal product of capital, MP_K, gives equation 7:

$$\frac{MP_L}{MP_K} = -\frac{\Delta K}{\Delta L} \qquad (7)$$

Equation 7 shows that when Neat Knits remains on an isoquant, the decrease in its capital, $-\Delta K$, divided by the increase in its labour, ΔL, is equal to the marginal product of labour, MP_L, divided by the marginal product of capital, MP_K. The decrease in capital divided by the increase in labour when the firm remains on a given isoquant is the *marginal rate of substitution of labour for capital*. What we have shown is that the marginal rate of substitution of labour for capital equals the ratio of the marginal product of labour to the marginal product of capital.

Marginal Cost

We can use the fact that the marginal rate of substitution of labour for capital equals the ratio of the marginal product of labour to the marginal product of capital to examine marginal cost.

We know that when the least-cost technique is used, the slope of the isoquant and the isocost line are equal as shown in equation 8:

$$\frac{MP_L}{MP_K} = \frac{P_L}{P_K} \qquad (8)$$

We can now show that the total cost is minimized when the marginal product of labour per pound spent on labour equals the marginal product of capital per pound spent on capital.

Rearrange equation 8 by multiplying both sides by the marginal product of capital and then dividing both sides by the price of labour, you get equation 9:

$$\frac{MP_L}{P_L} = \frac{MP_K}{P_K} \qquad (9)$$

Equation 9 says that the marginal product of labour per pound spent on labour is equal to the marginal product of capital per pound spent on capital. In other words, the extra output produced by the last pound spent on labour equals the extra output produced by the last pound spent on capital. If the extra output produced by the last pound spent on labour exceeds the extra output produced by the last pound spent on capital, it pays a firm to use less capital and more labour. The firm can produce the same output at a lower total cost. Conversely, if the extra output produced by the last pound spent on capital exceeds the extra output produced by the last pound spend on labour, the firm can

lower its cost of producing a given output by using less labour and more capital. A firm achieves the least-cost technique of production only when the extra output produced by the last pound spent on all the factors is the same.

Finally, we can show that the marginal cost with fixed capital and variable labour equals marginal cost with labour and variable capital. To see why, invert equation 9 to give equation 10:

$$\frac{P_L}{MP_L} = \frac{P_K}{MP_K} \qquad (10)$$

Equation 10 shows that the price of labour divided by its marginal product equals the price of capital divided by its marginal product. The price of labour divided by the marginal product of labour is marginal cost when the quantity of capital is held constant. Remember that marginal cost is the change in total cost resulting from a unit increase in output. If output increases because one more unit of labour is employed, total cost increases by the marginal product of labour. So marginal cost is the price of labour divided by the marginal product of labour. For example, if labour costs £25 a day and the marginal product of labour is 2 jumpers, then the marginal cost of a jumper is £12.50 (£25 divided by 2).

The price of capital divided by the marginal product of capital has a similar interpretation. The price of capital divided by the marginal product of capital is marginal cost when the quantity of labour is constant. You can see from equation 10 that with the least-cost technique, marginal cost is the same regardless of whether the quantity of capital is constant and more labour is used, or the quantity of labour is constant and more capital is used.

Making Connections

You're probably thinking that what you've learned in this Appendix looks a lot like what you learned in Chapter 8 about a consumer's decision. You are right. In a graph, an isoquant is like an indifference curve; an isocost line is like a budget line; and the least-cost production technique is like the consumer's best affordable point.

But there is an important difference between the two models. The consumer's problem is to get to the highest attainable indifference curve with a given budget. The firm's problem is to get to the lowest attainable isocost line for a given output. Nonetheless, the two models share similar techniques of analysis.

Chapter 11

Perfect Competition

After studying this chapter you will be able to:

◆ Define perfect competition

◆ Explain how price and output are determined in a competitive industry and why firms sometimes shut down temporarily and lay off workers

◆ Explain why firms enter and leave the industry

◆ Predict the effects of a change in demand and of a technological advance

◆ Explain why perfect competition is efficient

Rivalry in Personal Computers

Competition is fierce in the PC business and over the past few years, prices have tumbled. How do firms operate when they face the fiercest competition from other firms? Does competition bring efficiency? Why do firms sometimes shut down temporarily and lay off their workers? Why do firms enter or leave an industry? How do firms react when there is a permanent change in the demand for what they produce or a change in their costs of production? Find out in this chapter. And apply what you learn to the world's competitive tea market in the *Reading Between the Lines* on pp. 246–247.

What is Perfect Competition?

The firms that you study in the chapter face the force of raw competition. This type of extreme competition is called perfect competition. **Perfect competition** is industry in which:

1 Many firms sell identical products to many buyers.
2 There are no restrictions on entry into the industry.
3 Existing firms have no advantage over new ones.
4 Sellers and buyers are well informed about prices.

Farming, fishing, wood pulping and paper milling, the manufacture of paper cups and plastic shopping bags, grocery retailing, photo finishing, plumbing and dry cleaning are examples of highly competitive industries.

How Perfect Competition Arises

Perfect competition arises if the firm's minimum efficient scale is small relative to the demand for the good. A firm's *minimum efficient scale* is the smallest quantity of output at which long-run average cost reaches its lowest level. (See Chapter 10, p. 215.) If the firm's minimum efficient scale is small relative to demand, there is room for many firms in the industry.

Perfect competition also arises if each firm is perceived to produce a good or service that has no unique characteristics so that consumers don't care which firm they buy from.

Price Takers

Firms in perfect competition are price takers. A **price taker** is a firm that cannot influence the market price and that sets its own price at the market price.

The key reason why a perfectly competitive firm is a price taker is that it produces a tiny fraction of the total output of a particular good and buyers are well informed about the prices of other firms.

Imagine you are a wheat farmer with a hundred hectares under cultivation, which sounds like a lot. But when compared to the millions of hectares in Ukraine, Canada, Australia, Argentina and the United States, your hundred hectares is a drop in the ocean. Nothing makes your wheat any better than any other farmer's and all the buyers of wheat know the price at which they can do business.

If the market price of wheat is £85 a tonne and you ask £90 a tonne, no one will buy from you. People can go to the next farmer and the next and the one after that and buy all they need for £85 a tonne. If you set you price at £84 a tonne, you'll have lots of buyers. But you can sell all your output for £85 a tonne, so you're just giving away £1 a tonne. You can do no better than sell for the market price – you are a *price taker*.

Economic Profit and Revenue

A firm's goal is to maximize *economic profit*, which is equal to total revenue minus total cost. Total cost is the *opportunity cost* of production, which includes *normal profit*, the return that the firm's entrepreneur can expect to receive on average in an alternative business (see Chapter 9, p. 181).

A firm's **total revenue** equals the price of its output multiplied by the number of units of output sold (price × quantity). **Marginal revenue** is the change in total revenue that results from a one-unit increase in the quantity sold. Marginal revenue is calculated by dividing the change in total revenue by the change in the quantity sold.

Figure 11.1 illustrates these concepts in the market for jumpers. In part (a), the market demand curve, D, and the supply curve, S, determine the market price. The market price remains at £25 a jumper regardless of the quantity that Neat Knits, one small firm, produces, and the best that it can do is to sell its jumpers at £25.

Total Revenue

Total revenue is equal to the price multiplied by the quantity sold. In the table in Figure 11.1, if Neat Knits sells 9 jumpers, the firms total revenue is 9 × £25, which equals £225.

Figure 11.1(b) shows the firm's total revenue curve (*TR*), which graphs the relationship between total revenue and quantity sold. At point *A* on the *TR* curve, Neat Knits sells 9 jumpers and has total revenue of £225. Because each additional jumper sold brings in a constant amount – £25 – the total revenue curve is an upward-sloping straight line.

Marginal Revenue

Marginal revenue is the change in total revenue that results from a one-unit increase in quantity. In the table in Figure 11.1, when the quantity sold increases from 8 to 9 jumpers, total revenue increases from £200 to £225. Marginal revenue is £25. Marginal revenue is

Figure 11.1

Demand, Price and Revenue in Perfect Competition

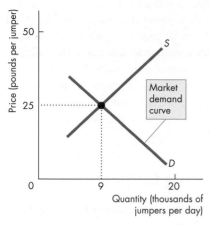

(a) Jumper industry

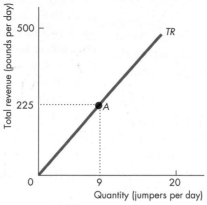

(b) Neat Knits' total revenue

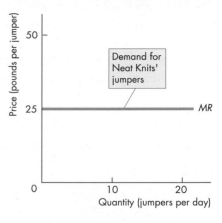

(c) Neat Knits' marginal revenue

Quantity sold (Q) (jumpers per day)	Price (P) (pounds per jumper)	Total revenue (TR = P × Q) (pounds)	Marginal revenue (MR = ΔTR/ΔQ) (pounds per jumper)
8	25	200	
			 25
9	25	225	
			 25
10	25	250	

In part (a), market demand and supply determine the market price (and quantity). Part (b) shows Neat Knits' total revenue curve (*TR*). Point *A* corresponds to the second row of the table – Neat Knits sells 9 jumpers at £25 a jumper, so total revenue is £225. Part (c) shows Neat Knits' marginal revenue curve (*MR*). This curve is the demand curve for jumpers produced by Neat Knits. Neat Knits faces a perfectly elastic demand for its jumpers at the market price of £25 a jumper.

£25 a jumper. Because the price remains constant when the quantity sold changes, the change in total revenue that results from a one-unit increase in the quantity sold equals price – in perfect competition, marginal revenue equals price.

Figure 11.1(c) shows Neat Knits' marginal revenue curve (*MR*), which is a horizontal line at the going market price.

Demand for Firm's Product and Market Demand

A horizontal demand curve is perfectly elastic. So the firm faces a perfectly elastic demand for its output. But the *market* demand for jumpers, in Figure 11.1(a), is not perfectly elastic. The market demand curve is down-ward sloping. How can the demand for Neat Knits' jumpers be perfectly elastic while the market demand for jumpers is not perfectly elastic?

The answer is that the elasticity of demand depends on the closeness of substitutes for a good. Neat Knits' jumpers are perfect substitutes for other firms' jumpers but jumpers in general are not perfect substitutes for other goods and services.

Review Quiz

1. Explain why a firm in perfect competition is a price taker.
2. In perfect competition, what is the relationship between the demand for the firm's output and the market demand?
3. In perfect competition, why is a firm's marginal revenue curve also the demand curve for the firm's output?
4. Why is the total revenue curve in perfect competition an upward-sloping straight line?

The Firm's Decisions in Perfect Competition

Firms in a perfectly competitive industry face a given market price and have the revenue curves that you've just studied. These revenue curves summarize the market constraint that the firm in perfect competition faces.

Firms also face a technology constraint, which is described by the product curves (total product, average product and marginal product) that you studied in Chapter 10. The technology available to the firm determines its costs, which are described by the cost curves (total cost, average cost and marginal cost) that you also studied in Chapter 10.

The goal of the competitive firm is to make the maximum profit possible, given the market constraints and technology constraints it faces. To achieve this objective, a firm must make four key decisions, two in the short run and two in the long run.

Short-run Decisions

The short run is a time frame in which the number of firms in the industry is fixed and each firm has a given plant size. But many things change in the short run and the firm must react to these changes. For example, the price for which the firm can sell its output might change with the seasons or it might fluctuate with general business conditions. The firm must react to such short-run price fluctuations and decide:

1 Whether to produce or to temporarily shut down

2 If the decision is to produce, what quantity to produce

Long-run Decisions

The long run is a time frame in which each firm can change the size of its plant and can decide whether to leave an industry or enter an industry. So in the long run, both the plant size of each firm and the number of firms in the industry can change. Also in the long run, the constraints that the firm faces can change. For example, the demand for a good can permanently fall, or a technological advance can change an industry's costs. Firms react to these long-run changes and decide:

1 Whether to increase or decrease their plants size

2 Whether to remain in an industry or leave it

The Firm and the Industry in the Short Run and the Long Run

To study a competitive industry, we begin by looking at an individual firm's short-run decisions. We then see how the short-run decisions of all the firms in a competitive industry combine to determine the industry price, output and economic profit. We then turn to the long run and study the effects of long-run decisions on the industry price, output and economic profit. All the decisions we study are driven by the pursuit of a single objective: maximization of profit.

Profit-maximizing Output

A perfectly competitive firm maximizes economic profit by choosing its output level. One way of finding the profit-maximizing output is to study a firm's total revenue and total cost curves and to find the output level at which total revenue exceeds total cost by the largest amount.

Figure 11.2 shows you how to find the profit-maximizing output for Neat Knits. The table lists Neat Knits' total revenue and total cost at different outputs, and part (a) of the figure shows its total revenue and total cost curves. These curves are graphs of the numbers shown in the first three columns of the table. The total revenue curve (*TR*) is the same as that in Figure 11.1(b). The total cost curve (*TC*) is similar to the one that you met in Chapter 10. As output increases, so does total cost.

Economic Profit and Economic Loss

Economic profit equals total revenue minus total cost. The fourth column of the table in Figure 11.2 shows Neat Knits' economic profit and part (b) of the figure illustrates these numbers as Neat Knits' profit curve. This curve shows that Neat Knits makes an economic profit at outputs between 4 and 12 jumpers a day. At outputs of fewer than 4 jumpers a day, Neat Knits incurs a loss. It also incurs a loss if it produces more than 12 jumpers a day. If Neat Knits produces either 4 jumpers or 12 jumpers a day, its total cost equals its total revenue and its economic profit is zero.

An output at which total cost equals total revenue is called a *break-even point*. The firm's economic profit is zero, but because normal profit is part of total cost, a firm makes normal profit at a break-even point. That is, at the break-even point, the entrepreneur makes an income equal to the best alternative return forgone.

Figure 11.2

Total Revenue, Total Cost and Economic Profit

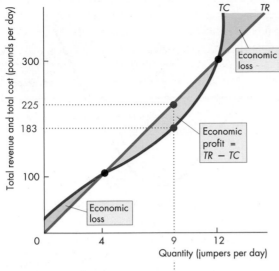

(a) Revenue and cost

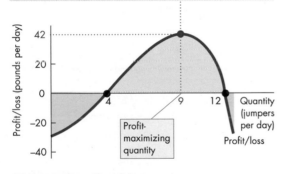

(b) Economic profit and loss

Quantity (Q) (jumpers per day)	Total revenue (TR) (pounds)	Total cost (TC) (pounds)	Economic profit (TR – TC) (pounds)
0	0	22	–22
1	25	45	–20
2	50	66	–16
3	75	85	–10
4	100	100	0
5	125	114	11
6	150	126	24
7	175	141	34
8	200	160	40
9	**225**	**183**	**42**
10	250	210	40
11	275	245	30
12	300	300	0
13	325	360	–35

The table lists Neat Knits' total revenue, total cost and economic profit. Part (a) graphs the total revenue and total cost curves. Economic profit, in part (a), is the height of the blue area between the total cost and total revenue curves. Neat Knits makes maximum economic profit, £42 a day (£225 – £183), when it produces 9 jumpers – the output at which the vertical distance between the total revenue and total cost curves is at its largest. At outputs of 4 jumpers a day and 12 jumpers a day, Neat Knits makes zero economic profit – these are break-even points. At outputs less than 4 and greater than 12 jumpers a day, Neat Knits incurs an economic loss. Part (b) shows Neat Knits' profit curve. The profit curve is at its highest when economic profit is at a maximum and cuts the horizontal axis at the break-even points.

Notice the relationship between the total revenue, total cost and economic profit curves. Economic profit is measured by the vertical distance between the total revenue and total cost curves. When the total revenue curve in Figure 11.2(a) is above the total cost curve, between 4 and 12 jumpers, the firm is making an economic profit and the profit curve in Figure 11.2(b) is above the horizontal axis.

At the break-even point, where the total cost and total revenue curves intersect, the profit curve intersects the horizontal axis. The profit curve is at its highest when the distance between the total revenue and total cost curves is greatest. In this example, profit maximization occurs at an output of 9 jumpers a day. At this output, Neat Knits makes an economic profit of £42 a day.

Marginal Analysis

Another way of finding the profit-maximizing output is to use *marginal analysis*, by comparing marginal cost, *MC*, with marginal revenue, *MR*. As output increases, marginal revenue remains constant but marginal cost changes. At low output levels, marginal cost decreases as output increases but eventually marginal cost increases. So where the marginal cost curve intersects the marginal revenue curve, marginal cost is rising – the marginal cost curve is upward sloping.

If marginal revenue exceeds marginal cost (if $MR > MC$), then the extra revenue from selling one more unit exceeds the extra cost incurred to produce it. The firm makes an economic profit on the marginal unit, so economic profit increases if output *increases*.

If marginal revenue is less than marginal cost (if $MR < MC$), then the extra revenue from selling one more unit is less than the extra cost incurred to produce it. The firm incurs an economic loss on the marginal unit, so its economic profit decreases if output increases and its economic profit increases if output *decreases*.

If marginal revenue equals marginal cost ($MR = MC$), the firm makes maximum economic profit. The rule $MR = MC$ is an example of marginal analysis. Let's check that this rule works to find the profit-maximizing output, by returning to Neat Knits.

Look at Figure 11.3. The table records Neat Knits' marginal revenue and marginal cost. Marginal revenue is constant at £25 per jumper. Over the range of outputs shown in the table, marginal cost increases from £19 a jumper to £35 a jumper. The graph shows Neat Knits' marginal revenue and marginal cost curves.

Focus on the highlighted rows of the table. If output increases from 8 jumpers to 9 jumpers, marginal revenue is £25 and marginal cost is £23. Because marginal revenue exceeds marginal cost, economic profit increases. The last column of the table shows that economic profit increases from £40 to £42, an increase of £2. This profit from the ninth jumper is shown as the blue area in the figure.

If Neat Knits increases output from 9 jumpers to 10 jumpers, marginal revenue is still £25 but marginal cost is £27. Because marginal revenue is less than marginal cost, economic profit decreases. The last column of the table shows that economic profit decreases from £42 to £40. This loss from the tenth jumper is shown as the red area in the figure.

Neat Knits maximizes economic profit by producing 9 jumpers a day, the quantity at which marginal revenue equals marginal cost.

Figure 11.3

Profit-maximizing Output

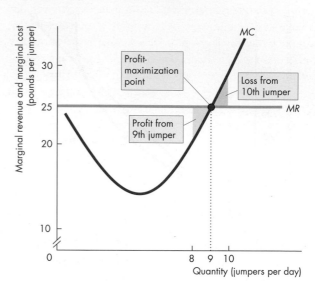

Quantity (Q) (jumpers per day)	Total revenue (TR) (pounds)	Marginal revenue (MR) (pounds per jumper)	Total cost (TC) (pounds)	Marginal cost (MC) (pounds per jumper)	Economic profit (TR – TC) (pounds)
7	175		141		34
		 25		 19	
8	200		160		40
		 25		 23	
9	**225**	 25	**183**	 27	**42**
10	250		210		40
		 25		 35	
11	275		245		30

Another way of finding the profit-maximizing output is to determine the output at which marginal revenue equals marginal cost. The table shows that if output increases from 8 to 9 jumpers, marginal cost is £23, which is less than the marginal revenue of £25. If output increases from 9 to 10 jumpers, marginal cost is £27, which exceeds the marginal revenue of £25.

The graph shows that marginal cost and marginal revenue are equal when Neat Knits produces 9 jumpers a day. If marginal revenue exceeds marginal cost, an increase in output increases economic profit. If marginal revenue is less than marginal cost, an increase in output decreases economic profit. If marginal revenue equals marginal cost, economic profit is maximized.

Profits and Losses in the Short Run

In the short run, although the firm produces the profit-maximizing output, it does not necessarily end up making an economic profit. It might do so, but it might alternatively break even (earn a normal profit) or incur an economic loss. Economic profit (or loss) per jumper is price, P, minus average total cost, ATC. So economic profit is $(P - ATC) \times Q$. If price equals average total cost, a firm breaks even – makes normal profit. If price exceeds average total cost, a firm makes an economic profit. If price is less than average total cost, the firm incurs an economic loss. Figure 11.4 shows these three possible short-run profit outcomes.

Three Possible Profit Outcomes

In Figure 11.4(a), the price of a jumper is £20. Neat Knits produces 8 jumpers a day. Average total cost is £20. Price equals average total cost, so Neat Knits breaks even and makes normal profit (zero economic profit).

In Figure 11.4(b), the price of a jumper is £25. Neat Knits maximizes profit by producing 9 jumpers a day.

Here price exceeds average total cost, so Neat Knits makes an economic profit. Economic profit is £42 a day. It is made up of £4.67 a jumper (£25.00 – £20.33), multiplied by the number of jumpers (£4.67 × 9), which is £42 a day. The blue rectangle in Figure 11.4(b) shows this economic profit. The height of the rectangle is profit per jumper, £4.67, and the length is the quantity of jumpers produced, 9 a day, so the area of the rectangle measures Neat Knits' economic profit of £42 a day.

In Figure 11.4(c), the price of a jumper is £17. Here, price is less than average total cost and Neat Knits incurs an economic loss. Price and marginal revenue are £17 a jumper, and the profit-maximizing (in this case, loss-minimizing) output is 7 jumpers a day. Neat Knits' average total cost is £20.14 a jumper, so its economic loss is £3.14 per jumper (£20.14 – £17.00). Neat Knits' economic loss equals this loss per jumper multiplied by the number of jumpers (£3.14 × 7), which equals is £22 a day. The red rectangle shows this economic loss. The height of that rectangle is economic loss per jumper, £3.14, and the length is the quantity of jumpers produced, 7 a day, so the area of the rectangle is Neat Knits' economic loss of £22 a day.

Figure 11.4

Three Possible Profit Outcomes in the Short-Run

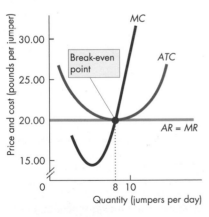

(a) Normal profit

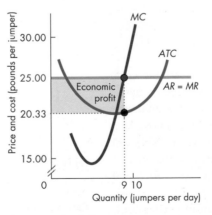

(b) Economic profit

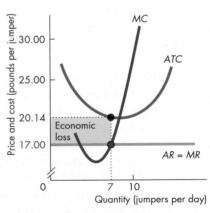

(c) Economic loss

In the short run, firms might break even (making a normal profit), make an economic profit or incur an economic loss. If price equals minimum average total cost, the firm breaks even and makes a normal profit (part a). If the market price is higher than the average total cost of producing the profit-maximizing output, the firm makes an economic profit – the blue rectangle in part (b). If the price is below minimum average total cost, the firm incurs an economic loss – the red rectangle in part (c).

The Firm's Short-run Supply Curve

A perfectly competitive firm's supply curve shows how the firm's profit-maximizing output varies as the market price varies, other things remaining the same. Figure 11.5 shows you how to derive Neat Knits' supply curve. Part (a) shows Neat Knits' marginal cost and average variable cost curves and part (b) shows its supply curve. There is a direct link between these cost curves and the supply curve. Let's see what that link is.

Temporary Plant Shutdown

In the short run, a firm cannot avoid its fixed costs. But it can avoid variable costs by temporarily laying off workers and shutting down. If a firm shuts down and produces no output, it incurs an economic loss equal to its total fixed cost. This loss is the largest that a firm need incur. A firm shuts down if price falls below the minimum average variable cost. A firm's **shutdown point** is the output and price at which the firm just covers its total *variable* costs, point T in Figure 11.5(a). If the price is £17, the marginal revenue curve is MR_0, and the profit-maximizing output is 7 jumpers a day at point T. But both price and average variable cost equal £17, so Neat Knits' total revenue equals its total variable cost. Neat Knits incurs an economic loss equal to total fixed cost. If the price falls below £17, no matter what quantity Neat Knits produces, average variable cost exceeds price and its loss exceeds total fixed cost. So Neat Knits shuts down temporarily.

The Short-run Supply Curve

If the price is above minimum average variable cost, Neat Knits maximizes profit by producing the output at which marginal cost equals price. We can determine the quantity produced from the marginal cost curve. At a price of £25, the marginal revenue curve is MR_1 and Neat Knits maximizes profit by producing 9 jumpers. At a price of £31, the marginal revenue curve is MR_2 and Neat Knits produces 10 jumpers.

Neat Knits' supply curve, shown in Figure 11.5(b), has two parts: At prices above minimum average variable cost, the supply curve is the same as the marginal cost curve above the shutdown point (T). At prices below minimum average variable cost, Neat Knits shuts down and produces nothing. Its supply curve runs along the vertical axis. At a price of £17, Neat Knits is indifferent between shutting down and producing 7 jumpers a day. Either way, it incurs a loss of £25 a day.

Figure 11.5

A Firm's Supply Curve

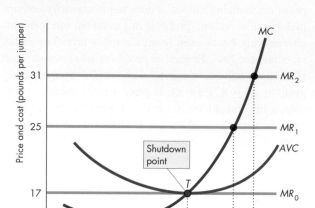

(a) Marginal cost and average variable cost

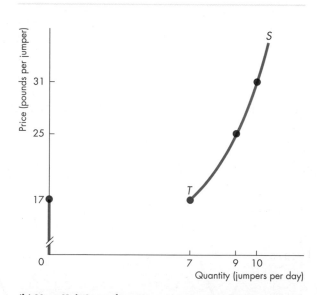

(b) Neat Knits' supply curve

Part (a) shows Neat Knits' profit-maximizing output at each market price. At £25 a jumper, Neat Knits produces 9 jumpers. At £17 a jumper, Neat Knits produces 7 jumpers. At any price below £17 a jumper, Neat Knits produces nothing. Neat Knits' shutdown point is T. Part (b) shows Neat Knits' supply curve – the number of jumpers Neat Knits will produce at each price. It is made up of the marginal cost curve (part a) at all points above minimum average variable cost and the vertical axis at all prices below minimum average variable cost.

Short-run Industry Supply Curve

The **short-run industry supply curve** shows how the quantity supplied by the industry varies as the market price varies when the plant size of each firm and the number of firms in the industry remain the same. The quantity supplied by the industry at a given price is the sum of the quantities supplied by all firms in the industry at that price.

Figure 11.6 shows the supply curve for the competitive jumper industry. In this example, the industry consists of 1,000 firms exactly like Neat Knits. At each price, the quantity supplied by the industry is 1,000 times the quantity supplied by a single firm.

The table in Figure 11.6 shows the firm's and the industry's supply schedule and how the industry supply curve is constructed. At prices below £17, every firm in the industry shuts down and produces nothing. The quantity supplied by the industry is zero. At a price of £17, each firm is indifferent between shutting down and producing nothing or producing 7 jumpers. Some firms will shut down and other will produce 7 jumpers a day. The quantity supplied by each firm is *either* 0 or 7 jumpers, but the quantity supplied by the industry is *between* 0 (all firms shut down) and 7,000 (all firms produce 7 jumpers a day each).

To construct the industry supply curve, we sum the quantities supplied by the individual firms at each price. Every of the 1,000 firms in the industry has a supply schedule like Neat Knits. At prices below £17, the industry supply curve runs along the price axis. At a price of £17, the industry supply curve is horizontal – supply is perfectly elastic. As the price rises above £17, each firm increases its quantity supplied and the quantity supplied by the industry increases by 1,000 times that of each individual firm. Figure 11.6 shows the industry supply curve S_I.

Review Quiz

1 Why does a firm in perfect competition produce the quantity at which marginal cost equals price?
2 What is the lowest price at which a firm will produce its output? Explain why.
3 What is the largest economic loss that a firm will incur in the short run?
4 What is the relationship between a firm's supply curve, its marginal cost curve and its average variable cost curve?
5 Explain how we derive an industry supply curve?

Figure 11.6

Industry Supply Curve

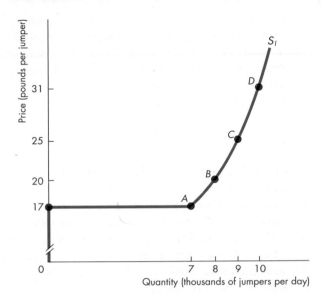

	Price (pounds per jumper)	Quantity supplied by Neat Knits (jumpers per day)	Quantity supplied by industry (jumpers per day)
A	17	0 or 7	0 to 7,000
B	20	8	8,000
C	25	9	9,000
D	31	10	10,000

The industry supply schedule is the sum of the supply schedules of all individual firms. An industry that consists of 1,000 identical firms has a supply schedule similar to that of the individual firm, but the quantity supplied by the industry is 1,000 times as large as that of the individual firm (see the table).

The industry supply curve is S_I. Points *A*, *B*, *C* and *D* correspond to the rows of the table. At the shutdown price of £17, each firm produces either 0 or 7 jumpers per day. The industry supply is perfectly elastic at the shutdown price.

So far, we have studied a single firm in isolation. We have seen that the firm's profit-maximizing actions depend on the market price, which the firm takes as given. But how is the market price determined? Let's find out.

Output, Price and Profit in Perfect Competition

To determine the market price and the quantity bought and sold in a perfectly competitive market, we need to study how market demand and market supply interact. We begin this process by studying a perfectly competitive market in the short run when the number of firms is fixed and each firm has a given plant size.

Short-run Equilibrium

Industry demand and supply determine market price and industry output. Figure 11.7 shows the short-run equilibrium. The supply curve, S, is the same as S_I in Figure 11.6. If demand is shown by the demand curve D_1, the equilibrium price is £20. Each firm takes this price as given and produces its profit-maximizing output, which is 8 jumpers a day. Because the industry has 1,000 firms, industry output is 8,000 jumpers a day.

A Change in Demand

Changes in demand bring changes to short-run industry equilibrium. Figure 11.7 shows these changes.

If demand increases, the demand curve shifts rightward to D_2. The price rises to £25. At this price, each firm maximizes profit by increasing output. The new output level is 9 jumpers a day for each firm and 9,000 jumpers a day for the industry. If demand decreases, the demand curve shifts leftward to D_3. The price now falls to £17. At this price, each firm maximizes profit by decreasing its output. The new output level is 7 jumpers a day for each firm and 7,000 jumpers a day for the industry.

If the demand curve shifts further leftward than D_3, the price remains constant at £17 because the industry supply curve is horizontal at that price. Some firms continue to produce 7 jumpers a day and others temporarily shut down. Firms are indifferent between these two activities, and whichever they choose, they incur an economic loss equal to total fixed cost. The number of firms continuing to produce is just enough to satisfy the market demand at a price of £17.

Figure 11.7

Short-run Equilibrium

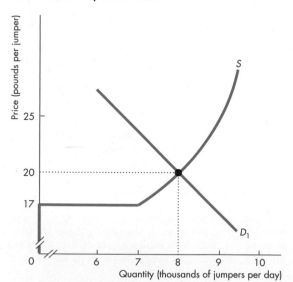

(a) Equilibrium

(b) Change in equilibrium

In part (a), the competitive jumper industry's supply curve is S. Demand is D_1 and the price is £20 a jumper. At this price, each firm produces 8 jumpers a day and the industry produces 8,000 jumpers a day. In part (b), when demand increases to D_2, the price rises to £25 and each firm increases its output to 9 jumpers a day. Industry output is 9,000 jumpers a day. When demand decreases to D_3, the price falls to £17 and each firm decreases its output to 7 jumpers a day. Industry output is 7,000 jumpers a day.

Long-run Adjustments

In short-run equilibrium, a firm might make an economic profit, incur an economic loss or break even (make normal profit). Although each of these three situations is a short-run equilibrium, only one of them is a long-run equilibrium. To see why, we need to examine the forces at work in a competitive industry in the long run.

In the long run, an industry adjusts in two ways:

◆ Entry and exit

◆ Changes in plant size

We'll look at entry and exit first.

Entry and Exit

In the long run, firms respond to economic profit and economic loss by either entering or exiting an industry. Firms enter an industry in which firms are making an economic profit; and firms exit an industry in which firms are incurring an economic loss. Temporary economic profit and temporary economic loss do not trigger entry and exit. But the prospect of persistent economic profit or loss does.

Entry and exit influence the market price, the quantity produced and economic profit. The immediate effect of entry and exit is to shift the industry supply curve. If more firms enter an industry, supply increases and the industry supply curve shifts rightward. If firms exit an industry, supply decreases and the industry supply curve shifts leftward.

Let's see what happens when new firms enter an industry.

The Effects of Entry

Figure 11.8 shows the effects of entry. Suppose that all the firms in this industry have cost curves like those in Figure 11.4. At any price greater than £20, firms make an economic profit. At any price less than £20, firms incur an economic loss. And at a price of £20, firms make zero economic profit. Also suppose that the demand curve for jumpers is D. If the industry supply curve is S_1, jumpers sell for £23 and 7,000 jumpers a day are produced. Firms in the industry make an economic profit. This economic profit is a signal for new firms to enter the industry. As these events unfold, supply increases and the industry supply curve shifts rightward to S_0. With the greater supply and unchanged demand, the market price falls from £23 to £20 a jumper and the quantity produced by the industry increases from 7,000 to 8,000 jumpers a day.

Industry output increases, but Neat Knits, like each other firm in the industry, *decreases* output! Because the price falls, each firm moves down along its supply curve and produces less. But because the number of firms in the industry increases, the industry as a whole produces more.

Because the price falls, each firm's economic profit decreases. When the price falls to £20, economic profit disappears and each firm makes a normal profit.

You have just discovered a key proposition:

> **As new firms enter an industry, the price falls and the economic profit of each existing firm decreases.**

An example of this process has occurred during the 1980s in the personal computer industry. When IBM introduced its first personal computer, there was little competition and the price of a PC gave IBM a big profit. But new firms such as Amstrad, Dell, Elonex and a

Figure 11.8

Entry and Exit

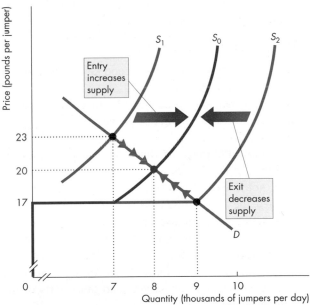

When new firms enter the jumper industry, the industry supply curve shifts rightward, from S_1 to S_0. The equilibrium price falls from £23 to £20 a jumper and the quantity produced increases from 7,000 to 8,000 jumpers. When firms exit the jumper industry, the industry supply curve shifts leftward, from S_2 to S_0. The equilibrium price rises from £17 to £20 a jumper, and the quantity produced decreases from 9,000 to 8,000 jumpers.

host of others soon entered the industry with machines technologically identical to the IBM PC. In fact, they were so similar that they came to be called "clones". The massive wave of entry into the personal computer industry shifted the supply curve rightward and lowered the price and the economic profit.

Let's now look at the effects of exit.

The Effects of Exit

Figure 11.8 shows the effects of exit. Suppose that firms' costs and the market demand are the same as before. But now suppose that the supply curve is S_2. The market price is £17 and 9,000 jumpers a day are produced. Firms in the industry are now incurring an economic loss. This economic loss is a signal for some firms to exit the industry. As firms exit, the industry supply curve shifts leftward to S_0. With the decrease in supply, industry output decreases from 9,000 to 8,000 jumpers and the price rises from £17 to £20.

As the price rises, Neat Knits, like each other firms in the industry, moves up along its supply curve and increases output. That is, for each firm remaining in the industry, the profit-maximizing output increases. Because the price rises and each firm sells more, economic loss decreases. When the price rises to £20, economic loss disappears and each firm makes a normal profit.

You have just discovered a second key proposition:

As firms leave an industry, the price rises and so do the economic profits of the remaining firms.

The same PC industry that saw a large amount of entry during the 1980s and 1990s is now beginning to see some exit. In 2001, IBM, the firm that first launched the PC, announced that it would no longer produce PCs. The intense competition from Compaq, Gateway, Dell and the host of others that entered the industry following IBM's lead has lowered the price and eliminated the economic profit on PCs. So IBM will now concentrate on servers and other parts of the computer market.

IBM exited the PC market because it was incurring economic losses on that line of business. Its exit decreased supply and made it possible for the remaining firms in the industry to earn normal profit.

You've now seen how economic profits induce entry, which in turn lowers economic profits. And you've seen how economic losses induce exit, which in turn eliminates economic losses. Let's now look at changes in plant size.

Changes in Plant Size

A firm changes its plant size if, by doing so, it can lower its costs and increase its economic profit. You can probably think of lots of examples of firms that have changed their plant size.

One example that has almost certainly happened near your university in recent years is a change in the plant size of copy shops. Another is the number of courier vans that you see on the streets and highways. And another is the number of square feet of retail space devoted to selling computers and video games. These are examples of firms increasing their plant size to seek larger profits.

There are also many examples of firms that have decreased their plant size to avoid economic losses. One example is the change in the plant size of many airlines. After 11 September 2001, as demand for air travel crashed, most European airlines cut their services – see the *Business Case Study* in Chapter 10. In recent years, many firms have scaled back their operations – a process called *downsizing*.

Figure 11.9 shows a situation in which Neat Knits can increase its profit by increasing its plant size. With its current plant, Neat Knits' marginal cost curve is MC_0 and its short-run average total cost curve is $SRAC_0$. The market price is £25 a jumper, so Neat Knits' marginal revenue curve is MR_0 and Neat Knits maximizes profit by producing 6 jumpers a day.

Neat Knits' long-run average cost curve is *LRAC*. By increasing its plant size – installing more knitting machines – Neat Knits can move along its long-run average cost curve. As Neat Knits increases its plant size, its short-run marginal cost curve shifts rightward.

Recall that a firm's short-run supply curve is linked to its marginal cost curve. As Neat Knits' marginal cost curve shifts rightward, so does its supply curve. If Neat Knits and the other firms in the industry increase their plant size, the short-run industry supply curve shifts rightward and the market price falls. The fall in the market price limits the extent to which Neat Knits can profit from increasing its plant size.

Figure 11.9 also shows Neat Knits in a long-run competitive equilibrium. This situation arises when the market price has fallen to £20 a jumper. Marginal revenue is MR_1, and Neat Knits maximizes profit by producing 8 jumpers a day. In this situation, Neat Knits cannot increase its profit by changing its plant size. It is producing at minimum long-run average cost (point *M* on *LRAC*).

Figure 11.9

Plant Size and Long-run Equilibrium

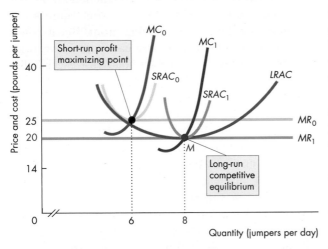

Initially, Neat Knits' plant has marginal cost curve MC_0 and short-run average total cost curve $SRAC_0$. The market price is £25 a jumper and Neat Knits' marginal revenue is MR_0. The short-run profit-maximizing quantity is 6 jumpers a day. Neat Knits can increase its profit by increasing its plant size. If all firms in the jumper industry increase their plant sizes, the short-run industry supply increases and the market price falls.

In long-run equilibrium, a firm operates with the plant size that minimizes its average cost. Here, Neat Knits operates the plant with short-run marginal cost MC_1 and short-run average total cost $SRAC_1$. Neat Knits is also on its long-run average cost curve $LRAC$ and produces at point M. Its output is 8 jumpers a day and average total cost equals the price of a jumper at £20.

Because Neat Knits is producing at minimum long-run average cost, it has no incentive to change its plant size. Either a bigger plant or a smaller plant has a higher long-run average cost. If Figure 11.9 describes the situation of all firms in the jumper industry, the industry is in long-run equilibrium. No firm has an incentive to change its plant size. Also, because each firm is making zero economic profit (normal profit), no firm has an incentive to enter the industry or to leave it.

Long-run Equilibrium

Long-run equilibrium occurs in a competitive industry when economic profit is zero (firms are earning normal profit). If the firms in a competitive industry are making an economic profit, new firms enter the industry. If firms can lower their costs by increasing their plant size, they expand. Each of these actions increases industry supply,

shifts the industry supply curve rightward, lowers the market price and decreases economic profit.

Firms continue to enter and economic profit continues to decrease as long as firms in the industry are earning positive economic profits. When economic profit has been eliminated, firms stop entering the industry. And when firms are operating with the least-cost plant size, they stop expanding.

If the firms in a competitive industry are incurring an economic loss, some firms exit the industry. If firms can lower these average costs by decreasing their plant size, they downsize. Each of these actions decreases industry supply, shifts the industry supply curve leftward, raises the market price and decreases economic loss.

Firms continue to leave and economic loss continues to decrease as long as firms in the industry are incurring economic losses. When the economic losses have been eliminated, firms stop exiting the industry. And when firms are operating with the least-cost plant size, they stop downsizing.

So in long-run equilibrium in a competitive industry, firms neither enter nor exit the industry and old firms neither expand nor downsize. Each firm earns a normal profit.

Review Quiz

1 When a firm in perfect competition maximizes its profit, what is the relationship between the firm's marginal cost, marginal revenue and price?
2 If the firms in a competitive industry earn an economic profit, what happens to the industry supply, the market price, the firm's output, the number of firms and economic profit?
3 If the firms in a competitive industry incur an economic loss, what happens to the industry supply, the market price, the firm's output, the number of firms and economic profit?
4 Under what conditions would a firm choose to change its plant size?

You've seen how a competitive industry adjusts towards its long-run equilibrium. But a competitive industry is rarely in a state of long-run equilibrium. A competitive industry is constantly and restlessly evolving towards such an equilibrium. But the constraints that firms in the industry face are constantly changing. The two most persistent sources of change are in tastes and technology. Let's see how a competitive industry reacts to such changes.

Changing Tastes and Advancing Technology

Increased awareness of the health hazard of smoking has caused a decrease in the demand for tobacco and cigarettes. The development of inexpensive cars and air travel has caused a huge decrease in the demand for long-distance trains and buses. Solid-state electronics have caused a large decrease in the demand for TV and radio repair. The development of good-quality inexpensive clothing has decreased the demand for sewing machines. What happens in a competitive industry when there is a permanent decrease in the demand for its products?

The development of the microwave oven has produced an enormous increase in the demand for paper, glass and plastic cooking utensils, and for plastic wrap. The widespread use of the personal computer has brought a huge increase in the demand for CD-Rs. What happens in a competitive industry when the demand for its product increases?

Advances in technology are constantly lowering the costs of production. New biotechnologies have dramatically lowered the costs of producing many food and pharmaceutical products. New electronic technologies have lowered the cost of producing just about every good and service. What happens in a competitive industry when technological change lowers its production costs?

Let's use the theory of perfect competition to answer these questions.

A Permanent Change in Demand

Figure 11.10(a) shows an industry that initially is in long-run competitive equilibrium. The demand curve is D_0, the supply curve is S_0, the market price is P_0 and industry output is Q_0. Figure 11.10(b) shows a single firm in this initial long-run equilibrium. The firm produces q_0 and makes a normal profit and zero economic profit.

Now suppose that demand decreases and the demand curve shifts leftward to D_1, as shown in Figure 11.10(a). The market price falls to P_1 and the quantity supplied by the industry decreases from Q_0 to Q_1 as the industry slides down its short-run supply curve S_0. Figure 11.10(b) shows the situation facing a firm. Price is now below minimum average total cost so the firm incurs an economic loss. But to keep its loss to a minimum, the firm adjusts its output to keep marginal cost equal to the market price. At a price of P_1, each firm produces an output of q_1.

The industry is now in short-run equilibrium but not long-run equilibrium. It is in short-run equilibrium because each firm is maximizing profit. But it is not in long-run equilibrium because each firm is incurring an economic loss – its average total cost exceeds the market price.

The economic loss is a signal for some firms to leave the industry. As they do so, short-run industry supply decreases and the supply curve shifts leftward.

As the industry supply decreases, the market price rises – as shown by the arrows along the demand curve labelled D_1 in Figure 11.10(a). At each higher price, a firm's profit-maximizing output is greater, so the firms remaining in the industry increase their output as the price rises. Each firm slides up its marginal cost or supply curve in Figure 11.10(b) – as shown by the arrows along the MC curve. That is, as some firms exit the industry, industry output decreases but the output of the firms that remain in the industry increases.

Eventually, enough firms leave the industry for the industry supply curve to have shifted to S_1 in Figure 11.10(a). At this time, the price has returned to its original level, P_0. At this price, the firms remaining in the industry produce q_0 (in part b), the same quantity that they produced before the decrease in demand. Because firms are now making normal profit (zero economic profit), no firm wants to enter or exit the industry. The industry supply curve remains at S_1, and industry output is Q_2. The industry is again in long-run equilibrium.

The difference between the initial long-run equilibrium and the final long-run equilibrium is the number of firms in the industry. A permanent decrease in demand has decreased the number of firms. Each remaining firm produces the same output in the new long-run equilibrium as it did initially and earns a normal profit. In the process of moving from the initial equilibrium to the new one, firms that remain in the industry incur economic losses.

We've just worked out how a competitive industry responds to a permanent *decrease* in demand. A permanent increase in demand triggers a similar response, except in the opposite direction. The increase in demand brings a higher market price, increased economic profit and entry. As new firms enter, the industry supply increases and the market price starts to fall. And as the market price falls, firms' profits start to decrease. Eventually, the market price returns to its original level and economic profit falls to zero. Each firm makes normal profit.

The demand for Internet service increased perma-

Figure 11.10

A Decrease in Demand

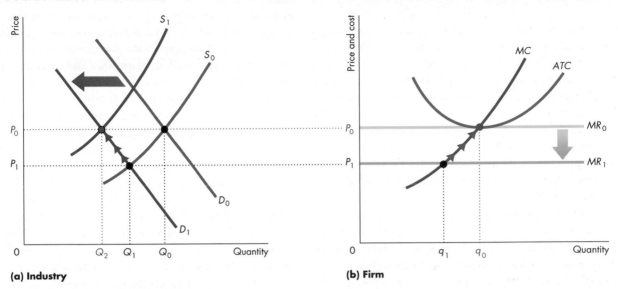

(a) Industry

(b) Firm

An industry starts out in long-run competitive equilibrium. Part (a) shows the industry demand curve D_0 and the industry supply curve S_0, the equilibrium quantity Q_0 and the market price P_0. Each firm sells at price P_0, so its marginal revenue curve is MR_0 in part (b). Each firm produces q_0 and makes a normal profit.

Demand decreases from D_0 to D_1 (part a). The equilibrium price falls to P_1, each firm decreases its output to q_1 (part b), and industry output decreases to Q_1 (part a). In this

new situation, firms are incurring losses and some firms leave the industry. As they do so, the industry supply curve gradually shifts leftward, from S_0 to S_1. This shift gradually raises the industry price from P_1 back to P_0. While the price is below P_0, firms are incurring losses and some leave the industry. Once the price has returned to P_0, each firm makes a normal profit. Firms have no further incentive to leave the industry. Each firm produces q_0 and industry output is Q_2.

nently during the 1990s and huge profit opportunities arose in this industry. The result was a massive rate of entry of Internet service providers. The process of competition and change in the Internet service industry is similar to what we have just studied but with an increase in demand rather than a decrease in demand.

We've now studied the effects of a permanent change in demand for a good. In doing so, we began and ended in a long-run equilibrium and we examined the process that takes a market from one equilibrium to another. It is this process, not the equilibrium points, that describes the real world.

One feature of the predictions that we have just generated seems odd. In the long run, regardless of whether the change in demand is a permanent increase or a permanent decrease, the market price returns to its original level. Is this outcome inevitable? In fact, it is not. It is possible for the market price in long-run equilibrium to remain the same, rise or fall.

Let's see why.

External Economies and Diseconomies

The change in the long-run equilibrium price depends on external economies and external diseconomies. **External economies** are factors beyond the control of an individual firm that lower its costs as *industry* output increases. **External diseconomies** are factors outside the control of a firm that raise its costs as industry output increases. With no external economies or external diseconomies, a firm's costs remain constant as industry output changes.

Figure 11.11 illustrates these three cases and introduces a new supply concept, the long-run industry supply curve.

A **long-run industry supply curve** shows how the quantity supplied by an industry varies as the market price varies, after all the possible adjustments have been made, including changes in plant size and changes in the number of firms in the industry.

Figure 11.11(a) shows the case we have just studied – no external economies or external diseconomies. The long-run industry supply curve (LS_A) is perfectly elastic. In this case, a permanent increase in demand from D_0 to D_1 has no effect on the price in the long run. The increase in demand brings a temporary increase in price to P_S and a short-run quantity increase from Q_0 to Q_S. Entry increases short-run supply from S_0 to S_1, which lowers the price to its original level, P_0, and increases the quantity to Q_1.

Figure 11.11(b) shows the case of external diseconomies. The long-run supply industry curve (LS_B) slopes upward. A permanent increase in demand from D_0 to D_1 increases the price in both the short run and the long run. As in the previous case, the increase in demand brings a temporary increase in price to P_S, and a short-run quantity increase from Q_0 to Q_S. Entry increases short-run supply from S_0 to S_2, which lowers the price to P_2 and increases the quantity to Q_2.

One source of external diseconomies is congestion. The airline industry in the 1990s provides a good illustration. With bigger airline industry output, there was more congestion of both airports and airspace,

which resulted in longer delays and extra waiting time for passengers and aircraft. These external diseconomies mean that as the output of air travel services increased (in the absence of technological advances), the airline's average cost increases. As a result, the long-run supply curve is upward-sloping. So a permanent increase in demand brings an increase in quantity and a rise in the price. Technological advances decrease average costs and *shift* the long-run supply curve downward. So even an industry that experiences external diseconomies might have falling prices over the long run.

Figure 11.11(c) shows the case of external economies. In this case, the long-run industry supply curve (LS_C) slopes downward. A permanent increase in demand from D_0 to D_1, increases the price in the short run and lowers it in the long run. Again, the increase in demand brings a temporary increase in price to P_S, and a short-run quantity increase from Q_0 to Q_S. Entry increases short-run supply from S_0 to S_3, which lowers the price to P_3 and increases the quantity to Q_3.

One of the best examples of external economies is the growth of specialist support services for an industry as it expands. As farm output increased in the nineteenth

---

Figure 11.11

Long-run Changes in Price and Quantity

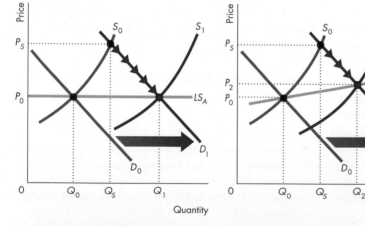

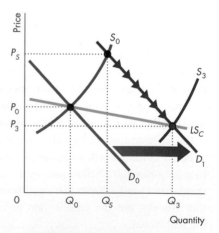

(a) Constant-cost industry

(b) Increasing-cost industry

(c) Decreasing-cost industry

Three possible changes in price and quantity occur in the long run. When demand increases from D_0 to D_1, entry occurs and the industry supply curve shifts from S_0 to S_1. In part (a), the long-run supply curve LS_A is horizontal. The quantity increases from Q_0 to Q_1 and the price remains constant at P_0.

In part (b), the long-run supply curve is LS_B; the price increases to P_2 and the quantity increases to Q_2. This case occurs in industries with external diseconomies. In part (c), the long-run supply curve is LS_C; the price decreases to P_3 and the quantity increases to Q_3. This case occurs in an industry with external economies.

and early twentieth centuries, the services available to farmers expanded and their costs fell. New firms specialized in the development and marketing of farm machinery and fertilizers. As a result, average farm costs decreased. Farms enjoyed the benefits of external economies. As a consequence, as the demand for farm products increased, the output increased but the price fell.

Over the long term, the prices of many goods and services have fallen, not because of external economies but because of technological change. Let's now study this influence on a competitive market.

Technological Change

Industries are constantly discovering lower-cost techniques of production. Most cost-saving production techniques cannot be implemented, however, without investing in new plant and equipment. As a consequence, it takes time for a technological advance to spread through an industry. Some firms whose plants are on the verge of being replaced will be quick to adopt the new technology, while other firms whose plants have recently been replaced will continue to operate with an old technology until they can no longer cover their average variable cost. Once average variable cost cannot be covered, a firm will scrap even a relatively new plant (embodying an old technology) in favour of a plant with a new technology.

New technology allows firms to produce at a lower cost and to make a larger profit than the existing technology. As a result, as firms adopt a new technology, their average total cost curve and marginal cost curve shift downward. With lower costs, firms are willing to supply a given quantity at a lower price or, equivalently, they are willing to supply a larger quantity at a given price. In other words, when a firm adopts a new technology it increases its supply and its supply curve shifts rightward. With a given demand, the quantity produced increases and the price falls.

Two forces are at work in an industry undergoing technological change:

1 Firms that adopt the new technology make an economic profit. So there is entry by new-technology firms.

2 Firms that stick with the old technology incur economic losses. They either exit the industry or switch to the new technology.

As old-technology firms disappear and new-technology firms enter, the price falls and the quantity produced increases. Eventually, the industry arrives at a long-run equilibrium in which all the firms use the new technology, produce at minimum long-run average cost and make zero economic profit (a normal profit). Because in the long run competition eliminates economic profit, technological change brings only temporary gains to producers. But the lower prices and better products that technological advances bring are permanent gains for consumers.

The process that we've just described is one in which some firms experience economic profits and others experience economic losses. It is a period of dynamic change for an industry. Some firms do well, and others do badly. Often, the process has a geographical dimension – the expanding new technology firms bring prosperity to what was once a backwater and traditional industrial regions decline. Sometimes, the new-technology firms are in another country, while the old-technology firms are in the domestic economy.

The information revolution of the 1990s produced many examples of changes like these. Commercial banking, which was traditionally concentrated in large cities such as London and Frankfurt, has decentralized with data processing centres in small Yorkshire towns. Scotland's "silicon glen" has displaced traditional agricultural production. And even in the agricultural sector, bio-technological advances are revolutionizing milk and crop production.

Review Quiz

1 Describe the course of events in a competitive industry following a permanent decrease in demand. What happens to output, market price and economic profit in the short run and in the long run?

2 Describe the course of events in a competitive industry following a permanent increase in demand. What happens to output, market price and economic profit in the short run and in the long run?

3 Describe the course of events in a competitive industry following the adoption of a new technology. What happens to output, market price and economic profit in the short run and in the long run?

We've seen how a competitive industry works in the short run and the long run. But does a competitive industry achieve an efficient use of resources?

Competition and Efficiency

A competitive industry can achieve an efficient use of resources. You studied efficiency in Chapter 5 using only the concepts of demand, supply and consumer surplus. But with your knowledge of what lies behind demand and supply curves in a competitive market, you can now gain a deeper understanding of how a competitive market achieves efficiency.

Efficient Use of Resources

Resource use is efficient when we produce the goods and services that people value most highly (see Chapter 5, pp. 98–99). If someone can become better off without anyone else becoming worse off, resources are *not* being used efficiently. For example, suppose we produce a computer that no one uses but many people want and demand more video games. If we produce one less computer and reallocate the unused resources to produce more video games, some people will become better off and no one will be worse off. So the initial resource allocation was inefficient.

In the more technical language you have learned, resource use is efficient when marginal benefit equals marginal cost. In the computer and video games example, the marginal benefit of video games exceeds the marginal cost. And the marginal cost of a computer exceeds its marginal benefit. So by producing fewer computers and more video games, we move resources towards a higher-value use.

Choices, Equilibrium and Efficiency

You can use what you have learned about the decisions made by consumers and competitive firms and market equilibrium to describe an efficient use of resources.

Choices

Consumers allocate their resources to get the most value possible out of them. Consumer demand is derived by finding how the best budget allocation changes as the price of a good changes. So consumers get the most value out of their resources at all points along their demand curves, which are also their marginal benefit curves.

Competitive firms produce the quantity that maximizes profit. And we derive the firm's supply curve by finding the profit-maximizing quantities at each price. So firms get the most value out of their resources at all points along their supply curves, which are also their marginal cost curves. Remember, when firms are on their supply curves they are *technologically efficient* – they get the maximum possible output from given inputs – and also *economically efficient* – they combine resources to minimize cost (see Chapter 9, pp. 183–184).

Equilibrium

In competitive equilibrium, the quantity demanded equals the quantity supplied. So the price equals the consumers' marginal benefit and the producers' marginal cost. In this situation, the gains from trade between consumers and producers are maximized. These gains from trade are the consumer surplus plus the producer surplus.

The gains from trade for consumers are measured by *consumer surplus*, which is the area below the demand curve and above the price paid. (See Chapter 5, p. 101.) The gains from trade for producers are measured by *producer surplus*, which is the area above the marginal cost curve and below the price received. The total gains from trade are the sum of consumer surplus and producer surplus.

Efficiency

If the people who consume and produce a good or service are the only ones affected by it, and if the market for the good or service is in equilibrium, then resources have been used efficiently. They cannot be reallocated to increase their value.

In such a situation, there is no external benefit or external costs. **External benefits** are benefits that accrue to people other than the buyer of a good. For example, you might get a benefit from your neighbour's expenditure on her garden. Your neighbour buys the quantities of garden plants that make her as well off as possible, not her and you.

In the absence of external benefits, the market demand curve measures marginal *social* benefit – the value that *everyone* places on one more unit of a good or service.

External costs are costs that are borne by someone other than the producer of a good or service. For example, a firm might lower its costs by polluting. The cost of pollution is an external cost. Firms produce the output that maximizes their profit. They do not count the cost of pollution as a charge against their profit.

In the absence of external costs, the market supply curve measures marginal social cost – the entire marginal cost that *anyone* bears to produce one more unit of a good or service.

Figure 11.12

Efficiency of Perfect Competition

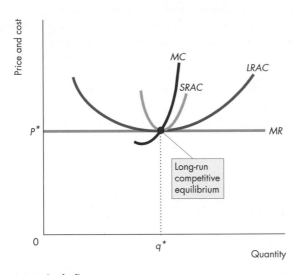

(a) A single firm

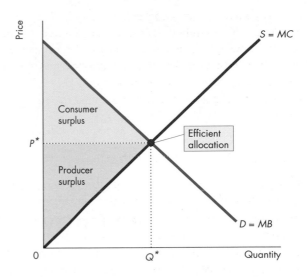

(b) A market

In part (a), a firm in perfect competition produces at the lowest possible long-run average total cost q^*. In part (b), consumers have made their best available choices and are on their demand curves. Firms are producing at least cost and are on their supply curves. With no external benefits or external costs, resources are used efficiently at the quantity Q^* and the price P^*. Perfect competition achieves an efficient allocation of resources.

An Efficient Allocation

Figure 11.12(a) shows an efficient allocation in perfect competition in long-run equilibrium. Part (a) shows the situation of an individual firm and part (b) shows the market. The equilibrium market price is P^*. At that price, each firm earns normal profit (zero economic profit). Each firm has a plant size that enables it to produce at the lowest possible average total cost. In this situation, consumers are as well off as possible because the good cannot be produced at a lower cost and the price equals that least possible cost.

In part (b), consumers have made their best available choices at all points along their demand curves, so on the market demand curve, D (which is also the marginal benefit curve MB), consumers are efficient. Producers are efficient at all points on the supply curve, S (which is also the marginal cost curve MC). Resources are used efficiently at the quantity Q^* and price P^*. At this point, marginal benefit equals marginal cost, and the sum of producer surplus (blue area) and consumer surplus (green area) is maximized.

When firms in perfect competition are away from long-run equilibrium, either entry or exit is taking place and the market is moving towards the situation depicted in Figure 11.12. But the market is still efficient. So long

as marginal benefit (on the demand curve) equals marginal cost (on the supply curve), the market is efficient. But it is only in long-run equilibrium that consumers pay the lowest possible price.

Review Quiz

1. Explain why a perfectly competitive industry achieves an efficient use of resources.
2. What are external benefits and external costs? Give two examples of each.
3. What is the marginal social benefit?
4. What is a marginal social cost?

You've now completed your study of perfect competition. *Reading Between the Lines* on pp. 246–247 gives you an opportunity to use what you have learned to understand recent events in the world market for tea.

Many markets are close to perfect competition, but many are not. In Chapter 12, we study the extreme of market power: monopoly. And in Chapter 13, we study monopolistic competition and oligopoly – varieties of real-world markets that lie between these two extremes.

Reading Between the Lines
Perfect Competition: Kenyan Tea

The BBC, 18 March 2003

Tea Growers Fear Price Falls

James Whittington

Kenya's tea exporters are struggling to cope with falling prices which they fear could threaten the viability of their industry. Tea is a major export crop for Kenya, outflanking coffee and contributing 20% of the country's foreign earnings.

But a mix of falling demand and rising output has caused a sustained drop in prices. Part of the problem, Kenyan tea traders say, is that South East Asian countries such as Indonesia and Vietnam have increased the amount of tea they are growing. . . . Mombasa is Kenya's main tea market and the site of weekly auctions. Tea brokers buy the crop from producers and sell it on for export. If Vietnamese and Indonesian growers continue to undercut Kenyan tea prices "obviously Kenya is going to suffer enormously," says Mr Wilson (managing director of Africa Tea Brokers in Mombasa). Many big growers are casting around for alternative crops, says Nigel Sandys-Lumsdaine, managing director of planters Williamson Tea Kenya. Timber, which is in short supply in Kenya, is a popular choice.

Source: http://news.bbc.co.uk/go/pr/fr//1/hi/business/2860239.stm

The Essence of the Story

◆ Kenya is a major producer of tea.

◆ Decreasing world demand and increasing world output has caused a sustained drop in world tea prices.

◆ The increase in output comes from East Asian countries.

◆ Some Kenyan tea growers are looking around for alternative crops such as timber.

Economic Analysis

◆ The world tea market is an example of a perfectly competitive market.

◆ Figure 1(a) shows that in 2002, the market price of tea was £0.88 per kilogram.

◆ At £0.88 per kilogram, each Kenyan tea garden produced Q_1 kilograms of tea and made an economic profit, as shown by the blue rectangle in Figure 1(b).

◆ The economic profits earned in 2002 were a signal for new tea growers to enter the market, especially from East Asia.

◆ Figure 2(a) shows that with the increase in the supply in 2003 and the decrease in world demand, the price fell to £0.85 per kilogram.

◆ Figure 2(b) shows that in 2003, Kenyan tea gardens incurred economic losses.

◆ If the economic losses persist, some tea growers will leave the tea industry and turn to other crops, such as timber.

◆ As tea growers exit the industry, the price will rise back to its long-run equilibrium and tea gardens will make zero economic profit.

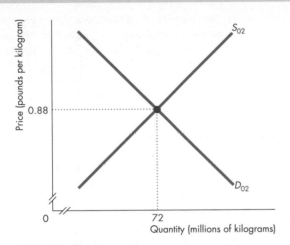

(a) Tea market

Figure 1 In 2002

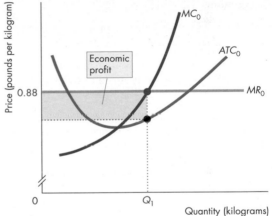

(b) Tea garden

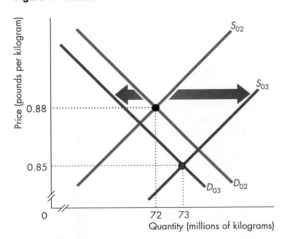

(a) Tea market

Figure 2 In 2003

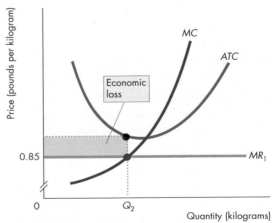

(b) Tea garden

Summary

Key Points

What is Perfect Competition?
(pp. 228–229)

◆ A perfectly competitive firm is a price taker.

The Firm's Decision in Perfect Competition (pp. 230–235)

◆ The firm produces the output at which marginal revenue (price) equals marginal cost.

◆ In short-run equilibrium, a firm can make an economic profit, incur an economic loss or break even.

◆ If price is less than minimum average variable cost, the firm temporarily shuts down.

◆ A firm's supply curve is the upward-sloping part of its marginal cost curve above minimum average variable cost.

◆ An industry supply curve shows the sum of the quantities supplied by each firm at each price.

Output, Price and Profit in Perfect Competition (pp. 236–239)

◆ Market demand and supply determine price.

◆ The firm produces the output at which price equals marginal cost.

◆ Economic profit induces entry. Economic loss induces exit.

◆ Entry and plant expansion increase supply and lower price and profit. Exit and plant contraction decrease supply and raise price and profit.

◆ In the long-run equilibrium, economic profit is zero (firms earn normal profit). There is no entry, exit, plant expansion or downsizing.

Changing Tastes and Advancing Technology (pp. 240–243)

◆ A permanent decrease in demand leads to a smaller industry output and a smaller number of firms.

◆ A permanent increase in demand leads to a larger industry output and a larger number of firms.

◆ The long-run effect of a change in demand on price depends on whether there are external economies (price falls), external diseconomies (price rises) or neither (price remains constant).

◆ New technologies increase supply and in the long run lower the price and increase the quantity.

Competition and Efficiency
(pp. 244–245)

◆ Resources are used efficiently when we produce goods and services in the quantities that everyone values most highly.

◆ When there are no external benefits or external costs, perfect competition achieves an efficient allocation. In long-run equilibrium, consumers pay the lowest possible price. Marginal benefit equals marginal cost, and the sum of consumer and producer surplus is maximized.

Key Figures

Key Terms

Problems

*1 Quick Copy is one of the many copy shops in London. The figure shows Quick Copy's cost curves.

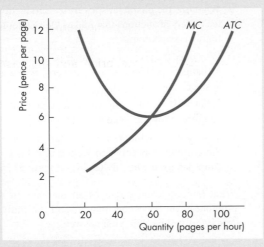

a If the market price of copying one page is 10 pence, what is Quick Copy's profit-maximizing output?

b Calculate Quick Copy's profit.

c With no change in demand or technology, how will the price change in the long run?

2 Bob's is one of many burger stands at Leeds United football stadium. The figure shows Bob's cost curves.

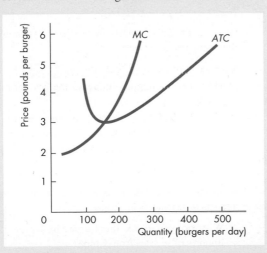

a If the market price of a burger is £4, what is Bob's profit-maximizing output?

b Calculate the profit that Bob's makes.

c With no change in demand or technology, how will the price change in the long run?

---

*Solutions to odd-numbered problems are available on *Parkin Interactive*.

*3 Pat's Pizza Restaurant is a price taker. It has the following hourly costs:

Output (pizza per hour)	Total cost (pounds per hour)
0	10
1	21
2	30
3	41
4	54
5	69

a What is Pat's profit-maximizing output and how much profit does Pat make if the market price is (i) €14 a pizza, (ii) €12 a pizza and (iii) €10 a pizza?

b What is Pat's shutdown point?

c Derive Pat's supply curve.

d What is the long-run equilibrium price of pizzas?

4 Luigi's Lasagna is a price taker. Its costs are:

Output (plates per hour)	Total cost (euros per hour)
0	14
1	38
2	48
3	62
4	80
5	102
6	128

a What is Luigi's profit-maximizing output and how much profit does he make if the market price is (i) €24 a plate, (ii) €20 a plate and (iii) €12 a plate?

b What is Luigi's shutdown point and what is his profit?

c Over what price range will firms with costs identical to Luigi's enter the lasagna industry?

*5 The EU market demand schedule for pop CDs is:

Price (euros per CD)	Quantity demanded (CDs per week)
3.65	500,000
4.40	475,000
5.20	450,000
6.00	425,000
6.80	400,000
7.60	375,000
8.40	350,000
9.20	325,000
10.00	300,000
10.80	275,000
11.60	250,000
11.40	225,000
13.20	200,000
14.00	175,000

The market is perfectly competitive and each firm has the same cost structure described by the following table:

Output (CDs per week)	Marginal cost	Average variable cost	Average total cost
		(euros per CD)	
150	6.00	8.80	15.47
200	4.60	7.80	11.80
250	7.00	7.00	11.00
300	7.65	7.10	10.43
350	8.40	7.20	10.06
400	10.00	7.50	10.00
450	12.40	8.00	10.22
500	20.70	9.00	11.00

There are 1,000 firms in the industry.

a What is the market price?

b What is the industry's output?

c What is the output produced by each firm?

d What is the economic profit made by each firm?

e Do firms enter or exit the industry?

f What is the number of firms in the long run?

6 The same demand conditions as those in Problem 5 prevail and there are still 1,000 firms in the industry, but fixed costs increase by €980. What now are your answers to the questions in problem 5?

7* In problem 5, a fall in the price of digital tapes decreases the demand for CDs permanently and the demand schedule becomes:

Price (euros per CD)	Quantity demanded (CDs per week)
2.95	500,000
4.13	450,000
5.30	400,000
6.48	350,000
7.65	300,000
8.83	250,000
10.00	200,000
11.18	150,000

Rework your answers for the questions in problem 5 using this demand schedule.

8 In problem 6, a fall in the price of digital tapes decreases the demand for CDs permanently and the demand schedule becomes that given in problem 7. Now rework your answer to the questions in problem 6.

Critical Thinking

1 Study the *Reading between the Lines* on pp. 244–245 and then answer the following questions:

a What are the characteristics of tea production and tea buyers at auctions that makes the market for tea highly competitive?

b Why does the price of tea change so rapidly? Is such a change a problem for tea growers? Explain your answer.

c What will be the long-run effect of East Asian countries growing more tea?

e Who are the winners and who are the losers in the competition between Kenya and East Asian countries for the quality tea export market?

2 What has been the effect of an increase in world population on the wheat market and the individual wheat farmer? Explain your answer.

3 Why have the prices of pocket calculators and VCRs fallen? What do you think has happened to the costs and economic profits of the firms that make these products?

Web Exercises

Use the links on *Parkin Interactive* to work the following exercises.

1 Read about "grey imports from Japan". Then answer the following questions:

a What is meant by a "grey import"?

b How do grey imports influence the UK car market in the short run?

c Do you think grey imports will increase the efficiency of the UK car market? Explain your answer.

d What effect will grey imports have on the UK car market in the long run?

2 Read about the EU decision to increase the quotas on imports of textiles from China.

a Why do you think the European Union limits imports of textiles from China?

b Draw a graph to illustrate the EU market for textiles and the situation facing an individual textile producer. In these graphs, show the equilibrium price, the equilibrium quantity, the quantity produced by a firm and its profit.

c On your graphs, show the effect of increasing the textiles import quota?

d Who benefits and who bears costs from the EU quotas on imports of textiles from China?

Chapter 12

Monopoly

After studying this chapter you will be able to:

◆ Explain how monopoly arises and distinguish between single-price monopoly and price-discriminating monopoly

◆ Explain how a single-price monopoly determines its output and price

◆ Compare the performance and efficiency of single-price monopoly and competition

◆ Explain how a price discriminating increases profit

◆ Explain how monopoly regulation influences output, price, economic profit and efficiency

Dominating the Internet

eBay and Google are dominant players in the markets they serve. How do firms like these behave? How do they choose the quantities to produce and the prices to charge? Do they charge too much and produce too little? Would more competition among Internet auctioneers and search engines bring greater efficiency? Find out in this chapter.

Advertising Programs - Business Solutions - About Google

Make Google Your Homepage!

©2004 Google - Searching 4,285,199,774 web pages

Market Power

Market power and competition are the two forces that operate in markets. **Market power** is the ability to influence the market, and in particular the market price, by influencing the total quantity offered for sale.

Firms in perfect competition have no market power. They face the force of raw competition and are price takers. A monopoly firm exercises raw market power. A **monopoly** is a firm that produces a good or service for which no close substitute exists and which is protected by a barrier that prevents other firms from selling that good or service. In monopoly, the firm is the industry.

Examples of monopoly include the firms that operate the pipelines and cables that bring gas, water, and electricity to your home, and Microsoft Corporation, the US software giant is close to being a monopoly.

How Monopoly Arises

Monopoly has two key features:

◆ No close substitutes
◆ Barriers to entry

No Close Substitutes

If a good has a close substitute, even though only one firm produces it, that firm effectively faces competition from the producers of substitutes. Water supplied by a local water board is an example of a good that does not have close substitutes. While it does have a close substitute for drinking – bottled spring water – it has no effective substitutes for bathing or washing a car.

Monopolies are constantly under attack from new products and ideas that substitute for products produced by monopolies. For example, DHL, the fax machine, and e-mail have ended the monopoly of the Post Office.

Barriers to Entry

Legal or natural constraints that protect a firm from potential competitors are called **barriers to entry**. A firm can sometimes create its own barrier to entry by acquiring a significant portion of a key resource. For example, De Beers controls more than 80 per cent of the world's supply of natural diamonds. But most monopolies arise from two other types of barriers: legal barriers and natural barriers.

Legal Barriers to Entry

Legal barriers to entry create legal monopoly. A **legal monopoly** is a market in which competition and entry are restricted through ownership of a resource, by the granting of a monopoly franchise, a government licence, a patent or a copyright.

A *monopoly franchise* is an exclusive right granted to a firm to supply a good or service. An example is the exclusive right granted to the Post Office to carry first-class mail.

A *government licence* controls entry into particular occupations, professions and industries. Examples of this type of barrier to entry occur in medicine, law, dentistry and many other professional services. A government licence doesn't always create a monopoly, but it does restrict competition.

A *patent* is an exclusive right granted to the inventor of a product or service. A *copyright* is an exclusive right granted to the author or composer of a literary, musical, dramatic or artistic work. Patents and copyrights are valid for a limited time period that varies from country to country. In the United Kingdom, a patent is valid for 16 years. Patents encourage the *invention* of new products and production methods.

Patents also stimulate *innovation* – the use of new inventions – by encouraging inventors to publicize their discoveries and offer them for use under licence. Patents have stimulated innovations in areas as diverse as soybean seeds, pharmaceuticals, memory chips, and video games.

Natural Barriers to Entry

Natural barriers to entry create **natural monopoly**, an industry in which one firm can supply the entire market at a lower price than two or more firms can.

Figure 12.1 shows a natural monopoly in the distribution of electric power. Here, the market demand curve for electric power is D, and the long-run average cost curve is $LRAC$. Because long-run average cost decreases as output increases, economies of scale prevail over the entire length of the $LRAC$ curve. One firm can produce 4 million kilowatt-hours at 5 pence a kilowatt-hour. At this price, the quantity demanded is 4 million kilowatt-hours. So if the price was 5 pence, one firm could supply the entire market. If two firms shared the market, it would cost each of them 10 pence a kilowatt-hour to produce a total of 4 million kilowatt-hours. If four firms shared the market, it would cost each of them 15 pence a kilowatt-hour to produce a total of 4 million kilowatt-hours. So in conditions like those shown in Figure 12.1, one firm can supply the entire market at a lower cost than two or more firms can. The distribution of electric power, water and gas are examples of natural monopoly.

Most monopolies are regulated in some way by government agencies. We will study such regulation at the end of this chapter. But for two reasons, we'll begin by studying unregulated monopoly. First, we can better understand why governments regulate monopolies and the effects of regulation if we also know how an unregulated monopoly behaves.

Second, even in industries with more than one producer, firms often have a degree of monopoly power, and the theory of monopoly sheds light on the behaviour of such firms and industries.

A major difference between monopoly and competition is that a monopoly sets its own price. But in doing so, it faces a market constraint. Let's see how the market limits a monopoly's pricing choices.

Figure 12.1

Natural Monopoly

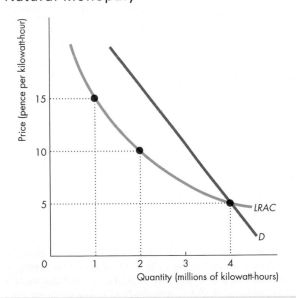

The market demand curve for electric power is *D*, and the long-run average cost curve is *LRAC*. Economies of scale exist over the entire *LRAC* curve. One firm can distribute 4 million kilowatt-hours at a cost of 5 pence a kilowatt-hour. This same total output costs 10 pence a kilowatt-hour with two firms and 15 pence a kilowatt-hour with four firms. So one firm can meet the market demand at a lower cost than two or more firms can, and the market is a natural monopoly.

Monopoly Price-setting Strategies

All monopolies face a trade-off between price and the quantity sold. To sell a larger quantity, the monopolist must charge a lower price. But there are two broad monopoly situations that create different trade-offs. They are:

◆ Price discrimination
◆ Single price

Price Discrimination

Price discrimination is the practice of selling different units of a good or service for different prices. Different customers might pay different prices for the same item. For example, airlines offer a dizzying array of different prices for the same trip so different passengers on the same flight end up paying different prices. Or one customer might pay different prices for different quantities bought. For example, pizza producers often charge one price for a single pizza and almost give away a second pizza. These are all examples of price discrimination.

Most of the firms that price discriminate are *not* monopolies. But they are firms that have some market power and it is easier to see how price discrimination works in the monopoly case than in other cases.

When a firm price discriminates, it looks as though it is doing its customers a favour by offering low prices to some of them. In fact, as you'll see later in this chapter, the firm is doing the opposite. It is charging the highest possible price for each unit that it sells and making the largest possible profit.

Not all monopolies can price discriminate. The main obstacle to price discrimination is resale by customers who buy for a low price. Because of resale possibilities, price discrimination is limited to monopolies that sell services that cannot be resold.

Single Price

A **single-price monopoly** is a monopoly that must sell each unit of its output for the same price to all its customers. De Beers is an example of a *single-price* monopoly. It sells diamonds (of a given size and quality) for the same price to all its customers. If it tried to sell at a higher price to some customers than to others, only the low-price customers would buy from De Beers. Others would buy from De Beers' low-price customers.

We'll look first at single-price monopoly.

A Single-price Monopoly's Output and Price Decision

To understand how a single-price monopoly makes its output and price decision, we must first study the link between price and marginal revenue.

Price and Marginal Revenue

Because in a monopoly there is only one firm, the demand curve facing the firm is the market demand curve. Let's look at Gina's Cut and Dry, the only hairdressing salon within a 15 mile radius of a North Yorkshire town. The table in Figure 12.2 shows the market demand schedule. At a price of £20, she sells no haircuts. The lower the price, the more haircuts per hour Gina can sell. For example, at £12, consumers demand 4 haircuts per hour (row E).

Total revenue (TR) is the price (P) multiplied by the quantity sold (Q). For example, in row D, Gina sells 3 haircuts at £14 each, so total revenue is £42. *Marginal revenue* (MR) is the change in total revenue (ΔTR) resulting from a one-unit increase in the quantity sold. For example, if the price falls from £16 (row C) to £14 (row D), the quantity sold increases from 2 to 3 haircuts. Total revenue rises from £32 to £42, so the change in total revenue is £10. Because the quantity sold increases by 1 haircut, marginal revenue equals the change in total revenue and is £10. Marginal revenue is placed between the two rows to emphasize that marginal revenue relates to the *change* in the quantity sold.

Figure 12.2 shows the market demand curve and marginal revenue curve (MR) and also illustrates the calculation we've just made. Notice that at each level of output, marginal revenue is less than price – the marginal revenue curve lies below the demand curve.

Why is marginal revenue *less* than price? It is because when the price is lowered to sell one more unit, two opposing forces affect total revenue. The lower price results in a revenue loss and the increased quantity sold results in a revenue gain. For example, at a price of £16, Gina sells 2 haircuts (point C). If she lowers the price to £14, she sells 3 haircuts and has a revenue gain of £14 on the third haircut. But she now receives only £14 on the first two – £2 less than before. She loses £4 of revenue on the first 2 haircuts. To calculate marginal revenue, she must deduct this amount from the revenue gain of £14. So her marginal revenue is £10, which is less than the price.

Figure 12.2 ◈

Demand and Marginal Revenue

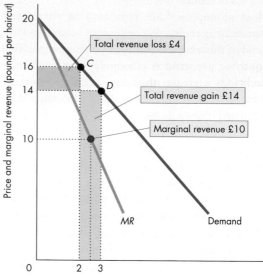

	Price P (pounds per haircut)	Quantity demanded Q (haircuts per hour)	Total revenue $TR = P \times Q$ (pounds)	Marginal revenue $MR = \Delta TR/\Delta Q$ (pounds per haircut)
A	20	0	0	
				18
B	18	1	18	
				14
C	**16**	**2**	**32**	
				10
D	**14**	**3**	**42**	
				6
E	12	4	48	
				2
F	10	5	50	

The table shows the demand schedule. Total revenue (TR) is price multiplied by quantity sold. For example, in row C, the price is £16 a haircut, Cut and Dry sells 2 haircuts and its total revenue is £32. Marginal revenue (MR) is the change in total revenue that results from a one-unit increase in the quantity sold. For example, when the price falls from £16 to £14 a haircut, the quantity sold increases by 1 haircut and total revenue increases by £10. Marginal revenue is £10. The demand curve and the marginal revenue curve, MR, are based on the numbers in the table and illustrate the calculation of marginal revenue when the price falls from £16 to £14 a haircut.

Marginal Revenue and Elasticity

A single-price monopoly's marginal revenue is related to the *elasticity of demand* for its good. The demand for a good can be *elastic* (the elasticity of demand is greater than 1), *inelastic* (the elasticity of demand is less than 1), or *unit elastic* (the elasticity of demand is equal to 1). Demand is *elastic* if a 1 per cent fall in price brings a greater than 1 per cent increase in the quantity demanded. Demand is *inelastic* if a 1 per cent fall in price brings a less than 1 per cent increase in the quantity demanded. And demand is *unit elastic* if a 1 per cent fall in price brings a 1 per cent increase in the quantity demanded. (See Chapter 4, p. 82.)

If demand is elastic, a fall in price brings an increase in total revenue – the increase in revenue from the increase in quantity sold outweighs the decrease in revenue from the lower price – and marginal revenue is positive. If demand is inelastic, a fall in price brings a decrease in total revenue – the increase in revenue from the increase in quantity sold is outweighed by the decrease in revenue from the lower price – and marginal revenue is negative. If demand is unit elastic, total revenue does not change – the increase in revenue from the increase in quantity sold offsets the decrease in revenue from the lower price – and marginal revenue is zero.

Figure 12.3 illustrates the relationship between marginal revenue, total revenue and elasticity. As the price of a haircut gradually falls from £20 to £10, the quantity of haircuts demanded increases from 0 to 5 an hour. Over this output range, marginal revenue is positive (part a), total revenue increases (part b) and the demand for haircuts is elastic. As the price falls from £10 to £0 a haircut, the quantity of haircuts demanded increases from 5 to 10 an hour. Over this output range, marginal revenue is negative (part a), total revenue decreases (part b) and the demand for haircuts is inelastic. When the price is £10 a haircut, marginal revenue is zero, total revenue is a maximum and the demand for haircuts is unit elastic.

In Monopoly, Demand is Always Elastic

The relationship between marginal revenue and elasticity that you've just discovered implies that a profit-maximizing monopoly never produces an output in the inelastic range of its demand curve. If it did so, it could produce a smaller quantity, charge a higher price and increase its profit. Let's now look at a monopoly's price and output decision.

Figure 12.3

Marginal Revenue and Elasticity

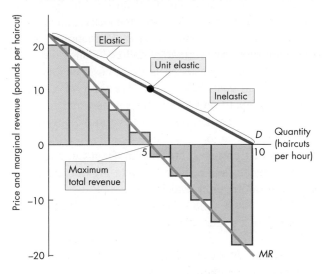

(a) Demand and marginal revenue curves

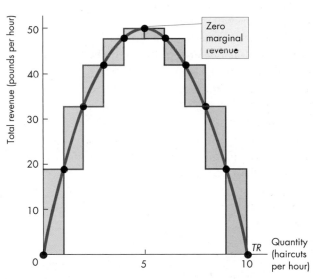

(b) Total revenue curve

In part (a), the demand curve is *D* and the marginal revenue curve is *MR*. In part (b), the total revenue curve is *TR*. Over the range from 0 to 5 haircuts an hour, a price cut increases total revenue, so marginal revenue is positive – as shown by the blue bars. Demand is elastic. Over the range from 5 to 10 haircuts an hour, a price cut decreases total revenue, so marginal revenue is negative – as shown by the red bars. Demand is inelastic. At 5 haircuts an hour, total revenue is maximized and marginal revenue is zero. Demand is unit elastic.

Price and Output Decision

A monopoly sets its price and output at the levels that maximize economic profit. To determine this price and output level, we need to study the behaviour of both cost and revenue as output varies. A monopoly faces the same types of technology and cost constraints as a competitive firm. So its costs (total cost, average cost, and marginal cost) behave just like those of a firm in perfect competition. And its revenues (total revenue, price, and marginal revenue) behave in the way we've just described.

Table 12.1 provides information about Cut and Dry's costs, revenues and economic profit. Figure 12.4 shows the same information graphically.

Maximizing Economic Profit

You can see in the table and part (a) of the figure that total cost (*TC*) and total revenue (*TR*) both rise as output increases, but *TC* rises at an increasing rate and *TR* rises at a decreasing rate.

Economic profit, which equals *TR* minus *TC*, increases at small output levels, reaches a maximum and then decreases. The maximum profit (£12) occurs when Gina sells 3 haircuts for £14 each. If she sells 2 haircuts for £16 each or 4 haircuts for £12 each, her economic profit will be only £8.

Marginal Revenue Equals Marginal Cost

You can see in the table and part (b) of the figure Gina's marginal revenue (*MR*) and marginal cost (*MC*). When Cut and Dry increases output from 2 to 3 haircuts, *MR* is £10 and *MC* is £6. *MR* exceeds *MC* by £4 and Cut and Dry's profit increases by that amount. If Cut and Dry increases output yet further, from 3 to 4 haircuts, *MR* is £6 and *MC* is £10. In this case, *MC* exceeds *MR* by £4, so profit decreases by that amount.

When *MR* exceeds *MC*, profit increases if output increases. When *MC* exceeds *MR*, profit increases if output *decreases*. When *MC* equals *MR*, profit is maximized.

Figure 12.4(b) shows the maximum profit as price (on the demand curve *D*) minus average total cost (on the *ATC* curve) multiplied by the quantity produced – the blue rectangle.

Maximum Price the Market will Bear

Unlike a firm in perfect competition, a monopoly influences the price of what it sells. But a monopolist doesn't set the price at the maximum *possible* price. At the maximum possible price, the firm would be able to sell only one unit of output, which in general is less than the profit-maximizing quantity. Rather, a monopoly produces the profit-maximizing quantity and sells that quantity for the highest price it can get.

Table 12.1

A Monopoly's Output and Price Decision

Price (*P*) (pounds per haircut)	Quantity demanded (*Q*) (haircuts per hour)	Total revenue (*TR* = *P* × *Q*) (pounds)	Marginal revenue (*MR* = Δ*TR*/Δ*Q*) (pounds per haircut)	Total cost (*Q*) (pounds)	Marginal cost (*MC* = Δ*TC*/Δ*Q*) (pounds per haircut)	Profit (*TR* − *TC*) (pounds)
20	0	0		20		−20
			 18		 1	
18	1	18		21		−3
			 14		 3	
16	2	32		24		8
			 10		 6	
14	**3**	**42**		**30**		**+12**
			 6		 10	
12	4	48		40		+8
			 2		 15	
10	5	50		55		−5

This table gives the information needed to find the profit-maximizing output and price. Total revenue (*TR*) equals price multiplied by the quantity sold. Profit equals total revenue minus total cost (*TC*). Profit is maximized when the price is £14 and 3 haircuts are sold. Total revenue is £42 an hour, total cost is £30 an hour and economic profit is £12 an hour.

Figure 12.4

A Monopoly's Output and Price

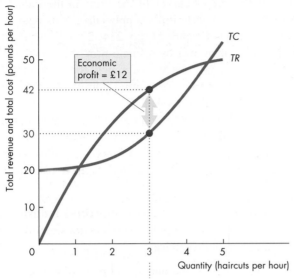

(a) Total revenue and total cost curves

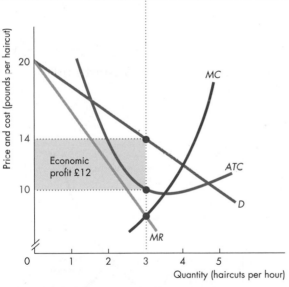

(b) Demand and marginal revenue and cost curves

In part (a), economic profit is the vertical distance equal to total revenue (*TR*) minus total cost (*TC*) and it is maximized at 3 haircuts an hour.

In part (b), economic profit is maximized when marginal cost (*MC*) equals marginal revenue (*MR*). The profit-maximizing output is 3 haircuts an hour. The price is determined by the demand curve (*D*) and is £14 a haircut. The average total cost is £10 a haircut, so economic profit, the blue rectangle, is £12 – the profit per haircut (£4) multiplied by 3 haircuts.

All firms maximize profit by producing the output at which marginal revenue equals marginal cost. For a competitive firm, price equals marginal revenue, so price also equals marginal cost. For a monopoly, price exceeds marginal revenue, so price also exceeds marginal cost.

A monopoly charges a price that exceeds marginal cost, but does it always make an economic profit? In Gina's case, when she produces 3 haircuts an hour, her average total cost is £10 (read from the *ATC* curve) and her price is £14 (read from the *D* curve). Her profit per haircut is £4 (£14 minus £10). Gina's economic profit is shown by the blue rectangle, which equals the profit per haircut (£4) multiplied by the number of haircuts (3), for a total of £12 an hour.

If firms in a perfectly competitive industry make a positive economic profit, new firms enter. That does not happen in monopoly. Barriers to entry prevent new firms from entering an industry in which there is a monopoly. So a monopoly can make a positive economic profit and might continue to do so indefinitely. Sometimes that profit is large, as in the international diamond business.

Gina makes a positive economic profit. But suppose that the owner of the shop that Gina rents increases Cut and Dry's rent. If Gina pays an additional £12 an hour, her fixed cost increases by £12 an hour. Her marginal cost and marginal revenue don't change, so her profit-maximizing output remains at 3 haircuts an hour. Her profit decreases by £12 an hour to zero. If Gina pays more than an additional £12 an hour for her shop rent, she incurs an economic loss. If this situation were permanent, Gina would go out of business.

Review Quiz

1. What is the relationship between marginal cost and marginal revenue when a single-price monopoly maximizes profit?
2. How does a single-price monopoly determine the price it will charge its customers?
3. What is the relationship between price, marginal revenue and marginal cost when a single-price monopoly is maximizing profit?
4. Why can a monopoly make a positive economic profit even in the long run?

Single-price Monopoly and Competition Compared

Imagine an industry that is made up of many small firms operating in perfect competition. Then imagine that a single firm buys out all these small firms and creates a monopoly.

What will happen in this industry? Will the price rise or fall? Will the quantity produced increase or decrease? Will economic profit increase or decrease? Will either the original competitive situation or the new monopoly situation be efficient?

These are the questions we're now going to answer. First, we look at the effects of monopoly on the price and quantity produced. Then we turn to the questions about efficiency.

Comparing Output and Price

Figure 12.5 shows the market we'll study. The market demand curve is D. The demand curve is the same regardless of how the industry is organized. But the supply side and the equilibrium are different in monopoly and competition. First, let's look at the case of perfect competition.

Perfect Competition

Initially, with many small, perfectly competitive firms in the market, the market supply curve is S. This supply curve is obtained by summing the supply curves of all the individual firms in the market.

In perfect competition, equilibrium occurs where the supply curve and the demand curve intersect. The quantity produced by the industry is Q_C, and the price is P_C. Each firm takes the price P_C and maximizes its profit by producing the output at which its own marginal cost equals the price. Because each firm is a small part of the total industry, there is no incentive for any firm to try to manipulate the price by varying its output.

Monopoly

Now suppose that this industry is taken over by a single firm. Consumers do not change, so the demand curve remains the same as in the case of perfect competition. But now the monopoly recognizes this demand curve as a constraint on its sales.

The monopoly's marginal revenue curve is MR. The monopoly maximizes profit by producing the quantity at which marginal revenue equals marginal cost. To find the monopoly's marginal cost curve, first recall that in perfect competition, the industry supply curve is the sum of the supply curves of the firms in the industry. Also recall that each firm's supply curve is its marginal cost curve (see Chapter 11, pp. 234–235). So when the industry is taken over by a single firm, the competitive industry's supply curve becomes the monopoly's marginal cost curve. To remind you of this fact, the supply curve is also labelled MC.

The output at which marginal revenue equals marginal cost is Q_M. This output is smaller than the competitive output Q_C. And the monopoly charges the price P_M, which is higher than P_C. We have established that:

> **Compared to a perfectly competitive industry, a single-price monopoly restricts its output and charges a higher price.**

We've seen how the output and price of a monopoly compare with those in a competitive industry. Let's now compare the efficiency of the two types of market.

Figure 12.5

Monopoly's Smaller Output and Higher Price

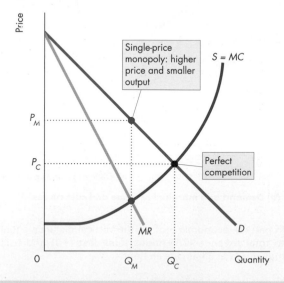

A competitive industry produces the quantity Q_C at price P_C. A single-price monopoly produces the quantity Q_M at which marginal revenue equals marginal cost and sells that quantity for the price P_M. Compared to perfect competition, a single-price monopoly restricts output and raises the price.

Efficiency Comparison

You saw in Chapter 11 (pp. 244–245) that (with no external costs and benefits) perfect competition is efficient. Figure 12.6(a), illustrates the efficiency of perfect competition and serves as a benchmark against which to measure the inefficiency of monopoly.

Along the demand curve and marginal benefit curve ($D = MB$), consumers are efficient. Along the supply curve and marginal cost curve ($S = MC$), producers are efficient. In competitive equilibrium, the price is P_C, the quantity is Q_C, and marginal benefit equals marginal cost.

Consumer surplus is the green triangle under the demand curve and above the equilibrium price (see Chapter 5, p. 101). *Producer surplus* is the blue area above the supply curve and below the equilibrium price (see Chapter 5, p. 103). The sum of the consumer surplus and producer surplus is maximized.

Also, in long-run competitive equilibrium, entry and exit ensure that each firm produces its output at the minimum possible long-run average cost.

To summarize: At the competitive equilibrium, marginal benefit equals marginal cost; the sum of consumer surplus and producer surplus is maximized; firms produce at the lowest possible long-run average cost; and resource use is efficient.

Figure 12.6(b) illustrates the inefficiency of monopoly and the sources of that inefficiency. A monopoly restricts output to Q_M and sells its output for P_M. The smaller output and higher price drive a wedge between marginal benefit and marginal cost and create a *deadweight loss*. The grey triangle shows the deadweight loss and its magnitude is a measure of the inefficiency of monopoly.

Consumer surplus shrinks for two reasons. First, consumers lose by having to pay more for the good. This loss to consumers is a gain for the producer and increases the producer surplus. Second, consumers lose by getting less of the good, and this loss is part of the deadweight loss.

Although the monopoly gains from a higher price, it loses some of the original producer surplus because of the smaller monopoly output. That loss is another part of the deadweight loss.

Because a monopoly restricts output below the level in perfect competition and faces no competitive threat, it does not produce at the minimum possible long-run average cost. As a result, monopoly damages the consumer interest in three ways: it produces less, it increases the cost of production, and it increases the price above the increased cost of production.

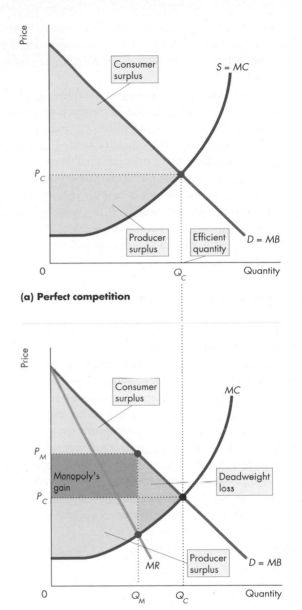

Figure 12.6

Inefficiency of Monopoly

(a) Perfect competition

(b) Monopoly

In perfect competition (part a), output is Q_C and the price is P_C. Marginal benefit (*MB*) equals marginal cost (*MC*); consumer surplus (the green triangle) plus producer surplus (the blue area) is maximized; and in the long-run, firms produce at the lowest possible average cost.

A monopoly (part b) restricts output to Q_M and raises the price to P_M. Consumer surplus shrinks, the monopoly gains and a deadweight loss (the grey triangle) arises.

Redistribution of Surpluses

You've seen that monopoly is inefficient because marginal benefit exceeds marginal cost and there is deadweight loss – a social loss. But monopoly also brings a *redistribution* of surpluses. And this redistribution is a further reason why monopoly might require regulation.

Some of the lost consumer surplus goes to the monopoly. In Figure 12.6(b), the monopoly gets the difference between the higher price, P_M, and the competitive price, P_C, on the quantity sold, Q_M. So the monopoly takes the part of the consumer surplus shown by the darker blue rectangle. This portion of the loss of consumer surplus is not a loss to society. It is a redistribution from consumers to the monopoly producer. If the monopoly owner is wealthier than most of the consumers, this redistribution will generally be regarded as unfair.

Rent Seeking

You've seen that monopoly creates a deadweight loss and is inefficient. But the social cost of monopoly exceeds the deadweight loss because of an activity called rent seeking. **Rent seeking** is any attempt to capture a consumer surplus, a producer surplus, or an economic profit. The activity is not confined to monopoly. But attempting to capture the economic profit of a monopoly is a major form of rent seeking.

You've seen that a monopoly makes its economic profit by diverting part of consumer surplus to itself. Thus the pursuit of an economic profit by a monopolist is rent seeking. It is the attempt to capture consumer surplus.

Rent seekers pursue their goals in two main ways. They might:

◆ Buy a monopoly

◆ Create a monopoly

Buy a Monopoly

To rent seek by buying a monopoly, a person searches for a monopoly that is for sale at a lower price than the monopoly's economic profit. Trading of taxi licences is an example of this type of rent seeking. In some cities, taxis are regulated. The city restricts both the fares and the number of taxis that can operate so that operating a taxi results in economic profit or rent. A person who wants to operate a taxi must buy a licence from someone who already has one. People rationally devote time and effort to seeking out profitable monopoly businesses to buy. In the process, they use up scarce resources that could otherwise have been used to produce goods and services. The value of this lost production is part of the social cost of monopoly. The amount paid for a monopoly is not a social cost because the payment is just a transfer of an existing producer surplus from the buyer to the seller.

Create a Monopoly

This type of rent seeking activity takes the form of lobbying and seeking to influence the political process. Such influence is sometimes sought by making political contributions in exchange for legislative support or by indirectly seeking to influence political outcomes through publicity in the media or more direct contacts with politicians and bureaucrats. An example would be the donations to political parties that the alcohol and tobacco companies make in an attempt to avoid a tightening of legislation on activities such as advertising and licensing, which might affect their profits.

This type of rent seeking is a costly activity that uses up scarce resources. In aggregate, firms spend millions of pounds lobbying Parliament in the pursuit of licences and laws that create barriers to entry and establish a monopoly right. Everyone has an incentive to rent seek, and because there are no barriers to entry into the rent-seeking activity, there is a great deal of competition for new monopoly rights.

Rent-seeking Equilibrium

How much will a person be willing to give up to acquire a monopoly right? The answer is the entire value of a monopoly's economic profit. Barriers to entry create monopoly, but rent-seeking activity is like perfect competition. There is no barrier to rent seeking. As long as the value of the resources used to create a monopoly falls short of the monopoly's economic profit, there is an economic profit to be earned. There is an incentive to rent seek. Rent seeking continues until all the potential for economic profit through monopoly is exhausted.

Figure 12.7 shows a rent-seeking equilibrium. The cost of rent seeking is a fixed cost that must be added to a monopoly's other costs. Rent-seeking costs increase to the point at which economic profit is zero. The average total cost curve, which includes the fixed cost of rent seeking, shifts upward until it just touches the demand curve. Producer surplus is zero. Consumer surplus is

Figure 12.7

Rent-seeking Equilibrium

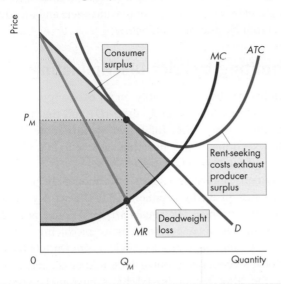

With competitive rent seeking, a monopoly uses all its economic profit to prevent another firm from taking its economic rent. The firm's rent-seeking costs are fixed costs. They add to total fixed cost and to average total cost. The *ATC* curve shifts upward until, at the profit-maximizing price, the firm breaks even.

unaffected. But the deadweight loss of monopoly now includes the original deadweight loss triangle plus the lost producer surplus, shown by the enlarged darker grey area in the figure.

1   Why does a single-price monopoly produce a smaller output and charge a higher price than what would prevail if the industry were perfectly competitive?
2   How does a monopoly transfer consumer surplus to itself?
3   Why is a single-price monopoly inefficient?
4   What is rent seeking and how does it influence the inefficiency of monopoly?

So far, we've considered only a single-price monopoly. But many monopolies do not operate with a single price. Instead, they price discriminate. Let's now see how price-discriminating monopoly works.

Price Discrimination

Price discrimination – selling a good or service at a number of different prices – is widespread. You encounter it when you travel, go to the cinema, go shopping or go out to eat. Most price discriminators are not monopolies, but monopolies price discriminate when they can do so.

To be able to price discriminate, a monopoly must:

1   Identify and separate different buyer types.
2   Sell a product that cannot be resold.

Price discrimination is charging different prices for a single good or service because of differences in buyers' willingness to pay and not because of differences in production costs. So not all price *differences* are price *discrimination*. Some goods that are similar but not identical have different prices because they have different production costs. For example, the cost of producing electricity depends on time of day. If an electric power company charges a higher price during the peak consumption periods from 7:00 to 9:00 in the morning and from 4:00 to 7:00 in the evening than it does at other times of the day, it is not price discriminating.

At first sight, it appears that price discrimination contradicts the assumption of profit maximization. Why would a railway company give a student discount? Why would a hairdresser charge students and senior citizens less? Aren't these producers losing profit by being so generous?

Deeper investigation shows that far from losing profit, price discriminators make a bigger profit than they would otherwise. So a monopoly has an incentive to find ways of discriminating and charging each buyer the highest possible price. Some people pay less with price discrimination, but others pay more.

Price Discrimination and Consumer Surplus

The key idea behind price discrimination is to convert consumer surplus into economic profit. Demand curves slope downward because the value that people place on any good decreases as the quantity consumed of that good increases. When all the units consumed are sold for a single price, consumers benefit. The benefit is the value the consumers get from each unit of the good minus the price actually paid for it. This benefit is *consumer surplus*. Price discrimination is an attempt by a monopoly to capture as much of the consumer surplus as possible for itself.

To extract every pound of consumer surplus from every buyer, the monopoly would have to offer each individual customer a separate price schedule based on that customer's own willingness to pay. Clearly, such price discrimination cannot be carried out in practice because a firm does not have enough information about each consumer's demand curve.

But firms try to extract as much consumer surplus as possible and to do so, they discriminate in two broad ways:

◆ Among units of a good
◆ Among groups of buyers

Discriminating Among Units of a Good

One method of price discrimination charges each buyer a different price on each unit of a good bought. A discount for bulk buying is an example of this type of discrimination. The larger the quantity bought, the larger is the discount – and the lower is the price. (Note that some discounts for bulk arise from lower costs of production for greater bulk. In these cases, such discounts are not price discrimination.)

Discriminating Among Groups of Buyers

Price discrimination often takes the form of discriminating among different groups of consumers on the basis of age, employment status or some other easily distinguished characteristic. This type of price discrimination works when each group has a different average willingness to pay for the good or service.

For example, a face-to-face meeting with a customer might bring in a large and profitable order. For salespeople and other business travellers, the marginal benefit from a trip is large (or the opportunity cost of *not* taking the trip might be large) so a business traveller is willing to pay a high price for a trip. In contrast, for a holiday traveller, any of several different destinations and even no holiday trip, are options. So for holiday travellers, the marginal benefit of a trip is small and the price that such a traveller is willing to pay for a trip is low.

Because business travellers are willing to pay more than holiday travellers are, it is possible for an airline to profit by price discriminating between these two groups. Similarly, because students have a lower willingness to pay for a haircut than a working person does, it is

possible for a hairdresser to profit by price discriminating between these two groups.

Let's see how an airline exploits the differences in demand by business and holiday travellers and increases its profit by price discriminating.

Profiting by Price Discriminating

Global Air has a monopoly on an exotic route. Figure 12.8 shows the demand curve (*D*) and the marginal revenue curve (*MR*) for travel on this route. It also shows Global Air's marginal cost curve (*MC*) and average total cost curve (*ATC*).

Initially, Global is a single-price monopoly and maximizes its profit by producing 8,000 trips a year (the quantity at which *MR* equals *MC*). The price is €1,200 per trip. The average total cost of producing a trip is €600, so economic profit is €600 a trip. On 8,000 trips, Global's economic profit is €4.8 million a year, shown by the blue rectangle. Global's customers enjoy a consumer surplus shown by the green triangle.

Figure 12.8

A Single Price of Air Travel

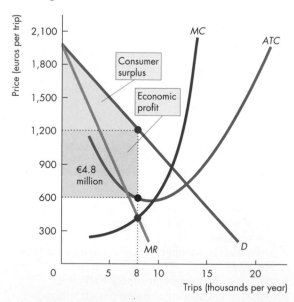

Global Airlines has a monopoly on an air route. The market demand curve is *D* and marginal revenue curve is *MR*. Global Air's marginal cost curve is *MC* and its average total cost curve is *ATC*. As a single-price monopoly, Global maximizes profit by selling 8,000 trips a year at €1,200 a trip. Its profit is €4.8 million a year – the blue rectangle. Global's customers enjoy a consumer surplus – the green triangle.

Global is struck by the fact that many of its customers are business travellers and it suspects they are willing to pay more than €1,200 a trip. So Global does some market research, which reveals that some business travellers are willing to pay as much as €1,800 a trip. Also, these customers frequently change their travel plans at the last moment. Another group of business travellers is willing to pay €1,600. These customers know a week ahead when they will travel and they never want to stay over a weekend. Yet another group would pay up to €1,400. These travellers know two weeks ahead when they will travel and also don't want to stay away over a weekend.

So Global announces a new fare schedule. No restrictions, €1,800; 7-day advance purchase, no cancellation, €1,600; 14-day advance purchase, no cancellation, €1,400; 14-day advance purchase, must stay over a weekend, €1,200.

Figure 12.9 shows the outcome with this new fare structure and also shows why Global is pleased with its new fares. It sells 2,000 seats at each of its four prices. Global's economic profit increases by the blue steps in Figure 12.9. Its economic profit is now its original €4.8 million a year plus an additional €2.4 million from its new higher fares. Consumer surplus has shrunk to the smaller green area.

Perfect Price Discrimination

Perfect price discrimination occurs if a firm is able to sell each unit of output for the highest price anyone is willing to pay for it. In such a case, the entire consumer surplus is eliminated and captured by the producer. To practise perfect price discrimination, a firm must be creative and come up with a host of prices and special conditions each one of which appeals to a tiny segment of the market.

With perfect price discrimination, something special happens to marginal revenue. For the perfect price discriminator, the market demand curve becomes the marginal revenue curve. The reason is that when the price is cut to sell a larger quantity, the firm sells only the marginal unit at the lower price. All the other units continue to be sold for the highest price that each buyer is willing to pay. So for the perfect price discriminator, marginal revenue *equals* price and the demand curve becomes the marginal revenue curve.

With marginal revenue equal to price, Global can obtain even greater profit by increasing output up to the point at which price (and marginal revenue) is equal to marginal cost.

So Global now seeks additional travellers who will not pay as much as €1,200 a trip but who will pay more than marginal cost. Global gets more creative and comes up with holiday specials and other fares that have combinations of advance reservation, minimum stay and other restrictions that make these fares unattractive to its existing customers but attractive to a different group of travellers. With all these fares and specials, Global increases sales, extracts the entire consumer surplus and maximizes economic profit.

Figure 12.10 shows the outcome with perfect price discrimination. The dozens of fares paid by the original travellers who are willing to pay between €1,200 and €2,000 have extracted the entire consumer surplus from this group and converted it into economic profit for Global.

The new fares between €900 and €1,200 have attracted 3,000 additional travellers but taken their entire consumer surplus also. Global is earning an economic profit of more than €9 million.

Figure 12.9

Price Discrimination

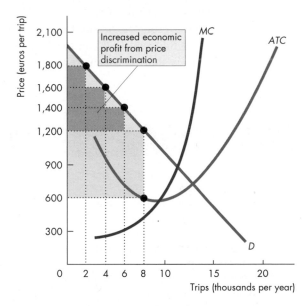

Global revises its fare structure: no restrictions at €1,800, 7-day advance purchase at €1,600, 14-day advance purchase at €1,400, and must stay over a weekend at €1,200. Global sells 2,000 trips at each of its four new fares. Its economic profit increases by €2.4 million a year to €7.2 million a year, which is shown by the original blue rectangle plus the blue steps. Global's customers' consumer surplus shrinks.

Figure 12.10

Perfect Price Discrimination

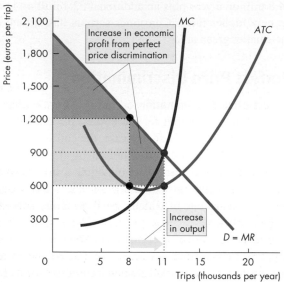

Dozens of fares discriminate among many different types of business travellers and many new low fares with restrictions appeal to holiday travellers. With perfect price discrimination, Global's demand curve becomes its marginal revenue curve. Economic profit is maximized when the lowest price equals marginal cost. Here, Global sells 11,000 trips and makes an economic profit of €9.35 million a year.

Real-world airlines are just as creative as Global, as you can see in the cartoon!

Would it bother you to hear how little I paid for this flight?

From William Hamilton, "Voodoo Economics," © 1992 by The Chronicle Publishing Company, p. 3. Reprinted with permission of Chronicle Books.

Efficiency and Rent Seeking with Price Discrimination

With perfect price discrimination, output increases to the point at which price equals marginal cost – where the marginal cost curve intersects the demand curve. This output is identical to that of perfect competition. Perfect price discrimination pushes consumer surplus to zero but increases producer surplus to equal the sum of consumer surplus and producer surplus in perfect competition. Deadweight loss with perfect price discrimination is zero. So perfect price discrimination achieves efficiency.

The more perfectly the monopoly can price discriminate, the closer its output gets to the competitive output and the more efficient is the outcome.

But there are two differences between perfect competition and perfect price discrimination. First, the distribution of the surplus is different. It is shared by consumers and producers in perfect competition, while the producer gets it all with perfect price discrimination. Second, because the producer grabs the surplus, rent seeking becomes profitable.

People use resources in pursuit of rents, and the bigger the rents, the more resources get used in pursuing them. With free entry into rent seeking, the long-run equilibrium outcome is that rent seekers use up the entire producer surplus.

You've seen that monopoly is profitable for the monopolist but costly for other people. It results in inefficiency. Because of these features of monopoly, it is subject to policy debate and regulation. We'll now study the key monopoly policy issues.

Monopoly Policy Issues

Monopoly looks bad when we compare it with competition. Monopoly is inefficient, and it captures consumer surplus and converts it into producer surplus or pure waste in the form of rent-seeking costs. If monopoly is so bad, why do we put up with it? Why don't we have laws that crack down on monopoly so hard that it never rears its head? We do indeed have laws that limit monopoly power and regulate the prices that monopolies are permitted to charge. But monopoly also brings some benefits. We begin this review of monopoly policy issues by looking at the benefits of monopoly. We then look at monopoly regulation.

Gains from Monopoly

The main reason why monopoly exists is that it has potential advantages over a competitive alternative. These advantages arise from:

◆ Incentives to innovation
◆ Economies of scale and economies of scope

Incentives to Innovation

Invention leads to a wave of innovation as new knowledge is applied to the production process. Innovation may take the form of developing a new product or a lower-cost way of making an existing product. Controversy has raged over whether large firms with market power or small competitive firms lacking such market power are the most innovative. It is clear that some temporary market power arises from innovation. A firm that develops a new product or process and patents it obtains an exclusive right to that product or process for the term of the patent.

But does the granting of a monopoly, even a temporary one, to an innovator increase the pace of innovation? One line of reasoning suggests that it does. Without protection, an innovator is not able to enjoy the profits from innovation for very long. Thus the incentive to innovate is weakened. A contrary argument is that monopolies can afford to be lazy while competitive firms cannot. Competitive firms must strive to innovate and cut costs even though they know that they cannot hang onto the benefits of their innovation for long. But that knowledge spurs them on to greater and faster innovation.

The evidence on whether monopoly leads to greater innovation than competition is mixed. Large firms do more research and development than do small firms. But research and development are inputs into the process of innovation. What matters is not input but output. Two measures of the output of research and development are the number of patents and the rate of productivity growth. On these measures, it is not clear that bigger is better. But as a new process or product spreads through an industry, the large firms adopt the new process or product more quickly than do small firms. So large firms help to speed the process of diffusion of technological change.

Economies of Scale and Scope

Economies of scale and economies of scope can lead to natural monopoly. And as you saw at the beginning of this chapter, in a natural monopoly, a single firm can produce at a lower average cost than a number of firms can.

A firm experiences *economies of scale* when an increase in its output of a good or service brings a decrease in the average total cost of producing it (see Chapter 10, p. 214). A firm experiences *economies of scope* when an increase in the *range of goods produced* brings a decrease in average total cost (see Chapter 9, p. 195). Economies of scope occur when different goods can share specialized (and usually costly) capital resources. For example, McDonald's can produce both hamburgers and chips at a lower average total cost than can two separate firms – a burger firm and a chips firm – because at McDonald's, hamburgers and chips share the use of specialized food storage and preparation facilities. A firm that produces a wide range of products can hire specialist computer programmers, designers, and marketing experts whose skills can be used across the product range, thereby spreading their costs and lowering the average total cost of production of each of the goods.

There are many examples in which a combination of economies of scale and economies of scope arise, but not all of them lead to monopoly. Some examples are the brewing of beer, the manufacture of refrigerators and other household appliances, the manufacture of pharmaceuticals, and the refining of petroleum.

Examples of industries in which economies of scale are so significant that they lead to a natural monopoly are becoming rare. Public utilities such as gas, electric power, local telephone service and waste collection once were natural monopolies. But technological advances now enable us to separate the *production* of electric power or gas from its *distribution*. The provision of water, though, remains a natural monopoly.

A large-scale firm that has control over supply and can influence price – and therefore behaves like the monopoly firm that you've studied in this chapter – can reap these economies of scale and scope.

Small, competitive firms cannot. Consequently, there are situations in which the comparison of monopoly and competition that we made earlier in this chapter is not valid. Recall that we imagined the takeover of a large number of competitive firms by a monopoly firm. But we also assumed that the monopoly would use exactly the same technology as the small firms and have the same costs. If one large firm can reap economies of scale and scope, its marginal cost curve will lie below the supply curve of a competitive industry made up of many small firms. It is possible for such economies of scale and scope to be so large as to result in a larger output and lower price under monopoly than a competitive industry would achieve.

Where significant economies of scale and scope exist, it is usually worth putting up with monopoly and regulating its price.

Regulating Natural Monopoly

Where demand and cost conditions create a natural monopoly, government either at the EU, national or local level usually steps in to regulate the price of the monopoly. By regulating a monopoly, some of the worst aspects of monopoly can be avoided or at least moderated. Let's look at monopoly price regulation.

Figure 12.11 shows the demand curve *D*, the marginal revenue curve *MR*, the long-run average cost curve *ATC*, and the marginal cost curve *MC* for a gas distribution company that is a natural monopoly.

The firm's marginal cost is constant at 10 cents per cubic metre. But average total cost decreases as output increases. The reason is that the gas company has a large investment in pipelines and so has high fixed costs. These fixed costs are part of the company's average total cost and appear in the *ATC* curve. The average total cost curve slopes downward because as the number of cubic metres sold increases, the fixed cost is spread over a larger number of units. (If you need to refresh your memory on how the average total cost curve is calculated, look back at Chapter 10, p. 208.)

This one firm can supply the entire market at a lower cost than two firms can because average total cost is falling even when the entire market is supplied. (Refer back to pp. 252–253 if you need a quick refresher on natural monopoly.)

Profit Maximization

First, suppose the gas company is not regulated and instead maximizes profit. Figure 12.11 shows the outcome. The company produces 2 million cubic metres a day, the quantity at which marginal cost equals marginal revenue. It prices this gas at 20 cents a cubic metre and makes an economic profit of 2 cents a cubic metre, or €40,000 a day.

This outcome is fine for the gas company, but it is inefficient. Gas costs 20 cents a cubic metre when its marginal cost is only 10 cents a cubic metre. Also, the gas company is making a big profit. What can regulation do to improve this outcome?

The Efficient Regulation

If the monopoly regulator wants to achieve an efficient use of resources, it must require the gas monopoly to produce the quantity of gas that brings marginal benefit into equality with marginal cost. Marginal benefit is what the consumer is willing to pay and is shown by the demand curve.

Marginal cost is shown by the firm's marginal cost curve. You can see in Figure 12.11 that this outcome occurs if the price is regulated at 10 cents per cubic foot and if 4 million cubic metres per day are produced.

The regulation that produces this outcome is called a marginal cost pricing rule. A **marginal cost pricing rule** sets price equal to marginal cost. It maximizes total surplus in the regulated industry. In this example, that surplus is all consumer surplus and it equals the area of the triangle beneath the demand curve and above the marginal cost curve.

The marginal cost pricing rule is efficient. But it leaves the natural monopoly incurring an economic loss. Because average total cost is falling as output increases, marginal cost is below average total cost.

And because price equals marginal cost, price is below average total cost. Average total cost minus price is the loss per unit produced. It's pretty obvious that a gas company that is required to use a marginal cost pricing rule will not stay in business for long. How can a company cover its costs and, at the same time, obey a marginal cost pricing rule?

One possibility is price discrimination. The company might charge a higher price to some customers but marginal cost to the customers who pay least. If the conditions required for marginal cost pricing are met, that solution is attractive. But price determination is not always feasible.

Figure 12.11

Regulating a Natural Monopoly

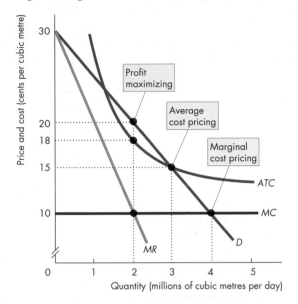

A natural monopoly is an industry in which average total cost is falling even when the entire market demand is satisfied. A gas producer faces the demand curve *D*. The firm's marginal cost is constant at 10 cents per cubic metre, as shown by the curve labelled *MC*. Fixed costs are large, and the average total cost curve, which includes average fixed cost, is shown as *ATC*. A marginal cost pricing rule sets the price at 10 cents per cubic metre. The monopoly produces 4 million cubic metres per day and incurs an economic loss. An average cost pricing rule sets the price at 15 cents per cubic metre. The monopoly produces 3 million cubic metres per day and makes normal profit.

Another possibility is to use a two-part price (called two-part tariff). For example, the gas company might charge a monthly fixed fee that covers its fixed cost and then charge for gas consumed at marginal cost.

But a natural monopoly cannot always cover its costs in these ways. If a natural monopoly cannot cover its total cost from its customers, and if the government wants it to follow a marginal cost pricing rule, the government must give the firm a subsidy. In such a case, the government raises the revenue for the subsidy by taxing some other activity. But as we saw in Chapter 6, taxes themselves generate deadweight loss. Thus the deadweight loss resulting from additional taxes must be subtracted from the efficiency gained by forcing the natural monopoly to adopt a marginal cost pricing rule. When the deadweight loss from taxes is taken into account, it might turn out to be better to abandon marginal cost pricing.

Average Cost Pricing

Regulators almost never impose efficient pricing because of its consequences for the firm's profit. Instead, they compromise by permitting the firm to cover its costs and to earn a normal profit. Recall that normal profit is a cost of production and we include it along with the firm's other fixed costs in the average total cost curve. So pricing to cover cost including normal profit means setting price equal to average total cost – called an **average cost pricing rule**.

Figure 12.11 shows the average cost pricing outcome. The gas company charges 15 cents a cubic metre and sells 3 million cubic metres per day. This outcome is better for consumers than the unregulated profit-maximizing outcome. The price is 5 cents a cubic metre lower, and the quantity consumed is 1 million cubic metres per day more. And the outcome is better for the producer than the marginal cost pricing rule outcome. The firm earns normal profit. The outcome is inefficient but less so than the unregulated profit-maximizing outcome.

Review Quiz

1   What are the two main reasons why monopoly is worth tolerating?
2   Can you provide some examples of economies of scale and economies of scope?
3   Why might the incentive to innovate be greater for a monopoly than for a small competitive firm?
4   What is the price that achieves an efficient outcome for a regulated monopoly? And what is the problem with this price?
5   Compare the consumer surplus, producer surplus and deadweight loss that arise from average cost pricing with those that arise from profit-maximization pricing and marginal cost pricing.

You've now have studied perfect competition and monopoly. *Reading Between the Lines* on pp. 268–269 looks at market power in the markets for Internet auctions and search. In the next chapter, we study markets that lie between the extremes of perfect competition and monopoly and that blend elements of the two.

Reading Between the Lines
eBay is a Monopoly but Google isn't!

The Economist, 30 October 2002

How Good is Google

. . . As search engines go . . . Google has clearly been a runaway success. Not only is its own site the most popular for search on the web, but it also powers the search engines of major portals, such as Yahoo! and AOL. All told, 75% of referrals to websites now originate from Google's algorithms. That is power.

For some time now, Google's board . . . has been deliberating how to translate that power into money. They appear to have decided to bring Google to the stock market next spring. Bankers have been overheard estimating Google's value at $15 billion or more. That could make Google Silicon Valley's first hot IPO since the dotcom bust, and perhaps its biggest ever.

. . . To be worth the rumoured $15 billion for longer than it takes a bubble to burst, it will need to raise its profitability substantially. That means matching such internet stars as eBay (market capitalisation $37 billion), but without the natural-monopoly advantages that have made eBay so dominant—the classic network effect of buyers and sellers knowing they do best by all trading in one place. For Google to stay permanently ahead of other search-engine technologies is almost impossible, since it takes so little—only a bright idea by another set of geeks—to lose the lead. In contrast to a portal such as Yahoo!, which also offers customers free e-mail and other services, a pure search engine is always but a click away from losing users.

The Essence of the Story

◆ Google is the most popular search engine and 75 per cent of referrals to websites originate from its searches.

◆ Some bankers estimate Google's value at $15 billion or more.

◆ It is almost impossible for Google to stay permanently ahead of other search-engine technologies because it takes only a bright idea by another set of programmers to lose its lead.

◆ Google does not have the natural-monopoly advantages that have made eBay dominant—network effect of buyers and sellers knowing they do best by all trading in one place.

Economic Analysis

◆ Almost all the costs of eBay or Google are fixed costs. When all costs are fixed, average fixed cost equals average total cost, and average variable cost and marginal cost are zero. Figure 1 shows eBay's cost curves. (Google's cost curves look just like these.)

◆ A natural monopoly has two features:
1. Economies of scale at the output that meet the entire market demand, and
2. No close substitutes.

◆ Both eBay and Google have the first feature but only eBay has the second.

◆ If another firm developed a better search engine than Google, it would take the market for Internet search. But Google can prevent this outcome by constantly improving its search engine and keeping it the best available.

◆ Because it enjoys the benefit of a network externality, as the article says, "buyers and sellers knowing they do best by all trading in one place", eBay has no close substitute and is unlikely to be confronted with one.

◆ The demand for eBay's services is D in Figure 1. The firm maximizes profit by setting a price, P, that generates a quantity demanded, Q, where marginal revenue is zero and equal to the zero marginal cost.

◆ eBay users enjoy a consumer surplus, eBay earns a large economic profit (capital value at an estimated $37 billion), but there is a deadweight loss.

◆ Although as a monopoly, eBay is inefficient and creates a deadweight loss, the world is better off with eBay than it would be without it. Figure 2 shows why.

◆ In the market for a rarely traded item such as carved bone fishes, the supply including the cost of finding a buyer was S_0 before eBay began to operate. The cost of finding a buyer was so large that none of these items were traded.

◆ Supply increases to S_1 when eBay lowers the cost of finding a buyer. Now the item is

traded. The buyer pays PB and receives a consumer surplus, the seller receives PS and a seller's surplus and eBay makes an economic profit.

◆ A deadweight loss arises because eBay doesn't set the price equal to marginal cost. So the market is inefficient. But compared to the situation before eBay existed, a huge consumer surplus and a surplus for the seller arise.

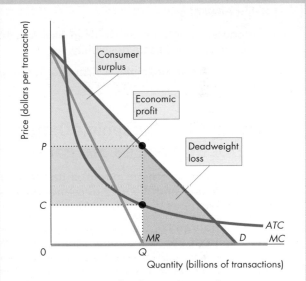

Figure 1 eBay's market for auction services

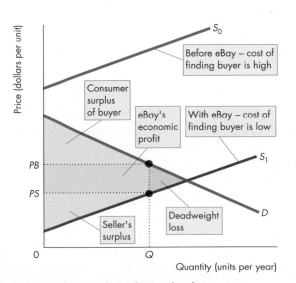

Figure 2 The view from the market for carved bone fishes

Summary

Key Points

Market Power (pp. 252–253)

◆ A monopoly is an industry with a single supplier of a good or service that has no close substitutes and in which barriers to entry prevent competition.

◆ Barriers to entry may be legal (public franchise, licence, patent, copyright, firm owns control of a resource) or natural (created by economies of scale).

◆ A monopoly might be able to price discriminate when there is no resale possibility.

◆ Where resale is possible, a firm charges one price.

A Single-Price Monopoly's Output and Price Decision (pp. 254–257)

◆ A monopoly's demand curve is the market demand curve and a single-price monopoly's marginal revenue is less than price.

◆ A monopoly maximizes profit by producing the output at which marginal revenue equals marginal cost and by charging the maximum price that consumers are willing to pay for that output.

Single-Price Monopoly and Competition Compared (pp. 258–261)

◆ A single-price monopoly charges a higher price and produces a smaller quantity than a perfectly competitive industry.

◆ A single-price monopoly restricts output and creates a deadweight loss.

◆ Monopoly imposes costs that equal its deadweight loss plus the cost of the resources devoted to rent seeking.

Price Discrimination (pp. 261–264)

◆ Price discrimination is an attempt by the monopoly to convert consumer surplus into economic profit.

◆ Perfect price discrimination extracts the entire consumer surplus. Such a monopoly charges a different price for each unit sold and obtains the maximum price that each consumer is willing to pay for each unit bought.

Monopoly Policy Issues (pp. 265–267)

◆ A monopoly with large economies of scale and economies of scope can produce a larger quantity at a lower price than a competitive industry can achieve, and monopoly might be more innovative than small competitive firms.

◆ Efficient regulation requires a monopoly to charge a price equal to marginal cost, but for a natural monopoly, such a price is less than average total cost.

◆ Average cost pricing is a compromise pricing rule that covers a firm's costs and provides a normal profit but is not efficient. It is more efficient than unregulated profit maximization.

Key Figures and Table

Key Terms

Problems

*1 Minnie's European Mineral Springs, a single-price monopoly, faces the market demand schedule:

Price (euros per bottle)	Quantity demanded (bottles)
10	0
8	1
6	2
4	3
2	4
0	5

a Calculate the total revenue schedule for Minnie's European Mineral Springs.

b Calculate the marginal revenue schedule.

2 Danny's Diamond Mines, a single-price monopoly, faces the market demand schedule:

Price (euros per diamond)	Quantity demanded (diamonds per day)
1,100	0
900	1
700	2
500	3
300	4

a Calculate the total revenue schedule for Danny's mine.

b Calculate the marginal revenue schedule.

*3 Minnie's European Mineral Springs in problem 1 has the following total cost:

Quantity produced (bottles)	Total cost (euros)
0	1
1	3
2	7
3	13
4	21
5	31

a Calculate the marginal cost of producing each output listed in the table.

---

*Solutions to odd-numbered problems are available on *Parkin Interactive*.

b Calculate the profit-maximizing output and price.

c Calculate economic profit.

d Does Minnie's European Mineral Springs use resources efficiently? Explain your answer.

4 Danny's Diamond Mines in problem 2 has the following total cost:

Quantity produced (diamonds per day)	Total cost (euros)
1	1,220
2	1,300
3	1,400
4	1,520

a Calculate the marginal cost of producing each output listed in the table.

b Calculate the profit-maximizing output and price.

c Calculate economic profit.

d Does Danny's Diamond Mine use resources efficiently? Explain your answer.

*5 The figure illustrates the situation facing the publisher of the only newspaper containing local news in an isolated UK community.

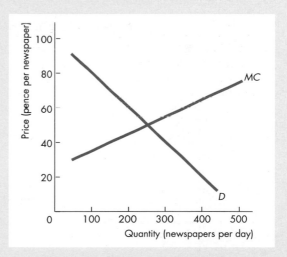

a What quantity of newspapers will maximize the publisher's profit?

b What price will the publisher charge?

c What is the publisher's daily total revenue?

d At the price charged for a newspaper, is the demand elastic or inelastic? Why?

e Might the newspaper try to price discriminate? Why or why not?

6 The figure illustrates the situation facing the only coffee bar in an isolated community:

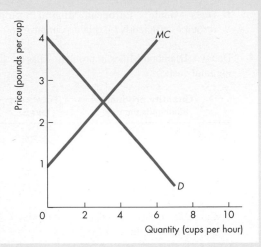

a What is the quantity of coffee that will maximize the firm's profit?

b What price will the coffee bar charge?

c What is the coffee bar's daily total revenue?

d At the price charged for a coffee, is the demand elastic or inelastic? Why?

e Might the coffee bar try to price discriminate? Explain why or why not.

*7 The figure illustrates the situation facing a natural monopoly that cannot price discriminate:

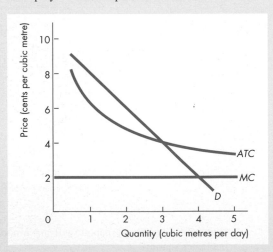

What quantity will the firm produce and what will be the deadweight loss if the firm is:

a An unregulated profit maximizer?

b Regulated to earn normal profit?

c Regulated to be efficient?

8 If in problem 7 marginal cost doubles, what now are your answers?

Critical Thinking

1. Study *Reading Between the Lines* on pp. 268–269 and then answer the following questions:

   a Why is eBay a monopoly but Google not a monopoly?

   b How would you regulate the Internet search engine business to ensure that resources are used efficiently?

   c How would you regulate the Internet auction business to ensure that resources are used efficiently?

   d "Anyone is free to buy stock in eBay, so everyone is free to share in eBay's economic profit, and the bigger that economic profit, the better for all." Evaluate this statement.

Web Exercises

Use the links on *Parkin Interactive* to work the following exercises.

1 Study the market for computer chips, then answer the following questions.

   a Is it correct to call Intel a monopoly? Explain why or why not.

   b How does Intel try to raise barriers to entry in this market?

2 Obtain information on Microsoft, then answer the following questions.

   a Is it correct to call Microsoft a monopoly? Explain why or why not.

   b How do you think that Microsoft set the price of Windows 98 and decided how many copies of the program to produce?

   c How is the expanding take up of Linux, the main alternative operating system to Windows, affecting Microsoft?

   d How is the constant threat of virus attacks on Windows affecting Microsoft?

   e "Anyone is free to buy shares in Microsoft, so everyone is free to share in Microsoft's economic profit, and the bigger that economic profit, the better for all." Evaluate this statement.

Chapter 13
Monopolistic Competition and Oligopoly

After studying this chapter you will be able to:

◆ Define and identify monopolistic competition

◆ Explain how price and output are determined in a monopolistically competitive industry

◆ Explain why advertising and branding costs are high in monopolistic competition

◆ Define and identify oligopoly

◆ Explain two traditional models of oligopoly

◆ Use game theory to explain how price and output are determined in oligopoly

◆ Use game theory to explain other strategic decisions

Fliers and Brand Names

Every week, all over Europe, people receive a newspaper stuffed with supermarket fliers that describe this week's specials and provide coupons and other enticements. How do Tesco, Carrefour, Metro, Macro and Delhaize compete in their markets? How do brand names change the competitive landscape? Find out in this chapter. How did Tesco beat Sainsbury in the UK supermarket wars? Find out in the *Business Case Study* on at the end of the chapter.

What is Monopolistic Competition?

You have studied two types of market structure: perfect competition and monopoly. In perfect competition, a large number of firms produce identical goods, there are no barriers to entry, and each firm is a price taker. In the long run, there is no economic profit and perfect competition is efficient. In monopoly, a single firm is protected from competition by barriers to entry and can make an economic profit, even in the long run.

Most real-world markets are competitive but not perfectly competitive because firms in these markets possess some market power to set their prices as monopolies do. We call this type of market *monopolistic competition*.

Monopolistic competition is a market structure in which:

◆ A large number of firms compete.

◆ Each firm produces a differentiated product.

◆ Firms compete on product quality, price, marketing and branding.

◆ Firms are free to enter and exit.

Large Number of Firms

In monopolistic competition, as in perfect competition, the industry consists of a large number of firms. The presence of a large number of firms has three implications for the firms in the industry.

Small Market Share

In monopolistic competition, each firm supplies a small part of the total industry output. Consequently, each firm has only limited market power to influence the price of its product. Each firm's price can deviate from the average price of other firms by a relatively small amount.

Ignore Other Firms

A firm in monopolistic competition must be sensitive to the average market price of the product. But each firm does not pay attention to any one individual competitor. Because all the firms are relatively small, no one firm can dictate market conditions and so no one firm's actions directly affect the actions of the other firms.

Collusion Impossible

Firms in monopolistic competition would like to be able to conspire to fix a higher price – called collusion. But because there are many firms, collusion is not possible.

Product Differentiation

A firm practices **product differentiation** if it makes a product that is slightly different from the products of competing firms. A differentiated product is one that is a close substitute but not a perfect substitute for the products of the other firms. Some people will pay more for one variety of the product, so when its price rises, the quantity demanded falls but it does not (necessarily) fall to zero. For example, Adidas, Asics, Diadora, Etonic, Fila, New Balance, Nike, Puma, and Reebok all make differentiated running shoes. Other things remaining the same, if the price of Adidas running shoes rises and the prices of the other shoes remain constant, Adidas sells fewer shoes and the other producers sell more. But Adidas shoes don't disappear unless the price rises by a large enough amount.

Competing on Quality, Price, Marketing and Branding

Product differentiation enables a firm to compete with other firms in four areas: product quality, price, marketing and branding.

Quality

The quality of a product is the physical attributes that make it different from the products of other firms. Quality includes design, reliability, the service provided to the buyer and the buyer's ease of access to the product. Quality lies on a spectrum that runs from high to low. Some firms – such as Dell Computer Corp. – offer high-quality products. They are well designed and reliable, and the customer receives quick and efficient service. Other firms offer a lower-quality product that is less well designed, that might not work perfectly and that the buyer must travel some distance to obtain.

Price

Because of product differentiation, a firm in monopolistic competition faces a downward-sloping demand curve. So, like a monopoly, the firm can set both its price and its output. But there is a trade-off between the product's quality and price. A firm that makes a high-quality product can charge a higher price than a firm that makes a low-quality product.

Marketing and Branding

Because of product differentiation, a firm in monopolistic competition must market its product. Marketing takes two main forms: advertising and packaging. A firm that produces a high-quality product wants to sell it for a suitably high price.

To be able to sell a high-quality product for a high price, a firm must advertise and package its product in a way that convinces buyers that they are getting the higher quality for which they are paying.

Branding is the main way in which firms seek to establish quality differences. For example, pharmaceutical companies create brand names for the drugs that they develop and patent the drugs and copyright the brand names. They then spend large sums to associate a brand name with high quality.

At the other end of the quality range, the producer of a low-quality version uses advertising and packaging to persuade buyers that although the quality is low, the low price more than compensates for this fact.

When branding and advertising work, they create a temporary monopoly in a specific version of a good or service.

Entry and Exit

In monopolistic competition, there is free entry and free exit. Consequently, a firm cannot make an economic profit in the long run. When firms make an economic profit, new firms enter the industry. This entry lowers prices and eventually eliminates economic profit. When firms incur economic losses, some firms leave the industry. This exit increases prices and profits and eventually eliminates the economic loss. In long-run equilibrium, firms neither enter nor leave the industry and the firms in the industry make zero economic profit.

Identifying Monopolistic Competition

Identifying monopolistic competition in the real world requires that we look for the four features we've just described. Some markets have some of these features but not all of them. These markets are *not* examples of monopolistic competition.

Examples of Monopolistic Competition

Some examples of monopolistic competition are audio and video equipment, computers, frozen foods, canned foods, book printing, clothing, sporting goods, fish and seafood, petrol stations, food stores, dry cleaners, haircutters and jewellers.

In these industries, a large number of firms compete, selling differentiated products that are heavily advertised, and firms come and go under the pressure of competition.

Product Differentiation and Branding *Not* Always Monopolistic Competition

Product differentiation and branding occurs in markets that do not fit the definition of monopolistic competition. And some of the best-known brands – indeed probably most of the best-known brands – are *not* monopolistic competition.

Some examples are three incredibly successful and very long lasting brands. The Coca-Cola brand, which was created in 1868, operates in a highly concentrated global market for soft drinks. Heinz Tomato Ketchup, created in 1875, is a dominant brand that does not face the type of competition present in monopolistic competition. And Kellogg's Corn Flakes, created in 1906, is another example of a brand and differentiated product line that operates in a concentrated market.

Long-lasting brands are the exception in monopolistic competition. For most companies, their brands are short lived. They come and go within a few months or years. To find out why, we need to look at the output and price decisions of firms in monopolistic competition and then examine their marketing strategies.

Review Quiz

1   What are the distinguishing characteristics of monopolistic competition?
2   Compare the characteristics of monopolistic competition and perfect competition.
3   Compare the characteristics of monopolistic competition and monopoly.
4   How do firms in monopolistic competition compete?
5   In addition to the examples given above, provide some examples of industries near your university that operate in monopolistic competition.

Price and Output in Monopolistic Competition

Suppose you've been employed by French Connection to manage the production and marketing of jackets. Think about the decisions that you must make at French Connection. First, you must decide on the design and quality of jackets and on your marketing plan. Second, you must decide on the quantity of jackets to produce and the price at which to sell them.

We'll suppose that French Connection has already made its decisions about design, quality and marketing, and now we'll concentrate on the output and pricing decision. We'll study quality and marketing decisions in the next section.

For a given quality of jackets and marketing activity, French Connection faces given costs and market conditions. How, given its costs and the demand for its jackets, does French Connection decide the quantity of jackets to produce and the price at which to sell them?

The Firm's Short-run Output and Price Decision

In the short run, a firm in monopolistic competition makes its output and price decision just like a monopoly firm does. Figure 13.1 illustrates this decision for French Connection jackets.

The demand curve for French Connection jackets is *D*. This demand curve tells us the quantity of French Connection jackets demanded at each price, given the prices of other jackets. It is not the demand curve for jackets in general.

The *MR* curve shows the marginal revenue curve associated with the demand curve for French Connection jackets. It is derived just like the marginal revenue curve of a single-price monopoly that you studied in Chapter 12.

The *ATC* curve and the *MC* curve show the average total cost and the marginal cost of producing French Connection jackets.

French Connection's goal is to maximize its economic profit. To do so, it will produce the output at which marginal revenue equals marginal cost. In Figure 13.1, this output is 125 jackets a day. French Connection charges the price that buyers are willing to pay for this quantity, which is determined by the demand curve. This price is £75 per jacket. When it produces 125 jackets a day, French Connection's average total cost is £25 per jacket and it makes an economic

Figure 13.1

Economic Profit in the Short Run

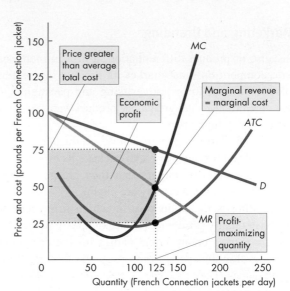

Profit is maximized where marginal revenue equals marginal cost. The profit-maximizing quantity is 125 jackets a day. The price of £75 a jacket exceeds the average total cost of £25 a jacket, so the firm makes an economic profit of £50 a jacket. The blue rectangle illustrates economic profit, which equals £6,250 a day (£50 a jacket multiplied by 125 jackets a day).

profit of £6,250 a day (£50 per jacket multiplied by 125 jackets a day). The blue rectangle shows French Connection's economic profit.

Profit Maximizing Might Be Loss Minimizing

Figure 13.1 shows that French Connection is making a healthy economic profit. But such an outcome is not inevitable. A firm might face a level of demand for its product that is too low for it to make an economic profit.

Excite@Home was such a firm. Offering high-speed Internet service, Excite@Home hoped to capture a large share of the Internet portal market in competition with AOL, MSN, Yahoo! and a host of other providers.

Figure 13.2 illustrates the situation facing Excite@Home in 2001. The demand curve for its portal service is *D*, the marginal revenue curve is *MR*, the average total cost curve is *ATC*, and the marginal cost curve is *MC*. Excite@Home maximized profit –

Figure 13.2

Economic Loss in the Short Run

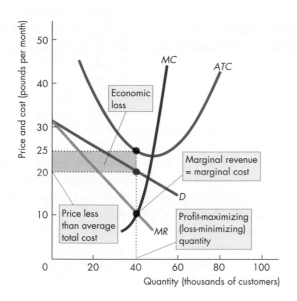

Profit is maximized where marginal revenue equals marginal cost. The loss-minimizing quantity is 40,000 customers. The price of £20 a month is less than the average total cost of £25 a month, so the firm incurs an economic loss of £5 a customer. The red rectangle illustrates economic loss, which equals £200,000 a month (£5 a customer multiplied by 40,000 customers).

equivalently, it minimized its loss – by producing the output at which marginal revenue equals marginal cost. In Figure 13.2, this output is 40,000 customers.

Excite@Home charged the price that buyers were willing to pay for this quantity, which was determined by the demand curve and which was £20 a month. With 40,000 customers, Excite@Home's average total cost was £25 per customer, so it incurred an economic loss of £200,000 a month (£5 a customer multiplied by 40,000 customers). The red rectangle shows Excite@Home's economic loss.

So far, the firm in monopolistic competition looks like a single-price monopoly. It produces the quantity at which marginal revenue equals marginal cost and then charges the price that buyers are willing to pay for that quantity, determined by the demand curve. The key difference between monopoly and monopolistic competition lies in what happens next when firms either make an economic profit or incur an economic loss.

Long Run: Zero Economic Profit

A firm like Excite@Home is not going to incur an economic loss for long. Eventually, it goes out of business. Also, there is no restriction on entry in monopolistic competition, so if firms in an industry are making an economic profit, other firms have an incentive to enter that industry.

As Burberry, Gap and other firms start to make jackets similar to those made by French Connection, the demand for French Connection jackets decreases. The demand curve for French Connection jackets and the marginal revenue curve shift leftward. And as these curves shift leftward, the profit-maximizing quantity and price fall.

Figure 13.3 shows the long-run equilibrium. The demand curve for French Connection jackets and the marginal revenue curve have shifted leftward. The firm produces 75 jackets a day and sells them for £50 each.

At this output level, average total cost is also £50 per jacket.

Figure 13.3

Output and Price in the Long Run

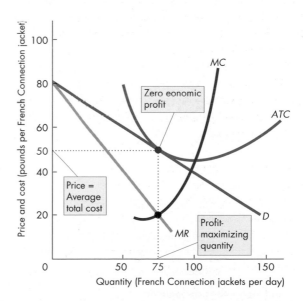

Economic profit encourages entry, which decreases the demand for each firm's product. When the demand curve touches the ATC curve at the quantity at which MR equals MC, the market is in long-run equilibrium. The output that maximizes profit is 75 jackets a day, and the price is £50 per jacket. Average total cost is also £50 per jacket, so economic profit is zero.

So French Connection is making zero economic profit on its jackets. When all the firms in the industry are making zero economic profit, there is no incentive for new firms to enter.

If demand is so low relative to costs that firms incur economic losses, exit will occur. As firms leave an industry, the demand for the products of the remaining firms increases and their demand curves shift rightward. The exit process ends when all the firms in the industry are making zero economic profit.

Monopolistic Competition and Perfect Competition

Figure 13.4 compares monopolistic competition and perfect competition and highlights two key differences between them:

◆ Excess capacity
◆ Mark up

Excess Capacity

A firm has excess capacity if it produces below its efficient scale, which is the quantity at which average total cost is a minimum – the quantity at the bottom of the U-shaped *ATC* curve. In Figure 13.4, the efficient scale is 100 jackets a day. French Connection (part a) produces 75 French Connection jackets a day and has *excess capacity* of 25 jackets a day. But if all jackets are alike and are produced by firms in perfect competition (part b) each firm produces 100 jackets a day, which is the efficient scale. Average total cost is the lowest possible only in *perfect* competition.

You can see the excess capacity in monopolistic competition all around you. Family restaurants (except for the truly outstanding ones) almost always have some empty tables. You can always get a pizza delivered in 30 minutes or so. It is rare that every pump at a petrol station is in use with customers queuing up to be served. There is always an abundance of estate agents ready to

---

Figure 13.4

Excess Capacity and Mark up

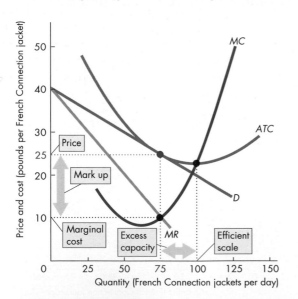

(a) Monopolistic competition

(b) Perfect competition

The efficient scale is 100 jackets a day. In monopolistic competition in the long run, because the firm faces a downward sloping demand curve for its product, the quantity produced is less than the efficient scale and the firm has excess capacity. Price exceeds marginal cost by the amount of the mark up.

In contrast, because in perfect competition the demand for each firm's product is perfectly elastic, the quantity produced equals the efficient scale and price equals marginal cost. The firm produces at the least possible cost and there is no mark up.

help find or sell a home. These industries are examples of monopolistic competition. The firms have excess capacity. They could sell more by cutting their prices, but they would then incur losses.

Mark Up

A firm's mark up is the amount by which price exceeds marginal cost. Figure 13.4(a) shows French Connection's mark up. In perfect competition, price always equals marginal cost and there is no mark up. Figure 13.4(b) shows this case. In monopolistic competition, buyers pay a higher price than in perfect competition and also pay more than marginal cost.

Is Monopolistic Competition Efficient?

You've learned that resources are used efficiently when marginal benefit equals marginal cost. You've also learned that price measures marginal benefit. So if the price of a French Connection jacket exceeds the marginal cost of producing it, the quantity of French Connection jackets produced is less than the efficient quantity. And you've just seen that in long-run equilibrium in monopolistic competition, price *does* exceed marginal cost. So is the quantity produced in monopolistic competition less than the efficient quantity?

Making the Relevant Comparison

Two economists meet in the street, and one asks the other how her husband is. "Compared to what?" is the quick reply. This bit of economic wit illustrates a key point: before we can conclude that something needs fixing, we must check out the available alternatives.

The mark up that drives a gap between price and marginal cost in monopolistic competition arises from product differentiation. It is because French Connection jackets are not quite the same as jackets from Banana Republic, Diesel, DKNY, Earl Jackets, Gap, Levi, Nautilus, Ralph Lauren, or any of the other dozens of producers of jackets that the demand for French Connection jackets is not perfectly elastic. The only way in which the demand for jackets from French Connection might be perfectly elastic is if there is only one kind of jacket and all firms make it. In this situation, French Connection jackets are indistinguishable from all other jackets. They don't even have identifying labels.

If there was only one kind of jacket, the marginal benefit of jackets would almost certainly be less than it

is with variety. People value variety. And people value variety not only because it enables each person to select what he or she likes best but also because it provides an external benefit. Most of us enjoy seeing variety in the choices of others. Contrast a scene from the China of the 1960s, when everyone wore a Mao tunic, with the China of today, where everyone wears the clothes of their own choosing. Or contrast a scene from the Germany of the 1930s, when almost everyone who could afford a car owned a first-generation Volkswagen Beetle, with the world of today with its enormous variety of styles and types of cars.

If people value variety, why don't we see infinite variety? The answer is that variety is costly. Each different variety of any product must be designed, and then customers must be informed about it. These initial costs of design and marketing – called setup costs – mean that some varieties that are too close to others already available are just not worth creating.

The Bottom Line

Product variety is both valued and costly. The efficient degree of product variety is the one for which the marginal benefit of product variety equals its marginal cost. The loss that arises because the marginal benefit of one more unit of a given variety exceeds marginal cost is offset by a gain that arises from having an efficient degree of product variety. So compared to the alternative – complete product uniformity – monopolistic competition is probably efficient.

Review Quiz

1   How does a firm in monopolistic competition decide how much to produce and at what price to offer its product for sale?
2   Why can a firm in monopolistic competition make an economic profit only in the short run?
3   Why do firms in monopolistic competition operate with excess capacity?
4   Why is there a price mark up over marginal cost in monopolistic competition?
5   Is monopolistic competition efficient?

You've seen how the firm in monopolistic competition determines its output and price when it produces a given product and undertakes a given marketing effort. But how does the firm choose its product quality and marketing effort? We'll now study these decisions.

Product Development and Marketing

When we studied French Connection's price and output decision, we assumed that it had already made its product quality and marketing decisions. We're now going to study these decisions and the impact they have on the firm's output, price and economic profit.

Innovation and Product Development

The prospect of new firms entering the industry keeps firms in monopolistic competition on their toes!

To enjoy economic profits, firms in monopolistic competition must be continually seeking ways of keeping one step ahead of imitators – other firms who imitate the success of the economically profitable firms.

One major way of trying to maintain economic profit is for a firm to seek out new products that will provide it with a competitive edge, even if only temporarily. A firm that introduces a new and differentiated product faces a less elastic demand for its product and so the firm is able to increase its price and make an economic profit. Eventually, imitators will enter the market and make close substitutes for the innovative product and they compete away the economic profit arising from an initial advantage. So to restore economic profit, the firm must again innovate.

Cost Versus Benefit of Product Innovation

The decision to innovate is based on the same type of profit-maximizing calculation that you've already studied. Innovation and product development are costly activities, but they also bring in additional revenues.

The firm must balance the cost and benefit at the margin. At a low level of product development, the marginal revenue from a better product exceeds the marginal cost. When the marginal pound of product development expenditure (the marginal cost of product development) brings in a pound of additional revenue (the marginal benefit of product development), the firm is spending the profit-maximizing amount on product development.

For example, when Microsoft releases a new version of Windows, it is not the best operating system that Microsoft could have created. Rather it is an operating system with features whose marginal benefit – and consumers' willingness to pay – equal the marginal cost of those features.

Efficiency and Product Innovation

Is product innovation an efficient activity? Does it benefit the consumer? There are two views about the answers to these questions. One view is that monopolistic competition brings to market many improved products that give great benefits to the consumer. Clothing, kitchen and other household appliances, computers, computer programs, cars, and many other products keep getting better every year, and the consumer benefits from these improved products.

An alternative view is that many so-called improvements are little more than changes in the appearance of a product or new-look packaging. In these cases, there is little objective benefit to the consumer.

Regardless of whether a product improvement is real or imagined, its value to the consumer is its marginal benefit, which equals the amount the consumer is willing to pay. In other words, the value of product improvements is the increase in price that the consumer is willing to pay. The marginal benefit to the producer is marginal revenue, which in equilibrium equals marginal cost. Because price exceeds marginal cost in monopolistic competition, product improvement is not pushed to its efficient level.

Advertising

Designing and developing products that are actually different from those of its competitors helps a firm achieve some product differentiation. But firms also attempt to create a consumer perception of product differentiation even when actual differences are small. Advertising and packaging are the principal means firms use to achieve this end. An American Express card is a different product from a Visa card. But the actual differences are not the main ones that American Express emphasizes in its marketing. The deeper message is that if you use an American Express card, you can be like Tiger Woods (or some other high-profile successful person).

Advertising Expenditures

Firms in monopolistic competition incur huge costs in order to persuade buyers to appreciate and value the differences between their own products and those of their competitors.

Figure 13.5 shows UK advertising expenditure for a range of industries in 2000. Advertising costs vary depending on the type of advertising used with the highest expenditures being in those sectors that rely on expensive television and national newspaper advertising.

Figure 13.5

Advertising Expenditures

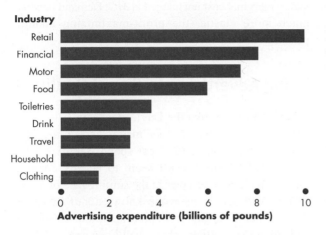

Advertising expenditures are highest for retailers and the finance, motor and food sectors, which rely on television and newspaper advertisements. Advertising expenditure is low by comparison on clothing.

While advertising in newspapers and magazines and on radio and television is the main selling cost, it is not the only one. Selling costs include the cost of rentals in splendid new shopping centres; the cost of glossy catalogues and direct mail advertising; the costs of promotions and exhibitions; and the salaries, airfares and hotel bills of sales staff.

Total selling costs today, on average, probably represent around 15 per cent of the price of most goods and services.

The proportion of the prices we pay that covers the cost of selling a good is not only large, it is also rising and dramatically. Advertising expenditure in the United Kingdom topped £17,000 million in 2000. Even after allowing for inflation, this level of spending is 35 per cent higher than it was in 1995 and a 56 per cent higher than in 1990.

Advertising expenditures and other selling costs affect the profits of firms in two ways. They increase costs and they change demand. Let's look at these effects.

Selling Costs and Total Costs

Selling costs such as advertising expenditures increase the costs of a monopolistically competitive firm above those of a perfectly competitive firm or a monopoly.

Advertising costs and other selling costs are fixed costs. They do not vary as total output varies. So, just like fixed production costs, advertising costs per unit decrease as production increases.

Figure 13.6 shows how selling costs and advertising expenditures change a firm's average total cost. The blue curve shows the average total cost of production. The red curve shows the firm's average total cost of production with advertising. The height of the red area between the two curves shows the average fixed cost of advertising. The *total* cost of advertising is fixed. But the *average* cost of advertising decreases as output increases.

The figure shows that if advertising increases the quantity sold by a large enough amount, it can lower average total cost. For example, if the quantity sold increases from 25 jackets a day with no advertising to 100 jackets a day with advertising, average total cost falls from £60 to £40 a jacket. The reason is that although the *total* fixed cost has increased, the greater fixed cost is spread over a greater output, so average total cost decreases.

Figure 13.6

Selling Costs and Total Cost

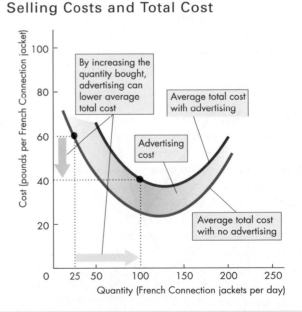

Selling costs such as the cost of advertising are fixed costs. When added to the average total cost of production, selling costs increase average total cost by a greater amount at small outputs than at large outputs. If advertising enables sales to increase from 25 jackets a day to 100 jackets a day, average total cost *falls* from £60 to £40 a jacket.

Selling Costs and Demand

Advertising and other selling efforts change the demand for a firm's product. But how? Does demand increase or does it decrease? The most natural answer is that advertising increases demand. By informing people about the quality of its products or by persuading people to switch from the products of other firms, a firm might expect to increase the demand for its own products.

But all firms in monopolistic competition advertise. And all seek to persuade customers that they have the best deal. If advertising enables a firm to survive, it might increase the number of firms in the market. And to the extent that it increases the number of firms, it *decreases* the demand faced by any one firm. It also makes the demand for any one firm's product more elastic. So advertising can end up not only lowering average total cost but also lowering the mark up and the price.

Figure 13.7 illustrates this possible effect of advertising. In part (a), with no advertising, the demand for French Connection jackets is not very elastic. Profit is

maximized at 75 jackets per day and the mark up is large. In part (b), advertising, which is a fixed cost, increases average total cost from ATC_0 to ATC_1 but leaves marginal cost unchanged at MC. Demand becomes much more elastic, the profit-maximizing quantity increases and the mark up shrinks.

Using Advertising to Signal Quality

Some advertising, like the David Beckham Gillette ads on television and in glossy magazines or the huge amounts that Coke and Pepsi spend, seems hard to understand. There doesn't seem to be any concrete information about a shaver in the smiling face of a footballer. And surely everyone knows about Coke and Pepsi. What is the gain from pouring millions of pounds a month into advertising these well-known colas?

One answer is that advertising is a signal to the consumer of a high-quality product. A **signal** is an action taken by an informed person (or firm) to send a message to uninformed people. Think about two shavers: Mach 3

Figure 13.7

Advertising and the Mark Up

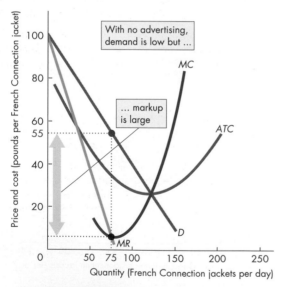

(a) No firms advertise

With no firms advertising, demand is low and not very elastic. The profit-maximizing output is small, the mark up is large and the price is high.

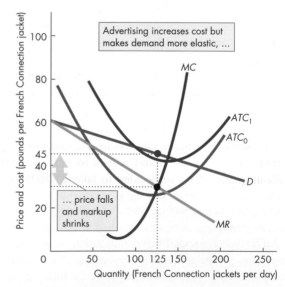

(b) All firms advertise

Advertising increases average total cost and shifts the ATC curve upward from ATC_0 to ATC_1. With all firms advertising, the demand for each firm's product becomes more elastic. Output increases, the price falls and the mark up shrinks.

and Bland. Bland knows that its blades are poor and of variable quality that depends on which cheap batch of unsold blades it happens to buy each week. So Bland knows that while it could get a lot of people to try Bland by advertising, they would all quickly discover what a poor product it is and switch back to the shaver they bought before. Gillette, in contrast, knows that its blade gives a high-quality consistent shave and that once consumers have tried it, there is a good chance they'll never use anything else. On the basis of this reasoning, Bland doesn't advertise but Gillette does.

And Gillette spends a lot of money to make a big splash. Mach 3 users who know that Gillette has done a $10 million deal with Beckham know that the firm would not spend so much money advertising if its product were not truly good. So consumers reason that a Gillette shaver is indeed a really good product. The flashy expensive ad has signalled that a Mach 3 is really good without saying anything about the shaver.

Notice that if advertising is a signal, it doesn't need any specific product information. It just needs to be expensive and hard to miss. That's what a lot of advertising looks like. So the signalling theory of advertising predicts much of the advertising that we see.

Brand Names

Many firms create and spend a lot of money promoting a brand name. Why? What benefit does a brand name bring to justify the sometimes high cost of establishing it?

The basic answer is that a brand name provides information about the quality of a product to consumers and an incentive to the producer to achieve a high and consistent quality standard.

To see how a brand name helps the consumer, think about how you use brand names to get information about quality. You've decided to take a holiday in the sun and you're trying to decide where to go. You see advertisements for Club Med and Sheraton Resorts and for Joe's Beachside Shack and Annie's Dive.

You know about Club Med and Sheraton Resorts because although you've not stayed in them before, you've seen their advertisements and you've heard about them from others. You know what to expect from them.

You have no information at all about Joe's and Annie's. They might be better than the places you do know about, but without that knowledge, you're not going to chance them. You use the brand name as information and choose Club Med.

This same story explains why a brand name provides an incentive to achieve high and consistent quality. Because no one would know whether they were offering a high standard of service, Joe's and Annie's have no incentive to do so. But equally, because everyone expects a given standard of service from Club Med, a failure to meet a customer's expectation would almost surely lose that customer to a competitor. So Club Med has a strong incentive to deliver what it promises in the advertising that creates its brand name.

Efficiency of Advertising and Brand Names

To the extent that advertising and brand names provide consumers with information about the precise nature of product differences and about product quality, they benefit the consumer and enable a better product choice to be made. But the opportunity cost of the additional information must be weighed against the gain to the consumer.

The final verdict on the efficiency of monopolistic competition is ambiguous. In some cases, the gains from extra product variety unquestionably offset the selling costs and the extra cost arising from excess capacity. The tremendous varieties of books and magazines, clothing, food and drinks are examples of such gains. It is less easy to see the gains from being able to buy a brand-name drug that has a chemical composition identical to that of a generic alternative. But many people do willingly pay more for the brand-name alternative.

Review Quiz

1   What are the two main ways, other than by adjusting price, in which a firm in monopolistic competition competes with other firms?
2   Why might product innovation and development be efficient and why might it be inefficient?
3   How does a firm's advertising expenditure influence its cost curves? Does average total cost increase or decrease?
4   How does a firm's advertising expenditure influence the demand for its product? Does demand increase or decrease?
5   Why is it difficult to determine whether monopolistic competition is efficient or inefficient? What is your opinion about the bottom line and why?

What is Oligopoly?

Oligopoly, like monopolistic competition, lies between perfect competition and monopoly. The firms in oligopoly might produce an identical product and compete only on price, or they might produce a differentiated product and compete on price, product quality and marketing. The distinguishing features of oligopoly are that:

◆ Natural or legal barriers prevent the entry of new firms.

◆ A small number of firms compete.

Barriers to Entry

Either natural or legal barriers to entry can create oligopoly. You saw in Chapter 12 how economies of scale and demand form a natural barrier to entry that can create a *natural monopoly*. These same factors can create a natural oligopoly.

Figure 13.8 illustrates two natural oligopolies. The demand curve, *D* (in both parts of the figure), shows the demand for taxi rides in a town. If the average total cost curve of a taxi company is ATC_1 in part (a), the market is a natural **duopoly** – an oligopoly with two firms. You can probably see some examples of duopoly where you live. Some cities have only two suppliers of milk, two local newspapers, two taxi companies, two car rental firms, two copy centres or two bookshops.

Notice that the efficient scale of one firm is 30 rides a day. The lowest price at which the firm would remain in business is £10 a ride. At that price, the quantity of rides demanded is 60 a day, the quantity that can be provided by just two firms.

There is no room in this market for three firms. To sell more than 60 rides, the price would have to fall below £10 a ride. But then the firms would incur an economic loss and one of them would exit. If there were only one firm, it would make an economic profit and a second firm would enter to take some of the business and economic profit. If the average total cost curve of a taxi company is ATC_2 in part (b), the efficient scale of one firm is 20 rides a day. This market is large enough for three firms.

Figure 13.8

Natural Oligopoly

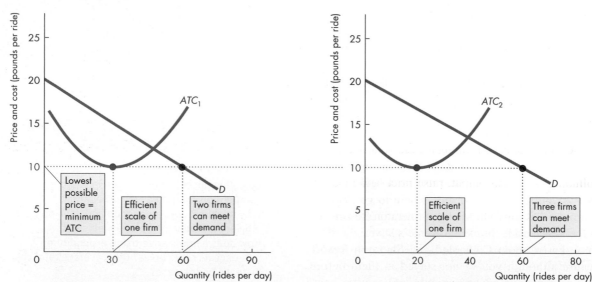

(a) Natural duopoly

(b) Natural oligopoly with three firms

The lowest possible price is £10 a ride, which is the minimum average total cost. When a firm produces 30 rides a day, the efficient scale, two firms can satisfy the market demand. This natural oligopoly has two firms – a natural duopoly.

When the efficient scale of one firm is 20 rides per day, three firms can satisfy the market demand at the lowest possible price. This natural oligopoly has three firms.

A legal oligopoly arises when a legal barrier to entry protects the small number of firms in a market. A city might license two taxi firms or two bus companies, for example, even though the combination of demand and economies of scale leaves room for more than two firms.

Small Number of Firms

Because barriers to entry exist, oligopoly consists of a small number of firms each of which has a large share of the market. Such firms are interdependent and they face a temptation to cooperate to increase their joint economic profit.

Interdependence

With a small number of firms in a market, each firm's actions influence the profits of the other firms. To see how, suppose you run one of the three petrol stations in a small town. If you cut your price, your market share increases, and your profits might increase too.

But the market share and profits of the other two firms fall. In this situation, the other firms most likely cut their prices too. If they do cut their prices, your market share and profit take a tumble. So before deciding to cut your price, you must predict how the other firms will react and take into account the effects of those reactions on your own profit.

Your profit depends on the actions of the other firms and their profit depends on your actions. You are interdependent.

Temptation to Cooperate

When a small number of firms share a market, they can increase their profits by forming a cartel and acting like a monopoly. A **cartel** is a group of firms acting together – colluding – to limit output, raise price and increase economic profit.

Cartels are illegal in the European Union and in most other regions and countries. But some international cartels exist. The best known is the Organization of Petroleum Exporting Countries, or OPEC, an international cartel of crude oil producers.

Even when there is no formal cartel, firms in an oligopoly market might try to operate as if they were in a cartel. That is, they might try behaving as they would if they were in a formal cartel.

For reasons that you'll discover in this chapter, cartels are hard to maintain and even formal cartels tend to break down.

Examples of Oligopoly

Identifying oligopoly is the flip side of identifying monopolistic competition. But the borderline between the two market types is hard to pin down.

As a practical matter, we try to identify oligopoly by looking at the five-firm concentration ratio qualified with other information about the geographical scope of the market and barriers to entry.

As we noted in Chapter 9 (see p. 191), the five-firm concentration ratio helps us measure the degree of competitiveness of a market. A concentration ratio that exceeds 60 per cent almost certainly indicates an oligopoly and a degree of market power that could enable a cartel to operate.

A concentration ratio between 40 and 60 per cent indicates that the market structure is probably oligopoly, although if entry is easy, such an industry might more nearly approximate monopolistic competition.

Examples of oligopoly include cigarettes, glass bottles and jars, washing machines, dryers and refrigerators, batteries, light bulbs, breakfast cereals, cars, motorcycles, and chocolate.

Duopoly, the special case of oligopoly that has just two firms, is common in local markets. There are some spectacular global examples as well. Two firms compete in the global market for personal computer processor chips – Intel and AMD. And two firms compete in the market for long-distance large airplanes – Boeing and Airbus. The markets for these products are highly competitive, but the competition is quite unlike that in perfect competition. The firms are able to influence the market price and the fortunes of each other.

Review Quiz

1   What are the distinguishing characteristics of oligopoly?
2   What arrangement are firms in oligopoly tempted to try to make?
3   In addition to the examples given above, provide some examples of industries with which you are familiar that operate in oligopoly.

Understanding how firms in oligopoly behave is a bit more complicated than the case of perfect competition and we look at two approaches in the rest of the chapter.

Two Traditional Oligopoly Models

In oligopoly, the quantity sold by one firm depends on that firm's price *and* on the other firms' prices and quantities sold. To see why, suppose you run one of the three petrol stations in a small town. If you cut your price and your two competitors don't cut theirs, your sales increase and the sales of the other two firms decrease. With lower sales, the other firms most likely cut their prices too. If they do cut their prices, your sales and profits take a tumble. So before deciding to cut your price, you must predict how the other firms will react and attempt to calculate the effects of those reactions on your own profit.

Several models have been developed to explain the prices and quantities in oligopoly markets. But no one theory has been found that can explain all the different types of behaviour that we observe in such markets. The models fall into two broad groups: traditional models and game theory models. We'll look at examples of both types, starting with two traditional models.

The Kinked Demand Curve Model

The kinked demand curve model of oligopoly is based on the assumption that each firm believes that if it raises its price, others will not follow, but if it cuts its price, other firms will cut theirs.

Figure 13.9 shows the demand curve (*D*) that a firm believes it faces. The demand curve has a kink at the current price, *P*, and quantity, *Q*. At prices above *P*, a small price rise brings a big decrease in the quantity sold. The other firms hold their current price and the firm has the highest price for the good, so it loses market share. At prices below *P*, even a large price cut brings only a small increase in the quantity sold. In this case, other firms match the price cut, so the firm gets no price advantage over its competitors.

The kink in the demand curve creates a break in the marginal revenue curve (*MR*). To maximize profit, the firm produces the quantity at which marginal cost equals marginal revenue. That quantity, *Q*, is where the marginal cost curve passes through the gap *AB* in the marginal revenue curve. If marginal cost fluctuates between *A* and *B*, like the marginal cost curves MC_0 and MC_1, the firm does not change its price or its output. Only if marginal cost fluctuates outside the range *AB* does the firm change its price and output. So the kinked demand curve model predicts that price and quantity are insensitive to small cost changes. A problem with the

Figure 13.9

The Kinked Demand Curve Model

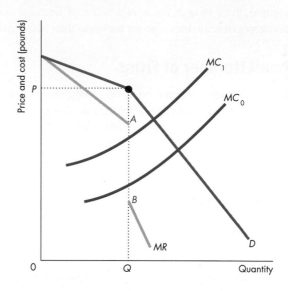

The price in an oligopoly market is *P*. Each firm believes it faces the demand curve *D*. At prices above *P*, a small price rise brings a big decrease in the quantity sold because other firms do not raise their prices. At prices below *P*, even a big price cut brings only a small increase in the quantity sold because other firms also cut their prices. Because the demand curve is kinked, the marginal revenue curve, *MR*, has a break *AB*. Profit is maximized by producing *Q*. The marginal cost curve passes through the break in the marginal revenue curve. Marginal cost changes inside the range *AB* leave the price and quantity unchanged.

kinked demand curve model is that the firms' beliefs about the demand curve are not always correct and firms can figure out that they are not correct. If marginal cost increases by enough to cause the firm to increase its price and if all firms experience the same increase in marginal cost, they all increase their prices together. The firm's belief that others will not join it in a price rise is incorrect. A firm that bases its actions on beliefs that are wrong does not maximize profit and might even end up incurring an economic loss.

The Dominant Firm Model

A second traditional model explains a dominant firm oligopoly, which arises when one firm – the dominant firm – has a big cost advantage over the other firms and produces a large part of the industry output. The dominant firm sets the market price and the other firms are

Figure 13.10

A Dominant Firm Model

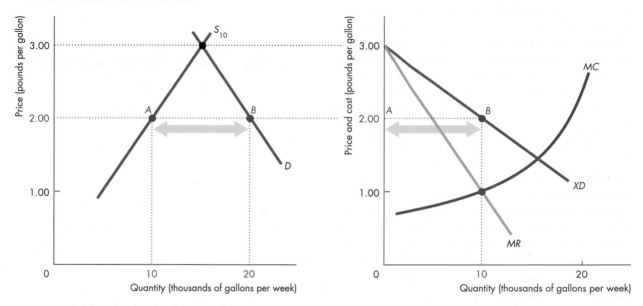

(a) Ten small firms and market demand

(b) Big-G's price and output decision

The demand curve for petrol in a city is *D* in part (a). There are 10 small competitive firms that together have a supply curve of S_{10}. In addition, there is 1 large firm, Big-G, shown in part (b). Big-G faces the demand curve *XD*, determined as the market demand *D* minus the supply of the 10 small firms S_{10} – the demand that is not satisfied by the small firms. Big-G's marginal revenue is *MR* and marginal cost is *MC*. Big-G sets its output to maximize profit by equating marginal cost, *MC*, and marginal revenue, *MR*. This output is 10,000 gallons per week. The price at which Big-G can sell this quantity is £2 a gallon. The 10 small firms take this price and each firm sells 1,000 gallons per week, point *A* in part (a).

price takers. Examples of dominant firm oligopoly are a large petrol retailer or a big video rental store that dominates its local market.

To see how a dominant firm oligopoly works, suppose that 11 firms operate petrol stations in a city.

Big-G is the dominant firm. Figure 13.10 shows the market for petrol in this city. In part (a), the demand curve *D* tells us the total quantity of petrol demanded in the city at each price. The supply curve S_{10} is the supply curve of the 10 small suppliers. Part (b) shows the situation facing Big-G. Its marginal cost curve is *MC*. Big-G faces the demand curve *XD* and its marginal revenue curve is *MR*. The demand curve *XD* shows the excess demand not met by the 10 small firms. For example, at a price of £1 a gallon, the quantity demanded is 20,000 gallons, the quantity supplied by the 10 small firms is 10,000 gallons, and the excess quantity demanded is 10,000 gallons, measured by the distance *AB* in both parts of the figure. To maximize profit, Big-G operates like a monopoly. It sells 10,000 gallons a week, where

marginal revenue equals marginal cost, for a price of £2 a gallon. The 10 small firms take the price of £2 a gallon. They behave just like firms in perfect competition. The quantity of petrol demanded in the entire city at £2 a gallon is 20,000 gallons, as shown in part (a). Of this amount, Big-G sells 10,000 gallons and the 10 small firms each sell 1,000 gallons.

Review Quiz

1 What does the kinked demand curve model predict and why must it sometimes make a prediction that contradicts its basic assumption?
2 Do you think a market with a dominant firm is in long-run equilibrium? Explain why or why not.

The traditional models don't enable us to understand all oligopoly markets and we're now going to study some newer models based on game theory.

Oligopoly Games

Economists think about oligopoly as a game and to study oligopoly markets they use a set of tools called game theory. **Game theory** is a tool for studying *strategic behaviour* – behaviour that takes into account the expected behaviour of others and the recognition of mutual interdependence. Game theory was invented by John von Neumann in 1937 and extended by von Neumann and Oskar Morgenstern in 1944. Today, it is one of the major research fields in economics.

Game theory seeks to understand oligopoly as well all other forms of economic, political, social, and even biological rivalries, by using a method of analysis specifically designed to understand games of all types, including the familiar games of everyday life. We will begin our study of game theory and its application to the behaviour of firms by thinking about familiar games.

What is a Game?

What is a game? At first thought, the question seems silly. After all, there are many different games. There are ball games and parlour games, games of chance and games of skill. But what is it about all these different activities that make them games? What do all these Games have in common? All games share four features:

1   Rules
2   Strategies
3   Payoffs
4   Outcome

Let's see how these common features of games apply to a game called "the prisoners' dilemma". This game, it turns out, captures some of the essential features of oligopoly and gives a good illustration of how game theory works and how it generates predictions.

The Prisoners' Dilemma

Art and Bob have been caught red-handed, stealing a car. Facing airtight cases, they will receive a sentence of 2 years each for their crime. During his interviews with the two prisoners, the police sergeant begins to suspect that he has stumbled on the two people who were responsible for a multimillion-pound bank robbery some months earlier. But this is just a suspicion. The policeman has no evidence on which he can convict them of the greater crime unless he can get them to confess. The police sergeant decides to make the prisoners play a game with the following rules.

Rules

Each prisoner (player) is placed in a separate room and cannot communicate with the other prisoner. Each is told that he is suspected of having carried out the bank robbery and that if both of them confess to the larger crime, each will receive a sentence of 3 years for both crimes. If he alone confesses and his accomplice does not, he will receive an even shorter sentence of 1 year while his accomplice will receive a 10-year sentence.

Strategies

In game theory, **strategies** are all the possible actions of each player. Art and Bob each have two possible actions:

1   Confess to the bank robbery.
2   Deny having committed the bank robbery.

Payoffs

Because there are two players, each with two strategies, there are four possible outcomes:

1   Both confess.
2   Both deny.
3   Art confesses and Bob denies.
4   Bob confesses and Art denies.

Each prisoner can work out exactly what happens to him – his *payoff* – in each of these four situations. We can tabulate the four possible payoffs for each of the prisoners in what is called a payoff matrix for the game. A **payoff matrix** is a table that shows the payoffs for every possible action by each player for every possible action by each other player.

Table 13.1 shows a payoff matrix for Art and Bob. The squares show the payoffs for each prisoner – the red triangle in each square shows Art's and the blue triangle shows Bob's. If both prisoners confess (top left), each gets a prison term of 3 years. If Bob confesses but Art denies (top right), Art gets a 10-year sentence and Bob gets a 1-year sentence. If Art confesses and Bob denies (bottom left), Art gets a 1-year sentence and Bob gets a 10-year sentence. Finally, if both of them deny (bottom right), neither can be convicted of the bank robbery charge but both are sentenced for the car theft – a 2-year sentence.

Outcome

The choices of both players determine the outcome of the game. To predict that outcome, we use an equilibrium idea proposed by John Nash of Princeton University (who received the Nobel Prize for Economic Science in 1994 and was the subject of the 2001 film *A Beautiful Mind*). In **Nash equilibrium**, player *A* takes the best possible action given the action of player *B* and player *B* takes the best possible action given the action of player *A*.

In the case of the prisoners' dilemma, the Nash equilibrium occurs when Art makes his best choice given Bob's choice and when Bob makes his best choice given Art's choice.

To find the Nash equilibrium, we compare all the possible outcomes associated with each choice and eliminate those that are dominated – that are not as good as some other choice. Let's find the Nash equilibrium for the prisoners' dilemma game.

Finding the Nash Equilibrium

Look at the situation from Art's point of view. If Bob confesses, Art's best action is to confess because in that case, he is sentenced to 3 years rather than 10 years. If Bob does not confess, Art's best action is still to confess because in that case he receives 1 year rather than 2 years. So Art's best action is to confess.

Now look at the situation from Bob's point of view. If Art confesses, Bob's best action is to confess because in that case, he is sentenced to 3 years rather than 10 years. If Art does not confess, Bob's best action is still to confess because in that case, he receives 1 year rather than 2 years. So Bob's best action is to confess.

Because each player's best action is to confess, each does confess, each gets a 3-year prison term, and the police sergeant has solved the bank robbery. This is the Nash equilibrium of the game.

The Dilemma

Now that you have found the solution to the prisoners' dilemma, you can better see the dilemma. The dilemma arises as each prisoner contemplates the consequences of denying. Each prisoner knows that if both of them deny, they will receive only a 2-year sentence for stealing the car. But neither has any way of knowing that his accomplice will deny.

Each poses the following questions: Should I deny and rely on my accomplice to deny so that we will both get only 2 years? Or should I confess in the hope of

Table 13.1

Prisoners' Dilemma Payoff Matrix

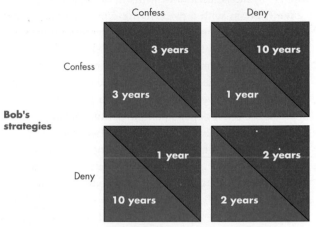

Each square shows the payoffs for the two players, Art and Bob, for each possible pair of actions. In each square, the red triangle shows Art's payoff and the blue triangle shows Bob's. For example, if both confess, the payoffs are in the top left square. The equilibrium of the game is for both players to confess and each gets a 3-year sentence.

getting just 1 year (provided that my accomplice denies) knowing that if my accomplice does confess, we will both get 3 years in prison? The dilemma is resolved by finding the equilibrium of the game.

A Bad Outcome

For the prisoners, the equilibrium of the game, with each confessing, is not the best outcome. If neither of them confesses, each gets only 2 years for the lesser crime. Isn't there some way in which this better outcome can be achieved? It seems that there is not, because the players cannot communicate with each other. Each player can put himself in the other player's place, and so each player can figure out that there is a best strategy for each of them. The prisoners are indeed in a dilemma. Each knows that he can serve 2 years only if he can trust the other to deny. But each prisoner also knows that it is not in the best interest of the other to deny. So each prisoner knows that he must confess, thereby delivering a bad outcome for both.

The firms in an oligopoly are in a similar situation to Art and Bob in the prisoners' dilemma game. Let's see how we can use this game to understand oligopoly.

An Oligopoly Price-fixing Game

We can use game theory and a game like the prisoners' dilemma to understand price fixing, price wars and other aspects of the behaviour of firms in oligopoly.

We'll begin with a price-fixing game. To understand price fixing, we're going to study the special case of duopoly – an oligopoly with two firms. Duopoly is easier to study than oligopoly with three or more firms, and it captures the essence of all oligopoly situations. Somehow, the two firms must share the market. And how they share it depends on the actions of each. We're going to describe the costs of the two firms and the market demand for the item they produce. We're then going to see how game theory helps us to predict the prices charged and the quantities produced by the two firms in a duopoly.

Cost and Demand Conditions

Two firms, Trick and Gear, produce switchgears. They have identical costs. Figure 13.11(a) shows their average total cost curve (*ATC*) and marginal cost curve (*MC*). Figure 13.11(b) shows the market demand curve for switchgears (*D*). The two firms produce identical switchgears, so one firm's switchgear is a perfect substitute for the other's. So the market price of each firm's product is identical. The quantity demanded depends on that price – the higher the price, the smaller is the quantity demanded.

This industry is a natural duopoly. Two firms can produce this good at a lower cost than either one firm or three firms can. For each firm, average total cost is at its minimum when production is 3,000 units a week. And when price equals minimum average total cost, the total quantity demanded is 6,000 units a week. So two firms can just produce that quantity.

Collusion

We'll suppose that Trick and Gear enter into a collusive agreement. A **collusive agreement** is an agreement between two (or more) producers to form a cartel to restrict output, raise the price and increase profits. Because such an agreement is illegal in the EU, it is undertaken in secret. The strategies that firms in a cartel can pursue are to:

1 Comply.

2 Cheat.

A firm that complies carries out the agreement. A firm that cheats breaks the agreement to its own benefit and to the cost of the other firm.

Because each firm has two strategies, there are four possible combinations of actions for the firms:

1 Both firms comply.

2 Both firms cheat.

3 Trick complies and Gear cheats.

4 Gear complies and Trick cheats.

Figure 13.11

Costs and Demand

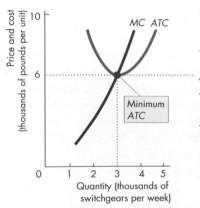

(a) Individual firm

(b) Industry

The average total cost curve for each firm is *ATC* and the marginal cost curve is *MC* (part a). Minimum average total cost is £6,000 a unit, and it occurs at a production of 3,000 units a week.

Part (b) shows the market demand curve. At a price of £6,000, the quantity demanded is 6,000 units per week. The two firms can produce this output at the lowest possible average cost. If the market had one firm, it would be profitable for another to enter. If the market had three firms, one would exit. There is room for only two firms in this industry. It is a natural duopoly.

Colluding to Maximize Profits

Let's work out the payoffs to the two firms if they collude to make the maximum profit for the cartel by acting like a monopoly. The calculations that the two firms perform are the same calculations that a monopoly performs. (You can refresh your memory of these calculations by looking at Chapter 12, pp. 256–257.)

The only thing that the duopolists must do beyond what a monopolist does is to agree on how much of the total output each of them will produce.

Figure 13.12 shows the price and quantity that maximize industry profit for the duopolists. Part (a) shows the situation for each firm and part (b) shows the situation for the industry as a whole. The curve labelled MR is the industry marginal revenue curve. This marginal revenue curve is like that of a single price monopoly (Chapter 12, p. 254). The curve labelled MC_I is the industry marginal cost curve if each firm produces the same level of output. That curve is constructed by adding together the outputs of the two firms at each level of marginal cost. That is, at each level of marginal cost, industry output is twice the output of each individual firm. Thus the curve MC_I in part (b) is twice as far to the right as the curve MC in part (a).

To maximize industry profit, the duopolists agree to restrict output to the rate that makes the industry marginal cost and marginal revenue equal. That output rate, as shown in part (b), is 4,000 units a week.

The highest price for which the 4,000 switchgears can be sold is £9,000 each. Trick and Gear agree to charge this price.

To hold the price at £9,000 a unit, production must not exceed 4,000 units a week. So Trick and Gear must agree on production levels for each of them that total 4,000 units a week. Let's suppose that they agree to split the market equally so that each firm produces 2,000 switchgears a week. Because the firms are identical, this division is the most likely. The average total cost (ATC) of producing 2,000 switchgears a week is £8,000, so the profit per unit is £1,000 and economic profit is £2 million (2,000 units × £1,000 per unit). The economic profit of each firm is represented by the blue rectangle in Figure 13.12(a).

We have just described one possible outcome for a duopoly game: the two firms collude to produce the monopoly profit-maximizing output and divide that output equally between them. From the industry point of view, this solution is identical to a monopoly. A duopoly that operates in this way is indistinguishable from a monopoly. The economic profit that is made by a monopoly is the maximum total profit that can be made by colluding duopolists.

But with price greater than marginal cost, either firm might think of trying to increase profit by cheating on the agreement and producing more than the agreed amount. Let's see what happens if one of the firms does cheat in this way.

Figure 13.12

Colluding to Make Monopoly Profits

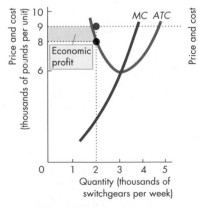

(a) Individual firm

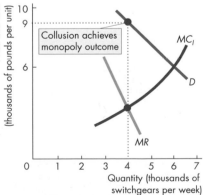

(b) Industry

The industry marginal cost curve, MC_I in part (b), is the horizontal sum of the two firms' marginal cost curves, MC in part (a). The industry marginal revenue curve is MR. To maximize profit, the firms produce 4,000 units a week (the quantity at which marginal revenue equals marginal cost). They sell that output for £9,000 a unit. Each firm produces 2,000 units a week. Average total cost is £8,000 a unit, so each firm makes an economic profit of £2 million (blue rectangle) – 2,000 units multiplied by £1,000 profit a unit.

One Firm Cheats on a Collusive Agreement

To set the stage for cheating on their agreement, Trick convinces Gear that demand has decreased and that it cannot sell 2,000 units a week. Trick tells Gear that it plans to cut its price in order to sell the agreed 2,000 units each week. Because the two firms produce an identical product, Gear matches Trick's price cut but still produces only 2,000 units a week.

In fact, there has been no decrease in demand. Trick plans to increase output, which it knows will lower the price, and Trick wants to ensure that Gear's output remains at the agreed level.

Figure 13.13 illustrates the consequences of Trick's cheating. Part (a) shows Gear (the complier); part (b) shows Trick (the cheat); and part (c) shows the industry as a whole. Suppose that Trick increases output to 3,000 units a week. If Gear sticks to the agreement to produce only 2,000 units a week, total output is 5,000 a week, and given demand in part (c), the price falls to £7,500 a unit.

Gear continues to produce 2,000 units a week at a cost of £8,000 a unit and incurs a loss of £500 a unit, or £1 million a week. This economic loss is represented by the red rectangle in part (a). Trick produces 3,000 units a week at an average total cost of £6,000 each.

With a price of £7,500, Trick makes a profit of £1,500 a unit and therefore an economic profit of £4.5 million. This economic profit is the blue rectangle in part (b).

We've now described a second possible outcome for the duopoly game: One of the firms cheats on the collusive agreement. In this case, the industry output is larger than the monopoly output and the industry price is lower than the monopoly price. The total economic profit made by the industry is also smaller than the monopoly's economic profit. Trick (the cheat) makes an economic profit of £4.5 million and Gear (the complier) incurs an economic loss of £1 million. The industry makes an economic profit of £3.5 million. Thus the industry profit is £0.5 million less than the economic profit a monopoly would make. But the profit is distributed unevenly. Trick makes a bigger economic profit than it would under the collusive agreement, while Gear incurs an economic loss.

A similar outcome would arise if Gear cheated and Trick complied with the agreement. The industry profit and price would be the same, but in this case, Gear (the cheat) would make an economic profit of £4.5 million and Trick (the complier) would incur an economic loss of £1 million. Let's next see what happens if both firms cheat.

Figure 13.13

One Firm Cheats

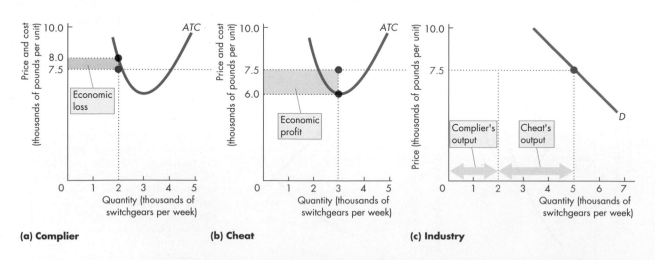

(a) Complier   **(b) Cheat**   **(c) Industry**

One firm, shown in part (a), complies with the agreement and produces 2,000 units. The other firm, shown in part (b), cheats on the agreement and increases its output to 3,000 units. Given the market demand curve, shown in part (c), and with a total production of 5,000 units a week, the price falls to £7,500. At this price, the complier in part (a) incurs an economic loss of £1 million (£500 per unit × 2,000 units), shown by the red rectangle. In part (b), the cheat makes an economic profit of £4.5 million (£1,500 per unit × 3,000 units), shown by the blue rectangle.

Both Firms Cheat

Suppose that both firms cheat and that each firm behaves like the cheating firm that we have just analyzed. Each tells the other that it is unable to sell its output at the going price and that it plans to cut its price. But because both firms cheat, each will propose a successively lower price. As long as price exceeds marginal cost, each firm has an incentive to increase its production – to cheat. Only when price equals marginal cost is there no further incentive to cheat. This situation arises when the price has reached £6,000. At this price, marginal cost equals price. Also, price equals minimum average total cost. At a price less than £6,000, each firm incurs an economic loss. At a price of £6,000, each firm covers all its costs and makes zero economic profit (makes normal profit). Also, at a price of £6,000, each firm wants to produce 3,000 units a week, so the industry output is 6,000 units a week. Given the demand conditions, 6,000 units can be sold at a price of £6,000 each.

Figure 13.14 illustrates the situation just described. Each firm, in part (a), produces 3,000 units a week, and its average total cost is a minimum (£6,000 per unit). The market as a whole, in part (b), operates at the point at which the market demand curve (D) intersects the industry marginal cost curve (MC_I). Each firm has lowered its price and increased its output to try to gain an advantage over the other firm. Each has pushed this process as far as it can without incurring an economic loss.

We have now described a third possible outcome of this duopoly game: Both firms cheat. If both firms cheat

on the collusive agreement, the output of each firm is 3,000 units a week and the price is £6,000. Each firm makes zero economic profit.

The Payoff Matrix

Now that we have described the strategies and payoffs in the duopoly game, we can summarize the strategies and the payoffs in the form of the game's payoff matrix. Then we can find the Nash equilibrium.

Table 13.2 sets out the payoff matrix for this game. It is constructed in the same way as the payoff matrix for the prisoners' dilemma in Table 13.1. The squares show the payoffs for the two firms – Gear and Trick. In this case, the payoffs are profits. (For the prisoners' dilemma, the payoffs were losses.)

The table shows that if both firms cheat (top left), they achieve the perfectly competitive outcome – each firm makes zero economic profit. If both firms comply (bottom right), the industry makes the monopoly profit and each firm makes an economic profit of £2 million. The top right and bottom left squares show what happens if one firm cheats while the other complies. The firm that cheats collects an economic profit of £4.5 million, and the one that complies incurs a loss of £1 million.

Nash Equilibrium in the Duopolists' Dilemma

The duopolists have a dilemma like the prisoners' dilemma. Do they comply or cheat? To answer this question, we must find the Nash equilibrium.

Figure 13.14

Both Firms Cheat

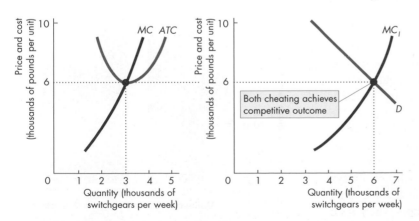

(a) Individual firm   (b) Industry

If both firms cheat by increasing production, the collusive agreement collapses. The limit to the collapse is the competitive equilibrium. Neither firm will cut price below £6,000 (minimum average total cost) because to do so will result in losses. In part (a), each firm produces 3,000 units a week at an average total cost of £6,000. In part (b), with a total production of 6,000 units, the price falls to £6,000. Each firm now makes zero economic profit. This output and price are the ones that would prevail in a competitive industry.

Table 13.2

◈

Duopoly Payoff Matrix

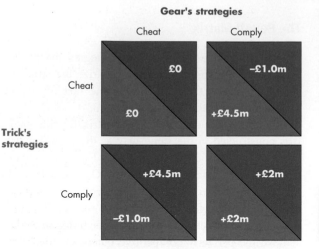

Gear's strategies

	Cheat	Comply
Cheat	£0 / £0	–£1.0m / +£4.5m
Comply	+£4.5m / –£1.0m	+£2m / +£2m

Trick's strategies

Each square shows the payoffs from a pair of actions. For example, if both firms comply with the collusive agreement, the payoffs are recorded in the bottom right square. The red triangle shows Gear's payoff, and the blue triangle shows Trick's. In Nash equilibrium, both firms cheat.

Look at things from Gear's point of view. Gear reasons as follows. Suppose that Trick cheats. If I comply, I will incur an economic loss of £1 million. If I also cheat, I will make zero economic profit. Zero is better than *minus* £1 million, so I'm better off if I cheat. Now suppose Trick complies. If I cheat, I will make an economic profit of £4.5 million, and if I comply, I will make an economic profit of £2 million.

A £4.5 million profit is better than a £2 million profit, so I'm better off if I cheat. So regardless of whether Trick cheats or complies, it pays Gear to cheat. Cheating is Gear's best strategy.

Trick comes to the same conclusion as Gear because the two firms face an identical situation. So both firms cheat. The Nash equilibrium of the duopoly game is that both firms cheat. And although the industry has only two firms, they charge the same price and produce the same quantity as those in a competitive industry. Also, as in perfect competition, each firm makes zero economic profit.

This conclusion is not general and will not always arise. We'll see why not first by looking at some other games that are like the prisoners' dilemma. Then we'll broaden the types of games we consider.

Other Oligopoly Games

Firms in oligopoly must decide whether to mount expensive advertising campaigns; whether to modify their product; whether to make their product more reliable and more durable; whether to price discriminate and, if so, among which groups of customers and to what degree; whether to undertake a large research and development (R&D) effort aimed at lowering production costs; and whether to enter or leave an industry.

All of these choices can be analyzed as games that are similar to the one that we've just studied. The box looks at an R&D game that is playing out today.

Box 13.1
A Prisoners' Dilemma in Soap Powder

Laundry detergent is big business and two firms, Procter & Gamble and Unilever, are the dominant players in Europe's €9 billion a year market.

In 2000, Unilever held 50 per cent of the UK market and Procter & Gamble 44 per cent. Unilever's share has fluctuated between 38 per cent in 1995 and 52 per cent in 1998. Procter and Gamble's share has mirrored that of Unilever and ranged between 40 per cent in 1998 and 50 per cent in 1995. Figure 1 shows the swings in these market shares.

The key to success in this industry (as in any other) is to create a product that people value highly relative to the cost of producing it. The firm that creates the most highly valued product and also develops the

Figure 1

Market Share for the UK soap powder

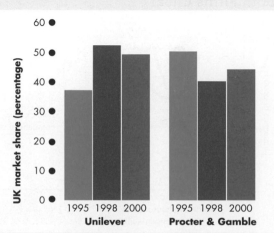

least-cost technology for producing it gains a competitive edge. It can undercut the rest of the market, increase its market share and increase its profit. But the R&D that must be undertaken to achieve product improvements and cost reductions is costly. So the cost of R&D must be deducted from the profit resulting from the increased market share that lower costs achieve. If neither firm does R&D, both firms might be better off, but if one firm initiates an R&D activity, the other must follow.

Table 1 illustrates (with hypothetical numbers) the dilemma for the R&D game that Unilever and Procter & Gamble play. Each firm has two strategies: engage in a €25 million a year R&D programme and the costly advertising needed to support it, or spend nothing on R&D. If neither firm spends on R&D, they each make a profit of €70 million a year. (bottom right of the payoff matrix). If each firm conducts R&D, market shares are maintained but each firm's profit is lower by the amount spent on R&D and each firm now makes €45 million a year (top left square of Table 1).

If Unilever does R&D but Procter & Gamble does not, Unilever gains a large part of Procter & Gamble's market. Unilever's profit jumps to €100 million and Procter & Gamble's drops to €15 million a year (top right square of the payoff matrix). Finally, if Procter & Gamble conducts R&D and Unilever does not, Procter & Gamble gains market share from Unilever, Procter & Gamble increases its profit to €100 million a year, while Unilever makes only €15 million a year (bottom left square).

Confronted with the payoff matrix in Table 1, the two firms calculate their best strategies. Unilever reasons as follows. If Procter & Gamble does not undertake R&D, we will make €100 million if we do and €70 million if we do not; so it pays us to conduct R&D. If Procter & Gamble conducts R&D, we will make €15 million if we don't and €45 million if we do. Again, R&D pays off. Thus conducting R&D is the best strategy for Unilever – regardless of Procter & Gamble's decision.

Procter & Gamble reasons similarly. If Unilever does not undertake R&D, we will make €100 million if we do R&D and €70 million if we don't. It therefore pays to conduct R&D. If Unilever does undertake R&D, we will make €45 million by doing the same and only €15 million if we don't do R&D. Again, it pays us to conduct R&D. So for Procter & Gamble, R&D is also the best strategy.

Because R&D is the best strategy for both players, it is the Nash equilibrium. The outcome of this game is that both firms conduct R&D. They make less profit than they would if they could collude to achieve the cooperative outcome of no R&D.

This steady ongoing R&D activity brings infrequent launches of new products that account for the swings in market shares. When Unilever launched liquids, its market share jumped. When Procter & Gamble launched biological agents, it gained share. And when Unilever introduced detergent tablets in 1997, its share increased again.

Table 1

Unilever Versus Procter & Gamble: An R&D Game

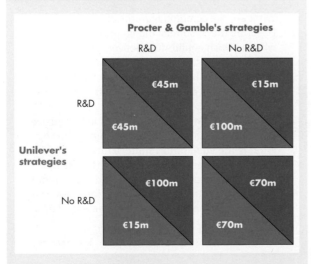

The Disappearing Invisible Hand

All the games that we've studied are versions of the prisoners' dilemma. The essence of that game lies in the structure of its payoffs. The worst possible outcome for each player arises from cooperating when the other player cheats. The best possible outcome, for each player to cooperate, is not a Nash equilibrium because it is in neither player's *self-interest* to cooperate if the other one cooperates. It is this failure to achieve the best outcome for both players – the best social outcome if the two players are the entire economy – that led John Nash to claim (as he was portrayed as doing in the movie *A Beautiful Mind*) that he had challenged Adam Smith's idea that we are always guided, as if by an invisible hand, to promote the social interest when we are pursuing our self-interest.

A Game of Chicken

The Nash equilibrium for the prisoners' dilemma is called a **dominant strategy equilibrium**, which is an equilibrium in which the best strategy of each player is to cheat (deny) *regardless of the strategy of the other player*. Not all games have such an equilibrium, and one that doesn't is a game called "chicken".

In a graphic, if disturbing, version of this game, two cars race towards each other. The first driver to swerve and avoid a crash is "chicken". The payoffs are a big loss for both if no one "chickens", zero for the chicken and a gain for the player who hangs tough.

If player 1 chickens, player 2's best strategy is to hang tough. And if player 1 hangs tough, player 2's best strategy is to chicken.

For an economic form of this game, suppose the R&D that creates a new nappy technology results in information that cannot be kept secret or patented, so both firms benefit from the R&D of either firm. The chicken in this case is the firm that does the R&D.

Table 13.3 illustrates a payoff matrix for an R&D game of chicken between Kimberly-Clark and Procter & Gamble. Each firm has two strategies: do the R&D (and "chicken") or don't do the R&D (and hang tough).

If neither "chickens", there is no R&D and each firm makes zero additional profit. If each firm conducts R&D – each "chickens" – each firm makes £5 million (the profit from the new technology minus the cost of the research). If one of the firms does the R&D, the payoffs are £1 million for the chicken and £10 million for the one who hangs tough.

Confronted with the payoff matrix in Table 13.3, the two firms calculate their best strategies. Kimberly-Clark is better off doing R&D if Procter & Gamble does not undertake it. Procter & Gamble is better off doing R&D if Kimberly-Clark doesn't do it. There are two equilibrium outcomes: one firm does the R&D, but we can't predict which firm it will be. The game of chicken has no dominant strategy and no unique Nash equilibrium.

You can see that it isn't a Nash equilibrium if no firm does the R&D because one firm would then be better off doing it. And you can see that it isn't a Nash equilibrium if both firms do the R&D because then one firm would be better off not doing it.

The firms could toss a coin or use some other random device to make a decision in this game. In some circumstances, such a strategy – called a mixed strategy – is actually better for both firms than choosing any of the strategies we've considered.

Table 13.3

An R&D Game of Chicken

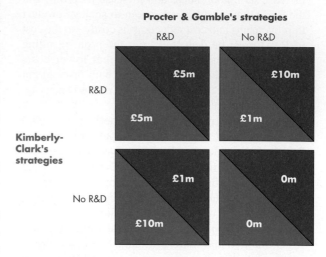

If both firms undertake R&D, their payoffs are those shown in the top left square. If neither firm undertakes R&D, their payoffs are in the bottom right square. When one firm undertakes R&D and the other one does not, their payoffs are in the top right and bottom left squares. The red triangle shows Procter & Gamble's payoff, and the blue triangle shows Kimberly-Clark's. The Nash equilibrium for this R&D game of chicken is for only one firm to undertake R&D. We cannot tell which firm will do the R&D and which will not.

Review Quiz

1   What are the common features of all games?
2   Describe the prisoners' dilemma game and explain why the Nash equilibrium delivers a bad outcome for both players.
3   Why does a collusive agreement to restrict output and raise price create a game like the prisoners' dilemma?
4   What creates an incentive for firms in a collusive agreement to cheat and increase production?
5   What is the equilibrium strategy for each firm in a duopolists' dilemma and why do the firms not succeed in colluding to raise the price and profits?
6   Describe two structures of payoffs for an R&D game and contrast the prisoners' dilemma and chicken game.

Repeated Games and Sequential Games

The games that we've studied are played just once. In contrast, many real-world games are played repeatedly. This feature of games turns out to enable real-world duopolists to cooperate, collude, and make a monopoly profit.

Another feature of the game that we've studied is that the players move simultaneously. But in many real-world situations, one player moves first and then the other moves – the play is sequential rather than simultaneous. This feature of real-world games creates a large number of possible outcomes.

We're now going to examine these two aspects of strategic decision making.

A Repeated Duopoly Game

If two firms play a game repeatedly, one firm has the opportunity to penalize the other for previous "bad" behaviour. If Gear cheats this week, perhaps Trick will cheat next week. Before Gear cheats this week, won't it consider the possibility that Trick will cheat next week? What is the equilibrium of this game?

Actually, there is more than one possibility. One is the Nash equilibrium that we have just analyzed. Both players cheat, and each makes zero economic profit forever. In such a situation, it will never pay one of the players to start complying unilaterally because to do so would result in a loss for that player and a profit for the other. But a **cooperative equilibrium** in which the players make and share the monopoly profit is possible.

A cooperative equilibrium might occur if cheating is punished. There are two extremes of punishment. The smallest penalty is called "tit for tat". A *tit-for-tat strategy* is one in which a player cooperates in the current period if the other player cooperated in the previous period but cheats in the current period if the other player cheated in the previous period. The most severe form of punishment is called a *trigger strategy*. A *trigger strategy* is one in which a player cooperates if the other player cooperates but plays the Nash equilibrium strategy forever thereafter if the other player cheats.

In the duopoly game between Gear and Trick, a tit-for-tat strategy keeps both players cooperating and making monopoly profits. Let's see why with an example.

Table 13.4 shows the economic profit that Trick and Gear will make over a number of periods under two alternative sequences of events: colluding and cheating with a tit-for-tat response by the other firm.

If both firms stick to the collusive agreement in period 1, each makes an economic profit of £2 million. Suppose that Trick contemplates cheating in period 1. The cheating produces a quick £4.5 million economic profit and inflicts a £1 million economic loss on Gear. But a cheat in period 1 produces a response from Gear in period 2. If Trick wants to get back into a profit-making situation, it must return to the agreement in period 2 even though it knows that Gear will punish it for cheating in period 1. So in period 2, Gear punishes Trick and Trick cooperates. Gear now makes an economic profit of £4.5 million, and Trick incurs an economic loss of £1 million. Adding up the profits over two periods of play, Trick would have made more profit by cooperating – £4 million compared with £3.5 million.

What is true for Trick is also true for Gear. Because each firm makes a larger profit by sticking with the collusive agreement, both firms do so and the monopoly price, quantity, and profit prevail.

In reality, whether a cartel works like a one-play game or a repeated game depends primarily on the number

Table 13.4

Cheating with Punishment

Period of play	Collude Trick's profit (millions of pounds)	Gear's profit	Cheat with tit-for-tat Trick's profit (millions of pounds)	Gear's profit
1	2	2	4.5	–1.0
2	2	2	–1.0	4.5
3	2	2	2.0	2.0
4	.	.	.	.

If duopolists repeatedly collude, each makes an economic profit of £2 million per period of play. If one player cheats in period 1, the other player plays a tit-for-tat strategy and cheats in period 2. The profit from cheating can be made for only one period and must be paid for in the next period by incurring a loss. Over two periods of play, the best that a duopolist can achieve by cheating is an economic profit of £3.5 million, compared to an economic profit of £4 million by colluding.

of players and the ease of detecting and punishing cheating. The larger the number of players, the harder it is to maintain a cartel.

Games and Price Wars

A repeated duopoly game can help us understand real-world behaviour and, in particular, price wars. Some price wars can be interpreted as the implementation of a tit-for-tat strategy. But the game is a bit more complicated than the one we've looked at because the players are uncertain about the demand for the product.

Playing a tit-for-tat strategy, firms have an incentive to stick to the monopoly price. But fluctuations in demand lead to fluctuations in the monopoly price, and sometimes, when the price changes, it might seem to one of the firms that the price has fallen because the other has cheated. In this case, a price war will break out. The price war will end only when each firm is satisfied that the other is ready to cooperate again. There will be cycles of price wars and the restoration of collusive agreements. Fluctuations in the world price of oil might be interpreted in this way.

Some price wars arise from the entry of a small number of firms into an industry that had previously been a monopoly. Although the industry has a small number of firms, the firms are in a prisoners' dilemma and they cannot impose effective penalties for price cutting.

A Computer Chip Price War

The prices of computer chips during 1995 and 1996 can be explained by the game you've just examined. Until 1995, the market for chips for IBM-compatible computers was dominated Intel Corporation. Intel was able to make maximum economic profit by producing the quantity of chips at which marginal cost equalled marginal revenue. The price of Intel's chips was set to ensure that the quantity demanded equalled the quantity produced. Then in 1995 and 1996, with the entry of a small number of new firms, the industry became an oligopoly. If the firms had maintained Intel's price and shared the market, together they could have made economic profits equal to Intel's profit. But the firms were in a prisoners' dilemma. So prices fell toward the competitive level.

Let's now study a sequential game. There are many such games, and the one we'll examine is among the simplest. It has an interesting implication and it will give you the flavour of this type of game.

The sequential game that we'll study is an entry game in a contestable market.

A Sequential Entry Game in a Contestable Market

If two firms play a sequential game, one firm makes a decision at the first stage of the game and the other makes a decision at the second stage.

We're going to study a sequential game in a **contestable market** – a market in which firms can enter and leave so easily that firms in the market face competition from *potential* entrants. Examples of contestable markets are routes served by airlines and by barge companies that operate on Europe's major waterways.

These markets are contestable because firms could enter if an opportunity for economic profit arose and could exit with no penalty if the opportunity for economic profit disappeared.

If the five-firm concentration ratio (p. 190) is used to determine the degree of competition, a contestable market appears to be uncompetitive. But a contestable market can behave as if it were perfectly competitive. To see why, let's look at an entry game for a contestable air route.

A Contestable Air Route

Agile Air is the only firm operating on a particular route. Demand and cost conditions are such that there is room for only one airline to operate. Wanabe, Inc. is another airline that could offer services on the route.

We describe the structure of a sequential game by using a *game tree* like that in Figure 13.15. At the first stage, Agile Air must set a price. Once the price is set and advertised, Agile can't change it. That is, once set, Agile's price is fixed and Agile can't react to Wanabe's entry decision. Agile can set its price at either the monopoly level or the competitive level.

At the second stage, Wanabe must decide whether to enter or to stay out. Customers have no loyalty (there are no frequent flyer programmes) and they buy from the lowest-price firm. So if Wanabe enters, it sets a price just below Agile's and takes all the business.

Figure 13.15 shows the payoffs from the various decisions (Agile's in the red triangles and Wanabe's in the blue triangles).

To decide on its price, Agile's CEO reasons as follows. Suppose that Agile sets the monopoly price. If Wanabe enters, it earns 90 (think of all payoff numbers as thousands of pounds). If Wanabe stays out, it earns nothing. So Wanabe will enter. In this case Agile will lose 50.

Figure 13.15

Agile Versus Wanabe: A Sequential Entry Game in a Contestable Market

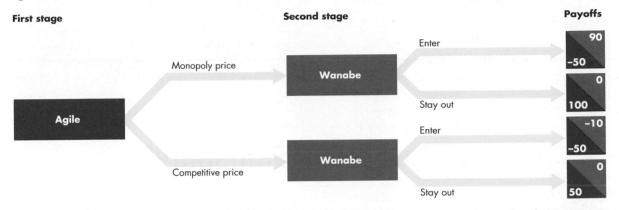

If Agile sets the monopoly price, Wanabe makes 90 (thousand pounds) by entering and earns nothing by staying out. So if Agile sets the monopoly price, Wanabe enters. If Agile sets the competitive price, Wanabe earns nothing if it stays out and incurs a loss if it enters. So if Agile sets the competitive price, Wanabe stays out.

Now suppose that Agile sets the competitive price. If Wanabe stays out, it earns nothing and if it enters, it loses 10, so Wanabe will stay out. In this case, Agile will earn 50. Agile's best strategy is to set its price at the competitive level and earn 50 (normal profit). The option of earning 100 by setting the monopoly price with Wanabe staying out is not available to Agile. If Agile sets the monopoly price, Wanabe enters, undercuts Agile, and takes all the business.

In this example, Agile sets its price at the competitive level and earns normal profit. A less costly strategy, called *limit pricing*, sets the price at the highest level that inflicts a loss on the entrant. Any loss is big enough to deter entry, so it is not always necessary to set the price as low as the competitive price. In the example of Agile and Wanabe, at the competitive price, Wanabe incurs a loss of 10 if it enters. A smaller loss would still keep Wanabe out.

This game is interesting because it points to the possibility of a monopoly behaving like a competitive industry and serving the consumer interest without regulation. But the result is not general and depends on one crucial feature of the setup of the game: at the second stage, Agile is locked into the price set at the first stage.

If Agile could change its price in the second stage, it would want to set the monopoly price if Wanabe stayed out – 100 with the monopoly price beats 50 with the competitive price. But Wanabe can figure out what Agile would do, so the price set at the first stage has no effect on Wanabe. Agile sets the monopoly price and Wanabe might either stay out or enter.

We've looked at two of the many possible repeated and sequential games, and you've seen how these types of game can provide insights into the complex forces that determine prices and profits.

Review Quiz

1   If a prisoners' dilemma game is played repeatedly, what punishment strategies might the players employ and how does playing the game repeatedly change the equilibrium?
2   If a market is contestable, how does the equilibrium differ from that of a monopoly?

So far, we've been studying the way in which consumers and firms interact in markets to determine the quantities and prices of goods and services. Your next task is to see how governments interact with households and firms. But first, take a look at the *Business Case Study* on pp. 300–301, which examines a marketing game that Tesco and Sainsbury's are playing.

Business Case Study
Marketing Game

Tesco versus Sainsbury's

The Companies

The UK supermarket sector is dominated by three companies that share 60 per cent of the market. They are Tesco, Asda and Sainsbury's. The total revenue of UK supermarkets exceeds £100 million. In 1997, Sainsbury's was the market leader and Tesco was in second position. By 2003, Tesco was market leader and Sainsbury's was in third position behind Asda. The battle for market share between Tesco and Sainsbury's was fought and won on strategic marketing decisions.

The Strategies

Two strategies have been used in the supermarket game: loyalty cards and non-food retailing. Loyalty cards aim to encourage repeat buying. Expanding into non-food retailing aims to lower the cost of shopping by providing more variety in one place.

In 1997, Tesco introduced a customer loyalty card but Sainsbury's did not follow immediately. In 2000, Tesco increased its floor space and expanded into non-food retailing. Again, Sainsbury's didn't follow.

The Payoffs

Tesco's marketing strategies aimed to increase sales and market share at the expense of its competitors. The table shows the growth of sales for the top three firms. Tesco (and Asda) achieved a more rapid increase in sales than Sainsbury's and Sainsbury's lost market share to both competitors.

Supermarket Sales
(millions of pounds)

Year	2000	2001	2002	2003
Tesco	29.6	30.3	33.6	41.6
Sainsbury's	25.9	24.4	24.5	27.4
Asda	13.2	14.5	15.3	18.1

Economic Analysis

◆ Tesco and Sainsbury's are two of the leading UK supermarkets, battling for an increasing share of the £100 billion market.

◆ Figure 1 shows the market share of these two firms along with that of Asda, the other major player, between 1997 and 2003. In 1997, Sainsbury's was the market leader with 17 per cent of the market and Tesco was in close second place with 15 per cent.

◆ The game between Tesco and Sainsbury's has involved the two strategies: loyalty cards and non-food retailing. Here we'll focus on the loyalty card strategy but the other plays out in a similar way.

◆ In 1997, Tesco introduced customer loyalty cards but Sainsbury's did not copy the strategy immediately. Tesco's sales and market share increased at the expense of Sainsbury's. Tesco's gain persisted and by 2003 it held a 27 per cent market share.

◆ Table 1 represents the competition as a strategic game. If neither supermarket introduces a loyalty card, both save marketing costs, market shares are similar and profits increase for both companies by 8 per cent (bottom-right). Marketing costs lower profits, so if both companies introduce a loyalty card, market shares are similar and economic profits are cut by 4 per cent (top-left).

◆ The Nash equilibrium is for both firms to introduce a loyalty card. But Sainsbury's did not play its Nash equilibrium strategy and lost market share. Profit increased by 12 per cent for Tesco and fell by 4 per cent for Sainsbury's (bottom-left of table).

◆ Sainsbury's paid a high price for not following Tesco's marketing lead in 1997 and by 2003, had slipped to third place behind the fast-growing Asda.

◆ Today, Tesco and Asda are locked in a similar strategic game to that played previously by Tesco and Sainsbury's. So far, Tesco and Asda have matched each others' moves.

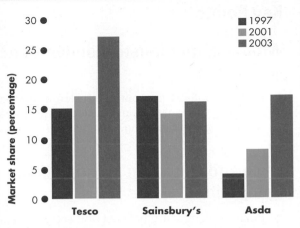

Figure 1 Market share

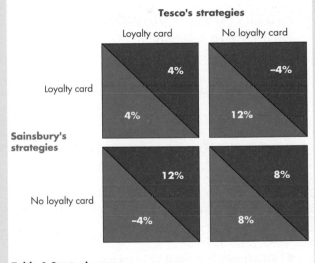

Table 1 Strategic game

Summary

Key Points

What Is Monopolistic Competition?
(pp. 274–275)

◆ In monopolistic competition, a large number of firms compete on product quality, price, marketing and branding.

Price and Output in Monopolistic Competition (pp. 276–279)

◆ Price exceeds marginal cost and entry and exit result in zero economic profit and excess capacity.

Product Development and Marketing (pp. 280–283)

◆ Advertising increases total cost but might lower *average* total cost by increasing the quantity sold.

◆ Advertising might increase or decrease the demand for a firm's product.

◆ Whether monopolistic competition is inefficient depends on the value we place on product variety.

What is Oligopoly? (pp. 284–285)

◆ Oligopoly is a market in which a small number of firms compete behind a barrier to entry.

Two Traditional Oligopoly Models
(pp. 286–287)

◆ If rivals match price cuts but do not match price hikes, they face a kinked demand curve and change price only when a large cost change occurs.

◆ If one firm dominates a market, it acts like a monopoly and the small firms take its price.

Oligopoly Games (pp. 288–296)

◆ Game theory is used to study strategic behaviour.

◆ In a prisoners' dilemma game, two prisoners acting in their self-interest harm their joint interest.

◆ An oligopoly price-fixing game is a prisoners' dilemma with a Nash equilibrium in which output and price are the same as in perfect competition.

Repeated Games and Sequential Games (pp. 297–299)

◆ In a repeated oligopoly game, punishment can produce a cooperative equilibrium in which price and output are the same as in monopoly.

◆ A small number of firms in a contestable market behave like firms in perfect competition.

Key Figures and Tables

Key Terms

Problems

*1 The figure shows the situation facing Lite and Kool plc., a European producer of running shoes.

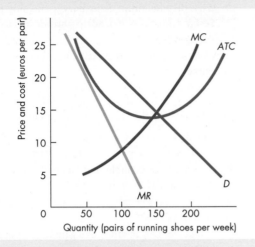

a What quantity does Lite and Kool produce?

b What does it charge?

c How much profit does Lite and Kool make?

2 The figure shows the situation facing Well Done plc., a European producer of steak sauce.

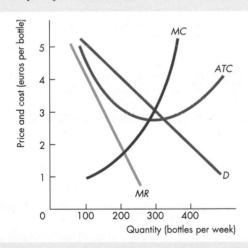

a What quantity does Well Done produce?

b What does it charge?

c How much profit does Well Done make?

*3 A firm in monopolistic competition produces running shoes. If it spends nothing on advertising, it can sell no shoes at €100 a pair and, for each €10 cut in price, the quantity of shoes it can sell increases by 25 pairs a day so that at €20 a pair, it can sell 200 pairs a day. The firm's total fixed cost is €4,000 a day. Its average variable cost and marginal cost is a constant €20 per pair. If the firm spends €3,000 a day on advertising it can double the quantity of shoes sold at each price

a If the firm doesn't advertise, what is the quantity of shoes produced and what is the price per pair?

b What is the firm's economic profit or economic loss?

c If the firm does advertise, what is the quantity of shoes produced and what is the price per pair?

d What is the firm's economic profit or economic loss?

e Will the firm advertise or not? Why?

4 The firm in problem 3 has the same demand and costs as before if it does not advertise. But it hires a new advertising agency. If the firm spends €3,000 a day on advertising with the new agency, it can double the amount that consumers are willing to pay at each quantity demanded.

a If the firm hires the new agency, what is the quantity of shoes produced and what is the price per pair?

b What is the firm's economic profit or economic loss?

c Will the firm advertise or not? Why?

d What is the firm's economic profit in the long run?

*5 A firm with a kinked demand curve experiences an increase in its fixed costs. Explain the effects on the firm's price, output and economic profit/loss.

6 A firm with a kinked demand curve experiences an increase in its variable cost. Explain the effects on the firm's price, output and economic profit/loss.

*7 An industry with one very large firm and 100 very small firms experiences an increase in the demand for its product. Use the dominant firm model to explain the effects on the price, output and economic profit of:

a The large firm.

b A typical small firm.

8 An industry with one very large firm and 100 very small firms experiences an increase in total variable cost. Use the dominant firm model to explain the effects on the price, output and economic profit of:

a The large firm.

b A typical small firm.

*9 Consider the following game. The game has two players, and each player is asked a question. The players can answer the question truthfully or they can lie. If both answer truthfully, each receives a payoff of €100. If one answers truthfully and the other lies, the liar gains at the expense of the honest player. In that event, the liar receives a payoff of €500 and the honest player gets nothing. If both lie, then each receives a payoff of €50.

a Describe this game in terms of its players, strategies and payoffs.

b Construct the payoff matrix.

c What is the equilibrium for this game?

10 Describe the game known as the prisoners' dilemma. In describing the game:

a Make up a story that motivates the game.

b Work out a payoff matrix.

c Describe how the equilibrium of the game is arrived at.

*11 Two firms, Soapy and Suddsies plc., are the only producers of soap powder. They collude and agree to share the market equally. If neither firm cheats on the agreement, each makes €1 million economic profit. If either firm cheats, the cheater increases its economic profit to €1.5 million while the firm that abides by the agreement incurs an economic loss of €0.5 million. Neither firm has any way of policing the other's actions.

a Describe the best strategy for each firm in a game that is played once.

b What is the economic profit for each firm if both cheat?

c Construct the payoff matrix of a game that is played just once.

d What is the equilibrium if the game is played once?

e If this duopoly game can be played many times, describe some of the strategies that each firm might adopt.

12 Two firms, Faster and Quicker, are the only two producers of sports cars on an island that has no contact with the outside world. The firms collude and agree to share the market equally. If neither firm cheats on the agreement, each firm makes €3 million economic profit. If either firm cheats, the cheater can increase its economic profit to €4.5 million, while the firm that abides by the agreement incurs an economic loss of €1 million. Neither firm has any way of policing the actions of the other.

a What is the economic profit for each firm if they both cheat?

b What is the payoff matrix of a game that is played just once?

c What is the best strategy for each firm in a game that is played once?

d What is the equilibrium if the game is played once?

e If this game can be played many times, what are two strategies that could be adopted?

Critical Thinking

1 Read the *Business case Study* on pp. 300–301 and answer the following questions:

a Why do you think Sainsbury's did not follow Tesco's innovative lead to introduce customer loyalty cards?

b What impact did this decision have on Sainsbury's market share?

2 Read Box 13.1 about soap market game on pp. 294–295 and then answer the following questions:

a Why do Procter & Gamble and Unilever spend huge amounts of money on washing powder products?

b Do Procter & Gamble and Unilever benefit from advertising? If so, in what way?

c Do consumers benefit from advertising and if so in what way?

d Would there be an efficiency gain from eliminating this type of advertising? Explain your answer.

e Would you expect these companies to spend as much on advertising their packaged snack or hair care products. Explain why or why not.

3 Explain the behaviour of the prices of computer chips in 1994 and 1995 by using the prisoners' dilemma game. Describe the types of strategies that individual firms in the industry have adopted.

Web Exercises

Use the links on *Parkin Interactive* to work the following exercises.

1 Obtain information about the market for vitamins.

a In what type of market are vitamins sold?

b What illegal act occurred in the vitamins market during the 1990s?

c Describe the actions of BASF and Roche as a game and set out a hypothetical payoff matrix for the game.

d Is the game played by BASF and Roche a one-shot game or a repeated game? How do you know which type of game it is?

2 Obtain information about the market for art and antiques.

a What illegal act occurred in the art and antiques auction market during the 1990s?

b Describe the game played by Sotheby's and Christie's and set out a payoff matrix.

Part 4
Government in the Economy

Constitutions, Government, Laws and Regulations

Valery Giscard d'Estaing knows better than most people the hazards of trying to define the rules by which governments play. As Chairman of the Convention that drafted the new EU constitution, he has struggled to craft a set of arrangements that will enable a large and still growing number of national European governments to work together and achieve better economic outcomes for their people.

A constitution that makes despotic and tyrannical rule impossible is relatively easy. The constitutions of Australia, France, Germany, Japan, Switzerland and the United States are all examples of political arrangements based on sound economics. They are sophisticated systems of incentives – of carrots and sticks – designed to make the government responsive to public opinion and to limit the ability of individual special interests to gain at the expense of the majority.

But no one has yet managed to design a constitution that effectively blocks the ability of special interest groups to capture the consumer and producer surpluses that result from specialization and exchange.

We face four economic problems that cannot be solved by self-interested individual action. The first is that the market economy would produce too small a quantity of those public goods and services that we must consume together, such as security and public health. The second problem is that the market economy enables monopoly to restrict production and charge too high a price. The third problem is that the market economy produces too large a quantity of those goods and services that create pollution and degrade our environment. And fourth, the market economy generates a distribution of income and wealth that most people believe is unfair because it is too unequal.

To deal with these four problems, we need a government. But as the drafters of all constitutions know, when govern-ments get involved in the economic life, people try to steer the government's actions in directions that bring personal gains at the expense of the general interest.

The three chapters in this part explain the problems with which the market has a hard time coping. Chapter 14 over-views the entire range of problems and studies one of them: competition law and the regulation of natural monopoly and oligopoly. Chapter 15 deals with externalities. It examines the costs imposed by pollution and the benefits that come from education and research, and it describes some of the ways in which externalities can be dealt with. This chapter also explains that one way of coping with externalities is to strengthen the market and "internalize" the externalities rather than to intervene in the market. Chapter 16 studies the problems created by public goods and services – items enjoyed by all but paid for directly by none – and common resources – resources owned by no one but used by all.

Chapter 14

Government Regulation and Competition Policy

After studying this chapter you will be able to:

◆ Explain why and how governments intervene to regulate monopoly and oligopoly and distinguish between the social interest and capture theories of regulation

◆ Explain how regulation affects prices, outputs, profits and the distribution of the gains from trade between consumers and producers

◆ Explain how monopoly control laws are applied in Europe

◆ Explain how public ownership affects prices, output and allocative efficiency

Social Interest or Special Interest

Why are the firms that produce our drinking water, electric power, natural gas and telephone services regulated? Why are European railways and pharmaceutical companies subject to anti-monopoly laws? Do regulations and anti-monopoly laws serve the social interest – the interest of all consumers and producers – or do they serve special interests – the interest of the regulated firms themselves? Can EU regulation make Europe's electricity and gas markets more competitive? Find out in the *Business Case Study* at the end of the chapter.

The Economic Theory of Government

The economic theory of government explains why governments exist, the economic roles of government, the economic choices they make and the consequences of those choices.

Why Governments Exist

Governments exist for three major reasons. First, they establish and maintain property rights. Second, they provide mechanisms for allocating scarce resources. Third, they implement arrangements that redistribute income and wealth.

Property rights are the fundamental foundation of the market economy. By establishing property rights and the legal system that enforces them, governments enable markets to function. In many situations, markets function well and help us to allocate our scarce resources efficiently.

But the market economy sometimes results in inefficiency – a situation called **market failure**. When market failure occurs, too many of some things and too few of some other things are produced. Choices made in the pursuit of self-interest have not served the social interest. By reallocating resources, it is possible to make some people better off while making no one worse off.

Also the market economy delivers a distribution of income and wealth that most people regard as being unfair. Equity requires some redistribution.

The Economic Roles of Government

In this chapter and in Chapters 15, 16 and 18, we're going to study the economic roles of government in five areas. They are:

◆ Monopoly and oligopoly regulation

◆ Externalities regulation

◆ Provision of public goods

◆ Use of common resources

◆ Income redistribution

Monopoly and Oligopoly Regulation

Monopoly and oligopoly can prevent resources from being allocated efficiently. Every business tries to maximize profit, and when monopoly or oligopoly exists, firms try to increase profit by restricting output and keeping the price high.

For example, until a few years ago, most European national telecommunication companies had a monopoly on telephone services and the price of business and domestic telephone services was higher and the quality of service was lower than it is today.

Although some monopolies arise from *legal barriers to entry* – barriers to entry created by governments – a major activity of government is to regulate monopoly and to enforce laws that prevent cartels and other restrictions on competition.

We'll study competition law and monopoly regulations in this chapter.

Externalities Regulation

When a chemical factory (perhaps legally) dumps its waste into a river and kills the fish, it imposes a cost – called an *external cost* – on the members of a fishing club who fish downstream. When a homeowner fills her garden with spring bulbs, she generates an external benefit for all the passers-by.

External costs and external benefits are not usually taken into account by the people whose actions create them. The chemical factory does not take the fishing club's wishes into account when it decides whether to dump waste into the river. The homeowner does not take her neighbours' views into account when she decides to fill her garden with flowers. Because self-interested choices ignore or place a low weight on the wishes of others, externalities can result in the over-provision or under-provision of some goods and services. Government actions can try to overcome these sources of market failure.

We study externalities in Chapter 15.

Provision of Public Goods

Some goods and services are consumed by everyone and no one can be excluded from the benefits that arise from their provision. Examples are national defence, law and order, and sewage and waste disposal services. A national defence system can't isolate individuals and refuse to protect them. Airborne diseases from untreated sewage don't favour some people and hit others. A good or service that is consumed by everyone is called a *public good*.

The market economy fails to deliver the efficient quantity of public goods because of a *free-rider problem*. Everyone tries to free ride on everyone else because the good is available to all whether they pay for it or not. We'll provide a more thorough description of public goods and the free-rider problem in Chapter 16. We'll also study the factors that influence the scale of provision of public goods in that chapter.

Use of Common Resources

Some resources are owned by no one and used by everyone. Examples are the Pennine Way and fish in the North Sea. Every week, hundreds of boats scoop up tonnes of fish from the North Sea. The consequence is that the stocks of some species – cod is one of them – are dangerously depleted. The market economy fails to use common resources efficiently because no one has an incentive to conserve what everyone else is free to use.

We'll describe this problem more thoroughly in Chapter 16, where we'll also review some ideas for coping with the problem.

Income Redistribution

The market economy delivers an unequal distribution of income and wealth. Most people regard the market outcome as being unfair – it creates too much inequality. (We reviewed ideas about fairness in Chapter 5, pp. 108–111.)

Governments redistribute income by using income support systems and progressive income taxes. You've already seen, in Chapter 6, how taxes affect markets and create deadweight losses. We'll look at the role of taxes in redistributing income in Chapter 18 after learning how factor markets operate.

Before we begin to study these problems from which government activity arises, let's look at the arena in which governments operate: the "political marketplace".

Public Choice and the Political Marketplace

Government is a complex organization made up of many individuals, each with his or her own economic objectives. Government policy is the outcome of the choices made by these individuals. To analyze these choices, economists have developed a *public choice theory* of the political marketplace.

Figure 14.1 shows the actors in and the anatomy of the political marketplace. The actors are:

◆ Voters
◆ Firms
◆ Politicians
◆ Civil servants

Voters

Voters are the consumers of the political process. In the political marketplace, voters express their demands by voting, campaigning, lobbying and making financial contributions. Public choice theory assumes that people support policies that they believe will make them better off and oppose policies that they believe will make them worse off. They neither oppose nor support (they are

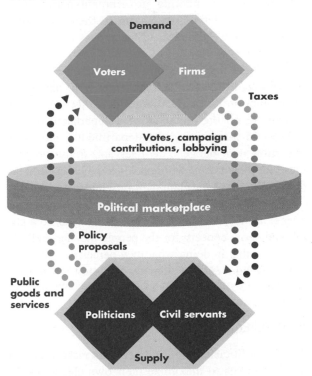

Figure 14.1

The Political Marketplace

Voters express their demands for policies with their votes, and voters and firms express demands by making campaign contributions and lobbying. Politicians propose policies that appeal to a majority of voters and to firms whose campaign contributions they seek. Civil servants try to maximize the budgets of their departments. A political equilibrium is a situation in which no group can improve its position by making a different choice.

indifferent towards) policies that they believe have no effect on them. Voters' *perceptions* of policy outcomes are what guide their choices.

Politicians

Politicians are the elected administrators and legislators at all levels of government. Economic models of public choice assume that the objective of a politician is to get elected and to remain in office. Votes, to a politician, are like profits to a firm. To get enough votes, politicians form political parties to develop policy proposals, which they expect will appeal to a majority of voters.

Civil Servants

Civil servants are the people who work in government departments: some are selected by senior civil servants and others are selected by politicians. They are responsible for enacting government policy. Civil servants are assumed to maximize their own utility, by maximizing the budget of the agency or department in which they work.

The bigger the budget of a department, the greater is the prestige of its chief and the larger is the opportunity for promotion for people farther down the bureaucratic ladder. So all the members of a department have an interest in maximizing the department's budget. To maximize their budgets, civil servants devise programmes that they expect will appeal to politicians and they help politicians to explain their programmes to voters.

The economic model of the political market place does not imply that civil servants don't try to do a good job and show concern for the people they serve. Rather it implies that in doing what they perceive to be a good job, they take care of their own interests as much as possible.

Political Equilibrium

Voters, politicians and civil servants make their economic choices to maximize their own objectives. But each group is constrained by the preferences of the other groups and by what is technologically feasible. The outcome of the choices of voters, politicians and civil servants is the **political equilibrium**, which is a situation in which the choices of voters, politicians and civil servants are all compatible and in which no group can improve its position by making a different choice.

The rest of this chapter looks at the public choices that we make in regulating monopoly and oligopoly.

Monopoly and Oligopoly Regulation

The economic theory of monopoly and oligopoly regulation is an application of the broader theory of public choice theory. In the political market place, there is a demand for regulation, a supply of regulation and the political equilibrium amount and type of regulation.

The Demand for Regulation

People and firms demand the regulation that makes them better off and they express this demand through political activity: voting, lobbying, and making campaign contributions. Consumers demand regulation that increases consumer surplus and firms demand regulation that increases producer surplus. The greater the number of people or firms that can benefit from a regulation, the greater is the demand for it. But numbers alone do not always translate into an effective political force because it is costly to organize for political action. A more powerful influence on the demand for regulation is the gain per person or per firm that results from it.

The Supply of Regulation

Politicians supply the regulations that increase their campaign funds and that get them enough votes to achieve and maintain office. If a regulation benefits a large number of people and by enough for it to be noticed, that regulation appeals to politicians and is supplied. If a regulation benefits a large number of people but by too small an amount per person to be noticed, that regulation does not appeal to politicians and is not supplied. If a regulation benefits a *small* number of people but by a large amount per person, that regulation also appeals to politicians because it helps them to get campaign funds from those who gain.

Equilibrium Regulation

In political equilibrium, regulation might be in the social interest or in the self-interest of producers. The **social interest theory** of regulation is that politicians supply the regulation that achieves an efficient allocation of resources.

According to this view, the political process works well, relentlessly seeks out deadweight loss and introduces regulations that eliminate it. For example, where monopoly practices exist, the political process introduces price regulations to ensure that outputs increase and prices fall to their competitive levels.

The **capture theory** of regulation is that regulation is in the self-interest of producers. The key idea of capture theory is that the cost of political organization is high and the political process will supply only those regulations that increase the surplus of small, easily identified groups that have low organization costs. Such regulations are supplied even if they impose costs on others, provided that those costs are spread thinly and widely enough that they do not decrease votes.

People who stand from the centre to the left of the political spectrum (socialists and social democrats) tend to believe that regulation is in the social interest and that when it is not, sufficient goodwill and hard work can ensure that it is changed. People who stand from the centre to the right of the political spectrum (conservatives and libertarians) tend to believe that most regulation is in the self-interest of producers and that no regulation is better for the social interest than the regulation that we have.

The predictions of the capture theory are less clear cut than those of the social interest theory. According to capture theory, regulations benefit cohesive interest groups by large and visible amounts and impose small costs on everyone else. Because these costs per person are small, no one feels it is worthwhile to incur the cost of organizing an interest group to avoid them.

Alternative Intervention Methods

Governments intervene in monopoly and oligopoly markets to influence prices, quantities produced and the distribution of the gains from economic activity – the distribution of consumer surplus and producer surplus – in three main ways:

◆ Regulation
◆ Monopoly control laws
◆ Pubic ownership

Regulation

Regulation consists of rules administered by a government agency to influence economic activity by determining prices, product standards and types and the conditions under which new firms may enter an industry. Price and entry condition regulations are typically applied at the industry level and product regulation is more often applied at the firm level. **Deregulation** is the process of removing previously imposed regulation.

Monopoly Control Laws

Monopoly control laws are laws that regulate and prohibit monopoly and monopolistic practices. These laws cover practices that the creation of barriers to entry, collusion over prices, restriction of consumer choice and mergers to enhance market power.

Public Ownership

Public ownership is the ownership (and sometimes operation) of a firm or industry by a government or a government controlled agency. Public ownership was popular during the 1940s and 1950s when much of what was called the "commanding heights" of industry was placed in public ownership in much of Europe.

Today, the opposite process is more common – **privatization** – the sale of a government-owned enterprise to private owners. Most European governments are in the process of selling firms and industries to private owners.

To understand why governments intervene in markets and to examine the impact of this intervention, we need to identify the gains and losses that these actions create. These gains and losses are the consumer and producer surpluses associated with different levels of output and prices. We'll start with the economic theory of regulation.

Review Quiz

1 What are the three main reasons why governments exist?
2 Describe five areas in which government choices influence economic life.
3 Describe the political marketplace. Who are the demanders and who are the suppliers? How do the demanders "pay" the suppliers?
4 How do consumers and producers express their demand for economic regulation? What are their objectives? What are the costs of expressing a demand for regulation?
5 When politicians and civil servants supply regulation, what are they trying to achieve? Do politicians and civil servants have the same objectives? Explain your answer.
6 What is a political equilibrium? When does the political equilibrium achieve economic efficiency?

We're now going to look at the regulation of monopoly and oligopoly today and see how they try to serve the social interest but might serve self-interest.

Regulating and Deregulating Monopoly and Oligopoly

The past 20 years have seen dramatic changes in the way in which European economies are regulated by government. We're going to examine some of these changes. To begin we'll look at what is regulated and also at the scope of regulation. Then we'll turn to the regulatory process itself and examine how regulators control prices and other aspects of market behaviour. Finally, we'll tackle the more difficult and controversial questions: Why do we regulate some things but not others? Who benefits from this regulation – consumers or producers?

The Scope of Regulation

Table 14.1 shows some of the main regulatory agencies that operate in the United Kingdom. At the top are institutions created by agreement among countries. These institutions regulate firms indirectly by restricting government protection of domestic industry. The World Trade Organization oversees and monitors international trade agreements and aims to avoid trade wars among its 124 participating countries. Below this is the European Commission, responsible for ensuring its member states comply with EU-level regulation of industries and markets, based on its legal treaties. EU directives control many aspects of business activity both directly and indirectly. For example, EU directives determine standards of production and marketing, the pricing of agricultural products, employment practices, health and safety, industrial pollution, market power, collusive practices and mergers.

Firms are also subject to regulation by agencies at the national level and local level. Some regulatory agencies cover all industries, for example, the Health and Safety Executive and the Environment Agency. Other agencies regulate specific activities within specific industries, such as the Office of Gas and Electricity Markets and the Office of Water Services. Local and regional governments also regulate firms, for example in relation to waste management and building planning regulations.

Table 14.1

Regulatory Agencies

Level	Agency	Activity
Global	World Trade Organization	Monitors and enforces rules on international trade
European Union	European Commission	Monitors and enforces EU rules on member states
UK central government	Departments/Ministries	Monitor and control public provision of health, agriculture, industry, education, and so on
	Monopolies and Mergers Commission	Investigates monopoly and recommends action
	Health and Safety Executive	Investigates breaches of health and safety law
	Environment Agency	Monitors and enforces environmental law
	Finance and Securities Agency	Regulates financial investment firms and other financial agencies
	Bank of England	Regulates banks and building societies
	Civil Aviation Authority	Monitors and regulates airlines, airports and air-traffic control
	Office of Gas and Electricity Markets	Monitors and regulates gas and electricity markets
	Office of Water Services	Monitors and regulates water companies
UK local and regional government	Departments	Control and monitor planning, waste management, and so on

The Regulatory Process

Although regulatory agencies vary in size and scope and in the detailed aspects of economic life that they control, there are certain features common to all agencies.

First, the civil servants, who are the key decision makers in the main regulatory agencies, are appointed by central and local governments. In addition, all agencies have a permanent bureaucracy made up of experts in the industry being regulated and often recruited from the regulated firms. Agencies are allocated financial resources by government to cover the costs of their operations.

Second, each agency adopts a set of practices or operating rules for controlling prices and other aspects of economic or professional performance. Regulation usually involves limiting the power of firms to determine one or more of the following: the price of output, the quantities sold, the quality of the product, or the markets served. The regulatory agency grants certification to a company to serve a particular market with a particular line of products, and it determines the level and structure of prices that will be charged. In some cases, the agency also determines the scale and quality of output permitted.

To analyze the way in which industry-specific regulation works, we will focus on the regulation of natural monopoly and cartels. Let's begin with natural monopoly.

Natural Monopoly

Natural monopoly was defined in Chapter 12 (p. 252) as an industry in which one firm can supply the entire market at a lower price than can two or more firms. As a consequence, a natural monopoly experiences economies of scale, no matter how high an output rate it achieves. Examples of natural monopolies include telephone and cable TV companies, local electricity and water companies, and rail infrastructure. It is much more expensive to have two or more competing sets of wires, pipes and railway lines serving every area than it is to have a single set.

Let's consider the example of UK cable TV shown in Figure 14.2. The demand curve for cable TV is *D*. The cable TV company's marginal cost curve is *MC*. That marginal cost curve is (assumed to be) horizontal at £10 per household per month – that is, the cost of providing each additional household with a month of cable programming is £10. The cable TV company has a heavy investment in satellite receiving dishes, cables

Figure 14.2

Natural Monopoly: Marginal Cost Pricing

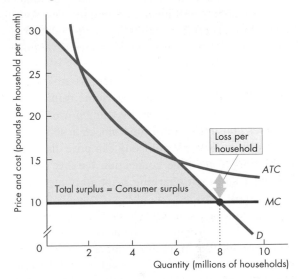

A cable TV company is a natural monopoly and it faces the demand curve *D*. The firm's marginal cost is constant at £10 per household per month, as shown by the curve *MC*. Fixed costs are large and the average total cost curve, which includes average fixed cost, is shown as *ATC*. A marginal cost pricing rule sets the price at £10 a month, with 8 million households being served. Consumer surplus is shown by the green area. The firm incurs a loss on each household, indicated by the red arrow. To remain in business, the cable TV company must either price discriminate or receive a subsidy.

and control equipment and so has high fixed costs. These fixed costs are part of the company's average total cost curve, shown as *ATC*. The average total cost curve slopes downward because as the number of households served increases, the fixed cost is spread over a larger number of households.

Regulating Monopoly in the Social Interest

According to the social interest theory, the cable TV company will be regulated to maximize **total surplus** – the sum of consumer surplus and producer surplus. Regulation will be in the social interest if the price equals marginal cost. In Figure 14.2, this outcome occurs if the price is regulated at £10 per household per month and 8 million households are served. This regulation is called a marginal cost pricing rule. A **marginal cost pricing rule** sets price equal to marginal cost. It maximizes total surplus in the regulated industry.

Figure 14.2 shows the average total cost curve is always falling for a natural monopoly, so marginal cost is below average total cost. If the regulator sets price equal to marginal cost, price is below average total cost and the monopoly will incur an economic loss. Average total cost minus price is the loss per unit produced. This cable TV company will go out of business eventually if it cannot cover its costs.

One way to avoid this problem is to allow the monopoly to price discriminate. Some natural monopolies can price discriminate by using a two-part tariff that gives consumers a bill for connection and a bill for units used. A cable TV company can price discriminate by charging a one-time connection fee that covers its fixed cost and then charging a monthly fee equal to marginal cost.

But a natural monopoly cannot always price discriminate. It is difficult to operate a two-part tariff on a rail network. When a natural monopoly cannot price discriminate, it can cover its total cost and follow a marginal cost pricing rule only if it receives a subsidy from the government. In this case, the government raises the revenue for the subsidy by taxing some other

activity. But we saw in Chapter 6, taxes themselves generate deadweight loss. The deadweight loss resulting from additional taxes must be offset against the allocative efficiency gained by forcing the natural monopoly to adopt a marginal cost pricing rule.

The regulatory agency could also avoid the problem if it used an average cost pricing rule. An **average cost pricing rule** sets the price equal to average total cost. Figure 14.3 shows the average cost pricing solution. The cable TV company charges £15 a month and serves 6 million households. A deadweight loss arises, shown by the grey triangle in the figure, but consumer surplus is less than under marginal cost pricing regulation.

The major obstacle to implementing these pricing rules is that the regulator knows less than the regulated firm about the cost of production. The regulator does not directly observe the firm's costs and doesn't know how hard the firm is trying to minimize cost. For this reason, regulators use one of two practical rules:

◆ Rate of return regulation

◆ Price cap regulation

Let's see whether these rules deliver an outcome that is in the social interest or the private interest.

Figure 14.3   ◆

Natural Monopoly: Average Cost Pricing

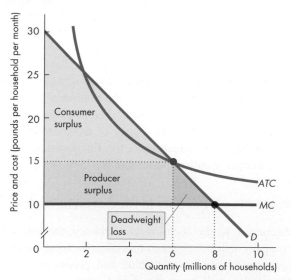

Average cost pricing sets price equal to average total cost. The cable TV company charges £15 a month and serves 6 million households. In this situation the firm breaks even – average total cost equals price. Deadweight loss, shown by the grey triangle, is generated. Consumer surplus is reduced to the green area.

Rate of Return Regulation

Under **rate of return regulation**, a regulated firm must justify its price by showing that its percentage return on its capital is in line with what is normal in competitive industries. If the regulator could observe the firm's costs and also know that the firm had minimized total cost, it would accept only a price proposal from the firm that was equivalent to average cost pricing.

The outcome would be like that in Figure 14.3. But the managers of a regulated firm have an incentive to inflate costs and raise price. One way to inflate the firm's costs is to spend on inputs that are not strictly required for the production of the good. On-the-job luxury in the form of sumptuous office suites, big cars, Premier League football tickets (disguised as public relations expenses), company jets, lavish international travel and entertainment are all ways in which managers can inflate costs.

If the cable TV operator in our example manages to persuade the regulator that its true average total cost curve is that shown as *ATC (inflated)* in Figure 14.4, then the regulator, applying the normal rate of return principle, will accept the firm's proposed price of £20 a month. In this example, the price and quantity will be the same as those under unregulated monopoly.

Figure 14.4

Natural Monopoly: Inflating Costs

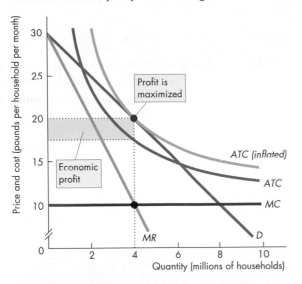

If the cable TV company is able to inflate its costs to *ATC (inflated)* and persuade the regulator that these are genuine minimum costs of production, rate of return regulation results in a price of £20 a month – the profit-maximizing price. To the extent that the producer can inflate costs above average total cost, the price rises, output decreases and deadweight loss increases. The profit is captured by the managers, not the shareholders (owners) of the firm.

Figure 14.5

Price Cap Regulation

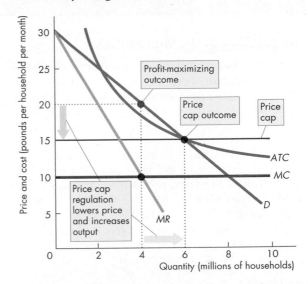

If the cable TV company is subject to a price cap regulation, the price cap limits the price that may be charged. At all quantities less than 6 million, the firm incurs a loss. At all quantities greater than 6 million, the firm also incurs a loss. Only at an output of 6 million can the firm break even and earn a normal rate of return. The firm has an incentive to keep costs as low as possible and to produce the quantity demanded at the price cap.

Price Cap Regulation

For the reason we've just examined, rate of return regulation is increasingly being replaced by price cap regulation. A **price cap regulation** is a price ceiling – a rule that specifies the highest price the firm is permitted to set. This type of regulation gives a firm an incentive to operate efficiently and keep costs under control. Price cap regulation has become common for the electricity and telecommunications industries and is replacing rate of return regulation.

To see how a price cap works, let's suppose that the cable TV company in our example is subject to this type of regulation. Figure 14.5 shows what happens.

Without regulation, the firm maximizes profit by serving 4 million households and charging a price of £20 a month. If a price cap is set at £15 a month, the firm is permitted to sell any quantity it chooses at that price or at a lower price. At 4 million households, the firm now incurs an economic loss. It can decrease the loss by *increasing* output to 6 million households.

But at more than 6 million households, the firm incurs losses. So the profit-maximizing quantity is 6 million households – the same as with average cost pricing.

Notice that a price cap lowers the price and increases output. This outcome is in sharp contrast to the effect of a price ceiling in a competitive market – see Chapter 6 (pp. 118–121). The reason is that in an unregulated monopoly, the equilibrium output is less than the competitive equilibrium output and the price cap regulation replicates the conditions of a competitive market.

Social Interest or Capture?

We cannot be sure whether the regulator gets captured or whether regulation works to serve the social interest. But we can examine some of the implications of each theory. One test of the two theories is based on rates of return before and after privatization, which you can take a look at in Box 14.1 on the next page. After

Box 14.1
Regulation in Action

Regulation of UK Monopolies

The social interest theory predicts that because regulation is efficient, there will be no change in the rate of return in an industry if it is privatized and deregulated. In contrast, capture theory predicts that privatization and deregulation will decrease the rate of return by forcing the industry to compete rather than be protected from competition by the regulator.

Table 1 compares the rates of return of British Gas, British Telecom, and British Airways before and after privatization. By 1992 they were all privatized, but British Gas and British Telecom were subject to price regulation. After privatization, the rates of return of both British Gas and British Telecom increased while that of British Airways decreased.

These changes in rates of return deliver an ambiguous verdict but point toward the conclusion that regulation has to some degree been in the social

interest. Price caps were used, and this type of regulation is more likely to operate in the social interest than target rates of return.

Table 1

Regulated UK Monopolies

	British Gas	British Telecom	British Airways
Rate of return before privatization (1979)	5%	14%	14%
Rate of return after privatization (1992)	7%	21%	12%
Productivity increase (1979–1992)	71%	180%	11%

Source: D. Parker, 'Privatization and Business Restructuring: Change and Continuity in the Privatized Industries', *The Review of Policy Issues*, 1994, 1 (2).

---

privatization, most government monopolies become industries with an oligopoly structure. Oligopoly is also regulated. So now we turn to regulation in oligopoly – the regulation of cartels.

Cartel Regulation

A *cartel* is a collusive agreement among a number of firms designed to restrict output and achieve a higher profit for the cartel's members. Cartels are illegal in the United Kingdom, the European Union and most other countries. International cartels can sometimes operate legally, such as the international cartel of oil producers known as OPEC (the Organization of Petroleum Exporting Countries).

Cartels can operate in oligopolistic industries if several firms agree to act like a monopoly to reap monopoly profit. So how is oligopoly regulated? Does regulation prevent monopoly practices or does it encourage those practices?

According to social interest theory, oligopoly is regulated to ensure a competitive outcome. Consider, for example, the market for road haulage of carrots from East Anglia to Yorkshire in the United Kingdom, illustrated in Figure 14.6. The demand curve for trips is *D*. The industry marginal cost curve – and the competitive supply curve – is *MC*. Social interest regulation will regulate the price of a trip at £20 and there will be 300 trips a week.

Figure 14.6

Collusive Oligopoly

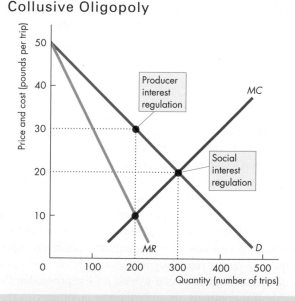

Ten firms transport carrots from East Anglia to Yorkshire. The demand curve is *D* and the industry marginal cost curve is *MC*. Under competition, the *MC* curve is the industry supply curve. If the industry is competitive, the price of a trip will be £20 and 300 trips will be made each week. The firms will demand regulation that restricts entry and limits output to 200 trips a week. This regulation raises the price to £30 a trip and results in each firm making maximum profit – as if it were a monopoly.

According to the capture theory, regulation of an oligopoly in the producer interest will maximize profit. In Figure 14.6, profit is maximized when the quantity produced is 200 trips a week (marginal cost, *MC*, equals marginal revenue, *MR*) and the price is set at £30 a trip. The regulator can achieve this outcome by placing an output limit on each firm in the industry. If there are 10 haulage companies, an output limit of 20 trips per company ensures that the total number of trips in a week is 200. Penalties can be imposed to ensure that no single producer exceeds its output limit.

All the firms in the industry would support this type of output regulation because it helps to prevent cheating and to maintain a monopoly outcome. Each firm knows that without the regulation, every firm has an incentive to increase output. (For each firm, price exceeds marginal cost so a greater output brings a larger profit.) So each firm wants a method of preventing output from increasing above the industry profit-maximizing level and the regulation achieves this. With this type of cartel regulation, the regulator enables a cartel to operate legally and in its own best interest.

What does cartel regulation do in practice? Although there is disagreement about the matter, the consensus view is that regulation tends to favour the producer. Regulating taxis (by local authorities) and airlines (by the Civil Aviation Authority) are specific examples in which profits of producers increased as a result of regulation.

Making Predictions

Most industries have a few producers and many consumers. In these cases, public choice theory predicts that regulation will protect producer interests because a small number of people stand to gain a large amount and so they will be fairly easy to organize as a cohesive lobby. Under such circumstances, politicians will be rewarded with political contributions rather than votes. But there are situations in which the consumer interest is sufficiently strong and well-organized and thus able to prevail. There are also cases in which the balance switches from producer to consumer, as seen in the deregulation process that began in the late 1970s.

Deregulation raises some hard questions for economists seeking to understand and make predictions about regulation. Why were so many sectors deregulated across Europe in the 1980 and 1990s? If producers gained from regulation and if the producer lobby was strong enough to achieve regulation, what happened in the 1980s to change the equilibrium to one in which the consumer interest prevailed? We do not have a complete answer to this question at present. But regulation had become so costly to consumers, and the potential benefits to consumers from deregulation so great, that the cost of organizing the consumer voice became a price worth paying.

One factor that increased the cost of regulation borne by consumers in the airline sector, eventually bringing deregulation, was the large increase in energy prices in the 1970s. These price hikes made route regulation extremely costly and changed the balance in favour of consumers in the political equilibrium. Another factor was technological change, which affected the airline sector and many other sectors such as finance and telecommunications as well. Computerized accounts, automatic tellers, satellite communications and mobile phones enabled smaller producers to offer low-cost services, which forced deregulation.

In the case of EU airlines, most member states allowed only two airlines to operate each route and regulated fares and traffic in such a way that airlines could not compete. These restrictions were lifted in 1997 to encourage competition. Now, airlines from one European country can launch domestic services in another. Ryanair and EasyJet operate dramatic cut-price services, which make economic profits when the big flag-ship carriers incur economic losses. How is it done? These airlines use direct telephone sales technology, pick the cheapest airports to serve, cut red tape and adopt a 'no frills' service approach. Customers get what they pay for, but low quality is accepted on short haul flights. If rapid technological change continues, we could expect to see more consumer-oriented regulation in future.

Review Quiz

1 Why does a natural monopoly need to be regulated?
2 What pricing rule enables a natural monopoly to operate in the social interest?
3 Why is a marginal cost pricing rule difficult to implement?
4 What pricing rule is typically used to regulate a natural monopoly and what problems does it create?
5 Why is it necessary to regulate a cartel and how could cartels be regulated in the social interest?

We can now turn to monopoly control laws.

Monopoly Control Laws

Monopoly control laws give powers to courts and to
government agencies to investigate monopolies and
ensure competitive practices. Like regulation, monopoly
control law can operate in the social interest, maximizing total surplus, or in the private interest, maximizing
the surpluses of particular interest groups such as
producers.

European monopoly control laws cover three aspects
of firm activity:

◆ Monopoly
◆ Mergers
◆ Restrictive practices

Monopoly

Monopoly control law began in the United Kingdom in
1948 when the Monopolies and Restrictive Practices
Act created an agency called the Monopolies and
Restrictive Practices Commission. Its role was to
investigate the activities of reported monopolies to
assess whether they act against the social interest.

The interpretation of social interest is still a political
rather than a judicial matter. Several subsequent Acts of
Parliament have adapted the law, and monopoly is now
defined as a firm with a 25 per cent share of a local
or national market. UK monopoly investigations are
triggered by the existence of monopoly, defined as a
market structure, and the UK government has the power
to break up monopolies or impose restrictions on
activities of UK firms.

Box 14.2
European Regulation in Action

Monopoly, Restrictive Practice and Mergers

Table 1 shows some examples of EU investigations and
actions concerning monopoly, restrictive practices and
mergers. It is rare for monopolies to be fined but
Microsoft, an exception, was fined for illegal monopolistic practices. More commonly, the EU requires
changes in monopolistic practice. For example, in 2001
the Italian government-owned rail monopoly was
ordered to allow German rail operators to run trains on
their tracks. Fines for companies operating in oligopoly
markets who abuse market power through collusive
agreements are more common. The record fine for cartel
activity stands at €478 million for the EU-wide price
agreement on plasterboard. Merger investigations are
common, 212 in 2003, but it is rare for mergers to be
blocked. The European Union usually negotiates a
settlement with companies after raising objections.

Table 1

Examples of EU Regulation Cases

Regulation	Date	Fine or action	Main companies	Countries	Product
Monopoly	2004	€500 million	Microsoft	United States	Software
	2001	Required to remove restrictive practice	Ferrovie dello Stato	Italy	State-owned railway
	2001	Objections raised	BskyB	United Kingdom	Premier League Football TV
Restrictive practices	2003	€138.4 million	Hoechst and others	Germany, Japan	Food preservative
	2002	€478 million	Lafarge, BPB, Knauf	France, Germany United Kingdom	Plasterboard
	2002	€149 million	Nintendo	United States	Computer games
	2001	€462 million	Hoffman La Roche, BASF and others	Switzerland Germany	Vitamins
Mergers	2004	Merger agreed	Aventis and Sanofi-Synthelabo	France Germany	Pharmaceuticals
	2004	Merger objections	Sony and BMG	Japan, Germany	Music

Source: Europea.eu.int/enterprise.

EU monopoly control laws define monopoly in a different way. Monopoly investigations, under EU law, are triggered by indications of abuse of power by a firm in a dominant position. Market power is illegal if it affects trade among member states by creating unfair trading conditions. Abuse includes imposing unfair price and purchase conditions, limiting production, applying different conditions in different countries and imposing restrictive contracts. The European Commission has wide-ranging powers to enforce its decisions with fines for the offending firms operating in the European Union.

Examples of recent cases are shown in Box 14.2: European Regulation in Action.

Mergers

A **merger** occurs when the assets of two or more firms are combined to form a single, new firm. In 1965, the UK Monopolies Commission became the Monopolies and Mergers Commission, which extended its powers to investigate any merger likely to create a monopoly or might lead to abuse of market power and would not be in "the social interest". According to the 1973 Fair Trading Act, "social interest" means any practice that maintains and promotes effective competition, which suggests that consumer surplus is given a higher weighting than producer surplus in evaluating merger proposals.

In contrast, the EU Merger Control Regulation of 1990 allows the European Commission to investigate mergers between firms that have dominant positions in European markets. The Commission only allows proposed mergers if any strengthening of a dominant position does not lead to a reduction in competition.

The number of mergers investigated by the European Union increased from just 12 in 1990 to a peak of 345 in 2000. Despite the large number of investigations, few EU mergers are ever blocked. Box 14.2: European Regulation in Action gives some recent examples of EU merger investigations.

Restrictive Practices

The UK 1973 Fair Trading Act defines **restrictive practices** as agreements between firms on prices, terms and conditions of sale and market share. Such practices are illegal unless the parties can prove to the Restrictive Practices Court that the agreements are in the social interest. The law sets out eight possible defences. Firms must prove at least one defence and that on balance, the benefits of the agreement to consumers outweigh the costs.

A restrictive practice under EU law is any agreement that affects trade among member states and reduces competition. Firms can but don't have to register their agreements. Restrictive practices are illegal unless they improve production and distribution or technical progress and do not reduce competition.

EU law is concerned with the *effect* of the agreement, while UK law is focused on its *form*. Focusing on the effect reduces the cost of investigation and increases the chance that anti-competitive agreements are identified. The European Commission has greater powers of enforcement than the UK Restrictive Practices Court and can impose fines of up to 10 per cent of a firm's worldwide annual turnover.

The European Union regularly fines companies operating in oligopoly markets for restrictive practices that raise prices. Box 14.2 European Regulation in Action gives some recent examples. In some cases, the restrictive practice is a simple cartel agreement; in others it is a distribution practice as in the case of Nintendo, which increased prices.

Social or Special Interest?

It appears that monopoly control law has evolved to protect the social interest and to restrain profit-seeking and the anti-competitive actions of producers. Although the interests of the producer can influence the way in which the national law is interpreted and applied, the overall thrust of EU law is towards achieving allocative efficiency and serving the social interest. The European Commission is now more proactive and forceful in its application of monopoly control laws in a drive to increase competition in the European single market.

Review Quiz

1   What main aspects of firms' activities do monopoly control laws cover?
2   What are the main differences between the UK and EU monopoly control laws?

Let's now look at the impact of public ownership and privatization.

Public Ownership and Privatization

The main type of public ownership is in the form of nationalized companies. Nationalization involves the 100 per cent ownership of companies by governments, either through compulsory purchase or share purchase. Most European governments followed a continuous programme of nationalization and purchase after the Second World War. But during the 1980s and 1990s many nationalized companies throughout Europe were privatized. Governments also sold off the part-shares that they held in many private companies.

The UK case is an interesting example because it is extreme. The range of UK public companies in 1979 included the main utilities, transport systems, key industries such as coal and steel, and many firms from relatively competitive industries. Between 1979 and 1999, nearly all of the publicly owned companies were sold. So why were so many UK firms brought into public ownership and then sold again? Let's look at an economic model of public ownership to find out.

Efficient Public Ownership

Public ownership is another way in which government can influence the behaviour of a natural monopoly. Suppose that an industry under public ownership is operated in a manner that results in economic efficiency – maximization of total surplus.

Let's consider the example of a railway that offers a freight service. Figure 14.7(a) illustrates the demand for freight service and the railway's costs. The demand curve is *D*. The marginal cost curve, *MC*, is horizontal at £2 a tonne. The railway has large fixed costs that feature in the company's average total cost curve, *ATC*. The average total cost curve slopes downward because as the number of tonnes of freight carried increases, the fixed costs are spread over a larger number of tonnes. To be efficient, a publicly owned railway adopts the rule:

Produce an output such that price equals marginal cost.

Figure 14.7

Public Ownership

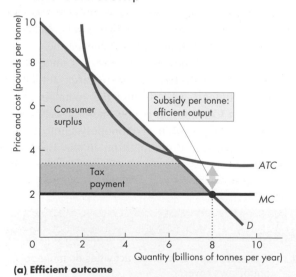

(a) Efficient outcome

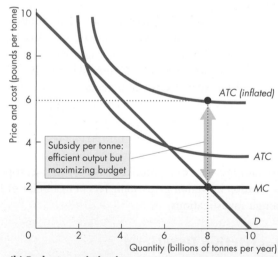

(b) Budget maximization

Part (a) shows a railway in public ownership that produces the output at which price equals marginal cost. Its output is 8 billion tonnes a year and the price is £2 a tonne. The railway receives a subsidy that enables it to cover its total cost and that cost is the minimum possible cost of providing the efficient quantity.

Part (b) shows what happens if the managers of the railway under public ownership pursue their own interest and maximize their budget by inflating costs. Average total cost now increases to *ATC* (*inflated*). If the railway is required to keep price equal to marginal cost, the quantity produced is efficient, but the managers divert the consumer surplus to themselves.

In this example, that output level is 8 billion tonnes of freight a year at a price – and marginal cost – of £2 a tonne. To be able to operate in this manner, a publicly owned railway has to be subsidized; and the subsidy on each unit of output must equal the difference between average total cost and marginal cost. So the subsidy must be collected through taxation rather than through the price of the good or service. If the government taxes each household by a fixed amount, the consumer surplus will shrink to the green triangle shown Figure 14.7(a), but consumer surplus will be at its maximum.

The situation depicted in Figure 14.7(a) achieves an efficient outcome because consumer surplus is maximized. But this outcome might not be in the interests of the managers of a publicly owned railway. The behaviour of managers in companies under public ownership can be predicted using the economic theory of bureaucracy. We'll look at this now.

A Bureaucratic Model of Public Ownership

The basic assumption of the economic theory of bureaucracy is that civil servants aim to maximize their departmental budgets. The equivalent assumption for managers in a company under public ownership is that they seek to maximize the company budget. The effect on the company under public ownership depends on the pricing constraints under which the managers operate. We will consider two alternative cases:

◆ Budget maximization with marginal cost pricing
◆ Budget maximization at a zero price

Budget Maximization with Marginal Cost Pricing

If managers maximize the budget but follow the marginal cost pricing rule, the outcome is efficient. In our case, the railway moves 8 billion tonnes of freight a year at a cost of £2 a tonne, as Figure 14.7(b) illustrates. But the railway managers do not minimize production costs because the internal control mechanisms that ensure efficiency in a private company are weak. So the railway pads its costs and becomes inefficient. The managers hire more workers than are required to move the efficient quantity and average total costs rise to *ATC* (*inflated*).

How far can the railway inflate its costs? The answer is the maximum that railway freight customers can be made to pay through taxation. That maximum is the total consumer surplus – the area beneath the demand curve and above the marginal cost curve. From Figure 14.7(b), this amount is £32 billion (1/2 × £8 billion × £8). This amount will be the upper limit that any government – in a political democracy – can extract from the taxpaying consumers of the output of the publicly owned company. Spread over 8 billion tonnes, £32 billion gives a subsidy of £4 a tonne, the amount shown in the figure.

Budget Maximization at Zero Price

What happens if a government department provides its goods or services free? There are many examples all over Europe of health and education services provided or funded by government. As you saw in Chapter 15, governments provide goods and services in kind such as health and education, as a method of redistributing income. The goods and services are provided free at the point of demand to everyone, but they are not free. The government uses general taxation to pay for them. If the poor pay less tax on average and demand similar quantities of these goods and services, then redistribution occurs from the rich to the poor.

Of course, it is improbable that a publicly owned railway would be able to persuade politicians and taxpayers that its activities should be expanded to the point of providing its freight service free. But to maintain the comparison with Figure 14.7, we'll continue with the example of the railway.

If freight transport is provided free, consumers maximize their surplus by demanding the largest quantity, which is 10 billion tonnes a year. Their maximum consumer surplus is the whole area under the demand curve *D* in Figure 14.7(b). If the price is zero, the transport department increases output to the point at which the price that consumers are willing to pay for the last unit produced is zero and output increases to 10 billion tonnes a year.

Providing freight transport services is not without costs. If the price of freight transport is zero, a dead-weight loss is created. Figure 14.7(b) shows that at an output of 10 billion tonnes, the marginal cost of production, £2 a tonne, is higher than the marginal benefit or willingness to pay, £0 per tonne. To provide the service free, the government will have to subsidize the railway.

There may also be additional bureaucratic inefficiency. The railway might inflate its costs so that its budget increases. The subsidy would increase with the inflated costs. The consumer surplus is the maximum subsidy that taxpayers are willing to pay.

Box 14.3
Budget Maximization in Action

UK Health Operation Costs

The National Health Service (NHS) in the United Kingdom provides healthcare free at the point of demand. But the cost of providing the service has been rising faster than the prices of goods and service on the average. The rising real cost of NHS provision is partly due to the rising cost of providing operations. Economic theory predicts that providing the NHS free at the point of demand may lead to budget maximization and the inflating of costs.

If some hospitals are inflating costs, we would expect to see large variation in the prices of similar operations across different hospitals. The figures in Table 1 show some of the range of prices charged by NHS hospitals for three common operations in 2003. Prices can vary by up to 70 per cent for the same operation.

Table 1

NHS Average Costs

Operation	Price range in 2003 (pounds)	Fixed price in 2005 (pounds)
Heart bypass	2,540 to 6,911	8,080
Hip replacement	4,111 to 5,319	5,568
Cataracts	763 to 1,164	786

Source: http://news.bbc.co.uk/1/hi/health/3461585.stm, Department of Health.

To reduce the burden of rising costs on the taxpayer, the UK government successfully imposed strict budget controls. By 2001, UK healthcare spending per person was below the EU average and below that in some European private healthcare systems. But in 2001, the UK government announced plans to increased real expenditure on the NHS after public opinion favoured tax increases for this purpose.

With increasing real expenditure, the government feared that further increases in costs would bring a higher tax burden. In 2004, to fight cost increases, the government announced that all hospitals would charge the same fixed price for similar operations from 2005. Table 1 shows the fixed prices that will be introduced. The government argues that efficient hospitals with prices today below the fixed prices will gain while inefficient hospitals with prices today above the fixed prices will be forced to cut costs.

Privatization

The reasons for privatization are derived from the predictions of our bureaucracy model. According to this model, firms in public ownership tend to overproduce and to inflate costs, although realistically not to the extent suggested in Figure 14.7(b). As the subsidy increases, consumer interest shifts towards supporting privatization as a means of increasing efficiency.

Many publicly owned companies are not natural monopolies. Privatization exposes these companies to the forces of market competition, which forces average total costs down, reduces prices, and removes the need for subsidies and taxes.

Some economists have questioned the benefits of privatizing natural monopolies. Natural monopolies must be regulated even if they are privately owned. As you have seen, the capture theory of regulation means that regulation of private monopoly might not be more effective than public ownership. But as privatized monopolies have the extra monitoring of shareholders, they might be less likely to inflate costs.

Pressure from shareholders to cut costs might work in the social interest but it might work against other aspects of social interest such as safety and equity. This concern has been raised in debate about the provision of rail and health services in the United Kingdom. The UK government took the provision of the rail infrastructure out of the private sector and placed it under the control of a non-profit making organization in 2001, after a series of rail disasters highlighted safety concerns.

Other economists argue that competition following the privatization of natural monopolies can also be achieved by separating the service part of the business from the ownership of physical networks. For example, the retail supply of gas and electricity, telecommunications and rail services are retail activities and can be highly competitive. The real natural monopoly lies in the network of pipes, lines and track.

Box 14.4 Privatization in Action gives an example of the problems that can arise when a government privatizes a natural monopoly. This box assesses the success of the privatization of gas and electricity markets in the United Kingdom and the impact of privatization on EU competitiveness. The European Union is pressing countries such as France and Italy to privatize and deregulate monopolies to promote competition. You can read more about the reasons for privatizing Europe's gas and electricity markets in the *Business Case Study* on pp. 324–325.

Box 14.4
Privatization in Action

The UK Gas Market

British Gas was the state-owned monopoly in the market for gas until 1997 when it was privatized. The company is now called Centrica. Ownership of the network of pipes is held by one company, privatization promoted competition between gas suppliers. But by 2001, British Gas still supplied 70 per cent of domestic gas customers.

In 2001, 57,000 households a week switched gas suppliers. Centrica's prices have fallen and since privatization, Centrica's average domestic bill has fallen 23 per cent from £397.69 to £301.67. Over the same period, the average bill across all gas suppliers has fallen 17 per cent despite the fact that wholesale prices more than doubled. The National Audit Office estimated that customers saved £1 billion between 1997 and 2001.

The UK Electricity Market

The UK electricity network and supply was privatized in 1997 in stages. There is now competition between suppliers for electricity. In 2001, 139,000 customers each week switched electricity suppliers. The average electricity bill has fallen has fallen 22 per cent.

The National Audit Office estimates that electricity consumers saved £750 million since privatization, but they could have saved more. The 35 per cent cuts in electricity generation prices have not been passed on to customers.

Competition in service has driven prices down, but regulation of the natural monopoly of the network and generation has been less successful.

Comparing Competition Across Europe

There is a strong association in Europe between the degree of competition and the extent of state ownership of natural monopolies.

Table 1 shows how members of the enlarged European Union rank on a competitiveness scale calculated by the World Economic Fund. The countries with high levels of privatization and deregulation are those at the top of the table. The countries with low levels of privatization and deregulation are at the bottom. The United Kingdom ranks fourth.

In a broader world ranking, the United States is more competitive than Europe with the exceptions of Finland, Denmark and Sweden that rank above the United States.

Table 1

European Competitiveness

Country	Competitiveness rank
Finland	1
Denmark	2
Sweden	3
United Kingdom	4
Netherlands	5
Germany	6
France	7
Austria	8
Belgium	9
Ireland	10
Estonia	11
Spain	12
Slovenia	13
Italy	14
Latvia	15
Portugal	16
Malta	17
Czech Republic	18
Hungary	19
Lithuania	20
Greece	21
Slovak Republic	22
Poland	23
Romania	24

Source: http://news.bbc.co.uk/go/pr/fr/-/1/hi/business/3661517.stm, *Global Competitiveness Report*, World Economic Forum.

Review Quiz

1 How might a company under public ownership operate efficiently?
2 What are the effects of budget maximization by managers in publicly owned companies?
3 How can governments fight the padding of costs?
4 Why might governments want to privatize a publicly owned company?
5 When might privatization be successful and why?

In the next chapter, we will see how governments regulate markets in which externalities arise.

Business Case Study
Regulation and Competition

Europe's Electricity and Gas Market

The European Industries

The electricity and gas industries in the European Union have traditionally been state-owned monopolies. During the 1990s, some countries, such as Sweden and the United Kingdom privatized the whole of these industries and introduced price regulation to limit market power. Other countries, such as Greece and France, have maintained state ownership and allowed only limited competition.

Progress on EU Deregulation

Despite the EU directives to increase competition, only about 75 per cent of the EU gas market and about 66 per cent of the electricity market is open to competition. The bar chart shows that electricity markets in the United Kingdom, Sweden, Finland and Germany are highly competitive markets while those in France, Greece and Ireland are the least competitive.[1]

The Impact of Limited Competition

When gas and electricity industries are state owned, they are not subject to the same costs of borrowing as are privatized companies. The state can subsidize the cost of capital. Such subsidization can help state-owned monopolies such as

Electricité de France to buy up other companies, including some of those privatized in the United Kingdom. So privatized gas and electricity companies in the European Union are not competing on the same terms as those protected by state ownership and regulation.

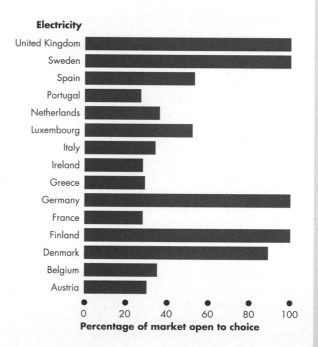

[1] The Guardian, 11 May 2001, "Hain plays national champion", D Gow and M Milner.

Economic Analysis

◆ Before privatization, the UK electricity market (and the gas market) was a monopoly market.

◆ Figure 1 shows this market. The demand curve for domestic electricity is D and the marginal revenue curve is MR. The marginal cost curve is MC.

◆ The UK monopoly maximizes profit by setting $MR = MC$ and supplying quantity Q_M at price P_M. The UK consumer surplus is the green area and the deadweight loss is the grey area.

◆ After privatization, the UK domestic electricity market is deregulated to remove barriers to entry. The market becomes competitive.

◆ Figure 2 shows the effect of deregulation if the market becomes perfectly competitive. The marginal cost curve, MC, becomes the supply curve. Market forces lower the price from P_M to P_C and the quantity increases from Q_M to Q_C. Consumer surplus increases and the deadweight loss is eliminated.

◆ One of the new entrants into the UK market is the French state monopoly, (Electricité de France). In France, this firm acts as a monopoly with price P_F and the quantity Q_F in Figure 3.

◆ Without access to the UK market, the French producer generates a deadweight loss similar to that in Figure 1.

◆ Figure 3 shows the impact on Electricité de France when it has access to the UK market but is subject to a price cap in that market. The firm maximizes profit by selling in France at P_F and selling in the United Kingdom at the capped price (assumed here to be the competitive price) of P_{UK}. The French consumer surplus in unchanged, but producer surplus increases and the deadweight loss decreases.

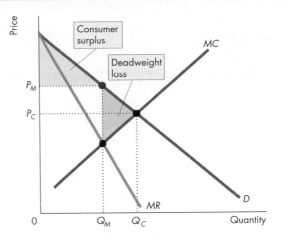

Figure 1 UK national monopoly

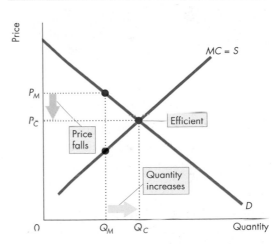

Figure 2 UK privatization and deregulation

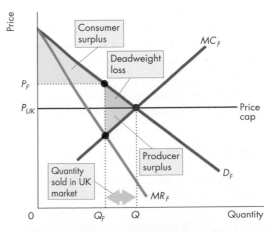

Figure 3 French monopoly sells in UK market

Summary

Key Points

Economic Theory of Government
(pp. 308–311)

◆ Governments regulate monopoly and oligopoly, regulate externalities, provide public goods, control the use of common resources and reduce income inequality.

◆ Public choice theory explains how voters, politicians and civil servants interact in a political marketplace.

◆ Consumers demand regulation that increases consumer surplus and firms demand regulation that increases producer surplus.

◆ Equilibrium regulation might be in the social interest and eliminate deadweight loss or in the self-interest of producers who capture the regulators.

Regulating and Deregulating Monopoly and Oligopoly (pp. 312–317)

◆ Regulated firms must comply with agency rules about price, product quality and output levels.

◆ Although the number of regulatory agencies continues to grow with the creation of special agencies to control privatized monopolies, there has been a tendency to deregulate many areas of the economy.

◆ Regulation in the social interest would set price equal to marginal cost. In practice, price at best equals average cost.

◆ Price cap regulation is replacing target rate of return regulation as the preferred way of regulating natural monopoly.

◆ Social interest theory predicts that deregulation occurs because the balance of power has shifted to consumers who demand lower prices.

Monopoly Control Laws (pp. 318–319)

◆ Monopoly control laws define monopoly in terms of the market structure and market power.

◆ Monopoly control laws allow governments to control monopoly and monopolistic practices.

◆ The overall thrust of European monopoly control law is directed towards serving the social interest.

Public Ownership and Privatization
(pp. 320–323)

◆ European countries have a long history of public ownership of firms, but many of these firms have now been privatized – sold to private investors.

◆ Privatization is in the consumer interest if regulatory costs fall and firms are exposed to competition but against consumer interest if social interest factors such as equity and safety are compromised.

Key Figures

Key Terms

Problems

*1 Elixir Springs, Inc., is an unregulated European natural monopoly that bottles Elixir, a unique health product with no substitutes. The total fixed cost incurred by Elixir Springs is €150,000, and its marginal cost is 10 cents a bottle. The figure illustrates the demand for Elixir.

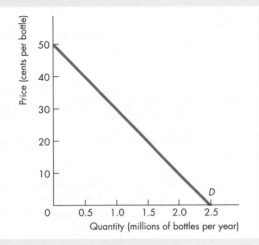

a What is the price of a bottle of Elixir?

b How many bottles does Elixir Springs sell?

c Does Elixir Springs maximize total surplus or producer surplus?

2 Cascade Springs, Inc., is a natural monopoly that bottles water from a spring high in the Alps. The total fixed cost it incurs is €120,000, and its marginal cost is 20 cents a bottle. The figure illustrates the demand for Cascade Springs bottled water.

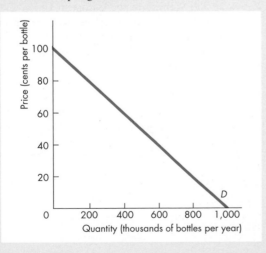

a What is the price of Cascade Springs water?

b How many bottles does Cascade Springs sell?

c Does Cascade Springs maximize total surplus or producer surplus?

*3 The EU Commission regulates Elixir Springs in problem 1 by imposing a marginal cost pricing rule.

a What is the price of a bottle of Elixir?

b How many bottles does Elixir Springs sell?

c Is the regulation in the social interest? Explain.

4 The EU Commission regulates Cascade Springs in problem 2 by imposing a marginal cost pricing rule.

a What is the price of Cascade Springs water?

b How many bottles does Cascade Springs sell?

c Is the regulation in the social interest? Explain.

5* The EU Commission regulates Elixir Springs in problem 1 by imposing an average cost pricing rule.

a What is the price of a bottle of Elixir?

b How many bottles does Elixir Springs sell?

c Is the regulation in the social interest? Explain.

6 The EU Commission regulates Cascade Springs in problem 2 by imposing an average cost pricing rule.

a What is the price of Cascade Springs water?

b How many bottles does Cascade Springs sell?

c Is the regulation in the social interest? Explain.

*7 Two airlines share an international route. The figure shows the demand curve for trips on this route and the marginal cost curve that each firm faces.

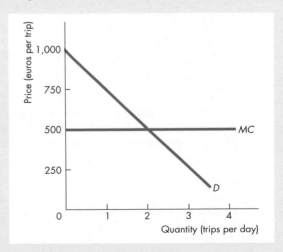

a What is the price of a trip and what is the number of trips per day if the regulation is in the social interest?

b What is the price of a trip and what is the number of trips per day if the airlines capture the regulator?

c What is the deadweight loss in part (b)?

d What do you need to know to predict whether the regulation will be in the social interest or the producer interest?

8 Two telephone companies offer local calls in an area. The figure shows the market demand curve for calls and the marginal cost curves of each firm. These firms are regulated.

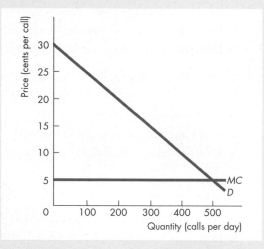

a What is the price of a call and what is the number of calls per day if the regulation is in the social interest?

b What is the price of a call and what is the number of calls per day if the telephone companies capture the regulator?

c What is the deadweight loss in part (b)?

d What do you need to know to predict whether the regulation will be in the social interest or the producer's interest?

9* Explain the main differences between regulation and monopoly law. In which situations does each apply? Provide examples of the use of each approach to regulating monopoly and oligopoly in Europe.

10 Explain the main differences between a regulated private monopoly and a monopoly in public ownership. Which do you think provides the best way of achieving an efficient use of resources and why.

Critical Thinking

1 Read the *Business Case Study* on pp. 324–325, answer the following questions.

a Why does the European Union want deregulation and liberalization in the electricity and gas markets?

d Why does the European Union want to convert the 15 national electricity markets into one integrated market?

e Would a fully integrated European electricity market still need regulation? If so, what type of regulation?

Web Exercises

Use the links on *Parkin Interactive* to work the following exercises.

1 Visit the *Financial Times* Website and read the surveys on the telecoms sector and British Telecom's local loop monopoly. Then answer the following questions.

a How can British Telecom generate economic profit from charging for calls to the Internet?

b Why has British Telecom focused on developing its dominance in domestic calls to the Internet?

c What effect would "local loop unbundling" have on competition and price for local calls.

d What effect would "local loop unbundling" have on British Telecom's profits?

e Is it better to regulate price for calls or open access to new entrants into line supply? Explain your answer.

2 Visit the Website of the European Union and find information on three cases: one of a merger, one of abuse of market power and one of cartel activity. In each case, explain why the activities are thought to reduce competition.

Figure 15.4

Property Rights Achieve an Efficient Outcome

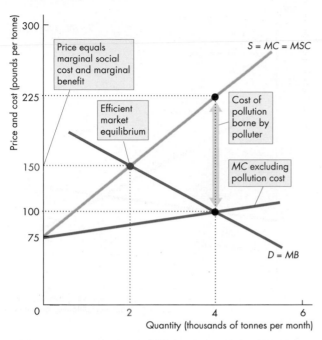

With property rights, the marginal cost curve that excludes pollution costs shows only part of the producers' marginal cost. The marginal private cost curve includes the cost of pollution, and the supply curve is $S = MC = MSC$. Market equilibrium is a price of £150 a tonne and a quantity of 2,000 tonnes a month. This equilibrium is efficient because marginal social cost equals marginal benefit.

The Coase Theorem

Does it matter how property rights are assigned? Does it matter whether the polluter or the victim of the pollution owns the resource that might be polluted? Until 1960, everyone – including economists who had thought long and hard about the problem – thought that it did matter. But in 1960, Ronald Coase had a remarkable insight, now called the Coase theorem.

The **Coase theorem** is the proposition that if property rights exist, if only a small number of parties are involved, and if transactions costs are low, then private transactions are efficient. There are no externalities because the transacting parties take all the costs and benefits into account. Furthermore, it doesn't matter who has the property rights.

Application of the Coase Theorem

In the example that we've just studied, the factories own the river and the homes. Suppose that instead, the residents own their homes and the river. Now the factories must pay a fee to the homeowners for the right to dump their waste. The greater the quantity of waste dumped into the river, the more the factories must pay. So again, the factories face the opportunity cost of the pollution they create. The quantity of chemicals produced and the amount of waste dumped are the same whoever owns the homes and the river. If the factories own them, they bear the cost of pollution because they receive a lower income from home rents. And if the residents own the homes and the river, the factories bear the cost of pollution because they must pay a fee to the homeowners. In both cases, the factories bear the cost of their pollution and dump the efficient amount of waste into the river.

The Coase solution works only when transactions costs are low. **Transactions costs** are the opportunity costs of conducting a transaction. For example, when you buy a house, you incur a series of transactions costs. You might pay an estate agent to help you find the best place and a lawyer to run checks that assure you that the seller owns the property and that after you've paid for it, the ownership has been properly transferred to you.

In the example of the homes alongside a river, the transactions costs that are incurred by a small number of chemical factories and a few homeowners might be low enough to enable them to negotiate the deals that produce an efficient outcome. But in many situations, transactions costs are so high that it would be inefficient to incur them. In these situations, the Coase solution is not available.

Suppose, for example, that everyone owns the airspace above their homes up to, say, 10 miles. If someone pollutes your airspace, you can charge a fee. But to collect the fee, you must identify who is polluting your airspace and persuade them to pay you. Imagine the costs of negotiating and enforcing agreements with the more than 50 million people who live in the United Kingdom (and perhaps those that live in Europe) and the several thousand factories that emit sulphur dioxide and create acid rain that falls on your property! In this situation, we use public choices to cope with externalities. But the transactions costs that block a market solution are real costs, so attempts by the government to deal with externalities offer no easy solution. Let's look at some of these attempts.

Government Actions in the Face of External Costs

The three main methods that governments use to cope with externalities are:

◆ Taxes

◆ Emission charges

◆ Marketable permits

Taxes

The government can use taxes as an incentive for producers to cut back on pollution. Taxes used in this way are called **Pigovian taxes**, in honour of Arthur Cecil Pigou, the British economist who first worked out this method of dealing with externalities during the 1920s.

By setting the tax rate equal to the marginal external cost, firms can be made to behave in the same way as they would if they bore the cost of the externality directly. To see how government actions can change market outcomes in the face of externalities, let's return to the example of the chemical factories and the river.

Assume that the government has assessed the marginal external cost accurately and imposes a tax on the factories that exactly equals this marginal external cost. Figure 15.5 illustrates the effects of this tax.

The demand curve and marginal benefit curve, $D = MB$, and the firms' marginal private cost curve, MC, are the same as in Figure 15.3. The government sets the pollution tax equal to the marginal external cost of the pollution. We add this tax to the marginal private cost to find the market supply curve. This curve is the one labelled $S = MC + tax = MSC$. This curve is the market supply curve because it tells us the quantity of chemicals supplied at each price given the firms' marginal private cost and the tax they must pay.

The curve $S = MC + tax = MSC$ is also the marginal social cost curve because the pollution tax has been set equal to the marginal external cost.

Demand and supply now determine the market equilibrium price at £150 a tonne and the equilibrium quantity at 2,000 tonnes a month. At this scale of chemical production, the marginal social cost is £150 a tonne and the marginal benefit is £150 a tonne, so the outcome is efficient. The firms incur a marginal private cost of £88 a tonne and pay a pollution tax of £62 a tonne. The government collects tax revenue of £124,000 a month, which is shown by the purple rectangle.

Figure 15.5

A Pollution Tax

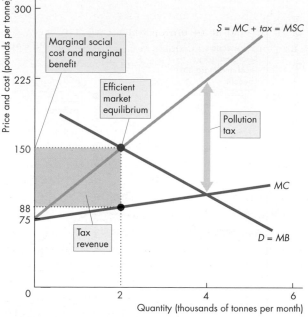

A pollution tax is imposed equal to the marginal external cost of pollution. The supply curve becomes the marginal private cost curve, *MC*, plus the tax: $S = MC + tax$. Market equilibrium is at a price of £150 a tonne and a quantity of 2,000 tonnes a month. This equilibrium is efficient because marginal social cost equals marginal benefit. The government collects a tax revenue shown by the purple rectangle.

Emission Charges

Emission charges are an alternative to a tax for confronting a polluter with the external cost of pollution. The government sets a price per unit of pollution. The more pollution a firm creates, the more it pays in emission charges. This method of dealing with pollution externalities is common in Europe where, for example, France, Germany and the Netherlands make water polluters pay a waste disposal charge. But to work out the emission charge that achieves efficiency, the government needs a lot of information about the polluting industry that, in practice, is rarely available.

The European Union introduced the idea of a tax on carbon emissions as part of its sustainable environmental policy in 1992. The issue is still pressing. Today, annual carbon emissions worldwide are a staggering

6 billion tonnes. By 2050, with current policies, that annual total is predicted to be 24 billion tonnes. If the rich countries used carbon taxes to keep emissions to their 1990 level and the developing countries remove subsidies from coal and oil, total emissions in 2050 might be held at 14 billion tonnes. So why have the European Union and other rich countries worldwide failed to introduce taxes on carbon emissions?

Marketable Permits

Instead of taxing or imposing emission charges on polluters, each potential polluter might be assigned a permitted pollution limit. Each firm knows its own costs and benefits of pollution, and making pollution limits marketable is a clever way of using this private information that is unknown to the government. The government issues each firm a permit to emit a certain amount of pollution, and firms can buy and sell these permits. Firms that have a low marginal cost of reducing pollution sell their permits, and firms that have a high marginal cost of reducing pollution buy permits. The market in permits determines the price at which firms trade permits. And firms buy or sell permits until their marginal cost of pollution equals the market price.

This method of dealing with pollution provides an even stronger incentive than do emission charges to find technologies that pollute less because the price of a permit to pollute rises as the demand for permits increases.

Review Quiz

1   What is the distinction between a negative production externality and a negative consumption externality?
2   What is the distinction between private cost and social cost?
3   How does an externality prevent a competitive market from allocating resources efficiently?
4   How can an externality be eliminated by assigning property rights? How does this method of coping with an externality work?
5   How do taxes help us to cope with externalities? At what level must a pollution tax be set if it is to induce firms to produce the efficient quantity of pollution?
6   How do emission charges and marketable pollution permits work?

Positive Externalities: Knowledge

Knowledge comes from education and research. To study the economics of knowledge, we must distinguish between private benefits and social benefits.

Private Benefits and Social Benefits

A *private benefit* is a benefit that the consumer of a good or service receives. *Marginal benefit* is the benefit from an *additional unit* of a good or service. So a **marginal private benefit** (*MB*) is the benefit from an additional unit of a good or service that the consumer of that good or service receives.

The *external benefit* from a good or service is the benefit that someone other than the consumer of the good or service receives. A **marginal external benefit** is the benefit from an additional unit of a good or service that people other than the consumer enjoy.

Marginal social benefit (*MSB*) is the marginal benefit enjoyed by society – by the consumer of a good or service (marginal private benefit) plus the marginal benefit enjoyed by others (the marginal external benefit). That is:

$$MSB = MB + \text{Marginal external benefit}$$

Figure 15.6 shows an example of the relationship between marginal private benefit, marginal external benefit and marginal social benefit. The marginal benefit curve, *MB*, describes the marginal private benefit – such as expanded job opportunities and higher incomes – enjoyed by graduates. Marginal private benefit decreases as the quantity of education increases.

But university graduates generate external benefits. On the average, they tend to be better citizens. Their crime rates are lower and they are more tolerant of the views of others. A society with a large number of graduates can support activities such as high-quality newspapers and television channels, music, theatre, and other organized social activities.

In the example in Figure 15.6, the marginal external benefit is £15,000 per student per year when 15 million students attend university. The marginal social benefit curve, *MSB*, is the sum of marginal private benefit and marginal external benefit. For example, when 15 million students a year attend university, the marginal private benefit is £10,000 per student and the marginal external

Figure 15.6

An External Benefit

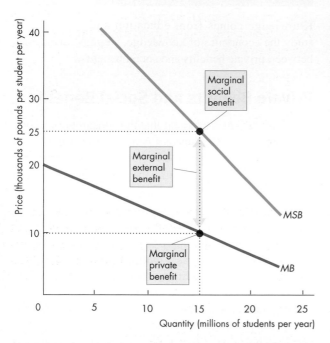

The *MB* curve shows the marginal private benefit enjoyed by the people who receive a university education. The *MSB* curve shows the sum of marginal private benefit and marginal external benefit. When 15 million students attend university, marginal private benefit is £10,000 per student, marginal external benefit is £15,000 per student and marginal social benefit is £25,000 per student.

Figure 15.7

Inefficiency with an External Benefit

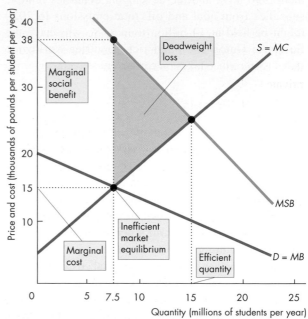

The market demand curve is the marginal private benefit curve, *D = MB*. The supply curve is the marginal cost curve, *S = MC*. Market equilibrium at a tuition fee of £15,000 a year and 7.5 million students is inefficient because marginal social benefit exceeds marginal cost. The efficient quantity is 15 million students. The grey triangle shows the deadweight loss created because too few students attend university.

benefit is £15,000 per student, so the marginal social benefit is £25,000 per student.

When people make decisions about how much education to take, they ignore its external benefits and consider only the private benefits that education brings. So if education were provided by private universities that charged full-cost tuition, we would produce too few graduates.

Figure 15.7 illustrates the underproduction if the government left education to the private market. The supply curve is the marginal cost curve of the private universities, *S = MC*. The demand curve is the marginal private benefit curve, *D = MB*. Market equilibrium occurs at a tuition fee of £15,000 per student per year and 7.5 million students per year. At this equilibrium, marginal social benefit is £38,000 per student, which exceeds marginal cost by £23,000. There are too few students in university. The efficient number is 15 million, where

marginal social benefit equals marginal cost. The grey triangle shows the deadweight loss.

Underproduction similar to that in Figure 15.7 would occur in primary school and high school if an unregulated market produced it. When children learn basic reading, writing and number skills, they receive the private benefit of increased earning power. But even these basic skills bring the external benefit of developing better citizens.

External benefits also arise from the discovery of new knowledge. When Isaac Newton worked out the formulas for calculating the rate of response of one variable to another – calculus – everyone was free to use his method. When a spreadsheet program called VisiCalc was invented, Lotus Corporation and Microsoft were free to copy the basic idea and create 123 and Excel. When the first shopping mall was built and found to be a successful way of arranging retailing, everyone was free to copy the idea, and malls spread like mushrooms.

Once someone has discovered how to do something, others can copy the basic idea. They do have to work to copy an idea, so they face an opportunity cost. But they do not usually have to pay a fee to the person who made the discovery to use it. When people make decisions, they ignore the external benefits and consider only the private benefits.

When people make decisions about the quantity of education or the amount of research to undertake, they balance the marginal private cost against the marginal private benefit. They ignore the external benefit. As a result, if we left education and research to unregulated market forces, we would get too little of these activities.

To get closer to producing the efficient quantity of a good or service that generates an external benefit, we make public choices, through governments, to modify the market outcome.

Government Actions in the Face of External Benefits

Four devices that governments can use to achieve a more efficient allocation of resources in the presence of external benefits are:

◆ Public provision
◆ Private subsidies
◆ Vouchers
◆ Patents and copyrights

Public Provision

Under **public provision**, a public authority that receives its revenue from the government produces the good or service. The education services produced by the public universities and schools are examples of public provision.

Figure 15.8

Public provision or Private Subsidy to Achieve an Efficient Outcome

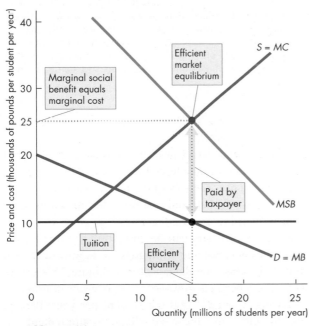

(a) Public provision

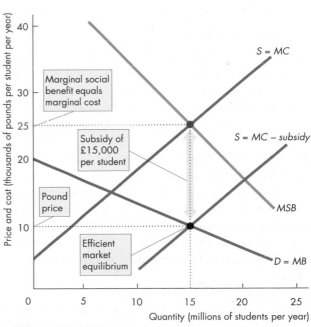

(b) Private subsidy

In part (a), marginal social benefit equals marginal cost with 15 million students attending university, the efficient quantity. Tuition is set at £10,000 per student and the taxpayers cover the other at £15,000 of marginal cost per student.

In part (b) with a subsidy of £15,000 per student, the supply curve is $S = MC - subsidy$. The equilibrium price is £10,000 and the market equilibrium is efficient with 15 million students attending university. Marginal social benefit equals marginal cost.

Figure 15.8(a) shows how public provision might overcome the underproduction that arises in Figure 15.7. Public provision cannot lower the cost of production, so marginal cost is the same as before. Marginal private benefit and marginal external benefit are also the same as before.

The efficient quantity occurs where marginal social benefit equals marginal cost. In Figure 15.8(a), this quantity is 15 million students. Tuition is set to ensure that the efficient number of students attend. That is, tuition is set at the level that equals the marginal private benefit at the efficient quantity. In Figure 15.8(a), tuition is £10,000 a year. The rest of the cost of the public university is borne by the taxpayers and, in this example, is £15,000 per student per year.

Private Subsidies

A **subsidy** is a payment that the government makes to private producers. By making the subsidy depend on the level of output, the government can induce private decision makers to consider external benefits when they make their choices.

Figure 15.8(b) shows how a subsidy to private colleges works. In the absence of a subsidy, the marginal cost curve is the market supply curve of private college education, $S = MC$. The marginal benefit is the demand curve, $D = MB$. In this example, the government provides a subsidy to universities of £15,000 per student per year. We must subtract the subsidy from the marginal cost of education to find the universities' supply curve. That curve is $S = MC - subsidy$ in the figure. The equilibrium tuition (market price) is £10,000 a year, and the equilibrium quantity is 15 million students. To educate 15 million students, universities incur a marginal cost of £25,000 a year. The marginal social benefit is also £25,000 a year. So with marginal cost equal to marginal social benefit, the subsidy has achieved an efficient outcome. The tuition and the subsidy just cover the universities' marginal cost.

Vouchers

A **voucher** is a token that the government provides to households, which they can use to buy specified goods or services. Food stamps are examples of vouchers. The vouchers (stamps) can be spent only on food and are designed to improve the diet and health of extremely poor families. School vouchers have been advocated as a means of improving the quality of education.

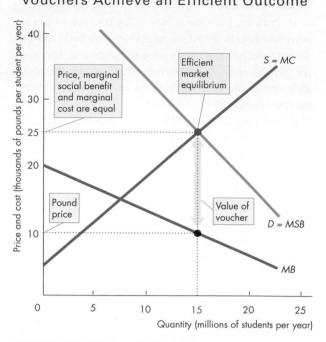

Figure 15.9

Vouchers Achieve an Efficient Outcome

With vouchers, buyers are willing to pay *MB* plus the value of the voucher, so the demand curve becomes the marginal social benefit curve, *D = MSB*. Market equilibrium is efficient with 15 million students in university because price, marginal social benefit and marginal cost are equal. The tuition consists of the pound price of £10,000 a year and the value of the voucher.

A school voucher allows parents to choose the school their children will attend and to use the voucher to pay part of the cost. The school cashes the vouchers to pay its bills. A voucher could be provided to a university student in a similar way.

Because vouchers can be spent only on a specified item, they increase the willingness to pay for that item and so increase the demand for it. Figure 15.9 shows how a voucher system works. The government provides vouchers worth £15,000 per student per year. Parents (or students) use these vouchers to supplement the pounds they pay for university education. The marginal social benefit curve becomes the demand for university education, $D = MSB$. The market equilibrium occurs at a price of £25,000 per student per year, and 15 million students attend university. Each student pays £10,000 tuition, and universities collect an additional £15,000 per student from the voucher.

If the government estimates the value of the external benefit correctly and makes the value of the voucher equal the marginal external benefit, the outcome from the voucher scheme is efficient. Marginal cost equals marginal social benefit, and the deadweight loss is eliminated.

Vouchers are similar to subsidies, but their advocates say that they are more efficient than subsidies because the consumer can monitor school performance more effectively than the government can.

Patents and Copyrights

Knowledge might be an exception to the principle of diminishing marginal benefit. Additional knowledge (about the right things) makes people more productive. And there seems to be no tendency for the additional productivity from additional knowledge to diminish.

For example, in just 15 years, advances in knowledge about microprocessors have given us a sequence of processor chips that has made our personal computers increasingly powerful. Each advance in knowledge about how to design and manufacture a processor chip has brought apparently ever larger increments in performance and productivity. Similarly, each advance in knowledge about how to design and build an airplane has brought apparently ever larger increments in performance. Orville and Wilbur Wright's 1903 Flyer was a one-seat plane that could hop a farmer's field. The Lockheed Constellation, designed in 1949, was an airplane that could fly 120 passengers from New York to London, but with two refuelling stops in Newfoundland and Ireland. Since June 2004, an Airbus 340 is transporting 200 people non-stop from Singapore to New York, a distance of 10,000 miles, in 18.5 hours. Similar examples can be found in agriculture, biogenetics, communications, engineering, entertainment and medicine.

One reason why the stock of knowledge increases without diminishing returns is the sheer number of different techniques that can in principle be tried. Paul Romer explains this fact. "Suppose that to make a finished good, 20 different parts have to be attached to a frame, one at a time. A worker could proceed in numerical order, attaching part one first, then part two . . . Or the worker could proceed in some other order, starting with part 10, then adding part seven . . . With 20 parts, . . . there are [more] different sequences . . . than the total number of seconds that have elapsed since the big bang created the universe, so we can be confident that in all activities, only a very small fraction of the possible sequences have ever been tried."[1]

Think about all the processes, all the products, and all the different bits and pieces that go into each, and you can see that we have only begun to scratch around the edges of what is possible.

Because knowledge is productive and generates external benefits, it is necessary to use public policies to ensure that those who develop new ideas have incentives to encourage an efficient level of effort. The main way of providing the right incentives uses the central idea of the Coase theorem and assigns property rights – called **intellectual property rights** – to creators. The legal device for establishing intellectual property rights is the patent or copyright. A **patent** or **copyright** is a government-sanctioned exclusive right granted to the inventor of a good, service or productive process to produce, use and sell the invention for a given number of years. A patent enables the developer of a new idea to prevent others from benefiting freely from an invention for a limited number of years.

Although patents encourage invention and innovation, they do so at an economic cost. While a patent is in place, its holder has a monopoly. And monopoly is another source of inefficiency (which is explained in Chapter 12). But without a patent, the effort to develop new goods, services or processes is diminished and the flow of new inventions is slowed. So the efficient outcome is a compromise that balances the benefits of more inventions against the cost of temporary monopoly in newly invented activities.

Review Quiz

1. What is special about knowledge that creates external benefits?
2. How might governments use public provision, private subsidies and vouchers to achieve an efficient amount of education?
3. How might governments use public provision, private subsidies, vouchers, and patents and copyrights to achieve an efficient amount of research and development?

Reading Between the Lines on pp. 342–343 looks at the debate over whether the Irish government's tax on chewing gum will reduce the negative externality that gum creates.

---

[1] Paul Romer, "Ideas and Things", in *The Future Surveyed*, supplement to *The Economist*, 11 September 1993, pp. 71–72.

Reading Between the Lines
Tax and Inefficiency:
A Sticky Tax

The Business, 3 November 2003

Ireland plans to stick a tax on chewing gum

Neil Thapar

Ireland is considering imposing the world's first tax on chewing gum, a move that could be followed by other European countries and beyond. A three-month study ordered by the Irish government into ways to curb litter will be handed to officials at the environmental department later this week, leading to speculation of a tax of up to €0.15 ($0.10) on a pack of gum. . . .

Advisors to the Irish government acknowledge that a tax would set a precedent. . . . A tax on gum – which manufacturers says aids dental hygiene and helps smokers to beat addiction – opens up a new front. It was once banned in Singapore . . . but that country's laws have been relaxed after intense pressure from the industry.

Ireland has set the pace in Europe in introducing environmental laws in recent years. It imposed a highly successful tax on plastic shopping bags three years ago, leading to a big fall in their use. . . .

The gum tax is part of a three-pronged attach to reduce litter from a variety of sources such as fast-food packaging and receipts from bank cash machines. Consultants say chewing gum causes a unique litter problem . . . "It is hard to enforce proper disposal of used gum as it is discarded surreptitiously. It sticks to the pavement and is very costly to clean as it requires highly specialised equipment. Why should the state have to pay millions?" (said a source).

The Essence of the Story

◆ The Irish government is considering introducing a tax on chewing gum to reduce the amount of litter.

◆ Chewing gum creates a major litter problem, which costs millions of euros every year to clean up.

◆ The Irish government has already put a tax on plastic carrier bags, which has reduced the quantity of bags used.

◆ The Irish government wants to use a tax because it is difficult to enforce careful disposal of chewing gum by the public.

Economic Analysis

◆ Figure 1 shows the market for chewing gum in Ireland. The demand curve for chewing gum is *D* and the supply curve for chewing gum is *S*. The newspaper article does not provide information on quantities purchased in Ireland so the quantities are hypothetical.

◆ With no tax on chewing gum, Figure 1 shows the equilibrium price of chewing gum is €0.50 per packet and the equilibrium quantity is 1 million packets a week.

◆ A tax of €0.15 a packet shifts the supply curve leftward to *S + tax* and raises the price that buyers pay to €0.57 a packet. The price received by sellers falls to €0.42 a packet and quantity decreases to 0.8 million packets a week.

◆ The tax brings in a tax revenue, the purple area, of €120,000 a week (€0.15 × 800,000 packets).

◆ The grey triangle shows the deadweight loss created by the tax. The deadweight loss represents the inefficiency of a tax in an efficient chewing gum market.

◆ Figure 2 shows why a chewing gum tax might increase efficiency. The demand for chewing gum is *D* and the manufacturer's supply of gum without no clean-up costs is *S*.

◆ The clean-up cost is an external cost, so the market outcome is inefficient.

◆ If a tax of €0.15 a packet is set equal to the marginal external cost, the supply of gum decreases to the curve labelled *S + tax*. The new supply curve is the same as the marginal social cost curve *MSC*.

◆ The price rises to €0.57 a packet and the quantity decreases to 0.8 million packets a week. This outcome is efficient because the marginal social cost equals the marginal benefit (€0.57 a packet).

◆ The tax raises the same amount of tax revenue but avoids creating a deadweight loss.

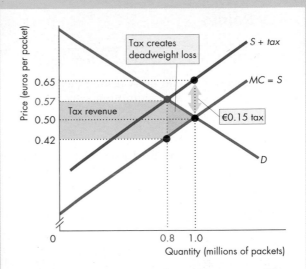

Figure 1 A chewing gum market with no externalities

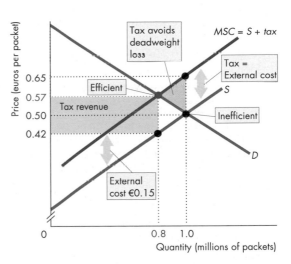

Figure 2 A chewing gum market with external cost

Summary

Key Points

Externalities in Our Lives (p. 330)

◆ An externality can arise from either a production activity or a consumption activity.

◆ A negative externality imposes an external cost.

◆ A positive externality provides an external benefit.

Negative Externalities: Pollution
(pp. 331–337)

◆ External costs are costs of production that fall on people other than the producer of a good or service. Marginal social cost equals marginal private cost plus marginal external cost.

◆ Producers take account only of marginal private cost and produce more than the efficient quantity when there is a marginal external cost.

◆ Sometimes it is possible to overcome a negative externality by assigning a property right.

◆ When property rights cannot be assigned, governments might overcome externalities by using taxes, emission charges or marketable permits.

Positive Externalities: Knowledge
(pp. 337–341)

◆ External benefits are benefits that are received by people other than the consumer of a good or service. Marginal social benefit equals marginal private benefit plus marginal external benefit.

◆ External benefits from education arise because better-educated people tend to be better citizens, commit fewer crimes and support social activities.

◆ External benefits from research arise because once someone has worked out a basic idea, others can copy it.

◆ Vouchers or subsidies to schools or the provision of public education below cost can achieve a more efficient provision of education.

◆ Patents and copyrights create intellectual property rights and an incentive to innovate. But they do so by creating a temporary monopoly, the cost of which must be balanced against the benefit of more inventive activity.

Key Figures

Figure 15.3 Inefficiency with an External Cost, 334
Figure 15.4 Property Rights Achieve an Efficient Outcome, 335
Figure 15.5 A Pollution Tax, 336
Figure 15.7 Inefficiency with an External Benefit, 338
Figure 15.8 Public Provision or Private Subsidy to Achieve an Efficient Outcome, 339
Figure 15.9 Vouchers Achieve an Efficient Outcome, 340

Key Terms

Coase theorem, 335
Copyright, 341
Externality, 330
Intellectual property rights, 341
Marginal external benefit, 337
Marginal external cost, 333
Marginal private benefit, 337
Marginal private cost, 333
Marginal social benefit, 337
Marginal social cost, 333
Negative externality, 330
Patent, 341
Pigovian taxes, 336
Positive externality, 330
Property rights, 334
Public provision, 339
Subsidy, 340
Transactions costs, 335
Voucher, 340

Problems

*1 The table provides information about costs and benefits from the production of pesticide that pollutes a lake used by a trout farmer.

Total product of pesticide (tonnes per week)	Pesticide producer's MC	Trout farmer's MC from pesticide production	Marginal benefit of pesticide
		(euros per tonne)	
0	0	0	250
1	5	33	205
2	15	67	165
3	30	100	130
4	50	133	100
5	75	167	75
6	105	200	55
7	140	233	40

a If no one owns the lake and if there is no regulation of pollution, what is the quantity of pesticide produced per week and what is the marginal cost of pollution borne by the trout farmer?

b If the trout farm owns the lake, how much pesticide is produced per week and what does the pesticide producer pay the farmer per tonne?

c If the pesticide producer owns the lake, and if a pollution-free lake rents for €1,000 a week, how much pesticide is produced per week and how much rent per week does the farmer pay the pesticide producer for the use of the lake?

d Compare the quantities of pesticide produced in parts (b) and (c) and explain the relationship between them.

2 The table at the top of the next column provides information about the costs and benefits of steel smelting that pollutes the air of a city.

a With no property rights in the city's air and no regulation of pollution, what is the quantity of steel produced per week and what is the marginal cost of pollution borne by the citizens?

b If the city owns the steel plant, how much steel is produced per week and what does the city charge the steel producer per tonne?

c If the steel firm owns the city, and if the residents of a pollution-free city are willing to pay €15,000 a week in property taxes, how much steel is produced per week and how much are the citizens willing to pay in property taxes to live in the polluted city?

d Compare the quantities of steel produced in parts (b) and (c) and explain the relationship between them.

Total product of steel (tonnes per week)	Steel producer's MC	Marginal external cost	Marginal benefit of steel
		(euros per tonne)	
0	0	0	1,200
10	100	15	1,100
20	200	25	1,000
30	300	50	900
40	400	100	800
50	500	200	700
60	600	300	600
70	700	400	500
80	800	500	400

*3 Back at the pesticide plant and trout farm described in problem 1, suppose that no one owns the lake and that the government introduces a pollution tax.

a What is the tax per tonne of pesticide produced that achieves an efficient outcome?

b Explain the connection between your answer to (a) and the answer to problem 1.

4 Back at the steel smelter and city in problem 2, suppose that the city government introduces a pollution tax.

a What is the tax per tonne of steel produced that will achieve an efficient outcome?

b Explain the connection between your answer to (a) and the answer to problem 2.

*5 Using the information provided in problem 1, suppose that no one owns the lake and that the government issues two marketable pollution permits, one to the farmer and one to the factory. Each may pollute the lake by the same amount, and the total amount of pollution is the efficient amount.

a What is the quantity of pesticide produced?

b What is the market price of a pollution permit? Who buys and who sells a permit?

c What is the connection between your answer and the answers to problems 1 and 3?

---

*Solutions to odd-numbered problems appear on *Parkin Interactive*.

6 Using the information given in problem 2, suppose that the city government issues two marketable pollution permits, one to the city government and one to the smelter. Each may pollute the air by the same amount, and the total is the efficient amount.

a How much steel is produced?

b What is the market price of a permit? Who buys and who sells a permit?

c What is the connection between your answer and the answers to problems 2 and 4?

*7 The marginal cost of educating a student is €4,000 a year and is constant. The figure shows the marginal private benefit curve.

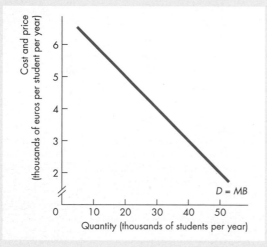

a With no government involvement and if the schools are competitive, how many students are enrolled and what is the tuition?

b The external benefit from education is €2,000 per student per year and is constant. If the government provides the efficient amount of education, how many school places does it offer and what is the tuition?

8 Online learning aids cuts the marginal cost of educating a student to €2,000 a year. The marginal private benefit is the same as that in problem 7. The external benefit from education increases to €4,000 per student per year.

a With no government involvement and if the schools are competitive, how many students are enrolled and what is the tuition?

b If the government provides the efficient amount of education, how many school places does it offer and what is the tuition?

c Compare the outcomes in problem 8 with those in problem 7. Explain the differences.

Critical Thinking

1 After you have studied *Reading Between the Lines* on pp. 342–343, answer the following questions:

a What reasons has the Irish government given for introducing a tax on chewing gum?

b What are the external costs associated with chewing gum?

c Who should pay the costs of clearing up chewing gum, the producer, the consumer or both? Explain your answer.

d Why do you think the Irish government did not ban chewing gum as it has done smoking in public places?

Web exercises

Use the links on *Parkin Interactive* to work the following exercises.

1 Obtain two viewpoints on global warming. Then answer the following questions:

a What are the benefits and costs of greenhouse gas emissions?

b Do you agree with environmentalists that greenhouse gas emissions must be cut or do you think the costs of reducing greenhouse gas emissions exceed the benefits? Explain your answer.

c If greenhouse gas emissions are to be reduced, will assigning quotas or using prices achieve the reduction?

2 Visit the Website of the UK Environment Agency and then answer the following questions:

a Describe the trend in UK emissions of carbon dioxide and sulphur dioxide over the past 20 years.

b Describe the trend in UK nitrogen oxides and volatile organic compounds over the past 20 years.

c Do these figures give any indication of the success of environmental policies to control emissions?

3 Visit the Website of the UK government's Department of Education. Read about the introduction of top-up fees for students in higher education and then answer the following questions.

a To what extent does higher education generate private benefits for graduate students?

b To what extent does higher education generate external benefits for society?

c Do you think top-up fees are efficient based on your answers to part (a) and (b)?

d Do you think top-up fees are fair based on your answers to parts (a) and (b)?

Chapter 16

Public Goods and Common Resources

After studying this chapter you will be able to:

◆ Distinguish among private goods, public goods and common resources

◆ Explain how the free-rider problem arises and how the quantity of public goods is determined

◆ Explain the problem of the commons and its possible solutions

Government: the Solution or the Problem?

Governments provide some goods and services but not all. What determines the proper scope and scale of government? Are our local, national, and EU governments too bureaucratic? Do we need as much government as we've got? Or have governments grown too big? Find out in this chapter. Also find out what we can do about the overuse of resources that no one owns and to which everyone has access. In *Reading Between the Lines* at the end of the chapter, find out about the serious overuse of tropical rain forests.

Classifying Goods and Resources

What's the difference between Scotland Yard and Brinks Security; between fish in the North Sea and fish produced by a Scottish fish farm; and between a live UB40 concert and a show on network television? Each pair differs in the extent to which people can be excluded from them and in the extent to which one person's consumption rivals the consumption of others.

A good or service or a resource is **excludable** if it is possible to prevent someone from enjoying its benefits. Brinks's security services, East Coast's fish, and a UB40's concert are examples. You must pay to consume them.

A good or service or a resource is **non-excludable** if it is impossible (or extremely costly) to prevent someone from benefiting from it. The services of Scotland Yard, fish in the North Sea and a concert on network television are examples.

A good or service or a resource is **rival** if its use by one person decreases the quantity available for someone else. A Brinks's truck can't deliver cash to two banks at the same time. A fish can be consumed only once. And one seat at a concert can hold only one person at a time. These items are rival.

A good or service or a resource is **non-rival** if its use by one person does not decrease the quantity available for someone else. The services of Scotland Yard and a concert on network television are non-rival. The arrival of one more person in a neighbourhood doesn't lower the police protection enjoyed by the community. When one more person switches on the TV, no other viewer is affected.

A Four-Fold Classification

Figure 16.1 classifies goods, services, and resources into four types.

Private Goods

A **private good** is both rival and excludable. A can of Coke and a fish on East Coast's farm are examples of private goods.

Public Goods

A **public good** is both non-rival and non-excludable. A public good can be consumed simultaneously by everyone and no one can be excluded from enjoying its benefits. National defence is the best example.

Figure 16.1

Four Classification of Goods

	Private goods	**Common resources**
Rival	Food and drink Car House	Fish in ocean Atmosphere City parks
	Natural monopolies	**Public goods**
Non-rival	Internet Cable television Bridge or tunnel	National defence The law Air traffic control
	Excludable	**Non-excludable**

A private good is one for which consumption is rival and from which consumers can be excluded. A public good is one for which consumption is non-rival and from which it is impossible to exclude a consumer. A common resource is one that is rival but non-excludable. And a natural monopoly is non-rival but excludable.

Common Resources

A **common resource** is rival and non-excludable. A unit of a common resource can be used only once, but no one can be prevented from using what is available. Ocean fish are a common resource. They are rival because a fish taken by one person isn't available for anyone else and they are non-excludable because it is difficult to prevent people from catching them.

Natural Monopolies

In a natural monopoly, economies of scale exist over the entire range of output for which there is a demand (see Chapter 12, p. 252). A special case of natural monopoly has zero marginal cost. Buyers can be excluded but are non-rival. The Internet and cable TV are examples.

Two Problems

Public goods create a **free-rider problem** – the absence of an incentive for people to pay for what they consume. *Common resources* create the **problem of the commons** – the absence of incentives to prevent the overuse and depletion of a resource.

The rest of this chapter looks more closely at the free-rider problem and the problem of the commons and examines public choice solutions to them.

Public Goods and the Free-rider Problem

Suppose that for its defence, a country must launch some surveillance satellites. The benefit provided by a satellite is the *value* of its services. The *value* of a *private* good is the maximum amount that a person is willing to pay for one more unit, which is shown by the person's demand curve. The *value* of a *public* good is the maximum amount that *all* the *people* are willing to pay for one more unit of it. To calculate the value placed on a public good, we use the concepts of total benefit and marginal benefit.

The Benefit of a Public Good

Total benefit is the euro value that a person places on a given quantity of a good. The greater the quantity of a good, the larger is a person's total benefit. *Marginal benefit* is the increase in total benefit that results from a one-unit increase in the quantity of a good.

Figure 16.2 shows the marginal benefit that arises from defence satellites for a society with only two people, Lisa and Max, whose marginal benefits are graphed as MB_L and MB_M, respectively, in parts (a) and (b) of the figure. The marginal benefit from a public good (like that from a private good) diminishes as the quantity of the good increases. For Lisa, the marginal benefit from the first satellite is €80 and that from the second is €60. By the time five satellites are deployed, Lisa's marginal benefit is zero. For Max, the marginal benefit from the first satellite is €50 and that from the second is €40. By the time five satellites are deployed, Max perceives only €10 worth of marginal benefit.

Figure 16.2(c) shows the economy's marginal benefit curve, *MB*. The economy's marginal benefit curve for a public good is different from the market demand curve for a private good. To obtain the market demand curve for a private good, we sum the quantities demanded by all individuals at each price – we sum the individual demand curves horizontally (see Chapter 7, p. 142). But to find the economy's marginal benefit curve of a public good, we sum the marginal benefits of each individual at each quantity – we sum the individual marginal benefit curves *vertically*. So the curve *MB* in part (c) is the marginal benefit curve for the economy made up of Lisa and Max. Lisa's marginal benefit from each satellite gets added to Max's marginal benefit from each satellite because they *both* consume the services of each satellite.

Figure 16.2

Benefits of a Public Good

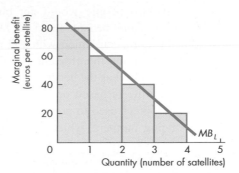

(a) Lisa's marginal benefit

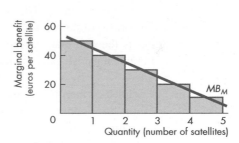

(b) Max's marginal benefit

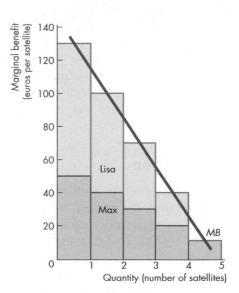

(c) Economy's marginal benefit

The marginal benefit to the economy at each quantity of the public good is the sum of the marginal benefits of all individuals. The marginal benefit curves are MB_L for Lisa, MB_M for Max and *MB* for the economy.

The Efficient Quantity of a Public Good

An economy with two people would not buy any satellites – because the total benefit would fall far short of the cost. But the European Union with 300 million people might. To determine the efficient quantity, we need to take the cost as well as the benefit into account.

The cost of a satellite is based on technology and the prices of the resources used to produce it (just like the cost of producing jumpers, which you studied in Chapter 10).

Figure 16.3 sets out the benefits and costs. The second and third columns of the table show the total and marginal benefits. The next two columns show the total and marginal costs of producing satellites. The final column shows net benefit. Total benefit, *TB*, and total cost, *TC*, are graphed in part (a) of the figure.

The efficient quantity is the one that maximizes *net benefit* – total benefit minus total cost – and occurs when two satellites are provided.

The fundamental principles of marginal analysis that you have used to explain how consumers maximize utility and how firms maximize profit can also be used to calculate the efficient scale of provision of a public good. Figure 16.3(b) shows this alternative approach. The marginal benefit curve is *MB*, and the marginal cost curve is *MC*. When marginal benefit exceeds marginal cost, net benefit increases if the quantity produced increases. When marginal cost exceeds marginal benefit, net benefit increases if the quantity produced decreases. Marginal benefit equals marginal cost with two satellites. So making marginal cost equal to marginal benefit maximizes net benefit and uses resources efficiently.

Private Provision

We have now worked out the quantity of satellites that maximizes net benefit. Would a private firm – Eurozone Protection, Inc. – deliver that quantity? It would not. To do so, it would have to collect €15 billion to cover its costs – or €50 from each of the 300 million people in the European Union. But no one would have an incentive to buy his or her "share" of the satellite system. Everyone would reason as follows. The number of satellites provided by Eurozone Protection, Inc., is not affected by my €50. But my own private consumption is greater if I free ride and do not pay my share of the cost of the satellite system. If I do not pay, I enjoy the same level of security and I can buy more private goods.

Therefore I will spend my €50 on other goods and free ride on the public good. This is the free-rider problem.

If everyone reasons the same way, Eurozone Protection has zero revenue and so provides no satellites. Because two satellites is the efficient level, private provision is inefficient.

Public Provision

Suppose there are two political parties, the Blues and the Greens, and they agree with each other on all issues except for the quantity of satellites. The Blues would like to provide 4 satellites. Figure 16.3(a) show that with 4 satellites, total cost is €50 billion, total benefit is €50 billion and net benefit is zero. The Greens would like to provide 1 satellite. Figure 16.3(a) shows that with 1 satellite, total cost is €5 billion, total benefit is €20 billion and net benefit is €15 billion.

Before deciding on their policy proposals, the two political parties do a "what-if" analysis. Each party reasons as follows. If each party offers the satellite programme it wants – the Blues 4 satellites and Greens 1 satellite – the voters will see that they will get a net benefit of €15 billion from the Greens and zero net benefit from the Blues. The Greens will win the election.

Contemplating this outcome, the Blues realize that they are too blue to get elected. They must scale back their proposal to 2 satellites. Figure 16.3(a) shows that with 2 satellites, total cost is €15 billion, total benefit is €35 billion, and net benefit is €20 billion. So if the Greens stick with 1 satellite, the Blues will win the election.

Contemplating this outcome, the Greens realize that they must match the Blues. They too propose to provide 2 satellites. If the two parties offer the same number of satellites, the voters are indifferent between the parties. They flip coins to decide their votes, and each party receives around 50 per cent of the vote.

The result of the politicians' "what-if" analysis is that each party offers 2 satellites, so regardless of who wins the election, this is the quantity of satellites installed. Figure 16.3(b) shows that this quantity is efficient. It maximizes the perceived net benefit of the voters – marginal benefit equals marginal cost.

In this example, competition in the political market-place results in the efficient provision of a public good. But for the efficient outcome to occur, voters must be well informed and evaluate the alternatives. As you will see below, they do not always have an incentive to achieve this outcome.

Figure 16.3

The Efficient Quantity of a Public Good

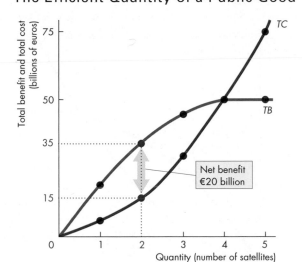

(a) Total benefit and total cost

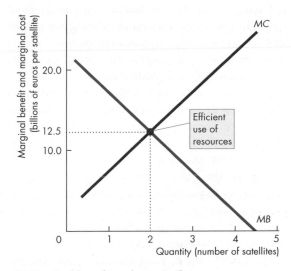

(b) Marginal benefit and marginal cost

Quantity (number of satellites)	Total benefit (billions of euros)	Marginal benefit (billions of euros per satellite)	Total cost (billions of euros)	Marginal cost (billions of euros per satellite)	Net benefit (billions of euros)
0	0		0		0
		20		5	
1	20		5		15
		15		10	
2	**35**		**15**		**20**
		10		15	
3	45		30		15
		10		20	
4	50		50		0
		5		25	
5	50		75		−25

Net benefit – the vertical distance between total benefit, *TB*, and total cost, *TC* – is maximized when 2 satellites are installed (part a) and where marginal benefit, *MB*, equals marginal cost, *MC* (part b). The Greens would like 1 satellite, and the Blues would like 4. But each party recognizes that is its only hope of being elected is to provide 2 satellites – the quantity that maximizes net benefit and so leaves no room for the other party to improve on.

The Principle of Minimum Differentiation

In the example we've just studied, both parties propose identical policies. This tendency towards identical policies is an example of the **principle of minimum differentiation**, which is the tendency for competitors to make themselves similar so as to appeal to the maximum number of clients or voters. This principle not only describes the behaviour of political parties, but it also explains why fast-food restaurants cluster in the same block and even why new models of cars have similar features. If McDonald's opens a restaurant in a new location, it is likely that Burger King will open next door to McDonald's rather than a mile down the road. If Chrysler designs a new van with a sliding door on the driver's side, most likely Ford will too.

The Role of Civil Servants

We have analyzed the behaviour of politicians but not that of the civil servants who translate the choices of the politicians into programmes and who control the day-to-day activities that deliver public goods. Let's now see how the economic choices of civil servants influence the political equilibrium.

To do so, we'll stick with the previous example. We've seen that competition between two political parties delivers the efficient quantity of satellites. But will the European Commission's civil servants cooperate and accept this outcome?

Suppose the EU Directorate General for Defence's objective is to maximize the defence budget. With two satellites being provided at minimum cost, the defence budget is €15 billion (see Figure 16.3). To increase its budget, the Directorate General might do two things. First, it might try to persuade the politicians that two satellites cost more than €15 billion. As Figure 16.4 shows, if possible, the Directorate General would like to convince Parliament that two satellites cost €35 billion – the entire benefit. Second, and pressing its position even more strongly, the Directorate General might argue for more satellites. It might press for four satellites and a budget of €50 billion. In this situation, total benefit and total cost are equal and net benefit is zero.

The Directorate General wants to maximize its budget, but won't the politicians prevent it from doing so because the Directorate General's preferred outcome costs votes? They will if voters are well informed and know what is best for them. But voters might be rationally ignorant. In this case, well-informed interest groups might enable the Directorate General to achieve its objective.

Rational Ignorance

A principle of public choice theory is that it is rational for a voter to be ignorant about an issue unless that issue has a perceptible effect on the voter's income. **Rational ignorance** is the decision *not* to acquire information because the cost of doing so exceeds the expected benefit. For example, each voter knows that he or she can make virtually no difference to the defence policy of the EU government. Each voter also knows that it would take an enormous amount of time and effort to become even moderately well informed about alternative defence technologies. So voters remain relatively uninformed about the technicalities of defence issues. (Though we are using defence policy as an

---

Figure 16.4

Bureaucratic Overprovision

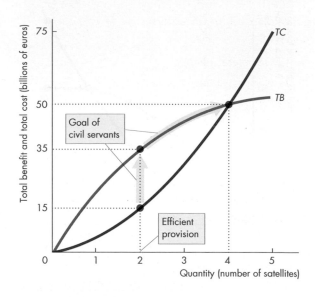

The goal of civil servants is to maximize the department's budget. A department that maximizes its budget will seek to increase its budget until its total cost equals total benefit. Then it will use its budget and expenditure. Here the EU Directorate General of Defence tries to get €35 billion to provide satellites. It would like to increase the quantity of satellites to four with a budget of €50 billion.

---

example, the same applies to all aspects of government economic activity.)

All voters are consumers of national defence. But not all voters are producers of national defence. Only a small number are in this latter category. Voters who own or work for firms that produce satellites have a direct personal interest in defence because it affects their incomes. These voters have an incentive to become well informed about defence issues and to operate a political lobby aimed at furthering their own interests. In collaboration with the defence bureaucracy, these voters exert a larger influence than do the relatively uninformed voters who only consume this public good.

When the rationality of the uninformed voter and special interest groups are taken into account, the political equilibrium provides public goods in excess of the efficient quantity. So in the satellite example, three or four satellites might be installed rather than the efficient quantity, which is two satellites.

Two Types of Political Equilibrium

We've seen that two types of political equilibrium are possible: efficient and inefficient. These two types of political equilibrium correspond to two theories of government:

◆ Social interest theory
◆ Public choice theory

Social Interest Theory

Social interest theory predicts that governments make choices that achieve efficiency. This outcome occurs in a perfect political system in which voters are fully informed about the effects of policies and refuse to vote for outcomes that can be improved upon.

Public Choice Theory

Public choice theory predicts that governments make choices that result in inefficiency. This outcome occurs in political markets in which voters are rationally ignorant and base their votes only on issues that they know affect their own net benefit. Voters pay more attention to their interests as producers than their interests as consumers, and public officials also act in their own best interest. The result is *government failure* that parallels market failure.

Why Government is Large and Grows

Now that we know how the quantity of public goods is determined, we can explain part of the reason for the growth of government. Government grows in part because the demand for some public goods increases at a faster rate than the demand for private goods. There are two possible reasons for this growth:

◆ Voter preferences
◆ Inefficient overprovision

Voter Preferences

The growth of government can be explained by voter preferences in the following way. As voters' incomes increase (as they do in most years), the demand for many public goods increases more quickly than income. (Technically, the *income elasticity of demand* for many public goods is greater than 1 – see Chapter 4, pp. 86–87.) These goods include public health, education, national defence, highways and air-traffic control

systems. If politicians did not support increases in expenditures on these items, they would not get elected.

Inefficient Overprovision

Inefficient overprovision might explain the size of government but not its growth rate. It (possibly) explains why government is larger than its efficient scale, but it does not explain why governments use an increasing proportion of total resources.

Voters Strike Back

If government grows too large relative to the value that voters place on public goods, there might be a voter backlash against government programmes and a large bureaucracy. Electoral success during the 1990s required politicians of all parties to embrace smaller, leaner and more efficient government. The September 11 attacks have led to a greater willingness to pay for security but have probably not lessened the desire for lean government.

Another way in which voters – and politicians – can try to counter the tendency of civil servants to expand their budgets is to privatize the production of public goods. Government *provision* of a public good does not automatically imply that a government-operated department must *produce* the good. Prisons are a public good and experiments are being conducted with private prisons in the United Kingdom. Garbage collection is often done by a private firm.

Review Quiz

1 What is the free-rider problem and why does it make the private provision of a public good inefficient?
2 Under what conditions will competition for votes among politicians result in an efficient quantity of a public good?
3 How do rationally ignorant voters and budget maximizing civil servants prevent competition in the marketplace from producing the efficient quantity of a public good? Do they result in too much or too little public provision of public goods?

You've seen how public goods create a free-rider problem that would result in the underprovision of such goods. We're now going to learn about common resources and see why they result in the opposite problem – the overuse of such resources.

Common Resources

North Sea cod stocks have been declining since the 1950s and some marine biologists fear that this species is in danger of becoming extinct in some regions. The whale population of the South Pacific has been declining also and some groups are lobbying to establish a whale sanctuary in the waters south of Australia and New Zealand to regenerate the population. Since the start of the Industrial Revolution in 1750, the concentration of carbon dioxide in the atmosphere has steadily increased. Scientists have estimated that it is about 30 per cent higher today than it was in 1750.

These situations involve common property, and the problem that we have identified is called the problem of the commons.

The Problem of the Commons

The *problem of the commons* is the absence of incentives to prevent the overuse and depletion of a commonly owned resource. If no one owns a resource, no one considers the effects of her or his use of the resource on others.

The Original Problem of the Commons

The term "problem of the commons" comes from fourteenth century England where areas of rough grassland surrounded villages. The commons were open to all and used for grazing cows and sheep owned by the villagers.

Because the commons were open to all, no one had an incentive to ensure that the land was not over grazed. The result was a severe over-grazing situation. Because the commons were over grazed, the quantity of cows and sheep that they could feed kept on falling.

During the sixteenth century, the price of wool increased and England became a wool exporter to the world. Sheep farming became profitable and sheep owners wanted to gain more effective control of the land they used. So the commons were gradually enclosed and privatized. Overgrazing ended and land use became more efficient.

A Problem of the Commons Today

One of today's pressing problems of the commons is overfishing. Several fish species have been seriously over fished, and one of them is Atlantic Cod.

To study the problem of the commons, we'll use the Atlantic Cod as an example.

Sustainable Production

Sustainable production is the rate of production that can be maintained indefinitely. In the case of ocean fish, the sustainable rate of production is the quantity of fish (of a given species) that can be caught each year into the indefinite future.

This production rate depends on the existing stock of fish and the number of boats that go fishing. For a given stock of fish, sending more boats to sea increases the quantity of fish caught. But sending too many boats to sea depletes the stock. So as the number of boats increases, the quantity of fish caught increases as long as the stock is maintained. But above some crucial level, as more boats go fishing, the stock of fish decreases and the number of fish caught also decreases.

Table 16.1 illustrates the relationship between the number of boats that go fishing and the quantity of fish caught. The numbers in this example are hypothetical.

Table 16.1

Sustainable Production: Total, Average and Marginal Catch

	Boats (thousands)	Total catch (thousands of tonnes)	Average catch (tonnes per boat)	Marginal catch (tonnes per boat)
A	0	0		
				90
B	1	90	90	
				70
C	2	160	80	
				50
D	3	210	70	
				30
E	4	240	60	
				10
F	5	250	50	
				−10
G	6	240	40	
				−30
H	7	210	30	
				−50
I	8	160	20	
				−70
J	9	90	10	
				−90
K	10	0	0	

As the number of fishing boats increases, the quantity of fish caught increases up to the maximum sustainable catch and then decreases. The average catch and marginal catch decrease as the number of boats increases.

Total Catch

The total catch is the sustainable rate of production. The numbers in the first two columns of Table 16.1 show the relationship between the number of fishing boats and the total catch, and Figure 16.5 illustrates this relationship.

You can see that as the number of boats increases from zero to 5,000, the sustainable catch increases to a maximum of 250,000 tonnes a month. As the number of boats increases above 5,000, the sustainable catch begins to decrease. By the time 10,000 boats are fishing, the fish stock is depleted to the point at which no fish can be caught.

With more than 5,000 boats, there is overfishing. Overfishing arises if the number of boats increases to the point at which the fish stock begins to fall and the remaining fish are harder to find and catch.

Average Catch

The average catch is the catch per boat and equals the total catch divided by the number of boats. The numbers in the third column of Table 16.1 show the average catch.

One boat catches 100 tonnes a month. With 1,000 boats, the total catch is 90,000 tonnes and the catch per

boat is 90 tonnes. With 2,000 boats, the total catch is 160,000 tonnes, and the catch per boat 80 tonnes. As more boats take to the ocean, the catch per boat decreases. By the time 8,000 boats are fishing, each boat is catching just 20 tonnes a month.

The decreasing average catch is an example of the principle of diminishing returns.

Marginal Catch

The marginal catch is the change in the total catch that occurs when one more boat joins the existing number. It is calculated as the change in the total catch divided by the increase in the number of boats. The numbers in the fourth column of Table 16.1 show the marginal catch.

For example, in rows C and D of the table, when the number of boats increases by 1,000, the catch increases by 50,000 tonnes, so the increase in the catch per boat equals 50 tonnes. In the table, we place this amount mid-way between the two rows because it is the marginal catch at 2,500 boats, mid-way between the two levels that we used to calculate it.

Notice that the marginal catch, like the average catch, decreases as the number of boats increases. Also notice that the marginal catch is always less than the average catch.

When the number of boats reaches that at which the sustainable catch is a maximum, the marginal catch is zero. At a larger number of boats, the marginal catch becomes negative – the total catch decreases.

An Overfishing Equilibrium

The problem of the commons is that common resources are overused. Why might the fish stock be overused? Why might overfishing occur? Why isn't the maximum number of boats that take to the sea the number that maximizes the sustainable catch – 5,000 in this example?

To answer this question, we need to look at the marginal cost and marginal private benefit to an individual boat owner.

Suppose that the marginal cost of a fishing boat is the equivalent of 20 tonnes of fish a month. That is, to cover the opportunity cost of maintaining and operating a boat, the boat must catch 20 tonnes of fish a month. This quantity of fish also provides the boat owner with normal profit (part of the cost of operating the boat), so the boat owner is willing to go fishing.

The marginal private benefit of operating a boat is the quantity of fish the boat can catch. This quantity is the average catch that we've just calculated.

Figure 16.5

Sustainable Production of Fish

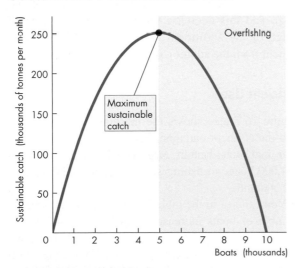

As the number of boats increases, the sustainable catch increases up to a maximum. Beyond that number, more boats will diminish the fish stock and the sustainable catch decreases. Overfishing occurs when the maximum sustainable catch decreases.

The average catch is the marginal private benefit because that is the quantity of fish that the boat owner gets by taking the boat to sea.

The boat owner will go fishing as long as the average catch (marginal private benefit) exceeds the marginal cost. And the boat owner will maximize profit when marginal private benefit equals marginal cost.

Figure 16.6 shows the marginal cost curve, *MC*, and the marginal private benefit curve, *MPB*. The *MPB* curve is based on the numbers for the average catch in Table 16.1.

You can see in Figure 16.6 that with fewer than 8,000 boats, each boat catches more fish than it costs to catch them. Because boat owners can gain from fishing, the number of boats is 8,000 and there is an overfishing equilibrium.

If one boat owner stopped fishing, the overfishing would be less severe. But that boat owner would be giving up an opportunity to make an economic profit.

The private interest is to fish, but the social interest is to limit fishing. The quantity of fish caught by each boat decreases as additional boats are introduced. But

when individual boat owners are deciding whether to fish, they ignore this decrease. They consider only the marginal private benefit. The result is an *inefficient* overuse of the resource.

The Efficient Use of the Commons

What is the efficient use of a common resource? It is the use of the resource that makes the marginal cost of using the resource equal to the marginal *social* benefit from its use.

Marginal Social Benefit

The marginal *social* benefit of a boat is the boat's marginal catch – the increase in the total catch that results from an additional boat. The reason is that when an additional boat puts to sea, it catches the average catch but it decreases the average catch for itself and for every other boat. The social benefit is the increase in the quantity of fish caught, not the average number of fish caught.

We calculated the marginal catch in Table 16.1 and we repeat part of that table for convenience in Figure 16.7. This figure also shows marginal social benefit curve, *MSB* and the marginal private benefit curve, *MPB*.

Notice that at any given number of boats, marginal social benefit is less than marginal private benefit. Each boat benefits privately from the average catch, but the addition of one more boat *decreases* the catch of every boat, and this decrease must be subtracted from the catch of the additional boat to determine the social benefit from the additional boat.

Efficient Use

Figure 16.7 also shows the marginal cost curve, *MC*, and the efficient outcome. Efficiency is achieved when marginal social benefit, *MSB*, equals marginal cost, *MC* – 4,000 boats go fishing and each catches 60 tonnes of fish a month.

You can see in the table in Figure 16.7 that when the number of boats increases from 3,000 to 4,000 (with 3,500 being the mid-point), marginal social benefit is 30 tonnes, which exceeds marginal cost. When the number of boats increases from 4,000 to 5,000 (with 4,500 being the mid-point), marginal social benefit is 10 tonnes, which is less than marginal cost. At 4,000 boats, marginal social benefit is 20 tonnes, which equals marginal cost.

Figure 16.6

Why Overfishing Occurs

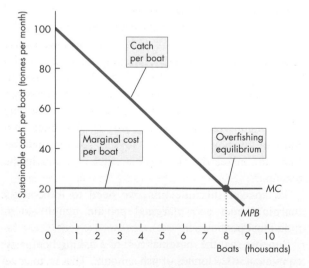

The average catch decreases as the number of boats increases. The average catch per boat is the marginal private benefit, *MPB*, of a boat. The marginal cost of a boat is equivalent to 20 tonnes of fish, shown by the curve *MC*. The equivalent number of boats is 8,000 – an overfishing equilibrium.

Figure 16.7

Efficient Use of a Common Resource

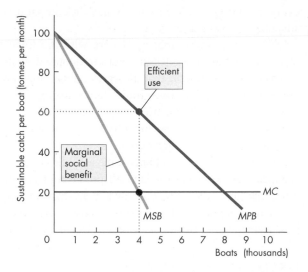

	Boats (thousands)	Total catch (thousands of tonnes)	MPB (tonnes per boat)	MSB (tonnes per boat)
A	0	0		
				90
B	1	90	90	
				70
C	2	160	80	
				5
D	3	210	70	
				30
E	4	240	60	
				10
F	5	250	50	

The marginal social benefit, *MSB*, of a fishing boat is the change in total benefit that results from an additional boat. The table shows the *MSB* calculations. When the number of boats increases from 2,000 to 3,000 (from row *C* to row *D*), the total catch increases from 160,000 to 210,000 tonnes per month and marginal catch and *MSB* is 50 tonnes.

The graph shows the *MSB* curve as well as the *MPB* curve. Marginal social benefit is less than marginal private benefit and decreases as the number of boats increases. The efficient quantity of boats is that at which *MSB* equals *MC* and is 4,000. The efficient use of a common resource does not overuse the resource.

Achieving an Efficient Outcome

Defining the conditions under which a common resource is used efficiently is easier than bringing those conditions about. To use a common resource efficiently, it is necessary to design an incentive mechanism that confronts users of the resource with the marginal social consequences of their actions. The same principles apply to common resources as those that you met when you studied externalities in Chapter 15.

Three main methods might be used to achieve the efficient use of a common resource. They are

◆ Property rights

◆ Quotas

◆ Individual transferable quotas (ITQs)

Property Rights

A common resource that no one owns and that anyone is free to use contrasts with private property, which is a resource that someone owns and has an incentive to use in the way that maximizes its value. One way of overcoming the problem of the commons is to remove the commons and make the resource private property. By assigning private property rights, each owner faces the same conditions as society faces. The *MSB* curve of Figure 16.7 becomes the marginal private benefit curve, and the use of the resource is efficient.

The private property solution to the problem of the commons is available in some cases. It was the solution to the original problem of the commons in England's Middle Ages. It is also a solution that has been used to prevent the airwaves that we use to carry our cell phone messages from being overused. The right to use this space – called the frequency spectrum – has been auctioned by governments to the highest bidders, and the owner of a particular part of the spectrum is the only one permitted to use it (or license someone else to use it).

But assigning private property rights is not always feasible. It would be difficult, for example, to assign private property rights to the oceans. It would not be impossible, but the cost of enforcing private property rights over thousands of square miles of ocean would be high. And it would be even harder to assign and protect property rights to the atmosphere.

In some cases, there is an emotional objection to assigning private property rights. When private property rights are too costly to assign and enforce, some form of government intervention is used and quotas are the simplest.

Quotas

You studied the effects of a quota in Chapter 6 (p. 132) and learned that a quota can drive a wedge between marginal benefit and marginal cost and create dead-weight loss. But in that earlier example, the market was efficient without a quota. In the case of the use of common property, the market is inefficient and is overproducing. So a quota that limits production can bring a move towards a more efficient outcome.

Figure 16.8 shows a quota that achieves an efficient use of a common resource. A quota is set for total production at the quantity at which marginal social benefit equals marginal cost. Here, that quantity is what 4,000 boats can catch. Individual boat owners are assigned their own share of the total permitted catch. If everyone sticks to the assigned quota, the outcome is efficient.

There are two problems in implementing a quota. First, it is in everyone's self-interest to cheat and use more of a common resource than the amount based on the assigned quota. The reason is that marginal private benefit exceeds marginal cost. So by catching more than

the allocated quota, each boat owner gets a higher income. If everyone breaks the quota, overproduction returns and the problem of the commons remains.

Second, marginal cost is not, in general, the same for every producer. Some producers have a comparative advantage in using a resource.

Efficiency requires that producers with the lowest marginal cost are the ones that get the quotas. But the government department that allocates quotas does not possess information about individual marginal cost. Even if the government tried to get this information, producers would have an incentive to lie about their costs in order to get a bigger quota.

So a quota can work, but only if the activities of every producer can be monitored and all producers have the same marginal cost. Where producers are hard or very costly to monitor or where marginal costs vary across producers, a quota cannot achieve an efficient outcome.

Individual Transferable Quotas

Where producers are hard to monitor and where marginal costs differ across producers, a more sophisticated quota system can be used. An **individual transferable quota (ITQ)** is a production limit that is assigned to an individual who is free to transfer the quota to someone else. A market in ITQs emerges and ITQs are transferred at their market price.

Figure 16.9 shows how ITQs work. In the market for ITQs, the price is the highest price that an ITQ is worth. If the number of ITQs issued equals the efficient production level, then the price of an ITQ will equal the amount shown in the figure. This price equals the marginal private benefit at the production limit minus the private marginal cost of using a boat. The price rises to this level because people who don't have an ITQ would be willing to pay this amount to acquire the right to fish. And people who do own an ITQ could sell it for this price, so not to sell it is to incur an opportunity cost. The result is that the marginal cost, which now includes the price of the ITQ, rises from MC_0 to MC_1. The equilibrium is efficient.

Individual differences in marginal cost do not prevent an ITQ system from delivering the efficient outcome. Producers that have a low marginal cost are willing and able to pay more for a quota than are producers that have a high marginal cost. The market price of a quota will equal the marginal cost of the marginal producer at the efficient quantity. Producers with higher marginal costs will not produce.

Figure 16.8

Using a Quota to Use a Common Resource Efficiently

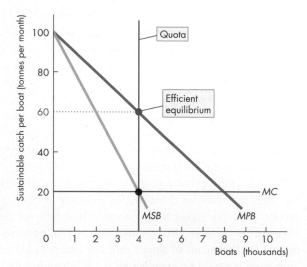

A quota is set at the efficient quantity, which makes the number of boats equal to the quantity at which marginal social benefit, *MSB*, equals marginal cost, *MC*. If the quota is not broken, the outcome is efficient.

Figure 16.9

Individual Transferable Quotas to Use a Common Resource Efficiently

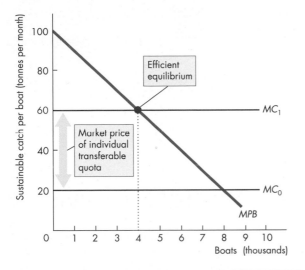

ITQs are issued on a scale that keeps output at the efficient level, the quantity of fish that 4,000 boats can catch. The market price of an ITQ equals the marginal private benefit minus marginal cost. With 4,000 boats, the marginal private benefit is 60 tonnes and the marginal cost is 20 tonnes of fish plus the price of the ITQ. So the price of an ITQ is 40 tonnes of fish. Because each user of the common resource faces the opportunity cost of using the resource, self-interest achieves the social interest.

Public Choice and the Political Equilibrium

You saw in the previous part of this chapter where we studied the provision of public goods that a political equilibrium might be inefficient – that there might be government failure.

This same political outcome might arise in the face of a problem of the commons. Defining an efficient allocation of resources and designing an ITQ system to achieve that allocation is not sufficient to ensure that the political process delivers the efficient outcome. In the case of the wild ocean fish stock, some countries have achieved an efficient political equilibrium, but not all have done so.

There is wide agreement among economists that ITQs offer the most effective tool for dealing with overfishing and achieving an efficient use of the stock of ocean fish. So a political commitment to ITQs is an

efficient outcome and an unwillingness to use ITQs is an inefficient political outcome.

Australia and New Zealand have introduced ITQs to conserve fish stocks in the South Pacific Ocean. The evidence from these examples suggests that ITQs work well. Fishing boat operators have an incentive to cheat and produce more than the amount for which they have a quota. But such cheating seems to be relatively rare. And producers that have paid for a quota have an incentive to monitor and report on cheating by others who have not paid the market price for a quota.

So ITQs do the job they are designed to do: help to maintain fish stocks. But they also reduce the size of the fishing industry. This consequence of ITQs puts them against the self-interest of fishers.

In all countries, the fishing industry opposes restrictions on its activities. But in Australia and New Zealand, the opposition is not strong enough to block ITQs. In contrast, in the United States the opposition is so strong that the fishing industry has persuaded Congress to outlaw ITQs. In 1996, the US Congress passed the Sustainable Fishing Act that puts a moratorium on ITQs. The result of this act is that earlier attempts to introduce ITQs in the Gulf of Mexico and the Northern Pacific have been abandoned.

Review Quiz

1 What is the problem of the commons?
2 Provide two examples of the problem of the commons, including one from your own neighbourhood.
3 Describe the conditions under which a common resource is used efficiently.
4 Review three methods that might achieve the efficient use of a common resource and explain the obstacles to efficiency.

Reading Between the Lines on pp. 360–361 looks at the overuse of tropical rainforests.

The next chapter begins a new part of your study of microeconomics and examines the third big question – for whom are goods and services produced? We examine the markets for factors of production and discover how wage rates and other incomes are determined.

Reading Between the Lines

Rainforests: A Problem of the Commons

BBC News, 22 May 2002

Malaysia laundering rainforest logs

Environmental campaigners in Malaysia are accusing the government of involvement in the criminal destruction of the endangered forests of Indonesia.

Their concerns come as the United Nations publishes its Global Environment Outlook report, in which it warns that 15% of the earth's land cover has now been degraded by human activity – and nearly a third of that is due to deforestation.

An investigation by the BBC has revealed that Malaysia is importing timber which has been felled illegally in nearby Indonesia, and then disguising its origin by using it for the manufacture of garden furniture or other products which are labelled as of Malaysian origin.

. . .

Just a few miles south of Malaysia's capital Kuala Lumpur there is a brand new port where boats with Indonesian flags are unloading the banned round logs.

And stacking them on the dockside where they will be turned into Malaysian doors or Malaysian garden furniture.

A junior manager at the Kuala Lumpur-based company Harvest, admitted that some of the timber coming in was from Indonesia and it was being stamped by the state government as an official import. . . .

© BBC. Reprinted with permission.

The Essence of the story

◆ A United Nations report says that 15 per cent of the earth's land cover has been degraded by human activity, almost a third of which is due to deforestation.

◆ Malaysia has been accused of importing timber felled illegally in Indonesia, disguising its origin, and using it to manufacture garden furniture or other products which are labelled as of Malaysian origin.

Economic Analysis

- The tropical rainforests of Indonesia grow valuable hardwood timber. These forests are also home to many rare species and a carbon-dioxide sink that helps maintain the earth's atmosphere.

- The forests are common property but their use is subject to the laws and international agreements.

- The private incentive to exploit these forest resources is strong. And because no one owns the forests, there is no incentive to conserve the resources and use them on a sustainable basis.

- The result is overuse, just like the overuse of the commons of England in the Middle Ages.

- The figures illustrate the problem of the commons in a tropical rainforest.

- Figure 1 shows the relationship between the sustainable production of wood from a rainforest and the number of lumber producers working the forest.

- Figure 2 shows the marginal benefit and marginal cost of a producer and the social marginal benefit and cost.

- The marginal cost of felling a tree incurred by a producer is assumed to be zero.

- As a common resource, the marginal benefit received by a producer is *MB* and *LD* producers acting in their self-interest deplete the resource. Sustainable production falls to zero.

- As a privately owned resource, the marginal social benefit curve, *MSB*, becomes the marginal private benefit curve. Self-interest results in *LP* producers who maximize the sustainable output of the rainforest.

- If the only benefit from the rainforest were its timber, maximum sustainable timber output would be efficient.

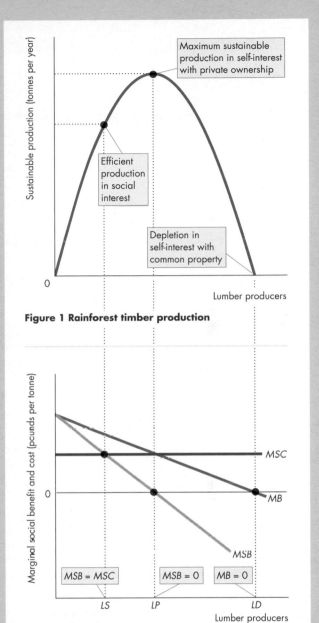

Figure 1 Rainforest timber production

Figure 2 Marginal benefit and marginal cost

- But external benefits arise from the diversity of the wildlife supported by the forest, so marginal social cost exceeds the zero marginal private cost.

- Production in the social interest – the efficient level of production – is achieved with *LS* producers and is less than the maximum sustainable production.

Summary

Key Points

Classifying Goods and Resources
(p. 348)

◆ A private good is a good or service that is rival and excludable.

◆ A public good is a good or service that is non-rival and non-excludable.

◆ A common resource is a resource that is rival but non-excludable.

Public Goods and the Free-Rider Problem (pp. 349–353)

◆ A public good is a good or service that is consumed by everyone and that is *non-rival* and *non-excludable*.

◆ A public good creates a *free-rider* problem: no one has an incentive to pay their share of the cost of providing a public good.

◆ The efficient level of provision of a public good is that at which net benefit is maximized. Equivalently, it is the level at which marginal benefit equals marginal cost.

◆ Competition between political parties, each of which tries to appeal to the maximum number of voters, can lead to the efficient scale of provision of a public good and to both parties proposing the same policies – the principle of minimum differentiation.

◆ Civil servants try to maximize the department's budget, and if voters are rationally ignorant, producer interests might result in voting to support taxes that provide public goods in quantities that exceed those that maximize net benefit.

Common Resources (pp. 354–359)

◆ Common resources create the problem of the commons – no one has a private incentive to conserve the resources and use them at an efficient rate.

◆ A common resource is used to the point at which the marginal private benefit equals the marginal cost.

◆ A common resource might be used efficiently by creating a private property right, setting a quota or issuing individual transferable quotas.

Key Figures

Figure 16.1 Four-Fold Classification of Goods, 348
Figure 16.2 Benefits of a Public Good, 349
Figure 16.3 The Efficient Quantity of a Public Good, 351
Figure 16.4 Bureaucratic Overprovision, 352
Figure 16.6 Why Overfishing Occurs, 356
Figure 16.7 Efficient Use of a Common Resource, 357

Key Terms

Common resource, 348
Excludable, 348
Free-rider problem, 348
Individual transferable quota (ITQ), 358
Non-excludable, 348
Non-rival, 348
Principle of minimum differentiation, 351
Private good, 348
Problem of the commons, 348
Public good, 348
Rational ignorance, 352
Rival, 348

Problems

*1 You are provided with the following information about a sewage disposal system that a city of 1 million people is considering installing.

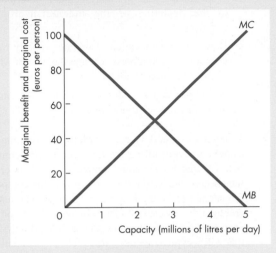

a What is the capacity that achieves maximum net benefit?

b How much will each person have to pay in taxes to pay for the efficient capacity level?

c What is the political equilibrium if voters are well informed?

d What is the political equilibrium if voters are rationally ignorant and civil servants achieve the highest attainable budget?

2 You are provided with the following information about a mosquito control programme.

Quantity (squares miles sprayed per day)	Marginal cost	Marginal benefit
	(euros per day)	
0	0	0
1	1,000	5,000
2	2,000	4,000
3	3,000	3,000
4	4,000	2,000
5	5,000	1,000

a What is the quantity of spraying that achieves maximum net benefit?

---

*Solutions to odd-numbered problems are available on *Parkin Interactive*.

b What is the total tax revenue needed to pay for the efficient quantity of spraying?

c What is the political equilibrium if voters are well informed?

d What is the political equilibrium if voters are rationally ignorant and civil servants achieve the highest attainable budget?

*3 The table shows the value of cod caught in the North Atlantic Ocean by American and European fishing boats. It also shows the value that concerned citizens of America, Canada and Europe place on the Atlantic Cod stock. The marginal cost of operating a boat is €70,000 a month.

Number of boats	Value of cod caught (thousands of euros per month)	Value placed on cod stock by concerned citizens (thousands of euros per month)
0	0	10,000
10	2,000	9,000
20	3,500	8,000
30	4,500	7,000
40	4,800	6,000
50	5,000	5,000
60	4,800	4,000
70	4,200	3,000
80	2,400	2,000

a What is the marginal private benefit of each fishing boat?

b What is the marginal social cost of each fishing boat?

c With no regulation of cod fishing, what is the equilibrium number of boats and the approximate value of cod caught?

d Is the equilibrium in part (c) an overfishing equilibrium?

e What is the marginal social benefit of each fishing boat?

f What is the efficient number of boats?

g What is the efficient value of the cod catch?

h Do you think that the concerned citizens of America, Canada and Europe and the fishing industry will agree about how much cod should be caught?

i If the United States, Canada and the European Union issued ITQs to fishing boats to limit the catch to the efficient quantity, what would be the price of an ITQ?

4 The table shows the value of salmon caught in the Pacific Ocean by US, Canadian and Japanese fishing boats. It also shows the value that concerned citizens of the United States, Canada and Japan place on the Pacific Salmon stock. The marginal cost of operating a boat is €100,000 a month.

Number of boats	Value of salmon caught (thousands of dollars per month)	Value placed on salmon stock by concerned citizens (thousands of dollars per month)
0	0	10,000
5	500	9,500
10	1,000	9,000
15	1,500	8,500
20	2,000	8,000
25	1,750	7,500
30	1,500	7,000
35	1,000	6,500
40	500	6,000

a What is the marginal private benefit of each fishing boat?

b What is the marginal social cost of each fishing boat?

c With no regulation of salmon fishing, what is the equilibrium number of boats and the approximate value of salmon caught?

d Is the equilibrium in part (c) an overfishing equilibrium?

e What is the marginal social benefit of each fishing boat?

f What is the efficient number of boats?

g What is the efficient value of the salmon catch?

h Do you think that the concerned citizens of the United States, Canada and Japan and the fishing industry will agree about how much salmon should be caught in the Pacific Ocean?

i If the United States, Canada and Japan issued ITQs to fishing boats to limit the catch to the efficient quantity, what would be the price of an ITQ?

Critical Thinking

1 After you have studied *Reading Between the Lines* on pp. 360–361, answer the following questions:

a What is happening in Malaysia that is contributing to the depletion of the Indonesian tropical rainforest?

b How would the creation of private property rights in Indonesian rainforests change the way in which the forest resources are used?

c Would private ownership solve all the problems of resource overuse? If not, why not?

2 Your city council is contemplating upgrading its system for controlling traffic signals. The council believes that by installing computers, it can improve the speed of the traffic flow. The bigger the computer the council buys, the better job it can do. The mayor and the other elected officials who are working on the proposal want to determine the scale of the system that will win them the most votes. The city councillors want to maximize the budget. Suppose that you are an economist who is observing this public choice. Your job is to calculate the quantity of this public good that uses resources efficiently.

a What data would you need to reach your own conclusions?

b What does the public choice theory predict will be the quantity chosen?

c How could you, as an informed voter, attempt to influence the choice?

Web Exercise

Use the links on *Parkin Interactive* to work the following exercise.

1 Read the article on demand revealing processes.

a What is a demand revealing process and what is its purpose?

b Why might using a demand revealing process deliver a more efficient level of public goods than our current political system?

c Why might our current political system deliver a more efficient level of public goods than would a demand revealing process?

Chapter 17

Demand and Supply in Factor Markets

After studying this chapter you will be able to:

◆ Explain the relationship between factor prices and factor incomes

◆ Explain how firms choose the quantity of labour to employ, how households choose the quantity of labour to supply, and how labour markets determines wage rates

◆ Explain how firms calculate the present value of future revenue from capital and how the capital market determines the interest rate

◆ Explain how natural resource markets work and why the price of non-renewable resources can be expected to rise

◆ Explain the concept of economic rent and distinguish between economic rent and opportunity cost

Many Happy Returns

The returns we get from our work vary a lot. Julie Adams does vital work as a nurse for £8.20 an hour while David Beckham earns a cool £3,500 an hour just for playing football. Why are some jobs well paid and others not? How can it be that a nurse who saves people's lives earns so much less than someone who merely provides entertainment? Why does Vodaphone pay its chief executive £10.9 million a year? Find out in this chapter and in the *Business Case Study* at the end of the chapter.

Factor Prices and Incomes

Goods and services are produced by using the four factors of production – *labour*, *capital*, *land* and *entrepreneurship*. (These factors of production are defined in Chapter 1, pp. 5–6.) Incomes are determined by the quantities of the factors used and by factor prices. The factor prices are the *wage* rate earned by labour, the *interest* rate earned by capital, the *rental* rate earned by land and *the normal profit* rate earned by entrepreneurship.

In addition to the four factor incomes, a residual income *economic profit* (or *economic loss*) is earned (or borne) by the firm's owners, who might be the entrepreneur or the shareholders.

Factors of production, like goods and services, are traded in markets. Some factor markets are competitive and behave similarly to competitive markets for goods and services. Other factor markets have monopoly elements. Our focus in this chapter is on competitive factor markets but an appendix (pp. 391–394) examines monopoly elements in labour markets. Demand and supply is the main tool used to understand a competitive factor market.

Firms demand factors of production and households supply them. The quantity demanded of a factor of production is the quantity that firms plan to employ during a given time period and at a given factor price. The law of demand applies to factors of production just as it does to goods and services. The lower the factor price, other things remaining the same, the greater is the quantity demanded of that factor. The demand for a factor of production is called a **derived demand** because it is *derived* from the demand for the goods and services produced by the factor.

The quantity supplied of a factor also depends on its price. With a possible exception that we'll identify later in this chapter, the law of supply applies to factors of production. The higher the price of a factor of production, other things remaining the same, the greater is the quantity supplied of the factor.

Figure 17.1 shows the market for a factor of production. The demand curve for the factor is the curve labelled *D*, and the supply curve of the factor is the curve labelled *S*. The equilibrium factor price is *PF*, and the equilibrium quantity is *QF*. The income earned by the factor is its price multiplied by the quantity used. In Figure 17.1, the factor income equals the area of the blue rectangle.

A change in demand or supply changes the equilibrium price, quantity and income. An increase in demand

Figure 17.1

Demand and Supply in a Factor Market

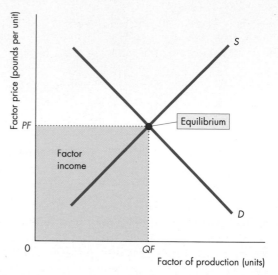

The demand curve for a factor of production (*D*) slopes downward, and the supply curve of a factor (*S*) slopes upward. Where the demand and supply curves intersect, the factor price (*PF*) and the quantity of a factor used (*QF*) are determined. The factor income is the product of the factor price and the quantity of the factor, as represented by the blue rectangle.

shifts the demand curve rightward and increases income. An increase in supply shifts the supply curve rightward and income might increase, decrease or remain constant depending on the elasticity of demand for the factor. If demand is elastic, income rises; if demand is inelastic, income falls; and if demand is unit elastic, income remains constant (see Chapter 4, p. 82).

Review Quiz

1   Why do we call the demand for a factor of production a *derived demand*? From what is it derived?
2   Why does an increase in the supply of a factor of production have an ambiguous effect on the factor's income?

In the rest of this chapter, we explore the influences on the demand for and supply of factors of production. We begin with the market for labour.

Labour Markets

For most people, the labour market is the major source of income. And for many people, it is the only source of income. In a typical year, labour income represents around 55 per cent of total income in the United Kingdom.

Average weekly earnings of full-time employees before tax were £476 in 2003. Part-time employees earned £152 a week. These earnings average around £13 an hour.

The average earnings rate hides a lot of diversity across individual occupations. You can see some of that diversity in Box 17.1, which shows a sample of wage rates in the 10 highest paid and 10 lowest paid jobs in 2000. The numbers in the box don't contain any major surprises, but they do show some interesting facts, so spend a minute looking at them.

Earnings rise most years and bring rising living standards. In 2003, they rose by an average of around 2.5 per cent. Although the average wage rate rises, the distribution of wage rates around the average changes, and some wage rates rise rapidly while some even fall.

To understand what determines wage rates, why some are high and some are low, and why some rise and some fall, we must probe the forces that influence the demand for labour and the supply of labour.

We begin on the demand side of the labour market.

The Demand for Labour

There is a link between the quantity of labour that a firm employs and the quantity of output that it plans to produce. The *total product curve* shows that link (Chapter 10, p. 204). A consequence of this link is that a firm's demand for labour is the flip side of its supply of output. To produce more output in the short run, a firm must employ more labour. In the long run, a firm can increase its output by using more capital and does not necessarily have to employ more labour.

A firm tries to produce the quantity of output that maximizes profit. And the profit-maximizing output is that at which marginal revenue equals marginal cost. To produce the profit-maximizing output, a firm must employ the profit-maximizing quantity of labour.

What is the profit-maximizing quantity of labour? And how does it change as the wage rate changes? We can answer these questions by comparing the marginal revenue earned by employing one more worker with the marginal cost of that worker. Let's look first at the marginal revenue side of this comparison.

Box 17.1
Wage Rates in Action

The Diversity of UK Wage Rates

The average wage rate in 2003 was about £13 an hour. But the variation around that average was very large. The lowest paid workers, a group that includes petrol pump attendants and hairdressers earn less than £6 an hour. At the other extreme, company financial officers and doctors earn up to £30 an hour. Figure 1 shows these wage rates along with those of some other high-paid and low-paid jobs. Most people have jobs that lie between these groups. They include lorry drivers and school teachers. A few people earn incomes that are off the scale of the figure. David Beckham's £20 million a year, for example, translates to several thousand pounds an hour!

Figure 1

10 High-paid and 10 Low-paid Jobs

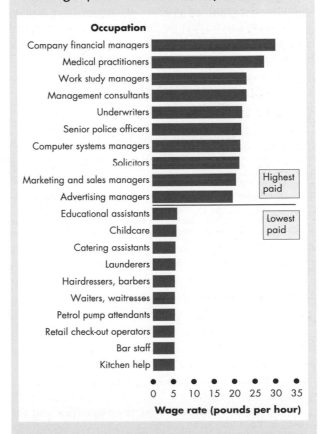

Source: New Earnings Survey, Office for National Statistics.

Marginal Revenue Product

The change in total revenue resulting from employing one worker, holding the quantity of all other factors constant, is called **marginal revenue product**. Table 17.1 shows you how to calculate marginal revenue product for a perfectly competitive firm.

The first two columns show the total product schedule for Max's Wash 'n' Wax car wash business. The numbers tell us how the number of car washes per hour varies as the quantity of labour increases. The third column shows the *marginal product of labour* – the change in total product that results from a one unit increase in the quantity labour employed. (Look back at Chapter 10, p. 203 for a quick refresher on this concept.)

The car wash market in which Max operates is perfectly competitive, and he can sell as many car washes as he chooses at £4 a wash, the (assumed) market price. So Max's *marginal revenue* is £4 a wash.

Given this information, we can calculate Max's *marginal revenue product* (fourth column). It equals marginal product multiplied by marginal revenue. For example, the marginal product of employing a second worker is 4 car washes an hour and because marginal revenue is £4 a wash, the marginal revenue product of the second worker is £16 (4 washes at £4 each).

The last two columns of Table 17.1 show an alternative way to calculate the marginal revenue product of labour. Total revenue is equal to total product multiplied by price. For example, two workers produce 9 washes per hour and generate a total revenue of £36 (9 washes at £4 each). One worker produces 5 washes per hour and generates a total revenue of £20 (5 washes at £4 each). Marginal revenue product, in the sixth column, is the change in the total revenue from employing one more worker. When the second worker is employed, total revenue increases from £20 to £36, an increase of £16. So the marginal revenue product of the second worker is £16, which agrees with the previous calculation.

Diminishing Marginal Revenue Product

As the quantity of labour rises, the marginal revenue product of labour diminishes. For a firm in perfect competition, marginal revenue product diminishes because marginal product diminishes. For a monopoly (or in monopolistic competition), marginal revenue product diminishes for a second reason. When more labour is employed and total product increases, the firm must cut its price to sell the extra product. So marginal product and marginal revenue decrease, both of which bring decreasing marginal revenue product.

Table 17.1

Marginal Revenue Product at Max's Wash 'n' Wax

	Quantity of labour (L) (workers)	Total product (TP) (car washes per hour)	Marginal product ($MP = \Delta TP/\Delta L$) (washes per worker)	Marginal revenue product ($MRP = MR \times MP$) (pounds per workers)	Total revenue ($TR = P \times TP$) (pounds)	Marginal revenue product ($MRP = \Delta TR/\Delta L$) (pounds per worker)
A	0	0			0	
			5	20		20
B	1	5			20	
			4	16		16
C	2	9			36	
			3	12		12
D	3	12			48	
			2	8		8
E	4	14			56	
			1	4		4
F	5	15			60	

The car wash market is perfectly competitive and the price is £4 a wash, so marginal revenue is £4 a wash. Marginal revenue product equals marginal product multiplied by marginal revenue. For example, the marginal product of the second worker is 4 washes, so the marginal revenue product of the second worker is £16. Alternatively, if Max employs 1 worker (row *B*), total product is 5 washes an hour and total revenue is £20. If he employs 2 workers (row *C*), total product is 9 washes an hour and total revenue is £36. By employing the second worker, total revenue rises by £16 – the marginal revenue product of labour is £16.

The Labour Demand Curve

Figure 17.2 shows how the labour demand curve is derived from the marginal revenue product curve. The *marginal revenue product curve* graphs the marginal revenue product of a factor at each quantity of the factor employed. Figure 17.2(a) illustrates the marginal revenue product curve for workers employed by Max. The horizontal axis measures the number of workers that Max employs and the vertical axis measures the marginal revenue product of labour. The blue bars show the marginal revenue product of labour as Max employs more workers. These bars correspond to the numbers in Table 17.1. The curve labelled *MRP* is Max's marginal revenue product curve.

A firm's marginal revenue product curve is also its demand for labour curve. Figure 17.2(b) shows Max's demand for labour curve (*D*). The horizontal axis measures the number of workers employed – the same as in part (a). The vertical axis measures the wage rate in pounds per hour. In Figure 17.2(a), when Max increases the quantity of labour employed from 2 workers an hour to 3 workers an hour, his marginal revenue product is £12 an hour. In Figure 17.2(b), at a wage rate of £12 an hour, Max employs 3 workers an hour.

The marginal revenue product curve is also the demand for labour curve because the firm employs the profit-maximizing quantity of labour. If the wage rate is *less* than marginal revenue product, the firm can increase its profit by employing one more worker. Conversely, if the wage rate is *greater* than marginal revenue product, the firm can increase its profit by employing one fewer worker. But if the wage rate *equals* marginal revenue product, the firm cannot increase its profit by changing the number of workers it employs. The firm is making the maximum possible profit. Thus the quantity of labour demanded by the firm is such that the wage rate equals the marginal revenue product of labour.

Because the marginal revenue product curve is also the demand curve, and because marginal revenue product diminishes as the quantity of labour employed increases, the demand for labour curve slopes downward. The lower the wage rate, other things remaining the same, the more workers a firm employs.

When we studied firms' output decisions, we discovered that a condition for maximum profit is that marginal revenue equals marginal cost. We've now discovered another condition for maximum profit: marginal revenue product of a factor equals the factor's price. Let's study the connection between these two conditions.

Figure 17.2

The Demand for Labour at Max's Wash 'n' Wax

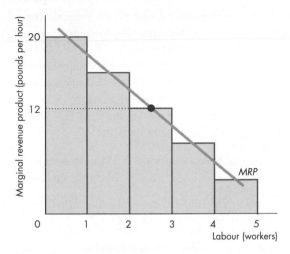

(a) Marginal revenue product

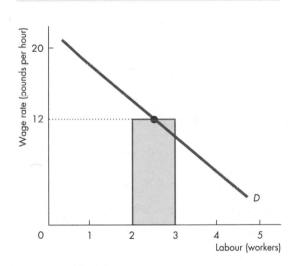

(b) Demand for labour

Max's Wash 'n' Wax operates in a perfectly competitive car wash market and can sell any quantity of washes at the market price of £4 a wash. The blue bars in part (a) represent the firm's marginal revenue product of labour. They are based on the numbers in Table 17.1. The orange line is the firm's marginal revenue product of labour curve.

Part (b) shows Max's demand for labour curve. This curve is identical to Max's marginal revenue product curve. Max demands the quantity of labour that makes the wage rate equal to the marginal revenue product of labour. The demand for labour curve slopes downward because marginal revenue product diminishes as the quantity of labour employed increases.

Equivalence of Two Conditions for Profit Maximization

Profit is maximized when at the quantity of labour employed, *marginal revenue product* equals the wage rate and when, at the quantity produced, *marginal revenue* equals *marginal cost*.

These two conditions for maximum profit are equivalent. The quantity of labour that maximizes profit produces the output that maximizes profit.

To see the equivalence of the two conditions for maximum profit, first recall that:

$$\text{Marginal revenue product} = \text{Marginal revenue} \times \text{Marginal product}$$

If we call marginal revenue product *MRP*, marginal revenue *MR* and marginal product *MP*, we have:

$$MRP = MR \times MP$$

If we call the wage rate *W*, the first condition for maximum profit is:

$$MRP = W$$

But $MRP = MR \times MP$, so:

$$MR \times MP = W$$

This equation tells us that when profit is maximized, marginal revenue multiplied by marginal product equals the wage rate.

Divide the last equation by *MP* to obtain:

$$MR = W \div MP$$

This equation states that when profit is maximized, marginal revenue equals the wage rate divided by the marginal product of labour.

The wage rate divided by the marginal product of labour equals marginal cost. It costs the firm *W* to employ one more hour of labour. But the labour produces *MP* units of output. So the cost of producing one of those units of output, which is marginal cost, is *W* divided by *MP*.

If we call marginal cost *MC*, then:

$$MR = MC,$$

which is the second condition for maximum profit.

Because the first condition for maximum profit implies the second condition, these two conditions are equivalent. Table 17.2 summarizes the reasoning and calculations that show the equivalence between the two conditions for maximum profit.

Table 17.2

Two Conditions for Maximum Profit

Symbols

Marginal product	**MP**
Marginal revenue	**MR**
Marginal cost	**MC**
Marginal revenue product	**MRP**
Wage rate	**W**

Two Conditions for Maximum Profit

1	**MR = MC**	2	**MRP = W**

Equivalence of Conditions

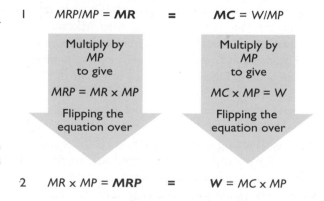

1    $MRP/MP = \mathbf{MR}$ = $\mathbf{MC} = W/MP$

Multiply by MP to give

$MRP = MR \times MP$ · $MC \times MP = W$

Flipping the equation over

2    $MR \times MP = \mathbf{MRP}$ = $\mathbf{W} = MC \times MP$

The two conditions for maximum profit are that marginal revenue product (*MR*) equals marginal cost (*MC*) and marginal revenue product (*MRP*) equals the wage rate (*W*). These two conditions for maximum profit are equivalent because marginal revenue product (*MRP*) equals marginal revenue (*MR*) multiplied by marginal product (*MP*), and the wage rate (*W*) equals marginal cost (*MC*) multiplied by marginal product (*MP*).

Max's Numbers

Check that the numbers for Max's Wash 'n' Wax and confirm that the conditions you've just examined work. Max's profit-maximizing labour decision is to employ 3 workers if the wage rate is £12 an hour. When Max employs 3 hours of labour, marginal product is 3 washes per hour. Max sells the 3 washes an hour for a marginal revenue of £4 a wash. So marginal revenue product is 3 washes multiplied by £4 a wash, which equals £12 per hour. At a wage rate of £12 an hour, Max is maximizing profit.

Equivalently, Max's marginal cost is £12 an hour divided by 3 washes per hour, which equals £4 per wash. At a marginal revenue of £4 a wash, Max is maximizing profit.

You've just discovered that the law of demand applies to labour as it does fro goods and services. Other things remaining the same, the lower the wage rate (the price of labour), the greater is the quantity of labour demanded.

Let's now study the influences that change the demand for labour and shift the demand for labour curve.

Changes in the Demand for Labour

The demand for labour changes and the demand curve for labour shifts when any of the following three factors change:

◆ The price of the firm's output
◆ Other factor prices
◆ Technology

The Price of the Firm's Output

The higher the price of a firm's output, the greater is the firm's demand for labour. The price of output affects the demand for labour through its influence on marginal revenue product. A higher price for the firm's output increases marginal revenue which, in turn, increases the marginal revenue product of labour. A change in the price of a firm's output leads to a shift in the firm's demand for labour curve. If the output price increases, the demand for labour curve shifts rightward.

Other Factor Prices

If the price of some other factor of production changes, the demand for labour changes, but only in the *long run* when all factors of production can be varied. The effect of a change in some other factor price depends on whether that factor is a *substitute* for or a *complement* of labour. For example, computers are substitutes for telephone operators but complements of word processor operators. So if computers become less costly to use, the demand for telephone operators decreases but the demand for word processor operators increases.

Technology

An advance in technology that changes the marginal product of labour changes the demand for labour. There is a general belief that advances in technology destroy jobs and therefore decrease the demand for labour. In fact, the opposite is true. Advances in technology destroy *some* jobs and create others. But the number of jobs created exceeds the number destroyed.

New technologies are substitutes for some types of labour and complements of other kinds. For example, the electronic telephone exchange is a substitute for telephone operators, so the arrival of this new technology has decreased the demand for telephone operators. This same new technology is a complement of systems managers, programmers and electronic engineers. So its arrival has increased the demand for these types of labour. Again, these effects on the demand for labour are long-run effects that occur when a firm adjusts all its resources and incorporates new technologies into its production process.

Table 17.3 summarizes the influences on a firm's demand for labour.

Table 17.3
A Firm's Demand for Labour

The Law of Demand
(Movements along the demand for labour curve)

The quantity of labour demanded by a firm

Decreases if:	Increases if:
◆ The wage rate increases	◆ The wage rate decreases

Changes in Demand
(Shifts in the demand for labour curve)

A firm's demand for labour

Decreases if:	Increases if:
◆ The firm's output price decreases	◆ The firm's output price increases
◆ The price of a substitute for the factor falls	◆ The prices of a substitute for the factor rises
◆ The price of a complement of the factor rises	◆ The price of a complement of the factor falls
◆ A new technology decreases the marginal product of labour	◆ A new technology increases the marginal product of labour

Market Demand

So far we have studied only the demand for labour by an individual firm. The market demand for labour is the total demand for labour by all firms in the market. The market demand for labour curve is found by adding together the quantities of labour demanded by all firms at each wage rate. Because each firm's demand for labour curve slopes downward, so does the market demand for labour curve.

Elasticity of Demand for Labour

This elasticity is important because it tells us how labour income changes when the supply of labour changes. An increase in supply (other things remaining the same) brings a lower wage rate. If demand is inelastic, it also brings lower labour income. But if demand is elastic, an increase in supply brings a lower wage rate and an increase in labour income. And if the demand for labour is unit elastic, a change in supply leaves labour income unchanged.

The demand for labour is less elastic in the short run, when only the quantity of labour can be varied, than in the long run, when the quantities of labour and other factors of production can be varied. The elasticity of demand for labour depends on:

◆ The labour intensity of the production process
◆ The elasticity of demand for the product
◆ The substitutability of capital for labour

Labour Intensity of the Production Process

A labour-intensive production process is one that uses a lot of labour and little capital – a process that has a high ratio of labour to capital. Home building is an example. The larger the degree of labour intensity, the more elastic is the demand for labour, other things remaining the same. To see why, suppose wages are 90 per cent of total cost. A 10 per cent increase in the wage rate increases total cost by 9 per cent. Firms will be extremely sensitive to such a large change in total cost, so if the wage rate increases, firms will decrease the quantity of labour demanded by a relatively large amount. But if wages are 10 per cent of total cost, a 10 per cent increase in the wage rate increases total cost by only 1 per cent. Firms will be less sensitive to this increase in cost, so if the wage rate increases in this case, firms will decrease the quantity of labour demanded by a small amount.

The Elasticity of Demand for the Product

The greater the elasticity of demand for the good, the larger is the elasticity of demand for labour used to produce it. An increase in the wage rate increases marginal cost of producing the good and decreases the supply of it. The decrease in the supply of the good increases the price of the good and decreases the quantity demanded of the good and the factors of production used to produce it. The greater the elasticity of demand for the good, the larger is the decrease in the quantity demanded of the good and so the larger is the decrease in the quantities of the factors of production used to produce it.

The Substitutability of Capital for Labour

The more easily capital can be used instead of labour in production, the more elastic is the long-run demand for labour. For example, it is fairly easy to use robots rather than assembly-line workers in car factories and grape-picking machines rather than labour in vineyards. So the demand for these types of labour is elastic. At the other extreme, it is difficult (though not impossible) to substitute computers for newspaper reporters, bank loan officers and teachers. So the demand for these types of labour is inelastic. The more readily capital can be substituted for labour, the more elastic is the firm's demand for labour in the long run.

We can now turn from the demand side of the labour market to the supply side and examine the decisions people make about how to allocate their time between working and other activities.

Supply of Labour

People can allocate their time to two broad activities – labour supply and leisure. (Leisure is a term that includes all activities other than supplying labour.) For most people, leisure is more enjoyable than supplying labour. We'll look at the labour supply decision of Amy, who is like most people. She enjoys her leisure time, and she would be pleased if she didn't have to spend her weekends working in a supermarket.

But Amy has chosen to work weekends because she is offered a wage rate that exceeds her *reservation wage*. Amy's reservation wage is the lowest wage at which she is willing to supply labour. If the wage rate exceeds her reservation wage, she supplies some labour. But how much labour will she supply? The quantity of labour that Amy is willing to supply depends on the wage rate.

Substitution Effect

Other things remaining the same, the higher the wage rate Amy is offered, at least over a range, the greater is the quantity of labour that she supplies. The reason is that Amy's wage rate is her *opportunity cost of leisure*. If she takes an hour off work to go shopping, the cost of that extra hour of leisure is the wage forgone. The higher the wage rate, the less willing is Amy to forgo the income and take the extra leisure time. This tendency for a higher wage rate to induce Amy to work longer hours is a *substitution effect*.

But there is also an *income effect* that works in the opposite direction to the substitution effect.

Income Effect

The higher Amy's wage rate, the higher is her income. A higher income, other things remaining the same, induces Amy to increase her demand for most goods. Leisure is one of these goods. Because an increase in income creates an increase in the demand for leisure, it also creates a decrease in the quantity of labour supplied.

Backward-Bending Labour Supply Curve

As the wage rate rises, the substitution effect brings an increase in the quantity of labour supplied while the income effect brings a decrease in the quantity of labour

supplied. At low wage rates, the substitution effect is larger than the income effect, so as the wage rate rises, people supply more labour. But as the wage rate continues to rise, the income effect eventually becomes larger than the substitution effect and the quantity of labour supplied decreases. The labour supply curve is *backward bending*.

Figure 17.3(a) shows the labour supply curves for Amy, and two friends, Jack and Lisa. Each labour supply curve is backward bending, but the three people have different reservation wage rates.

Market Supply

The market supply of labour curve is the sum of the individual supply curves. Figure 17.3(b) shows the market supply curve (S_M) derived from the supply curves of Amy, Jack and Lisa (S_A, S_B, S_C respectively). At wage rates of less than £1 an hour, no one supplies any labour. At a wage rate of £1 an hour, Amy works but Jack and Lisa don't. At £7 an hour, all three will work. The market supply curve S_M eventually bends backward, but it has a long upward-sloping section.

Changes in the Supply of Labour

The supply of labour changes when influences other than the wage rate change. The key factors that change the supply of labour and that have increased it are:

Figure 17.3

The Supply of Labour

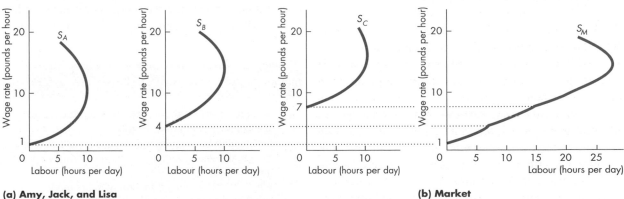

(a) Amy, Jack, and Lisa

(b) Market

Part (a) shows the labour supply curves of Amy (S_A), Jack (S_B) and Lisa (S_C). Each person has a reservation wage below which he or she will supply no labour. As the wage rises, the quantity of labour supplied rises to a maximum. If the wage continues to rise, the quantity of labour supplied begins to decrease. Each person's supply curve eventually bends backward.

Part (b) shows how, by adding together the quantities of labour supplied by each person at each wage rate, we derive the market supply of labour curve (S_M).

1 The size of the adult population

2 Technological change and capital accumulation

An increase in the adult population increases the supply of labour. So does a technological change or increase in capital in home production (of meals, laundry services and cleaning services). These factors that increase the supply of labour shift the labour supply curve rightward.

Let's now build on what we've learned about the demand for labour and the supply of labour and study labour market equilibrium and the trends in wage rates and employment.

Labour Market Equilibrium

Wages and employment are determined by equilibrium in the labour markets. You saw, in Box Figure 1 (p. 367), that the wage rate has risen and that total hours of employment in most European countries have also risen. But this picture hides some important differences between different types of labour market. Now you can see why.

Trends in the Demand for Labour

The demand for labour had *increased* in most European countries because of technological change and capital accumulation, and the demand for labour curve has shifted rightward.

Many people are surprised that technological change and capital accumulation *increase* the demand for labour. They see new technologies *destroying jobs*, not creating them. Downsizing has become a catchword as the use of computers has eliminated millions of "good" jobs, even those of managers. So how can it be that technological change *creates* jobs and increases the demand for labour?

Technological change destroys some jobs and creates others. But it creates more jobs than it destroys, and *on average*, the new jobs pay more than the old ones did. But to benefit from the advances in technology, people must acquire new skills and change their jobs. For example, during the past 20 years, the demand for typists has fallen almost to zero. But the demand for people who can type (on a computer rather than a typewriter) and do other tasks as well has increased. And the output of these people is worth more than that of a typist. So the demand for people with typing (and other) skills has increased.

Trends in the Supply of Labour

The supply of labour has increased because of population growth and technological change as well as capital accumulation in the home. The mechanization of home production of fast-food preparation services (the freezer and the microwave oven) and laundry services (the automatic washer and dryer and wrinkle-free fabrics) has decreased the time spent on activities that once were full-time jobs and have led to a large increase in the supply of labour. As a result, the supply labour curve has shifted steadily rightward, but at a slower pace than the shift in the demand curve.

Trends in Equilibrium

Because technological advances and capital accumulation have increased demand by more than population growth and technological change in home production have increased supply, both wage rates and employment have increased. But not everyone has shared in the increased prosperity. Some groups have been left behind, and seen their wage rates fall. Why?

Two key reasons can be identified. First, technological change affects the marginal productivity of different groups in different ways. High-skilled computer-literate workers have benefited from the information revolution while low-skilled workers have suffered. The demand for the services of the first group has increased, and the demand for the services of the second group has decreased. (Draw a supply and demand graph, and you will see that these changes widen the wage difference between the two groups.) Second, international competition has lowered the marginal revenue product of low-skilled workers and so has decreased the demand for their labour.

Review Quiz

1 What links the quantity that a firm produces and the quantity of labour it employs?

2 Distinguish between marginal revenue product and marginal revenue and illustrate the distinction with an example.

3 Why is it that when a firm's marginal revenue product equals the wage rate, marginal revenue also equals marginal cost?

4 What determines the amount of labour that households plan to supply?

5 Describe and explain the trends in wages and employment.

Capital Markets

Capital markets are the channels through which firms obtain *financial* resources to buy *physical* capital. *Physical capital* is the *stock* of tools, instruments, machines, buildings and other constructions that firms use to produce goods and services. Physical capital also includes the inventories of raw material and semi-finished and finished goods that firms hold. These capital resources are called *physical capital* to emphasize that they are real physical objects. They are goods that have been produced by some firms and bought by other firms. Physical capital is a *stock* – a quantity of objects that exists at a given time. But each year, that stock changes. It is depleted as old capital wears out and it is replenished and added to as firms buy new items of capital.

The markets in which each item of physical capital is traded are not the capital markets. They are goods markets just like the ones that you've studied in Chapters 11, 12 and 13. For example, the prices and quantities of tower cranes and earth movers are determined in the markets for those items.

A firm buys many different items of capital during a given time period. The pound value of those capital goods is called the firm's *investment*. But it is the objects themselves that are the capital, not the pounds of value that they represent.

The financial resources used to buy physical capital are called *financial capital*. These financial resources come from saving. The "price of capital", which adjusts to make the quantity of capital supplied equal to the quantity demanded, is the interest rate.

For most of us, capital markets are where we make our biggest-ticket transactions. We borrow in a capital market to buy a home. And we lend in capital markets to build up a fund on which to live when we retire.

Because we make our biggest transactions in capital markets, we are very concerned about the interest rate. When we save, we want to receive the highest possible interest rate. And when we borrow, we want to pay the lowest possible rate.

Does the interest rate in a capital markets increase as wage rates do? Box 17.2 answers this question.

Some of the ideas you've already met in your study of the labour market apply to the capital market as well. But capital has some special features. Its main special feature is that people must compare *present* costs with *future* returns. We'll discover how these comparisons are made by studying the demand for capital.

Box 17.2
The Real Interest Rate in Action

A *real interest rate* is an interest rate that is measured after removing the effects of inflation. If prices are rising by 5 per cent a year, money is losing value at 5 per cent a year. So if you lend a pound and get repaid after a year, or if you borrow a pound and repay the loan after a year, the value of the money that repays the loan is worth 5 per cent less than the original amount. We must subtract this amount from the market interest rate to find the real, or true, interest rate.

Figure 1 shows the real interest rate during the period from 1981 to 2004. You can see that the real interest rate fluctuates, but it does not tend to increase year after year like the real wage rate does.

Capital markets, unlike labour markets, are global. Funds move from one country to another in search of the highest return and the lowest borrowing cost. These movements tend to keep interest rates similar, though not identical, around the world.

Figure 1

The Real Interest Rate: 1981–2004

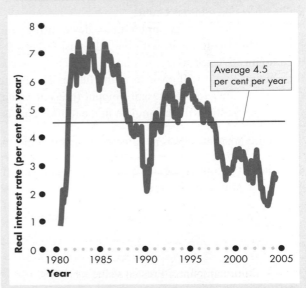

The real interest rate (the interest rate adjusted for inflation) expressed as a rate per year fluctuated between about 1 per cent in 1981 and more than 7 per cent in 1983. On the average, the real interest rate has been 4.5 per cent per year.

Source: Bank of England and Office for National Statistics.

The Demand for Capital

A firm's demand for *financial* capital stems from its demand for *physical* capital, and the amount that a firm plans to *borrow* in a given time period is determined by its planned investment – purchases of new capital. This decision is driven by the firm's attempt to maximize profit. As a firm increases the quantity of physical capital employed, other things remaining the same, the marginal revenue product of physical capital diminishes. To maximize profit, a firm increases its plant size and uses more capital if the marginal revenue product of the capital exceeds the price of capital. But the marginal revenue product comes in the *future*, and the capital must be paid for in the *present*. So the firm must convert *future* marginal revenue products into a *present value*, so that it can be compared with the present price of new equipment. To make this conversion, we use the technique of discounting.

Discounting and Present Value

Discounting is converting a future amount of money to its present value. The **present value** of a future amount of money is the amount that, if invested today, will grow to be as large as that future amount when the interest it will earn is taken into account.

The easiest way to understand discounting and present value is to begin with the relationship between an amount invested today, the interest that it earns and the amount that it will grow to in the future. The future amount is equal to the present amount (present value) plus the interest it will accumulate in the future. That is:

Future amount = Present value + Interest income

The interest income is equal to the present value multiplied by the interest rate, r, so:

Future amount = Present value + ($r \times$ Present value)

or:

Future amount = Present value $\times$ (1 + r)

If you have £100 today and the interest rate is 10 per cent a year ($r = 0.1$), one year from today you will have £110 – the original £100 plus £10 interest. Check that the above formula delivers that answer: £100 × 1.1 = £110.

The formula that we have just used calculates a future amount one year from today from the present value and

an interest rate. To calculate the present value, we just work backward. Instead of multiplying the present value by (1 + r), we divide the future amount by (1 + r). That is:

$$\text{Present value} = \frac{\text{Future amount}}{(1 + r)}$$

Let's check that we can use the present value formula by calculating the present value of £110 one year from now when the interest rate is 10 per cent a year. You'll be able to guess that the answer is £100 because we just calculated that £100 invested today at 10 per cent a year becomes £110 in one year. Thus it follows immediately that the present value of £110 in one year's time is £100. But let's use the formula. Putting the numbers into the above formula, we have:

$$\text{Present value} = \frac{110}{(1 + 0.1)}$$
$$= \frac{110}{1.1} = £100$$

Calculating the present value of an amount of money one year from now is the easiest case. But we can also calculate the present value of an amount any number of years in the future. As an example, let's see how we calculate the present value of an amount of money that will be available two years from now.

Suppose that you invest £100 today for two years at an interest rate of 10 per cent a year. The money will earn £10 in the first year, which means that by the end of the first year, you will have £110. If the interest of £10 is invested, then the interest earned in the second year will be a further £10 on the original £100 plus £1 on the £10 interest. Thus the total interest earned in the second year will be £11. The total interest earned overall will be £21 (£10 in the first year and £11 in the second year). After two years, you will have £121. From the definition of present value, you can see that the present value of £121 two years hence is £100. That is, £100 is the present amount that, if invested at an interest rate of 10 per cent a year, will grow to £121 two years from now.

To calculate the present value of an amount of money two years in the future, we use the formula:

$$\text{Present value}$$
$$= \frac{\text{Amount of money two years in future}}{(1 + r)^2}$$

Use this formula to calculate the present value of £121 two years from now at an interest rate of 10 per cent a year. With these numbers the formula gives:

$$\text{Present value} = \frac{£121}{(1 + 0.1)^2}$$

$$= \frac{£121}{(1.1)^2}$$

$$= \frac{£121}{1.21} = £100$$

We can calculate the present value of an amount of money any number of years in the future by using a formula based on the two that we've already used. The general formula is:

$$\text{Present value}$$

$$= \frac{\text{Amount of money } n \text{ years in future}}{(1 + r)^2}$$

For example, if the interest rate is 10 per cent a year, £100 to be received 10 years from now has a present value of £38.55. That is, if £38.55 is invested today at an interest rate of 10 per cent a year, it will accumulate to £100 in 10 years. (You might check that calculation on your pocket calculator.)

You've seen how to calculate the present value of an amount of money one year in the future, two years in the future, and n years in the future. Most practical applications of present value calculate the present value of a sequence of future amounts of money that spread over several years. To calculate the present value of a sequence of amounts over several years, we use the formula you have learned and apply it to each year. We then sum the present values for each year to find the present value of the sequence of amounts.

For example, suppose that a firm expects to receive £100 a year for each of the next five years. And suppose that the interest rate is 10 per cent per year (0.1 per year). The present value of these five payments of £100 each is calculated by using the following formula:

$$PV = \frac{£100}{1.1} + \frac{£100}{1.1^2} + \frac{£100}{1.1^3} + \frac{£100}{1.1^4} + \frac{£100}{1.1^5}$$

which equals:

$$PV = £90.91 + £82.64 + £75.13 + £68.30 + £62.09$$

$$= £379.07$$

You can see that the firm receives £500 over five years. But because the money arrives in the future, it is not worth £500 today. Its present value is only £379.07. And the further in the future it arrives, the smaller is its present value. The £100 received one year in the future is worth £90.91 today. And the £100 received five years in the future is worth only £62.09 today.

The Present Value of a Computer

Let's see how a firm decides how much capital to buy by calculating the present value of a new computer. Tina runs Taxfile plc, a UK firm that sells advice to taxpayers. Tina is considering buying a new computer that costs £2,000. The computer has a life of two years, after which it will be worthless. If Tina buys the computer, she will pay out £2,000 now and she expects to generate business that will bring in an additional £1,150 at the end of each of the next two years.

To calculate the present value, PV, of the marginal revenue product of a new computer, Tina uses the formula:

$$PV = \frac{MRP_1}{(1 + r)} + \frac{MRP_2}{(1 + r)^2}$$

Here, MRP_1 is the marginal revenue product received by Tina at the end of the first year. It is converted to a present value by dividing it by $(1 + r)$. The term MRP_2 is the marginal revenue product received at the end of the second year. It is converted to a present value by dividing it by $(1 + r)^2$.

If Tina can borrow or lend at an interest rate of 4 per cent a year, the present value (PV) of her marginal revenue product is given by:

$$PV = \frac{£1,150}{(1 + 0.04)} + \frac{£1,150}{(1 + 0.04)^2}$$

$$PV = £1,106 + £1,063$$

$$PV = £2,169$$

The present value (PV) of £1,150 one year in the future is £1,150 divided by 1.04 (4 per cent as a proportion is 0.04). The present value of £1,150 two years in the future is £1,063 divided by $(1.04)^2$. Working out these two present values and then adding them gives Tina the present value of the future stream of marginal revenue products, which is £2,169.

Table 17.4 summarizes the data. Part (b) puts Tina's numbers into the present value formula and calculates the present value of the marginal revenue product of a computer.

Tina's Decision to Buy

Tina decides whether to buy the computer by comparing the present value of its flow of marginal revenue product with its purchase price. She makes this comparison by calculating the net present value (*NPV*) of the computer. **Net present value** is the present value of the future return – the future flow of marginal revenue product generated by the capital minus the price of the capital. If net present value is positive, the firm buys additional capital. If net present value is negative, the firm does not buy additional capital.

Table 17.4(c) shows the calculation of Tina's net present value of a computer. The net present value is £169 – greater than zero – so Tina buys the computer. Tina can buy any number of computers that cost £2,000 and have a life of two years. But like all other factors of production, capital is subject to diminishing marginal returns. The greater the amount of capital employed, the smaller is its marginal revenue product. So if Tina buys a second computer or a third one, she gets successively smaller marginal revenue products from the additional computers.

Table 17.5(a) sets out Tina's marginal revenue products for one, two and three computers. The marginal revenue product of one computer (the case just reviewed) is £1,150 a year. The marginal revenue product of a second computer is £1,100 a year and the marginal revenue product of a third computer is £1,050 a year. Table 17.5(b) shows the calculations of the present values of the marginal revenue products of the first, second and third computers.

You've seen that with an interest rate of 4 per cent a year, the net present value of one computer is positive. At an interest rate of 4 per cent a year, the present value of the marginal revenue product of a second computer is £2,075, which exceeds its price by £75. So Tina buys a second computer. But at an interest rate of 4 per cent a year, the present value of the marginal revenue product of a third computer is £1,980, which is £20 less than

---

Table 17.4

Net Present Value of an Investment – Taxfile plc

(a) Data

Price of computer	2,000
Life of computer	2 years
Marginal revenue product	£1,150 at end of each year
Interest rate	4% a year

(b) Present value of the flow of marginal revenue product:

$$PV = \frac{MRP_1}{(1+r)} + \frac{MRP_2}{(1+r)^2}$$

$$= \frac{£1,150}{1.04} + \frac{£1,150}{(1.04)^2}$$

$$= £1,106 + £1.063$$

$$= £2,169$$

(c) Net present value of investment:

$NPV = PV$ of marginal revenue product – Price of computer

$$= £2,169 - £2,000$$

$$= £169$$

Table 17.5

Taxfile's Investment Decision

(a) Data

Price of computer	£2,000
Life of computer	2 years
Marginal revenue product:	
Using 1 computer	£1,150 a year
Using 2 computers	£1,100 a year
Using 3 computers	£ 1,050 a year

(b) Present value of the flow of marginal revenue product

If *r* = 0.04 (4% a year):

Using 1 computer: $PV = \dfrac{£1,150}{1.04} + \dfrac{£1,150}{(1.04)^2} = £2,169$

Using 2 computers: $PV = \dfrac{£1,100}{1.04} + \dfrac{£1,100}{(1.04)^2} = £2,075$

Using 3 computers: $PV = \dfrac{£1,050}{1.04} + \dfrac{£1,050}{(1.04)^2} = £1,980$

If *r* = 0.08 (8% a year):

Using 1 computer: $PV = \dfrac{£1,150}{1.08} + \dfrac{£1,150}{(1.08)^2} = £2,051$

Using 2 computers: $PV = \dfrac{£1,100}{1.08} + \dfrac{£1,100}{(1.08)^2} = £1,962$

If *r* = 0.12 (12% a year):

Using 1 computer: $PV = \dfrac{£1,150}{1.12} + \dfrac{£1,150}{(1.12)^2} = £1,944$

the price of a computer. So Tina does not buy a third computer.

A Change in the Interest Rate

We've seen that at an interest rate of 4 per cent a year, Tina buys two computers but not three. Suppose that the interest rate is 8 per cent a year. In this case, the present value of the first computer is £2,051 (see Table 17.5b), so Tina still buys one machine because it has a positive net present value. At an interest rate of 8 per cent a year, the present value of the second computer is £1,962, which is less than £2,000, the price of the computer. So at an interest rate of 8 per cent a year, Tina buys only one computer.

Suppose that the interest rate is even higher, 12 per cent a year. In this case, the present value of the marginal revenue product of one computer is £1,944 (see Table 17.5b). At this interest rate, Tina buys no computers.

These calculations trace Taxfile's demand schedule for capital, which shows the value of computers demanded by Taxfile at each interest rate. Other things remaining the same, as the interest rate rises, the quantity of capital demanded decreases. The higher the interest rate, the smaller is the quantity of *physical* capital demanded. But to finance the purchase of *physical* capital, firms demand *financial* capital. So the higher the interest rate, the smaller is the quantity of *financial* capital demanded.

Demand Curve for Capital

A firm's demand curve for capital shows the relationship between the quantity of financial capital demanded by the firm and the interest rate, other things remaining the same. Figure 17.4(a) shows Tina's demand curve for capital and the four points on it that we've just found. If Tina can buy other capital items so that her demand for capital is divisible into one-dollar units (not restricted to jumping in £2,000 units), her demand curve for capital would look like the entire blue curve in Figure 17.4(a).

Figure 17.4(b) shows the market demand curve for capital, *KD*, which is the horizontal sum of the demand curves of each firm. In the figure, the quantity of capital demanded in the entire capital market is £150 billion when the interest rate is 6 per cent a year.

You've seen how the demand for capital is determined. Let's now look at the supply side of the capital market.

Figure 17.4

A Firm's Demand and the Market Demand for Capital

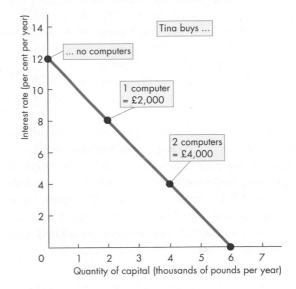

(a) Tina's demand curve for capital

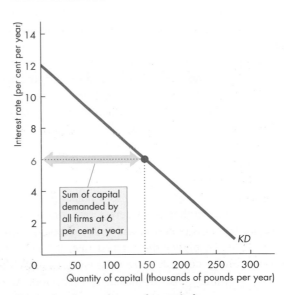

(b) Market demand curve for capital

Part (a) shows Tina's demand for capital. As the interest rate falls, the quantity of capital Tina demands increases. That is, for each firm, the lower the interest rate, the greater is the quantity of capital demanded.

Part (b) illustrates the market demand for capital. The market demand for capital curve is the horizontal sum of the firms' demand curves.

The Supply of Capital

The quantity of capital supplied results from people's saving decisions. The main factors that determine household saving are:

◆ Current income

◆ Expected future income

◆ The interest rate

Current Income

Saving is the act of converting *current* income into *future* consumption. When Aaron's income increases, he plans to consume more both now and in the future. But to increase *future* consumption, Aaron must save today. So, other things remaining the same, the higher Aaron's current income, the more he saves. The relationship between saving and current income is remarkably stable.

Expected Future Income

If Aaron's current income is high and his expected future income is low, he will have a high level of saving. But if Aaron's current income is low and his expected future income is high, he will have a low (perhaps even negative) level of saving.

Students have low current incomes compared with expected future incomes, so they tend to consume more than they earn. In middle age, most people are earning more than they expect to earn when they retire, so they save for their retirement years.

The Interest Rate

A pound saved today grows into a pound plus interest tomorrow. The higher the interest rate, the greater is the amount that a pound saved today becomes in the future. Thus the higher the interest rate, the greater is the opportunity cost of current consumption. With a higher opportunity cost of current consumption, Aaron cuts his current consumption and increases his saving.

Supply Curve of Capital

The supply curve of capital shows the relationship between the quantity of capital supplied and the interest rate, other things remaining the same. The curve KS_0 in Figure 17.5 is a supply curve of capital. Let's now use what we've learned about the demand for and supply of capital and see how the interest rate is determined.

The Interest Rate

The interest rate coordinates people's saving and investment plans through capital markets. If saving exceeds investment, the interest falls and if saving is less than investment, the interest rate rises. By adjusting in response to a surplus or shortage of funds, the interest rate makes saving and investment plans compatible.

Figure 17.5 illustrates these adjustments in the capital market. The demand for capital is KD_0 and the supply of capital is KS_0. The equilibrium real interest rate is 6 per cent a year, and the quantity of capital – amount of investment by firms and saving by households – is £150 billion.

If the interest rate exceeded 6 per cent a year, the quantity of capital supplied would exceed the quantity demanded and the interest rate would fall. The interest rate would keep falling until the capital surplus was eliminated.

If the interest rate were less than 6 per cent a year, the quantity of capital demanded would exceed the quantity supplied and the interest rate would rise. The interest rate would keep rising until the capital shortage was eliminated.

Figure 17.5

Capital Market Equilibrium

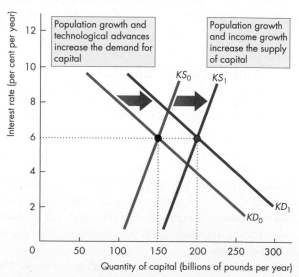

Initially, the demand for capital is KD_0 and the supply of capital is KS_0. The equilibrium interest rate is 6 per cent a year and the capital stock is £150 billion.

Over time, both the demand and supply of capital increase, to KD_1 and KS_1. The quantity of capital increases, but the interest rate is constant.

Changes in Demand and Supply

Over time, both the demand for capital and the supply of capital increase. In Figure 17.5, the demand curve shifts rightward to KD_1 and the supply curve shifts to KS_1. Both curves shift because the same or related forces influence them. Population growth increases both demand and supply. Technological advances increase demand and bring higher incomes, which in turn increase supply. Because both demand and supply increase over time, the quantity of capital increases but the real interest rate remains constant.

In reality, the real interest rate fluctuates, as you can see in Box 17.2 Figure 1 on p. 375. The reason is that the demand for capital and the supply of capital do not change in step. Sometimes rapid technological change brings an increase in the demand for capital *before* it brings the higher incomes that increase the supply of capital. When this sequence of events occurs, the real interest rate rises. The 1990s was such a time.

At other times, the demand for capital grows slowly or even decreases temporarily. In this situation, supply outgrows demand and the real interest rate falls and may even become negative. The mid-1970s was such a period.

The lessons we've just learned about capital markets can be used to understand the prices of non-renewable natural resources. Let's see how.

Natural Resource Markets

Natural resources, or what economists call *land*, fall into two categories:

1 Renewable.
2 Non-renewable.

Renewable natural resources are natural resources that are repeatedly replenished by nature. Examples are land (in its everyday sense), rivers, lakes, rain, forests and sunshine.

Non-renewable natural resources are natural resources that nature does not replenish. Once used, they are no longer available. Examples are coal, natural gas and oil – the so-called hydrocarbon fuels.

The demand for natural resources as inputs into production is based on the same principle of marginal revenue product as the demand for labour (and the demand for capital). But the supply of natural resources is special. Let's look first at the supply of renewable natural resources.

The Supply of a Renewable Natural Resource

The quantity of land and other renewable natural resources is fixed. The quantity supplied cannot be changed by individual decisions. People can vary the amount of land they own. But when one person buys some land, another person sells it. The aggregate quantity of land supplied of any particular type and in any particular location is fixed, regardless of the decisions of any individual. This fact means that the supply of each particular piece of land is perfectly inelastic.

Figure 17.6 illustrates such a supply. Regardless of the rent available, the quantity of land supplied in Oxford Street, London is a fixed number of square metres.

Because the supply of land is fixed regardless of its price, price is determined by demand. The greater the demand for a specific piece of land, the higher is its price.

Expensive land can be, and is, used more intensively than inexpensive land. For example, high-rise buildings enable land to be used more intensively. However, to use land more intensively, it has to be combined with another factor of production: capital. An increase in the amount of capital per block of land does not change the supply of land itself.

Figure 17.6

The Supply of Land

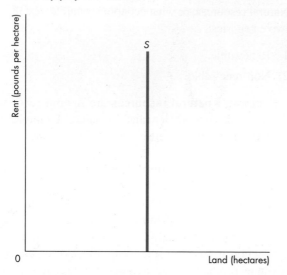

The supply of a given piece of land is perfectly inelastic. No matter what the rent, no more land than exists can be supplied.

Although the supply of each type of land is fixed and its supply is perfectly inelastic, each individual firm, operating in competitive land markets, faces an elastic supply of land. For example, Oxford Street, London has a fixed amount of land, but McDonald's could rent space from Selfridges, the department store, if they want to open a new outlet. Each firm can rent the quantity of land that it demands at the going rent, as determines in the marketplace. So provided land markets are highly competitive, firms are price takers in these markets, just as they are in the markets for other factors of production.

The Supply of Non-renewable Natural Resource

The *stock* of a natural resource is the quantity in existence at a given time. This quantity is fixed and is independent of the price of the resource. The *known* stock of a natural resource is the quantity that has been discovered. This quantity increases over time because advances in technology enable ever less accessible sources to be discovered. Both of these *stock* concepts influence the price of a non-renewable natural resource. But the influence is indirect. The direct influence on price is the rate at which the resource is supplied for use in production – called the flow supply.

The flow supply of a non-renewable natural resource is *perfectly elastic* at a price that equals the present value of the expected price next period.

To see why, think about the economic choices of Saudi Arabia, a country that possesses a large inventory of oil. Saudi Arabia can sell an additional billion barrels of oil right now and use the income it receives to buy US or EU bonds. Or it can keep the billion barrels in the ground and sell them next year. If it sells the oil and buys bonds, it earns the interest rate on the bonds. If it keeps the oil and sells it next year, it earns the amount of the price increase or loses the amount of the price decrease between now and next year.

If Saudi Arabia expects the price of oil to rise next year by a percentage that equals the current interest rate, the price that it expects next year equals $(1 + r)$ multiplied by this year's price. For example, if this year's price is £30 a barrel and the interest rate is 5 per cent ($r = 0.5$), then next year's expected price is $1.05 \times £30$, which equals £31.50 a barrel.

With the price expected to rise to £31.50 next year, Saudi Arabia is indifferent between selling now for £30 and not selling now but waiting until next year and selling for £31.50. Saudi Arabia expects to make the same return either way. So at £30 a barrel, Saudi Arabia will sell whatever quantity is demanded.

But if Saudi Arabia expects the price to rise next year by a percentage that exceeds the current interest rate, then Saudi Arabia expects to make a bigger return by hanging onto the oil than by selling the oil and buying bonds. So it keeps the oil and sells none.

And if Saudi Arabia expects the price to rise next year by a percentage that is less than the current interest rate, the bond gives a bigger return than the oil, so Saudi Arabia sells as much oil as it can.

Recall the idea of discounting and present value. The minimum price at which Saudi Arabia is willing to sell oil is the present value of the expected future price. At this price, it will sell as much oil as buyers demand. So its supply is perfectly elastic.

Price and the Hotelling Principle

Figure 17.7 shows the equilibrium in a natural resource market. Because supply is perfectly elastic at the present value of next period's expected price, the actual price of the natural resource equals the present value of next period's expected price. Also, because the current price is the present value of the expected future price, the price of the resource is expected to rise at a rate equal to the interest rate.

Figure 17.7

A Non-renewable Natural Resource

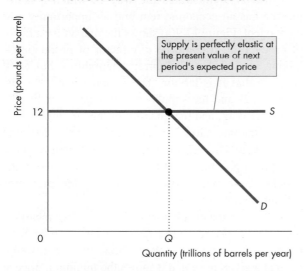

Supply is perfectly elastic at the present value of next period's expected price

Quantity (trillions of barrels per year)

The supply of a non-renewable natural resource is perfectly elastic at the *present value* of next period's expected price. The demand for a non-renewable natural resource is determined by its marginal revenue product. The price is determined by supply and equals the *present value* of next period's expected price.

The proposition that the price of a resource is expected to rise at a rate equal to the interest rate is called the **Hotelling Principle**. It was first realized by Harold Hotelling, a mathematician and economist at Columbia University. But as Figure 17.8 shows, *actual* prices do not follow the path *predicted* by the Hotelling Principle. Why do the prices of non-renewable natural resources sometimes fall rather than follow their expected path and increase over time?

The key reason is that the future is unpredictable. Expected technological change is reflected in the price of a natural resource. But a previously unexpected new technology that leads to the discovery or the more efficient use of a non-renewable natural resource causes its price to fall. Over the years, as technology has advanced, we have become more efficient in our use of non-renewable natural resources. And we haven't just become more efficient. We've become more efficient than we expected to. We have repeatedly been surprised by our good fortune in discovering more fuel-efficient technologies and in discovering previously unexpected sources of fuels.

When this period of pleasant surprises comes to an end, prices will begin to rise as predicted by the Hotelling rule.

Figure 17.8

Falling Metal Prices

The prices of metals (here an average of the prices of aluminium, copper, iron ore, lead, manganese, nickel, silver, tin and zinc) have tended to fall over time, not rise as predicted by the Hotelling Principle. The reason is that unanticipated advances in technology have decreased the cost of extracting metals and greatly increased the exploitable known reserves.

Source: *International Financial Statistics*, International Monetary Fund, Washington, DC (various issues).

Review Quiz

1   Define a renewable natural resource and a non-renewable natural resource and provide some examples of each.
2   Why is the supply of a renewable natural resource such as land perfectly inelastic?
3   At what price is the flow supply of a non-renewable natural resource perfectly elastic and why?
4   Why is the price of a non-renewable natural resource expected to rise at a rate equal to the interest rate?
5   Why do the prices of non-renewable natural resources not follow the path predicted by the Hotelling Principle?

People supply resources to earn income. But some peoples earn enormous incomes. Are such incomes necessary to induce people to work and supply other resources? Let's now answer this question.

Income, Economic Rent and Opportunity Cost

You've now seen how factor prices are determined by the interaction of demand and supply. And you've seen that demand is determined by marginal productivity and supply is determined by the resources available and by people's choices about their use. The interaction of demand and supply in factor markets determines who receives a large income and who receives a small income.

Large and Small Incomes

A chief executive earns a large income because she has a high marginal revenue product – reflected in the demand for her services – and the supply of people with the combination of talents needed for this kind of job is small – reflected in the supply. Equilibrium occurs at a high wage rate and a small quantity employed.

People who work at fast-food restaurants earn a low wage rate because they have a low marginal revenue product – reflected in the demand for their services – and many people are able and willing to supply their labour for these jobs. Equilibrium occurs at a low wage rate and a large number of fast-food workers employed.

If the demand for chief executives increases, their incomes increase by a large amount and the number of chief executives barely changes. If the demand for fast-food workers increases, the number of people doing these jobs increases by a large amount and the wage rate barely changes.

Another difference between a chief executive and a fast-food worker is that if the chief executive were hit with a pay cut, she would probably still supply her services, but if a fast-food worker were hit with a pay cut, he would probably quit. This difference arises from the interesting distinction between economic rent and opportunity cost.

Economic Rent and Opportunity Cost

The total income of a factor of production is made up of its economic rent and its opportunity cost. **Economic rent** is an income received by the owner of a factor over and above the amount required to induce that owner to offer the factor for use. Any factor of production can receive an economic rent. The income required to induce the supply of a factor of production is the oppor-

tunity cost of using a factor of production – the value of the factor in its next best use.

Figure 17.9 illustrates the way in which a factor income has an economic rent and an opportunity cost component. Figure 17.9(a) shows the market for a factor of production. It could be *any* factor of production – labour, capital, land or entrepreneurship – but we'll suppose that it is labour. The demand curve for the labour is D and the supply curve of labour is S. The wage rate is W, and the quantity of labour employed is C. The income earned is the sum of the yellow and green areas. The yellow area below the supply curve measures opportunity cost. The green area above the supply curve but below the factor price measures economic rent.

To see why the area below the supply curve measures opportunity cost, recall that a supply curve can be interpreted in two different ways. It shows the quantity supplied at a given price and it shows the minimum price at which a given quantity is willingly supplied. If suppliers receive only the minimum amount required to induce them to supply each unit of the factor, they will be paid a different price for each unit. The prices will trace the supply curve and the income received will be entirely opportunity cost – the yellow area in Figure 17.9(a).

The concept of economic rent is similar to the concept of producer surplus that you met in Chapter 5. The economic rent is the price a person receives for the use of a factor minus the minimum price at which a given quantity of the factor is willingly supplied.

Economic rent is *not* the same thing as the "rent" that a farmer pays for the use of some land or the "rent" that you pay on your flat. Everyday "rent" is a price paid for the services of land or a building. *Economic rent* is a component of the income received by any factor of production.

The portion of factor income that consists of economic rent depends on the elasticity of the supply of the factor. When the supply of a factor is perfectly inelastic, its entire income is economic rent. A large part of the income received by a chief executive is economic rent. When the supply of a factor of production is perfectly elastic, none of its income is economic rent. Most of the income earned by low-skilled workers is opportunity cost. In general, when the supply curve is neither perfectly elastic nor perfectly inelastic, some part of the factor income is economic rent and the other part opportunity cost – as Figure 17.9(a) illustrates.

Figures 17.9(b) and 17.9(c) show the other two possibilities. Part (b) shows the market for a particular

Figure 17.9

Economic Rent and Opportunity Cost

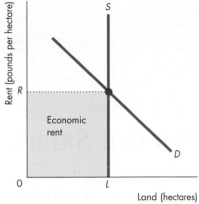

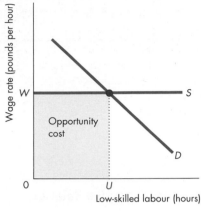

(a) General case

(b) All economic rent

(c) All opportunity cost

When the supply curve of a factor slopes upward – the general case – as in part (a), part of the factor income is economic rent (the green area) and part is opportunity cost (the yellow area). When the supply of a factor is perfectly inelastic (the supply curve is vertical), as in part (b), the entire factor income is economic rent. When the supply of a factor is perfectly elastic (the supply curve is horizontal), as in part (c), the entire factor income is opportunity cost.

block of land in London. The quantity of land is fixed in size at L hectares. So the supply curve of land is vertical – perfectly inelastic. No matter what the rent on the land is, there is no way of increasing the quantity supplied.

The demand for that block of land is determined by its marginal revenue product, which depends on the uses to which the land can be put. In central London, the marginal revenue product is high because there is a great deal of capital and business there. The marginal revenue product of this land is shown by the demand curve in Figure 17.9(b). The entire income accruing to the owner of the land is the green area in the figure. This income is economic rent. The rent charged for this piece of land depends entirely on its marginal revenue product – on the demand curve. If the demand curve shifts rightward, the rent rises. If the demand curve shifts leftward, the rent falls. The quantity of land supplied remains constant at L.

Figure 17.9(c) shows the market for a factor of production that is in perfectly elastic supply. An example of such a market might be unskilled labour in India or China. In these countries, lots of people flock to the cities and are available for work at the going wage rate (in this case, W). In these labour markets, the supply of

labour is almost perfectly elastic. The entire income earned by these unskilled workers is opportunity cost. They receive no economic rent at all.

Review Quiz

1. Why do premier league football players earn larger incomes than bus drivers?
2. What is the distinction between an economic rent and an opportunity cost?
3. Is the income that Manchester United pays Wayne Rooney an economic rent, compensation for his opportunity cost, or a combination of economic rent and opportunity cost? Explain.
4. Is coffee more expensive in London than in Lincoln because rents are higher in London or are rents higher in London because people in London are willing to pay more for a coffee?

The *Business Case Study* on pp. 386–387 looks at the market for chief executives. And the next chapter looks at how the market economy distributes income. The chapter also looks at the efforts by governments to redistribute income and modify the market outcome.

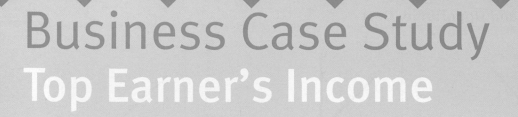

Business Case Study
Top Earner's Income

Fat Cat Salaries

Chief Executive Salaries

Every year the record salary for company fat cats is broken. The table shows that chief executives in the United States were paid most on average, followed by chief executives in the United Kingdom. Chief executives in Germany, Sweden and Spain are paid half that in the United Kingdom.

Country	Chief executive pay (pounds per year)
United States	1,182,256
United Kingdom	408,993
Australia	334,691
France	317,566
Japan	310,863
Germany	278,360
Sweden	253,205

Source: http://news.bbc.co.uk/go/pr/fr/-/1/hi/business/3023254.stm, Towers Perrin

Chief Executives' Actual Income

The stated salary of chief executives is just a small fraction of their total payment package. In 2004, a report by Independent Remuneration Solutions (IRS)[1] found that basic salaries comprised only 16 per cent of the total pay to UK chief executives. Additional payments include bonuses, share options and pension payments. IRS found that the actual average payment to a UK company executive in 2003 was £5.4 million. Vodafone's chief executive received the highest pay – £10.9 million.

Reasons for Fat Cat Salaries

Companies state that additional payments to chief executives reflect their huge positive impact on profits, share value and growth. IRS estimated UK chief executive payments rose 24 per cent in 2003, whereas the value of shares in the top 100 UK companies increased by only 10 per cent. But another factor identified for high payments is competition for the best chief executives. Chief executives with good track records are difficult to find.

Are Shareholder's Happy?

A 2003 report by Mori and the Investor Relations Society found that 73 per cent of investors thought that current pay deals were bad for business[2]. Almost all shareholders – 94 per cent – thought pay should be more clearly linked to performance. Shareholders are becoming proactive. In 2003, a wave of shareholder revolts made UK companies rethink their chief executive pay deals.

[1] http://news.bbc.co.uk/go/pr/fr/-/1/hi/business/3622643.stm

[2] http://news.bbc.co.uk/go/pr/fr/-/1/hi/business/3243290.stm

Economic Analysis

◆ The marginal revenue product of chief executives is large because they generate huge
revenues for their companies.

◆ The supply of chief executives is limited. No
one would be willing to qualify and get the
experience to be a chief executive for an
income below the managerial average. But
plenty of executives are willing to be chief
executives at incomes above the managerial
average.

◆ Very few executives have the talent to perform at the highest level. No matter how
much executives' compensation rises above
the managerial average, the quantity of
best-performing chief executives does not
increase. The supply is inelastic.

◆ In Figure 1, the supply of best-performing
executives is the curve labelled S. The average managerial payment is at A. As managerial payments rise above A, the quantity
of chief executives supplied increases. The
maximum quantity, Q_0, is determined by the
limited pool of talent.

◆ The demand for the best 100 chief executives is determined by their marginal revenue
product, shown by the curve D_0 in Figure 1.

◆ Equilibrium in the market for these chief
executives occurs at an average payment
of about £5.4 million. They earn at least
£1 million and as much as £10.9 million
a year – Vodaphone's chief executive's pay.

◆ Most of the executive's income is economic
rent, the green area in Figure 1, and only
a small proportion is opportunity cost, the
yellow area.

◆ The marginal revenue product of the majority
of chief executives, D_1 is not as high as that
of the high fliers. The equilibrium wage for
this group is about £1 million a year and
their economic rent is less than that of the
high fliers.

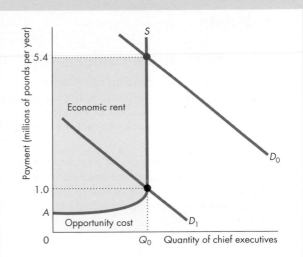

Figure 1 The market for chief executives

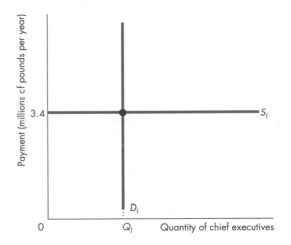

Figure 2 The individual firm

◆ Figure 2 shows the situation facing an individual company. The company faces a perfectly elastic supply of chief executives, S_l,
at the equilibrium payment of $3.4 million
a year. If the company wants Q_l chief executives, its demand curve is D_l, and it pays the
going rate.

Summary

Key Points

Factor Prices and Incomes (p. 366)

♦ An increase in the demand for a factor of production increases the factor's price and total income; a decrease in the demand for a factor of production decreases the factor's price and total income.

♦ An increase in the supply of a factor of production increases the quantity used but decreases its price and might increase or decrease its total income depending on whether demand is elastic or inelastic.

Labour Markets (pp. 367–374)

♦ The demand for labour is determined by the marginal revenue product.

♦ The demand for labour increases if the price of the firm's output rises or if technological change and capital accumulation increase marginal product.

♦ The elasticity of demand for labour depends on labour intensity in production, the elasticity of demand for the product and the ease with which labour can be substituted for capital.

♦ The quantity of labour supplied increases as the real wage rate increases, but at high wage rates, the supply curve eventually bends backwards.

♦ The supply of labour increases as the population increases and with technological change and capital accumulation.

♦ Wage rates increase because the demand for labour increases by more than the supply of labour.

Capital Markets (pp. 375–381)

♦ To make an investment decision, firms compare the *present value* of the marginal revenue product of capital with the price of capital.

♦ The higher the interest rate, the greater is the amount of saving and the quantity of capital supplied.

♦ Capital market equilibrium determines interest rates.

♦ Common and related factors influence both demand and supply, so the interest rate fluctuates but doesn't rise or fall over time.

Natural Resource Markets
(pp. 381–383)

♦ The demand for a natural resource is determined by marginal revenue product.

♦ The supply of land is inelastic.

♦ The supply of non-renewable natural resources is perfectly elastic at a price equal to the present value of the expected future price.

♦ The price of non-renewable natural resources is expected to rise at a rate equal to the interest rate but fluctuates and might fall.

Income, Economic Rent and Opportunity Cost (pp. 384–385)

♦ Economic rent is the income received by a factor over and above the amount needed to induce the factor owner to supply the resource for use.

♦ The rest of a factor's income is opportunity cost.

♦ When the supply of a factor is perfectly inelastic, its entire income is made up of economic rent. When the supply of a factor is perfectly elastic, its entire income is made up of opportunity cost.

Key Figures and Tables

Key Terms

Problems

*Solutions to odd-numbered problems are available on *Parkin Interactive*.

*1 The figure illustrates a European market for straw-berry pickers:

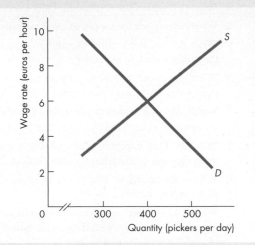

a What is the wage rate paid to strawberry pickers?

b How many strawberry pickers get employed?

c What is the income received by strawberry pickers?

2 In problem 1, if the demand for strawberry pickers increases by 100 a day,

a What is the new wage rate paid to the pickers?

b How many additional pickers get employed?

c What is the total income paid to pickers?

*3 The European fish packing industry is competitive and Wanda owns a fish shop. She employs students to sort and pack the fish. Students can pack the following amounts of fish in an hour:

Number of students	Quantity of fish (kilograms)
1	20
2	50
3	90
4	120
5	145
6	165
7	180
8	190

The market price of fish is 50 cents a kilogram and the wage rate of packers is €7.50 an hour.

a Calculate the marginal product of the students and draw the marginal product curve.

b Calculate the marginal revenue product of the students and draw the marginal revenue product curve.

c Find Wanda's demand for labour curve.

d How many students does Wanda employ?

4 The European ice market is competitive and Barry makes bags of ice. He employs workers to bag the ice who can produce the following quantities in an hour:

Number of workers	Quantity of ice (bags)
1	40
2	100
3	180
4	240
5	290
6	330
7	360
8	380

The market price of ice is 25 cents a bag and the wage rate for bagging ice is €5.00 an hour.

a Calculate the marginal product of the workers and draw the marginal product curve.

b Calculate the marginal revenue product of the workers and draw the marginal revenue produce curve.

c Find Barry's demand for labour curve.

d How much ice does Barry sell?

*5 Back at Wanda's fish shop described in problem 3, the price of fish falls to €33.33 a kilogram but fish packers' wages remain at €7.50 an hour, what happens to:

a Wanda's marginal product?

b Wanda's marginal revenue product?

c Wanda's demand for labour curve?

d Number of students Wanda employs?

6 Back at Barry's ice making plant described in problem 4, the price of ice falls to 10 cents a bag but baggers' wages remain at €5.00 an hour, what happens to:

a Barry's marginal product?

b Barry's marginal revenue product?

c Barry's demand for labour curve?

d Number of students Barry employs?

*7 Back at Wanda's fish shop described in problem 3, packers' wages increase to €10 an hour, but the price of fish remains at 50 cents a kilogram.

  a What happens to marginal revenue product?

  b What happens to Wanda's demand for labour curve?

  c How many students does Wanda employ?

8 Back at Barry's ice shop described in problem 4, baggers' wages increase to €10 an hour, but the price of ice remains at 25 cents a bag.

  a What happens to marginal revenue product?

  b What happens to Barry's demand for labour curve?

  c How many baggers does Barry employ?

*9 Using the information in problem 3, calculate Wanda's marginal revenue, marginal cost, and marginal revenue product. Show that when Wanda is making maximum profit, marginal cost equals marginal revenue and marginal revenue product equals the wage rate.

10 Using the information in problem 4, calculate Barry's marginal revenue, marginal cost, and marginal revenue product. Show that when Barry is making maximum profit, marginal cost equals marginal revenue and marginal revenue product equals the wage rate.

*11 Greg has found an oil well in his backyard. A geologist estimates that a total of 10 million barrels can pump for a pumping cost of €1 a barrel. If the price of oil is €20 a barrel, how many barrels of oil does Greg sell each year? If you can't predict how many, what extra information do you need to be able to do so?

12 Orley has a wine cellar in which he keeps choice wines from around the world. What does Orley expect to happen to the prices of the wines he keeps in his cellar? Explain your answer. How does Orley decide which wine to drink and when to drink it?

*13 Use the graph in problem 1 and show on the graph the strawberry pickers':

  a Economic rent.

  b Opportunity cost.

14 Use the graph in problem 1 and the information in problem 2 and show on the graph the strawberry pickers':

  a Economic rent.

  b Opportunity cost.

Critical Thinking

1 Study the *Business Case Study* on pp. 386–387 and then answer the following questions:

  a What determines the demand for chief executives?

  b What determines the supply of chief executives?

  c What do you think chief executives would do if they didn't work in industry?

  d What does your answer to part (c) tell you about the opportunity cost of these chief executives?

  e What does your answer to part (c) tell you about the economic rent received by these chief executives?

  f Why don't top executives have contracts that give them their entire marginal revenue product?

  g Why is the economic rent of most executives less than the top chief executives?

  h Would an inexperienced executive gain as much economic rent as executives with good track records? Explain your answer?

2 "We are running out of natural resources and must take urgent action to conserve our precious reserves." "There is no shortage of resources that the market cannot cope with." Identify the pros and cons for each view, and discuss each in turn. What is your view and why?

3 Why do we keep finding new reserves of oil? Why don't we do a big once-and-for-all survey to catalogue the earth's entire inventory of natural resources?

Web Exercise

Use the links on *Parkin Interactive* to work the following exercises.

1 Find data on the earnings of leading golfers, tennis players, and footballers. Then answer the following questions:

  a What determines the demand for a top-performing professional sports person?

  b What determines the supply of a top-performing professional sports person?

  c What do you think Lee Westwood, Tim Henman and David Beckham would do if they didn't play their sports?

  d What does your answer to part (c) tell you about the opportunity cost of these players?

  e What does your answer to part (c) tell you about the economic rent received by these players?

Chapter 17 APPENDIX
Market Power in the Labour Market

After studying this appendix you will be able to:

◆ Explain why union workers earn more than non-union workers

◆ Explain how a minimum wage can increase both the wage rate and employment in a monopsony labour market

Trade Unions

Just as a monopoly firm can restrict output and raise price, so a monopoly owner of a resource can restrict supply and raise the price of the resource. The main source of market power in the labour market is the trade union. A **trade union** is an organized group of workers that aims to increase wages and influence other job conditions.

A union's ability to pursue its objectives is restricted by two sets of constraints – one on the supply side of the labour market and the other on the demand side. On the supply side, the union's activities are limited by how well it can restrict non-union workers from offering their labour in the same market as union labour. The larger the fraction of the work force controlled by the union, the more effective the union can be in this regard. It is difficult for unions to operate in markets in which the supply of willing non-union labour is abundant. For example, the market for hotel workers is tough for a union to organize because of the ready flow of non-union labour from Eastern Europe.

At the other extreme, unions in the construction industry can better pursue their goals because they can influence the number of people who can obtain skills as electricians, plasterers and joiners. The professional associations of dentists and doctors are best able to restrict supply. These groups control the number of qualified workers by controlling either the examinations that new entrants must pass or entrance into professional degree programmes.

On the demand side of the labour market, the union faces a trade-off that arises from firms' profit-maximizing decisions. Because labour demand curves slope downward, anything a union does that increases the wage rate or other employment costs decreases the quantity of labour demanded.

Let's see how a trade union operates in competitive labour markets.

A Union in a Competitive Labour Market

Figure A17.1 illustrates a competitive labour market that a union enters. The demand curve is D_C, and the supply curve is S_C. Before the union enters the market, the wage rate is £7 an hour and 100 hours of labour are employed.

Now suppose that a union is formed to organize the workers in this market. The union can attempt to increase wages in this market in two ways. It can try to

Figure A17.1

A Union in a Competitive Labour Market

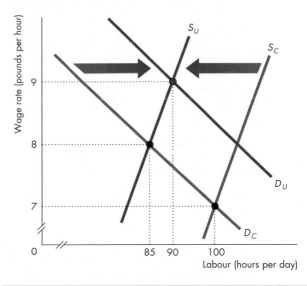

In a competitive labour market, the demand curve is D_C and the supply curve is S_C. Competitive equilibrium occurs at a wage rate of £7 an hour with 100 hours employed. By restricting employment below the competitive level, the union shifts the supply of labour to S_U. If the union can do no more than that, the wage rate will increase to £8 an hour but employment will fall to 85 hours. If the union can increase the demand for labour (by increasing the demand for the good produced by union members or by raising the price of substitute labour) and shift the demand curve to D_U, then it can increase the wage rate still higher, to £9 an hour, and achieve employment of 90 hours.

restrict the supply of labour or it can try to stimulate the demand for labour. First, look at what happens if the union has sufficient control over the supply of labour to be able to artificially restrict that supply below its competitive level – to S_U. If that is all the union is able to do, employment falls to 85 hours of labour and the wage rate rises to £8 an hour. The union simply picks its preferred position along the demand curve that defines the trade-off it faces between employment and the wage rate. You can see that if the union can only restrict the supply of labour, it raises the wage rate but decreases the number of jobs available. Because of this outcome, unions try to increase the demand for labour and shift the demand curve rightward. Let's see what they might do to achieve this outcome.

How Unions Try to Change the Demand for Labour

The union tries to operate on the demand for labour in two ways. First, it tries to make the demand for union labour inelastic. Second, it tries to increase the demand for union labour. Making the demand for labour less elastic does not eliminate the trade-off between employment and the wage rate. But it does make the trade-off less unfavourable. If a union can make the demand for labour less elastic, it can increase the wage rate at a lower cost in terms of lost employment opportunities. But if the union can increase the demand for labour, it might even be able to increase both the wage rate and the employment opportunities of its members.

Unions try to increase the marginal product of their members, which in turn increases the demand for their labour, by organizing and sponsoring training schemes, by encouraging apprenticeship and other on-the-job training activities, and by professional certification.

Figure A17.1 illustrates the effects of an increase in the demand for the labour of a union's members. If the union can also take steps that increase the demand for labour to D_U, it can achieve an even bigger increase in the wage rate with a smaller fall in employment.

By maintaining the restricted labour supply at S_U, the union increases the wage rate to £9 an hour and achieves an employment level of 90 hours of labour.

Because a union restricts the supply of labour in the market in which it operates, its actions increase the supply of labour in non-union markets. Workers who can't get union jobs must look elsewhere for work. This increase in the supply of labour in non-union markets lowers the wage rate in those markets and further widens the union–non-union differential.

Monopsony

A market in which there is a single buyer is called **monopsony**. This market type is unusual, but it does exist. With the growth of large-scale production over the last century, large manufacturing plants such as coal mines, steel and textile mills, and car manufacturers became the major employer in some regions, and in some places a single firm employed almost all the labour. Today, in some parts of the country, managed healthcare organizations are the major employer of healthcare professionals. These firms have market power.

In monopsony, the employer determines the wage rate and pays the lowest wage at which it can attract the labour it plans to employ. A monopsony makes a bigger profit than a group of firms that compete with each other for their labour. Let's find out how they achieve this outcome.

Like all firms, a monopsony has a downward-sloping marginal revenue product curve, which is *MRP* in Figure A17.2. This curve tells us the extra revenue the monopsony receives by selling the output produced by an extra hour of labour. The supply of labour curve is *S*. This curve tells us how many hours are supplied at each wage rate. It also tells us the minimum wage for which a given quantity of labour is willing to work.

A monopsony recognizes that to employ more labour, it must pay a higher wage; equivalently, by employing less labour, it can pay a lower wage. Because a monopsony controls the wage rate, the marginal cost of labour exceeds the wage rate. The marginal cost of labour is shown by the curve *MCL*. The relationship between the marginal cost of labour curve and the supply curve is similar to the relationship between the marginal cost and average cost curves that you studied in Chapter 10.

The supply curve is like the average cost of labour curve. In Figure A17.2, the firm can employ 49 hours of labour for a wage rate of just below £4.90 an hour. The firm's total labour cost is £240. But suppose that the firm employs 50 hours of labour. It can employ the 50th hour of labour for £5 an hour. The total cost of labour is now £250 an hour. So employing the 50th hour of labour increases the cost of labour from £240 to £250, which is a £10 increase. The marginal cost of labour is £10 an hour. The curve *MCL* shows the £10 marginal cost of employing the 50th hour of labour.

To calculate the profit-maximizing quantity of labour to employ, the firm sets the marginal cost of labour equal to the marginal revenue product of labour. That is, the firm wants the cost of the last worker employed to equal the extra total revenue brought in. In Figure A17.2, this outcome occurs when the monopsony employs 50 hours of labour. What is the wage rate that the monopsony pays? To employ 50 hours of labour, the firm must pay £5 an hour, as shown by the supply of labour curve. So workers are paid £5 an hour. But the marginal revenue product of labour is £10 an hour, so the firm makes an economic profit of £5 on the last hour of labour that it employs. Compare this outcome with that in a competitive labour market.

If the labour market shown in Figure A17.2 were competitive, equilibrium would occur at the point of intersection of the demand curve and the supply curve. The wage rate would be £7.50 an hour, and 75 hours of labour a day would be employed. So compared with a competitive labour market, a monopsony decreases both the wage rate and employment.

The ability of a monopsony to cut the wage rate and employment and make an economic profit depends on the elasticity of labour supply. If the supply of labour is highly elastic, a monopsony has little power to cut the wage rate and employment to boost its profit.

Figure A17.2

A Monopsony Labour Market

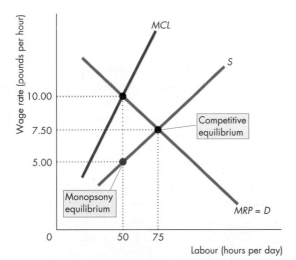

A monopsony is a market structure in which there is a single buyer. A monopsony in the labour market has value of marginal revenue product curve *MRP* and faces a labour supply curve *S*. The marginal cost of labour curve is *MCL*. Making the marginal cost of labour equal to marginal revenue product maximizes profit. The monopsony employs 50 hours of labour and pays the lowest wage for which that labour will work, which is £5 an hour.

Monopsony and a Union

Suppose that a union operates in a monopsony labour market. A union is like a monopoly. If the union (monopoly seller) faces a monopsony buyer, the situation is called **bilateral monopoly**. In bilateral monopoly, the wage rate is determined by bargaining.

In Figure A17.2, if the monopsony is free to determine the wage rate and employment, it employs 50 hours of labour for a wage rate of £5 an hour. But suppose that a union represents the workers. The union agrees to maintain employment at 50 hours but seeks the highest wage rate that the employer can be forced to pay. That wage rate is £10 an hour – the wage rate that equals the marginal revenue product of labour. The union might not be able to get the wage rate up to £10 an hour, but it won't accept £5 an hour. The monopsony firm and the union bargain over the wage rate, and the result is an outcome between £10 and £5 an hour.

The outcome of the bargaining depends on the costs that each party can inflict on the other as a result of a failure to agree on the wage rate. The firm can shut down the plant and lock out its workers, and the workers can shut down the plant by striking. Each party knows the other's strength and knows what it will lose if it does not agree to the other's demands. If the two parties are equally strong and they realize it, they will split the gap between £5 and £10 and agree to a wage rate of £7.50 an hour. If one party is stronger than the other – and both parties know that – the agreed wage will favour the stronger party.

Usually, an agreement is reached without a strike or a lockout. The threat is usually enough to bring the bargaining parties to an agreement. When a strike or lockout does occur, it is usually because one party has misjudged the costs each party can inflict on the other.

Minimum wage laws have interesting effects in monopsony labour markets as you'll now see.

Monopsony and the Minimum Wage

In a competitive labour market, a minimum wage that exceeds the equilibrium wage decreases employment (see Chapter 6, p. 123). In a monopsony labour market, a minimum wage can *increase* both the wage rate and employment. Figure A17.3 shows how.

The wage rate is £5 an hour and 50 hours of labour are employed. A minimum wage of £7.50 an hour is imposed. The monopsony now faces a perfectly elastic supply of labour at £7.50 an hour up to 75 hours. Above 75 hours, a wage above £7.50 an hour must be paid to employ additional hours of labour. The marginal cost of labour is also constant at £7.50 up to 75 hours. Beyond 75 hours, the marginal cost of labour rises above £7.50 an hour. To maximize profit, the monopsony sets the marginal cost of labour equal to the marginal revenue product of labour. It employs 75 hours of labour at £7.50 an hour. The minimum wage law has succeeded in raising the wage rate by £2.50 an hour and increasing the amount of labour employed by 25 hours.

Figure A17.3

Minimum Wage Law in Monopsony

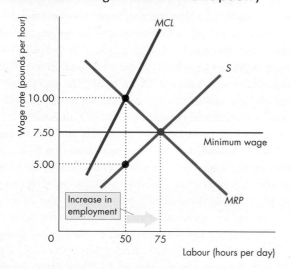

In a monopsony labour market, the wage rate is £5 an hour and 50 hours are employed. If a minimum wage law increases the wage rate to £7.50 an hour, employment increases to 75 hours.

Summary

Key Points

Trade Unions (pp. 391–392)

◆ In competitive labour markets, unions obtain higher wages only at the expense of lower employment but they try to influence the demand for labour.

Monopsony (pp. 392–394)

◆ A monopsony employs less labour and pays a wage rate lower than that in a competitive labour market.

◆ In bilateral monopoly, the wage rate is determined by bargaining.
◆ In monopsony, a minimum wage law can raise the wage rate and increase employment.

Key Terms

Bilateral monopoly, 393
Monopsony, 392
Trade union, 391

Problems

*1   A monopsony gold mining firm operates in an isolated region. The table shows the firm's labour supply schedule (columns 1 and 2) and total product schedule (columns 2 and 3). The price of gold is €1.40 a grain.

Wage rate (euros per day)	Number of workers	Quantity produced (grains per day)
5	0	0
6	1	10
7	2	25
8	3	45
9	4	60
10	5	70
11	6	75

a What wage rate does the company pay?

b How many workers does the gold mine employ?

2   A monopsony logging firm operates in an isolated part of the Alps. The table shows the firm's labour supply schedule (columns 1 and 2) and total product schedule (columns 2 and 3). The price of logs is €2 a tonne.

Wage rate (euros per day)	Number of workers	Quantity produced (tonnes per day)
5	0	0
6	1	9
7	2	17
8	3	24
9	4	30
10	5	35
11	6	39
12	7	42

a What wage rate does the company pay?

b How many workers does the gold mine employ?

Chapter 18

Economic Inequality and Redistribution

After studying this chapter you will be able to:

◆ Describe the inequality in income and wealth in the United Kingdom and Europe and the trends in inequality

◆ Explain the features of the labour market that contribute to economic inequality

◆ Describe the scale of income redistribution by governments and the effects of taxes and benefits on economic inequality

Rags to Riches

J. K. Rowling earns more than £20 million a year and is Britain's highest-earning woman. But before she had the inspiration to write the Harry Potter stories, she was a typical single mother. Many single mothers earn almost nothing and rely on government benefits for their survival. Why are some people incredibly rich while others are abjectly poor? Can governments redistribute income and wealth to moderate the amount of poverty in our society? Find out in this chapter. Do European health services reduce the impact of income inequality without harming efficiency? Find out in the *Policy Case Study* at the end of this chapter.

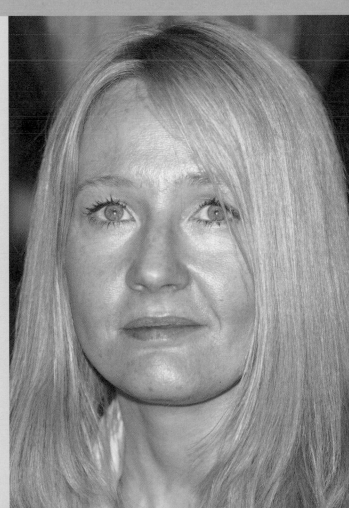

Measuring Economic Inequality

The most commonly used measure of economic inequality is the distribution of annual income. The Office for National Statistics defines as **original income** the income that households receive from market activity before government intervention. Original income equals wages, interest, rent, and profit earned in factor markets and before paying income taxes.

The Distribution of Original Income

Figure 18.1 shows the distribution of original income across the 25 million households in the United Kingdom in 1999–2000. Note that the *x*-axis measures household income and the *y*-axis is percentage of households. The income numbers are expressed as average weekly incomes (annual income divided by 52).

The most common household original income, called the *mode* income, was received by the 9 per cent of the households whose incomes fell between £100 and £149 a week. The value of £125 marked on Figure 18.1 is the middle of that range.

The income that separates households into two equal groups, called the *median* income, was about £330 a week. One half of UK households had incomes greater than this amount, and the other half had incomes less than this amount.

The average household original income in 1999–2000, called the *mean* income, was £510 a week.

You can see in Figure 18.1 that the mode income is less than the median income and the median income is less than the mean income. This feature of the distribution of income tells us that there are more households with low incomes than with high incomes. And some of the high incomes are very high – well off the scale shown in the figure.

The income distribution in Figure 18.1 is called a *positively skewed* distribution, which means that it has a long tail of high values. This distribution shape contrasts with a *bell-shaped* distribution such as the distribution of people's heights. In a bell-shaped distribution, the mean, median and mode are all equal.

Another way of looking at the distribution of income is to measure the percentage of total income received by each given percentage of households. Data are reported for five groups – called *quintiles* or fifth shares – each consisting of 20 per cent of households.

Figure 18.2 shows the distribution based on these shares in 1999–2000. The poorest 20 per cent of house-

Figure 18.1

The Distribution of Original Income in the United Kingdom in 1999–2000

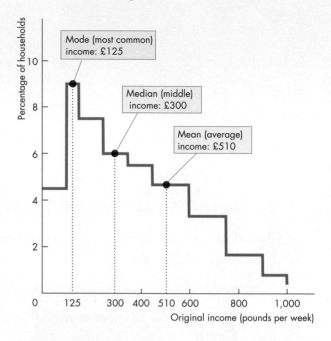

The distribution of original income – income from market activity and before government intervention – is positively skewed. The mode (most common) income is less than the median (middle) income, which in turn is less than the mean (average) income. The percentage of households with an income above £1,000 a week (not shown) falls off slowly and the highest incomes are more than £100,000 a week.

Source: "The effects of taxes and benefits on household income, 1999–2000" by Caroline Lakin, Office for National Statistics.

holds received 2 per cent of total income; the second poorest 20 per cent received 7 per cent of total income; the middle 20 per cent received 15 per cent of total income; the next highest 20 per cent received 25 per cent of total income; and the highest 20 per cent received 52 per cent of total income. (These numbers are rounded to the nearest whole number and don't quite sum to 100.)

The distribution of income in Figure 18.1 and the quintile shares in Figure 18.2 tell us that income is distributed unequally. But we need a way of comparing the distribution of income in different periods and using different measures. A neat graphical tool called the *Lorenz curve* enables us to make such comparisons.

Figure 18.2

UK Quintile Shares in 1999–2000

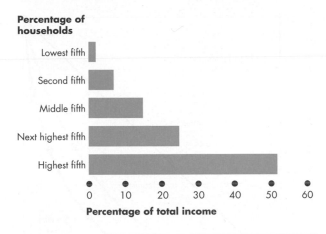

Households (percentage)	Income (percentage of total income)
Lowest 20	2
Second 20	7
Middle 20	15
Next highest 20	25
Highest 20	52

In 1999–2000, the poorest 20 per cent of households received 2 per cent of total income; the second poorest 20 per cent received 7 per cent; the middle 20 per cent received 15 per cent; the next highest 20 per cent received 25 per cent; and the highest 20 per cent received 52 per cent. (These numbers are rounded to the nearest whole number and don't quite sum to 100.)

Source: Office for National Statistics (see Figure 18.1).

The Income Lorenz Curve

The income **Lorenz curve** graphs the cumulative percentage of income against the cumulative percentage of households. Figure 18.3 shows the income Lorenz curve using the quintile shares from Figure 18.2. The table shows the percentage of income of each quintile group. For example, row *A* tells us that the lowest quintile of households receives 2 per cent of total income. The table also shows the *cumulative* percentages of households and income. For example, row *B* tells us that the lowest two quintiles (lowest 40 per cent) of households receive 9 per cent of total original income – 2 per cent for the lowest quintile and 7 per cent for the next lowest.

If income were distributed equally across all the households, each quintile would receive 20 per cent of

Figure 18.3

The Income Lorenz Curve in 1999–2000

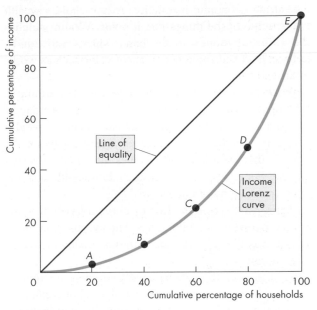

	Households		Income	
	Percentage	Cumulative percentage	Percentage	Cumulative percentage
A Lowest 20	20	20	2	2
B Second 20	40	40	7	9
C Middle 20	60	60	15	24
D Next highest 20	80	80	25	49
E Highest 20	100	100	52	100*

The cumulative percentage of income is graphed against the cumulative percentage of households. Points *A* to *E* on the Lorenz curve correspond to the rows of the table. If incomes were distributed equally, each 20 per cent of households would receive 20 per cent of total income and the Lorenz curve would fall along the line of equality. The Lorenz curve shows that income is unequally distributed.

*The numbers sum to 101 because they are rounded to the nearest whole percentage.

Source: Office for National Statistics (see Figure 18.1).

total income and the cumulative percentages of income received by the cumulative percentages of households would fall along the straight line labelled "Line of equality". The actual distribution of income is shown by the curve labelled "Income Lorenz curve". The closer the Lorenz curve is to the line of equality, the more equal is the distribution.

The Distribution of Wealth

The distribution of wealth provides another way of measuring economic inequality. A household's wealth is the value of the things that it owns. Wealth includes the value of money in the bank, shares and bonds, houses, land and any other assets of value such as works of art and cars.

Wealth is measured at a *point in time*. For example, we might value a household's wealth on the last day of the year. The point-in-time measurement of wealth contrasts with the measurement of income, which is the amount that the household receives *over a given period of time*. For example, we measure a household's income over a week, a month or a year.

Figure 18.4 shows the Lorenz curve for wealth in the United Kingdom in 2002–2003. The average household wealth was £58,385. But the variation around this value was enormous.

Because wealth is distributed extremely unequally, the quintile shares data on the distribution of wealth are not very revealing. The lowest quintile owns nothing, and the next lowest quintile owns almost nothing. It is more revealing to look at the distribution of wealth by placing households in *unequal* groups. That is what we do in Figure 18.4. The poorest 50 per cent of households own only 5 per cent of total wealth (row A' in the table in Figure 18.4). The next 25 per cent of households own 20 per cent of total wealth (row B' in the table). So the bottom 75 per cent of households own only 25 per cent of total wealth and the richest 25 per cent of households own 75 per cent of total wealth. Because this group owns such a large percentage of total wealth, we break it into smaller bits in rows C' to E'. The richest 1 per cent of households own 23 per cent of total wealth (row E').

Figure 18.4 shows the income Lorenz curve (from Figure 18.3) alongside the wealth Lorenz curve. You can see that the Lorenz curve for wealth is much farther away from the line of equality than is the Lorenz curve for income, which means that the distribution of wealth is much more unequal than the distribution of income.

Wealth versus Income

We've seen that wealth is much more unequally distributed than income. Which distribution provides the better description of the degree of inequality? To answer this question, we need to think about the connection between wealth and income.

Wealth is a stock of assets and income is the flow of earnings that results from the stock of wealth. Suppose

Figure 18.4

Lorenz Curves for Income and Wealth

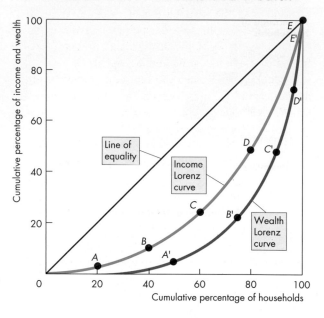

	Households		Wealth	
	Percentage	Cumulative percentage	Percentage	Cumulative percentage
A'	Lowest 50	50	5	5
B'	Next 25	75	20	25
C'	Next 15	90	19	44
D'	Next 9	99	33	77
E'	Highest 1	100	23	100

The cumulative percentage of wealth is graphed against the cumulative percentage of households. Points A' to E' on the Lorenz curve for wealth correspond to the rows of the table. By comparing the Lorenz curves for income and wealth, we can see that wealth is distributed much more unequally than income.

Sources: *Social Trends, 2003*, Office for National Statistics, The Stationery Office, London (2004).

that a person owns assets worth £1 million – has a wealth of £1 million. If the rate of return on assets is 5 per cent a year, then this person receives an income of £50,000 a year from those assets. We can describe this person's economic condition by using either the wealth of £1 million or the income of £50,000. When the rate of return is 5 per cent a year, £1 million of wealth equals

£50,000 of income in perpetuity. Wealth and income are just different ways of looking at the same thing.

But in Figure 18.4, the distribution of wealth is more unequal than the distribution of income. Why? It is because the wealth data do not include the value of human capital, while the income data measure income from all wealth, including human capital.

Table 18.1 illustrates the consequence of omitting human capital from the wealth data. Lee has twice the wealth and twice the income of Peter. But Lee's human capital is less than Peter's – £200,000 compared with £499,000. And Lee's income from human capital of £10,000 is less than Peter's income from human capital of £24,950. Lee's other capital is larger than Peter's – £800,000 compared with £1,000. And Lee's income from other capital of £40,000 is larger than Peter's income from other capital of £50.

When Lee and Peter are surveyed by the Office for National Statistics in a national wealth and income survey, their incomes are recorded as £50,000 and £25,000, respectively, which implies that Lee is twice as well off as Peter. And their tangible assets are recorded as £800,000 and £1,000, respectively, which implies that Lee is 800 times as wealthy as Peter.

Because the national survey of wealth excludes human capital, the income distribution is a more accurate measure of economic inequality than the wealth distribution.

Annual or Lifetime Income and Wealth?

A household's income changes over time. It starts out low, grows to a peak when the household's workers reach retirement age and then falls after retirement.

Also, a typical household's wealth changes over time. Like income, wealth starts out low, grows to a peak at the point of retirement and then falls.

Suppose we look at three households that have identical lifetime incomes. One household is young, one is middle-aged and one is retired. The middle-aged household has the highest income and wealth, the retired household has the lowest and the young household falls in the middle.

The distributions of annual income and wealth in a given year are unequal, but the distributions of lifetime income and wealth are (by assumption) equal.

Although some of the inequality in annual income arises because different households are at different stages in the life cycle, after allowing for this factor, a substantial amount of inequality remains.

Table 18.1

Capital, Wealth and Income

	Lee		Peter	
	Wealth	**Income**	**Wealth**	**Income**
Human capital	200,000	10,000	499,000	24,950
Other capital	800,000	40,000	1,000	50
Total	£1,000,000	£50,000	£500,000	£25,000

When wealth is measured to include the value of human capital as well as other forms of capital, the distribution of income and the distribution of wealth display the same degree of inequality.

So far, we have examined the extent of inequality in income and wealth in a few recent years. What are the trends in inequality? Is the distribution of income becoming less equal or more equal? We can see trends in the income distribution by looking at a number of years.

Trends in Inequality

To see trends in the income distribution, we need a measure that enables us to rank distributions on the scale of more equal and less equal. No perfect scale exists, but one that is much used is called the Gini coefficient.

The **Gini coefficient** is based on the Lorenz curve and equals the area between the line of equality and the Lorenz curve as a percentage of the entire area beneath the line of equality. If income is distributed equally, the Lorenz curve is the same as the line of equality, so the Gini coefficient is zero. If one person has all the income and everyone else has none, the Gini coefficient is 100. Gini coefficients based on the distribution of original (or market) income are typically between 40 and 50 in most rich industrial countries today.

Figure 18.5 shows the UK Gini coefficient from 1980 to 2003. The Gini coefficient has clearly increased, which means that on this measure, incomes have become more unequal.

The major increase in inequality occurred during the 1980s, but inequality continued to increase into the early 1990s. Since 1994, inequality has been roughly constant.

No one knows for sure why these changes in inequality have occurred, but a possibility that we'll explore in the next section is that they are the result of technological change in the information-age economy.

Figure 18.5

The UK Gini Coefficient: 1980–2003

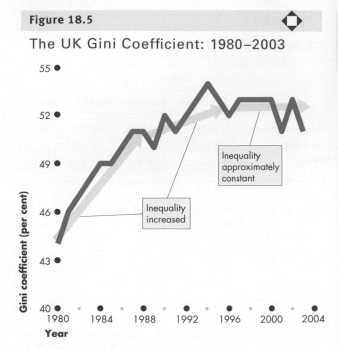

Measured by the Gini coefficient, the distribution of income in the United Kingdom became more unequal between 1980 and 1994. During the past 10 years, inequality has remained approximately constant.

Source: Office for National Statistics.

Who are the Rich and the Poor?

The lowest-income household in the United Kingdom today is likely to be a retired person over 75 years of age, living alone in low-cost rented accommodation, somewhere in Northern Ireland. The highest-income household is likely to comprise two adults aged between 30 and 50, both graduates with professional or managerial jobs, living with two children somewhere in the south east of England.

These snapshot profiles are the extremes of the characteristics shown in Figure 18.3. The figure illustrates the role of household size, age, education and economic status of the householder and the region of residence in influencing the likelihood that a household is poor and living on an income well below average.

The poorest households are considered to be living in **poverty**, a state in which a household's income is too low for it to be able to buy the quantities of food, shelter and clothing that are deemed necessary. The *poverty line* is a benchmark that determines when people become poor. One such definition is the number of people living at or below 60 per cent of median income.

Box 18.1
Poverty in Action

Poverty in the European Union

Defining the poverty line as 60 per cent of median EU income, poverty rates vary throughout the European Union. Figure 1 shows that more than 40 per cent of people in Portugal and Greece live in poverty, but fewer than 15 per cent do in most member states. The accession of the ten new EU members in 2004 will lower the median income but will increase the number of member states with relatively high poverty rates.

Poverty in the United Kingdom

Defining the poverty line as 60 per cent of median EU income, 15 per cent of UK households lived in poverty in 2002. But defining the poverty line as 60 per cent of median UK income, 18 per cent of UK households lived in poverty in 2000. Using this UK-based measure, poverty rates were at their highest in 1991, when 21 per cent of households lived in poverty, and at their lowest in 1977, when just 10 per cent lived in poverty.

Figure 1

Poverty in the European Union

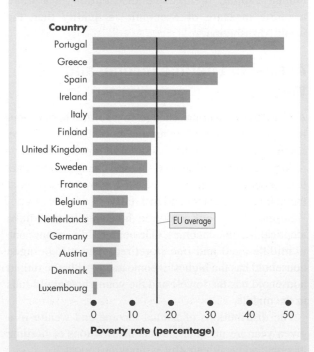

Source: Social Trends, May 2003. Office for National Statistics, The Stationery Office, London.

Figure 18.6

The Distribution of Income by Selected Household Characteristics in 2002–2003

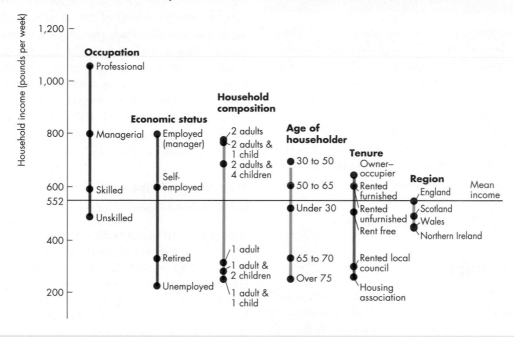

Single adults, single parents, those who are unemployed and those aged over 75 are likely to be among the poorest households in the United Kingdom. Other poor households are those in which the main earner is employed as a manual worker and those that live in local council accommodation. Households in Northern Ireland and Wales are on average poorer than those in England and Scotland.

Source: Office for National Statistics, *Family Spending: A Report on the 2002/2003 Family Expenditure Survey*, 2004, London, The Stationery Office.

The box on the previous page shows some numbers on poverty in the European Union and the United Kingdom. It also highlights a difficulty with measuring poverty. If we define the poverty line in the United Kingdom as 60 per cent of the median UK income, we find about 18 per cent of UK households live in poverty. If we define the poverty line as 60 per cent of EU income, 15 per cent of UK households live in poverty. The difference arises because the median UK income is greater than the median EU income. If we expressed the poverty line in the United Kingdom as 60 per cent of *world* average income – about £85 a week – almost no UK households would be living in poverty. And if we defined the poverty line as 60 per cent of income in the United States – around £425 a week – almost 60 per cent of UK households would be living in poverty.

Measures of poverty are useful for helping to identify trends that might need correcting. But as absolute measures, they provide little information of value.

Review Quiz

1   Which is distributed more unequally: income or wealth? Why? Which is the better measure of inequality?
2   What does a Lorenz curve show and how do we use it to gauge the degree of inequality?
3   What is the Gini coefficient and how is it used to measure inequality?
4   Has the distribution of income in the United Kingdom become more unequal or less unequal? When did the largest changes occur?
5   What are the main characteristics of low-income households?
6   Describe one measure of the poverty line and explain how it is used.

The Sources of Economic Inequality

We've described economic inequality in the United Kingdom. Our task now is to explain it. We began this task in Chapter 17 by learning about the forces that influence demand and supply in the markets for labour, capital and land. We're now going to deepen our understanding of these forces.

Economic inequality arises from unequal labour market outcomes and from unequal ownership of capital. We'll begin by looking at labour markets and two features of them that contribute to differences in income:

◆ Human capital

◆ Discrimination

Human Capital

A clerk in a barrister's office earns less than a tenth of the amount earned by the barrister he assists. An operating room assistant earns less than a tenth of the amount earned by the surgeon she works with. A bank clerk earns less than a tenth of the amount earned by the bank's managing director. These differences in earnings arise from differences in human capital. We can explain these differences by using a model of competitive labour markets.

We'll study a model economy with two levels of human capital, which we'll call high-skilled labour and low-skilled labour. The low-skilled labour might represent the barrister's clerk, the operating room assistant or the bank clerk, and the high-skilled labour might represent the barrister, the surgeon or the bank's managing director.

We'll first look at the demand side of the markets for these two types of labour.

The Demand for High-skilled and Low-skilled Labour

High-skilled workers can perform tasks that low-skilled labour would perform badly or perhaps cannot perform at all. Imagine an untrained person doing open-heart surgery. High-skilled labour has a higher marginal revenue product than low-skilled labour. As we learned in Chapter 17, a firm's demand for labour curve is the same as the marginal revenue product of labour curve.

Figure 18.7(a) shows the demand curves for high-skilled and low-skilled labour. The demand curve for high-skilled labour is D_H, and that for low-skilled labour is D_L. At any given level of employment, firms are willing to pay a higher wage rate to a high-skilled worker than to a low-skilled worker. The gap between the two wage rates measures the marginal revenue product of skill; for example, at an employment level of 2,000 hours, firms are willing to pay £12.50 an hour for a high-skilled worker and only £5 for a low-skilled worker, a difference of £7.50 an hour. So the marginal revenue product of skill is £7.50 an hour.

The Supply of High-skilled and Low-skilled Labour

High-skilled labour contains more human capital than low-skilled labour, and human capital is costly to acquire. The opportunity cost of acquiring human capital includes actual expenditures on such things as tuition fees and room and board and costs in the form of lost or reduced earnings while the skill is being acquired. When a person goes to school, college or university full time, that cost is the total earnings forgone. But some people acquire skills on the job – on-the-job training.

Usually, a worker undergoing on-the-job training is paid a lower wage than one doing a comparable job but not undergoing training. In such a case, the cost of acquiring the skill is the wage paid to a person not being trained minus that paid to a person being trained.

The position of the supply curve of high-skilled labour reflects the cost of acquiring human capital. Figure 18.7(b) shows two supply curves: one for high-skilled labour and the other for low-skilled labour. The supply curve for high-skilled labour is S_H, and that for low-skilled labour is S_L.

The high-skilled labour supply curve lies above the low-skilled labour supply curve. The vertical distance between the two supply curves is the compensation that high-skilled labour requires for the cost of acquiring the skill. For example, suppose that the quantity of low-skilled labour supplied is 2,000 hours at a wage rate of £5 an hour. This wage rate compensates the low-skilled workers mainly for their time on the job.

To induce high-skilled workers to supply 2,000 hours of labour, firms must pay a wage rate of £8.50 an hour. This wage rate for high-skilled labour is higher than that for low-skilled labour because high-skilled workers must be compensated not only for the time on the job but also for the time and other costs of acquiring the skill.

Figure 18.7

Skill Differentials

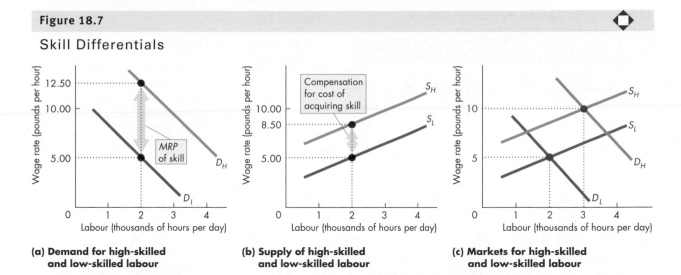

(a) Demand for high-skilled and low-skilled labour

(b) Supply of high-skilled and low-skilled labour

(c) Markets for high-skilled and low-skilled labour

Part (a) illustrates the marginal revenue product of skill. Low-skilled workers have a marginal revenue product that gives rise to the demand curve marked D_L. High-skilled workers have a higher marginal revenue product than low-skilled labour. So the demand curve for high-skilled labour, D_H, lies to the right of D_L. The vertical distance between these two curves is the marginal revenue product of the skill.

Part (b) shows the effects of the cost of acquiring skills on the supply curves of labour. The supply curve for low-skilled labour is S_L. The supply curve for high-skilled labour is S_H. The vertical distance between these two curves is the required compensation for the cost of acquiring a skill.

Part (c) shows the equilibrium employment and the wage differential. Low-skilled workers earn £5 an hour and 2,000 hours of low-skilled labour are employed. High-skilled workers earn £10 an hour and 3,000 hours of high-skilled labour are employed. The wage rate for high-skilled labour always exceeds that for low-skilled labour.

Wage Rates of High-skilled and Low-skilled Labour

To work out the wage rates of high-skilled and low-skilled labour, we have to bring together the effects of skill on the demand for and supply of labour.

Figure 18.7(c) shows the demand curves and the supply curves for high-skilled and low-skilled labour. These curves are exactly the same as those plotted in parts (a) and (b). Equilibrium occurs in the market for low-skilled labour where the supply and demand curves for low-skilled labour intersect. The equilibrium wage rate is £5 an hour and the quantity of low-skilled labour employed is 2,000 hours. Equilibrium in the market for high-skilled labour occurs where the supply and demand curves for high-skilled labour intersect. The equilibrium wage rate is £10 an hour and the quantity of high-skilled labour employed is 3,000 hours.

As you can see in part (c), the equilibrium wage rate of high-skilled labour is higher than that of low-skilled labour. There are two reasons why this occurs. First, high-skilled labour has a higher marginal revenue product than low-skilled labour, so at a given wage rate, the quantity of high-skilled labour demanded exceeds that of low-skilled labour. Second, skills are costly to acquire, so at a given wage rate, the quantity of high-skilled labour supplied is less than that of low-skilled labour. The wage differential (in this case, £5 an hour) depends on both the marginal revenue product of the skill and the cost of acquiring it. The higher the marginal revenue product of the skill, the larger is the vertical distance between the demand curves. The more costly it is to acquire a skill, the larger is the vertical distance between the supply curves. The higher the marginal revenue product of the skill and the more costly it is to acquire, the larger is the wage differential between high-skilled and low-skilled labour.

Do Education and Training Pay?

Rates of return on a university education have been estimated to be as high as 35 per cent for women and 17.5 per cent for men. A solid secondary education ending with 5 or more O-levels generates returns that exceed 20 per cent. These returns suggest that a degree is a better investment than almost any other that a person can undertake!

Inequality Explained by Human Capital Differences

Human capital differences help to explain some of the inequality that we observe. You saw in Figure 18.6 that high-income households tend to be better educated and middle-aged. Human capital differences are correlated with these household characteristics. Education contributes directly to human capital. Age contributes indirectly to human capital because older workers have more experience than do younger workers.

Human capital differences can also explain some of the inequality associated with sex and race. A larger proportion of men than of women and a larger proportion of whites than of visible minorities have a university degree. These differences in education levels among the sexes and the races are becoming smaller, but they have not yet been eliminated.

Interruptions to a career reduce the effectiveness of job experience in contributing to human capital. Historically, job interruptions have been more common for women than for men because women's careers have been interrupted for bearing and rearing children. This factor is a possible source of lower wages, on average, for women. Although maternity leave and day-care facilities are making career interruptions for women less common, this factor remains a problem for many women.

Trends in Inequality Explained by Human Capital Trends

You've seen that income inequality increased during the 1980s and 1990s. Human capital differences are a possible explanation for this trend, and Figure 18.8 illustrates how. The supply of low-skilled labour (part a) and that of high-skilled labour (part b) are S, and initially, the demand in each market is D_0. The low-skilled wage rate is £5 an hour, and the high-skilled wage rate is £10 an hour.

Information technologies such as computers and laser scanners are *substitutes* for low-skilled labour: they perform tasks that previously were performed by low-skilled labour. The introduction of these technologies has decreased the demand for low-skilled labour (part a), decreased the number of low-skilled jobs and lowered the wage rate of low-skilled workers.

These same technologies require high-skilled labour to design, programme and run them. Information technologies and high-skilled labour are *complements*, so the introduction of these technologies has increased the demand for high-skilled labour (part b), increased the number of high-skilled jobs and raised the wage rate of high-skilled workers.

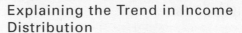

Figure 18.8

Explaining the Trend in Income Distribution

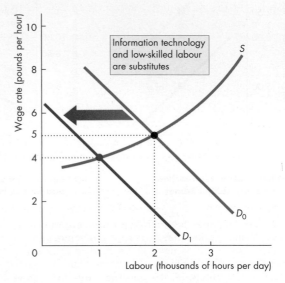

(a) A decrease in demand for low-skilled labour

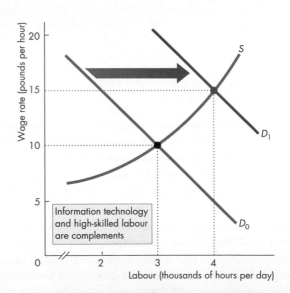

(b) An increase in demand for high-skilled labour

Low-skilled labour in part (a) and information technologies are substitutes. When these technologies were introduced, the demand for low-skilled labour decreased and the quantity of this type of labour employed and its wage rate decreased. High-skilled labour in part (b) and information technologies are complements. When these technologies were introduced, the demand for high-skilled labour increased and the quantity of this type of labour employed and its wage rate increased.

Discrimination

Human capital differences can explain some of the economic inequality that we observe. But it can't explain all of it. Discrimination is another possible source of inequality.

An Example of Discrimination

Suppose that women and men have identical abilities as investment advisors. Figure 18.9 shows the supply curves of women, S_W (in part a), and of men, S_M (in part b). The marginal revenue product of investment advisors shown by the two curves labelled *MRP* is the same for both groups.

If everyone is free of sex prejudice, the market determines a wage rate of £40,000 a year for investment advisors. But if the customers are prejudiced against women, this prejudice is reflected in the wage rate and employment. Suppose that the perceived marginal revenue product of the women, when discriminated against, is MRP_{DA}. Suppose that the perceived marginal revenue product for men, the group discriminated in favour of, is MRP_{DF}. With these *MRP* curves, women earn £20,000 a year and only 1,000 women work as investment advisors. Men earn £60,000 a year, and 3,000 of them work as investment advisors.

Counteracting Forces

Economists disagree about whether prejudice actually causes wage differentials and one line of reasoning implies that it does not. In the example you've just studied, customers who buy from men pay a higher service charge for investment advice than do the customers who buy from women. This price difference acts as an incentive to encourage people who are prejudiced to buy from the people against whom they are prejudiced.

This force could be strong enough to eliminate the effects of discrimination altogether. Suppose, as is true in manufacturing, that a firm's customers never meet its workers. If such a firm discriminates against women, it can't compete with firms that hire women because its costs are higher than those of the non-prejudiced firms. Only firms that do not discriminate survive in a competitive industry.

Whether because of discrimination or from some other source, women do earn lower incomes than men. Another possible source of lower wage rates of women arises from differences in the relative degree of specialization of women and men.

Figure 18.9

Discrimination

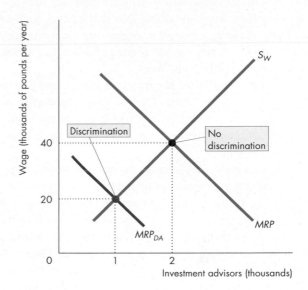

(a) Females

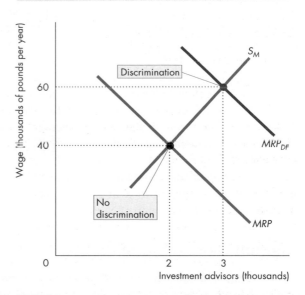

(b) Males

With no discrimination, the wage rate is £40,000 a year and 2,000 of each group are employed. With discrimination against women, the marginal revenue product curve in part (a) is MRP_{DA}. With discrimination in favour of men, the marginal revenue product curve in part (b) is MRP_{DF}. The wage rate for women falls to £20,000 a year, and only 1,000 are employed. The wage rate for men rises to £60,000 a year, and 3,000 are employed.

Differences in the Degree of Specialization

Couples must choose how to allocate their time between working for a wage and doing jobs in the home, such as cooking, cleaning, shopping, organizing vacations and, most important, bearing and rearing children. Let's look at the choices of Bob and Sue.

Bob might specialize in earning an income and Sue in taking care of the home. Or Sue might specialize in earning an income and Bob in taking care of the home. Or both of them might earn an income and share home production jobs.

The allocation they choose depends on their preferences and on the earning potential of each of them. The choice of an increasing number of households is for each person to diversify between earning an income and doing some home chores. But in most households, Bob will specialize in earning an income and Sue will both earn an income and bear a larger share of the task of running the home. With this allocation, Bob will probably earn more than Sue. If Sue devotes time and effort to ensuring Bob's mental and physical well-being, the quality of Bob's market labour will be higher than it would be if he were diversified. If the roles were reversed, Sue would be able to supply market labour that earns more than Bob.

To test whether the degree of specialization accounts for earnings differences between the sexes, economists have compared the incomes of never-married men and women. They have found that, on the average, with equal amounts of human capital, the wages of these two groups are the same.

We've examined some sources of inequality in the labour market. Let's now look at the way inequality arises from unequal ownership of capital.

Unequal Ownership of Capital

You've seen that inequality in wealth (excluding human capital) is much greater than inequality in income. This inequality arises from saving and transfers of wealth from one generation to the next.

The higher a household's income, the more that household tends to save and pass on to the next generation. Saving is not always a source of increased inequality. If a household's saving redistributes an uneven income over the household's life, consumption will fluctuate less than its income and saving decreases inequality. If a lucky generation that has a high income saves a large part of that income and leaves capital to a succeeding generation that is unlucky, this act of saving also decreases the degree of inequality. But two features of intergenerational transfers of wealth lead to increased inequality: people can't inherit debts, and marriage tends to concentrate wealth.

Can't Inherit Debt

Although a person may die in debt – with negative wealth – a debt can't be forced onto the next generation of a family. So inheritance only adds to a future generation's wealth; it cannot decrease it.

Most people inherit nothing or a very small amount. A few people inherit an enormous fortune. As a result, intergenerational transfers make the distribution of income persistently more unequal than the distribution of ability and job skills. A household that is poor in one generation is more likely to be poor in the next. A household that is wealthy in one generation is more likely to be wealthy in the next. And marriage reinforces this tendency.

Marriage and Wealth Concentration

People tend to marry within their own socioeconomic class – a phenomenon called *assortative mating*. In everyday language, "like attracts like". Although there is a good deal of folklore that "opposites attract", perhaps such Cinderella tales appeal to us because they are so rare in reality. Wealthy people seek wealthy partners.

Because of assortative mating, wealth becomes more concentrated in a small number of families and the distribution of wealth becomes more unequal.

Review Quiz

1. What role does human capital play in accounting for income inequality?
2. What role might discrimination play in accounting for income inequality?
3. What are the possible reasons for income inequality by sex and age group?
4. Does inherited wealth make the distribution of income less equal or more equal?
5. Why does wealth inequality persist across generations?

Next we're going to see how taxes and government policies redistribute income and wealth and decrease the degree of economic inequality.

Income Redistribution

Governments use three main types of policies to redistribute income. They are:

◆ Income taxes
◆ Benefit payments
◆ Subsidized welfare services

Income Taxes

Income taxes may be progressive, regressive or proportional. A **progressive income tax** is one that taxes income at an average rate that increases with income. A **regressive income tax** is one that taxes income at an average rate that decreases with income. A **proportional income tax** (also called a *flat-rate income tax*) is one that taxes income at a constant average rate regardless of the level of income.

Income taxes are progressive in all EU member states. For example, in 2003 in the United Kingdom, people who earned £4,615 or less paid no income tax. A tax of 10 per cent is paid on the first £1,960 earned over £4,615a tax of 22 per cent is paid on the next £30,500 earned. Any income above this amount is taxed at 40 per cent.

Benefit Payments

Benefit payments redistribute income by making direct payments to people with low incomes. In 2003, the UK government paid out £120 billion in benefits, 28.5 per cent of total government expenditure. The main types of benefit payments are:

◆ Income support payments
◆ Tax credits
◆ State pensions

Income Support Payments

Governments use a wide range of income support payments to raise household incomes and reduce poverty. These include income support, unemployment benefits, disability payments and child support payments. For example, in the United Kingdom, the Job Seekers' Allowance is paid for a limited period to individuals who have lost their jobs involuntarily and have no other main source of income. This allowance was £54.65 a week for people over 25 years of age in 2003.

Tax Credits

Tax credits are a method of helping low-income employed individuals and families. A tax credit increases a household's disposable income. For example, in 2003, the Working Families Tax Credit provided £69.90 a week to families in which at least one person was in work, but the family wage fell below a specified level.

State Pensions

State pensions for the elderly are the main component of government benefit payments in all the EU member states. These pensions are paid for out of current taxes, so they result in redistribution from people currently working to those retired. In the United Kingdom in 2003, 7 million people received a pension of £77.45 a week for a single person (more for a couple).

Subsidized Welfare Services

A great deal of redistribution takes place in most European countries through the subsidized provision of welfare goods and services. These are the goods and services provided by the government at prices below marginal cost. Taxpayers who consume these goods and services receive a transfer in kind from taxpayers who do not consume them. The two most important areas in which this form of redistribution takes place are education – from nursery care through to university – and healthcare.

In the United Kingdom, 50 per cent of government expenditure is on benefits in kind: 24 per cent on the National Health Service, 21 per cent on education and the remainder on other services. The National Health Service provides almost all healthcare services free at the point of demand. Primary and secondary education is provided free for all children in the United Kingdom.

In the European Union, the extent and method of subsidizing education and healthcare services varies greatly across member states. For example, in some countries healthcare is free at the point of demand, and in other countries healthcare is privately provided and the government reimburses patients' costs. In some countries, people are required to pay into compulsory health insurance systems.

Whatever the method, subsidized provision of services improves access to good-quality healthcare and education and reduces inequality in health status and basic human capital.

Box 18.2
EU Redistribution in Action

The governments of the EU member states redistribute income using both progressive income taxes and benefit payments.

The role of income tax in the redistribution policies varies a great deal. Income taxes constitute just 14 per cent of all taxes in the United Kingdom and Ireland, 19 per cent in Spain and Portugal, 25 per cent in Finland and the Netherlands and more than 30 per cent in Sweden and Denmark.

Benefit payments also vary across the EU members. Figure 1 compares government spending per person on cash benefit payments across the EU members (expressed as a percentage of total income).

Benefit spending as a percentage of income is much higher in Germany, France and the rich northern countries than in the poorer southern countries of the European Union. Benefit spending increases with country wealth and is associated with lower poverty rates.

Figure 1

Benefits in the European Union

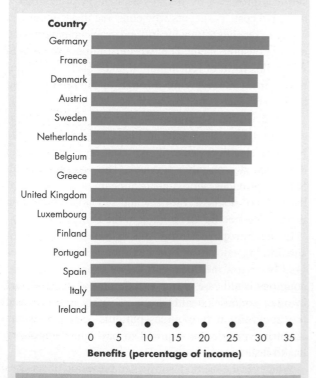

Source: Europe at a glance.

Box 18.3
UK Redistribution in Action

Figure 1 shows the impact of taxes and benefits in the United Kingdom for the five quintile income groups, from poorest fifth to richest fifth.

On average, the poorest fifth received £5,250 in cash benefits each year, while the richest fifth received only £2,650. (The richest group receives benefits because some benefits, such as pensions, are universally available.) The effect of cash benefits and tax credits is limited by low take-up rates. Means testing on income and form filling bureaucracy put some people off claiming benefits to which they are entitled.

Benefits in kind – mainly health benefits provide by the National Health Service and free or heavily subsidized education – are strongly progressive and represent 50 per cent of post-tax income for the poorest fifth but only 6 per cent of post-tax income for the richest fifth.

Income taxes have a strong effect on the distribution of income. The richest fifth pay £15,200 in income taxes each year and the poorest fifth pay £1,040 each year.

Figure 1

The Effect of Taxes and Benefits on the Distribution of Income

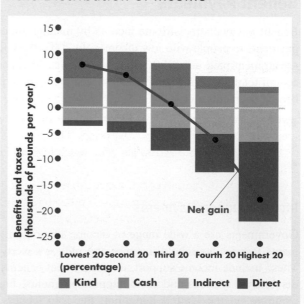

Source: Office of National Statistics, Social Trends, 2003, London, The Stationery Office, 2004.

Expenditure taxes such at the VAT have a less dramatic effect because the poorest groups spend proportionately more of their total income on goods and services.

Overall, the net impact of UK taxes and benefits is a redistribution of income from the top 40 per cent to the bottom 40 per cent, with a small net loss to the middle 20 per cent.

The Big Trade-off

All redistribution runs up against the *big trade-off* between equity and efficiency – see Chapter 5, p. 109.

Taxes are inefficient because they drive a wedge between marginal cost and marginal benefit and create deadweight loss. (Pigovian taxes that correct an externality are an exception – see Chapter 15, p. 336.) Government can only redistribute income by taxing richer people to pay for benefits to poorer people. Taxes on the rich reduce their incentive to work and save. And benefits for the poor reduce their incentive to work and save. The result is less output and consumption for everybody – rich and poor.

The disincentive effect of the benefits system is so severe that it gives rise to what is called a benefit trap.

The Benefit Trap

The benefits system can catch people in a *benefit trap* that arises because, in some cases, if a person take a job or works longer hours, the loss of benefits exceeds the income earned. If a person loses £1 of benefit for every extra £1 earned – a *withdrawal rate* of 100 per cent – there is no gain from working. The person in effect faces a tax rate of 100 per cent, much higher than all other taxpayers!

There are two main types of benefit trap – the unemployment trap and the poverty trap. In the unemployment trap, people make decisions based on the expected wage they might earn compared to the benefits they will lose if they take a job. If the expected wage is only slightly higher than the level of unemployment benefit, the rational choice is to remain unemployed.

In the poverty trap, people are in low-paid work but are receiving benefits. They may want to work longer hours to earn an extra £10, but they will pay tax on the extra £10 and lose up to £10 of benefit. Again, the rational choice is often not to work more hours.

Box 18.4
Breaking the Benefit Trap in the United Kingdom

Before 1986, many people receiving benefits lost £1.20 of benefits for every extra £1 earned. If you were receiving benefits because you were very poor and tried to improve your situation by working, for every extra pound you earned, you lost £1.20 of your benefits.

The 1986 Social Security Act removed this aspect of the poverty trap by allowing benefits to be calculated on post-tax income rather than on before-tax income. The change eased the severity of the poverty trap, but it left many more people facing extremely high marginal tax rates of between 60 and 90 per cent.

In 1998, the UK government raised benefit levels, cut the rate at which benefits are withdrawn as extra income is earned and introduced a system of paying benefits as tax credits. The lower withdrawal rate and higher levels of benefits reduced the poverty trap further.

Review Quiz

1. What are the methods that governments use to redistribute income?
2. To what extent does government policy succeed in redistributing income in the United Kingdom?
3. Why has the UK government introduced a system of tax credits to replace many cash benefits?
4. Can you explain what is meant by a benefit trap? Can you give an example?
5. Why is the UK government unlikely to introduce a full scale negative income tax?

You have now completed your study of microeconomics. In the chapters that follow, you will shift your focus to the aggregate economy and apply the principles you've learned in microeconomics to the working of the economy as a whole.

But before moving on to macroeconomics, spend a few minutes with the *Policy Case Study* on pp. 410–411 and learn about efficiency and equity issues in health-care systems.

Policy Case Study
Efficiency and Equity in Healthcare

Comparing Healthcare Systems

Healthcare Provision in Europe

Healthcare in the European Union is provided and financed in a variety of ways, but all EU countries subsidize healthcare to improve health and to redistribute income. In the United Kingdom and eight other member states of the EU15 (before the 2004 expansion), the government provides and finances the majority of healthcare. In Austria, Belgium, France, Germany and Luxembourg there is a broad mix of government and private supply, but backed by government finance. The Netherlands has a broad mix of government and private provision and finance.[1]

Efficiency and Equity

In a recent World Health Organization (WHO) report, the UK health system came 24th on the global list in terms of efficiency, behind countries like Oman, Italy, France and Spain, which were in the top ten. Efficiency was measured as the amount of healthcare provided for resources spent.

In a WHO report including equity as well as efficiency measures, the United Kingdom fared slightly better at 18th, with France at the top.[2] In the European Union, only Luxembourg spends a smaller percentage of income on healthcare (5.9 per cent compared to the UK's 6.7 per cent). The EU average is 9.2 per cent.

UK Spending Trend

The real level of spending on healthcare in the United Kingdom has grown every year since 1979. Both public and private spending have contributed to this upward trend. (Private healthcare spending has increased in all but three years over this period.)[3] The government has pledged to continue this trend and increase healthcare spending to 8 per cent of income by 2006.

---

[1] C. Propper (2001), "Expenditure on Healthcare in the UK: A Review of the Issues", *Fiscal Studies*, vol. 22, no. 2, pp. 151–183.

[2] S. Bosely, "NHS healthcare lags in world efficiency list", *The Guardian*, 10 August 2001, p. 8.
[3] See note 1.

Economic Analysis

◆ The efficiency of a healthcare system is measured by comparing health outcomes achieved for resources spent. Figure 1 shows a comparison of one widely used measure of health outcome, infant mortality, against *public* healthcare spending as a percentage of income.

◆ Higher spending countries generally have higher outcome measures (lower infant mortality), but the relationship is not perfect.

◆ The fairness of a healthcare system is measured by the distribution of access to healthcare between groups, such as equal treatment for equal need, or by the distribution of payment among different income groups.

◆ Figure 2 shows the percentage of UK National Health Service (NHS) expenditure, standardized for need, received from the poorest 20 per cent to the richest 20 per cent and the average expenditure on each group. The NHS benefits all income groups but favours the poorest 40 per cent.

◆ Figure 3 shows measures of fairness in the financing and delivery of healthcare. A value of zero for the financing measure means everyone pays the same proportion of income for healthcare. A positive value means the rich pay a larger proportion of their income than do the poor; and a negative value means the rich pay a smaller proportion of their income than do the poor.

◆ The United Kingdom and Finland are the fairest. Many countries have the poor paying a larger proportion of their income for healthcare than the rich. But the UK system delivers a smaller proportion of healthcare services to the poor than to the rich.

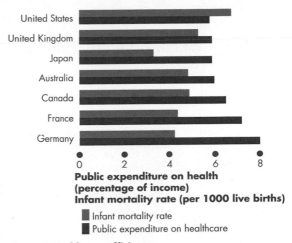

Public expenditure on health (percentage of income)
Infant mortality rate (per 1000 live births)

Infant mortality rate
Public expenditure on healthcare

Figure 1 Healthcare efficiency

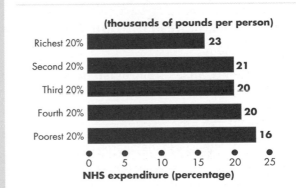

NHS expenditure (percentage)

Figure 2 NHS equity

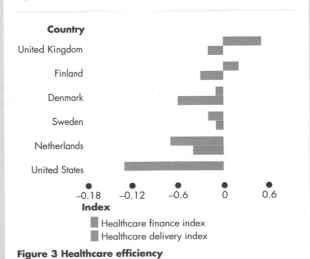

Healthcare finance index
Healthcare delivery index

Figure 3 Healthcare efficiency

Source: C. Propper (2001), "Expenditure on Healthcare in the UK: A Review of the Issues", *Fiscal Studies*, vol. 22, no. 2, p. 15.

Summary

Key Points

Measuring Economic Inequality
(pp. 396–401)

◆ Income is distributed less unequally than wealth.

◆ Income inequality was reduced in the early 1960s and 1970s but increased in all other periods.

◆ The poorest people tend to be older, out of work and living in low-income areas.

◆ The distribution of income is a more accurate measure of inequality than the distribution of wealth.

The Sources of Economic Inequality
(pp. 402–406)

◆ Inequality arises from differences in human capital.

◆ Inequality might arise from discrimination.

◆ Inequality between men and women might arise from differences in the degree of specialization.

◆ Intergenerational transfers of wealth lead to increased inequality because people can't inherit debts and assortative mating tends to concentrate wealth.

Income Redistribution (pp. 407–409)

◆ Governments redistribute income through progressive income taxes and the payment of cash benefits and benefits in kind.

◆ Redistribution in the United Kingdom transfers income from the richest 40 per cent to the poorest 40 per cent and has little effect on the middle 20 per cent.

◆ Redistribution suffers from the big trade-off between equity and efficiency because the process uses resources and weakens incentives to work and save.

◆ Reforms to the benefits system try to lessen the severity of the benefit trap.

Key Figures

Figure 18.1 The Distribution of Original Income in the United Kingdom in 1999–2000, 396

Figure 18.4 Lorenz Curves for Income and Wealth, 398

Figure 18.5 The UK Gini Coefficient: 1980–2003, 400

Figure 18.6 The Distribution of Income by Selected Household Characteristics in 2002–2003, 401

Figure 18.7 Skill Differentials, 403

Figure 18.8 Explaining the Trend in Income Distribution, 404

Figure 18.9 Discrimination, 405

Key Terms

Gini coefficient, 399
Lorenz curve, 397
Original income, 396
Poverty, 400
Progressive income tax, 407
Proportional income tax, 407
Regressive income tax, 407

Problems

*1 The table shows shares of original (or market) income in the United States in 2002.

Households (percentage)	Income (per cent of total)
Lowest 20	1
Second 20	7
Third 20	14
Fourth 20	23
Highest 20	55

a Draw a Lorenz curve for the United States and compare it with the Lorenz curve for the United Kingdom shown in Figure 18.3.

b Which country has the higher Gini coefficient?

c Was US income distributed more equally or less equally than UK income?

d Can you think of some reasons for the differences in the distribution of income in the United States and United Kingdom?

2 The table shows shares of income in Australia.

Households (percentage)	Income (per cent of total)
Lowest 20	7
Second 20	13
Third 20	18
Fourth 20	24
Highest 20	38

a Draw the Lorenz curve for the income distribution in Australia.

b Use the information in Figure 18.2 on the distribution of income in the United Kingdom in 1999/2000. Was income distributed more equally or less equally than in Australia?

c Is the Gini Coefficient for Australia larger or smaller than that for the United Kingdom? Explain your answer.

d Was Australian income distributed more equally or less equally than UK income?

*3 The table shows the demand for and supply of low-skilled labour. High-skilled workers have three times the marginal product of low-skilled workers. (The marginal product at each employment level is three times the marginal product of a low-skilled worker.)

But the cost of acquiring the skill adds £6 an hour to the wage that must be offered to attract high-skilled labour.

Wage rate (pounds per hour)	Quantity demanded	Quantity supplied
	(thousands of hours a week)	
1	10	2
2	9	3
3	8	4
4	7	5
5	6	6
6	5	7
7	4	8
8	3	9
9	2	10
10	1	11

a What is the wage rate of low-skilled labour and what is the quantity of low-skilled labour employed?

b What is the wage rate of high-skilled labour and what is the quantity of high-skilled labour employed?

4 The following table shows the demand for low-skilled labour. The supply of low-skilled labour is perfectly elastic at a wage rate of £6 an hour. The marginal productivity of a high-skilled worker is £8 an hour greater than that of a low-skilled worker. The cost of acquiring the skill adds £6 an hour to the wage that must be offered to attract high-skilled labour.

Wage rate (pounds per hour)	Quantity demanded (thousands of hours per week)
1	7
2	6
3	5
4	4
5	3
6	2
7	1
8	0

a What is the wage rate of low-skilled labour and what is the quantity of low-skilled labour employed?

b What is the wage rate of high-skilled labour and what is the quantity of high-skilled labour employed?

c Why does the wage rate of a high-skilled worker exceed that of a low-skilled worker by exactly the cost of acquiring the skill?

*Solutions to odd-numbered problems are available on *Parkin Interactive*.

*5 The table shows the final income shares after government redistribution in the United Kingdom in 1999–2000.

Households (percentage)	Income (per cent of total)
Lo\west 20	6
Second 20	11
Third 20	16
Fourth 20	22
Highest 20	45

a Draw the Lorenz curve for final income in the United Kingdom in 1999–2000.

b Use the information in Figure 18.2 on the distribution of original income in the United Kingdom in 1999–2000. Was final income distributed more equally or less equally than original income?

c Compare the Gini Coefficient for final income with that for original income? Explain your answer.

d Explain how taxes contribute to the differences in the distribution of original income and final income.

e Explain how benefits contribute to the differences in the distribution of original income and final income.

6 The table shows the final income (after government redistribution) shares in the United States in 2002.

Households (percentage)	Final income shares (per cent of total)
Lowest 20	5
Second 20	11
Third 20	16
Fourth 20	23
Highest 20	45

a Draw the Lorenz curve for final income in the United States in 2002.

b Was final income distributed more equally or less equally than original income in problem 1?

c Is the Gini Coefficient for final income larger or smaller than that for original income? Explain why.

d Compare the original distribution and final distribution of income in the United States with those of the United Kingdom shown in Figure 18.2 and problem 5. Which country has the larger amount of income redistribution?

e Which country begins with the more equal distribution and which country ends up with the more equal distribution? Can you think of reasons why?

Critical Thinking

1 Read the *Policy Case Study* on pp. 410–411 and then answer the following questions:

a How can efficiency be measured in a healthcare service?

b How can equity or fairness be measured in a healthcare service?

c What is meant by the "big trade-off" in the UK NHS?

d Are healthcare systems in Europe generally progressive, regressive or proportionate in financing?

e In your opinion, which European country has the best healthcare system? Explain your answer.

2 Many professional footballers earn huge salaries, but most earn modest salaries.

a Which do you predict is the more unequal distribution: that for the United Kingdom as a whole or that for professional footballers?

b Which distribution do you predict has the higher average: that for the United Kingdom as a whole or that for professional footballers?

Web Exercises

Use the links on *Parkin Interactive* to work the following exercises.

1 Visit the Website of the Office for National Statistics, and look through *Social Trends*, 2004.

a What is the poverty line used in *Social Trends*?

b How has the distribution of income changed over time? Which groups are getting richer and which groups poorer?

c What other ways are there of measuring poverty?

d Do the poorest have access to the same level of goods and services as the richest? Does it matter?

2 Download the World Bank's Deininger and Squire Data Set on income distribution in a large number of countries.

a Which country in the data set has the most unequal distribution? Which country has the least unequal distribution?

b Can you think of reasons for the differences in income distribution in the two countries you've identified?

Part 5
Macroeconomic Basics

Talking with Jürgen von Hagen

Jürgen von Hagen is Professor of Economics and Director of the Centre for European Integration Studies at the University of Bonn in Germany. He has previously held academic appointments at the University of Mannheim in Germany and the Indiana University in the United States. Professor von Hagen's main areas of research are in monetary theory and policy, European economic integration, international finance and public finance. He has held visiting appointments at the Federal Reserve Bank of St. Louis, the Board of Governors of the Federal Reserve System, the International Monetary Fund, the EU Commission, World Bank and the Bank of Japan.

Professor von Hagen took his Diploma and PhD at the University of Bonn. He has published over a hundred monographs and chapters in books and over sixty papers in leading scholarly journals.

Kent Mathews talked with Jürgen von Hagen about his work, the European Central Bank and the EU Stability and Growth Pact.

What is the Centre for European Integration?

It is a research institute of the University of Bonn with a brief to examine problems associated with European integration. The institute has three areas: Political, Legal and Institutional; European values, Culture and Languages; and Economic and Social. The main research of the Economic section examines macroeconomic issues relating to Europe in general but also issues of monetary policy and public finance within the European Monetary Union.

The European Central Bank (ECB) has recently downgraded the role of money in its policy framework. Why do you think this is?

On the one hand, monetary analysis has lost recognition in the international research community in the past 15 years. Thus, the ECB is following what is trendy in macroeconomics. On the other hand, monetary analysis focuses on the medium- to long-term consequences of current monetary policy actions. Thus the ECB's move reflects a shift in its attention away from the longer term and towards the shorter term, where monetary policy is able to influence the business cycle.

Do you think it is an appropriate policy move for the ECB?

Such a shift of policy from the long term to the short term is common for central banks in times of low inflation. My hope is that it will be reversed when inflation goes up again, which is sure to happen at some point in the future.

Would you describe the Stability and Growth Pact and its rationale?

The Stability and Growth Pact sets out the policy guidelines for member states of the European Monetary Union (EMU) – the EU countries that have adopted the euro as its currency. The Pact was adopted to ensure that member states continue to carry out sound budgetary policies after they join the EMU.

The main rationale of the Pact is to avoid a free-rider problem. All countries want the EU as a whole to have a low overall government budget deficit and debt to ensure the stability of the common currency. But individually each country wants to free-ride on the stability efforts of the others and run a large deficit.

Is the Stability and Growth Pact working well?

The Stability and Growth Pact is flawed, because it relies on an oversight of government policies by other governments. It had some bite, when countries violating the fiscal criteria of the Maastricht Treaty faced the threat of being excluded from entering the EMU. Now countries are in the EMU, the Pact has become rather powerless. The main reason is that, as long as the governments themselves decide who should be punished and who should be excused for having a large deficit, the Pact cannot be enforced effectively. So there are strong incentives to cheat and to find cheap excuses.

Do you think the Stability and Growth Pact should remain as a central plank of macroeconomic policy?

Political economy tells us that governments will not be harsh on fellow governments that breach the deficit limit. The reason is that they expect to be treated in the same way should they run high deficits. This argument suggests that fiscal discipline in the EMU needs an independent monitoring institution, which has no incentives to play political games.

Interestingly, under the Maastricht Treaty the European Commission largely had that position. The Pact, however, has severely curtailed the Commission's role and authority in this context. While it looks like a tough regime at first sight, the Pact was actually a political trick to soften the fiscal framework of EMU.

How did you get into economics?

By way of doing some policy-oriented work on Latin American countries. That first research experience really wetted my appetite for more serious work in macroeconomics.

Who are the macroeconomists that have inspired you most and why?

Manfred Neumann, who supervised my PhD dissertation, engaged me in many hours of critical and inspiring discussion of empirical methodology, research design and economic policy. Karl Brunner, who invited me to the Konstanz Seminar in the early 1980s, was a very critical and constructive mind. Both taught me that dialogue between academics must be critical, taking no hostages, but at the same time friendly at the personal level.

What advice would you give a student of economics?

My advice would be to always look for interesting applications of what you learn in class, and, later on if you do a PhD, try to make contact with quality institutions like the Bank of England or the Treasury Department.

What is really fascinating about economics is that it has a lot to do with the real world. Do not just read textbooks, read newspapers like the *Financial Times* and news magazines like *The Economist* because what is going to keep you excited by economics is the translation of the economic model into the practical.

◆ ◆ ◆ ◆ ◆ ◆ ◆ ◆ ◆ ◆ ◆

Chapter 19

A First Look at Macroeconomics

After studying this chapter you will be able to:

◆ Describe the origins of macroeconomics and the problems with which it deals

◆ Describe the trends and fluctuations in economic growth

◆ Describe the trends and fluctuations in jobs and unemployment

◆ Describe the trends and fluctuations in inflation

◆ Describe the trends and fluctuations in government and international deficits

◆ Identify the macroeconomic policy challenges and describe the tools available for meeting them

Boom or Bust

Are we better off today than our parents were in the swinging 60s and our Victorian great grandparents were 100 years ago? Are the booms and busts of economic life getting better or worse? Is mass unemployment a horror of the past that we need no longer fear? Have we conquered inflation – rising prices that wipe out people's savings? Can the government manage the economy to make it perform better? Are government and international deficits becoming a problem? This chapter takes a first look at these questions and sets the scene for your study of macroeconomics. And *Reading Between the Lines* at the end of the chapter (pp. 432–433) looks at the global expansion of 2004 and the interplay between economic expansion and the price of oil.

Origins and Issues of Macroeconomics

Economists began to study economic growth, inflation and international payments as long ago as the 1750s, and this work was the forerunner of macroeconomics. But macroeconomics did not emerge until the **Great Depression**, a decade (1929–1939) of high unemployment and stagnant production throughout the world economy. In the depression's worst year, 1931, total UK production fell by more than 5 per cent and in the following year unemployment reached a record 15 per cent of the workforce. The entire period between the two World Wars of the last century (1919–1930) were years of human misery on a scale that is hard to imagine today. A state of pessimism about the ability of the market economy to work properly led many people to the view that private enterprise, free markets and democratic political institutions could not survive.

The science of economics had no solutions to the Great Depression. An alternative economic system of central planning and the political system of socialism seemed increasingly attractive to many people.

It was in this climate of economic depression and political and intellectual turmoil that macroeconomics was born. Its origin was the publication in 1936 of John Maynard Keynes' *The General Theory of Employment, Interest, and Money*.

Short-term versus Long-term Goals

Keynes' theory was that depression and high unemployment result from insufficient spending and that to cure these problems, the government must increase its own spending or try to stimulate private spending. Keynes' focus was on the *short term*. He wanted to cure an immediate and serious problem almost regardless of what the *long-term* consequences of the cure might be. 'In the long run,' said Keynes, 'we're all dead'.

But Keynes believed that after his cure for depression had restored the economy to a normal condition, the long-term problems of inflation and economic growth would become the central ones. He even suspected that his cure for depression, increased government spending, might trigger inflation and also might lower the long-term growth rate of production. With a lower long-term growth rate, the economy would create fewer jobs. If this outcome did occur, a policy aimed at lowering unemployment in the short term might end up increasing it in the long term.

By the late 1960s and through the 1970s, Keynes' predictions became a reality. Full employment was achieved but inflation increased and economic growth slowed. Later, unemployment became stubbornly high in many countries. The causes of these developments are complex. But they point to an inescapable conclusion: the long-term problems of inflation, slow growth and persistent unemployment, and the short-term problems of depression and economic fluctuations intertwine and are most usefully studied together. So although macroeconomics was reborn during the Great Depression, its emphasis today is broader than depression economics. The macroeconomics that you will learn is a subject that tries to understand long-term economic growth and inflation as well as short-term economic fluctuations and unemployment.

The Road Ahead

There is no unique way to study macroeconomics. Because its rebirth was a product of economic depression, it was common for many years to pay most attention to short-term output fluctuations and unemployment, but never to lose sight of the long-term issues completely.

When a rapid inflation emerged during the late 1960s and 1970s, inflation returned to prominence. During the 1980s, when long-term economic growth slowed in the United Kingdom and other rich industrial countries, economists redirected their energy towards economic growth. During the 1990s, when information technologies further shrank the globe, the international dimension of macroeconomics became more prominent.

The result of all these events is that modern macroeconomics is a broad subject that pays attention to all the issues we've just identified: economic growth and fluctuations, unemployment, inflation and government and international deficits.

Over the past 40 years, economists have developed a clearer understanding of the forces that determine macroeconomic performance and they have devised policies that they hope will improve performance and prevent the extremes of depression and inflation.

Your main goal is to become familiar with the theories of macroeconomics and the policies they make possible. To set you on your path towards this goal, we're going to take a first look at the issues of economic growth, unemployment, inflation and government and international surpluses and deficits, and learn why these phenomena merit our attention.

Economic Growth

Your parents are richer than your grandparents were when they were young. But are you going to be richer than your parents are? And are your children going to be richer than you? The answers depend on the rate of economic growth.

Economic growth is the expansion of the economy's production possibilities. It can be pictured as an outward shift of the production possibilities frontier (*PPF*) – see Chapter 2, pp. 38–39.

We measure economic growth as the increase in real gross domestic product. **Real gross domestic product** (also called **real GDP**) is the value of the total production of the country's farms, factories, shops and offices, measured in the prices of a single year. Real GDP in the United Kingdom is currently measured in prices that prevailed in 2001 (called 2001 pounds). We use the pound prices of a single year so that we can eliminate the influence of *inflation* – the increase in the average level of prices – and determine how much production has grown from one year to another. (The concept of real GDP is explained more fully in Chapter 20 on pp. 438–442.)

Real GDP is not a perfect measure of total production because it does not include everything that is produced. It excludes the things we produce for ourselves at home (preparing meals, doing laundry, cleaning, gardening and doing odd jobs). It also excludes production that people hide to avoid taxes or because the activity is illegal – the underground economy. But despite its shortcomings, real GDP is the best measure of total production available. Let's see what it tells us about economic growth.

Economic Growth in the United Kingdom

Figure 19.1 shows real GDP in the United Kingdom from 1963 to 2003 and it highlights two features of economic growth:

◆ The growth of potential GDP
◆ Fluctuations of real GDP around potential GDP

The Growth of Potential GDP

When all the economy's labour, capital, land and entrepreneurial ability are fully employed, the value of production is called **potential GDP**. Real GDP fluctuates around potential GDP and the rate of long-term economic growth is measured by the growth rate of potential GDP.

It is shown by the steepness of the potential GDP line – the black line in Figure 19.1.

You can see that the potential GDP line is steeper in the 1960s than in the 1970s and becomes steeper in the early 1980s and again in the late 1990s and 2000s.

During the 1960s, potential GDP grew at 2.9 per cent a year. The growth rate slowed during the 1970s to 1.5 per cent a year. The growth rate of output per person sagged during the 1970s in a phenomena called the **productivity growth slowdown**. The growth rate of potential GDP increased briefly to 3 per cent a year during the mid-1980s, slowed to 1.7 per cent and then increased to 2.8 per cent a year during the late 1990s and 2000s.

Why did the productivity growth slowdown occur? This question is controversial. We explore the causes of the productivity growth slowdown in Chapter 30. Whatever its cause, the slowdown means that we have smaller incomes today than we would have had if the economy had kept growing at its 1960s rate.

Let's now look at real GDP fluctuations around potential GDP.

Figure 19.1

Economic Growth in the United Kingdom: 1963–2003

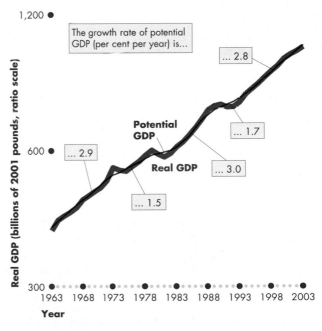

The long-term economic growth rate, measured by the growth of potential GDP, was 2.9 per cent a year in the 1960s but slowed to 1.5 per cent a year in the 1970s, 3.0 in the 1980s and 1.7 per cent before increasing to 2.8 per cent in the 1990s and the 2000s. Real GDP fluctuates around potential GDP.

Sources: Office for National Statistics, International Monetary Fund, *World Economic Outlook*, and authors' assumptions.

Fluctuations Around Potential GDP

Real GDP fluctuates around potential GDP in a business cycle. A **business cycle** is the periodic but irregular up and down movement in economic activity.

Business cycles are not regular, predictable or repeating cycles like the phases of the moon. Their timing changes unpredictably. But cycles do have some things in common. Every business cycle has two phases:

1 Recession
2 Expansion

and two turning points:

1 A peak
2 A trough

Figure 19.2 shows these features of the most recent business cycle in the United Kingdom.

A **recession** is a period during which real GDP decreases – the growth rate of real GDP is negative – for at least two successive quarters. A recession, highlighted in the figure, began in the second quarter of 1990 and ended in the first quarter of 1992. This recession was unusually

long and brought an overall decrease in real GDP of 2.5 per cent over the two-year period that it lasted.

An **expansion** is a period during which real GDP increases. An expansion began in the second quarter of 1992. This expansion was an unusually long one. By the end of 2003, it had run for almost 12 years and real GDP had expanded by almost 40 per cent.

When a business cycle expansion ends and a recession begins, the turning point is called a *peak*. A peak occurred in the second quarter of 1990. When a business cycle recession ends and an expansion begins, the turning point is called a *trough*. A trough occurred in the first quarter of 1992.

The long expansion of the past 12 years is unusual. Let's put this expansion and the most recent business cycle into a longer term perspective.

The Most Recent Recession in Historical Perspective

The recession of 1990–1992 seemed pretty severe while we were passing through it, but compared with some earlier recessions it was mild. You can see how mild it

---

Figure 19.2

The Most Recent UK Business Cycle

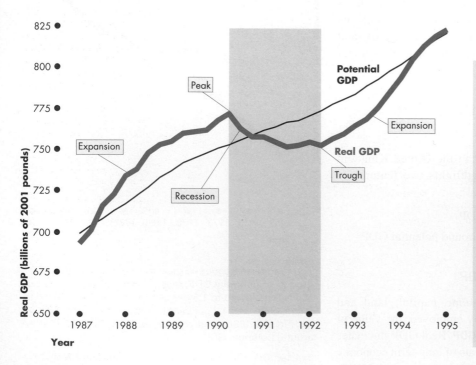

A business cycle has two phases: recession and expansion. The most recent recession (highlighted) ran from the second quarter of 1990 to the trough in first quarter of 1992. Then a new expansion began in the second quarter of 1992. A business cycle has two turning points: a peak and a trough. In the most recent business cycle, the peak occurred in the second quarter of 1990 and the trough occurred in the first quarter of 1992.

Source: Office for National Statistics, International Monetary Fund, *World Economic Outlook* and authors' assumptions.

was by looking at Figure 19.3, which shows a longer history of economic growth. The biggest decreases in real GDP occurred immediately after the First World War, ten years later during the Great Depression and in the period immediately following the Second World War. In more recent times, milder decreases in real GDP occurred during the mid-1970s – the time of oil price hikes by OPEC – and during the early 1980s and early 1990s. You can see that the downturns that occurred before the Second World War were more severe and prolonged than the recessions that came in the post-war years.

The fact is that the last truly great depression occurred before governments started taking policy actions to stabilize the economy. It also occurred before the birth of modern macroeconomics. Is the absence of another great depression a sign that macroeconomics has contributed to economic stability? Some people believe it is. Others doubt it. We'll evaluate these opinions on a number of occasions in this book.

We've seen that real GDP in the United Kingdom has increased over the long term. We've seen that long-term growth slowed during the 1970s. We've seen that recessions have interrupted the broad upward sweep

of real GDP. Is the UK experience typical? Do other countries share this experience? Let's see if they do.

Economic Growth Around the World

All countries experience economic growth, but the growth rate varies both over time and across countries. The fluctuations in economic growth rates over time tend to be correlated across countries, but some countries experience greater volatility in growth rates than others. And some growth rate differences across countries persist over a number of years.

We'll compare UK economic growth over time with that in other countries. And we'll look at longer term differences in growth rates among countries and groups of countries.

Growth Rates over Time

First, we'll compare the growth rate of real GDP in the United Kingdom with that for the rest of the world as a whole. Figure 19.4(a) (overleaf) shows these two growth rates from 1973 to 2003. (Note that this figure

---

Figure 19.3

Long-term Economic Growth in the United Kingdom

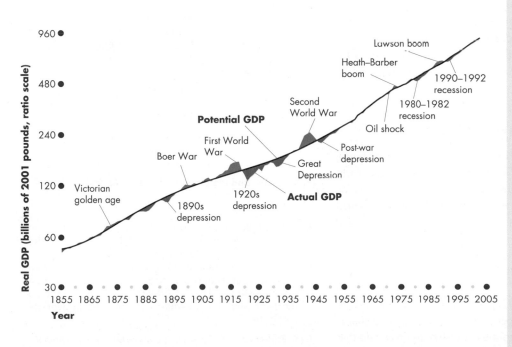

The thin black line shows potential GDP. Along that line, real GDP grew at an average rate of 2 per cent per year between 1855 and 2003. The blue areas show when real GDP was above potential GDP and the red areas show when it was below potential GDP. The labels indicate the events associated with some of the major deviations from potential GDP.

Sources: Real GDP 1855–1947: C. H. Feinstein, *National income Expenditure and Output of the United Kingdom, 1955–1965*, 1972, Cambridge, Cambridge University Press. Real GDP 1948–2003: Office for National Statistics. Potential GDP: Lombard Street Research Ltd and authors' assumptions.

graphs *growth rates* of real GDP and not *levels* of real GDP that the three previous figures showed. So the number on the *y*-axis of this graph is a growth rate expressed as per cent per year.)

You can see a striking fact in Figure 19.4(a). The UK real GDP growth rate fluctuates much more than the real GDP growth rate in the world as a whole. In several years, UK real GDP actually fell – a negative growth rate – but the world economy didn't experience negative growth during the 30 years shown in the figure.

Persistent Different Growth Rates

Second, we'll look at longer term persistent differences across countries. Figure 19.4(b) compares the growth of the UK economy with that of several other countries and regions on average from 1993 to 2003. Among the industrial economies (the red bars), Japan has grown the slowest and the newly industrialized Asian economies have grown fastest. The United Kingdom is in the middle of these two growth rates.

Among the developing economies (the green bars), the most rapid growth has occurred in Asia where the average growth rate was more than 7 per cent a year – China and India are the main economies in this group. The slowest growing developing countries are in the Western Hemisphere (Central and South America).

The transition economies (purple bar) grew at a moderate rate during the ten years to 2003. These are countries such as Russia and the other countries of Central and Eastern Europe that are making a transition from a state-managed economy to a market economy.

World average growth (the blue bar) has been a bit more than 3.5 per cent a year, somewhat greater than the UK growth rate.

Consequences of Persistent Differences

The persistent differences in growth rates are bringing dramatic change to the share of some nations in world real GDP. Because the UK real GDP growth rate is below that of the rest of the world, the UK share of world real GDP is falling. The UK share of world real GDP decreased from 4 per cent in 1983 to 3 per cent in 2003. Some fast-growing nations such as China and India are becoming a significantly bigger part of the global economy. China's share of world real GDP increased from 4 per cent in 1983 to 13 per cent in 2003 and India's share increased from 4 per cent to 6 per cent. The shares of these two Asian economies continue to grow and that of the United Kingdom continues to shrink.

Figure 19.4

Economic Growth Around the World

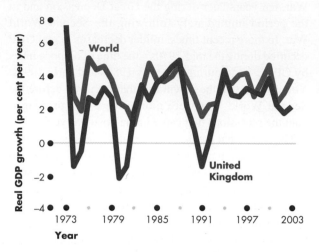

(a) The United Kingdom and the world: 1973–2003

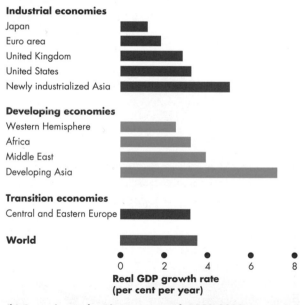

(b) Countries and regions compared: 1993–2003 average

In part (a), economic growth fluctuates much more in the United Kingdom than in the world economy, but the fluctuations across countries are correlated.

In part (b), growth rate differences persist. Between 1993 and 2003, Asian economies grew fastest and transition economies shrank. The UK growth rate is in the middle of the pack and is somewhat below the world average growth rate.

Source: International Monetary Fund, *World Economic Outlook.*

The Lucas Wedge and the Okun Gap

You've seen that productivity growth slowed during the 1970s. And you've seen that real GDP growth fluctuates, so from time to time real GDP falls below potential GDP. How costly are the growth slowdown and lost output over the business cycle?

Two measures provide the answers:

◆ The Lucas wedge
◆ The Okun gap

The Lucas Wedge

The **Lucas wedge** is the accumulated loss of output that results from a slowdown in the growth rate of real GDP. It is given this name because Robert E. Lucas Jr., a leading macroeconomist and Nobel Laureate, drew attention to it and remarked that once you begin to think about the benefits of faster economic growth, it is hard to think about anything else!

Figure 19.5(a) shows the Lucas wedge that arises from the productivity growth slowdown of the 1970s. The black line in the figure tracks the path that potential GDP would have followed if its 1960s growth rate had been maintained through the years to 2003.

The Lucas wedge is a staggering £4 trillion – about four years' real GDP at the 2003 level. This number is a measure of the cost of slower productivity growth.

The Okun Gap

The **Okun gap** is the gap between real GDP and potential GDP and so is another name for the *output gap*. It is given this name because Arthur M. Okun, a policy economist who was chairman of President Lyndon Johnson's council of economic advisors during the 1960s, drew attention to it as a source of loss from economic fluctuations.

Figure 19.5(b) shows the Okun gap from the recessions that occurred during the same years for which we've just calculated the Lucas wedge.

The Okun gaps in the four recessions since 1970 sum to £98 billion – about one-tenth of real GDP in 2003. This number is a measure of the cost of business cycle fluctuations.

You can see that the Lucas wedge is a much bigger deal than the Okun gap – more than 40 times as big a deal! Smoothing the business cycle saves spells of high unemployment and lost output. But maintaining a high productivity growth rate makes a dramatic and persistent difference to the standard of living.

Figure 19.5

The Lucas Wedge and the Okun Gap

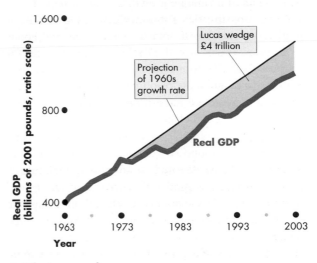

(a) The Lucas wedge

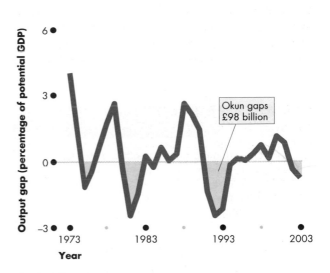

(b) The Okun gap

In part (a), the Lucas wedge that arises from the productivity growth slowdown of the 1970s is a staggering £4 trillion or almost 4 times the real GDP of 2003.

In part (b), the Okun gap that arises from the lost production in the recessions since the early 1970s amounts to £98 billion or about one-tenth of real GDP in 2003. Over this 33-year period, the Lucas wedge is more than 40 times as large as the Okun gap.

Source: Office for National Statistics, International Monetary Fund, *World Economic Outlook* and authors' assumptions.

Benefits and Costs of Economic Growth

The benefits of economic growth are the increased consumption possibilities for individuals and societies. Faster economic growth translates into more real goods and services. Faster growth provided more resources for healthcare for the poor and elderly, more cancer and AIDS research and more resources to improve our roads and houses. We even have more to spend on cleaner rivers, more trees and cleaner air.

But fast growth is also costly. Its main cost is forgone *current* consumption. To sustain a high growth rate, resources must be devoted to advancing technology and accumulating capital rather than to *current* consumption. This cost cannot be avoided. But it brings the benefit of greater consumption in the future – see Chapter 2, p. 38.

Two other possible costs of faster growth are a more rapid depletion of non-renewable natural resources such as oil and natural gas and increased pollution of the air, rivers and oceans. But neither of these two costs is inevitable. The technological advances that bring economic growth help us to economize on our use of natural resources and to clean up the environment. For example, more efficient car engines cut petrol use and carbon emissions.

Review Quiz

1   What is economic growth and how is the long-term economic growth rate measured?
2   What is the distinction between real GDP and *potential* GDP?
3   What is a business cycle and what are its phases?
4   What is a recession?
5   In what phase of the business cycle was the UK economy during 2003?
6   What happened to economic growth in the United Kingdom and other countries during the 1970s?
7   What is the Lucas wedge and what is the Okun gap? How big are they?
8   What are the benefits and the costs of long-term economic growth?

We've seen that real GDP grows and that it also fluctuates over the business cycle. Business cycles bring fluctuations in jobs available and unemployment. Let's now examine these core macroeconomic problems.

Jobs and Unemployment

What kind of labour market will you enter when you graduate? Will there be plenty of good jobs to choose from, or will there be so much unemployment that you will be forced to take a low-paying job that doesn't use your education? The answer depends, to a large degree, on the total number of jobs available and on the unemployment rate.

Jobs

Between 1979 and 2003, 10.4 million jobs were created in the European Union. This number may appear to be impressive but let's put it in an international perspective. In the United States – a comparably sized economy – 42.3 million jobs were created over the same period. In the United Kingdom the number of jobs created were 2.5 million. But these figures hide the details – a general switch from manufacturing jobs to service jobs, from male to female workers and from full-time to part-time jobs.

New jobs are created every month, but many jobs are destroyed. The pace of job creation and destruction fluctuates over the business cycle. More jobs are destroyed than created during a recession, so the number of jobs decreases. But more jobs are created than destroyed during a recovery and expansion, so the number of jobs increases. For example, in the United Kingdom 1.7 million jobs were lost between 1979 and 1983. In the long recovery to 1989, 3.2 million jobs were created, in the recession of 1990–1992 the number of jobs fell by nearly 1.9 million and in the recovery from 1993 to 2003, 2.9 million jobs were created.

Unemployment

Not everyone who wants a job can find one. On one day in any recent year, around 900,000 men and 600,000 women in the United Kingdom are unemployed. During a recession, unemployment rises above this level and during an expansion, it falls below this level.

An internationally recognized definition of **unemployment** is a state in which a person does not have a job but is available for work, willing to work and has made some effort to find work within the previous four weeks. The total number of people who are unemployed on this criterion plus the number of people employed is called the **workforce**. The **unemployment rate** is the percentage of the people in the workforce who are unemployed. (The concepts of the workforce and unemployment are explained more fully in Chapter 21, pp. 460–461.)

The unemployment rate is not a perfect measure of the underutilization of labour for two main reasons. First, it excludes discouraged workers. A **discouraged worker** is a person who does not have a job, is available for work and willing to work, but who has given up the effort to find work. Many people switch between the unemployment and discouraged worker categories in both directions every month. Second, the unemployment rate measures unemployed persons rather than unemployed labour hours. It excludes those people who have a part-time job but who want a full-time job.

Despite these two limitations, the unemployment rate is the best available measure of underused labour resources. Let's look at some facts about unemployment.

Unemployment in the United Kingdom

Figure 19.6 shows the unemployment rate in the United Kingdom from 1855 to 2003. Three features stand out.

First, the United Kingdom has had some spells of very high unemployment. During the entire period between the two World Wars (1919–1939) unemployment was extremely high and reached a peak of 15.6 per cent at the depths of the Great Depression. The unemployment rate was also high on the average during the 1980s and early 1990s.

Second, the unemployment rate has fluctuated a great deal. The fluctuations were pronounced during the nineteenth century Victorian trade cycles. But unemployment has fluctuated in an unending sequence of business cycles. After a period of mild fluctuations during the 1960s and early 1970s, the swings in the unemployment rate became large again during the 1980–1982 recession and the 1990–1992 recession and the expansions that followed.

Figure 19.6

Unemployment in the United Kingdom: 1855–2003

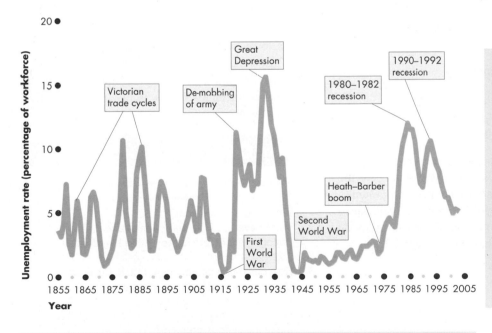

Unemployment is a persistent feature of economic life, but its rate varies. At its worst – during the Great Depression – nearly 16 per cent of the workforce was unemployed. Even in recent recessions, the unemployment rate climbed to 11 per cent. Between 1945 and the late 1960s, the unemployment rate remained steady. During the 1970s, the unemployment rate increased and during the late 1990s and 2000s, it tended to decrease.

Sources: C. H. Feinstein, *National Income Expenditure and Output of the United Kingdom, 1855–1965*, 1972, Cambridge, Cambridge University Press; and Office for National Statistics.

Third, there have been periods of extremely low unemployment. The lowest rates occurred during the two World Wars and throughout the 1950s and 1960s.

How does UK unemployment compare with unemployment in other countries?

Unemployment Around the World

Figure 19.7 shows the unemployment rate in the United States, the European Union and Japan. Over the period shown in this figure, US unemployment averaged 6.3 per cent, much higher than Japanese unemployment, which averaged 3.2 per cent, but lower than unemployment in the European Union, which averaged 8.9 per cent.

The figure shows that unemployment fluctuates over the business cycle. It increases during a recession and decreases during an expansion. The US unemployment cycle is out of phase with the EU unemployment cycle. Japanese unemployment has been remarkably stable but has risen steadily in the 1990s and by 2003 was only just below that in the United States.

We've looked at some facts about unemployment in the United Kingdom and in other countries. Let's now look at some of the consequences of unemployment that make it the serious problem that it is.

Why Unemployment is a Problem

Unemployment is a serious economic, social and personal problem for two main reasons:

◆ Lost production and incomes
◆ Lost human capital

Lost Production and Incomes

The loss of a job brings an immediate loss of income and production. These losses can be devastating for the people who bear them and make unemployment a frightening propect for everyone. Jobseeker's allowance creates a short-term safety net, but it does not provide the same living standard as having a job does.

Lost Human Capital

Prolonged unemployment can permanently damage a person's job prospects. For example, a middle-aged manager loses his job when his firm downsizes. Short of income, he takes a job as a taxi driver. After a year he discovers that he cannot compete with young MBA graduates. He eventually finds a job as a shop manager

Figure 19.7

Unemployment in the Advanced Economies

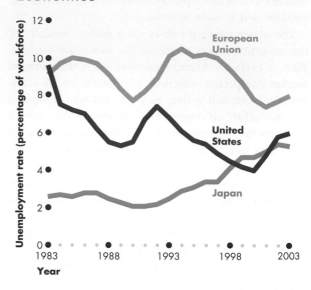

The unemployment rate in the European Union has in general been higher than that in the United States, but it has fallen in recent years. EU unemployment has a cycle that is out of phase with the US unemployment cycle. Unemployment in Japan barely changed in the 1980s but has risen in the 1990s and is now just below that in the United States.

and at a lower wage than his previous managerial job. He has lost some of his human capital.

The costs of unemployment are spread unequally, which makes unemployment a highly charged political problem as well as a serious economic problem.

Review Quiz

1   How many new jobs have been created in the United Kingdom between 1979 and 2003?
2   What is unemployment?
3   What have been the main trends and cycles in the unemployment rate in the United Kingdom since 1933?
4   How has the unemployment rate in the European Union compared with the unemployment rates in the United States and Japan?
5   What are the main costs of unemployment that make it a serious problem?

Let's now turn to the third major macroeconomic issue: inflation.

Inflation

Prices on average can be rising, falling or stable. **Inflation** is a process of rising prices. We measure the *inflation rate* as the percentage change in the *average* level of prices or **price level**. A common measure of the price level is the *Retail Price Index* (RPI). The RPI tells us how the average price of all the goods and services bought by a typical household changes from month to month. (The RPI is explained in Chapter 20, p. 470.) Every month the television news and the newspapers report the inflation rate. How is the inflation rate calculated?

So that you can see in a concrete way how the inflation rate is measured, let's do a calculation. In February 2004, the RPI was 183.8 and in February 2003, it was 179.3, so the inflation rate over the year from February 2003 to February 2004 was:

$$\text{Inflation rate} = \frac{183.8 - 179.3}{179.3} \times 100$$

$$= 2.5 \text{ per cent}$$

Inflation in the United Kingdom

Figure 19.8 shows the UK inflation rate from 1963 to 2003. You can see from this figure that during the early 1960s the inflation rate was between 2 and 3 per cent a year. Inflation began to increase in the late 1960s, but the largest increases occurred in 1975 and 1980. These were years in which the actions of the Organization of the Petroleum Exporting Countries (OPEC) resulted in exceptionally large increases in the price of oil, but domestic policies also contributed to the inflation process. Inflation was brought under control in the early 1980s when the Thatcher government instructed the Bank of England to push interest rates up and people cut back on their spending. Since the early 1990s, the UK inflation rate has remained low.

The inflation rate rises and falls over the years, but it rarely becomes negative. If the inflation rate is negative, the price *level* is falling and we have **deflation**. Since the 1930s, the price level has generally risen – the inflation rate has been positive. So even when the inflation rate is low, as it was in 1963 and 1993, the price level is rising.

Figure 19.8

Inflation in the United Kingdom: 1963–2003

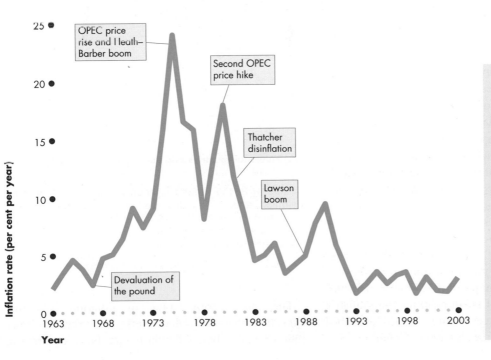

Inflation is a persistent feature of economic life in the United Kingdom. The inflation rate was low in the first half of the 1960s, but it increased during the second half with the rise in the world inflation rate. It increased further with the OPEC oil price hikes in the 1970s but declined during the Thatcher years of the 1980s. The inflation rate has remained low since the early 1990s.

Source: Office for National Statistics.

Inflation Around the World

Figure 19.9 shows inflation in the major industrial economies since 1973. You can see in part (a) that the inflation rates in the United States, the European Union and Japan have had a similar pattern. You can see that they all shared the burst of double-digit inflation during the 1970s, the fall in inflation during the 1980s and low inflation in the 1990s.

You can see in Figure 19.9(b) that the average inflation rate of the industrial economies has been very low compared with that of the developing countries. Among the industrial economies, Japan's inflation rate has been close to zero in recent years. Among the developing countries, the most recent extreme inflation has occurred in the former Yugoslavia, where its rate exceeded 6,000 per cent per year.

Why is Inflation a Problem?

A very low inflation rate is not much of a problem. But a high inflation rate is a serious problem. It makes inflation hard to predict, and unpredictable inflation makes the economy behave like a giant casino in which some people gain and some lose and no one can accurately predict where the gains and losses will fall.

Gains and losses occur because of unpredictable changes in the value of money. Money is used as a measuring rod of value in the transactions that we undertake. Borrowers and lenders, workers and employers all make contracts in terms of money. If the value of money varies unpredictably over time, then the amounts really paid and received – the quantity of goods that the money will buy – also fluctuate unpredictably. Measuring value with a measuring rod whose units vary is a bit like trying to measure a piece of cloth with an elastic ruler. The size of the cloth depends on how tightly the ruler is stretched.

In a period of rapid unpredictable inflation, resources are diverted from productive activities to forecasting inflation. It becomes more profitable to forecast the inflation rate correctly than to invent a new product. Doctors, lawyers, accountants, farmers – just about everyone – can make themselves better off, not by specializing in the profession for which they have been trained but by spending more of their time dabbling as amateur economists and inflation forecasters and managing their investment portfolios. From a social perspective, this diversion of talent resulting from inflation is like throwing our scarce resources on to the rubbish heap. This waste of resources is a cost of inflation.

Figure 19.9

Inflation Around the World

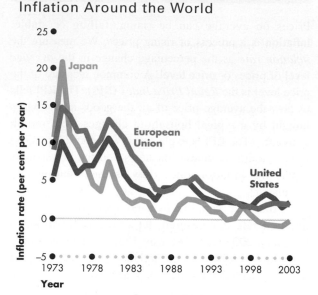

(a) Inflation in industrial economies

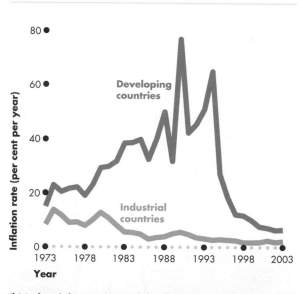

(b) Industrial countries and developing countries

Inflation in the industrial economies has followed a similar pattern. They all shared the burst of double-digit inflation in the 1970s and low inflation in the 1990s. Compared with the developing countries, inflation in the industrial economies is low.

Source: International Monetary Fund, *World Economic Outlook*.

The most serious type of inflation is called *hyperinflation* – an inflation rate that exceeds 50 per cent a month. Hyperinflation is rare, but it occurred in

Germany, Poland and Hungary during the 1920s and Hungary and China during the 1940s. At the height of these hyperinflations, workers were paid twice a day because money lost its value so quickly. As soon as they were paid, people rushed off to spend their wages before they lost too much value.

Hyperinflation is rare but it is not just a historical curiosity. There have been some specular examples of hyperinflation. In 1994, the African country of Zaire had a hyperinflation that peaked at a *monthly* inflation rate of 76 per cent. Also during 1994, Brazil almost reached the hyperinflation stratosphere with a monthly inflation rate of 40 per cent. A cup of coffee that cost 15 cruzeiros in 1980 cost 22 *billion* cruzeiros in 1994. With numbers this big, Brazil twice changed the name of its currency and twice lopped off three zeros to keep the magnitudes of monetary values manageable.

Inflation imposes costs, but lowering the inflation rate is also costly. Policies that lower the inflation rate increase the unemployment rate. Most economists think that the increase in the unemployment rate that accompanies a fall in the inflation rate is temporary. But some economists say that higher unemployment is a permanent cost of low inflation. The cost of lowering inflation must be evaluated when an anti-inflation policy is followed. You will learn more about inflation and the costs of curing it in Chapter 29.

Review Quiz

1   What is inflation and how does it influence the value of money?
2   How is inflation measured?
3   What has been the UK inflation record since 1963?
4   How does inflation in the United Kingdom compare with inflation in other industrial countries and in developing countries?
5   What are some of the costs of inflation that make it a serious economic problem?

We've now looked at economic growth and fluctuations, unemployment and inflation. Let's turn to the fourth macroeconomic issue: surpluses and deficits. What happens when a government spends more than it collects in taxes? And what happens when a nation buys more from other countries than it sells to them? Do governments and nations face the problem that you and I would face if we spent more than we earned? Do they run out of funds? Let's look at these questions.

Surpluses and Deficits

In only 8 of the past 30 years has the UK government had a budget surplus. And for the past 20 years, the United Kingdom has had a persistent international deficit. What exactly are a government budget deficit and a nation's international deficit?

Government Budget Surplus and Deficit

If a government collects more in taxes than it spends, it has a surplus – a **government budget surplus**. If a government spends more than it collects in taxes, it has a deficit – a **government budget deficit**. The UK government had a surplus from 1987 to 1990 and again from 1998 to 2000. Aside from these two brief spells of surplus, the government has generally had a budget deficit.

Figure 19.10(a) shows the government surplus and deficit since 1973 measured as a percentage of GDP. (The concept of GDP, which is explained more fully in Chapter 20, equals total income in the economy.)

We measure the budget surplus or deficit as a percentage of GDP so that we can make comparisons over a number of years. You can think of this measure as the number of pence of surplus or deficit per pound of income earned by an average person.

When the government had a budget surplus, it was modest, rising to a maximum of about 4 per cent of GDP in 2000. But when the government has a budget deficit, it was on occasion extremely large. For example, in 1975, the deficit was 5 per cent of GDP. The deficit was even larger during the recession of the early 1990s. The government deficit generally has swelled during recessions.

International Deficit

When we import goods and services from the rest of the world, we make payments to the rest of the world. When we export goods and services to the rest of the world, we receive payments from the rest of the world. If our imports exceed our exports, we have an international deficit.

Figure 19.10(b) shows the UK international balance from 1963 to 2003. The figure shows the balance on the **current account**, which includes UK exports minus UK imports but also takes into account interest payments paid to and received from the rest of the world.

Figure 19.10

The UK Government Budget and International Surpluses and Deficits: 1973–2003

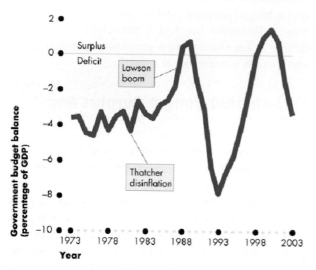

(a) Government budget balance

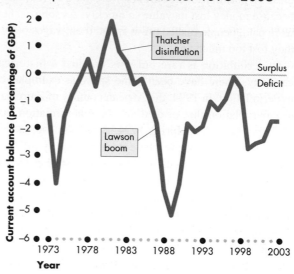

(b) Current account balance

In part (a), the UK government had a persistent budget deficit during the 1970s and most of the 1980s. The deficit became large during the recession of the early 1990s. A surplus emerged in 1998, but since 2001 the government budget has again been in deficit.

In part (b), the UK current account shows the balance of UK exports minus UK imports. In the mid-1980s, a current account deficit emerged. The current account balance has fluctuated, but the balance has remained a deficit for twenty years.

Source: Office for National Statistics.

To compare one year with another, Figure 19.10(b) shows the current account as a percentage of GDP. The United Kingdom has had a persistent current account deficit since the time of the OPEC oil crisis in the mid-1970s and has now been in deficit for twenty years.

Do Surpluses and Deficits Matter?

Why do deficits cause anxiety? What happens when a government cannot cover its spending with taxes, or when a country buys more from other countries than it sells to them?

If you spend more than you earn, you have a deficit. And to cover your deficit, you go into debt. But when you borrow, you must pay interest on your debt. Just like you, if a government or a nation has a deficit, it must borrow. And like you, the government and the nation must pay interest on their debts.

Whether borrowing and paying out huge amounts of interest is a good idea depends on what the borrowed funds are used for. If you borrow to finance a holiday, you must eventually tighten your belt, cut spending and repay your debt, as well as pay interest on the debt. But

if you borrow to invest in a business that earns a large profit, you might be able to repay your debt and pay the interest on it while increasing your spending. It is the same with a government and a nation.

A government or a nation that borrows to increase its consumption might be heading for trouble later. But a government or a nation that borrows to buy assets that earn a profit might be making a sound investment.

You will learn more about the government budget in Chapter 25 and about the international current account deficit in Chapter 34.

Review Quiz

1   What determines a government's budget deficit or budget surplus?
2   How has the budget of the UK government evolved since 1973?
3   What is a country's international deficit?
4   How has the UK current account changed since 1973?

Macroeconomic Policy Challenges and Tools

From the time of Adam Smith's *The Wealth of Nations* in 1776 until the publication of Keynes' *General Theory of Employment, Interest, and Money* in 1936, it was widely believed that the proper role of government in economic life was to provide the legal framework to enforce property rights and enable people to freely pursue their self-interest. The economy behaved best, it was believed, if the government left people free to pursue their own best interests – a doctrine called *laissez faire*.

The economic hardship of the 1920s and 1930s challenged this traditional view of the role of government. Everyone wanted governments to act to alleviate the economic suffering. But there was no economic theory to guide such actions. It was a bit like the situation today with a disease such as AIDS/HIV for which we have no cure. We want action but we don't know what to do.

The macroeconomics of Keynes provided the missing theory and the action checklist. Keynes' central proposition was that the economy does not always fix itself. *Laissez faire* works most of the time but not all of the time. And when it fails, government actions are needed to achieve and maintain full employment.

The Second World War brought full employment but it did not erase the memory of the years of economic depression that preceded it. So when the war ended, governments began to embrace the ideas of Keynes and develop active macroeconomic policies.

The UK government was among the first to declare full employment as a policy goal. Other governments quickly followed and by the early 1970s even an American president (Richard Nixon) was ready to declare that "We are all Keynesians now".

Policy Challenges and Tools

Today, the widely agreed challenges for macroeconomic policy in all countries are to:

1 Boost long-term growth.
2 Stabilize the business cycle.
3 Lower unemployment.
4 Keep inflation low.
5 Reduce government and international deficits.

How can we do all these things? What are the tools available to pursue the macroeconomic policy challenges?

Macroeconomic policy tools are divided into two broad categories:

◆ Fiscal policy
◆ Monetary policy

Fiscal Policy

Making changes in taxes and in government spending is called **fiscal policy**. This range of actions are under the control of the government. Fiscal policy can be used to try to boost long-term growth by creating incentives that encourage saving, investment and technological change. Fiscal policy can also be used to try to smooth out the business cycle. When the economy is in a recession, the government might cut taxes or increase its spending. Conversely, when the economy is in a rapid expansion, the government might increase taxes or cut its spending in an attempt to slow real GDP growth and prevent inflation from increasing. Fiscal policy is discussed in Chapter 25.

Monetary Policy

Changing interest rates and changing the quantity of money in the economy is called **monetary policy**. These actions are under the control of the Bank of England in the United Kingdom and the European Central Bank (ECB) in the Eurozone economies. The principal aim of monetary policy is to keep inflation in check. To achieve this objective, the Bank of England and the ECB prevents the quantity of money from expanding too rapidly. Monetary policy can also be used to smooth the business cycle. When the economy is in recession, the Bank of England and the ECB might lower interest rates and inject money into the economy. And when the economy is in a rapid expansion, the Bank of England and the ECB might increase interest rates in an attempt to slow real GDP growth and prevent inflation from increasing. We study the roles of money and monetary policy in Chapters 26 and 27.

Review Quiz

1 What are the main macroeconomic policy challenges?
2 What are the main tools of macroeconomic policy?
3 Distinguish between fiscal policy and monetary policy?

Reading Between the Lines

Oil prices and the Global Economy

The Financial Times, 4 May 2004

FT

High oil prices hitting world recovery

Andrew Balls

High oil prices over the past five years are dampening the global economic recovery and causing inflation and fiscal problems in oil-importing countries, a report from the International Energy Agency [IEA] said on Monday.

The IEA, which monitors the oil market for the Organisation of Economic Co-operation and Development countries, said: "Higher prices are contributing to stubbornly high levels of unemployment and exacerbating budget deficit problems in many OECD and other oil-importing countries."

It said high energy prices had also exacerbated the world economic downturn in 2000–2001, and warned that the worst effects of high prices are felt in developing countries.

The OECD countries imported more than half of their oil needs in 2003 at a cost of more than $260bn (€218bn, £147bn) – 20 per cent above the 2001 total.

Analysis by the IEA, the OECD and the International Monetary Fund suggests that a sustained increase in oil prices from $25 to $35 per barrel subtracts 0.4 per cent from the gross domestic product of the OECD countries in the first and second year. It pushes inflation up by half a percentage point.

A $10 rise in oil prices subtracts at least 0.5 per cent from world GDP – even taking into account the impact on consumption in the oil exporting countries.

The eurozone countries suffer the most among the OECD countries because they are highly dependent on oil imports, while the US suffers the least owing to a greater share of domestic production. Japan falls in between, owing to a high proportion of imported oil but low energy-intensity in its economy. The impact on developing countries is more severe because their economies are more dependent on imported oil and more energy-intensive and because energy is used less efficiently, the IEA says.

The Essence of the Story

◆ The International Energy Agency (IEA) suggests that high oil prices are contributing to stubbornly high levels of unemployment in the OECD countries.

◆ High oil prices have also exacerbated the economic downturn in the world economy in 2000–2001.

◆ Analysis by the IEA suggests that a sustained rise in oil prices by $10 a barrel will subtract at least 0.5 per cent from world GDP.

◆ Within the OECD, the Eurozone countries will suffer the most because they import oil and the United States will suffer least because it produces oil.

Economic Analysis

◆ World oil prices have been rising because of growing world demand (particularly in China), cuts in supply by the oil-producing countries and uncertainties about the political situation in Iraq.

◆ The rise in oil prices raises the prices of energy and costs in the energy-intensive industries of the OECD economies.

◆ Rising energy costs might weaken productivity growth in the same way as high oil prices slowed world productivity growth in the 1970s.

◆ Figure 1 shows the price of oil during 2003 and 2004. In May 2004, the price of oil touched $40 a barrel.

◆ Figure 2 shows the growth rate of real GDP in Eurozone and OECD economies along with forecasts for 2004–2005. Growth in the Eurozone area has been slower than the average in the OECD economies and is not expected to recover as quickly.

◆ Figure 3 shows the unemployment rate in the Eurozone and the OECD economies along with forecasts for 2004–2005. Unemployment remains high partly because the high price of oil will slow productivity growth and slow the fall in unemployment.

◆ But we should be sceptical about the gloomy forecasts based on high oil prices. The world economy today is less dependent on oil than it was in the 1970s and early 1980s when oil prices also rose sharply. Furthermore, oil prices rose five-fold in 1973 and three-fold in 1979. Adjusting for UK inflation, the real price of oil in 2004 is one-third of what it was in 1979.

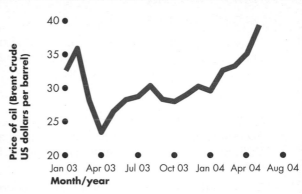

Figure 1 The price of oil

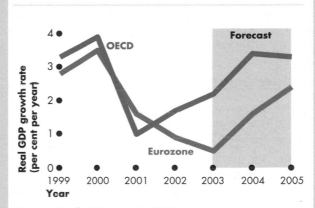

Figure 2 Real GDP growth: OECD and Eurozone

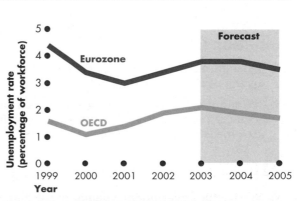

Figure 3 Unemployment: OECD and Eurozone

Summary

Key Points

Origins and Issues of Macroeconomics (p. 418)

◆ Macroeconomics studies economic growth and fluctuations, jobs and unemployment, inflation and surpluses and deficits.

Economic Growth (pp. 419–424)

◆ Economic growth is the expansion of potential GDP. Real GDP fluctuates around potential GDP in a business cycle.

◆ Slow productivity growth (the Lucas wedge) is more costly than the business cycle (the Okun gap).

◆ The main benefit of long-term economic growth is higher future consumption and the main cost is lower current consumption.

Jobs and Unemployment (pp. 424–426)

◆ The economy creates more jobs than it loses in an expansion and loses more jobs than it creates in a recession.

◆ The unemployment rate increases during a recession and decreases during an expansion.

◆ The unemployment rate is higher in the United Kingdom than in Japan and the United States.

◆ Unemployment can permanently damage a person's job prospects.

Inflation (pp. 427–429)

◆ Inflation, a process of rising prices, is measured by the percentage change in the RPI.

◆ Inflation is a problem because it lowers the value of money and makes money less useful as a measuring rod of value.

Surpluses and Deficits (pp. 429–430)

◆ When the government spends more than it collects in taxes, it has a budget deficit. When the government collects more in taxes than it spends, it has a budget surplus.

◆ When imports exceed exports, a nation has a current account deficit.

Macroeconomic Policy Challenges and Tools (p. 431)

◆ The macroeconomic policy challenge is to use fiscal policy and monetary policy to boost long-term growth, stabilize the business cycle, lower unemployment, maintain low inflation and prevent large deficits.

Key Figures

Figure 19.1   Economic Growth in the United Kingdom: 1963–2003, 419
Figure 19.2   The Most Recent UK Business Cycle, 420
Figure 19.3   Long-term Economic Growth in the United Kingdom, 421
Figure 19.5   The Lucas Wedge and the Okun Gap, 423
Figure 19.6   Unemployment in the United Kingdom: 1855–2003, 425
Figure 19.8   Inflation in the United Kingdom: 1963–2003, 427
Figure 19.10 The UK Government Budget and International Surpluses and Deficits: 1973–2003, 430

Key Terms

Business cycle, 420
Current account, 429
Deflation, 427
Discouraged worker, 425
Economic growth, 419
Expansion, 420
Fiscal policy, 431
Government budget deficit, 429
Government budget surplus, 429
Great Depression, 418
Inflation, 427
Lucas wedge, 423
Monetary policy, 431
Okun gap, 423
Potential GDP, 419
Price level, 427
Productivity growth slowdown, 419
Real gross domestic product (real GDP), 419
Recession, 420
Unemployment, 424
Unemployment rate, 425
Workforce, 425

Problems

*1 Use Data Graphing in Chapter 19 resources on *Parkin Interactive* to answer the following questions. In which country in 1992 was

   a The growth rate of real GDP highest: Canada, France, Japan or the United States?

   b The unemployment rate highest: Canada, Japan, the United Kingdom or the United States?

   c The inflation rate lowest: Canada, Germany, the United Kingdom or the United States?

   d The government budget deficit (as a percentage of GDP) largest: Canada, Japan, the United Kingdom or the United States?

2 Use Data Graphing in Chapter 19 resources on *Parkin Interactive* to answer the following questions.

   a In which country in 2000 was the growth rate of real GDP highest: Canada, Japan or the United States?

   b In which country in 2000 was the unemployment rate lowest: Canada, Japan, the United Kingdom or the United States?

   c In which country in 2000 was the inflation rate lowest: Canada, Japan, the United Kingdom or the United States?

   d In which country in 2000 was the government budget deficit (as a percentage of GDP) smallest: Canada, the United Kingdom or the United States?

   e Is it possible to say in which country consumption possibilities are growing faster? Why or why not?

*3 The graph shows real GDP growth rate in Greece and Turkey from 1998 to 2002.

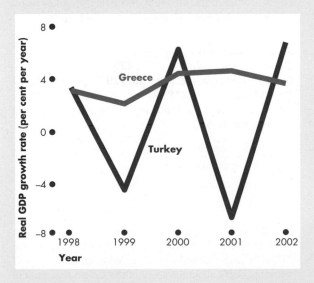

   a In which years did economic growth in Greece increase? And in which year was growth the fastest?

   b In which years did economic growth in Turkey decrease? And in which year was growth the slowest?

   c Compare the paths of economic growth in Greece and Turkey during this period.

4 The figure shows real GDP per person in Australia and Japan from 1992 to 2002.

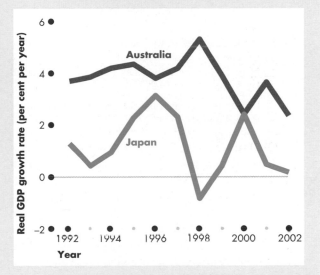

   a In which years did economic growth in Australia increase? And in which year was growth the fastest?

   b In which years did economic growth in Japan decrease? And in which year was growth the slowest?

   c Compare the paths of economic growth in Australia and Japan during this period.

*5 The graph shows real GDP in Germany from 1989 to 2003.

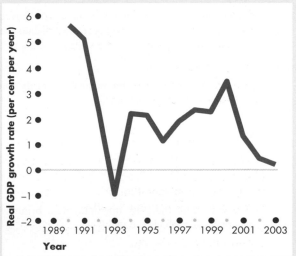

*Solutions to odd-numbered problems are available on *Parkin Interactive*.

a How many recessions did Germany experience during this period?

b In which years, if any, did Germany experience a business cycle peak and a business cycle trough?

c In which years, if any, did Germany experience an expansion?

6 Use the links on *Parkin Interactive* to obtain data on quarterly real GDP for the United Kingdom since the fourth quarter of 2003 and update Figure 19.2.

a Is the UK economy now in a recession or an expansion?

b If the economy is still in an expansion, how long has the expansion lasted? If the economy is now in recession, how long has the economy been in recession?

c During the last year, has the growth rate sped up or slowed down?

*7 Use Data Graphing in Chapter 19 resources on *Parkin Interactive* to answer the following questions. Which country, in 1998, had

a The largest government budget deficit (as a percentage of GDP): Canada, Japan, the United Kingdom or the United States?

b A current account surplus (as a percentage of GDP): Canada, Japan, Germany or the United States?

8 Use Data Graphing in Chapter 19 resources on *Parkin Interactive* to answer the following questions. Which country, in 2002, had

a The largest government budget surplus (as a percentage of GDP): Canada, Japan, the United Kingdom or the United States?

b The largest current account deficit (as a percentage of GDP): Canada, Japan, Germany or the United States?

*9 Use Data Graphing in Chapter 19 resources on *Parkin Interactive* to make a scatter diagram of the inflation rate and the unemployment rate in the United Kingdom.

a Describe the relationship.

b Do you think that low unemployment brings an increase in the inflation rate?

10 Use Data Graphing in Chapter 19 resources on *Parkin Interactive* to make a scatter diagram of the government budget deficit as a percentage of GDP and the unemployment rate in the United States.

a Describe the relationship.

b Do you think that low unemployment brings a decrease in the budget deficit?

Critical Thinking

1 Study *Reading Between the Lines* on pp. 432–433 and then answer the following questions:

a Why did the price of oil rise prior to 2004?

b Why might a rise in oil prices slow down growth in the Eurozone economies more than in the United States?

c How much does a rise of $10 a barrel in the oil price decrease world GDP?

Web Exercises

Use the links on *Parkin Interactive* to work the following exercises.

1 Obtain the latest data on real GDP, unemployment and inflation in the Eurozone countries (countries that use the euro).

a Draw a graph of GDP growth, inflation and unemployment since 2001.

b What dangers does the Eurozone economy face today?

c What actions, if any, do you think might be needed by the European Central Bank to keep the economy strong?

2 Obtain data on the unemployment rate for your region of the country.

a Compare the unemployment rate in your region with that in the United Kingdom as a whole.

b Compare the unemployment rate in your region with that in the neighbouring regions.

3 Obtain data on the following variable for the United Kingdom for the most recent period available. Describe how the following variables have changed over the the last year:

a The unemployment rate

b The inflation rate

c The government budget surplus or deficit

d The international deficit

4 Obtain data on the the growth rate of real GDP for the United Kingdom and for the world economy for the most recent period available. What do these growth rates imply about the share of the United Kingdom in the global economy?

Chapter 20

Measuring GDP and Economic Growth

After studying this chapter you will be able to:

◆ Define GDP and use the circular flow model to explain why GDP equals aggregate expenditure and aggregate income

◆ Explain two ways of measuring GDP

◆ Explain how we measure economic growth, *real* GDP and the GDP deflator

◆ Explain how real GDP is used as an indicator of economic welfare and describe its limitations

Economic Barometers

Every three months, you read and hear a news report about the country's gross domestic product or GDP. How do economic statisticians add up all the economic activity in a country to arrive at the GDP number, and what does the number tell us? How can we use it to compare how well off we are today compared to previous periods? You know that some countries are rich and some poor. How do we compare economic well-being in one country with that in another?

Gross Domestic Product

What exactly is GDP, how is it calculated, what does it mean and why do we care about it? You are going to discover the answers to these questions in this chapter. First, what is GDP?

GDP Defined

GDP or **gross domestic product** is the market value of all the final goods and services produced within a country in a given time period – usually a year. This definition has four parts:

◆ Market value

◆ Final goods and services

◆ Produced within a country

◆ In a given time period

We examine each in turn.

Market Value

To measure total production, we must add together the production of apples and oranges, computers and popcorn. Just counting the items doesn't get us very far. For example, which is the greater total production: 100 apples and 50 oranges, or 50 apples and 100 oranges?

GDP answers this question by valuing items at their *market values* – at the prices at which each item is traded in markets. If the price of an apple is 10 pence, the market value of 50 apples is £5. If the price of an orange is 20 pence, the market value of 100 oranges is £20. By valuing production at market prices, we can add the apples and oranges together. The market value of 50 apples and 100 oranges is £5 plus £20, or £25.

Final Goods and Services

To calculate GDP, we value the *final goods and services* produced. A **final good** (or service) is an item that is bought by its final user during a specified time period. It contrasts with an **intermediate good** (or service), which is an item that is produced by one firm, bought by another firm and used as a component of a final good or service.

For example, a Ford Focus is a final good, but a tyre on the Ford Focus is an intermediate good. A Dell computer is a final good, but an Intel Pentium chip inside it is an intermediate good. If we were to add the value of intermediate goods and services produced to the value

of final goods and services, we would count the same thing many times – a problem called *double counting*. The value of a Ford Focus already includes the value of the tyres, and the value of a Dell PC already includes the value of the Pentium chip inside it.

Some goods can be an intermediate good in some situations and a final good in other situations. For example, the ice cream that you buy on a hot summer day is a final good, but the ice cream that a café buys and uses to make sundaes is an intermediate good. The sundae is the final good. So whether a good is an intermediate good or a final good depends on what it is used for, not on what it is.

Produced Within a Country

Only goods and services that are produced *within a country* count as part of that country's GDP. When James Dyson, a British entrepreneur who makes vacuum cleaners, produces them in Malaysia, the market value of those cleaners is part of Malaysia's GDP, not part of GDP in the United Kingdom. Toyota, a Japanese firm, produces cars in Deeside, Wales and the value of this production is part of UK GDP, not part of Japan's GDP.

In a Given Time period

GDP measures the value of production *in a given time period* – normally either a quarter of a year (called the quarterly GDP data) or a year (called the annual GDP data). Some components of GDP are measured for a period as short as a month, but we have no reliable monthly GDP data.

Businesses such as British Airways and HSBC and governments use the quarterly GDP data to keep track of the short-term evolution of the economy. They use the annual GDP data to examine long-term trends and changes in production and the standard of living.

GDP measures not only the value of total production but also total income and total expenditure. The equality between the value of total production and total income is important because it shows the direct link between productivity and living standards. Our standard of living rises when our incomes rise and we can afford to buy more goods and services. But we must produce more goods and services if we are to be able to buy more goods and services.

Rising incomes and a rising value of production go together. To see why, we study the circular flow of expenditure and income.

GDP and the Circular Flow of Expenditure and Income

Figure 20.1 illustrates the circular flow of expenditure and income. The economy consists of households, firms, governments and the rest of the world (the purple diamonds), which trade in factor markets, goods (and services) markets and financial markets. Let's focus first on households and firms.

Households and Firms

Households sell and firms buy the services of labour, capital and land in factor markets. For these factor services, firms pay income to households: wages for labour services, interest for the use of capital and rent for the use of land. A fourth factor of production, entrepreneurship, receives profit.

Firms' retained earnings – profits that are not distributed to households – are also part of the household sector's income. You can think of retained earnings as being income that households save and lend back to firms. Figure 20.1 shows the *aggregate income* received by all households in payment for factor services by the blue dots labelled *Y*.

Firms sell and households buy consumption goods and services – such as beer, pizzas and dry cleaning services – in the markets for goods and services. Total payment for these goods and services is **consumption expenditure**, shown by the red dots labelled *C*.

Firms buy and sell new capital equipment in the goods market. For example, Compaq sells 1,000 PCs to Virgin or BAC sells an aircraft to British Airways. Some of what firms produce is not sold but is added to stock. For example, if MG Rover produces 1,000 cars and sells 950 of them, the other 50 cars remain unsold and the firm's stock of cars increases by 50. When a firm adds unsold output to its stocks (or inventories), we can think of the firm as buying goods from itself. The purchase of new plant, equipment and buildings, and the additions to stocks, are **investment**, shown by the red dots labelled *I*.

Figure 20.1

The Circular Flow of Expenditure and Income

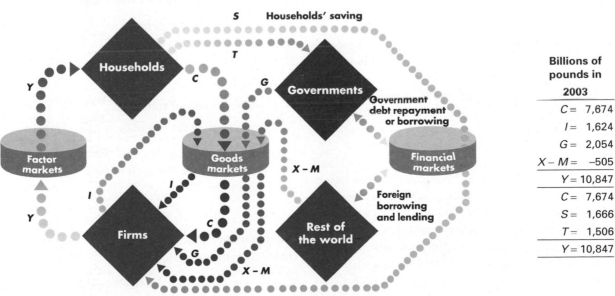

Billions of pounds in 2003	
C =	7,674
I =	1,624
G =	2,054
X – M =	–505
Y =	10,847
C =	7,674
S =	1,666
T =	1,506
Y =	10,847

In the circular flow of expenditure and income, households make consumption expenditures (*C*); firms make investment expenditures (*I*); governments purchase goods and services (*G*); the rest of the world purchases net exports (*X – M*) (red flows). Households receive incomes (*Y*) from firms (blue flow).

Aggregate income (blue flow) equals aggregate expenditure (red flows). Households use their income to consume (*C*), save (*S*) and pay net taxes (*T*). Firms borrow to finance their investment expenditures and governments and the rest of the world borrow to finance their deficits or lend their surpluses – (green flows).

Governments

Governments buy goods and services, **government expenditures**, from firms. In Figure 20.1, government expenditures on goods and services are shown as the red flow G. Governments use taxes to pay for their purchases. Figure 20.1 shows taxes as net taxes by the green dots T. **Net taxes** are taxes paid to governments minus transfer payments received from governments. Transfer payments are cash transfers from governments to households and firms such as social security benefits, unemployment compensation, subsidies and interest on the government's debt.

Rest of World

Firms sell goods and services to the rest of the world, **exports**, and buy goods and services from the rest of the world, **imports**. The value of exports minus the value of imports is called **net exports**. Figure 20.1 shows net exports by the red flow $X - M$.

If net exports are positive, there is a net flow from the rest of the world to domestic firms. If net exports are negative, there is a net flow from firms to the rest of the world.

GDP Equals Expenditure Equals Income

GDP can be determined in two ways: by the total expenditure on goods and services or by the total income earned by producing goods and services.

The total expenditure – *aggregate expenditure* – is the sum of the red flows in Figure 20.1. Aggregate expenditure equals consumption expenditure plus investment plus government expenditures plus net exports.

Aggregate income earned producing goods and services is equal to the total amount paid for the factors used – wages, interest, rent and profit. This amount is shown by the blue flow in Figure 20.1. Because firms pay out as incomes (including retained profits) everything they receive from the sale of their output, income (the blue flow) equals expenditure (the sum of the red flows). That is:

$$Y = C + I + G + X - M$$

The table in Figure 20.1 shows the UK numbers for 2003. You can see that the sum of the expenditures is £1,100 billion, which also equals aggregate income.

Because aggregate expenditure equals aggregate income, these two methods of valuing GDP give the same answer. So:

GDP equals aggregate expenditure and equals aggregate income.

The circular flow model is the foundation on which the national economic accounts are built.

Financial Flows

The circular flow model enables us to see the link between the expenditure and income flows and the flows through the financial markets that finance deficits and pay for investment. These flows are shown in green in Figure 20.1. Households' **saving** (S) is the amount that households have left after they have paid their net taxes and bought their consumption goods and services. Government borrowing finances a government budget deficit. (Government lending occurs if the government has a budget surplus.) Foreign borrowing pays for a deficit with the rest of the world. These financial flows are the sources of the funds that firms use to pay for their investment. Let's look a bit more closely at how investment is financed.

How Investment Is Financed

Investment, which adds to the stock of capital, is one of the determinants of the rate at which aggregate output grows. Investment is financed from three sources:

1 Private saving
2 Government budget surplus
3 Borrowing from the rest of the world

Private saving is the green flow labelled S in Figure 20.1. Households' income is consumed, saved or paid in taxes. That is:

$$Y = C + S + T$$

But you have seen that Y also equals the sum of the components of aggregate expenditure. That is:

$$Y = C + I + G + X - M$$

Use these two equations to obtain:

$$I + G + X - M = S + T$$

Now subtract G and X from both sides of the last equation and add M to both sides to obtain:

$$I = S + (T - G) + (M - X)$$

In this equation, $(T - G)$ is the government budget surplus and $(M - X)$ is borrowing from the rest of the world.

If net taxes (T) exceed government expenditures (G), the government budget surplus equals $(T - G)$ and the surplus contributes towards paying for investment. If net taxes are less than government expenditures the government has a budget deficit equal to $(T - G)$, which is negative. This deficit subtracts from the sources that finance investment.

If we import more than we export, we borrow an amount equal to $(M - X)$ from the rest of the world. So part of the rest of the world's saving finances investment in the United Kingdom. If we export more than we import, the United Kingdom lends an amount equal to $(X - M)$ to the rest of the world. So part of saving in the United Kingdom finances investment in other countries.

The sum of private saving (S) and government saving $(T - G)$ is called **national saving**. So investment is financed by national saving and foreign borrowing.

In 2003, UK investment was £181 billion. This investment was paid for out of a national saving of £149 billion and borrowing from the rest of the world $(M - X)$, of £32 billion.

Gross and Net Domestic Product

What does "gross" in GDP mean? Gross means before accounting for the depreciation of capital. The opposite of gross is net, which means after accounting for the depreciation of capital. To understand what the depreciation of capital is and how it affects aggregate expenditure and income, we need to expand the accounting framework that we use and distinguish between flows and stocks.

Flows and Stocks in Macroeconomics

A **flow** is a quantity per unit of time. The water running from an open tap into a bath is a flow. So is the number of CDs you buy in a month and the amount of income you earn in a month. GDP is another flow. It is the value of production in a country in a given time period. Saving and investment are flows.

A **stock** is a quantity that exists at a point in time. The water in a bath is a stock. So is the number of CDs that you own and the amount of money in your bank account. The two key stocks in macroeconomics are wealth and capital. The flows of saving and investment change these stocks.

Wealth and Saving

The value of all the things that people own is called **wealth**. What people own (a stock) is related to what they earn (a flow). People earn an income, which is the amount they receive during a given time period from supplying the services of factors of production. Income that is left after paying net taxes is either consumed or saved. Consumption expenditure is the amount spent on consumption goods and services. Saving is the amount of income remaining after meeting consumption expenditures. So saving adds to wealth.

For example, at the end of the year, you have £50 in your bank account and computer equipment worth £1,000. That's all you own. Your wealth is £1,050. Suppose that over the summer you earn an income of £3,000. You are extremely careful and spend only £500 on consumption goods and services. When university starts again, you have £2,550 in your bank account. Your wealth is now £3,550. Your wealth has increased by £2,500, which equals your saving of £2,500. And your saving of £2,500 equals your income during the summer of £3,000 minus your consumption expenditure of £500.

National wealth and national saving work just like this personal example. The wealth of a nation at the start of a year equals its wealth at the start of the previous year plus its saving during the year. Its saving equals its income minus its consumption.

Capital and Investment

Capital is the plant, equipment, buildings and stocks of raw materials and semifinished goods that are used to produce other goods and services. The amount of capital in the economy exerts a big influence on GDP.

Two flows change the stock of capital: investment and depreciation. *Investment*, the purchase of new capital, increases the stock of capital. **Depreciation** is the decrease in the stock of capital that results from wear and tear and obsolescence. The total amount spent on purchases of new capital and on replacing depreciated capital is called **gross investment**. The amount by which the stock of capital increases is called **net investment**.

Net investment = Gross investment − Depreciation

Figure 20.2 illustrates these concepts. On 1 January 2004, Tom's Tapes Inc. had 3 machines. This quantity was its initial capital. During 2004, Tom's scrapped an older machine. This quantity is its depreciation. After depreciation, Tom's stock of capital was down to

2 machines. But also during 2004, Tom's bought 2 new machines. This amount is its gross investment. By 31 December 2004, Tom's Tapes had 4 machines so its capital had increased by 1 machine. This amount is Tom's net investment. Tom's net investment equals its gross investment (the purchase of 2 new machines) minus its depreciation (1 machine scrapped).

The example of Tom's Tapes factory can be applied to the economy as a whole. The nation's capital stock decreases because capital depreciates and increases because of gross investment. The change in the nation's capital stock from one year to the next equals its net investment.

Back to the Gross in GDP

We can now see the distinction between gross domestic product and net domestic product. On the income side of the flows that measure GDP, a firm's *gross* profit is

its *profit* before subtracting *depreciation*. A firm's gross profit is part of aggregate income and GDP. Similarly, on the expenditure side of the flows that measure GDP, *gross investment* includes depreciation. So depreciation is counted as part of aggregate expenditure and total expenditure is a gross measure.

Net domestic product excludes depreciation. Like GDP, net domestic product can be viewed as the sum of incomes or expenditures. Net income includes firms' net profit – profits after subtracting depreciation. Net expenditure includes net investment, which also excludes depreciation.

The Short Term Meets the Long Term

The flows and stocks that you have just studied influence GDP growth and fluctuations. One of the reasons why GDP grows is that the capital stock grows. And one of the reasons that real GDP fluctuates is that investment fluctuates. Investment adds to capital, so GDP grows because of investment. But investment fluctuates, which brings fluctuations to GDP. So capital and investment along with wealth and saving are part of the key to understanding both the growth and fluctuations of GDP.

Investment and saving interact with income and consumption expenditure in a circular flow of expenditure and income. In this circular flow, income equals expenditure, which also equals the value of production. This equality is the foundation on which a nation's economic accounts are built and from which its GDP is measured.

Figure 20.2

Capital and Investment

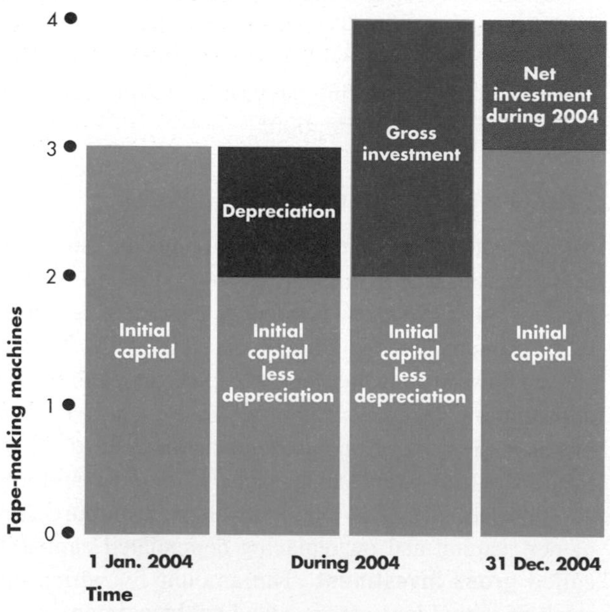

At the end of 2004, Tom's Tapes has a capital stock that equals its capital stock at the beginning of 2004 plus its net investment during 2004.

Net investment is equal to gross investment less depreciation. Tom's Tapes gross investment is the 2 new machines bought during the year, and its depreciation is the 1 machine that it scrapped during the year. Tom's net investment was 1 machine.

Review Quiz

1 Define GDP and distinguish between a final good and an intermediate good. Provide some examples.
2 Why does GDP equal aggregate income and also equal aggregate expenditure?
3 How can investment be financed? What determines national saving?
4 What is the distinction between gross and net?
5 Define capital and explain how the flows of investment and depreciation change the stock of capital.

Let's now see how the ideas that you have just studied can be used in practice. We'll see how to use the circular flow of expenditure and income to measure GDP.

Measuring UK GDP

The Office for National Statistics uses the concepts that you met in the circular flow model to measure GDP and its components, which it publishes in the *United Kingdom National Accounts Blue Book*.

Because the value of aggregate output equals aggregate expenditure and aggregate income, there are two approaches available for measuring GDP, and both are used. They are:

◆ The expenditure approach

◆ The income approach

The Expenditure Approach

The *expenditure approach* measures GDP as the sum of consumption expenditure (C), investment (I), government expenditures on goods and services (G) and net exports of goods and services ($X - M$), corresponding to the red flows in the circular flow model in Figure 20.1. Table 20.1 shows the results of this approach for 2003. The table also shows the terms used in the *United Kingdom National Accounts*.

Consumption expenditure is the expenditure by households on goods and services produced in the United Kingdom and the rest of the world. It includes goods such as beer, CDs, books and magazines; and services such as insurance, banking and legal advice. It does *not* include the purchase of new houses, which is counted as part of investment.

Investment is expenditure on capital equipment and buildings by firms and expenditure on new residential houses by households. It also includes the change in firms' stocks or inventories.

Government expenditures is the purchase of goods and services by all levels of government – from Westminster to the local town hall. This item includes expenditure on national defence, law and order, street lighting and refuse collection. It does *not* include *transfer payments* because they are not purchases of goods and services.

Net exports are the value of UK exports minus the value of UK imports. When a UK company sells a car to a buyer in the United States, the value of that car is part of UK exports. When your local VW dealer stocks up on the latest model, its expenditure is part of UK imports.

Table 20.1 shows the relative magnitudes of the four items of aggregate expenditure.

Table 20.1

GDP: The Expenditure Approach

Item	Symbol	Amount in 2003 (billions) of pounds)	Percentage of GDP
Consumption expenditure (Final consumption expenditure: personal)	C	721	65.5
Investment (Gross capital formation)	I	181	16.5
Government expenditures (Final consumption expenditure: governments)	G	230	20.9
Net exports (External balance of goods and services)	$X - M$	−32	−2.9
Gross domestic product	Y	£1,100	100.0

The expenditure approach measures GDP as the sum of consumption expenditure, investment, government expenditures and net exports. In 2003, GDP was £1,100. Almost two-thirds of aggregate expenditure is consumption expenditure.

Source: Office for National Statistics, *United Kingdom National Accounts: The Blue Book 2004*, London: The Stationery Office.

The Income Approach

The *income approach* measures GDP by summing all the incomes paid by firms to households for the services of the factors of production they hire – wages for labour, interest for capital, rent for land and profits for entrepreneurship. Let's see how the income approach works.

In the *United Kingdom National Accounts*, incomes are divided into three categories:

1 Compensation of employees

2 Gross operating surplus

3 Mixed incomes

Compensation of employees is the total payments by firms for labour services. This item includes the net wages and salaries (called take-home pay) plus taxes withheld plus fringe benefits such as social security and pension fund contributions.

Gross operating surplus is the total profit made by companies and the surpluses generated by publicly owned enterprises. Some of these profits are paid to households in the form of dividends, and some are retained by companies as undistributed profits. The surpluses from public enterprises are either retained by the enterprises or paid to the government as part of its general revenue. They are all income.

Mixed income is a combination of rental income and income from self-employment. *Rental income* is the payment for the use of land and other rented inputs. It includes payments for rented housing and imputed rent for owner-occupied housing. (Imputed rent is an estimate of what homeowners would pay to rent the housing they own and use themselves. By including this item in the *National Accounts*, we measure the total value of housing services, whether they are owned or rented.)

Income from self-employment is a mixture of the elements that we have just reviewed. The proprietor of an owner-operated business supplies labour, capital and perhaps land and buildings to the business.

Table 20.2 shows these three components of aggregate income and their relative magnitudes.

The sum of the incomes is called *gross domestic income at factor cost*. The term *factor cost* is used because it is the cost of the *factors of production* used to produce final goods and services. When we sum all the expenditures on final goods and services, we arrive at a total called *domestic product at market prices*. Market prices and factor cost would be the same except for indirect taxes and subsidies.

An *indirect tax* is a tax paid by consumers when they buy goods and services. (In contrast, a *direct tax* is a tax on income.) Sales taxes, VAT and taxes on alcohol, petrol and tobacco products are indirect taxes. Because of indirect taxes, consumers pay more for some goods and services than producers receive. Market price exceeds factor cost. For example, with VAT at 17.5 per cent, the purchase of a CD at a cost of £12.99 means you will have paid £11.06 as the cost price and £1.93 VAT.

A *subsidy* is a payment by the government to a producer. Payments made to farmers under the EU Common Agricultural Policy are subsidies. Because of subsidies, consumers pay less for some goods and services than producers receive. Factor cost exceeds market price.

To get from factor cost to market price, we add indirect taxes and subtract subsidies. Making this adjustment brings us GDP – the value of production in market prices.

Table 20.2

GDP: The Income Approach

Item	Amount in 2003 (billions of pounds)	Percentage of GDP
Compensation of employees	615	55.9
Gross operating surplus	276	25.1
Mixed income	69	6.3
Indirect taxes *less* Subsidies	140	12.7
Gross domestic product	**1,100**	**100.0**

The sum of all factor incomes equals domestic income at factor cost. GDP equals net domestic income plus indirect taxes less subsidies. In 2003, GDP measured by the factor incomes approach was £1,100 billion. Compensation of employees was by far the largest part of total factor income.

Source: Office for National Statistics, *United Kingdom National Accounts: The Blue Book 2004*, London: The Stationery Office.

Review Quiz

1 Why does GDP measured by the expenditure approach equal GDP measured by the income approach?
2 What is the distinction between expenditure on final goods and expenditure on intermediate goods?
3 What is value added? How is it calculated?

You now know how the national income statisticians value all the goods and services produced to calculate GDP. But as you've seen GDP is measured in pounds – units of money. But the money value of GDP can change for two reasons: prices change or because the volume of goods and services produced changes. It is the quantities of goods and services produced rather than just their money value that contributes to our standard of living. So we need a way of separately identifying when real GDP changes because prices have changed and when it changes because the quantities produced have changed. We need a measure of *real* GDP.

Measuring Economic Growth

You've seen that GDP measures total expenditure on final goods and services in a given period. In 2003, GDP was £1,100 billion. A year before, in 2002, GDP was £1,044 billion. Because GDP was greater in 2003 than in 2002, we know that one or two things must have happened during 2003:

1 We produced more goods and services in 2003 than in 2002.

2 We paid higher prices in 2003 than in 2002.

Producing more goods and services contributes to an improvement in our standard of living. The expansion of production is *economic growth*. Paying higher prices means that our cost of living has increased. The ballooning of prices is called *inflation*.

It matters a great deal whether GDP has increased because of economic growth or because of inflation. So the economic statisticians at the Office for National Statistics separate the change in GDP into two parts: one that reveals the amount of economic growth and another that reveals the amount of inflation.

You're now going to learn how this separation is done. We'll describe and illustrate the method by working through an example using an economy that produces only two goods: balls and bats. Table 20.3 shows the data for this economy in 2002 and 2003. We begin by defining nominal GDP.

Nominal GDP

Nominal GDP is the value of the final goods and services produced in a given year valued at the prices that prevailed in that same year. Nominal GDP is just a more precise name for GDP that reminds us that the prices used to calculate GDP change every year – they are the prices of the current year.

We can calculate nominal GDP for the ball and bat economy described in Table 20.3 in both 2002 and 2003.

To find nominal GDP in 2002, we sum the expenditures on balls and bats in that year as follows:

Expenditure on balls = 100 balls × £1 = £100.

Expenditure on bats = 20 bats × £5 = £100.

Nominal GDP in 2002 = £100 + £100 = £200.

In 2003, the quantity of balls produced increased to 160, and the quantity of bats produced increased to 22.

Table 20.3

GDP Quantities and Prices Data

Quantities and prices in 2002

Item	Quantity	Price
Balls	100	£1.00
Bats	20	£5.00

Quantities and prices in 2003

Item	Quantity	Price
Balls	160	£0.50
Bats	22	£22.50

The price of a ball fell to 50 pence, and the price of a bat increased to £22.50. To find nominal GDP in 2003, we sum the expenditures on balls and bats in that year as follows:

Expenditure on balls = 160 balls × £0.50 = £80

Expenditure on bats = 22 bats × £22.50 = £495

Nominal GDP in 2003 = £80 + £495 = £575.

We now know that GDP was £200 in 2002 and £575 in 2003, so GDP increased by £375 between these two years. The percentage increase is (£375 ÷ £200) × 100 = 187.5 per cent. (This example is using big numbers for the rate of increase to make the point of the exercise jump out!)

How much of this 187.5 per cent increase is an increase in production and how much is just the effect of higher average prices? The answer is found by revaluing the 2003 quantities at the 2002 prices.

Current year Production at Previous-year Prices

We can compare the quantities produced in 2002 and 2003 by valuing the production in 2003 at the 2002 prices.

Table 20.4 (overleaf) brings together the data from Table 20.3 to show the prices in 2002 and the quantities in 2003 that we need for this calculation.

The value of the 2003 quantities at the 2002 prices is calculated as follows:

Table 20.4

2003 Quantities and 2002 Prices

Item	Quantity	Price	Value
Balls	160	£1.00	£160
Bats	22	£5.00	£110
Total			£270

Expenditure on balls = 160 balls × £1.00 = £160

Expenditure on bats = 22 bats × £5.00 = £110

Value of the 2003 quantities at 2002 prices = £270

We can now compare the two years using the 2002 prices. Holding prices constant, GDP was £200 in 2002 and £270 in 2003. So the volume of production increased by £70 and the percentage increase in production is (£70 ÷ £200) × 100, which is 35 per cent. Production has expanded by 35 per cent.

We know that GDP in 2003 valued in 2003 prices was £575 compared with £270 when valued in 2002 prices. So the increase from £270 to £575 is due to the higher prices of 2003.

We've separated the £375 change in GDP into an economic growth component of £70 and an inflation component of £305.

Chain Linking

The calculations that we've just done for 2002 and 2003 can be done for any pair of years for which we have data on the quantities produced and prices. So we can calculate the growth rate of production between every pair of years. But we'd like to have an easy way of comparing the current year with *every* previous year, not just the most recent one.

To make comparisons across a number of years, we calculate **real GDP**, which is the volume of final goods and services produced in a given year expressed in pounds that are linked back to the value of the pound in a *base year*. The linking of each year to a base year is called *chain linking* and the resulting measure of real GDP is called a **chained volume measure**.

The base year used by the Office for National Statistics is currently 2001 and the current plan is to change the base year every year so that in any current year the base year is to be three years before the current year.

Table 20.5

Chain Linking to the Base Year

GDP in	Valued in prices of			Real GDP in 2001 pounds
	2001	**2002**	**2003**	
2001	£50			£50
2002	£100	£200		£100
2003		£270	£575	£135

Table 20.5 above shows how the chain linking works. We've calculated nominal GDP for 2002 and 2003 and you can find those values in the table: £200 for 2002 and £575 for 2003.

We've also calculated the value of 2003 production in 2002 prices. You can also find that value in the table: £270.

Suppose that we have done similar calculations for 2001 and 2002 and obtained the numbers in the table. That is, nominal GDP is £50 in 2001 and the value of 2002 production at 2001 prices is £100.

By definition, real GDP equals nominal GDP in the base year. So real GDP in 2001 is £50, the same as nominal GDP for 2001 in the table.

Real GDP in 2002 is £100. That is the 2002 production valued at 2001 prices.

Real GDP for 2003 is £135. That is the value of 2003 production in 2002 prices chain linked back to 2001 prices. To link 2003 back to 2001, we apply the growth rate we calculated for 2003 – 35 per cent – to the level of real GDP in 2002. Because real GDP in 2002 is £100, real GDP in 2003 being 35 per cent higher is £135.

By applying the calculated percentage change to the real GDP of the preceding year, each year is linked back, like the links in a chain, to the pounds of the base year.

Calculating the Price Level

The average level of prices is called the **price level**. One measure of the price level is the **GDP deflator**, which is an average of current-year prices expressed as a percentage of base-year prices. We calculate the GDP deflator by using nominal GDP and real GDP in the formula:

GDP deflator = (Nominal GDP ÷ Real GDP) × 100

You can see why the GDP deflator is a measure of the price level. If nominal GDP rises but real GDP remains unchanged, it must be that the price level has risen. The formula gives a higher value for the GDP deflator. The larger the nominal GDP for a given real GDP, the higher is the price level and the larger is the GDP deflator.

Let's calculate the GDP deflator. In 2001, the deflator is 100 by definition. In 2002, it is 200, which equals nominal GDP of £200 divided by real GDP of £100 and then multiplied by 100. And in 2003, the GDP deflator is 425.9, which equals nominal GDP of £575 divided by real GDP of £135 and then multiplied by 100.

Deflating the GDP Balloon

You can think of GDP as a balloon that is blown up by growing production and rising prices. In Figure 20.3, the GDP deflator lets the inflation air out of the nominal GDP balloon – the contribution of rising prices – so that we can see what has happened to *real* GDP. The red balloon for 1983 shows real GDP in that year. The green balloon shows *nominal* GDP in 2003. The red balloon for 2003 shows real GDP for that year.

To see real GDP in 2003, we *deflate* nominal GDP using the GDP deflator.

Review Quiz

1   What is the distinction between nominal GDP and real GDP?
2   What is the chained volume measure of real GDP?
3   What is the chained volume measure of real GDP calculated?
4   How is the GDP deflator calculated?

You now know how to calculate economic growth, real GDP and the GDP deflator. Your next task is to learn how to use real GDP to make economic welfare comparisons. We also look at some limitations of real GDP as a measure of economic welfare and as a tool for comparing living standards across countries.

Figure 20.3

The UK GDP Balloon

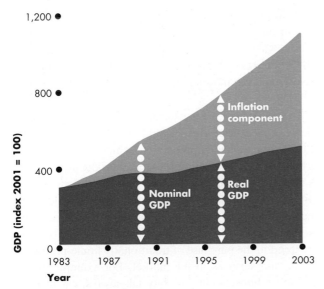

(a) Nominal GDP and real GDP

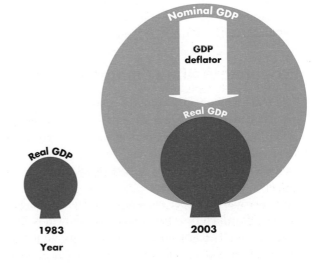

(b) Deflating nominal GDP

Part of the rise in GDP comes from inflation and part from increased production – an increase in real GDP. The GDP deflator lets some air out of the GDP balloon so that we can see the extent to which production has increased.

Source: Office for National Statistics and authors' calculations.

Uses and Limitations of Real GDP

Every country calculates GDP and real GDP and international agencies such as the International Monetary Fund (IMF) publishes these data on a regular basis. We use these estimates of real GDP for three main purposes.

First, we use them to make comparisons of living standards and economic welfare across generations. This exercise enables us to determine whether or by how much our standard of living today has improved on that of our parents and grandparents.

Second, we use GDP numbers to make international comparisons of living standards. This type of comparison enables us to estimate whether or by how much the standard of living in one country exceeds that in another.

Third, we use both real GDP and the GDP deflator to assess the current and likely future state of the economy to guide the actions of stabilization policies of the Bank of England, the European Central Bank and governments. Determining whether the economy is heading for recession or an overheating boom is vital for a successful stabilization policy.

Although real GDP is used for these three purposes, it is not a perfect measure for any of them. But nor is it a totally misleading measure. We'll evaluate the limitations of real GDP for making economic welfare comparisons across generations and across countries and for guiding stabilization policy.

Economic Welfare Comparisons

Economic welfare is a comprehensive measure of the general state of well-being. Economic welfare improves when the production per person of all the goods and services grows. The goods and services that make up real GDP growth are only a part of all the items that influence economic welfare.

Today, real GDP per person in the United Kingdom is £17,250, which because of real GDP growth is 75 per cent higher that it was in 1973. But are we 75 per cent better off?

Does this growth of real GDP provide a full and accurate measure of the change in economic welfare?

It does not. The reason is that economic welfare depends on many factors that are not measured by real GDP or that are not measured accurately by real GDP. Some of these factors are:

◆ Quality improvements
◆ Household production
◆ Underground economic activity
◆ Health and life expectancy
◆ Leisure time
◆ Environmental quality
◆ Political freedom and social justice

Quality Improvements

The price indices that are used to measure inflation give an upward-biased estimate of true inflation. (You will learn about the sources of this bias on p. 473.) If we overestimate the rise in prices, we underestimate the growth of real GDP. When car prices rise because cars have become better (safer, more fuel efficient, more comfortable), the GDP deflator counts the price increase as inflation. So what is really an increase in production is counted as an increase in price rather than an increase in real GDP. It is deflated away by the wrongly measured higher price level. The magnitude of this bias is probably less than 1 percentage point a year, but its exact magnitude is not known.

Household Production

An enormous amount of production takes place every day in our homes. Changing a light bulb, cutting the grass, washing the car and growing vegetables are all examples of productive activities that do not involve market transactions and are not counted as part of GDP.

If these activities grew at the same rate as real GDP, then not measuring them would not be a problem. But it is likely that market production, which is part of GDP, is increasingly replacing household production, which is not part of GDP. Two trends point in this direction. One is the trend in female employment, which has increased from 38 per cent of the female population of working age in 1963 to 53 per cent in 2003. The other is the trend in the purchase of traditionally home-produced goods and services in the market. For example, more and more households now buy takeaways, eat in fast-food restaurants and use childcare services. This trend means that increasing proportions of food preparation and childcare that used to be part of household production are now measured as part of GDP. So real GDP grows more rapidly than does real GDP plus home production.

Underground Economic Activity

The *underground economy* is the part of the economy purposely hidden from view by the people operating in it to avoid taxes and regulations or because the goods and services they are producing are illegal. Because underground economic activity is unreported, it is omitted from GDP.

The underground economy is easy to describe, even if it is hard to measure. It includes the production and distribution of drugs, prostitution, production that uses illegal labour that is paid less than the minimum wage, and jobs done for cash to avoid paying income taxes. This last category might be quite large and includes tips earned by taxi drivers, hairdressers and hotel and restaurant workers.

Estimates of the scale of the underground economy range between 3.5 and 13.5 per cent of GDP (£38 billion to £148 billion) in the United Kingdom and much more in some countries. In *Reading Between the Lines* (pp. 452–453) we examine the implication of VAT fraud and the underground economy for the measurement of imports and consumption expenditure.

If the underground economy is a constant proportion of the total economy, the growth rate of real GDP provides a useful estimate of *changes* in economic welfare. But production can shift from the underground economy to the rest of the economy, and it can shift the other way. The underground economy expands relative to the rest of the economy if taxes rise sharply or if regulations become especially restrictive. And the underground economy shrinks relative to the rest of the economy if the burdens of taxes and regulations ease.

During the 1980s, when tax rates were cut, there was an increase in tax revenues. Some of this increase may have been due to the existing workforce, particularly high-paid labour, working harder, taking greater risks and being more productive, but some of it could have been due to a switch from what was previously underground activity to recorded activity. So some part (but probably a small part) of the expansion of real GDP during the 1980s represented a shift of economic activity from the underground economy rather than an increase in production.

Health and Life Expectancy

Good health and a long life – the hopes of everyone – do not show up in real GDP, at least not directly. A higher real GDP does enable us to spend more on medical research, healthcare, healthy food and exercise equipment. And as real GDP has increased, our life expectancy has lengthened – from 70 years at the end of the Second World War to approaching 80 years today. Infant deaths and death in childbirth, two fearful scourges of the nineteenth century, have almost been eliminated.

But we face new health and life expectancy problems every year. AIDS, drug abuse, suicide and murder are taking young lives at a rate that causes serious concern. When we take these negative influences into account, we see that real GDP growth overstates the improvements in economic welfare.

Leisure Time

Leisure time is an economic good that adds to our economic welfare. Other things remaining the same, the more leisure we have, the better off we are. Our time spent working is valued as part of GDP, but our leisure time is not. Yet from the point of view of economic welfare, that leisure time must be at least as valuable to us as the wage that we earn for the last hour worked. If it were not, we would work instead of taking the leisure. Over the years, leisure time has steadily increased. The working week has become shorter and the number and length of holidays have increased. These improvements in economic well-being are not reflected in GDP.

Environmental Quality

Economic activity directly influences the quality of the environment. The burning of hydrocarbon fuels is the most visible activity that damages our environment. But it is not the only example. The depletion of non-renewable resources, the mass clearing of forests, and the pollution of lakes and rivers are other major environmental consequences of industrial production.

Resources used to protect the environment are valued as part of GDP. For example, the value of catalytic converters that help to protect the atmosphere from carbon emissions are part of GDP. But if we did not use such pieces of equipment and instead polluted the atmosphere, we would not count the deteriorating air that we were breathing as a negative part of GDP.

An industrial society possibly produces more atmospheric pollution than does an agricultural society. But pollution does not always increase as we become wealthier. Wealthy people value a clean environment and are willing to pay for one. Compare the pollution in East Germany in the late 1980s with pollution in the United Kingdom. East Germany, a poor country, polluted its rivers, lakes and atmosphere in a way that is unimaginable in the United Kingdom or in wealthy West Germany.

Political Freedom and Social Justice

Most people value political freedoms such as those provided by the western democracies. They also value social justice or fairness – equality of opportunity and of access to social security safety nets that protect people from the extremes of misfortune.

A country might have a very large real GDP per person but have limited political freedom and equity. For example, an elite might enjoy political liberty and extreme wealth, while the vast majority are effectively enslaved and live in abject poverty. Such an economy would generally be regarded as having less economic welfare than one that had the same amount of real GDP but in which political freedoms were enjoyed by everyone. Today, China has rapid real GDP growth but limited political freedoms, while Russia has slow real GDP growth and an emerging democratic political system. Economists have no easy way to determine which of these countries is better off.

The Bottom Line

Do we get the wrong message about the growth in economic welfare by looking at the growth of real GDP? The influences that are omitted from real GDP are probably important and could be large. Developing countries have a larger underground economy and a larger amount of household production than do developed countries. So as an economy develops and grows, part of the apparent growth might reflect a switch from underground to regular production and from home production to market production. This measurement error overstates the rate of economic growth and the improvement in economic welfare.

Other influences on living standards include the amount of leisure time available, the quality of the environment, the security of jobs and homes, the safety of city streets, and so on. It is possible to construct broader measures that combine the many influences that contribute to human happiness. Real GDP will be one element in these broader measures, but it will by no means be the whole of them.

International Comparisons

All the problems we've just reviewed affect the economic welfare of every country, so to make international comparisons of economic welfare, factors additional to real

Box 20.1
How Much Poorer is China than the United States?

In 2003, real GDP per person in the United States was $39,000. The official Chinese statistics say that real GDP per person in China in 2003 was 9,500 yuan (the yuan is the currency of China). In 2003, $1 was worth 8.276 yuan. If we use this exchange rate to convert Chinese yuan into US dollars, we get a value of $1,150. This comparison of China and the United States makes China looks extremely poor. In 2003, GDP per person in the United States was 34 times that in China.

Figure 1 shows the story of real GDP in China from 1983 to 2003 based on converting the yuan to the US dollar at the market exchange rate. The figure also shows another story based on prices called *purchasing power parity* (PPP) *prices*.

GDP in the United States is measured by using prices that prevail in the United States. China's GDP is measured by using prices that prevail in China. But some goods that are expensive in the United States cost very little in China. These items have a small weight in China's real GDP. If, instead of using China's prices, the goods and services produced in China are valued at the prices prevailing in the United States, then a more valid comparison can be made.

GDP must be used. But real GDP comparisons are a major component of international welfare comparisons and two special problems arise in making these comparisons. First, the real GDP of one country must be converted into the same currency units as the real GDP of the other country. Second, the same prices must be used to value the goods and services in the countries being compared. Box 20.1 looks at these two problems with a striking comparison between the United States and China.

Forecasts for Stabilization Policy

If policymakers plan to raise interest rates to slow an expansion that they believe is too strong, they look at the latest estimates of real GDP. But suppose that for the reasons that we've just discussed, real GDP is mis-measured. Does this mis-measurement hamper our ability to identify the phases of the business cycle? It does not. The reason is that although the omissions from real GDP do change over time, they probably do not change

Figure 1

Two Views of Real GDP in China

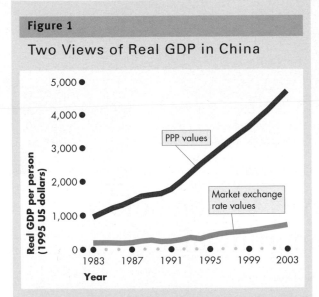

Valuing GDP at the market exchange rate, China is a poor developing country in which income per person is less than 3 per cent of the US level. But valuing GDP at purchasing power parity prices, China's real GDP is 16 per cent of the US level. Some China scholars think that even the market exchange rate numbers are too big. So there is much uncertainty about China's real GDP.

Source: International Monetary Fund, *World Economic Outlook.*

Robert Summers and Alan Heston, economists in the Center for International Comparisons at the University of Pennsylvania, have used PPP prices to construct real GDP data for more than 100 countries. And the IMF now uses methods similar to those of Summers and Heston to calculate PPP estimates of GDP in all countries. The PPP comparisons tell a remarkable story about China. According to the PPP comparisons, GDP per person in the United States in 2003 was 6 times that of China, not the 34 times shown at the market exchange rate

A prominent China scholar, Thomas Rawski of the University of Pittsburgh, doubts both sets of data shown in the figure. He believes that the growth rate of China's real GDP has been exaggerated for some years and that even the market exchange rate data overstate real GDP in China. The truth about real GDP in China is not known. But China is expanding and many businesses are paying close attention to the prospects of expanding their activities in China and other fast-growing Asian economies.

in a systematic way with the business cycle. So inaccurate measurement of real GDP does not necessarily cause a wrong assessment of the phase of the business cycle.

The fluctuations in economic activity measured by real GDP tell a reasonably accurate story about the phase of the business cycle that the economy is in. When real GDP grows, the economy is in a business cycle expansion; when real GDP shrinks (for two quarters), the economy is in a recession. Also, as real GDP fluctuates, so do production and jobs.

But real GDP fluctuations probably exaggerate or overstate the fluctuations in total production and economic welfare. The reason is that when business activity slows in a recession, household production increases and so does leisure time. When business activity speeds up in an expansion, household production and leisure time decrease. Because household production and leisure time increase in a recession and decrease in an expansion, real GDP fluctuations tend to overstate the fluctuations in both total production and economic welfare. But the directions of change of real GDP, total production and economic welfare are probably the same.

Review Quiz

1 Does real GDP measure economic welfare? If not, why not?
2 Does real GDP measure total production of goods and services? If not, what are the main omissions?
3 How can we make valid international comparisons of real GDP?
4 Does the growth rate of real GDP measure the economic growth rate accurately? If not, why not?
5 Do the fluctuations in real GDP measure the business cycle accurately? If not, why not?

You've now studied the methods used to measure GDP, real GDP and economic growth and you've learned about some of the limitations of these measures. In *Reading Between the Lines* on pp. 452–453, you can take a look at a recent example of the way illegal activities can distort (or as it turns out, not distort very much) some of the national accounts numbers.

Your next task is to learn how we monitor employment and unemployment and inflation.

Reading Between the Lines
Measuring the Economy

The Financial Times, 10 July 2003

FT

VAT scam leaves £23 bn hole in UK's import figures

Lydia Adetunji and James Chisholm

A Europe-wide scam involving mobile phones and computer parts has led to billions of pounds of imports going missing from official data in the past four years, the Office for National Statistics [ONS] said yesterday.

The ONS was forced to make huge revisions to its trade numbers to reflect the "missing trader" VAT fraud.

The scheme was perpetrated by traders obtaining registration to acquire goods VAT-free from other European Union countries, before selling them on in Britain at VAT inclusive prices and pocketing the difference.

The ONS revised up import data by £1.7bn in 1999, £2.8bn in 2000, £7.1bn in 2001 and £11.1bn in 2002 – meaning that the UK's goods trade deficit in those years was larger than reported at the time.

Customs and Excise first became alarmed by the growth in "missing trader" fraud in 1999. Last year, it recognised that there were implications for trade figures but it took a further year for the ONS and Customs to quantify the effect.

The scale of the fraud provides an explanation for a statistical anomaly; other EU countries' reported exports to Britain have been higher than Britain's recorded imports from the same countries. The 2002 current account deficit will be doubled from 1 per cent to about 2 per cent of gross domestic product.

The ONS said the revisions would leave gross domestic product broadly unchanged. But the news has implications for the Bank of England's monetary policy committee, which decides on interest rates this morning.

The Essence of the Story

◆ Illegal operators in the underground economy have been importing mobile phones and computer parts from other countries in the European Union.

◆ These goods were imported VAT free, but they were sold in the United Kingdom with VAT added on.

◆ The operators have pocketed the VAT and not remitted the VAT to the tax authorities.

◆ Consumers have paid the full price including VAT.

◆ The VAT fraud means that imports and consumption spending have been under-measured.

◆ The mis-measurement of imports means that the true trade deficit in the period 1999–2002 was larger than originally thought.

Economic Analysis

◆ The import of computer parts and mobile phones from other countries in the European Union had not been recorded in the import figures because of fraud.

◆ Figure 1 shows the imports of goods and services before and after the fraud was discovered.

◆ The Office for National Statistics periodically revises data as new information is obtained. The scale of the revisions on the discovery of the VAT fraud was major.

◆ In the revised data, the expenditure on mobile phones is included in the revised consumption expenditure (C) and the expenditure on computer parts is included in the revised investment (I). Some mobile phones were re-exported and are included in exports (X).

◆ Figure 2 shows that the revision barely changed GDP (Y).

◆ Figure 3 shows the changes to C, I and X created by the revisions to the data. In the equation,

$$Y = C + I + G + X - M$$

M decreased, C, I and X increased.

◆ The increases in consumption expenditure, investment and exports have matched the decrease in imports, so real GDP barely changed.

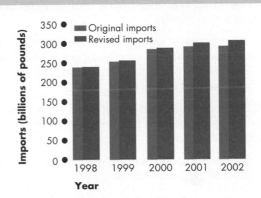

Figure 1 Original and revised measures of imports

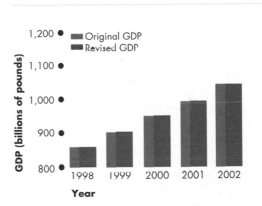

Figure 2 Original and revised measures of GDP

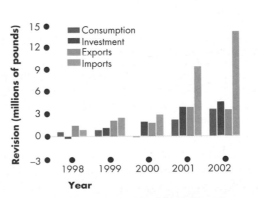

Figure 3 Revisions to consumption expenditure, investment, exports and imports

Summary

Key Points

Gross Domestic Product (pp. 438–442)

◆ GDP, or gross domestic product, is the market value of all the final goods and services produced in a country in a year.

◆ A final good is an item that is bought by its final user during a specified period and contrasts with an intermediate good, which is a component of a final good.

◆ GDP is calculated by using the expenditure and income totals in the circular flow of expenditure and income.

◆ Aggregate expenditure on goods and services equals aggregate income.

Measuring UK GDP (pp. 443–444)

◆ Because aggregate expenditure, aggregate income and the value of aggregate output are equal, we can measure GDP by either the expenditure approach or the income approach.

◆ The expenditure approach adds together consumption expenditure, investment, government purchases of goods and services and net exports.

◆ The income approach adds together the incomes paid to the factors of production – wages, interest, rent and profit – and indirect taxes less subsidies.

Measuring Economic Growth (pp. 445–447)

◆ We measure economic growth by comparing real GDP across a number of years.

◆ We calculate real GDP by using a chained volume measure, which is the volume of final goods and services produced in a given year expressed in pounds that are linked back to the value of the pound in a base year.

◆ The GDP deflator measures the price level based on the prices of the items that make up GDP.

Uses and Limitations of Real GDP (pp. 448–451)

◆ Real GDP is not a perfect measure of economic welfare because it excludes quality improvements, household production, underground production, environmental damage and the contribution to economic welfare of health and life expectancy, leisure time, and political freedom and social justice.

◆ Changes in real GDP provide a good indication of the phases of the business cycle.

Key Figures and Tables

Key Terms

Problems

*1 The figure shows the flows of expenditure and income on Lotus Island. During 2000: *A* was £10 million; *B* was £30 million; *C* was £12 million; *D* was £15 million; and *E* was £3 million. Calculate

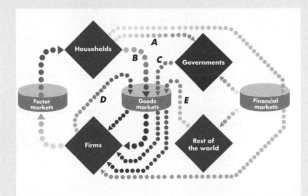

a Aggregate expenditure.

b Aggregate income.

c GDP.

d Government budget deficit.

e Household saving.

f Government saving.

g Foreign borrowing.

h National saving.

2 In problem 1, during 2001: *A* was £10 million; *B* was £50 million; *C* was £15 million; *D* was £15 million; and *E* was –£5 million. Calculate the quantities in problem 1 during 2001.

*3 Martha owns a copy shop that has 5 copiers. One copier wears out each year and is replaced. In addition, this year Martha will expand her business to 7 copiers. Calculate Martha's initial capital stock, depreciation, gross investment, net investment and final capital stock.

4 Wendy operates a weaving shop with 10 looms. One loom wears out each year and is replaced. But this year, Wendy will expand her business to 12 looms. Calculate Wendy's initial capital stock, depreciation, gross investment, net investment and final capital stock.

*Solutions to odd-numbered problems are available on *Parkin Interactive*.

*5 The transactions in Ecoland last year were:

Item	Euros
Wages paid to labour	800,000
Consumption expenditure	600,000
Taxes	250,000
Transfer payments	50,000
Profits	200,000
Investment	250,000
Government expenditures	200,000
Exports	300,000
Saving	300,000
Imports	250,000

a Calculate Ecoland's GDP.

b Did you use the expenditure approach or the income approach to make this calculation?

c How is investment financed?

6 The transactions in Highland last year were:

Item	Euros
Wages paid to labour	800,000
Consumption expenditure	650,000
Net taxes	200,000
Profits	250,000
Investment	300,000
Government expenditures	250,000
Exports	250,000
Saving	300,000
Imports	300,000

a Calculate Highland's GDP.

b What extra information do you need to calculate net domestic product?

c Where does Highland get the funds to finance its investment?

*7 Bananaland produces only bananas and sunscreen. The tables give the quantities produced and the prices in 2002 and 2003.

	Quantity	
Good	**2002**	**2003**
Bananas	1,000 bunches	1,100 bunches
Sunscreen	500 bottles	525 bottles

Good	Price	
	2002	**2003**
Bananas	£2 a bunch	£3 a bunch
Sunscreen	£10 a bottle	£8 a bottle

Calculate Bananaland's:

a Nominal GDP in 2002 and 2003.

b Real GDP in 2003 in 2002 prices.

8 Sea Island produces only lobsters and crabs. The base year is 2003 and the tables give the quantities produced and the prices.

Good	Quantity	
	2003	**2004**
Lobsters	1,200	1,300
Crabs	500	525

Good	Price	
	2003	**2004**
Lobsters	£20 each	£25 each
Crabs	£10 each	£12 each

Calculate Sea Island's:

a Nominal GDP in 2003 and 2004.

b Real GDP in 2004 using the prices of 2003.

*9 Bananaland (in problem 7) uses the chain volume measure to calculate real GDP. The base year is 2001 and nominal GDP in that year was £6,500. GDP in 2002 valued at 2001 prices was £6,750. Calculate:

a Real GDP in 2001, 2002 and 2003.

b The GDP deflator in 2001, 2002 and 2003.

c The growth rate of real GDP and the inflation rate in 2002 and 2003.

10 Sea Island (in problem 8) uses the chain volume measure to calculate real GDP. The base year is 2001 and nominal GDP in that year was £28,000. GDP in 2002 valued at 2001 prices was £30,000. Calculate:

a Real GDP in 2001, 2002 and 2003.

b The GDP deflator in 2001, 2002 and 2003.

c The growth rate of real GDP and the inflation rate in 2002 and 2003.

Critical Thinking

1 Study *Reading Between the Lines* on pp. 452–453 and then answer the following questions:

a What is the implication of the VAT fraud for the aggregate measure of imports?

b What is the implication of the VAT fraud for the aggregate measure of consumption?

c How much is the aggregate measure of GDP affected by the VAT fraud?

d Why did the discovery of the VAT fraud have such a small effect on the measure of GDP?

e How would the allowance for the VAT fraud affect the measure of net exports?

f How might the information discovered about the VAT fraud influence economic policy?

2 Think about the VAT fraud described in *Reading Between the Lines* on pp. 452–453 from the point of view of the EU country that exported the mobile phones and computer parts. Assume that only one country, Finland, is involved.

a What is the implication of the VAT fraud for Finland's aggregate measure of exports?

b What is the implication of the VAT fraud for Finland's aggregate measure of GDP?

c Can you think of other implications of the VAT fraud for Finland's national income accounts?

Web Exercise

Use the links on *Parkin Interactive* to work the following exercise.

1 Visit the National Statistics Website and obtain data on real GDP and nominal GDP (expenditure based at market prices) for the United Kingdom. In the most recent quarter available

a What is the value of nominal GDP?

b What is the value of real GDP using the chain volume measure?

c What is the GDP deflator?

d What is the value of real GDP in the same quarter the previous year?

e By how much has real GDP changed over the past year? (Express your answer as a percentage.)

f Did real GDP increase or decrease and what does the change tell you about the state of the economy over the past year?

Chapter 21

Monitoring Cycles, Jobs and Inflation

After studying this chapter you will be able to:

◆ Explain how we date business cycles

◆ Define the workforce, the unemployment rate, the economic activity rate and aggregate hours

◆ Describe the sources of unemployment, its duration, the groups most affected by it and how it fluctuates over the business cycle

◆ Explain how we measure the price level and the inflation rate using the RPI

Vital Signs

Each month, we track the unemployment rate as a measure of economic health. How do we measure the unemployment rate and what does it tell us? Is it a reliable vital sign for the economy? How long does it take an unemployed person to find a new job? Why does unemployment affect young people and ethnic minorities more severely than other groups? Why is the unemployment rate higher in the European Union than in the United States?

Having a good job that pays a decent wage is only one half of the equation that translates into a good standard of living. The other half is the cost of living. We track the cost of the items we buy with another number that is published every month, the RPI. What is the RPI, how is it calculated, and does it provide a good guide to the changes in our cost of living?

The Business Cycle

The business cycle is a periodic but irregular up-and-down movement in production and jobs (see p. 420). There is no official, government-sponsored record of the dating of business cycles. Instead, business cycles are identified by independent research agencies and individual economic researchers. The National Bureau of Economic Research (NBER) in the United States is the pioneer of business cycle dating and other agencies use the NBER methods. The Economic Cycle Research Institute (ECRI) identifies and dates the business cycle in the United Kingdom and 18 other countries and the NBER dates the US business cycle. The working definition of the business cycle used by the ECRI is as follows:

> . . . pronounced, pervasive and persistent advances and declines in aggregate economic activity, which cannot be defined by any single variable, but by the consensus of key measures of output, income, employment and sales.[1]

A business cycle has two phases – expansion and recession – and two turning points – peak and trough. The NBER defines the phases and turning points of the cycle as follows.

> A *recession* is a significant decline in activity spread across the economy, lasting more than a few months, visible in industrial production, employment, real income, and wholesale–retail trade. A recession begins just after the economy reaches a *peak* of activity and ends as the economy reaches its *trough*. Between trough and peak, the economy is in an *expansion*.[2]

Real GDP is the broadest measure of economic activity, and another popular working definition of a recession is a decrease in real GDP that lasts for at least two quarters.

The people who date the business cycle want to pin down the turning points as closely as possible. For this purpose, the real GDP data are of limited use because they are calculated only on a quarterly basis.

So instead of using real GDP data, the NBER and ECRI look at employment, which is the broadest indicator of *monthly* economic activity. They also look at other monthly indicators that include estimates of personal income, sales of manufactures and industrial production. But employment is the major indicator.

Business cycle dating cannot be done until sufficient time has elapsed after a turning point to be reasonably sure that a recession has actually started or ended.

UK Business Cycle Dates

Table 21.1 summarizes the ECRI dates for the UK business cycle since 1952. What is most striking about the information in this table is the infrequency of cycle turning points. In the 624 months between August 1952 and August 2004 (the time of this writing), the UK economy was in an expansion phase of the business cycle for 568 months (or 91 per cent of the time). Of the three recessions, two lasted for about two years and one for about a year.

Glance back at Figure 19.3 (p. 421) and you can refresh your memory of this business cycle record and see it in its historical perspective.

Although the ECRI business cycle dates are determined with joint reference to output, income, employment and sales, there is a strong correlation between the dates identified as recessions and periods in which real GDP decreases for at least two successive quarters. Only one "recession" was missed by the ECRI method compared to the GDP method and that was in 1973 when real GDP decreased for three successive quarters.

Table 21.1

UK Business Cycle Reference Dates

Trough	Peak	Expansion (months)	Recession (months)
August, 1952	September, 1974	265	
August, 1975	June, 1979	46	11
May, 1981	May, 1990	108	23
March, 1992		149	22

Four expansions between 1952 and 2004 lasted for an average of 142 months (almost 12 years) and the current expansion is ongoing. Three recessions lasted for an average of 19 months. Historically, recessions have been getting shorter and less frequent.

Source: Economic Cycle Research Institute (ECRI), New York.

---

[1] You can find this definition and the dates of business cycles in 18 countries at the ECRI Website (www.businesscycle.com).
[2] "The NBER's Business Cycle Dating Procedure", 10 January 2002, NBER Website (www.nber.org). (Italisizing of key terms added.)

Growth Rate Cycles

Because recessions are rare and becoming rarer, just looking at expansions and recessions misses a lot of the volatility in our economy. If the growth rate of real GDP slows to a crawl but keeps growing, the unemployment rate rises and people notice hard times. The standard method of identifying a recession counts such a period as part of an expansion.

A newer alternative and more sensitive criterion for identifying a cycle is to look at growth rates rather than levels of cycle indicators. A **growth rate cycle downturn** is a:

> ... pronounced, pervasive and persistent decline in the *growth rate* of aggregate economic activity. The procedures used to identify peaks and troughs in the growth rate cycle are analogous to those used to identify business cycle turning points, except that they are applied to the growth rates of the same time series, rather than their levels.[3]

Figure 21.1 illustrates the business cycle in the United Kingdom using the growth rate of real GDP. The shaded regions highlight the growth recessions identified by the ECRI.

Using this method, there have been 13 recessions in the period since 1955. (The quarterly GDP data in the United Kingdom begins in that year.) The most pronounced recessions occurred in the mid-1970s, early 1980s, and early 1990s and are the recessions identified by the traditional dating method.

The growth rate cycle method of identifying recessions, expansions and turning points makes economic fluctuations look much more severe than the traditional method. But it provides a description of the business cycle that more closely aligns with how people are affected by economic fluctuations.

Review Quiz

1 What are the phases of the business cycle?
2 How do we know when a recession has begun?
3 How do we know when a recession has ended?
4 Have recessions been getting worse?
5 Describe and compare the two methods of identifying a recession.

Figure 21.1

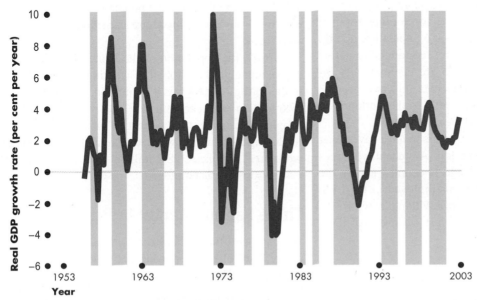

UK Growth Rate Cycles

The growth rate of real GDP fluctuates and reveals 13 growth rate recessions since 1955. The most severe growth rate recessions in the mid-1970s, early 1980s and early 1990s are the ones identified by the traditional business cycle dating method.

Sources: Real GDP: Office for National Statistics. Growth recessions: Economic Cycles Research Institute.

---

[3] This definition is from the ECRI Website (with small changes).

Employment and Wages

You have seen that employment is a key feature of the economy that helps to identify the month in which a recession begins and ends. The state of the labour market has a large impact on our incomes and our lives. We become concerned when jobs are hard to find and more relaxed when they are plentiful. But we want a good job, which means that we want a well-paid and interesting job. You are now going to learn how economists monitor the health of the labour market.

Labour Force Survey

Every working day, interviewers employed by the Social and Vital Statistics Division of the Office for National Statistics contact, either face to face or by telephone, close to 1,000 households (60,000 in a three-month period) and ask them questions about the age and labour market status of the household's members. This continuous data gathering activity is called the Labour Force Survey (LFS). The Office for National Statistics (ONS) uses the information obtained from the LFS to describe the changing anatomy of the labour market.

Figure 21.2 shows the population categories used by the ONS and the relationships among them. The population divides into two groups: the working-age population and others. The **working-age population** is the total number of people aged between 16 years and retirement who are not in jail, hospital or some other form of institutional care. The working-age population divides into two groups: those who are economically active (the workforce) and those who are economically inactive. The workforce also divides into two groups: the employed and the unemployed. So the **workforce** is the sum of the employed and the unemployed.

To be counted as employed, a person must have either a full-time job or a part-time job. A student who does part-time work while at college is counted among the employed. To be counted as *un*employed in the LFS, people must be available for work within the two weeks following their interview and must be in one of three categories:

1 Without work, but having made specific efforts to find a job within the previous four weeks.

2 Waiting to be called back to a job from which they have been laid off.

3 Waiting to start a new job within 30 days.

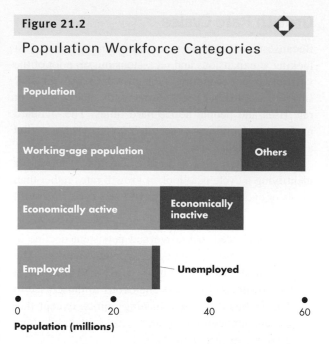

Figure 21.2

Population Workforce Categories

The population is divided into the working-age population and the young and institutionalized. The working-age population is divided into the workforce and those not in the workforce. The workforce is divided into the employed and the unemployed.

Source: Office for National Statistics.

People in the working-age population who are neither employed nor unemployed are classified as not in the workforce.

In 2004, the population of the United Kingdom was approximately 60 million. The working-age population in the spring of 2004 was 47.2 million. Of this number, 17.6 million were economically inactive. Most of these people were in full-time education or had retired. The remaining 29.6 million were economically active (in the workforce). Of these, 28.2 million were employed and 1.4 million were unemployed.

Three Labour Market Indicators

We can use official data to calculate three indicators of the state of the labour market which are shown in Figure 21.3. They are:

◆ The unemployment rate

◆ The economic activity rate

◆ The employment rate

The Unemployment Rate

The amount of unemployment is an indicator of the extent to which people who want jobs can't find them. The **unemployment rate** is the percentage of the people in the workforce who are unemployed. That is:

$$\text{Unemployment rate} = \frac{\text{Number of people unemployed}}{\text{Workforce}} \times 100$$

and

$$\text{Workforce} = \text{Number of people employed}$$
$$+ \text{Number of people unemployed}$$

In the spring of 2004, the number of people employed in the United Kingdom was 28.2 million and the number unemployed was 1.4 million. By using the above equations, you can verify that the workforce was 29.6 million and the unemployment rate was 4.7 per cent.

Figure 21.3 shows the unemployment rate (orange line) between 1963 and 2003. The average unemployment rate was 2.5 per cent during the 1960s and 1970s but 9 per cent during the 1980s and 1990s.

The Economic Activity Rate

The number of people in the workforce is an ind....or of the willingness of the people of working age to take jobs. The **economic activity rate** is the percentage of the working-age population who are members of the workforce. That is:

$$\frac{\text{Economic}}{\text{activity rate}} = \frac{\text{Workforce}}{\text{Working-age population}} \times 100$$

In the spring of 2004, the workforce was 29.6 million and the working-age population was 47.2 million. By using the above equation, you can calculate the economic activity rate. It was 62.7 per cent.

Figure 21.3 shows the economic activity rate (graphed in red and plotted against the left scale). It has increased a little, rising from 61.1 per cent in 1963 to 63.1 per cent in 2003. It has also had some mild fluctuations, which result from unsuccessful job seekers becoming discouraged workers.

Discouraged workers are people who are available and willing to work but have stopped actively looking for jobs. Fluctuations in the economic activity rate give an estimate of the number of discouraged workers.

Figure 21.3

Employment, Unemployment and Economic Activity Rates: 1963–2003

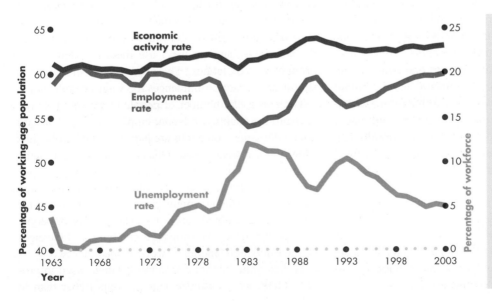

The state of the labour market is indicated by the economic activity rate, the employment rate and the unemployment rate. The economic activity rate has increased a little since 1960. The employment rate has increased slightly and fluctuates with the business cycle, but it has fluctuated more in the 1980s and 1990s. The unemployment rate has fallen steadily during the 1990s.

Sources: Office for National Statistics, *Annual Abstract of Statistics*, 2004.

The Employment Rate

The number of people of working age who have jobs is an indicator of the availability of jobs and the degree of match between people's skills and jobs. The **employment rate** is the percentage of the people of working age who have jobs. That is:

$$\text{Employment rate} = \frac{\text{Number of people employed}}{\text{Working-age population}} \times 100$$

In the spring of 2004, employment in the United Kingdom was 28.2 million and the working-age population was 47.2 million. By using the above equation, you can calculate the employment rate. It was 59.7 per cent.

Figure 21.3 shows the UK employment rate (graphed in blue and plotted against the left scale). It has increased slightly from 58.8 per cent in 1963 to 59.9 per cent in 2003, but it has fluctuated and reached a trough of 54 per cent in 1983. The increase in the employment rate since 1983 means that the economy has created jobs at a faster rate than the working-age population has grown. This labour market indicator also fluctuates, and its fluctuations coincide with but are opposite to those in the unemployment rate. The employment rate falls during a recession and increases during a recovery and expansion.

The economic activity rate has increased while the employment rate has remained roughly constant because the unemployment rate has increased. In other words, the total number of jobs has not kept up with the increase in the working-age population.

The aggregate economic activity rate and employment rate obscure an interesting and important difference between the labour market activity of women and men. Figure 21.4 reveals this information.

The female economic activity rate and employment rate have increased. Shorter working hours, higher productivity and an increased emphasis on white-collar work expanded the job opportunities and wages available to women. At the same time, technological advances increased productivity in the home and freed women from some of their more traditional work outside the job market.

Figure 21.4 also shows another remarkable fact: the male economic activity rate and employment rate have *decreased*. Increasing numbers of men are in full-time higher education, some are retiring earlier and some are specializing in the household work that previously was done almost exclusively by women.

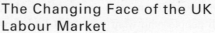

Figure 21.4

The Changing Face of the UK Labour Market

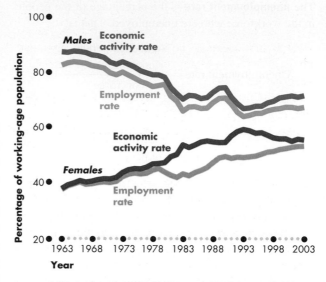

The female economic activity rate and employment rate have increased as more women have taken new white-collar jobs and part-time jobs. The male economic activity rate and employment rate have decreased as more men have remained in higher education, retired earlier and specialized in household work.

Source: Office for National Statistics, *Labour Market Trends*, June 2004.

Aggregate Hours

The three labour market indicators that we've just examined are useful signs of the health of the economy and directly measure what matters to most people: jobs. But they don't tell us the quantity of labour used to produce GDP, and we can't use them to calculate the productivity of labour. The productivity of labour is significant because it influences the wages people earn.

The reason the number of people employed does not measure the quantity of labour employed is that jobs are not all the same. Some jobs are part time and involve just a few hours of work a week. Others are full time, and some of these involve regular overtime work. For example, one shop might hire six students who each work for three hours a day. Another might hire two full-time workers who each work nine hours a day. The number of people employed in these two shops is eight, but six of the eight do the same total amount of work as the other two.

To determine the total amount of labour used to produce GDP, we measure labour in hours rather than in jobs. **Aggregate hours** are the total number of hours worked by all the people employed, both full time and part time, during a year.

Figure 21.5(a) shows aggregate hours in the UK economy from 1973 to 2003. You can see in the figure that aggregate hours fluctuate a great deal. You can also see what at first seems to be a surprising fact: aggregate hours in 2003 are almost the same as they were thirty years earlier in 1973.

Why is this fact surprising? Because there were 3 million more people employed in 2003 than in 1973. You saw in Figure 21.3 that the employment rate has been roughly constant at about 60 per cent of the working-age population. But the working-age population has increased every year, so the number of people employed has increased. The increase of 3 million people is a 16 per cent increase.

Why, when the number of people employed has increased by 3 million have aggregate hours barely changed? The answer is that average weekly hours per worker have fallen.

Figure 21.5(b) shows average weekly hours per worker. Average hours per worker decreased from around 36.4 hours a week in 1973 to 32.1 hours a week in 2003. The largest decreases were during the 1980–1982 and 1990–1992 recessions.

The shortening of the average working week has occurred partly because the average hours worked by full-time workers has decreased slightly. But the main reason for the fall in average weekly hours per worker is that the number of part-time jobs has increased faster than the number of full-time jobs.

Fluctuations in aggregate hours and average hours per worker line up with the business cycle. Figure 21.5 highlights the past three recessions during which aggregate hours decreased and average hours per worker decreased more quickly than the trend. While both measures show a fall that corresponds with the downturn of the economy in a recession, aggregate hours fall by more because people lose their jobs.

The Real Wage Rate

The **real wage rate** is the quantity of goods and services that an hour's work can buy. It is equal to the money wage rate (pounds per hour) divided by the price level. If we use the GDP deflator as the price level, the real wage rate is expressed in 2001 pounds because the GDP deflator is 100 in 2001. The real wage rate is a significant economic variable because it measures the cost of and reward for labour.

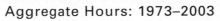

Figure 21.5

Aggregate Hours: 1973–2003

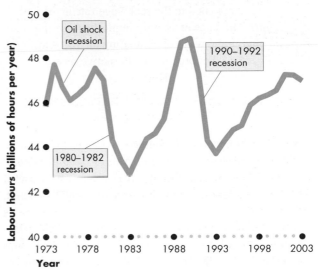

(a) Aggregate hours

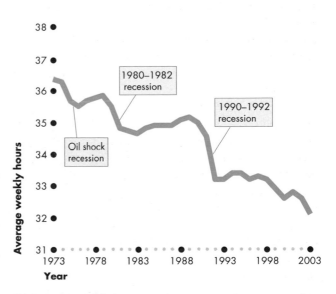

(b) Average weekly hours per person

Aggregate hours, part (a), measure the total labour used to produce real GDP more accurately than does the number of people employed because an increasing proportion of jobs are part time. Aggregate hours barely changed between 1973 and 2003. Fluctuations in aggregate hours coincide with business cycle fluctuations. Aggregate hours have changed little, while the number of jobs has increased because the average working week has shortened, part (b).

Sources: Office for National Statistics, *Labour Market Trends*, June 2004; and authors' calculations.

Changes in the real wage rate reflect changes in what an hour of work will buy and any effects of inflation have been removed.

What has happened to the real wage rate in the United Kingdom? The answer is not simple because there are several alternative ways of estimating the real wage rate. We will look at the three main alternative measures.

Average Hourly Earnings of Adult Manual Workers

The Office for National Statistics conducts a periodic survey of the *average hourly earnings of adult manual workers*. This measure of the real wage rate is useful because it is readily available and frequently updated. But it does not cover the entire workforce, so is not as useful as broader measures. In 2001 pounds, this measure of the hourly real wage was £5.29 in 1973 and £8.06 in 2003 – an increase of almost 50 per cent over the 30 years or an average increase of 1.34 per cent per year. Figure 21.6 shows the history of this wage rate.

Figure 21.6

Real Wage Rates in the United Kingdom: 1973–2003

The average hourly real wage rate of adult manual workers kept pace with the other two measures based on national income accounts. It accelerated in the late 1980s but slowed in the 1990s. All three measures of average hourly real wage rates reflect the productivity growth slowdown of the mid-1970s.

Source: Office for National Statistics and author's assumptions and calculations.

Total Wages and Salaries per Hour

A second measure of the hourly real wage rate is based on the national income accounts. It is calculated by dividing total wages and salaries by aggregate hours. This measure of the hourly wage rate is broader than the first and includes the incomes of all types of labour, whether their rate of pay is calculated by the hour or not. It includes managers and supervisors as well as manual workers. Figure 21.6 shows this measure in a sustained upward trend over the 30-year period.

Total Labour Compensation per Hour

An increasing proportion of labour cost takes the form of employer's add-on costs, such as employer's National Insurance contributions, and graduated pension contributions. To take this trend into account, we use a third measure of the hourly real wage rate, which equals *real labour compensation* – wages, salaries and supplements – divided by aggregate hours. This measure is the most comprehensive one available, and it shows that the average hourly wage rate has increased.

All three measures show that there was a common slowdown coinciding with the productivity slowdown of the mid-1970s.

Review Quiz

1 What are the trends in the economic activity rate, the employment rate and the unemployment rate?
2 What are the trends in the female economic activity rate and male economic activity rate?
3 Why has the economic activity rate increased, but the employment rate not increased by much?
4 Why have aggregate hours not grown while total employment has?
5 How have average hourly real wage rates changed since 1973?

You've now seen how we measure employment, unemployment, aggregate hours and the real wage rate. You've also seen how employment grows and how employment and unemployment fluctuate with the business cycle. Your next task is to study the anatomy of the labour market a bit more deeply and see why unemployment is ever present, even at full employment.

Unemployment and Full Employment

How do people become unemployed, how long do they remain unemployed and who is at greatest risk of becoming unemployed? Let's answer these questions by looking at the anatomy of unemployment.

The Anatomy of Unemployment

People become unemployed if they:

1 Lose their jobs.

2 Leave their jobs.

3 Enter or re-enter the workforce.

People end a spell of unemployment if they:

1 Are hired or recalled.

2 Withdraw from the workforce.

People who are laid off, either permanently or temporarily, from their jobs are called *job losers*. Some job losers become unemployed but some immediately withdraw from the workforce. People who voluntarily leave their jobs are called *job leavers*. Like job losers, some job leavers become unemployed and search for a better job, while others withdraw from the workforce temporarily or permanently retire from work.

People who enter or re-enter the workforce are called *entrants* and *re-entrants*. Entrants are mainly people who have just left school. Some entrants get a job straight away and are never unemployed, but many spend time searching for their first job and during this period they are unemployed.

Re-entrants are people who have previously withdrawn from the workforce. Most of these people are formerly discouraged workers or women returning to the labour market after an extended absence while raising a family. Figure 21.7 shows these labour market categories.

Let's see how much unemployment arises from the three different ways in which people can become unemployed.

The Sources of Unemployment

Figure 21.8 (overleaf) shows the proportion of unemployment by reason for becoming unemployed. Job losers are the biggest source of unemployment. These are the people who make up the redundancy statistics

Figure 21.7

Labour Market Flows

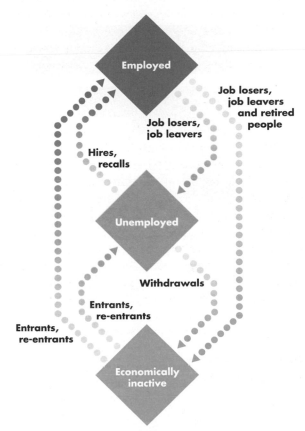

Unemployment results from employed people losing or leaving their jobs (job losers and job leavers) and from people entering the workforce (entrants and re-entrants). Unemployment ends because people get hired or recalled or because they withdraw from the workforce.

we hear about so regularly on the television news and read in the newspapers. Their number fluctuates a great deal. During the 1980s, when the average unemployment rate was almost 10 per cent, over half of the unemployed were job losers. During the 1990s, job losers represented 46 per cent of the unemployed.

Entrants are also a significant component of the unemployed. They are picked up in the Labour Force Survey as school leavers. On any given day during the 1990s, more than 25 per cent of those recently unemployed were entrants to the labour market.

Job leavers are the smallest and most stable source of unemployment. On any given day during the 1990s, fewer than 15 per cent of people unemployed were job leavers. But the willingness to leave a job and look for a

| Figure 21.8 | Figure 21.9 |

Unemployment by Reason

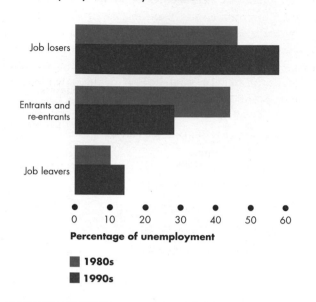

Most unemployment results from job loss. The number of job losers fluctuates more closely with the business cycle than do the numbers of job leavers and entrants and re-entrants. Entrants and re-entrants are the second most common type of unemployed people. Their number fluctuates with the business cycle because of discouraged workers. Job leavers are the least common type of unemployed people.

Source: The Labour Force Survey.

Unemployment by Duration

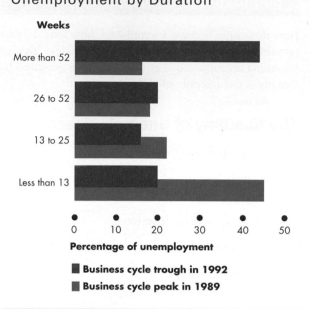

At a business cycle peak, when unemployment is at its lowest level, 45 per cent of unemployment lasts for under 13 weeks, 22 per cent lasts for 13–25 weeks, 18 per cent lasts for 26–52 weeks and 16 per cent lasts for one year or more. At a business cycle trough, when unemployment is at its highest level, only 20 per cent of unemployment lasts for under 13 weeks, 16 per cent lasts for 13–25 weeks, 20 per cent lasts for 26–52 weeks and 44 per cent lasts for one year or more.

Sources: The Labour Force Survey and Quantime Ltd.

new one varies slightly with the unemployment rate. In the 1980s, when the unemployment rate averaged close to 10 per cent, fewer people left their jobs than in the 1990s when the unemployment rate was a bit lower.

The Duration of Unemployment

Some people are unemployed for a week or two, and others are unemployed for periods of a year or more. Figure 21.9 examines the duration of unemployment at the peak and the trough of the business cycle. We can see that the proportion of the unemployed who were jobless for under 13 weeks is higher in the peak than in the trough and the proportion who were jobless for more than 13 weeks is lower in the peak than in the trough.

People who have been unemployed for over one year experience **long-term unemployment**. In the peak of 1989, 16 per cent of the jobless population were classified as long-term unemployed; in the trough of 1992, that proportion increased to 44 per cent. The proportion of the long-term unemployed has remained stubbornly in

excess of 16 per cent over the business cycle. The high proportion of people who experience long-term unemployment presents a serious social problem both in the United Kingdom and in the European Union.

The Demographics of Unemployment

Figure 21.10 shows unemployment for different demographic groups. Figure 21.10(a) shows that the high unemployment rates occur among young workers, especially young men, and ethnic minority groups, especially blacks. In the summer of 2003, the unemployment rate of all ethnic minorities was 13 per cent; for blacks as a whole it was 14 per cent compared with whites for whom it was only 5 per cent. Teenagers also have a higher than average unemployment rate. In summer 2003, the unemployment rate of all 16–17 year-olds was 21.0 per cent, while that of teenage men was 24 per cent. Figure 21.10(b) shows that the gap between white and non-white unemployment rates increases in the trough and decreases in the peak.

Figure 21.10

Unemployment by Demographic Group

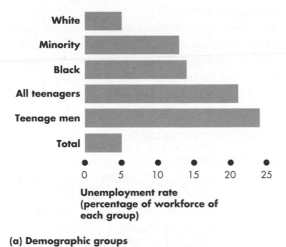

(a) Demographic groups

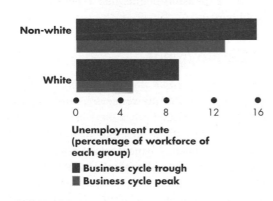

Unemployment rate
(percentage of workforce of
each group)

■ Business cycle trough
■ Business cycle peak

(b) Ethnic groups

Teenagers experience unemployment rates nearly five times higher than the average, and unemployment among blacks is nearly three times the average. Even at a business cycle trough, when unemployment is at its highest rate, the ratio of non-white to white unemployment is 1.7.

Source: *Labour Market Trends*; December 2003.

Why are teenage unemployment rates so high? There are three reasons. First, young people are still in the process of discovering what they are good at and trying different lines of work. So they leave their jobs more frequently than older workers. Second, firms sometimes hire teenagers on a short-term trial basis. So the rate of job loss is higher for teenagers than for other people. Third, most teenagers are not in the workforce but are at school. If we count being in full-time education as having a job, the true teenage unemployment rate is much lower than the reported teenage unemployment rate.

Ethnic minorities' unemployment rates are higher than white unemployment rates. One reason is that ethnic minorities face unequal opportunities and possible discrimination in the labour market. In the peak of the business cycle, unemployment among non-whites is 2.6 times higher than unemployment among whites. Even in the trough of the business cycle, when unemployment is higher all round, the ratio of non-white to white unemployment falls to only 1.7.

Types of Unemployment

Unemployment is classified into three types that are based on its sources. They are:

◆ Frictional unemployment
◆ Structural unemployment
◆ Cyclical unemployment

Frictional Unemployment

Frictional unemployment is the unemployment that arises from normal labour turnover. Frictional unemployment is not usually regarded as a problem, but it is a permanent, long term phenomenon.

Normal labour turnover arises for two reasons. First, people are constantly entering the workforce – young people leave school, mothers return to the workforce and previously discouraged workers try once more to find jobs. At the same time, other people retire and create job vacancies for the new entrants and re-entrants to fill. This constant churning of the individuals in the workforce is the first reason for normal labour turnover.

The second reason is the constant churning of individual businesses. Some businesses fail, close down and lay off their workers. Other new businesses start up and hire workers. The people who lose their jobs in this process are frictionally unemployed and are trying to match their skills to jobs that are opening up.

The unending flow of people into and out of the workforce and of job creation and job destruction creates the need for people to search for jobs and for businesses to search for workers. Always there are businesses with unfilled jobs and people seeking jobs. Look in your local newspaper and you will see that there are always some jobs being advertised. Businesses don't usually hire the first person who applies for a job, and unemployed people don't usually take the first job that comes their way. Instead, both firms and workers spend time searching out what they believe will be the best match available. By this process of search, people can match their own skills and interests with the available jobs and find a satisfying job and income. While these unemployed people are searching, they are frictionally unemployed.

The amount of frictional unemployment depends on the rate at which people enter and re-enter the workforce and on the rate at which jobs are created and destroyed. During the 1960s, the amount of frictional unemployment increased as a consequence of the post-war baby boom that began during the 1940s.

The amount of frictional unemployment is also influenced by the level of unemployment benefits. The greater the number of people covered by unemployment benefits and the more generous the benefits, the longer is the average time taken in job search and the greater is the amount of frictional unemployment. Studies of variations in unemployment rates and benefits across the member states of the European Union show this factor to be important.

Structural Unemployment

Structural unemployment is the unemployment that arises when changes in technology or international competition destroy jobs that use different skills or are located in different regions from the new jobs that are created. Structural unemployment usually lasts longer than frictional unemployment because it is often necessary to retrain and possibly relocate to find a job. For example, on the day the shipyards in the Upper Clyde announced the loss of 600 jobs, a computer chip company in Gwent announced the creation of 750 new jobs. The unemployed former shipyard workers remain unemployed for several months until they move home, retrain and get one of the new jobs being created in other parts of the country.

Structural unemployment is painful, especially for older workers for whom the best available option might be to retire early, but with a lower income than they had expected. For example, a shipyard worker from Humberside who is made redundant may reluctantly accept to remain unemployed rather than retrain, accept a lower wage for another type of job, or move south where new jobs are being created. Such a person has opted to join the ranks of the long-term unemployed. The decision to accept long-term unemployment is governed by the options available to and the constraints on the structurally unemployed person. A person with different circumstances may make an entirely different decision. A younger person with family commitments may retrain, or take a job as a taxi driver in the short term until a better opportunity turns up, or relocate to take advantage of job opportunities elsewhere. One of

the many factors that influence a person's decision is the level of unemployment benefit. The higher the benefit, the less incentive there is to accept the alternatives to long-term unemployment.

Structural unemployment can be a serious long-term problem. It began to increase in the 1970s during the period of stagflation, when an increasingly competitive international environment brought a decline in the number of jobs in traditional industries.

Cyclical Unemployment

Cyclical unemployment is the fluctuating unemployment that coincides with the business cycle. It is a repeating short-term problem. The amount of cyclical unemployment increases during a recession and decreases during an expansion. A worker in a car component factory who is laid off because the economy is in a recession and who gets rehired some months later when the expansion begins has experienced cyclical unemployment.

Full Employment

There is always *some* unemployment – even at full employment. So what do we mean by full employment? **Full employment** occurs when there is no cyclical unemployment – when all the unemployment is frictional and structural. The unemployment rate at full employment is called the **natural rate of unemployment**.

There can be quite a lot of unemployment at full employment, and the terms "full employment" and "natural rate of unemployment" are examples of technical economic terms that do not correspond with everyday language. For most people – and especially for unemployed workers – there is nothing natural about unemployment. So why do economists call a situation with a lot of unemployment one of "full employment" and "natural unemployment"?

The reason is that the economy is a complex mechanism that is always changing. In 2003, the UK economy employed 28 million people. About a half a million workers retired during that year and more than half a million new workers entered the labour force. All these people worked in several million businesses that produced goods and services valued at more than £1 trillion. Some of these businesses downsized and failed, and others expanded.

This process of change creates frictions and dislocations that are unavoidable. And the unemployment the process creates is unavoidable. Natural unemployment and full employment refer to that state of the world in which the unemployment that exists stems from the natural frictions and dislocations that constantly bombard our lives.

Real GDP and Unemployment Over the Business Cycle

The quantity of real GDP at full employment is called *potential GDP*. You will study the forces that determine potential GDP in Chapter 22 (p. 480). Over the business cycle, real GDP fluctuates around potential GDP and the unemployment rate fluctuates around the natural rate of unemployment.

Figure 21.11 illustrates these fluctuations in the United Kingdom between 1983 and 2003 – real GDP in part (a) and the unemployment rate in part (b). When the economy is at full employment, the unemployment rate equals the natural rate of unemployment and real GDP equals potential GDP. When the unemployment rate is less than the natural rate of unemployment, real GDP is greater than potential GDP. And when the unemployment rate is greater than the natural rate of unemployment, real GDP is less than potential GDP.

Economists do not know the magnitude of the natural rate of unemployment and the natural rate shown in the figure is only one estimate. In the figure, the natural rate of unemployment is 10.4 per cent in 1983 and it falls steadily through the 1980s and 1990s to 5.1 per cent by 2003. This estimate of the natural rate of unemployment in the United Kingdom is one that many, but not all, economists would accept.

Review Quiz

1   What are the categories of people who become unemployed?
2   Define frictional, structural and cyclical unemployment and provide an example of each type of unemployment.
3   What is the natural rate of unemployment?
4   What factors might make the natural rate of unemployment change?
5   How does the unemployment rate fluctuate over the business cycle?

Your final task in this chapter is to learn about another vital sign that gets monitored every month, the Retail Prices Index (RPI). What is the RPI, how do we measure it and what does it mean?

Figure 21.11

UK Real GDP and Unemployment: 1983–2003

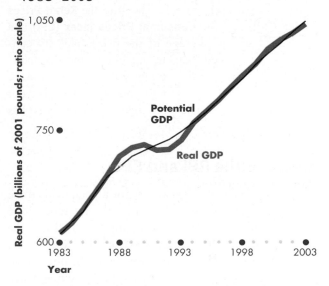

(a) Real GDP and potential GDP

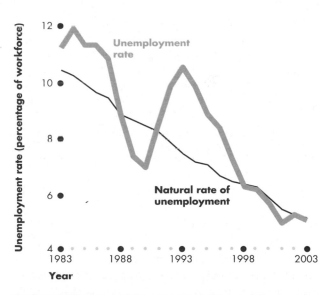

(b) Unemployment and the natural rate of unemployment

As real GDP fluctuates around potential GDP in part (a), the unemployment rate fluctuates around the natural rate of unemployment in part (b). In the recession of 1990–1992, the unemployment rate peaked at 10 per cent. The labour market reforms of the 1980s helped to reduce the natural rate of unemployment, but we don't know how far it has fallen.

Sources: Office for National Statistics and authors' assumptions and calculations.

Price Indexes

The Office for National Statistics (ONS) calculates two price indexes every month. They are the **Retail Prices Index (RPI)** and the **Consumer Prices Index (CPI)** and both measure an average of the prices paid by consumers for a fixed "basket" of goods and services.[4] What you learn in this section will help you to make sense of the RPI and the CPI and relate them to your own economic life. The price indexes tell you what has happened to the value of the money in your pocket.

Reading the RPI and CPI

The RPI is defined to equal 100 for a period called the **reference base period**. Currently, the reference base period is January 1987. That is, for January 1987, the RPI equals 100. In January 2004, the RPI was 183.1. This number tells us that the average of the prices paid by households for a particular basket of consumer goods and services was 83.1 per cent higher in January 2003 than it was in January 1987.

In 2003, the RPI was 183.1 and in January 2002, it was 178.5. Comparing the 2003 RPI with the 2002 RPI tells us that the average of the prices paid by households for a particular basket of consumer goods and services increased between 2002 and 2003 by 4.6 index points – from 178.5 to 183.1 – or by 2.6 per cent.

The reference base period for the CPI is 1996 and in January 2004, the CPI was 110.1. We read the CPI and calculate percentage changes in it in the same way that you've just seen for the RPI.

Constructing the RPI and CPI

Constructing the RPI and the CPI is a huge operation that costs millions of pounds and involves three stages:

◆ Selecting and updating the basket

◆ Conducting a monthly price survey

◆ Calculating the price index

Selecting and Updating the Basket

The first stage in constructing a price index is to select the "basket" of goods and services that the index will cover. The RPI basket contains the goods and services

bought by an average household in the United Kingdom. The idea is to make the relative importance of the items in the RPI basket the same as that in the budget of an average household. For example, because people spend more on housing than on bus rides, the RPI places more weight on the price of housing than on the price of a bus ride.

To be representative of typical households, the RPI basket does not take account of the spending patterns of the 4 per cent of households with the highest incomes or of pensioner households.

The CPI basket is a bit different from the RPI basket and covers *all* expenditure on consumer goods and services made in the United Kingdom by private households, residents of institutions and tourists.

To determine the spending patterns of households and to select the RPI and CPI baskets, the Office for National Statistics conducts periodic expenditure surveys. These surveys are costly and so are undertaken infrequently. Figure 22.12 shows the RPI and CPI baskets in 2004.

For the RPI, there are five major categories of which by far the largest is housing and household expenditure. Travel and leisure comes next and is larger than food, alcoholic drinks and tobacco combined.

The ONS breaks down each of these categories into ever smaller ones, right down to distinguishing between packaged and loose new potatoes!

The CPI basket contains 12 major categories of which transport, and recreation and culture, are the largest.

As you look at the relative importance of the items in the RPI and CPI baskets, remember that they apply to an *average* household. *Individual* households are spread around the average. Think about your own expenditure and compare the basket of goods and services you buy with the RPI basket.

Conducting a Monthly Price Survey

Each month, ONS employees check 110,000 prices of more than 550 types of goods and services. They visit shops in about 150 places throughout the United Kingdom to see the goods and the prices to ensure accuracy. Because the RPI aims to measure price *changes*, it is important that the prices recorded each month refer to exactly the same item. For example, suppose the price of a packet of biscuits has decreased but a packet now contains fewer biscuits. Has the price of biscuits decreased, remained the same or increased? The ONS price checker must record the details of changes in quality or packaging so that price changes can be isolated from other changes.

---

[4] A third price index, the Retail Prices Index Excluding Mortgage Interest (RPIX), is also published.

Figure 21.12

The RPI and CPI baskets

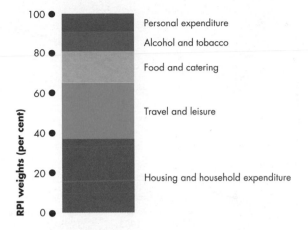

(a) The RPI basket

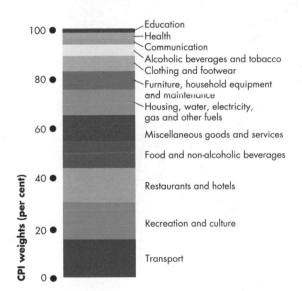

(b) The CPI basket

The RPI basket contains items that a typical household buys. The CPI basket is broader and contains all the consumer items bought in the United Kingdom.

Source: Office for National Statistics.

Calculating the Price Index

The RPI and CPI calculations have three steps:

1 Find the cost of the basket at base-period prices.

2 Find the cost of the basket at current-period prices.

3 Calculate the index for the base period and the current period.

We'll work through these three steps for a simple example. Suppose the basket contains only two goods and services: oranges and haircuts. We'll construct an annual price index rather than a monthly index with the reference base period 2003 and the current period 2004.

Table 22.2 shows the quantities in the basket and the prices in the base period and current period. Part (a) contains the data for the base period. In that period, consumers bought 10 oranges at £1 each and 5 haircuts at £8 each. To find the cost of the basket in the base-period prices, multiply the quantities in the basket by the base-period prices. The cost of oranges is £10 (10 at £1 each), and the cost of haircuts is £40 (5 at £8 each). So total cost of the basket in the base period is £50 (£10 + £40).

Part (b) contains the price data for the current period. The price of an orange increased from £1 to £2, which is a 100 per cent increase (£1 ÷ £1 × 100 = 100). The price of a haircut increased from £8 to £10, which is a 25 per cent increase (£2 ÷ £8 × 100 = 25).

A price index provides a way of averaging these price increases by comparing the cost of the basket rather than the price of each item. To find the cost of the basket in the current period, 2004, multiply the quantities in the basket by their 2004 prices. The cost of oranges is £20 (10 at £2 each), and the cost of haircuts is £50 (5 at £10 each). So total cost of the basket at current-period prices is £70 (£20 + £50).

Table 22.2

The RPI: A Simplified Calculation

(a) The cost of the basket at base-period prices: 2003

Basket			
Item	Quantity	Price	Cost of basket
Oranges	10	£1	£10
Haircuts	5	£8	£40
Cost of the basket at base-period prices			£50

(b) The cost of the basket at current-period prices: 2004

Basket			
Item	Quantity	Price	Cost of basket
Oranges	10	£2	£20
Haircuts	5	£10	£50
Cost of the basket at current-period prices			£70

You've now taken the first two steps towards calculating a price index: calculating the cost of the basket in the base period and the current period. The third step uses the numbers you've just calculated to find the price index (the RPI or CPI) for 2003 and 2004.

The formula for the price index is:

$$\text{RPI} = \frac{\text{Cost of basket at current-period prices}}{\text{Cost of basket at base-period prices}} \times 100$$

In Table 22.2, you have established that in 2003, the cost of the basket was £50 and in 2004, it was £70. You also know that the base period is 2003. So the cost of the basket at base-period prices is £50. If we use these numbers in the RPI formula, we can find the RPI for 2003 and 2004. For 2003:

$$\text{RPI in 2003} = \frac{£50}{£50} \times 100 = 100$$

For 2004:

$$\text{RPI in 2004} = \frac{£70}{£50} \times 100 = 140$$

The principles that you've applied in this simplified price index calculation apply to the more complex calculations performed every month by the ONS.

Measuring Inflation

A major purpose of the RPI is to measure *changes* in the cost of living and in the value of money. To measure these changes, we calculate the **inflation rate**, which is the percentage change in the price level from one year to the next. To calculate the inflation rate, we use the formula:

$$\text{Inflation rate} = \frac{(\text{RPI this year} - \text{RPI last year})}{\text{RPI last year}} \times 100$$

We can use this formula to calculate the inflation rate in 2003. The RPI in January 2004 was 183.1, and the RPI in January 2003 was 178.5. So the inflation rate during 2003 was:

$$\text{Inflation rate} = \frac{(183.1 - 178.5)}{178.5} \times 100$$

$$= 2.6 \text{ per cent}$$

Figure 21.13

The RPI and the Inflation Rate

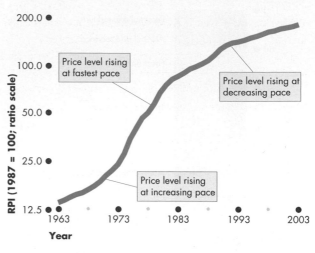

(a) RPI: 1963–2003

(b) Inflation rate: 1963–2003

In part (a), the RPI (the price level) has increased every year. In part (b), the inflation rate has averaged 5.5 per cent a year. During the 1970s and early 1980s, the inflation rate was high and peaked at 25 per cent a year. But after 1983, the inflation rate fell to an average of 3 per cent a year.

Source: Office for National Statistics.

Figure 21.13 shows the RPI and the inflation rate in the United Kingdom during the 40 years between 1963 and 2003. The two parts of the figure are related. The figure shows that when the price *level* in part (a) rises rapidly, the inflation rate in part (b) is high, and when the price level in part (a) rises slowly, the inflation rate in part (b) is low. Notice in part (a) that the RPI increased every year during this period. During the late 1970s and 1980s, the RPI was increasing rapidly, but its rate of increase slowed during the late 1980s and 1990s.

The RPI is not a perfect measure of the price level, and changes in the RPI can overstate the inflation rate. Let's look at the sources of bias in the RPI against which the ONS must guard.

Biased Price Indexes

The main sources of bias in a price index are:

◆ New goods bias
◆ Quality change bias
◆ Substitution bias

New Goods Bias

New goods keep replacing old goods. For example, CDs have replaced LP records and PCs have replaced typewriters. If you want to compare the price level in 2005 with that in 1975, you somehow have to compare the price of a CD and a computer today with that of an LP and typewriter in 1975. Because CDs and PCs are more expensive today than LPs and typewriters, the arrival of these new goods puts an upward bias into the estimate of the price level.

Quality Change Bias

Most goods undergo constant quality improvement. Cars, computers, CD players and even textbooks get better year after year. Quality improvements often increase the price, but such price increases are not inflation. For example, suppose that a 1999 car is 5 per cent better and costs 5 per cent more than a 1995 car. Adjusted for the quality change, the price of the car has not changed. But in calculating the RPI, the price of the car will have increased by 5 per cent.

Estimates have been made of the quality change bias, especially for obvious changes such as those in cars and computers. Allowing for quality improvements changes the inflation picture by 1 percentage point a year, on average, according to some economists.[5] That is, correctly

---

[5] S Checchetti and M Wynne, "Inflation measurement and the ECB's pursuit of price stability: a first assessment", *Economic Policy*, 37, 2003.

measured, the inflation rate might be as much as 1 percentage point a year less than the published numbers.

Substitution Bias

A change in the price index measures the percentage change in the price of a *fixed* basket of goods and services. But changes in relative prices lead consumers to seek less costly items. For example, by shopping more frequently at discount shops and less frequently at corner shops, consumers can cut the prices they pay. By using discount fares on airlines, they can cut the cost of travel. This kind of substitution of cheaper items for more costly items is not picked up by the price index. Because consumers make such substitutions, a price index based on a fixed basket overstates the effects of a given price change on the inflation rate.

Some Consequences of Bias in the RPI and CPI

The RPI is also used to calculate increases in pensions and other government outlays. So a bias in the RPI could end up swelling government expenditure (and taxes). The CPI is used by the Bank of England to determine whether the interest rate needs to be raised or lowered. So a bias in the CPI could lead to an inappropriate policy decision.

Mindful of these potentially harmful effects, our price indexes are constructed with the greatest possible care to minimize the biases we've just examined.

Review Quiz

1 What are the RPI and CPI and how are they calculated?
2 What is the relationship between the RPI and the inflation rate?
3 How might a price index be biased?
4 What problems arise from biased RPI and CPI?

You've now completed your study of the measurement of macroeconomic performance. Your task in the following chapters is to learn what determines that performance and how policy actions might improve it. But first, take a close-up look at the jobless recovery of 2002 and 2003 in *Reading Between the Lines* on pp. 474–475.

Reading Between the Lines

Unemployment and the Business Cycle

The Financial Times, 17 June 2004

Buoyant jobs market boosts case for rate rise

David Turner

Employment has risen to a record high and underlying earnings growth has accelerated bolstering the case for further interest rate rises to damp down heady consumer and homebuyer optimism.

Simon Rubinsohn, economist at Gerrard, the fund manager, said "the employment figures play a significant role in driving consumer confidence".

The total number of people in work rose by 30,000 to 28.302 million in the three months to April, according to the Office for National Statistics, although the employment rate remained stuck at 74.8 per cent.

The number of people seeking work but unable to find it – the generally preferred measure of unemployment – fell by 9,000 to 1.427 million in the three months to April, 4.8 per cent of the potential labour force. The unemployment claimant count fell by 12,000 last month to 862,000.

But economic inactivity – which includes many people on benefits whom the government is trying to get back to work – rose by 36,000 to 7.806 million in the three months to April.

The ONS also revealed that there were only 3.371 million jobs in manufacturing industries in April, down 106,000 in a year and less than half of 25 years ago.

Britain's overall rate of employment is the highest of any of the Group of Seven leading economic powers.

The Essence of the Story

◆ Employment increased by 30,000 in February–April 2004.

◆ Unemployment measured by the unemployment benefits claimant count fell by 12,000 in May 2004.

◆ Unemployment measured by the Labour Force Survey fell by 9,000 to 4.8 per cent of the workforce.

◆ Despite the increase in employment, jobs were lost in manufacturing.

◆ Lower unemployment boosts consumer confidence and strengthens the case for actions to dampen the expanding economy.

Economic Analysis

◆ With the increase in employment and the decrease in unemployment in early 2004, it is likely, as Figure 1 shows, that real GDP has risen above potential GDP.

◆ At the same time, as Figure 2 shows, the unemployment rate has fallen below the natural rate of unemployment.

◆ The rise in employment has been matched by a fall in unemployment, which means that more jobs have been created than lost.

◆ Employment jumped sharply in the first quarter of 2004, as Figure 3 shows.

◆ The information provided in the news article about the decrease in the number of unemployment benefit claimants does not add much to what the Labour Force Survey (LFS) data tell us.

◆ The change in the number of unemployment benefit claimants is a poor estimate of the change in the unemployment rate, which is why the news article describes the LFS data as "the generally preferred measure" of unemployment.

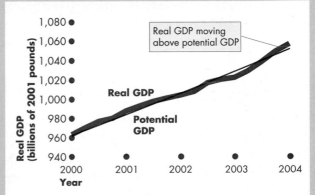

Figue 1 Real GDP and potential GDP

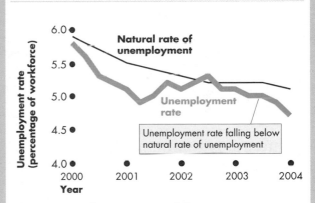

Figure 2 Unemployment rate and the natural rate of unemployment

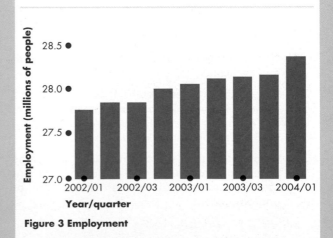

Figure 3 Employment

Summary

Key Points

The Business Cycle (pp. 458–459)

◆ A recession is a significant decline in economic activity spread across the economy and lasting more than a few months.

◆ Another definition of recession is a decrease in real GDP that lasts for at least two quarters.

◆ The ECRI has identified only three recessions in the United Kingdom since 1950.

Employment and Wages (pp. 460–464)

◆ The economic activity rate, the employment rate and the unemployment rate fluctuate with the business cycle.

◆ The female economic activity rate has increased, but the male economic activity rate has decreased.

◆ Aggregate hours fluctuate in line with the business cycle. Average weekly hours per worker have decreased.

◆ Real hourly wage rates have increased but at a pace that slowed during the 1970s.

Unemployment and Full Employment (pp. 465–469)

◆ People are constantly entering and leaving the state of unemployment.

◆ The duration of unemployment fluctuates over the business cycle, but the phase of the business cycle makes little difference to the demographic patterns in unemployment.

◆ Unemployment can be frictional, structural and cyclical.

◆ When all the unemployment is frictional and structural, unemployment is at its natural rate, the economy is at full employment and real GDP equals potential GDP.

◆ Over the business cycle, real GDP fluctuates around potential GDP and the unemployment rate fluctuates around the natural rate of unemployment.

Price Indexes (pp. 470–473)

◆ The Retail Prices Index (RPI) and the Consumer Prices Index (CPI) measure the average prices paid for a specified basket in a current period as a percentage of the cost of the same basket in a base period.

◆ The inflation rate is the percentage change in the RPI (or CPI) from one year to the next.

◆ A price index might be biased and measures must be taken to estimate and eliminate the bias.

Key Figures

Figure 21.2   Population Workforce Categories, 460
Figure 21.7   Labour Market Flows, 465
Figure 21.11 UK Real GDP and Unemployment: 1983–2003, 469
Figure 21.12 The RPI and CPI Baskets, 471

Key Terms

Aggregate hours, 463
Consumer Prices Index (CPI), 470
Cyclical unemployment, 468
Economic activity rate, 461
Employment rate, 462
Frictional unemployment, 467
Full employment, 468
Growth rate cycle downturn, 459
Inflation rate, 472
Long-term unemployment, 466
Natural rate of unemployment, 468
Real wage rate, 463
Reference base period, 470
Retail Prices Index (RPI), 470
Structural unemployment, 468
Unemployment rate, 461
Workforce, 460
Working-age population, 460

Problems

*1 In 2001, the Labour Force Survey measured the UK workforce at 29,088,000, employment at 27,660,000, and the working-age population at 46,351,000. Calculate for 2001 the

   a Unemployment rate.

   b Economic activity rate.

   c Employment rate.

2 In 2003, the Labour Force Survey measured the UK workforce at 29,580,000, employment at 28,095,000 and the working-age population at 46,903,000. Calculate for 2003 the

   a Unemployment rate.

   b Economic activity rate.

   c Employment rate.

*3 During 2002, the working-age population increased by 277,000, employment increased by 156,000 and the economically active labour force increased by 41,000. Use the data in problem 1 to calculate the change in unemployment and the change in the number of discouraged workers during 2002.

4 During the first quarter of 2004, the working-age population increased by 234,000, employment increased by 251,000, and the workforce increased by 180,000. Use the data in problem 2 to calculate the change in unemployment and the change in the number of discouraged workers during the first quarter of 2004.

*5 In January 2003, the unemployment rate was 5.1 per cent. In January 2004, the unemployment rate was 4.7 per cent. What do you predict happened between January 2003 and January 2004 to the numbers of:

   a Job losers and job leavers?

   b Entrants and re-entrants into the workforce?

6 In March 2003, the unemployment rate in Sweden was 5.3 per cent. In March 2004, the unemployment rate was 6.4 per cent. (These are seasonally adjusted rates that exclude the winter seasonal unemployment.) What do you predict happened in 2003 to the numbers of:

   a Job losers and job leavers?

   b Entrants and re-entrants into the workforce?

*7 In July 2002, in the economy of Sandy Island, 10,000 people were employed, 1,000 were unemployed, and 5,000 of working age were not in the workforce. During

August 2002, 80 people lost their jobs, 20 people left their jobs, 150 people were hired or recalled, 50 people withdrew from the workforce, and 40 people entered or re-entered the workforce. Calculate for July 2002:

   a The workforce.

   b The unemployment rate.

   c The working-age population.

   d The economic activity rate.

And calculate for the end of August 2002

   e The number of people unemployed.

   f The number of people employed.

   g The workforce.

   h The unemployment rate.

8 In July 2003, in the economy of Sandy Island, 11,000 people were employed, 900 were unemployed, and 5,000 of working age were not in the workforce. During August 2002, 40 people lost their jobs, 10 people left their jobs, 180 people were hired or recalled, 20 people withdrew from the workforce, and 60 people entered or re-entered the workforce. Calculate for July 2003.

   a The workforce.

   b The unemployment rate.

   c The working-age population.

   d The economic activity rate.

And calculate for the end of August 2003

   e The number of people unemployed.

   f The number of people employed.

   g The workforce.

   h The unemployment rate.

*9 A typical family on Sandy Island consumes only juice and cloth. Last year, which was the reference base period, the family spent £40 on juice and £25 on cloth. Last year, juice was £4 a bottle and cloth was £5 a length. This year, juice is £4 a bottle and cloth is £6 a length. Calculate

   a The RPI basket.

   b The RPI in the current year.

   c The inflation rate in the current year.

10 A typical family on Lizard Island consumes only mangoes and nuts. Last year, which was the reference base period, the family spent £60 on nuts and £10 on mangoes. Last year, mangoes were £1 each and nuts were £3 a bag. This year, mangoes are £1.50 each and nuts are £4 a bag. Calculate

   a The RPI basket.

   b The RPI in the current year.

   c The inflation rate in the current year.

---

*Solutions to odd-numbered problems are available on *Parkin Interactive*.

Critical Thinking

1 Study *Reading Between the Lines* on pp. 474–475 and then answer the following questions:

a What is the labour market signalling about the trend in unemployment in 2001?

b Why does the claimant count give a different picture about the trend in unemployment than the LFS measure?

c What is the reason for the rise in unemployment?

d Which sectors are particularly hit by job losses and why?

2 The figures below show the unemployment rate and the OECD estimate of the natural rate of unemployment for five large economies of the OECD for 2001 and 2002. The countries are the United States, United Kingdom, Germany, France and Italy. The first column shows the unemployment rate (U) for 2001, the second column shows the natural rate of unemployment (U^*) for 2001, the third column shows the unemployment rate in 2003 and the fourth column shows the natural rate of unemployment in 2003.

Country	U 2001	U^* 2001	U 2003	U^* 2003
United States	4.7	5.1	6.0	5.1
United Kingdom	5.0	5.5	4.9	5.2
Germany	7.8	7.2	9.3	7.2
France	8.5	9.2	9.4	9.0
Italy	9.4	9.0	8.6	8.8

a In which countries did the unemployment rate fall between 2001 and 2003?

b In which countries is the unemployment rate above the natural rate? And in which countries is it below the natural rate?

c In which countries is real GDP above potential GDP? And in which countries is it below potential GDP?

d If the unemployment rate is below the natural rate, what do you think will happen to the economy if the government does nothing?

e If unemployment rate is above the natural rate, what do you think the government of that country should do about it ?

3 You've seen in this chapter that the average working week has shortened over the years. Do you think that shorter work hours are a problem or a benefit? Do you expect the average working week to keep getting shorter? Why or why not?

Web Exercises

Use the links on *Parkin Interactive* to work the following exercises.

1 Obtain data on business cycle turning points in the European Union.

a Which countries have experienced the most recessions during the past twenty years?

b Compare the cycles in the United Kingdom with those in the rest of the European Union. Does the United Kingdom experience recession more frequently, less frequently or just as frequently as the rest of the European Union?

2 Obtain data on unemployment in your economic region of the United Kingdom.

a What have been the changes in the employment rate, unemployment rate and the economic activity rate in your own region during the past two years?

b On the basis of what you know about your own region, how would you set about explaining these trends?

c Compare unemployment in your region with that in the United Kingdom as a whole.

d Why do you think your region might have a higher or a lower unemployment rate than the UK average?

e Try to identify those industries that have expanded most and those that have shrunk in your region.

f What are the problems in your region's labour market that you think local government and Development Agencies can do to solve?

3 Obtain data on the RPI for the United Kingdom and the CPI for the United Kingdom and the other EU countries.

a What have been the changes in the inflation rates of the EU countries during the past two years?

b Which EU countries have had the lowest inflation rates and which have had the highest?

c Why might the price index for one country differ from that of another?

d What are the differences in the inflation rate measured by the RPI and the CPI for the United Kingdom?

e Why do you think the RPI and CPI inflation measures are different? Is either "correct"? Why or why not?

f Suppose that someone proposed replacing the RPI with the CPI for the purpose of linking wage rates and pensions. Who would be in favour of this proposal, who would oppose it and why?

Chapter 22

Aggregate Supply and Aggregate Demand

After studying this chapter you will be able to:

◆ Explain what determines aggregate supply

◆ Explain what determines aggregate demand

◆ Explain macroeconomic equilibrium and the effects of changes in aggregate supply and aggregate demand on economic growth, inflation and the business cycle

◆ Explain UK economic growth, inflation and the business cycle by using the *AS–AD* model

◆ Explain the main schools of thought in macroeconomics today

Catching the Wave

If you want a good economic ride, you must catch the wave like a champion surfer. But economic waves are hard to read. What makes the economy ebb and flow in waves around its long-term growth trend? Why do the waves sometimes rise high and then crash, and sometimes rise and roll on a long high? How do the waves in the global economy spread around the world?

Aggregate Supply

The aggregate supply–aggregate demand model enables us to understand three features of macroeconomic performance:

1 Growth of potential GDP
2 Inflation
3 Business cycle fluctuations

The model uses the concepts of *aggregate* supply and *aggregate* demand to determine *real GDP* and the *price level* (GDP deflator). We begin by looking at the limits to production that influence aggregate supply.

Aggregate Supply Fundamentals

The *quantity of real GDP supplied* (*Y*) depends on three factors:

1 The quantity of labour (*L*)
2 The quantity of capital (*K*)
3 The state of technology (*T*)

The influence of these three factors on the quantity of real GDP supplied is described by the **aggregate production function**, which is written as the equation:

$$Y = F(L, K, T)$$

In words, the quantity of real GDP supplied is determined by (is a function *F* of) the quantities of labour and capital and the state of technology. The larger any *L, K* or *T*, the greater is *Y*.

At any given time, capital and the state of technology are fixed. They depend on decisions made in the past. The population is also fixed. But the quantity of labour is not fixed. It will depend on the decisions made by people and firms about the supply of and demand for labour.

The labour market can be in any one of three states: at full employment, above full employment or below full employment.

Even at full employment, there are always some people looking for jobs and some firms looking for people to hire. The reason is that there is a constant churning of the labour market. Every day, some jobs are destroyed as businesses reorganize or fail. Some jobs are created as new businesses start up or existing ones expand. Some workers decide, for any of a thousand personal reasons, to leave their jobs. And other people decide to start looking for a job. This constant churning in the labour market prevents unemployment from ever disappearing. The unemployment rate at full employment is called the **natural rate of unemployment**.

Another way to think about full employment is as a state of the labour market in which the quantity of labour demanded equals the quantity supplied. Firms demand labour only if it is profitable to do so. And the lower the wage rate, which is the cost of labour, the greater is the quantity of labour demanded. People supply labour only if doing so is the most valuable use of their time. And the higher the wage rate, which is the return to labour, the greater is the quantity of labour supplied. The wage rate that makes the quantity of labour demanded equal to the quantity of labour supplied is the equilibrium wage rate. At this wage rate, there is full employment.

The quantity of real GDP supplied at full employment is *potential GDP*. Potential GDP depends on the full employment quantity of labour, the quantity of capital and the state of technology.

Over the business cycle, employment fluctuates around full employment and real GDP fluctuates around potential GDP. Real GDP goes below potential GDP in a recession and above potential GDP in an expansion.

To study aggregate supply in different states of the labour market, we distinguish two time frames:

◆ Long-run aggregate supply
◆ Short-run aggregate supply

Long-run Aggregate Supply

The economy is constantly bombarded by events that move real GDP away from potential GDP and, equivalently, the unemployment rate away from the natural rate. Following such an event, forces operate to push real GDP back towards potential GDP and restore full employment. The **macroeconomic long run** is a time-frame that is sufficiently long for these forces to succeed so that real GDP equals potential GDP and full employment prevails.

The **long-run aggregate supply curve** is the relationship between the quantity of real GDP supplied and the price level when real GDP equals potential GDP. Figure 22.1 illustrates this relationship as the vertical line labelled *LAS*. Along the long-run aggregate supply curve, as the price level changes, real GDP remains at potential GDP, which in Figure 22.1 is £1,000 billion. The long-run aggregate supply curve is always vertical and located at potential GDP.

Figure 22.1

Long-run Aggregate Supply

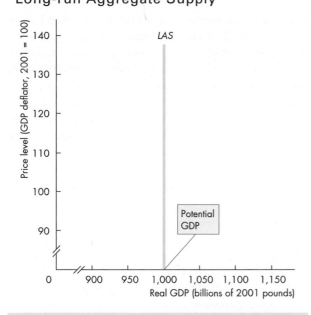

The long-run aggregate supply curve (*LAS*) shows the relationship between potential GDP and the price level. Potential GDP is independent of the price level, so the *LAS* curve is vertical at potential GDP.

The long-run aggregate supply curve is vertical because potential GDP is independent of the price level. The reason for this independence is that a movement along the long-run aggregate supply curve is accompanied by changes in *two* sets of prices: the prices of goods and services (the price level) and the prices of factors of production. Along the long-run aggregate supply curve, a 10 per cent increase in the prices of goods and services is matched by a 10 per cent increase in the money wage rate and the prices of other factors of production. That is, the price level, wage rate and other factor prices all change by the same percentage and so *relative prices* and the *real wage rate* are unchanged. When the price level changes but relative prices and the real wage rate remain constant, real GDP also remains constant.

Production at Liz's Meat Pies

You can see why real GDP remains constant when all prices change by the same percentage if you think about production decisions at Liz's meat pie plant. The plant is producing the quantity of pies that maximizes profit.

The plant can increase production but only by incurring a higher *marginal cost* (see Chapter 2, p. 35). So the firm has no incentive to change production.

Short-run Aggregate Supply

The **macroeconomic short run** is a period during which real GDP has fallen below or risen above potential GDP. At the same time, the unemployment rate has risen above or fallen below the natural rate of unemployment.

The **short-run aggregate supply curve** is the relationship between the quantity of real GDP supplied and the price level in the short run, when the money wage rate, the prices of other factors of production, and potential GDP remain constant.

Figure 22.2 (overleaf) illustrates this short-run aggregate supply curve as the upward-sloping curve labelled *SAS*. This curve is based on the short-run aggregate supply schedule, and each point on the aggregate supply curve corresponds to a row of the aggregate supply schedule. For example, point *A* on the short-run aggregate supply curve and row *A* of the schedule tell us that if the price level is 100, the quantity of real GDP supplied is £900 billion.

At point *C*, the price level is 110 and the quantity of real GDP supplied is $1,000 billion, which equals potential GDP. If the price level is higher than 110, real GDP exceeds potential GDP; if the price level is below 110, real GDP is less than potential GDP.

Back at Liz's Meat Pies

You can see why the short-run aggregate supply curve slopes upward by returning to Liz's meat pie plant. The plant produces the quantity of pies that maximizes profit. If the price of a pie rises and the money wage rate and Liz's other costs don't change, the *relative price* of a pie rises and Liz has an incentive to increase her production. The higher relative price of a pie covers the higher *marginal cost* of producing more pies, so Liz increases production.

Similarly when the price of a pie falls and the money wage rate and Liz's other costs don't change, the lower relative price of a pie is not sufficient to cover the marginal cost of a pie, so Liz decreases production.

Again, what's true for meat pie producers is true for the producers of all goods and services. So when the price level rises and the money wage rate and prices of other factors of production remain constant, the quantity of real GDP supplied increases.

Figure 22.2

Short-run Aggregate Supply

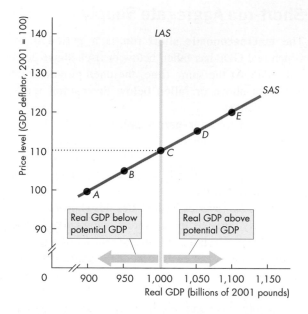

	Price level (GDP deflator)	Real GDP (billions of 2001 pounds)
A	100	900
B	105	950
C	110	1,000
D	115	1,050
E	120	1,100

The short-run aggregate supply curve shows the relationship between the quantity of real GDP supplied and the price level when the money wage rate, other resource prices and potential GDP remain the same. The short-run aggregate supply curve, *SAS*, is based on the schedule in the table.

The *SAS* curve is upward-sloping because firms' marginal costs increase as output increases, so a higher price is needed, relative to the prices of productive resources, to bring forth an increase in the quantity produced.

On the *SAS* curve, when the price level is 110, real GDP equals potential GDP (£1,000 billion). If the price level is greater than 110, real GDP exceeds potential GDP; if the price level is below 110, real GDP is less than potential GDP.

Movements along the *LAS* and *SAS* Curves

Figure 22.3 summarizes what you've just learned about the *LAS* and *SAS* curves. When the price level, the money wage rate, and the prices of other factors of production rise by the same percentage, relative price remains constant and real GDP remains at potential GDP. There is a *movement along* the *LAS* curve.

When the price level rises but the money wage rate and the prices of other factors of production remain the same, the quantity of real GDP supplied increases and there is a *movement along* the *SAS* curve.

Let's next study the influences that bring changes in aggregate supply.

Figure 22.3

Movements along the Aggregate Supply Curves

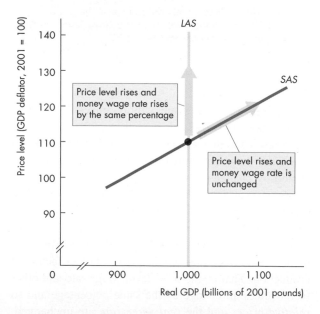

A rise in the price level with no change in the money wage rate and other resource prices brings an increase in the quantity of real GDP supplied and a movement along the short-run aggregate supply curve, *SAS*.

A rise in the price level with equal percentage increases in the money wage rate and other resource prices keeps the quantity of real GDP supplied constant at potential GDP and brings a movement along the long-run aggregate supply curve, *LAS*.

Changes in Aggregate Supply

You've just seen that a change in the price level brings a movement along the aggregate supply curves but does not change aggregate supply. Aggregate supply changes when any influence on production plans other than the price level changes. Let's begin by looking at factors that change potential GDP.

Changes in Potential GDP

When potential GDP changes, both long-run aggregate supply and short-run aggregate supply change. Potential GDP changes for three reasons:

◆ A change in the full-employment quantity of labour

◆ A change in the quantity of capital

◆ An advance in technology

An increase in the full-employment quantity of labour, an increase in the quantity of capital, or an advance in technology increases potential GDP. And an increase in potential GDP changes both the long-run aggregate supply and short-run aggregate supply.

Figure 22.4 shows these effects of a change in potential GDP. Initially, the long-run aggregate supply curve is LAS_0 and the short-run aggregate supply curve is SAS_0. If an increase in the quantity of capital or a technological advance increases potential GDP to $1,100 billion, long-run aggregate supply increases and the long-run aggregate supply curve shifts rightward to LAS_1. Short-run aggregate supply also increases, and the short-run aggregate supply curve shifts rightward to SAS_1.

Let's look more closely at the influences on potential GDP and the aggregate supply curves.

A Change in the Full-employment Quantity of Labour

A meat pie production plant that employs 100 workers produces more pies than an otherwise identical plant that employs 10 workers. The same is true for the economy as a whole. The larger the quantity of labour employed, the greater is GDP.

Over time, potential GDP increases because the labour force increases. But (with constant capital and technology) *potential* GDP increases only if the full-employment quantity of labour increases. Fluctuations in employment over the business cycle bring fluctuations in real GDP. But these changes in real GDP are fluctuations around potential GDP and long-run aggregate supply.

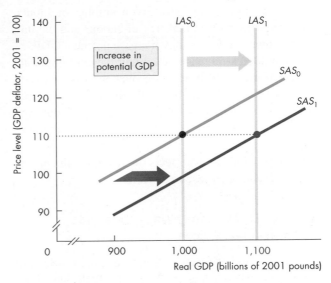

Figure 22.4

A Change in Potential GDP

An increase in potential GDP increases both long-run aggregate supply and short-run aggregate supply and shifts both aggregate supply curves rightward from LAS_0 to LAS_1 and from SAS_0 to SAS_1.

Change in the Quantity of Capital

A meat pie plant that has two production lines has more capital and produces more output than an otherwise identical plant that has one production line. For the economy, the larger the quantity of capital, the more productive is the workforce, the greater is its potential GDP. Potential GDP per person in capital-rich EU economies is vastly greater than that in capital-poor China and Russia.

Capital includes *human capital*. One pie production plant is managed by an economics graduate with an MBA and has a workforce with an average of 10 years of experience. This plant produces a much larger output than an otherwise identical plant that is managed by someone with no business training or experience and that has a young workforce that is new to bottling. The first plant has a greater amount of human capital than the second. For the economy as a whole, the larger the quantity of *human capital* – the skills that people have acquired in school and through on-the-job-training – the greater is potential GDP.

An Advance in Technology

A meat pie production plant that has a pre-computer age kitchen produces less than one that uses the latest robot technology. Technological change enables firms to produce more from any given amount of inputs. So even with fixed quantities of labour and capital, improvements in technology increase potential GDP.

Technological advances are by far the most important source of increased production over the past two centuries. Because of technological advances, one farmer in the United Kingdom today can feed 100 people and one auto worker can produce almost 14 cars and trucks in a year.

Let's now look at the effects of changes in the money wage rate and other resource prices.

Changes in the Money Wage Rate and Other Resource Prices

When the money wage rate or the money prices of other resources (such as the price of oil) change, short-run aggregate supply changes but long-run aggregate supply does not change.

Figure 22.5 shows the effect on aggregate supply of an increase in the money wage rate. Initially, the short-run aggregate supply curve is SAS_0. A rise in the money wage rate *decreases* short-run aggregate supply and shifts the short-run aggregate supply curve leftward to SAS_2.

The money wage rate (and other resource prices) affect short-run aggregate supply because they influence firms' costs. The higher the money wage rate, the higher are firms' costs and the smaller is the quantity that firms are willing to supply at each price level. So an increase in the money wage rate decreases short-run aggregate supply.

A change in the money wage rate does not change long-run aggregate supply because on the *LAS* curve, a change in the money wage rate is accompanied by an equal percentage change in the price level. With no change in *relative* prices, firms have no incentive to change production and real GDP remains constant at potential GDP. With no change in potential GDP, the long-run aggregate supply curve remains at *LAS*.

What Makes the Money Wage Rate Change?

The money wage rate can change for two reasons: departures from full employment and expectations about inflation. Unemployment above the natural rate puts downward pressure on the money wage rate, and unemployment below the natural rate puts upward pressure on the money wage rate. An expected increase in the inflation rate makes the money wage rate rise faster,

Figure 22.5

A Change in the Money Wage Rate

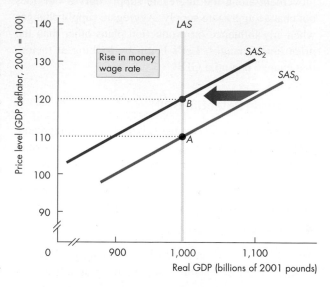

A rise in the money wage rate decreases short-run aggregate supply and shifts the short-run aggregate supply curve leftward from SAS_0 to SAS_2. A rise in the money wage rate does not change potential GDP, so the long-run aggregate supply curve does not shift.

and an expected decrease in the inflation rate slows the rate at which the money wage rate rises.

Review Quiz

1 If the price level rises and if the money wage rate also rises by the same percentage, what happens to the quantity of real GDP supplied? Along which aggregate supply curve does the economy move?

2 If the price level rises and the money wage rate remains constant, what happens to the quantity of real GDP supplied? Along which aggregate supply curve does the economy move?

3 If potential GDP increases, what happens to aggregate supply? Is there a shift of or a movement along the *LAS* curve and the *SAS* curve?

4 If the money wage rate rises and potential GDP remains the same, what happens to aggregate supply? Is there a shift of or a movement along the *LAS* curve and the *SAS* curve?

Aggregate Demand

The quantity of real GDP demanded is the sum of the real consumption expenditure (*C*), investment (*I*), government expenditures (*G*), and exports (*X*) minus imports (*M*). That is:

$$Y = C + I + G + X - M$$

The *quantity of real GDP demanded* is the total amount of final goods and services produced in the United Kingdom that people, businesses, governments and foreigners plan to buy.

These buying plans depend on many factors. The four main ones are:

1 The price level
2 Expectations
3 Fiscal policy and monetary policy
4 The world economy

We first focus on the relationship between the quantity of real GDP demanded and the price level. To study this relationship, we keep all other influences on buying plans the same and ask: How does the quantity of real GDP demanded vary as the price level varies?

The Aggregate Demand Curve

Other things remaining the same, the higher the price level, the smaller is the quantity of real GDP demanded. This relationship between the quantity of real GDP demanded and the price level is called **aggregate demand**. Aggregate demand is described by an aggregate demand schedule and an aggregate demand curve.

Figure 22.6 shows an aggregate demand curve (*AD*) and an aggregate demand schedule. Each point on the *AD* curve corresponds to a row of the schedule. For example, point *C'* on the *AD* curve and row *C'* of the schedule tell us that if the price level is 110, the quantity of real GDP demanded is $1,000 billion.

The aggregate demand curve slopes downward for two reasons:

◆ Wealth effect
◆ Substitution effects

Wealth Effect

When the price level rises but other things remain the same, *real* wealth decreases. Real wealth is the amount

Figure 22.6

Aggregate Demand

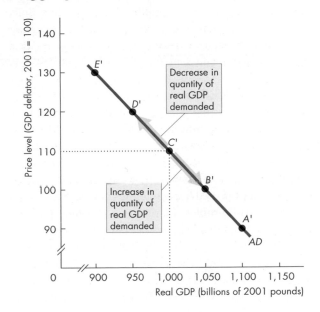

	Price level (GDP deflator)	Real GDP (billions of 2001 pounds)
A'	90	1,100
B'	100	1,050
C'	110	1,000
D'	120	950
E'	130	900

The aggregate demand curve (*AD*) is based on the aggregate demand schedule in the table. Each point *A'* to *E'* on the curve corresponds to the row in the table identified by the same letter. For example, when the price level is 110, the quantity of real GDP demanded is £1,000 billion, shown by point *C'* in the figure. A change in the price level with all other influences on aggregate buying plans remaining the same brings a change in the quantity of real GDP demanded and a movement along the *AD* curve.

of money in the bank, bonds, stocks and other assets that people own, measured not in dollars but in terms of the goods and services that this money, bonds and shares will buy.

People save and hold money, bonds and shares for many reasons. One reason is to build up funds for education expenses. Another reason is to build up enough funds to meet possible medical or other big bills. But the biggest reason is to build up enough funds to provide a retirement income.

If the price level rises, real wealth decreases. People then try to restore their wealth. To do so, they must increase saving and, equivalently, decrease current consumption. Such a decrease in consumption is a decrease in aggregate demand.

Maria's Wealth Effect

You can see how the wealth effect works by thinking about Maria's buying plans. Maria lives in Moscow, Russia. She has worked hard all summer and saved 20,000 rubles (the ruble is the currency of Russia), which she plans to spend attending graduate school when she has finished her economics degree. So Maria's wealth is 20,000 rubles. Maria has a part-time job, and her income from this job pays her current expenses. The price level in Russia rises by 100 percent, and now Maria needs 40,000 rubles to buy what 20,000 once bought. To try to make up some of the fall in value of her savings, Maria saves even more and cuts her current spending to the bare minimum.

Substitution Effects

When the price level rises and other things remain the same, interest rates rise. The reason is related to the wealth effect that you've just studied. A rise in the price level decreases the real value of the money in people's pockets and bank accounts. With a smaller amount of real money around, banks can get a higher interest rate on loans. But faced with higher interest rates, people and businesses delay plans to buy new capital and consumer durable goods and cut back on spending.

This substitution effect involves substituting goods in the future for goods in the present and is called an *intertemporal* substitution effect – a substitution across time. Saving increases to increase future consumption.

To see this intertemporal substitution effect more clearly, think about your own plan to buy a new computer. At an interest rate of 5 per cent a year, you might borrow £1,000 and buy the new machine you've been researching. But at an interest rate of 10 per cent a year, you might decide that the payments would be too high. You don't abandon your plan to buy the computer, but you decide to delay your purchase.

A second substitution effect works through international prices. When the UK price level rises and other things remain the same, UK-made goods and services become more expensive relative to foreign-made goods and services. This change in *relative prices* encourages people to spend less on UK-made items and more on foreign-made items. For example, if the UK price level rises relative to the Swedish price level, Swedes buy fewer UK-made cars (UK exports decrease) and Britons buy more Swedish-made cars (UK imports increase). GDP in the United Kingdom decreases.

Maria's Substitution Effects

In Moscow, Russia, Maria makes some substitutions. She was planning to trade in her old motor scooter and get a new one. But with a higher price level and faced with higher interest rates, she decides to make her old scooter last one more year. Also, with the prices of Russian goods sharply increasing, Maria substitutes a low-cost dress made in Malaysia for the Russian-made dress she had originally planned to buy.

Changes in the Quantity of Real GDP Demanded

When the price level rises and other things remain the same, the quantity of real GDP demanded decreases – a movement up the *AD* curve as shown by the arrow in Figure 22.6. When the price level falls and other things remain the same, the quantity of real GDP demanded increases – a movement down the *AD* curve.

We've now seen how the quantity of real GDP demanded changes when the price level changes. How do other influences on buying plans affect aggregate demand?

Changes in Aggregate Demand

A change in any factor that influences buying plans other than the price level brings a change in aggregate demand. The main factors are:

◆ Expectations
◆ Fiscal policy and monetary policy
◆ The world economy

Expectations

Expectations about future disposable income, inflation and profit influence people's decisions about spending today. An increase in expected future disposable income, other things remaining the same, increases the amount of consumption goods (especially items such as cars) that people plan to buy today and increases aggregate demand today.

An increase in the expected future inflation rate increases aggregate demand today because people decide to buy more goods and services at today's relatively lower prices. An increase in expected future profit increases the investment that firms plan to undertake today and increases aggregate demand today.

Fiscal Policy and Monetary Policy

The government's attempt to influence the economy by setting and changing taxes, making transfer payments, and purchasing goods and services is called **fiscal policy**. A tax cut or an increase in transfer payments – for example, unemployment benefits or welfare payments – increases aggregate demand. Both of these influences operate by increasing households' disposable income. **Disposable income** is aggregate income minus taxes plus transfer payments. The greater the disposable income, the greater is the quantity of consumption goods and services that households plan to buy and the greater is aggregate demand.

Government expenditures on goods and services are one component of aggregate demand. So if the government spends more on hospitals, schools and motorways, aggregate demand increases.

Monetary policy consists of changes in interest rates and in the quantity of money in the economy. The quantity of money in the United Kingdom is determined by the Bank of England and the banks (in a process described in Chapters 25 and 26). An increase in the quantity of money increases aggregate demand.

To see why money affects aggregate demand, imagine that the Bank of England borrows the army's helicopters, loads them with millions of new £5 notes and sprinkles these notes like confetti across the nation.

People gather the newly available money and plan to spend some of it. So the quantity of goods and services demanded increases. But people don't plan to spend all the new money. They save some of it and lend it to others through the banks. Interest rates fall, and with lower interest rates, people plan to buy more consumer durables and firms plan to increase their investment.

The World Economy

Two main influences that the world economy has on aggregate demand are the foreign exchange rate and foreign income. The *foreign exchange rate* is the amount of a foreign currency that you can buy with a pound. Other things remaining the same, a rise in the foreign exchange rate decreases aggregate demand. To see how the foreign exchange rate influences aggregate demand,

Figure 22.7

Changes in Aggregate Demand

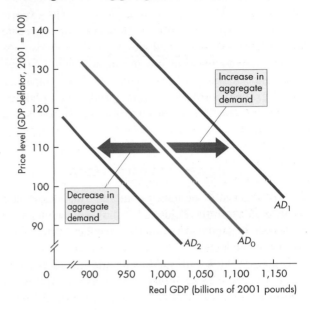

Aggregate demand

Decreases if:

◆ Expected future disposable income, inflation or profit decreases

◆ Fiscal policy decreases government expenditures on goods and services, increases taxes or decreases transfer payments

◆ Monetary policy decreases the quantity of money and increases interest rates

◆ The foreign exchange rate increases or foreign income decreases

Increases if:

◆ Expected future disposable income, inflation or profit increases

◆ Fiscal policy increases government expenditures on goods and services, decreases taxes or increases transfer payments

◆ Monetary policy increases the quantity of money and decreases interest rates

◆ The foreign exchange rate decreases or foreign income increases

suppose that £1 is worth 2,000 South Korean won. You can buy a Samsung TV (made in South Korea) that costs 400,000 won for £200. If the price of a Ferguson TV (made in the United Kingdom) is the same, you may be willing to buy the Ferguson TV.

Now suppose the foreign exchange rate rises to 2,200 won per pound. At 2,200 won per pound, the Samsung TV now costs only £18.82 and is now cheaper than the Ferguson TV. People around the world will switch from the UK-made TV to the South Korean-made TV. UK exports will decrease and UK imports will increase. UK aggregate demand will decrease.

An increase in foreign income increases UK exports and increases the UK aggregate demand – the aggregate demand for UK-produced goods and services. For example, an increase in income in the United States, Japan and Germany increases the American, Japanese and German consumers' and producers' planned expenditures on UK-produced consumption goods and capital goods.

Shifts of the Aggregate Demand Curve

When aggregate demand changes, the aggregate demand curve shifts. Figure 22.7 shows two changes in aggregate demand and summarizes the factors that bring about such changes.

Aggregate demand increases and the aggregate demand curve shifts rightward from AD_0 to AD_1 when expected future disposable income, inflation or profit increases; government expenditures increase; taxes are cut; transfer payments increase; the quantity of money increases and interest rates fall; the foreign exchange rate falls; or foreign income increases.

Aggregate demand decreases and the aggregate demand curve shifts leftward from AD_0 to AD_2 when expected future disposable income, inflation or profit decreases; government expenditures decrease; taxes increase; transfer payments decrease; the quantity of money decreases and interest rates rise; the foreign exchange rate rises; or foreign income decreases.

Review Quiz

1 What factors change and what factors remain the same when there is a movement along the aggregate demand curve?
2 Why does the aggregate demand curve slope downward?
3 How do changes in expectations about future income, inflation and profits change aggregate demand and shift the aggregate demand curve?
4 How do changes in fiscal policy and monetary policy change aggregate demand and shift the aggregate demand curve?
5 How do changes in foreign exchange rate and foreign incomes change aggregate demand and shift the aggregate demand curve?

Macroeconomic Equilibrium

The purpose of the aggregate supply–aggregate demand model is to explain changes in real GDP and the price level. To achieve this purpose, we combine aggregate supply and aggregate demand and determine macroeconomic equilibrium. There is a macroeconomic equilibrium for each of the time frames for aggregate supply: a long-run equilibrium and a short-run equilibrium. Long-run equilibrium is the state towards which the economy is heading. Short-run equilibrium is the normal state of the economy as it fluctuates around potential GDP.

We'll begin our study of macroeconomic equilibrium by looking at the short run.

Short-run Macroeconomic Equilibrium

The aggregate demand curve tells us the quantity of real GDP demanded at each price level, and the short-run aggregate supply curve tells us the quantity of real GDP supplied at each price level. **Short-run macroeconomic equilibrium** occurs when the quantity of real GDP demanded equals the short-run quantity of real GDP supplied at the point of intersection of the *AD* curve and the *SAS* curve. Figure 22.8 illustrates such an equilibrium at a price level of 110 and real GDP of £1,000 billion (point *C* and *C'*).

To see why this position is the equilibrium, think about what happens if the price level is something other than 110. Suppose, for example, that the price level is 120 and that real GDP is £1,100 billion (at point *E* on the *SAS* curve). The quantity of real GDP demanded is less than £1,100 billion, so firms are unable to sell all their output. Unwanted inventories (stocks) pile up, and firms cut both production and prices. Production and prices are cut until firms can sell all their output. This situation occurs only when real GDP is £1,000 billion and the price level is 110.

Now suppose that the price level is 100 and real GDP is £900 billion (at point *A* on the *SAS* curve). The quantity of real GDP demanded exceeds £900 billion, so firms are unable to meet demand for their output. Inventories (stock) decrease and customers clamour for goods and services. So firms increase production and raise prices. Production and prices increase until firms can meet demand. This situation occurs only when real GDP is £1,000 billion and the price level is 110.

Figure 22.8

Short-run Macroeconomic Equilibrium

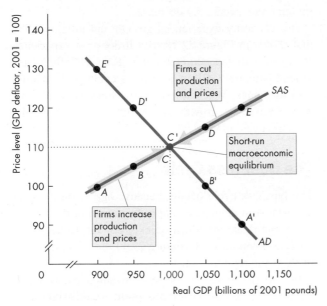

Long-run Macroeconomic Equilibrium

Long-run macroeconomic equilibrium occurs when real GDP equals potential GDP – equivalently, when the economy is on its *long-run* aggregate supply curve. Figure 22.9 shows *long-run* equilibrium, which occurs at the intersection of the aggregate demand curve and the long-run aggregate supply curve (the blue curves). Long-run equilibrium comes about because the money wage rate adjusts. Potential GDP and aggregate demand determine the price level, and the price level influences the money wage rate. In long-run equilibrium, the money wage rate has adjusted to put the (green) short-run aggregate supply curve through the long-run equilibrium point.

We'll look at this money wage adjustment process later in this chapter. But first, let's see how the *AS–AD* model helps us to understand economic growth and inflation.

Short-run macroeconomic equilibrium occurs when real GDP demanded equals real GDP supplied – at the intersection of the aggregate demand curve (*AD*) and the short-run aggregate supply curve (*SAS*). Here, such an equilibrium occurs at points *C* and *C'* where the price level is 110 and real GDP is £1,000 billion.

If the price level was 120 and real GDP was £1,100 billion (point *E*), firms would not be able to sell all their output. They would decrease production and cut prices. If the price level was 100 and real GDP was £900 billion (point *A*), people would not be able to buy all the goods and services they demanded. Firms would increase production and raise their prices.

Only when the price level is 110 and real GDP is £1,000 billion can firms sell all they produce and people buy all they demand. The economy is in short-run macroeconomic equilibrium.

Figure 22.9

Long-run Macroeconomic Equilibrium

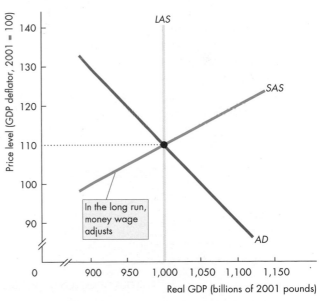

In long-run macroeconomic equilibrium, real GDP equals potential GDP. So long-run equilibrium occurs where the aggregate demand curve *AD* intersects the long-run aggregate supply curve *LAS*. In the long run, aggregate demand determines the price level and has no effect on real GDP. The money wage rate adjusts in the long run, so the *SAS* curve intersects the *LAS* curve at the long-run equilibrium price level.

In short-run macroeconomic equilibrium, the money wage rate is fixed. It does not adjust to bring full employment. So in the short run, real GDP can be greater than or less than potential GDP. But in the long run, the money wage rate does adjust and real GDP moves towards potential GDP. We are going to study this adjustment process. But first, let's look at the economy in long-run equilibrium.

Economic Growth and Inflation

Economic growth occurs because over time, the quantity of labour grows, capital is accumulated and technology advances. These changes increase potential GDP and shift the long-run aggregate supply curve rightward. Figure 22.10 shows such a shift. The growth rate of potential GDP is determined by the pace at which labour grows, capital is accumulated and technology advances.

Inflation occurs when, over time, aggregate demand increases by more than long-run aggregate supply. That is, inflation occurs if the aggregate demand curve shifts rightward by more than the rightward shift in the long-run aggregate supply curve. Figure 22.10 shows such shifts.

If aggregate demand increased at the same pace as long-run aggregate supply, we would experience real GDP growth with no inflation.

In the long run, the main influence on aggregate demand is the growth rate of the quantity of money.

Figure 22.10

Economic Growth and Inflation

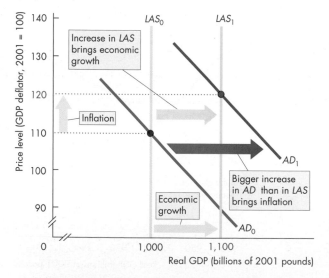

Economic growth is the persistent increase in potential GDP. Economic growth is shown as an ongoing rightward movement in the *LAS* curve. Inflation is the persistent rise in the price level. Inflation occurs when aggregate demand increases by more than the increase in long-run aggregate supply.

At times when the quantity of money increases rapidly, aggregate demand increases quickly and the inflation rate is high. When the growth rate of the quantity of money slows, other things remaining the same, the inflation rate eventually decreases.

Our economy experiences growth and inflation, like that shown in Figure 22.10. But it does not experience *steady* growth and *steady* inflation. Real GDP fluctuates around potential GDP in a business cycle, and inflation also fluctuates. When we study the business cycle, we ignore economic growth. By doing so, we can see the business cycle more clearly.

The Business Cycle

The business cycle occurs because aggregate demand and short-run aggregate supply fluctuate but the money wage rate does not adjust quickly enough to keep real GDP at potential GDP. Figure 22.11 shows three types of short-run equilibrium.

In part (a) there is a below full-employment equilibrium. A **below full-employment equilibrium** is a macroeconomic equilibrium in which potential GDP exceeds real GDP. The amount by which potential GDP exceeds real GDP is the *Okun gap* that you saw in Chapter 19 (p. 423). This gap is also called a **recessionary gap**, a name that reminds us that the gap has opened either because the economy has experienced a recession – a decrease in real GDP – or a growth recession – a slowdown in the growth rate associated with rising unemployment (see Chapter 21, pp. 458–459).

The below full-employment equilibrium illustrated in Figure 22.11(a) occurs where aggregate demand curve AD_0 intersects short-run aggregate supply curve SAS_0 at a real GDP of £980 billion and a price level of 110. The recessionary gap is £20 billion. The UK economy was in a situation similar to that shown in Figure 22.11(a) in 1980–1981 and again in 1990–1992. In those years, real GDP was less than potential GDP.

Figure 22.11(b) is an example of long-run equilibrium. *Long-run equilibrium* is a macroeconomic equilibrium in which real GDP equals potential GDP. In this example, the equilibrium occurs where the aggregate demand curve AD_1 intersects the short-run aggregate supply curve SAS_1 at an actual and potential GDP of £1,000 billion. The economy was in a situation such as that shown in Figure 22.11(b) in 2003.

Figure 22.11(c) illustrates an above full-employment equilibrium. An **above full-employment equilibrium** is a macroeconomic equilibrium in which real GDP exceeds potential GDP. The amount by which real GDP exceeds potential GDP is called an **inflationary gap**. This name reminds us that a gap has opened up between real GDP and potential GDP and that this gap creates inflationary pressure – a tendency for the price level to rise more quickly.

The above full-employment equilibrium shown in Figure 22.11(c) occurs where the aggregate demand curve AD_2 intersects the short-run aggregate supply curve SAS_2 at a real GDP of £1,020 billion and a price level of 110. There is an inflationary gap of £20 billion. The UK economy was last in a situation similar to that depicted in Figure 22.11(c) in 1987–1990.

The economy moves from one type of equilibrium to another as a result of fluctuations in aggregate demand and in short-run aggregate supply. These fluctuations produce fluctuations in real GDP and the price level. Figure 22.11(d) shows how real GDP fluctuates around potential GDP.

Let's now look at some of the sources of these fluctuations around potential GDP.

Figure 22.11

The Business Cycle

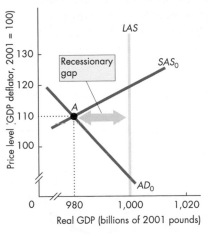

(a) Below full-employment equilibrium

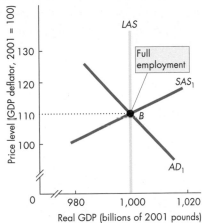

(b) Long-run equilibrium

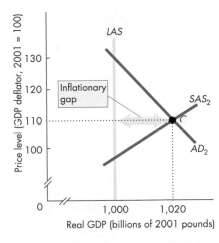

(c) Above full-employment equilibrium

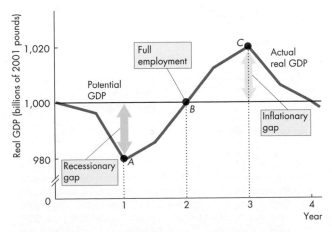

(d) Fluctuations in real GDP

Part (a) shows a below full-employment equilibrium in year 1, part (b) shows long-run equilibrium in year 2, and part (c) shows an above full-employment equilibrium in year 3. Part (d) shows how real GDP fluctuates around potential GDP in a business cycle.

In year 1, a recessionary gap exists and the economy is at point *A*, in parts (a) and (d). In year 2, the economy is in long-run equilibrium and the economy is at point *B* in parts (b) and (d). In year 3, an inflationary gap exists and the economy is at point *C* in parts (c) and (d).

Fluctuations in Aggregate Demand

One reason real GDP fluctuates around potential GDP is that aggregate demand fluctuates. Let's see what happens when aggregate demand increases.

Figure 22.12(a) shows an economy in long-run equilibrium. The aggregate demand curve is AD_0, the short-run aggregate supply curve is SAS_0, and the long-run aggregate supply curve is LAS. Real GDP equals potential GDP at £1,000 billion, and the price level is 110.

Now suppose that the world economy expands and that the demand for UK-made goods increases in Japan, Canada and the United States. The increase in UK exports increases aggregate demand and the aggregate demand curve shifts rightward from AD_0 to AD_1 in Figure 22.12(a).

Faced with an increase in demand, firms increase production and raise prices. Real GDP increases to £1,050 billion and the price level rises to 115. The economy is now in an above full-employment equilibrium. Real

GDP exceeds potential GDP, and there is an inflationary gap. Such a situation is examined in *Reading Between the Lines* in pp. 498–499.

The increase in aggregate demand has increased the prices of all goods and services. Faced with higher prices, firms have increased their output rates. At this stage, prices of goods and services have increased but the money wage rate has not changed. (Recall that as we move along a short-run aggregate supply curve, the money wage rate is constant.)

Because the price level has increased and the money wage rate is unchanged, workers have experienced a fall in the buying power of their wages and firms' profits have increased. In these circumstances, workers demand higher wages and firms, anxious to maintain their employment and output levels, meet those demands. If firms do not raise the money wage rate, they will either lose workers or have to hire less productive ones.

As the money wage rate rises, the short-run aggregate supply curve begins to shift leftward. In Figure 22.12(b), the short-run aggregate supply curve shifts

---

Figure 22.12

An Increase in Aggregate Demand

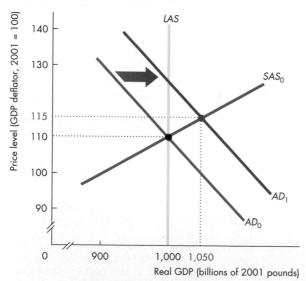

(a) Short-run effect

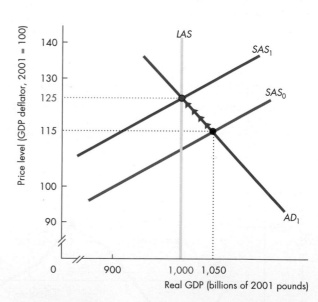

(b) Long-run effect

An increase in aggregate demand shifts the aggregate demand curve from AD_0 to AD_1. In the short run (part a), real GDP increases from £1,000 billion to £1,050 billion and the price level rises from 110 to 115. The economy has moved up along the SAS curve. In this situation, an inflationary gap exists.

In the long run (part b), with an inflationary gap, the money wage rate starts to rise. The short-run aggregate supply curve starts to shift leftward from SAS_0 to SAS_1. As the SAS curve shifts leftward, it intersects the aggregate demand curve AD_1 at higher price levels and real GDP decreases. Eventually, the price level rises to 125 and real GDP decreases to £1,000 billion – potential GDP.

from SAS_0 towards SAS_1. The rise in the money wage rate and the shift in the SAS curve produce a sequence of new equilibrium positions. Along the adjustment path, real GDP decreases and the price level rises. The economy moves up along its aggregate demand curve as the arrowheads show.

Eventually, the money wage rate rises by the same percentage as the price level. At this time, the aggregate demand curve AD_1 intersects SAS_1 at a new long-run equilibrium. The price level has risen to 125, and real GDP is back where it started, at potential GDP.

A decrease in aggregate demand has similar but opposite effects to those of an increase in aggregate demand. That is, a decrease in aggregate demand shifts the aggregate demand curve leftward. Real GDP decreases to less than potential GDP and a recessionary gap emerges. Firms cut prices. The lower price level increases the purchasing power of wages and increases firms' costs relative to their output prices because the money wage rate remains unchanged. Eventually, the money wage rate falls and the short-run aggregate supply curve shifts rightward. But the money wage rate changes slowly, so real GDP slowly returns to potential GDP and the price level falls slowly.

Let's now work out how real GDP and the price level change when aggregate supply changes.

Fluctuations in Aggregate Supply

Fluctuations in short-run aggregate supply can bring fluctuations in real GDP around potential GDP. Suppose that initially, real GDP equals potential GDP. Then there is a large but temporary rise in the price of oil. What happens to real GDP and the price level?

Figure 22.13 answers this question. The aggregate demand curve is AD_0, the short-run aggregate supply curve is SAS_0 and the long-run aggregate supply curve is LAS. Equilibrium real GDP is £1,000 billion, which equals potential GDP, and the price level is 110. Then the price of oil rises. Faced with higher energy and transportation costs, firms decrease production. Short-run aggregate supply decreases and the short-run aggregate supply curve shifts leftward to SAS_1. The price level rises to 120 and real GDP decreases to £950 billion.

Because real GDP decreases, the economy experiences recession. Because the price level increases, the economy experiences inflation. A combination of recession and inflation, called *stagflation*, actually occurred in the United Kingdom in the mid-1970s following a jump in the price of oil.

Figure 22.13

A Decrease in Aggregate Supply

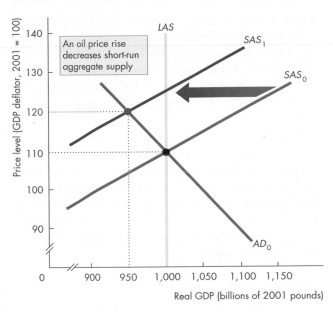

An increase in the price of oil decreases short-run aggregate supply and shifts the short-run aggregate supply curve leftward from SAS_0 to SAS_1. Real GDP decreases from £1,000 billion to £950 billion, and the price level increases from 110 to 120. The economy experiences both recession and inflation – a situation know as stagflation.

Review Quiz

1　Does economic growth result from increases in aggregate demand, short-run aggregate supply or long-run aggregate supply?
2　Does inflation result from increases in aggregate demand, short-run aggregate supply or long-run aggregate supply?
3　Describe the three types of short-run macroeconomic equilibrium.
4　How do fluctuations in aggregate demand and short-run aggregate supply bring fluctuations in real GDP around potential GDP?

Let's put our new knowledge of aggregate supply and aggregate demand to work and see how we can explain recent macroeconomic performance in the United Kingdom.

Economic Growth, Inflation and Cycles in the UK Economy

The economy is continually changing. If you imagine the economy as a video, then an aggregate supply–aggregate demand figure such as Figure 22.13 is a freeze-frame. We're going to run the video – an instant replay – but keep our finger on the freeze-frame button and look at some important parts of the previous action. Let's run the video from 1963.

Figure 22.14 shows the state of the economy in 1963 at the point where the aggregate demand curve AD_{63} and the short-run aggregate supply curve SAS_{63} intersect. Real GDP was £395 billion and the price level was 8. By 2003, the economy had reached the intersection aggregate demand curve AD_{03} and short-run aggregate supply curve SAS_{03}. Real GDP was £1,035 billion and the price level was 106.

The path traced by the blue and red dots between 1963 and 2003 in Figure 22.14 shows three key features:

◆ Economic growth

◆ Inflation

◆ Business cycles

Economic Growth

The rightward movement of the points in Figure 22.14 shows economic growth. The faster the growth rate, the larger is the horizontal distance between successive dots. The force generating economic growth is an increase in long-run aggregate supply, which occurs because the quantity of labour grows, we accumulate physical capital and human capital and our technologies advance.

Figure 22.14

Aggregate Supply and Aggregate Demand: 1963–2003

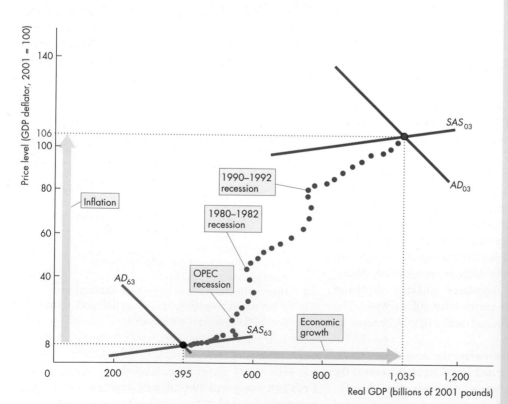

Each point indicates the price level and real GDP in a given year. In 1963, these variables were determined by the intersection of AD_{63} and SAS_{63}. Each point is generated by the gradual shifting of the AD and SAS curves. By 2003, these curves were AD_{03} and SAS_{03}. Real GDP grew and the price level increased. But growth and inflation did not proceed smoothly.

Real GDP grew quickly and inflation was moderate in the 1960s; real GDP growth sagged in 1974–1975 and again in 1980–1982. The 1974–1975 slowdown was the aftermath of the OPEC oil price rise in 1973–1974. The 1980–1982 recession caused by a sharp slow-down in the growth of aggregate demand, which resulted from tough monetary policy. Inflation was rapid during the 1970s but slowed after the 1980–1982 recession. The period from 1982 to 1989 was one of strong, persistent expansion. After the 1990–1992 recession, the economy returned to steady growth.

Source: Office for National Statistics.

Inflation

The price level rises over the years – shown in Figure 22.14 by the upward movement of the points. The more rapid the inflation rate, the larger is the vertical distance between successive dots in the figure. The main force generating the persistent increase in the price level is a tendency for aggregate demand to increase at a faster pace than the increase in long-run aggregate supply. All of the factors that increase aggregate demand and shift the aggregate demand curve influence the pace of inflation. But one factor – the growth of the quantity of money – is the main source of *persistent* increases in aggregate demand and persistent inflation.

Business Cycles

Over the years, the economy grows and shrinks in cycles – shown in Figure 22.14 by the wavelike pattern made by the points, with recessions highlighted in red. The cycles arise because both the expansion of short-run aggregate supply and the growth of aggregate demand do not proceed at a fixed, steady pace. Although the economy has cycles, recessions do not usually follow quickly on the heels of their predecessors; "double-dip" recessions like the one in the cartoon are rare.

The Evolving Economy: 1963–2003

During the 1960s, real GDP growth was rapid and inflation was low. This was a period of rapid increases in aggregate supply and of moderate increases in aggregate demand.

The 1970s were years of rapid inflation and slow growth. The major sources of these developments were a series of massive oil price increases that slowed the rightward shift of the long-run aggregate supply curve and rapid increases in the quantity of money that shifted the aggregate demand curve rightward. The short-run aggregate supply curve shifted leftward at a faster pace than the aggregate demand shifted rightward.

The rest of the 1970s saw high inflation – the price level increased quickly – and only moderate growth in real GDP. By 1979, inflation was a major problem and the Bank of England decided to take strong action against inflation. The Bank of England permitted interest rates to rise to previously unknown levels. Consequently, aggregate demand decreased. The decrease in aggregate demand put the UK economy in a deep recession.

"Please stand by for a series of tones. The first indicates the official end of the recession, the second indicates prosperity, and the third the return of the recession."

The economy began to expand after 1982, with improved aggregate supply policies, which increased potential GDP. Steady growth moved the UK economy to above full-employment in 1987 to 1990. Inflation increased during this period and the UK economy was in this condition when a decrease in aggregate demand led to the 1990–1992 recession. The economy again embarked on a path of expansion over the rest of the 1990s up until 2003.

Review Quiz

1 How does the *AS–AD* model explain the economic growth and inflation of the past forty years?
2 How does the *AS–AD* model explain the business cycles of the 1970s, 1980s and 1990s?

You've now reviewed the *AS–AD* model and seen how that model can provide an account of the forces that move real GDP and the price level to bring economic growth, inflation and the business cycle. The account that we've just given is the consensus account. But it isn't the only one. We're going to end this chapter by using the *AS–AD* model as a framework for a quick look at the alternative schools of thought in macroeconomics.

...onomic Schools of ...t

Macroeconomics is an active field of research and much remains to be learned about the forces that make our economy grow and fluctuate. There is a greater degree of consensus and certainty about economic growth and inflation – the longer term trends in real GDP and the price level – than there is about the business cycle – the short-term fluctuations in these variables. Here, we'll look only at differences of view about short-term fluctuations.

The aggregate supply–aggregate demand model that you've studied in this chapter provides a good foundation for understanding the range of views that macroeconomists hold about this topic. But what you will learn here is just a first glimpse at the scientific controversy and debate. We'll return to these issues at various later points in the text and deepen your appreciation of the alternative views.

Classification usually requires simplification. And classifying macroeconomists is no exception to this general rule. The classification that we'll use here is simple, but it is not misleading. We're going to divide macroeconomists into three broad schools of thought and examine the views of each group in turn. The groups are:

◆ The Keynesian View
◆ The Classical View
◆ The Monetarist View

The Keynesian View

A **Keynesian** macroeconomist believes that left alone, the economy would rarely operate at full employment and that to achieve and maintain full employment, active help from fiscal policy and monetary policy is required. The term "Keynesian" derives from the name of one of the twentieth century's most famous economists, John Maynard Keynes.

The Keynesian view is based on beliefs about the forces that determine aggregate demand and short-run aggregate supply.

Aggregate Demand Fluctuations

In the Keynesian view, expectations are the most significant influence on aggregate demand. And expectations are based on herd instinct or, what Keynes himself called "animal spirits". A wave of pessimism about future profit prospects can lead to a fall in aggregate demand and plunge the economy into recession.

Aggregate Supply Response

In the Keynesian view, the money wage rate that lies behind the short-run aggregate supply curve is extremely sticky downward. Basically, the money wage rate doesn't fall. So if there is a recessionary gap, there is no automatic mechanism for getting rid of it. If it were to happen, a fall in the money wage rate would increase short-run aggregate supply and restore full employment. But the money wage rate doesn't fall, so the economy remains stuck in recession.

A modern version of the Keynesian view known as the **new Keynesian** view holds that not only is the money wage rate sticky but that prices of goods and services are also sticky. With a sticky price level, the short-run aggregate supply curve is horizontal at a fixed price level.

Policy Response Needed

The Keynesian view calls for fiscal policy and monetary policy to actively offset the changes in aggregate demand that bring recession. By stimulating aggregate demand in a recession, full employment can be restored.

The Classical View

A **classical** macroeconomist believes that the economy is self-regulating and that it is always at full employment. The fluctuations that occur are efficient responses of a well-functioning market economy that is bombarded by shocks, mainly coming from the uneven pace of technological change.

The term "classical" derives from the name of the founding school of economics that includes Adam Smith, David Ricardo, and John Stuart Mill.

Like the Keynesian view, the classical view can be understood in terms of beliefs, different from those of a Keynesian, about aggregate demand and aggregate supply.

Aggregate Demand Fluctuations

In the classical view, technological change is the most significant influence on both aggregate demand and aggregate supply. For this reason, classical macroeconomists don't use the *AS–AD* framework. But their views can be interpreted in this framework. A technological change that increases the productivity of capital brings an increase in aggregate demand because firms increase their expenditure on new plant and equipment. A technological change that lengthens the useful life of existing capital decreases the demand for new capital, which decreases aggregate demand.

Aggregate Supply Response

In the classical view, the money wage rate that lies behind the short-run aggregate supply curve is instantly and completely flexible. The money wage rate adjusts so quickly to maintain equilibrium in the labour market that real GDP always adjusts to equal potential GDP.

Potential GDP itself fluctuates for the same reasons that aggregate demand fluctuates – technological change. When the pace of technological change is rapid, potential GDP increases quickly and so does real GDP. And when the pace of technological change slows, so does the growth rate of potential GDP.

Classical Policy

The classical view of policy emphasizes the potential for taxes to stunt incentives and create inefficiency. By minimizing the disincentive effects of taxes, employment, investment and technological advance are at their efficient levels and the economy expands at an appropriate and rapid pace.

The Monetarist View

A **monetarist** is a macroeconomist who believes that the economy is self-regulating and that it will normally operate at full employment, provided that monetary policy is not erratic and that the pace of money growth is kept steady.

The term "monetarist" was coined by an outstanding twentieth century economist, Karl Brunner, to describe his own views and those of Milton Friedman.

The monetarist view can be interpreted in terms of beliefs about the forces that determine aggregate demand and short-run aggregate supply.

Aggregate Demand Fluctuations

In the monetarist view, the quantity of money is the most significant influence on aggregate demand. And the quantity of money is determined by the Bank of England. If the Bank of England keeps money growing at a steady pace, aggregate demand fluctuations will be minimized and the economy will operate close to full employment. But if the Bank of England decreases the

quantity of money or even just slows its growth rate too abruptly, the economy will go into recession. In the monetarist view, all recessions result from inappropriate monetary policy.

Aggregate Supply Response

The monetarist view of short-run aggregate supply is the same as the Keynesian view – the money wage rate is sticky. If the economy is in recession, it will take an unnecessarily long time for it to return unaided to full employment.

Monetarist Policy

The monetarist view of policy is the same as the classical view on fiscal policy. Taxes should be kept low to avoid disincentive effects that decrease potential GDP. Provided that the quantity of money is kept on a steady growth path, no active stabilization is needed to offset changes in aggregate demand.

The Way Ahead

In the chapters that follow, you're going to encounter Keynesian, classical, and monetarist views again. The popular way to study macroeconomics today is to begin with the classical model and that's what we do in the next chapter. Then we study the Keynesian model. From there, we study money and inflation and lay the foundation for a deeper look at the sources of macroeconomic fluctuations and economic growth.

And we finish with a closer look at fiscal policies and monetary policies that try to achieve faster growth, stable prices and a smoother cycle. This order for learning macroeconomics was not always followed. And some lecturers today prefer to move to a study of economic growth after the classical model. That sequence can be followed in this text. To do so, the reader will jump to Chapter 30 and then backtrack through money, inflation and business cycles.

The *AS–AD* model explains economic growth, inflation and the business cycle. The *AS–AD* model enables us to keep our eye on the big picture, but it lacks detail. It does not tell us as much as we need to know about the deeper forces that lie behind aggregate supply and aggregate demand. The chapters that follow begin to fill in some details on the forces that influence aggregate demand. But first take a look at *Reading Between the Lines* on pp. 498–499, which shows how the *AS–AD* model illuminates the expansion of the UK economy during 2003 and the first quarter of 2004.

Reading Between the Lines
Aggregate Supply and Aggregate Demand in Action

The Times, 1 July 2004

Economy gives signs of robust condition

Gary Duncan

Britain's economy grew at its fastest annual pace for nearly four years in the first quarter in a healthier performance than previously believed, revised official figures showed.

In growth that was both stronger and better balanced than shown in earlier estimates, the economy expanded by 3.4 per cent from a year earlier, up from a previous figure of 3 per cent, to give its best showing since the autumn of 2000.

The stronger first performance came despite cuts in the strength of household spending, implying that the economy has become less dependent upon the consumer boom than was thought.

With business investment also revised up sharply, economists said yesterday's rejig of the national accounts pointed to more balanced growth that should prove more sustainable than an expansion propelled by the consumer.

Business investment is now thought to have jumped by 1.9 per cent in the first three months of the year, compared with an initial estimate showing a rise of just 0.3 per cent.

Most analysts agreed that with the more potent growth now reported likely to have eaten up much of the limited spare capacity left in the economy . . .

The Essence of the Story

◆ Real GDP in the first quarter of 2004 was 3.4 per cent higher than the same quarter in 2003.

◆ The stronger growth resulted from stronger growth in investment expenditure, which increased by 1.9 per cent in the first quarter.

◆ The more rapid growth has probably left the economy with little spare capacity.

Economic Analysis

◆ Figure 1 shows the real GDP growth rate from the first quarter of 2000 to the first quarter of 2004. You can see that the growth rate increased during 2003 and the first quarter of 2004.

◆ Figure 2 shows the economy in the first quarter of 2003. The long-run aggregate supply curve was LAS_{03} with potential GDP at £257 billion (per quarter).

◆ The short-run aggregate supply curve was SAS_{03}, the aggregate demand curve was AD_{03} and equilibrium real GDP was £255 billion.

◆ There was a recessionary gap in the first quarter of 2003 of £2 billion or a bit less than 1 per cent of potential GDP.

◆ Figure 3 shows the changes in the economy during the year to the first quarter of 2004. The long-run aggregate supply curve shifted rightward to LAS_{04} with potential GDP at £264 billion. This increase in potential GDP represents an economic growth rate of 2.7 per cent a year.

◆ The short-run aggregate supply curve shifted to SAS_{04}, the aggregate demand curve shifted to AD_{04} and equilibrium real GDP increased to £264 billion.

◆ In the first quarter of 2004, real GDP equalled potential GDP – a situation described in the news article as one with little "spare capacity".

◆ If aggregate demand grows faster than potential GDP during 2004, an inflationary gap might arise.

◆ The news article reports a strong increase in investment, which will eventually speed economic growth. But this effect comes over a longer period and does not contribute much to increased aggregate supply in the immediate future.

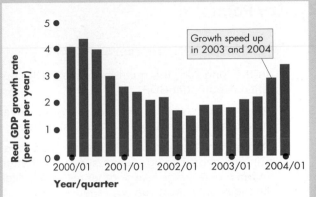

Figure 1 Real GDP growth rate: 2000–2004

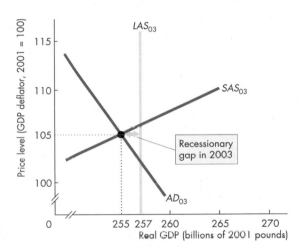

Figure 2 The economy in 2003 first quarter

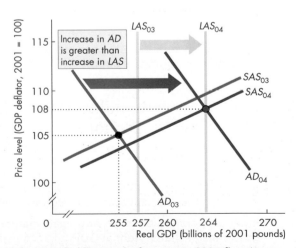

Figure 3 The changes in the year to 2004 first quarter

Summary

Key Points

Aggregate Supply (pp. 480–484)

◆ In the long run, the quantity of real GDP supplied is potential GDP.

◆ In the short run, a rise in the price level increases the quantity of real GDP supplied.

◆ A change in potential GDP changes both long-run and short-run aggregate supply. A change in the money wage rate or other resource prices changes only short-run aggregate supply.

Aggregate Demand (pp. 485–488)

◆ A rise in the price level decreases the quantity of real GDP demanded because of wealth and substitution effects.

◆ Changes in expectations, fiscal policy, monetary policy and the world economy change aggregate demand.

Macroeconomic Equilibrium

(pp. 488–493)

◆ Aggregate demand and short-run aggregate supply determine real GDP and the price level.

◆ In the long run, real GDP equals potential GDP and aggregate demand determines the price.

◆ Economic growth occurs because potential GDP increases and inflation occurs because aggregate demand grows more quickly than potential GDP.

◆ Business cycles occur because aggregate demand and aggregate supply fluctuate.

Economic Growth, Inflation and Cycles in the UK Economy

(pp. 494–495)

◆ Potential GDP grew fastest during the 1960s, mid-1980s, and late 1990s and 2000s, and slowest during the late 1970s, early 1980s and 1990s.

◆ Inflation persists because aggregate demand grows faster than potential GDP.

◆ Business cycles occur because aggregate supply and aggregate demand change at an uneven pace.

Macroeconomic Schools of Thought

(pp. 496–497)

◆ Keynesian economists believe that full employment can be achieved only with active policy.

◆ Classical economists believe that the economy is self-regulating and always at full employment.

◆ Monetarist economists believe that recessions result from inappropriate monetary policy.

Key Figures

Key Terms

Problems

*1 The following events occur that influence the economy of Toughtimes:

i A deep recession hits the world economy.

ii Oil prices rise sharply.

iii Businesses expect huge losses in the near future.

a Explain the separate effects of each of these events on real GDP and the price level in Toughtimes, starting from a position of long-run equilibrium.

b Explain the combined effects of these events on real GDP and the price level in Toughtimes, starting from a position of long-run equilibrium.

c Explain what the Toughtimes government and central bank can do to overcome the problems faced by the economy.

2 The following events occur that influence the economy of Coolland:

i A strong expansion in the world economy.

ii Businesses expect huge profits in the near future.

iii The Coolland government cuts its expenditures on goods and services.

a Explain the separate effects of each of these events on real GDP and the price level in Coolland, starting from a position of long-run equilibrium.

b Explain the combined effects of these events on real GDP and the price level in Coolland, starting from a position of long-run equilibrium.

c Explain why the Coolland government or central bank might want to take action to influence the Coolland economy.

*3 The economy of Mainland has the following aggregate demand and supply schedules:

Price level	Real GDP demanded	Real GDP supplied in the short run
	(billions of 2001 euros)	
90	450	350
100	400	400
110	350	450
120	300	500
130	250	550
140	200	600

*Solutions to odd-numbered problems are available on *Parkin Interactive*.

a In a figure, plot the aggregate demand curve and short-run aggregate supply curve.

b What are the values of real GDP and the price level in Mainland in a short-run macroeconomic equilibrium?

c Mainland's potential GDP is €500 billion. Plot the long-run aggregate supply curve in the same figure in which you answered part (a).

4 The economy of Miniland has the following aggregate demand and supply schedules:

Price level	Real GDP demanded	Real GDP supplied in the short run
	(billions of 2001 euros)	
90	600	150
100	500	200
110	400	250
120	300	300
130	200	350
140	100	400

a In a graph, plot the aggregate demand curve and short-run aggregate supply curve.

b What are the values of real GDP and the price level in Miniland in a short-run macroeconomic equilibrium?

c Miniland's potential GDP is €250 billion. Plot the long-run aggregate supply curve in the same figure in which you answered part (a).

*5 In problem 3, aggregate demand is increased by €100 billion. How do real GDP and the price level change in the short run?

6 In problem 4, aggregate demand is decreased by €150 billion. How do real GDP and the price level change in the short run?

*7 In problem 3, aggregate supply decreases by €100 billion. What now is the short-run macroeconomic equilibrium?

8 In problem 4, aggregate supply increases by €150 billion. What now is the short-run macroeconomic equilibrium?

*9 In the economy shown in the graph (overleaf), initially the short-run aggregate supply is SAS_0 and aggregate demand is AD_0. Then some events change aggregate demand and the aggregate demand curve shifts rightward to AD_1. Later, some other events change aggregate supply and shift the short-run aggregate supply curve leftward to SAS_1.

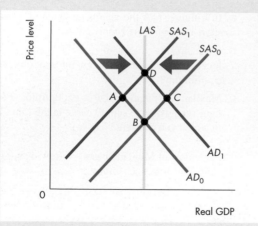

a What is the equilibrium point after the change in aggregate demand?

b What is the equilibrium point after the change in aggregate supply?

c What events could have changed aggregate demand from AD_0 to AD_1?

d What events could have changed aggregate supply from SAS_0 to SAS_1?

10 In the economy shown in the figure, initially long-run aggregate supply is LAS_0, short-run aggregate supply is SAS_0, and aggregate demand is AD. Then some events change aggregate supply and the aggregate supply curves shift rightward to LAS_1 and SAS_1.

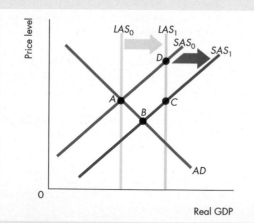

a What is the equilibrium point after the change in aggregate supply?

b What events could have changed long-run aggregate supply from LAS_0 to LAS_1?

c What events could have changed short-run aggregate supply from SAS_0 to SAS_1?

d After the increase in aggregate supply, is the real GDP greater than or less than potential GDP?

e What change in aggregate demand will make real GDP equal to potential GDP?

Will there be a recessionary gap or an inflationary gap? By how much?

Critical Thinking

1 After you have studied *Reading Between the Lines* on pp. 498–499, answer the following questions.

   a Describe the growth of the UK economy during the period between 2000 and the first quarter of 2004.

   b Did the UK have a recessionary gap, an inflationary gap or full employment in the first quarter of 2003?

   c Use the *AS–AD* model to illustrate the UK economy during the first years of the 2000s.

   d Suppose that aggregate demand continues to expand rapidly through the rest of 2004 and that the Bank of England does not act strongly enough to dampen the expansion. Illustrate using an *AS–AD* figure the state of the economy at the beginning of 2005. Indicate whether there is full employment, a recessionary gap or an inflationary gap.

   e Suppose that aggregate demand continues to expand rapidly through the rest of 2004 but that the Bank of England *does* act strongly enough to dampen the expansion. Illustrate using an *AS–AD* figure the state of the economy at the beginning of 2005. Indicate whether there is full employment, a recessionary gap or an inflationary gap.

Web Exercises

Use the links on *Parkin Interactive* to work the following exercises.

1 Visit the Website of the Office for National Statistics to obtain the data on real GDP and the price level for the United Kingdom. Then:

   a Use the data to update Figure 22.14.

   b What has happened to real GDP and the price level?

   c What has happened to aggregate demand and short-run aggregate supply since 2003?

   d Use this information to assess whether real GDP in 2004 was above, below or at potential GDP.

2 Find data on recent change in and forecasts of real GDP and the price level in the European Union. Then:

   a What is your forecast of EU real GDP for the coming year?

   b What is your forecast of the EU price level for the coming year?

   c What is your forecast of the EU real GDP growth rate for the coming year?

   d What is your forecast of the EU inflation rate for the coming year?

Chapter 23

At Full Employment: The Classical Model

After studying this chapter you will be able to:

◆ Describe the purpose of the classical model

◆ Describe the relationship between the quantity of labour employed and real GDP

◆ Explain what determines the demand for labour and the supply of labour and how labour market equilibrium determines employment, the real wage rate and potential GDP

◆ Derive the long-run and short-run aggregate supply curves

◆ Explain what determines the natural rate of unemployment

◆ Use the classical model to explain the forces that change potential GDP

Our Economy's Gyroscope

The progress of a liner through the ocean is like economic growth that brings an ever rising standard of living. The rocking and rolling of the liner as it is battered by waves and winds is like the alternation of the economy between recessionary gap and inflationary gap over the business cycle. But the ship has a gyroscope that helps to keep it stable and avoid too much rocking and rolling for the passengers' safety and comfort. The ship's gyroscope is like the forces that prevent the economy from fluctuating too wildly and keep returning it to its forward path. These are the forces that determine full-employment economy that you study in this chapter.

The Classical Model: A Preview

Economists have made progress in understanding how the economy works by dividing the variables that describe macroeconomic performance into two lists:

1 Real variables

2 Nominal variables

Real variables describe the physical state of the economy and tell us what is *really* happening to economic well-being. The real variables include real GDP, employment and unemployment, the real wage rate, consumption, saving and investment.

Nominal variables describe money values and tell us how *pound values* and the cost of living are changing. The nominal variables include the price level (RPI, CPI and GDP deflator), the inflation rate, nominal GDP and the nominal wage rate.

This separation of macroeconomic performance into a real part and a nominal (or money) part is the basis of a huge insight called the **classical dichotomy**, which states:

> **At full employment, the forces that determine real variables are independent of those that determine nominal variables.**

In practical terms, the classical dichotomy means that we can explain why real GDP per person in the United Kingdom is 30 times that in Burundi by looking only at the real parts of the two economies and ignoring differences in their price levels and inflation rates.

Similarly, we can explain why real GDP per person in the United Kingdom in 2003 was more than twice that in 1963 without considering what has happened to the value of the pound between those two years.

The **classical model** is a model of an economy that determines the real variables – real GDP, employment and unemployment, the real wage rate, consumption, saving, investment and the real interest rate – at full employment.

Most economists believe that the economy is rarely at full employment and that the business cycle is a fluctuation around full employment. Classical economists think that the economy is always at full employment and that the business cycle is a fluctuation of the full-employment economy.

Regardless of which view of the cycle an economist takes, all agree that the classical model that you're now going to study provides powerful insights into macroeconomic performance.

Real GDP and Employment

To produce more output, we must use more inputs. We can increase real GDP by employing more labour, increasing the quantity of capital or developing technologies that are more productive. In the short term, the quantity of capital and the state of technology are fixed. So to increase real GDP in the short term, we must increase the quantity of labour employed. Let's look at the relationship between real GDP and the quantity of labour employed.

Production Possibilities

When you studied the limits to production in Chapter 2 (see p. 32) you learned about the *production possibilities frontier*, which is the boundary between those combinations of goods and services that can be produced and those that cannot. In Chapter 2, we looked at the production possibilities frontier for pizzas and CDs. But we can think about the production possibilities for *any* pair of goods or services when we hold the quantities of all other goods and services constant. Let's think about the production possibilities frontier between two special items – real GDP and the quantity of leisure time.

Real GDP is a measure of all the final goods and services produced in the economy in a given time period (see Chapter 20, p. 438). We measure real GDP as a number of 2001 pounds, but the measure is a *real* one. Real GDP is not a quantity of pounds. It is a quantity of goods and services. Think of it as a number of big shopping carts filled with goods and services. Each cart contains some of each of the different goods and services produced and one cartload of items costs £1 billion. To say that real GDP is £1,000 billion means that real GDP is 1,000 big shopping carts of goods and services.

The quantity of leisure time is the number of hours we spend not working. It is the time we spend playing or watching sports, seeing movies, going to concerts and hanging out with friends. Leisure time is a special type of good or service.

Each hour that we spent pursuing fun could have been an hour spent working. So when the quantity of leisure time increases by one hour, the quantity of labour employed decreases by one hour.

If we spent all our time having fun rather than working we would not produce anything. Real GDP would be zero. The more leisure time we forgo to work, the greater is the quantity of labour employed and the greater is real GDP.

The relationship between leisure time and real GDP is a *production possibilities frontier* (*PPF*). Figure 23.1(a) shows an example of this frontier. Here, an economy has 110 billion hours of leisure time available. If people use all these hours to pursue leisure, no labour is employed and real GDP is zero. As people forgo leisure and work more, real GDP increases. If people took 60 billion hours in leisure and spent 50 billion hours working, real GDP would be £1,000 billion at point *A*. If people spent all the available hours working, real GDP would be £1,500 billion.

The bowed out *PPF* displays increasing opportunity cost. In this case, the opportunity cost of a given amount of real GDP is the amount of leisure time forgone to produce the real GDP. The additional hours of leisure forgone to produce a given additional amount of real GDP increases as real GDP increases. The reason is that we use the most productive labour first and, as we use more labour, we use increasingly less productive labour.

The Production Function

The **production function** is the relationship between real GDP and the quantity of labour employed when all other influences on production remain the same. The production function shows how real GDP varies as the quantity of labour employed varies, other things remaining the same.

Because one more hour of labour employed means one less hour of leisure, the production function is like a mirror image of the leisure time–real GDP *PPF*. Figure 23.1(b) shows the production function (*PF*) for the economy whose *PPF* is shown in Figure 23.1(a). You can see that when the quantity of labour employed is zero, real GDP is also zero. And as the quantity of labour employed increases, so does real GDP. When 50 billion labour hours are employed, real GDP is £1,000 billion (at point *A*).

A decrease in leisure hours and the corresponding increases in the quantity of labour employed and real GDP bring a movement along the production possibilities frontier and along the production function. The arrows along the *PPF* and the *PF* curves in Figure 23.1 show these movements. Such movements occurred when employment and real GDP surged during the first four years of the Second World War.

The production function tells us how real GDP and employment are linked. We're now going to see how the levels of employment and real GDP are determined.

Figure 23.1

Production Possibilities and the Production Function

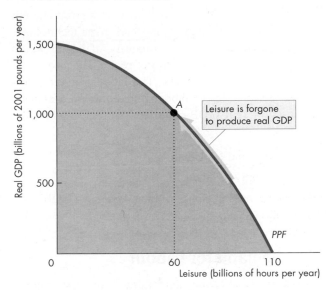

(a) Production possibilities frontier

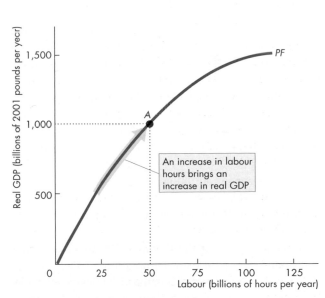

(b) Production function

On the *PPF* in part (a), if we enjoy 110 billion hours of leisure, we produce no real GDP. If we forgo 50 billion hours of leisure and take only 60 billion hours of leisure, we produce a real GDP of £1,000 billion, at point *A*.

The production function (*PF*) in part (b) is like a mirror image of the *PPF*. At point *A* on the *PF*, we use 50 billion hours of labour to produce £1,000 billion of real GDP.

The Labour Market and Potential GDP

You've seen that in a given year, with a given amount of physical and human capital and given technology, real GDP depends on the quantity of labour hours employed. To produce more real GDP, we must employ more labour hours. The labour market determines the quantity of labour hours employed and the quantity of real GDP supplied. We'll learn how by studying:

◆ The demand for labour

◆ The supply of labour

◆ Labour market equilibrium and potential GDP

◆ Aggregate supply

The Demand for Labour

The **quantity of labour demanded** is the labour hours hired by all the firms in the economy. The **demand for labour** is the relationship between the quantity of labour demanded and the real wage rate when all other influences on firms' hiring plans remain the same. The **real wage rate** is the quantity of goods and services that an hour of labour earns. In contrast, the **money wage rate** is the number of pounds that an hour of labour earns. A real wage rate is equal to a money wage rate divided by the price of a good. For the economy as a whole, the average real wage rate equals the average money wage rate divided by the price level multiplied by 100. So we express the real wage rate in constant pounds. (Today, we express this real wage rate in 2001 pounds.)

The *real* wage rate influences the quantity of labour demanded because what matters to firms is how much output they must sell to earn the number of pounds they pay (the money wage rate).

We can represent the demand for labour as either a demand schedule or a demand curve. The table in Figure 23.2 shows part of a demand for labour schedule. It tells us the quantity of labour demanded at three different real wage rates. For example, if the real wage rate falls from £20.00 an hour to £17.50 an hour, the quantity of labour demanded increases from 40 billion hours a year to 50 billion hours a year. (You can find these numbers in rows *A* and *B* of the table.) The labour demand curve is *LD*. Points *A*, *B* and *C* on the curve correspond to rows *A*, *B* and *C* of the demand schedule.

Figure 23.2

The Demand for Labour

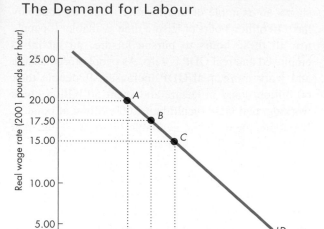

	Real wage rate (2001 pounds per hour)	Quantity of labour demanded (billions of hours per year)
A	20.00	40
B	17.50	50
C	15.00	60

The table shows part of a demand for labour schedule. Points *A*, *B* and *C* on the demand for labour curve correspond to the rows of the table. The lower the real wage rate, the greater is the quantity of labour demanded. The demand for labour curve slopes downward.

Why does the quantity of labour demanded *increase* as the real wage rate *decreases*? That is, why does the demand for labour curve slope downward? To answer these questions, we must learn about the marginal product of labour.

The Marginal Product of Labour

The **marginal product of labour** is the additional real GDP produced by an additional hour of labour when all other influences on production remain the same. The marginal product of labour is governed by the **law of diminishing returns**, which states that as the quantity of labour increases, other things remaining the same, the marginal product of labour decreases.

The Law of Diminishing Returns

Diminishing returns arise because the amount of capital is fixed. Two people operating one machine are not twice as productive as one person operating one machine. Eventually, as more labour is hired, workers get in each other's way and output barely increases.

Marginal Product Calculation

We calculate the marginal product of labour as the change in real GDP divided by the change in the quantity of labour employed. Figure 23.3(a) shows some marginal product calculations and Figure 23.3(b) shows the marginal product curve.

In Figure 23.3(a), when the quantity of labour employed increases from 30 billion hours to 50 billion hours, an increase of 20 billion hours, real GDP increases from £600 billion to £1,000 billion, an increase of £400 billion. The marginal product of labour equals the increase in real GDP (£400 billion) divided by the increase in the quantity of labour employed (20 billion hours), which is £20 an hour.

When the quantity of labour employed increases from 50 billion hours to 70 billion hours, an increase of 20 billion hours, real GDP increases from £1,000 billion to £1,300 billion, an increase of £300 billion. The marginal product of labour equals £300 billion divided 20 billion hours, which is £15 an hour.

In Figure 23.3(b), as the quantity of labour employed increases, the marginal product of labour diminishes. Between 30 billion and 50 billion hours (at 40 billion hours), marginal product is £20 an hour – at point *A*. And between 50 billion and 70 billion hours (at 60 billion hours), marginal product is £15 an hour – at point *C*.

The diminishing marginal product of labour limits the demand for labour.

Diminishing Marginal Product and the Demand for Labour

Firms are in business to maximize profits. Each hour of labour that a firm hires increases output and adds to costs. Initially, an extra hour of labour produces more output than the real wage that the labour costs. Marginal product exceeds the real wage rate. But each additional hour of labour produces less additional output than the previous hour – the marginal product of labour diminishes.

As a firm hires more labour, eventually the extra output from an extra hour of labour is exactly what that hour of labour costs. At this point, marginal product

Figure 23.3

The Marginal Product and the Demand for Labour

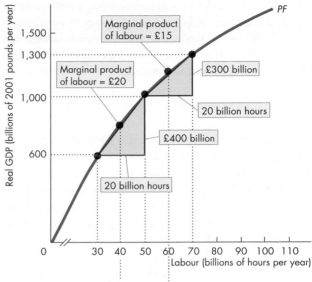

(a) Calculating marginal product

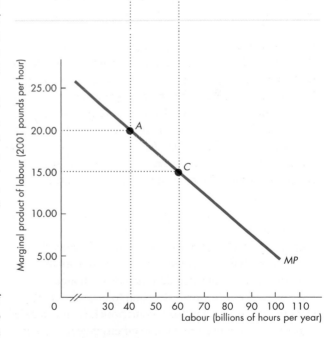

(b) The marginal product curve

Between 30 billion and 50 billion hours, the marginal product of labour is £20 an hour. Between 50 billion and 70 billion hours, the marginal product of labour is £15 an hour. At point *A* on the *MP* curve, the marginal product of labour is £20 an hour at 40 billion hours. At point *C*, the marginal product of labour is £15 an hour at 60 billion hours. The *MP* curve is the demand for labour curve.

equals the real wage rate. Hire one less hour and marginal product exceeds the real wage rate. Hire one more hour and the real wage rate exceeds the marginal product. In either case, profit is less.

Because marginal product diminishes as the quantity of labour employed increases, the lower the real wage rate, the greater is the quantity of labour that a firm can profitably hire. The marginal product curve is the same as the demand for labour curve.

You might gain a clearer understanding of the demand for labour by looking at an example.

The Demand for Labour at Liz's Meat Pie Plant

Suppose that when Liz employs one additional hour of labour, output increases by 3 pies an hour. Marginal product is 3 pies an hour. If the money wage rate is £6 an hour and if meat pies sell for £2 each, the real wage rate is 3 pies an hour. (We calculate the real wage rate as the money wage rate of £6 an hour divided by a price of a pie, £2, which equals a real wage rate of 3 pies an hour.) Because marginal product diminishes, we know that if Liz did not hire this hour of labour, marginal product would exceed 3 pies. Because Liz can hire the hour of labour for a real wage rate of 3 pies, it pays Liz to do so.

If the price of a meat pie remains at £2 and the money wage rate falls to £4 an hour, the real wage rate falls to 2 pies an hour and Liz increases the quantity of labour demanded. Similarly, if the money wage rate remains at £6 an hour and the price of a meat pie rises to £3, the real wage rate falls to 2 pies an hour and Liz increases the quantity of labour demanded.

When the firm pays a real wage rate equal to the marginal product of labour, it is maximizing profit.

Changes in the Demand for Labour

A change in the real wage rate brings a change in the quantity of labour demanded, which is shown by a movement along the demand curve. A change in any other influence on a firm's decision to hire labour brings a change in the demand for labour, which is shown by a shift of the demand curve. These other influences are the quantities of physical and human capital and technology. An increase in capital or an advance in technology shifts the production function upward. These same forces increase the marginal product of labour and shift the demand for labour curve rightward. Labour-saving technological change decreases the demand for some types of labour, but overall advances in technology increase the demand for labour.

The Supply of Labour

The **quantity of labour supplied** is the number of labour hours that all the households in the economy plan to work. The **supply of labour** is the relationship between the quantity of labour supplied and the real wage rate when all other influences on work plans remain the same.

We can represent the supply of labour as either a supply schedule or a supply curve. The table in Figure 23.4 shows a supply of labour schedule. It tells us the quantity of labour supplied at three different real wage rates. For example, if the real wage rate rises from £7.50 an hour (row A) to £17.50 an hour (row B), the quantity of labour supplied increases from 40 billion hours to 50 billion hours a year.

Figure 23.4

The Supply of Labour

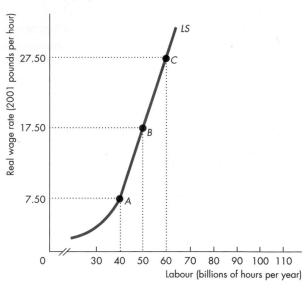

	Real wage rate (2001 pounds per hour)	Quantity of labour supplied (billions of hours per year)
A	7.50	40
B	17.50	50
C	27.50	60

The table shows part of a supply of labour schedule. Points A, B and C on the supply of labour curve correspond to the rows of the table. The higher the real wage rate, the greater is the quantity of labour supplied.

The curve *LS* is a labour supply curve. Points *A*, *B* and *C* on the curve correspond to rows *A*, *B* and *C* of the supply schedule.

The *real* wage rate influences the quantity of labour supplied because what matters to people is not the number of pounds they earn (the money wage rate) but what those pounds will buy.

The quantity of labour supplied increases as the real wage rate increases for two reasons:

◆ Hours per person increase
◆ Economic activity rate increases

Hours per Person Increase

In choosing how many hours to work, a household considers the opportunity cost of not working. This opportunity cost is the real wage rate. The higher the real wage rate, the greater is the opportunity cost of taking leisure and not working. And as the opportunity cost of taking leisure rises, other things remaining the same, the more the household chooses to work.

But other things don't remain the same. The higher the real wage rate, the greater is the household's income. And the higher the household's income, the more it wants to consume. One item that it wants to consume more of is leisure.

So a rise in the real wage rate has two opposing effects. By increasing the opportunity cost of leisure, it makes the household want to consume less leisure and to work more. And by increasing the household's income, it makes the household want to consume more leisure and to work fewer hours. For most households, the opportunity cost effect is stronger than the income effect. So the higher the real wage rate, the greater is the amount of work that the household chooses to do.

Economic Activity Rate Increases

Almost everyone has productive opportunities outside the labour force. If the value of one of these other productive activities exceeds the real wage rate, a person will not join the labour force. For example, a parent might work full time caring for her or his child. The alternative is to pay for the child to attend a childcare centre. The parent will choose to work only if he or she can earn a high enough wage rate per hour to pay the cost of childcare, pay the transport costs and taxes involved and have income enough left over to make the work effort worthwhile.

The higher the real wage rate, the more likely it is that a person will choose to work and so the greater is the economic activity rate.

Labour Supply Response

The quantity of labour supplied increases as the real wage rate rises. But the quantity of labour supplied is not highly responsive to the real wage rate. A large percentage change in the real wage rate brings only a small percentage change in the quantity of labour supplied.

Changes in the Supply of Labour

A change in the real wage rate brings a change in the quantity of labour supplied, which is shown by a movement along the supply curve. A change in any other influence on a household's decision to work brings a change in the supply of labour, which is shown by a shift of the supply curve.

The other major influence on the supply of labour is the working-age population. Over time, as the working-age population increases – either because the number of births exceeds the number of deaths, or from immigration – the supply of labour increases.

Other factors that include technology in the home and social attitudes also influence the supply of labour and especially the supply of female labour. Advances in technology in the home along with greater opportunities for women have shifted the supply of labour curve rightward.

Let's now see how the labour market determines employment, the real wage rate and potential GDP.

Labour Market Equilibrium and Potential GDP

The forces of supply and demand operate in labour markets just as they do in the markets for goods and services. The price of labour is the real wage rate. A rise in the real wage rate eliminates a shortage of labour by decreasing the quantity demanded and increasing the quantity supplied. A fall in the real wage rate eliminates a surplus of labour by increasing the quantity demanded and decreasing the quantity supplied. If there is neither a shortage nor a surplus, the labour market is in equilibrium.

In macroeconomics, we study the economy-wide labour market to determine the total quantity of labour employed and the average real wage rate.

Labour Market Equilibrium

Figure 23.5(a) shows a labour market in equilibrium. The demand curve *LD* and the supply curve *LS* are the same as those in Figure 23.2 and Figure 23.4, respectively.

Figure 23.5

The Labour Market and Potential GDP

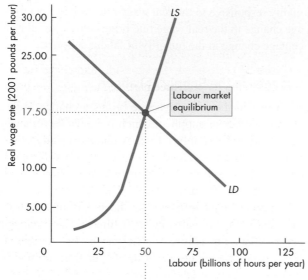

(a) The labour market

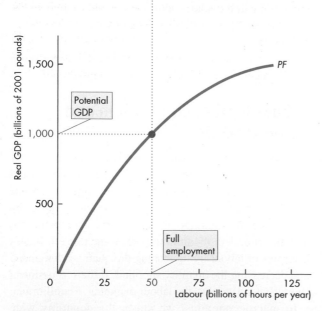

(b) Potential GDP

Full employment occurs in part (a) when the quantity of labour demanded equals the quantity of labour supplied. The equilibrium real wage rate is £17.50 an hour and equilibrium employment is 50 billion hours a year.

Part (b) shows potential GDP. It is the quantity of real GDP determined by the production function and the full-employment quantity of labour.

If the real wage rate exceeds £17.50 an hour, the quantity of labour supplied exceeds the quantity demanded and there is a surplus of labour. In this situation, the real wage rate falls.

If the real wage rate is less than £17.50 an hour, the quantity of labour demanded exceeds the quantity supplied and there is a shortage of labour. In this situation, the real wage rate rises.

If the real wage rate is £17.50 an hour, the quantity of labour demanded equals the quantity supplied and there is neither a shortage nor a surplus of labour. In this situation, the labour market is in equilibrium and the real wage rate remains constant.

The equilibrium level of employment is 50 billion hours a year. This equilibrium level of employment is *full employment*.

Potential GDP

You've seen that the quantity of real GDP depends on the quantity of labour employed. The production function tells us how much real GDP a given amount of employment can produce. At the labour market equilibrium, employment is at its full-employment level. And the quantity of real GDP produced by the full-employment quantity of labour is *potential GDP*. So the equilibrium level of employment produces potential GDP.

Figure 23.5(b) shows potential GDP. The equilibrium level of employment in Figure 23.5(a) is 50 billion hours. The production function in Figure 23.5(b) tells us that 50 billion hours of labour can produce a real GDP of £1,000 billion. This amount is potential GDP.

Review Quiz

1 What is the relationship between the leisure time–real GDP *PPF* and the production function?
2 What does the outward-bowed shape of the leisure time–real GDP *PPF* imply about the opportunity cost of real GDP and why is the *PPF* bowed outward?
3 Why does a rise in the real wage rate bring a decrease in the quantity of labour demanded, other things remaining the same?
4 Why does a rise in the real wage rate bring an increase in the quantity of labour supplied, other things remaining the same?
5 What happens in the labour market if the real wage rate is above or below the full-employment level?
6 How is potential GDP determined?

Aggregate Supply

You can use what you've just learned about the labour market and potential GDP to derive the long-run aggregate supply curve and short-run aggregate supply curve that you met in Chapter 22 (pp. 480–482). Figure 23.6 explains how these two aggregate supply curves are derived from the labour market and production function.

Along the long-run aggregate supply curve, as the price level changes, the money wage rate changes to keep the real wage rate at the full-employment equilibrium level in Figure 23.6(a). With no change in the real wage rate and no change in employment, real GDP remains at potential GDP. So regardless of the price level, the quantity of real GDP supplied in the long run is £1,000 billion.

Along the short-run aggregate supply curve, the money wage rate remains fixed, so as the price level changes the real wage rate changes.

Figure 23.6(a) shows the three short-run equilibrium levels of the real wage rate and employment. The money wage rate is fixed at £17.50 an hour. If the price level is 100, the real wage rate is £17.50 an hour and 50 billion hours of labour are employed – point B. If the price level is 87.5, the real wage rate is £20 an hour and employment is 38 billion hours – point A. If the price level is 116.7, the real wage rate is £15 an hour and employment is 60 billion hours – point C.

Figure 23.6(b) shows the production function and the quantities of real GDP produced at each employment level. For example, when employment is 40 billion hours, real GDP is £820 billion – point A. When employment is 50 billion hours, real GDP is £1,000 billion – point B. And when employment is 60 billion hours, real GDP is £1,170 billion – point C.

Figure 23.6(c) shows the short-run aggregate supply curve. At point B in all three parts of the figure, the price level is 100. From the labour market in part (a) we know that when the price level is 100, the real wage is £17.50 an hour and 50 billion hours of labour are employed. At this employment level, we know from the production function in part (b) that real GDP is £1,000 billion and the economy is at full employment.

If the price level falls to 87.5, the real wage rises to £20 an hour and the quantity of labour demanded decreases to 40 billion hours in part (a). At this employment level, we know from the production function in part (b) that real GDP decreases to £820 billion. The economy moves to point A on the SAS curve in part (c).

If the price level rises to 116.7, the real wage falls to £15 an hour and the quantity of labour demanded increases to 60 billion hours in part (a). At this employment level, we know from the production function in part (b) that real GDP increases to £1,170 billion. The economy moves to point C on the SAS curve in part (c).

Figure 23.6

The Labour Market and the Aggregate Supply Curves

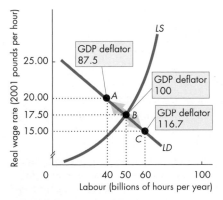

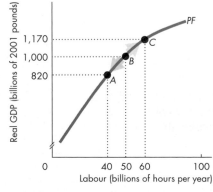

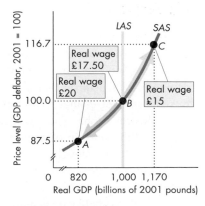

(a) The labour market

(b) Production function

(c) Aggregate supply curves

The money wage rate is fixed at £17.50 an hour. If the GDP deflator is 100, the economy operates at point B on its long-run aggregate supply curve LAS. If the GDP deflator is 87.5, the real wage rate is £20 an hour and the economy is at point A. If the GDP deflator is 116.7, the real wage rate is £15 an hour and the economy is at point C.

Unemployment at Full Employment

So far, we've focused on the forces that determine the real wage rate, the quantity of labour employed and potential GDP. And we've studied the effects of changes in population, capital and technology on these variables. We're now going to bring unemployment into the picture.

In Chapter 21, we learned how unemployment is measured. We described how people become unemployed – they lose jobs, leave jobs and enter or re-enter the workforce – and we classified unemployment – it can be frictional, structural and cyclical. We also learned that we call the unemployment rate at full employment the *natural rate of unemployment*.

But measuring, describing and classifying unemployment do not *explain* it. Why is there always some unemployment? Why does its rate fluctuate? Why was the unemployment rate lower during the 1960s and the late 1990s than during the 1980s and early 1990s?

The forces that make the unemployment rate fluctuate around the natural rate take some time to explain and we study these forces in Chapters 24 to 31. Here, we look at the churning economy and the reasons why we have unemployment at full employment – why the natural rate of unemployment is *not* zero.

Unemployment is ever present for two broad reasons:

◆ Job search
◆ Job rationing

Job Search

Job search is the activity of looking for an acceptable vacant job. There are always some people who have not yet found a suitable job and who are actively searching for one. The reason is that the labour market is in a constant state of change. The failure of existing businesses destroys jobs. The expansion of existing businesses and the start up of new businesses that use new technologies and develop new markets create jobs. As people pass through different stages of life, some enter or re-enter the labour market. Others leave their jobs to look for better ones and still others retire. This constant churning in the labour market means that there are always some people looking for jobs and these people are the unemployed.

The amount of job search depends on a number of factors, one of which is the real wage rate. In Figure 23.7,

when the real wage rate is £17.50 an hour, the economy is at full employment. The amount of job search that takes place at this wage rate generates unemployment at the natural rate. If the real wage rate is above the full-employment real wage rate – for example, at £22.50 an hour – there is a surplus of labour. At this higher real wage rate, more job search takes place and the unemployment rate rises above the natural rate. If the real wage rate is below the full-employment real wage rate – for example, at £12.50 an hour – there is a shortage of labour. At this real wage rate, less job search takes place and the unemployment rate falls below the natural rate.

The market forces of supply and demand move the real wage rate towards the full-employment equilibrium. And these same forces move the amount of job search towards the level that creates unemployment at the natural rate.

Figure 23.7

Job Search Unemployment

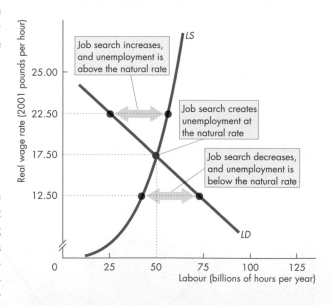

When the real wage rate is at its full-employment level – £17.50 an hour in this example – job search puts unemployment at the natural rate. If the real wage rate is above its full-employment level, there is a surplus of labour. Job search increases and unemployment rises above the natural rate. If the real wage rate is below its full-employment level, there is a shortage of labour. Job search decreases and unemployment falls below the natural rate.

But other influences on the amount of job search bring changes, over time, in the natural rate of unemployment. The main sources of these changes are:

◆ Demographic change
◆ Unemployment benefits
◆ Technological change
◆ Hysteresis

Demographic Change

An increase in the proportion of the working-age population brings an increase in the entry rate into the workforce and an increase in the unemployment rate. A bulge in the birth rate occurred in the late 1940s and early 1950s, following the Second World War. This bulge increased the proportion of new entrants into the workforce during the 1970s and brought an increase in the unemployment rate. Another demographic trend is an increase in the number of households with two working adults. If unemployment hits one person but the income from the second income continues, the unemployed person might spend more time in job search, which increases frictional unemployment.

Unemployment Benefits

The length of time that an unemployed person spends searching for a job depends, in part, on the opportunity cost of job search. With no income during a period of unemployment, an unemployed person faces a high opportunity cost of job search. In this situation, search is likely to be short and an unattractive job is likely to be accepted as a better alternative to continuing a costly search process. With generous unemployment benefits, the opportunity cost of job search is low. In this situation, search is likely to be prolonged. An unemployed worker will hold out for the ideal job.

The opportunity cost of job search has fallen over the years as unemployment benefits have increased. In 1966, unemployment benefits included a flat-rate component and an earnings-related component. As a result of these changes, the natural rate of unemployment was on an upward trend during the 1970s.

But not all of the changes in unemployment benefits have been increases. Concern over the incentive effects of high benefits has brought some decreases. For example, in 1982, earnings-related benefit was abolished in the United Kingdom and during the 1990s the conditions for the receipt of benefit were tightened.

These changes contributed to a decrease rate during the 1980s and 1990s.

Technological Change

Labour market flows and unemployment are influenced by the pace and direction of technological change. Sometimes technological change brings a *structural slump*, in which some industries die and regions suffer and other industries are born and regions flourish. When these events occur, labour turnover is high – the flows between employment and unemployment and the pool of unemployed people increases. The decline of traditional heavy industries such as shipbuilding, steel and coal and the rapid expansion of industries in the electronics and car components sectors are examples of the effects of technological change and sources of the increase in unemployment during the 1970s and early 1980s. While these changes were taking place, the natural rate of unemployment increased. Supply-side policies that increased job market flexibility in the 1980s resulted in the labour market being able to adjust more rapidly to technological shocks.

Hysteresis

The unemployment rate fluctuates around the natural rate of unemployment. But it is possible that the natural rate itself depends on the path of the actual unemployment rate. So where the unemployment rate ends up depends on where it has been. Such a process is called **hysteresis**.

If hysteresis is present, then an increase in the unemployment rate brings an increase in the natural rate. A possible source of hysteresis is that the human capital of unemployed workers depreciates and people who experience long bouts of unemployment usually find it difficult to get new jobs as good as the ones they have lost. An increase in the number of long-term unemployed workers means an increase in the amount of human capital lost and possibly a permanent increase in the natural rate of unemployment. The hysteresis theory is controversial and has not yet been thoroughly tested, but it is also consistent with the view that the long-term unemployed are willing to remain on state benefits indefinitely.

Job-search unemployment is present even when the quantity of labour demanded equals the quantity supplied. The other possible explanations of unemployment are based on the view that the quantity of labour demanded does not always equal the quantity supplied.

Job Rationing

You've learned that markets *allocate* scarce resources by adjusting the market price to make buying plans and selling plans agree. Another word that has a meaning similar to "allocate" is "ration". Markets *ration* scarce resources by adjusting prices. In the labour market, the real wage rate rations employment and therefore rations jobs. Changes in the real wage rate keep the number of people seeking work and the number of jobs available in balance.

But the real wage rate is not the only possible instrument for rationing jobs. And in some industries, the real wage rate is set above the market equilibrium level. **Job rationing** is the practice of paying a real wage rate above the equilibrium level and then rationing jobs by some method. Three reasons why the real wage rate might be set above the equilibrium level are:

◆ Efficiency wage
◆ Insider interest
◆ Minimum wage

Efficiency Wage

In some circumstances, a firm can increase its labour productivity by paying wages above the competitive wage rate. The higher wage attracts a higher quality of labour, encourages greater work effort and cuts down on the firm's labour turnover rate and recruiting costs. But the higher wage also adds to the firm's costs. So a firm offers a wage rate that balances productivity gains and additional costs. The wage rate that maximizes profit is called the **efficiency wage**.

The efficiency wage will be higher than the competitive equilibrium wage. If it was lower than the competitive wage rate, competition for labour would bid the wage rate up. With an efficiency wage above the competitive wage rate, some labour is unemployed and employed workers have an incentive to perform well to avoid being fired.

The payment of efficiency wages is another reason the natural rate of unemployment is not zero.

Insider Interest

Why don't firms cut their wage costs by offering jobs to unemployed workers at a lower wage rate than that paid to existing workers? One explanation, called **insider-outsider theory**, is that to be productive, new workers – outsiders – must receive on-the-job training from existing workers – insiders. If insiders provide such training to outsiders who are paid a lower wage, the insiders' bargaining position is weakened. So insiders will not train outsiders unless outsiders receive the same rate of pay as insiders.

When bargaining for a wage deal, unions represent only the interests of insiders, so the wage rate agreed exceeds the competitive wage rate and there are always outsiders unable to find work. So the pursuit of rational self-interest by insiders is another reason the natural rate of unemployment is positive. The weakening of trade union power through legislation may have reduced the insiders' bargaining position.

The Minimum Wage

A minimum wage is legislated by the government at a level higher than the one the market would determine. As a result, the quantity of labour supplied exceeds the quantity demanded and jobs are rationed. The minimum wage from 1 October 2004 for the United Kingdom is £4.85 an hour for workers aged 22 and over. A lower minimum wage of £4.10 exists for 18–21 year-olds and £3 for 16-17 year-olds. It is estimated that the minimum wage will affect only 4.3 per cent of employees in London but 11.6 per cent of employees in the Northeast. It will also affect nearly one-third of employees in the hotel and restaurant business and a quarter of security guards and cleaners. A recent survey suggested that nearly 13 per cent of UK businesses would suffer a fall in profits if minimum wages were raised to £5 an hour.

Review Quiz

1   Why does the economy experience unemployment at full employment?
2   Why does the natural rate of unemployment fluctuate?
3   What is job search and why does it occur?
4   What factors have changed the amount of job-search unemployment in the United Kingdom?
5   What is job rationing and why does it occur?
6   How does an efficiency wage influence the real wage rate, employment and unemployment?
7   How do insider interests influence the amount of job-rationing unemployment?
8   How does the minimum wage create unemployment?

In the next section, we'll see how the classical model explains some of the major changes in our economy.

The Dynamic Classical Model

The classical model has rich implications for how the economy changes over time in response to population growth and technological change and an increasing quantity of capital. We're now going to look at some of these dynamic aspects of the full-employment economy. We'll begin by looking at the sources and effects of changes in productivity.

Changes in Productivity

When we talk about *productivity*, we usually mean labour productivity. **Labour productivity** is real GDP per hour of labour. Three factors influence labour productivity:

◆ Physical capital
◆ Human capital
◆ Technology

Physical Capital

A farm worker equipped with only a stick and primitive tools can cultivate almost no land and grow barely enough food to feed a single family. A farmer equipped with a steel plough pulled by an animal can cultivate more land and produce enough food to feed a small village. A farmer equipped with a modern tractor, plough and harvester can cultivate thousands of hectares and produce enough food to feed hundreds of people.

By using physical capital on our farms and in our factories, shops and offices, we enormously increase labour productivity.

Human Capital

An economy's *human capital* is the knowledge and skill that people have obtained from education and on-the-job training. The average university graduate has a greater amount of human capital than the average school leaver. Consequently, the university graduate is able to perform some tasks that are beyond the ability of the school leaver. The university graduate is more productive. For the nation as a whole, the greater the amount of education its citizens complete, the greater is its real GDP, other things remaining the same.

Regardless of how much education a person has completed, not much production is accomplished on the first day at work. Learning about the new work environment consumes the newly hired worker. But as time passes and experience accumulates, the worker becomes more productive. We call this on-the-job training activity **learning-by-doing**.

Learning-by-doing can bring incredible increases in labour productivity. The more experienced the workforce, the greater is its labour productivity and other things remaining the same, the greater is real GDP.

Technology

A student equipped with a pen can complete a readable page of writing in perhaps 10 minutes. This same task takes 5 minutes with a typewriter and 2 minutes with a computer. This is an example of the enormous impact of technology on labour productivity.

Any influence on production that increases labour productivity shifts the production function upward. Real GDP increases at each level of labour hours. In Figure 23.8, the production function is initially PF_0. Then an increase in physical capital or human capital or an advance in technology occurs. The production function shifts upward to PF_1.

Labour productivity in the United Kingdom increases, on average, by almost 2 per cent a year.

Figure 23.8

An Increase in Labour Productivity

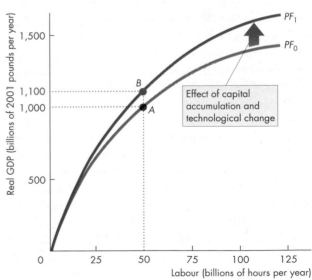

On PF_0, 50 billion labour hours produce a real GDP of $1,000 billion (point *A*). An increase in capital or an advance in technology increases labour productivity and shifts the production function upward to PF_1. Now, 50 billion labour hours produce a real GDP of $1,100 billion (point *B*).

The classical model helps us to understand how changes in labour productivity and other factors change real GDP. Real GDP increases if:

1   The economy recovers from recession.
2   Potential GDP increases.

Recovery from recession means the economy moves along the real GDP–leisure PPF from a point at which real GDP is less than potential GDP to one that is closer to it. Equivalently, the economy moves along the short-run aggregate supply curve. Economists have a lot to say about such a move. You can learn about this type of short-term change in real GDP in Chapter 22.

Increasing potential GDP means expanding production possibilities. We're going to study such an expansion in the rest of this chapter and in Chapter 30. We begin this process here by examining two influences on potential GDP:

◆   An increase in population

◆   An increase in labour productivity

An Increase in Population

As the population increases and additional people reach working age, the supply of labour increases. With more labour available and with capital and technology remaining the same, production possibilities expand. But does the expansion of production possibilities mean that potential GDP increases? And does it mean that potential GDP *per person* increases?

The answers to these questions have intrigued economists for many years. And they cause heated political debate today. In China, for example, families are under enormous pressure to limit the number of children they have. In other countries, an example of which is France, the government encourages large families. We can study the effects of an increase in population by using the classical model.

In Figure 23.9(a), the demand for labour is LD and initially the supply of labour is LS_0. At full employment, the real wage rate is £17.50 an hour and employment is 50 billion hours a year. In Figure 23.9(b), the production function (PF) shows that with 50 billion hours of labour employed, potential GDP is £1,000 billion. We're now going to work out what happens when the population increases.

An increase in the population increases the number of people of working age and the supply of labour increases. The labour supply curve shifts rightward to

Figure 23.9

The Effects of an Increase in Population

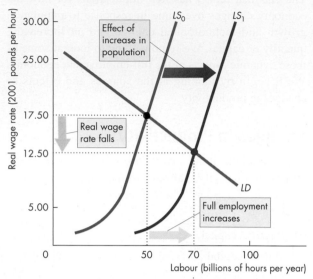

(a) The labour market

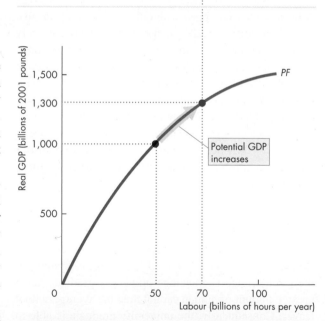

(b) Potential GDP

An increase in population increases the supply of labour. In part (a), the supply of labour curve shifts rightward from LS_0 to LS_1. The real wage rate falls and the quantity of labour employed at full employment increases. In part (b), the increase in full employment increases potential GDP. Because the marginal product of labour diminishes, the increased population increases potential GDP but potential GDP per hour of work decreases.

LS_1. At a real wage rate of £17.50 an hour, there is now a surplus of labour. So the real wage rate falls. In this example, it falls until it reaches £12.50 an hour. At £12.50 an hour, the quantity of labour demanded equals the quantity of labour supplied. Equilibrium employment increases to 70 billion hours a year.

Figure 23.9(b) shows the effect of the increase in equilibrium employment on real GDP. As the full-employment quantity of labour increases from 50 billion hours to 70 billion hours, potential GDP increases from £1,000 billion to £1,300 billion.

So at full employment, an increase in population increases employment, increases potential GDP and lowers the real wage rate.

An increase in population also decreases potential GDP per hour of work. You can see this decrease by dividing potential GDP by total labour hours. Initially, with potential GDP at £1,000 billion and labour hours at 50 billion, potential GDP per hour of work was £20. With the increase in population, potential GDP is £1,300 billion and labour hours are 70 billion. Potential GDP per hour of work is £18.57. Diminishing returns is the source of the decrease in potential GDP per hour of work.

You've seen that an increase in population increases potential GDP and decreases potential GDP per work hour. Some people challenge this conclusion and argue that people are the ultimate economic resource. They claim that a larger population brings forth a greater amount of scientific discovery and technological advance. Consequently, these people argue that an increase in population never takes place in isolation. It is always accompanied by an increase in labour productivity. Let's now look at the effects of this influence on potential GDP.

An Increase in Labour Productivity

We've seen that three factors increase labour productivity:

◆ An increase in physical capital
◆ An increase in human capital
◆ An advance in technology

Saving and investment increase the quantity of physical capital over time. Education and on-the-job training and experience increase human capital. Research and development efforts bring advances in technology. In Chapter 30, we study how all these forces interact to determine the growth rate of potential GDP.

Here, we study the *effects* of an increase in physical capital, an increase in human capital, or an advance in technology on the labour market and potential GDP. We'll see how the real wage rate, employment and potential GDP change when any of these three influences on labour productivity changes.

An Increase in Physical Capital

If the quantity of physical capital increases, labour productivity increases. With labour being more productive, the economy's production possibilities expand. How does such an expansion of production possibilities change the equilibrium real wage rate, employment and potential GDP?

The additional capital increases the real GDP that each quantity of labour can produce. It also increases the marginal product of labour and so increases the demand for labour. Some physical capital replaces some types of labour. So the demand for those types of labour decreases when capital increases. But an increase in physical capital creates a demand for the types of labour that build, sell and maintain the additional capital. The increases in demand for labour are always larger than the decreases in demand and the economy-wide demand for labour increases.

With an increase in the economy-wide demand for labour, the real wage rate rises and the quantity of labour supplied increases. Equilibrium employment increases.

Potential GDP now increases for two reasons. First, a given level of employment produces more real GDP. Second, equilibrium employment increases.

An Increase in Human Capital

If the quantity of human capital increases, labour productivity increases. Again, with labour being more productive, the economy's production possibilities expand. And this expansion of production possibilities changes the equilibrium real wage rate, employment and potential GDP in a similar manner to the effects of a change in physical capital.

An Advance in Technology

As technology advances, labour productivity increases. And exactly as in the case of an increase in capital, the economy's production possibilities expand. Again, just as in the case of an increase in capital, the new technology increases the real GDP that each quantity of labour can produce and increases the marginal product of labour and the demand for labour.

With an increase in the demand for labour, the real wage rate rises, the quantity of labour supplied increases and equilibrium employment increases. And again, potential GDP increases because a given level of employment produces more real GDP and because equilibrium employment increases.

Illustrating the Effects of an Increase in Labour Productivity

Figure 23.10 shows the effects of an increase in labour productivity that result from an increase in capital or an advance in technology. In part (a), the demand for labour initially is LD_0 and the supply of labour is LS. The real wage rate is £17.50 an hour and full employment is 50 billion hours a year.

In part (b), the production function initially is PF_0. With 50 billion hours of labour employed, potential GDP is £1,000 billion.

Now an increase in capital or an advance in technology increases the labour productivity. In Figure 23.10(a), the demand for labour increases and the demand curve shifts rightward to LD_1. In Figure 23.10(b), the increase in labour productivity shifts the production function upward to PF_1.

In Figure 23.10(a), at the original real wage rate of £17.50 an hour, there is now a shortage of labour. So the real wage rate rises. In this example, it keeps rising until it reaches £22.50 an hour. At £22.50 an hour, the quantity of labour demanded equals the quantity of labour supplied and full employment increases to 56 billion hours a year.

Figure 23.10(b) shows the effects on potential GDP of an increase in full employment combined with the new production function. As full employment increases from 50 billion hours to 56 billion hours, potential GDP increases from £1,000 billion to £1,500 billion.

Potential GDP per hour of work also increases. Initially, with potential GDP at £1,000 billion and labour hours at 50 billion, potential GDP per hour of work was £20. With the increase in labour productivity, potential GDP is £1,500 billion and labour hours are 56 billion, so potential GDP per hour of work is £26.79.

We've just studied the effects of a change in population and an increase in labour productivity separately. In reality, these changes occur together. Real GDP and employment both increase. And the real wage rate typically increases because the effects of increases in labour productivity are greater than the effects of an increase in the population. Box 23.1 examines these combined effects in the UK economy.

Figure 23.10

The Effects of an Increase in Labour Productivity

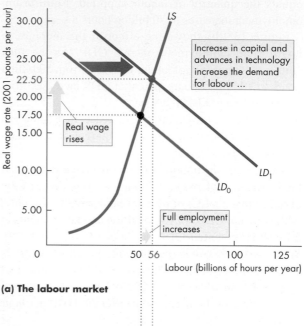

(a) The labour market

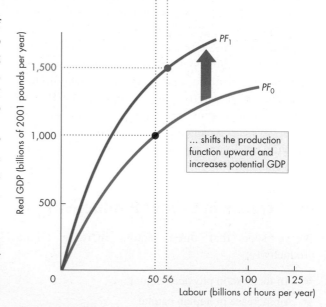

(b) Potential GDP

An increase in labour productivity shifts the demand for labour curve rightward from LD_0 to LD_1 in part (a) and the production function upward from PF_0 to PF_1 in part (b). The real wage rate rises from £17.50 to £22.50 an hour, full employment increases from 50 billion to 56 billion hours. Potential GDP increases from £1,000 billion to £1,500 billion.

Box 23.1
Population and Productivity in the United Kingdom

Between 1973 and 2003, aggregate hours of labour barely changed but real GDP increased from £550 billion to £1,034 billion and the real wage rate increased from £7.12 an hour to £12.30 an hour.

Figure 1 shows how these changes came about. In 1973, the labour demand curve was LD_{73} and the labour supply curve was LS_{73}. The equilibrium real wage rate was £7.12 an hour and 47 billion hours of labour were employed.

Labour productivity increased because capital per worker increased and technology advanced. The demand for labour shifted rightward to LD_{03} in part (a) and the production function shifted upward from PF_{73} to PF_{03} in part (b).

An increase in the population increased the supply of labour, but an increase in trade union militancy, higher income taxes and more generous unemployment benefits decreased the supply of labour. The net effect was a decrease in supply to LS_{03}.

The equilibrium real wage rate increased to £12.30 an hour in part (a) and equilibrium real GDP increased to £1,034 billion in part (b). But equilibrium employment remained constant at 47 billion hours.

These aggregate changes hide some structural changes that were going on at the same time. Technological change and stiffer international competition during the 1980s and 1990s brought a decrease in the demand for labour in manufacturing. But the same forces that destroyed jobs in manufacturing created jobs in services and in the high-tech parts of the economy. The increase in demand for labour in these growing sectors brought higher wages in those sectors. The decrease in demand for labour in manufacturing kept wages in that part of the economy low. But the average wage rate increased sharply.

Figure 1

Trends in Employment and the Real Wage Rate

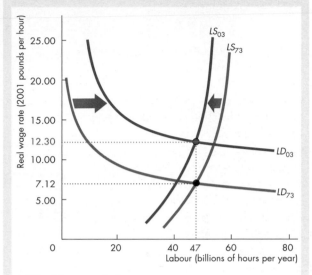

(a) The labour market

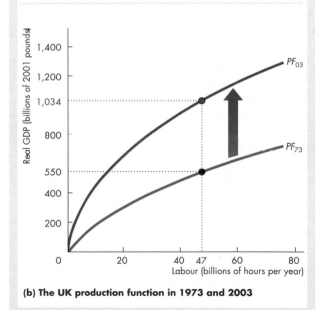

(b) The UK production function in 1973 and 2003

Review Quiz

1. When the population increases but nothing else changes, why does real GDP per hour of work decrease?
2. How does an increase in capital change the real wage rate, full employment and potential GDP?
3. How do advances in technology change the real wage rate, full employment and potential GDP?

In this chapter, you've seen how the economy operates at full employment. In *Reading Between the Lines* on pp. 520–521, we examine the effect of immigration from the new EU member states into the United Kingdom.

Reading Between the Lines

Labour Market in the United Kingdom

The Financial Times, 30 July 2004

FT

Workers from New EU states set to ease staff shortages

David Turner

Citizens of the new members of the European Union are set to ease labour shortages in key industries where employers cannot fill the gaps through British workers, figures from Britain's biggest private sector employment website revealed. The numbers from reed.co.uk suggest the 10 accession countries will increase the potential for overseas workers to act as a safety valve for labour market pressure. Many industries have long relied on large numbers of foreign staff.

Hospitality and catering – where business leaders claim 100,000 vacancies – tops the list of sectors where would-be workers from the 10 accession countries are looking for work. Five per cent are looking for employment in each of the three fields of construction, engineering and transport and logistics while 4 per cent are seeking work in accountancy, the figures reveal. Reed added that

registrations on its website by jobseekers from the 10 new states had increased sixfold in a year. One in nine of the workers wants a job in IT, where employers say there is strong demand for certain highly qualified technical staff, despite a surplus in some areas. . . .

Reed says that workers from the new EU member states account for 5 per cent of job seekers using its website. The other EU countries account for another 7 per cent.

About 24,000 workers from the new member states signed up to the Home Office's compulsory Worker Registration Scheme in May and June, according to official figures. James Reed, chief executive of the Reed recruitment group, said: "The UK is suffering skills shortages in a number of specific areas, so an increase in registrations from the EU may well ease this problem."

The Essence of the Story

◆ Labour shortages in key industries are being increasingly filled by foreign workers from the EU accession countries.

◆ EU rules enable workers from any part of the European Union to work and reside in any other part.

◆ The hospitality and catering industry has the highest demand for labour with 100,000 vacancies.

◆ Five per cent of job seekers who use the Reed site are from the new EU countries and 7 per cent are from the old EU countries.

Economic Analysis

◆ The unemployment rate in the United Kingdom has been falling steadily for a number of years.

◆ Figure 1 shows that the UK unemployment rate fell from 4.1 per cent in January 2002 to 3.7 per cent in May 2004.

◆ The United Kingdom has a relatively flexible labour market, which makes it easy to hire workers in good times and lay them off in bad times.

◆ Figure 2 shows the total number of jobs created in the UK economy and in the hotel and catering sector from 2002 to the first quarter of 2004.

◆ More jobs have been created than lost in each quarter. And since 2002, the hotel and catering industry has generated one-third of the jobs created in the whole economy.

◆ Figure 3 shows the UK labour market in 2003 and 2004. Increased productivity, especially in the hotel and catering sector, has increased the demand for labour from LD_{03} to LD_{04}.

◆ With no change in the supply of labour, the real wage rate (in 2001 pounds) would rise from £12.30 an hour in 2003 to £12.60 an hour in 2004.

◆ With an enlarged European Union, the supply of foreign workers increases. (The UK market is especially attractive to young Eastern Europeans who value the opportunity to practise and improve their English.) The labour supply curve shifts rightward from LS_{03} to LS_{04}.

◆ The real wage rate rises to £12.50 an hour and employment increases.

◆ The enlarged European Union keeps a lid on UK wage rates but increases UK employment and increases UK real GDP.

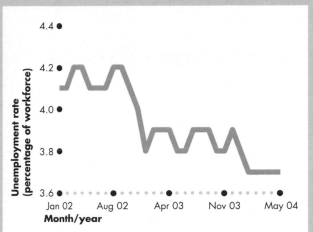

Figure 1 The unemployment rate: 2002–2004

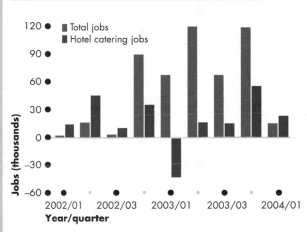

Figure 2 The increase in jobs: 2002–2004

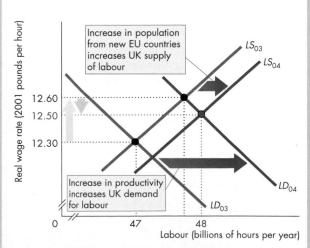

Figure 3 The labour market: 2003 and 2004

Summary

Key Points

The Classical Model: A Preview
(p. 504)

◆ The classical model explains how real GDP, employment and the real wage are determined at full employment.

Real GDP and Employment
(pp. 504–505)

◆ To produce real GDP, we must forgo leisure time and as the quantity of labour increases, real GDP increases.

The Labour Market and Potential GDP (pp. 506–510)

◆ Other things remaining the same, a fall in the real wage rate increases the quantity of labour demanded and decreases the quantity of labour supplied.

◆ At full employment equilibrium, the quantity of labour demanded equals the quantity of labour supplied and real GDP equals potential GDP.

Aggregate Supply (p. 511)

◆ In the long-run, when the price level changes, the money wage rate changes and the real wage rate, employment and real GDP remain constant.

◆ In the short-run, the money wage rate is constant so when the price level changes the real wage rate, employment and real GDP change.

Unemployment at Full Employment
(pp. 512–514)

◆ The unemployment rate at full employment is the natural unemployment rate.

◆ Persistent unemployment arises from job search and job rationing.

The Dynamic Classical Model
(pp. 515–519)

◆ An increase in capital or a technological advance increases both employment and the real wage rate and increases potential GDP.

◆ An increase in population increases the supply of labour, lowers the real wage rate, increases the quantity of labour employed and increases potential GDP. It decreases potential GDP per work hour.

Key Figures

Key Terms

Problems

*1 Robinson Crusoe lives on a desert island on the equator. He has 12 hours of daylight every day to allocate between leisure and work. The table shows seven alternative combinations of leisure and real GDP in the economy of Crusoe:

Possibility	Leisure (hours per day)	Real GDP (euros per day)
A	12	0
B	10	10
C	8	18
D	6	24
E	4	28
F	2	30
G	0	30

a Make a graph of Crusoe's production possibilities frontier for leisure and real GDP.

b Make a table and a graph of Crusoe's production function.

c Find Crusoe's marginal product of labour at different quantities of labour.

2 The people of Nautica have 100 hours every day to allocate between leisure and work. The table shows the combinations of real GDP and leisure in the economy of Nautica:

Possibility	Leisure (hours per day)	Real GDP (euros per day)
A	0	1,500
B	20	1,400
C	40	1,200
D	60	900
E	80	500
F	100	0

a Make a table and a graph of Nautica's production function.

b Find Nautica's marginal product of labour at different quantities of labour.

*3 Use the information provided in problem 1 about the economy of Crusoe. Also, use the information that Crusoe must earn €4.50 an hour. If he earns less than this amount, he does not have enough food on which

to live. He has no interest in earning more than €4.50 an hour. At a real wage rate of €4.50 an hour he is willing to work any number of hours between zero and the total available to him.

a Make a table that shows Crusoe's demand for labour schedule and draw Crusoe's demand for labour curve.

b Make a table that shows Crusoe's supply of labour schedule and draw Crusoe's supply of labour curve.

c What is the full-employment equilibrium real wage rate and quantity of labour in Crusoe's economy?

d Find Crusoe's potential GDP.

4 Use the information provided in problem 2 about the economy of Nautica. Also, use the information that the people of Nautica are willing to work 20 hours a day for a real wage rate of €10 an hour. And for each €0.50 an hour *increase* in the real wage, they are willing to work an *additional* hour a day.

a Make a table that shows Nautica's demand for labour schedule and draw Nautica's demand for labour curve.

b Make a table that shows Nautica's supply of labour schedule and draw Nautica's supply of labour curve.

c Find the full-employment equilibrium real wage rate and quantity of labour in Nautica's economy.

d Find Nautica's potential GDP.

*5 Crusoe, whose economy is described in problems 1 and 3, gets a bright idea. He diverts a stream and increases his food production by 50 per cent. That is, each hour that he works produces 50 per cent more real GDP than before.

a Make a table that shows Crusoe's new production function and new demand for labour schedule.

b Find the new full-employment equilibrium real wage rate and quantity of labour in Crusoe's economy.

c Find Crusoe's new potential GDP.

d Explain and interpret the results you have obtained in parts (a), (b) and (c).

6 Nautica's economy, described in problems 2 and 4, experiences a surge in its population. The supply of labour increases and 50 per cent more hours are supplied at each real wage rate.

a Make a table that shows Nautica's new supply of labour schedule.

b Find the new full-employment equilibrium real wage rate and quantity of labour in Nautica's economy.

---

*Solutions to odd-numbered problems are available on *Parkin Interactive*.

c Find Nautica's new potential GDP.

d Explain and interpret the results you have obtained in parts (a), (b) and (c).

*7 The figure describes the labour market in Cocoa Island. In addition (not shown in the figure) a survey tells us that when Cocoa Island is at full employment, people spend 1,000 hours a day in job search.

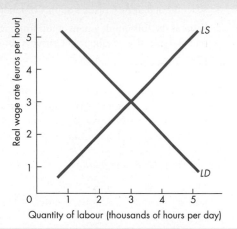

a Find the full-employment equilibrium real wage rate and quantity of labour employed.

b Find potential GDP in Cocoa Island. [Hint: the demand for labour curve tells you the *marginal* product of labour. How do we calculate the marginal product of labour?]

c Calculate the natural rate of unemployment on Cocoa Island.

8 In problem 7, the government of Cocoa Island introduces a minimum wage of €4 an hour.

a Find the new equilibrium real wage rate and quantity of labour employed.

b What now is the potential GDP in Cocoa Island?

c How much of the unemployment results from the minimum wage?

d Calculate the new natural rate of unemployment on Cocoa Island.

Critical Thinking

1 Study *Reading Between the Lines* on pp. 520–521 and then answer the following questions:

a How are labour shortages in key industries in the United Kingdom to be satisfied in the coming years?

b Which sector has the highest demand for labour?

c What is the likely effect of the influx of foreign workers on the aggregate real wage and hours worked in the economy?

2 You are working as an Economic Assistant in the Treasury and must write a memo for the Chancellor that provides a checklist of policy initiatives that will increase potential GDP. Be as imaginative as possible but justify each of your suggestions with reference to the concepts and tools that you have learned about in this chapter.

Web Exercises

Use the links on *Parkin Interactive* to work the following exercises.

1 Obtain information about the economy of Russia during the 1990s. Try to figure out what has happened to the production possibilities frontier and production function and to the demand for labour and supply of labour in Russia during the 1990s. Tell a story about the Russian economy during these years using only the concepts and tools that you have learned about in this chapter.

2 Obtain information about the economy of China during the 1990s. Try to figure out what has happened to the production possibilities frontier and production function and to the demand for labour and supply of labour in China during the 1990s. Tell a story about the Chinese economy during these years using only the concepts and tools that you have learned about in this chapter.

Chapter 24

Expenditure Multipliers: The Keynesian Model

After studying this chapter you will be able to:

◆ Explain the consumption function and the saving function

◆ Explain how equilibrium real GDP is determined when the price level is fixed

◆ Explain the expenditure multiplier

◆ Explain the relationship between equilibrium expenditure and aggregate demand and the influence of changes in the price level on the multiplier

Economic Amplifier or Shock Absorber

Investment and exports fluctuate like the volume of Pavarotti's voice and the uneven surface of a country road. How does the economy react to these fluctuations? Does it react like a BMW to absorb the shocks and provide a smooth ride for its passengers? Or does it react like the amplifier that carries Pavarotti's voice around an open air stadium and enlarge and spread the shocks to affect the millions of participants in an economic opera?

Expenditure Plans and GDP

The model that we study in this chapter describes the economy in the very short run. In this model, all the firms are like your local supermarket. They set their prices, advertise their products and services and sell the quantities their customers are willing to buy. If they persistently sell a greater quantity than they plan to and are constantly running out of stock, they eventually raise their prices. And if they persistently sell a smaller quantity than they plan to and have stocks piling up, they eventually cut their prices. But in the very short term their prices are fixed. They hold the prices they have set and the quantities they sell depend on demand, not supply.

Fixed prices have two implications for the economy as a whole:

1 Because each firm's price is fixed, the *price level* is fixed.

2 Because demand determines the quantities that each firm sells, *aggregate demand* determines the aggregate quantity of goods and services sold, which equals real GDP.

So to understand the fluctuations in real GDP when the price level is fixed, we must understand aggregate demand fluctuations. The aggregate expenditure model is also called the **Keynesian model** because it was first proposed by John Maynard Keynes in his book *The General Theory of Employment, Interest and Money*. Keynes believed that recessions and depressions occur because of insufficient aggregate demand. So Keynes set out to explain fluctuations in aggregate demand by identifying the forces that determine expenditure plans.

Expenditure Plans

Aggregate expenditure has four components:

1 Consumption expenditure

2 Investment

3 Government expenditures on goods and services

4 Net exports: exports minus imports.

These four components of aggregate expenditure sum to real GDP (see Chapter 20, p. 440).

Aggregate planned expenditure is equal to *planned* consumption expenditure plus *planned* investment plus *planned* government expenditures plus *planned* exports minus *planned* imports.

In the very short run, planned investment, planned government expenditures and planned exports are fixed. But planned consumption expenditure and planned imports depend on the level of real GDP itself.

A Two-Way Link between Aggregate Expenditure and GDP

If people spend more or import less, real GDP increases. But if real GDP increases people have higher incomes, some of which they spend on consumption goods and services and imported items. So there is a two-way link between aggregate expenditure and real GDP. Other things remaining the same,

1 An increase in real GDP increases aggregate expenditure.

2 An increase in aggregate expenditure increases real GDP.

You are going to learn how this two-way link between aggregate expenditure and real GDP determines real GDP when the price level is fixed. The starting point is to consider the first piece of the two-way link: the influence of real GDP on planned consumption expenditure and saving.

Consumption Function and Saving Function

Several factors influence consumption expenditure and saving. Among the more important of them are:

1 Disposable income

2 The real interest rate

3 Wealth

4 Expected future income

Disposable income is the most direct influence on consumption plans and saving plans. **Disposable income** equals aggregate income minus taxes plus transfer payments. Aggregate income equals real GDP. So to explore the two-way link between real GDP and planned consumption expenditure, we focus on the relationship between consumption expenditure and disposable income when the other factors are constant.

Real GDP is Y, taxes minus transfer payments are net taxes (T), so the equation for disposable income (YD) is:

$$YD = Y - T$$

Disposable income is either spent on consumption goods and services – consumption expenditure (C) – or saved (S). So planned consumption expenditure plus planned saving equals disposable income. That is:

$$YD = C + S$$

The table in Figure 24.1 shows some examples of planned consumption expenditure and planned saving at different levels of disposable income.

The greater is disposable income, the greater is consumption expenditure and the greater is saving. Also, at each level of disposable income, consumption expenditure plus saving equals disposable income.

The relationship between consumption expenditure and disposable income, with other things remaining the same, is the **consumption function**. The relationship between saving and disposable income, with other things remaining the same, is the **saving function**.

Figure 24.1

Consumption Function and Saving Function

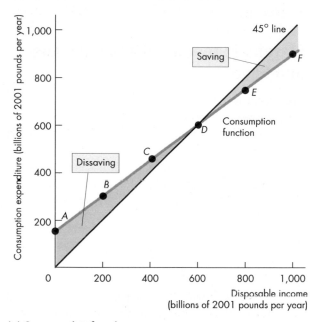

(a) Consumption function

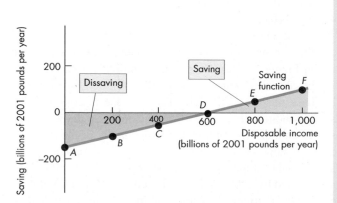

(b) Saving function

	Disposable income	Planned consumption expenditure	Planned saving
		(billions of 2001 pounds per year)	
A	0	150	–150
B	200	300	–100
C	400	450	–50
D	600	600	0
E	800	750	50
F	1,000	900	100

The table shows consumption expenditure and saving plans at various levels of disposable income. When disposable income is £800 (row *E*) planned consumption expenditure is £750 and planned saving is £50.

Part (a) of the figure shows the consumption function (the relationship between consumption expenditure and disposable income). The height of the consumption function measures consumption expenditure at each level of disposable income.

Part (b) shows the saving function (the relationship between saving and disposable income). The height of the saving function measures saving.

Points *A* to *F* on the consumption and saving functions correspond to the rows in the table.

The height of the 45° line in part (a) measures disposable income. So along the 45° line, consumption expenditure equals disposable income. Consumption expenditure plus saving equals disposable income. When the consumption function is above the 45° line, saving is negative (dissaving occurs). When the consumption function is below the 45° line, saving is positive. At the point where the consumption function intersects the 45° line, all disposable income is consumed, saving is zero and the saving function intersects the horizontal axis.

Consumption Function

Figure 24.1(a) shows a consumption function. The y-axis measures consumption expenditure and the x-axis measures disposable income. Along the consumption function, the points labelled A through F correspond to the rows of the table. For example, point E shows that when disposable income is £800 billion, consumption expenditure is £750 billion. Along the consumption function, as disposable income increases, consumption expenditure also increases.

At point A on the consumption function, consumption expenditure is £150 billion even though disposable income is zero. This consumption expenditure is called *autonomous consumption* and is the amount of consumption expenditure that would take place in the short run even if people had no current income. You can think of this amount as the expenditure on the vital necessities of life.

When consumption expenditure exceeds disposable income, past savings are used to pay for current consumption. Such a situation cannot last forever, but it can occur temporarily.

Consumption expenditure in excess of autonomous consumption is called *induced consumption* – expenditure that is induced by an increase in disposable income.

45° Line

Figure 24.1(a) also contains a 45° line, the height of which measures disposable income. At each point on this line, consumption expenditure equals disposable income. In the range over which the consumption function lies above the 45° line – between A and D – consumption expenditure exceeds disposable income. In the range over which the consumption function lies below the 45° line – between D and F – consumption expenditure is less than disposable income. And at the point at which the consumption function intersects the 45° line – at point D – consumption expenditure equals disposable income.

Saving Function

Figure 24.1(b) shows a saving function. The x-axis is exactly the same as that in part (a). The y-axis measures saving. Again, the points marked A through F correspond to the rows of the table. For example, point E shows that when disposable income is £800 billion, saving is £50 billion. Along the saving function, as disposable income increases, saving also increases. At disposable incomes less than £600 billion (point D), saving is

negative. Negative saving is called dissaving. At disposable incomes greater than £600 billion, saving is positive, and at £600 billion, saving is zero.

Notice the connection between the two parts of Figure 24.1. When consumption expenditure exceeds disposable income in part (a), saving is negative in part (b). When consumption expenditure is less than disposable income in part (a), saving is positive in part (b). And when consumption expenditure equals disposable income in part (a), saving is zero in part (b).

When saving is negative (when consumption expenditure exceeds disposable income), past savings are used to pay for current consumption. Such a situation cannot last forever, but it can occur if disposable income falls temporarily.

Marginal Propensities to Consume and Save

The extent to which consumption expenditure changes when disposable income changes depends on the marginal propensity to consume. The **marginal propensity to consume** (*MPC*) is the fraction of a *change* in disposable income that is consumed. It is calculated as the *change* in consumption expenditure (ΔC) divided by the *change* in disposable income (ΔYD) that brought it about. That is:

$$MPC = \frac{\Delta C}{\Delta YD}$$

In the table in Figure 24.1, when disposable income increases from £600 billion to £800 billion, consumption expenditure increases from £600 billion to £750 billion. The £200 billion increase in disposable income increases consumption expenditure of £150 billion. The *MPC* is £150 billion divided by £200 billion, which equals 0.75.

The marginal propensity to consume is the slope of the consumption function. You can check this fact out in Figure 24.2(a). Here, a £200 billion increase in disposable income from £600 billion to £800 billion is the base of the red triangle. The increase in consumption expenditure that results from this increase in disposable income is £150 billion and is the height of the triangle. The slope of the consumption function is given by the formula "slope equals rise over run" and is £150 billion divided by £200 billion, which equals 0.75: the *MPC*.

The amount by which saving changes when disposable income changes depends on the marginal propensity to save. The **marginal propensity to save**

(*MPS*) is the fraction of a *change* in disposable income that is saved. It is calculated as the *change* in saving (Δ*S*) divided by the *change* in disposable income (Δ*YD*) that brought it about. That is:

$$MPS = \frac{\Delta S}{\Delta YD}$$

In the table in Figure 24.1, an increase in disposable income from £600 billion to £800 billion increases saving from zero to £50 billion. The £200 billion change in disposable income increases saving of £50 billion. The *MPS* is £50 billion divided by £200 billion, which equals 0.25.

The marginal propensity to save is the slope of the saving function. You can check this fact out in Figure 24.2(b). Here, a £200 billion increase in disposable income from £600 billion to £800 billion (the base of the red triangle) increases saving by £50 billion (the height of the triangle). The slope of the saving function is £50 billion divided by £200 billion, which equals 0.25 – the *MPS*.

The marginal propensity to consume plus the marginal propensity to save always equals 1. They sum to 1 because consumption expenditure and saving exhaust disposable income. Part of each pound increase in disposable income is consumed, and the remaining part is saved. You can see that these two marginal propensities sum to 1 by using the equation:

$$\Delta C + \Delta S = \Delta YD$$

Divide both sides of the equation by the change in disposable income to obtain:

$$\frac{\Delta C}{\Delta YD} + \frac{\Delta S}{\Delta YD} = 1$$

Δ*C*/Δ*YD* is the *marginal propensity to consume (MPC)* and Δ*S*/Δ*YD* is the *marginal propensity to save (MPS)*, so:

$$MPC + MPS = 1$$

Other Influences on Consumption Expenditure and Saving

You've seen that a change in disposable income leads to changes in consumption expenditure and saving. A change in disposable income brings movements along the consumption function and saving function. A change in other influences on consumption expenditure and

Figure 24.2

Marginal Propensities to Consume and Save

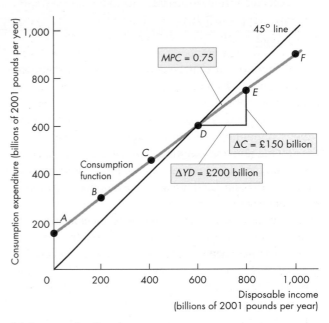

(a) Consumption function

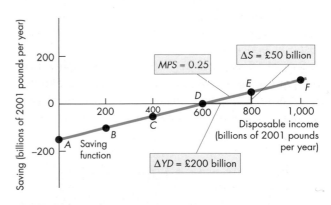

(b) Saving function

The marginal propensity to consume, *MPC*, is equal to the change in consumption expenditure divided by the change in disposable income, other things remaining the same. It is measured by the slope of the consumption function. In part (a), the *MPC* is 0.75.

The marginal propensity to save, *MPS*, is equal to the change in saving divided by the change in disposable income, other things remaining the same. It is measured by the slope of the saving function. In part (b), the *MPS* is 0.25.

saving shifts both the consumption function and the saving function as shown in Figure 24.3.

The other main influences are:

1. Expected future disposable income
2. The real interest rate
3. Wealth

An increase in expected future disposable income makes people feel better off and leads to an increase in current consumption expenditure and a decrease in current saving. A fall in the real interest rate, other things remaining the same, encourages an increase in borrowing and consumption expenditure and a decrease in saving. And an increase in wealth, other things remaining the same, stimulates consumption expenditure and decreases saving.

When expected future disposable income increases, the real interest rate falls, or when wealth increases, consumption expenditure increases and saving decreases. In Figure 24.3 the consumption function shifts upward from CF_0 to CF_1, and the saving function shifts downward from SF_0 to SF_1.

When expected future disposable income decreases, the real interest rate rises, or when wealth decreases, consumption expenditure decreases and saving increases. The consumption function shifts downward from CF_0 to CF_2, and the saving function shifts upward from SF_0 to SF_2. Such shifts often occur when a recession begins because at such a time, expected future disposable income decreases.

Box 24.1 looks at shifts in the UK consumption function and *Reading Between the Lines* on pp. 546–547 examines the effects of changes in the real interest rate on the consumption functions of the Netherlands and Portugal.

Consumption as a Function of Real GDP

You've seen that consumption expenditure changes when disposable income changes. Disposable income changes when either real GDP changes or net taxes change. But net taxes – taxes minus transfer payments – are themselves related to real GDP. When real GDP increases, taxes increase and transfer payments decrease. Because net taxes depend on real GDP, disposable income depends on real GDP and so consumption expenditure depends not only on disposable income but also on real GDP. We use this link between consumption expenditure and real GDP to determine equilibrium expenditure. But before we do so, we need

Figure 24.3

Shifts in the Consumption and Saving Functions

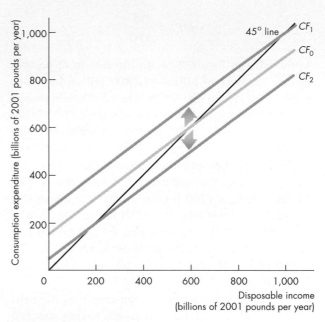

(a) Consumption function

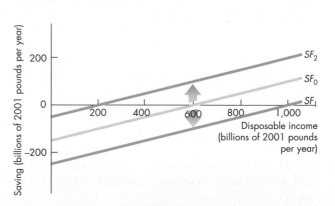

(b) Saving function

A fall in the real interest rate, an increase in wealth or an increase in expected future disposable income increases consumption expenditure, shifts the consumption function upward from CF_0 to CF_1 and shifts the saving function downward from SF_0 to SF_1.

Similarly, a rise in the real interest rate, a decrease in wealth, or a decrease in expected future disposable income shifts the consumption function downward from CF_0 to CF_2 and shifts the saving function upward from SF_0 to SF_2.

Box 24.1
The UK Consumption Function

Figure 1 shows some data on consumption expenditure and disposable income in the United Kingdom. Each blue dot represents consumption expenditure and disposable income for a particular year between 1973 and 2003. The numbers on the dots indicate the year to which the dot refers.

The orange line labelled CF_{73} is an estimate of the UK consumption function in 1973, and the line labelled CF_{03} is an estimate of the UK consumption function in 2003.

The slope of the consumption function in the figure is 0.84, which means that a £100 billion increase in disposable income brings a £84 billion increase in consumption expenditure. This slope, which is an estimate of the marginal propensity to consume, is the average over the period 1997–2003 and it is the middle of the range of values that economists have estimated for the marginal propensity to consume.

The consumption function shifts upward over time as other influences on consumption expenditure change. Of these other influences, expected future disposable income, the real interest rate, and wealth fluctuate and so bring upward *and* downward shifts in the consumption function. But rising wealth and

rising expected future disposable income brings a steady upward shift in the consumption function. As the consumption function shifts upward, autonomous consumption expenditure increases.

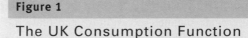

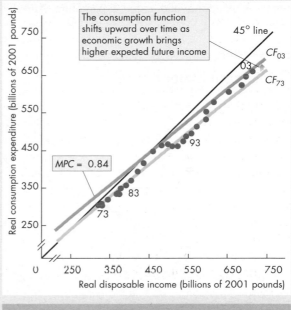

The UK Consumption Function

Source: Office for National Statistics.

---

to look at one further component of aggregate expenditure: imports. Like consumption expenditure, imports also are influenced by real GDP.

Import Function

UK imports are determined by a number of factors, but in the short run with fixed prices, one factor dominates: real GDP in the United Kingdom. Other things remaining the same, the greater the UK real GDP, the larger is the quantity of UK imports. So an increase in UK real GDP brings an increase in UK imports.

The relationship between imports and real GDP is determined by the marginal propensity to import. The **marginal propensity to import** is the fraction of an increase in real GDP that is spent on imports. It is calculated as the change in imports divided by the change in real GDP that brought it about, other things remaining the same. For example, if a £100 billion increase in real GDP increases imports by £30 billion, the marginal propensity to import is 0.3.

Review Quiz

1 Which components of aggregate planned expenditure are influenced by real GDP?
2 Define the marginal propensity to consume.
3 What is your estimate of your own marginal propensity to consume? After you graduate and begin work, will your marginal propensity to consume change? Why or why not?
4 How do we calculate the effects of real GDP on consumption expenditure and imports?

Real GDP influences consumption and imports. But consumption and imports – along with investment, government expenditures and exports – influence real GDP. Your next task is to study this second piece of the two-way link between aggregate expenditure and real GDP and see how all the components of aggregate planned expenditure interact to determine real GDP.

Equilibrium Expenditure at a Fixed Price Level

You are now going to discover how aggregate expenditure plans interact to determine real GDP when the price level is fixed. First, we will study the relationship between aggregate planned expenditure and real GDP. Second, we'll learn about the key distinction between *planned* expenditure and *actual* expenditure. And third,

we'll study equilibrium expenditure, a situation in which aggregate planned expenditure and actual expenditure are equal.

The relationship between aggregate planned expenditure and real GDP can be described by either an aggregate expenditure schedule or an aggregate expenditure curve. The *aggregate expenditure schedule* lists aggregate planned expenditure generated at each level of real GDP. The *aggregate expenditure curve* is a graph of the aggregate expenditure schedule.

Figure 24.4

Aggregate Expenditure

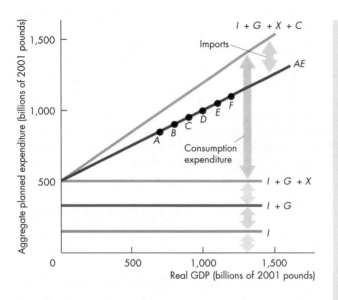

The aggregate expenditure schedule shows the relationship between aggregate planned expenditure and real GDP. Aggregate planned expenditure is the sum of planned consumption expenditure, investment, government expenditure on goods and services, and exports minus imports. For example, in row *B* of the table, when real GDP is £800 billion, planned consumption expenditure is £560 billion, planned investment is £150 billion, planned government expenditures on goods and services are £180 billion, planned exports are £170 billion, and planned imports are £160 billion. So when real GDP is £800 billion, aggregate planned expenditure is £900 billion (£560 + £150 + £180 + £170 − £160). The schedule shows that aggregate planned expenditure increases as real GDP increases.

This relationship is graphed as the aggregate expenditure curve *AE*. The components of aggregate expenditure that increase with real GDP are consumption expenditure and imports. The other components – investment, government expenditures and exports – do not vary with real GDP.

		Planned expenditure					
	Real GDP **(Y)**	**Consumption** **expenditure** **(C)**	**Investment** **(I)**	**Government** **expenditures** **(G)**	**Exports** **(X)**	**Imports** **(M)**	**Aggregate** **planned** **expenditure** **(AE = C + I + G + X − M)**
				(billions of 2001 pounds)			
	0	0	150	180	170	0	500
A	700	490	150	180	170	140	850
B	800	560	150	180	170	160	900
C	900	630	150	180	170	180	950
D	1,000	700	150	180	170	200	1,000
E	1,100	770	150	180	170	220	1,050
F	1,200	840	150	180	170	240	1,100

Aggregate Planned Expenditure and Real GDP

The table in Figure 24.4 sets out an aggregate expenditure schedule together with the components of aggregate planned expenditure. To calculate aggregate planned expenditure at a given real GDP, we add the various components together. The first column of the table shows real GDP and the second column shows the consumption expenditure generated by each level of real GDP. A £700 billion increase in real GDP generates a £490 billion increase in consumption expenditure – the *MPC* is 0.7.

The next two columns show investment and government expenditures on goods and services. Investment depends on factors such as the real interest rate and the expected future profit. But at a given point in time, these factors generate a particular level of investment. Suppose this level of investment is £150 billion. Also, suppose that government expenditures on goods and services are £180 billion.

The next two columns show exports and imports. Exports are influenced by income in the rest of the world, prices of foreign-made goods and services relative to the prices of similar goods and services produced in the United Kingdom, and foreign exchange rates. But exports are not directly affected by real GDP in the United Kingdom. In the table, exports appear as a constant £180 billion. In contrast, imports increase as real GDP increases. A £100 billion increase in real GDP generates a £20 billion increase in imports – the marginal propensity to import is 0.2.

The final column of the table shows aggregate planned expenditure – the sum of planned consumption expenditure, investment, government expenditures on goods and services, and exports minus imports.

Figure 24.4 plots an aggregate expenditure curve. Real GDP is shown on the *x*-axis and aggregate planned expenditure on the *y*-axis. The aggregate expenditure curve is the red line *AE*. Points *A* to *F* on this curve correspond to the rows of the table. The *AE* curve is a graph of aggregate planned expenditure (the last column) plotted against real GDP (the first column).

Figure 24.4 also shows the components of aggregate expenditure. The constant components – investment (*I*), government expenditures on goods and services (*G*), and exports (*X*) – are shown by the horizontal lines in the figure. Consumption expenditure (*C*) is the vertical gap between the lines labelled *I* + *G* + *X* + *C* and *I* + *G* + *X*.

To construct the *AE* curve, subtract imports (*M*) from the *I* + *G* + *X* + *C* line. Aggregate expenditure is

expenditure on UK-made goods and services. But the components of aggregate expenditure, *C*, *I* and *G*, include expenditure on imported goods and services. For example, if you buy a new mobile phone, your expenditure is part of consumption expenditure. But if the mobile phone is a Nokia made in Finland, your expenditure on it must be subtracted from consumption expenditure to find out how much is spent on goods and services produced in the United Kingdom – on UK real GDP. Money paid to Nokia for mobile phone imports from Finland does not add to aggregate expenditure in the United Kingdom.

Because imports are only a part of aggregate expenditure, when we subtract imports from the other components of aggregate expenditure, aggregate planned expenditure still increases as real GDP increases, as you can see in Figure 24.4.

Consumption expenditure minus imports, which varies with real GDP, is called **induced expenditure**. The sum of investment, government expenditures and exports, which does not vary with real GDP, is called **autonomous expenditure**. Consumption expenditure and imports can also have an autonomous component – a component that does not vary with real GDP. Another way of thinking about autonomous expenditure is that it would be the level of aggregate planned expenditure if real GDP were zero.

In Figure 24.4, autonomous expenditure is £500 billion – aggregate planned expenditure when real GDP is zero. For each £100 billion increase in real GDP, induced expenditure increases by £50 billion.

The aggregate expenditure curve summarizes the relationship between aggregate planned expenditure and real GDP. But what determines the point on the aggregate expenditure curve at which the economy operates? What determines *actual* aggregate expenditure?

Actual Expenditure, Planned Expenditure and Real GDP

Actual aggregate expenditure is always equal to real GDP, as we saw in Chapter 20 (p. 440). But aggregate *planned* expenditure does not necessarily equal actual aggregate expenditure and real GDP. How can actual expenditure and planned expenditure differ from each other? Why don't expenditure plans get implemented? The main reason is that firms might end up with greater inventories or stocks or with smaller inventories or stocks than planned. People carry out their consumption expenditure plans, the government implements its planned expenditures on goods and services, and net exports are as planned. Firms carry out their plans to purchase new buildings, plant and equipment. But one component of investment is the increase in firms' stocks of goods. If aggregate planned expenditure is less than real GDP, firms don't sell all the goods and services they produce and they end up with stocks they hadn't planned. If aggregate planned expenditure is less than real GDP, firms sell more goods and services than they produce and they end up with smaller stocks than they had planned.

Equilibrium Expenditure

Equilibrium expenditure is the level of aggregate expenditure that occurs when aggregate *planned* expenditure equals real GDP. It is a level of aggregate expenditure and real GDP at which everyone's spending plans are fulfilled. When the price level is fixed, equilibrium expenditure determines real GDP. When aggregate planned expenditure and actual aggregate expenditure are unequal, a process of convergence towards

---

Figure 24.5

Equilibrium Expenditure

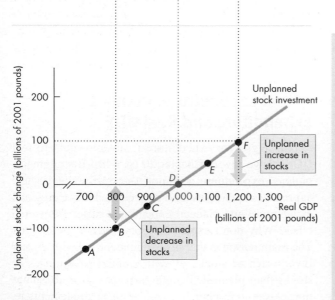

(a) Equilibrium expenditure

	Real GDP (*Y*)	Aggregate planned expenditure (*AE*)	Unplanned stock change (*Y* – *AE*)
	(billions of 2001 pounds)		
A	700	850	−150
B	800	900	−100
C	900	950	−50
D	**1,000**	**1,000**	**0**
E	1,100	1,050	50
F	1,200	1,100	100

(b) Unplanned stock changes

The table shows expenditure plans at different levels of real GDP. When real GDP is £1,000 billion, aggregate planned expenditure equals real GDP.

Part (a) of the figure illustrates equilibrium expenditure, which occurs when aggregate planned expenditure equals real GDP at the intersection of the 45° line and the *AE* curve. Part (b) of the figure shows the forces that bring about equilibrium expenditure.

When aggregate planned expenditure exceeds real GDP, firms' stocks decrease – for example, point *B* in both parts of the figure. Firms increase production and real GDP increases. When aggregate planned expenditure is less than real GDP, firms' stocks increase – for example, point *E* in both parts of the figure. Firms decrease production and real GDP decreases. When aggregate planned expenditure equals real GDP, there are no unplanned stock changes and real GDP remains constant at equilibrium expenditure.

equilibrium expenditure occurs. And throughout this convergence process real GDP adjusts. Let's examine equilibrium expenditure and the process that brings it about.

Figure 24.5(a) illustrates equilibrium expenditure. The table sets out aggregate planned expenditure at various levels of real GDP. These values are plotted as points A through F along the AE curve. The 45° line shows all the points at which aggregate planned expenditure equals real GDP. Thus where the AE curve lies above the 45° line, aggregate planned expenditure exceeds real GDP; where the AE curve lies below the 45° line, aggregate planned expenditure is less than real GDP; and where the AE curve intersects the 45° line, aggregate planned expenditure equals real GDP. Point D illustrates equilibrium expenditure. At this point, real GDP is £1,000 billion.

Convergence to Equilibrium

What are the forces that move aggregate expenditure towards its equilibrium level? To answer this question, we must look at a situation in which aggregate expenditure is away from its equilibrium level. Suppose that in Figure 24.5, actual aggregate expenditure is also £800 billion. But aggregate *planned* expenditure is £900 billion, point B in Figure 24.5(a). Aggregate planned expenditure exceeds *actual* expenditure. When people spend £900 billion, and firms produce goods and services worth £800 billion, firms' inventories (stocks) fall by £100 billion, point B in Figure 24.5(b). Because the change in stocks is part of investment, *actual* investment is £100 billion less than *planned* investment.

Real GDP doesn't remain at £800 billion for long. Firms have inventory (stock) targets based on their sales. When stocks fall below target, firms increase production to restore stocks to their target levels. To increase stocks, firms hire additional labour and increase production.

Suppose that firms increase production in the next period by £100 billion. Real GDP increases by £100 billion to £900 billion. But again, aggregate planned expenditure exceeds real GDP. When real GDP is £900 billion, aggregate planned expenditure is £950 billion, point C in Figure 24.5(a). Again, stocks decrease, but this time by less than before. With real GDP of £900 billion and aggregate planned expenditure of £950 billion, stocks decrease by £50 billion, point C in Figure 24.5(b). Again, to restore stocks, firms hire additional labour and production increases; real GDP increases yet further.

The process that we have just described – planned expenditure exceeds real GDP, stocks decrease and production increases to restore the stocks back to their target levels – ends when real GDP has reached £1,000 billion. At this real GDP, there is equilibrium. Unplanned stock changes are zero. Firms do not change their production.

You can do a similar experiment to the one we've just done, but starting with a level of real GDP greater than equilibrium expenditure. In this case, planned expenditure is less than actual expenditure, stocks pile up and firms cut production. As before, real GDP keeps on changing (decreasing this time) until it reaches its equilibrium level of £1,000 billion.

This process of convergence to equilibrium is driven by changes in output and real GDP, not by changes in prices. Throughout the entire process the price level (and the price of every firm's output) remains constant.

Review Quiz

1   Explain the relationship between aggregate planned expenditure and real GDP.

2   Distinguish between autonomous expenditure and induced expenditure.

3   What is the relationship between aggregate planned expenditure and real GDP at equilibrium expenditure?

4   What adjusts to achieve equilibrium expenditure?

5   If real GDP and aggregate expenditure are less than their equilibrium levels, what happens to firms' inventories or stocks? How do firms change their production? What happens to real GDP?

6   If real GDP and aggregate expenditure are greater than their equilibrium levels, what happens to firms' inventories or stocks? How do firms change their production? What happens to real GDP?

We've learned that when the price level is fixed, real GDP is determined by equilibrium expenditure. And we have seen how unplanned changes in inventories or stocks and the production response they generate bring a convergence towards equilibrium expenditure. We're now going to study *changes* in equilibrium expenditure and discover an economic amplifier called the *multiplier*.

The Multiplier

Investment and exports can change for many reasons. A fall in the real interest rate might induce firms to increase their planned investment. A wave of innovation, such as occurred with the spread of multimedia computers in the 1990s, might increase expected future profits and lead firms to increase their planned investment. With stiff competition in the world car market, UK car producers might increase their investment in robotic assembly lines. An economic boom in the United States and Canada might lead to a large increase in their expenditure on UK exports. These are all examples of increases in autonomous expenditure in the United Kingdom.

When autonomous expenditure increases, aggregate expenditure increases, and so do equilibrium expenditure and real GDP. But the increase in equilibrium expenditure and real GDP is *larger* than the change in autonomous expenditure. The **multiplier** is the amount by which a change in autonomous expenditure is magnified or multiplied to determine the change in equilibrium expenditure and real GDP.

It is easiest to get the basic idea of the multiplier if we work with an example economy in which there are no income taxes and no imports. So we'll first assume that these factors are absent. Then, when you understand the basic idea, we'll bring these factors back into play and see what difference they make to the multiplier.

The Basic Idea of the Multiplier

Suppose that investment increases. The additional expenditure by businesses means that aggregate expenditure and real GDP increases. The increase in real GDP increases disposable income, and with no income taxes, real GDP and disposable income increase by the same amount. The increase in disposable income brings an increase in consumption expenditure. And the increased consumption expenditure adds even more to aggregate expenditure. Real GDP and disposable income increase further, and so does consumption expenditure. The initial increase in investment brings an even bigger increase in aggregate expenditure because it induces an increase in consumption expenditure. The magnitude of the increase in aggregate expenditure that results from an increase in autonomous expenditure is determined by the *multiplier*.

The table in Figure 24.6 sets out aggregate planned expenditure. Initially, when real GDP is £900 billion,

aggregate planned expenditure is £925 billion. For each £100 billion increase in real GDP, aggregate planned expenditure increases by £75 billion. This aggregate expenditure schedule is shown in the graph as the aggregate expenditure curve AE_0.

Initially, equilibrium expenditure is £1,000 billion. You can see this equilibrium in row B of the table, and in the graph where the curve AE_0 intersects the 45° line at the point marked B.

Now suppose that autonomous expenditure increases by £50 billion. What happens to equilibrium expenditure? You can see the answer in Figure 24.6. When this increase in autonomous expenditure is added to the original aggregate planned expenditure, aggregate planned expenditure increases by £50 billion at each level of real GDP. The new aggregate expenditure curve is AE_1. The new equilibrium expenditure, highlighted in the table (row D'), occurs where AE_1 intersects the 45° line and is £1,200 billion (point D'). At this point, aggregate planned expenditure equals real GDP. Equilibrium expenditure is £1,200 billion.

The Multiplier Effect

In Figure 24.6, the increase in autonomous expenditure of £50 billion increases equilibrium expenditure from £1,000 billion to £1,200 billion – an increase of £200 billion. That is, the change in autonomous expenditure leads to an amplified change in equilibrium expenditure. This amplified change is the *multiplier effect* – equilibrium expenditure increases by *more than* the increase in autonomous expenditure. The multiplier is greater than 1.

Initially, when autonomous expenditure increases, aggregate planned expenditure exceeds real GDP. As a result, stocks decrease. Firms respond by increasing production so as to restore their stocks to thir target levels. As production increases, so does real GDP. With a higher level of real GDP, *induced expenditure* increases. So equilibrium expenditure increases by the sum of the initial increase in autonomous expenditure and the increase in induced expenditure. In this example, the initial increase in autonomous expenditure is £50 billion and induced expenditure increases by £150 billion, so equilibrium expenditure increases by £200 billion.

Although we have just analyzed the effects of an *increase* in autonomous expenditure, the same analysis applies to a decrease in autonomous expenditure. If initially the aggregate expenditure curve is AE_1, equilibrium expenditure and real GDP are £1,200 billion. A decrease in autonomous expenditure of £50 billion

Figure 24.6

The Multiplier

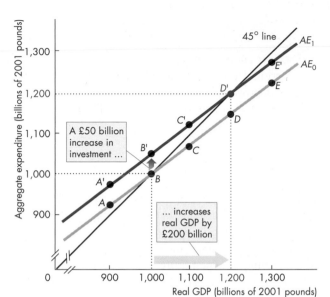

Real GDP (Y)	Aggregate planned expenditure			
	Original (AE₀)		New (AE₁)	
	(billions of 2001 pounds)			
900	A	925	A'	975
1,000	**B**	**1,000**	B'	1,050
1,100	C	1,075	C'	1,125
1,200	**D**	**1,150**	**D'**	**1,200**
1,300	E	1,225	E'	1,275

A £50 billion increase in autonomous expenditure shifts the *AE* curve upward by £50 billion from *AE*₀ to *AE*₁. Equilibrium expenditure increases by £200 billion from £1,000 billion to £1,200 billion. The increase in equilibrium expenditure is 4 times the increase in autonomous expenditure, so the multiplier is 4.

shifts the aggregate expenditure curve downward by £50 billion to *AE*₀. Equilibrium expenditure decreases from £1,200 billion to £1,000 billion. The decrease in equilibrium expenditure (£200 billion) is larger than the decrease in autonomous expenditure that brought it about (£50 billion).

Why is the Multiplier Greater than 1?

We've seen that equilibrium expenditure increases by more than the increase in autonomous expenditure. This makes the multiplier greater than 1. How come? Why does equilibrium expenditure increase by more than the increase in autonomous expenditure?

The multiplier is greater than 1 because of induced expenditure – an increase in autonomous expenditure *induces* further increases in expenditure. If Vodafone spends £10 million on a new telephone-video system, aggregate expenditure and real GDP immediately increase by £10 million. But that is not the end of the story. Electrical engineers and video-system designers now have more income, and they spend part of the extra income on cars, microwave ovens, holidays, DVDs and a host of other consumption goods and services.

Real GDP now increases by the initial £10 million plus the extra consumption expenditure induced by the £10 million increase in income. The producers of cars, microwave ovens, holidays, DVDs and other consumption goods and services now have increased incomes, and they, in turn, spend part of the increase in their incomes on consumption goods and services. Additional income induces additional expenditure, which creates additional income.

We've seen that a change in autonomous expenditure has a multiplier effect on real GDP. But how big is the multiplier?

The Size of the Multiplier

The *multiplier* is the amount by which a change in autonomous expenditure is multiplied to determine the change in equilibrium expenditure that it generates. To calculate the multiplier, we divide the change in equilibrium expenditure by the change in autonomous expenditure. Let's calculate the multiplier for the example in Figure 24.6.

Initially, equilibrium expenditure is £1,000 billion. Then autonomous expenditure increases by £50 billion, and equilibrium expenditure increases by £200 billion to £1,200 billion. So:

$$\text{Multiplier} = \frac{\text{Change in equilibrium expenditure}}{\text{Change in autonomous expenditure}}$$

$$= \frac{£200 \text{ billion}}{£50 \text{ billion}} = 4$$

The Multiplier and the Slope of the *AE* Curve

What determines the magnitude of the multiplier? The answer is the slope of the *AE* curve. The steeper the slope of the *AE* curve, the larger is the multiplier. To see why, think about what the slope of the *AE* curve tells you. It tells you by how much induced expenditure increases when real GDP increases. The steeper the *AE* curve, the greater is the increase in induced expenditure that results from a given increase in real GDP. Let's do a calculation to show the relationship between the slope of the *AE* curve and the multiplier.

The change in real GDP (ΔY) equals the change in induced expenditure (ΔN) plus the change in autonomous expenditure (ΔA). That is:

$$\Delta Y = \Delta N + \Delta A.$$

The slope of the *AE* curve equals the "rise", ΔN, divided by the "run", ΔY. That is:

$$\text{Slope of } AE \text{ curve} = \Delta N \div \Delta Y$$

So:

$$\Delta N = \text{Slope of } AE \text{ curve} \times \Delta Y$$

Now use this equation to replace ΔN in the first equation above to give:

$$\Delta Y = (\text{Slope of } AE \text{ curve} \cdot \Delta Y) + \Delta A.$$

Now, solve for ΔY as:

$$(1 - \text{Slope of } AE \text{ curve}) \times \Delta Y = \Delta A$$

and rearrange to give:

$$\Delta Y = \frac{\Delta A}{1 - \text{Slope of the } AE \text{ curve}}$$

Finally, divide both sides of the previous equation by ΔA to give:

$$\text{Multiplier} = \frac{\Delta Y}{\Delta A}$$

$$= \frac{1}{1 - \text{Slope of the } AE \text{ curve}}$$

Using the numbers for Figure 24.6, the slope of the *AE* curve 0.75, so the multiplier is:

$$\text{Multiplier} = \frac{1}{1 - 0.75} = \frac{1}{0.25} = 4$$

When there are no income taxes and no imports, the slope of the *AE* curve equals the marginal propensity to consume (*MPC*). So the multiplier is:

$$\text{Multiplier} = \frac{1}{(1 - MPC)}$$

There is another formula for the multiplier. Because the marginal propensity to consume (*MPC*) plus the marginal propensity to save (*MPS*) adds up to 1, the term $(1 - MPC)$ equals *MPS*. Therefore, another formula for the multiplier is:

$$\text{Multiplier} = \frac{1}{MPS}$$

Because the marginal propensity to save (*MPS*) is a fraction – a number lying between 0 and 1 – the multiplier is greater than 1.

Figure 24.7 illustrates the multiplier process. In round 1, autonomous expenditure increases by £50 billion (shown by the green bar). At this time, induced expenditure does not change, so aggregate expenditure and real GDP increase by £50 billion. In round 2, the larger real GDP induces more consumption expenditure. Induced expenditure increases by 0.75 times the increase in real GDP, so the increase in real GDP of £50 billion induces a further increase in expenditure of £37.5 billion. This change in induced expenditure (the green bar in round 2), when added to the previous increase in expenditure (the blue bar in round 2), increases aggregate expenditure and real GDP by £87.5 billion. The round 2 increase in real GDP induces a round 3 increase in expenditure. The process repeats through successive rounds. Each increase in real GDP is 0.75 times the previous increase. The cumulative increase in real GDP gradually approaches £200 billion.

So far, we've ignored imports and income taxes. Let's now see how these two factors influence the multiplier.

Imports and Income Taxes

The multiplier is determined, in general, not only by the marginal propensity to consume but also by the marginal propensity to import and by the marginal tax rate.

Imports make the multiplier smaller than it otherwise would be. To see why, think about what happens following an increase in investment in the United Kingdom. An increase in investment increases real GDP, which in turn increases consumption expenditure

Figure 24.7

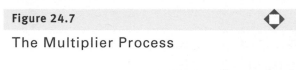

The Multiplier Process

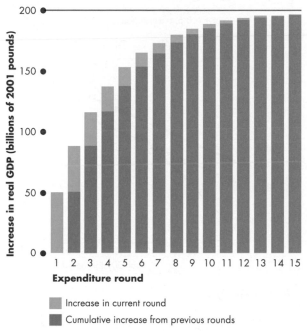

Autonomous expenditure increases in round 1 by £50 billion. As a result, real GDP increases by the same amount. With a marginal propensity to consume of 0.75, each additional pound of real GDP induces an additional 0.75 of a pound of aggregate expenditure.

The round 1 increase in real GDP induces an increase in consumption expenditure of £37.5 billion in round 2. At the end of round 2, real GDP has increased by £87.5 billion. The extra £37.5 billion of real GDP in round 2 induces a further increase in consumption expenditure of £28.1 billion in round 3. Real GDP increases yet further to £115.6 billion.

This process continues with real GDP increasing by ever smaller amounts. When the process comes to an end, real GDP has increased by a total of £200 billion.

in the United Kingdom. But part of this increase in consumption expenditure is expenditure on imported goods and services, not expenditure on UK-produced good and services. Only expenditure on goods and services produced in the United Kingdom increases real GDP in the United Kingdom. The larger the marginal propensity to import, the smaller is the change in UK real GDP.

Income taxes also make the multiplier smaller than it otherwise would be. Again, think about what happens following an increase in investment. An increase in investment increases real GDP. But because income taxes increase with income, disposable income increases by less than the increase in real GDP. Consequently, consumption expenditure increases by less than it would if taxes had not changed. The larger the marginal tax rate, the smaller is the change in disposable income and real GDP.

The marginal propensity to import and the marginal tax rate together with the marginal propensity to consume determine the slope of the *AE* curve and the multiplier. The multiplier is equal to 1 divided by (1 minus the slope of the *AE* curve).

Figure 24.8 (overleaf) compares two situations. In Figure 24.8(a) there are no imports and no taxes. The marginal propensity to consume, which also equals the slope of the *AE* curve, is 0.75 and the multiplier is 4. In Figure 24.8(b), imports and income taxes decrease the slope of the *AE* curve to 0.5. In this case, the multiplier is 2.

Over time, changes in the marginal propensity to consume, the marginal propensity to import and tax rates change the value of the multiplier. These changes make the multiplier hard to predict. But they do not alter the fundamental fact that an initial change in autonomous expenditure leads to a magnified change in aggregate expenditure and real GDP.

The Mathematical Note on pp. 548–549 shows the effects of taxes, imports, and the *MPC* on the multiplier.

Now that we've studied the multiplier and the factors that influence its magnitude, let's use what we've learned to gain some insights into the most critical points in the life of an economy: business cycle turning points.

Business Cycle Turning Points

At business cycle turning points, the economy moves from expansion to recession or from recession to expansion. Economists understand these business cycle turning points like seismologists understand earthquakes. They know quite a lot about the forces and mechanisms that produce them, but they can't predict them. The forces that bring business cycle turning points are the swings in investment and exports. The mechanism that gives momentum to the economy's new direction is the multiplier. Let's use what we've now learned to examine these turning points.

Figure 24.8

The Multiplier and the Slope of the *AE* Curve

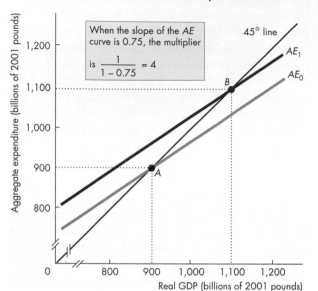

When the slope of the *AE* curve is 0.75, the multiplier is $\dfrac{1}{1-0.75} = 4$

(a) Multiplier is 4

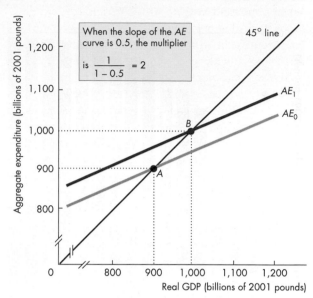

When the slope of the *AE* curve is 0.5, the multiplier is $\dfrac{1}{1-0.5} = 2$

(b) Multiplier is 2

Imports and income taxes make the *AE* curve less steep and reduce the value of the multiplier. In part (a), with no imports and income taxes the slope of the *AE* curve is 0.75 (the marginal propensity to consume) and the multiplier is

4. But with imports and income taxes, the slope of the *AE* curve is less than the marginal propensity to consume. In part (b), the slope of the *AE* curve is 0.5. In this case, the multiplier is 2.

An Expansion Begins

An expansion is triggered by an increase in autonomous expenditure. At the moment the economy turns the corner into an expansion, aggregate planned expenditure exceeds real GDP. In this situation, firms see their inventories or stocks taking an unplanned dive. The expansion now begins. To meet their stock targets, firms increase production and real GDP begins to increase. This initial increase in real GDP brings higher incomes that stimulate consumption expenditure. The multiplier process kicks in and the expansion picks up speed.

A Recession Begins

The process we've just described works in reverse at a business cycle peak. A recession is triggered by a decrease in autonomous expenditure. At the moment the economy turns the corner into recession, real GDP exceeds aggregate planned expenditure. In this situation, firms see unplanned stocks piling up. The recession now begins. To decrease their stocks, firms cut production and real GDP begins to decrease. This initial decrease in real

GDP brings lower incomes that cut consumption expenditure. The multiplier process reinforces the initial cut in autonomous expenditure and the recession takes hold.

The 2003–2004 Expansion

During 2003–2004, the UK economy picked up speed. During this expansion, in the second quarter of 2003, stocks fell by £514 million. With stocks falling, firms increased production. By the beginning of 2004, stocks were probably close to target and the expansion during 2004 would be expected to pull back from its rapid 2003 rate.

Review Quiz

1   What is the multiplier? What does it determine?
2   Why does the multiplier matter?
3   How do the marginal propensity to consume, the marginal tax rate and the marginal propensity to import influence the multiplier?
4   If autonomous expenditure decreases, which phase of the business cycle does the economy enter?

The Multiplier and the Price Level

When firms can't keep up with sales and their inventories or stocks fall below target, they increase production, but at some point they raise their prices. Similarly, when firms find unwanted stocks piling up, they decrease production, but eventually they cut their prices.

So far, we've studied the macroeconomic consequences of firms changing their production levels when their sales change, but we've not looked at the effects of price changes. When individual firms change their prices, the economy's price level changes.

To study the simultaneous determination of real GDP and the price level, we use the *aggregate supply– aggregate demand model*, which is explained in Chapter 22. But to understand how aggregate demand adjusts, we need to work out the connection between the aggregate supply–aggregate demand model and the equilibrium expenditure model that we've used in this chapter. The key to understanding the relationship between these two models is the distinction between the aggregate expenditure and aggregate demand and the related distinction between the aggregate expenditure curve and the aggregate demand curve.

Aggregate Expenditure and Aggregate Demand

The aggregate expenditure curve is the relationship between the aggregate planned expenditure and real GDP, when all other influences on aggregate planned expenditure remain the same. The aggregate demand curve is the relationship between the aggregate quantity of goods and services demanded and the price level, when all other influences on aggregate demand remain the same. Let's explore the links between these two relationships.

Aggregate Expenditure and the Price Level

When the price level changes, aggregate planned expenditure changes and the quantity of real GDP demanded changes. The aggregate demand curve slopes downward. Why?

There are two main reasons:

◆ Wealth effect
◆ Substitution effects

Wealth Effect

Other things remaining the same, the higher the price level, the smaller is the purchasing power of people's real wealth. For example, suppose you have £100 in the bank and the price level is 110. If the price level rises to 130, your £100 buys fewer goods and services. You are less wealthy. With less wealth, you will probably want to spend a bit less and save a bit more. The higher the price level, other things remaining the same, the lower is aggregate planned expenditure.

Substitution Effects

A rise in the price level today, other things remaining the same, makes current goods and services more costly relative to future goods and services and results in a delay in purchases – an *intertemporal substitution*. A rise in the price level, other things remaining the same, makes UK-produced goods more expensive relative to foreign-produced goods and services and increases imports and decreases exports – an *international substitution*.

When the price level rises, each of these effects reduces aggregate planned expenditure at each level of real GDP. As a result, when the price level *rises*, the *AE* curve shifts *downward*. A fall in the price level has the opposite effect. When the price level *falls*, the *AE* curve shifts *upward*.

Figure 24.9(a) illustrates the shifts of the *AE* curve. When the price level is 110, the aggregate expenditure curve is AE_0, which intersects the 45° line at point *B*. Equilibrium expenditure and real GDP are £1,000 billion. If the price level increases to 130, the aggregate expenditure curve shifts downward to AE_1, which intersects the 45° line at point *A*. Equilibrium expenditure and real GDP are £900 billion. If the price level decreases to 90, the aggregate expenditure curve shifts upward to AE_2, which intersects the 45° line at point *C*. Equilibrium expenditure and real GDP are £1,100 billion.

We've just seen that when the price level changes, other things remaining the same, the aggregate expenditure curve shifts and equilibrium expenditure changes. And when the price level changes, other things remaining the same, there is a movement along the aggregate demand curve. Figure 24.9(b) illustrates these movements. At a price level of 110, the aggregate quantity of goods and services demanded is £1,000 billion – point *B* on the aggregate demand curve *AD*. If the price level increases to 130, the aggregate quantity of goods and

Figure 24.9

Aggregate Demand

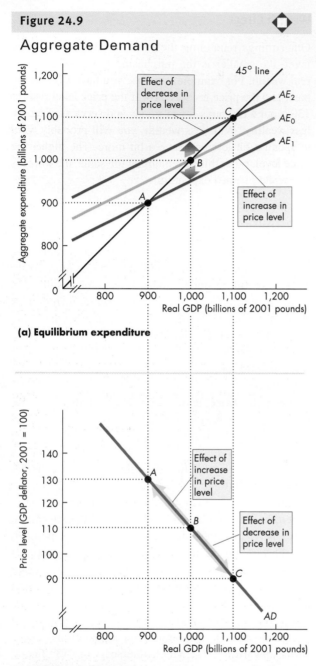

(a) Equilibrium expenditure

(b) Aggregate demand

A change in the price level *shifts* the *AE* curve and results in a *movement along* the *AD* curve. When the price level is 110, the *AE* curve is AE_0. Equilibrium expenditure is £1,000 billion at point *B*. When the price level rises to 130, the *AE* curve shifts downward to AE_1 and equilibrium expenditure is £900 billion at point *A*. When the price level falls to 90, the *AE* curve shifts upward to AE_2, and equilibrium expenditure is £1,100 billion at point *C*. Points *A*, *B* and *C* on the *AD* curve correspond to the equilibrium expenditure points *A*, *B* and *C* in part (a).

services demanded decreases to £900 billion. There is a movement along the aggregate demand curve from point *B* to point *A*. If the price level decreases to 90, the aggregate quantity of goods and services demanded increases to £1,100 billion. There is a movement along the aggregate demand curve from point *B* to point *C*.

Each point on the *AD* curve corresponds to a point of equilibrium expenditure. The equilibrium expenditure points *A*, *B* and *C* in Figure 24.9(a) correspond to points *A*, *B* and *C* on the *AD* curve in Figure 24.9(b).

A change in the price level, other things remaining the same, shifts the *AE* curve and brings a movement along the *AD* curve. A change in any other influence on aggregate planned expenditure shifts *both* the *AE* curve and the *AD* curve. For example, an increase in investment or in exports increases both aggregate planned expenditure and aggregate demand and shifts both the *AE* curve and the *AD* curve. Figure 24.10 illustrates the effect of such an increase.

Initially, the aggregate expenditure curve is AE_0 in part (a) and the aggregate demand curve is AD_0 in part (b). The price level is 110, real GDP is £1,000 billion, and the economy is at point *A* in both parts of the figure. Now suppose that investment increases by £100 billion. At a constant price level of 110, the aggregate expenditure curve shifts upward to AE_1. This curve intersects the 45° line at an equilibrium expenditure of £1,200 billion (point *B*).

This equilibrium expenditure of £1,200 billion is the aggregate quantity of goods and services demanded at a price level of 110, as shown by point *B* in part (b). Point *B* lies on a new aggregate demand curve. The aggregate demand curve has shifted rightward to AD_1.

But how do we know by how much the *AD* curve shifts? The multiplier determines the answer. The larger the multiplier, the larger is the shift in the *AD* curve that results from a given change in autonomous expenditure. In this example, the multiplier is 2. A £100 billion increase in investment produces a £200 billion increase in the aggregate quantity of goods and services demanded at each price level. That is, a £100 billion increase in autonomous expenditure shifts the *AD* curve rightward by £200 billion.

A decrease in autonomous expenditure shifts the *AE* curve downward and shifts the *AD* curve leftward. You can see these effects by reversing the change that we've just studied. Suppose that the economy is initially at point *B* on the aggregate expenditure curve AE_1 and the aggregate demand curve AD_1. A decrease in autonomous expenditure shifts the aggregate planned expenditure curve downward to AE_0. The aggregate

Figure 24.10

A Change in Aggregate Demand

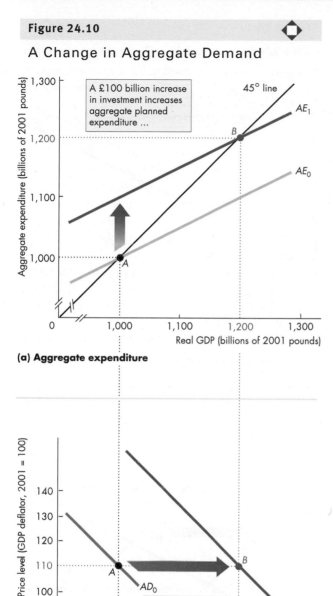

A £100 billion increase in investment increases aggregate planned expenditure ...

(a) Aggregate expenditure

... and increases aggregate demand. The multiplier in this example is 2

(b) Aggregate demand

The price level is 110. When the aggregate expenditure curve is AE_0 in part (a), the aggregate demand curve is AD_0 in part (b). An increase in autonomous expenditure shifts the AE curve upward to AE_1. In the new equilibrium, real GDP is £1,200 billion (point B). Because the quantity of real GDP demanded at a price level of 110 increases to £1,200 billion, the AD curve shifts rightward to AD_1.

quantity of goods and services demanded falls from £1,200 billion to £1,000 billion and the aggregate demand curve shifts leftward to AD_0.

Let's summarize what we have discovered:

> **If some factor other than a change in the price level increases autonomous expenditure, the AE curve shifts upward and the AD curve shifts rightward.**
>
> **The size of the shift of the AD curve depends on the change in autonomous expenditure and the multiplier.**

Equilibrium GDP and the Price Level

In Chapter 22, we learned that aggregate demand and short-run aggregate supply determine equilibrium real GDP and the price level. We've now put aggregate demand under a more powerful microscope and discovered that a change in investment (or in any component of autonomous expenditure) changes aggregate demand and shifts the aggregate demand curve. The magnitude of the shift depends on the multiplier. But whether a change in autonomous expenditure results ultimately in a change in real GDP, or a change in the price level, or some combination of the two depends on aggregate supply and the initial state of the economy. We'll look at two cases of an increase in autonomous expenditure: starting from a recessionary gap and starting from full employment.

An Increase in Aggregate Demand with a Recessionary Gap

Figure 24.11 (overleaf) describes the economy. In part (a), the aggregate expenditure curve is AE_0, and equilibrium expenditure is £800 billion – point A. In part (b), aggregate demand is AD_0 and the short-run aggregate supply curve is SAS. (Chapter 22, pp. 481–482 explains the SAS curve.) Equilibrium is at point A, where the aggregate demand and short-run aggregate supply curves intersect. The price level is 110 and real GDP is £800 billion. Potential GDP is £1,000 billion so there is a recessionary gap of £200 billion.

Now investment increases by £100 billion. With the price level fixed at 110, the aggregate expenditure curve shifts upward to AE_1. Equilibrium expenditure increases to £1,000 billion – point B in part (a). In part (b), the aggregate demand curve shifts rightward by £200 billion, from AD_0 to AD_1. How far the AD curve shifts is determined by the multiplier when the price level is fixed. But with this new AD curve, the price level does not remain fixed. The price level rises and as it does so, the *AE* curve shifts downward. The short-run equilibrium occurs when the aggregate expenditure curve has shifted downward to AE_2 and the new aggregate demand curve, AD_1, intersects the short-run aggregate supply curve. Real GDP is £930 billion and the price level is 123 (at point *C*).

When the price level effects are taken into account, the increase in investment still has a multiplier effect on real GDP, but the multiplier effect is smaller than it would be if the price level were fixed. The steeper the slope of the *SAS* curve, the larger is the increase in the price level and the smaller is the multiplier effect on real GDP.

An Increase in Aggregate Demand at Full Employment

Figure 24.12 illustrates the effect of an increase in aggregate demand starting at full employment. Real GDP equals potential GDP, which is $1,000 billion. The long-run aggregate supply curve is *LAS*. Initially, the economy is at point *A* in part (a) and part (b).

Investment increases by £100 billion. The aggregate expenditure curve shifts upward to AE_1 and the aggregate demand curve shifts rightward to AD_1. With no change in the price level, the economy would move to point *B* and real GDP would increase to $1,200 billion. But in the short run, the price level rises to 123 and real GDP increases to $1,130 billion. With the higher price level, the aggregate expenditure curve shifts from AE_1 to AE_2. The economy is now in a short-run equilibrium at point *C*.

But real GDP is now above potential GDP – an inflationary gap has opened up. The workforce is more than fully employed, and there is a shortage of labour. The money wage rate begins to rise. The higher money wage rate increases costs, which decreases short-run aggregate supply. The *SAS* curve begins to shift leftward towards SAS_1. There is a movement along AD_1, and the *AE* curve shifts downward from AE_2 towards AE_0. When the money wage rate and the price level have increased by the same percentage, real GDP again equals potential GDP and the economy is at point *A'*. Starting from full employment, in the long run, the multiplier is zero.

Closing and Opening Gaps

We've just seen how an increase in autonomous expenditure changes real GDP and the price level starting from a recessionary gap and starting from full employment. The effects of a decrease in autonomous

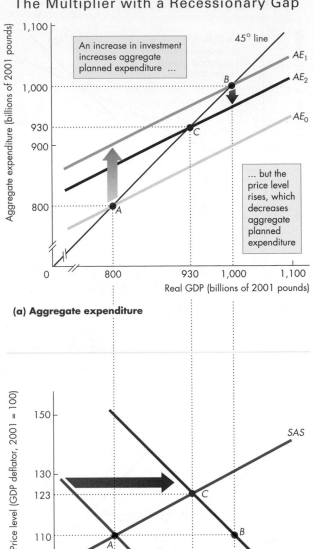

Figure 24.11

The Multiplier with a Recessionary Gap

(a) Aggregate expenditure

(b) Aggregate demand

An increase in investment shifts the *AE* curve from AE_0 to AE_1 in part (a) and shifts the *AD* curve from AD_0 to AD_1 in part (b). The price level does not remain at 110 but rises, and the higher price level shifts the *AE* curve downward from AE_1 to AE_2. The economy moves to point *C* in both parts. In the short run, when prices are flexible, the multiplier effect is smaller than when the price level is fixed.

Figure 24.12

The Multiplier at Full Employment

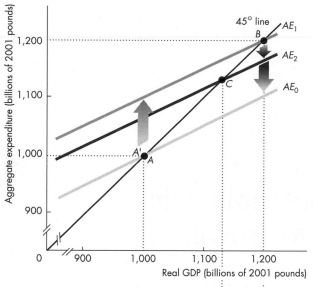

(a) Aggregate expenditure

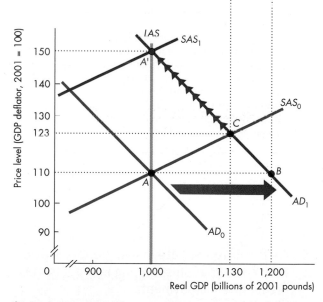

(b) Aggregate demand

Starting from point *A*, an increase in investment shifts the *AE* curve to AE_1 and shifts the *AD* curve to AD_1. In the short run, the economy moves to point *C*. In the long run, the money wage rate rises, the *SAS* curve shifts to SAS_1, the price level rises, the *AE* curve shifts back to AE_0 and real GDP decreases. The economy moves to point *A'* and in the long run, the multiplier is zero.

expenditure like those of an increase, depend on the starting point. Starting at full employment, a decrease in autonomous expenditure opens up a recessionary gap. Such a gap might persist for some time because the adjustment to long-run equilibrium requires a fall in the money wage rate, a process that is slow.

Starting from an existing recessionary gap, a decrease in autonomous expenditure widens the gap by decreasing real GDP and lowering the price level. Starting from an inflationary gap – an above full-employment equilibrium – a decrease in autonomous expenditure decreases real GDP, lowers the price level and moves the economy towards full employment.

Review Quiz

1   How does a change in the price level influence the *AE* curve and the *AD* curve?
2   If autonomous expenditure increases with no change in the price level, what happens to the *AE* curve and the *AD* curve? Which curve shifts by an amount that is determined by the multiplier?
3   How does real GDP change in the short run when there is an increase in autonomous expenditure? Does real GDP change by the same amount as the change in aggregate demand? Why or why not?
4   How does real GDP change in the long run when there is an increase in autonomous expenditure? Does real GDP change by the same amount as the change in aggregate demand? Why or why not?

We've seen that when the price level is fixed, changes in investment and exports are amplified. But we've also seen that when the price level changes, the amplification effect is smaller and that starting from full employment, the shocks are absorbed as the economy eventually returns to full employment.

You are now ready to build on what you've learned about aggregate expenditure and aggregate demand and study the roles of fiscal policy and monetary policy in smoothing the business cycle. In Chapter 25, we study fiscal policy and in Chapters 26 and 27, we study monetary policy – interest rates and the quantity of money. But before you leave the current topic, look at *Reading Between the Lines* on pp. 546–547, which looks at the effects of interest rates on the consumption function in the Netherlands and Portugal.

Reading Between the Lines
Shifts in the Consumption Function

The Financial Times, 2 July 2004

FT

Heavy household debt 'a threat to growth'

Jenny Wiggins

Record levels of global household debt are threatening economic growth and affecting some countries' ability to borrow cheaply, say the credit agency Fitch Ratings.

Household debt has risen sharply over the past decade, with the ratio of debt to disposable income in advanced countries now at around 115 per cent compared with 90 per cent in 1990.

Households were able to absorb more mortgage and consumer debt while interest rates remained low. But as governments have started to raise rates, economists have grown concerned that consumers may need to scale back spending to make interest payments. "It is a reason to think that consumer spending ought to be softer over the next few years," said Cary Leahey, senior economist at Deutsche Bank.

Portugal and the Netherlands, two of the most highly leveraged countries in the eurozone, both suffered falls in real gross domestic product in 2003. Economists are particularly concerned about the impact of higher interest rates in countries with floating mortgage rates, such as Australia, Portugal, Spain and the UK.

The Essence of the Story

◆ Global household debt increased from 90 per cent of income in 1990 to 115 per cent of income in 2004.

◆ Households were able to increase their consumer debt and mortgage debt when the interest rate was low.

◆ As the interest rate rises, people will cut their consumption spending in order to make higher interest payments.

◆ The effect of a higher interest rate on consumption expenditure will be greater in countries such as the Netherlands and Portugal which have particularly high consumer debt levels.

Economic Analysis

◆ The *real* interest rate is the opportunity cost of consumption. If you spend £1 today, you forgo spending £1 plus the real interest it would earn one year from today.

◆ A low *real* interest rate provides an incentive to increase consumption, decrease saving and increase debt by borrowing more.

◆ A high *real* interest rate provides the opposite incentive to decrease consumption, increase saving and pay off debt.

◆ It is not the case (as claimed in the article) that people cannot afford to spend when the interest rate is high because they must make larger interest payments. They *chose* to spend less because the opportunity cost of spending and borrowing has increased.

◆ Figure 1 shows the average real interest rate faced by borrowers in the Eurozone. The real interest rate rose sharply in 2001–2002.

◆ A rise in the real interest rate leads to a decrease in planned consumption expenditure, which means that the consumption function shifts downward.

◆ Figures 2 and 3 show the effects of the rise in the real interest rate in 2000 and 2001 in the Netherlands. The blue dots show actual consumption expenditure and real GDP between 1999 and 2004. (The numbers on the dots identify the years.)

◆ As the real interest rate increased in 2000 and 2001, the consumption function shifted downward from CF_0 down to CF_1 in both countries.

◆ As the real interest rate fell in 2002–2004, the consumption function began to shift upward again in the Netherlands (Figure 2) but remained at CF_1 in Portugal (Figure 3), where other factors must have influenced consumption expenditure in 2004.

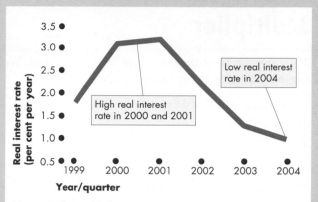

Figure 1 The real interest rate

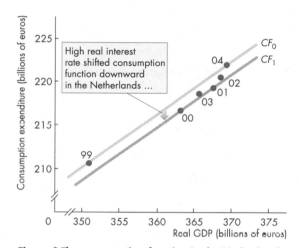

Figure 2 The consumption function in the Netherlands

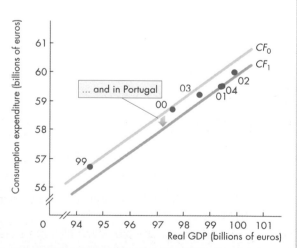

Figure 3 The consumption function in Portugal

Mathematical Note The Algebra of the Multiplier

This note explains the multiplier in greater detail. We begin by defining the symbols we need:

◆ Aggregate planned expenditure, *AE*

◆ Real GDP, *Y*

◆ Consumption expenditure, *C*

◆ Investment, *I*

◆ Government expenditures, *G*

◆ Exports, *X*

◆ Imports, *M*

◆ Net taxes, *T*

◆ Disposable income, *YD*

◆ Autonomous expenditure, *A*

◆ Autonomous consumption expenditure, *a*

◆ Marginal propensity to consume, *b*

◆ Marginal propensity to import, *m*

◆ Marginal tax rate, *t*

Aggregate Expenditure

Aggregate planned expenditure (*AE*) is the sum of planned consumption expenditure (*C*), investment (*I*), government expenditures (*G*), and exports (*X*) minus the planned amount of imports (*M*). That is:

$$AE = C + I + G + X - M$$

Consumption Function

Consumption expenditure (*C*) depends on disposable income (*YD*) and we write the consumption function as:

$$C = a + bYD$$

Disposable income (*YD*) equals real GDP minus net taxes (*Y* − *T*). So replacing *YD* with (*Y* − *T*), the consumption function becomes:

$$C = a + b(Y - T)$$

Net taxes equal real GDP (*Y*) multiplied by the marginal tax rate (*t*). That is:

$$T = tY$$

Use this equation in the previous one to obtain:

$$C = a + b(1 - t)Y$$

This equation describes consumption expenditure as a function of real GDP.

Import Function

Imports depend on real GDP and the import function is:

$$M = mY$$

Aggregate Expenditure Curve

Use the consumption function and the import function to replace *C* and *M* in the aggregate planned expenditure equation. That is:

$$AE = a + b(1 - t)Y + I + G + X - mY$$

Collect the terms on the right-side of the equation that involve *Y* to obtain:

$$AE = [a + I + G + X] + [b(1 - t) - m]Y$$

Autonomous expenditure (*A*) is [*a* + *I* + *G* + *X*], and the slope of the *AE* curve is [*b*(1 − *t*) − *m*]. So the equation for the *AE* curve, which is shown in Figure 1, is:

$$AE = A + [b(1 - t) - m]Y$$

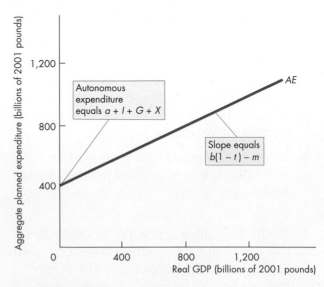

Figure 1 The AE curve

Equilibrium Expenditure

Equilibrium expenditure occurs when aggregate planned expenditure (AE) equals real GDP (Y). That is:

$$AE = Y$$

In Figure 2, the scales of the x-axis (real GDP) and the y-axis (aggregate planned expenditure) are identical, so the 45° line shows the points at which aggregate planned expenditure equals real GDP. That is, along the 45° line, AE equals Y.

Figure 2 shows the point of equilibrium expenditure at the intersection of the AE curve and the 45° line.

To calculate equilibrium expenditure and real GDP, we solve the equations for the AE curve and the 45° line for the two unknown quantities AE and Y. So, starting with:

$$AE = A + [b(1 - t) - m]Y$$

$$AE = Y$$

replace AE with Y in the AE equation to obtain:

$$Y = A + [b(1 - t) - m]Y$$

The solution for Y is:

$$Y = \frac{1}{1 - [b(1 - t) - m]}A$$

The Multiplier

The multiplier equals the change in equilibrium expenditure and real GDP (Y) that results from a change in autonomous expenditure (A) divided by the change in autonomous expenditure. A change in autonomous expenditure (ΔA) changes equilibrium expenditure and real GDP (ΔY) by:

$$\Delta Y = \frac{1}{1 - [b(1 - t) - m]}\Delta A$$

$$\text{Multiplier} = \frac{1}{1 - [b(1 - t) - m]}$$

The size of the multiplier depends on the slope of the AE curve and the larger the slope, the larger is the multiplier. So the multiplier is larger,

1   The greater the marginal propensity to consume (b)

2   The smaller the marginal tax rate (t)

3   The smaller the marginal propensity to import (m)

An economy with no imports and no marginal taxes has $m = 0$ and $t = 0$. In this special case, the multiplier equals $1/(1 - b)$. If b is 0.75, then the multiplier is 4 as shown in the Figure 3. In an economy with $b = 0.75$, $t = 0.2$, and $m = 0.1$, the multiplier is 1 divided by 1 minus $0.75(1 - 0.2) - 0.1$, which equals 2. Make up some more examples to show the effects of b, t, and m on the multiplier.

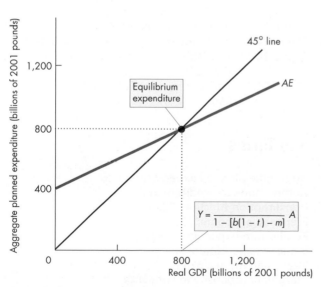

Figure 2 Equilibrium expenditure

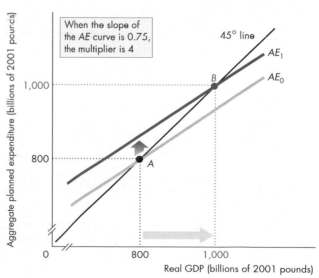

Figure 3 The multiplier

Summary

Key Points

Expenditure Plans and GDP
(pp. 526–531)

◆ When the price level is fixed, aggregate expenditure determines real GDP.

◆ Consumption expenditure is determined by disposable income; and the marginal propensity to consume (*MPC*) determines the change in consumption expenditure brought about by a change in disposable income. Real GDP is the main influence on disposable income.

◆ Imports are determined by real GDP; and the marginal propensity to import determines the change in imports brought about by a change in real GDP.

Equilibrium Expenditure at a Fixed Price Level (pp. 532–535)

◆ Aggregate *planned* expenditure depends on real GDP.

◆ Equilibrium expenditure occurs when aggregate planned expenditure equals real GDP.

The Multiplier (pp. 536–540)

◆ The multiplier is the magnified effect of a change in autonomous expenditure on real GDP.

◆ The multiplier is equal to 1 divided by (1 minus the slope of the *AE* curve).

◆ The multiplier is also influenced by the marginal propensity to consume, the marginal propensity to import and the marginal tax rate.

The Multiplier and the Price Level
(pp. 541–545)

◆ The aggregate demand curve is the relationship between the quantity of real GDP demanded and the price level, other things remaining the same.

◆ The aggregate expenditure curve is the relationship between aggregate planned expenditure and real GDP, other things remaining the same.

◆ At a given price level, there is a given aggregate expenditure curve. A change in the price level changes aggregate planned expenditure and shifts the aggregate expenditure curve. A change in the price level also creates a movement along the aggregate demand curve.

◆ A change in autonomous expenditure that is not caused by a change in the price level shifts the aggregate expenditure curve and shifts the aggregate demand curve. The magnitude of the shift of the aggregate demand curve depends on the multiplier and on the change in autonomous expenditure.

◆ The multiplier decreases as the price level changes and starting from full employment is zero in the long run.

Key Figures

Key Terms

Problems

*1 You are given the following information about the economy of Heron Island:

Disposable income	Consumption expenditure
(millions of euros per year)	
0	5
10	10
20	15
30	20
40	25

Calculate Heron Island's

a Marginal propensity to consume.

b Saving at each level of disposable income.

c Marginal propensity to save.

2 You are given the following information about the economy of Spendthrift Island:

Disposable income	Saving
(millions of euros per year)	
0	−100
500	−50
1,000	0
1,500	50
2,000	100
2,500	150
3,000	200

Calculate Spendthrift Island's

a Marginal propensity to save.

b Consumption expenditure at each level of disposable income.

c Marginal propensity to consume.

*3 Turtle Island has no imports or exports, the people of Turtle Island pay no income taxes, and the price level is fixed. The figure illustrates the components of aggregate planned expenditure on Turtle Island.
On Turtle Island, what is:

a Autonomous expenditure?

b The marginal propensity to consume?

c Equilibrium expenditure?

d Happening to inventories or stocks if real GDP is €4 billion?

e Happening to inventories or stocks if real GDP is €6 billion?

f The multiplier?

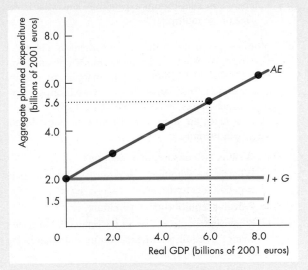

4 The spreadsheet figure lists the components of aggregate planned expenditure in Spice Bay. The numbers are in billions of cloves, the currency of the Bay.

	A	B	C	D	E	F	G
1		Y	C	I	G	X	M
2	A	100	110	50	60	60	15
3	B	200	170	50	60	60	30
4	C	300	230	50	60	60	45
5	D	400	290	50	60	60	60
6	E	500	350	50	60	60	75
7	F	600	410	50	60	60	90

In Spice Bay, what is:

a Autonomous expenditure?

b The marginal propensity to consume?

c Aggregate planned expenditure when real GDP is 200 billion cloves?

d Happening to inventories or stocks if real GDP is 200 billion cloves?

e Happening to inventories or stocks if real GDP is 500 billion cloves?

f The multiplier in Spice Bay?

*5 In the economy of Zee, autonomous consumption expenditure is €100 billion and the marginal propensity to consume is 0.9. Investment is €460 billion, government expenditures on goods and services are €400 billion, and net taxes are €400 billion and do not vary with income. Zee has no imports or exports.

---

*Solutions to odd-numbered problems are available on *Parkin Interactive*.

a What is the consumption function?

b What is the equation that describes the aggregate expenditure curve?

c Calculate equilibrium expenditure.

d If investment decreases to €360 billion, what is the change in equilibrium expenditure and what is the size of the multiplier?

6 You are given the following information about the economy of Antarctica: autonomous consumption expenditure is €1 billion, and the marginal propensity to consume is 0.95. Investment is €4 billion, government expenditures on goods and services are €4 billion, and net taxes are a constant €4 billion – they do not vary with income.

a What is the consumption function?

b What is the equation that describes the aggregate expenditure curve?

c Calculate equilibrium expenditure.

d If investment decreases to €3 billion, what is the change in equilibrium expenditure and what is the size of the multiplier?

*7 Suppose that in problem 5 the price level is 100 and real GDP equals potential GDP. If investment increases by €100 billion,

a What is the change in the quantity of real GDP demanded?

b In the short run, does equilibrium real GDP increase by more than, less than or the same amount as the increase in the quantity of real GDP demanded?

c In the long run, does equilibrium real GDP increase by more than, less than or the same amount as the increase in the quantity of real GDP demanded?

d In the short run, does the price level in Zee rise, fall or remain unchanged?

e In the long run, does the price level in Zee rise, fall or remain unchanged?

8 Suppose that in problem 6 the price level is 100 and real GDP equals potential GDP. If investment increases by €50 billion,

a What is the change in the quantity of real GDP demanded?

b In the short run, does equilibrium real GDP increase by more than, less than or the same amount as the increase in the quantity of real GDP demanded?

c In the long run, does equilibrium real GDP increase by more than, less than or the same amount as the increase in the quantity of real GDP demanded?

d In the short run, does the price level in Antarctica rise, fall or remain unchanged?

e In the long run, does the price level in Antarctica rise, fall or remain unchanged?

Critical Thinking

1 Study *Reading Between the Lines* on pp. 546–547 and then answer the following questions.

a What has happened to the real interest rate in the Eurozone economies between 1999 and 2002?

b What is the effect of the rise in the real interest rate on the consumption function?

c What is the effect of the rise in the real interest rate on the savings function?

d What happened to consumer spending in the Netherlands and Portugal?

e What is your prediction for the real rate of interest and consumer spending in 2004 for these two countries?

f Use the links on *Parkin Interactive* to obtain data on real consumer spending growth in 2004 for Portugal and Netherlands and check your prediction.

2 You are a research assistant working for the government. You've been asked to draft a note for the Minister of Finance that explains the power and limitations of the multiplier. The Minister wants only 250 words of crisp, clear, jargon-free explanation together with a lively example by tomorrow morning.

Web Exercise

Use the link on *Parkin Interactive* to work the following exercise.

1 Visit the Penn World Table and obtain data on real GDP per person and consumption as a percentage of real GDP for the United States, China, South Africa and Mexico since 1960.

a In a spreadsheet, multiply your real GDP data by the consumption percentage and divide by 100 to obtain data on real consumption expenditure per person.

b Make graphs like the figure in Box 24.1 on p. 531 to show the relationship between consumption and real GDP for these four countries.

c Based on the numbers you've obtained, in which country do you expect the multiplier to be largest (other things remaining the same)?

d What other data do you need to calculate the multipliers for these countries?

Part 6
Macroeconomic Policy

Improving Economic Health

To cure a disease, doctors must first understand how it responds to different treatments. It helps to understand the mechanisms that operate to cause the disease, but sometimes, a workable cure can be found even before the full story of the cause has been told.

Curing economic ills is similar to curing our medical ills. We need to understand how the economy responds to the treatments we might prescribe for it. And sometimes, we want to try a cure even though we don't fully understand the reasons for the problem we're trying to control.

You've seen how the pace of capital accumulation and technological change determine the long-term growth trend. You've learned how fluctuations around the long-term trend can be generated by changes in aggregate demand and aggregate supply. And you've learned about the key sources of fluctuations in aggregate demand and aggregate supply.

The chapters in this part build on everything you've studied in macroeconomics. The central tools they use are the demand and supply model of Chapter 3 and the *AS–AD* model of Chapter 22. But they use these models to explain the big picture or grand vision that different schools of thought hold concerning the way the economy operates and what is important.

Chapter 25 reviews a range of fiscal policy issues and problems, and Chapters 26 and 27 describes the monetary system and explain the effects of monetary policy. Chapter 28 brings fiscal policy and monetary policy together and examines their interactions.

Chapters 29 to 31 examine the three major policy problems of inflation, economic growth and the business cycle. In these chapters, you will learn what is known about the causes of inflation and the way to prevent it and the sources of faster growth and the policies that can foster it.

Finally, in Chapter 32 you will explore the current state of the macroeconomic policy debate. You will meet the alternative approaches that have been proposed to contain inflation, sustain economic growth and smooth the business cycle.

Chapter 25

Fiscal Policy

After studying this chapter you will be able to:

◆ Describe the recent history of UK government revenues, outlays and the budget deficits

◆ Define and explain the fiscal policy multipliers

◆ Explain the demand-side effects of fiscal policy in the short run and the long run

◆ Explain the supply-side effects of fiscal policy

Balancing Acts in Westminster

What are the effects of government spending on the economy? Does it create jobs? Or does it destroy them? Does a pound spent by the government have the same effects as a pound spent by someone else? What happens if governments spend more than they receive in revenue and run into debt? Does government debt damage economic growth and the well-being of future generations?

Government Budgets

A government's **budget** is an annual statement of projected outlays and revenues during the next year together with the laws and regulations that will support those outlays and revenues. The finance minister – the Chancellor of the Exchequer in Britain – presents the budget to Parliament in what is often a piece of political theatre and always a major media event.

A government's budget has three major purposes:

1 To state the scale and allocation of the government's outlays and its plans to finance its activities

2 To stabilize the economy

3 To encourage the economy's long-term growth and balanced regional development

Before the Second World War, the budget had only the first of these goals – to plan and finance the business of government.

But during the late 1940s and early 1950s, the budget began to assume its second purpose – stabilization of the economy.

In more recent years, the budget has assumed its third goal of helping to secure faster sustained economic growth and to seek balance across regions.

Today, the role of the budget is the tool used by a government in pursuit of its fiscal policy. *Fiscal policy is a government's use of its budget to achieve macroeconomic objectives such as full employment, sustained economic growth and price level stability. It is the fiscal policy aspects of the budget that we focus on in this chapter.*

Government budgets differ in size and detail, but they all have the same components. Here, we'll illustrate a government budget by looking at the United Kingdom.

Highlights of the UK Budget in 2004

Table 25.1 shows the main items in the UK government's budget. The numbers are projections for the fiscal year beginning in April 2004. The three main items in the budget are:

◆ Revenues

◆ Outlays

◆ Budget balance

Table 25.1

The Government Budget in 2004/05

Item		Projections (billions of pounds)
Revenues		**455**
Taxes on income and wealth		173
Taxes on expenditure		122
Other receipts and royalties		82
National Insurance contributions		78
Outlays		**488**
Expenditures on goods and services		325
Health	88	
Education	63	
Law and order	29	
Defence	27	
Other	118	
Transfer payments		138
Debt interest		25
Budget balance (surplus +/deficit –)		**–33**

Source: HM Treasury, *Budget 2004.*

Revenues

Revenues come from four sources:

1 Taxes on income and wealth

2 Taxes on expenditure

3 National Insurance contributions

4 Other receipts and royalties

The largest source of revenue is *taxes on income and wealth*, which were projected to be £173 billion in 2004/05. These are the taxes paid by individuals on their incomes and wealth and the taxes paid by businesses on their profits.

The second largest source of revenue is *taxes on expenditure*, which in 2004/05 were projected at £122 billion. These taxes include VAT and special duties and taxes on gambling, alcoholic drinks, petrol, luxury items and imported goods.

Third in size are *other receipts and royalties*. This item included oil royalties, stamp duties, car taxes, miscellaneous rents, dividends from abroad and profits from nationalized industries.

Fourth in size are *National Insurance contributions*, projected to be £78 billion in 2004/05. This revenue comes from contributions paid by workers and employers to fund the welfare and healthcare programmes.

Outlays

Outlays are classified in three broad categories:

1   Expenditures on goods and services
2   Transfer payments
3   Debt interest

Expenditures on goods and services are by far the largest item at £325 billion in 2004/05.

The table lists some of the larger components of these expenditures. Health (expenditure on the National Health Service) took £88 billion and education took another £66 billion. The provision of law and order and defence, the two traditional roles of government, took only £56 billion between them.

Transfer payments – £138 billion in 2004/05 – are payments to individuals, businesses, other levels of government and the rest of the world. These payments include National Insurance benefits, healthcare benefits, unemployment benefits, welfare supplements, grants to local authorities and aid to developing countries.

Debt interest, which in 2004/05 is projected to be £25 billion, is the interest on the government debt minus interest received by the government on its own investments.

The bottom line of the government budget is the balance – the surplus or deficit.

Budget Balance

The government's budget balance is equal to its revenues minus its outlays. That is:

Budget balance = Revenues − Outlays

If revenues exceed outlays, the government has a **budget surplus**. If outlays exceed revenues, the government has a **budget deficit**. If revenues equal outlays, the government has a **balanced budget**. In fiscal year 2004/05, with projected outlays of £488 billion and revenue of £455 billion, the projected government deficit is £33 billion.

How typical is the budget of 2004/05? Let's look at its recent history.

The Budget in Historical Perspective

Figure 25.1 shows the government's revenues, outlays and budget balance since fiscal year 1973/74. The figure expresses the revenues, outlays and the budget balance as percentages of GDP. Expressing them in this way lets us see how large government is relative to the size of the

Figure 25.1

The UK Government Revenues, Outlays and Budget Balance

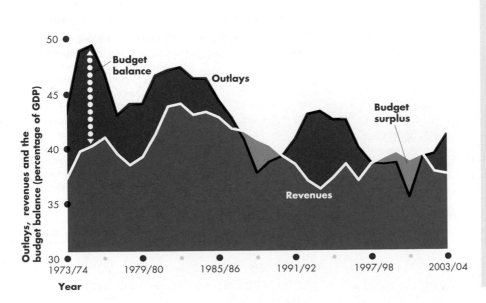

The figure records the UK government's revenues, outlays and budget deficit as percentages of GDP. During the 1970s, the budget deficit became large and persisted well into the 1980s. A budget surplus appeared in the late 1980s, but income taxes cuts and an increase in outlays turned the budget into a deficit again in the early 1990s. The budget was in balance in 1997/98, in surplus in 1998/99 and 1999/00, but once again returned to a deficit in the early 2000s.

Source: HM Treasury, *Budget 2004*.

economy, and it helps us to study *changes* in the scale of government over time. You may think of these percentages of GDP as telling you how many pence of each pound that we earn get paid to and spent by the government.

Throughout most of this period there was a budget deficit. The deficit increases in recessions and decreases in expansions. The deficit rose to a peak following the recession of the 1970s. Government revenues were actually higher than outlays in the fiscal years 1987/89. But the budget deficit increased again during the 1990s but has fallen sharply and turned into a budget surplus in recent years.

Why did the government deficit grow so sharply in the 1990s? The immediate answer is that outlays increased and revenues decreased. But which components of outlays increased and which sources of revenues decreased? Let's look at revenues and outlays in a bit more detail.

Revenues

Figure 25.2 shows the components of revenues received by the government as a percentage of GDP, between 1989 and 2003. Government revenues as a percentage of GDP increased from 1989 to 1991 and then decreased in the following three years. This decrease occurred

because the 1990–1992 recession decreased tax revenues. Firms' profits fell, which lowered the taxes on business profits, and as the unemployment rate increased, the revenue from personal income taxes decreased. Tax revenues increased from 1994 to 2000 as the economy settled into a long boom. They then settled to a plateau as the economy grew at a steady rate.

Outlays

Figure 25.3 shows the components of government outlays as percentages of GDP, between 1989 and 2003. Total outlays increased as a proportion of GDP during the first half of the 1990s. The main source of the increased outlays was a large increase in transfer payments that resulted from the recession. A sharp rise in unemployment and in early retirements increased benefit and welfare payments.

A small part of UK government outlays is the interest payment on government debt. The amount of interest paid depends on the debt. A large debt means a high interest payment. A small debt means a low interest payment. Compared to many other EU countries, the United Kingdom has a relatively low ratio of debt to GDP, so its interest payments are modest. But for some countries, high interest payments on debt make controlling the deficit a challenge.

Figure 25.2

UK Government Revenues

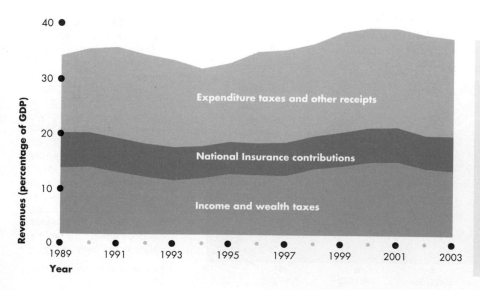

The figure shows the three components of government revenues: income and wealth taxes (including taxes on business profits), expenditure taxes (including VAT) and national insurance contributions. Revenues from income and wealth taxes declined in 1993 but rose in 1994. Revenues from expenditure taxes fell in 1994 and rose consistently through to 2001.

Source: HM Treasury, *Budget 2004*.

Figure 25.3

UK Government Outlays

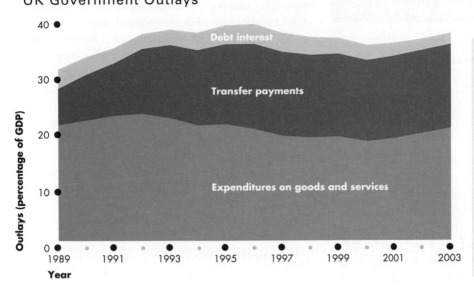

The figure shows three components of government outlays: expenditures on goods and services, transfer payments and debt interest. Expenditures on goods and services fell steadily from 1992 until 2000 when they begun to rise again. Transfer payments increased during the 1990–1991 recession and have remains steady. Debt interest has fallen since 1996.

Source: HM Treasury, *Budget 2004*.

Deficit, Debt and Capital

Government debt is the total amount of borrowing by the government. It is the sum of past deficits minus the sum of past surpluses minus the receipts from the sale of assets.

When the government has a budget deficit, its debt increases, and when it has a budget surplus, its debt decreases. If a government sells state-owned assets, it can reduce its debt even though its tax revenues are less than its outlays.

Figure 25.4 shows the history of government debt in the United Kingdom since 1973. The United Kingdom started the period as a high debt country. It steadily reduced its debt in the 1970s and accelerated the reduction in the 1980s through an aggressive programme of sales of state assets.

Like individuals and businesses, governments borrow to buy assets. Governments own public assets such as roads, bridges, schools and universities, public libraries and defence equipment. The value of UK government assets exceeded £450 billion in 2004, while its debt was £387 billion.

So although the UK government has some debt, that debt is not a problem and is not out of line with the assets it owns.

But how do the UK deficit and debt compare with deficits and debts in other major economies and the European Union?

Figure 25.4

UK Government Debt

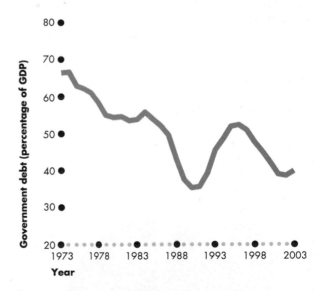

In 1973, UK government debt was 67 per cent of GDP. During the 1970s and 1980s the government lowered its debt. An aggressive programme of privatization of state assets hastened the reduction in debt during the 1980s. The United Kingdom saw a sharp rise in debt after the 1990–1992 recession, but as a per cent of GDP, UK debt has fallen since 1996.

Source: HM Treasury.

Box 25.1
Budgets in the European Union

Each of the 25 member states of the European Union has a budget that has similar categories of revenues and outlays to the UK budget that we've just described. In addition to the national budgets, there is an EU budget drawn up by the Council of the European Union and approved by the European Parliament.

The European Union receives 85 per cent of its revenue from the member states and 15 per cent from EU tariffs on imports from non-member countries. Member states' contributions are based on VAT, which provides 35 per cent of revenue, and on gross national product, which produces 50 per cent of revenue. (A country's gross *national* product is equal to its gross *domestic* product plus net property income from the rest of the world.)

The total EU budget in 2003 was €100 billion – equivalent to only 1.1 per cent of EU GDP.

Figure 1 shows how the European Union spends its resources. Agriculture – the Common Agricultural Policy – takes the biggest slice of the budget pie. Structural measures – grants to weaker economic regions – take another large slice.

Despite its small size relative to GDP, the EU budget is hotly debated and makes a significant difference to economic life in many EU countries. For

example, Ireland has been a major beneficiary of both the Common Agricultural Policy and the structural programmes of the European Union.

Most government revenue and outlays in the European Union remain with the member states. The 25 members of the enlarged European Union span a huge range of budgetary outcomes. Two aspects of these budgets are budget balances and government debt. Figure 2 shows the budget balances of the 25 EU members in 2003. They range from a deficit of 13 per cent of GDP in the Czech Republic to a surplus of 2.6 per cent in Estonia. The EU average is a deficit at 2.8 per cent of GDP, a bit below the UK deficit of

Figure 2

EU Budget Balances in 2003

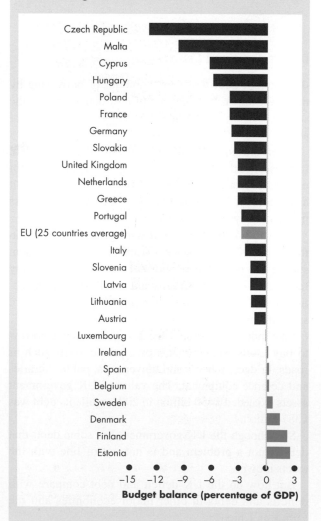

Figure 1

EU Budget Outlays in 2003

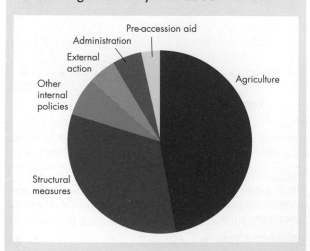

3.2 per cent of GDP. Two other large EU members, France and Germany, have deficits greater than the UK deficit. Figure 3 shows the government debt of the 25 EU members in 2003. It ranges from a high of 106 per cent of GDP in Italy to a low of 5 per cent in Luxembourg. The EU average debt is 63 per cent of GDP, which is substantially above the UK debt of 40 per cent of GDP. Three other large EU members, France, Germany and Italy, each have debt greater than the UK debt.

There is no correlation between debts and deficits. Some EU countries with large debt levels are running low deficits to bring the debt down.

EU Government Debts in 2003

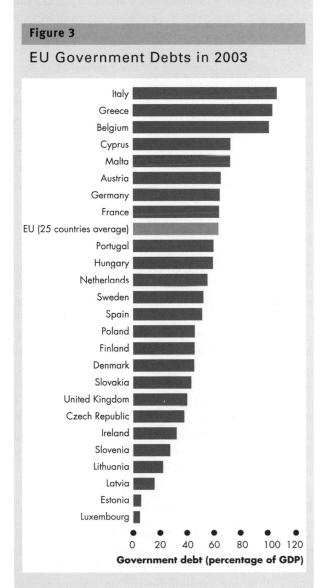

UK and EU Budget Deficits and Debts in a Global Perspective

You've seen that the United Kingdom had a budget deficit in 2004 of £33 billion (a bit more than 3 per cent of GDP) and that the EU average budget deficit is 2.8 per cent of the GDP of the EU members. How do these deficits stack up against the rest of the world?

The answer is that the UK and other EU member's budget deficits are among the smallest. Japan has been running a budget deficit of more than 6 per cent of GDP for some years. The developing countries of Africa and Asia have deficits of about 4 per cent of their GDPs. The United States has a larger deficit than the EU average.

Among the few countries that have smaller deficits that the European average are the newly industrialized Asian economies (Hong Kong, Singapore, South Korea and Taiwan), Australia and Canada, all of which have surpluses.

There is nothing inherently wrong with a government running a deficit, provided the resources are being used to add to the stock of social capital. There is also a case for a government running a deficit if it wants to try to lift its economy from recession.

Review Quiz

1   What are the functions of a government's budget?
2   What are the goals of fiscal policy?
3   Describe the main sources of revenues and outlays in the budget of the UK government?
4   Under what circumstances does a government have a budget surplus?
5   Which members of the European Union ran a budget deficit in 2003?
6   Which members of the European Union had the largest debt levels in 2003?
7   Explain the connection between a government's budget deficit and its debt.

We have now described the government budget. Your next task is to study the effects of fiscal policy on the economy. We'll begin by learning about its effects on expenditure plans when the price level is fixed. You will see that fiscal policy has multiplier effects like the multiplier explained in Chapter 24. Then we'll study the influences of fiscal policy on aggregate demand and aggregate supply and look at its short-run and long-run effects on real GDP and the price level.

Fiscal Policy Multipliers

Fiscal policy actions can be either automatic or discretionary. **Automatic fiscal policy** is a change in fiscal policy that is triggered by the state of the economy. For example, an increase in unemployment triggers an *automatic* increase in payments to unemployed workers. A fall in incomes triggers an *automatic* decrease in tax revenues. That is, fiscal policy adjusts automatically. **Discretionary fiscal policy** is a policy action that is initiated by the Chancellor of the Exchequer. It requires a change in tax laws or in some spending programme. For example, a cut in tax rates and an increase in defence spending are discretionary fiscal policy actions. That is, discretionary fiscal policy is a deliberate policy action.

We begin by studying the effects of *discretionary* changes in government spending and taxes. To focus on the essentials, we'll initially study a model economy that is simpler than the one in which we live. In our model economy, there is no international trade and the taxes are autonomous. **Autonomous taxes** are taxes that do not vary with real GDP. They are fixed by the government and they change only when the government changes them.

Autonomous taxes are rare in reality and they are generally considered to be unfair because rich people and poor people pay the same amount of tax. (It is said that the former Prime Minister, Margaret Thatcher, lost her job because of the unpopularity of an autonomous tax called the 'poll tax', which was a fixed tax per person to pay for local government services.)

We use autonomous taxes in our model economy because they make the principles we are studying easier to understand. Once we've grasped the principles, we'll explore our real economy with its international trade and income taxes – taxes that *do* vary with real GDP.

Like our real economy, the model economy we study is constantly bombarded by spending fluctuations. Business investment in new buildings, plant and equipment and inventories fluctuate because of swings in profit expectations and interest rates. These fluctuations set up multiplier effects that begin a recession or an expansion. If a recession takes hold, unemployment increases and incomes fall. If an expansion becomes too strong, inflationary pressures build up. To minimize the effects of these swings in spending, the government might change either its expenditures on goods and services or taxes. By changing either of these items, the government can influence aggregate expenditure and

real GDP, but the government's budget deficit or surplus also changes. An alternative fiscal policy action is to change both expenditures and taxes together so that the budget balance does not change. We are going to study the initial effects of these discretionary fiscal policy actions in the very short run when the price level is fixed. Each of these actions creates a multiplier effect on real GDP. These multipliers are the:

◆ Government expenditures multiplier

◆ Autonomous tax multiplier

◆ Balanced budget multiplier

Government Expenditures Multiplier

The **government expenditures multiplier** is the amount by which a change in government expenditures on goods and services is multiplied to determine the change in equilibrium expenditure that it generates.

Government expenditures are a component of aggregate expenditure. So when government expenditures on goods and services change, aggregate expenditure and real GDP change. The change in real GDP induces a change in consumption expenditure, which brings an additional change in aggregate expenditure. A multiplier process ensues. This multiplier process is like the one described in Chapter 24, pp. 536–539. Let's look at an example.

Peace Dividend Multiplier

After end of the Cold War, the NATO countries looked forward to a reduction in defence spending. In the United Kingdom, part of the reduction in government expenditures has been the downgrading of the Rosyth naval base in Scotland. The cut in government expenditures reduce the region's GDP and increase unemployment in the area. Because military personnel and workers spend most of their incomes locally, consumption expenditure in the region will decrease. Retail shops and hotels will experience falling trade and will lay off workers. In the long term, the Rosyth area will develop alternative industries, but in the short term, it will experience a negative multiplier effect.

The Size of the Multiplier

Table 25.2 illustrates the government expenditures multiplier with a numerical example. The first column lists various possible levels of real GDP. Our task is to find equilibrium expenditure and the change in real

Table 25.2

The Government Expenditures Multiplier

	Real GDP (Y)	Taxes (T)	Disposable income ($Y - T$)	Consumption expenditure (C)	Investment (I)	Initial government expenditures (G)	Initial aggregate planned expenditure ($AE = C + I + G$)	New government expenditures (G')	New aggregate planned expenditure ($AE' = C + I + G'$)
					(billions of pounds)				
A	900	200	700	525	200	200	925	250	975
B	1,000	200	800	600	200	200	1,000	250	1,050
C	1,100	200	900	675	200	200	1,075	250	1,125
D	1,200	200	1,000	750	200	200	1,150	250	1,200
E	1,300	200	1,100	825	200	200	1,225	250	1,275

GDP when government expenditures change. The second column shows taxes. They are fixed at £200 billion, regardless of the level of real GDP. (This is an assumption that keeps your attention on the key idea and makes the calculations easier to do.) The third column calculates disposable income. Because taxes are autonomous, disposable income equals real GDP minus the £200 billion of taxes. For example, in row B, real GDP is £1,000 billion and disposable income is £800 billion. The next column shows consumption expenditure. In this example, the *marginal propensity to consume* is 0.75. That is, a £1 increase in disposable income brings a 75 pence increase in consumption expenditure. Check this fact by calculating the increase in consumption expenditure when disposable income increases by £100 billion from row B to row C. Consumption expenditure increases by £75 billion. The next column shows investment, which is a constant of £200 billion. And the next column shows the initial level of government expenditures, which is £200 billion. Aggregate planned expenditure is the sum of consumption expenditure, investment and government expenditures.

Equilibrium expenditure and real GDP occur when aggregate planned expenditure equals real GDP. In this example, equilibrium expenditure is £1,000 billion (highlighted in row B of the table).

The final two columns of the table show what happens when government expenditures increase by £50 billion to £250 billion. Aggregate planned expenditure increases by £50 billion at each level of real GDP. For example, at the initial real GDP of £1,000

billion, aggregate planned expenditure increases to £1,050 billion.

Because aggregate planned expenditure now exceeds real GDP, inventories decrease. So firms increase production. Increased incomes further increase consumption expenditure, which is less than the increase in income. Aggregate planned expenditure increases and eventually a new equilibrium is reached. In this example, the new equilibrium expenditure is at a real GDP of £1,200 billion (highlighted in row D).

A £50 billion increase in government expenditures has increased equilibrium expenditure and real GDP by £200 billion. Therefore the government expenditures multiplier is 4. The size of the multiplier depends on the marginal propensity to consume, which in this example is 0.75. The following formula shows the connection between the government expenditures multiplier and the marginal propensity to consume (MPC):

$$\text{Government expenditures multiplier} = \frac{1}{(1 - MPC)}$$

Let's check this formula by using the numbers in the above example. The marginal propensity to consume is 0.75, so the government expenditures multiplier is 4.

Figure 25.5 (overleaf) illustrates the government expenditures multiplier. Initially, aggregate planned expenditure is shown by the curve labelled AE_0. The points on this curve, labelled A to E, correspond with the rows of Table 25.2. This aggregate expenditure curve intersects the 45° line at the equilibrium level of real GDP, which is £1,000 billion.

Figure 25.5

The Government Expenditures Multiplier

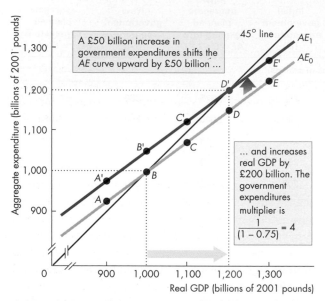

A £50 billion increase in government expenditures shifts the AE curve upward by £50 billion ...

... and increases real GDP by £200 billion. The government expenditures multiplier is

$$\frac{1}{(1 - 0.75)} = 4$$

Initially, the aggregate expenditure curve is AE_0 and real GDP is £1,000 billion (at point *B*). An increase in government expenditures of £50 billion increases aggregate planned expenditure at each level of real GDP by £50 billion. The aggregate expenditure curve shifts upward from AE_0 to AE_1 – a parallel shift.

At the initial real GDP of £1,000 billion, aggregate planned expenditure is now £1,050 billion. Because aggregate planned expenditure is greater than real GDP, real GDP increases. The new equilibrium is reached when real GDP is £1,200 billion – the point at which the AE_1 curve intersects the 45° line (at *D'*). In this example, the government expenditures multiplier is 4.

When government expenditures increase by £50 billion, the aggregate expenditure curve shifts upward by that amount to AE_1. With this new aggregate expenditure curve, equilibrium real GDP increases to £1,200 billion. The increase in real GDP is 4 times the increase in government expenditures. The government expenditures multiplier is 4.

You've seen that in the very short term, when the price level is fixed, an increase in government expenditures increases real GDP. But to produce more output, more people must be employed, so in the short term, an increase in government expenditures can create jobs.

Increasing its expenditures on goods and services is one way in which the government can try to stimulate the economy. A second way in which the government might act to increase real GDP in the very short run is by decreasing autonomous taxes. Let's see how this action works.

Autonomous Tax Multiplier

The **autonomous tax multiplier** is the magnification effect of a change in autonomous taxes on equilibrium expenditure and real GDP. An *increase* in taxes *decreases* disposable income, which decreases in consumption expenditure. The amount by which consumption expenditure initially changes is determined by the marginal propensity to consume. The marginal propensity to consume in our example is 0.75, so a £1 tax cut increases disposable income by £1 and increases aggregate expenditure initially by 75 pence.

This initial change in aggregate expenditure has a multiplier just like the government expenditures multiplier. We've seen that the government expenditures multiplier is $1/(1 - MPC)$. Because a tax *increase* leads to a *decrease* in expenditure, the autonomous tax multiplier is *negative*. And because a change in autonomous taxes changes aggregate expenditure initially by only the *MPC* multiplied by the tax change, the autonomous tax multiplier is equal to:

$$\text{Autonomous tax multiplier} = \frac{-MPC}{(1 - MPC)}$$

In our example, the marginal propensity to consume is 0.75, so:

$$\text{Autonomous tax multiplier} = \frac{-0.75}{(1 - 0.75)} = -3$$

Figure 25.6 illustrates the autonomous tax multiplier. Initially, the aggregate expenditure curve is AE_0 and equilibrium expenditure is £1,000 billion. Taxes increase by £100 billion and disposable income falls by that amount. With a marginal propensity to consume of 0.75, aggregate expenditure decreases initially by £75 billion and the aggregate expenditure curve shifts downward by that amount to AE_1. Equilibrium expenditure and real GDP fall by £300 billion to £700 billion. The autonomous tax multiplier is −3.

The autonomous tax multiplier also tells us the effects of a change in autonomous transfer payments – negative taxes. An *increase* in transfer payments has the same effect as a *decrease* in taxes. So the autonomous transfer

Figure 25.6

The Autonomous Tax Multiplier

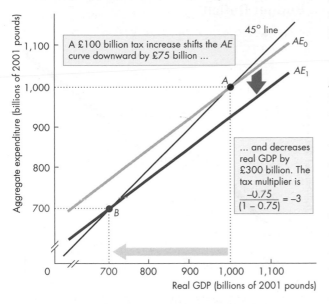

A £100 billion tax increase shifts the AE curve downward by £75 billion ...

... and decreases real GDP by £300 billion. The tax multiplier is
$$\frac{-0.75}{(1-0.75)} = -3$$

Initially, the aggregate expenditure curve is AE_0, and equilibrium expenditure is £1,000 billion. The marginal propensity to consume is 0.75. Autonomous taxes increase by £100 billion, so disposable income decreases by £100 billion. The decrease in aggregate expenditure is found by multiplying this change in disposable income by the marginal propensity to consume: this is £100 billion × 0.75, which equals £75 billion. The aggregate expenditure curve shifts *downward* by this amount to AE_1. Equilibrium expenditure decreases by £300 billion, and the autonomous tax multiplier is –3.

payments multiplier equals the negative of the autonomous tax multiplier.

Balanced Budget Multiplier

The **balanced budget multiplier** is the multiplier that arises from a fiscal policy action that changes *both* government expenditures and taxes by the *same* amount so that the government's budget deficit or surplus remains *unchanged*.

Because the tax multiplier is smaller than the government expenditures multiplier, the balanced budget multiplier is greater than zero. With no imports and no income taxes, the balanced budget multiplier is one. But this special case does not apply when there are imports and income taxes. Nonetheless, the balanced budget multiplier is always greater than zero.

Induced Taxes and Transfer Payments

In the examples we've studied so far, taxes are autonomous. But in reality, net taxes (taxes minus transfer payments) vary with the state of the economy.

On the revenue side of the budget, tax laws define the tax *rates* to be paid, not the tax *pounds* to be paid. Tax *pounds* paid depend on tax *rates* and incomes. But incomes vary with real GDP, so tax revenues depend on real GDP. Taxes that vary as real GDP are called **induced taxes**. When the economy expands, induced taxes increase because real GDP increases. When the economy is in a recession, induced taxes decrease because real GDP decreases.

On the outlays side of the budget, the government creates programmes that entitle suitably qualified people and businesses to receive benefits. For example, the government pays unemployed workers a job-seeker's allowance. The spending on such programmes is not fixed in pounds and it results in transfer payments that depend on the economic state of individual citizens and businesses. When the economy is in a recession, unemployment is high, the number of people experiencing economic hardship increases and a larger number of firms and farms experience hard times. Transfer payments increase. When the economy expands, transfer payments decrease.

Induced taxes and transfer payments decrease the multiplier effects of changes in government expenditures and autonomous taxes. The reason is that they weaken the link between real GDP and disposable income and so dampen the effect of a change in real GDP on consumption expenditure. When real GDP increases, induced taxes increase and transfer payments decrease, so disposable income does not increase by as much as the increase in real GDP. As a result, consumption expenditure does not increase by as much as it otherwise would have done and the multiplier effect is reduced.

The extent to which induced taxes and transfer payments decrease the multiplier depends on the *marginal tax rate*. The marginal tax rate is the proportion of an additional pound of real GDP that flows to the government in net taxes (taxes minus transfer payments). The higher the marginal tax rate, the larger is the proportion of an additional pound of real GDP that is paid to the government and the smaller is the induced change in consumption expenditure. The smaller the change in consumption expenditure induced by a change in real GDP, the smaller is the multiplier effect of a change in government expenditures or autonomous taxes.

International Trade and Fiscal Policy Multipliers

Not all expenditure on final goods and services in the United Kingdom is expenditure on UK-produced goods and services. Some of it is on imports – foreign-produced goods and services. Imports affect the fiscal policy multipliers in the same way as they influence the investment multiplier, as explained in Chapter 24 (see pp. 538–539). The extent to which as additional pound of real GDP is spent on imports is determined by the *marginal propensity to import.* Expenditure on imports does not generate UK real GDP and so does not lead to an increase in UK consumption expenditure. The larger the marginal propensity to import, the smaller is the increase in consumption expenditure induced by an increase in real GDP and the smaller are the government expenditures and autonomous tax multipliers. (The mathematical note on pp. 576–577 explains the details of the effects of induced taxes and transfer payments and imports on the fiscal policy multipliers.)

So far, we've studied *discretionary* fiscal policy. Let's look at *automatic* stabilizers.

Automatic Stabilizers

Automatic stabilizers are mechanisms that operate without the need for explicit action by the government. Their name is borrowed from engineering and conjures up images of shock absorbers, thermostats and sophisticated devices that keep aircraft and ships steady in turbulent air and seas. But automatic fiscal stabilizers do not actual stabilize. They just make fluctuations less severe. These stabilizers operate because income taxes and transfer payments fluctuate with real GDP. As real GDP falls, tax revenues fall, transfer payments rise and the budget deficit changes. Let's look at the budget deficit over the business cycle.

Budget Deficit over the Business Cycle

Figure 25.7 shows the business cycle and fluctuations in the budget deficit between 1985 and 2000. Part (a) shows the fluctuations of real GDP around potential GDP. Part (b) shows the government budget deficit. Both parts highlight the most recent recession by shading this period. By comparing the two parts of the figure, you can see the relationship between the business cycle and the budget deficit. As a rule, when the economy is in the expansion phase of a business cycle, the budget deficit declines.

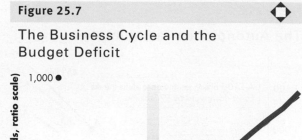

Figure 25.7

The Business Cycle and the Budget Deficit

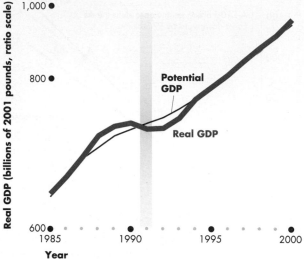

(a) Real GDP and potential GDP

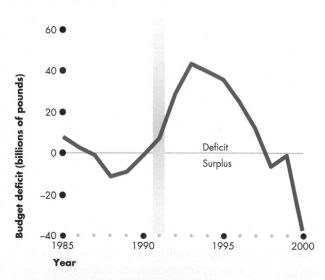

(b) The UK government budget deficit

As real GDP fluctuates around potential GDP in part (a), the budget deficit fluctuates in part (b). During a recession (shaded areas), the budget deficit increases. The deficit also increases *before* a recession as real GDP growth slows and *after* a recession before real GDP growth speeds up. When the growth rate of real GDP is high during an expansion, the budget deficit decreases.

Sources: Office for National Statistics.

As the expansion slows and before the recession begins, the budget deficit increases. It continues to increase during the recession and for a further period after the recession is over. Then, when the expansion is well underway, the budget deficit declines again.

The budget deficit fluctuates with the business cycle because both revenues and outlays fluctuate with real GDP. As real GDP increases during an expansion, tax revenues increase and transfer payments decrease, so the budget deficit automatically decreases. As real GDP decreases during a recession, tax revenues decrease and transfer payments increase, so the budget deficit automatically increases.

Fluctuations in investment or exports have a multiplier effect on real GDP. But automatic fluctuations in tax revenues (and the budget deficit) act as an automatic stabilizer. They decrease the swings in disposable income and make the multiplier smaller. They dampen both the expansions and recessions.

Cyclical and Structural Balances

Because the government budget balance fluctuates with the business cycle, we need a method of measuring the balance so that we know whether it is a temporary cyclical phenomenon or a persistent structural phenomenon. A temporary and cyclical surplus or deficit vanishes when full employment returns. A persistent structural surplus or deficit requires government action to remove it.

To determine whether the budget balance is persistent and structural, or temporary and cyclical, economists have developed the concepts of the structural budget balance and the cyclical budget balance. The **structural surplus or deficit** is the budget balance that would occur if the economy were at full employment and real GDP were equal to potential GDP. The **cyclical surplus or deficit** is the actual surplus or deficit minus the structural surplus or deficit. That is, the cyclical surplus or deficit is the part of the budget balance that arises purely because real GDP does not equal potential GDP.

For example, suppose that the budget deficit is £10 billion and the structural deficit is £2.5 billion. Then the cyclical deficit is £7.5 billion.

Figure 25.8 illustrates the concepts of cyclical and structural deficits. The blue curve shows government outlays. The outlays curve slopes downward because transfer payments, a component of government outlays, decrease as real GDP increases. The green curve shows revenues. The revenues curve slopes upward because most tax revenues increase as income and real GDP increases.

Figure 25.8

Cyclical and Structural Deficits and Surpluses

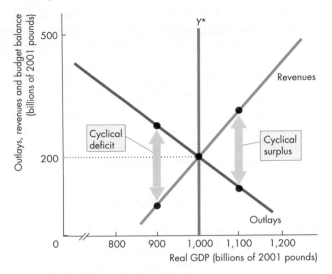

(a) Cyclical deficit and cyclical surplus

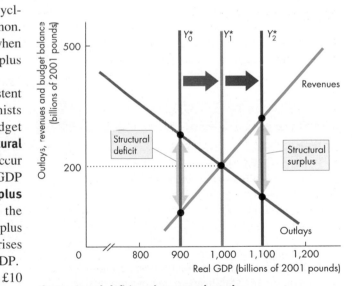

(b) Structural deficit and structural surplus

In part (a), potential GDP is £1,000 billion. When real GDP is less than potential GDP, the budget is in a *cyclical deficit*. When real GDP exceeds potential GDP, the budget is in a *cyclical surplus*. The government has a *balanced budget* when real GDP equals potential GDP.

In part (b), when potential GDP is £900 billion, the budget deficit is a *structural deficit*. But when potential GDP is £1,100 billion, the budget surplus is a *structural surplus*.

In this example, potential GDP is £1,000 billion. If real GDP equals potential GDP, the government has a *balanced budget*. Outlays and revenues each equal £200 billion. If real GDP is less than potential GDP, outlays exceed revenues and there is a *cyclical deficit*. If real GDP is greater than potential GDP, outlays are less than revenues and there is a *cyclical surplus*.

In Figure 25.8(b), potential GDP grows but the revenues curve and the outlays curve do not change. When potential GDP is £900 billion (Y_0^*), the deficit is a *structural deficit*. When potential GDP grows to £1,000 billion (Y_1^*), there is a structural balance of zero. And when potential GDP grows to £1,100 billion, the budget surplus is a *structural surplus*.

Estimates of Structural Balances

The Organization for Economic Cooperation and Development (OECD) estimates that the United Kingdom had a structural deficit of 2.3 per cent of potential GDP in 2003. Other EU members that have significant structural deficits include Sweden, Portugal, Finland, Denmark and Germany. Greece and Ireland have large structural surpluses.

A country with a structural deficit needs to take steps either to bring outlays under control or increase revenues. Countries with a structural surplus have room for spending increases or tax cuts.

Review Quiz

1 What are the government expenditures multiplier and the autonomous taxes multiplier?
2 Which multiplier effect is larger: the multiplier effect of a change in government expenditures or the multiplier effect of a change in autonomous taxes?
3 How do income taxes and imports influence the size of the fiscal policy multipliers?
4 How do income taxes and transfer payments work as automatic stabilizers to dampen the business cycle?
5 How do we tell whether a budget deficit needs government action to remove it?

Your next task is to see how the passage of time and price level adjustments change the values of the multipliers.

Fiscal Policy Multipliers and the Price Level

We've seen how real GDP responds to changes in fiscal policy when the price level is fixed and all the adjustments that take place are in spending, income and production. Once production starts to change, prices also start to change. The price level and real GDP change together, and the economy moves to a new short-run equilibrium.

To study the simultaneous changes in real GDP and the price level that result from fiscal policy, we use the *AS–AD* model of Chapter 22. In the long run, both the price level and the money wage rate respond to fiscal policy. As these further changes take place, the economy gradually moves towards a new long-run equilibrium. We also use the *AS–AD* model to study these adjustments.

We begin by looking at the effects of fiscal policy on aggregate demand and the aggregate demand curve.

Fiscal Policy and Aggregate Demand

You learned about the relationship between aggregate demand, aggregate expenditure, and equilibrium expenditure in Chapter 24, pp. 541–543. You are now going to use what you learned to work out what happens to aggregate demand, the price level and real GDP when fiscal policy changes. We'll start by looking at the effects on aggregate demand.

Figure 25.9 shows the effects of an increase in government expenditures on aggregate demand. Initially, the aggregate expenditure curve is AE_0 in part (a) and the aggregate demand curve is AD_0 in part (b). The price level is 110, real GDP is £1,000 billion and the economy is at point *A* in both parts of the figure.

Now suppose that government expenditures increase by £50 billion. At a constant price level of 110, the aggregate expenditure curve shifts upward from AE_0 to AE_1. This curve intersects the 45° line at an equilibrium expenditure of £1,200 billion at point *B*. This amount is the aggregate quantity of goods and services demanded at a price level of 110, as shown by point *B* in part (b). Point *B* lies on a new aggregate demand curve. The aggregate demand curve has shifted rightward to AD_1.

The government expenditures multiplier determines the distance by which the aggregate demand curve shifts rightward. The larger the multiplier, the larger is the

Figure 25.9

Changes in Government Expenditures and Aggregate Demand

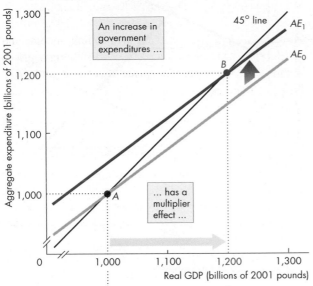

(a) Aggregate expenditure

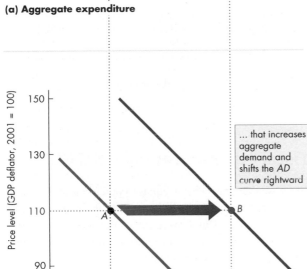

(b) Aggregate demand

The price level is 110. When the aggregate expenditure curve is AE_0 in part (a), the aggregate demand curve is AD_0 in part (b). An increase in government expenditures shifts the AE curve to AE_1 and real GDP increases to £1,200 billion. The aggregate demand curve shifts rightward to AD_1.

shift of the aggregate demand curve that results from a given change in government expenditures. In this example, a £50 billion increase in government expenditures produces a £200 billion increase in the aggregate quantity of goods and services demanded at each price level. The multiplier is 4. So the £50 billion increase in government expenditures shifts the aggregate demand curve rightward by £200 billion.

Figure 25.9 shows the effects of an increase in government expenditures. But a similar effect occurs for *any* expansionary fiscal policy. An **expansionary fiscal policy** is an increase in government expenditures on goods and services or a decrease in net taxes. But the distance that the aggregate demand curve shifts is smaller for a decrease in taxes than for an increase in government expenditures of the same size.

Figure 25.9 can also be used to illustrate the effects of a **contractionary fiscal policy** – a decrease in government expenditures on goods and services or an increase in net taxes. In this case, start at point B in each part of the figure and decrease government expenditures or increase taxes. Aggregate demand decreases and the aggregate demand curve shifts leftward from AD_1 to AD_0.

Equilibrium GDP and the Price Level in the Short Run

We've seen how an increase in government expenditures increases aggregate demand. Let's now see how it changes real GDP and the price level. Figure 25.10(a) – overleaf – describes the economy. Aggregate demand is AD_0 and the short-run aggregate supply curve is SAS. (Check back to Chapter 22, pp. 481–483 if you need to refresh your understanding of the short-run aggregate supply curve.) Equilibrium is at point A, where the aggregate demand and short-run aggregate supply curves intersect. The price level is 110, and real GDP is £1,000 billion.

An increase in government expenditures of £50 billion shifts the aggregate demand curve rightward from AD_0 to AD_1. While the price level is fixed at 110, the economy moves towards point B and real GDP increases towards £1,200 billion. But during the adjustment process, the price level does not remain constant. It gradually rises and the economy moves along the short-run aggregate supply curve to the point of intersection of the short-run aggregate supply curve and the new aggregate demand curve – point C. The price level rises to 123 and real GDP increases to £1,130 billion.

Figure 25.10

Fiscal Policy, Real GDP and the Price Level

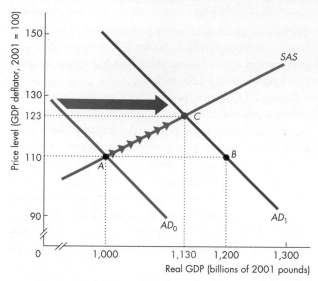

(a) Fiscal policy with unemployment

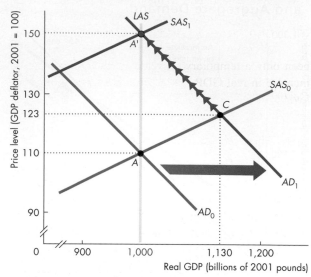

(b) Fiscal policy at full employment

An increase in government expenditures shifts the *AD* curve from AD_0 to AD_1 in part (a). With a fixed price level, the economy would have moved to point *B*. But the price level rises. And in the short run, the economy moves along the *SAS* curve to point *C*. The price level increases to 123, and real GDP increases to £1,130 billion.

At point *C*, real GDP exceeds potential GDP and unemployment is below the natural rate in part (b). The money wage rate starts to rise, and short-run aggregate supply decreases. The *SAS* curve shifts towards SAS_1. In the long run, the economy moves to point *A'*. The price level rises to 150 and real GDP returns to £1,000 billion.

When we take the price-level effect into account, the increase in government expenditures still has a multiplier effect on real GDP, but the effect is smaller than it would be if the price level remained constant. The steeper the short-run aggregate supply curve, the larger is the increase in the price level and the smaller is the increase in real GDP. So the steeper the short-run aggregate supply curve, the smaller is the government expenditures multiplier but it is not zero.

In the long run, real GDP equals potential GDP – the economy is at full employment. When real GDP equals potential GDP, an increase in aggregate demand has the same short-run effect as we have just worked out, but the long-run effect is different. The increase in aggregate demand raises the price level but in the long-run, real GDP remains at potential GDP.

To study this case, let's see what happens if the government embarks on an expansionary fiscal policy at full employment, when real GDP equals potential GDP.

Fiscal Expansion at Potential GDP

Suppose that real GDP is equal to potential GDP, which means that unemployment is equal to the natural rate of unemployment. But suppose also that both the unemployment rate and the natural rate are high and that most people, including the government, mistakenly think that the unemployment rate exceeds the natural rate. In this situation, the government tries to lower the unemployment rate by using an expansionary fiscal policy.

Figure 25.10(b) shows the effect of an expansionary fiscal policy when real GDP equals potential GDP. In this example, potential GDP is £1,000 billion. Aggregate demand increases and the aggregate demand curve shifts rightward from AD_0 to AD_1. The short-run equilibrium, point *C*, is an above full-employment equilibrium. The money wage rate begins to increase. The higher wage rate increases firms' costs, and short-run aggregate supply decreases. The *SAS* curve begins to shift leftward from SAS_0 to SAS_1. The economy moves up along the aggregate demand curve AD_1 towards point A'.

When all adjustments to the money wage rate and the price level have been made, the price level is 150 and real GDP is again at potential GDP of £1,000 billion. The multiplier in the long run is zero. There has been only a temporary decrease in unemployment and increase in real GDP, but a permanent rise in the price level.

Limitations of Fiscal Policy

Because the short-run fiscal policy multipliers are not zero, expansionary fiscal policy can be used to increase real GDP and decrease the unemployment rate in a recession. Contractionary fiscal policy can also be used, if the economy is overheating, to decrease real GDP and help to keep inflation in check. But two factors limit the use of fiscal policy.

First, the legislative process is slow, which means that it is difficult to take fiscal policy actions in a timely way. The economy might be able to benefit from fiscal stimulation right now, but it will take Parliament many months, perhaps more than a year, to act. By the time the action is taken, the economy might need an entirely different fiscal medicine.

Second, it is not always easy to tell whether real GDP is below (or above) potential GDP. A change in aggregate demand can move real GDP away from potential GDP, or a change in aggregate supply can change real GDP and change potential GDP. This difficulty is a serious one because, as you've seen, fiscal stimulation might occur too close to full employment, in which case it will increase the price level and have no long-run effect on real GDP.

Review Quiz

1. How do changes in the price level influence the multiplier effects of fiscal policy on real GDP?
2. What is the long-run fiscal multiplier effect on real GDP and the price level?

So far, we've ignored any potential effects of fiscal policy on aggregate supply. Yet many economists believe that the supply-side effects of fiscal policy are the biggest. Let's now look at these effects.

Supply-side Effects of Fiscal Policy

Tax cuts increase disposable income and increase aggregate demand. But tax cuts also strengthen incentives and increase aggregate supply. The strength of the supply-side effects of tax cuts is not known with certainty. Some economists believe that the supply-side effects are large and exceed the demand-side effects. Other economists, while agreeing that supply-side effects are present, believe that they are relatively small.

The controversy over the magnitude of the effects of taxes on aggregate supply is a political controversy. Generally speaking, people on the conservative or right wing of the political spectrum believe that supply-side effects are powerful, and people on the liberal or left wing of the political spectrum view supply-side effects as being small.

Regardless of which view is correct, we can study the supply-side effects of tax cuts by using the AS–AD model. Let's study the effects of taxes on potential GDP and then see how the supply-side effects and demand-side effects together influence real GDP and the price level.

Fiscal Policy and Potential GDP

Potential GDP depends on the full-employment quantity of labour, the quantity of capital, and the state of technology. Taxes can influence all three of these factors. The main tax to consider is the income tax. By taxing the incomes people earn when they work or save, the government weakens the incentives to work and save. The result is a smaller quantity of labour and capital and a smaller potential GDP. Also, the income tax weakens the incentive to develop new technologies that increase income. So the pace of technological change might be slowed, which slows the growth rate of potential GDP. Let's look at the effect of the income tax on both the quantity of labour and the quantity of capital.

Labour Market Taxes

The quantity of labour is determined by demand and supply in the labour market. Figure 25.11(a) – overleaf – shows the demand for labour is LD and the supply is LS. The equilibrium real wage rate is £15 an hour and 60 billion hours of labour per year are employed.

Figure 25.11

Supply-side Effects of Taxes

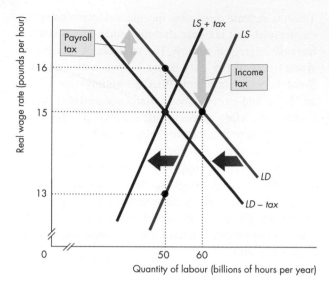

(a) The labour market

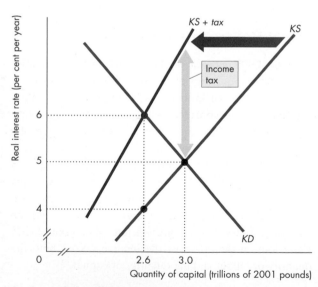

(b) The capital market

In part (a), an income tax decreases the supply of labour from *LS* to *LS + tax* and a payroll tax decreases the demand for labour from *LD* to *LD – tax*. The quantity of labour decreases. In part (b), the income tax decreases the supply of capital from *KS* to *KS + tax*. The quantity of capital decreases. With less labour and less capital, potential GDP decreases.

Now suppose that two taxes are introduced. An income tax weakens the incentive to work and decreases the supply of labour. The supply curve shifts leftward to *LS + tax*. A payroll tax makes it more costly to employ labour and decreases the demand for labour. The demand curve shifts leftward to *LD – tax*. With the new decreased supply and demand, the quantity of labour employed decreases to 50 billion hours a year. The *before-tax* real wage rate remains at £15 an hour (but it might rise or fall depending on whether demand or supply decreases more). The *after-tax* real wage rate falls to £13 an hour, and the cost of hiring labour rises to £16 an hour.

Capital and the Income Tax

The quantity of capital is determined by demand and supply in the capital market. Figure 25.11(b) shows the capital market. The demand for capital is *KD* and the supply is *KS*. The equilibrium real interest rate is 5 per cent a year and the quantity of capital is £3 trillion.

A tax on the income from capital weakens the incentive to save and decreases the supply of capital. The supply curve shifts leftward to *KS + tax*. With the new decreased supply, the quantity of capital decreases to £2.6 trillion. The *before-tax* interest rate rises to 6 per cent a year, and the *after-tax* interest rate falls to 4 per cent a year.

Potential GDP and the *LAS* Curve

Because the income tax decreases the equilibrium quantities of labour and capital, it also decreases potential GDP. But potential GDP determines long-run aggregate supply. So the income tax decreases long-run aggregate supply and shifts the *LAS* curve leftward.

Supply Effects and Demand Effects

Let's now bring the supply-side effects and demand-side effects of fiscal policy together. Figure 25.12(a) shows the most likely effects of a tax cut. The tax cut increases aggregate demand and shifts the *AD* curve rightward, just as before. But a tax cut that increases the incentive to work and save also increases aggregate supply. It shifts the long-run and short-run aggregate supply curves rightward. Here we focus on the short run and show the effect on the *SAS* curve, which shifts rightward to *SAS₁*. In this example, the tax cut has a large effect on aggregate demand and a small effect on aggregate supply. The aggregate demand curve shifts rightward by

Figure 25.12

Supply-side Effects of Fiscal Policy

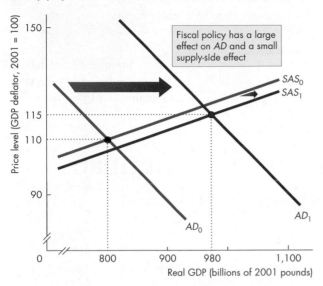

Fiscal policy has a large effect on *AD* and a small supply-side effect

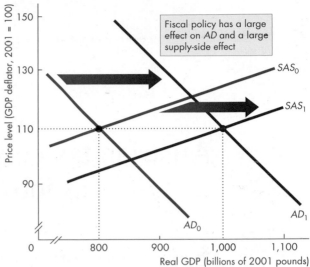

Fiscal policy has a large effect on *AD* and a large supply-side effect

(a) The traditional view

(b) The supply-side view

An expansionary fiscal policy such as a tax cut increases aggregate demand and shifts the *AD* curve rightward from AD_0 to AD_1 (both parts). Such a policy change also has a supply-side effect. If the supply-side effect is small, the *SAS* curve shifts rightward from SAS_0 to SAS_1 in part (a). In this case, the demand-side effect dominates the supply-side effect, real GDP increases and the price level rises.

If the supply-side effect of a tax cut is large, the *SAS* curve shifts rightward from SAS_0 to SAS_1 in part (b). In this case, the supply-side effect is as large as the demand-side effect. Real GDP increases and the price level remains constant. But if the supply-side effect was larger than the demand-side effect, the price level would actually fall.

a larger amount than the rightward shift in the short-run aggregate supply curve. The outcome is a rise in the price level and an increase in real GDP. But notice that the price level rises by *less* and real GDP increases by *more* than would occur if there were no supply-side effect.

Figure 25.12(b) shows the effects that supply-siders believe occur. A tax cut has a large effect on aggregate demand, but it has a similarly large effect on aggregate supply. The aggregate demand curve and the short-run aggregate supply curve shift rightward by similar amounts. In this particular case, the price level remains constant and real GDP increases. A slightly larger increase in aggregate supply would have brought a fall in the price level, a possibility that some supply-siders believe could occur.

The general point with which everyone agrees is that a tax cut that strengthens incentives increases real GDP by more and is less inflationary than an equal-size expansionary fiscal policy that does not change incentives or that weakens them.

Review Quiz

1   How do income taxes and payroll taxes influence the labour market, and how would a cut in these taxes influence real GDP?
2   How would an income tax cut influence aggregate supply and aggregate demand?
3   How would an income tax cut influence real GDP and the price level?

You've seen how fiscal policy influences the way real GDP fluctuates around its trend and how it influences the long-term growth rate of real GDP. *Reading Between the Lines* on pp. 574–575 looks at the very different fiscal policies of Germany and Austria.

Your next task is to study the other main arm of macroeconomic policy: monetary policy.

Reading Between the Lines
Supply-side Policy in Austria

The Financial Times, 24 June 2004

FT

Austrian tax cuts worry the Germans as jobs disappear

Haig Simonian

Germany could do worse than look south to Austria – its smaller, more dynamic neighbour – to help revive its sluggish economy. While Germany struggles with inflexible labour laws and high taxation, Austria has pushed through tax reforms that will bring (tax) rates down close to east European levels, to run alongside already business-friendly employment measures.

The results have been dramatic. Since January this year, when the first phase of Austria's two-step reforms kicked in with big income tax cuts and some relief for small and medium-size companies, the country has enjoyed a rash of high-profile investment. Businesses have been enticed not just by the current reforms but by the prospect of corporate (tax) rates falling from 34 to 25 per cent, or less than 22 per cent including

allowances, from January next year as part of the second stage.

However, Austria's success has been at Germany's expense, as companies relocate from the German border region of Bavaria. Infineon, the semiconductor group spun off from Siemens, has relocated its automotive industrial division from Munich to the southern Austrian province of Carinthia. Escada, the Bavarian fashion group, has shifted its logistics activities from Munich to Upper Austria.

The second stage of reforms will bring corporate taxation in line with the 21–22 per cent of the Czech Republic or Slovenia. While Germany is still struggling, for example, to liberalise inflexible labour laws, Austrian employment legislation is much more business-friendly, particularly on shedding staff.

The Essence of the Story

◆ A number of high profile German companies have relocated to Austria.

◆ Low taxes and business-friendly legislation has attracted this relocation.

◆ High taxes and inflexible labour markets in Germany has encouraged firms to leave Germany.

◆ Austria has cut corporate tax in two stages. Stage one cut the tax rate from 34 per cent to 25 per cent and stage two cut the rate to 21–22 per cent.

Economic Analysis

◆ Cuts in corporate taxes and business-friendly legislation in Austria have led to an increase in investment.

◆ The investment has increased Austria's capital and increased its potential GDP.

◆ Figure 1 compares the real GDP growth rates of Austria and Germany. (The figures for 2004 and 2005 are forecasts.) Austria has generally outperformed Germany.

◆ Figure 2 shows how Austria's tax cuts increase the supply of capital, increase the equilibrium quantity of capital and raise the after-tax real interest rate in Austria. These effects are on the supply side of the economy.

◆ The demand for capital is KD. Initially, the supply of capital is KS + tax before. The tax cuts increase the supply of capital to KS + tax after. The equilibrium quantity of capital increases from €600 billion to €650 billion (hypothetical but ball-park, reasonable numbers).

◆ Figure 3 shows the effects of the tax cuts on aggregate demand and aggregate supply.

◆ The tax cuts stimulate investment in Austria, which shifts the aggregate demand curve rightward from AD_0 to AD_1.

◆ The tax cuts also increase the quantity of capital in Austria, which increases potential GDP and short-run aggregate supply. The SAS curve shifts rightward from SAS_0 to SAS_1.

◆ The increase in investment and capital have a bigger impact on aggregate demand than on aggregate supply, so the price level rises. But real GDP increases by a large amount.

◆ With no supply-side stimulus, Germany does not enjoy the large increase in aggregate demand and aggregate supply that bring faster growth to Austria.

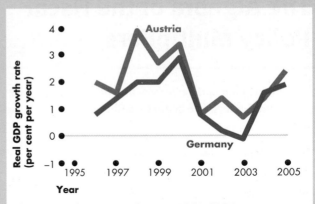

Figure 1 Real GDP growth rates: 1996–2005

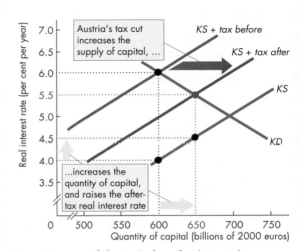

Figure 2 Taxes and the capital market in Austria

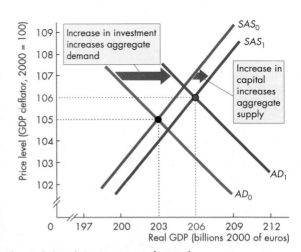

Figure 3 Austria's aggregate demand and aggregate supply

Mathematical Note The Algebra of the Fiscal Policy Multipliers

This mathematical note derives the formula for the fiscal policy multipliers. We begin by defining the symbols we need:

◆ Aggregate planned expenditure, AE

◆ Real GDP, Y

◆ Consumption expenditure, C

◆ Investment, I

◆ Government expenditures, G

◆ Exports, X

◆ Imports, M

◆ Net taxes, T

◆ Autonomous expenditure, A

◆ Autonomous consumption expenditure, a

◆ Autonomous taxes, T_a

◆ Marginal propensity to consume, b

◆ Marginal propensity to import, m

◆ Marginal tax rate, t

Equilibrium Expenditure

Aggregate planned expenditure is:

$$AE = C + I + G + X - M$$

The consumption function is:

$$C = a + b(Y - T)$$

Net taxes equals autonomous taxes plus induced taxes, which is:

$$T = T_a + tY$$

Use the last equation in the consumption function to give consumption expenditure as a function of GDP:

$$C = a - bT_a + b(1 - t)Y$$

The import function is:

$$M = mY$$

Use the consumption function and the import function to replace C and M in the aggregate planned expenditure

equation to obtain:

$$AE = a - bT_a + b(1 - t)Y + I + G + X - mY$$

Collect the terms on the right side of the equation that involve Y to obtain:

$$AE = [a - bT_a + I + G + X] + [b(1 - t) - m]Y$$

Autonomous expenditure (A) is given by:

$$A = a - bT_a + I + G + X$$

so:

$$AE = A + [b(1 - t) - m]Y$$

Equilibrium expenditure occurs when aggregate planned expenditure (AE) equals real GDP (Y). That is:

$$AE = Y$$

To calculate equilibrium expenditure we solve the equation:

$$Y = A + [b(1 - t) - m]Y$$

to obtain:

$$Y = \frac{1}{1 - [b(1 - t) - m]}A$$

Government Expenditures Multiplier

The government expenditures multiplier equals the change in equilibrium expenditure (Y) that results from a change in government expenditures (G) divided by the change in government expenditures. Because autonomous expenditure is:

$$A = a - bT_a + I + G + X$$

the change in autonomous expenditure equals the change in government expenditures. That is:

$$\Delta A = \Delta G$$

The government expenditures multiplier is found by working out the change in Y that results from the change in A. You can see from the solution for Y that:

$$\Delta Y = \frac{1}{1 - [b(1 - t) - m]}\Delta G$$

The government expenditures multiplier equals:

$$\frac{1}{1 - [b(1 - t) - m]}$$

In an economy in which $t = 0$ and $m = 0$, the government expenditures multiplier is $1/(1 - b)$. With $b = 0.75$, the government expenditures multiplier equals 4, as part (a) of the figure shows. Make up some examples and use the above formula to show how b, m, and t influence the government expenditures multiplier.

Autonomous Tax Multiplier

The autonomous tax multiplier equals the change in equilibrium expenditure (Y) that results from a change in autonomous taxes (T_a) divided by the change in autonomous taxes. Because autonomous expenditure is:

$$A = a - bT_a + I + G + X$$

the change in autonomous expenditure equals *minus b* multiplied by the change in autonomous taxes. That is:

$$\Delta A = -b\Delta T_a$$

You can see from the solution for Y that:

$$\Delta Y = \frac{-b}{1 - [b(1 - t) - m]}\Delta T_a$$

The autonomous tax multiplier equals:

$$\frac{-b}{1 - [b(1 - t) - m]}$$

In an economy in which $t = 0$ and $m = 0$, the autonomous tax multiplier is $-b/(1 - b)$. With $b = 0.75$, the autonomous tax multiplier equals -3, as part (b) of the figure shows. Make up some examples and use the above formula to show how b, m, and t influence the autonomous tax multiplier.

Balanced Budget Multiplier

The balanced budget multiplier equals the change in equilibrium expenditure that results from a fiscal policy action that changes *both* government expenditures and taxes by the *same* amount so that the government's budget balance remains *unchanged*.

If government expenditures increase by ΔG and autonomous taxes increase by ΔT_a and $\Delta G = \Delta T_a$, then the budget balance does not change.

The change in government expenditures (ΔG) changes equilibrium expenditure (Y) by:

$$\Delta Y = \frac{1}{1 - [b(1 - t) - m]}\Delta G$$

and the change in autonomous taxes (ΔT_a) changes equilibrium expenditure (Y) by:

$$\Delta Y = \frac{-b}{1 - [b(1 - t) - m]}\Delta T_a$$

So when government expenditures and taxes change together, the change in equilibrium expenditure is:

$$\Delta Y = \frac{1}{1 - [b(1 - t) - m]}\Delta G + \frac{-b}{1 - [b(1 - t) - m]}\Delta T_a$$

But $\Delta G = \Delta T_a$, so:

$$\Delta Y = \frac{1 - b}{1 - [b(1 - t) - m]}\Delta G$$

The balanced budget multiplier is:

$$\frac{1 - b}{1 - [b(1 - t) - m]}$$

In an economy in which $t = 0$ and $m = 0$, the balanced budget multiplier is $(1 - b)/(1 - b)$, which equals 1.

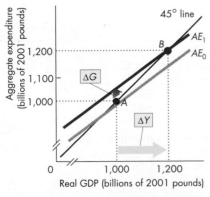

(a) Government expenditures multiplier

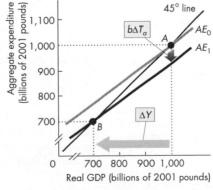

(b) Autonomous tax multiplier

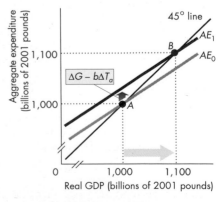

(c) Balanced budget multiplier

Summary

Key Points

Government Budgets (pp. 556–561)

◆ The government budget finances the activities of the government and is used to conduct fiscal policy.

◆ Government revenues come from taxes on income and wealth, taxes on expenditure and social security contributions.

◆ When government outlays exceed revenues, the government has a budget deficit.

Fiscal Policy Multipliers (pp. 562–568)

◆ Fiscal policy actions are either discretionary or automatic.

◆ Government expenditures, taxes and transfer payments have multiplier effects on real GDP.

◆ The government expenditures multiplier equals $1/(1 - MPC)$. The autonomous tax multiplier equals $-MPC/(1 - MPC)$.

◆ The autonomous transfer payments multiplier is equal to the magnitude of the tax multiplier but is positive.

◆ Induced taxes and transfers payments and imports make the fiscal policy multipliers smaller.

◆ Income taxes and transfer payments act as automatic stabilizers.

Fiscal Policy Multipliers and the Price Level (pp. 568–571)

◆ An expansionary fiscal policy increases aggregate demand and shifts the aggregate demand curve rightward. It increases real GDP and raises the price level. (A contractionary fiscal policy has the opposite effects.)

◆ Price level changes dampen fiscal policy multiplier effects.

◆ At potential GDP, an expansionary fiscal policy increases the price level but leaves real GDP unchanged. The fiscal policy multipliers are zero.

Supply-side Effects of Fiscal Policy (pp. 571–573)

◆ Fiscal policy has supply-side effects because increases in taxes weaken the incentives to work and save.

◆ A tax cut increases both aggregate demand and aggregate supply and increases real GDP, but the tax cut has an ambiguous effect on the price level.

Key Figures

Figure 25.5   The Government Expenditures Multiplier, 564
Figure 25.6   The Autonomous Tax Multiplier, 565
Figure 25.7   The Business Cycle and the Budget Deficit, 566
Figure 25.8   Cyclical and Structural Deficits and Surpluses, 567
Figure 25.9   Changes in Government Expenditures and Aggregate Demand, 569
Figure 25.10 Fiscal Policy, Real GDP and the Price Level, 570
Figure 25.11 Supply-side Effects of Taxes, 572
Figure 25.12 Supply-side Effects of Fiscal Policy, 573

Key Terms

Automatic fiscal policy, 562
Automatic stabilizers, 566
Autonomous taxes, 562
Autonomous tax multiplier, 564
Balanced budget, 557
Balanced budget multiplier, 565
Budget, 556
Budget deficit, 557
Budget surplus, 557
Contractionary fiscal policy, 569
Cyclical surplus or deficit, 567
Discretionary fiscal policy, 562
Expansionary fiscal policy, 569
Government debt, 559
Government expenditures multiplier, 562
Induced taxes, 565
Structural surplus or deficit, 567

Problems

*1 In the economy of Zap, the marginal propensity to consume is 0.9. Investment is €50 billion, government expenditures on goods and services are €40 billion, and autonomous taxes are €40 billion. Zap has no exports, no imports and no income taxes.

   a The government cuts its expenditures on goods and services to €30 billion. What is the change in equilibrium expenditure?

   b What is the value of the government expenditures multiplier?

   c The government continues to buy €40 billion worth of goods and services and cuts autonomous taxes to €30 billion. What is the change in equilibrium expenditure?

   d What is the value of the autonomous tax multiplier?

   e The government simultaneously cuts both its expenditures on goods and services and autonomous taxes to €30 billion. What is the change in equilibrium expenditure? Why does equilibrium expenditure decrease?

   f If the government wants to increase equilibrium expenditure by €500 billion, but wants to keep its budget balanced, by how much must it increase its expenditures and taxes?

2 In the economy of Zip, the marginal propensity to consume is 0.8. Investment is €60 billion, government expenditures on goods and services are €50 billion and autonomous taxes are €60 billion. Zip has no exports, no imports and no income taxes.

   a The government increases its expenditures on goods and services to €60 billion. What is the change in equilibrium expenditure?

   b What is the value of the government expenditures multiplier?

   c The government continues to purchase €60 billion worth of goods and services and increases autonomous taxes to €70 billion. What is the change in equilibrium expenditure?

   d What is the value of the autonomous tax multiplier?

   e The government simultaneously increases both its expenditures on goods and services and autonomous taxes by €10 billion. What is the change in equilibrium expenditure? Why does equilibrium expenditure increase?

   f If the government wants to increase equilibrium expenditure by €800 billion, but wants to keep its budget balanced, by how much must it increase its expenditures and taxes?

*3 Suppose that the price level in the economy of Zap as described in problem 1 is 100. The economy is also at full employment.

   a If the government of Zap increases its expenditures on goods and services by €10 billion, what happens to the quantity of real GDP demanded?

   b How does Zap's aggregate demand curve change? Draw a two-part graph that is similar to Figure 25.9 to illustrate the change in both the *AE* curve and the *AD* curve.

   c In the short run, does equilibrium real GDP increase by more than, less than or the same amount as the increase in the quantity of real GDP demanded?

   d In the long run, does equilibrium real GDP increase by more than, less than or the same amount as the increase in the quantity of real GDP demanded?

   e In the short run, does the price level in Zap rise, fall or remain unchanged?

   f In the long run, does the price level in Zap rise, fall or remain unchanged?

4 Suppose that the price level in the economy of Zip as described in problem 2 is 100. The economy is also at full employment.

   a If the government of Zip decreases its expenditures on goods and services by €5 billion, what happens to the quantity of real GDP demanded?

   b How does Zip's aggregate demand curve change? Draw a two-part diagram that is similar to Figure 25.9 to illustrate the change in both the *AE* curve and the *AD* curve.

   c In the short run, does equilibrium real GDP decrease by more than, less than or the same amount as the decrease in the quantity of real GDP demanded?

   d In the short run, does the price level in Zip rise, fall or remain unchanged?

   e Why does real GDP in the short run decrease by a smaller amount than the decrease in aggregate demand?

*5 The figure shows revenues and outlays of the government of Dreamland. Potential GDP is €40 million.

---

*Solutions to odd-numbered problems are available on *Parkin Interactive*.

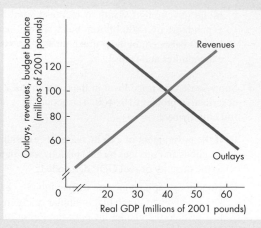

a What is the government's budget balance if real GDP is €40 million?

b Does Dreamland have a structural surplus or deficit if its real GDP is €40 million? What is its size? Explain why.

c What is the government's budget balance if real GDP is €30 million?

d If Dreamland's real GDP is €30 million, does Dreamland have a structural surplus or deficit? What is its size? Explain why.

e If Dreamland's real GDP is €50 million, does Dreamland have a structural surplus or deficit? What is its size? Explain why.

6 In problem 5, if Dreamland's real GDP is €40 million:

a What is the government's budget balance?

b If potential GDP is €30 million, does Dreamland have a cyclical surplus or deficit? What is its size? Explain why.

c If potential GDP is €40 million, does Dreamland have a cyclical surplus or deficit? What is its size? Explain why.

d If potential GDP is €50 million, does Dreamland have a cyclical surplus or deficit? What is its size? Explain why.

e How can the Dreamland government eliminate a structural deficit/surplus and avoid a cyclical deficit/surplus if potential GDP is €40 million?

Critical Thinking

1 Study *Reading Between the Lines* on pp. 574–575 and then answer the following questions.

a What policy has the Austrian government conducted with its expansionary fiscal policy?

b Why have Bavarian firms relocated from Munich to Austria?

c What is the economic argument for the type of supply-side policy conducted by the Austrian government?

d If the supply-side policy in Austria is successful what do you expect to happen to real GDP in the long run?

e In the long run, is the multiplier in Austria zero or positive?

f In the long run, is the multiplier in Germany zero or positive?

Web Exercises

Use the link on *Parkin Interactive* to work the following exercises.

1 Obtain data on the components of government outlays in the main industrial countries. Then use the fiscal policy multiplier to predict which countries have strong automatic stabilizers and which have weak ones. Explain the reasons for your predictions.

2 Visit the Office for National Statistics and obtain the most recent data you can find on the revenues, outlays, and budget surplus or deficit for the United Kingdom.

a Compare the data you obtain with that in Table 25.1.

b Is the most recent budget more or less expansionary or than that in Table 25.1? Explain why?

c Predict the effects of the most recent budget on real GDP and the price level.

Chapter 26

Money, Banks and Interest Rate

After studying this chapter you will be able to:

◆ Define money and describe its functions

◆ Explain the economic functions of banks and other financial institutions

◆ Explain how banks create money

◆ Explain what determines the demand for money

◆ Explain how the interest rate is determined

Money Makes the World Go Round

When you want to buy something, you use coins, notes, write a cheque, or present a debit or credit card. Are all these things money? When you deposit some coins or notes in the bank, is it still money? What happens when the bank lends your money to someone else? How can you still get it back if it's been lent out? Why does the amount of money in the economy matter? How does it affect the interest rate? And how does the interest rate affect spending plans?

What is Money?

What do cowrie shells, wampum, whales' teeth, tobacco, cattle and pennies have in common? The answer is that all of them are (or have been) forms of money. **Money** is any commodity or token that is generally acceptable as a means of payment. A **means of payment** is a method of settling a debt. When a payment has been made there is no remaining obligation between the parties to a transaction. So what cowrie shells, wampum, whales' teeth, cattle and pennies have in common is that they have served (or still do serve) as the means of payment. But money has three other functions as:

◆   A medium of exchange

◆   A unit of account

◆   A store of value

Medium of Exchange

A *medium of exchange* is an object that is generally accepted in exchange for goods and services. Money acts as such a medium. Without money, it would be necessary to exchange goods and services directly for other goods and services – an exchange called **barter**. Barter requires a *double coincidence of wants*, a situation that rarely occurs. For example, if you want a pizza, you might offer a CD in exchange for it. But you must find someone who is selling pizza and who wants your CD.

A medium of exchange overcomes the need for a double coincidence of wants. And money acts as a medium of exchange because people with something to sell will always accept money in exchange for it. But money isn't the only medium of exchange. You can buy with a credit card. But a credit card isn't money. It doesn't make a final payment and the debt it creates must eventually be settled by using money.

Unit of Account

A *unit of account* is an agreed measure for stating the prices of goods and services. To get the most out of your budget you have to work out, among other things, whether seeing one more film is worth the price you have to pay, not in pounds and pence, but in terms of the number of ice creams, beers and cups of tea that you have to give up. It's easy to do such calculations when all these goods have prices in terms of pounds and pence (see Table 26.1). If a cinema ticket costs £4 and a pint of

beer in the Students' Union costs £1, you know straight away that seeing one more film costs you 4 pints of beer. If a cup of tea costs 50 pence, one more cinema ticket costs 8 cups of tea. You need only one calculation to work out the opportunity cost of any pair of goods and services.

But imagine how troublesome it would be if your local cinema posted its price as 4 pints of beer; and if the Students' Union announced that the price of a pint of beer was 2 ice creams; and if the corner shop posted the price of an ice cream as 1 cup of tea; and if the café priced a cup of tea as 5 rolls of mints!

Now how much running around and calculating do you have to do to work out how much that film is going to cost you in terms of the beer, ice cream, tea or mints that you must give up to see it? You get the answer for beer from the sign posted at the cinema, but for all the other goods you're going to have to visit many different shops to establish the prices you need to work out the opportunity costs you face.

Cover up the column labelled "price in money units" in Table 26.1 and see how hard it is to work out the number of local telephone calls it costs to see one film.

It is much simpler for everyone to express their prices in terms of pounds and pence.

Table 26.1

The Unit of Account Function of Money Simplifies Price Comparisons

Good	Price in money units	Price in units of another good
Cinema ticket	£4.00 each	4 pints of beer
Beer	£1.00 per pint	2 ice creams
Ice cream	£0.50 per cone	1 cup of tea
Tea	£0.50 per cup	5 rolls of mints
Mints	£0.10 per roll	1 local phone call

Money as a unit of account. 1 cinema ticket costs £4 and 1 cup of tea costs 50 pence, so a film costs 8 cups of tea (£4.00/£0.5 = 8).

No unit of account. You go to a cinema and learn that the price of a film is 4 pints of beer. You go to a café and learn that a cup of tea costs 5 rolls of mints. But how many rolls of mints does it cost you to see a film? To answer that question, you go to the Students' Union bar and find that a pint of beer costs 2 ice creams. Now you head for the ice cream shop, where an ice cream costs one cup of tea. Now you get out your pocket calculator: 1 film costs 4 pints of beer, or 8 ice creams, or 8 cups of tea, or 40 rolls of mints!

Sometimes we use a unit of account that is not money. An example is the European Currency Unit that preceded the euro. Also, the euro existed as a unit of account before it became money – a means of payment – on 1 January 2002.

Store of Value

Money is a *store of value* in the sense that it can be held and exchanged later for goods and services. If money were not a store of value, it could not serve as a means of payment.

Money is not alone in acting as a store of value. A physical object such as a house, a car, a work of art or a computer can act as a store of value. The most reliable and useful stores of value are items that have a stable value. The more stable the value of a commodity or token, the better it can act as a store of value and the more useful it is as money. No store of value has a completely stable value. The value of a house, a car or a work of art fluctuates over time. The value of the commodities and tokens that are used as money also fluctuate over time. And when there is inflation, their values persistently fall.

Because inflation brings a falling value of money, a low inflation rate is needed to make money as useful as possible as a store of value.

Money in the United Kingdom Today

In the United Kingdom today, money consists of:

◆ Currency

◆ Deposits at banks and other financial institutions

Currency

The notes and coins that we use in the United Kingdom today are known as **currency**. They are money because the government declares them to be so. The Royal Mint maintains the inventory of coins in circulation and the Bank of England issues notes. (In Scotland and Northern Ireland, private banks also issue notes, but they must hold £1 of Bank of England notes for every £1 they issue.)

Deposits at banks and other financial institutions

Deposits at banks and building societies are also money. This type of money is an accounting entry in an electronic database in the banks' and building societies' computers.

They are money because they can be converted instantly into currency and because they are used directly to settle debts. In fact, deposits are the main means of settling debts in modern societies. The owner of a deposit transfers ownership to another person simply by writing a cheque – an instruction to a bank – that tells the bank to change its database, debiting the account of one depositor and crediting the account of another.

The Official UK Measure of Money

The official measure of money in the United Kingdom today is known as M4. **M4** consists of currency held by the public plus bank deposits and building society deposits. M4 does *not* include currency held by banks and building societies and it does not include currency or bank deposits owned by the UK government. Figure 26.1 shows the components that make up M4.

Figure 26.1

The Official UK Measure of Money

£ billions in 2003

M4   1,064.6

	£ billions in 2003	%
Large time deposits at banks and building societies (Wholesale deposits)	269.3	25%
Sight and time deposits at building societies (Retail deposits of building societies)	141.4	13%
Sight and time deposits at banks (Retail deposits of banks)	567.9	53%
Sight deposits (Non-interest bearing deposits)	53.2	5%
Currency held by the public	32.8	3%

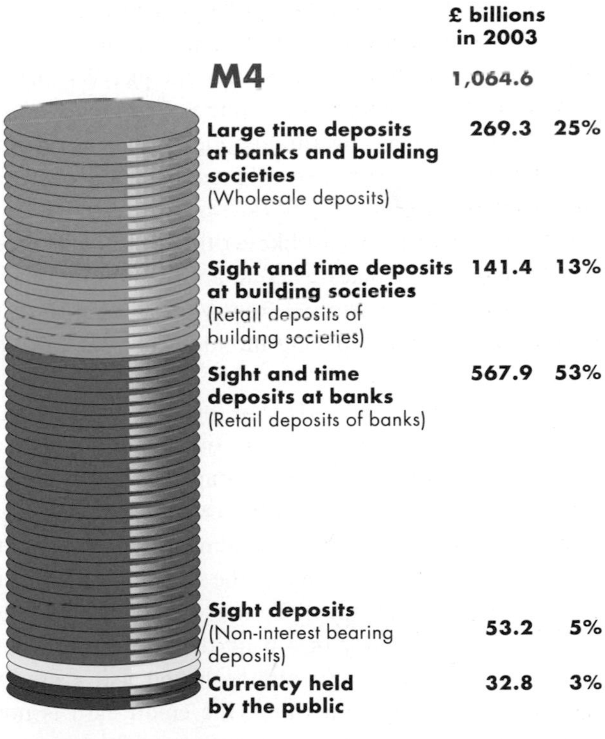

M4 is the official measure of money in the United Kingdom. It is the sum of currency held by the public, bank deposits and building society deposits. Currency represents only 3 per cent of the money in the UK economy.

Source: Bank of England.

Are all the Components of M4 Really Money?

Money is the means of payment. So the test of whether something is money is whether it serves as a means of payment. Currency passes the test.

Deposits are divided into two types: sight deposits and time deposits. A *sight deposit* (sometimes called a chequeable deposit) can be transferred from one person to another by writing a cheque or using a debit card. So it is clearly money. A *time deposit* is a deposit that has a fixed term to maturity. Although not usually a chequeable deposit, technological advances in the banking industry have made it easy to switch funds from a time deposit to a sight deposit. Because of the ease with which funds in a time deposit can be switched into a sight deposit, time deposits are included in the definition of money.

Cheques, Debit Cards and Credit Cards are not Money

The funds you've got in the bank are your money. When you write a cheque, you are telling your bank to move some funds from your account to the account of the person to whom you've given the cheque. Writing a cheque doesn't create more money. The money was there before you wrote the cheque. And when your cheque is paid, the money is still there but it moves from you to someone else.

Using a debit card is just like writing a cheque except that the transaction takes place in an instant. The funds are electronically transferred from your account to that of the person you are paying the moment your card is read.

A credit card is just an ID card, but one that lets you take a loan at the instant you buy something. When you sign a credit card sales slip, you are saying: "I agree to pay for these goods when the credit card company bills me." Once you get your statement from the credit card company, you must make the minimum payment due (or clear your balance). To make that payment you need money – currency or a bank deposit – to pay the credit card company. So although you use a credit card when you buy something, the credit card is not the *means of payment* and it is not money. The currency or the bank deposit that you use is money.

We've seen that the main component of money is deposits at banks and building societies. These institutions play a crucial role in our economic life and we're now going to examine that role.

Box 26.1
Money in the Eurozone

The official Eurozone measure of money is called M3, but the items included in the Eurozone M3 are very similar to those in M4 in the United Kingdom. The figure shows the numbers. The most interesting feature of euro money is the large amount of currency held by the public, 6 per cent of the total, compared to 3 per cent in the United Kingdom. Think about the reasons for this huge difference!

Figure 1

Official Eurozone Measure of Money

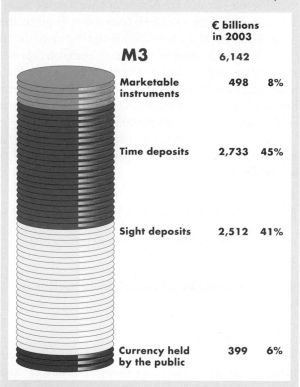

	€ billions in 2003	
M3	6,142	
Marketable instruments	498	8%
Time deposits	2,733	45%
Sight deposits	2,512	41%
Currency held by the public	399	6%

Review Quiz

1 What makes something money? What are the functions that money performs? Why do you think polo mints don't serve as money?
2 What are the largest components of money in the United Kingdom and in the Eurozone today?
3 Are all the components of M4 really money?
4 Why are cheques, debit cards and credit cards not money?

Financial Intermediaries

A firm that takes deposits from households and firms and makes loans to other households and firms is called a **financial intermediary**. There are many types of financial intermediary in different countries whose deposits are components of money. The main financial intermediaries whose deposits are money are commercial banks. In the United Kingdom, deposits at building societies are money.

Commercial Banks

A **bank** is a private firm, licensed to take deposits and make loans. In the United Kingdom banks are licensed by the Bank of England under the Banking Act of 1987. More than 400 commercial banks operate in the United Kingdom today. In 2003, total deposits at commercial banks were more than £800 billion. A commercial bank's business is summarized in its balance sheet.

A bank's *balance sheet* lists its assets, liabilities and net worth. *Assets* are what the bank owns, *liabilities* are what the bank owes and *net worth*, which is equal to assets minus liabilities, is the value of the bank to its shareholders – its owners. A bank's balance sheet is described by the equation:

$$\text{Liabilities} + \text{Net worth} = \text{Assets}$$

Among a bank's liabilities are the deposits that are the main component of money. Your deposit at the bank is a liability to your bank (and an asset to you) because the bank must repay your deposit (and sometimes the interest on it too) whenever you decide to take your money out of the bank.

Profit and Prudence: A Balancing Act

The aim of a bank is to maximize its net worth – its value to its shareholders. To achieve this objective, a bank makes loans at interest rates higher than those it pays for deposits. But a bank must perform a delicate balancing act. Lending is risky, and the more the bank ties up its deposits in high-risk, high-interest rate loans, the bigger is its chance of not being able to repay its depositors. And if depositors perceive a high risk of not being repaid, they withdraw their funds and create a crisis for the bank. So a bank must be prudent in the way it uses its deposits, balancing security for the depositors against profit for its shareholders.

Reserves and Loans

To achieve security for its depositors, a bank divides its funds into two parts: reserves and loans. **Reserves** are cash in a bank's vault plus its deposits at the central bank. (The Bank of England is the central bank in the United Kingdom.) The cash in a bank's vaults is a reserve to meet the demands that its customers place on it – it keeps that ATM replenished every time you and your friends need to use it for a midnight pizza. A commercial bank's deposit at the central bank is similar to your deposit at your own bank. Commercial banks use these deposits in the same way that you use your bank account. A commercial bank deposits cash into or draws cash out of its account at the central bank and writes cheques on that account to settle debts with other banks.

If a bank kept all its assets as cash in its vault or as deposits at the central bank, it wouldn't make any profit. In fact it keeps only a small fraction of its funds in reserves and lends the rest. A bank makes three different types of loan, or equivalently, holds three different types of asset:

1 *Liquid assets* are government Treasury bills and commercial bills. These assets can be sold and instantly converted into cash with virtually no risk of loss. Because liquid assets are virtually risk free, they earn a low interest rate.

2 *Investment securities* are longer-term government bonds and other bonds. These assets can be sold quickly and converted into cash but at prices that fluctuate. Because their prices fluctuate, these assets are riskier than liquid assets and they have a higher interest rate.

3 *Loans* are lines of credit extended to companies to finance the purchase of capital equipment and stocks and to households – personal loans – to finance consumer durable goods, such as cars or boats. The outstanding balances on credit card accounts are also bank loans. Loans are the riskiest assets of a bank because they cannot be converted into cash until they are due to be repaid. And some borrowers default and never repay. Because they are the riskiest of a bank's assets, they carry the highest interest rate.

Commercial bank deposits are only one component of money. Other financial institutions also take deposits and make loans. And although they differ from banks in important details, their economic functions are similar to those of banks that you've just reviewed. Box 26.2 looks at the UK building societies whose deposits are a component of money.

Box 26.2
Building Societies

A *building society* is a financial intermediary that historically obtained its funds from savings deposits (sometimes called share accounts) and made long-term mortgage loans to home buyers.

The first building societies were founded in the late eighteenth century as mutuals. A *mutual* is an organization that belongs to its members. In the case of a building society, its mutual status means that by law it belongs to its depositors and borrowers.

Until the 1980s, building societies concentrated on their traditional function of lending to home buyers. But their role began to change during the late 1970s when they offered depositors accounts that gave them instant access to their funds but paid interest. This type of account put the banks under pressure.

The Building Societies Act of 1986 allowed for the deregulation of the building societies, which enabled them to offer financial products that brought them into direct competition with the banks. The act also enabled building societies to give up their mutual status and become banks.

The Abbey National took this route in 1989 and became a bank. The merged Halifax/Leeds Building Society did the same in 1997. Many other building societies have *demutualized* recently.

The structure and balance sheets of building societies are similar to those of banks. Like banks, they have developed a branch network and have liabilities that are deposits. Like bank deposits, building society deposits are sight deposits (chequeable deposits) and are accepted in shops in exchange for goods. Building societies also offer similar services to banks, such as credit cards, personal lending and foreign currency.

The building societies' assets include reserves, but unlike the banks they do not hold deposits at the Bank of England. Instead, they hold deposits that act as their reserves at commercial banks. Building societies also hold liquid assets such as Treasury bills and like banks, they hold government bonds.

Unlike banks most of building society lending is for house purchases. These assets have a much longer maturity than the normal lending of the commercial banks. Mortgage loans are typically for 25 years.

Despite their long term, building society loans for home purchases are extremely safe assets.

The Economic Functions of Financial Intermediaries

All financial intermediaries make a profit from the spread between the interest rate they pay on deposits and the interest rate at which they lend. Why can financial intermediaries borrow at a low interest rate and lend at a higher one? What services do they perform that make their depositors willing to put up with a low interest rate and their borrowers willing to pay a higher one?

Financial intermediaries provide four main services that people are willing to pay for:

◆ Creating liquidity
◆ Minimizing the cost of obtaining funds
◆ Minimizing the cost of monitoring borrowers
◆ Pooling risk

Creating Liquidity

Financial intermediaries create liquidity. *Liquid* assets are those that are easily and with certainty convertible into money. Some of the liabilities of financial intermediaries are themselves money; others are highly liquid assets that are easily converted into money.

Financial intermediaries create liquidity by borrowing short and lending long. Borrowing short means taking deposits but standing ready to repay them at short notice (and even at no notice in the case of sight deposits). Lending long means making loan commitments for a prearranged, and often quite long, period of time. For example, when a person makes a deposit with a UK building society, that deposit can be withdrawn at any time. But the building society makes a lending commitment for perhaps up to 25 years to a home buyer.

Minimizing the Cost of Obtaining Funds

Finding someone from whom to borrow can be a costly business. Imagine how troublesome it would be if there were no financial intermediaries. A firm that was looking for £1 million to buy a new production plant would probably have to hunt around for several dozen people from whom to borrow in order to acquire enough funds for its capital project. Financial intermediaries lower such costs. A firm needing £1 million can go to a single financial intermediary to obtain those funds. The financial intermediary has to borrow from a large number of people, but it's not doing that just for this one firm and the £1 million it wants to borrow. The financial intermediary can establish an organization capable of raising funds from a large number of depositors and can spread the cost of this activity over a large number of borrowers.

Minimizing the Cost of Monitoring Borrowers

Lending money is a risky business. There's always a danger that the borrower may not repay. Most of the money lent gets used by firms to invest in projects that they hope will return a profit. But sometimes these hopes are not fulfilled. Checking up on the activities of a borrower and ensuring that the best possible decisions are being made for making a profit and avoiding a loss is a costly and specialized activity. Imagine how costly it would be if each and every household that lent money to a firm had to incur the costs of monitoring that firm directly. By depositing funds with a financial intermediary, households avoid those costs. The financial intermediary performs the monitoring activity by using specialized resources that have a much lower cost than that which each household would incur if it had to undertake the activity individually.

Pooling Risk

As we noted above, lending money is risky. There is always a chance of not being repaid – of default. The risk of default can be reduced by lending to a large number of different individuals. In such a situation, if one person defaults on a loan it is a nuisance but not a disaster. In contrast, if only one person borrows and that person defaults on the loan, the entire loan is a write-off. Financial intermediaries enable people to pool risk in an efficient way. Thousands of people lend money to any one financial intermediary and, in turn, the financial intermediary re-lends the money to hundreds, and perhaps thousands, of individual firms. If any one firm defaults on its loan, that default is spread across all the depositors with the intermediary and no individual depositor is left exposed to a high degree of risk.

Review Quiz

1   What is a financial intermediary?
2   What are the three main types of assets held by banks on their balance sheet?
3   What are the main economic functions of a financial intermediary?

How Banks Create Money

Banks create money.[1] But this doesn't mean that they have smoke-filled back rooms in which counterfeiters are busily working. Remember that most money is deposits, not currency. What banks create is deposits and they do so by making loans. But the amount of deposits they can create is limited by their reserves.

Reserves: Actual and Required

We've seen that banks don't have £100 in notes for every £100 that people have deposited with them. In fact, a typical bank today has about 60 pence in currency and another 26 pence on deposit at the central bank, a total reserve of less than £1, for every £100 deposited in it. But there is no need for panic. These reserve levels are adequate for ordinary business needs.

The fraction of a bank's total deposits that are held in reserves is called the **reserve ratio**. The value of the reserve ratio is influenced by the actions of a bank's depositors. If a depositor withdraws currency from a bank, the reserve ratio decreases. If a depositor puts currency into a bank, the reserve ratio increases.

The **required reserve ratio** is the ratio of reserves to deposits that banks are required, by regulation, to hold. A bank's **desired reserve ratio** is the ratio of reserves to deposits that banks consider to be prudent to hold. A bank's desired reserve ratio exceeds the required reserve ratio. A bank's desired reserves are equal to its deposits multiplied by the desired reserve ratio. Actual reserves minus *desired reserves* are **excess reserves**. Whenever banks have excess reserves, they are able to create money.

To see how banks create money we are going to look at two model banking systems. In the first model there is only one bank. In the second model there are many banks.

Creating Deposits by Making Loans in a One-bank Economy

In the model banking system that we'll study, there is only one bank and its desired reserve ratio is 25 per cent. That is, for each £1 deposited, the bank keeps 25 pence in reserves and lends the rest. The balance sheet of One-and-Only Bank is shown in Figure 26.2(a). Its deposits are £400 million and its reserves are 25 per cent of this

---

[1] In this section, we'll use the term *banks* to refer to all the financial intermediaries whose deposits are money: commercial banks and building societies.

amount – £100 million. Its loans are equal to deposits minus reserves and are £300 million.

The story begins with Silas Marner, who has decided that it is too dangerous to keep on hiding his fortune under his mattress. Silas has been holding his fortune in currency and has a nest egg of £1 million. He decides to put his £1 million on deposit at the One-and-Only Bank. On the day that Silas makes his deposit, the One-and-Only Bank's balance sheet changes and the new situation is shown in Figure 26.2(b). The bank now has £101 million in reserves and £401 million in deposits. It still has loans of £300 million.

Figure 26.2

Creating Money at the One-and-Only Bank

(a) Balance sheet on January 1

Assets (millions of pounds)		**Liabilities** (millions of pounds)	
Reserves	£100	Deposits	£400
Loans	£300		
Total	£400	Total	£400

(b) Balance sheet on January 2

Assets (millions of pounds)		**Liabilities** (millions of pounds)	
Reserves	£101	Deposits	£401
Loans	£300		
Total	£401	Total	£401

(c) Balance sheet on January 3

Assets (millions of pounds)		**Liabilities** (millions of pounds)	
Reserves	£101	Deposits	£404
Loans	£303		
Total	£404	Total	£404

In part (a), the One-and-Only Bank has deposits of £400 million, loans of £300 million and reserves of £100 million. The bank's desired reserve ratio is 25 per cent. When the bank receives a deposit of £1 million in part (b), it has excess reserves. It lends £3 million and creates a further £3 million of deposits. Deposits increase by £3 million and loans increase by £3 million in part (c).

The bank now has *excess reserves*. With reserves of £101 million, the bank would like to have deposits of £404 million and loans of £303 million. And being the One-and-Only Bank, the manager knows the reserves will remain at £101 million. That is, she knows that when she makes a loan, the amount lent remains on deposit at the One-and-Only Bank. She knows, for example, that all the suppliers of Sky's-the-Limit Construction, her biggest borrower, are also depositors of One-and-Only. So she knows that if she makes the loan that Sky's-the-Limit has just requested, the deposit she lends will never leave One-and-Only. When Sky's-the-Limit uses part of its new loan to pay £100,000 to I-Dig-It Building Company for some excavations, the One-and-Only Bank simply moves the funds from Sky's-the-Limit's account to I-Dig-It's account.

So the manager of One-and-Only calls Sky's-the-Limit's accountant and offers to lend the maximum that she can. How much does she lend? She lends £3 million. By lending £3 million, One-and-Only's balance sheet changes to the one shown in Figure 26.2(c). Loans increase by £3 million to £303 million. The loan shows up in Sky's-the-Limit's deposit initially and total deposits increase to £404 million – £400 million plus Silas Marner's deposit of £1 million plus the newly created deposit of £3 million. The bank now has no excess reserves and has reached the limit of its ability to create money.

The Deposit Multiplier

The **deposit multiplier** is the amount by which an increase in bank reserves is multiplied to calculate the increase in bank deposits. That is:

$$\text{Deposit multiplier} = \frac{\text{Change in deposits}}{\text{Change in reserves}}$$

In the example we've just worked through, the deposit multiplier is 4. The £1 million increase in reserves created a £4 million increase in deposits. The deposit multiplier is linked to the desired reserve ratio by the following equation:

$$\text{Deposit multiplier} = \frac{1}{\text{Desired reserve ratio}}$$

In the example, the desired reserve ratio is 25 per cent, or 0.25. That is:

$$\text{Deposit multiplier} = 1/0.25$$
$$= 4$$

Creating Deposits by Making Loans with Many Banks

If you told the student loans officer at your own bank that she creates money, she wouldn't believe you. Bankers see themselves as lending the money they receive from others, not creating money. But in fact, even though each bank only lends what it receives, the banking *system* creates money. To see how, let's look at another example.

The model banking system that we'll now study has many banks. Like before, each bank has a desired reserve ratio of 25 per cent.

The process begins when Alan, who has just had a lucky run in Monte Carlo, decides to decrease his currency holding and put £100,000 into his bank deposit. Alan's bank now has £100,000 of new deposits and £100,000 of additional reserves.

With a desired reserve ratio of 25 per cent, the bank keeps £25,000 on reserve. So it lends £75,000. Amy is looking for a loan to buy a photocopy shop franchise and the bank lends her the £75,000 she needs. At this point, Alan's bank has a new deposit of £100,000, new loans of £75,000 and new reserves of £25,000.

For Alan's bank, that is the end of the story. But it's not the end of the story for the entire banking system.

Amy writes a cheque for £75,000 to buy the photocopy shop franchise from Barbara. Barbara deposits her cheque for £75,000 in another bank, which now has an increase in deposits and reserves of £75,000.

Barbara's bank keeps 25 per cent of its increase in deposits, £18,750, in reserve and lends £56,250. It makes a loan to Bob. So Barbara's bank now has a new deposit of £75,000, new loans of £56,250 and additional reserves of £18,750.

Bob writes a cheque for £56,250 to pay Carl for an antique car. When Carl takes the cheque to his bank, its deposits and reserves increase by £56,250.

Carl's bank keeps 25 per cent of its increase in deposit, £14,060, in reserve and lends £42,190.

Notice that at each stage in the story we've told, a bank has excess reserves. But the excess reserves keep getting smaller – £75,000 for the first bank, £56,250 for the second bank and £42,190 for the third bank.

This process continues until the excess reserves in the entire banking system have been eliminated. But this outcome takes a lot of further steps.

To work out the entire process, look closely at the numbers we've just worked out. At each stage, the loan is 75 per cent (0.75) of the previous loan and the deposit is 0.75 of the previous deposit. Call that proportion L ($L = 0.75$). The complete sequence is:

$$1 + L + L^2 + L^3 + \ldots$$

Remember, L is a fraction, so at each stage in this sequence the amount of new loans gets smaller. The total number of loans made at the end of the process is the above sum which is:[2]

$$\frac{1}{(1 - L)}$$

Using the numbers from the example, the total increase in deposits is:

$$£100,000 + 75,000 + 56,250 + 42,190 + \ldots$$

$$= £100,000 \times (1 + 0.75 + 0.5625 + 0.42187 + \ldots)$$

$$= £100,000 \times (1 + 0.75 + 0.75^2 + 0.75^3 + \ldots)$$

$$= £100,000 \times (1 \div [1 - 0.75])$$

$$= £100,000 \times (1 \div 0.25)$$

$$= £100,000 \times 4$$

$$= £400,000$$

So even though each bank only lends the money it receives, the banking system as a whole does create money by making loans. And the amount created is the same in a multi-bank system as in a one-bank system.

Figure 26.3 (overleaf) tracks the process we've just described and summarizes the events that end up creating £400,000 out of an initial deposit of £100,000. Work through this figure and check that the running tallies and the final tallies agree with the above formula.

---

[2] Both here and in the expenditure multiplier process in Chapter 24, the sequence of values is called a convergent geometric series. To find the sum of such a series, begin by calling the sum S. Then write out the sum as:

$$S = 1 + L + L^2 + L^3 + \ldots$$

Multiply by L to give:

$$LS = L + L^2 + L^3 + \ldots$$

and then subtract the second equation from the first to give:

$$S(1 - L) = 1$$

or:

$$S = 1/(1 - L)$$

Figure 26.3

The Multiple Creation of Bank Deposits

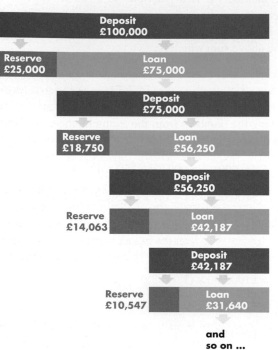

	Reserves	Loans	Deposits
	£25,000	£75,000	£100,000
	£43,750	£131,250	£175,000
	£57,813	£173,437	£231,250
	£68,360	£205,077	£273,437
	•	•	•
	•	•	•
	▼	▼	▼
	£100,000	£300,000	£400,000

When a bank receives deposits, it keeps 25 per cent in reserves and lends 75 per cent. The amount lent becomes a new deposit at another bank. The next bank in the sequence keeps 25 per cent and lends 75 per cent, and the process continues until the banking system has created enough deposits to eliminate its excess reserves. The running tally tells us the amount of deposits and loans created at each stage. At the end of the process, an additional £100,000 of reserves creates an additional £400,000 of deposits.

The deposit multiplier in the United Kingdom works in the same way as the deposit multiplier you've just seen for a model economy. But the actual deposit multiplier differs from the one we've just calculated for two reasons. First, the banks' desired reserve ratio is much smaller than the 25 per cent we've used. Second, not all the loans made by banks return to them as reserves. Some of the loans remain outside the banks and are held as currency. The smaller desired reserve ratio makes the UK deposits multiplier larger than the above example. But the drain of currency from the banking system makes the UK deposit multiplier smaller.

Review Quiz

1   How do banks create deposits by making loans and what factors limit the amount of deposits and loans that banks can create?
2   A bank manager tells you that he doesn't create money. He just lends the money that people deposit in the bank. How do you explain to him that he's wrong and that he does create money?
3   What is the relationship between the desired reserve ratio and the deposit multiplier?

We've now seen how banks create money. Money has a powerful influence on the economy and this influence begins with interest rates. To understand how money influences interest rates, we must study the demand for money.

The Demand for Money

The amount of money we *receive* each week in payment for our labour is income – a flow. The amount of money that we hold in our wallets or in a sight deposit account at our local bank is an inventory – a stock. There is no limit to how much income – or flow – we would like to receive each week. But there is a limit to how big a stock of money each of us would like to hold, on average.

The Influences on Money Holding

The quantity of money that people choose to hold depends on four main factors. They are:

◆ The price level
◆ The interest rate
◆ Real GDP
◆ Financial innovation

Let's look at each of them.

The Price Level

The quantity of money measured in current pounds is called the quantity of *nominal money*. The quantity of nominal money demanded is proportional to the price level, other things remaining the same. That is, if the price level (GDP deflator) increases by 10 per cent from 100 to 110, people will want to hold 10 per cent more nominal money than before, other things remaining the same. What matters is not the number of pounds that you hold but their buying power. If you hold £50 to buy your weekly groceries, you will increase your money holding to £55 pounds if the prices of groceries – and your income – increase by 10 per cent.

The quantity of money measured in constant pounds (for example, in 2001 pounds) is called *real money*. Real money is equal to nominal money divided by the price level (multiplied by 100).

The quantity of real money demanded is independent of the price level. In the above example, you held an average of £50 at the original price level. When the price level increased by 10 per cent, you increased your average cash holding by 10 per cent to keep your *real* cash holding constant. Your £55 at the new price level is the same quantity of *real money* as your £50 at the original price level. That is, £50 divided by 1 equals £55 divided by 1.1.

The Interest Rate

A fundamental principle of economics is that as the opportunity cost of something increases, people try to find substitutes for it. Money is no exception. The higher the opportunity cost of holding money, other things remaining the same, the smaller is the quantity of real money demanded.

The interest rate is the opportunity cost of holding money. To see why, recall that the opportunity cost of any activity is the value of the best alternative forgone. The alternative to holding money is holding a savings bond or a Treasury bill that earns interest. By holding money instead, you forgo the interest that you otherwise would have received. This forgone interest is the opportunity cost of holding money.

Money loses value because of inflation. Why isn't the inflation rate part of the cost of holding money? It is. Other things remaining the same, the higher the expected inflation rate, the higher is the interest rate and so the higher is the opportunity cost of holding money.

Real GDP

The quantity of money that households and firms plan to hold depends on the amount they spend, and the quantity of money demanded in the economy as a whole depends on aggregate expenditure – real GDP.

Again, suppose that you hold an average of £50 to finance your weekly purchases of goods. Now imagine that the prices of these goods and of all other goods remain constant, but that your income increases. As a consequence, you now spend more and you also keep a larger amount of money on hand to finance your higher volume of expenditure.

Financial Innovation

Technological change and the arrival of new financial products – called **financial innovation** – change the quantity of money held. The major financial innovations are the widespread use of:

1   Interest-bearing sight deposits
2   Automatic transfers between sight and time deposits
3   Automatic teller machines
4   Credit cards and debit cards

These innovations have occurred because of the development of computing power that has lowered the cost of calculations and record keeping.

The Demand for Money Curve

We summarize the effects of the influences on money holding by using the demand for money curve. The **demand for money** is the relationship between the quantity of real money demanded and the interest rate – the opportunity cost of holding money – all other influences on the amount of money that people wish to hold remaining the same.

Figure 26.4 shows a demand for money curve, *MD*. When the interest rate rises, everything else remaining the same, the opportunity cost of holding money rises and the quantity of money demanded decreases – there is a movement along the demand for money curve. Similarly, when the interest rate falls, the opportunity cost of holding money falls and the quantity of money demanded increases – there is a downward movement along the demand for money curve.

When any influence on the amount of money that people plan to hold changes, there is a change in the demand for money and the demand for money curve shifts. Let's look at these shifts.

Shifts in the Demand for Money Curve

A change in real GDP or a financial innovation changes the demand for money and shifts the demand for money curve. Figure 26.5 illustrates the changes in the demand for money.

A decrease in real GDP decreases the demand for money and shifts the demand curve leftward from MD_0 to MD_1. An increase in real GDP has the opposite effect. It increases the demand for money and shifts the demand curve rightward from MD_0 to MD_2.

The influence of financial innovation on the demand for money curve is more complicated. Financial innovation might increase the demand for some types of deposit and decrease the demand for others and decrease the demand for currency.

Box 26.4 looks at the effects of changes in real GDP and financial innovation on the demand for money in the United Kingdom.

Figure 26.4 ◆

The Demand for Money

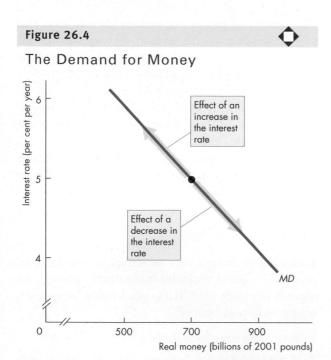

The demand for money curve, *MD*, shows the relationship between the quantity of real money that people plan to hold and the interest rate, other things remaining the same. The interest rate is the opportunity cost of holding money. A change in the interest rate leads to a movement along the demand for money curve.

Figure 26.5 ◆

Changes in the Demand for Money

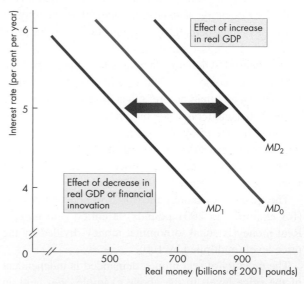

A decrease in real GDP decreases the demand for money and shifts the demand curve leftward from MD_0 to MD_1. An increase in real GDP increases the demand for money and shifts the demand curve rightward from MD_0 to MD_2. Financial innovation can either increase or decrease the demand for money depending on the specific innovation.

Box 26.4
The Demand for Money in the United Kingdom

Figure 1 shows the relationship between the interest rate and the quantity of real M4 money held in the United Kingdom between 1963 and 2003. Each dot shows the interest rate and the amount of real money held in a given year (with a year identified by a two digit number near a dot).

The figure also shows four demand curves. In 1963, the demand for real M4 was MD_{63}. During the rest of the 1960s and the 1970s, the demand for M4 increased and the demand curve shifted rightward to MD_{79}. During the 1980s, the demand for M4 increased further and the demand curve shifted rightward to MD_{89}. The demand for real M4 increased yet further during the 1990s and early 2000s when the demand curve shifted rightward to MD_{03}.

Why did these shifts in the demand for M4 money occur? They occurred first because real GDP increased and second because of financial innovation.

On average, with no financial innovation, we would expect the demand for real M4 to increase at a rate close to the rate of increase in real GDP.

The magnitude of the increase in the demand for real M4 during the 1960s and 1970s was in fact similar to the increase in real GDP. But during the 1980s, demand for real M4 increased at a pace more than three times that of real GDP. And during the 1990s and early 2000s, the demand for real M4 increased at about a half of the increase in real GDP.

The 1980s was a period of major financial innovation and deregulation. The introduction of interest-bearing sight deposits and of automatic transfers between sight deposits and time deposits, as well as the deregulation of financial intermediaries that compete with banks, led to a surge in the demand for deposits and so an increase in the demand for M4.

You can see the effects of financial innovation more dramatically by looking at the demand for one component of M4, the demand for currency. Figure 2 shows some relevant data. This figure shows the relationship between the interest rate and the demand for real currency. You can see that during the 1980s, when the demand for bank deposits was increasing fastest, the demand for currency was decreasing.

Figure 1

The Demand for M4 in the United Kingdom

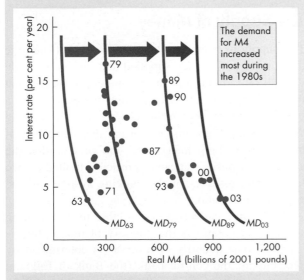

Source: Bank of England and authors' assumptions and calculations.

Figure 2

The Demand for Currency in the United Kingdom

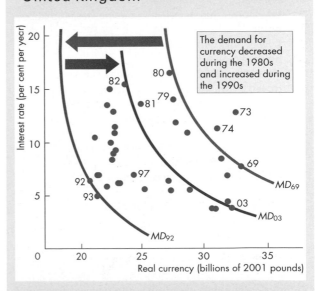

Source: Bank of England and authors' assumptions and calculations.

Figure 2 tells an interesting story that reinforces the interpretation of the shifts in the demand for M4 in Figure 1.

From 1969 to 1979, the demand for currency remained roughly constant at MD_{69}. Then, during the 1980s and into the 1990s, the demand for currency decreased and the demand curve shifted leftward. By 1992, the demand for real currency was MD_{92}.

This decrease in the demand for currency resulted from the same financial innovations that increased the demand for M4. As banks and other financial institutions provided ever more convenient means of payment that could earn interest, people found ways of getting by with less currency in their purses and more plastic to access their bank deposits. The demand for deposits swelled and the demand for currency decreased.

This process slowed during the rest of the 1990s and 2000s and the demand for currency increased. But even by 2003, the demand for real currency had not returned to its 1969 level. The new non-currency means of payment have displaced currency completely for many types of transactions.

Review Quiz

1   What are the main influences on the quantity of real money that people and businesses plan to hold?
2   Why is the interest rate the opportunity cost of holding money?
3   What does the demand for money curve show?
4   How does an increase in the interest rate change the quantity of money demanded and how would you use the demand for money curve to show the effects?
5   How does an increase in real GDP change the demand for money and how would you use the demand for money curve to show the effects?
6   How has financial innovation altered the demand for money?

We now know what determines the demand for money. And we've seen that a key factor is the interest rate – the opportunity cost of holding money. But what determines the interest rate? Let's find out.

Interest Rate Determination

You've seen that the interest rate is the opportunity cost of holding money. You learned in Chapter 3 (p. 54) to think of an opportunity cost as a price. And you also learned how a price gets determined in a market. We're now going to see how the interest rate as the opportunity cost (or price) of holding money is determined in the *money market*.

The Money Market

The money market isn't a market in the everyday sense of the word. You don't go to a shop to buy or sell money. But you do demand money – you chose to hold an inventory of currency and bank deposits. And banks supply money – the Bank of England supplies currency and the commercial banks and building societies create or supply deposits. So we can think of the demand for money by individuals and firms and the supply of money by banks and other financial institutions as taking place in a market that determines the interest rate.

You've just seen that the quantity of money demanded varies inversely with the interest rate (other things remaining the same) – that the demand for money curve slopes downward. To see how the interest rate is determined, we need to look at the supply of money and equilibrium in the money market.

The Supply of Money

The **supply of money** is the relationship between the quantity of real money supplied and the interest rate with all other influences on the amount of money that the banking system creates remaining the same.

You've seen earlier in this chapter that the banking system creates deposits, which are the major part of money, by making loans. And you've seen that the amount of deposits that can be created is limited by two factors: the reserves of the banking system and the desired reserve ratio.

The greater the reserves available to the banking system, the greater is the quantity of money that is supplied. The quantity of reserves is determined by decisions of the central bank (the Bank of England in the United Kingdom and the European Central Bank in the Eurozone part of the European Union). You will learn about those decisions in Chapter 27. For now, we'll take the quantity of reserves as given.

The desired reserve ratio influences the quantity of money supplied because the deposit multiplier – the amount by which we multiply reserves to find the total deposits – is equal to the inverse of the desired reserve ratio (one divided by the desired reserve ratio).

Reserves for a bank play a role similar to that played by money for you. You hold money so that you can make payments. A bank holds reserves so that it can make payments. Banks must pay currency when depositors want to withdraw their funds. And they must pay other banks when the cheques paid by their customers sum to a greater total than the cheques received by their customers.

A bank's desired reserve (and its desired reserve ratio) is determined in a similar way to your demand for money. The opportunity cost of reserves is the interest rate the bank could earn if it bought a bond or made a loan.

Banks are like all other economic decision makers. They respond to incentives. The higher the interest rate, other things remaining the same, the greater the percentage of their deposits the banks want to lend and the smaller the percentage they want to hold as reserves – the higher the interest rate, the smaller is the desired reserve ratio.

Because the money multiplier is the inverse of the desired reserve ratio, the higher the interest rate, the greater is the money multiplier and the greater is the quantity of money supplied.

For a given amount of reserves in the banking system, the quantity of money supplied increases as the interest rate rises. The supply of money curve is upward sloping.

Money Market Equilibrium

Figure 26.7 illustrates money market equilibrium, which determines the interest rate. The demand for real money curve is *MD* and the supply of real money curve is *MS*.

Equilibrium is achieved by changes in the interest rate. If the interest rate is too high, people demand a smaller quantity of money than the banking system wants to supply. They are holding too much money. In this situation, they try to get rid of money by buying

Figure 26.6

The Supply of Money

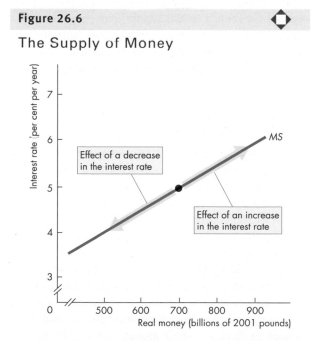

The supply of money curve, *MS*, shows the relationship between the quantity of real money that the banking system supplies and the interest rate, other things remaining the same. The interest rate is the opportunity cost of reserves for the banks. A rise in the interest rate brings a lower desired reserve ratio and a greater quantity of money supplied.

Figure 26.7

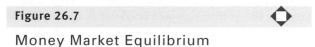

Money Market Equilibrium

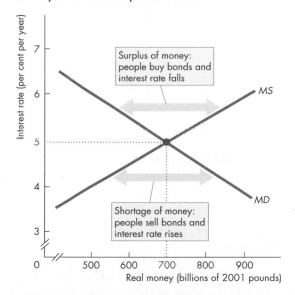

Money market equilibrium occurs when the interest rate has adjusted to make the quantity of money demanded equal to the quantity supplied. Here, equilibrium occurs at an interest rate of 5 per cent a year. At interest rates above 5 per cent a year, the quantity of money demanded is less than the quantity supplied, so people buy bonds, and the interest rate falls. At interest rates below 5 per cent a year, the quantity of real money demanded exceeds the quantity supplied, so people sell bonds and the interest rate rises. Only at 5 per cent a year is the quantity of real money in existence willingly held.

bonds. Conversely, if the interest rate is too low, people demand a larger quantity of money than the quantity that the banking system wants to supply. They are holding too little money. In this situation, they try to get more money by selling bonds.

The Interest Rate and the Price of a Bond

Buying bonds makes the price of a bond rise and selling bonds makes the price of a bond fall. And the interest rate changes in the opposite direction to the price of a bond. Let's see why.

A bond is a promise to make a sequence of future payments. There are many different possible sequences but the simplest one is the case of a bond called a perpetuity – a bond that promises to pay a specified fixed amount of money each year forever. The issuer of perpetuity will never buy the bond back (redeem it); the bond will remain outstanding forever and will earn a fixed number of pounds each year.

Because the payment each year is a fixed money amount, the interest rate on a bond varies as the price of the bond varies. In the case of a perpetuity, the formula that links the interest rate to the price of the bond is a particularly simple one. That formula is:

$$\text{Interest rate} = \frac{\text{Money payment per year}}{\text{Price of a bond}} \times 100$$

This formula states that the higher the price of a bond, other things remaining the same, the lower is the interest rate.

An example will make this relationship clear. Suppose the UK government sells a bond that promises to pay £10 a year. If the price of the bond is £100, the interest rate is 10 per cent a year – £10 is 10 per cent of £100. If the price of the bond is £50, the interest rate is 20 per cent a year – £10 is 20 per cent of £50. If the price of the bond is £200, the interest rate is 5 per cent a year – £10 is 5 per cent of £200.

You can now see why buying bonds, which raises the price of a bond, sends the interest rate down and why selling bonds, which lowers the price of a bond, sends the interest rate up.

Speculative Demand for Money

The link between the price of a bond and the interest rate provides a further explanation for why people hold money even though it pays either no interest or, in the case of some bank deposits, a low interest rate.

The link works two ways. A change in the price of a bond changes the interest rate. But a change in the interest rate changes the price of a bond. If the interest rate is expected to rise in the near future, then the price of a bond must be expected to fall. Similarly, if the interest rate is expected to fall in the near future, then the price of a bond must be expected to rise.

People try to anticipate fluctuations in the interest rate because of its effect on the price of a bond. When the interest rate is expected to rise, holding money is better than holding bonds. Money pays no interest but avoids a loss on the fall of the price of bonds. When the interest rate is expected to fall, holding bonds is better than holding money because in this situation bonds not only pay interest but are also expected give a gain from the rise in their price.

Holding money in anticipation of a fall in the price of bonds is called the speculative demand for money.

Fluctuating Interest Rate

The interest rate fluctuates a great deal. Between 1963 and 2003, the average interest rate on UK Government Treasury bills was close to 9 per cent a year. But the rate fluctuated between a low of 4 per cent a year in 2001 and a high of almost 17 per cent a year in 1979.

The interest rate can fluctuate because either the demand for money or the supply of money fluctuates. Figure 26.8 illustrates the two cases. Initially, the demand for money curve is MD_0 and the supply of money curve is MS_0 and the equilibrium interest rate is 5 per cent a year.

In Figure 26.8(a), the demand for money increases and the demand curve shifts rightward to MD_1. At an interest rate of 5 per cent a year, there is a shortage of money. People are holding less money than they would like to hold. They attempt to increase their money holding by selling bonds. As they do so, the price of a bond falls and the interest rate rises. When the interest rate has risen to 6 per cent a year, the quantity of money supplied has increased and money market equilibrium has been restored.

A decrease in the demand for money shifts the demand curve leftward to MD_2. At an interest rate of 5 per cent a year, there is a surplus of money. People are holding more money than they would like to hold. They attempt to decrease their money holding by buying bonds. As they do so, the price of a bond rises and the interest rate falls. When the interest rate has fallen to 4 per cent a year, the quantity of money supplied has decreased and money market equilibrium has been restored.

In Figure 26.8(b), the supply of money increases and the supply of money curve shifts rightward to MS_1. At

Figure 26.8

The Fluctuating Interest Rate

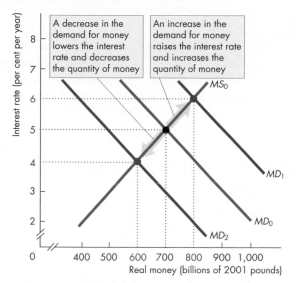

(a) Fluctuations in the demand for money

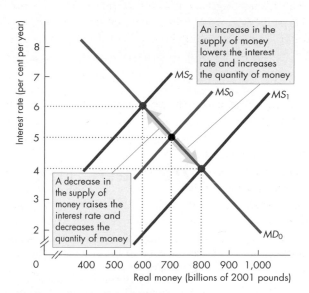

(b) Fluctuations in the supply of money

Fluctuations in the demand for money bring fluctuations in the interest rate and equilibrium quantity of money. When the demand for money fluctuates, the interest rate and quantity of money fluctuate in the same direction.

Fluctuations in the supply of money bring fluctuations in the interest rate and equilibrium quantity of money. When the supply of money fluctuates, the interest rate and quantity of money fluctuate in opposite directions.

an interest rate of 5 per cent a year, there is a surplus of money. People are holding more money than they would like to hold. They attempt to decrease their money holding by buying bonds. As they do so, the price of a bond rises and the interest rate falls. When the interest rate has fallen to 4 per cent a year, the quantity of money demanded has increased and money market equilibrium has been restored.

A decrease in the supply of money shifts the supply curve leftward to MS_2. At an interest rate of 5 per cent a year, there is a shortage of money. People are holding less money than they would like to hold. They attempt to increase their money holding by selling bonds. As they do so, the price of a bond rises and the interest rate falls. When the interest rate has risen to 6 per cent a year, the quantity of money demanded has decreased and money market equilibrium has been restored.

UK Interest Rate Fluctuations

Interest rate fluctuations in the United Kingdom have come from fluctuations in both the demand for money and the supply of money. But most of the fluctuations originate on the supply side of the money market.

In the late 1970s, when the interest rate climbed to almost 17 per cent a year, it was a decrease in the supply

of money that brought about the rise. And when the interest rate fell during the early 2000s, an increase in the supply of money was at work. Even when a change in demand would change the interest rate, the central bank does not have to stand idly by. It can take actions to offset the effect of the change in demand.

Review Quiz

1　What is a bond and what is the relationship between the price of a bond and the interest rate?
2　How is the interest rate determined?
3　What do people do if they are holding *less* money than they plan to hold and what happens to the interest rate?
4　What do people do if they are holding *more* money than they plan to hold and what happens to the interest rate?
5　What happens to the interest rate if the quantity of money increases or decreases?

Your task in the next chapter is to study the actions that the central bank can take. But before moving on, take a look at *Reading Between the Lines* on pp. 598–599 and see how the way we make payments is changing.

Reading Between the Lines
Electronic Money

Telegraph.co.uk, 30 July 2004

Dramatic rise of the 'flexible friend'

By Richard Alleyne

It has taken less than 40 years for the credit card to revolutionise the way we spend and borrow.

Pioneered by Barclaycard, itself a copy of the American Diners Club, the product appeared in Britain in 1966 and, within a year, more than a million people had acquired one.

But "plastic" really took off the following decade when Access, the first rival to Barclaycard, was launched and sparked a fierce battle to win customers which dramatically boosted the number of card carriers and all but killed off the cheque book transaction.

Now, nearly 30 million people are said to have a "flexible friend" and, with 63 million cards in circulation, most have more than one.

This year, credit and debit cards are expected to overtake cash as our preferred method of payment. In 2003, credit and debit cards accounted for £244 billion of spending. . . .

Spending is increasing at a tremendous pace. In the three months to June 1993, spending on credit cards reached a record £8 billion. In the same period this year, it topped £35 billion. . . .

The Essence of the Story

◆ The Barclaycard was launched in 1966 and in one year more than a million people had a card.

◆ When Access appeared, competition between card issuers increased the number of card holders and plastic began to replace cheques.

◆ By 2004, nearly 30 million people held 63 million cards and credit and debit cards were about to overtake cash as the preferred method of payment.

◆ In 2003, credit and debit cards accounted for £244 billion of spending

◆ In the three months to June 1993, credit card spending was £8 billion. In the same period in 2004, it was £35 billion.

Economic Analysis

◆ The news article reports changes in the way we make payments.

◆ Figure 1 provides a graphic description of the changes between 1965 and 2005: cash down from 67 per cent to 33 per cent; cheques down from 33 per cent to 17 per cent; credit cards up from zero to 23 per cent; and debit cards up from zero to 27 per cent.

◆ Cheques and debit cards are alternative ways of paying with a bank deposit. For these methods of payment, it is the bank deposit that is money.

◆ Credit cards are not a method of *payment*. Payment occurs when the credit card balance is paid off. These payments are made by writing a cheque or by making an electronic transfer from a bank deposit. Again, it is a bank deposit that is the means of payment.

◆ The choice of a transaction technology is like any other economic choice: it is driven by cost and people choose the least-cost technology for each transaction.

◆ All forms of payment incur a transaction cost.

◆ The main cost of using cash arises from theft. Carrying cash is more risky than carrying a plastic card that needs a PIN to be used.

◆ Electronic forms of payment are used only if they provide a lower transaction cost than cash or a cheque.

◆ Transaction costs make a huge difference to the way a market works.

◆ Figure 2 shows the effects of transaction costs in the market for music downloads.

◆ The demand curve for downloads is D, and the supply curve, which includes a transaction cost of 20p per transaction, is S_0. The equilibrium number of downloads is 2 million tracks per week.

◆ If the transaction cost were zero, the supply curve would be S_1. The equilibrium number of downloads would increase to 3 million tracks per week. (The numbers are hypothetical.)

◆ As the cost of electronic transactions falls, we can expect the use of these methods of transaction to increase and the use of cash and cheques to decrease further.

◆ As an example, the price of a PayPal (e-money) transaction has fallen.

◆ Improved transactions technologies increase the quantities of goods and services that we are able to consume.

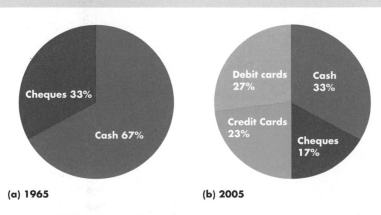

(a) 1965   (b) 2005

Figure 1 The changing methods of payment

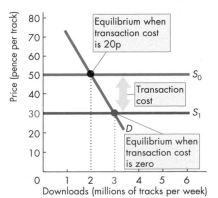

Figure 2 How transactions costs change market outcomes

Summary

Key Points

What is Money? (pp. 582–584)

◆ Money is the means of payment and it has three functions. It is a medium of exchange, a unit of account and a store of value.

◆ The main measure of money in the United Kingdom today is M4, which is currency held by the public and all bank and building society sight and time deposits.

Financial Intermediaries (pp. 585–587)

◆ The main UK financial intermediaries whose liabilities are money are commercial banks and building societies.

◆ These institutions take in deposits, hold cash and liquid assets as reserves so that they can meet their depositors' demands and use the rest either to buy securities or to make loans.

◆ Financial intermediaries provide four main economic services. They create liquidity, minimize the cost of obtaining funds, minimize the cost of monitoring borrowers and pool risks.

How Banks Create Money (pp. 587–590)

◆ Banks create money by making loans.

◆ The total quantity of deposits that can be supported by a given amount of reserves (the deposit multiplier) is equal to 1 divided by the desired reserve ratio.

The Demand for Money (pp. 591–594)

◆ The quantity of money demanded is the amount of money that people plan to hold.

◆ The quantity of real money equals the quantity of nominal money divided by the price level.

◆ The quantity of real money demanded depends on the interest rate and real GDP. As the interest rate rises, the quantity of real money demanded decreases.

Interest Rate Determination (pp. 594–597)

◆ The interest rate adjusts to achieve equilibrium in the markets for money and bonds (financial assets).

◆ Money market equilibrium achieves an interest rate (and an asset price) that makes the quantity of real money supplied willingly held.

◆ If the demand for money increases, the interest rate rises, the prices of bonds fall, and the quantity of money decreases.

◆ If the supply of money increases, the interest rate falls, the prices of bonds rise, and the quantity of money increases.

Key Figures

Figure 26.1 The Official UK Measure of Money, 583
Figure 26.2 Creating Money at the One-and-Only Bank, 588
Figure 26.3 The Multiple Creation of Bank Deposits, 590
Figure 26.4 The Demand for Money, 592
Figure 26.5 Changes in the Demand for Money, 592
Figure 26.6 The Supply of Money, 595
Figure 26.7 Money Market Equilibrium, 595
Figure 26.8 The Fluctuating Interest Rate 597

Key Terms

Bank, 585
Barter, 582
Currency, 583
Demand for money, 592
Deposit multiplier, 588
Desired reserve ratio, 587
Excess reserves, 587
Financial innovation, 591
Financial intermediary, 585
M4, 583
Means of payment, 582
Money, 582
Required reserve ratio, 587
Reserve ratio, 587
Reserves, 585
Supply of money, 594

Problems

*1 Which of the following items are money?

a Bank of England notes in the commercial banks' cash machines.

b Your Visa card.

c The coins inside public phones.

d Pound coins in your wallet.

e The cheque you have just written to pay for your rent.

f The student loan you took out in September to pay for your tuition fees.

2 Which of the following items are money? Which are deposit money?

a Deposits at the Bank of England.

b British Telecom shares held by individuals.

c The £5 commemorative crown for the Queen's Jubilee.

d UK Government securities.

*3 Sara withdraws £1,000 from her savings account at her building society, keeps £50 in cash, and deposits the balance in her chequable account at her commercial bank. What is the immediate change in currency and in M4?

4 Monica takes €10,000 from her account at a commercial bank in Spain and puts the funds into her building society account in the United Kingdom. What changes occur in Eurozone M3 and UK M4?

*5 The banks in Zap have:

Reserves	£250 million
Loans	£1,000 million
Deposits	£2,000 million
Total assets	£2,500 million

a Construct the banks' balance sheet. If you are missing any assets, call them 'other assets'; if you are missing any liabilities, call them 'other liabilities'.

b Calculate the banks' reserve ratio.

c If banks hold no excess reserves, calculate the deposit multiplier.

6 The banks in Zip have:

Reserves	£125 million
Loans	£1,875 million
Deposits	£2,000 million
Total assets	£2,100 million

a Construct the banks' balance sheet. If you are missing any assets, call them 'other assets'; if you are missing any liabilities, call them 'other liabilities'.

b Calculate the banks' reserve ratio.

c If banks hold no excess reserves, calculate the deposit multiplier.

*7 The spreadsheet figure provides information about the demand for money and supply of it in Minland. Column A is the interest rate, R. Columns B, C, and D show the quantity of money demanded at three different levels of real GDP: Y_0 is £10 billion, Y_1 is £20 billion, and Y_2 is £30 billion. Column E shows the supply of money. Initially, real GDP is £20 billion.

	A	B	C	D	E
1	R	Y_0	Y_1	Y_2	MS
2	6	1	3	5	7
3	5	2	4	6	6
4	4	3	5	7	5
5	3	4	6	8	4
6	2	5	7	9	3
7	1	6	8	10	2

Draw a graph to show the demand for money, supply of money and money market equilibrium in Minland and explain what happens in Minland if the interest rate:

a Exceeds 4 per cent a year?

b Is less than 4 per cent a year?

c Equals 4 per cent a year?

8 In problem 7, Minland experiences a severe recession. Real GDP falls to £10 billion.

a What happens in Minland if the interest rate is 4 per cent a year?

b What is the equilibrium interest rate?

c Compared with the situation in problem 7, does the interest rate in Minland rise or fall? Why?

*9 In problem 7, Minland experiences a strong expansion. Real GDP rises to £30 billion. Then a recession hits and real GDP falls to £10 billion. What happens to the interest rate in Minland during the:

a Expansion phase of the cycle?

b Recession phase of the cycle?

*Solutions to odd-numbered problems are available on *Parkin Interactive*.

10 In problem 7, a financial innovation changes the demand for money. People plan to hold £0.5 billion less than the numbers in the spreadsheet.

  a What happens to the interest rate?

  b What happens to the interest rate if at the same time as the change in the demand for money, the supply of money decreases by £0.5 billion? Explain.

*11 In problem 7, Real GDP in Minland is £20 billion. The supply of money increases by £1 billion above the numbers shown in the spreadsheet.

  a What happens in Minland if the interest rate is 4 per cent a year?

  b What is the equilibrium interest rate?

  c Compared with the situation in problem 7, does the interest rate in Minland rise or fall? Why?

12 In problem 7, Real GDP in Minland is £20 billion. The supply of money decreases by £1 billion above the numbers shown in the spreadsheet.

  a What happens in Minland if the interest rate is 4 per cent a year?

  b What is the equilibrium interest rate?

  c Compared with the situation in problem 7, does the interest rate in Minland rise or fall? Why?

*13 In Minland in problem 7, a new smart card replaces currency and the demand for money changes. Also, the new smart card causes business to boom and real GDP increases.

  a Modify the numbers in the spreadsheet by making up your own numbers that are consistent with the events just described.

  b Draw the demand for money curve and supply of money curve that describe the initial situation and the situation based on your numbers.

  c What would have to happen to the supply of money in Minland if the interest rate was to remain constant through these events?

14 In Minland in problem 7, a financial crisis occurs. The people begin to distrust the banks and withdraw their deposits. At the same time, they cut up their smart cards and start using currency again. The financial crisis brings a deep recession.

  a Modify the numbers in the spreadsheet by making up your own numbers that are consistent with the events just described.

  b Draw the demand for money curve and supply of money curve that describe the initial situation and the situation based on your numbers.

  c What would have to happen to the supply of money in Minland if the interest rate was to remain constant through these events?

Critical Thinking

1 Study *Reading Between the Lines* on pp. 598–599 and then answer the following questions:

  a What changes in the payments technology are described in the news article?

  b What does the news article imply has happened to the amount of currency held?

  c What are the trends in currency holding? [Hint: you can find the answer in this chapter.]

  d Why do you think currency holdings increased during the 1990s?

  e Why doesn't the increased holding of currency during the 1990s contradict the news article?

  f What do you expect the future trends in the use of currency to be and why?

  g Based on information that you can find in this chapter, do you predict that credit cards and debit cards are used more widely or less widely in the Eurozone than in the United Kingdom? Explain.

2 Rapid inflation in Brazil caused the cruzeiro, the former currency of Brazil, to lose its ability to function as money. People were unwilling to accept it because it lost value too fast. Which of the following commodities do you think would be most likely to take the place of the cruzeiro and act as money in the Brazilian economy?

  a Tractor parts.

  b Packs of cigarettes.

  c Loaves of bread.

  d Impressionist paintings.

  e Baseball trading cards.

Web Exercise

Use the link on Parkin Interactive to work the following exercise.

1 Visit Roy Davies's Web site, "Money – Past, Present, and Future", and study the section on e-money. Then answer the following questions:

  a What is e-money and what are the alternative forms that it takes?

  b Do you think that the widespread use of e-money will lead to an increase or a decrease in the demand for money? Explain.

  c When you buy an item on the Internet and pay for it using PayPal, are you using money? Explain why or why not.

  d Why might e-money be superior to cash as a means of payment?

withdraws currency when it needs additional funds to top up its cash dispensers.

The Bank of England does *not* provide banking services for businesses and individual citizens.

Lender of Last Resort

The Bank of England is the **lender of last resort** to the banking system – the source of funds when all other sources have been exhausted.

If the banking system as a whole or an individual bank is short of funds and unable to get them from any other source, the Bank of England can step in to enable payments to be made. The purpose of last-resort loans is to ensure confidence in the financial system's ability to always make payments.

Regulator of Banks

The Bank of England licenses the firms that operate in the United Kingdom as banks. And with the Financial Services Authority, which supervises individual banks, it ensures that the banks maintain levels of cash and capital that are adequate for them to operate safely and in the interests of their depositors.

Maker of Monetary Policy

Monetary policy-making involves two activities:

1 Setting the goals
2 Setting the instruments

A few central banks – America's Federal Reserve is one of them – set both the goals and the instruments. But most central banks, including the Bank of England and the ECB, set only the instruments in pursuit of goals laid down by the government.

The goal set by the government for UK monetary policy is to achieve an inflation rate between 1.5 and 2.5 per cent a year. The goal set by the European Parliament for Eurozone monetary policy is to keep the inflation rate below 2 per cent a year.

Making monetary policy is like driving a very strange car. The car has an accelerator (lower interest rates) and a brake (higher interest rates). The accelerator and the brake work, but not very predictably. The driver (the Bank of England) cannot be sure how strong or how delayed the response to its actions will be. Also, to make the ride more interesting, the driver has only a rear view. The road just travelled can be seen, but the road ahead is invisible.

The objective is to drive the car at a constant speed over a terrain that alternates between uphill (tough economic times with falling inflation along with decreasing real GDP growth rate and rising unemployment) and downhill (easy economic times with rising inflation, an increasing real GDP growth rate and falling unemployment). So sometimes the accelerator must be applied, sometimes the brake and sometimes neither. You can see that to have a smooth ride, the driver must read the current situation and try to predict what lies ahead.

So to make monetary policy, the Bank of England must anticipate the future course of the economy and try to read that course from current economic conditions.

To appreciate the instruments available to the Bank of England, we must first learn about its financial structure, summarized in its balance sheet.

The Bank of England's Balance Sheet

Table 27.1 shows the Bank of England's balance sheet – a statement of the Bank's liabilities and assets. Its largest liability is notes held by the public. These are the £5, £10, £20 and £50 pound notes that we use in our cash transactions. Some of these notes are part of *currency* – a component of the M4 definition of money (see p. 583). And some of them are in the tills and vaults of the commercial banks – part of the banks' reserves.

The Bank of England's other main liability is the reserves of commercial banks. These liabilities – all the Bank of England's liabilities except for government deposits – along with the coins held by the public make up the **monetary base**. Coins do not appear in the Bank of England balance sheet because they are issued by the

Table 27.1

Balance sheet of the Bank of England, 28 May 2004

Assets (billions of pounds)		Liabilities (billions of pounds)	
Government bonds	15.3	Notes held by the public	34.5
Repo loans to banks	20.0	Government deposits	0.6
Eligible bills	0.7	Bank reserves	1.9
Other	1.0		
Total	**37.0**	**Total**	**37.0**

Source: Bank of England (Author calculations).

Mint, a branch of the government, and not the Bank of England.

The Bank's main assets are government bonds (mainly in the form of Treasury bills) and loans to banks under repurchase agreements called **repo loans**. Under a repurchase agreement, a commercial bank sells a government bond to the Bank of England and simultaneously agrees to repurchase it (buy it back) at a higher price usually two weeks later. This type of agreement is a major source of reserves for the banks.

Let's see how the Bank of England uses the items in its balance as part of its monetary policy toolkit.

The Bank of England's Policy Tools

The Bank of England uses two policy tools to influence the supply of money and the interest rate. They are:

◆ Repo rate
◆ Open market operations

Repo Rate

The **repo rate** is the interest rate at which the Bank of England stands ready to make loans to commercial banks. The Bank of England uses repurchase agreements (*repos*) to make these loans. A rise in the repo rate makes it more costly for banks to borrow from the Bank of England and encourages them to cut their lending, which decreases the supply of money and increases other interest rates. A fall in the repo rate makes it less costly for banks to borrow from the Bank of England and stimulates bank lending, which increases the supply of money and lowers other interest rates.

Open Market Operations

An **open market operation** is the purchase or sale of government bonds by the central bank in the open market. The term "open market" refers to commercial banks and the general public but not the government. So when the Bank of England conducts an open market operation, it does a transaction with a bank or some other business but it does not transact with the government.

Open market operations influence the supply of money. We'll study the details of this influence in the next section. Briefly, when the central bank sells government bonds it receives payment with bank deposits and bank reserves, which creates tighter monetary and credit conditions. With lower reserves, the banks cut their lending, and the supply of money decreases. When

the central bank buys government bonds, it pays for them with bank deposits and bank reserves, which creates looser monetary and credit conditions. With extra reserves, the banks increase their lending, and the supply of money increases.

The Monetary Policy Process: An Overview

There is a big distance between the goal of monetary policy and the instruments available for achieving it. The goal is a target inflation rate. The instruments are changes in the repo rate and open market operations.

The instruments work by changing the interest rate and the quantity of money. These changes influence spending plans. As businesses and household change their spending plans, so, eventually, does production, employment and unemployment change.

Changes in spending, production and employment change the inflationary pressure in the markets for labour and goods and services. Eventually, these changes in inflationary pressure bring a change in the inflation rate.

The time from an action by a central bank to a change in the inflation rate is variable but almost never less than one year and usually around two years. The central bank can forecast at best a few months ahead.

The rest of this chapter spells out the details of how each of the steps just outlined work. We begin by learning how a central bank influences the reserves of the banking system and through that influence changes the supply of money and the interest rate. We then go on to study the ripple effects of monetary policy.

Review Quiz

1 What is a central bank?
2 How do the responsibilities of the European Central Bank differ from those of the Bank of England?
3 What is the lender of last resort? Why do we need one?
4 What are the main items in the balance sheet of a central bank?
5 What policy tools are available to a central bank to conduct a nation's monetary policy?

Let's now see how a central bank influences the supply of money and the interest rate.

Influencing the Supply of Money

Every working day, the Bank of England takes actions that influence the supply of money. Open market operations are the most powerful of these actions. When the Bank of England *buys* bonds in an open market operation, the monetary base *increases*, commercial banks *increase* their lending and the supply of money *increases*. When the Bank of England *sells* bonds in an open market operation, the monetary base *decreases*, commercial banks *decrease* their lending and the supply of money *decreases*.

We're going to study these changes in the supply of money, beginning with the effects of open market operations on the monetary base.

How an Open Market Operation Changes the Monetary Base

When the Bank of England conducts an open market operation, the reserves of the banking system, a component of the monetary base, change. To see why this outcome occurs, we'll trace the effects of an open market operation when the Bank of England *buys* bonds.

Suppose the Bank of England buys £100 million of government bonds in the open market. There are two cases to consider: when the Bank of England buys from a commercial bank and when it buys from the public (a person or business that is not a commercial bank). The outcome is essentially the same in either case, but you'll need to be convinced of this fact. So we'll look at both cases, starting with the simplest in which the Bank of England buys bonds from a commercial bank.

Buy from a Commercial Bank

When the Bank of England buys £100 million of government bonds from Barclays Bank, two things happen:

1 Barclays has £100 million fewer bonds and the Bank of England has £100 million more bonds.

2 The Bank of England pays for the bonds by crediting Barclay's deposit account at the Bank of England with £100 million.

Figure 27.1 shows the effects of these actions on the balance sheets of the Bank of England and Barclays. Ownership of the bonds passes from the Barclays to the Bank of England, so Barclays' assets decrease by £100 million and the Bank of England's assets increase

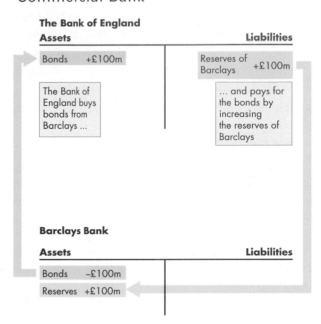

Figure 27.1

The Bank of England Buys Bonds from a Commercial Bank

When the Bank of England buys bonds in the open market, bank reserves increase. If the Bank of England buys from a commercial bank, bank reserves increase when the Bank pays the commercial bank for the bonds.

by £100 million – shown by the blue arrow running from Barclays to the Bank of England. The Bank of England pays for the bonds by crediting the Barclays Banks' deposit account – its reserves – at the Bank of England £100 million – shown by the green arrow running from the Bank of England to Barclays Bank. This action increases the monetary base and increases the reserves of the banking system.

The Bank of England's assets increase by £100 million and its liabilities also increase by £100 million. The commercial banks' total assets remain constant but their composition changes. Barclays' deposits (reserves) at the Bank of England increase by £100 million and its holdings of government bonds decrease by £100 million. So the commercial bank has additional reserves, which it can use to make loans.

We've just seen that when the Bank of England buys government bonds from Barclays Bank, the reserves of Barclays increase. But what happens if the Bank of England buys government bonds from the public – from an investment bank such as Goldman Sachs International, a financial services company?

Buy from Public

When the Bank of England buys £100 million of bonds from Goldman Sachs, three things happen:

1   Goldman Sachs has £100 million fewer bonds and the Bank of England has £100 million more bonds.

2   The Bank of England pays for the bonds with a cheque for £100 million drawn on itself, which Goldman Sachs deposits in its account at Barclays Bank.

3   Barclays collects payment of this cheque from the Bank of England, and £100 million is deposited in Barclays' account (reserves) at the Bank of England.

Figure 27.2 shows the effects of these actions on the balance sheets of the Bank of England, Goldman Sachs International and Barclays Bank. Ownership of the bonds passes from Goldman Sachs to the Bank of England, so Goldman Sachs' assets decrease by £100 million and the Bank of England's assets increase by £100 million – shown by the blue arrow running from Goldman Sachs to the Bank of England.

The Bank of England pays for the bonds with a cheque payable to Goldman Sachs. This payment increases Goldman Sachs' deposit at Barclays by £100 million and it also increases Barclays' reserves by £100 million – shown by the red arrow running from Barclays to Goldman Sachs and the green arrow running from the Bank of England to Barclays.

Just as when the Bank of England buys bonds directly from Barclays Bank, this open market purchase increases the monetary base and increases the reserves of the banking system.

Again, the Bank of England assets increase by £100 million and its liabilities also increase by £100 million. Goldman Sachs has the same total assets as before, but their composition has changed. It now has more money and fewer bonds. The Barclays' total assets increase and so do its liabilities. Its deposits at the Bank of England – its reserves – increase by £100 million and its deposit liability to Goldman Sachs increases by £100 million. Because its reserves have increased by the same amount as its deposits, Barclays has excess reserves, which it can use to make loans.

We've now studied what happens when the Bank of England *buys* government bonds from either a commercial bank or the public. If the Bank *sells* bonds, all the stages that you have studied are reversed. Reserves decrease and the commercial banks are short of reserves.

The effects of an open market operation on the balance sheets of the Bank of England and the commercial banks that we have just described are only the beginning of the story. With an increase in their reserves, the

Figure 27.2

The Bank of England Buys Bonds from the Public

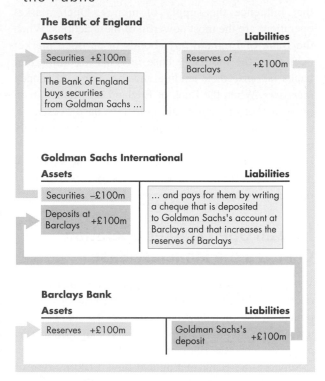

When the Bank of England buys bonds in the open market, bank reserves increase. If the Bank of England buys from the public, bank deposits and bank reserves increase when the seller of the bonds deposits the Bank of England's cheque and the commercial bank collects payment from the Bank of England.

commercial banks are able to make more loans, which increase the quantity of money. Conversely, with a decrease in reserves, the commercial banks must cut loans, which decrease the quantity of money.

You learned how loans create deposits in Chapter 27. Here, we build on that basic idea but instead of studying the link between bank reserves and bank deposits, we examine the related broader link between the monetary base and the quantity of money.

Monetary Base and Bank Reserves

The *monetary base* is the sum of notes and coins and commercial banks' reserves held at the Bank of England. The monetary base is held either by banks as *reserves* or outside the banks as *currency* held by the public. When the monetary base increases, both bank reserves and currency held by the public increase. But only the increase in bank reserves can be used by banks to make loans and create additional money. An increase in currency held by the public is called a **currency drain**. A currency drain reduces the amount of additional money that can be created from a given increase in the monetary base.

The **money multiplier** is the amount by which a change in the monetary base is multiplied to determine the resulting change in the quantity of money. That is, the money multiplier is equal to the change in the quantity of money, ΔM, divided by the change in the monetary base, ΔMB:

$$\text{Money multiplier} = \frac{\Delta M}{\Delta MB}$$

The money multiplier is related to but differs from the *deposit multiplier* that we studied in Chapter 27. Recall that the deposit multiplier is the amount by which a change in bank reserves is multiplied to determine the change in bank deposits.

Let's examine the money multiplier.

The Money Multiplier

Following an open market purchase of bonds, the sequence of events shown in Figure 27.3 takes place. These events are:

1   Banks have excess reserves.

2   Banks lend excess reserves.

3   Bank deposits increase.

4   The quantity of money increases.

5   New money is used to make payments.

6   Some of the new money remains on deposit.

7   Some of the new money is a *currency drain*.

8   Desired reserves increase because deposits increase.

9   Excess reserves decrease but remain positive.

The sequence repeats in a series of rounds, but each round begins with a smaller quantity of excess reserves than did the previous one. The process continues until excess reserves have finally been eliminated.

Figure 27.3

A Round in the Multiplier Process Following an Open Market Purchase

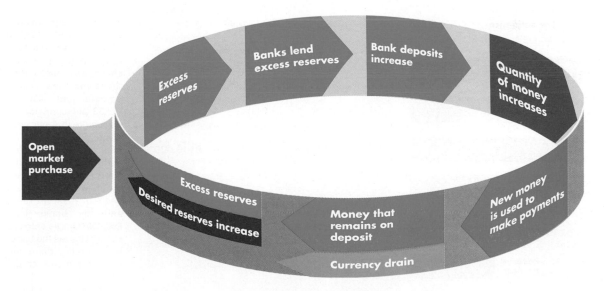

An open market purchase increases bank reserves and creates excess reserves. Banks lend the excess reserves, new bank deposits are created, and the quantity of money increases. New money is used to make payments. Households and firms receiving payments keep some of the receipts as currency – a currency drain – and place the rest on deposit in banks. The increase in bank deposits increases banks' reserves but also increases banks' desired reserves. Desired reserves increase by less than the increase in actual reserves, so the banks still have some excess reserves, though less than before. The process repeats until excess reserves have been eliminated.

You've seen that an open market purchase creates excess reserves for the banks and that the reaction of the banks to this situation increases the quantity of money. But you've not seen the magnitude of the increase in the quantity of money.

Figure 27.4 illustrates these rounds and keeps track of the magnitudes of the increases in reserves, loans, deposits, currency and money that result from an open market purchase of £100,000. In this figure, the *currency drain* is 50 per cent of deposits and the *desired reserve ratio* is 10 per cent of deposits.

The Bank of England buys £100,000 of bonds from the banks. The banks' reserves increase by this amount but deposits do not change. The banks have excess reserves of £100,000, and they lend those reserves. When the banks lend £100,000 of excess reserves, £66,667 remains in the banks as deposits and £33,333 drains off and is held outside the banks as currency. The quantity of money has now increased by £100,000 – the increase in deposits plus the increase in currency.

The increased bank deposits of £66,667 generate an increase in required reserves of 10 per cent of that amount, which is £6,667. Actual reserves have increased by the same amount as the increase in deposits – £66,667. So the banks now have excess reserves of £60,000. At this stage we have gone around the circle shown in Figure 27.3 once. The process we've just described repeats but begins with excess reserves of £60,000. Figure 27.4 shows the next two rounds. At the end of the process, the quantity of money has increased by £250,000, which is 2.5 times the increase in the monetary base.

An open market *sale* works similarly to an open market purchase, but it *decreases* the quantity of money. (Trace the process again but with the Bank of England selling and the banks or public buying bonds.)

The Size of the Money Multiplier

In the example we've just worked through, the money multiplier is 2.5. Why? The size of the money multiplier depends on the magnitudes of the required reserve ratio and the ratio of currency to deposits. To see how these two ratios influence the size of the money

---

Figure 27.4

The Multiplier Effect of an Open Market Purchase

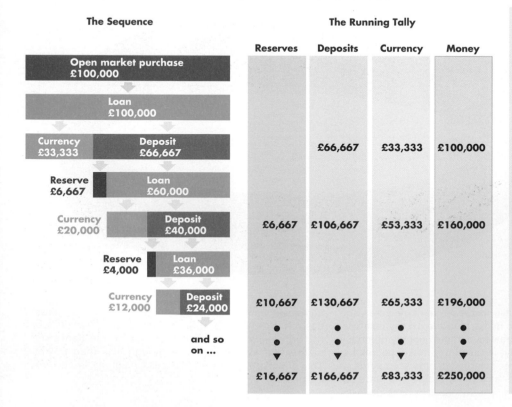

The Sequence	The Running Tally			
	Reserves	Deposits	Currency	Money
Open market purchase £100,000				
Loan £100,000				
Currency £33,333 / Deposit £66,667		£66,667	£33,333	£100,000
Reserve £6,667 / Loan £60,000				
Currency £20,000 / Deposit £40,000	£6,667	£106,667	£53,333	£160,000
Reserve £4,000 / Loan £36,000				
Currency £12,000 / Deposit £24,000	£10,667	£130,667	£65,333	£196,000
and so on ...	£16,667	£166,667	£83,333	£250,000

When the Bank provides the banks with £100,000 of additional reserves in an open market purchase, the banks lend those reserves. Of the amount lent, £33,333 (33.33 per cent) leaves the banks in a currency drain and £66,667 remains on deposit. With additional deposits, desired reserves increase by £6,667 (10 per cent desired reserve ratio) and the banks lend £60,000. Of this amount, £20,000 leaves the banks in a currency drain and £40,000 remains on deposit. The process keeps repeating until the banks have created enough deposits to eliminate their excess reserves. An additional £100,000 of reserves creates an additional £250,000 of money.

multiplier, call desired reserves R, the desired reserve ratio r, currency C, the ratio of currency to deposits c, deposits D, the quantity of money M, and the monetary base MB.

Desired reserves $R = rD$ and currency $C = cD$. The quantity of money M, which equals $C + D$, or:

$$M = (1 + c)D \qquad (1)$$

The monetary base MB, which equals $R + C$, or:

$$MB = (r + c)D \qquad (2)$$

Divide equation (1) by equation (2) to get:

$$\frac{M}{MB} = \frac{(1 + c)}{(r + c)}$$

or

$$M = \left[\frac{(1 + c)}{(r + c)} \right] \times MB$$

With $r = 0.1$ (10 per cent) and $c = 0.5$ (50 per cent), $(1 + c)/(r + c) = (1.5/0.6) = 2.5$.

Changing the Supply of Money

You learned in Chapter 26 (p. 594) that the *supply of money* is the relationship between the quantity of real money supplied and the interest rate, when all other influences on the quantity of money that the banking system creates remains the same.

You can now see that the *quantity of money supplied* depends on two things: the money multiplier and the monetary base. An increase in either increases the quantity of money supplied.

The higher the interest rate, other things remaining the same, the smaller is the desired reserve ratio and the greater is the money multiplier. So the higher the interest rate, the greater is the quantity of money supplied – the supply of money curve slopes upward.

Also, the greater the monetary base, the greater is the *supply of money* – that is, the greater is the quantity of money supplied *at each interest rate*. A change in the monetary base shifts the supply of money curve.

Figure 27.5 illustrates the effects of an open market operation in the money market. An open market purchase increases the monetary base and increases the supply of money. The supply curve shifts rightward

Box 27.1
The UK Money Multiplier

In the United Kingdom in 2003, monetary base was £39 billion and M4 was £1,006 billion, so M4 is approximately 26 times monetary base. Currency was £37 billion, bank reserves were £2 billion and deposits in M4 were £969 billion.

In round numbers in 2003, the desired reserve ratio, r, was 0.002 (about 0.2 per cent) and the currency to deposits ratio, d, was 0.038 (about 3.8 per cent). Using these numbers in the formula for the money multiplier gives:

$$\frac{(1 + 0.038)}{(0.002 + 0.038)} \approx 26$$

That is, a £1 million change in the monetary base brings approximately a £26 million change in M4. The UK money multiplier is about 26.

Figure 27.5

How an Open Market Operation Changes the Interest Rate

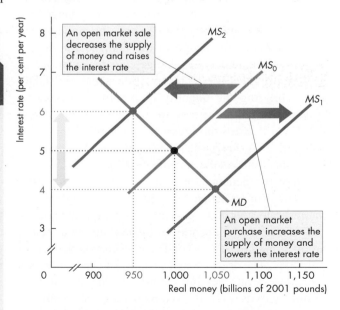

An open market purchase increases the supply of money from MS_0 to MS_1. The quantity of money increases and the interest rate falls. An open market sale decreases the supply of money from MS_0 to MS_2. The quantity of money decreases and the interest rate rises.

from MS_0 to MS_1. At the original interest rate of 5 per cent a year, there is surplus of money. People buy bonds, which drives up the price of a bond and lowers the interest rate. When the interest rate has fallen to 4 per cent a year, money market equilibrium is restored. The quantity of money has increased.

An open market sale has the opposite effect. It decreases the supply of money to MS_2. The interest rate rises and the quantity of money decreases.

In Figure 27.5, the monetary base changes for no particular reason. But the Bank of England might conduct open market operations to achieve specific objectives in the money market. Two special cases are interesting. They are the cases in which the Bank of England conducts open market operations:

◆ Targeting the quantity of money
◆ Targeting the interest rate

Targeting the Quantity of Money

Some economists say that the Bank of England should set a target for the quantity of money and then use open market operations to hit that target.

We'll review the pros and cons of such a monetary policy strategy in Chapter 32, (pp. 731–741) but here is the idea in brief. If the quantity of money changes and the Bank of England knows that it has not changed the supply of money, then the demand for money must have changed. A change in the demand for money occurs when real GDP changes, so the quantity of money provides useful information about real GDP. By stabilizing the quantity of money, the Bank of England might contribute to the stabilization of real GDP. We'll assess this argument in Chapter 32.

Figure 27.6 shows what the Bank of England must do if it wants to target the quantity of money.

When the demand for money increases from MD_0 to MD_1, with no action from the Bank of England, the interest rate rises and the quantity of money increases.

To stabilize the quantity of money, the Bank makes an open market sale of bonds and decreases the supply of money. The decrease in the supply of bonds increases the interest rate yet further but returns the quantity of money to its original level. Stabilizing the quantity of money brings a bigger change in the interest rate than would occur by permitting the quantity of money to rise.

The Bank of England would respond with a decrease in the demand for money with the opposite action: an open market purchase.

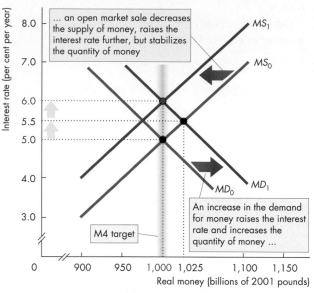

Figure 27.6

Targeting the Quantity of Money

... an open market sale decreases the supply of money, raises the interest rate further, but stabilizes the quantity of money

An increase in the demand for money raises the interest rate and increases the quantity of money ...

M4 target

An increase in the demand for money shifts the demand for money curve from MD_0 to MD_1. The interest rate rises and the quantity of money increases. An open market sale decreases the supply of money from MS_0 to MS_1. The quantity of money returns to its original level but the interest rate rises further.

Targeting the Interest Rate

The larger fluctuations in the interest rate that come from targeting the quantity of money would be appropriate if the changes in the demand for money correctly indicated changes in real GDP.

But the demand for money changes for other reasons such as financial innovation. If the demand for money decreased because of a technological change with no change in real GDP, offsetting the change in the quantity of money could induce interest rate changes that are the opposite of those needed to stabilize the economy.

Some economists think that such fluctuations in the demand for money are so frequent and large that the quantity of money provides no information about the state of the economy. These economists suggest that the Bank of England should target the interest rate to minimize inappropriate changes in the interest rate.

Figure 27.7 shows what the Bank of England must do if it wants to target the interest rate. When the demand for money increases from MD_0 to MD_1, as before, with no action from the Bank of England, the quantity of money would increase and the interest rate would rise.

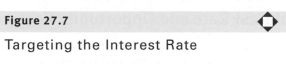

Figure 27.7

Targeting the Interest Rate

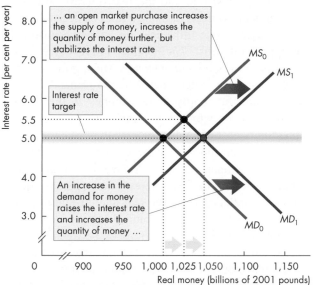

... an open market purchase increases the supply of money, increases the quantity of money further, but stabilizes the interest rate

Interest rate target

An increase in the demand for money raises the interest rate and increases the quantity of money ...

An increase in the demand for money shifts the demand curve from MD_0 to MD_1. The interest rate rises and the quantity of money increases. An open market purchase increases the supply of money from MS_0 to MS_1. The quantity of money increases further, but the interest rate returns to its original level.

To stabilize the interest rate, the Bank makes an open market purchase of bonds and increases the supply of money. The increase in supply increases the quantity of money yet further but returns the interest rate to its original level. Stabilizing the interest rate brings a bigger change in the quantity of money than would occur by permitting the interest rate to rise.

The Bank of England would respond to a decrease in the demand for money with the opposite action: an open market sale that would decrease the quantity of money to stabilize the interest rate.

The Trade-off Between Money and Interest Rate Stabilization

Every central bank faces a trade-off between stabilizing the quantity of money and smoothing the interest rate. And as in all situations that involve a trade-off, the central bank must make a choice. It does not have to choose either of the extremes – perfectly stable quantity of money versus a perfectly stable interest rate. But it does have to choose the degree to which it will permit one to fluctuate while pursuing stability of the other.

In practice, the Bank of England (along with all the other central banks) opts for stabilizing the interest rate on a day to day basis and considering and possibly revising the interest rate target approximately once a month.

There is good reason for this choice – the interest rate is the only variable that the Bank of England can observe day by day. The quantity of money is a hard number to measure. It requires a survey of banks and such a survey is costly to conduct. So the quantity of money is monitored each month rather than each day.

Evaluating the most recent numbers on the quantity of money, the labour market, the CPI and GDP, the Bank of England's Monetary Policy Committee decides whether to change its interest rate target.

You can think of Figure 27.7 as showing us how the money market works day by day as the demand for money fluctuates. But the interest rate target changes from time to time as information becomes available that the current target is not appropriate for achieving the ultimate target – an inflation rate close to 2 per cent a year.

You've seen how money market equilibrium determines the interest rate and how the actions of the Bank of England influence it. We are now going to examine the ripple effects of monetary policy starting with the influence of the interest rate on expenditure plans.

The Ripple Effects of Monetary Policy

You've seen that the interest rate affects the quantity of money that people plan to hold and the quantity of reserves that banks choose to hold. The interest rate also influences spending decisions. The reason is the same in both cases. The interest rate is an opportunity cost. But the interest rate that is relevant for the money-holding decision is not quite the same as the one that is relevant for a spending decision. Let's find out why.

Nominal Interest and Real Interest

We distinguish between two interest rates: the nominal interest rate and the real interest rate. The **nominal interest rate** is the percentage return on an asset such as a bond expressed in terms of money. It is the interest rate that is quoted in everyday transactions and news reports. The **real interest rate** is the percentage return on an asset expressed in terms of what money will buy. It is the nominal interest rate adjusted for inflation and is approximately equal to the nominal interest rate minus the inflation rate.[1]

Suppose that the nominal interest rate is 10 per cent a year and the inflation rate is 4 per cent a year. The real interest rate is 6 per cent a year (10 per cent minus 4 per cent).

To see why the real interest rate is 6 per cent a year, think about the following example. Jackie lends Joe £1,000 for a year. At the end of the year, Joe repays Jackie the £1,000 plus interest. At 10 per cent a year, the interest is £100, so Jackie receives £1,100.

Because of inflation, the money that Joe uses to repay Jackie is worth less than the money that Jackie originally loaned to Joe. At an inflation rate of 4 per cent a year, Jackie needs an extra £40 a year to compensate her for the fall in the value of money. So when Joe repays the loan, Jackie needs £1,040 to buy the same items that she could have bought for £1,000 when she made the loan. Because Joe pays Jackie £1,100, the interest that she *really* earns is £60, which is 6 per cent of the £1,000 that she lent to Joe.

[1] The exact calculation allows for the change in the purchasing power of the interest as well as the amount of the loan. To calculate the *exact* real interest rate, use the formula: *real interest rate* = (*nominal interest rate – inflation rate*) divided by (1 + *inflation rate*/100). If the nominal interest rate is 10 per cent and the inflation rate is 4 per cent, the real interest rate is (10 − 4)/(1 + 0.04) = 5.77 per cent. The lower the inflation rate, the better is the approximation.

Interest Rate and Opportunity Cost

Now that you understand the distinction between the nominal interest rate and the real interest rate, let's think about the effects of interest rates on decisions.

The interest rate influences decisions because it is an opportunity cost. *The nominal interest rate is the opportunity cost of holding money.* And it is the nominal interest rate that is determined by the demand for real money and the supply of real money in the money market. To see why the nominal interest rate is the opportunity cost of holding money, think about the *real* interest rate on money compared with the real interest rate on other financial assets. Money loses value at the inflation rate. So the real interest rate on money equals *minus* the inflation rate. The real interest rate on other financial assets equals the nominal interest rate minus the inflation rate. So the difference between the real interest rate on money and the real interest rate on other financial assets is the nominal interest rate. By holding money rather than some other financial asset, we incur a *real* opportunity cost equal to the nominal interest rate.

The real interest rate is the opportunity cost of spending. Spending more today means spending less in the future. But spending one additional pound today means cutting future spending by more than a pound. And the *real* interest rate determines the real amount by which future spending must be cut.

A change in the real interest rate changes the opportunity cost of three components of aggregate expenditure:

◆ Consumption expenditure
◆ Investment
◆ Net exports

Consumption Expenditure

Other things remaining the same, the lower the real interest rate, the greater is the amount of consumption expenditure and the smaller is the amount of saving.

You can see why the real interest rate influences consumption expenditure and saving by thinking about the effect of the interest rate on a student loan. If the real interest rate on a student loan fell to 1 per cent a year, students would be happy to take larger loans and spend more. But if the real interest rate on a student loan jumped to 20 per cent a year, students would cut their expenditure, buying cheaper food and finding lower rent accommodation, for example, to pay off their loans as quickly as possible.

The effect of the real interest rate on consumption expenditure is probably not large. And it is certainly not as powerful as the effect of disposable income that we studied in Chapter 24 (pp. 526–530). You can think of the real interest rate as influencing *autonomous consumption expenditure*. The lower the real interest rate, the greater is autonomous consumption expenditure.

Investment

Other things remaining the same, the lower the real interest rate, the greater is the amount of investment.

The funds used to finance investment might be borrowed, or they might be the financial resources of the firm's owners (the firm's retained earnings). But regardless of the source of the funds, the opportunity cost of the funds is the real interest rate. The real interest paid on borrowed funds is an obvious cost. The real interest rate is also the cost of using retained earnings because these funds could be loaned to another firm. The real interest rate forgone is the opportunity cost of using retained earnings to finance an investment project.

To decide whether to invest in new capital, firms compare the real interest rate with the expected profit rate from the investment. For example, suppose that MG-Rover expects to earn 20 per cent a year from a new car assembly plant. It is profitable for MG-Rover to invest in this new plant as long as the real interest rate is less than 20 per cent a year. That is, at a real interest rate below 20 per cent a year, MG-Rover will build this assembly line, but at a real interest rate in excess of 20 per cent a year, it will not. Some projects are profitable at a high real interest rate, but other projects are profitable only at a low real interest rate. So the higher the real interest rate, the smaller is the number of projects that are worth undertaking and the smaller is the amount of investment.

Net Exports

The interest rate is not the opportunity cost of net exports. But a change in the interest rate changes the exchange rate. The exchange rate is the price of a unit of foreign currency in terms of the pound – the number of pounds (or pence) it costs for a euro is an exchange rate. And the exchange rate is part of the opportunity cost of exports and imports. A change in the exchange rate changes net exports.

Net Exports and the Exchange Rate

Let's first see why the exchange rate influences exports and imports. When a student at Salford University buys a Dell PC that is shipped from Ireland, the price of the PC equals the euro price converted into pounds. The price of the PC is €1,500 and the exchange rate is 70 pence per euro, so the price of the PC in Salford is £1,050. If the euro falls to 60 pence per euro, the price of the PC in Salford falls to £900. When the price of a PC made in Ireland falls, UK residents import more PCs.

Similarly, when a Dublin retailer buys a consignment of Burberry raincoats from London, the price of the consignment of 100 raincoats equals the price in pounds converted into euros. If the price of the 100 coats is £7,000 and the exchange rate is 70 pence per euro, the price in Dublin is €10,000 for the consignment. If the euro falls to 60 pence per euro, the price of the raincoats in Dublin rises to €11,667. When the price of a UK-made raincoat rises, UK residents export fewer raincoats.

So when the euro falls, the pound buys more euros, imports increase, exports decrease and net exports decrease. Similarly, when the euro rises and the pound falls, imports decrease, exports increase and net exports increase.

The Interest Rate and the Exchange Rate

When the interest rate in the United Kingdom rises, and other things remain the same, the pound exchange rate rises. The reason is that more people move funds into pounds to take advantage of the higher interest rate. But when money flows into the United Kingdom, the demand for pounds increases, so the pound exchange rate (the price) rises. And when the interest rate in the United Kingdom falls, and other things remain the same, the pound exchange rate falls.

Because the interest rate influences the exchange rate, it also influences net exports. A rise in the interest rate decreases net exports and a fall in the interest rate increases net exports, other things remaining the same.

Interest-sensitive Expenditure Curve

Figure 27.8 illustrates the effects of the real interest rate on expenditure plans and summarizes those effects in the interest-sensitive expenditure curve. The **interest-sensitive expenditure curve** (the *IE* curve) shows the relationship between aggregate expenditure plans and the real interest rate when all other influences on expenditure plans remain the same.

Figure 27.8

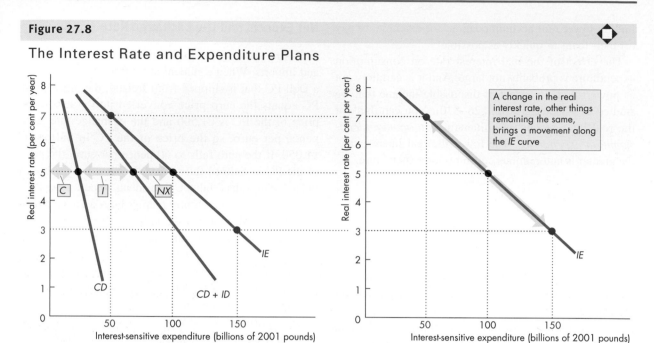

The Interest Rate and Expenditure Plans

(a) The components of expenditure

(b) Aggregate expenditure plans

When the interest rate is 5 per cent a year, autonomous consumption expenditure is £20 billion, investment is £50 billion, net exports are £30 billion, and interest-sensitive expenditure is £100 billion on the *IE* curve. Other things remaining the same, when the interest rate falls to 3 per cent a year, interest-sensitive expenditure increases to £150 billion a year. And when the interest rate rises to 7 per cent a year, interest-sensitive expenditure decreases to £50 billion a year.

Figure 27.8(a) shows the components of interest-sensitive expenditure: autonomous consumption expenditure, investment and net exports. When the real interest rate is 5 per cent a year, autonomous consumption expenditure is £20 billion on the curve *CD*. Investment is £50 billion, so when we add investment and autonomous consumption expenditure together, we get £70 billion on the curve *CD + ID*. Net exports are £30 billion, so when we add this amount to £100 billion, we obtain the sum of all the interest-sensitive components of aggregate expenditure, which is £100 billion on the *IE* curve.

In Figure 27.8(b), as the real interest rate changes, interest-sensitive expenditure changes along the *IE* curve. Other things remaining the same, when the real interest rate falls to 3 per cent a year, interest-sensitive expenditure increases to £150 billion. And when the real interest rate rises to 7 per cent a year, interest-sensitive expenditure decreases to £50 billion.

We can use the interest-sensitive expenditure curve to see how monetary policy affects spending plans. When the interest rate falls, planned expenditure increases and when the interest rate rises, planned expenditure decreases. These changes don't occur immediately but after a delay that varies and is impossible to predict.

Real GDP and the Price Level

The final part of the ripple effect is a change in real GDP and the price level. We'll look at two cases. In the first case, the Bank of England seeks to avoid inflation and in the second, to avoid recession. To keep the story as clear as possible, we'll suppose (unrealistically) that the Bank can control the economy with enormous precision, so it takes exactly the correct actions to restore full employment.

The Bank Tightens to Avoid Inflation

Suppose that real GDP exceeds potential GDP – there is an inflationary gap – and the Bank of England decides to try to eliminate the gap and return real GDP to potential GDP. Figure 27.9 shows how the Bank would achieve this outcome if it were able to control the economy.

Figure 27.9(a) shows the money market. Initially, the supply of money curve is MS_0 and with the demand for money curve *MD*, the interest rate is 5 per cent a year.

Figure 27.9(b) shows the interest-sensitive expenditure curve *IE*. At an interest rate of 5 per cent a year, interest-sensitive expenditure is £100 billion.

Figure 27.9

Monetary Stabilization: Avoiding Inflation

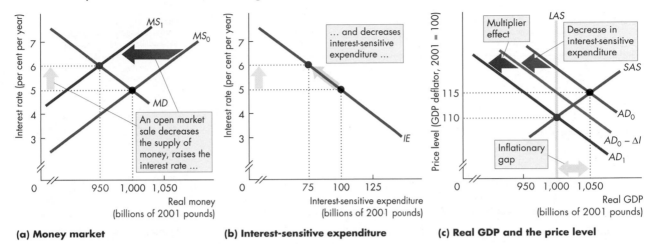

(a) Money market **(b) Interest-sensitive expenditure** **(c) Real GDP and the price level**

Real GDP is £1,050 billion, which exceeds potential GDP of £1,000 billion in part (c). The Bank of England raises the interest rate in part (a), interest-sensitive expenditure decreases in part (b), and aggregate demand decreases with a multiplier effect in part (c).

Figure 27.9(c) shows the aggregate supply and aggregate demand curves. With interest-sensitive expenditure at £100 billion, aggregate demand is AD_0. The aggregate supply curve is SAS, so equilibrium real GDP is £1,050 billion, which exceeds potential GDP. An inflationary gap exists.

The Bank now conducts an open market sale that decreases the supply of money to MS_1 in part (a). The interest rate rises to 6 per cent a year. Interest-sensitive expenditure decreases to £75 billion in part (b). In part (c), aggregate demand decreases to $AD_0 - \Delta I$. With the decrease in aggregate demand, real GDP, aggregate expenditure and aggregate income decrease. The decrease in income induces a further decrease in consumption expenditure, and a multiplier effect decreases aggregate demand further. The aggregate demand curve shifts further leftward to AD_1.

The Bank of England's actions have eliminated an inflation threat and brought real GDP to equal potential GDP at £1,000 billion and the price level to 110.

In reality, because real GDP is growing and the price level is rising, the Bank's actions would slow real GDP growth and slow inflation rather than decrease real GDP and lower the price level as they do in this example. Also, the effects would occur over a period that lasts up to two years or more.

And finally, in reality, the Bank can only dream of having the accuracy we've just given it!

The Bank Eases to Avoid Recession

Now suppose that real GDP is less than potential GDP – there is a recessionary gap – and the Bank of England decides to try to eliminate the recessionary gap and return real GDP to potential GDP.

Figure 27.10 shows how the Bank would achieve this outcome (again if it were able to control the economy with precision). The starting point is the same as in Figure 27.9. The interest rate is 5 per cent a year, and interest-sensitive expenditure is £100 billion.

In part (c), the aggregate demand curve is AD_0, the aggregate supply curve is SAS, and equilibrium real GDP is £950 billion, which is less than potential GDP.

The Bank now conducts an open market purchase that increases the supply of money. The MS curve shifts rightward to MS_2. The interest rate falls to 4 per cent a year. In part (b), interest-sensitive expenditure increases to £125 billion. And in part (c), aggregate demand increases to $AD_0 + \Delta I$.

With the increase in aggregate demand, real GDP, aggregate expenditure and aggregate income increase. The increase in income induces a further increase in consumption expenditure, and aggregate demand increases further. The aggregate demand curve shifts further rightward to AD_1.

The Bank's actions have avoided a recession and brought real GDP to equal potential GDP at £1,000 billion and the price level to 110.

Figure 27.10

Monetary Stabilization: Avoiding Recession

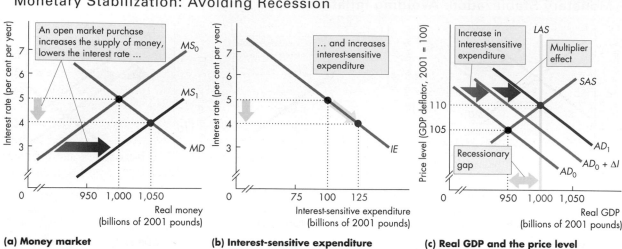

(a) Money market

(b) Interest-sensitive expenditure

(c) Real GDP and the price level

Real GDP is £950 billion, which is below potential GDP of £1,000 billion in part (c). The Bank of England lowers the interest rate in part (a), interest-sensitive expenditure increases in part (b), and aggregate demand increases with a multiplier effect in part (c).

Figure 27.11

The Ripple Effects of Monetary Policy: A Summary

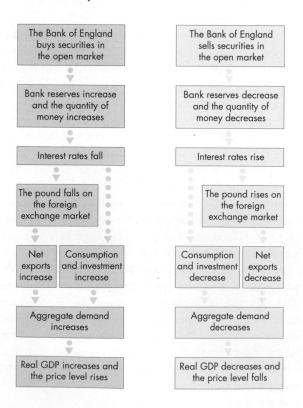

Figure 27.11 provides a schematic summary of the effects that we've just studied. The left half of the figure describes the actions aimed at avoiding recession and the right half describes the actions that avoid inflation.

Review Quiz

1 What is the real interest rate and how does it differ from the nominal interest rate?
2 Which interest rate influences the quantity of money that people plan to hold and why?
3 Which interest rate influences expenditure decisions and why?
4 How does the interest rate influence the exchange rate?
5 How does the exchange rate influence net exports?
6 What does the interest-sensitive expenditure curve show?

You have now learned how the Bank of England can influence the economy by using open market operations to change the interest rate. But you are possibly thinking: all this sounds nice in theory, but does it really happen? Does the Bank of England actually do the things we've learned about in this chapter? Indeed, it does happen, as you can see in the next section.

Monetary Policy in Action

You've seen the connection between the Bank of England's actions and interest rates in Figures 27.9 and 27.10 and a summary of the ripple effects in Figure 27.11. Do actions by the Bank of England that change the interest rate ultimately change real GDP and the price level? Yes they do. You can see the effects on real GDP in Figure 27.12.

The blue line shows the short-term interest rate minus the long-term interest rate. The short-term interest rate is influenced by the Bank of England in the way that you've studied earlier in this chapter. The long-term interest rate is slower to change because it is more strongly influenced by saving and investment plans and by long-term inflation expectations. The red line in Figure 27.12 is the real GDP growth rate *one year later*.

You can see that when the short-term interest rate rises relative to the long-term interest rate, the real GDP growth rate slows down in the following year. These fluctuations in the short-term interest rate are the direct consequence of actions by the Bank of England like those we've described in this chapter. Monetary policy works and is powerful. The price level (and inflation rate) also changes, but it changed later and is more long-drawn out than the changes in real GDP.

Figure 27.12

Interest Rates and Real GDP Growth

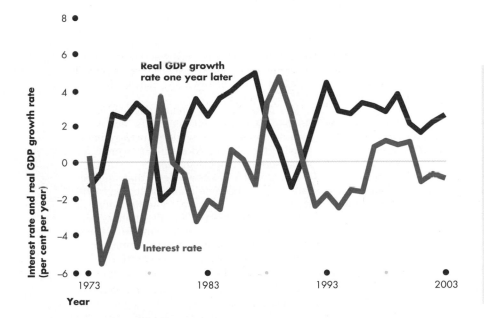

When the Bank of England increases the short-term interest rate, the short-term interest rate rises above the long-term interest rate and a year later the real GDP growth rate slows. Similarly, when the Bank of England decreases the short-term interest rate, the short-term interest rate falls below the long-term interest rate and a year later the real GDP growth rate speeds up.

Source: Office for National Statistics and Bank of England.

Review Quiz

1   Do interest rates fluctuate in response to the Bank of England's actions?
2   How do the Bank of England's actions influence real GDP and how long does it take for real GDP to respond to the Bank's policy actions?

You've seen how the Bank of England's open market operations change the interest rate, how the interest rate influence expenditure plans and how these changes ripple through the economy to change real GDP and the price level. In the next chapter, we're going to explore how interactions of fiscal policy and monetary policy influence the economy. But first, take a look at *Reading Between the Lines* on pp. 620–621 and see the ECB in action in the Eurozone.

Reading Between the Lines

Monetary Policy in the Eurozone

The Financial Times, 27 July 2004

Easy does it on rate rises, says ECB

Tony Major and Mark Schieritz

The European Central Bank has hinted that it will not rush into raising interest rates despite inflationary pressures and the risk it will miss its price stability goal for the fourth year running. Guy Quaden, the governor of the Belgian central bank and an ECB governing council member, said the bank saw no reason to start tightening monetary policy because inflation would subside next year. Eurozone interest rates have been held at 2 per cent since June last year.

The ECB is worried that workers may demand higher pay rises to compensate for inflation, thereby turning a temporary rise in prices into a more permanent one. "So far we do not see any second-round effects from the rise in oil prices," Mr. Quaden said. "Wage growth remains moderate. Inflation expectations have risen slightly but are subdued".

Inflation eased slightly to 2.4 per cent last month after hitting 2.5 per cent in May because of oil prices. This week's "flash" estimate for July should show inflation, which economists forecast to be 2.1 per cent for the full year, remaining well above the ECB's price stability goal of "below but close to 2.00 per cent". Mr. Quaden said that while the inflation rate was disappointing, inflationary pressure seemed to be "limited to surging oil prices and indirect taxes and public [government controlled] prices". He expected inflation to fall below 2 per cent in the first half of next year.

Mr. Quaden's comments suggest more dovish ECB council members are keen to hold rates steady while growth remains fragile. But ECB hawks are likely to press for a rise sooner rather than later.

Mr. Quaden acknowledged that another rate cut had become improbable as growth was starting to pick up. "The first quarter was better than expected. Preliminary second quarter figures are favourable." It was likely that Eurozone growth would soon approach its long-term potential rate of 2.00–2.50 per cent.

The Essence of the Story

- The ECB's inflation target is a rate of below 2.00 per cent a year. In May 2004 the inflation rate was 2.5 per cent and in June it fell to 2.4 per cent but still above the target level.

- It is claimed that the breach in the target was due to a temporary rise in the price level caused by the rise in the price of oil.

- The ECB is worried that the temporary rise in inflation would spark further rises, but the evidence is that inflation continues to fall.

- The ECB is reluctant to raise the interest rate because although inflation is above target its pace is slowing and real GDP growth is beginning to improve.

- The ECB target is inflation, but it does not want to jeopardize real GDP growth with a rise in the interest rate.

Economic Analysis

◆ Inflation in the Eurozone economies has been above 2 per cent during 2003 and has only fallen below 2 per cent briefly in 2004.

◆ The ECB is reluctant to raise the interest rate to bring inflation down below the official upper limit of 2 per cent a year because it believes the inflation rate is falling.

◆ Figure 1 shows that the growth rate of M3 (the Eurozone definition of money) has fallen during the second half of 2003 and in 2004. Inflation is expected to follow and fall below the 2 per cent upper limit in the coming months.

◆ Figure 2 shows that Eurozone real GDP growth was low during 2003. Despite being required to target the inflation rate, the ECB has lowered the interest rate in an attempt to stimulate real GDP growth.

◆ While the Eurozone economy remains weak, the ECB is reluctant to raise the interest rate to lower inflation because this action would slow real GDP growth.

◆ In Figure 3, the Eurozone long-run aggregate supply curve is *LAS* at potential GDP. The short-run aggregate supply curve is *SAS*.

◆ In 2003, aggregate demand was AD_{03}. Equilibrium real GDP was below potential GDP.

◆ Real GDP growth in the first quarter of 2004 was better than expected and aggregate demand in 2004 was AD_{04}.

◆ Real GDP increased and the recessionary gap narrowed.

◆ As Eurozone real GDP approaches potential GDP, the case for raising the interest rate strengthens.

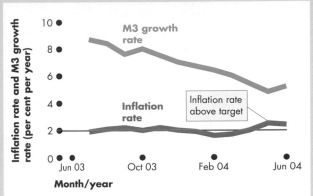

Figure 1 Eurozone inflation and M3 growth

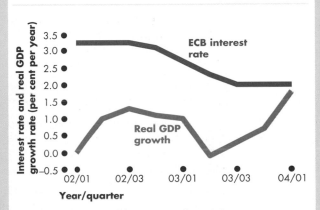

Figure 2 Eurozone real GDP growth and the ECB interest rate

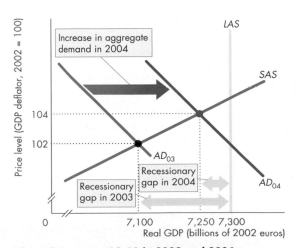

Figure 3 Eurozone *AS–AD* in 2003 and 2004

Summary

Key Points

Central Banking (pp. 604–606)

◆ The Bank of England is the central bank of the United Kingdom.

◆ The central banks of the Eurozone are the European Central Bank (ECB) and the national central banks.

◆ A central bank sets the interest rate at which it is willing to lend to the banking system and conducts open market operations.

Influencing the Supply of Money (pp. 607–613)

◆ An open market purchase of bonds by the central bank increases the monetary base. An open market sale of bonds by the central bank decreases the monetary base.

◆ A change in the monetary base changes the supply of money with a multiplier effect.

◆ The money multiplier depends on the desired reserve ratio and the currency to deposits ratio.

◆ Open market operations can be used to target either the quantity of money or the interest rate.

The Ripple Effects of Monetary Policy (pp. 614–618)

◆ The real interest rate is (approximately) the nominal interest rate minus the inflation rate.

◆ The nominal interest rate is the opportunity cost of holding money.

◆ The real interest rate is the opportunity cost of consumption expenditure and investment.

◆ A fall in the interest rate increases interest sensitive expenditure. (A rise in the interest rate decreases interest-sensitive expenditure.)

◆ A fall in the interest rate lowers the exchange rate and increases net exports. (A rise in the interest rate raises the exchange rate and decreases net exports.)

Monetary Policy in Action (p. 619)

◆ When the Bank of England lowers the interest rate, it increases aggregate demand, which speeds real GDP growth about a year later and speeds inflation later.

◆ When the Bank of England raises the interest rate, it decreases aggregate demand, which slows real GDP growth about a year later and slows inflation later.

Key Figures

Key Terms

Problems

1 You are given the following information about the economy of Nocoin: the banks have deposits of €300 billion. Their reserves are €15 billion, two-thirds of which is in deposits with the central bank. There are €30 billion notes outside the banks. There are no coins!

   a Calculate the monetary base.

   b Calculate the quantity of money.

   c Calculate the banks' reserve ratio.

   d Calculate the currency drain as a percentage of the quantity of money.

2 You are given the following information about the economy of Freezone: the people and businesses in Freezone have bank deposits of €500 billion and hold €100 billion in notes and coin. The banks hold deposits at the Freezone central bank of €50 billion and they keep €5 billion in notes and coin in their vaults and ATM machines.

   a Calculate the monetary base.

   b Calculate the quantity of money.

   c Calculate the banks' reserve ratio.

   d Calculate the currency drain as a percentage of the quantity of money.

*3 In problem 1, suppose that the Bank of Nocoin, the central bank, undertakes an open market purchase of bonds of €1 billion.

   a What happens to the monetary base?

   b What happens to the reserves of the banks?

   c After one round of bank lending, what is the change in the quantity of loans, deposits, reserves and currency in circulation?

   d After two rounds of bank lending, what is the change in the quantity of loans, deposits, reserves and currency in circulation?

   e When excess reserves are zero, what is the change in the quantity of loans, deposits, reserves and currency in circulation?

   f What is the magnitude of the money multiplier in Nocoin?

4 In problem 2, suppose that the Freezone central bank undertakes an open market sale of bonds of €1 billion.

   a What happens to the monetary base?

   b What happens to the reserves of the banks?

   c After one round of bank lending, what is the change in the quantity of loans, deposits, reserves and currency in circulation?

   d After two rounds of bank lending, what is the change in the quantity of loans, deposits, reserves and currency in circulation?

   e When excess reserves are zero, what is the change in the quantity of loans, deposits, reserves and currency in circulation?

   f What is the magnitude of the money multiplier in Freezone?

*5 In problem 3, when the Bank of Nocoin has done its open market operation and the commercial banks have no excess reserves:

   a How has the supply of money changed?

   b What has happened to the interest rate?

   c What has happened to the quantity of money?

   Draw a graph to illustrate these changes in the Nocoin money market.

6 In problem 4, when the Bank of Freezone has done its open market operation and the commercial banks have no excess reserves:

   a How has the supply of money changed?

   b What has happened to the interest rate?

   c What has happened to the quantity of money?

   Draw a figure to illustrate these changes in the Freezone money market.

*7 In Nocoin, the central bank decides that it wants to keep the quantity of money constant. If the demand for money in Nocoin increases, what must the Bank of Nocoin do?

   a Explain whether it buys or sells bonds on the open market?

   b Explain how the Bank of Nocoin's actions achieve its goal of a stable quantity of money.

   c What happens to the interest rate in Nocoin?

   Draw a graph to illustrate these changes in the Nocoin money market.

8 In Freezone, the central bank decides that it wants to keep the interest constant. If the demand for money in Freezone increases, what must the Bank of Freezone do?

   a Explain whether it buys or sells bonds on the open market?

   b Explain how the Bank of Freezone's actions achieve its goal of a stable interest rate.

   c What happens to the quantity of money in Freezone?

---

*Solutions to odd-numbered problems are available on *Parkin Interactive*.

Draw a graph to illustrate these changes in the Freezone money market.

*9 What is the nominal interest rate and why is it *not* the opportunity cost of consumption and investment?

10 What is the real interest rate and why is it the opportunity cost of consumption and investment? How can a central bank change the real interest rate?

*11 In Minland, the central bank lowers the interest rate from 5 per cent a year to 3 per cent a year.

a Describe in detail the steps that the Bank of Minland must follow to make the interest rate fall?

b Describe the effects of the lower interest rate on consumption expenditure and investment.

c Describe the effects of the lower interest rate on the exchange rate of the Minland dollar for the UK pound.

d Describe the effects of the change in the Minland dollar exchange rate on Minland's net exports.

e Explain whether the change in the interest rate shifts or brings a movement along Minland's interest-sensitive expenditure curve.

f Explain the full set of ripple effects of the interest rate cut ending with the changes in real GDP and the price level.

12 In Minland, the central bank conducts an open market purchase of bonds.

a Describe in detail the effects of this action on the interest rate in Minland?

b Describe the effects of the change in the interest rate on consumption expenditure and investment.

c Describe the effects of the change in the interest rate on the exchange rate of the Minland dollar for the UK pound.

d Describe the effects of the change in the Minland dollar exchange rate on Minland's net exports.

e Explain whether the change in the interest rate shifts or brings a movement along Minland's interest-sensitive expenditure curve.

f Explain the full ripple effects of the open market operation through to the changes in real GDP and the price level.

Critical Thinking

1 Study *Reading Between the Lines* on pp. 620–621 and then answer the following questions:

a What was inflation in May 2004 in the Eurozone and what is the inflation target for the ECB?

b Why has the inflation rate risen in the Eurozone? Is it expected to continue rising?

c Why is the ECB not raising the interest rate?

d Why is the governing council of the ECB divided on whether to raise the interest rate or not?

2 Suppose that the United Kingdom joined the Eurozone:

a What functions would the Bank of England retain and what functions would move to the ECB?

b What would happen to the current inflation targets?

c Would this change benefit the United Kingdom?

d Would the United Kingdom incur any cost?

e Explain why you favour or oppose the United Kingdom joining the Eurozone.

3 Gordon Brown, the Chancellor of the Exchequer, tells Mervyn King, Governor of the Bank of England, to keep the interest rate stable and the quantity of money stable. The Governor asks you to draft a reply to the Chancellor explaining why the Bank is unable to do what he asks. Make your report crisp and clear so that the Chancellor is in no doubt about the impossibility of the task he has set.

Web Exercise

Use the links on *Parkin Interactive* to work the following exercise.

1 Visit the Bank of England Website. Find the latest data on the monetary base (M0), M4 and the base interest rate, and the minutes of the Monetary Policy Committee.

a Is the Bank trying to slow economic growth or speed it up? How can you tell?

b What has the MPC decided about interest rates in the past month?

c Skim the MPC minutes and see if you can discover which way interest rates will move at the next meeting by the voting behaviour of its members.

d In light of the Bank's recent actions, what ripple effects do you expect over the coming months?

e What do you think the effects of the Bank's recent actions will be on bond prices and stock prices?

Chapter 28

Fiscal and Monetary Interactions

After studying this chapter, you will be able to:

◆ Describe macroeconomic equilibrium for a given fiscal policy and monetary policy

◆ Explain how fiscal policy influences aggregate demand given monetary policy

◆ Explain how monetary policy influences aggregate demand given fiscal policy

◆ Explain the relative effectiveness of fiscal policy and monetary policy

◆ Explain the interaction of monetary policy and fiscal policy at full employment

◆ Explain the effects of fiscal policy and monetary policy that are coordinated or in conflict

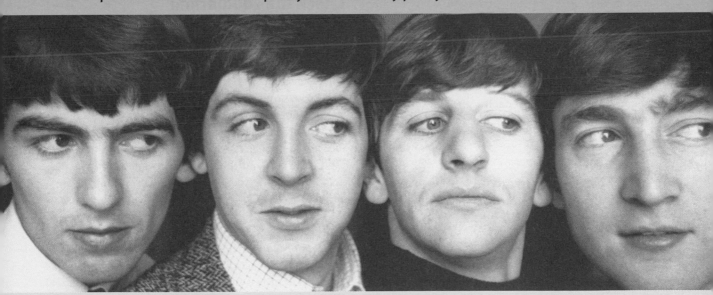

Harmony and Discord

Do fiscal and monetary policies need to be coordinated so that they work in harmony? Or can the government's fiscal policy and the Bank of England's monetary policy play their own tunes in discord? If a recession is looming, is a tax cut just as good as an interest rate cut to get the economy moving? Or is one more powerful than the other? And to rein in inflation, is a tax rise just as good as a rise in the interest rate? When the government has a budget deficit, must the interest rate rise or can the Bank of England just print more money to cover the deficit?

Macroeconomic Equilibrium

Our goal in this chapter is to learn how changes in government expenditure and changes in the quantity of money interact to change real GDP, the price level and the interest rate. But before we study the effects of *changes* in these policy variables, we must describe the state of the economy with a given level of government expenditure and a given quantity of money.

The Basic Idea

Aggregate demand and short-run aggregate supply determine real GDP and the price level. And the demand for and supply of real money determine the interest rate. But aggregate demand and the money market are linked together.

Other things remaining the same, the greater the level of aggregate demand the higher is real GDP and the price level. A higher real GDP means a greater demand for money; a higher price level means a smaller supply of real money; so a greater level of aggregate demand means a higher interest rate.

Aggregate demand depends on the interest rate. The reason is that consumption expenditure, investment and net exports are influenced by the interest rate (see Chapter 27, pp. 614–616). So, other things remaining the same, the lower the interest rate, the greater is aggregate demand.

Only one level of aggregate demand and one interest rate are consistent with each other in macroeconomic equilibrium. Figure 28.1 describes this unique equilibrium.

AS–AD Equilibrium

In Figure 28.1(a) the intersection of the aggregate demand curve, *AD*, and the short-run aggregate supply curve, *SAS*, determines real GDP at £1,000 billion and the price level at 110.

The equilibrium amounts of consumption expenditure, investment, government expenditures and net exports lie behind the *AD* curve. But some components of these expenditures are influenced by the interest rate. And the interest rate, in turn, is determined by equilibrium in the money market. Assume that interest-sensitive expenditures total £100 billion, government expenditure is £100 billion, and the rest of real GDP totals £800 billion.

Money Market Equilibrium and Interest-sensitive Expenditure

In Figure 28.1(b) the intersection of the demand for money curve, *MD*, and the supply of money curve, *MS*, determines the interest rate at 5 per cent a year. (We're assuming that the central bank targets the quantity of money so that the *MS* curve is vertical.)

The position of the *MD* curve depends on the level of real GDP. Suppose that the demand for money curve shown in the figure describes the demand for money when real GDP is £1,000 billion, which is equilibrium real GDP in Figure 28.1(a).

The position of the *MS* curve depends on the quantity of nominal money and the price level. Suppose that the supply of money curve shown in the figure describes the supply of real money when the price level is 110, which is the equilibrium price level in Figure 28.1(a).

In Figure 28.1(c), the *IE* curve determines the level of interest-sensitive expenditure at the equilibrium interest rate of 5 per cent a year. Interest-sensitive expenditure is £100 billion, which is the level of this expenditure that lies behind the aggregate demand curve *AD* in Figure 28.1(a).

Check the Equilibrium

The *AS–AD* equilibrium in Figure 28.1(a), the money market equilibrium in Figure 28.1(b), and interest-sensitive expenditure in Figure 28.1(c) are consistent with each other. And there is no other equilibrium.

To check this claim, assume that aggregate demand is less than *AD* in Figure 28.1(a) so that real GDP is less than £1,000 billion. If this assumption is correct, the demand for money curve lies to the left of *MD* in Figure 28.1(b) and the equilibrium interest rate is less than 5 per cent a year. With an interest rate less than 5 per cent a year, interest-sensitive expenditure exceeds the £100 billion in Figure 28.1(c). If interest-sensitive expenditure exceeds £100 billion, the *AD* curve lies to the right of the one shown in Figure 28.1(a) and equilibrium real GDP exceeds £1,000 billion. So if we assume a real GDP of less than £1,000 billion, equilibrium real GDP is greater than £1,000 billion. There is an inconsistency. The assumed equilibrium real GDP is too small.

Now assume that aggregate demand is greater than *AD* in Figure 28.1(a) so that real GDP exceeds £1,000 billion. If this assumption is correct, the demand for money curve lies to the right of *MD* in Figure 28.1(b) and the equilibrium interest rate exceeds 5 per cent a year. With an interest rate above 5 per cent a year,

Figure 28.1

Equilibrium Real GDP, Price Level, Interest Rate and Expenditure

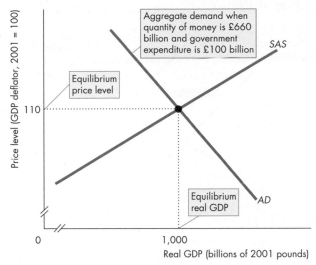

(a) Aggregate supply and aggregate demand

In part (a), the intersection of the aggregate demand curve, *AD*, and the short-run aggregate supply curve, *SAS*, determines real GDP at £1,000 billion and the price level at 110. Behind the *AD* curve, interest-sensitive expenditure is £100 billion, government expenditure is £100 billion and the rest of real GDP is £800 billion.

In part (b), when real GDP is £1,000 billion, the demand for money is *MD* and when the price level is 110, the supply of (real) money is *MS*. The intersection of the demand for money curve, *MD*, and the supply of money curve, *MS*, determines the interest rate at 5 per cent a year. In part (c), on the *IE* curve, interest-sensitive expenditure is £100 billion at the equilibrium interest rate of 5 per cent a year.

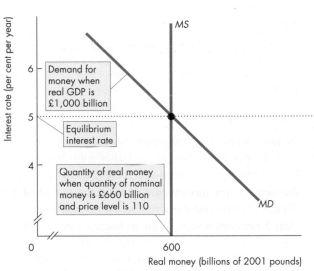

(b) Money and the interest rate

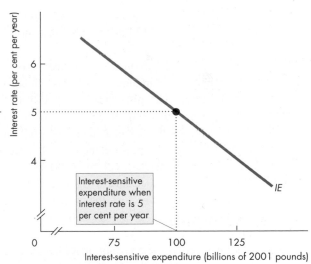

(c) Expenditure and the interest rate

interest-sensitive expenditure is less than the £100 billion in Figure 28.1(c), in which case the *AD* curve must lie to the left of the one shown in Figure 28.1(a) and equilibrium real GDP must be smaller than £1,000 billion. So if we assume that real GDP exceeds £1,000 billion, equilibrium real GDP is less than £1,000 billion. There is another inconsistency. The assumed equilibrium real GDP is too large.

Only one level of aggregate demand delivers the same money market equilibrium and *AS–AD* equilibrium. In

this example, it is the aggregate demand curve *AD* in Figure 28.1(a). Assuming this level of aggregate demand implies this level of aggregate demand. Assuming a smaller level of aggregate demand implies a larger level. And assuming a larger level of aggregate demand implies a smaller level.

Now that you understand how aggregate demand and the interest rate are simultaneously determined, let's study the effects of a change in government expenditures.

Fiscal Policy in the Short Run

Real GDP growth is slowing, and the government is concerned that a recession is likely. So the government decides to head off the recession by using fiscal policy to stimulate aggregate demand. A fiscal policy that increases aggregate demand is called an *expansionary fiscal policy*.

The effects of an expansionary fiscal policy are similar to those of throwing a pebble into a pond. There's an initial splash followed by a series of ripples that become ever smaller. The initial splash is the "first round effect" of the fiscal policy action. The ripples are the "second round effects". You've already met the first round effects in Chapter 25, pp. 566–569, so here is a refresher.

First Round Effects of Fiscal Policy

The economy starts out in the position shown in Figure 28.1. Real GDP is £1,000 billion, the price level is 110, the interest rate is 5 per cent a year, and interest-sensitive expenditure is £100 billion.

The government now increases its expenditures on goods and services by £100 billion. Figure 28.2 shows the first round effects of this action.

The increase in government expenditures has a multiplier effect because it induces an increase in consumption expenditure. (The government expenditures multiplier is explained in Chapter 25, pp. 560–562.) Let's assume that the multiplier is 2, so a £100 billion increase in government expenditure increases aggregate demand at a given price level by £200 billion. The aggregate demand curve shifts rightward from AD_0 to AD_1. At a price level of 110, the quantity of real GDP demanded increases from £1,000 billion to £1,200 billion.

If the price level remained constant, real GDP would increase to £1,200. But the price level does rise and the economy heads off in the direction of the intersection of AD_1 and SAS. Real GDP starts to increase and the price level starts to rise.

These are the first round effects of expansionary fiscal policy.

Second Round Effects of Fiscal Policy

Increasing real GDP and rising price level bring changes in the money market that creates second round effects. Through the second round, real GDP increases and

Figure 28.2

First Round Effects of an Expansionary Fiscal Policy

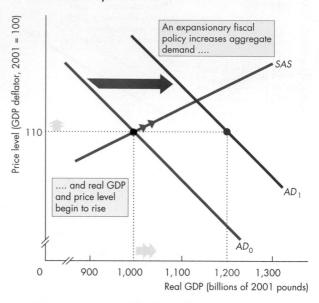

Initially, the aggregate demand curve is AD_0, real GDP is £1,000 billion and the price level is 110. A £100 billion increase in government expenditures on goods and services has a multiplier effect and increases aggregate demand by £200 billion. The aggregate demand curve shifts rightward to AD_1. Real GDP begins to increase and the price level begins to rise. These are the first round effects of an expansionary fiscal policy.

the price level rises until a new macroeconomic equilibrium is reached. But to find that equilibrium and to describe the changes that result from the initial increase in government expenditures, we must keep track of further changes in the money market and in expenditure plans.

It is easier to keep track of the second round effects if we split them into two parts: one that results from the increasing real GDP and the other that results from the rising price level. We follow these effects in Figure 28.3.

First, the increasing real GDP increases the demand for money. In Figure 28.3(b), the demand for money curve shifts rightward. Eventually, it shifts to MD_1 and the interest rate rises to 6 per cent a year. At this interest rate, interest-sensitive expenditure decreases to £75 billion in Figure 28.3(c). The decrease in planned expenditure decreases aggregate demand and the aggregate demand curve shifts leftward to AD_2 in Figure 28.3(a).

Figure 28.3

Second Round Effects of an Expansionary Fiscal Policy

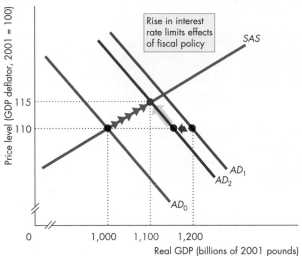

(a) Aggregate supply and aggregate demand

Initially, the demand curve for money is MD_0, the supply curve of real money is MS_0 and the interest rate is 5 per cent a year in part (b). With an interest rate of 5 per cent a year, interest-sensitive expenditure is £100 billion on the curve IE in part (c). With the increased government expenditures, the aggregate demand curve is AD_1 in part (a). Real GDP is increasing, and the price level is rising.

The increasing real GDP increases the demand for money and the demand for money curve shifts rightward to MD_1 in part (b). The higher interest rate decreases interest-sensitive expenditure in part (c), which decreases aggregate demand to AD_2 in part (a). The rising price level brings a movement along the new AD curve. It does so because the rising price level decreases the supply of real money to MS_1, which in turn raises the interest rate further and decreases expenditure. The new equilibrium occurs when real GDP has increased to £1,100 billion and the price level has risen to 115.

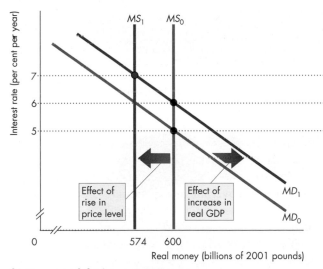

(b) Money and the interest rate

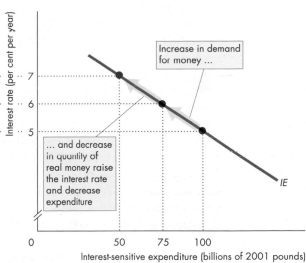

(c) Expenditure and the interest rate

Second, with a given quantity of nominal money, the rising price level decreases the quantity of real money. In Figure 28.3(b), the money supply curve shifts leftward to MS_1. The decrease in the quantity of real money raises the interest rate further to 7 per cent a year. In Figure 28.3(c), the higher interest rate decreases interest-sensitive expenditure to £50 billion. Because this decrease in spending plans is induced by rise in the price level, it decreases the quantity of real GDP

demanded and is shown as a movement along the aggregate demand curve AD_2 in Figure 28.3(c).

During this second round process, real GDP is increasing and the price level is rising in a gradual movement up along the short-run aggregate supply curve as indicated by the arrows. In the new equilibrium, real GDP is £1,100 billion, the price level is 115, the interest rate is 7 per cent a year, and interest-sensitive expenditure is £50 billion.

Figure 28.4

How the Economy Adjusts to an Expansionary Fiscal Policy

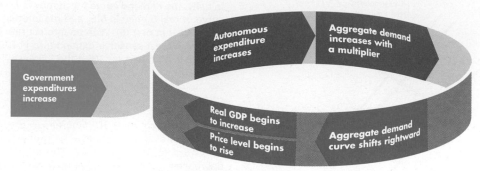

(a) First round effect of expansionary fiscal policy

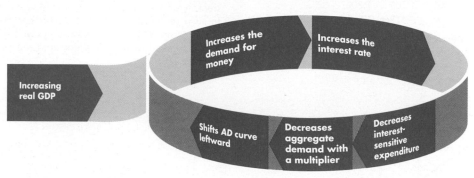

(b) Second round real GDP effect

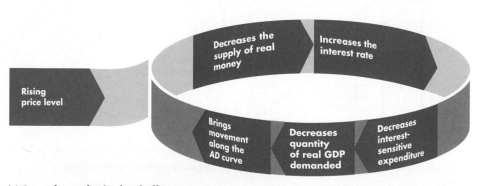

(c) Second round price level effect

Just as the initial equilibrium in Figure 28.1 was consistent, so the new equilibrium is consistent. The *AS–AD* equilibrium in Figure 28.3(a), the money market equilibrium in Figure 28.3(b) and interest-sensitive expenditure in Figure 28.3(c) are consistent with each

other. And there is no other equilibrium.

Figure 28.4(a) summarizes the first round of an expansionary fiscal policy action. Figure 28.4(b) summarizes the two parts of the second round adjustments as the economy responds.

Other Fiscal Policies

A change in government expenditures is only one possible fiscal policy action. Others are a change in transfer payments, such as an increase in unemployment benefits, and a change in taxes. All fiscal policy actions work by changing expenditure. But the magnitude of the initial change in expenditure differs for different fiscal actions. For example, changes in taxes and transfer payments change expenditure by smaller amounts than does a change in government expenditures. But fiscal policy actions that change autonomous expenditure by a given amount and in a given direction have similar effects on real GDP, the price level and the interest rate regardless of the initial fiscal policy action. Let's look more closely at the effect of the rise in the interest rate.

Crowding Out and Crowding In

Because an expansionary fiscal policy increases the interest rate, it decreases all the interest-sensitive components of aggregate expenditure. One of these components is investment and the decrease in investment that results from an expansionary fiscal action is called **crowding out**.

Crowding out may be partial or complete. Partial crowding out occurs when the decrease in investment is less than the increase in government expenditures. This is the normal case – and the case we've just seen.

Complete crowding out occurs if the decrease in investment equals the initial increase in government expenditures. For complete crowding out to occur, a small change in the demand for real money must lead to a large change in the interest rate, and the change in the interest rate must lead to a large change in investment.

But another potential influence of government expenditures on investment works in the opposite direction to the crowding-out effect and is called "crowding in". **Crowding in** is the tendency for expansionary fiscal policy to *increase* investment. This effect works in three ways.

First, in a recession, an expansionary fiscal policy might create expectations of a more speedy recovery and bring an increase in expected profits. Higher expected profits might increase investment despite a higher interest rate.

Second, government expenditures might be productive and lead to more profitable business opportunities. For example, a new motorway might cut the cost of transporting a farmer's produce to a market and induce the farmer to invest in a new fleet of trucks.

Third, if an expansionary fiscal policy takes the form of a cut in taxes on business profits, firms' after-tax profits increase and firms might increase investment.

The Exchange Rate and International Crowding Out

We've seen that an expansionary fiscal policy leads to higher interest rates. But a change in interest rates also affects the exchange rate. Higher interest rates make the pound rise in value against other currencies. With interest rates higher in the United Kingdom than in the rest of the world, funds flow into the United Kingdom and people around the world demand more pounds sterling. As the pound rises in value, foreigners find UK-produced goods and services more expensive and UK residents find imports less expensive. Exports decrease and imports increase – net exports decrease. The tendency for an expansionary fiscal policy to decrease net exports is called **international crowding out**. The decrease in net exports offsets, to some degree, the initial increase in aggregate expenditure brought about by an expansionary fiscal policy.

Review Quiz

1 Describe macroeconomic equilibrium. What conditions are met in such an equilibrium? What are the links between aggregate demand, the money market and investment?

2 What is an expansionary fiscal policy and what are its first round effects? What is happening at the end of the first round?

3 What are the second round effects of an expansionary fiscal policy action? Describe the forces at work and the changes that occur in the interest rate, investment, real GDP and the price level.

4 What is crowding out? How does crowding out influence the outcome of a fiscal policy action?

5 What is crowding in? How does crowding in influence the outcome of a fiscal policy action?

6 How does an expansionary fiscal policy affect the exchange rate? What happens to imports and exports?

You've seen how the money market and the goods market interact when the government changes its fiscal policy. Next we'll study these same interactions when the Bank of England changes its monetary policy.

Monetary Policy in the Short Run

Figure 28.5 describes the economy initially. The quantity of money is £660 billion, the interest rate is 5 per cent a year, interest-sensitive expenditure is £100 billion, real GDP is £1,000 billion and the price level is 110. The Bank of England now increases the quantity of money to £1,155 billion. With a price level of 110, the quantity of real money increases to £1,050 billion.

First Round Effects

Figure 28.5(a) shows the immediate effect. The real money supply curve shifts rightward from MS_0 to MS_1, and the interest rate falls from 5 per cent to 1 per cent a year. The lower interest rate increases interest-sensitive expenditure to £200 billion in part (b). The increase in interest-sensitive expenditure sets off a multiplier process and increases aggregate demand. The aggregate demand curve shifts rightward from AD_0 to

Figure 28.5

First Round Effects of an Expansionary Monetary Policy

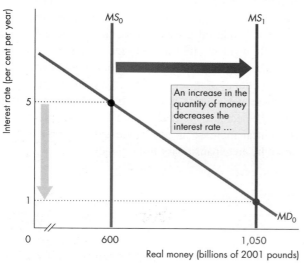

(a) Change in quantity of money

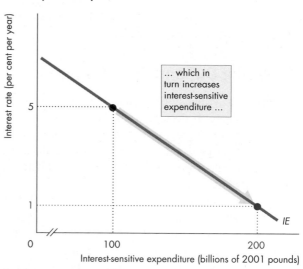

(b) Change in expenditure

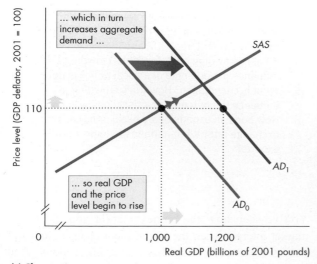

(c) Change in aggregate demand

Initially, the demand curve for real money is MD_0, the supply curve of real money is MS_0, and the interest rate is 5 per cent a year in part (a). With an interest rate of 5 per cent a year, interest-sensitive expenditure is £100 billion on the IE curve in part (b). The aggregate demand curve is AD_0 in part (c). Equilibrium real GDP is £1,000 billion and the price level is 110.

An increase in the quantity of money shifts the supply of real money curve rightward to MS_1 in part (a). The increased supply of money lowers the interest rate to 1 per cent a year and interest-sensitive expenditure increases to £200 billion in part (b). This increase in expenditure increases aggregate demand to AD_1 in part (c). Real GDP begins to increase and the price level begins to rise.

AD_1 in part (c). As aggregate demand increases, real GDP and the price level begin to increase along the SAS curve towards a new macroeconomic equilibrium.

These are the first round effects of an expansionary monetary policy. An increase in the quantity of money decreases the interest rate and increases aggregate demand. Real GDP and the price level begin to increase.

Let's now look at the second round effects.

Second Round Effects

The increasing real GDP and rising price level set off the second round, which Figure 28.6(b) illustrates. And as in the case of fiscal policy, it is best to break the second round into two parts: the consequence of increasing real GDP and the consequence of the rising price level.

The increasing real GDP increases the demand for money from MD_0 to MD_1 in Figure 28.6(a). The

---

Figure 28.6

Second Round Effects of an Expansionary Monetary Policy

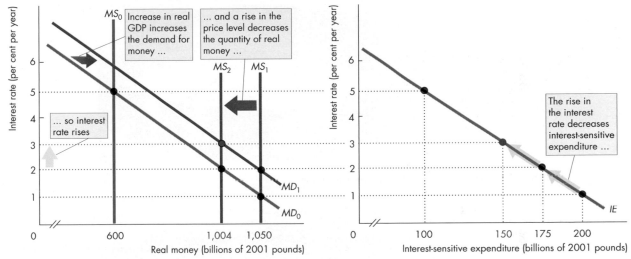

(a) Money and the interest rate

(b) Decrease in expenditure

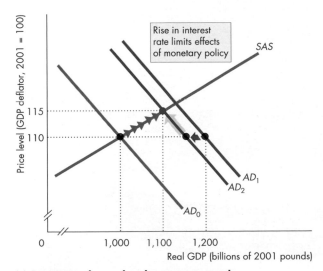

(c) Aggregate demand and aggregate supply

At the start of the second round, the demand curve for money is still MD_0 in part (a), the supply curve of real money is MS_1, and the interest rate is 1 per cent a year. With an interest rate of 1 per cent a year, interest-sensitive expenditure is £200 billion on the curve IE in part (b). With the increased quantity of money and expenditure, the aggregate demand curve is AD_1 in part (c). Real GDP is increasing and the price level is rising.

The increasing real GDP increases the demand for money and the demand for money curve shifts rightward to MD_1. The higher interest rate decreases interest-sensitive expenditure, which decreases aggregate demand to AD_2. The rising price level brings a movement along the new AD curve. It does so because it decreases the supply of real money to MS_2, which in turn raises the interest rate further and decreases expenditure. The new equilibrium occurs when real GDP has increased to £1,100 billion and the price level has risen to 115.

increased demand for money raises the interest rate to 2 per cent a year. The higher interest rate brings a decrease in interest-sensitive expenditure from £200 billion to £175 billion in Figure 28.6(b). And the lower level of expenditure decreases aggregate demand and shifts the aggregate demand curve leftward to AD_2 in Figure 28.6(c).

The rising price level brings a movement along the new aggregate demand curve in Figure 28.6(c). This movement occurs because the rising price level decreases the real money supply. As the price level rises, the real money supply decreases to £1,004 billion and the money supply curve shifts leftward to MS_2 in part (a). The interest rate rises further to 3 per cent a year. And interest-sensitive expenditure decreases to £150 billion in part (b).

In the new short-run equilibrium, real GDP has increased to £1,100 billion, and the price level has risen

Figure 28.7

How the Economy Adjusts to an Expansionary Monetary Policy

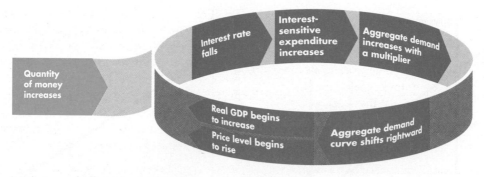

(a) First round effect of expansionary monetary policy

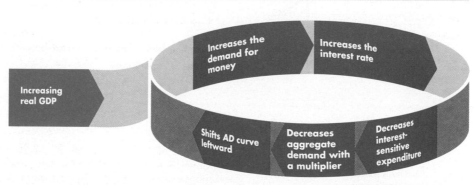

(b) Second round real GDP effect

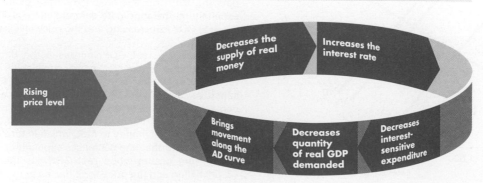

(c) Second round price level effect

to 115, where the aggregate demand curve AD_2 intersects the short-run aggregate supply curve SAS.

The demand for money curve is MD_1, the money supply curve is MS_2, and the interest rate is 3 per cent a year in part (a). With an interest rate of 3 per cent a year, interest-sensitive expenditure is $150 billion in part (b).

The new equilibrium is the only consistent one and is like that of Figure 28.1. Figure 28.7 summarizes the adjustments that occur to bring the economy to this new equilibrium.

Money and the Exchange Rate

An increase in the quantity of money lowers the interest rate. If the interest rate falls in the United Kingdom but does not fall in the United States, Japan and Asia, international investors buy the now higher-yielding foreign assets and sell the relatively lower-yielding UK assets. As they make these transactions, they sell pounds. So the pound depreciates against other currencies. (This mechanism is explained in greater detail in Chapter 34, pp. 781–784.)

With a cheaper pound, foreigners face lower prices for UK-produced goods and services and people and firms in the United Kingdom face higher prices for foreign-produced goods and services. UK exports increase and UK imports decrease. UK net exports increase, and real GDP and the price level in the United Kingdom increase further.

Review Quiz

1   What are the first round effects of an expansionary monetary policy? What happens to the interest rate, investment and other components of interest-sensitive expenditure, aggregate demand, the demand for money, real GDP and the price level in the first round?
2   What are the second round effects of an expansionary monetary policy? What happens to the interest rate, investment and other components of interest-sensitive expenditure, aggregate demand, the demand for money, real GDP and the price level in the second round?
3   How does an expansionary monetary policy influence the exchange rate, imports and exports?

Let's now see which policy is more effective.

Relative Effectiveness of Policies

We've seen that aggregate demand and real GDP are influenced by both fiscal and monetary policy. But which policy is the more potent? This question was once at the centre of a controversy among macro-economists. Later in this section we'll look at that controversy and see how it was settled. But we begin by discovering what determines the effectiveness of fiscal policy.

Effectiveness of Fiscal Policy

The effectiveness of fiscal policy is measured by the magnitude of the increase in aggregate demand that results from a given increase in government expenditures (or decrease in taxes). The effectiveness of fiscal policy depends on the strength of the crowding-out effect. Fiscal policy is most powerful if no crowding out occurs. Fiscal policy is impotent if there is complete crowding out. And the strength of the crowding-out effect depends on two things:

1   The responsiveness of expenditure to the interest rate
2   The responsiveness of the quantity of money demanded to the interest rate

If expenditure is not very responsive to a change in the interest rate, the crowding-out effect is small. But if expenditure is highly responsive to a change in the interest rate, the crowding-out effect is large. Other things remaining the same, the smaller the responsiveness of expenditure to the interest rate, the smaller is the crowding-out effect and the bigger is the change in aggregate demand. So the less responsive expenditure is to the interest rate, the more effective is fiscal policy.

The responsiveness of the quantity of money demanded to the interest rate also affects the size of the crowding-out effect. An increase in real GDP increases the demand for money and with no change in the supply of money, the interest rate rises. But the extent to which the interest rate rises depends on the responsiveness of the quantity of money demanded to the interest rate. Other things remaining the same, the greater the responsiveness of the quantity of money demanded to the interest rate, the smaller is the rise in the interest rate, the smaller is the crowding-out effect and the bigger is the change in aggregate demand. So the more responsive the quantity of money demanded is to the interest rate, the more effective is fiscal policy.

Effectiveness of Monetary Policy

The effectiveness of monetary policy is measured by the magnitude of the increase in aggregate demand that results from a given increase in the money supply. The effectiveness of monetary policy depends on the same two factors that influence the effectiveness of fiscal policy:

1 The responsiveness of the quantity of money demanded to the interest rate

2 The responsiveness of expenditure to the interest rate

The starting point for monetary policy is a change in the quantity of money that changes the interest rate. A given change in the quantity of money might bring a small change or a large change in the interest rate. Other things remaining the same, the larger the initial change in the interest rate, the more effective is monetary policy. The initial change in the interest rate will be greater, the less responsive is the quantity of money demanded to the interest rate.

But effectiveness of monetary policy also depends on how much expenditure changes. If expenditure is not very responsive to a change in the interest rate, monetary actions do not have much effect on expenditure. But if expenditure is highly responsive to a change in the interest rate, monetary actions have a large effect on aggregate expenditure. The greater the responsiveness of expenditure to the interest rate, the more effective is monetary policy.

The effectiveness of fiscal policy and monetary policy that you've just studied were once controversial. During the 1950s and 1960s, this issue lay at the heart of what was called the Keynesian–monetarist controversy. Let's look at the dispute and see how it was resolved.

The Keynesian–Monetarist Controversy

The Keynesian–monetarist controversy was an ongoing dispute in macroeconomics between two broad groups of economists. A **Keynesian** macroeconomist believes that left alone, the economy would rarely operate at full employment and that to achieve and maintain full employment, active help from fiscal policy and monetary policy is required. Keynesian views about the functioning of the economy are based on the theories of John Maynard Keynes, published in Keynes' *The General Theory of Employment, Interest and Money*. Traditionally, Keynesians assigned a low degree of

importance to monetary policy and a high degree of importance to fiscal policy. Modern Keynesians assign a high degree of importance to both types of policy. A **monetarist** is a macroeconomist who believes that most macroeconomic fluctuations are caused by fluctuations in the quantity of money and that the economy is inherently stable and requires no active government intervention. Monetarist views about the functioning of the economy are based on theories most forcefully set forth by Milton Friedman. Traditionally, monetarists assigned a low degree of importance to fiscal policy. But modern monetarists, like modern Keynesians, assign a high degree of importance to both types of policy.

The nature of the Keynesian–monetarist debate has changed over the years. During the 1950s and 1960s, it was a debate about the relative effectiveness of fiscal policy and monetary policy in changing aggregate demand. We can see the essence of that debate by making three points of view distinct:

◆ Extreme Keynesianism

◆ Extreme monetarism

◆ Intermediate position

Extreme Keynesianism

The extreme Keynesian hypothesis is that a change in the quantity of money has no effect on aggregate demand and that a change in government expenditures on goods and services or taxes has a large effect on aggregate demand. The two circumstances in which a change in the quantity of money has no effect on aggregate demand are:

1 Expenditure demand is completely insensitive to the interest rate.

2 The demand for real money is highly sensitive to the interest rate.

If expenditure is completely insensitive to the interest rate (if the *IE* curve is vertical), a change in the quantity of money changes interest rates, but those changes do not affect aggregate planned expenditure. Monetary policy is impotent.

If the demand for real money is highly sensitive to the interest rate (if the *MD* curve is horizontal), people are willing to hold any amount of money at a given interest rate – a situation called a *liquidity trap*. With a liquidity trap, a change in the quantity of money affects only the amount of money held. It does not affect interest rates. With an unchanged interest rate, expenditure remains constant. Monetary policy is impotent. Some people claim (incorrectly) that Japan has been in a liquidity trap since the late 1990s.

Extreme Monetarism

The extreme monetarist hypothesis is that a change in government expenditures on goods and services or taxes has no effect on aggregate demand and that a change in the quantity of money has a large effect on aggregate demand. Two circumstances give rise to these predictions:

1 Expenditure is highly sensitive to the interest rate.
2 The demand for real money is completely insensitive to the interest rate.

If an increase in government expenditures on goods and services induces an increase in interest rates that is sufficiently large to reduce expenditure by the same amount as the initial increase in government expenditures, then fiscal policy has no effect on aggregate demand. This outcome is complete crowding out. For this result to occur, either the demand for real money must be insensitive to the interest rate – a fixed amount of money is held regardless of the interest rate – or expenditure must be highly sensitive to the interest rate – any amount of expenditure will be undertaken at a given interest rate.

The Intermediate Position

The intermediate position is that both fiscal policy and monetary policy affect aggregate demand. Crowding out is not complete, so fiscal policy does have an effect. There is no liquidity trap and expenditure responds to the interest rate, so monetary policy does indeed affect aggregate demand. This intermediate position is the one that now appears to be correct and is the one that we've spent most of this chapter exploring. Let's see how economists came to this conclusion.

Sorting Out the Competing Claims

The dispute between monetarists, Keynesians and those taking an intermediate position was essentially a disagreement about the magnitudes of two economic parameters:

1 The responsiveness of expenditure to the interest rate
2 The responsiveness of the demand for real money to the interest rate

If expenditure is highly sensitive to the interest rate or the demand for real money is barely sensitive to the interest rate, then monetary policy is powerful and fiscal policy relatively ineffective. In this case, the world looks similar to the claims of extreme monetarists. If expenditure is very insensitive to the interest rate or the demand for real money is highly sensitive, then fiscal policy is powerful and monetary policy is relatively ineffective. In this case, the world looks similar to the claims of the extreme Keynesians.

By using statistical methods to study the demand for real money and expenditure and data from a wide variety of historical and national experiences, economists were able to settle this dispute. Neither extreme position is supported by the evidence. There is no liquidity trap, not even in Japan. Expenditure *is* interest sensitive. Neither the demand for money curve nor interest-sensitive expenditure curve is vertical or horizontal, so the extreme Keynesian and extreme monetarist hypotheses are rejected.

Interest Rate and Exchange Rate Effectiveness

Although fiscal policy and monetary policy are alternative ways of changing aggregate demand, they have opposing effects on the interest rate and the exchange rate. A fiscal policy action that increases aggregate demand raises the interest rate and increases the exchange rate. A monetary policy action that increases aggregate demand lowers the interest rate and decreases the exchange rate. Because of these opposing effects on interest rates and the exchange rate, if the two policies are combined to increase aggregate demand, their separate effects on the interest rate and the exchange rate can be minimized.

Review Quiz

1 What two macroeconomic parameters influence the relative effectiveness of fiscal policy and monetary policy?
2 Under what circumstances is the Keynesian view correct and under what circumstances is the monetarist view correct?
3 How can fiscal policy and monetary policy be combined to increase aggregate demand yet at the same time keep the interest rate constant?

We're now going to look at expansionary fiscal and monetary policy at full employment.

Policy Actions at Full Employment

An expansionary fiscal policy or monetary policy can bring the economy to full employment. But it is often difficult to determine whether the economy is below full employment. So an expansionary fiscal policy or monetary policy might be undertaken when the economy is at full employment. What happens then? Let's answer this question starting with an expansionary fiscal policy.

Expansionary Fiscal Policy at Full Employment

Suppose the economy is at full employment and the government increases expenditure. All the effects that we worked out earlier in this chapter occur. Except that these effects determine only a *short-run equilibrium*. That is, both the first round and second round effects of policy occur in the short run. There is a third round, which is the long-run adjustment.

Starting out at full employment, an expansionary fiscal policy will create an above full-employment equilibrium in which there is an *inflationary gap*. The money wage rate begins to rise, short-run aggregate supply decreases, and a long-run adjustment occurs in which real GDP decreases to potential GDP and the price level rises.

Figure 28.8 illustrates the combined first and second round short-run effects and the third round long-run adjustment.

In Figure 28.8, potential GDP is £1,000 billion. Real GDP equals potential GDP on aggregate demand curve AD_0 and short-run aggregate supply curve SAS_0. An expansionary fiscal policy action increases aggregate demand. The combined first round and second round effect increases aggregate demand to AD_1. Real GDP increases to £1,100 billion and the price level rises to 115. There is an inflationary gap of £100 billion.

With the economy above full-employment, a shortage of labour puts upward pressure on the money wage rate, which now begins to rise. And a third round of adjustment begins. The rising money wage rate decreases short-run aggregate supply and the *SAS* curve starts moving leftward towards SAS_1.

As the short-run aggregate supply decreases, real GDP decreases and the price level rises. This process continues until the inflationary gap has been eliminated and the economy has returned to full employment. At

Figure 28.8

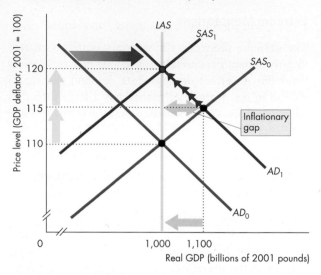

Fiscal Policy at Full Employment

The long-run aggregate supply curve is *LAS* and initially the aggregate demand curve is AD_0 and the short-run aggregate supply curve is SAS_0. Real GDP is £1,000 billion and the price level is 110. Changes in fiscal policy and monetary policy shift the aggregate demand curve to AD_1. At the new short-run equilibrium, real GDP is £1,100 billion and the price level is 115. Because real GDP exceeds potential GDP, the money wage rate begins to rise and the short-run aggregate supply curve begins to shift leftward to SAS_1. At the new long-run equilibrium, the price level is 120 and real GDP is back at its original level.

long-run equilibrium, real GDP is £1,000 billion, which is potential GDP, and a price level of 120.

Crowding Out at Full Employment

You've just seen that when government expenditures increase at full employment, the long-run change in real GDP is zero. The entire effect of the increase in aggregate demand is to increase the price level. This outcome implies that at full employment, an increase in government expenditures *completely crowds out investment* or *creates an international (net exports) deficit*, or results in a combination of the two.

The easiest way to see why is to recall that aggregate expenditure, which equals consumption expenditure, C, plus investment, I, plus government expenditures, G, plus net exports, NX, equals real GDP. That is:

$$Y = C + I + G + NX$$

Comparing the initial situation with the outcome, real GDP has not changed. So aggregate expenditure, $C + I + G + NX$, is constant between the two situations.

But government expenditures have increased, so the sum of consumption expenditure, investment, and net exports must have decreased. If net exports don't change, consumption expenditure plus investment decreases by the full amount of the increase in government expenditures. If consumption expenditure and investment don't change, net exports decrease by an amount equal to the increase in government expenditures. A decrease in net exports is an increase in our international deficit.

You've now seen that the effects of expansionary fiscal policy are extremely sensitive to the state of the economy when the policy action is taken. At less than full employment, an expansionary fiscal policy can move the economy towards full employment. At full employment, an expansionary fiscal policy raises the price level, crowds out private expenditure, and creates an international deficit.

You've now seen that the effects of expansionary fiscal policy are extremely sensitive to the state of the economy when the policy action is taken. At less than full employment, an expansionary fiscal policy can move the economy towards full employment. At full employment, an expansionary fiscal policy raises the price level, crowds out investment and creates an international deficit.

Expansionary Monetary Policy at Full Employment

Now suppose the economy is at full employment and the Bank of England increases the quantity of money. Again, all the effects that we worked out earlier in this chapter occur. But again, these effects determine only a *short-run equilibrium*. That is, the first round and second round effects of monetary policy both occur in the short run. And again, there is a third round, which is the long-run adjustment.

Starting out at full employment, an expansionary monetary policy will create an above full-employment equilibrium in which there is an *inflationary gap*. The money wage rate begins to rise, short-run aggregate supply decreases and a long-run adjustment occurs in which real GDP decreases to potential GDP and the price level rises.

Figure 28.8, which illustrates the effects of an expansionary fiscal policy at full employment, also illustrates the effects of an expansionary monetary policy at full employment.

In the short run, an expansionary monetary policy increases real GDP and the price level. But in the long run, it increases only the price level and leaves real GDP unchanged at potential GDP.

Long-run Neutrality

In the long run, a change in the quantity of money changes only the price level and leaves real GDP unchanged. The independence of real GDP from the quantity of money is an example of the long-run neutrality of money.

But **long-run neutrality** applies not only to real GDP but also to all real variables. The so-called long-run neutrality proposition is that in the long run, a change in the quantity of money changes the price level and leaves all real variables unchanged.

You can see this outcome in the case of real GDP in Figure 28.8. Because a change in the quantity of money leaves real GDP unchanged, it also leaves consumption expenditure unchanged. With no change in real GDP, the demand for money does not change. The price level rises by the same percentage as the increase in the quantity of money, so the supply of real money does not change. With no change in the demand for money and no change in the supply of real money, the interest rate does not change. And with no change in the interest rate, expenditure remains the same. Finally, with no change in real GDP, consumption expenditure, investment, government expenditures and net exports are unchanged.

Review Quiz

1 Contrast the short-run effects of an expansionary fiscal policy on real GDP and the price level with its long-run effects when the policy action occurs at full employment.
2 Contrast the short-run effects of an expansionary monetary policy on real GDP and the price level with its long-run effects when the policy action occurs at full employment.
3 Explain crowding out at full employment.
4 Explain the long-run neutrality of money.

You've seen how fiscal policy and monetary policy interact. Do they need to be coordinated and if uncoordinated, do they come into conflict?

Policy Coordination and Conflict

So far, we've studied fiscal policy and monetary policy in isolation from each other. We are now going to consider what happens if the two branches of policy are coordinated and if they come into conflict.

Policy coordination occurs when the government and central bank work together to achieve a common set of goals. **Policy conflict** occurs when the government and the central bank pursue different goals and the actions of one make it harder (perhaps impossible) for the other to achieve its goals.

Policy Coordination

The basis for policy coordination is the fact that either fiscal policy or monetary policy can be used to increase aggregate demand. Starting from a position of *unemployment equilibrium*, an increase in aggregate demand increases real GDP and decreases unemployment. If the size of the policy action is well judged, it can restore full employment. Similarly, starting from a position of *above full-employment equilibrium*, a decrease in aggregate demand decreases real GDP and can, if the size of the policy action is well judged, eliminate an *inflationary gap*. Because either a fiscal policy or a monetary policy action can achieve these objectives, the two policies can (in principle) be combined to also achieve the same outcome.

If either or both policies can restore full employment and eliminate inflation, why does it matter which policy is used? It matters because the two policies have different side effects – different effects on other variables about which people care. These side effects of policy work through two key variables and have:

◆ Interest rate effects
◆ Exchange rate effects

Interest Rate Effects

An expansionary fiscal policy *raises* the interest rate while an expansionary monetary policy *lowers* the interest rate. When the interest rate changes, investment changes, so an expansionary fiscal policy decreases investment (crowding out) while an expansionary monetary policy increases investment. So if an expansionary fiscal policy increases aggregate demand, consumption expenditure increases and investment decreases. But if an expansionary monetary policy increases aggregate

demand, consumption expenditure and investment increase.

By coordinating fiscal policy and monetary policy and increasing aggregate demand with an appropriate combination of the two, it is possible to increase real GDP and lower unemployment with either no change in the interest rate or with any desired change in the interest rate. A big dose of fiscal expansion and a small dose of monetary expansion raises the interest rate and decreases investment, while a small dose of fiscal expansion and a big dose of monetary expansion lowers the interest rate and increases investment.

The interest rate affects our long-term growth prospects because the growth rate of potential GDP depends on the amount of investment. The connection between investment, capital and growth is explained in Chapter 23, pp. 515–517.

Exchange Rate Effects

An expansionary fiscal policy raises not only the interest rate but also the exchange rate. In contrast, an expansionary monetary policy *lowers* the exchange rate. When the exchange rate changes, net exports change. An expansionary fiscal policy decreases net exports (international crowding out), while an expansionary monetary policy increases net exports. So if full employment is restored by expansionary policy, net exports decrease with fiscal expansion and increase with monetary expansion.

Policy Conflict

Policy conflicts are not planned. But they can happen. When they arise, it is usually because of a divergence of the political priorities of the government and the objectives of the central bank.

Governments pay a lot of attention to employment and production over a short time horizon. They look for policies that make their re-election chances high. Central banks pay a lot of attention to price level stability and have a long time horizon. They don't have an election to worry about.

So a situation might arise in which the government wants the central bank to pursue an expansionary monetary policy but the central bank wants to keep its foot on the monetary brake. The government says that a lower interest rate and exchange rate are essential to boost investment and exports. The central bank says that the problem is with fiscal policy. Spending is too high and revenues too low. With fiscal policy too expansionary, the interest rate and the exchange rate are high and they cannot be lowered permanently by monetary policy. To lower the interest rate and give investment and exports a boost, fiscal policy must become contractionary. Only then can an expansionary monetary policy be pursued.

A further potential conflict between a government and its central bank concerns the financing of the government deficit. A government deficit can be financed either by borrowing from the general public or by borrowing from the central bank. If the government borrows from the general public, it must pay interest on its debt. If it borrows from the central bank, it pays interest to the bank. But the government owns the bank, so the interest comes back to the government.

But when the central bank buys government debt, it pays for the debt with a newly created monetary base. The quantity of money increases. And such finance leads to inflation. In many countries, for example in Eastern Europe, Latin America and Africa, government deficits have been financed by the central bank.

In the United Kingdom, government deficits have not been financed by the Bank of England. Indeed, the requirement for the Bank of England to achieve an inflation target along with its independence to pursue that target makes it very unlikely that a United Kingdom government would easily follow the Latin American path.

The "Stability and Growth Pact" of the Eurozone (see Box 28.1) is an attempt to avoid conflict.

Box 28.1
EU Stability and Growth Pact

The potential for conflict between fiscal policy and monetary policy is greater in the Eurozone than in the United Kingdom. The key reason is that in the United Kingdom, the government ultimately controls the central bank while in the Eurozone, the governments of the member states do not control the European Central Bank (ECB). To avoid conflict, membership of the European Monetary Union (EMU) imposes fiscal constraints on individual countries.

In 1997, the European Council resolved by treaty to ensure that the national budgetary policies of EMU countries will support the ECB's monetary policy of a target inflation rate of less than 2 per cent a year.

The Stability and Growth Pact states that member countries of the Eurozone will aim to have a balanced fiscal budget. Countries that have a budget deficit in excess of 3 per cent of GDP will be fined up to 0.5 per cent of GDP, except if a natural disaster or a severe recession occurs and real GDP falls by more than 2 per cent in a year.

The provisions of the Stability and Growth Pact appear draconian in its measure, but there are good arguments as to why fiscal policy might need to be constrained in the EMU.

For example, if one country conducts an expansionary fiscal policy, aggregate demand in that country will increase and so will the demand for money in both that country and the whole Eurozone. The increase in the demand for money will raise the interest rate, which will lead to an appreciation of the euro exchange rate against the US dollar. Exports from all Eurozone countries will decrease. In addition, the higher interest rate will reduce interest-sensitive expenditure in all Eurozone countries, not only the country with expansionary fiscal policy. So the country that adopts an expansionary fiscal policy will gain at the expense of those that do not.

If the expansionary fiscal policy creates a budget deficit, the increased borrowing to cover the deficit will lead to a higher interest rate in the Eurozone. Countries hurt by the higher interest rate might attempt to pressure the ECB into increasing the quantity of money and lowering the interest rate. The Stability and Growth Pact can interfere with the automatic fiscal policy that occurs as the economy goes into a downturn.

Creating a Stability and Growth Pact is easy. Enforcing it is turning out to be harder. France and Germany, the two largest members of the EMU, are in breach of the Stability and Growth Pact.

Review Quiz

1   What are the main things that can be achieved by coordinating fiscal policy and monetary policy?

2   What are the main sources of conflict in policy between the central bank and the government?

3   Explain what happens if the government pursues an expansionary fiscal policy while the central bank pursues a contractionary monetary policy.

4   Explain how inflation can be avoided despite a government building up a large budget deficit.

Reading Between the Lines on pp. 642–643 looks at the interaction of the Bank of England's monetary policy and the UK government's fiscal policy in 2004.

Reading Between the Lines

Fiscal and Monetary Policy Conflict

The Economist, 31 July 2004

Boom, bust and hubris

Gordon Brown, Britain's chancellor of the exchequer, has recently developed a worrying tendency to boast about his economic record. It's the longest period of sustained growth in the past 200 years, he says, extolling the "British model" to other countries as an example of how to run an economy properly, with monetary and fiscal policy working together to achieve stability and growth.

But every triumph has a price tag. The success in avoiding recession meant that the economy built up little spare capacity during the slowdown. So this time, unlike in previous recoveries, there is less scope for a bout of rapid growth in which excess supply keeps inflation at bay.

That is why the latest economic figures will worry the Bank of England's monetary policy committee when it considers its next decision on interest rates. GDP increased by 3.7% in the year to the second quarter. That was not just the fastest growth in almost four years, it was also well above the underlying economic growth rate of around 2.5%.

June figures show . . . monetary and fiscal policy are no longer working together to achieve stability. Instead they are pulling in different directions. Fiscal policy remains highly expansionary, the budget deficit will remain around 3% of GDP this year and the next. That's because, with an election looming in summer 2005, the chancellor has run scared of new tax increases. This shifts the burden of reining in the economy to the Bank of England, which has to raise interest rates more than would otherwise be the case.

The Essence of the Story

◆ Mr. Gordon Brown, the British Minister of Finance, is saying that UK fiscal and monetary policy are working together to achieve stability and growth.

◆ The success of avoiding recession means that the UK economy has built up little spare capacity during the slowdown.

◆ The UK government fiscal policy has remained expansionary with the government budget expected to remain at 3 per cent of GDP in 2004.

◆ An election is expected in 2005, so Mr. Brown is reluctant to raise taxes, which shifts the burden of reining in the economy to the Bank of England.

643

Economic Analysis

◆ The Bank of England's objective is to keep the inflation rate below 2.5 per cent a year.

◆ The UK government has embarked on a strong expansionary fiscal policy before the election in 2005.

◆ Figure 1 shows the growth rate of real GDP and the government forecast of real GDP growth the last quarter of 2004. The figure also shows the Bank of England's interest rate and the consensus forecast for interest rates for the last quarter of 2004.

◆ Expansionary fiscal policy will increase aggregate demand. If the economy is at potential GDP, the increase in aggregate demand will shift the aggregate demand curve in Figure 2 from AD_{03} to AD_{04}.

◆ To achieve its inflation target, the Bank of England will be forced to decrease the supply of money and raise the interest rate, which will decrease aggregate demand and shift the aggregate demand curve leftward.

◆ The contractionary monetary policy will offset the expansionary fiscal policy. Monetary policy and fiscal policy will be in conflict.

◆ The policy conflict will result in complete crowding out and no increase in real GDP – the higher interest rate decreases interest-sensitive expenditure by the same amount as fiscal policy has increased autonomous expenditure.

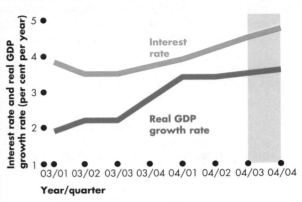

Figure 1 Interest rate and real GDP growth

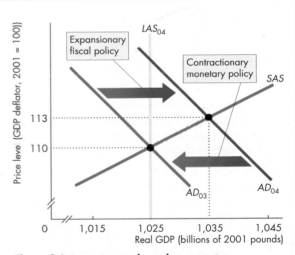

Figure 2 Aggregate supply and aggregate demand in 2004

Summary

Key Points

Macroeconomic Equilibrium
(pp. 626–627)

◆ Equilibrium real GDP, the price level and the interest rate are determined simultaneously by equilibrium in the money market and equality of aggregate demand and aggregate supply.

Fiscal Policy in the Short Run
(pp. 628–631)

◆ The first round effects of an expansionary fiscal policy are an increase in aggregate demand, increasing real GDP, and a rising price level.

◆ The second round effects are an increasing demand for money and a decreasing supply of (real) money that limit the increase in real GDP and the rise in the price level.

◆ Interest-sensitive expenditure, which includes investment and net exports, decreases.

Monetary Policy in the Short Run
(pp. 632–635)

◆ The first round effects of an expansionary monetary policy are a fall in the interest rate, an increase in aggregate demand, an increasing real GDP and a rising price level.

◆ The second round effects are an increasing demand for money and a decreasing supply of (real) money that limit the increase in real GDP and the rise in the price level.

◆ Interest-sensitive expenditure, which includes investment and net exports, increases.

Relative Effectiveness of Policies
(pp. 635–637)

◆ The relative effectiveness of fiscal and monetary policy depends on the interest-sensitivity of expenditure and the demand for money.

◆ The extreme Keynesian position is that only fiscal policy affects aggregate demand. The extreme monetarist position is that only monetary policy affects aggregate demand. Neither extreme is correct.

◆ The mix of fiscal and monetary policy influences the composition of aggregate demand.

Policy Actions at Full Employment
(pp. 638–639)

◆ An expansionary fiscal policy at full employment increases real GDP and the price level in the short run but increases only the price level in the long run. Complete crowding of investment occurs or the international deficit increases.

◆ An expansionary monetary policy at full employment increases real GDP and the price level in the short run but increases only the price level in the long run. Money is neutral – has no real effects – in the long run.

Policy Coordination and Conflict
(pp. 640–641)

◆ Policy coordination can make changes in the interest rate and the exchange rate small.

◆ Policy conflict can avoid inflation in the face of a government deficit.

Key Figures

Key Terms

Problems

*1 In the economy described in Figure 28.1, suppose the government decreases its expenditures on goods and services by £100 billion.

   a Work out the first round effects.

   b Explain how real GDP and the interest rate change.

   c Explain the second round effects that take the economy to a new equilibrium.

2 In the economy described in Figure 28.1, suppose the government increases its expenditures on goods and services by £25 billion.

   a Work out the first round effects.

   b Explain how real GDP and the interest rate change.

   c Explain the second round effects that take the economy to a new equilibrium.

   d Compare the equilibrium in this case with the one described in the chapter on pp. 628–629. In which case does the interest rate change by most? Why?

*3 In the economy described in Figure 28.1, suppose the Bank of England decreases the money supply by £450 billion.

   a Work out the first round effects.

   b Explain how real GDP and the interest rate change.

   c Explain the second round effects that take the economy to a new equilibrium.

4 In the economy described in Figure 28.1, suppose the Bank of England increases the supply of real money by £250 billion.

   a Work out the first round effects.

   b Explain how real GDP and the interest rate change.

   c Explain the second round effects that take the economy to a new equilibrium.

   d Compare the equilibrium in this case with the one described in the chapter on pp. 632–634. In which case does real GDP change by most? In which case does the interest rate change by most? Why?

*5 The economies of two countries, Alpha and Beta, are identical in every way except the following: in Alpha, a change in the interest rate of 1 percentage point

(e.g. from 5 per cent to 6 per cent) results in a €1 billion change in the quantity of real money demanded. In Beta, a change in the interest rate of 1 percentage point results in a €0.1 billion change in the quantity of real money demanded.

   a In which economy does an increase in government expenditures on goods and services have a larger effect on real GDP?

   b In which economy is the crowding-out effect weaker?

   c In which economy does a change in the money supply have a larger effect on equilibrium real GDP?

   d Which economy, if either, is closer to the Keynesian extreme and which is closer to the monetarist extreme?

6 The economies of two countries, Gamma and Delta, are identical in every way except the following: in Gamma, a change in the interest rate of 1 percentage point (e.g. from 5 per cent to 6 per cent) results in a €0.1 billion change in interest-sensitive expenditure. In Delta, a change in the interest rate of 1 percentage point results in a €10 billion change in interest-sensitive expenditure.

   a In which economy does an increase in government expenditures on goods and services have a larger effect on real GDP?

   b In which economy is the crowding-out effect weaker?

   c In which economy does a change in the money supply have a larger effect on equilibrium real GDP?

   d Which economy, if either, is closer to the Keynesian extreme and which is closer to the monetarist extreme?

*7 The economy is in a recession and the government wants to increase aggregate demand, stimulate exports and increase investment. It has three policy options: increase government expenditures on goods and services, decrease taxes and increase the supply of money.

   a Explain the mechanisms at work under each alternative policy.

   b What is the effect of each policy on the composition of aggregate demand?

   c What are the short-run effects of each policy on real GDP and the price level?

   d Which policy would you recommend that the government adopt? Why?

---

*Solutions to odd-numbered problems are available on *Parkin Interactive*.

8 The economy has an inflationary gap and the government wants to decrease aggregate demand, cut exports and decrease investment. It has three policy options: decrease government expenditures on goods and services, increase taxes and decrease the supply of money.

a Explain the mechanisms at work under each alternative policy.

b What is the effect of each policy on the composition of aggregate demand?

c What are the short-run effects of each policy on real GDP and the price level?

d Which policy would you recommend and why?

*9 The economy is at full employment, but the government is disappointed with the growth rate of real GDP. It wants to increase real GDP growth by stimulating investment. At the same time, it wants to avoid an increase in the price level.

a Suggest a combination of fiscal and monetary policies that will achieve the government's objective.

b Which policy would you recommend that the government adopt?

c Explain the mechanisms at work under your recommended policy.

d What is the effect of your recommended policy on the composition of aggregate demand?

e What are the short-run and long-run effects of your recommended policy on real GDP and the price level?

10 The economy is at full employment, and the government is worried that the growth rate of real GDP is too high because it is depleting the country's natural resources. The government wants to lower real GDP growth by lowering investment. At the same time it wants to avoid a fall in the price level.

a Suggest a combination of fiscal and monetary policies that will achieve the government's objective.

b Which policy would you recommend that the government adopt?

c Explain the mechanisms at work under your recommended policy.

d What is the effect of your recommended policy on the composition of aggregate demand?

e What are the short-run and long-run effects of your recommended policy on real GDP and the price level?

Critical Thinking

1 Study *Reading Between the Lines* on pp. 642–643 and then answer the following questions:

a What is happening to fiscal policy in the United Kingdom? What is the budget deficit expected to be in 2004 and 2005 as per cent of GDP?

b What is the objective of the Bank of England's monetary policy?

c What happened to real GDP growth in the United Kingdom in 2003 and 2004?

d Has the increase in real GDP been caused by the expansionary fiscal policy alone?

e What policy has the Bank of England taken in response to increasing growth?

d What in your opinion is the likely outcome of both the government and Bank of England policies on real GDP and inflation?

Web Exercise

Use the link on *Parkin Interactive* to work the following exercise.

1 Visit the website of Office for National Statistics and look at the current economic conditions. On the basis of the current state of the UK economy, and in the light of what you now know about fiscal and monetary policy interaction, what do you predict would happen to real GDP and the price level:

a If the Bank of England conducted an expansionary monetary policy?

b If the Bank of England conducted a contractionary monetary policy?

c If the government conducted an expansionary fiscal policy?

d If the government conducted a contractionary fiscal policy?

e If the Bank of England conducted an expansionary monetary policy and the government conducted a contractionary fiscal policy?

f If the Bank of England conducted a contractionary monetary policy and the government conducted an expansionary fiscal policy.

CHAPTER 28 APPENDIX
The *IS–LM* Model of Aggregate Demand

After studying this appendix, you will be able to:

◆ Explain the purpose and origin of the *IS–LM* model

◆ Define and derive the *IS* curve

◆ Define and derive the *LM* curve

◆ Define and derive *IS–LM* equilibrium

◆ Use the *IS–LM* model to analyze the relative effectiveness of fiscal policy and monetary policy

◆ Use the *IS–LM* model to derive the aggregate demand curve

Purpose and Origin of the *IS–LM* Model

This appendix explains a neat way of summarizing what you've learned about aggregate demand. Before we get into the details of the *IS–LM* model, we'll examine its purpose and origin.

Purpose of the *IS–LM* Model

The purpose of the *IS–LM* model is two-fold:

1 To provide a tool for analyzing fiscal policy and monetary policy

2 To derive the aggregate demand curve

In Chapter 22, you saw the importance of distinguishing between aggregate demand and the quantity of real GDP demanded at a given price level. And you learned why the aggregate demand curve slopes downward and what makes it shift.

In Chapter 24, you learned that each point on the aggregate demand curve corresponds to a point of equilibrium expenditure – a point at which the *AE* curve intersects the 45 degree line (Figure 24.9, p. 542). In deriving the *AD* curve, we noted that there is a different

AE curve for each price level. The *IS–LM* model breaks the source of the shift in the *AE* curve into two parts:

1 The effect of the interest rate on spending plans

2 The effect of the price level on the interest rate.

In Chapter 25, you saw how fiscal policy influences aggregate demand. Then in Chapters 26 and 27 you saw that spending plans depend on the interest rate. We summarized this effect with the interest-sensitive expenditure curve. You also saw how monetary policy influences the interest rate and spending.

Once money becomes a central part of the story about how aggregate demand is determined, things get a bit complicated. The source of the complication is that everything seems to depend on everything else! Spending plans depend on real GDP and the interest rate. In equilibrium, planned spending equals real GDP but because planned spending depends on the interest rate, we need to know how the interest rate is determined.

You've seen how the demand for money and the supply of money determine the interest rate. But the quantity of real money that people plan to hold depends on real GDP. So to determine the interest rate, that we need to determine real GDP, we need to know real GDP! We seem to be going around in a circle.

The *IS–LM* model cuts through the complexity of combining spending plans and money holding plans and shows us how both real GDP and the interest rate are determined simultaneously by equilibrium expenditure and money market equilibrium.

By using a model that simultaneously determines real GDP and the interest rate, we can see how fiscal policy and monetary policy influence both these variables. We can also see why fiscal policy and monetary policy might come into conflict and need to be coordinated.

Origin of the *IS–LM* Model

The *IS–LM* model was invented by John Hicks, of Oxford University, one of the greatest economists of the twentieth century. The model is a logically coherent clarification of the confusing prose written by John Maynard Keynes in his *General Theory of Employment, Interest and Money*. Hicks cut through the mystery of the *General Theory* and although Keynes never acknowledged that Hick had correctly interpreted his words, almost every other economist believed that he had done so. Hicks' *IS–LM* model became the core model for macroeconomic policy analysis.

The *IS* Curve

The **IS curve** shows combinations of real GDP and the interest rate at which aggregate planned expenditure equals real GDP. Figure A28.1 derives the *IS* curve.

Each row of the table is an aggregate expenditure schedule. Aggregate expenditure depends on the interest rate: as the interest rate decreases aggregate expenditure increases. Part (a) shows an *AE* curve for each interest rate. When the interest rate is 6 per cent a year (row *A*), the aggregate expenditure curve is AE_A. The curves AE_B

and AE_C correspond to rows *B* and *C* of the table. Each *AE* curve generates equilibrium expenditure. On AE_A, equilibrium expenditure is £800 billion at point *A*. On AE_B and AE_C, equilibrium expenditure is at points *B* and *C*.

Part (b) shows the *IS* curve – equilibrium expenditure at each interest rate. Point *A* on the *IS* curve corresponds to point *A* in part (a). It tells us that if the interest rate is 6 per cent a year, the equilibrium expenditure occurs at a real GDP of £800 billion. Points *B* and *C* on the *IS* curve illustrate the equilibrium expenditure at points *B* and *C* in part (a).

Figure A28.1

Aggregate Planned Expenditure and the *IS* Curve

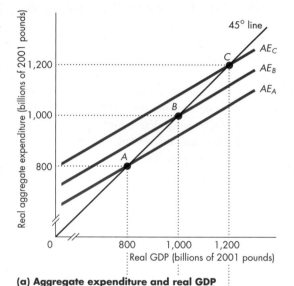

(a) Aggregate expenditure and real GDP

The table shows aggregate planned expenditure that occurs at different combinations of the interest rate and real GDP. Each of rows *A*, *B* and *C* represents an aggregate expenditure schedule, which is plotted as the aggregate expenditure curves AE_A, AE_B and AE_C, respectively, in part (a).

Equilibrium expenditure occurs in part (a), where these *AE* curves intersect the 45° line and are marked *A*, *B* and *C*. Part (b) shows these same equilibrium positions but highlights the combinations of the interest rate and the real GDP at which they occur. The green squares show equilibrium expenditure. The line connecting these points is the *IS* curve.

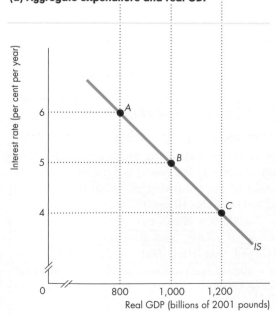

	Interest rate (per cent per year)	Autonomous expenditure (billions of 2001 pounds)		Aggregate planned expenditure (billions of 2001 pounds)		
A	6	200		800	950	1,100
B	5	250		850	1,000	1,150
C	4	300		900	1,050	1,200

Induced expenditure		600	750	900
Real GDP (billions of 2001 pounds)		800	1,000	1,200

(b) The *IS* curve

The *LM* Curve

The **LM curve** shows the combinations of real GDP and the interest rate at which the quantity of real money demanded equals the quantity of real money supplied. Figure A28.2 derives the *LM* curve.

Each column of the table is a demand for money schedule. The demand for money depends on real GDP: as real GDP increases the demand for money increases. Part (a) shows an *MD* curve for each real GDP. When real GDP is £800 billion (column *D*), the demand for money curve is MD_D. Demand for money curves MD_E and MD_F correspond to columns *E* and *F* of the table.

Each *MD* curve generates an equilibrium interest rate. On MD_D, money market equilibrium is at point *D*, where the interest rate is 4 per cent a year. On MD_E and MD_F, money market equilibrium is at points *E* and *F*.

Part (b) shows the *LM* curve – equilibrium real GDP at each interest rate. Point *D* on the *LM* curve corresponds to point *D* in part (a). It tells us that if the interest rate is 4 per cent a year, the quantity of money demanded equals the quantity of money supplied at a real GDP of £800 billion. Points *E* and *F* in part (b) on the *LM* curve illustrate money market equilibrium at points *E* and *F* in part (a).

Figure A28.2

The Money Market and the *LM* Curve

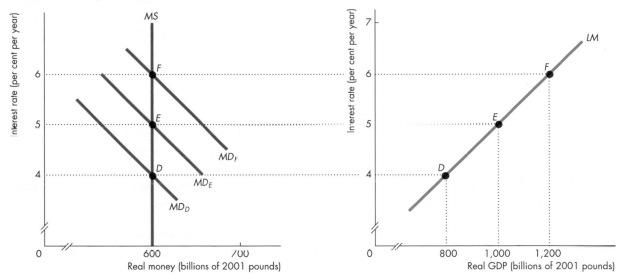

(a) Money market equilibrium

(b) The *LM* curve

The table shows the quantity of real money demanded at different combinations of the interest rate and real GDP. Money market equilibrium – equality between the quantity of real money demanded and supplied – is shown by the green squares. Each of the columns *D*, *E* and *F* represents a demand for real money schedule, plotted as the demand for real money curves MD_D, MD_E and MD_F, respectively, in part (a). Money market equilibrium occurs at points *D*, *E* and *F*. Part (b) shows these equilibrium points but highlights the combinations of the interest rate and real GDP at which they occur. The line connecting these points is the *LM* curve.

Interest rate (per cent per year)	Quantity of real money demanded (billions of 2001 pounds)		
6	500	540	600
5	550	600	660
4	600	660	730
Real GDP	800	1,000	1,200

Real money supply (billions of 2001 pounds)	600	600	600
	D	*E*	*F*

IS–LM Equilibrium

The *IS* curve and the *LM* curve determine the equilibrium interest rate and real GDP at a given price level. Figure A28.3 brings together the *IS* curve and the *LM* curve and shows the *IS–LM* equilibrium – at the intersection of the *IS* curve and *LM* curve.

At point *B* on the *IS* curve, aggregate planned expenditure equals real GDP. At point *E* on the *LM* curve, the quantity of real money demanded equals the quantity of real money supplied. At this intersection point, the equilibrium interest rate is 5 per cent a year and real GDP is £1,000 billion.

All other points are either off the *IS* curve or off the *LM* curve. At points off the *IS* curve, aggregate planned expenditure does not equal real GDP. And at points off the *LM* curve are points at which the money market is not in equilibrium.

Figure A28.3

IS–LM Equilibrium

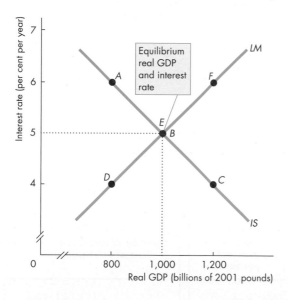

All points on the *IS* curve are points where aggregate planned expenditure equals real GDP. All points on the *LM* curve are points at which the quantity of real money demanded equals the quantity of real money supplied. The intersection of the *IS* curve on the *LM* curve determines the equilibrium interest rate and real GDP – 5 per cent a year and £1,000 billion. At this interest rate and real GDP, there is equilibrium in the goods market and the money market.

IS–LM Policy Analysis

We can use the *IS–LM* model to analyse the effects of fiscal policy and monetary policy on real GDP and the interest rate (at a given price level).

Fiscal Policy

A change in government expenditures or autonomous taxes shifts the *IS* curve, but with a given monetary policy, the *LM* curve does not change. If the government conducts an expansionary fiscal policy, the *IS* curve shifts rightward from IS_0 to IS_1 in Figure A28.4(a). The interest rate rises and real GDP increases.

The increase in real GDP is less than the shift in the *IS* curve. The reason is that the rise in the interest rate leads to a decrease in interest-sensitive expenditure, which partially offsets the increase in aggregate expenditure created by the expansionary fiscal policy – what is called partial crowding out.

Monetary Policy

Along the *LM* curve the quantity of money supplied is constant. If the Bank of England changes the quantity of money, the *LM* curve shifts and the interest rate adjusts to restore money market equilibrium. But other changes occur when the Bank of England conducts an expansionary monetary policy and the *IS–LM* model shows these changes.

An increase in the quantity of money shifts the *LM* curve rightward and with a given fiscal policy, the *IS* curve does not change. The *LM* curve shifts from LM_0 to LM_1 in Figure 28.4(b). The interest rate falls and real GDP increases. Real GDP increases because the lower interest rate induced by the expansionary monetary policy increases the amount of interest-sensitive expenditure.

Two Extreme Cases

An extreme Keynesian outcome occurs when the *LM* curve is horizontal (LM_H). The *LM* curve is horizontal only if there is a "liquidity trap" – a situation when people are willing to hold any quantity of money at a specific rate of interest. The extreme monetarist case occurs when the *LM* curve is vertical (LM_V) – the demand for money is insensitive to the interest rate. Expansionary fiscal policy shifts the *IS* curve rightward from IS_0 to IS_1 in parts (c) and (d) of Figure A28.4.

Figure A28.4

Fiscal Policy and Monetary Policy

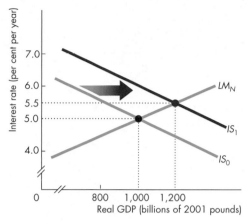

(a) Fiscal policy: normal case

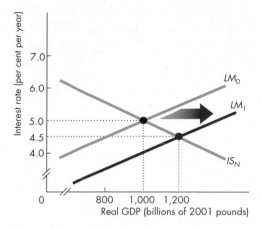

(b) Monetary policy: normal case

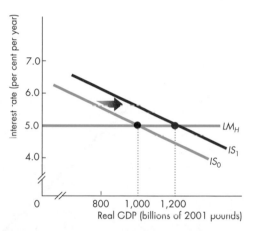

(c) Fiscal policy: maximum effect on GDP

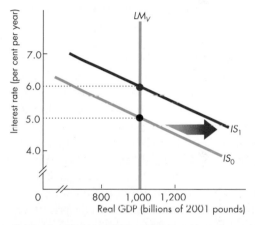

(d) Fiscal policy: no effect on GDP

In part (a), expansionary fiscal policy shifts the *IS* curve rightward. The interest rate rises and real GDP increases. In part (b), expansionary monetary policy shifts the *LM* curve rightward. The interest rate falls and real GDP increases. In part (c), the *LM* curve is horizontal – extreme Keynesian case. Expansionary fiscal policy does not change the interest rate and no crowding out occurs. In part (d), the *LM* curve is vertical – extreme monetarist case. Expansionary fiscal policy increases the interest rate and complete crowding out occurs.

In the extreme Keynesian case in part (c), the interest rate does not change and real GDP increases by the same amount as the shift of the *IS* curve. Crowding out does not occur.

In the extreme monetarist case in part (d), the interest rate rises and real GDP does not change. The higher interest rate reduces interest-sensitive expenditure by an amount equal to the initial increase in aggregate expenditure. Complete crowding out occurs because the demand for money is completely insensitive to the interest rate.

The extreme monetarist case shows that fiscal policy is completely ineffective and the extreme Keynesian case shows that fiscal policy is fully effective.

In contrast to fiscal policy, you can see that in the extreme Keynesian case monetary policy is ineffective. In Figure A28.4(c), the *LM* curve is horizontal, which tells us that any increase in the quantity of money is willingly held – the demand for money is perfectly elastic – at the specific interest rate. So an increase in the quantity of money with a given fiscal policy (*IS* curve) will not bring about a fall in the interest rate. Real GDP will remain the same.

In the extreme monetarist case in Figure A28.4(d), an increase in the quantity of money shifts the *LM* curve rightward. With a given fiscal policy (*IS* curve), the interest rate falls and real GDP increases.

The Aggregate Demand Curve

We can use the *IS–LM* model to derive the aggregate demand curve. In the example on pp. 648–650, the quantity of real money is £600 billion. Suppose that the quantity of *nominal* money is £660 billion and the price level is 110. If the price level was 120, the quantity of real money would be £550 billion. (£660 billion divided by 120 multiplied by 100 = £550 billion.) And if the price level was 100, the quantity of real money would be £660.

Because there is a different quantity of real money for each price level, there is a different *LM* curve at each price level. Figure A28.5(a) illustrates the *LM* curves for the three price levels we've just considered.

The initial *LM* curve has the price level of 110. This *LM* curve is labelled LM_0 in Figure A28.5(a). When the price level is 120 and real GDP is £1,000 billion, the interest rate that achieves money market equilibrium is 6 per cent a year at point *G*. The entire *LM* curve shifts leftward to LM_1 to pass through point *G*.

When the price level is 100 and real GDP is £1,000 billion, the interest rate that achieves money market equilibrium is 4 per cent a year at point *H* in Figure A28.5(a). Again, the entire *LM* curve shifts rightward to LM_2 to pass through point *H*.

Because there are three *LM* curves in Figure A28.5, there are three *IS–LM* equilibrium points. When the price level is 110 and the *LM* curve is LM_0, equilibrium is at point *E* where real GDP is £1,000 billion and the interest rate is 5 per cent a year. When the price level is 120 and the *LM* curve is LM_1, equilibrium is at point *J* where real GDP is £900 billion and the interest rate is 5.5 per cent a year. And when the price level is 90 and the *LM* curve is LM_2, equilibrium is at point *K* where real GDP is £1,100 billion and the interest rate is 4.5 per cent a year.

At each price level there is a different equilibrium real GDP and interest rate.

Figure A28.5(b) traces the aggregate demand curve. Notice that the price level is measured on the vertical axis of part (b) and real GDP on the horizontal axis. When the price level is 110, equilibrium real GDP is £1,000 billion (point *E*). When the price level is 120, equilibrium real GDP is £900 billion (point *J*). And when the price level is 100, real GDP demanded is £1,100 billion (point *K*). Each of these points corresponds to the same point in part (a).

The line passing through points *J*, *E* and *K* in part (b) is the aggregate demand curve.

Figure A28.5

Deriving the Aggregate Demand Curve

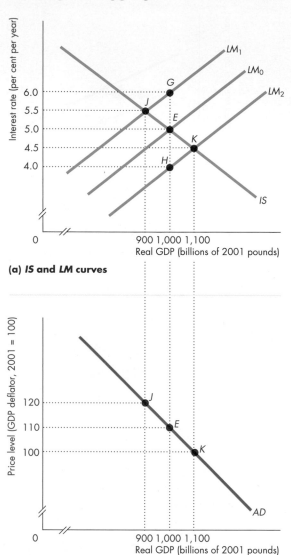

(a) *IS* and *LM* curves

(b) Aggregate demand curve

In part (a), if the price level is 110, the *LM* curve is LM_0 and *IS–LM* equilibrium occurs at point *E*. The quantity of real GDP demanded is £1,000 billion. This combination of the price level of 110 and the quantity of real GDP demanded of £1,000 billion is point *E* on the *AD* curve in part (b).

If the price level rises to 120, the *LM* curve shifts leftward to LM_1. The *IS–LM* equilibrium occurs at point *J* and a quantity of real GDP demanded of £900 billion – point *J* on the *AD* curve in part (b).

If the price level falls to 100, the *LM* curve shifts rightward to LM_2. The *IS–LM* equilibrium occurs at point *K* and a quantity of real GDP demanded of £1,100 billion – point *K* on the *AD* curve in part (b).

Chapter 29

Inflation

After studying this chapter you will be able to:

◆ Distinguish between inflation and a one-time rise in the price level and explain how demand-pull inflation and cost-push inflation are generated

◆ Explain the quantity theory of money

◆ Describe the effects of inflation

◆ Explain the short-run and long-run relationships between inflation and unemployment

◆ Explain the short-run and long-run relationships between inflation and interest rates

◆ Describe the political origins of inflation

From Rome to Russia

In the dying days of the Roman Empire (at the end of the third century AD) and in Russia's transition to a market economy (during the early 1990s), inflation ripped away at rates of more than 300 per cent a year. What causes rapid inflation? What are the effects of inflation? Does inflation bring only costs and no benefits? How can inflation be controlled? You can find the answers in this chapter and, in *Reading Between the Lines* at the end of the chapter, you'll see how Zimbabwe is struggling to contain inflation today.

Demand-pull and Cost-push Inflation

We don't have much inflation today, but during the 1970s and the late 1980s, it was a major problem. **Inflation** is a process in which the *price level is rising* and *money is losing value*.

If the price level rises persistently, then people need more and more money to make transactions. Incomes rise, so firms must pay out more in wages and other payments to owners of factors of production.

And prices rise, so consumers must take more money with them when they go shopping. But the value of money gets smaller and smaller.

Some persistent price rises occur that are not inflation. And sometimes a jump in the price level occurs that is not inflation.

Inflation versus a Rising Relative Price

A persistent tendency for a price to rise is not always a sign of inflation. For example, suppose the price of a gallon of petrol rises by 5 per cent a year but all other prices fall slightly so that the price level remains constant. In this situation, the *relative price* of petrol *is rising* but there is no inflation. Inflation is a process in which the *price level is rising*, not the price of a single (or small number) of items.

Inflation versus a Rise in the Price Level

A one-time jump in the price level is not inflation. Instead, inflation is an ongoing *process*. Figure 29.1 illustrates this distinction. The blue line shows a one-time jump in the price level. Such a jump might occur if a broad tax such as the GST increases. It might also occur if there is a one-time rise in the price of a widely used commodity such as oil. An economy in which the price level jumps like the blue line in the figure is not experiencing inflation. Its price level is constant most of the time.

The red line in Figure 29.1 shows a continuously rising price level. That is inflation. The steeper the rise of the price level, the faster is the inflation rate.

We calculate the inflation rate as the percentage increase in the price level and we generally measure the price level either as the Consumer Prices Index or the

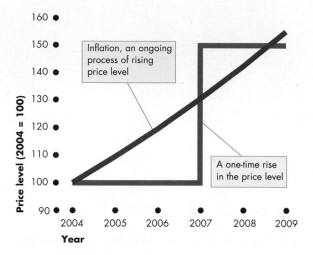

Figure 29.1

Inflation versus a One-time Rise in the Price Level

Along the red line, an economy experiences inflation because the price level rises persistently. Along the blue line, an economy experiences a one-time rise in the price level if some disturbance increases the price level but does not set off an ongoing process of a rising price level. To measure the inflation *rate*, we calculate the annual percentage change in the price level.

GDP deflator. Call the price level in the current year P_1 and the price level in the previous year P_0, then:

$$\text{Inflation rate} = \frac{P_1 - P_0}{P_0} \times 100$$

For example, if this year's price level is 111.3 and last year's price level was 106, the inflation rate is 5 per cent per year. That is:

$$\text{Inflation rate} = \frac{111.3 - 106}{106} \times 100$$

$$= 5 \text{ per cent per year}$$

This equation shows the connection between the *inflation rate* and the *price level*. For a given price level last year, the higher the price level in the current year, the higher is the inflation rate.

If the price level is *rising*, the inflation rate is *positive*. If the price level rises at a *faster* rate, the inflation rate *increases*.

Inflation can result from an increase in aggregate demand, a decrease in aggregate supply, or both. To study the forces that generate inflation, we distinguish two types of impulse that can get inflation started. These impulses are called:

◆ Demand-pull

◆ Cost-push

We'll first study a demand-pull inflation.

Demand-pull Inflation

An inflation that results from an initial increase in aggregate demand is called **demand-pull inflation**. Such an inflation may arise from any individual factor that increases aggregate demand such as:

1 An increase in the money supply

2 An increase in government expenditures

3 An increase in exports

Initial Effect of an Increase in Aggregate Demand

Suppose that last year the price level was 110, real GDP was £1,000 billion and potential GDP was also £1,000

billion. Figure 29.2(a) illustrates this situation. The aggregate demand curve is AD_0, the short-run aggregate supply curve is SAS_0 and the long-run aggregate supply curve is LAS.

In the current year, aggregate demand increases and the aggregate demand curve shifts rightward to AD_1. Such a situation arises if, for example, the Bank of England loosens its grip on the quantity of money, the government increases its expenditure on goods and services or exports increase.

With no change in potential GDP and with no change in the money wage rate, the long-run aggregate supply curve and the short-run aggregate supply curve remain at LAS and SAS_0 respectively.

The price level and real GDP are determined at the point where the aggregate demand curve AD_1 intersects the short-run aggregate supply curve. The price level rises to 113 and real GDP increases above potential GDP to £1,050 billion. The economy experiences a 2.7 per cent rise in the price level (a price level of 113 compared with 110 in the previous year) and a rapid expansion of real GDP. Unemployment falls below its natural rate. The next step in the unfolding story is a rise in the money wage rate.

Figure 29.2

A Demand-pull Rise in the Price Level

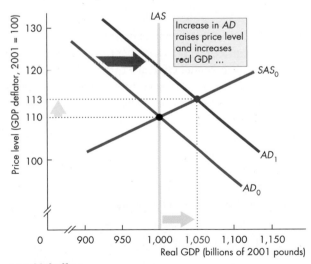

(a) Initial effect

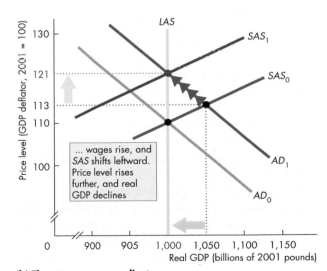

(b) The money wage adjusts

In part (a), the aggregate demand curve is AD_0, the short-run aggregate supply curve is SAS_0 and the long-run aggregate supply curve is LAS. The price level is 110 and real GDP is £1,000 billion, which equals potential GDP. Aggregate demand increases to AD_1. The price level rises

to 113 and real GDP increases to £1,050 billion. In part (b), starting from above full employment, the money wage rate begins to rise and the short-run aggregate supply curve shifts leftward towards SAS_1. The price level rises further and real GDP returns to potential GDP.

Money Wage Response

Real GDP cannot remain above potential GDP forever. With unemployment below its natural rate, there is a shortage of labour. In this situation, the money wage rate begins to rise. As the money wage rate rises, the short-run aggregate supply starts to decrease and the *SAS* curve starts to shift leftward. The price level rise further and real GDP begins to decrease.

With no further change in aggregate demand – the aggregate demand curve remains at AD_1 – this process comes to an end when the short-run aggregate demand curve has shifted to SAS_1 in Figure 29.2(b). At this time, the price level has increased to 121 and real GDP has returned to potential GDP of £1,000 billion, the level from which it started.

A Demand-pull Inflation Process

The process we've just studied eventually ends when, for a given increase in aggregate demand, the money wage rate has adjusted enough to restore the real wage rate to its full-employment level. We've studied a one-time rise in the price level like that described in Figure 29.1. For inflation to proceed, aggregate demand must persistently increase.

The only way in which aggregate demand can persistently increase is if the quantity of money persistently increases. Suppose the government has a large budget deficit that it finances by selling bonds. Also suppose that the Bank of England buys these bonds. When the Bank of England buys bond, it creates more money. In this situation, aggregate demand increases year after year. The aggregate demand curve keeps shifting rightward. This persistent increase in aggregate demand puts continual upward pressure on the price level. The economy now experiences demand-pull inflation.

Figure 29.3 illustrates the process of demand-pull inflation. The starting point is the same as that shown in Figure 29.2. The aggregate demand curve is AD_0, the short-run aggregate supply curve is SAS_0, and the long-run aggregate supply curve is *LAS*. Real GDP is £1,000 billion and the price level is 110. Aggregate demand increases, shifting the aggregate demand curve to AD_1. Real GDP increases to £1,050 billion and the price level rises to 113. The economy is at an above full-employment equilibrium. There is a shortage of labour and the money wage rate rises. The short-run aggregate supply curve shifts leftward to SAS_1. The price level rises to 121 and real GDP returns to potential GDP.

But the Bank of England increases the quantity of money again and aggregate demand continues to

Figure 29.3

A Demand-pull Inflation Spiral

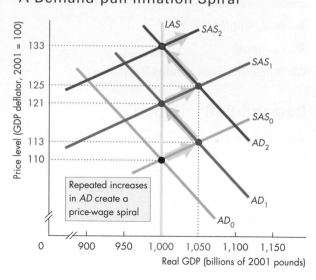

Each time the quantity of money increases, aggregate demand increases and the aggregate demand curve shifts rightward from AD_0 to AD_1 to AD_2 and so on. Each time real GDP goes above potential GDP, the money wage rate rises and the short-run aggregate supply curve shifts leftward from SAS_0 to SAS_1 to SAS_2 and so on. The price level rises from 110 to 113, 121, 125, 133 and so on. There is a perpetual demand-pull inflation. Real GDP fluctuates between £1,000 billion and £1,050 billion.

increase. The aggregate demand curve shifts rightward to AD_2. The price level rises further to 125 and real GDP again exceeds potential GDP at $1,050 billion.

Yet again, the money wage rate rises and decreases short-run aggregate supply. The *SAS* curve shifts to SAS_2 and the price level rises further to 133. As the money supply continues to grow, aggregate demand increases and the price level rises in an ongoing demand-pull inflation process.

The process you have just studied generates inflation – an ongoing process of a rising price level.

Demand-pull Inflation in Hartlepool

You may better understand the inflation process that we've just described by considering what is going on in an individual part of the economy, such as a Hartlepool soft drinks factory. Initially, when aggregate demand increases, the demand for soft drinks increases and the price of soft drinks rises. Faced with a higher price, the soft drink factory works overtime and increases production. Conditions are good for workers in Hartlepool and the soft drinks factory finds it hard to hang on to its best people. To do so it has to offer higher money wages. As money wages increase, so do the soft drinks factory's costs.

What happens next depends on what happens to aggregate demand. If aggregate demand remains unchanged, as in Figure 29.2(b), the firm's costs are increasing but the price of soft drinks is not increasing as quickly as the factory's costs. Production is scaled back. Eventually, the money wage rate and costs increase by the same percentage as the price of soft drinks. In real terms, the soft drinks factory is in the same situation as it was initially – before the increase in aggregate demand. The soft drinks factory produces the same quantity of soft drinks and employs the same amount of labour as before the increase in aggregate demand.

But if aggregate demand continues to increase, so does the demand for soft drinks and the price of lemonade rises at the same rate as the money wage rate. The soft drinks factory continues to operate above full employment and there is a persistent shortage of labour. Prices and wages chase each other upward in an unending spiral.

Demand-pull Inflation in the United Kingdom

A demand-pull inflation like the one you've just studied occurred in the United Kingdom during the 1970s.

In 1972–1973, the government pursued an expansionary monetary and fiscal policy. Its goal was to lower the unemployment rate and boost the rate of economic growth. The aggregate demand curve shifted rightward, the price level increased quickly and real GDP moved above potential GDP. The money wage rate started to rise more quickly and the short-run aggregate supply curve shifted leftward.

The Bank of England responded with a further increase in the growth rate of the quantity of money. Aggregate demand increased even more quickly and a demand-pull inflation spiral unfolded.

By the mid-1970s, the inflation rate had reached more than 20 per cent a year. Contrary to the government's goal, the growth rate of real GDP didn't increase and the unemployment rate didn't decrease. On the contrary, the late 1970s were years of extremely high unemployment and slow real GDP growth.

You've seen how demand-pull inflation arises. Let's now see how a supply shock brings cost-push inflation.

Cost-push Inflation

An inflation that results from an initial increase in costs is called **cost-push inflation**. The two main sources of increases in costs are:

1 An increase in money wage rates
2 An increase in the money prices of raw materials

At a given price level, the higher the cost of production, the smaller is the amount that firms are willing to produce. So if the money wage rate rises or if the price of a raw material (e.g. oil) rises, firms decrease their supply of goods and services. Aggregate supply decreases and the short-run aggregate supply curve shifts leftward.[1] Let's trace the effects of such a decrease in short-run aggregate supply on the price level and real GDP.

Initial Effect of a Decrease in Aggregate Supply

Suppose that last year the price level was 110 and real GDP was £1,000 billion. Potential real GDP was also £1,000 billion. Figure 29.4 (overleaf) illustrates this situation. The aggregate demand curve was AD_0, the short-run aggregate supply curve was SAS_0 and the long-run aggregate supply curve was LAS.

In the current year, the world's oil producers form a price-fixing organization that strengthens their market power and increases the relative price of oil. They raise the price of oil by a large enough percentage to bring a huge decrease in short-run aggregate supply.

The short-run aggregate supply curve shifts leftward to SAS_1. The price level rises to 117, and real GDP decreases to £950 billion. The combination of a rise in the price level and a decrease in real GDP is called *stagflation*.

This event brings a change in the relative price of oil and a one-time change in the price level, like that in Figure 29.1. It is not inflation. In fact, a supply shock *on its own* cannot cause inflation. If aggregate demand remains at AD_0, a recessionary gap eventually forces the money wage rate and all other money factor prices down and short-run aggregate supply increases. The cost-push shock brings a temporary recession but no inflation.

Something more must happen to enable a one-time supply shock, which causes a one-time rise in the price

[1] Some cost-push forces, such as an increase in the price of oil accompanied by a decrease in the availability of oil, can also decrease long-run aggregate supply. We'll ignore such effects here and examine cost-push factors that change only short-run aggregate supply.

Figure 29.4

A Cost-push Rise in the Price Level

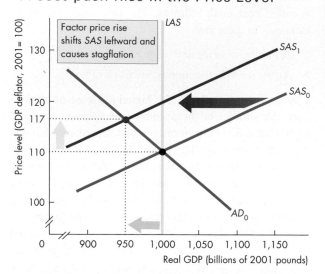

Initially, the aggregate demand curve is AD_0, the short-run aggregate supply curve is SAS_0 and the long-run aggregate supply curve is LAS. A decrease in aggregate supply (for example, resulting from an increase in the world price of oil) shifts the short-run aggregate supply curve to SAS_1. The economy moves to the point where the short-run aggregate supply curve SAS_1 intersects the aggregate demand curve AD_0. The price level rises to 117 and real GDP decreases to £950 billion. The economy experiences stagflation.

Figure 29.5

Aggregate Demand Response to Cost-push

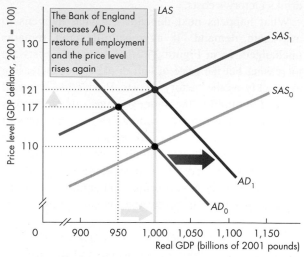

Following a cost–push increase in the price level, real GDP is below potential GDP and unemployment is above its natural rate. If the Bank of England responds by increasing aggregate demand to restore full employment, the aggregate demand curve shifts rightward to AD_1. The economy returns to full employment but the price level rises to 121.

---

level, to be converted into a process of ongoing inflation. That something more is a persistent increase in the quantity of money.

Aggregate Demand Response

When real GDP decreases, unemployment rises above the natural rate of unemployment. In such a situation, there is usually an outcry of concern and a call for action to restore full employment. Suppose that the Bank of England increases the quantity of money. Aggregate demand increases. In Figure 29.5, the aggregate demand curve shifts rightward to AD_1. The increase in aggregate demand has restored full employment. But the price level rises to 121, a 10 per cent rise over the original price level.

The beginnings of a cost-push inflation spiral are now in place. But we still don't have cost-push inflation. A further inflationary response on the cost side is needed.

A Cost-push Inflation Process

Oil producers now see the prices of everything that they buy is increasing. So they increase the price of oil again to restore its new high relative price. Figure 29.6 continues the story.

The short-run aggregate supply curve now shifts to SAS_2, and another bout of stagflation ensues. The price level rises further to 129 and real GDP decreases to £950 billion. Unemployment increases above its natural rate. If the Bank of England responds yet again with an increase in the quantity of money, aggregate demand increases and the aggregate demand curve shifts to AD_2. The price level rises even higher – to 133 – and full employment is again restored. A cost-push inflation spiral results. But if the Bank of England does not respond, the economy remains below full employment.

You can see that the Bank of England has a dilemma. If it increases the quantity of money to restore full employment, it invites another oil price hike that will call forth another increase in the quantity of money.

Figure 29.6

A Cost-push Inflation Spiral

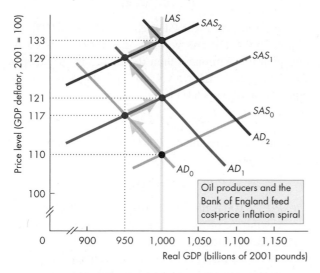

When a cost increase (for example, an increase in the world oil price) decreases short-run aggregate supply from SAS_0 to SAS_1, the price level rises to 117 and real GDP decreases to £950 billion. The central bank responds with an increase in the money supply that shifts the aggregate demand curve from AD_0 to AD_1. The price level rises again to 121 and real GDP returns to £1,000 billion. A further cost increase occurs, which shifts the short-run aggregate supply curve again, this time to SAS_2. Stagflation is repeated and the price level now rises to 129. The central bank responds again and the cost-push inflation spiral continues.

Inflation will rage along at a rate decided by the oil-exporting countries. If the Bank of England keeps the lid on money growth, the economy operates with a high level of unemployment.

Cost-push Inflation in Hartlepool

What is going on in the Hartlepool soft drinks factory when the economy is experiencing cost-push inflation? When the oil price increases, so do the costs of bottling soft drinks. These higher costs decrease the supply of soft drinks, increasing its price and decreasing the quantity produced. The soft drinks factory lays off some workers. This situation will persist until either the Bank of England increases aggregate demand or the price of oil falls. If the Bank of England increases aggregate demand, as it did in the United Kingdom in the mid-1970s, the demand for soft drinks increases and so does the price of soft drinks. The higher price of soft drinks

brings higher profits and the factory increases its production. The soft drinks factory re-hires the laid-off workers.

Cost-push Inflation in the United Kingdom

A cost-push inflation like the one you've just studied occurred in the United Kingdom during the 1970s. It began in 1974 when Organization of the Petroleum Exporting Countries (OPEC) raised the price of oil four-fold. The higher oil price decreased aggregate supply, which caused the price level to rise more quickly and real GDP to shrink. The Bank of England then faced a dilemma. Would it increase the quantity of money and accommodate the cost-push forces or would it keep aggregate demand growth in check by limiting money growth?

In 1975, 1976 and 1977, the Bank of England repeatedly allowed the quantity of money to grow fast and inflation proceeded rapidly. In 1979 and 1980, OPEC was again able to push oil prices higher. On that occasion, the Bank of England decided not to respond to the oil price hike with an increase in the quantity of money. The result was a recession but also, eventually, a fall in inflation.

Review Quiz

1 Distinguish between a rising relative price and inflation.
2 Distinguish between a one-time rise in the price level and inflation.
3 How does demand-pull inflation begin? What are the initial effects of demand-pull inflation on real GDP and the price level?
4 When real GDP exceeds potential GDP, what happens to the money wage rate and short-run aggregate supply? How do real GDP and the price level respond?
5 What must happen to create a demand-pull inflation spiral?
6 How does cost-push inflation begin? What are its initial effects on real GDP and the price level?
7 What is stagflation and why does cost-push inflation cause stagflation?
8 What must the Bank of England do to convert a one-time rise in the price level into a freewheeling cost-push inflation?

You've studied demand-pull inflation and cost-push inflation and seen that the quantity of money plays a central role. We're now going to focus on the role of money in generating inflation.

The Quantity Theory of Money

Regardless of whether it originates in a demand-pull or a cost-push impulse, to convert a one-time rise in the price level into an ongoing inflation, aggregate demand must increase. And although many factors can and do influence aggregate demand, only one factor can persistently keep aggregate demand increasing: the quantity of money. The special place of money gives rise to a special long-run theory of inflation, called the quantity theory of money.

The **quantity theory of money** is the proposition that in the long run, an increase in the quantity of money brings an equal percentage increase in the price level. The basis of the quantity theory of money is a concept known as *the velocity of circulation* and an equation called *the equation of exchange.*

The **velocity of circulation** is the average number of times a dollar of money is used annually to buy the goods and services that make up GDP. GDP equals the price level (P) multiplied by real GDP (Y). That is:

$$GDP = PY$$

Call the quantity of money M. The velocity of circulation, V, is determined by the equation:

$$V = PY/M$$

For example, if GDP is £1,000 billion ($PY = £1,000$ billion) and the quantity of money is £250 billion, the velocity of circulation is 4. (£1,000 billion divided by £250 billion equals 4.)

The **equation of exchange** states that the quantity of money (M) multiplied by the velocity of circulation (V) equals GDP. That is:

$$MV = PY$$

Given the definition of the velocity of circulation, this equation is always true – it is true by definition.

With M equal to £250 billion and V equal to 4, MV is equal to £1,000 billion, the value of GDP. The equation of exchange becomes the quantity theory of money by making two assumptions:

1 The velocity of circulation is not influenced by the quantity of money.

2 Potential GDP is not influenced by the quantity of money.

If these two assumptions are true, then the equation of exchange tells us that a change in the quantity of money brings about an equal proportional change in the price level. You can see why by solving the equation of exchange for the price level. Dividing both sides of the equation by real GDP (Y) gives:

$$P = (V/Y) \times M$$

In the long run, real GDP equals potential GDP, so if potential GDP and velocity are not influenced by the quantity of money, then the relationship between the change in the price level (ΔP) and the change in the quantity of money (ΔM) is:

$$(\Delta P) = (V/Y) \times \Delta M$$

Divide this equation by $P = (V/Y) \times M$, and multiply by 100 to get:

$$(\Delta P/P) \times 100 = (\Delta M/M) \times 100$$

$(\Delta P/P) \times 100$ is the inflation rate and $(\Delta M/M) \times 100$ is the growth rate of the quantity of money. So this equation is the quantity theory of money: the percentage increase in the price level and the percentage increase in the quantity of money are equal.

Does the Quantity Theory of Money Predict Inflation?

Figure 29.7 summarizes some UK evidence on the ability of the quantity theory of money to predict the inflation rate. The figure reveals that:

1 On average, the money growth rate exceeds the inflation rate.

2 The money growth rate is correlated with the inflation rate.

Money growth exceeds inflation because real GDP grows. Money growth that matches real GDP growth does not create inflation. But money growth in excess of real GDP growth does create inflation.

Money growth and inflation are correlated – they move up and down together. For example, the rise in the inflation rate during the 1970s and the slight rebound in inflation during the late 1980s were accompanied by a rise in the money growth rate. The decreases in the inflation rate during the 1980s and 1990s were accompanied by decreases in the money growth rate. But the correlation is not perfect. Nor does it tell us that money growth *causes* inflation.

Money growth might cause inflation; inflation might cause money growth; or some third variable might simultaneously cause inflation and money growth.

Figure 29.8 summarizes some international evidence on the quantity theory of money. It shows the inflation rate and the money growth rate for 60 countries.

Figure 29.7

Money Growth and Inflation in the United Kingdom

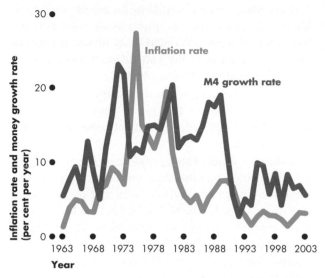

On average, the money growth rate exceeds the inflation rate because real GDP grows. Money growth and inflation are correlated – they rise and fall together.

Sources: Office for National Statistics and the Bank of England.

There is a clear tendency for high money growth to be associated with high inflation.

The evidence is strongest for the high-inflation countries shown in Figure 29.8(a), but it is also present for low-inflation countries, which are shown in Figure 29.8(b).

Review Quiz

1   What is the quantity theory of money?
2   What is the velocity of circulation of money and how is it calculated?
3   What is the equation of exchange? Can the equation of exchange be wrong?
4   What does the long-run historical evidence and international evidence on the relationship between money growth and inflation tell us about the quantity theory of money?

You've studied the *causes* of inflation and your next task is to examine its effects.

Figure 29.8

Money Growth and Inflation in the World Economy

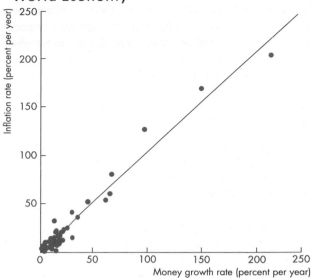

(a) Data for 60 countries during the 1980s

(in part a) and major countries and regions during the 1990s (in part b) show a positive relationship between money growth and inflation.

Sources: Federal Reserve Bank of St. Louis, *Review*, May/June 1988, p. 15 and *World Economic Outlook* data base, International Monetary Fund.

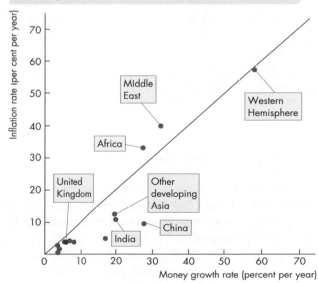

(b) 13 regions and countries during the 1990s

Inflation and money growth in 60 countries (in part a) and low-inflation countries (in part b) show a clear positive relationship between money growth and inflation.

Source: Federal Reserve Bank of St. Louis, *Review*, May/June 1988, p. 15.

Effects of Inflation

Regardless of whether inflation is demand-pull or cost-push, the failure to *anticipate* it correctly results in unintended consequences. These unintended consequences impose costs on firms and workers. Let's examine these costs.

Unanticipated Inflation in the Labour Market

Unanticipated inflation has two main consequences for the operation of the labour market. They are:

◆ Redistribution of income
◆ Departure from full employment

Redistribution of Income

Unanticipated inflation redistributes income between employers and workers. Sometimes employers gain at the expense of workers and sometimes they lose. If an unexpected increase in aggregate demand increases the inflation rate, then the money wage rate will not have been set high enough. Profits will be higher than expected and real wages will buy fewer goods than expected. In this case, employers gain at the expense of workers. But if aggregate demand is expected to increase rapidly and it fails to do so, workers gain at the expense of employers. Anticipating a high inflation rate, the money wage rate is set too high and profits are squeezed. Redistributions between employers and workers create an incentive for both firms and workers to try to forecast inflation correctly.

Departures from Full Employment

Redistribution brings gains to some and losses to others. But departures from full employment impose costs on everyone. To see why, let's return to the soft drinks factory in Hartlepool. If the soft drink factory and its workers do not anticipate inflation, but inflation occurs, the money wage rate does not rise to keep up with inflation. The real wage rate falls and the firm tries to hire more labour and increase production. But because the real wage rate has fallen, the firm has difficulty in attracting the labour it wants to employ. It pays overtime rates to its existing workforce and because it runs its factory at a faster pace, it incurs higher maintenance and parts replacement costs. But also, because the real wage

rate has fallen, workers begin to quit the soft drinks factory to find jobs that pay a real wage rate closer to that prevailing before the outbreak of inflation. This labour turnover imposes additional costs on the firm. So even though its production increases, the firm incurs additional costs and its profit does not increase. The workers incur additional costs of job search and those who remain at the soft drinks factory end up feeling cheated. They've worked overtime to produce the extra output and, when they come to spend their wages, they discover that prices have increased, so their wages buy a smaller quantity of goods and services than expected.

If the soft drinks factory and its workers anticipate a high inflation rate that does not occur, they increase the money wage rate by too much and the real wage rate rises. At the higher real wage rate, the firm lays off some workers and the unemployment rate increases. Those workers who keep their jobs gain, but those who become unemployed lose. The soft drinks factory also loses because its output and profits fall.

Unanticipated Inflation in the Capital Market

Unanticipated inflation has two consequences for the operation of the capital market. They are:

◆ Redistribution of income
◆ Too much or too little lending and borrowing

Redistribution of Income

Unanticipated inflation redistributes income between borrowers and lenders. Sometimes borrowers gain at the expense of lenders; sometimes they lose. When inflation is unexpected, interest rates are not set high enough to compensate lenders for the falling value of money and borrowers gain at the expense of lenders. If inflation is expected and does not occur, interest rates will have been set too high and lenders gain at the expense of borrowers. This unintended redistribution of income between borrowers and lenders provides incentives for both parties to try to forecast inflation correctly.

Too Much or Too Little Lending and Borrowing

If inflation turns out to be either higher or lower than expected, the interest rate does not incorporate a correct allowance for the falling value of money and the real interest rate is either lower or higher than it otherwise would be. When the real interest rate turns out to too low, which occurs when inflation is *higher* than expected, borrowers wish that they had borrowed more and lenders wish that they had lent less. Both groups would have made different lending and borrowing decisions with greater foresight about the inflation rate.

When the real interest rate turns out to too high, which occurs when inflation is *lower* than expected, borrowers wish that they had borrowed less and lenders wish that they had lent more. Again, both groups would have made different lending and borrowing decisions with greater foresight about the inflation rate.

So unanticipated inflation imposes costs regardless of whether the inflation turns out to be higher or lower than anticipated. The presence of these costs gives everyone an incentive to forecast inflation correctly. Let's see how people go about this task.

Forecasting Inflation

Inflation is difficult to forecast for two reasons. First, there are several sources of inflation – the demand-pull and cost-push sources you've just studied. Second, the speed with which a change in either aggregate demand or aggregate supply translates into a change in the price level varies. This speed of response also depends, as you will see below, on the extent to which the inflation is anticipated.

Because inflation is costly and difficult to forecast, people devote considerable resources to improving inflation forecasts. Some people specialize in forecasting, and others buy forecasts from specialists. The specialist forecasters are economists who work for public and private macroeconomic forecasting agencies and for banks, insurance companies, trade unions and large corporations. The returns these specialists make depend on the quality of their forecasts, so they have a strong incentive to forecast as accurately as possible. The most accurate forecast possible is the one that is based on all the relevant information available and is called a **rational expectation**.

A rational expectation is not necessarily a correct forecast. It is simply the best forecast available. It will often turn out to be wrong, but no other forecast that could have been made with the information available could be predicted to be better.

You've seen the effects of inflation when people fail to anticipate it. You've also seen why it pays to try and anticipate inflation. Let's now see what happens if inflation is correctly anticipated.

Anticipated Inflation

In the demand-pull and cost-push inflations that we studied earlier in this chapter, the money wage rate is sticky. When aggregate demand increases, either to set off a demand-pull inflation or to accommodate a cost-push inflation, the money wage rate does not change immediately. But if people correctly anticipate increases in aggregate demand, they will adjust the money wage rate so as to keep up with anticipated inflation.

In this case, inflation proceeds with real GDP equal to potential GDP and unemployment equal to the natural rate of unemployment. Figure 29.9 explains why. Suppose that last year the price level was 110 and real GDP was £1,000 billion, which is also potential GDP. The aggregate demand curve was AD_0, the aggregate supply curve was SAS_0 and the long-run aggregate supply curve was LAS.

Suppose that potential GDP does not change, so the LAS curve does not shift. Also suppose that aggregate demand is expected to increase and that the expected aggregate demand curve for this year is AD_1. In anticipation of the increase in aggregate demand, the money wage rate rises and the short-run aggregate supply curve shifts leftward. If the money wage rate rises by the same percentage as the price level rises, the short-run aggregate supply for next year is SAS_1.

If aggregate demand turns out to be the same as expected, the aggregate demand curve is AD_1. The short-run aggregate supply curve SAS_1 and AD_1 determine the actual price level at 121. Between last year and this year, the price level increased from 110 to 121 and the economy experienced an inflation rate of 10 per cent, the same as the inflation rate that was anticipated. If this anticipated inflation is ongoing, in the following year aggregate demand increases (as anticipated) and the aggregate demand curve shifts to AD_2. The money wage rate rises to reflect the anticipated inflation, and the short-run aggregate supply curve shifts to SAS_2. The price level rises by a further 10 per cent to 133.

What has caused this inflation? The immediate answer is that because people expected inflation, they increased wages and increased prices. But the expectation was correct. Aggregate demand was expected to increase and it did increase. Because aggregate demand was *expected* to increase from AD_0 to AD_1, the short-run aggregate supply curve shifted upward from SAS_0 to SAS_1. Because aggregate demand actually did increase by the amount that was expected, the actual aggregate demand curve shifted from AD_0 to AD_1. The combination of the anticipated and actual shifts of the aggregate demand curve rightward produced an increase in the price level that was anticipated.

Only if aggregate demand growth is correctly forecasted does the economy follow the course described in Figure 29.9. If the expected growth rate of aggregate demand is different from its actual growth rate, the expected aggregate demand curve shifts by an amount different from the actual aggregate demand curve. The inflation rate departs from its expected level and, to some extent, there is unanticipated inflation.

Figure 29.9

Anticipated Inflation

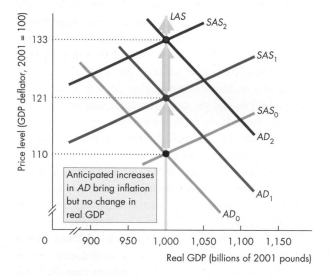

Potential real GDP is £1,000 billion. Last year, the aggregate demand curve was AD_0 and the short-run aggregate supply curve was SAS_0. The actual price level was the same as the expected price level – 110. This year, aggregate demand is expected to increase to AD_1. The rational expectation of the price level changes from 110 to 121. As a result, the money wage rate rises and the short-run aggregate supply curve shifts to SAS_1.

If aggregate demand actually increases as expected, the actual aggregate demand curve AD_1 is the same as the expected aggregate demand curve. Real GDP is £1,000 billion and the actual price level is 121. The inflation is correctly anticipated. Next year, the process continues with aggregate demand increasing as expected to AD_2 and the money wage rate rising to shift the short-run aggregate supply curve to SAS_2. Again, real GDP remains at £1,000 billion, and the price level rises, as anticipated, to 133.

Unanticipated Inflation

When aggregate demand increases by *more* than expected, there is some unanticipated inflation that looks just like demand-pull inflation that you examined earlier. Some inflation is expected and the money wage rate is set to reflect that expectation. The *SAS* curve intersects the *LAS* curve at the expected price level. Aggregate demand then increases, but by more than expected. The *AD* curve intersects the *SAS* curve at a level of real GDP that exceeds potential GDP. With real GDP above potential GDP and unemployment below the natural rate of unemployment, the money wage rate rises. So the price level rises further. If aggregate demand increases again, the demand-pull spiral unwinds.

When aggregate demand increases by *less* than expected, there is some unanticipated inflation that looks like cost-push inflation. Again, some inflation is expected and the money wage rate is set to reflect that expectation. The *SAS* curve intersects the *LAS* curve at that expected price level. Aggregate demand then increases, but by *less* than expected. So the *AD* curve intersects the *SAS* curve at a level of real GDP below potential GDP. Aggregate demand increases to restore full employment. But if aggregate demand is expected to increase by more than it actually does, the money wage rate again rises, short-run aggregate supply again decreases and a cost-push spiral unwinds.

We've seen that only when inflation is unanticipated does real GDP depart from potential GDP. When inflation is anticipated, real GDP remains at potential GDP. Does this mean that an anticipated inflation has no costs?

The Costs of Anticipated Inflation

The costs of an anticipated inflation depend on its rate. At a moderate rate of 2 to 3 per cent a year, the cost is probably small. But as the anticipated inflation rate rises, so does its cost and an anticipated inflation at a rapid rate is extremely costly.

Anticipated inflation decreases potential GDP and slows economic growth. These adverse consequences arise for three major reasons:

◆ Transactions costs

◆ Tax effects

◆ Increased uncertainty

Transactions Costs

The first transactions costs are known as the "shoe-leather costs". These are costs that arise from an increase in the velocity of circulation of money and an increase in the amount of running around that people do to try to avoid incurring losses from the falling value of money.

When money loses value at a rapid anticipated rate, it does not function well as a store of value and people try to avoid holding money. They spend their incomes as soon as they receive them, and firms pay out incomes – wages and dividends – as soon as they receive revenue from their sales. The velocity of circulation increases. During the 1920s in Germany, when inflation reached *hyperinflation* levels (rates more than 50 per cent a month), wages were paid and spent twice in a single day!

The range of estimates of the shoeleather costs is large. Some economists put them at close to zero. Others estimate them to be as much as 2 per cent of GDP for a 10 per cent inflation. For a rapid inflation, these costs are much more.

The shoeleather costs of inflation are just one of several transactions costs that are influenced by the inflation rate. At high anticipated inflation rates, people seek alternatives to money as means of payment and use tokens and commodities, or even barter, all of which are less efficient than money as a means of payment. For example, in Russia during the 1990s, when inflation reached 1,000 per cent a year, the US dollar started to replace the increasingly worthless Russian ruble. Consequently, people had to keep track of the exchange rate between the ruble and the US dollar hour by hour and had to engage in many additional and costly transactions in the foreign exchange market.

Because anticipated inflation increases transaction costs, it diverts resources from producing goods and services and it decreases potential GDP. The faster the anticipated inflation rate, the greater is the decrease in potential GDP and the further leftward does the *LAS* curve shift.

Tax Effects

Anticipated inflation interacts with the tax system and creates serious distortions in incentives. Its major effect is on real interest rates.

Anticipated inflation swells the pound returns on investments. But pound returns are taxed, so the effective tax rate rises. This effect becomes serious at even modest inflation rates. Let's consider an example.

Suppose the real interest rate is 4 per cent a year and the tax rate is 50 per cent. With no inflation, the nominal interest rate is also 4 per cent a year and 50 per cent of this rate is taxable. The real *after-tax* interest rate is 2 per cent a year (50 per cent of 4 per cent).

Now suppose the inflation rate is 4 per cent a year and the nominal interest rate is 8 per cent a year. The *after-tax* nominal rate is 4 per cent a year (50 per cent of 8 per cent). Now subtract the 4 per cent inflation rate from this amount, and you see that the *after-tax real interest rate* is zero! The true tax rate on interest income is 100 per cent.

The higher the inflation rate, the higher is the effective tax rate on income from capital. And the higher the tax rate, the higher is the interest rate paid by borrowers and the lower is the after-tax interest rate received by lenders.

With a low after-tax real interest rate, the incentive to save is weakened and the saving rate falls. With a high cost of borrowing, the amount of investment decreases. And with a fall in saving and investment, the pace of capital accumulation slows and so does the long-term growth rate of real GDP.

Increased Uncertainty

When the inflation rate is high, there is increased uncertainty about the long-term inflation rate. Will inflation remain high for a long time or will price stability be restored? This increased uncertainty makes long-term planning difficult and gives people a shorter-term focus. Investment falls and the growth rate slows.

But this increased uncertainty also misallocates resources. Instead of concentrating on the activities at which they have a comparative advantage, people find it more profitable to search for ways of avoiding the losses that inflation inflicts. As a result, inventive talent that might otherwise work on productive innovations works on finding ways of profiting from the inflation instead.

The implications of inflation for economic growth have been estimated to be enormous. Peter Howitt of Brown University, building on work by Robert Barro of Harvard University, has estimated that if inflation is lowered from 3 per cent a year to zero, the growth rate of real GDP will rise by between 0.06 and 0.09 percentage points a year. These numbers might seem small, but they are growth rates. After 30 years, real GDP would be 2.3 per cent higher and the present value of all the future output would be 85 per cent of current GDP – £850 billion! In the rapid anticipated inflations of Brazil and Russia, the costs are much greater than the numbers given here.

We've seen that an increase in aggregate demand that is not fully anticipated increases both the price level and real GDP. It also decreases unemployment. Similarly, a decrease in aggregate demand that is not fully anticipated decreases the price level and real GDP. It also increases unemployment. Do these relationships mean that there is a trade-off between inflation and unemployment? Does low unemployment always bring inflation and does low inflation bring high unemployment? Let's explore these questions.

Inflation and Unemployment: The Phillips Curve

The aggregate supply–aggregate demand model focuses on the price level and real GDP. Knowing how these two variables change, we can work out what happens to the inflation rate and the unemployment rate. But the model does not place inflation and unemployment at the centre of the stage.

A more direct way of studying inflation and unemployment uses a relationship called the Phillips curve. The Phillips curve approach uses the same basic ideas as the *AS–AD* model, but it focuses directly on inflation and unemployment. The Phillips curve is so named because it was popularized by a New Zealand economist, A.W. Phillips, when he was working at the London School of Economics in the 1950s. A **Phillips curve** is a curve showing the relationship between inflation and unemployment. There are two time-frames for Phillips curves:

◆ The short-run Phillips curve

◆ The long-run Phillips curve

The Short-run Phillips Curve

The **short-run Phillips curve** shows the relationship between inflation and unemployment, holding constant:

1 The expected inflation rate
2 The natural rate of unemployment

You've just seen what determines the expected inflation rate. The natural rate of unemployment and the factors that influence it are explained in Chapter 21, pp. 488–489.

Figure 29.10 shows a short-run Phillips curve, *SRPC*. Suppose that the expected inflation rate is 10 per cent a year and the natural rate of unemployment is 6 per cent, point *A* in the figure. A short-run Phillips curve passes through this point. If inflation rises above its expected rate, the unemployment rate falls below its natural rate.

Figure 29.10

A Short-run Phillips Curve

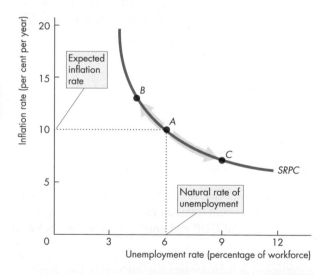

The short-run Phillips curve *SRPC* shows the relationship between inflation and unemployment at a given expected inflation rate and given natural rate of unemployment. With an expected inflation rate of 10 per cent a year and a natural rate of unemployment of 6 per cent, the short-run Phillips curve passes through point *A*. An unanticipated increase in aggregate demand lowers unemployment and increases inflation – a movement up the short-run Phillips curve. An unanticipated decrease in aggregate demand increases unemployment and lowers inflation – a movement down the short-run Phillips curve.

This joint movement in the inflation rate and the unemployment rate is illustrated as a movement up the short-run Phillips curve from point A to point B in the figure. Similarly, if inflation falls below its expected rate, unemployment rises above the natural rate. In this case, there is movement down the short-run Phillips curve from point A to point C.

This negative relationship between inflation and unemployment along the short-run Phillips curve is explained by the aggregate supply–aggregate demand model. Figure 29.11 explains the connection between the two approaches. Initially, the aggregate demand curve is AD_0, the short-run aggregate supply curve is SAS_0 and the long-run aggregate supply curve is LAS. Real GDP is £1,000 billion and the price level is 110. Aggregate demand is expected to increase and the aggregate demand curve is expected to shift rightward to AD_1.

In anticipation of this increase in aggregate demand, the money wage rate rises. The result is a leftward shift of the short-run aggregate supply curve from SAS_0 to SAS_1. What happens to actual inflation and real GDP depends on the *actual* change in aggregate demand.

First, suppose that aggregate demand actually increases by the amount expected, so the aggregate demand curve shifts to AD_1. The price level rises from 110 to 121, and the inflation rate is an anticipated 10 per cent a year. Real GDP remains at potential GDP, and unemployment remains at its natural rate – 6 per cent. The economy moves to point A in Figure 29.11 and it can equivalently be described as being at point A on the short-run Phillips curve in Figure 29.10.

Alternatively, suppose that aggregate demand is expected to increase to AD_1 but actually increases by more than expected to AD_2. The price level now rises to 124, a 13 per cent inflation rate and real GDP increases above potential GDP and unemployment falls below its natural rate. We can now describe the economy as being at point B in Figure 29.11 or at point B on the short-run Phillips curve in Figure 29.10.

Finally, suppose that aggregate demand is expected to increase to AD_1 but actually remains at AD_0. The price level now rises to 118, a 7 per cent inflation rate. Real GDP falls below potential GDP and unemployment rises above its natural rate. We can now describe the economy as being at point C in Figure 29.11 or at point C on the short-run Phillips curve in Figure 29.10.

The short-run Phillips curve is like the short-run aggregate supply curve. A movement along the SAS curve that brings a higher price level and an increase in real GDP is equivalent to a movement along the short-

Figure 29.11

AS–AD and the Short-run Phillips Curve

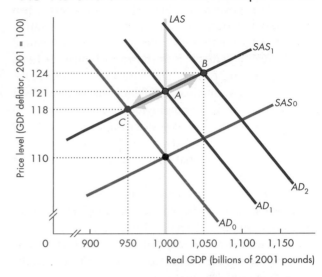

If aggregate demand is expected to increase and shift the aggregate demand curve from AD_0 to AD_1, then the money wage rate rises by an amount that shifts the short-run aggregate supply curve from SAS_0 to SAS_1. The price level rises to 121, a 10 per cent rise, and the economy is at point A in this figure and at point A on the short-run Phillips curve in Figure 29.10.

If with the same expectations, aggregate demand increases and shifts the aggregate demand curve from AD_0 to AD_2, the price level rises to 124, a 13 per cent rise, and the economy is at point B in this figure and at point B on the short-run Phillips curve in Figure 29.10. If with the same expectations, aggregate demand does not change, the price level rises to 118, a 7 per cent rise, and the economy is at point C in this figure and at point C on the short-run Phillips curve in Figure 29.10.

run Phillips curve that brings an increase in the inflation rate and a decrease in the unemployment rate.

Similarly, a movement along the SAS curve that brings a lower price level and a decrease in real GDP is equivalent to a movement along the short-run Phillips curve that brings a decrease in the inflation rate and an increase in the unemployment rate.

Because the SAS curve and the short-run Phillips curve tell the same story, we can use either to examine the inflation rate over the business cycle. The Phillips curve version is useful because it highlights fluctuations in the unemployment rate. The SAS curve version is useful because it highlights the central role of the sticky money wage rate.

The Long-run Phillips Curve

The **long-run Phillips curve** is a curve that shows the relationship between inflation and unemployment, when the actual inflation rate equals the expected inflation rate. The long-run Phillips curve is vertical at the natural rate of unemployment. It is shown in Figure 29.12 as the vertical line *LRPC*. The long-run Phillips curve tells us that any anticipated inflation rate is possible at the natural rate of unemployment. This proposition is the same as the one you discovered in the *AS–AD* model, which predicts that when inflation is anticipated, real GDP equals potential GDP and unemployment is at its natural rate.

When the expected inflation rate changes, the short-run Phillips curve shifts but the long-run Phillips curve does not shift. If the expected inflation rate is 10 per cent a year, the short-run Phillips curve is $SRPC_0$. If the expected inflation rate falls to 7 per cent a year, the short-run Phillips curve shifts downward to $SRPC_1$. The distance by which the short-run Phillips curve shifts downward when the expected inflation rate falls is equal to the change in the expected inflation rate.

To see why the short-run Phillips curve shifts when the expected inflation rate changes let's do a thought experiment. The economy is at full employment and a fully anticipated inflation is 10 per cent a year. The central bank now begins a permanent attack on inflation by slowing money supply growth. Aggregate demand growth slows down and the inflation rate falls to 7 per cent a year. At first, this decrease in inflation is unanticipated, so wages continue to rise at their original rate, shifting the short-run aggregate supply curve leftward at the same pace as before. Real GDP falls and unemployment increases. In Figure 29.12, the economy moves from point *A* to point *C* on the short-run Phillips curve $SRPC_0$.

If the actual inflation rate remains steady at 7 per cent a year, eventually this rate will come to be expected. As this happens, wage growth slows down and the short-run aggregate supply curve shifts leftward less quickly. Eventually it shifts leftward at the same pace at which the aggregate demand curve is shifting rightward. The actual inflation rate equals the expected inflation rate and full employment is restored. Unemployment is back at its natural rate. In Figure 29.12, the short-run Phillips curve has shifted from $SRPC_0$ to $SRPC_1$ and the economy is at point *D*.

Changes in expected inflation cause shifts in the Phillips curve. Another important source of shifts in the Phillips curve is a change in the natural rate of unemployment.

Changes in the Natural Rate of Unemployment

The natural rate of unemployment changes for many reasons that are explained in Chapter 21, pp. 468–469. A change in the natural rate of unemployment shifts both the short-run and the long-run Phillips curves. Such shifts are illustrated in Figure 29.13. If the natural rate of unemployment increases from 6 per cent to 9 per cent, the long-run Phillips curve shifts from $LRPC_0$ to $LRPC_1$, and if expected inflation is constant at 10 per cent a year, the short-run Phillips curve shifts from $SRPC_0$ to $SRPC_1$. Because the expected inflation rate is constant, the short-run Phillips curve $SRPC_1$ intersects the long-run curve $LRPC_1$ (point *E*) at the same inflation rate at which the short-run Phillips curve $SRPC_0$ intersects the long-run curve $LRPC_0$ (point *A*).

Figure 29.12

Short-run and Long-run Phillips Curves

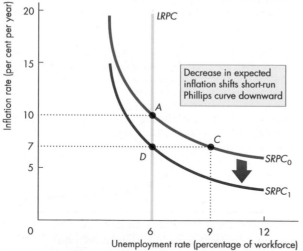

The long-run Phillips curve is *LRPC*, a vertical line at the natural rate of unemployment. A fall in inflation expectations shifts the short-run Phillips curve downward by the amount of the fall in the expected inflation rate. In this figure, when the expected inflation rate falls from 10 per cent a year to 7 per cent a year, the short-run Phillips curve shifts downward from $SRPC_0$ to $SRPC_1$. The new short-run Phillips curve intersects the long-run Phillips curve at the new expected inflation rate – point *D*. With the original expected inflation rate (of 10 per cent), an inflation rate of 7 per cent a year would occur at an unemployment rate of 9 per cent, at point *C*.

Figure 29.13

A Change in the Natural Rate of Unemployment

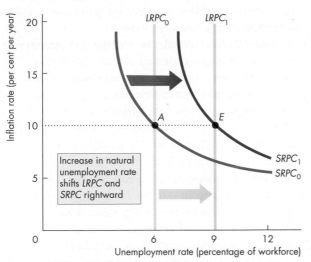

A change in the natural rate of unemployment shifts both the short-run and long-run Phillips curves. Here the natural rate of unemployment increases from 6 per cent to 9 per cent, and the two Phillips curves shift rightward to $SRPC_1$ and $LRPC_1$. The new Phillips curves intersect at the expected inflation rate – point F.

Box 29.1

Phillips Curves in the United Kingdom

When A.W. (Bill) Phillips first discovered the curve that bears his name, he was looking at data on wage inflation and unemployment between 1861 and 1957. It was hard to see the Phillips curve in the data. The scatter diagram of data covering almost 100 years was more like a snow storm than a neat inverse relationship.

Figure 1(a) continues the story that Phillips began by showing a scatter diagram of the inflation rate and the unemployment rate in the United Kingdom between 1960 and 2003. Each dot represents the combination of inflation and unemployment for a particular year. We certainly cannot see a Phillips curve similar to that shown in Figure 29.10.

But we can interpret the data in terms of a shifting short-run Phillips curve like those in Figures 29.12 and 29.13. Three short-run Phillips curves appear in Figure 1(b). The short-run Phillips curve of the 1960s is $SRPC_0$. At that time, the expected inflation rate was 2 per cent a year and the natural rate of unemployment was 2 per cent.

The short-run Phillips curve of the mid-1970s to mid-1980s is $SRPC_1$. During this period, the natural

Figure 1

Phillips Curves in the United Kingdom

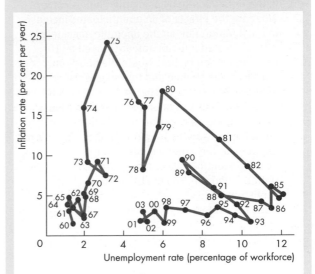

(a) Time sequence

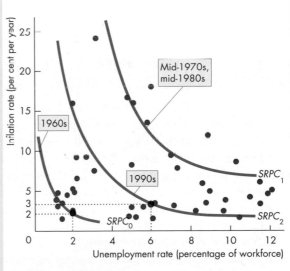

(b) Shifting Phillips curves

Source: Office for National Statistics.

rate of unemployment was higher than that of the 1960s and the expected inflation rate was much higher.

The short-run Phillips curve of the 1990s is $SRPC_2$. During the 1980s and 1990s the natural rate of unemployment fell and expected inflation declined. So the short-run Phillips curve shifted leftward and downward during this period.

Review Quiz

1 How would you illustrate an unanticipated change in the inflation rate by using the Phillips curve?
2 What are the effects of an unanticipated increase in the inflation rate on the unemployment rate?
3 If the expected inflation rate increased by 10 percentage points, how would the short-run Phillips curve change and how would the long-run Phillips curve change?
4 If the natural rate of unemployment increases, what happens to the short-run Phillips curve? What happens to the long-run Phillips curve? What happens to the expected inflation rate?
5 Can you identify a short-run Phillips curve for the United Kingdom? Has the UK short-run Phillips curve remained stable?
6 Does the United Kingdom have a stable long-run Phillips curve?

So far, we've studied the effects of inflation on real GDP, real wages, employment and unemployment. Inflation lowers the value of money and changes the real value of the amounts borrowed and repaid. As a result, inflation influences interest rates. Let's see how.

Interest Rates and Inflation

Today, low-risk companies in the United Kingdom can borrow at an interest rate of less than 6 per cent a year. In contrast, even a major company that is unlikely to default on its loans pays 250 per cent a year in Zimbabwe. While companies in the United Kingdom have never paid interest rates as high as those in Zimbabwe today, they did pay around 15 per cent a year during the early 1980s. Why do interest rates fluctuate so much across countries and over time?

Part of the answer is that the real interest rate varies across countries and over time. (The *real interest rate* equals the *nominal* interest rate minus the inflation rate – see Chapter 27, p. 614.) Risk differences bring international differences in the real interest rate and fluctuations in saving supply and investment demand bring fluctuations in the real interest rate.

But another part of the answer – a major part – is that the inflation rate varies across countries and fluctuates over time. High inflation in Zimbabwe today and in the United Kingdom during the 1980s is the source of high interest rates.

To see why inflation influences the interest rate, think about the decisions of borrowers and lenders.

The supply of loans is greater the higher the *real* interest rate. And the demand for loans is greater the lower the *real* interest rate. The forces of demand and supply determine an equilibrium *real* interest rate that makes the amount that people want to borrow equal to the amount that people want to lend.

Imagine there is no inflation and the real interest rate and nominal interest rate are 4 per cent a year. The amount that businesses and people want to borrow equals the amount that businesses and people want to lend at this real interest rate. British Petroleum (BP) is willing to pay an interest rate of 4 per cent a year to get the funds it needs to pay for its global investment in new oil exploration sites. Sue, who is saving to buy a new car, and thousands of people like her, are willing to lend BP the amount it needs for its exploration work if they can get a *real* return of 4 per cent a year.

Now suppose inflation breaks out at a steady 6 per cent a year. All prices and values, including oil exploration profits and car prices, rise by 6 per cent a year. If BP was willing to pay a 4 per cent interest rate when there was no inflation, it is now willing to pay 10 per cent interest. The reason is that its profits are rising by 6 per cent a year, owing to the 6 per cent inflation, so it is *really* paying only 4 per cent. Similarly, if Sue was willing to lend at a 4 per cent interest rate when there was no inflation, she is now willing to lend only if she gets 10 per cent interest. The price of the car Sue is planning to buy is rising by 6 per cent a year, owing to the 6 per cent inflation, so she is *really* getting only a 4 per cent interest rate.

Because borrowers are willing to pay the higher rate and lenders are willing to lend only if they receive the higher rate, when inflation is anticipated the *nominal interest rate* increases by an amount equal to the expected inflation rate. The *real interest rate* remains constant. The real interest rate might change because the supply of saving or investment demand has changed for some other reason. But a change in the expected inflation rate alone does not change the real interest rate.

Box 29.2 examines the real-world relationship between inflation and the interest rate and shows that the effect we've just described does occur.

Review Quiz

1 What is the relationship between the real interest rate, the nominal interest rate and the inflation rate?
2 Why does inflation change the nominal interest rate?

Box 29.2

Inflation and Interest Rates in the United Kingdom and Around the World

We can study the relationship between the inflation rate and the interest rate by looking at either changes over time in a given country or variations across countries at a given time.

Figure 1(a) shows the relationship between the inflation rate and the nominal interest rate in the United Kingdom between 1963 and 2003. The interest rate measured on the vertical axis is that paid by the UK government on 3-month Treasury bills. Each point on the graph represents a year (identified by the two-digit number). The blue line shows the relationship between the nominal interest rate and the inflation rate if the real interest rate is constant at 2.5 per cent a year. As you can see, there is a clear relationship between the inflation rate and the interest rate, but it is not exact. When the red dot lies above the blue line, the real interest rate exceeds 2.5 per cent a year. When the red dot lies below the blue line, the real interest rate is less than 2.5 per cent a year.

The reason the relationship between the inflation rate and the nominal interest rate isn't exact is that the real interest rate fluctuates. During the 1960s, both the inflation rate and the nominal interest rate were low. In the early 1970s, inflation began to increase, but it was not expected to increase much and certainly not to persist. As a result, the nominal interest rate did not rise much at that time. By the mid-1970s, there was a burst of unexpectedly high inflation. The interest rate increased somewhat but not by nearly as much as the inflation rate. During the late 1970s and early 1980s, inflation of between 15 and 20 per cent a year came to be expected as an ongoing and highly persistent phenomenon. As a result, the nominal interest rate increased to around 12–14 per cent a year. Then in 1982, the inflation rate fell – at first unexpectedly. Interest rates began to fall but not nearly as quickly as the inflation rate. Short-term interest rates fell more quickly than long-term interest rates because, at that time, it was expected that inflation would be lower in the short term but not so low in the longer term.

Figure 1(b) shows the relationship between the inflation rate and the nominal interest rate across a number of countries, some of which, such as Turkey and Russia, have had very high inflation – rates of 60 to 80 per cent a year. Again, you can see a strong relationship between the two variables but not a perfect relationship. The real interest rate, as well as the inflation rate, varies from one country to another for some of the reasons discussed on the previous page.

Figure 1

Inflation and the Interest Rates in the United Kingdom and Around the World

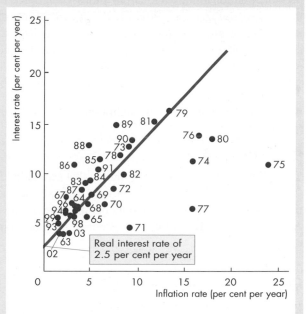

(a) United Kingdom

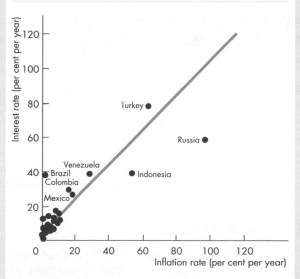

(b) Around the world

The graph in part (a) reveals that the influence of inflation on the interest rate in the United Kingdom is a powerful one. The graph in part (b) reveals a powerful influence of inflation on the interest rate across a number of countries.

Sources: Office for National Statistics, Bank of England and International Monetary Fund.

The Politics of Inflation

Inflation has plagued nations over many centuries, from the Roman Empire to modern Russia. (There are examples of inflation from even earlier times going back to the earliest civilizations.) What are the deeper sources of inflation that are common to all these vastly different societies? The answer lies in politics. There are two main political sources of inflation. They are:

◆ Inflation tax
◆ Poor reputation and weak credibility

Inflation Tax

The **inflation tax** is a tax on the money that people hold. Governments don't pass inflation tax laws like income tax and VAT laws. But governments do generate revenue from inflation just like they generate revenue from other taxes.

Origin of the Inflation Tax

Before the invention of banking, when money consisted of gold coins, the King had a monopoly on minting coins from gold. If you brought an ounce of gold to the King, he would mint coin to a value less than an ounce and keep some of the gold as a profit. This profit came to be known as *seigniorage*. The term derives from an old French word *seigneur* "a feudal lord or king". The more seigniorage the King took from an ounce of gold, the less valuable were the coins he minted and the higher were the prices of goods and services in terms of money. Collecting seigniorage generated inflation. We continue to call the revenue obtained from the inflation tax seigniorage, although we generate it today in a more subtle way than that used by feudal lords and kings.

Inflation Tax Today

Today, a government can finance its expenditure by selling bonds to the central bank. The central bank pays for these bonds with new money – with an increase in the monetary base. An increase in the monetary base gives the banks excess reserves, which they lend and which brings an increase in the quantity of money. The increase in the quantity of money increases aggregate demand and the price level rises. If the government routinely finances its expenditure in this way, inflation takes hold.

So the government gets revenues from inflation just as if it had increased taxes. Who pays the inflation tax? The holders of money pay. They pay because the real value of their money holdings decreases at a rate equal to the inflation rate.

The government creates additional money (ΔM) to finance its expenditure. The real value of its revenue is $\Delta M/P$, which we can express as $(\Delta M/M) \times (M/P)$ – the growth rate of money ($\Delta M/M$) multiplied by the quantity of real money (M/P). In the long run, the inflation rate equals the growth rate of money minus the growth rate of real GDP. At a high inflation rate, we can ignore the growth rate of real GDP and describe the real revenue obtained by the inflation tax as (approximately):

$$\frac{\Delta P}{P}\left(\frac{M}{P}\right)$$

The Inflation Tax and Inflation Rate

The amount of revenue that a government raises from a tax depends on the tax rate. At low tax rates, an increase in the tax rate increases tax revenue. But at high tax rates, an increase in the tax rate decreases tax revenue. The reason is that people find substitutes for items that are taxed at too high a rate.

In the case of the inflation tax, as the inflation rate ($\Delta P/P$) increases the quantity of real money held (M/P) decreases. So when the inflation tax rate increases, the inflation tax base decreases.

At low inflation rates, the interest rate is low and the quantity of real money demanded is large. The government can generate extra revenue from the inflation tax by creating more inflation. But at high inflation rates, the interest rate is high and the quantity of real money demanded is small. If the quantity of real money demanded decreases faster than the inflation rate rises, the government obtains less revenue from more inflation.

Figure 29.14 shows the relationship between inflation tax revenue and the inflation rate. Up to 550 per cent a year, a rise in the inflation rate brings more tax revenue. But beyond 550 per cent a year, the inflation tax revenue falls as the inflation rate rises.

Inflation is not used as a major source of tax revenue in the United Kingdom or in any developed economy. But it is used in some developing countries. The closing years of the Roman Empire and the transition years to a market economy in Russia and Eastern Europe are examples. Zimbabwe is also using the inflation tax as a source of real revenue for the government. In *Reading Between the Lines* on pp. 674–675, we examine the experience of high inflation in Zimbabwe.

Figure 29.14

The Inflation Tax and Inflation Rate

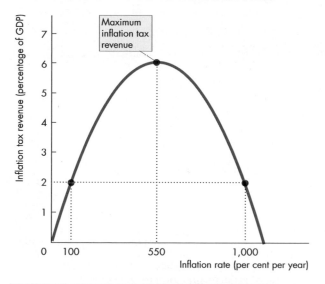

At an inflation rate of 100 per cent a year and at an inflation rate of 1,000 per cent a year, the revenue from the inflation tax is 2 per cent of GDP. The inflation tax revenue is maximized at an inflation rate of 550 per cent a year. (The numbers are hypothetical but approximate many actual high- (hyper-) inflation situations.)

Poor Reputation and Weak Credibility

One of the problems with conducting a low inflation policy is that people who need to forecast inflation and interest rates may have a different expectation of inflation from the central bank. The government, through the central bank, may conduct a policy that decreases the money growth rate and reduces inflation. Short-term interest rates may decline because inflation in the short term may be lower, but long-term interest rates may not decline because people expect long-term inflation to remain high. This outcome occurs if people anticipate that the policy of a low money growth rate now will be reversed at some point in the future. While current inflation may be low, bond holders may anticipate higher inflation in the future and decide to sell some bonds, which reduces the price of a bond and raises the long-term interest rate.

Why would people have such an expectation? The reason is that they do not believe that the central bank, and through it the government, will stick to its plans of keeping the inflation rate low. People may believe that once they adjust their expectations of inflation and anticipate low inflation, the government may be tempted to increase the money growth rate and increase aggregate demand by more than expected. In other words, people do not think that the policy has *credibility*. One reason people do not trust the government is that it may not have a *reputation* for trustworthiness. Too often governments have said one thing and done another.

A policy is credible if the cost to the government of following the policy is viewed as less than not following it. There is always an incentive for a government that has promised low inflation to expand the economy by increasing the money growth rate to temporarily reduce unemployment – particularly just before an election. The benefits of lower unemployment are reaped immediately, but the costs of higher inflation and unemployment are felt in the future. A government may avoid the temptation to increase aggregate demand after reducing inflation only if it values its reputation.

Some economists argue that independence of the central bank improves the credibility of a low inflation policy; others suggest that credibility is obtained by joining an exchange rate agreement such as the European Monetary System or the European Monetary Union. A good reputation for consistent macroeconomic policy can only be earned over a period of time. The German central bank, the Bundesbank, developed a good reputation for low inflation.

Reading Between the Lines on pp. 674–675 examines a rapid inflation in Zimbabwe and the difficulty that a central bank without a strong anti-inflation reputation has to bring inflation under control.

Review Quiz

1 What is an inflation tax and when is it used as a source of government revenue?
2 Why does a government find it hard to obtain a low inflation reputation?
3 When is a low inflation policy credible?

You have now completed your study of inflation and the aggregate demand side of the economy. Our next task in the following chapters is to focus more deeply on the supply side, long-term trends and the business cycle. Then, in Chapter 32, we'll study the policy challenges that make it difficult to achieve rapid growth and avoid excessive unemployment and inflation.

Reading Between the Lines

Inflation Tax in Zimbabwe

Financial Gazette, 22 July 2004

Zimbabwe's Inflation Slows Down

Charles Rukuni

Despite the forecast by the Reserve Bank of Zimbabwe to reduce inflation to a manageable level, what we are seeing on the ground is the reverse. While statistics being given are indicating a downward trend, the reality is that prices of basic commodities are rising. "This is confusing," so said Comfort Muchekeza, regional manager of the Consumer Council of Zimbabwe (CCZ) in Matabeleland. Muchekeza's sentiments are shared by many. It is indeed confusing, even baffling. Inflation is going down but prices are going up . . .

Central Bank Governor Gideon Gono, the architect of the current reform programme which aims to reduce inflation to below 200 per cent by the end of the year and to a single digit by 2008, is emphatic. Inflation is indeed going down. But he quickly adds that a decline in inflation does not necessarily translate into a decline in prices. Gono said that when inflation started declining, all that it meant was that prices were going up, but at a lower rate.

The drop in inflation has been remarkable – unbelievable, some would even say – considering the mess in which the country was in. From a peak of 622.8 per cent in January, it declined slightly to 602.5 per cent in February, then marginally to 587.7 per cent in March. Inflation dropped significantly to 505 per cent in April, then 448.8 per cent in May and 394.6 per cent in June. This has convinced even the worst sceptics that Gono's target of reducing inflation to 200 per cent by December is achievable.

Although Gono has declared inflation enemy number one, and the government is helping fight inflation, there are some who think that governments "love inflation" because they benefit tremendously. According to some, when governments "borrow" from you, they have no intention of repaying the money they have supposedly borrowed. This is much of what inflation is all about. Inflation is a trick to make you think you are being repaid money that you lend the government, when in fact they are stealing the money from you. The objective is that the longer you leave your money in savings, the less it will be worth.

Zimbabwe's domestic debt has, for example, ballooned from Z$375 billion in May last year to a staggering Z$1.4 trillion by June 26 this year. If this does not make any sense, just imagine: If you lent someone Z$10,000 in June last year, and they gave you back Z$10,000 today, or even Z$20,000, would you not feel robbed.

The Essence of the Story

◆ The inflation rate in Zimbabwe has fallen from a peak of 623 per cent a year in January 2004 and the Reserve Bank of Zimbabwe aims to lower it to below 200 per cent a year by December 2004 and to less than 10 per cent a year by 2008.

◆ The fall in the inflation rate during 2004 was unexpected.

◆ The Reserve Bank's governor notes that a fall in the inflation rate does not mean falling prices. It means that prices are going up, but at a slower rate.

◆ Some people think that governments like inflation because it lowers the value of their debts.

Economic Analysis

◆ Figure 1 shows Zimbabwe's inflation rate and money growth rate from 1999 to 2004.

◆ Figure 2 shows that the government's budget deficit, which jumped from 10 per cent of GDP in 1999 to 23 per cent in 2000 and since then has remained at 10 per cent.

◆ Figure 2 also shows that real GDP growth has been negative each year between 1999 and 2004. Negative growth means that real GDP has fallen each year.

◆ The Reserve Bank of Zimbabwe's plan is to slow the money growth rate during 2004, as shown in Figure 1, and cut the inflation rate to 200 per cent by December.

◆ Because the Reserve Bank of Zimbabwe has not established a reputation for fighting inflation and because the government has a large deficit and debt, it will be difficult for Zimbabwe to achieve the Bank's declared objective.

◆ Figure 3 illustrates what has been happening in Zimbabwe in terms of the *AS–AD* model.

◆ In 1999, long-run aggregate supply was LAS_{99}, short-run aggregate supply was SAS_{99} and aggregate demand was AD_{99}. Real GDP was Z$67 billion and the price level was 333.

◆ Extremely rapid money growth increased aggregate demand and by 2004, the aggregate demand curve had shifted rightward to AD_{04}.

◆ The high inflation rate increased uncertainty and decreased potential GDP to LAS_{04}. It also increased the money wage rate and decreased short-run aggregate supply to SAS_{04}.

◆ Real GDP decreased to Z$39 billion and the price level increased to 84,058.

◆ The decrease in the money growth rate in 2004 means that aggregate demand will continue to increase but at a slower rate.

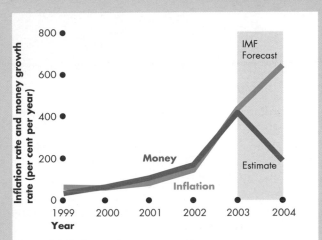

Figure 1 Inflation and money growth

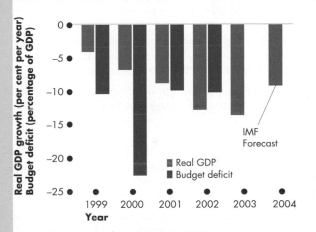

Figure 2 GDP growth and budget deficit

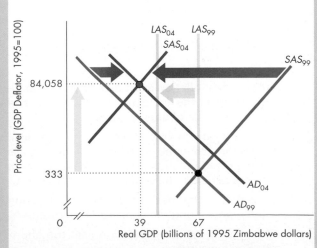

Figure 3 Aggregate supply and aggregate demand

Summary

Key Points

Demand-pull and Cost-push Inflation (pp. 654–659)

- Inflation is a process of persistently rising prices and falling value of money.
- Demand-pull inflation arises from increasing aggregate demand sustained by growth in the quantity of money.
- Cost-push inflation arises from a decrease in aggregate supply sustained by growth in the quantity of money.

The Quantity Theory of Money (pp. 660–661)

- The quantity theory of money is the proposition that money growth and inflation move up and down together in the long run.
- The UK and international evidence is consistent with the quantity theory on the average.

Effects of Inflation (pp. 662–666)

- Inflation is costly when it is unanticipated because it redistributes income and wealth and creates inefficiencies in the economy.
- A rapid anticipated inflation is costly because it decreases potential GDP and slows economic growth.

Inflation and Unemployment: The Phillips Curve (pp. 666–670)

- The short-run Phillips curve shows the trade-off between inflation and unemployment, holding constant the expected inflation rate and the natural rate of unemployment.
- The long-run Phillips curve which is vertical, shows that when the actual inflation rate equals the expected inflation rate, the unemployment rate equals the natural rate of unemployment.
- Unexpected changes in the inflation rate bring movements along the short-run Phillips curve.
- Changes in expected inflation shift the short-run Phillips curve.
- Changes in the natural rate of unemployment shift both the short-run and long-run Phillips curves.

Interest Rates and Inflation (pp. 670–671)

- The higher the expected inflation rate, the higher is the nominal interest rate.
- As the anticipated inflation rate rises, borrowers willingly pay a higher interest rate and lenders successfully demand a higher interest rate.
- The nominal interest rate adjusts to equal the real interest rate plus the expected inflation rate.

The Politics of Inflation (pp. 672–673)

- Inflation is a tax paid by holders of money.
- A government with a good reputation for controlling inflation can contain inflation more easily than a government with a poor reputation.

Key Figures

Key Terms

Problems

*1 The figure shows an economy's long-run aggregate supply curve, *LAS*, three aggregate demand curves AD_0, AD_1 and AD_2, and three short-run aggregate supply curves SAS_0, SAS_1 and SAS_2. The economy starts out on the curves AD_0 and SAS_0. Some events then occur that generate a demand-pull inflation.

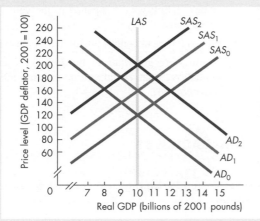

a List the events that might cause demand-pull inflation.

b Using the graph, describe the initial effects of demand-pull inflation.

c Using the graph, describe what happens as a demand-pull inflation spiral unwinds.

2 In the economy described in problem 1, some events then occur that generate a cost-push inflation.

a List the events that might cause cost-push inflation.

b Using the graph, describe the initial effects of cost-push inflation.

c Using the graph, describe what happens as a cost-push inflation spiral unwinds.

*3 Quantecon is a country in which the quantity theory of money operates. The country has a constant population, capital stock and technology. In year 1, real GDP was €400 million, the price level was 200, and the velocity of circulation of money was 20. In year 2, the quantity of money was 20 per cent higher than in year 1.

a What was the quantity of money in year 1?

b What was the quantity of money in year 2?

c What was the price level in year 2?

d What was the level of real GDP in year 2?

e What was the velocity of circulation in year 2?

4 In Quantecon, described in problem 3, in year 3, the quantity of money falls to one-fifth of its year 2 level.

a What is the quantity of money in year 3?

b What is the price level in year 3?

c What is the level of real GDP in year 3?

d What is the velocity of circulation in year 3?

e If it takes more than one year for the full quantity theory effect to occur, what do you predict happens in Quantecon in year 3 to real GDP? Why?

*5 In the economy described in problem 1, some events then occur that generate perfectly anticipated inflation.

a List the events that might cause a perfectly anticipated inflation.

b Using the graph, describe the initial effects of anticipated inflation.

c Using the graph, describe what happens as anticipated inflation proceeds.

6 In the economy described in problem 1, suppose that people anticipate deflation (a falling price level) but aggregate demand turns out to not change.

a What happens to the short-run and long-run aggregate supply curves? (Draw some new curves if you need to.)

b Using the graph, describe the initial effects of anticipated deflation.

c Using the graph, describe what happens as it becomes obvious to everyone that the anticipated deflation is not going to occur.

*7 An economy with a natural rate of unemployment of 4 per cent and an expected inflation rate of 6 per cent a year has the following inflation and unemployment history:

Year	Inflation rate (per cent per year)	Unemployment rate (percentage of workforce)
1999	10	2
2000	8	3
2001	6	4
2002	4	5
2003	2	6

---

*Solutions to odd-numbered problems are available on *Parkin Interactive*.

a Draw a diagram of the economy's short-run and long-run Phillips curves.

b If the actual inflation rate rises from 6 per cent a year to 8 per cent a year, what is the change in the unemployment rate? Explain why it occurs.

8 For the economy described in problem 7, the natural rate of unemployment rises to 5 per cent and the expected inflation rate falls to 5 per cent a year. Draw the new short-run and long-run Phillips curves in a diagram.

*9 An economy has an unemployment rate of 4 per cent and an inflation rate of 5 per cent a year at point A in the graph. Some events then occur that move the economy to point D.

a Describe the events that could move the economy from point A to point D.

b Draw in the graph the economy's short-run and long-run Phillips curves when the economy is at point A.

c Draw in the graph the economy's short-run and long-run Phillips curves when the economy is at point D.

10 In the economy described in problem 9, some events occur that move the economy from point B to point C.

a Describe the events that could move the economy from point B to point C.

b Draw in the graph the economy's short-run and long-run Phillips curves when the economy is at point B.

c Draw in the graph the economy's short-run and long-run Phillips curves when the economy is at point C.

Critical Thinking

1 Study *Reading Between the Lines* on pp. 674–675 and then answer the following questions.

a Why did the inflation rate take off in Zimbabwe in 2000?

b Try to think of reasons why the inflation rate increased to a higher rate than the growth rate of money. [Hint: what happened to the velocity of circulation and why?]

c Why is it hard to control inflation in Zimbabwe?

d If you were governor of the Reserve Bank of Zimbabwe, what would you do to bring inflation under control?

Web Exercises

Use the link on *Parkin Interactive* to work the following exercises.

1 Obtain data on the growth rate of the quantity of money and the inflation rate in the United Kingdom since 2000.

a Calculate the average growth rate of the quantity of money since 2000.

b Calculate the average inflation rate since 2000.

c Make a graph of the growth rate of the quantity of money and the inflation rate since 2000.

d Interpret your graph and explain what it tells you about the forces that generate inflation and the relationship between money growth and inflation.

2 Obtain data on the inflation rate and the unemployment rate in the United States during the 1990s and 2000s.

a Make a graph using the data you've obtained that is similar to the figure in Box 29.1.

b Describe the similarities and the differences in the relationship between inflation and unemployment in the United States and in the United Kingdom.

3 Obtain the latest data on inflation, unemployment and money growth in Japan, the United Kingdom, the United States and Canada. Then:

a Interpret the data for each country in terms of shifting Phillips curves.

b Which country do you think has the lowest expected inflation rate? Why?

Chapter 30

Economic Growth

After studying this chapter you will be able to:

◆ Describe the long-term growth trends in the United Kingdom and other countries and regions

◆ Identify the main sources of real GDP growth

◆ Explain the productivity growth slowdown in the United Kingdom during the 1970s and speed-up in the 1980s

◆ Explain the theories of economic growth

Economic Miracles

In China and India, and in some other smaller economies in East Asia, real GDP doubles in 7 years. In the United Kingdom, real GDP doubles every 25 years or so. In many African economies, real GDP barely changes from one year to the next. Why? What makes an economic miracle like the ones we see in East Asia today? Can China and India continue to expand at the current dizzying rate? Or will this growth come to an end? And if so, what kind of end: abrupt or gradual? And why do some countries stagnate?

Long-term Growth Trends

The long-term growth trends that we study in this chapter are the trends in *real GDP per person*. We are interested in long-term economic growth because it brings rising incomes and a rising standard of living. Let's begin by looking at some facts about the level and the growth rate of real GDP per person in the United Kingdom and around the world.

Growth in the UK Economy

Figure 30.1 shows real GDP per person in the United Kingdom for the 150 years from 1855 to 2005. The average growth rate over this period is 1.3 per cent a year. But the long-term growth rate has varied. For example, growth slowed during the 1970s to 1.3 per cent a year, down from 2.4 per cent a year during the 1960s. Growth picked up again in the 1980s and 1990s and returned to 2.6 per cent a year in the late 1990s.

You can see the growth slowdown of the 1970s in a longer perspective in Figure 30.1 and you can see that it is not unique. The interwar period (1919–1939) and the early years of the 1900s had even slower growth than the 1970s.

In the middle of the graph are two extraordinary events: a period of prolonged depression during the interwar years and a burst of rapid growth and higher than normal real GDP per person during the Second World War (1939–1945). The interwar depression and the Second World War growth bulge obscure changes in the long-term growth trend that occurred during those years. But between 1919 and 1953, averaging out the depression and the war, the long-term growth rate was 1.2 per cent a year.

A major goal of this chapter is to explain why our economy grows and why the long-term growth rate varies. Another goal is to explain variations in the economic growth rate across countries. Let's look at some facts about other country's growth rates.

Figure 30.1

A Hundred and Fifty Years of Economic Growth in the United Kingdom

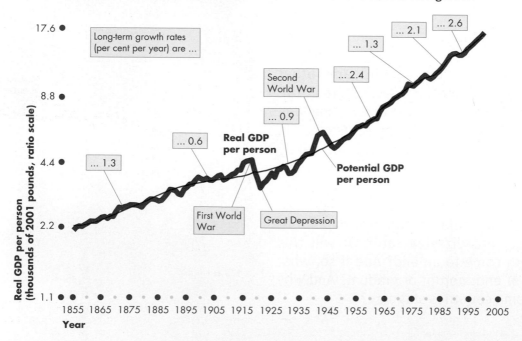

During the 150 years from 1855 to 2005, real GDP per person in the United Kingdom grew by 1.3 per cent a year, on average. The growth rate was above average during the 1950s, 1960s, 1980s and 1990s. It was below average in the 1900s, the interwar period and 1970s.

Source: Charles Feinstein, *National Income Expenditure and Output of the United Kingdom 1855–1965*, Cambridge, Cambridge University Press, 1972; National Statistics.

Real GDP Growth in the World Economy

Figure 30.2 shows real GDP per person in Europe Big 4 (France, Germany, Italy and the United Kingdom) and in other countries between 1964 and 2004. (The data in this figure are in 1996 US dollars.) Part (a) looks at the seven richest countries – known as the G7 nations. Among these nations, the United States has the highest real GDP per person. In 2004, Canada had the second-highest real GDP per person and Japan the third.

The gaps between the United States, Canada and Europe Big 4 have been roughly constant. Japan is the biggest mover in this group. Before the 1990s, Japan grew fastest, overtook Europe and Canada and was catching up on the United States. But during the 1990s, the Japanese economy stagnated while the other G7 economies continued to expand. Japan's real GDP per person has remained higher than Europe's, although it has slipped below that of Canada.

Not all countries are growing at the same pace as or catching up with the United States. Figure 30.2(b) looks at some of these. Western Europe (other than the Big 4) grew faster than the United States before 1975, but slowed during the 1980s and then fell further behind during the 1990s. After a brief period of catch-up, the former Communist countries of Central Europe fell increasingly behind the United States and in 2004 they were as far behind as they had been 30 years earlier.

Africa and Central and South America have grown more slowly than the United States. Real GDP per person in Central and South America slipped from 30 per cent of the US level of real GDP per person in 1963 to 20 per cent in 2004.

Figure 30.2

Economic Growth Around the World: Catch-up or Not?

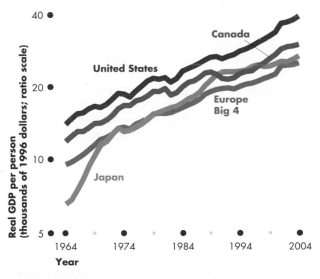

(a) Catch up?

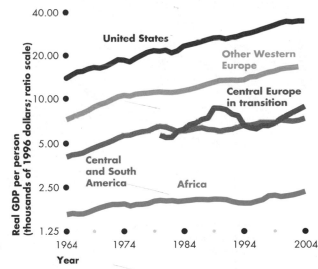

(b) No catch up?

Real GDP per person has grown throughout the world economy. The rich industrial countries in part (a) have grown at a similar pace with the exception of Japan. Japan grew fastest before 1990 and overtook the four big countries of Europe (France, Germany, Italy and the United Kingdom) and Canada. During the 1990s Japan stagnated.

Growth rates in the regions shown in part (b) have been lower than that of the United States and gaps between the levels of real GDP per person have widened. The gaps between the United States and Central Europe and Africa widened most.

Sources: (1964–2000) Alan Heston, Robert Summers and Bettina Aten, Penn World Table Version 6.1, Center for International Comparisons at the University of Pennsylvania (CICUP), October 2002; and (2001–2004) International Monetary Fund, *World Economic Outlook*, April 2004.

A group of Asian economies provides a strong contrast to the persistent and widening gaps between the United States and other economies shown in Figure 30.2. Hong Kong (now part of China), South Korea, Singapore and Taiwan have experienced spectacular growth, which you can see in Figure 30.3. During the 1960s, real GDP per person in these economies averaged 30 per cent of that in the United Kingdom and 22 per cent of that in the United States. But by 2004, real GDP per person in these counties had reached 70 per cent of that in the United States and more than 100 per cent of that in the United Kingdom.

Figure 30.3 shows that China is also catching up, but from a long way behind. China's real GDP per person increased from 5 per cent of the US level in 1964 to 14 per cent in 2004.

The Asian economies shown in Figure 30.3 are like fast trains running on the same track at similar speeds and with a roughly constant gap between them. Hong Kong is the lead train and runs about 15 years in front of South Korea and about 40 years in front of the rest of China, which is the last train. Real GDP per person in South Korea was similar to that of Hong Kong in 1986 and real GDP per person in China is similar to that of Hong Kong in 1963. Between 1963 and 2003, Hong Kong transformed itself from a poor developing country into one of the world's richest countries.

The rest of China is now doing what Hong Kong has done. If China continues its rapid growth, the world economy will be a dramatically different place. China has a population 200 times that of Hong Kong, more than 20 times that if the United Kingdom and almost 5 times that of the United States, so a rich China will have a huge impact on the global economy.

Figure 30.3

Catch-up in Asia

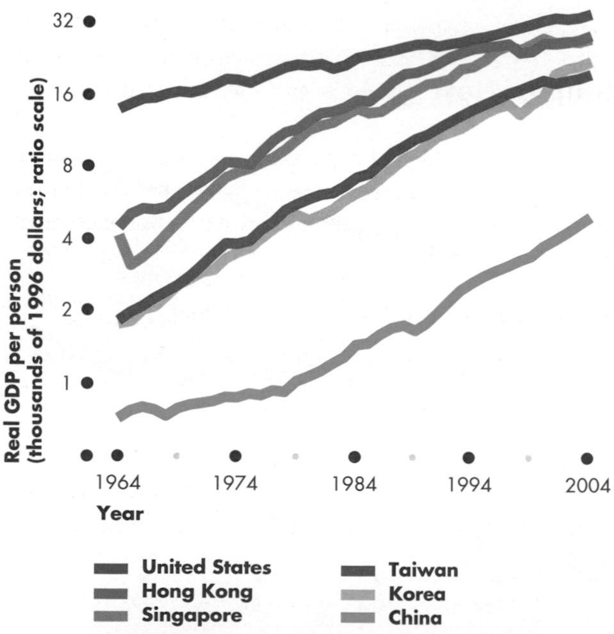

The clearest examples of catch-up have occurred in five economies in Asia. Starting out in 1964 with incomes as little as one-tenth of that in the United States, four Asian economies (Hong Kong, South Korea, Singapore and Taiwan) have substantially narrowed the gap on the United States. And from being a very poor developing country in 1964, China has caught up with the income level that Hong Kong had in 1964 and is growing at a rate that is enabling it to continue catching up with the rich G7 countries.

Source: See Figure 30.2.

Review Quiz

1   What has been the average growth rate in the United Kingdom over the past 150 years? In which period was growth the most rapid and in which was it the slowest?
2   Describe the gaps between the levels of real GDP per person in Europe Big 4 and other countries. For which countries are the gaps narrowing. For which countries are the gaps widening? For which countries are the gaps remaining unchanged?
3   Compare the growth rates and levels of real GDP per person in Hong Kong, Singapore, Taiwan, South Korea, China and the United States. How far is China behind the other Asian economies?

The facts about economic growth in the United Kingdom and around the world raise some big questions that we're now going to answer. We'll study the causes of economic growth in three stages. First, we'll look at the preconditions for growth and the activities that sustain it. Second, we'll learn how economists measure the relative contributions of the sources of growth – an activity called *growth accounting*. And third, we'll study three theories of economic growth that seek to explain how the influences on growth interact to determine the growth rate.

Let's take our first look at the causes of economic growth.

The Causes of Economic Growth: A First Look

Most human societies have lived for centuries and even thousands of years, with no economic growth. The key reason is that they have lacked some fundamental social institutions and arrangements that are essential preconditions for economic growth. Let's see what these preconditions are.

Preconditions for Economic Growth

The most basic precondition for economic growth is an appropriate *incentive* system. Three institutions are crucial to the creation of incentives. They are:

1 Markets

2 Property rights

3 Monetary exchange

Markets enable buyers and sellers to get information and to do business with each other, and market prices send signals to buyers and sellers that create *incentives* to increase or decrease the quantities demanded and supplied. Markets enable people to specialize and trade and to save and invest. But to work well, markets need property rights and monetary exchange.

Property rights are the social arrangements that govern the ownership, use and disposal of factors of production and goods and services. They include the right to physical property (land, buildings and capital equipment), to financial property (claims by one person against another) and to intellectual property (such as inventions). Clearly established and enforced property rights give people an assurance that a capricious government will not confiscate the income they earn and their savings.

Monetary exchange facilitates transactions of all kinds, including the orderly transfer of private property from one person to another. Property rights and monetary exchange create incentives for people to specialize and trade, to save and invest, and to discover new technologies.

No unique political system is necessary to deliver the preconditions for economic growth. Liberal democracy, founded on the fundamental principle of the rule of law, is the system that does the best job. It provides a solid base on which property rights can be established and enforced. But authoritarian political systems have some-times provided an environment in which economic growth has occurred.

Early human societies, based on hunting and gathering, did not experience economic growth because they lacked the preconditions we've just described. Economic growth began when societies evolved the three key institutions that create incentives. But the presence of an incentive system and the institutions that create it do not guarantee that economic growth will occur. They permit economic growth but do not make it inevitable.

The simplest way in which growth happens when the appropriate incentive system exists is that people begin to specialize in the activities at which they have a comparative advantage and trade with each other. You saw in Chapter 2, pp. 40–43, how everyone can gain from such activity. By specializing and trading, everyone can acquire goods and services at the lowest possible cost. Equivalently, everyone can obtain a greater volume of goods and services from their labour.

As an economy moves from one with little specialization to one that reaps the gains from specialization and trade, its production and consumption grows. Real GDP per person increases and the standard of living rises.

But for growth to be persistent, people must face incentives that encourage them to pursue three activities that generate ongoing economic growth. These activities are:

◆ Saving and investment in new capital

◆ Investment in human capital

◆ Discovery of new technologies

These three sources of growth, which interact with each other, are the primary sources of the extraordinary growth in productivity during the past 200 years. Let's look at each in turn.

Saving and Investment in New Capital

Saving and investment in new capital increase the amount of capital per worker and increase real GDP per hour of labour – labour productivity. Labour productivity took the most dramatic upturn when the amount of capital per worker increased during the Industrial Revolution. Production processes that use hand tools can create beautiful objects, but production methods that use large amounts of capital per worker, such as car plant assembly lines, are much more productive.

The accumulation of capital on farms, in textiles factories, in iron foundries and steel mills, in coal mines, on building sites, in chemical plants, in car plants, in banks and insurance companies, in retail stores and shopping malls have added incredibly to the productivity of our economy. The next time you see a film set in colonial times, look carefully at the small amount of capital around. Try to imagine how productive you would be in such circumstances compared with your productivity today.

Investment in Human Capital

Human capital – the accumulated skill and knowledge of human beings – is the most fundamental source of economic growth. It is a source of both increased productivity and technological advance.

The development of one of the most basic human skills – writing – was the source of some of the earliest major gains in productivity. The ability to keep written records made it possible to reap ever-larger gains from specialization and exchange. Imagine how hard it would be to do any kind of business if all the accounts, invoices and agreements existed only in people's memories.

Later, the development of mathematics laid the foundation for the eventual extension of knowledge about physical forces and chemical and biological processes. This base of scientific knowledge was the foundation for the technological advances of the Industrial Revolution 200 years ago and of today's information revolution.

But much human capital that is extremely productive is much more humble. It takes the form of millions of individuals learning and repetitively doing simple production tasks and becoming remarkably more productive in the tasks.

One carefully studied example illustrates the importance of this kind of human capital. Between 1941 and 1944 (during the Second World War), US shipyards produced some 2,500 units of a cargo ship, called the Liberty Ship, to a standardized design. In 1941, it took 1.2 million person-hours to build one ship. By 1942, it took 600,000 person-hours and, by 1943, it took only 500,000. Not much change occurred in the capital employed during these years. But an enormous amount of human capital was accumulated. Thousands of workers and managers learned from experience and accumulated human capital that more than doubled their productivity in two years.

Discovery of New Technologies

Saving and investment in new capital and the accumulation of human capital have made a large contribution to economic growth. But technological change – the discovery and the application of new technologies and new goods – has made an even greater contribution.

People are many times more productive today than they were a hundred years ago. We are more productive because we have more steam engines per person and more horse-drawn carriages per person. Rather, it is because we have engines and transport equipment that use technologies unknown hundred years ago, which are more productive than those old technologies were. Technological change makes an enormous contribution to our increased productivity. It arises from formal research and development programmes and from informal trial and error, and it involves discovering ways of getting more out of our resources.

To reap the benefits of technological change, capital must increase. Some of the most powerful and far-reaching fundamental technologies are embodied in human capital – for example, language, writing and mathematics. But most technologies are embodied in physical capital. For example, to reap the benefits of the internal combustion engine, millions of horse-drawn carriages and horses had to be replaced by cars; and, more recently, to reap the benefits of computerized word processing, millions of typewriters had to be replaced by PCs and printers.

Review Quiz

1   How do markets, property rights and monetary exchange facilitate economic growth? What are the economic activities that they make possible that lead to economic growth?
2   How do saving and investment in new capital, the growth of human capital and the discovery of new technologies generate economic growth?
3   Provide some examples of how human capital has created new technologies that are embodied in both human and physical capital.

We've described the sources of economic growth. What are the quantitative contributions of the sources of economic growth? To answer this question, economists use growth accounting.

Growth Accounting

The quantity of real GDP supplied (Y) depends on three factors:

1 The quantity of labour (L)
2 The quantity of capital (K)
3 The state of technology (T)

The purpose of **growth accounting** is to calculate how much real GDP growth results from growth of labour and capital and how much is attributable to technological change.

The key tool of growth accounting is the **aggregate production function**, which we write as:

$$Y = F(L, K, T)$$

In words, the quantity of real GDP supplied is determined by (is a function F of) the quantities of labour and capital and of the state of technology. The larger L, K or T, the greater is Y. And the faster L and K grow and T advances, the faster Y grows.

So understanding what makes labour and capital grow and technology advance is the key to understanding economic growth. Labour growth depends primarily on population growth. And the growth rate of capital and the pace of technological advance determine the growth rate of labour productivity.

Labour Productivity

Labour productivity is real GDP per hour of labour. Labour productivity is calculated by dividing real GDP Y by aggregate labour hours L.

Labour productivity determines how much income an hour of labour generates. Figure 30.4 shows labour productivity for the period 1963–2003. Productivity growth was most rapid during the 1960s. It slowed down in 1973 and remained low for about 6 years. Productivity growth then speeded up again in what has been called the new economy of the 1990s.

Why did productivity grow fastest during the 1960s and late 1990s? Why did it slow down in 1973 and then speed up again during the 1980s?

Growth accounting answers these questions by dividing the growth in labour productivity into two components and then measuring the contribution of each. The components are

1 Growth in capital per hour of labour
2 Technological change

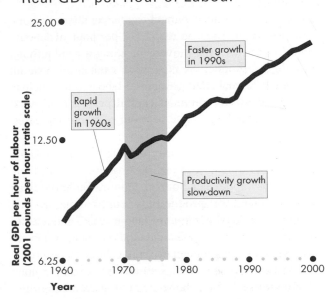

Figure 30.4

Real GDP per Hour of Labour

Real GDP divided by aggregate hours equals real GDP per hour of labour, which is a broad measure of productivity. During the 1960s, the productivity growth rate was high. It slowed during the 1970s and speeded up again during the 1990s.

Sources: Office for National Statistics, Labour Force Survey; R.C.O. Matthews, C.H. Feinstein and J.C. Odling-Smee, British Economic Growth 1856–1953, 1982, Oxford, Clarendon Press.

Capital is physical capital. Technological change includes everything that contributes to labour productivity growth that is not included in the growth in capital per hour. In particular, it includes human capital growth. Human capital growth and technological change are intimately related. Technology advances because knowledge advances. And knowledge is part of human capital. So "technological change" is a broad catchall concept.

The analytical engine of growth accounting is a relationship called the productivity curve. Let's learn about this relationship and see how it is used.

The Productivity Curve

The **productivity curve** is a relationship that shows how real GDP per hour of labour changes as the amount of capital per hour of labour changes with a given state of technology. Figure 30.5 illustrates the productivity curve. Capital per hour of labour is measured on the x-axis and real GDP per hour of labour is measured on the y-axis. The figure shows two productivity curves. One is the curve labelled PC_0 and the other is the curve labelled PC_1.

An increase in the amount of capital per hour of labour results in an increase in real GDP per hour of labour, which is shown by a movement along a productivity curve. For example, on PC_0, when capital per hour of labour is £20, real GDP per hour of labour is £5. On that same productivity curve, if capital per hour of work increases to £40, real GDP per hour of labour increases to £7.

Technological change increases the amount of GDP per hour of labour that can be produced by a given amount of capital per hour of labour. Technological change shifts the productivity curve upward. For example, if capital per hour of labour is £20 and a technological change increases real GDP per hour of labour from £5 to £7, the productivity curve shifts upward from PC_0 to PC_1 in Figure 30.5. Similarly, if capital per hour of labour is £40, the same technological change increases real GDP per hour of labour from £7 to £10 and shifts the productivity curve upward from PC_0 to PC_1.

To calculate the contributions of capital growth and technological change to productivity growth, we need to know the shape of the productivity curve. The shape of the productivity curve reflects a fundamental economic law – the law of diminishing returns. The **law of diminishing returns** states that as the quantity of one input increases with the quantities of all other inputs remaining the same, output increases but by ever smaller increments. For example, in a factory that has a given amount of capital, as more labour is hired, production increases. But each *additional* hour of labour produces less *additional* output than the previous hour produced. Two typists working with one computer type fewer than twice as many pages per day as one typist working with one computer.

Applied to capital, the law of diminishing returns states that if a given number of hours of labour use more capital (with the same technology), the *additional* output that results from the *additional* capital gets smaller as the amount of capital increases. One typist working with two computers types fewer than twice as many pages per day as one typist working with one computer. More generally, one hour of labour working with £40 of capital produces less than twice the output of one hour of labour working with £20 of capital. But how much less?

The answer is going to be different for every production process. But on the average for the economy as a whole, the answer is given by the "one-third rule" that we'll now study.

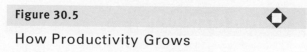

Figure 30.5

How Productivity Grows

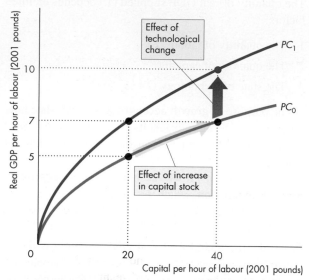

Productivity can be measured by real GDP per hour of labour. Productivity can grow for two reasons: (1) capital per hour of labour increases, and (2) technological advances occur. The productivity curve, *PC*, shows the effects of an increase in capital per hour of labour on productivity. Here, when capital per hour of labour increases from £20 to £40, real GDP per hour of labour increases from £5 to £7 along the productivity curve PC_0. Technological advance shifts the productivity curve upward. Here, an advance in technology shifts the productivity curve from PC_0 to PC_1. When capital per hour of labour is £40, real GDP per hour of labour increases from £7 to £10.

The One-third Rule

Robert Solow of MIT estimated a productivity curve and discovered the **one-third rule**: on average, with no change in technology, a 1 per cent increase in capital per hour of labour brings a *one-third of 1 per cent* increase in real GDP per hour of labour. This one-third rule is used to calculate the contributions of an increase in capital per hour of labour and technological change to the growth of real GDP. Let's do such a calculation.

Suppose that capital per hour of labour grows by 3 per cent a year and real GDP grows by 2.5 per cent a year. The one-third rule tells us that capital growth has contributed one-third of 3 per cent, which is 1 per cent. The rest of the 2.5 per cent growth of real GDP comes from technological change. That is, technological change has contributed 1.5 per cent.

Accounting for the Productivity Growth Slowdown and Speed-up

We can use the one-third rule to study the UK productivity growth and productivity slowdown. Figure 30.6 tells the story, starting in 1960.

1960 to 1973

In 1960, capital per hour of labour (measured in 2001 pounds) was £24.13. Real GDP per hour of labour was £6.98 at the point marked 60 on PC_{60} in Figure 30.6. Over the next 13 years, capital per hour grew at about 4.5 per cent a year to £42.87 and real GDP per hour increased at about 4.3 per cent a year to £12.01. With no change in technology, the economy would have moved to point A on PC_{60}. But rapid technological change increased productivity and shifted the productivity curve upward from PC_{60} to PC_{73}. The economy moved to the point marked 73.

1973 to 1979

Between 1973 and 1979, capital per hour of labour grew at 2 per cent a year to £48.18 and real GDP per hour of labour grew at 0.9 per cent a year to £12.68. With no change in technology, the economy would have moved to point B in Figure 30.6. And there was almost no change in technology. The productivity curve shifted from PC_{73} to PC_{79}, a shift that is almost invisible in the figure, and the economy moved to the point marked 79.

The reasons for the productivity growth slowdown have now been identified. It was partly the result of slower growth in capital per hour of labour – a slow down from 4.5 per cent a year to 2 per cent a year. But the productivity slowdown was mainly the result of a near zero contribution of technological change during this period.

1979 to 2003

Between 1979 and 2003, capital per hour of labour grew at 2.4 per cent a year to £84.23 and real GDP per hour of labour grew by 2.3 per cent to £22.06. With no change in technology, the economy would have moved to point C in Figure 30.6. But technological change shifted the productivity curve upward from PC_{79} to PC_{03} and the economy moved to the point marked 03.

Figure 30.6

Growth Accounting and the Productivity Changes

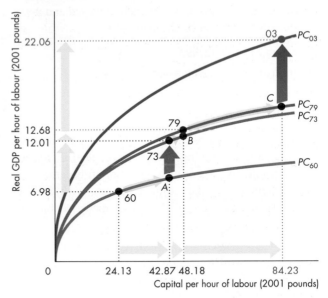

(a) The shifting productivity curve

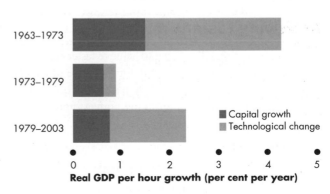

(b) The sources of growth

Part (a) shows the productivity curves for 1960, PC_{60}, 1973, PC_{73}, 1979, PC_{79}, and 2003, PC_{03}. The points labelled 60, 73, 79, and 03 show actual levels of capital per hour of labour and real GDP per hour of labour. The points labelled A, B and C show where the economy would have moved if there had been no technological change. Part (b) shows that growth slowed between 1973 and 1979 mainly because the contribution of technological change shrank to almost zero.

Sources: R.C.O. Matthews, C.H. Feinstein and J.C. Odling-Smee, *British Economic Growth 1856–1953*, 1982, Oxford, Clarendon Press; Angus Maddison, *Dynamic Forces in Capitalist Development*, 1991, Oxford, Oxford University Press; Office for National Statistics, and the authors' assumptions and calculations.

Technological Change During the Productivity Growth Slowdown

Technological change did not stop during the growth slowdown of the 1970s. But its focus changed and it was to some degree offset by the effects of:

◆ Energy price shocks
◆ Industrial relations tensions

Energy Price Shocks

Energy price increases in 1973–1974 and 1979 diverted research towards saving energy rather than increasing labour productivity. For example, aircraft became more fuel efficient, but they didn't operate with smaller crews. Real GDP per gallon of fuel increased but real GDP per hour of labour stagnated.

Industrial Relations Tensions

During the 1970s, trade union membership increased from 45 per cent to 59 per cent of the workforce. Restrictive labour practices, overmanning and strike activity increased. These negative factors are captured in the catch-all of "technological change".

Achieving Faster Growth

Growth accounting tells us that to achieve faster economic growth we must either increase the growth rate of capital per hour of labour or increase the pace of technological advance (which includes improving human capital). The main ways of achieving these objectives are:

◆ Stimulate saving
◆ Stimulate research and development
◆ Target high-technology industries
◆ Encourage international trade
◆ Improve the quality of education

Stimulate Saving

Saving finances investment and investment increases the quantity of capital. So stimulating saving can stimulate economic growth. The East Asian economies have the highest growth rates and the highest saving rates.

Tax incentives can increase saving. Tax incentives to stimulate saving already exist, but economists claim that a tax on consumption rather than income provides the best saving incentive.

Stimulate Research and Development

Everyone can use the fruits of basic research and development efforts. For example, all biotechnology firms can use advances in gene-splicing technology. Because basic inventions can be copied, the inventor's profit is limited, and the market allocates too few resources to this activity.

Governments can use public funds to finance basic research, but some mechanism is needed to allocate the funds to their highest-valued use. The universities and research councils are the main channels through which public funds are used to finance research in the United Kingdom.

Target High-Technology Industries

Some people say that by providing public funds to high-technology firms and industries, a country can become the first to exploit a new technology and can earn above-average profits for a period while others are busy catching up. This strategy is risky and just as likely to use resources inefficiently as to speed growth.

Encourage International Trade

Free international trade stimulates growth by extracting all the available gains from specialization and trade. The fastest-growing nations today are those with the fastest-growing exports and imports.

Improve the Quality of Education

The free market produces too little education because it brings benefits beyond those valued by the people who receive the education. By funding basic education and by ensuring high standards in basic skills such as language, mathematics and science, governments can contribute to a nation's growth potential. Education can also be stimulated and improved by using tax incentives to encourage improved private education.

Review Quiz

1 Explain the one-third rule and explain how the rule is used in growth accounting to isolate the contributions of capital growth and technological change to productivity growth.
2 Explain how growth accounting can be used to provide information about the factors that contributed to the productivity growth slowdown.

Growth Theories

We've seen that real GDP grows when the quantities of labour and capital (which includes human capital) grow and when technology advances. Does this mean that the growth of labour and capital *cause* economic growth It might mean that. But there are other possibilities. *One of these factors might be the cause of real GDP growth and the others might be the effect.* We must try to discover how the influences on economic growth interact with each other to make some economies grow quickly and others grow slowly. And we must probe the reasons why a country's long-term growth rate sometimes speeds up and sometimes slows down.

Growth theories are designed to study the interactions among the several factors that contribute to growth and to disentangle cause and effect. They are also designed to enable us to study the way the different factors influence each other.

Growth theories are also designed to be universal. They are not theories about the growth of poor countries only or rich countries only. They are theories about why and how poor countries become rich and rich countries continue to get richer.

We're going to study three theories of economic growth, each one of which gives some insights into the process of economic growth. But none provides a definite answer to the basic questions: what causes economic growth and why do growth rates vary? Economics has some way to go before it can provide a definite answer to these most important of questions. The three growth theories we study are:

◆ Classical growth theory

◆ Neoclassical growth theory

◆ New growth theory

Classical Growth Theory

Classical growth theory is the view that real GDP growth is temporary and that when real GDP per person rises above the subsistence level, a population explosion eventually brings real GDP per person back to the subsistence level. Adam Smith, Thomas Robert Malthus and David Ricardo, the leading economists of the late eighteenth century and early nineteenth century, proposed this theory, but the view is most closely associated with the name of Malthus and is sometimes called the *Malthusian theory.*

Many people today are Malthusians! They say that if today's global population of 6.2 billion explodes to 11 billion by 2200, we will run out of resources and return to a primitive standard of living. We must act, say the Malthusians, to contain the population growth.

The Basic Classical Idea

To understand classical growth theory let's transport ourselves back to the world of 1710. Many of the 5.3 million people who lived in England worked on farms or on their own land and performed their tasks using simple tools and animal power. They earned about 1 shilling and 4 pence for working a 10-hour day.

Then advances in farming technology brought new types of ploughs and seeds that increased farm productivity. As farm productivity increased, farm production rose and some farm workers moved from the land to the cities, where they got work producing and selling the expanding range of farm equipment. Incomes rose and the people seemed to be prospering. But would the prosperity last? Classical growth theory says it would not.

Advances in technology – in both agriculture and industry – lead to investment in new capital, which makes labour more productive. More and more businesses start up and hire the now more productive labour. The greater demand for labour raises the real wage rate and increases employment.

At this stage, economic growth has occurred and everyone has benefited from it. Real GDP has increased and real wage rate has increased. But the classical economists believed that this new situation can't last because it will induce a population explosion.

Classical Theory of Population Growth

When the classical economists were developing their ideas about population growth, an unprecedented population explosion was underway. In Britain and other Western European countries, improvements in diet and hygiene had lowered the death rate while the birth rate remained high. For several decades, population growth was extremely rapid. For example, after being relatively stable for several centuries, the population of Britain increased by 40 per cent between 1750 and 1800 and by a further 50 per cent between 1800 and 1830. Meanwhile, an estimated 1 million people (about 20 per cent of the 1750 population) left Britain for North America and Australia before 1800, and outward migration continued on a similar scale through the nineteenth century. These facts are the empirical basis for the classical theory of population growth.

To explain the high rate of population growth, the classical economists used the idea of a **subsistence real wage rate**, which is the minimum real wage rate needed to maintain life. If the actual real wage rate is less than the subsistence real wage rate, some people cannot survive and the population decreases. In the classical theory, whenever the real wage rate exceeds the subsistence real wage rate, the population grows. But a rising population brings diminishing returns to labour. So labour productivity eventually decreases. This dismal implication led to economics being called the *dismal science*. The dismal implication is that no matter how much technological change occurs, real wage rates are always pushed back towards the subsistence level.

Classical Theory and the Productivity Curve

Figure 30.7 illustrates the classical growth theory using the productivity curve. Initially, the productivity curve is PC_0. Subsistence real GDP is £10 an hour, shown by the horizontal line in the graph. The economy starts out at point *A*, with £30 of capital per hour of labour and £10 of real GDP per hour of labour, the subsistence level. Because real GDP is at the subsistence level, the population is constant.

Then a technological advance occurs, which shifts the productivity curve upward to PC_1. The economy now moves to point *B* on PC_1 and real GDP per hour of labour rises to £15. Now earning more than the subsistence wage, people have more children and live longer. The population grows.

A growing population means that labour hours grow, so capital per hour of labour falls. As capital per hour of labour falls, there is a movement down along the productivity curve PC_1. Real GDP per hour of labour falls and keeps falling as long as the population grows and capital per hour of labour falls.

This process ends when real GDP per hour of labour is back at the subsistence level at point *C* on productivity curve PC_1. The population stops growing and capital per hour of labour stops falling.

Repeated advances in technology play out in the same way as the advance that we've just studied. No matter how productive our economy becomes, population growth lowers capital per hour of labour and drives real GDP per hour of labour towards the subsistence level. Living standards temporarily improve while the population is expanding, but when the population expansion ends, the standard of living is back at the subsistence level.

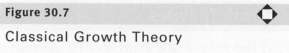

Figure 30.7

Classical Growth Theory

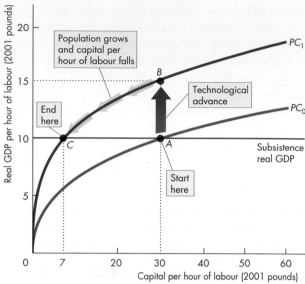

The economy starts out at point *A* with capital per hour of labour of £30 and real GDP per hour of labour of £10 – the subsistence level – on productivity curve PC_0. A technological advance shifts the productivity curve upward to PC_1 and the economy moves to point *B*. The population grows, and both capital and real GDP per hour of labour decrease. The process ends at point *C* when real GDP per hour of labour is back at its subsistence level.

Classical Theory and Capital Accumulation

In the story you've just worked through, the total quantity of capital didn't change. Suppose that people save and invest, so capital grows. Doesn't a growing quantity of capital prevent the dismal conclusion of classical theory? It does not. *Anything* that raises real GDP per hour of labour above the subsistence level triggers a population explosion that eventually wipes out the gains from greater productivity.

The dismal conclusion of classical growth theory is a direct consequence of the assumption that the population explodes if real GDP per hour of labour exceeds the subsistence level. To avoid this conclusion, we need a different view of population growth.

The neoclassical growth theory that we'll now study provides a different view.

Neoclassical Growth Theory

Neoclassical growth theory is the proposition that real GDP per person grows because technological change induces a level of savings and investment that makes capital per hour of labour grow. Growth ends only if technological change stops.

Robert Solow of MIT suggested the most popular version of neoclassical growth theory in the 1950s. But Frank Ramsey of Cambridge University first developed this theory in the 1920s.

Neoclassical theory's big break with its classical predecessor is its view about population growth. So we'll begin our account of neoclassical theory by examining its views about population growth.

The Neoclassical Economics of Population Growth

The population explosion of eighteenth century Europe that created the classical theory of population eventually ended. The birth rate fell and the population growth rate became moderate. This slowdown in population growth seemed to make the classical theory less relevant. It also eventually led to the development of a modern economic theory of population growth.

The modern view is that although the population growth rate is influenced by economic factors, the influence is not a simple and mechanical one like that proposed by the classical economists. Key among the economic influences on population growth is the opportunity cost of a woman's time. As women's wage rates increase and their job opportunities expand, the opportunity cost of having children increases. Faced with a higher opportunity cost, families choose to have fewer children and the birth rate falls.

A second economic influence works on the death rate. The technological advance that brings increased productivity and increased incomes brings advances in healthcare that extend lives.

These two opposing economic forces influence the population growth rate. As incomes increase, both the birth rate and the death rate decrease. It turns out that these opposing forces almost offset each other, so the rate of population growth is independent of the rate of economic growth.

This modern view of population growth and the historical trends that support it contradict the views of the classical economists and call into question the modern doomsday conclusion that the planet will one day be swamped with too many people to feed.

Neoclassical growth theory adopts this modern view of population growth. Forces other than real GDP and its growth rate determine population growth.

Technological Change

In the neoclassical theory, the rate of technological change influences the rate of economic growth but economic growth does not influence the pace of technological change. It is assumed that technological change results from chance. When we get lucky, we have rapid technological change, and when bad luck strikes, the pace of technological advance slows.

Target Rate of Return and Saving

The key assumption in the neoclassical growth theory concerns saving. Other things remaining the same, the higher the real interest rate, the greater is the amount that people save. To decide how much to save, people compare the rate of return with a *target rate of return*. If the rate of return exceeds the target rate of return, saving is sufficient to make capital per hour of labour grow. If the target rate of return exceeds the rate of return, saving is not sufficient to maintain the current level of capital per hour of labour, so capital per hour of labour shrinks. And if the rate of return equals a target rate of return, saving is just sufficient to maintain the quantity of capital per hour of labour at its current level.

The Basic Neoclassical Idea

To understand neoclassical growth theory, imagine the world of the late 1950s, just after Robert Solow has explained his idea. Prime Minister Harold Macmillan is running a General Election campaign with the slogan "You've never had it so good." Income per person is around £6,000 a year in today's money. The population is growing at about 1 per cent a year. People are saving and investing about 20 per cent of their incomes, enough to keep the quantity of capital per hour of labour constant. Income per person is growing, but not by much.

Then technology begins to advance at a more rapid pace. The transistor revolutionizes an emerging electronics industry. New plastics revolutionize the manufacture of household appliances. Motorways begin to revolutionize road transport. Jet airliners start to replace piston-engine planes and speed air transport.

These technological advances bring new profit opportunities. Businesses expand and new businesses are created to exploit the newly available profitable technologies. Investment and saving increase. The economy enjoys new levels of prosperity and growth. But will the prosperity last? And will the growth last?

Neoclassical growth theory says that the *prosperity* will last but the *growth* will not last unless technology keeps advancing.

According to the neoclassical growth theory, the prosperity will persist because there is no classical population growth to induce lower wages.

But growth will stop if technology stops advancing, for two related reasons. First, high profit rates that result from technological change bring increased saving and capital accumulation. But second, capital accumulation eventually results in diminishing returns that lower the rate of return, and that eventually decrease saving and slow the rate of capital accumulation.

Neoclassical Theory and the Productivity Curve

Figure 30.8 illustrates the neoclassical growth theory using the productivity curve. Initially, the productivity curve is PC_0 and the economy is at point A, with £30 of capital per hour of labour and real GDP of £10 an hour.

The slope of the productivity curve measures the additional output that results from an additional unit of capital – the marginal product of capital or rate of return on capital. People have a target rate of return that can be illustrated by a straight line with a slope equal to the target rate of return.

At point A on productivity curve PC_0, the slope of the PC curve equals the slope of the target rate of return line. If the quantity of capital per hour of labour were less than £30, the real interest rate would exceed the target rate of return and capital per hour of labour would grow. If the quantity of capital per hour of labour were greater than £30, the rate of return would be less than the target rate of return and capital per hour of labour would shrink. But when the quantity of capital per hour of labour is £30, the rate of return equals the target rate of return and capital per hour of labour is constant.

Now a technological advance occurs that shifts the productivity curve upward to PC_1. The economy now moves to point B on PC_1, and real GDP per hour of labour rises to £15. It is at this point in the classical theory that forces kick in to drive real GDP per hour of labour back to the subsistence level. But in the neoclassical theory, no such forces operate. Instead, at point B, the rate of return exceeds the target rate of return. (You can see why by comparing the slopes of PC_1 at point B and the target rate of return line.)

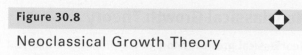

Figure 30.8

Neoclassical Growth Theory

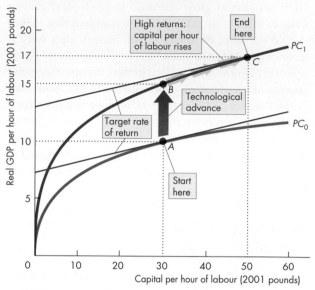

The economy starts on productivity curve PC_0 at point A. The slope of the productivity curve measures the rate of return, so at point A the rate of return equals the target rate of return. A technological advance shifts the productivity curve upward to PC_1 and the economy moves to point B. The rate of return exceeds the target rate of return, and the quantity of capital per hour of labour increases – a movement up along the productivity curve PC_1. Growth ends when the rate of return again equals the target rate of return at point C.

With a high rate of return available, saving and investment increase and the quantity of capital per hour of labour increases. There is a movement up along the productivity curve PC_1 and real GDP per hour of labour increases.

This growth process eventually ends because, as the quantity of capital per hour of labour increases, the rate of return falls. At point C, where the process ends, the real interest rate again equals the target rate of return.

Throughout the process you've just studied, real GDP per hour of labour grows but the growth rate gradually decreases and eventually growth ends.

But if another advance in technology occurs, the process you've just seen repeats. Ongoing advances in technology constantly increase the rate of return, inducing the saving that increases capital per hour of labour.

The growth process persists as long as technology advances. And the growth rate fluctuates because technological progress occurs at a variable rate.

A Problem with Neoclassical Growth Theory

All economies have access to the same technologies and capital is free to roam the globe seeking the highest available rate of return. Given these facts, neoclassical growth theory implies that growth rates and income levels per person around the globe will converge. While there is some sign of convergence among the rich countries, as Figure 30.2(a) shows, convergence is slow, and it does not appear to be imminent for all countries, as Figure 30.2(b) shows.

New growth theory attempts to overcome this shortcoming of neoclassical growth theory. It also attempts to explain how the rate of technological change is determined.

New Growth Theory

New growth theory holds that real GDP per person grows because of the choices people make in the pursuit of profit and that growth can persist indefinitely.

Paul Romer of Stanford University developed this theory during the 1980s, but the ideas go back to work by Joseph Schumpeter during the 1930s and 1940s.

The theory begins with two facts about market economies:

◆ Discoveries result from choices
◆ Discoveries bring profit and competition destroys profit

Discoveries and Choices

When someone discovers a new product or technique, they think of themselves as being lucky. They are right. But the pace at which new discoveries are made – at which technology advances – is not determined by chance. It depends on how many people are looking for a new way of doing something and how intensively they are looking.

Discoveries and Profits

Profit is the spur to technological change. The forces of competition are constantly squeezing profits, so to increase profit, people constantly seek either lower-cost methods of production or new and better products for which people are willing to pay a higher price. Inventors can maintain a profit for several years by taking out a patent or a copyright. But eventually, a new discovery is copied and profits disappear.

Two further facts play a key role in the new growth theory:

◆ Discoveries are a public capital good.
◆ Knowledge is capital that is not subject to the law of diminishing returns.

Discoveries are a Public Capital Good

Economists call a good a public good when no one can be excluded from using it and when one person's use does not prevent others from using it. National defence is one example of a public good. Knowledge is another.

When in 1992, Marc Andreesen and his friend Eric Bina developed a browser they called Mosaic, they laid the foundation for Netscape Navigator and Internet Explorer, two pieces of capital that have increased productivity unimaginably.

While patents and copyrights protect the inventors or creators of new products and production processes, and enable them to reap the returns from their innovative ideas, once a new discovery has been made, everyone can benefit from its use. And one person's use of a new discovery does not prevent others from using it. Your use of a Web browser doesn't prevent someone else from using that same browser simultaneously.

Because knowledge is a public good, as the benefits of a new discovery spread, free resources become available. These resources are free because nothing is given up when they are used. They have a zero opportunity cost. Knowledge is even more special because it is not subject to diminishing returns.

Knowledge Capital is not Subject to Diminishing Returns

Production is subject to diminishing returns when one resource is fixed and the quantity of another resource changes. Adding labour to a fixed amount of equipment or adding equipment to a fixed amount of labour both bring diminishing marginal product – diminishing returns.

But increasing the stock of knowledge makes labour and machines more productive. Knowledge capital does not bring diminishing returns.

The fact that knowledge capital does not experience diminishing returns is the central novel proposition of the new growth theory. And the implication of this simple and appealing idea is astonishing. The new growth theory has no growth-stopping mechanism like those of the other two theories. As physical capital accumulates, the rate of return falls. But the incentive to innovate and earn a higher profit becomes stronger. So innovation occurs, which increases the rate of return. Real GDP per hour of labour grows indefinitely as people find new technologies that yield a higher real interest rate.

The growth rate depends on people's ability to innovate and the rate of return. Over the years, the ability to innovate has changed. The invention of language and writing (the two most basic human capital tools) and later the development of the scientific method and the establishment of universities and research institutions brought huge increases in the rate of return. Today, a deeper understanding of genes is bringing profit in a growing biotechnology industry. And astonishing advances in computer technology are creating an explosion of profit opportunities in a wide range of information-age industries.

New Growth Theory and the Productivity Curve

Figure 30.9 illustrates new growth theory. Like Figure 30.8, which illustrates neoclassical growth theory, Figure 30.9 contains a productivity curve and a target rate of return curve.

But unlike in neoclassical theory, the productivity curve in the new growth theory never stands still. The pursuit of profit means that technology is always advancing and human capital is always growing. The result is an ever upward-shifting PC curve. As physical capital is accumulated, diminishing returns lower its rate of return. But ever-advancing productivity counteracts this tendency and keeps the rate of return above the target rate of return curve.

Advancing technology and human capital growth keep the PC curve shifting upward in Figure 30.9 from PC_0 to PC_1 to PC_2 and beyond. As the productivity curve shifts upward, capital per hour of labour and real GDP per hour of labour increase together along the line labelled "Ak line".

The new growth theory implies that although the productivity curve shows diminishing returns, if capital is interpreted more broadly as physical capital, human capital and the technologies they embody then real GDP per hour of labour grows at the same rate as the growth in capital per hour of labour. Real GDP per hour of labour is proportional to capital per hour of labour.

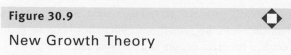

Figure 30.9

New Growth Theory

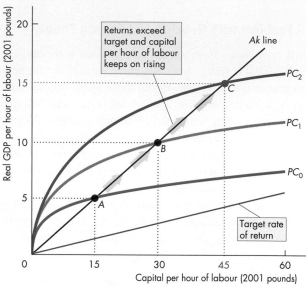

In new growth theory, economic growth results from incentives to innovate and from capital that does not experience diminishing returns. The productivity curve, PC, keeps shifting upward, and real GDP per hour of labour and capital per hour of labour grow along the Ak line.

Real GDP per hour of labour y is related to capital per hour of labour k by the equation:

$$y = Ak$$

In Figure 30.9, A is 1/3. When capital per hour of labour is £15, real GDP per hour of labour is £5 at point A. People look for yet more profit and accumulate yet more capital. The economy expands to point B, with capital per hour of labour of £30 and real GDP per hour of labour of £10. In pursuit of further profit, technology keeps advancing and capital per hour of labour rises to £45 with real GDP per hour of labour of £15, at point C. Real GDP per hour of labour and capital per hour of labour increase without limit.

A Perpetual Motion Economy

The new growth theory sees the economy as a perpetual motion machine, which Figure 30.10 illustrates. Insatiable wants lead us to pursue profit, innovate and create new and better products. New firms start up and old firms go out of business. As firms start up and die, jobs are created and destroyed. New and better jobs

Figure 30.10

A Perpetual Motion Machine

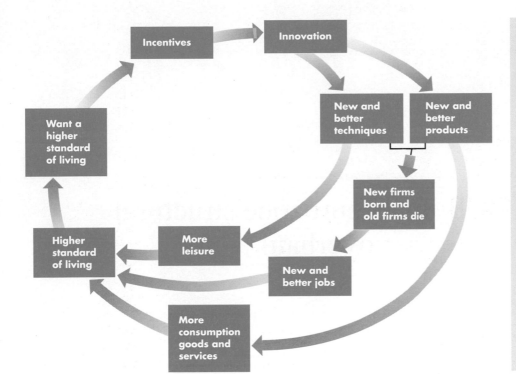

People want a higher standard of living and are spurred by profit incentives to make the innovations that lead to new and better techniques and new and better products, which in turn lead to the birth of new firms and the death of some old firms, new and better jobs, more leisure and more consumption of goods and services. The result is a higher standard of living. But people want a still higher standard of living and the growth process continues.

Source: Based on a similar figure in *These Are the Good Old Days: A Report on U.S. Living Standards*, Federal Reserve Bank of Dallas 1993 Annual Report.

lead to more leisure and more consumption. But our insatiable wants are still there, so the process continues, going around and around a circle of wants, profits, innovation and new products.

Sorting out the Theories

Which theory is correct? Probably none, but they all teach us something of value. The classical theory reminds us that our physical resources are limited and that with no advances in technology, we must eventually hit diminishing returns. Neoclassical theory reaches essentially the same conclusion, but not because of a population explosion. Instead, it emphasizes diminishing returns to capital and reminds us that we cannot keep growth going just by accumulating physical capital. We must also advance technology and accumulate human capital. We must become more creative in our use of scarce resources. New growth theory emphasizes the possible capacity of human resources to innovate at a pace that offsets diminishing returns.

Review Quiz

1   What is the central idea of classical growth theory that leads to the dismal outcome?
2   What, according to the neoclassical growth theory, is the fundamental cause of economic growth?
3   What is the key proposition of the new growth theory that makes growth persist?

Economic growth is the single most decisive factor influencing a country's living standard. But another is the extent to which the country fully employs its scarce resources. In the next chapter, we study economic fluctuations and recessions But before embarking on this topic, take a look at *Reading Between the Lines* on pp. 696–697, which compares recent economic growth in the Eurozone with that in the United States.

Reading Between the Lines
Productivity Growth Trends in the Eurozone

The Financial Times, 9 July 2004

ECB urges eurozone structural overhaul

Ralph Atkins

The European Central Bank yesterday stepped up pressure for structural reform in the eurozone, releasing a study of productivity growth trends it said made "rapid and forceful" implementation of the European Union's liberalisation plans "even more urgent".

The research, published in the ECB's monthly bulletin, followed concern expressed last week by Jean-Claude Trichet, the central bank's president, about the downward trend in labour productivity growth since the mid-1990s, which has contrasted with the rise in the US over the same period

The ECB argues that, without an improvement in the eurozone's medium-term growth prospects, the standard of living would decline as the population ages. Its productivity study calculates that real gross domestic product per capita increased by 1.6 per cent a year in the euro area between 1996 and 2003, compared with 2.2 per cent in the US. One explanation for the slowdown in productivity growth in the euro area, the study says, has been the stronger increase in employment as more people have joined the labour market. But it also says the impact of new technology has been "relatively subdued", partly because technology-intensive service sectors are still relatively small in the euro area.

Together such trends "make a rapid and forceful implementation of the (EU's) 'Lisbon' agenda (to make Europe the world's most competitive economy by 2010) even more urgent," the study concludes. "Only if the euro area can manage to reap the benefits of innovation and the widespread diffusion of new technologies will it be able to improve its long term prospects for productivity growth".

The Essence of the Story

◆ A slowdown in productivity growth in the Eurozone economies since the mid-1990s contrasts with strong productivity growth in the United States in the same period.

◆ The ECB report says that if the Eurozone does not increase productivity growth, the standard of living in the euro area will fall as the population ages.

◆ The ECB says that widespread adoption of new technologies is needed to improve long-term growth.

Economic Analysis

◆ Figure 1 shows the growth rates of real GDP per hour of labour in the Eurozone and in the United States.

◆ The growth of real GDP per hour in the Eurozone has fallen and from the mid-1990s it has fallen below that of the United States.

◆ The ECB report identifies two reasons for the slowdown in productivity growth:

   1 A stronger growth in the employment of low-skilled labour in the Eurozone than in the United States

   2 A greater impact of information technology (IT) investment in the United States than in the Eurozone.

◆ Figure 2 shows the growth of output per person employed in the IT-intensive sectors in the Eurozone and the United States.

◆ Except for telecoms, in all the other IT-intensive industries the United States has outpaced the Eurozone in the period 1996–2003.

◆ Figure 3 compares the productivity curves in the Eurozone and United States. Faster technological change in the United States has shifted the productivity curve up further and greater investment in the United States has increased the amount of capital per hour of labour by more than in the Eurozone.

◆ The new technology sectors are smaller in the Eurozone economies than in the United States. About one-quarter of the labour force in the Eurozone works in the IT-intensive sectors of the economy, compared with more than one-third of the work force in the United States.

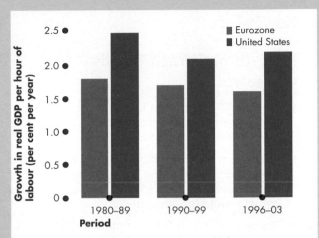

Figure 1 Growth in real GDP per hour of labour

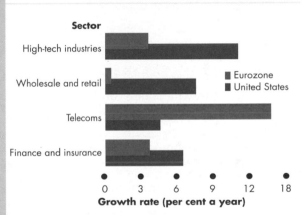

Figure 2 Labour productivity in IT-intensive sectors 1996–2003

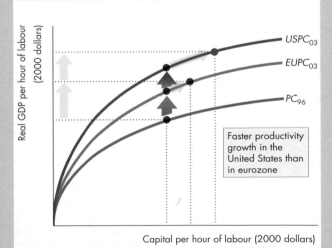

Figure 3 Productivity curves

Summary

Key Points

Long-term Growth Trends
(pp. 680–682)

◆ Real GDP per person in the United Kingdom has grown at an average rate of 1.3 per cent a year over the long term.

◆ Among the major industrial countries, the United States has the highest real GDP per person and the gaps among the rich countries remain roughly constant.

◆ Some poor countries are falling further behind the rich countries but others, notably Hong Kong, South Korea, Singapore, Taiwan and China are closing the gaps.

The Causes of Economic Growth: A First Look (pp. 683–684)

◆ Economic growth requires an *incentive* system created by markets, property rights and monetary exchange.

◆ Economic growth occurs when people save, invest in physical capital, and discover new technologies.

Growth Accounting (pp. 685–688)

◆ Growth accounting measures the contributions of capital accumulation and technological change to productivity growth.

◆ Growth accounting uses the productivity curve and the one-third rule: a 1 per cent increase in capital per hour of labour brings a one-third of 1 per cent increase in real GDP per hour of labour.

◆ During the productivity growth slowdown of the 1970s, technological change made almost no contribution to real GDP growth.

◆ It might be possible to achieve faster growth by stimulating saving, subsidizing research and development, targeting (and possibly subsidizing) high-technology industries, encouraging more international trade and encouraging more education and training.

Growth Theories (pp. 689–695)

◆ In the classical theory, when a technological advance increases real GDP per person above the *subsistence* level, a population explosion brings diminishing returns to labour and real GDP per person returns to the subsistence level.

◆ In neoclassical growth theory, when a technological advance increases saving and investment, an increase in the capital stock brings diminishing returns to capital and eventually, without further technological change, the capital stock and real GDP per person stop growing.

◆ In new growth theory, when a technological advance increases saving and investment, an increase in the capital stock *does not* bring diminishing returns to capital and growth persists indefinitely.

Key Figures

Figure 30.1 A Hundred and Fifty Years of Economic Growth in the United Kingdom, 680
Figure 30.5 How Productivity Grows, 686
Figure 30.6 Growth Accounting and the Productivity Changes, 687
Figure 30.7 Classical Growth Theory, 690
Figure 30.8 Neoclassical Growth Theory, 692
Figure 30.9 New Growth Theory, 694

Key Terms

Aggregate production function, 685
Classical growth theory, 689
Growth accounting, 685
Labour productivity, 685
Law of diminishing returns, 686
Neoclassical growth theory, 691
New growth theory, 693
One-third rule, 686
Productivity curve, 685
Subsistence real wage rate, 690

Problems

*1 The following information has been discovered about the economy of Longland: The economy's productivity curve is:

Capital per hour of labour (2001 pounds per hour)	Real GDP per hour of labour (2001 pounds per hour)
10	3.80
20	5.70
30	7.13
40	8.31
50	9.35
60	10.29
70	11.14
80	11.94

Does this economy conform to the one-third rule? If so, explain why. If not, explain why not and explain what rule, if any, it does conform to. Explain how you would do the growth accounting for this economy.

2 The following information has been discovered about the economy of Flatland: the economy's productivity curve is:

Capital per hour of labour (2001 pounds per hour)	Real GDP per hour of labour (2001 pounds per hour)
20	6.00
40	7.50
60	8.44
80	9.14
100	9.72
120	10.20
140	10.62
160	11.00

Does this economy conform to the one-third rule? If so, explain why. If not, explain why not and explain what rule, if any, it does conform to. Explain how you would do the growth accounting for this economy.

*3 In Longland, described in problem 1, capital per hour of labour in 1999 was £40 and real GDP per hour of labour was £8.31. In 2001, capital per hour of labour had increased to £50 and real GDP per hour of labour had increased to £10.29 an hour.

a Does Longland experience diminishing returns? Explain why or why not.

b Use growth accounting to find the contribution of the change in capital between 1999 and 2001 to the growth of productivity in Longland.

c Use growth accounting to find the contribution of technological change between 1999 and 2001 to the growth of productivity in Longland.

4 In Flatland, described in problem 2, capital per hour of labour in 1999 was £60 and real GDP per hour of labour was £8.44. In 2001, capital per hour of labour had increased to £1,200 and real GDP per hour of labour had increased to £12.74 an hour.

a Does Flatland experience diminishing returns? Explain why or why not.

b Use growth accounting to find the contribution of the change in capital between 1999 and 2001 to the growth of productivity in Flatland.

c Use growth accounting to find the contribution of technological change between 1999 and 2001 to the growth of productivity in Flatland.

*5 The following information has been discovered about the economy of Cape Despair. The subsistence real wage rate is £15 an hour. Whenever the real wage rate rises above this level the population grows, and when the real wage rate falls below this level the population decreases. The productivity curve in Cape Despair is as follows:

Capital per hour of labour (2001 pounds per hour)	Real GDP per hour of labour (2001 pounds per hour)
20	8
40	15
60	21
80	26
100	30
120	33
140	35
160	36

Initially, the population of Cape Despair is constant and real GDP is at its subsistence level. Then a technological advance shifts the productivity curve upward by £7 at each level of capital per hour of labour.

a What is the initial capital per hour of labour and real GDP per hour of labour?

b What happens to the real GDP per hour of labour immediately following the technological advance?

c What happens to the population growth rate following the technological advance?

d What is the eventually quantity of capital per hour of labour in Cape Despair?

6 Martha's Island is an economy that behaves according to the neoclassical growth model. The economy has no growth, a target rate of return of 10 per cent a year and the following productivity curve:

Capital per hour of labour (2001 pounds per year)	Real GDP per hour of labour (2001 pounds per hour)
40	16
80	30
120	42
160	52
200	60
240	66
280	70
320	72

a What is the initial real interest rate on Martha's Island?

b What is the target rate?

A technological advance increases the demand for capital by £2 billion at each real interest rate.

c What is the real interest rate immediately following the technological advance?

d What is the real interest rate and quantity of capital when Martha's Island returns to a long-run equilibrium?

*7 Romeria is a country that behaves according to the predictions of new growth theory. The target rate is 3 per cent a year. A technological advance increases the demand for capital and raises the real interest rate to 5 per cent a year. Describe the events that happen in Romeria and contrast them with the events in Martha's Island in problem 6.

8 Suppose that in Romeria, which is described in problem 7, technological advance slows and the real interest rate falls to 3 per cent a year. Describe what happens in Romeria.

Critical Thinking

1 After studying *Reading Between the Lines* on pp. 696–697, answer the following questions:

a What is the reason suggested by the ECB for the weaker growth in real GDP person in the Eurozone than in the United States between 1996 and 2003?

b What was the growth rate of real GDP per person in the Eurozone and the United States in 1996–2003?

c If the growth in hours per person in the same period in the Eurozone and the United States was 0.4 per cent a year and 0.3 per cent a year, calculate the growth in real GDP per hour for each economy.

2 Write a letter to your Member of Parliament in which you set out the policies you believe the UK government must follow to speed up the growth rate of real GDP in the United Kingdom.

Web Exercise

Use the link on *Parkin Interactive* to work the following exercise.

1 Visit the Penn World Table website and obtain data on real GDP per person for the United States, China, South Africa and Mexico since 1960.

a Draw a graph of the data.

b Which country has the lowest real GDP per person and which has the highest?

c Which country has experienced the fastest growth rate since 1960 and which the slowest?

d Explain why the growth rates in these four countries are ranked in the order you have discovered?

e Return to the Penn World Table website and obtain data for any four other countries that interest you. Describe and explain the patterns that you find for these countries.

Chapter 31

The Business Cycle

After studying this chapter you will be able to:

◆ Distinguish among different theories of the business cycle

◆ Explain the aggregate demand theories of the business cycle – Keynesian, monetarist and rational expectations

◆ Explain real business cycle theory

◆ Describe the origins of and the mechanisms at work during the 1990–1992 recession

◆ Describe the origins of and the mechanisms at work during the Great Depression

Must What Goes Up Always Come Down?

The twenty years between the two World Wars of the last century (1919–1939) were ones of extraordinary change. From the start of the Industrial Revolution in the mid-eighteenth century, the economy fluctuated in what came to be called a "trade cycle". But the general trend was steadily upward. The 1920s and 1930s raised doubts that our economy would continue its upward path. Deep and pro-longed depression brought appalling economic hardship. But not everyone suffered. For some, these were years of unparalleled prosperity. By the standards of the inter-war years, recent economic cycles have been mild. But recessions and expansions have not gone away. Our economy continues to cycle around its rising trend. What causes the business cycle? That is the major question that you study in this chapter.

Cycle Patterns, Impulses and Mechanisms

Cycles are a widespread physical phenomenon. In a tennis match, the ball cycles from one side of the court to the other and back again. Every day, the earth cycles from day to night and back to day. A child on a rocking horse creates a cycle as the horse swings back and forth.

The tennis ball cycle is the simplest. It is caused by the actions of the players. Each time the ball changes direction (at each turning point), the racquet (an outside force) is applied. The day–night–day cycle is the most subtle. The rotation of the earth causes this cycle. No new force is applied each day to make the sun rise and set. It happens because of the design of the objects that interact to create the cycle.

Nothing happens at a turning point (sunrise and sunset) that is any different from what is happening at other points except that the sun comes into or goes out of view. The child's rocking horse cycle is a combination of these two cases. To start the horse rocking, some outside force must be exerted (as in the tennis ball cycle). But once the horse is rocking, the to-and-fro cycle continues for some time with no further force being applied (as in the day–night–day cycle).

The rocking horse cycle eventually dies out unless the horse is pushed again, and each time the horse is pushed, the cycle temporarily becomes more severe.

The economy is a bit like all three of these examples. It can be hit by shocks (like a tennis ball) that send it in one direction or another, it can cycle indefinitely (like the turning of day into night), and it can cycle in swings that get milder until another shock sets off a new burst of bigger swings (like a rocking horse).

While none of these analogies is perfect, they all contain some insights into the business cycle. Different theories of the cycle emphasize different impulses (different tennis racquets) and different cycle mechanisms (different solar system and rocking horse designs).

Although there are several different theories of the business cycle, they all agree about one aspect of the cycle: the central role played by investment and the accumulation of capital.

The Role of Investment and Capital

Whatever the shocks are that hit the economy, they hit one crucial variable: investment. Recessions begin when investment in new capital slows down and they turn into expansions when investment speeds up. Investment and capital interact like the spinning earth and the moon to create an ongoing cycle.

In an expansion, investment proceeds at a rapid rate and the capital stock grows quickly. But rapid capital growth means that the amount of capital per hour of labour is growing. Equipped with more capital, labour becomes more productive. But the *law of diminishing returns* begins to operate. The law of diminishing returns states that as the quantity of capital increases, with the quantity of labour remaining the same, the gain in productivity from an additional unit of capital eventually diminishes. Diminishing returns to capital bring a fall in the profit rate and with a lower profit rate, the incentive to invest weakens.

As a result, investment eventually falls. When it falls by a large amount, recession begins. In a recession, investment is low and the capital stock grows slowly. In a deep recession, the capital stock might actually decrease. Slow capital growth (or even a decreasing capital stock) means that the amount of capital per hour of labour is decreasing.

With a low amount of capital per hour of labour, businesses begin to see opportunities for profitable investment and the pace of investment eventually picks up. As it does so, recession turns into expansion.

The *AS–AD* Model

Investment and capital are just part of the business cycle mechanism, but they are just one part. To study the broader business cycle mechanism, we need a broader framework – the *AS–AD* model. We can use the *AS–AD* model to describe all theories of the business cycle. Theories differ in what they identify as the impulse and the cycle mechanism. But all theories can be thought of as making assumptions about the factors that make either aggregate supply or aggregate demand fluctuate and about how those assumptions interact to create a business cycle. Business cycle impulses can affect either the supply side or the demand side of the economy or both. There are no pure supply-side theories, so we classify the theories as either:

1   Aggregate demand theories
2   Real business cycle theory

We'll study the aggregate demand theories first. Then we'll study real business cycle theory, which is the more recent approach that isolates a shock that has both aggregate supply and aggregate demand effects.

Aggregate Demand Theories of the Business Cycle

Three types of aggregate demand theories of the business cycle have been proposed. They are:

◆ Keynesian theory

◆ Monetarist theory

◆ Rational expectations theory

Keynesian Theory

The **Keynesian theory of the business cycle** regards volatile expectations as the main source of economic fluctuations. This theory is distilled from Keynes' *The General Theory of Employment, Interest and Money*. We'll explore the Keynesian theory by looking at its main impulse and the mechanism that converts this impulse into a real GDP cycle.

Keynesian Impulse

The *impulse* in the Keynesian theory of the business cycle is expected future sales and profits. A change in expected future sales and profits changes the demand for new capital and changes the level of investment.

Keynes reasoned that profit expectations would be volatile because most of the events that shape the future are unknown and impossible to forecast. So, he reasoned, news or even rumours about future influences on profit (such as tax rate changes, interest rate changes, advances in technology, global economic and political events, or any of the thousands of other relevant factors) have large effects on the expected profit rate.

To emphasize the volatility and diversity of sources of changes in expected sales and profits, Keynes described these expectations as *animal spirits*.

Keynesian Cycle Mechanism

In the Keynesian theory, once a change in animal spirits has changed investment, a cycle mechanism begins to operate that has two key elements. First, the initial change in investment has a multiplier effect. The change in investment changes *aggregate* expenditure, real GDP and disposable income. The change in disposable income changes consumption expenditure and aggregate demand changes by a multiple of the initial change in investment. (Chapter 24, p. 536 and pp. 541–544

describes this mechanism in detail.) The aggregate demand curve shifts leftward in a recession and rightward in an expansion.

The second element of the Keynesian cycle mechanism is a sticky money wage rate together with a horizontal *SAS* curve. With a horizontal *SAS* curve, swings in aggregate demand translate into swings in real GDP with no changes in the price level.

Figure 31.1 illustrates the Keynesian cycle. The long-run aggregate supply curve is *LAS*, the short-run aggregate supply curve is *SAS*, and the aggregate demand curve is AD_0. Initially, the economy is at full employment (point *A*) with real GDP at £1,000 billion and the price level at 110.

A fall in animal spirits decreases investment and a multiplier process decreases aggregate demand. The

Figure 31.1

The Keynesian Cycle

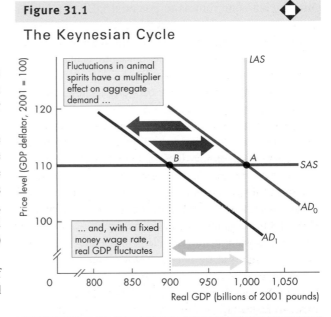

The economy is operating at point *A* at the intersection of the long-run aggregate supply curve (*LAS*), the short-run aggregate supply curve (*SAS*), and the aggregate demand curve (AD_0). A Keynesian recession begins when a fall in animal spirits decreases investment. Aggregate demand decreases and the *AD* curve shifts leftward to AD_1. With a fixed money wage rate, real GDP decreases to £900 billion and the price level does not change. The economy moves to point *B*. A rise in animal spirits has the opposite effect. A Keynesian expansion begins and takes the economy back to point *A*. The economy cycles by bouncing between point *A* and point *B*.

aggregate demand curve shifts leftward to AD_1. With a fixed money wage, real GDP decreases to £900 billion and the economy moves to point B.

Unemployment has increased and there is a surplus of labour, but the money wage rate does not fall and the economy remains at point B until some force moves it away.

That force is a rise in animal spirits, which increases investment. The AD curve shifts back to AD_0 and real GDP increases in an expansion to £1,000 billion again.

As long as real GDP remains below potential GDP (£1,000 billion in this example), the money wage rate and the price level remain constant. And real GDP cycles between points A and B.

Keynes at Above-full Employment

If animal spirits increase investment at full employment, an inflationary gap arises. Real GDP increases temporarily, but soon returns to potential GDP at a higher price level. Figure 31.2 shows this case.

Starting from full employment, at point A, an increase in aggregate demand shifts the aggregate demand curve rightward from AD_0 to AD_1. Real GDP increases to £1,100 billion at point C. The economy is now at above full-employment and there is now an inflationary gap. Once real GDP exceeds potential GDP and unemployment falls below the natural rate, the money wage rate begins to rise. As it does so, the short-run aggregate supply curve begins to shift from SAS_0 towards SAS_1. Real GDP now begins to decrease and the price level rises. The economy follows the arrows from point C to point D, the eventual long-run equilibrium.

The Keynesian business cycle is like a rally in a tennis match. It is caused by outside forces – animal spirits – that change direction and set off a process that ends at an equilibrium that must be hit again by the outside forces to disturb it.

On the downside, when aggregate demand decreases and unemployment rises, the money wage rate does not change. It is completely rigid in the downward direction. With a decrease in aggregate demand and no change in the money wage rate, the economy gets stuck in a below full-employment equilibrium. There are no natural forces operating to restore full employment. The economy remains in that situation until animal spirits are lifted and investment increases again.

On the upside, if an increase in aggregate demand creates an inflationary gap, the money wage rate rises and the price level also rises. Real GDP returns to potential GDP.

Figure 31.2

A Keynesian Inflationary Gap

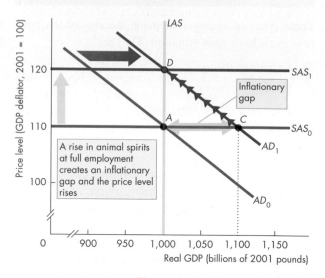

The economy is initially at full employment at point A. A Keynesian expansion begins when a rise in animal spirits increases investment. Aggregate demand increases and the AD curve shifts rightward from AD_0 to AD_1. With a fixed money wage rate, real GDP increases to £1,100 billion at point C.

The economy is now at above full-employment and there is now an inflationary gap. The money wage rate rises and the SAS curve shifts from SAS_0 towards SAS_1. Real GDP decreases and the price level rises as the economy heads towards point D.

Monetarist Theory

The **monetarist theory of the business cycle** regards fluctuations in the quantity of money as the main source of economic fluctuations. This theory is distilled from the writings of Milton Friedman and several other economists. We'll explore the monetarist theory as we did the Keynesian theory, by looking first at its main impulse and second at the mechanism that creates a cycle in real GDP.

Monetarist Impulse

The impulse in the monetarist theory of the business cycle is the *growth rate of the quantity of money*. A speed-up in money growth brings expansion, and a slow-down in money growth brings recession. The source of the change in the growth rate of quantity of money is the monetary policy actions of the Bank of England.

Monetarist Cycle Mechanism

In the monetarist theory, once the Bank of England has changed the money growth rate, a cycle mechanism begins to operate which, like the Keynesian mechanism, first affects aggregate demand.

When the money growth rate increases, the quantity of real money in the economy increases. Interest rates fall. The foreign exchange rate also falls – the pound loses value on the foreign exchange market. These initial financial market effects begin to spill over into other markets.

Interest-sensitive expenditure, which includes investment and consumer spending on durable goods as well as exports increases. These initial increases in expenditure have a multiplier effect, just as investment has in the Keynesian theory. Through these mechanisms, a speed-up in the money growth rate shifts the aggregate demand curve rightward and brings an expansion.

Similarly, a slowdown in the money growth rate has the effects just described but in the opposite direction, which shifts the aggregate demand curve leftward to bring a recession.

The second element of the monetarist cycle mechanism is the response of aggregate supply to a change in aggregate demand. The short-run aggregate supply curve is upward-sloping. With an upward-sloping *SAS* curve, swings in aggregate demand translate into swings in both real GDP and the price level. But monetarists think that real GDP deviations from full employment are temporary in both directions.

In monetarist theory, the money wage rate is only *temporarily sticky*. When aggregate demand decreases and unemployment rises above its natural rate, the money wage rate eventually begins to fall. As the money wage rate falls, so does the price level. And after a period of adjustment, real GDP returns to potential GDP and the unemployment rate returns to the natural rate. When aggregate demand increases and unemployment falls below the natural rate, the money wage rate begins to rise. As the money wage rate rises so does the price level. And after a period of adjustment, real GDP returns to potential GDP and the unemployment rate returns to the natural rate.

Figure 31.3 illustrates the monetarist recession and recovery. The economy is initially at full employment (point *A*) on the long-run aggregate supply curve (*LAS*), the aggregate demand curve (*AD*₀), and the short-run aggregate supply curve (*SAS*₀). A slowdown in the money growth rate decreases aggregate demand and the aggregate demand curve shifts leftward to *AD*₁. Real

GDP falls to £950 billion and the economy moves into recession (point *B*).

Unemployment increases and there is a surplus of labour. The money wage rate begins to fall. As the money wage rate falls, the short-run aggregate supply curve starts to shift rightward from *SAS*₀ to *SAS*₁. The price level falls and real GDP begins to expand as the economy moves to point *C*. Real GDP returns to potential GDP. Full employment is restored.

The monetarist business cycle is like a rocking horse. It needs an outside force to get it going but once going, it rocks to-and-fro (but just once). Starting from full employment, when the quantity of money decreases (or its growth rate slows), the economy cycles with a recession followed by expansion. And if the quantity of money increases (or its growth rate speeds) the economy also cycles but with an expansion followed by recession.

A Monetarist Recession

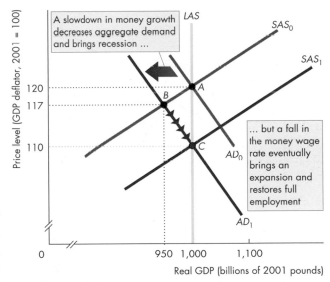

The economy is initially at full employment at point *A*. Real GDP is £1,000 billion and the price level is 120. A monetarist recession begins when a slowdown in the money growth rate decreases aggregate demand. The *AD* curve shifts leftward from *AD*₀ to *AD*₁. With a sticky money wage rate, real GDP decreases to £950 billion and the price level falls to 117 as the economy moves from point *A* to point *B*. With a surplus of labour, the money wage rate falls and the short-run aggregate supply curve shifts rightward from *SAS*₀ to *SAS*₁. The price level falls further and real GDP returns to potential GDP at point *C*.

Figure 31.4 shows the effects of this opposite case in which the quantity of money increases. Here, starting out at point *C*, an increase in the quantity of money increases aggregate demand and shifts the *AD* curve to *AD*$_2$. Both real GDP and the price level increase as the economy moves to point *D*, where *SAS*$_1$ and *AD*$_2$ intersect. With real GDP above potential GDP and unemployment below the natural rate, the money wage rate begins to rise and the *SAS* curve starts to shift leftward towards *SAS*$_2$. As the money wage rate rises, the price level also rises and real GDP decreases. The economy moves from point *D* to point *E*, its new full-employment equilibrium.

Although monetarists think that the money wage rate will fall when real GDP is less than potential GDP – when there is a recessionary gap – they do not see this process as being a rapid one.

Figure 31.4

A Monetarist Expansion

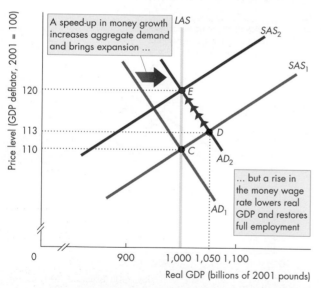

Starting at point *C*, a monetarist expansion begins when an increase in the money growth rate increases aggregate demand and shifts the *AD* curve rightward from *AD*$_1$ to *AD*$_2$. With a sticky money wage rate, real GDP increases to £1,050 billion, the price level rises to 113 and the economy moves to point *D*.

With a shortage of labour, the money wage rate rises and the *SAS* curve shifts towards *SAS*$_2$. The price level rises and real GDP decreases to potential GDP as the economy heads towards point *E*.

Rational Expectations Theories

A **rational expectation** is a forecast that is based on all the available relevant information. Rational expectations theories of the business cycle are theories based on the view that the money wage rate is determined by a rational expectation of the price level. Two distinctly different rational expectations theories of the business cycle have been proposed. A **new classical theory of the business cycle** regards *unanticipated* fluctuations in aggregate demand as the main source of economic fluctuations. This theory is based on the work of Robert E. Lucas Jr. and several other economists, including Thomas Sargent and Robert J. Barro. A different **new Keynesian theory of the business cycle** also regards *unanticipated* fluctuations in aggregate demand as the main source of economic fluctuations but it leaves room for *anticipated* fluctuations in aggregate demand to play a role. We'll explore these theories as we did the Keynesian and monetarist theories, by looking first at the main impulse and second at the cycle mechanism.

Rational Expectations Impulse

The impulse that distinguishes the rational expectations theories from the other aggregate demand theories of the business cycle is the *unanticipated change in aggregate demand*. A larger than anticipated increase in aggregate demand brings an expansion and a smaller than anticipated increase in aggregate demand brings a recession. Any factor that influences aggregate demand – for example, fiscal policy, monetary policy or developments in the world economy that influence exports – whose change is not anticipated, can bring a change in real GDP.

Rational Expectations Cycle Mechanisms

To describe the rational expectations cycle mechanisms, we'll deal first with the new classical version. When aggregate demand decreases, if the money wage rate doesn't change, real GDP and the price level both decrease. The fall in the price level increases the *real* wage rate. Employment decreases and unemployment increases. In the new classical theory, these events occur only if the decrease in aggregate demand is not anticipated. If the decrease in aggregate demand *is* anticipated, the price level is expected to fall and both firms and workers will agree to a lower money wage rate. By doing so, they can prevent the real wage from rising and avoid an increase in the unemployment rate.

Similarly, if firms and workers anticipate an increase in aggregate demand, they expect the price level to rise and will agree to a higher money wage rate. By doing so, they can prevent the real wage from falling and avoid a fall in the unemployment rate below the natural rate.

Only fluctuations in aggregate demand that are unanticipated and not taken into account in wage contracts bring changes in real GDP. *Anticipated* changes in aggregate demand change the price level, but they leave real GDP and unemployment unchanged and do not create a business cycle.

New Keynesian economists, like new classical economists, think that the money wage rate is influenced by rational expectations of the price level. But new Keynesians emphasize the long-term nature of most wage contracts. They say that *today's* money wage rate is influenced by *yesterday's* rational expectations. These expectations, which were formed in the past, are based on old information that might now be known to be incorrect. After they have made a long-term wage agreement, both firms and workers might anticipate a change in aggregate demand, which they expect will change the price level. But because they are locked into their agreement, they are unable to change the money wage rate. So the money wage rate is sticky in the new Keynesian theory and with a sticky money wage rate, even an *anticipated* change in aggregate demand changes real GDP.

New classical economists say that long-term contracts are renegotiated when conditions change to make them outdated. So they do not regard long-term contracts as an obstacle to money wage flexibility, provided both parties to an agreement recognize the changed conditions. If both firms and workers expect the price level to change, they will change the agreed money wage rate to reflect that shared expectation. In this situation, anticipated changes in aggregate demand change the money wage rate and the price level and leave real GDP unchanged.

The distinctive feature of both versions of the rational expectations theory of the business cycle is the role of *unanticipated* changes in aggregate demand. Figure 31.5 illustrates their effect on real GDP and the price level.

Potential GDP is £1,000 billion and the long-run aggregate supply curve is LAS. Aggregate demand is expected to be EAD. Given potential GDP and EAD, the money wage rate is set at the level that is expected to bring full employment. At this money wage rate, the short-run aggregate supply curve is SAS.

Imagine that, initially, aggregate demand equals expected aggregate demand, so there is full employment. In Figure 31.5, real GDP is £1,000 billion and the price level is 110. The economy is at point A.

Then, unexpectedly, aggregate demand turns out to be less than expected and the aggregate demand curve shifts leftward to AD_0. Many different aggregate demand shocks, such as a slowdown in the money growth rate or a collapse of exports, could have caused this shift. A recession begins. But aggregate demand is expected to be at EAD, so the money wage rate doesn't change and the short-run aggregate supply curve remains at SAS. Real GDP decreases to £950 billion and the price level falls to 107. The economy moves to point B. Unemployment increases and there is surplus of labour.

Figure 31.5

A Rational Expectations Business Cycle

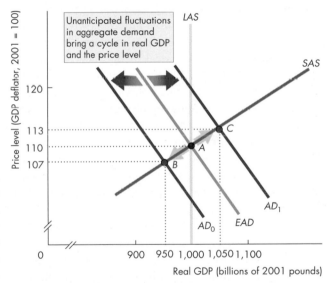

The economy is expected to be at point A at the intersection of the *expected* aggregate demand curve, EAD, the short-run aggregate supply curve, SAS, and the long-run aggregate supply curve, LAS. As long as aggregate demand is expected to be EAD, there is no change in the money wage rate and the SAS curve does not shift. A rational expectations recession begins when an unanticipated decrease in aggregate demand shifts the AD curve leftward to AD_0. Real GDP decreases to £950 billion and the price level falls to 107 as the economy moves to point B. A rational expectations expansion begins when an unanticipated increase in aggregate demand shifts the AD curve rightward to AD_1. Real GDP increases to £1,050 billion and the price level rises to 113 as the economy moves to point C.

A shock that takes aggregate demand to a level that exceeds *EAD* brings an expansion. The aggregate demand curve shifts rightward to AD_1. A speed-up in the money growth rate or an export boom might have increased aggregate demand. But aggregate demand is expected to be at *EAD*, so the money wage rate doesn't change and the short-run aggregate supply curve remains at *SAS*. Real GDP increases to £1,050 billion and the price level rises to 113. The economy moves to point *C*. Unemployment is below the natural rate.

Fluctuations in aggregate demand between AD_0 and AD_1 around expected aggregate demand *EAD* bring fluctuations in real GDP and the price level between points *B* and *C*.

The two versions of the rational expectations theory differ in their predictions about the effects of a change in expected aggregate demand. The new classical theory predicts that as soon as expected aggregate demand changes, the money wage rate also changes so the *SAS* curve shifts. The new Keynesian theory predicts that the money wage rate changes gradually when new contracts are made so that the *SAS* curve moves slowly. This difference between the two theories is crucial for policy. According to the new classical theory, anticipated policy actions change only the price level and have no effect on real GDP and unemployment. The reason is that when policy is expected to change, the money wage rate changes so the *SAS* curve shifts and offsets the effects of the policy action on real GDP. In contrast, in the new Keynesian theory, because money wages change only when new contracts are made, even anticipated policy actions change real GDP and can be used in an attempt to stabilize the cycle.

Like the monetarist business cycle, these rational expectations cycles are similar to rocking horses. They need an outside force to get going, but once going the economy rocks around its full-employment point. The new classical horse rocks faster and comes to rest more quickly than the new Keynesian horse.

AS–AD General Theory

All the theories of the business cycle that we've considered can be viewed as particular cases of a more general *AS–AD* theory. In this more general theory, the impulses of both the Keynesian and monetarist theories can change aggregate demand. A multiplier effect makes aggregate demand change by more than any initial change in one of its components. The money wage rate can be viewed as responding to changes in the rational expectation of the future price level. Even if the money

wage rate is flexible, it will change only to the extent that price level expectations change. As a result, the money wage rate will adjust gradually.

Although in all three types of business cycle theory that we've considered, the cycle is caused by fluctuations in aggregate demand, the possibility that an occasional aggregate supply shock might occur is not ruled out by the aggregate demand theories.

A recession could occur because aggregate supply decreases. For example, a widespread drought that cuts agricultural production could cause a recession in an economy that has a large agricultural sector. But these aggregate demand theories of the business cycle regard supply shocks as rare rather than normal events. Aggregate demand fluctuations are the normal ongoing sources of fluctuations.

Review Quiz

1 What, according to Keynesian theory, is the main business cycle impulse?
2 What, according to Keynesian theory, are the main business cycle mechanisms? Describe the roles of *animal spirits*, the multiplier, and a sticky money wage rate in this theory.
3 What, according to monetarist theory, is the main business cycle impulse?
4 What, according to monetarist theory, are the business cycle mechanisms? Describe the roles of the Bank of England and the quantity of money in this theory.
5 What, according to new classical theory and new Keynesian theory, causes the business cycle? What are the roles of rational expectations and unanticipated fluctuations in aggregate demand in these theories?
6 What are the differences between the new classical theory and the new Keynesian theory concerning the money wage rate over the business cycle?

For all their differences, the theories of the business cycle that we've just reviewed all have aggregate demand fluctuations at their core. A controversial new theory of the business cycle challenges these mainstream and traditional aggregate demand theories that you've just studied. It is called the real business cycle theory. Let's take a look at this new theory of the business cycle.

Real Business Cycle Theory

The newest theory of the business cycle, known as **real business cycle theory** (or RBC theory), suggests random fluctuations in productivity as the main source of economic fluctuations. These productivity fluctuations are assumed to result mainly from fluctuations in the pace of technological change, but they might also have other sources such as international disturbances, climate fluctuations or natural disasters. The origins of real business cycle theory can be traced to the rational expectations revolution set off by Robert E. Lucas Jr., but the first demonstration of the power of this theory was given by Edward Prescott and Finn Kydland and by John Long and Charles Plosser. Today, real business cycle theory is part of a broad research agenda called *dynamic general equilibrium analysis* and hundreds of young macroeconomists do research on this topic.

Like our study of the aggregate demand theories, we'll explore the RBC theory by looking first at its impulse and second at the mechanism that converts that impulse into a cycle in real GDP.

The RBC Impulse

The impulse in the RBC theory is the *growth rate of productivity that results from technological change*. Real business cycle theorists believe this impulse to be generated mainly by the process of research and development that leads to the creation and use of new technologies.

Most of the time, technological progress is steady and productivity grows at a moderate pace. But sometimes productivity growth speeds up and, occasionally, productivity *decreases* – labour becomes less productive, on average.

A period of rapid productivity growth brings a strong business cycle expansion and a *decrease* in productivity triggers a recession.

It is easy to understand why technological change brings productivity growth. But how does it *decrease* productivity? All technological change eventually increases productivity. But if initially technological change makes a sufficient amount of existing capital (especially human capital) obsolete, productivity temporarily decreases. At such a time, more jobs are destroyed than created and more businesses fail than start up.

Figure 31.6

The Real Business Cycle Impulse

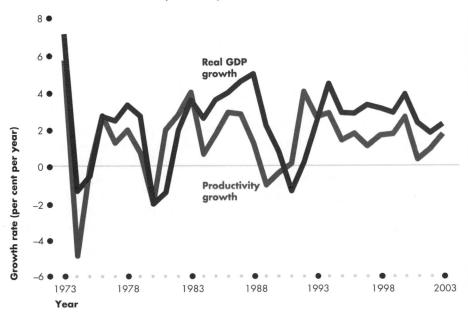

The real business cycle impulse is fluctuations in the growth rate of productivity that are caused by changes in technology. The fluctuations in productivity growth shown here are calculated by using growth accounting (the one-third rule) to remove the contribution of capital accumulation to productivity growth. Productivity fluctuations are correlated with real GDP fluctuations. Economists are not sure what the productivity variable actually measures or what causes it to fluctuate.

Sources: Office for National Statistics; and the authors' calculations.

To isolate the RBC theory impulse, economists use growth accounting, which is explained in Chapter 30, pp. 685–688. Figure 31.6 shows the RBC impulse for the United Kingdom from 1975 to 2003. This figure also shows that fluctuations in productivity growth are correlated with GDP fluctuations. This RBC productivity variable is a catch-all variable. Economists are not sure what it actually measures or what causes it to fluctuate.

The RBC Mechanism

According to the RBC theory, two immediate effects follow from a change in productivity that get an expansion or a contraction going. They are:

1 Investment demand changes.

2 Demand for labour changes.

We'll study these effects and their consequences during a recession. In an expansion, they work in the opposite direction to what is described here.

Technological change makes some existing capital obsolete and temporarily decreases productivity. Firms expect their future profit rate to fall and labour productivity to fall. With lower profit expectations, firms cut back their purchases of new capital, and with lower labour productivity they plan to lay off some workers. So the initial effect of a temporary fall in productivity is a decrease in investment demand and a decrease in the demand for labour.

Figure 31.7 illustrates these two initial effects of a decrease in productivity. Part (a) shows investment demand, ID, and saving supply, SS (in RBC theory saving depends on the real interest rate). Initially, investment demand is ID_0, and the equilibrium investment and saving is £100 billion at a real interest rate of 6 per cent a year. A decrease in productivity lowers the expected profit rate and decreases investment demand. The ID curve shifts leftward to ID_1. The real interest rate falls to 4 per cent a year, and investment and saving decrease to £70 billion.

Part (b) shows the demand for labour and the supply of labour (which are explained in Chapter 23, pp. 506–509). Initially, the demand for labour curve is LD_0, the supply of labour curve is LS_0 and employment is 50 billion hours a year at a real wage rate of £12 an hour. The decrease in productivity decreases the demand for labour and the LD curve shifts leftward to LD_1.

Before we can determine the new real wage rate and employment, we need to take a ripple effect into account – the key ripple effect in RBC theory.

The Key Decision: When to Work?

According to the RBC theory, people decide *when* to work by doing a cost–benefit calculation. They compare the return from working in the current period with the *expected* return from working in a later period. You make such a comparison every day at university. Suppose your goal in this course is to get a first. To achieve this goal, you work pretty hard most of the time. But during the few days before the mid-term and final exams, you work especially hard. Why? Because you think the return from studying close to the exam is greater than the return from studying when the exam is a long time away. So during the term you hang around the Students' Union bar, go to parties, play squash and enjoy other leisure pursuits, but at exam time you work every evening and weekend.

Real business cycle theory says that workers behave like you. They work fewer hours, and sometimes zero hours, when the real wage rate is temporarily low and they work more hours when the real wage rate is temporarily high. But to compare properly the current wage rate with the expected future wage rate, workers must use the real interest rate. If the real interest rate is 6 per cent a year, a real wage rate of £1 an hour earned this week will become £1.06 a year from now. If the real wage rate is expected to be £1.05 an hour next year, today's wage of £1 looks good. By working longer hours now and shorter hours a year from now, a person can get a 1 per cent higher real wage. But suppose the real interest rate is 4 per cent a year. In this case, £1 earned now is worth £1.04 next year. Working fewer hours now and more next year is the way to get a 1 per cent higher real wage.

So the when-to-work decision depends on the real interest rate. The lower the real interest rate, other things remaining the same, the smaller is the supply of labour. Many economists think this *intertemporal substitution effect* to be of negligible size. RBC theorists say the effect is large and it is the key element in the RBC mechanism.

You've seen in Figure 31.7(a) that the decrease in investment demand lowers the real interest rate. This fall in the real interest rate lowers the return to current work and decreases the supply of labour. In Figure 31.7(b), the labour supply curve shifts leftward to LS_1. The effect of a productivity shock on the demand for labour is larger than the effect of the fall in the real interest rate on the supply of labour. That is, the LD curve shifts further leftward than does the LS curve. As a result, the real wage rate falls to £11.50 an hour and employment decreases to 49 billion hours. A recession has begun and is intensifying.

Figure 31.7

Capital and Labour Markets in a Real Business Cycle

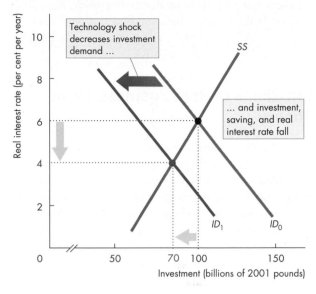

(a) Investment, saving and interest rate

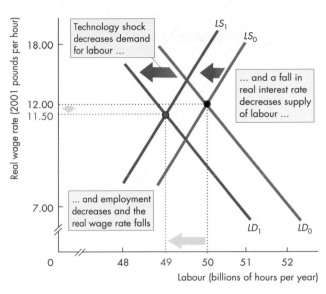

(b) Labour and wage rate

Saving supply is *SS* in part (a) and, initially, investment demand is ID_0. The real interest rate is 6 per cent a year and saving and investment are £100 billion. In the labour market in part (b), the demand for labour is LD_0 and the supply of labour is LS_0. The real wage rate is £12 an hour and employment is 50 billion hours.
A technological change decreases productivity and both investment demand and the demand for labour decrease.

The two demand curves shift leftward to ID_1 and LD_1. In part (a), the real interest rate falls to 4 per cent a year and investment and saving decrease. In part (b), the fall in the real interest rate decreases the supply of labour (the when-to-work decision) and the supply curve shifts leftward to LS_1. Employment decreases to 49 billion hours and the real wage rate falls to £11.50 an hour. A recession is underway.

Real GDP and the Price Level

The next part of the RBC story traces the consequences of the changes you've just seen for real GDP and the price level. With a decrease in employment, aggregate supply decreases; and with a decrease in investment demand, aggregate demand decreases. Figure 31.8 illustrates these effects, using the AS–AD framework. Initially, the aggregate demand curve is AD_0 and the long-run aggregate supply curve is LAS_0. The price level is 110 and real GDP is £1,000 billion. There is no short-run aggregate supply curve in this figure because in the RBC theory, the *SAS* curve has no meaning. The labour market moves relentlessly towards its equilibrium, and the money wage rate adjusts freely (either increases or decreases) to ensure that the real wage rate keeps the quantity of labour demanded equal to the quantity supplied. In RBC theory, unemployment is always at the

natural rate, and the natural rate fluctuates over the business cycle because the amount of job search fluctuates.

The decrease in employment decreases total production and aggregate supply decreases. The *LAS* curve shifts leftward to LAS_1. The decrease in investment demand decreases aggregate demand and the *AD* curve shifts leftward to AD_1. The price level falls to 107, and real GDP decreases to £950 billion. The economy has gone through a recession.

What Happened to Money?

The name *real* business cycle theory is no accident. It reflects the central prediction of the theory: real things, not nominal or monetary things, cause the business cycle. If the quantity of money changes, aggregate demand changes. But if there is no real change – no change in the productivity or use of the factors of

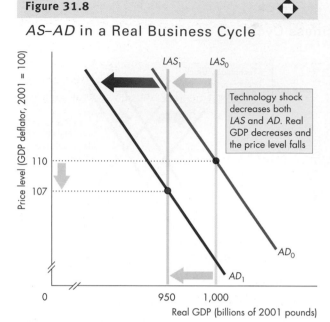

Figure 31.8

AS–AD in a Real Business Cycle

Initially, the long-run aggregate supply curve is LAS_0 and the aggregate demand curve is AD_0. Real GDP is £1,000 billion (which equals potential GDP) and the price level is 110. There is no SAS curve in the real business cycle theory because the money wage rate is flexible. The technological change described in Figure 31.7 temporarily decreases potential GDP and the LAS curve shifts leftward to LAS_1. The decrease in investment decreases aggregate demand and the AD curve shifts leftward to AD_1. Real GDP decreases to £950 billion and the price level falls to 107. The economy has gone into recession.

logy advances, productivity grows. But it grows at an uneven pace. You saw this fact when you studied growth accounting in Chapter 30. There, we focused on slow-changing trends in productivity growth. Real business cycle theory uses the same idea but says there are frequent shocks to productivity that are mostly positive but that are occasionally negative.

Criticisms of Real Business Cycle Theory

RBC theory is controversial and when economists discuss it they often generate more heat than light. Its detractors claim that its basic assumptions are just too incredible. Money wage rate *is* sticky, they claim, so to assume otherwise is at odds with a clear fact. Intertemporal substitution is too weak, they say, to account for large fluctuations in the supply of labour and employment with small changes in the real wage rate.

But what really kills the RBC story, say most economists, is an implausible impulse. Technology shocks are not capable of creating the swings in productivity that growth accounting reveals. These shocks are caused by something, they concede, but they are as likely to be caused by *changes in aggregate demand* as by technology. If fluctuations in productivity are caused by aggregate demand fluctuations, then the traditional aggregate demand theories are needed to explain these shocks. Fluctuations in productivity do not cause the business cycle but are caused by it!

Building on this theme, the critics point out that the so-called productivity fluctuations that growth accounting measures are correlated with changes in the growth rate of money and other indicators of changes in aggregate demand.

production, there is no change in potential GDP and the change in the quantity of money changes only the price level. In real business cycle theory, this outcome occurs because the aggregate supply curve is the *LAS* curve, which pins real GDP down at potential GDP.

According to real business cycle theory, correlation between money growth and real GDP arises from a reverse causation. A more rapid real expansion brings a faster growth rate of the quantity of money and a slowdown in the real growth rate slows the growth rate of the quantity of money. We describe this reverse causation mechanism below.

Cycles and Growth

The shock that drives the business cycle of the RBC theory is the same as the force that generates economic growth: technological change. On average, as techno-

Defence of Real Business Cycle Theory

The defenders of RBC theory claim that the theory works. It explains the macroeconomic facts about the business cycle and is consistent with the facts about economic growth. In effect, a single theory explains *both economic growth and business cycles*. The growth accounting exercise that explains slowly changing trends also explains the more frequent business cycle swings. Its defenders also claim that RBC theory is consistent with a wide range of *microeconomic* evidence about labour supply decisions, labour demand and investment demand decisions, and information on the distribution of income between labour and capital.

RBC theorists acknowledge that money growth and the business cycle are correlated. That is, rapid money growth and expansion go together, and slow money growth and recession go together. But, they argue, causation does not run from money to real GDP as the traditional aggregate demand theories state. Instead, RBC theorists view causation as running from real GDP to money – so-called reverse causation. In a recession, the initial decrease in investment demand that lowers the real interest rate decreases the demand for bank loans and lowers the profitability of banking. So banks increase their reserves and decrease their loans. The quantity of bank deposits and hence the quantity of money decreases. This reverse causation is responsible for the correlation between money growth and real GDP according to real business cycle theory.

Defenders of real business cycle theory also argue that the RBC view is significant because it at least raises the possibility that the business cycle is efficient. The business cycle does not signal an economy that is misbehaving; it is business as usual. If this view is correct, it means that policy to smooth the cycle is misguided. Only by taking out the peaks can the troughs be smoothed out. But peaks are bursts of investment to take advantage of new technologies in a timely way. So smoothing the business cycle means delaying the benefits of new technologies.

Review Quiz

1   According to real business cycle theory, what causes the business cycle? What is the role of fluctuations in the rate of technological change?
2   According to real business cycle theory, how does a fall in productivity growth influence investment demand, the real interest rate, the demand for labour, the supply of labour, employment and the real wage rate?
3   According to real business cycle theory, how does a fall in productivity growth influence long-run aggregate supply, aggregate demand, real GDP and the price level?

You've now reviewed the main theories of the business cycle. Your next task is to examine some actual business cycles. In pursuing this task, we will focus on the recession phase of the business cycle. We begin by looking at the 1990–1992 recession in the United Kingdom.

The 1990–1992 Recession

In the theories of the business cycle that you've studied, recessions can be triggered by a variety of forces, some on the aggregate demand side and some on the aggregate supply side. Let's identify the shocks that triggered the 1990–1992 recession.

The Origins of the 1990–1992 Recession

Three forces were at work in United Kingdom during the early 1990s that contributed to the recession and subsequent slow growth. They were:

◆   Bank of England's monetary policy
◆   German reunification
◆   A slowdown in the world economy

Bank of England's Monetary Policy

The Bank of England pursued an anti-inflationary monetary policy during the early 1990s that decreased aggregate demand and contributed to the start of a recession. This anti-inflationary monetary policy was a direct consequence of the United Kingdom joining the Exchange Rate Mechanism (ERM) of the European Monetary System (EMS).

The United Kingdom joined the ERM in October 1990. The ERM is a monetary system based on pegged exchange rates. If a central bank pegs its exchange rate, it stands ready to buy its currency on the foreign exchange market when market forces push the exchange rate downward. And it stands ready to sell its currency when market forces push the exchange rate upward.[1]

Under the ERM arrangements of 1990, the exchange rate for the pound was set at 2.95 deutschmarks (plus or minus a permitted spread around that value). To remain in the ERM, the Bank of England was required to take actions that prevented the exchange rate of the pound from moving outside the agreed range.

When the United Kingdom entered the ERM, the UK inflation rate was 10 per cent a year, which was much higher than the EU average. So the Bank of England was facing a one-way bet. It was clear to everyone that the Bank of England would have a hard time preventing the pound from falling. So speculators sold pounds and bought other currencies.

---

[1] You can learn more about the exchange rate in Chapter 34.

To try to convince speculators to keep holding pounds, the Bank of England increased the interest rate to a level higher than that in the rest of Europe. But the more the Bank of England resisted currency speculators by keeping the interest rate high, the stronger became the belief that devaluation could not be avoided. A game between the Bank of England and the currency speculators ensued. Like a game of "chicken", someone has to give way and be the chicken. In September 1992, the United Kingdom became the chicken and left the ERM. But by then, a lot of damage had been done.

The high interest rate lowered investment and expenditure on consumer durable goods. And with the exchange rate fixed, UK-made goods and services became increasingly more expensive in other EU countries. UK exports to other EU countries decreased. Also, other EU-made goods and services become increasingly cheaper in the United Kingdom and UK imports increased. All of these changes in expenditure decreased aggregate demand in the United Kingdom and sent the UK economy into recession.

Figure 31.9 shows the extent to which the Bank of England slowed the money growth rate and the consequences for real GDP growth.

Figure 31.9

M4 and Real GDP Growth: 1990–1992

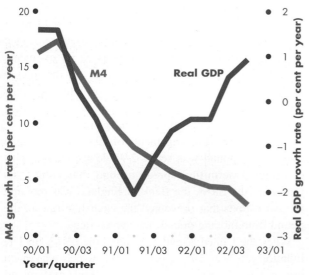

The UK entry into the ERM meant that the Bank of England had to pursue a contractionary monetary policy. The money growth rate began to slow during 1989. It slowed even further during 1990. A sharp slowdown in the money growth rate contributed to the decrease in real GDP.

Source: Bank of England and Office for National Statistics.

German Reunification

In November 1989, the Berlin Wall came down and in October 1990, East Germany was reunited with West Germany. The cost of the reunification was enormous and the German government's budget went into deficit. From being a net lender in the world capital market, the new Germany began its life as a net borrower. Afraid that this budget deficit would increase the money growth rate and fuel inflation, the German central bank, the Bundesbank, raised interest rates. With the deutschmark as the anchor currency for the ERM (which means that all the other currencies in the ERM were linked to it), the rise in German interest rates meant that other members of the ERM had to raise their interest rates to maintain their fixed exchange rates. The rise in interest rates contributed to the slowdown in UK aggregate demand.

A Slowdown in the World Economy

After its longest ever period of peacetime expansion, US real GDP growth began to slow in 1989 and 1990 and the United States went into recession in mid-1990. The slowdown of the US economy brought slower growth in the US demand for the rest of the world's exports, which resulted in lower export prices and smaller export volumes. The world economic activity began to slow down.

Let's see how the events we've just described influenced the UK economy in 1991.

AS–AD in the 1990–1992 Recession

Figure 31.10 describes the effects of the various events that triggered the 1990–1992 recession. In 1990, the aggregate demand curve was AD_{90} and the short-run aggregate supply curve was SAS_{90}. Real GDP was £765 billion and the price level was 73.

The 1990–1992 recession was caused by a decrease in both aggregate demand and aggregate supply. Aggregate demand decreased initially because of the high real interest rate, the overvalued exchange rate and the slowdown in the money growth rate. These factors were soon reinforced by the slowdown in the world economy that brought a further decline in the growth of exports. The combination of these factors triggered a massive decline in investment. The resulting decrease in aggregate demand is shown in Figure 31.11 by the shift of the aggregate demand curve leftward to AD_{91}. Aggregate supply decreased because the money wage rate continued to increase throughout 1990 at a rate similar to that in 1989. This decrease in aggregate supply

Figure 31.10

AS–AD in the 1990–1992 Recession

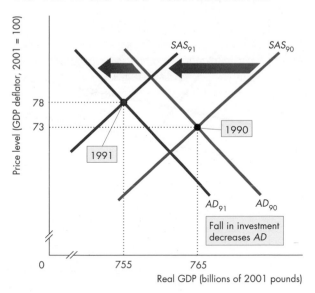

At the end of 1990, the economy was on its aggregate demand curve, AD_{90}, and its short-run aggregate supply curve, SAS_{90}, with real GDP at £765 billion and a GDP deflator of 73. The combination of a decrease in both aggregate supply and aggregate demand put the economy into recession. Real GDP decreased to £755 billion and the price level increased to 78.

Figure 31.11

The Labour Market in 1990–1992 Recession

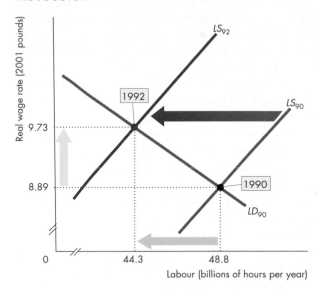

In 1990, the demand for labour was LD_{90} and the supply of labour was LS_{90}. The real wage was £8.89 an hour and employment was 48.8 billion of hours. The money wage rate continued to rise in 1991 and 1992 because people did not anticipate the fall in inflation and the LS curve shifted leftward to LS_{92}. The real wage rose to £9.73 an hour and employment decreased to 44.3 billion hours.

shifted the short-run aggregate supply curve leftward to SAS_{91}. (The figure does not show the long-run aggregate supply curve.)

The combined effect of the decreases in aggregate supply and aggregate demand was a decrease in real GDP to £755 billion – a 1.3 per cent decrease – and a rise in the price level to 78 – a 6.8 per cent increase.

You've seen how aggregate demand and aggregate supply changed during the 1990–1992 recession. What happened in the labour market during this recession?

The Labour Market in the 1990–1992 Recession

Figure 31.11 shows employment and the real wage rate during this period. As employment decreased in 1990, 1991 and 1992, the real wage rate increased. The money wage rate rose because people did not anticipate the slowdown in inflation. When inflation did slow down, the real wage rate increased and the quantity of labour demanded decreased.

As the expansion began in mid-1993, the demand for labour began to increase. Employment increased and the real wage rate decreased. These movements in employment and the real wage rate suggest that the forces of supply and demand do not operate smoothly in the labour market.

Review Quiz

1 What events triggered the 1990–1992 recession in the United Kingdom?
2 What role did external factors play and what role did UK policy play in the 1990–1992 recession?
3 What mechanisms translated the shocks into a recession?

You've seen how business cycle theory can be used to interpret the 1990–1992 recession. We'll now use business cycle theory to explain the Great Depression that engulfed the global economy during the 1930s.

The Great Depression

The late 1920s were years of economic revival in some parts of the UK economy. While the traditional industries like coal and shipbuilding stagnated, others like motor manufacturing were booming. New firms were created, and the capital stock of the nation expanded. At the beginning of 1929, real GDP in the United Kingdom nearly equalled potential GDP.

But as that eventful year unfolded, increasing signs of economic weakness began to appear. The most dramatic events occurred in October when the US stock market collapsed. Shares lost more than one-third of their value in two weeks. The four years that followed were years of monstrous economic depression across the world.

We'll describe the depression by using the *AS–AD* model and identify the forces that made aggregate demand and aggregate supply change.

Figure 31.12 shows the dimensions of the Great Depression. On the eve of the Great Depression in 1929, the economy was on aggregate demand curve AD_{29} and short-run aggregate supply curve SAS_{29}. Real GDP was £193 billion (2001 pounds) and the price level was 2.5 (GDP deflator, 2001 = 100).

In 1931, there was a widespread expectation that the price level would fall and the money wage rate fell. With a lower money wage rate, the short-run aggregate supply curve shifted from SAS_{29} to SAS_{31}. But increased pessimism and uncertainty decreased investment, the demand for consumer durables and international trade. Aggregate demand decreased to AD_{31}. In 1931, real GDP decreased to £182 billion and the price level fell to 2.4.

Although the Great Depression brought enormous hardship, the distribution of that hardship was uneven. At its worst point, 16 per cent of the workforce had no jobs at all. Although there were unemployment benefits and other forms of poor relief, there was a considerable level of poverty for those on the dole. But the wallets of those who kept their jobs barely noticed the Great Depression. It is true that wage rates fell. But at the same time, the price level fell by more, so real wage rates actually rose. So those who had jobs were paid a wage rate that had an increasing buying power during the Great Depression.

You can begin to appreciate the magnitude of the Great Depression if you compare it with the 1990–1992 recession. In 1991, real GDP decreased by 1.4 per cent, while in 1931, real GDP decreased by 5.7 per cent.

Figure 31.12

The Great Depression

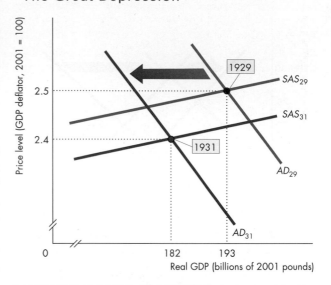

In 1929, real GDP was £193 billion and the GDP deflator was 2.5 – at the intersection of AD_{29} and SAS_{29}. Increased pessimism from a fall in world trade resulted in a drop in investment, resulting in a decrease in aggregate demand to AD_{31}. To some degree, this decrease was reflected in the labour market and the money wage rate fell, so the short-run aggregate supply curve shifted to SAS_{31}. Real GDP and the price level fell. By 1931, real GDP had fallen to £182 billion (94 per cent of its 1929 level) and the GDP deflator had fallen to 2.4 (96 per cent of its 1929 level).

Why the Great Depression Happened

The late 1920s were years of economic expansion in the world economy, but they were also years of increasing uncertainty. The main source of increased uncertainty was international. The world economy was going through tumultuous times. The patterns of world trade were changing as the United Kingdom began its period of relative economic decline and new economic powers such as Japan began to emerge. International currency fluctuations and the introduction of restrictive trade policies by many countries (see Chapter 33) further increased the uncertainty faced by firms. There was also domestic uncertainty arising from the restrictive monetary and fiscal policies followed by the government to ensure that the pound remained on the gold standard. Because prices in the United States fell, prices in the United Kingdom had to fall to maintain an exchange rate of £4.86 per pound and remain on the gold standard. So the UK expansion was good but not booming as in the United States.

In 1929, the stock market crashed and the slowdown in the world economy that followed fuelled the environment of uncertainty. It was this slowdown in the world economy, which led to a drop in exports, which in turn led to a fall in income, consumer spending and investment and to the initial leftward shift of the aggregate demand curve from AD_{29} to AD_{31} in Figure 31.12.

Can It Happen Again?

We cannot be sure about anything in economics, but some features of our economy today make a great depression less likely. They are:

◆ Bank of England's role as lender of last resort

◆ Taxes and government spending

◆ Multi-income families

Bank of England's Role as Lender of Last Resort

The Bank of England is the lender of last resort in the UK economy. If a single bank is short of reserves, it can borrow reserves from other banks. If the entire banking system is short of reserves, banks in the United Kingdom can borrow from the Bank of England. By making reserves available (at a suitable interest rate), the Bank of England is able to make the quantity of reserves in the banking system respond flexibly to the demand for those reserves. Bank failure can be prevented, or at least contained, to cases where bad management practices are the source of the problem. Widespread failures of the type that occurred in the Great Depression can be prevented.

Taxes and Government Spending

The government sector was a much smaller part of the economy in 1929 than it is today. On the eve of that earlier recession, government expenditures on goods and services were less than 25 per cent of GDP. Today, government expenditures on goods and services exceed 40 per cent of GDP. Government transfer payments were about 6 per cent of GDP in 1929. Today, they are 18 per cent of GDP.

A higher level of government expenditures on goods and services means that when recession hits, a large component of aggregate demand does not decline. But government transfer payments are the most sensitive economic stabilizer. When the economy goes into recession and depression, more people qualify for unemployment benefits and social assistance. As a consequence,

although disposable income decreases, the extent of the decrease is moderated by the existence of such programmes. Consumption expenditure, in turn, does not decline by as much as it would in the absence of such government programmes. The limited decline in consumption spending further limits the overall decrease in aggregate expenditure, thereby limiting the magnitude of an economic downturn.

Multi-income Families

At the time of the Great Depression, families with more than one wage earner were much less common than they are today. The economic activity rate in 1929 was around 45 per cent. Today, it is 75 per cent. So even if the unemployment rate increased to around 20 per cent today, 60 per cent of the adult population would actually have jobs. During the Great Depression, only 40 per cent of the adult population had work.

Multi-income families have greater security than single-income families. The chance of both (or all) income earners in a family losing their jobs simultaneously is much lower than the chance of a single earner losing work. With greater family income security, family consumption is likely to be less sensitive to fluctuations in family income that are seen as temporary. So when aggregate income falls, it does not induce an equivalent cut in consumption.

For the reasons we have just reviewed, it appears the economy has better shock-absorbing characteristics today than it had in the 1920s and 1930s. Even if there is a collapse of confidence leading to a decrease in investment, the recession mechanism that is now in place will not translate that initial shock into the large and prolonged decrease in real GDP and increase in unemployment that occurred more than 60 years ago.

We have now completed our study of the business cycle. In *Reading Between the Lines* on pp. 718–719, we examine the impact of expectations on consumer demand in South Korea and discuss the policy needed to stimulate demand in that economy.

We have also completed our study of the *science* of macroeconomics and learned about the influences on long-term economic growth and inflation as well as the business cycle. We have discovered that these issues pose huge policy challenges. How can we speed up the rate of economic growth while at the same time keeping inflation low and avoiding big swings of the business cycle? Our task in the next chapter is to study these macroeconomic policy challenges.

Reading Between the Lines

Downswing in Korea?

The Financial Times, 6 August 2004

South Korean Consumer Confidence Plummets

Jung-A Song

South Korea's consumer sentiment in July weakened to its lowest in nearly four years, reflecting the deepening sense of gloom surrounding Asia's fourth-largest economy. South Korea has been struggling since the consumer credit bubble burst last year. The consumer sentiment index fell to 89.6 in July, the lowest since December 2000, as South Koreans lost confidence in the economy because of higher oil prices, rising US interest rates and an expected cooling of the Chinese economy.

Opinion polls show many South Koreans believe economic conditions are worse now than during the 1997 economic crisis, when the country needed a Dollars 58bn (Euros 48bn, Pounds 32bn) bailout from the International Monetary Fund to avoid bankruptcy. . . .

A recovery in domestic spending is badly needed, as growth in exports, which have buttressed the fragile economy, is likely to slow in coming months along with an expected decline in overseas demand. South Korea's exports jumped 38 per cent in the year to the end of July but the momentum is likely to weaken, hurt by higher oil prices and Beijing's efforts to slow the economy. China is South Korea's largest export market, taking a fifth of its overseas sales. . . .

High oil prices are further damping the country' corporate investments, which have plunged in the past two years because of weak consumption, frequent labour strife and uncertainty over President Roh Moo-hyun's economic policies. Analysts said active corporate spending was crucial to compensate for stagnant consumption and to achieve economic growth of 5.2 per cent this year. But capital expenditure showed no sign of a recovery . . .

The Essence of the Story

◆ High oil prices, rising US interest rates and Beijing's efforts to cool the Chinese economy have pushed South Korea's consumer confidence to its lowest since December 2000.

◆ Many South Koreans believe economic conditions were worse in 2004 than during the 1997 economic crisis.

◆ South Korea's exports jumped 38 per cent in the year to the end of July 2004 but were expected to slow with a decrease in overseas demand.

◆ High oil prices, weak consumption growth, frequent labour strife and uncertainty over the government's economic policy have lowered business investment.

◆ A recovery in domestic spending is badly needed.

Economic Analysis

◆ Figure 1 shows the growth of consumer expenditure and investment in Korea during 2002 and 2003.

◆ Figure 2 shows a longer perspective on the growth of real GDP and the components of aggregate demand.

◆ China and the United States are South Korea's largest export markets and if a slowdown in these two countries occurs, South Korea's exports growth will slow. A rise in oil prices will increase South Korea's imports. The decrease in net exports will decrease (or slow the growth rate of) aggregate demand.

◆ Lower consumer and investor confidence can be interpreted either as a downturn in "animal spirits" – a Keynesian impulse – or as a rational expectation of the consequences of a slowdown in the US and Chinese economies.

◆ If the pessimistic picture painted in the article comes about, Figure 3 shows how it occurs. Potential GDP increases by about 4.7 per cent and shifts the long-run aggregate supply curve from LAS_{03} to LAS_{04}. The increase in potential GDP increases short-run aggregate supply, but the expected rise in oil prices leads to a rationally expected increase in the money wage rate, which decreases short-run aggregate supply. The net change is a small increase in short-run aggregate supply from SAS_{03} to SAS_{04}.

◆ Aggregate demand increases, but by less than the increase in potential GDP and the aggregate demand curve shifts rightward from AD_{03} to AD_{04}.

◆ Real GDP increases by only 3 per cent, the price level rises sharply and a recessionary gap opens up.

◆ This outcome might be avoided by stronger growth in the world economy, which will increase Korean exports or by expansionary monetary policy that lowers the interest rate to stimulate consumption and investment. In August 2004, the Bank of Korea lowered the interest rate with that objective in mind.

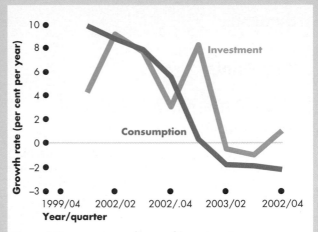

Figure 1 Consumer spending and investment growth in 2002 and 2003

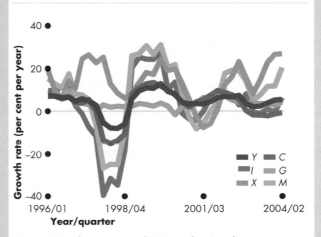

Figure 2 South Korean real GDP and expenditure components, 1996–2004

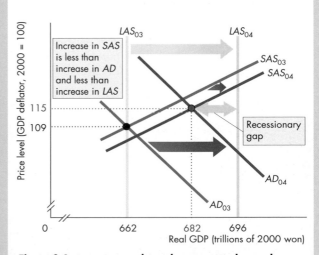

Figure 3 Aggregate supply and aggregate demand

Summary

Key Points

Cycle Patterns, Impulses and Mechanisms (p. 702)

◆ The economy can be hit (like a tennis ball), cycle indefinitely (like the turning of day into night), and cycle in swings that get milder until another shock hits (like a rocking horse).

Aggregate Demand Theories of the Business Cycle (pp. 703–708)

◆ Keynesian business cycle theory identifies volatile expectations about future sales and profits as the main source of economic fluctuations.

◆ Monetarist business cycle theory identifies fluctuations in the quantity of money as the main source of economic fluctuations.

◆ Rational expectations theories identify unanticipated fluctuations in aggregate demand as the main source of economic fluctuations.

Real Business Cycle Theory (pp. 709–713)

◆ In real business cycle (RBC) theory, economic fluctuations are caused by fluctuations in the influence of technological change on productivity growth.

◆ A temporary slowdown in the pace of technological change decreases investment demand and both the demand for labour and the supply of labour.

The 1990–1992 Recession (pp. 713–715)

◆ Three forces contributed to the weak performance of the UK economy in the early 1990s: the ERM, the reunification of Germany and a slowdown in the world economy.

The Great Depression (pp. 716–717)

◆ The Great Depression started with increased uncertainty and pessimism that brought a decrease in investment and spending.

◆ Increased uncertainty and pessimism also brought on the stock market crash. The crash added to the pessimistic outlook and further spending cuts occurred.

Key Figures

Figure 31.1   The Keynesian Cycle, 703
Figure 31.2   A Keynesian Inflationary Gap, 704
Figure 31.3   A Monetarist Recession, 705
Figure 31.5   A Rational Expectations Business
              Cycle, 707
Figure 31.7   Capital and Labour Markets in a
              Real Business Cycle, 711
Figure 31.8   *AS–AD* in a Real Business Cycle, 712
Figure 31.10 *AS–AD* in the 1990–1992 Recession,
              715

Key Terms

Keynesian theory of the business cycle, 703
Monetarist theory of the business cycle, 704
New classical theory of the business cycle, 706
New Keynesian theory of the business cycle, 706
Rational expectation, 706
Real business cycle theory, 709

Problems

*1 The figure shows the economy of Virtual Reality. When the economy is in a long-run equilibrium, it is at points *B*, *F* and *J*. When a recession occurs in Virtual Reality, the economy moves away from these points to one of the three other points identified in each part of the figure.

a If the Keynesian theory is the correct explanation for the recession, to which points does the economy move?

b If the monetarist theory is the correct explanation for the recession, to which points does the economy move?

c If the new classical rational expectations theory is the correct explanation for the recession, to which points does the economy move?

d If the new Keynesian rational expectations theory is the correct explanation for the recession, to which points does the economy move?

e If real business cycle theory is the correct explanation for the recession, to which points does the economy move?

2 The figure shows the economy of Vital Signs. When the economy is in a long-run equilibrium, it is at points *A*, *E* and *I*. When an expansion occurs in Vital Signs, the economy moves away from these points to one of the three other points identified in each part of the figure.

a If the Keynesian theory is the correct explanation for the recession, to which points does the economy move?

b If the monetarist theory is the correct explanation for the recession, to which points does the economy move?

c If the new classical rational expectations theory is the correct explanation for the recession, to which points does the economy move?

d If the new Keynesian rational expectations theory is the correct explanation for the recession, to which points does the economy move?

e If real business cycle theory is the correct explanation for the recession, to which points does the economy move?

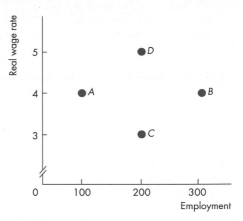

(a) Labour market

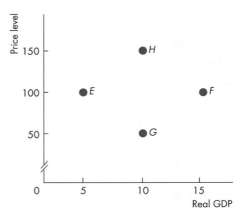

(b) AS–AD

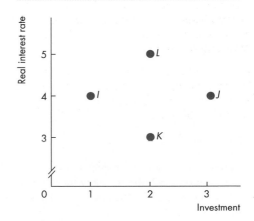

(c) Investment

---

*Solutions to odd-numbered problems are available on *Parkin Interactive*.

*3 Suppose that when the recession occurs in Virtual Reality in problem 1, the economy moves to *D*, *G* and *K*. Which theory of the business cycle, if any, explains this outcome?

4 Suppose that when the expansion occurs in Vital Signs in problem 2, the economy moves to *D*, *H* and *L*. Which theory of the business cycle, if any, explains this outcome?

*5 Suppose that when the recession occurs in Virtual Reality in problem 1, the economy moves to *C*, *G* and *K*. Which theory of the business cycle, if any, explains this outcome?

6 Suppose that when the expansion occurs in Vital Signs in problem 2, the economy moves to *C*, *H* and *L*. Which theory of the business cycle, if any, explains this outcome?

*7 Suppose that when the recession occurs in Virtual Reality in problem 1, the economy moves to *D*, *H* and *K*. Which theory of the business cycle, if any, explains this outcome?

8 Suppose that when the expansion occurs in Vital Signs in problem 2 the economy moves to *D*, *G* and *L*. Which theory of the business cycle, if any, explains this outcome?

*9 Suppose that when the recession occurs in Virtual Reality in problem 1, the economy moves to *C*, *H* and *K*. Which theory of the business cycle, if any, explains this outcome?

10 Suppose that when the expansion occurs in Vital Signs in problem 2, the economy moves to *C*, *G* and *L*. Which theory of the business cycle, if any, explains this outcome?

*11 Suppose that when the recession occurs in Virtual Reality in problem 1, the economy moves to *D*, *G* and *L*. Which theory of the business cycle, if any, explains this outcome?

12 Suppose that when the expansion occurs in Vital Signs in problem 2, the economy moves to *C*, *H* and *K*. Which theory of the business cycle, if any, explains this outcome?

*13 Suppose that when the recession occurs in Virtual Reality in problem 1, the economy moves to *C*, *G* and *L*. Which theory of the business cycle, if any, explains this outcome?

14 Suppose that when the expansion occurs in Vital Signs in problem 2, the economy moves to *D*, *H* and *K*. Which theory of the business cycle, if any, explains this outcome?

Critical Thinking

1 Study *Reading Between the Lines* on pp. 718–719 and then answer the following questions:

a What is the reason for the weakness in consumer confidence in Korea?

b Why would a slowdown in the Chinese economy influence growth in Korea?

c Why would a rise in US interest rates influence consumption in Korea?

d How does a rise in the world price of oil influence the Korean economy?

e What policy do you recommend the Bank of Korea conduct to avoid recession?

Web Exercise

Use the links on *Parkin Interactive* to work the following exercise.

1 Obtain information about the current state of the US economy. Then:

a List all of the features of the US economy during the current year that you think are consistent with a pessimistic outlook for the next two years.

b List all of the features of the US economy during the current year that you think are consistent with an optimistic outlook for the next two years.

c Describe how you think the US economy is going to evolve over the next year or two. Explain your predictions, drawing on the pessimistic and optimistic factors that you listed in parts (a) and (b) and on your knowledge of macroeconomic theory.

Chapter 32

Macroeconomic Policy Challenges

After studying this chapter you will be able to:

◆ Describe the goals of macroeconomic policy

◆ Describe the main features of fiscal and monetary policy in the European Union and the Eurozone in recent years

◆ Explain how fiscal policy and monetary policy influence long-term economic growth

◆ Distinguish between and evaluate fixed-rule and feedback-rule policies to stabilize the business cycle

◆ Evaluate fixed-rule and feedback-rule policies to contain inflation and explain why lowering inflation usually brings recession

What Can Policy Do?

What can monetary and fiscal policy do to improve macroeconomic performance? Can the government use fiscal policy to speed economic growth, maintain low unemployment and keep inflation in check? Can monetary policy achieve these same ends? Are some goals better achieved with monetary policy and some with fiscal policy? What specific policy actions and rules work best?

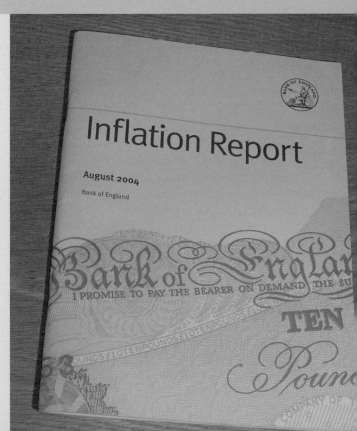

Policy Goals

Macroeconomic policy has four goals. They are to achieve:

◆ High sustainable potential GDP growth

◆ Moderate business cycle fluctuations

◆ Low unemployment

◆ Low inflation

Potential GDP Growth

Rapid sustained real GDP growth makes a profound contribution to economic well-being. A growth rate of 2.5 per cent a year doubles production in 28 years. A growth rate of 5 per cent a year doubles production in just over 14 years. The limits to *sustainable* growth are determined by the availability of natural resources, by environmental considerations and by the willingness of people to save and invest in new capital and new technologies rather than consume everything they produce.

Between 1987 and 2003, through one complete business cycle, UK potential GDP grew at a rate of 2.4 per cent a year. With population growth of 0.5 per cent a year that translates into a growth rate of real GDP per person of 1.9 per cent a year, which means that output per person doubles every 37 years. Improving on this long-term growth rate is of critical importance.

Business Cycle

Potential GDP probably does not grow at a constant rate. Fluctuations in the pace of technological advance and in the pace of investment in new capital bring fluctuations in potential GDP. So some fluctuations in real GDP represent fluctuations in potential GDP. But when real GDP grows less quickly than potential GDP, output is lost, and when real GDP grows more quickly than potential GDP, bottlenecks arise that create inefficiencies and inflationary pressures. Keeping real GDP growth steady and equal to potential growth avoids these problems.

It is not known how smooth real GDP can be made. Real business cycle theory regards all the fluctuations in real GDP as arising from fluctuations in potential GDP. The aggregate demand theories of the business cycle regard most of the fluctuations in real GDP as being avoidable deviations from potential GDP.

Unemployment

When real GDP growth slows, unemployment increases and rises above its natural rate. The higher the unemployment rate, the longer is the time it takes unemployed people to find jobs. Productive labour is wasted and there is a slowdown in the accumulation of human capital. If high unemployment persists, serious psychological and social problems arise for the unemployed workers and their families.

When real GDP growth speeds up, unemployment decreases and falls below the natural rate of unemployment. The lower the unemployment rate, the harder it becomes for expanding industries to get the labour they need to keep growing. If extremely low unemployment persists, serious bottlenecks and production dislocations occur, sucking in imports and creating inflationary pressure.

Keeping unemployment at the natural rate avoids both of these problems. But just what is the natural rate of unemployment? Assessments vary. The actual average unemployment rate in the United Kingdom over the most recent business cycle – 1987 to 2003 – was 7.7 per cent. Most economists would put the natural rate at about 5–6 per cent. But real business cycle theorists believe the natural rate fluctuates and equals the actual unemployment rate.

If the natural unemployment rate becomes high, then a goal of policy is to lower the natural rate itself. This goal is independent of smoothing the business cycle.

Inflation

When inflation fluctuates unpredictably, money becomes less useful as a measuring rod for conducting transactions. Borrowers and lenders and employers and workers must take on extra risks. Keeping the inflation rate steady and predictable avoids these problems.

What is the most desirable inflation rate? Some economists say that the *rate* of inflation doesn't matter much as long as the rate is *predictable*. So, say these economists, any predictable inflation rate will serve well as a target for policy. But most economists believe that price stability, which they translate as an inflation rate of between 0 and 2 per cent a year, is desirable. The reason zero is not the target is that some price increases are due to quality improvements – a measurement bias in the price index – so a positive average *measured* inflation rate is equivalent to price stability. It has been suggested that a good definition of price stability is a situation in which no one considers inflation to be a factor in the decisions they make.

Core Policy Indicators: Growth, Unemployment and Inflation

Although macroeconomic policy pursues the four policy goals we've just described, the goals are not dependent. Three of them – increasing potential GDP growth, smoothing the business cycle and maintaining low unemployment – are interlinked and they lie at the core of economic policy. The level of unemployment tells us about the state of the business cycle and the structural problems of the economy. The goal of reducing the number of long-term unemployed people is linked to the goal of high and sustainable long-term economic growth. If the unemployment rate is below the natural rate, then economic growth may be too rapid. If unemployment rises above the natural rate, then economic growth may be too slow. So maintaining unemployment at its natural rate is equivalent to avoiding business fluctuations and keeping real GDP growing steadily at its maximum sustainable rate.

Figure 32.1 shows the macroeconomic performance of 15 EU economies on average during 1994–2004. The shaded areas indicate a performance that gives some concern. The white areas indicate a performance that most people would regard as acceptable.

The dots in Figure 32.1(a) describe the combination of inflation and unemployment for each of economy. You can see that Austria, Denmark, Luxembourg, Netherlands, Sweden and the United Kingdom fall in the white area. Greece and Spain have the worst performance on this combination of variables.

The dots in Figure 32.1(b) describe the combination of inflation and real GDP growth. Here, you can see that Finland, Luxembourg, Sweden and the United Kingdom fall in the white area. Italy and Portugal are the two economies with the worst performance on this combination of variables.

Unemployment is high and a serious problem for Belgium, Finland, France, Germany, Greece, Italy and Spain. Slow growth is a serious problem for Austria, Germany and Italy. And inflation remains somewhat high in Greece, Ireland, Portugal and Spain.

Review Quiz

1 What are the objectives of macroeconomic policy?
2 Can macroeconomic policy keep the unemployment rate below the natural rate?
3 Why are GDP growth, inflation and unemployment the three core indicators of macroeconomic policy?

Figure 32.1

Macroeconomic Performance: EU Unemployment, Inflation and Growth: 1994–2004

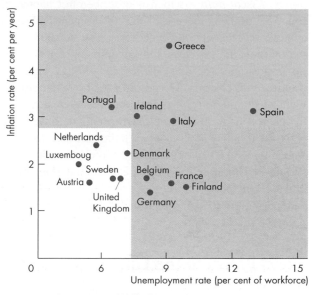

(a) Unemployment and inflation

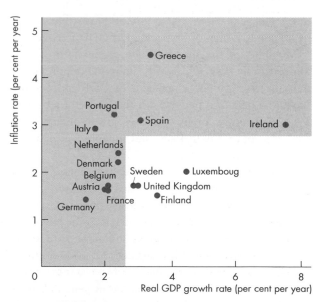

(b) Real GDP growth and inflation

Part (a) shows that Greece, Ireland, Italy and Spain have too much inflation combined with too much unemployment. Part (b) shows that Portugal and Italy have too much inflation combined with too little growth. Of the large EU economies, the United Kingdom has performed best on these three variables during the time period covered here.

Source: International Monetary Fund, *World Economic Outlook* database, April 2004.

Policy Tools and Performance

The tools used to try to achieve macroeconomic performance objectives are fiscal policy and monetary policy. *Fiscal policy*, which is described in Chapter 25 (pp. 555–580), is the use of the government budget to achieve macroeconomic objectives. The detailed fiscal policy tools are tax rates and government expenditures on goods and services. *Monetary policy*, which is described in Chapter 27 (pp. 603–624), is the adjustment of the quantity of money and the interest rate by the central bank to achieve macroeconomic objectives. How fiscal policy and monetary policy are used together is examined in Chapter 28 (pp. 625–652). How have the European Union and the European Central Bank actually used the policy tools? Let's answer this question by summarizing the main directions of fiscal and monetary policy in recent years.

Fiscal Policy in the European Union

Government plays a large role in all the member states of the European Union. General government expenditure averages 47 per cent of GDP across the enlarged union and ranges between a low of 34 per cent of GDP in Ireland to a high of 58 per cent of GDP in Sweden.

Members of the Eurozone are parties to a Stability and Growth Pact that limits their maximum budget deficits to less than 3 per cent of GDP and commits them to a balanced budget over the course of a business cycle. Currently, eight countries are in breach of the Stability and Growth Pact, and notably Germany and France are among them.

The degree of fiscal stimulus to the economy is signalled not by the *level* of government expenditures and the size of a government's budget deficit but by the *change* in expenditures and the deficit (or surplus).

Figure 32.2 provides a broad summary of these two features of fiscal policy in 2003 across the countries of the enlarged European Union.

Figure 32.2(a) shows the *change* in general government expenditure as a percentage of GDP. A positive change is expansionary and a negative change is contractionary. No change or a small change is neutral. You can see that fiscal policy has been expansionary in more than two-thirds of the countries.

Some of the increase arises from automatic fiscal policy induced by an increase in the unemployment rate and unemployment benefits. But discretionary fiscal policy has also increased in several countries.

Figure 32.2(b) shows the change in general government deficit (or surplus) as a percentage of GDP. Again, you can see that most countries increased their budget deficit or decreased their surplus.

Keynesian economists support the expansionary fiscal polices of 2003 and say they are exactly the actions needed to reduce unemployment.

Monetarist and classical economists worry that expansionary fiscal policy that breaches the Stability and Growth Pact will force the European Central Bank to drive the interest rate up and that such a move would decrease investment and increase unemployment.

Monetary Policy in the Eurozone

Since 1 January 1999, the countries that comprise the single currency area of the Eurozone have surrendered the conduct of monetary policy to the European Central Bank (ECB) in Frankfurt. The objective of the ECB is to maintain price stability, which is seen as the best contribution that monetary policy can make to achieving sustained economic growth.

Price stability in the Eurozone is defined as an inflation rate of below 2 per cent a year. To achieve this inflation target, the ECB monitors the growth rate of broad money (M3) and adjusts the interest rate. The ECB increases the interest rate if the quantity of M3 is growing too rapidly and Eurozone real GDP is expanding above potential GDP. The ECB lowers the interest rate in the opposite conditions.

There is concern as to whether one monetary policy can suit so many different countries. For example in the first quarter of 2004, real GDP growth was 6.1 per cent in Ireland and 0.9 per cent in Italy. And in June 2004, the inflation rate was 3.7 per cent in Portugal and 1.9 per cent in the Netherlands.

Should the ECB increase the interest rate to slow rapid growth in Ireland and inflation in Portugal or should it decrease the interest rate to boost economic growth in Italy?

As a practical matter, the ECB pays attention to the average inflation rate and the average real GDP growth rate in the Eurozone. But the ECB cannot be completely insensitive to the effects of its actions on the economies with performances substantially different from the average.

Most economists recommend that microeconomic adjustment polices be implemented to deal with wide regional differences in performance. Such policies work on the incentives to locate in particular regions and countries.

Figure 32.2

EU Fiscal Policy in 2003

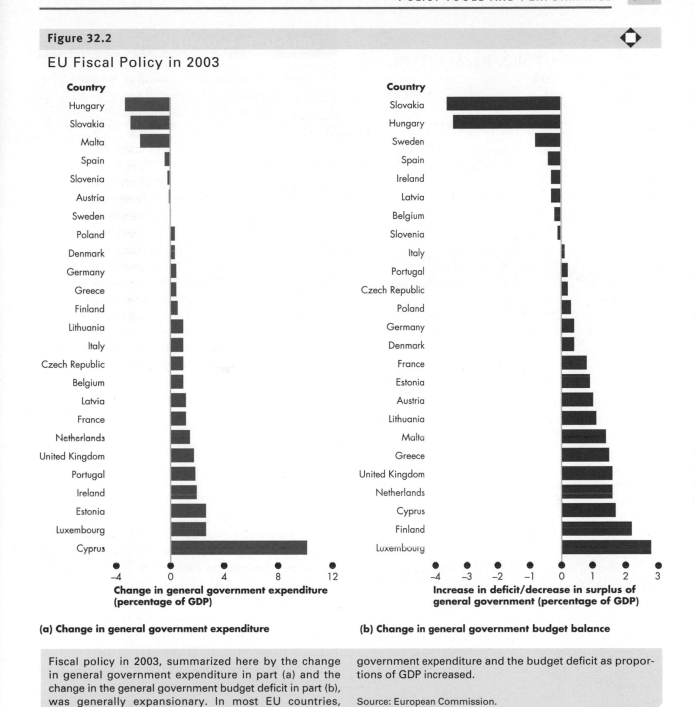

(a) Change in general government expenditure

(b) Change in general government budget balance

Fiscal policy in 2003, summarized here by the change in general government expenditure in part (a) and the change in the general government budget deficit in part (b), was generally expansionary. In most EU countries, government expenditure and the budget deficit as proportions of GDP increased.

Source: European Commission.

Figure 32.3 shows the monetary policy record of the ECB with the EU inflation rate between 2000 and 2004. The inflation rate moved above target in 2000 and the ECB responded by increasing the interest rate from 2.5 per cent to 3 per cent a year. During 2001, the inflation rate remained above 2 per cent a year and M3 growth increased. So the ECB pushed the interest rate yet higher, reaching 4.25 per cent a year by June 2001.

Money growth remained high, but the inflation rate was falling. In September 2001, following the terrorist attack in New York, the ECB lowered the interest rate. The timing of this move was coordinated with the Federal Reserve in the United States to maintain calm in global money markets.

With inflation almost on target, the interest rate was lowered to 2 per cent a year in 2003.

Figure 32.3

The Monetary Policy Record of the ECB: 2000–2004

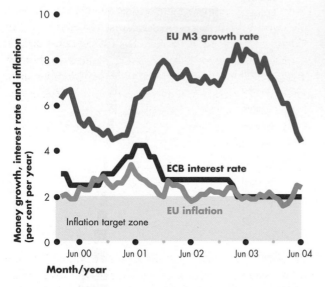

In 2000, the ECB increased the interest rate from 2.5 per cent to 3 per cent a year. The M3 growth rate decreased during 2000. The interest rate was increased during 2001 to slow the money growth rate, but after the terrorist attack on 11 September 2001 the interest rate was lowered even though money growth was high. With inflation on the edge of its target range, the interest rate was lowered in 2003.

Source: European Central Bank.

Review Quiz

1 What are the macroeconomic policy tools available for stabilization policy?
2 What happens to automatic fiscal policy in times of high unemployment? What happened to discretionary fiscal policy in the EU countries in 2002–2003?
3 What is the objective of monetary policy in the Eurozone economies?
4 What did the ECB do following the 11 September 2001 terrorist attack on New York? Why?

You've now studied the goals and recent trends in fiscal policy and monetary policy. Let's now see how policy might be better used to achieve the goals of macroeconomic policy. We'll begin by looking at long-term growth policy.

Long-term Growth Policy

The sources of the long-term growth of potential GDP, which are explained in Chapter 30 (pp. 683–684), are the accumulation of physical and human capital and the advance of technology. Chapter 30 also briefly examines the range of policies that might achieve faster growth (p. 688). Here, we probe more deeply into the problem of boosting the long-term growth rate.

The factors that determine long-term growth result from millions of individual decisions. The role of government in influencing growth is limited, but policy does influence the long-term growth rate.

Monetary policy can contribute to long-term growth by keeping the inflation rate low. (Chapter 29, pp. 662–666 explains some of the connections between inflation and economic growth.) Fiscal policy and other policies at both the national and EU level can also contribute to economic growth by influencing private decisions on which long-term growth depends in three areas. All growth policies increase:

◆ National saving

◆ Investment in human capital

◆ Investment in new technologies

National Saving

National saving equals private saving plus government saving. Figure 32.4 shows the scale of national saving within the European Union from 1963 to 2003 and its private and government components. The government component is obtained by subtracting private saving from national saving.

From 1963 to 1975, national saving fluctuated around an average of 25 per cent of GDP. Then national saving began a steady slide to 21 per cent in 1975. It then fluctuated between 21 and 18 per cent of GDP from 1982 to 2003.

Private saving has remained remarkably stable over a long period. It actually increased a little as a percentage of GDP between 1963 and 1979, when it peaked at 22 per cent of GDP. But over the whole period from 1963 to 2003, private saving has remained between 19 and 21 per cent of GDP.

Government saving became increasingly negative during the 1980s and 1990s but ended the decade with positive saving as members of the European Union brought budget deficits under control to meet the conditions of entry into the European Monetary Union.

EU investment, one of the engines of growth, is not limited by national saving in the European Union. The reason is that foreign saving can be harnessed to finance EU investment. By borrowing from the rest of the world, the EU economy can invest more and grow faster than EU national saving permits.

But by the same reasoning, EU investment is not the only potential use of EU saving. Europeans can invest in other parts of the world instead of in Europe. Such investment brings faster growth in other regions. But it can be beneficial for Europe too. The European Union has an ageing population with an increasing number of aged dependents who must be supported by the production of a shrinking working-age population. In such a situation, Europe can benefit by using some of its saving to build up a retirement nest egg by lending to the developing world and the emerging economies. Such lending benefits Europeans because it earns a return that might exceed that available in Europe. And it benefits the people of the developing and emerging world by helping them to meet their investment needs.

Figure 32.4

National Saving Rates in the European Union: 1963–2003

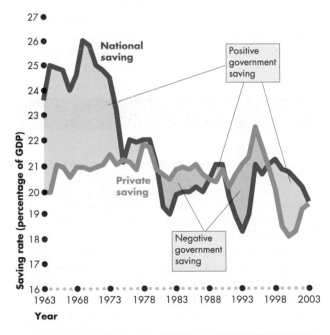

The EU national saving rate peaked in 1970 at 25.8 per cent of GDP. EU national saving has fallen since that year and government saving has been the largest source of the fall. Government saving became positive in the late 1990s in an effort to meet the fiscal conditions for joining the EMU.

Source: European Commission.

Boosting the EU saving rate can help to bring faster real GDP growth for two reasons. First, the European Union represents a significant proportion of the world economy, so an increase in EU saving would increase world saving and bring lower real interest rates around the world. With lower real interest rates, investment would be boosted everywhere. The EU economy and the world economy could grow faster. Second, with more domestic saving, there might be an increase in investment in domestic high-risk, high-return new technologies that could boost long-term EU growth.

How can national saving be increased? The two points of attack are:

◆ Increasing government saving
◆ Increasing private saving

Increasing Government Saving

Between 1981 and 1987 and again between 1991 and 1996, government saving was negative. Government budget deficits in many European countries combined to bring this negative drain on the national savings of the EU economy. During those 13 years of government deficits (negative government saving), 17 per cent of GDP was diverted from investment in new capital (or lending to the rest of the world) towards financing government deficits.

Increasing government saving means eliminating government deficits in the EU countries. They are one and the same action. Achieving a substantial cut in government deficits is part of the Stability and Growth Pact that Eurozone countries have accepted by Treaty as a condition of membership of the EMU. The reduction in the deficit in the EMU countries has been difficult and was achieved by privatization of some previous government-provided functions and cuts in sensitive areas such as welfare spending.

Increasing Private Saving

Private saving in the European Union as a whole has remained remarkably stable since 1963. The only way that government actions can boost private saving is by increasing the after-tax return on saving.

The most effective way of stimulating private saving is to cut taxes on interest income. But such a tax cut would be costly and could only be financed either by a further decrease in government expenditures or by increases in taxes on labour incomes or in Value Added Tax (VAT). This would be difficult politically and cannot be carried out at the EU level on existing political arrangements. So governments are limited to making minor changes to the taxation of interest income, which will have negligible effects on the saving rate.

Private Saving and Inflation

Inflation erodes the value of saving and uncertainty about future inflation is bad for saving. One further policy, therefore, that increases the saving rate is a monetary policy that preserves stable prices and minimizes uncertainty about the future value of money. Chapter 29, pp. 662–666, spells out the broader connection between inflation and real GDP and explains why low inflation may bring greater output and faster growth.

Human Capital Policies

The accumulation of human capital plays a crucial role in economic growth and two areas are relevant: attending school, college or university and on-the-job experience.

Economic research shows that education and training pay. On average, the greater the number of years a person remains at school, college or university or in training, the higher are that person's earnings. Primary, secondary and higher education as well as on-the-job training in Europe is good by international standards. But they are not the best. For example, the UK government wants to increase the number of university places to enable one-half of all school leavers to enter higher education. In the United States and Canada, that proportion is already greater than one-half and is creeping upward to two-thirds. So there is plenty of room for more resources being devoted to education.

If education and on-the-job training yield higher earnings, why does the government or the European Commission need a policy towards investment in human capital? Why can't people simply be left to get on with making their own decisions about how much human capital to acquire? The answer is that the *social* returns to human capital exceed the *private* returns. The extra productivity that comes from the interactions of well-educated and experienced people exceeds what each individual can achieve alone. So left on its own, a purely private market in education would seriously under invest in human capital.

Economic research has also shown that on-the-job training pays. This type of training can be formal, such as a school or at work, or informal, such as learning-by-doing. The scope for government involvement in these areas is limited, but it can set an example as an employer and it can encourage best-practice training programmes for workers.

Investment in New Technologies

Chapter 30 explains that investment in new technologies is special for two reasons. First, it appears not to run into the problem of diminishing returns that plague other factors of production. Second, the benefits of new technologies spill over to influence all parts of the economy, not just the firms undertaking the investment. For these reasons, a particularly promising way of boosting economic growth is to stimulate investment in the research and development efforts that create new technologies.

Governments can fund and provide tax incentives for research and development activities. Through the various research councils, the universities and research institutes, the governments of the European Union already fund a large amount of basic research.

The European Commission estimates that about 2 per cent of EU GDP, 2.8 per cent of US GDP and 3 per cent of Japanese GDP are spent on research and technological development.

Considering the large pay-off from economic growth, and the pay-off, therefore, from improved knowledge about the forces that bring growth, it is surprising that more is not spent, both on research and technological development and on economic research on the causes of growth.

Review Quiz

1 Why do long-term growth policies focus on increasing saving and increasing investment in human capital and new technologies?
2 What policies can governments in the European Union take to increase the national saving rate?
3 What actions can governments in the European Union take to increase investment in human capital?
4 What actions can governments in the European Union take to increase investment in new technologies?

We've seen how government might use fiscal policy and the central bank use monetary policy to influence long-term economic growth. How can the business cycle and unemployment be influenced? Let's now address this question.

Business Cycle and Unemployment Policies

Many different fiscal and monetary policies can be pursued to stabilize the business cycle and cyclical unemployment. But all these polices fall into three broad categories:

◆ Fixed-rule policies

◆ Feedback-rule policies

◆ Discretionary policies

Fixed-rule Policies

A **fixed-rule policy** specifies an action to be pursued independently of the state of the economy. An everyday example of a fixed rule is a stop sign. It says "stop regardless of the state of the road ahead – even if no other vehicle is trying to use the road".

Several fixed-rule policies have been proposed for the economy. One, proposed by Milton Friedman, is to keep the quantity of money growing at a constant rate year in and year out, regardless of the state of the economy, to make the *average* inflation rate zero. Another fixed-rule policy is to balance the government budget.

Fixed rules are rarely followed in practice, but they have some important benefits in principle. Later in this chapter we'll study the way they would work if they were pursued.

Feedback-rule Policies

A **feedback-rule policy** specifies how policy actions respond to changes in the state of the economy. A give way sign is an everyday feedback rule. It says "stop if another vehicle is attempting to use the road ahead but otherwise, proceed".

A macroeconomic feedback-rule policy is one that changes the money supply, or interest rates, or even tax rates, in response to the state of the economy. One feedback rule proposed by John Taylor that we'll examine later in this chapter provides direct guidance to the ECB and the Monetary Policy Committee of the Bank of England on when and by how much to change the interest rate in response to inflation and real GDP. Other feedback-rule policies are automatic. For example, the automatic rise in taxes during an expansion and the automatic fall in taxes during a recession are automatic feedback-rule policies.

Discretionary Policies

A **discretionary policy** responds to the state of the economy in a possibly unique way that uses all the information available, including perceived lessons from past "mistakes". An everyday discretionary policy occurs at an unmarked junction. Each driver uses discretion in deciding whether to stop and how slowly to approach the junction.

Most macroeconomic policy actions have an element of discretion because every situation is to some degree unique. For example, between 1994 and 1995 (before the Bank of England became independent), interest rates were raised three times but by half percentage points in each case to forestall an expansion in the economy. The government used discretion based on lessons learned from earlier expansions. The granting of independence to the Bank of England was in part to remove government discretion.

Despite the fact that all policy actions have an element of discretion, they can be regarded as modifications to a basic feedback-rule policy. Discretionary policy is sophisticated feedback policy, where the rules gradually evolve to reflect new knowledge about the way the economy works.

We'll study the effects of business cycle policy by comparing the performance of real GDP and the price level with a fixed rule and a feedback rule. Because the business cycle can result from demand shocks or supply shocks, we need to consider these two cases. We'll begin by studying demand shocks.

Stabilizing Aggregate Demand Shocks

We'll study an economy that starts out at full employment and has no inflation. Figure 32.5 illustrates this situation. The economy is on aggregate demand curve AD_0 and short-run aggregate supply curve SAS. These curves intersect at a point on the long-run aggregate supply curve, LAS. The price level is 110 and real GDP is £1,000 billion at point A. Now suppose that there is an unexpected and temporary decrease in aggregate demand. Let's see what happens.

Perhaps investment decreases because of a wave of pessimism about the future, or perhaps exports decrease because of a recession in the rest of the world. Regardless of the origin of the decrease in aggregate demand, the aggregate demand curve shifts leftward from AD_0 to AD_1 in Figure 32.5. The price level falls to 105 and real GDP decreases to £950 billion.

Figure 32.5

A Decrease in Aggregate Demand

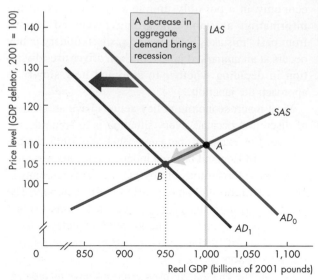

The economy starts out at full employment on aggregate demand curve AD_0 and short-run aggregate supply curve SAS, with the two curves intersecting on the long-run aggregate supply curve LAS. Real GDP is £1,000 billion and the price level is 110. A decrease in aggregate demand (owing to pessimism about future profits, for example) unexpectedly shifts the aggregate demand curve to AD_1. Real GDP decreases to £950 billion and the price level falls to 105. The economy is in a recession.

The economy is in a recession. Real GDP is below potential GDP and unemployment is above its natural rate.

Suppose that the decrease in aggregate demand from AD_0 to AD_1 is temporary. As confidence in the future improves, firms' investment picks up, or as economic expansion proceeds in the rest of the world, exports gradually increase. As a result, the aggregate demand curve gradually returns to AD_0, but it takes some time to do so.

We are going to work out how the economy responds under two alternative monetary policies during the period in which aggregate demand gradually increases to its original level: a fixed rule and a feedback rule.

Fixed Rule: Monetarism

The fixed rule that we'll study here is one in which the government expenditures on goods and services, taxes and the supply of money remain constant. Neither fiscal

policy nor monetary policy responds to the depressed economy. This is the rule advocated by monetarists. A **monetarist** is an economist who believes that fluctuations in the quantity of money are the main source of economic fluctuations – the monetarist theory of the business cycle (see Chapter 31, pp. 704–706).

Figure 32.6(a) shows the response of the economy under this fixed-rule policy. When aggregate demand decreases to AD_1, no policy measures are taken to bring the economy back to full employment. But the decrease in aggregate demand is only *temporary*. Starting from recession at point B, aggregate demand gradually returns to its original level and the aggregate demand curve shifts rightward to AD_0. Real GDP and the price level gradually increase as the economy returns to point A. The price level gradually returns to 110 and real GDP to potential GDP of £1,000 billion, as shown in Figure 32.6(a). Throughout this process, real GDP growth is more rapid than usual but beginning from below potential GDP. Throughout the adjustment, unemployment remains its natural rate.

Figure 32.6(b) illustrates the response of the economy under a fixed rule when the decrease in aggregate demand to AD_1 is *permanent*. Again starting from recession at point B and with unemployment above the natural rate, the money wage rate falls. Short-run aggregate supply increases and the SAS curve shifts rightward to SAS_1. As it does so, real GDP gradually increases towards £1,000 billion and the price level falls towards 95, at point C. Again, throughout the adjustment, real GDP is less than potential GDP and unemployment exceeds the natural rate. Let's contrast this adjustment with what occurs under a feedback-rule policy.

Feedback Rule: Keynesian Activism

The feedback rule that we'll study is one in which government expenditures on goods and services increase, taxes decrease and the supply of money increases when real GDP falls below potential GDP. In other words, both fiscal policy and monetary policy become expansionary when real GDP is less than potential GDP. When real GDP exceeds potential GDP, both policies operate in reverse, becoming contractionary. This rule is advocated by Keynesian activists. A **Keynesian activist** is an economist who believes that fluctuations in aggregate demand combined with sticky money wage rates (and/or sticky prices) are the main source of economic fluctuations – the Keynesian and new Keynesian theories of the business cycle (see Chapter 31, pp. 703–704 and pp. 706–707).

Figure 32.6

Two Stabilization Policies: Aggregate Demand Shock

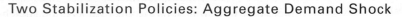

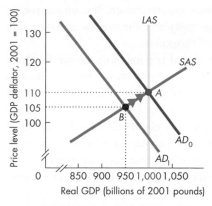

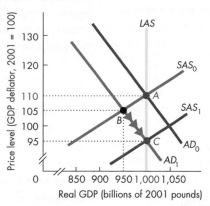

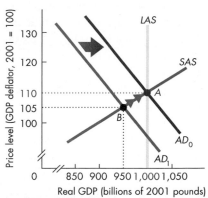

(a) Fixed rule: temporary demand shock   **(b) Fixed rule: permanent demand shock**   **(c) Feedback rule**

Aggregate demand is AD_1 and the economy is in a recession at point B. Real GDP is £950 billion, and the price level is 105. In part (a) the aggregate demand shock is temporary and a fixed-rule policy is pursued. Aggregate demand gradually increases to AD_0. Real GDP increases to £1,000 billion, and the price level increases to 110 at point A. In part (b), the demand shock is permanent and a fixed-rule policy is pursued. Aggregate demand remains at AD_1.

Eventually the money wage rate falls and the SAS curve shifts to SAS_1. The price level falls to 95, and real GDP increases to £1,000 billion at point C. In part (c), a feedback rule is pursued. With the economy in recession, expansionary fiscal and monetary policies increase aggregate demand and shift the aggregate demand curve from AD_1 to AD_0. Real GDP increases to £1,000 billion, and the price level increases to 110 at point A.

Figure 32.6(c) shows the response of the economy under this feedback-rule policy. Starting from the recession at point B, the expansionary fiscal and monetary policy increases aggregate demand immediately. The aggregate demand curve shifts to AD_0 and the economy moves back to point A. As other influences begin to increase aggregate demand, fiscal and monetary policy become contractionary to hold the aggregate demand curve steady at AD_0. Real GDP is held steady at £1,000 billion and the price level remains at 110.

The Two Rules Compared

Under a fixed-rule policy, the economy goes into a recession and stays there for as long as it takes for aggregate demand to increase again under its own steam. Only gradually does the aggregate demand curve return to its original position and the recession come to an end.

Under a feedback-rule policy, the policy action pulls the economy out of its recession. Once back at potential GDP, real GDP is held there by a gradual, policy-induced decrease in aggregate demand that exactly offsets the increase in aggregate demand coming from private spending decisions.

The price level and real GDP decrease and increase by exactly the same amounts under the two policies, but

real GDP stays below potential GDP for longer with a fixed rule than it does with a feedback rule.

So Feedback Rules are Better?

Isn't it obvious that a feedback rule is better than a fixed rule? Can't the government and the Bank of England use feedback rules to keep the economy close to full employment with a stable price level? Of course, unforecasted events – such as a collapse in business confidence – will hit the economy from time to time. But by responding with a change in tax rates, spending, interest rates and the supply of money, can't the government and the Bank minimize the damage from such a shock? It appears to be so from our analysis.

Despite the apparent superiority of a feedback rule, many economists remain convinced that a fixed rule stabilizes the economy more effectively than does a feedback rule. These economists argue that fixed rules are better than feedback rules because:

◆ Potential GDP is not known.

◆ Policy lags are longer than the forecast horizon.

◆ Feedback-rule policies are less predictable than fixed-rule policies.

Let's look at these arguments.

Knowledge of Potential GDP

To decide whether a feedback policy needs to stimulate aggregate demand or retard it, it is necessary to determine whether real GDP is currently above or below potential GDP. But potential GDP is not known with certainty. It depends on a large number of factors, one of which is the level of employment when unemployment is at its natural rate. But there is uncertainty and disagreement about how the labour market works, so we can only estimate the natural rate of unemployment. As a result, there is uncertainty about the *direction* in which a feedback policy should be pushing the level of aggregate demand.

Policy Lags and the Forecast Horizon

The effects of policy actions taken today are spread out over the next two years or even more. But no one is able to forecast that far ahead. The forecast horizon of the policy-makers is less than one year. Furthermore, it is not possible to predict the precise timing and magnitude of the effects of policy itself. So a feedback policy that reacts to today's economy may be inappropriate for the state of the economy at that uncertain future date when the policy's effects are felt.

For example, suppose that today the UK economy is in a recession. The Bank of England reacts with an increase in the money growth rate. When the Bank of England puts on the monetary accelerator, the first re-action is a fall in interest rates. Some time later, lower interest rates produce an increase in investment and the purchases of consumer durable goods. Some time still later, this increase in expenditure increases income. The higher income in turn induces higher consumption expenditure. Later still, the higher expenditure increases the demand for labour and eventually money wage rates and prices rise. The sectors in which the spending increases occur vary and so does the impact on employment. It can take from nine months to two years for an initial action by the Bank of England to cause a change in real GDP, employment and the inflation rate.

By the time the Bank of England's actions are having their maximum effect, the economy has moved on to a new situation. Perhaps a world economic slowdown has added a new negative effect on aggregate demand that is offsetting the Bank's expansionary actions. Or perhaps a boost in business confidence has increased aggregate demand yet further, adding to the Bank's own expansionary policy. Whatever the situation, the Bank of England can only take the appropriate actions today if it can forecast those future shocks to aggregate demand.

To smooth the fluctuations in aggregate demand, the Bank of England needs to take actions today, based on a forecast of what will be happening over a period stretching two or more years into the future. It is no use taking actions a year from today to influence the situation that then prevails. It will be too late.

If the Bank of England is good at economic forecasting and bases its policy actions on its forecasts, then it can deliver the type of aggregate demand-smoothing performance that we assumed in the model economy we studied earlier in this chapter. But if the Bank of England takes policy actions that are based on today's economy rather than on the forecasted economy a year into the future, then those actions will often be inappropriate ones.

When unemployment is high and the Bank of England puts its foot on the accelerator, it speeds the economy back to full employment. But the Bank of England cannot see far enough ahead to know when to ease off the accelerator and gently tap the brake, holding the economy at its full-employment point. Usually it keeps its foot on the accelerator for too long and, after the Bank of England has taken its foot off the accelerator pedal, the economy races through the full-employment point and starts to experience shortages and inflationary pressures. Eventually, when inflation increases and unemployment falls below its natural rate, the Bank of England steps on the brake, pushing the economy back below full employment.

The supporters of fixed rules believe that the Bank of England's own reaction to the current state of the economy are one of the major sources of fluctuations in aggregate demand and the major factor that people have to forecast in order to make their own economic choices.

During the past ten years or so, central banks have tried hard to avoid the problems just described. They have increased the interest rate in several small increments early in the expansion of a cycle before inflation has turned upwards. And they have begun to cut the interest rate when real GDP growth slows but before any serious signs of recession are on the horizon

Whether the Bank of England and the ECB now know enough to avoid some of the mistakes of the past is too early to tell. But their actions during the past few years have been gentler and better timed than those in earlier times.

The problems with feedback rules for fiscal policy are similar to those for monetary policy, but they are more severe because of the lags in the implementation of fiscal policy. The Bank of England can take actions fairly quickly. But before a fiscal policy action can be taken, the entire legislative process must be completed. So even before a fiscal policy action is implemented, the economy may have moved on to a new situation that calls for a different feedback from the one that is in the legislative pipeline.

Predictability of Policies

To make decisions about long-term contracts for employment (wage contracts) and for borrowing and lending, people have to anticipate the future course of prices – the future inflation rate. To forecast the inflation rate, it is necessary to forecast aggregate demand. And to forecast aggregate demand, it is necessary to forecast the policy actions of the government and the central bank.

If the government and the central bank stick to rock-steady, fixed rules for tax rates, spending programmes and money growth, then policy itself cannot be a contributor to unexpected fluctuations in aggregate demand.

In contrast, when a feedback rule is being pursued there is more scope for the policy actions to be unpredictable. The main reason is that feedback rules are not written down for all to see. Rather, they have to be inferred from the behaviour of the government and the central bank. The deliberations of the Bank of England's Monetary Policy Committee are published and the decision on the interest rate is explained in the minutes. This means that over time it becomes possible to predict the Bank of England's action by knowing what factors guided its policy in the past.

So with a feedback policy it is necessary to predict the variables to which the government and central bank react and the extent to which they react. Consequently, a feedback rule for fiscal and monetary policy can create more unpredictable fluctuations in aggregate demand than a fixed rule.

Economists disagree about whether these bigger fluctuations offset the potential stabilizing influence of the predictable changes the government and the central bank make. No agreed measurements have been made to settle this dispute. Nevertheless, the unpredictability of the government in its pursuit of feedback policies is an important fact of economic life and the government does not always go out of its way to make its reactions clear. This is one of the reasons for taking monetary policy out of the hands of the government.

To the extent that policy actions are discretionary and unpredictable, they lead to unpredictable fluctuations in aggregate demand. These fluctuations, in turn, produce fluctuations in real GDP, employment and unemployment.

It is difficult for the government to pursue a predictable feedback stabilization policy. Such policies are formulated in terms of spending programmes and tax laws announced at the time of the Budget. Because these programmes and tax laws are the outcome of a political process of negotiation between the Treasury or finance departments and the spending departments of government, there can be no effective way in which a predictable feedback fiscal policy can be adhered to.

We reviewed three reasons why feedback policies may not be more effective than fixed rules in controlling aggregate demand. But there is a fourth reason why some economists prefer fixed rules: not all shocks to the economy are on the demand side. Advocates of feedback rules believe that most fluctuations do come from aggregate demand. Advocates of fixed rules believe that aggregate supply fluctuations are the dominant ones. Let's now see how aggregate supply fluctuations affect the economy under a fixed rule and a feedback rule. We will also see why those economists who believe that aggregate supply fluctuations are the dominant ones also favour a fixed rule rather than a feedback rule.

Stabilizing Aggregate Supply Shocks

Real business cycle theorists believe that fluctuations in real GDP (and in employment and unemployment) are caused *not* by fluctuations in aggregate demand but by fluctuations in productivity growth. According to real business cycle theory (RBC theory), there is no useful distinction between long-run aggregate supply and short-run aggregate supply. Because money wage rates are flexible, the labour market is always in equilibrium and unemployment is always at its natural rate. The vertical long-run aggregate supply curve is also the short-run aggregate supply curve.

Fluctuations occur because of shifts in the long-run aggregate supply curve. Normally, the long-run aggregate supply curve shifts to the right – the economy expands. But the pace at which the long-run aggregate supply curve shifts to the right varies. Also, on occasion, the long-run aggregate supply curve shifts leftward, bringing a decrease in aggregate supply and a fall in real GDP.

If RBC theory is correct, economic policy that influences the aggregate demand curve has no effect on real GDP. But it does affect the price level. If a feedback-rule policy is used to increase aggregate demand every time real GDP decreases and if the RBC theory is correct, the feedback-rule policy will make price level fluctuations more severe than they otherwise would be. To see why, consider Figure 32.7 (overleaf).

Figure 32.7

Responding to a Productivity Growth Slowdown

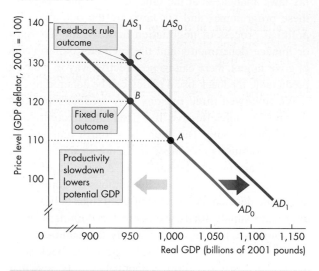

Initially, the economy is at point *A*. A productivity slowdown shifts the long-run aggregate supply curve from LAS_0 to LAS_1. Real GDP decreases to £950 billion and the price level rises to 120 at point *B*. With a fixed rule, there is no change in the supply of money, taxes or government spending, aggregate demand stays at AD_0 and that is the end of the matter. With a feedback rule, the Bank of England increases the supply of money and/or the government cuts taxes or increases spending, intending to increase real GDP. Aggregate demand shifts to AD_1, but the result is an increase in the price level – to 130 – with no change in real GDP at point *C*.

In Figure 32.7, the UK economy starts at point *A* on aggregate demand curve AD_0 and long-run aggregate supply curve LAS_0. The price level is 110 and real GDP is £1,000 billion. Now suppose that the long-run aggregate supply curve shifts to LAS_1. An actual decrease in long-run aggregate supply can occur as a result of a severe drought or other natural catastrophe, or perhaps as the result of a disruption of international trade such as the OPEC embargo of the 1970s.

Fixed Rule

With a fixed rule, the fall in the long-run aggregate supply has no effect on the Bank of England or the government and no effect on aggregate demand. The aggregate demand curve remains AD_0. Real GDP decreases to £950 billion and the price level rise to 120.

Feedback Rule

Now suppose that the Bank of England and the government use feedback-rule policies. In particular, suppose that when real GDP decreases, the Bank of England increases the supply of money and Parliament approves a tax cut to increase aggregate demand. In this example, the supply of money increases and the tax cut shifts the aggregate demand curve to AD_1. The policy goal is to bring real GDP back to £1,000 billion. But potential GDP has decreased to £950 billion and the long-run aggregate supply curve has shifted leftward. The increase in aggregate demand cannot bring forth an increase in output if the economy does not have the capacity to produce that output. So real GDP stays at £950 billion but the price level rises still further – to 130 at point *C*. You can see that in this case the attempt to stabilize real GDP using a feedback-rule policy has no effect on real GDP, but it generates a substantial price level increase.

Nominal GDP Targeting

A leading Keynesian activist economist, the late James Tobin of Yale University, has suggested that feedback rules should target not real GDP but nominal GDP. **Nominal GDP targeting** is the attempt to keep the growth rate of nominal GDP steady.

Nominal GDP growth equals the real GDP growth rate plus the inflation rate. When nominal GDP grows quickly, it is usually because the inflation rate is high. When nominal GDP grows slowly, it is usually because real GDP growth is negative – the economy is in recession. So if nominal GDP growth is held steady, excessive inflation and deep recession might be avoided.

Nominal GDP targeting uses feedback rules. Expansionary fiscal and/or monetary actions increase aggregate demand when nominal GDP is below target and contractionary fiscal and/or monetary actions decrease aggregate demand when nominal GDP is above target.

Nominal GDP targeting avoids taking a view of whether the economy has been hit by a demand shock or a supply shock. But it shares all the other problems of real GDP targeting that we've reviewed.

We've now seen some of the shortcomings of using feedback rules for stabilization policy. Some economists believe that these shortcomings are serious enough to discredit such rules and argue that simple fixed rules can deliver a better outcome. Others think the potential advantages of feedback rules as greater than their costs and advocate their continued use and the gradual evolution of better rules.

Natural-rate Policies

All the business cycle and unemployment policies we've considered have been directed at smoothing the business cycle and minimizing cyclical unemployment – keeping unemployment close to the natural rate. It is also possible to pursue policies directed towards lowering the natural rate of unemployment. But there are no simple costless ways of lowering the natural rate of unemployment.

The main policy tools that influence the natural rate of unemployment are supply-side factors dealing with tax rates, employers' additional costs of hiring labour, unemployment benefits, union regulation and minimum wages. But to use these tools the government faces tough trade-offs. To lower the natural rate of unemployment, the government could lower the tax rate on income or employers' social insurance contributions, or lower unemployment benefits or even shorten the period for which benefits are paid. These policy actions might create hardships and have costs that exceed the cost of a high natural rate of unemployment.

Some economists have argued that the supply-side policies of the 1980s in the United Kingdom had the effect of reducing the natural rate of unemployment. Taxes on income were reduced, trade union activity was regulated, employers' social insurance contributions were reduced and the eligibility for unemployment benefits restricted. The outcome of all these policies has been to make the labour market more flexible and labour less costly to employ.

Review Quiz

1 What is a fixed-rule fiscal policy and a fixed-rule monetary policy?
2 Can you provide two examples of fixed rules in everyday life (other than those in the text)?
3 What is a feedback-rule fiscal policy and a feedback-rule monetary policy?
4 When might a feedback-rule policy be used? Can you provide two examples of feedback rules in everyday life (other than those in the text)?
5 Why do some economists say that feedback rules do not necessarily deliver a better macroeconomic performance than fixed rules? Do you agree or disagree with them? Why?

We've studied growth policy and business cycle and unemployment policy. Let's next look at anti-inflation policy.

Anti-inflation Policy

There are two inflation policy problems. In times of price level stability, the problem is to prevent inflation from breaking out. In times of inflation, the problem is to reduce its rate and restore price stability. Preventing inflation from breaking out means avoiding both demand-pull and cost-push forces. Avoiding demand-pull inflation is just the opposite of avoiding demand-driven recession and is achieved by stabilizing aggregate demand. So the business cycle and unemployment policy we've just studied is also an anti-inflation policy. But avoiding cost-push inflation raises some special issues that we need to consider. So we will look at two issues for inflation policy:

◆ Avoiding cost-push inflation
◆ Slowing inflation

Avoiding Cost-push Inflation

Cost-push inflation is inflation that has its origins in cost increases. In 1973–1974, the world oil price exploded. Cost shocks such as these become inflationary if they are accommodated by an increase in the supply of money. Such an increase in the supply of money can occur if a monetary policy feedback rule is used. A fixed-rule policy for the supply of money makes cost-push inflation impossible. Let's see why.

Figure 32.8 shows the economy at full employment. Aggregate demand is AD_0, short-run aggregate supply is SAS_0 and long-run aggregate supply is LAS. Real GDP is £1,000 billion and the price level is 110 at point A. Now suppose that OPEC tries to gain a temporary advantage by increasing the price of oil. The short-run aggregate supply curve shifts leftward from SAS_0 to SAS_1.

Monetarist Fixed Rule

Figure 32.8(a) shows what happens if the Bank of England follows a fixed rule for monetary policy and the government follows a fixed rule for fiscal policy. Suppose that the fixed rule is for zero money growth and no change in taxes or government spending. With these fixed rules, the Bank and the government pay no attention to the fact that there has been an increase in the price of oil. No policy actions are taken. The short-run aggregate supply curve has shifted to SAS_1 but the aggregate demand curve remains at AD_0. The price level rises to 120 and real GDP decreases to £950 billion at

Figure 32.8

Responding to an OPEC Oil Price Increase

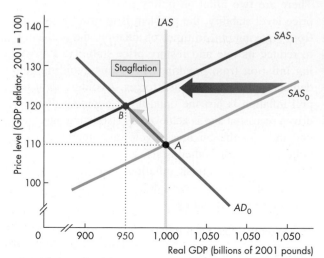

(a) Fixed rule

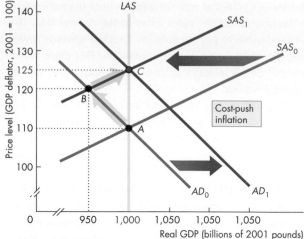

(b) Feedback rule

The economy starts out at point A on AD_0 and SAS_0, with a price level of 110 and real GDP of £1,000 billion. OPEC forces up the price of oil and the short-run aggregate supply curve shifts to SAS_1. Real GDP decreases to £950 billion and the price level increases to 120 at point B. With a fixed-rule policy (part a), the Bank of England makes no change to aggregate demand. The economy stays in a recession until the price of oil falls and the economy returns to its original position. With a feedback rule (part b), the Bank of England injects additional money and the government increases spending. The aggregate demand curve shifts to AD_1. Real GDP returns to £1,000 billion (potential GDP) but the price level increases to 125 at point C. The economy is set for another round of cost-push inflation.

point B. The economy experiences *stagflation*. With unemployment above the natural rate, the money wage rate eventually falls. The low level of real GDP and low sales will probably bring a fall in the price of oil. These events will shift the short-run aggregate supply curve back to SAS_0. The price level will fall to 110 and real GDP will increase to £1,000 billion. But this adjustment might take a long time.

Reading Between the Lines on pp. 742–743 looks at the policy dilemma faced by the European Central Bank in containing the potential inflationary consequences of an oil price increase in 2004.

Keynesian Feedback Rule

Figure 32.8(b) shows what happens if the Bank of England and the government operate a feedback rule. The starting point A is the same as before – the economy is on SAS_0 and AD_0 with a price level of 110 and real GDP of £1,000 billion. OPEC raises the price of oil and the short-run aggregate supply curve shifts to SAS_1. Real

GDP decreases to £950 billion and the price level rises to 120 at point B.

A feedback rule is followed. With potential GDP perceived to be £1,000 billion and with actual real GDP at £950 billion, the Bank of England pumps money into the economy and the government increases its spending and lowers taxes. Aggregate demand increases and the aggregate demand curve shifts rightward to AD_1. The price level rises to 125 and real GDP returns to £1,000 billion. The economy moves back to full employment but at a higher price level. The economy has experienced *cost-push inflation*.

What if the government and Bank of England reacted in a different way? Let's run through the example again. OPEC raises the price of oil again. Short-run aggregate supply decreases and the short-run aggregate supply curve shifts leftward once more. The Bank of England, realizing this danger, does *not* respond to the OPEC price increase. Instead, it holds firm and even slows down the growth of aggregate demand to dampen further the inflationary consequences of OPEC's actions.

Incentives to Push Up Costs

You can see that there are no checks on the incentives to push up *nominal* costs if the Bank of England accommodates price rises. If some groups see a temporary gain from pushing up the price at which they are selling their resources and if the Bank of England always accommodates to prevent unemployment and slack business conditions from emerging, then cost-push elements will have a free rein.

But when the Bank of England pursues a fixed-rule policy, the incentive to attempt to steal a temporary advantage from a price increase is severely weakened. The cost of higher unemployment and lower output is a consequence that each group will have to face and recognize.

So a fixed-rule policy can deliver a steady inflation rate (and even zero inflation), while a feedback-rule policy that places its main weight on keeping real GDP at potential GDP and unemployment at its natural rate leaves the inflation rate free to rise and fall at the whim of whichever group believes a temporary advantage to be available from pushing up its price.

Slowing Inflation

So far, we've concentrated on *avoiding* inflation. But often the problem is not to avoid inflation but to tame it. How can inflation, once it has set in, be cured? We'll look at two ways:

◆ A surprise inflation reduction

◆ A credible, announced inflation reduction

A Surprise Inflation Reduction

We'll use two equivalent approaches to study the problem of lowering inflation: the aggregate supply–aggregate demand model and the Phillips curve. The *AS–AD* model tells us about real GDP and the price level, while the Phillips curve, which is explained in Chapter 29, pp. 666–667, lets us keep track of inflation and unemployment.

Figure 32.9 illustrates the economy at full employment with inflation raging at 10 per cent a year. In part (a), the economy is on aggregate demand curve AD_0 and short-run aggregate supply curve SAS_0. Real GDP is £1,000 billion and, at a moment in time, the price level is 110. With real GDP equal to potential GDP on the *LAS* curve, the economy is at full employment. Equivalently, in part (b), the economy is on its long-run Phillips curve, *LRPC*, and short-run Phillips curve,

$SRPC_0$. The inflation rate of 10 per cent a year is anticipated, so unemployment is at its natural rate of 6 per cent of the workforce.

Next year, aggregate demand is *expected* to increase and the aggregate demand curve in Figure 32.9(a) is expected to shift rightward to AD_1. Expecting this increase in aggregate demand, the money wage rate increases and shifts the short-run aggregate supply curve from SAS_0 to SAS_1. If expectations are fulfilled, the price level rises to 121 – a 10 per cent inflation – and real GDP remains at potential GDP. In part (b), the economy remains at its original position – unemployment is at the natural rate and the inflation rate is 10 per cent a year.

Now suppose that people expect the Bank of England not to change its policy, but that the Bank actually tries to slow inflation. It increases interest rates and slows money growth. Aggregate demand growth slows and the aggregate demand curve in part (a) shifts rightward from AD_0 not to AD_1 as people expect but only to AD_2.

With no change in the expected inflation rate, the money wage rate rises by the same amount as before and the short-run aggregate supply curve shifts leftward from SAS_0 to SAS_1. Real GDP decreases to £950 billion and the price level rises to 118.8 – an 8 per cent a year inflation. In Figure 32.9(b), the economy moves along the short-run Phillips curve $SRPC_0$ as unemployment rises to 9 per cent and inflation falls to 8 per cent a year. The policy has slowed inflation, but at the cost of recession. Real GDP is below potential GDP and unemployment is above its natural rate.

A Credible, Announced Inflation Reduction

Suppose that instead of simply slowing the growth of aggregate demand, the Bank of England announces its intention ahead of its action in a credible and convincing way, so that its announcement is believed. That is, the Bank's policy is anticipated. Because the lower level of aggregate demand is expected, the money wage rate increases at a pace consistent with the lower level of aggregate demand. The short-run aggregate supply curve, in Figure 32.9(a), shifts leftward from SAS_0 but only to SAS_2. Aggregate demand increases by the amount expected and the aggregate demand curve shifts from AD_0 to AD_2. The price level rises to 115.5 – an inflation rate of 5 per cent a year – and real GDP remains at potential GDP.

In Figure 32.9(b), the lower expected inflation rate shifts the short-run Phillips curve downward to $SRPC_1$ and inflation falls to 5 per cent a year while unemployment remains at its natural rate.

Figure 32.9

Lowering Inflation

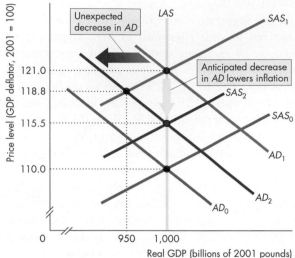

(a) Aggregate demand and aggregate supply

(b) Phillips curves

Initially, aggregate demand is AD_0 and short-run aggregate supply is SAS_0. Real GDP and potential GDP are £1,000 billion on the long-run aggregate supply curve, LAS. The aggregate demand curve is expected to shift and actually shifts to AD_1. The short-run aggregate supply curve shifts to SAS_1. The price level rises to 121, but real GDP remains at £1,000 billion. Inflation is proceeding at 10 per cent a year and this inflation is anticipated. In part (b), which shows the same situation, the economy is on the short-run Phillips curve $SRPC_0$ and on the long-run Phillips curve $LRPC$. Unemployment is at the natural rate of 6 per cent and inflation is 10 per cent a year.

An unexpected slowdown in aggregate demand growth means that the aggregate demand curve shifts from AD_0 to AD_2, real GDP decreases to £950 billion and inflation slows to 8 per cent (price level is 118.8). Unemployment increases to 9 per cent as the economy slides down $SRPC_0$. An anticipated, credible, announced slowdown in aggregate demand growth means that when the aggregate demand curve shifts from AD_0 to AD_2, the short-run aggregate supply curve shifts from SAS_0 to SAS_2. The short-run Phillips curve shifts to $SRPC_1$. Inflation slows to 5 per cent a year, real GDP remains at £1,000 billion and unemployment remains at its natural rate of 6 per cent.

Inflation Reduction in Practice

When the UK government slowed inflation in 1980, the economy paid a high price. This monetary policy action was unexpected. As a result, it occurred in the face of money wage rates that had been set at too high a level to be consistent with the growth of aggregate demand that the Bank of England subsequently allowed. The consequence was recession – a decrease in real GDP and a rise in unemployment. Couldn't the Bank of England have lowered inflation without causing recession by telling people far enough ahead of time that it did indeed plan to slow down the growth rate of aggregate demand?

The answer appears to be no. The main reason is that people form their expectation of the Bank's action (as they form expectations about anyone's actions) on the basis of actual behaviour, not on the basis of stated intentions. How many times have you told yourself that it is your firm intention to reduce weight, or to keep

within a budget and put a few pounds away for a rainy day, only to discover that, despite your best intentions, your old habits win out in the end?

Forming expectations about the Bank of England's behaviour is similar to forecasting your own behaviour. People look at the Bank's past *actions*, not its stated intentions. On the basis of such observations they try to work out what the government's policy is, to forecast its future actions and to forecast the effects of those actions on aggregate demand and inflation. When Mrs. Thatcher came to power in June 1979, the forecast for the Bank of England's policy was to do the same as it had done under all previous governments – that is, to say one thing and do another. The Thatcher government had no reputation for an anti-inflation policy. Its credibility was low. Over time, the Bank of England won credibility for its anti-inflation policies. But it lost this reputation by the end of the 1980s after allowing inflation to rise.

Balancing Inflation and Real GDP Objectives: The Taylor Rule

John Taylor, formerly an economics professor at Stanford University and now Undersecretary of the Treasury for International Affairs in the Bush administration in Washington, has suggested a policy feedback rule that he says would deliver a better performance than what central banks have achieved.

The idea is to target inflation but also to be explicit about the extent to which the interest rate will be changed in response to both inflation and deviations of real GDP from potential GDP. By being explicit and always following the same rule, central bank watching becomes a simpler task and smaller forecasting errors might be made, which translates into smaller deviations of real GDP from potential GDP and smaller deviations of the unemployment rate from the natural rate.

A central bank that uses a **Taylor rule** adjusts the overnight interest rate to equal the neutral real overnight interest rate plus the inflation rate plus one-half the deviation of the inflation rate from target plus one-half of the output gap. That is, with R the rate of interest, r^* the neutral real interest rate, π the inflation, π^* the inflation target, y real GDP and y^* potential GDP:

$$R = r^* + \pi + 0.5(\pi - \pi^*) + 0.5(y - y^*)/y^*$$

If the ECB followed the Taylor rule with a target inflation rate of 2 per cent a year and an average real (overnight) interest rate of 2.5 per cent a year, it would set a target for the interest rate equal to 4.5 per cent plus one-half of the amount by which the inflation rate exceeds 2 per cent a year plus one-half of the percentage gap between real GDP and potential GDP. There is uncertainty about the neutral real interest rate, which might be between 1 and 2 per cent a year.

Figure 32.10 shows the ECB interest rate and the range of the target rate if it followed the Taylor rule. You can see that the ECB's actual policy is similar to the Taylor rule. Sometimes the ECB rate is at the top of the range and sometimes at the bottom of the range but always it has been inside the Taylor rule range.

When inflation was below target, the interest rate was kept low. As inflation and real GDP increased in 2000, the interest rate was raised. The interest rate reached a peak in 2001 and then came down as Eurozone real GDP fell increasingly below potential GDP. Although the inflation rate remained at the upper bound of the target, the interest rate continued to fall because real GDP was below potential GDP.

Figure 32.10

ECB interest rate and the Taylor Rule: 1999–2004

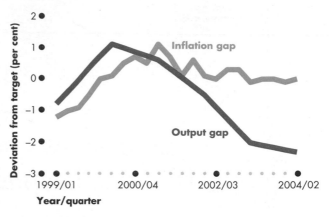

(a) Deviations from target

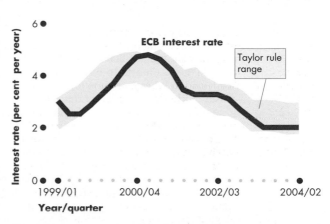

(b) ECB interest rate: actual and Taylor rule

The ECB interest rate changes are described well by the Taylor rule.

Source: ECB and authors' calculations.

Review Quiz

1 Why does a fixed rule provide more effective protection against cost-push inflation than a feedback rule?
2 Why does a recession usually result as inflation is being tamed?

Reading Between the Lines on pp. 742–743 looks at the ECB's challenge to contain inflationary pressures in 2004.

Reading Between the Lines
Stabilization Policy Dilemma

The Irish Times, 13 August 2004

ECB shows no sign of interest rate rise despite rising oil prices

The European Central Bank has expressed heightened concern about inflation risks from surging oil prices, but gave no sign it plans to tighten credit any time soon.

Inflation is likely to hold above the ECB's 2 per cent ceiling for the rest of this year and the early months of 2005 if oil prices stay at high levels as markets expect, the central bank said in its August monthly bulletin.

But with the recovery broadening only gradually, analysts said the ECB is showing it feels no pressure to follow other major central banks in ending the era of record low interest rates in the 12-nation eurozone. . . .

As long as higher oil costs do not spill over into higher wages and general prices analysts said the central bank can delay any monetary tightening until recovery is solid. "The risk is that the longer inflation stays above 2 per cent, the risk of second-round effects increases a little bit," said Rainer Guntermann, an economist at DKW in Frankfurt.

"But for fundamental inflationary pressure to happen, we would need to see investment and domestic consumption pick up," he said. "And we don't see that," he added. Indeed, the ECB said it expects price stability, defined as an inflation rate below but close to 2 per cent, to return next year despite current pressure from oil and indirect taxes.

"Looking further ahead, there are no indications as yet of a build-up of stronger general inflationary pressures," it said in the bulletin. . . .

The ECB urged governments to use the current economic upswing to push through reform of the labour and product markets, in order to build confidence in a sustainable recovery and boost jobs and growth.

The Essence of the Story

◆ The ECB, concerned about inflation risks from rising oil prices, says that inflation is likely to be above 2 per cent a year for the rest of 2004 and into 2005.

◆ But with weak real GDP growth, the ECB believes that rising oil prices will not translate into higher wages and general prices.

◆ So the ECB feels no pressure to raise the interest rate.

◆ Independently of inflation, the ECB urges governments to reform labour and goods markets and build confidence in sustainable growth.

Economic Analysis

◆ Figure 1 shows inflation in the Eurozone economy hovering at the upper bound target of 2 per cent a year

◆ Figure 2 shows the Eurozone output gap – the deviation of real GDP from potential GDP.

◆ With inflation at 2 per cent a year and a large recessionary gap, the Eurozone economy was hit with a rise in the price of oil to over $40 a barrel.

◆ If the ECB keeps the interest rate low to try to close the output gap, it might end up accommodating the oil price rise and triggering rising inflation.

◆ Figure 3 shows the ECB's dilemma in terms of the AS-AD model. In 2004, aggregate demand is AD_0 and short-run aggregate supply is SAS_0. Real GDP is €10.2 trillion and the price level is 115.5 at point A.

◆ The ECB would like to move the Eurozone economy to point B, by keeping the interest rate low and increasing aggregate demand from AD_0 to AD_1. With no change in short-run aggregate supply, the economy would move to full employment at a price level of 117.8 – a 2 per cent rise.

◆ Figure 3 shows the effect of the rise in the price of oil, which decreases short-run aggregate supply from SAS_0 to SAS_1. With an increase in the interest rate to keep aggregate demand at AD_0, the economy moves to point C. The inflation target is met but the output gap widens.

◆ A decrease in short-run aggregate supply from SAS_0 to SAS_1 combined with an increase in aggregate demand to AD_1 moves the economy to point D. The output gap narrows, but the price level rises to 120 taking the inflation rate well above the 2 per cent upper bound.

◆ The dilemma for the ECB is that if it does not increase the interest rate and lessen the increase in aggregate demand, inflation will go above the 2 per cent upper bound. If the ECB does increase the interest rate, the Eurozone economy will spend a third year with real GDP below potential GDP.

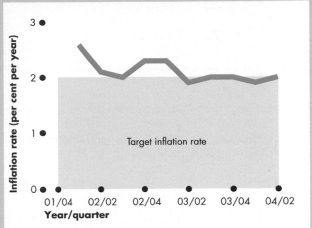

Figure 1 Inflation rate and target

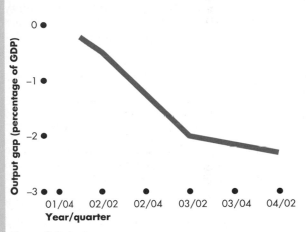

Figure 2 Output gap

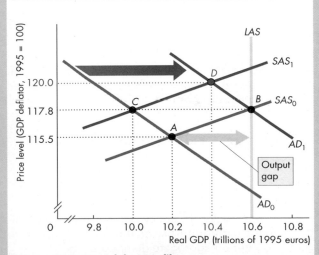

Figure 3 AS–AD and the ECB dilemma

Summary

Key Points

Policy Goals (pp. 724–725)

◆ The goals of macroeconomic policy are to achieve the highest sustainable rate of long-term real GDP growth, smooth out avoidable business fluctuations and maintain low unemployment and low inflation.

Policy Tools and Performance (pp. 726–728)

◆ The macroeconomic policy tools are fiscal policy and monetary policy.

◆ Within the EMU, fiscal policy and monetary policy are constrained by the Stability and Growth Pact and by an inflation target.

Long-term Growth Policy (pp. 728–730)

◆ The sources of the long-term growth of potential GDP are the accumulation of physical and human capital and the advance of technology.

◆ Policies to increase the long-term growth rate focus on increasing saving and investment in human capital and new technologies.

◆ The EU national saving rate has been on a generally falling path since 1970.

◆ Increased government saving and stronger incentives for private saving can boost the saving rate.

◆ Human capital investment might be increased with improved education and by improving on-the-job training programmes.

◆ Investment in new technologies can be encouraged by tax incentives and EU sponsored research programmes.

Business Cycle and Unemployment Policies (pp. 731–737)

◆ A fixed-rule policy takes no action to counter an aggregate demand shock.

◆ A feedback-rule policy adjusts taxes, government expenditures, or the money supply to counter an aggregate demand shock.

◆ A feedback rule does not always make the economy more stable because it requires greater knowledge of the state of the economy than we have.

Anti-inflation Policy (pp. 737–741)

◆ A fixed rule minimizes the threat of cost-push inflation.

◆ A feedback rule validates cost-push inflation and leaves the price level and inflation rate free to move to wherever they are pushed.

◆ Usually, when inflation is slowed down, a recession occurs.

Key Figures

Figure 32.1 Macroeconomic Performance: EU Unemployment, Inflation and Growth: 1994–2004, 725
Figure 32.2 EU Fiscal Policy in 2003, 727
Figure 32.3 The Monetary Policy Record of the ECB: 2000–2004, 728
Figure 32.6 Two Stabilization Policies: Aggregate Demand Shock, 733
Figure 32.7 Responding to a Productivity Growth Slowdown, 736
Figure 32.8 Responding to an OPEC Oil Price Increase, 738
Figure 32.9 Lowering Inflation, 740

Key Terms

Discretionary policy, 731
Feedback-rule policy, 731
Fixed-rule policy, 731
Keynesian activist, 732
Monetarist, 732
Nominal GDP targeting, 736
Taylor rule, 741

Problems

*1 A productivity growth slowdown has occurred. Explain its possible origins and describe a policy package that is designed to speed up growth again.

2 A nation is experiencing a falling saving rate. Explain its possible origins and describe a policy package that is designed to increase the saving rate?

*3 The economy shown in the graph is initially on aggregate demand curve AD_0 and short-run aggregate supply curve SAS. Then aggregate demand decreases and the aggregate demand curve shifts leftward to AD_1.

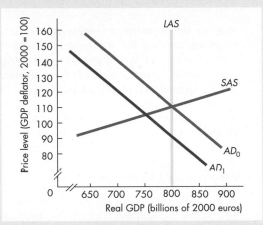

a What is the equilibrium real GDP and price level?

b If the decrease in aggregate demand is temporary and the government follows a fixed-rule fiscal policy, what happens to real GDP and the price level? Trace the immediate effects and the adjustment as aggregate demand returns to its original level.

c If the decrease in aggregate demand is temporary and the government follows a feedback-rule fiscal policy, what happens to real GDP and the price level? Trace the immediate effects and the adjustment as aggregate demand returns to its original level.

d If the decrease in aggregate demand is permanent and the government follows a fixed-rule fiscal policy, what happens to real GDP and the price level?

e If the decrease in aggregate demand is permanent and the government follows a feedback-rule fiscal policy, what happens to real GDP and the price level?

4 The economy shown in the graph is initially on aggregate demand curve AD and short-run aggregate supply curve SAS_0. Then short-run aggregate supply decreases and the short-run aggregate supply curve shifts upward to SAS_1.

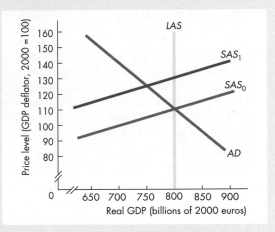

a What is the equilibrium real GDP and price level?

b What type of event could have caused the decrease in short-run aggregate supply?

c If the government follows a fixed-rule monetary policy, what happens to real GDP and the price level? Trace the immediate effects and the adjustment as short-run aggregate supply returns to its original level.

d If the government follows a feedback-rule monetary policy, what happens to real GDP and the price level? Trace the immediate effects and the adjustment as aggregate demand and short-run aggregate supply respond to the policy action.

*5 The economy is experiencing inflation of 10 per cent a year and unemployment of 7 per cent. Real GDP growth has sagged to 1 per cent a year. The stock market has crashed.

a Explain how the economy might have got into its current state.

b Set out policies for the Bank of England and the government to pursue that will lower inflation, lower unemployment and speed real GDP growth.

c Explain how and why your proposed policies will work.

6 The inflation rate has fallen to 1 per cent a year but the unemployment rate is stubborn and has not fallen much. Real GDP is growing at more than 3 per cent a year. The stock market is at a record high.

   a Explain how the economy might have got into its current state.

   b Set out policies for the Bank of England and the government to pursue that will keep inflation low, lower unemployment and maintain a high real GDP growth rate.

   c Explain how and why your proposed policies will work.

*7 When the economies of Indonesia, South Korea, Thailand, Malaysia and the Philippines entered into recession in 1997, the International Monetary Fund (IMF) made loans but only on condition that the recipients of the loans increased interest rates, raised taxes and cut government expenditures.

   a Would you describe the IMF prescription as a feedback-rule policy or a fixed-rule policy?

   b What do you predict the effects of the IMF policies would be?

   c Do you have any criticisms of the IMF policies? What would you have required these countries to do? Why?

8 As the UK economy continued to expand and its stock market soared to new record levels during 1998, the Bank of England cut the interest rate.

   a Would you describe the Bank of England's actions as a feedback-rule policy or a fixed-rule policy?

   b What do you predict the effects of the Bank of England's policies would be?

   c Do you have any criticisms of the Bank of England's policies? What monetary policy would you have pursued? Why?

Critical Thinking

1 Study *Reading Between the Lines* pp. 742–743 and then answer the following questions.

   a Why does the rise in oil prices pose a problem for the European Central Bank?

   b What is the response of the ECB to the negative output gap in the Eurozone economy?

   c What is the risk from current ECB policy to inflation in the near future?

   d What is the danger to the Eurozone economy if the ECB raises the interest rate in response to the oil price shock?

   e What do you think the ECB should do and why?

2 Suppose the economy is booming and inflation is beginning to rise, but it is widely agreed that a massive recession is just around the corner. Weigh the advantages and disadvantages of the government pursuing a fixed rule and a feedback rule for *fiscal* policy.

3 Suppose the economy is in a recession and inflation is falling. It is widely agreed that a strong recovery is just around the corner. Weigh the advantages and disadvantages of the Bank of England pursuing a fixed-rule policy and a feedback-rule policy.

Web Exercises

Use the links on *Parkin Interactive* to work the following exercises.

1 Visit the Bank of England's Web site and look at the latest *Inflation Report*. Write a summary and critique of this report.

2 Visit the IMF's *World Economic Outlook* Web database and review the latest data on real GDP growth and inflation in the global economy.

   a What are the major macroeconomic stabilization policy problems in the world today?

   b What is the general direction in which policy actions are pushing the global economy?

Part 7
Globalization and the International Economy

It's a Small World

The global economy is always in the headlines. The scale of international trade, borrowing and lending expands every year. International economic activity is large and fast-growing because today's economic world is small and because communication is so incredibly cheap and fast.

But today's world is not a new world. From the beginning of recorded history, people have traded over large and increasing distances. The great Western civilizations of Greece and Rome traded around the Mediterranean and into the Gulf of Arabia. The great Eastern civilizations traded around the Indian Ocean. By the Middle Ages, the East and the West were trading routinely overland on routes pioneered by

Venetian traders and explorers such as Marco Polo. When, in 1497, Vasco da Gama opened a sea route between the Atlantic and Indian Oceans around Africa, a new trade between East and West began, which brought tumbling prices of Eastern goods in Western markets. The European discovery of America and the subsequent opening up of Atlantic trade continued the process of steady globalization.

So, the developments of the 1990s and 2000s, amazing though many of them are, represent a continuation of an ongoing expansion of human horizons. The two chapters in this short but important part study the interaction of nations in today's global economy.

Chapter 33 describes and explains international trade in goods and services. In this chapter, you come face to face with one of the biggest policy issues of all ages, free trade versus protection and the globalization debate. The chapter explains how all nations benefit from free international trade.

Chapter 34 explains some of the fundamentals of international borrowing and lending and the exchange rate. It explains the poorly understood fact that the size of a nation's international deficit depends not on how efficient it is, but on how much its citizens save relative to how much they invest. Nations with low saving rates, everything else being the same, have international deficits. This chapter also explains why foreign exchange rates fluctuate so much.

Chapter 33

Trading With the World

After studying this chapter you will be able to:

◆ Describe the patterns and trends in international trade

◆ Explain comparative advantage and why all countries can gain from international trade

◆ Explain why international trade restrictions reduce the volume of imports and exports and reduce our consumption possibilities

◆ Explain the arguments used to justify international trade restrictions and show how they are flawed

◆ Explain why we have international trade restrictions

Silk Routes and Cargo Jets

Since ancient times, people have striven to expand their trading as far as technology would allow. Marco Polo opened up the silk route between Europe and China in the thirteenth century. Today, cargo jets and container ships carry billions of pounds worth of goods around the globe. Why? Why do people go to such lengths to trade with others in far away places? How can we compete with people whose wages are much lower than our own? Why don't we restrict international trade so that people will buy local products?

Patterns and Trends in International Trade

The goods and services that we buy from people in other countries are called **imports**. The goods and services that we sell to people in other countries are called **exports**. What are the most important things that we import and export? Most people would probably guess that a relatively rich country such as the United Kingdom imports raw materials and exports manufactured goods. While that is one feature of UK international trade, it is not its most important feature. The vast bulk of our merchandise exports *and* imports are manufactured goods. We sell people in other countries Land Rovers, aircraft, machines and scientific equipment, and we buy TV sets, video recorders, blue jeans, T-shirts and fruit and flowers from them. Also, we are a major exporter of primary materials, particularly North Sea oil, and we export chemical goods. We import and export a huge volume of services.

Trade in Goods

About 70 per cent of UK international trade is trade in goods and 30 per cent is trade in services. Of the categories of goods traded, by far the most important is manufactured goods. The total value of exports of manufactured goods is less than the total value of imports – the United Kingdom is a net importer of manufactured goods. The United Kingdom is also a net importer of textile fibres, metals and agricultural products. But the United Kingdom is a net exporter of chemical goods, oil and services.

Trade in Services

You may be wondering how a country can "export" and "import" services. Let's look at some examples.

Suppose that you decided to take a holiday in Spain, travelling there from Manchester on Iberian Airways. What you buy from Iberian Airways, a Spanish firm, is not a good but a transport service. Although the concept may sound odd at first, in economic terms you are importing that service from Spain. The money you spend in Spain on hotel bills, restaurant meals and other things is also classified as the import of services. Similarly, the holiday taken by a Spanish student in the United Kingdom counts as an export of UK services to Spain.

When we import TV sets from South Korea, the owner of the ship that carries these TV sets might be Greek and the company that insures the cargo might be with Lloyd's in London. The payment that we make for the transport to the Greek company is a payment for the UK import of services, and the payment the Greek ship-owner makes to the London insurance company is a payment for the UK export of a service. Similarly, when a UK shipping company transports Scotch whisky to Tokyo, the transport cost is a UK export of a service.

Geographical Patterns

The United Kingdom has trading links with almost every part of the world. The rest of the European Union is our largest trading partner. North America, which includes the United States, Canada and Mexico, takes a significant share of UK trade at 18 per cent of exports and 16 per cent of imports.

Trends in the Volume of Trade

In 1960, UK exports were 14 per cent of GDP and UK imports were 15 per cent of GDP. In 2003, UK exports had increased to 25 per cent of GDP and imports to 28 per cent of GDP.

On the export side, mechanical and electrical machinery and semi-manufactured goods have remained the largest components of exports and have roughly maintained their share in total exports. But export of fuel has increased from 4 per cent of exports in 1963 to 8 per cent in 2003.

The composition of imports has also changed. Food and raw materials imports have decreased, imports of fuel decreased after North Sea oil came on stream in the 1970s and imports of machinery and semi-manufactured goods increased dramatically, from 33 per cent of imports in 1963 to 72 per cent in 2003.

Net Exports and International Borrowing

The value of exports minus imports is called **net exports**. In 2003, UK net exports were a negative £33 billion. UK imports were £33 billion more than exports. When we import more than we export, we borrow from foreigners or sell some of our assets to them. When we export more than we import, we make loans to foreigners or buy some of their assets.

The Gains from International Trade

The fundamental force that determines international trade is *comparative advantage*. And the basis of comparative advantage is divergent *opportunity costs*. You met these ideas in Chapter 2, when we learned about the gains from specialization and exchange between Ace and Galaxy.

Ace and Galaxy each specialize in producing just one good and then trade with each other. Most nations do not go to the extreme of specializing in a single good and importing everything else. But nations can increase the consumption of all goods if they redirect their scarce resources towards the production of those goods and services in which they have a comparative advantage.

To see how this outcome occurs, we'll apply the same basic ideas that we learned in the case of Ace and Galaxy to trade among nations. We'll begin by recalling how we can use the production possibilities frontier to measure opportunity cost. Then we'll see how divergent opportunity costs bring comparative advantage and gains from trade for countries as well as for individuals even though no country completely specializes in the production of just one good.

Opportunity Cost in Farmland

Farmland (a fictitious country) can produce grain and cars at any point inside or along the production possibilities frontier, *PPF*, in Figure 33.1. (We're holding constant the output of all the other goods that Farmland produces.) The Farmers (the people of Farmland) are consuming all the grain and cars that they produce and they are operating at point *A* in the figure. That is, Farmland is producing and consuming 15 million tonnes of grain and 8 million cars each year. What is the opportunity cost of a car in Farmland?

We can answer this question by calculating the slope of the production possibilities frontier at point *A*. The magnitude of the slope of the *PPF* measures the opportunity cost of one good in terms of the other. To measure the slope of the frontier at point *A*, place a straight line tangential to the frontier at point *A* and calculate the slope of that straight line. Recall that the formula for the slope of a line is the change in the value of the variable measured on the *y*-axis divided by the change in the value of the variable measured on the *x*-axis as we move along the line. Here, the variable measured on the *y*-axis

is millions of tonnes of grain and the variable measured on the *x*-axis is millions of cars. So the slope is the change in the number of tonnes of grain divided by the change in the number of cars.

As you can see from the red triangle at point *A* in Figure 33.1, if the number of cars produced increases by 2 million, grain production decreases by 18 million tonnes. Therefore the magnitude of the slope is 18 million tonnes divided by 2 million cars, which equals 9 tonnes per car. To get one more car, the people of Farmland must give up 9 tonnes of grain. So the opportunity cost of 1 car is 9 tonnes of grain. Equivalently, the opportunity cost of 9 tonnes of grain is 1 car. For the people of Farmland, these opportunity costs are the prices they face. The price of a car is 9 tonnes of grain and the price of 9 tonnes of grain is 1 car.

Figure 33.1

Opportunity Cost in Farmland

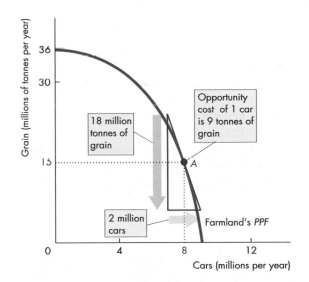

Farmland produces and consumes 15 million tonnes of grain and 8 million cars a year. That is, Farmland produces and consumes at point *A* on its production possibilities frontier.

Opportunity cost is equal to the magnitude of the slope of the production possibilities frontier. The red triangle tells us that at point *A*, 18 million tonnes of grain must be forgone to get 2 million cars. That is, at point *A*, 2 million cars cost 18 million tonnes of grain. Equivalently, 1 car costs 9 tonnes of grain or 9 tonnes of grain cost 1 car.

Opportunity Cost in Mobilia

Figure 33.2 shows the production possibilities frontier of Mobilia (another fictitious country). Like the Farmers, the Mobilians consume all the grain and cars that they produce. Mobilia consumes 18 million tonnes of grain a year and 4 million cars, at point A'.

Let's calculate the opportunity costs in Mobilia. At point A', the opportunity cost of a car is equal to the magnitude of the slope of the red line tangential to the production possibilities frontier, *PPF*. You can see from the red triangle that the magnitude of the slope of Mobilia's production possibilities frontier is 6 million tonnes of grain divided by 6 million cars, which equals 1 tonne of grain per car. To get one more car, the Mobilians must give up 1 tonne of grain. So the opportunity cost of 1 car is 1 tonne of grain, or equivalently, the opportunity cost of 1 tonne of grain is 1 car. These are the prices faced in Mobilia.

Comparative Advantage

Cars are cheaper in Mobilia than in Farmland. One car costs 9 tonnes of grain in Farmland but only 1 tonne of grain in Mobilia. But grain is cheaper in Farmland than in Mobilia – 9 tonnes of grain costs only 1 car in Farmland while that same amount of grain costs 9 cars in Mobilia.

Mobilia has a comparative advantage in car production. Farmland has a comparative advantage in grain production. A country has a **comparative advantage** in producing a good if it can produce that good at a lower opportunity cost than any other country. Let's see how opportunity cost differences and comparative advantage generate gains from international trade.

The Gains from Trade: Cheaper to Buy than to Produce

If Mobilia bought grain for what it costs Farmland to produce it, then Mobilia could buy 9 tonnes of grain for 1 car. That is much lower than the cost of growing grain in Mobilia, for there it costs 9 cars to produce 9 tonnes of grain. If the Mobilians can buy grain at the low Farmland price, they will reap some gains.

If the Farmers can buy cars for what it costs Mobilia to produce them, they will be able to obtain a car for 1 tonne of grain. Because it costs 9 tonnes of grain to produce a car in Farmland, the Farmers would gain from such an opportunity.

Figure 33.2

Opportunity Cost in Mobilia

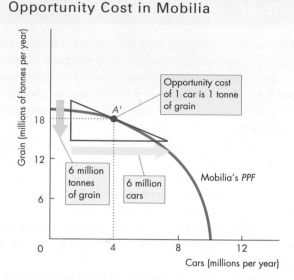

Mobilia produces and consumes 18 million tonnes of grain and 4 million cars a year. That is, Mobilia produces and consumes at point A' on its production possibilities frontier. Opportunity cost is equal to the magnitude of the slope of the production possibilities frontier. The red triangle tells us that at point A', 6 million tonnes of grain must be forgone to get 6 million cars. That is, at point A', 6 million cars cost 6 million tonnes of grain. Equivalently, 1 car costs 1 tonne of grain or 1 tonne of grain costs 1 car.

In this situation, it makes sense for Mobilia to buy their grain from Farmers and for Farmers to buy their cars from Mobilia.

The Terms of Trade

The quantity of grain that Farmland must pay Mobilia for a car is Farmland's **terms of trade** with Mobilia. We measure the terms of trade in the real world as an index number that averages the terms of trade over all the items we trade.

The forces of international supply and demand determine the terms of trade. Figure 33.3 illustrates these forces in the Farmland–Mobilia international car market. The quantity of cars *traded internationally* is measured on the *x*-axis. On the *y*-axis, we measure the price of a car. This price is expressed as the *terms of trade*: "tonnes of grain per car". If no international trade takes place, the price of a car in Farmland is 9 tonnes of grain, its opportunity cost, indicated by point A in the figure.

Figure 33.3

International Trade in Cars

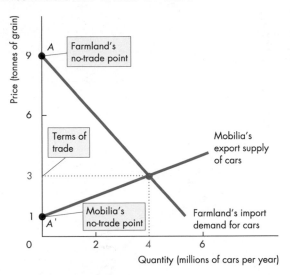

Farmland's import demand curve for cars is downward sloping, and Mobilia's export supply curve of cars is upward sloping. Without international trade, the price of a car is 9 tonnes of grain in Farmland (point A) and 1 tonne of grain in Mobilia (point A').

With free international trade, the price (terms of trade) is determined where the export supply curve intersects the import demand curve: 3 tonnes of grain per car. At that price, 4 million cars a year are imported by Farmland and exported by Mobilia. The value of grain exported by Farmland and imported by Mobilia is 12 million tonnes a year, the quantity required to pay for the cars imported.

Again, if no trade takes place, the price of a car in Mobilia is 1 tonne of grain, its opportunity cost, indicated by point A' in Figure 33.3.

The no-trade points A and A' in Figure 33.3 correspond to the points identified by those same letters in Figures 33.1 and 33.2.

The lower the price of a car (terms of trade), the greater is the quantity of cars that the Farmers are willing to import from the Mobilians. This fact is illustrated by the downward-sloping curve, which shows Farmland's import demand for cars.

The Mobilians respond in the opposite direction. The higher the price of a car (terms of trade), the greater is the quantity of cars that Mobilians are willing to export to Farmers. This fact is reflected in Mobilia's export supply of cars – the upward-sloping line in Figure 33.3.

The international market in cars determines the equilibrium terms of trade (price) and quantity traded. This

equilibrium occurs where the import demand curve intersects the export supply curve. In this case, the equilibrium terms of trade are 3 tonnes of grain per car. Mobilia exports and Farmland imports 4 million cars a year. Notice that the terms of trade are lower than the initial price in Farmland but higher than the initial price in Mobilia.

Balanced Trade

The number of cars exported by Mobilia – 4 million a year – is exactly equal to the number of cars imported by Farmland. How does Farmland pay for its cars? It pays by exporting grain. How much grain does Farmland export? You can find the answer by noticing that for 1 car, Farmland has to pay 3 tonnes of grain. So for 4 million cars, Farmland has to pay 12 million tonnes of grain. Farmland's exports of grain are 12 million tonnes a year. Mobilia imports this same quantity of grain.

Mobilia is exchanging 4 million cars for 12 million tonnes of grain each year and Farmland is doing the opposite, exchanging 12 million tonnes of grain for 4 million cars. Trade is balanced between these two countries. The value received from exports equals the value paid out for imports.

Changes in Production and Consumption

We've seen that international trade makes it possible for Farmers to buy cars at a lower price than they can produce them for themselves. Equivalently, Farmers can sell their grain for a higher price. International trade also enables Mobilia to sell their cars for a higher price. Equivalently, Mobilia can buy grain for a lower price. Everybody gains. How is it possible for *everyone* to gain? What are the changes in production and consumption that accompany these gains?

An economy that does not trade with other economies has identical production and consumption possibilities. Without trade, the economy can consume only what it produces. But with international trade, an economy can consume quantities of goods and services that differ from those that it produces. The production possibilities frontier describes the limit of what a country can produce, but it does *not* describe the limits to what it can consume. Figure 33.4 will help you to see the distinction between production possibilities and consumption possibilities when a country trades with other countries.

Figure 33.4

Expanding Consumption Possibilities

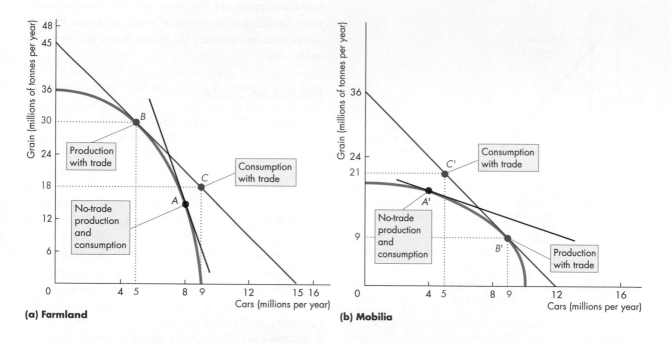

(a) Farmland

(b) Mobilia

With no international trade, Farmers produce and consume at point *A* and the opportunity cost of a car is 9 tonnes of grain – the slope of the black line in part (a). Also, with no international trade, the Mobilians produce and consume at point *A'* and the opportunity cost of 1 tonne of grain is 1 car – the slope of the black line in part (b).

Goods can be exchanged internationally at the world price of 3 tonnes of grain for 1 car along the red line in each part of the figure. In part (a), Farmland decreases its production of cars and increases its production of grain,

moving from *A* to *B*. It exports grain and imports cars, and it consumes at point *C*. Farmers have more of both cars and grain than they would if they produced all their own consumption goods – at point *A*.

In part (b), Mobilia increases car production and decreases grain production, moving from *A'* to *B'*. Mobilia exports cars and imports grain, and it consumes at point *C'*. Mobilians have more of both cars and grain than they would if they produced all their own consumption goods – at point *A'*.

First, notice that Figure 33.4 has two parts, part (a) for Farmland and part (b) for Mobilia. The production possibilities frontiers that you saw in Figures 33.1 and 33.2 are reproduced here. The slopes of the two black lines represent the opportunity costs in the two countries when there is no international trade. Farmland produces and consumes at point *A* and Mobilia produces and consumes at *A'*. Cars cost 9 tonnes of grain in Farmland and 1 tonne of grain in Mobilia.

Consumption Possibilities

The red line in each part of Figure 33.4 shows the country's consumption possibilities with international trade. These two red lines have the same slope and the

magnitude of that slope is the opportunity cost of a car in terms of grain on the world market – 3 tonnes of grain per car. The *slope* of the consumption possibilities line is common to both countries because its magnitude equals the *world* price.

But the position of a country's consumption possibilities line depends on the country's production possibilities. A country cannot produce outside its production possibilities curve so its consumption possibility curve touches its production possibilities curve. So Farmland could choose to consume at point *B* with no international trade or, with international trade, at any point on its red consumption possibilities line.

Let's now find the equilibrium amount of trade between the two countries.

Free Trade Equilibrium

With international trade, the producers of cars in Mobilia can get a higher price for their output. As a result, they increase the quantity of car production. At the same time, grain producers in Mobilia are getting a lower price for their grain and so they reduce production. Producers in Mobilia adjust their output by moving along their production possibilities frontier until the opportunity cost in Mobilia equals the world price (the opportunity cost in the world market). This situation arises when Mobilia is producing at point B' in Figure 33.4(b).

But the Mobilians do not consume at point B'. That is, they do not increase their consumption of cars and decrease their consumption of grain. Instead, they sell some of their car production to Farmland in exchange for some of Farmland's grain. They trade internationally. But to see how that works out, we first need to check in with Farmland to see what's happening there.

In Farmland, producers of cars now get a lower price and producers of grain get a higher price. As a consequence, producers in Farmland decrease car production and increase grain production. They adjust their outputs by moving along the production possibilities frontier until the opportunity cost of a car in terms of grain equals the world price (the opportunity cost on the world market). They move to point B in part (a). But the Farmers do not consume at point B. Instead, they exchange some of their additional grain production for the now cheaper cars from Mobilia.

Figure 33.4 shows us the quantities consumed in the two countries. We saw in Figure 33.3 that Mobilia exports 4 million cars a year and Farmland imports those cars. We also saw that Farmland exports 12 million tonnes of grain a year and Mobilia imports that grain. So Farmland's consumption of grain is 12 million tonnes a year less than it produces and its consumption of cars is 4 million a year more than it produces. Farmland consumes at point C in Figure 33.4(a).

Similarly, we know that Mobilia consumes 12 million tonnes of grain more than it produces and 4 million cars fewer than it produces. So Mobilia consumes at C' in Figure 33.4(b).

Calculating the Gains from Trade

You can now literally see the gains from trade in Figure 33.4. Without trade, Farmers produce and consume at A (part a) – a point on Farmland's production possibilities frontier. With international trade, Farmers consume at point C in part (a) – a point *outside* the production possibilities frontier. At point C, Farmers are consuming 3 million tonnes of grain a year and 1 million cars a year more than before. These increases in consumption of both cars and grain, beyond the limits of the production possibilities frontier, are the gains from international trade.

Mobilians also gain. Without trade, they consume at point A' in part (b) – a point on Mobilia's production possibilities frontier. With international trade, they consume at point C' – a point outside the production possibilities frontier. With international trade, Mobilia consumes 3 million tonnes of grain a year and 1 million cars a year more than without trade. These are the gains from international trade for Mobilia.

Gains from Trade in Reality

The gains from trade that we have just studied between Farmland and Mobilia in grain and cars occur in a model economy – in a world economy that we have imagined. But these same phenomena occur every day in the real global economy.

Comparative Advantage in the Global Economy

We buy cars made in Japan and Europe, shirts and fashion goods from the people of Sri Lanka, TV sets and video recorders from South Korea and Taiwan. In exchange we sell chemicals, pharmaceuticals and financial services to those countries. We make some kinds of machines, and Europeans and Japanese make other kinds, and we exchange one type of manufactured good for another.

These are all examples of international trade generated by comparative advantage, just like the international trade between Farmland and Mobilia in our model economy. All international trade arises from comparative advantage, even when it is trade in similar goods such as tools and machines. At first, it seems puzzling that countries exchange manufactured goods. Why doesn't each developed country produce all the manufactured goods its citizens want to buy? Let's look a bit more closely at this question.

Trade in Similar Goods

Why does it make sense for the United Kingdom to produce cars for export and at the same time to import large quantities of them from Japan, Germany, Italy and Sweden? Wouldn't it make more sense to produce all the cars that we buy here in the United Kingdom? After all, we have access to the best technology available for producing cars. Car workers in the United Kingdom are surely as productive as their fellow workers in Germany and Japan. Capital equipment, production lines, robots and so on used in the manufacture of cars are as available to UK car producers as they are to any others. This line of reasoning leaves a puzzle concerning the sources of international exchange of similar commodities produced by similar people using similar equipment. Why does it happen? Why does the United Kingdom have a comparative advantage in some types of cars and Japan and Europe in others?

Diversity of Taste and Economies of Scale

The first part of the answer to the puzzle is that people have a tremendous diversity of taste. Let's stick with the example of cars. Some people prefer sports cars, some prefer estates, some prefer hatchbacks and some prefer the urban jeep look. In addition to size and type of car, there are many other ways in which cars vary. Some have low fuel consumption, some have high performance, some are spacious and comfortable, some have a large boot, some have four-wheel drive, some have front-wheel drive, some have manual gears, some are durable, some are flashy, some have a radiator grill that looks like a Greek temple, others look like a wedge. People's preferences across these many variables differ. The tremendous diversity in tastes for cars means that people would be dissatisfied if they were forced to consume from a limited range of standardized cars. People value variety and are willing to pay for it in the marketplace.

The second part of the answer to the puzzle is *economies of scale* – the tendency for the average cost of production to be lower, the larger is the scale of production. In such situations, larger and larger production runs lead to ever lower average production costs. Many manufactured goods, including cars, experience economies of scale. For example, if a car producer makes only a few hundred (or perhaps a few thousand) cars of a particular type and design, the producer must use production techniques that are much more labour-intensive and much less automated than those employed to make hundreds of thousands of cars in a particular model. With low production runs and labour-intensive production techniques, costs are high. With very large production runs and automated assembly lines, production costs are much lower. But to obtain lower costs, the automated assembly lines have to produce a large number of cars.

It is the combination of diversity of taste and economies of scale that produces comparative advantages and generates such a large amount of international trade in similar commodities. With international trade, each manufacturer of cars has the whole world market to serve. Each producer can specialize in a limited range of products and then sell its output to the world market. This arrangement enables large production runs on the most popular cars and feasible production runs even on the most customized cars demanded by only a handful of people in each country.

The situation in the market for cars is also present in many other industries, especially those producing specialized equipment and parts. For example, the United Kingdom exports machines but imports machine tools, and it exports mainframe computers but imports PCs. Thus international exchange of similar but slightly differentiated manufactured products is a highly profitable activity.

Review Quiz

1. What is the fundamental source of the gains from international trade?
2. In what circumstances can countries gain from international trade?
3. What determines the goods and services that a country will export?
4. What determines the goods and services that a country will import?
5. What is comparative advantage and what role does it play in determining the amount and type of international trade that occurs?
6. How can it be that all countries gain from international trade and that there are no losers?
7. Provide some examples of comparative advantage in today's world.
8. Why does the United Kingdom both export and import cars?

You've now seen how free international trade brings gains for all. But trade is not free in our world. We'll now take a brief look at some of the international trade restrictions that exist and work out the effects of these trade restrictions. We'll see that free trade brings the greatest possible benefits and that international trade restrictions are costly.

International Trade Restrictions

Governments restrict international trade to protect domestic industries from foreign competition by using two main tools:

1 Tariffs
2 Non-tariff barriers

A **tariff** is a tax that is imposed by the importing country when an imported good crosses its international boundary. A **non-tariff barrier** is any action other than a tariff that restricts international trade. Examples of non-tariff barriers are quantitative restrictions and licensing regulations which limit imports. We'll consider non-tariff barriers in more detail below. First, let's look at tariffs.

The History of Tariffs

Tariffs have been used as a source of government revenue for centuries. They reached their peak during the 1930s, not as a source of government revenue but as a means of protecting domestic industry from foreign competition. Many countries including the United Kingdom and the United States hid behind enormous tariff barriers that restricted international trade and contributed to the severity of the Great Depression. These barriers to international trade were slowly dismantled after the Second World War.

Tariff Reduction in the Post-war Years

Determined to avoid the tariff wars of the 1920s and 1930s, the United States, Europe, and many other countries joined together in 1947 in a **General Agreement on Tariffs and Trade** (GATT). Since its formation, the GATT has organized several rounds of negotiations that have resulted in tariff reductions. One of these, the Kennedy Round that began in the early 1960s, resulted in large tariff cuts starting in 1967. Another, the Tokyo Round, resulted in further tariff cuts in 1979.

The Uruguay Round, which started in 1986 and was completed in 1994, was the most ambitious and comprehensive of the rounds and led to the creation of a new **World Trade Organization** (WTO). Membership of the WTO brings greater obligations on countries to observe the GATT rules.

Since 1994, the WTO has been involved in reducing tariffs in telecommunications, information technology and financial services. A new round of WTO negotiations started in 2000 in Doha, Qatar aims at further liberalising trade in agriculture and services by January 2005.

In other parts of the world, trade barriers have virtually been eliminated. The *Single European Market* (SEM) in the European Union has created the largest unified tariff-free market in the world. The SEM programme has simplified border formalities for the movement of goods; capital and labour have complete freedom of movement within the European Union; other forms of protection such as non-tariff barriers are to be eliminated; and public procurement is to be made open to all EU firms. In the longer term, the SEM programme provides for all indirect taxes within the European Union to be harmonized so that no individual country can tax a good differently from another country in the Union.

In 1994, discussions among the Asia-Pacific Economic group (APEC) led to an agreement in principle to work towards a free-trade area that embraces China, all the economies of East Asia and the South Pacific, and the United States and Canada. These countries include the fastest-growing economies and hold the promise of heralding a global free-trade area. But the Asia crisis of 1997 and other problems with China make it unlikely that free trade will come to APEC in the near term.

In the Americas, Canada, the United States and Mexico are parties to the North American Free Trade Agreement that is lowering tariffs among these countries.

Tariffs Today

A consequence of this persistent movement towards lower tariffs its that UK tariffs today stand at less than 1 per cent of total imports and tariffs on trade with other members of the European Union have been eliminated completely.

But despite the effort to achieve freer trade, most agricultural products are still subject to extremely high tariffs. In the European Union, buyers of agricultural products face prices that on average are 40 per cent above world prices. These high prices result from the **Common Agricultural Policy** (CAP), which is a price support programme for farmers in the European Union and acts as a tariff on non-EU agricultural products. The meat, cheese and sugar that you consume cost significantly more because of protection than they would with free international trade.

Figure 33.5 shows the average tariff the CAP imposes on world agricultural goods. The implied average tariff varies because the world price of agricultural goods varies from year to year.

The temptation for governments to impose tariffs is a strong one. They do, of course, provide revenue to the government, but this is not particularly large compared with other sources. Their most important attribute is that they enable the government to satisfy special interest groups in import-competing industries. But, as we'll see, free international trade brings enormous benefits that are reduced when tariffs are imposed. Let's see how.

How Tariffs Work

To analyse how tariffs work, let's return to the example of trade between Farmland and Mobilia. Figure 33.6 shows the international market for cars in which these two countries are the only traders. The volume of trade and the price of a car are determined at the point of intersection of Mobilia's export supply curve of cars and Farmland's import demand curve for cars.

In Figure 33.6, these two countries are trading cars and grain in exactly the same way that we analysed before in Figure 33.3. Mobilia exports cars and Farmland exports grain. The volume of car imports into Farmland is 4 million a year and the world market price of a car is 3 tonnes of grain. To make the example more concrete and real, Figure 33.6 expresses prices in pounds rather than in units of grain and is based on a money price of grain of £1,000 a tonne. With grain costing £1,000 a tonne, the money price of a car is £3,000.

Now suppose that the government of Farmland, perhaps under pressure from car producers, decides to impose a tariff on imported cars. In particular, suppose that a tariff of £4,000 per car is imposed. (This is a huge tariff, but the car producers of Farmland are pretty fed up with competition from Mobilia.) What happens?

Figure 33.5

Average Implied Tariffs on EU Agricultural Products 1979–2003

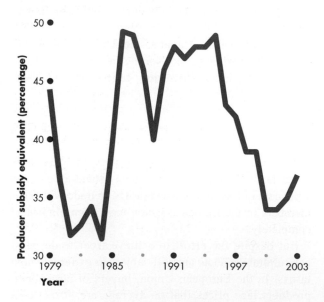

The OECD estimates the average percentage subsidy paid to EU farmers that would give them the same additional income as the actual CAP intervention price, which artificially holds agricultural prices above world prices. The graph is an estimate of the percentage by which EU prices are raised above world prices.

Source: OECD, *Agricultural Policies in OECD Countries: At a Glance*, 2004.

Figure 33.6

The Effects of a Tariff

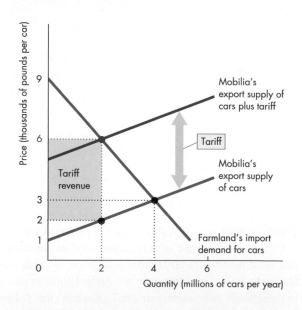

Farmland imposes a tariff on car imports from Mobilia. The tariff increases the price that Farmers have to pay for cars. The tariff shifts the supply curve of cars in Farmland upward. The distance between the original supply curve and the new one is the amount of the tariff, £4,000 per car. The price of cars in Farmland increases and the quantity of cars imported decreases. The government of Farmland collects a tariff revenue of £4,000 per car – total of £8 billion on the 2 million cars imported. Farmland's exports of grain decrease because Mobilia now has a lower income from its exports of cars.

When Farmland imposes a tariff on car imports, the following events happen in Farmland:

◆ The supply of cars decreases.

◆ The price of a car rises.

◆ Car imports decrease.

◆ The government collects the tariff revenue.

◆ Resource use is inefficient.

◆ Trade remains balanced.

The Supply of Cars Decreases

Cars are no longer available at Mobilia's export supply price. The tariff of £4,000 a car must be added to that price. So the supply curve in Farmland shifts leftward. The new supply curve is that labelled "Mobilia's export supply of cars plus tariff". The vertical distance between Mobilia's original export supply curve and the new supply curve is the tariff imposed of £4,000 a car.

The Price of a Car Rises

A new equilibrium occurs where the new supply curve intersects Farmland's import demand curve for cars. That equilibrium is at a price of £6,000 a car, up from £3,000 with free trade.

Car Imports Decrease

Car imports decrease from 4 million to 2 million cars a year. At the higher price of £6,000 a car, domestic car producers increase their production. Domestic grain production decreases as resources are moved into the expanding car industry.

Government Collects Tariff Revenue

Total expenditure on imported cars by the Farmers is £6,000 a car multiplied by the 2 million cars imported (£12 billion). But not all of that money goes to Mobilia. They receive £2,000 a car or £4 billion for the 2 million cars. The difference – £4,000 a car or a total of £8 billion for the 2 million cars – is collected by the government of Farmland as tariff revenue.

Resource Use is Inefficient

The people of Farmland are willing to pay £6,000 for the marginal car imported. But the opportunity cost of that car is £2,000. So there is a gain from trading an extra car. In fact, there are gains – willingness to pay exceeds opportunity cost – all the way up to 4 million cars a year. Only when 4 million cars are being traded is the maximum price that a Farmer is willing to pay equal to the minimum price that is acceptable to a Mobilian. So restricting international trade reduces the gains from trade and makes resource use inefficient.

Trade Remains Balanced

With free trade, Farmland was paying £3,000 a car and buying 4 million cars a year from Mobilia. The total amount paid to Mobilia for imports was £12 billion a year. With a tariff, Farmland's imports have been cut to 2 million cars a year and the price paid to Mobilia has also been cut to only £2,000 a car. The total amount paid to Mobilia for imports has been cut to £4 billion a year. Doesn't this fact mean that Farmland has a balance of trade surplus? It does not!

The price of a car in Mobilia has fallen. But the price of grain remains at £1,000 a tonne. So the relative price of a car has fallen and the relative price of grain has increased. With free trade, Mobilia could buy 3 tonnes of grain for the price of one car. Now they can buy only 2 tonnes for one car. With a higher relative price of grain, the quantity demanded by Mobilia decreases and Mobilia imports less grain. But because Mobilia imports less grain, Farmland exports less grain. In fact, Farmland's grain industry suffers from two sources. First, the quantity of grain sold to Mobilia decreases. Second, competition for inputs from the now expanded car industry increases. The tariff leads to a contraction in the scale of the grain industry in Farmland.

It seems paradoxical at first that a country imposing a tariff on cars would hurt its own export industry, decreasing its exports of grain. It may help to think of it this way: Mobilians buy grain with the money they make from exporting cars to Farmland. If Mobilians export fewer cars, they cannot afford to buy as much grain. In fact, in the absence of any international borrowing and lending, Mobilia must cut its imports of grain by exactly the same amount as the loss in revenue from its export of cars. Grain imports into Mobilia are cut back to a value of £4 billion, the amount that can be paid for by the new lower revenue from Mobilia's car exports. Trade is still balanced. The tariff cuts imports and exports by the same amount. The tariff has no effect on the *balance* of trade, but it reduces the *volume* of trade.

The result that we have just derived is perhaps one of the most misunderstood aspects of international economics. On countless occasions, politicians and others have called for tariffs to remove a balance of trade deficit or have argued that lowering tariffs would produce a balance of trade deficit. They reach this conclusion by failing to work out all the implications of a tariff. Let's now look at non-tariff barriers.

Non-tariff Barriers

There are two important forms of non-tariff barriers:

1 Quotas

2 Voluntary export restraints

A **quota** is a quantitative restriction on the import of a particular good. It specifies the maximum amount of the good that may be imported in a given period of time. A **voluntary export restraint** (VER) is an agreement between two governments in which the government of the exporting country agrees to restrain the volume of its own exports.

Quotas are especially important in textile and agriculture. Voluntary export restraints are used to regulate trade between Japan and the United States.

How Quotas and VERs Work

To see how a quota works, suppose that Farmland imposes a quota on car imports that restricts imports to not more than 2 million cars a year. Figure 33.7 shows the effects of this action. The quota is shown by the vertical red line at 2 million cars a year. Because it is illegal to import more than that number of cars, car importers buy only that quantity from Mobilia and they pay £2,000 a car. But because the import supply of cars is restricted to 2 million cars a year, people are willing to pay £6,000 per car. This is the price of a car in Farmland.

The value of imports falls to £4 billion, exactly the same as in the case of the tariff in Figure 33.6. So with lower incomes from car exports and with a higher relative price of grain, Mobilians cut their imports of grain in exactly the same way as they did under a tariff.

The key difference between a quota and a tariff lies in who collects the gap between the import supply price and the domestic price. In the case of a tariff, it is the government of the importing country. In the case of a quota, it goes to the person who has the right to import under the import-quota regulations.

A VER is like a quota arrangement where quotas are allocated to each exporting country. The effects of VERs are similar to those of quotas but differ from them in that the gap between the domestic price and the export price is captured not by domestic importers but by the foreign exporter. The government of the exporting country has to establish procedures for allocating the restricted volume of exports among its producers.

Figure 33.7

The Effects of a Quota

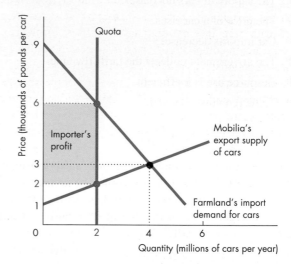

Farmland imposes a quota of 2 million cars a year on car imports from Mobilia. That quantity appears as the vertical line labelled "Quota". Because the quantity of cars supplied by Mobilia is restricted to 2 million, the price at which those cars will be traded increases to £6,000 per car. Importing cars is profitable because Mobilia is willing to supply cars at £2,000 each. There is competition for import quotas.

Review Quiz

1 What are the tools that a country can use to restrict international trade?

2 What do international trade restrictions do to the gains from international trade?

3 Which is best for a country: restricted trade, no trade, or free trade? Why?

4 What does a tariff on imports do to the volume of imports and the volume of exports?

5 In the absence of international borrowing and lending, how do tariffs and other international trade restrictions influence the total value of imports and exports and the balance of trade: the value of exports minus the value of imports?

Let's now look at some commonly heard arguments for restricting international trade and see why they are almost never correct.

The Case Against Protection

For as long as countries and international trade have existed, people have debated whether a country is better off with free international trade or with protection from foreign competition. The debate continues, but for most economists a verdict has been delivered and it is the one you have just explored. Free trade is the arrangement most conducive to prosperity, and protection creates more problems than it solves. We've seen the most powerful case for free trade in the example of how Farmland and Mobilia both benefit from their comparative advantage. But there is a broader range of issues in the free-trade versus protection debate. Let's review these issues.

Three arguments for restricting international trade are:

◆ The national security argument
◆ The infant-industry argument
◆ The dumping argument

Let's look at each in turn.

The National Security Argument

The national security argument for protection is that a country must protect the industries that produce defence equipment and armaments and those on which the defence industries rely for their raw materials and other intermediate inputs. This argument for protection does not withstand close scrutiny.

First, it is an argument for international isolation, for in time of war, there is no industry that does not contribute to national defence. Second, even if the case is made for increasing the output of a strategic industry, it is more efficient to achieve this outcome with a subsidy to the firms in the industry financed out of taxes. Such a subsidy would keep the industry operating at the scale judged appropriate and free international trade would keep the prices faced by consumers at their world market levels.

The Infant-Industry Argument

The so-called **infant-industry argument** for protection is that it is necessary to a new industry to enable it to grow into a mature industry that can compete in world markets. The argument is based on the idea of *dynamic comparative advantage* which can arise from *learning-by-doing* (see Chapter 2, p. 43).

Learning-by-doing is a powerful engine of productivity growth and comparative advantage does evolve and change because of on-the-job experience. But these facts do not justify protection.

First, the infant-industry argument is valid only if the benefits of learning-by-doing *not only* accrue to the owners and workers of the firms in the infant industry but also *spill over* to other industries and parts of the economy. For example, there are huge productivity gains from learning-by-doing in the manufacture of aircraft. But almost all of these gains benefit the shareholders and workers of BAe, Westland and other aircraft producers. Because the people making the decisions, bearing the risk and doing the work are the ones who benefit, they take the dynamic gains into account when they decide on the scale of their activities. In this case, almost no benefits spill over to other parts of the economy, so there is no need for government assistance to achieve an efficient outcome.

Second, even if the case is made for protecting an infant industry, it is more efficient to do so by a direct subsidy to the firms in the industry, with the subsidy financed out of taxes.

The Dumping Argument

Dumping occurs when a foreign firm sells its exports at a lower price than its cost of production. Dumping might be used by a firm that wants to gain a global monopoly. In this case, the firm sells at a price below its cost to drive domestic firms out of business. When the domestic firms have gone, the foreign firm takes advantage of its monopoly position and charges a higher price for its product. Dumping is usually regarded as a justification for temporary countervailing tariffs.

But there are powerful reasons to resist the dumping argument for protection. First, it is virtually impossible to detect dumping because it is hard to determine a firm's costs. As a result, the test for dumping is whether a firm's export price is below its domestic price. But this test is a weak one because it can be rational for a firm to charge a low price in markets in which the quantity demanded is highly sensitive to price and a higher price in markets in which demand is less price-sensitive.

Second, it is hard to think of a good that is produced by a natural *global* monopoly. So even if all the domestic firms in some industry were driven out of business, it would always be possible to find many alternative foreign sources of supply and to buy at prices determined in competitive markets.

Third, if a good or service were produced by a truly global natural monopoly, the best way of dealing with it would be by regulation – just as in the case of domestic monopolies. Such regulation would require international cooperation.

The three arguments for protection we've just examined have an element of credibility. The counter-arguments are in general stronger so these arguments do not make the case for protection. But they are not the only arguments that you might encounter. The many other arguments commonly heard are quite simply wrong. They are fatally flawed. The most common of them are that protection:

◆ Saves jobs
◆ Allows us to compete with cheap foreign labour
◆ Brings diversity and stability
◆ Penalizes lax environmental standards
◆ Safeguards national culture
◆ Prevents rich countries from exploiting developing countries

Saves Jobs

The argument that protection saves jobs goes as follows. When we buy shoes from Brazil or shirts from Taiwan, workers in Lancashire lose their jobs. With no earnings and poor prospects, these workers become a drain on the welfare state and they spend less, causing a ripple effect of further job losses. The proposed solution to this problem is to ban imports of cheap foreign goods and protect jobs at home. The proposal is flawed for the following reasons.

First, free trade does cost some jobs, but it also creates other jobs. It brings about a global rationalization of labour and allocates labour resources to their highest-value activities. Because of international trade in textiles, tens of thousands of workers in the United Kingdom have lost jobs because textile mills and other factories have closed. But tens of thousands of workers in other countries have got jobs because textile mills have opened there. And tens of thousands of workers in the United Kingdom have got better-paying jobs than textile workers because other industries have expanded and created more jobs than have been destroyed.

Second, imports create jobs. They create jobs for retailers which sell imported goods and for firms which service these goods. They also create jobs by creating incomes in the rest of the world, some of which are spent on UK-made goods and services.

Although protection does save particular jobs, it does so at an inordinate cost. For example, in the United States jobs in the textile industry are protected by quotas imposed under an international agreement called the Multi-Fibre Arrangement. It has been estimated that because of the quotas, 72,000 jobs existed in textiles in the United States that would otherwise disappear and the annual clothing expenditure in the United States is $15.9 million or $160 per family higher than it would be with free trade. Equivalently, each textile job saved cost $221,000 a year!

Allows Us to Compete with Cheap Foreign Labour

The late Sir James Goldsmith, multimillionaire and Euro MP, argued that if Europe does not build protective tariffs against cheap imports from the newly industrializing economies of East Asia, there will be a loss of jobs that will threaten the way of life in Europe. The loss of jobs will occur as firms relocate to the Far East to take advantage of cheap labour. Let's see what's wrong with this view.

The labour cost of a unit of output equals the wage rate divided by labour productivity. For example, if a UK production assembly worker earns £15 an hour and produces 10 units of output an hour, the average labour cost of a unit of output is £1.50. If a Chinese production assembly worker earns £2 an hour and produces 1 unit of output an hour, the average labour cost of a unit of output is £2. Other things remaining the same, the higher a worker's productivity, the higher is the worker's wage rate. High-wage workers have high productivity. Low-wage workers have low productivity.

Although high-wage UK workers are more productive, on average, than low-wage Chinese workers, there are differences across industries. UK labour is relatively more productive at some activities than others. For example, the productivity of UK workers in producing chemical products, financial services, luxury cars and high-quality engineering is relatively higher than in the production of metals and some standardized machine parts. The activities in which UK workers are relatively more productive than their Chinese counterparts are those in which the United Kingdom has a *comparative advantage*.

By engaging in free trade, increasing our production and exports of the goods in which the United Kingdom has a comparative advantage and decreasing UK production and increasing imports of the goods and services in which our trading partners have a comparative advantage, we can make ourselves and the citizens of other countries better off.

Brings Diversity and Stability

A diversified investment portfolio is less risky than one that has all its eggs in one basket. The same is true for an economy's production. A diversified economy fluctuates less than an economy that produces only one or two goods.

But big, rich, diversified economies like the United States, Japan and the European Union do not have this type of stability problem. Even a country such as Saudi Arabia, which produces almost only one good (oil), can benefit from specializing in the activity at which it has a comparative advantage and then investing in a wide range of other countries to bring greater stability to its income and consumption.

Penalizes Lax Environmental Standards

Another argument for protection is that many poor countries, such as Mexico, do not have the same environmental policies we have and, because they are willing to pollute and we are not, we cannot compete with them without tariffs. So if these countries with lax environmental standards want free trade with the richer and "greener" countries, they must clean up their environments to our standards. This argument was used extensively in the Uruguay Round of the GATT negotiations.

This argument for international trade restrictions is weak. First, it is not true that all poorer countries have significantly lower environmental standards than the United Kingdom has. Many poor countries, and the former communist countries of Eastern Europe, do have a bad environmental record. But some countries have strict environmental laws and they enforce them.

Second, a poor country cannot afford to be as concerned about its environment as a rich country can. The best hope for a better environment in developing countries is rapid income growth through free international trade. As their incomes grow, developing countries will have the *means* to match their desires to improve their environment.

Third, poor countries have a comparative advantage at doing "dirty" work, which helps rich countries achieve higher environmental standards than they otherwise could.

Safeguards National Culture

A national culture argument for protection is one that is frequently heard in Europe. The expressed fear is that free trade in books, magazines, film and television programmes means the erosion of local culture and the domination of US culture. So, the argument continues, it is necessary to protect domestic "culture" industries to ensure the survival of national cultural identity. This is an argument that the European film industry often uses.

Protection of these industries is common and usually takes the form of non-tariff barriers. For example, local content regulations on radio and television broadcasting and in magazines is often required.

The cultural identity argument for protection has no merit. Writers, publishers and broadcasters want to limit foreign competition so that they can earn larger economic profits. There is no actual danger to national culture. In fact, many of the creators of so-called American cultural products are not Americans but the talented citizens of other countries, ensuring the survival of their national culture in Hollywood! Also, if national culture is in danger, there is no surer way of helping it on its way out than by impoverishing the nation whose culture it is. Protection is an effective way of doing just that.

Prevents Rich Countries from Exploiting Developing Countries

Another new argument for protection is that international trade must be restricted to prevent the people of the rich industrial world from exploiting the poorer people of the developing countries, forcing them to work for slave wages.

Wage rates in some developing countries are, indeed, very low. But by trading with developing countries, we increase the demand for the goods that these countries produce and, more significantly, we increase the demand for their labour. When the demand for labour in developing countries increases, the wage rate also increases. So, far from exploiting people in developing countries, international trade improves their opportunities and increases their incomes.

We have reviewed the arguments commonly heard in favour of protection and the counter-arguments against them. There is one counter-argument to protection that is general and quite overwhelming. Protection invites retaliation and can trigger a trade war. The best example of a trade war occurred during the Great Depression of the 1930s when the United States introduced the Smoot-Hawley tariff. Country after country retaliated with its own tariff and, in a short time, world trade had almost disappeared. The costs to all countries were large and led to a renewed international resolve to avoid such self-defeating moves in future. They also led to the creation of the GATT and are the impetus behind the European Union, NAFTA and APEC.

Review Quiz

1   Is there any merit to the view that we should restrict international trade to achieve national security goals, to stimulate the growth of new industries or to restrain foreign monopoly?
2   Is there any merit to the view that we should restrict international trade to save jobs, compensate for low foreign wages, make the economy more diversified, compensate for costly environmental policies, protect national culture or protect developing countries from being exploited?
3   Is there any merit to the view that we should restrict international trade for any reason? What is the main argument against trade restrictions?

Why is International Trade Restricted?

Why, despite all the arguments against protection, is trade restricted? There are two key reasons:

◆   Tariff revenue
◆   Rent seeking

Tariff Revenue

Government revenue is costly to collect. In the developed economies such as the United Kingdom, a well-organized tax collection system is in place that can generate billions of pounds of income taxes, VAT and excise taxes revenues. This tax collection system is made possible by the fact that most economic transactions are done by firms that must keep properly audited financial records. Without such records, the revenue collection agencies (e.g. the Inland Revenue) would be severely hampered in their work. Even with audited financial accounts, some proportion of potential tax

revenue is lost. Nonetheless, for the industrialized countries, income taxes, VAT and excise taxes are the major sources of government revenue and the tariff plays a very small role.

But governments in developing countries have a difficult time collecting taxes from their citizens. Much economic activity takes place in an informal economy with few financial records. So only a small amount of revenue is collected from income taxes and sales taxes in these countries. The one area in which economic transactions are well recorded and audited is in international trade. So this activity is an attractive base for tax collection in these countries and is used much more extensively than in the developed countries.

Rent Seeking

Rent seeking is the major reason why international trade is restricted. **Rent seeking** is lobbying and other political activity that seeks to capture the gains from trade. Free international trade increases consumption possibilities *on average*, but not everyone shares in the gain and some people even lose. Free international trade brings benefits to some and imposes costs on others, with total benefits exceeding total costs. It is the uneven distribution of costs and benefits that is the principal source of impediment to achieving more liberal international trade.

Let's return to our example of international trade in cars and grain between Farmland and Mobilia. In Farmland, the benefits from free trade accrue to all the producers of grain and those producers of cars who would not have to bear the costs of adjusting to a smaller car industry. These costs are transition costs, not permanent costs. The costs of moving to free trade are borne by those car producers and their employees who have to become grain producers.

The number of people who gain will, in general, be enormous compared with the number who lose. The gain per person will, therefore, be rather small. The loss per person to those who bear the loss will be large. Because the loss that falls on those who bear it is large, it will pay those people to incur considerable expense in order to lobby against free trade. On the other hand, it will not pay those who gain to organize to achieve free trade. The gain from trade for any one individual is too small for that individual to spend much time or money on a political organization to achieve free trade. The loss from free trade will be seen as being so great by those bearing that loss that they *will* find it profitable to join a political organization to prevent free trade. Each group is optimizing – weighing benefits against costs and choosing the best action for themselves. The anti-free trade group will, therefore, undertake a larger quantity of political lobbying than the pro-free trade group.

Rent seeking accounts for the protection of sugar producers in the European Union as you can see in *Reading Between the Lines* on pp. 766–767.

Compensating Losers

If, in total, the gains from free international trade exceed the losses, why don't those who gain compensate those who lose so that everyone is in favour of free trade?

The main answer is that there are serious obstacles to providing direct and correctly calculated compensation. First, the cost of identifying the losers from free trade and of estimating the value of their losses would be enormous.

Second, it would never be clear whether a person who has fallen on hard times is suffering because of free trade or for other reasons, perhaps reasons that are largely under the control of the individual.

Third, some people who look like losers at one point in time may, in fact, end up gaining. The young steel worker in South Wales who loses his job and becomes a computer assembly worker resents the loss of work and the need to move. But a year or two later, looking back on events, he counts himself fortunate. He's made a move that has increased his income and given him greater job security.

Despite the absence of explicit compensation, those who lose from a change in protection do receive some compensation. But compensation is not restricted to the losers from changes in trade policy.

In the United Kingdom (and in all the other rich industrial countries) elaborate schemes are in place to ensure that people who suffer from economic change receive help during their transition to new activities.

Two major forms of compensation are fiscal transfers and employment insurance. Fiscal transfers result in tax pounds collected in the rich and expanding regions of the country being spent in the poorer regions. Employment insurance provides substantial compensation for workers who lose their jobs regardless of the reason for the job loss. Jobs lost because of changes in international protection are included among those for which benefits are paid.

But because we do not explicitly compensate the losers from free international trade, protectionism remains a popular and permanent feature of our national economic and political life.

Compensating Losers from Protection

There is no general presumption that it is the ones who lose from a tariff cut that should be compensated. Protection brings losses to the consumer and the view might be taken that the winners from protection should compensate the losers from protection. When this perspective is taken, the removal of protection would mean the removal of the compensation of the losers by the winners and no further adjustments would be needed. What is fair is a tricky matter (see Chapter 5, pp. 108–111).

Review Quiz

1 What are the two main reasons for imposing tariffs on imports?
2 What type of country benefits most from the revenue from tariffs? Do countries in the European Union need to use tariffs to raise revenue for the government?
3 If international trade restrictions are costly, why do we use them? Why don't the people who gain from international trade organize a political force that is strong enough to ensure their interests are protected?

You've now seen how free international trade enables all countries to gain from increased specialization and exchange. By producing goods at which we have a comparative advantage and exchanging some of our own production for that of others, we expand our consumption possibilities. Placing impediments on that decreases the gains from specialization and trade. By opening up our country to free international trade, the markets for the things that we sell expands and the relative price rises. The market for the things that we buy also expands and the relative price falls.

Reading Between the Lines overleaf shows how the EU and global sugar markets have been hijacked by a few producers who benefit greatly at the expense of millions who individually pay little but together pay a huge amount to successful rent seekers.

In the next chapter, we're going to study the ways in which international trade is financed, and also learn why international borrowing and lending, which permit unbalanced international trade, arise. We'll discover the forces that determine a country's balance of payments and the value of its money in the foreign exchange market.

Reading Between the Lines
EU Sugar Tariffs

The Times, 14 April 2004

EU sugar subsidies reward rich, says Oxfam

Carl Mortished

Britain's sugar barons are earning massive profits at the expense of consumers and taxpayers, thanks to an EU subsidy regime, according to a report by Oxfam, published today.

A group of 27 East Anglian beet farmers are gaining an annual subsidy of about euro 285,000 (£187,000) each from guaranteed EU sugar prices while Europe's sugar refiners claim up to 1.4 billion euros every year in export subsidies dumping surplus sugar abroad.

The Oxfam report, *Dumping on the World*, alleges that Tate & Lyle received a direct grant of 158 million euros from the taxpayer for sugar exports. Europe exports five million tonnes of sugar per year, half of which is eligible for a direct subsidy, representing the yawning gap between the world price of the commodity and the high cost of producing it in a cold northern climate. Oxfam calculates that the EU is spending 3.30 euro in subsidies to export sugar worth 1 euro. The report also names British Sugar, part of Associated British Foods and owner of the Silver Spoon brand, as a beneficiary of quotas and tariff barriers.

Oxfam called for a cut in the EU quotas that rewarded companies and rich farmers while hurting the poorest. Mozambique, Malawi and Ethiopia lost $238 million in potential earnings since 2001 because of EU quotas on imports. Tate and Lyle said yesterday it was not benefiting from the export subsidies but acting as agent for overseas cane sugar growers. British Sugar said it would not object to ending direct export subsidies but would not comment on the removal of quotas and tariffs.

The Essence of the Story

- Europe exports 5 million tonnes of sugar a year. An EU export subsidy fills the gap between the world price and the high cost of producing sugar in Europe and an import quota keeps foreign sugar out of Europe.

- An Oxfam report, *Dumping on the World*, provides some striking data on winners and losers and calls for a cut in the EU quotas.

- East Anglian beet farmers receive annual subsidies of £187,000 each.

- Europe's sugar refiners (Tate & Lyle and British Sugar, among them) receive €1.4 billion a year in export subsidies.

- The European Union spends an estimated €3.30 in subsidies to export sugar worth €1.

- Mozambique, Malawi and Ethiopia are among the big losers from EU restrictions on sugar imports.

Economic Analysis

◆ A tariff on sugar imports and a subsidy on sugar exports maintains the EU price at 22 US cents a pound compared to the world price of 6 US cents a pound.

◆ Figure 1 shows the EU market and Figure 2 shows the rest of the world market for sugar with free trade. The demand curves are D_{EU} and D_{RW} and the supply curves are S_{EU} and S_{RW}. The equilibrium price is 14 cents a pound and the European Union imports and the rest of the world exports 12 billion pounds a year.

◆ Figure 3 shows the effect of the EU sugar export subsidy in the European Union.

Supply from the European Union increases, the world price falls to 6 cents a pound and the EU price rises to 22 cents a pound. EU production increases, EU consumption decreases and the European Union switches from being a sugar importer to an exporter. EU producers collect €1.4 billion in subsidy.

◆ Figure 4 shows the effects in the rest of the world. A tariff of 16 cents a pound makes it unprofitable for the rest of the world to sell sugar to the European Union. Sugar production and the producer surplus earned by sugar farmers shrink.

◆ The EU sugar subsidy and tariff harm EU sugar consumers and foreign sugar producers. It benefits EU sugar producers but by less than the harm it does to others.

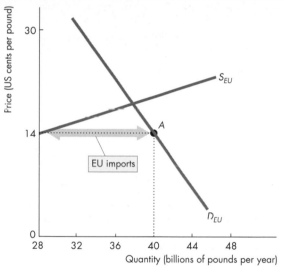

Figure 1 Free trade in sugar: EU imports sugar

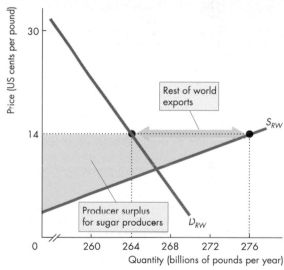

Figure 2 Free trade in sugar: rest of the world exports sugar

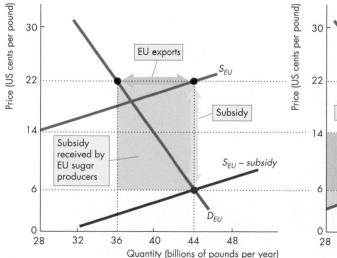

Figure 3 Subsidy benefits EU producers

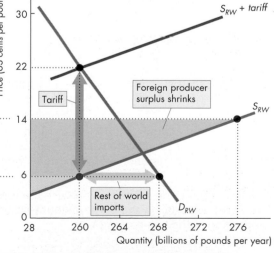

Figure 4 EU protection harms foreign producers

Summary

Key Points

Patterns and Trends in International Trade (p. 750)

◆ Large flows of trade take place between countries, most of which is in manufactured goods.

◆ Finished manufactured goods constitute the largest group of export items by the United Kingdom.

The Gains from International Trade (pp. 751–756)

◆ Comparative advantage is the fundamental source of the gains from trade.

◆ Comparative advantage exists when opportunity cost between countries diverge.

◆ By increasing its production of goods in which it has a comparative advantage and then trading some of the increased output, a country can consume at points outside its production possibilities frontier.

◆ In the absence of international borrowing and lending, trade is balanced as prices adjust to reflect the international supply of and demand for goods.

◆ The world price balances the production and consumption plans of the trading parties. At the equilibrium price, trade is balanced.

◆ Comparative advantage explains the enormous volume and diversity of international trade that takes place in the world.

◆ But trade in similar goods arises from economies of scale in the face of diversified tastes.

International Trade Restrictions (pp. 757–760)

◆ Countries restrict international trade by imposing tariffs or non-tariff barriers, such as quotas and VERs.

◆ International trade restrictions raise the domestic price of imported goods, reduce the volume of imports and reduce the total value of imports.

◆ International trade restrictions reduce the total value of exports by the same amount as the reduction in the value of imports.

The Case Against Protection (pp. 761–764)

◆ Arguments that protection is necessary for national security, to protect infant industries and to prevent dumping are weak.

◆ Arguments that protection is necessary to save jobs, allows us to compete with cheap foreign labour, makes the economy diversified and stable, penalizes lax environmental standards, protects national culture, and prevents exploitation of developing countries are fatally flawed.

Why is International Trade Restricted? (pp. 764–765)

◆ Trade is restricted because tariffs raise government revenue and because protection brings a small loss to a large number of people and a large gain per person to a small number of people.

Key Figures

Key Terms

Problems

*1 The table provides information about Virtual Reality's production possibilities.

TV sets (per day)		Computers (per day)
0	and	36
10	and	35
20	and	33
30	and	30
40	and	26
50	and	21
60	and	15
70	and	8
80	and	0

a Calculate Virtual Reality's opportunity cost of a TV set when it produces 10 sets a day.

b Calculate Virtual Reality's opportunity cost of a TV set when it produces 40 sets a day.

c Calculate Virtual Reality's opportunity cost of a TV set when it produces 70 sets a day.

d Using the answers to parts (a), (b), and (c), graph the relationship between the opportunity cost of a TV set and the quantity of TV sets produced in Virtual Reality.

2 The table provides information about Vital Signs' production possibilities.

TV sets (per day)		Computers (per day)
0	and	18.0
10	and	17.5
20	and	16.5
30	and	15.0
40	and	13.0
50	and	10.5
60	and	7.5
70	and	4.0
80	and	0

a Calculate Vital Signs' opportunity cost of a TV set when it produces 10 sets a day.

b Calculate Vital Signs' opportunity cost of a TV set when it produces 40 sets a day.

c Calculate Vital Signs' opportunity cost of a TV set when it produces 70 sets a day.

d Using the answers to parts (a), (b), and (c), sketch the relationship between the opportunity cost of a TV set and the quantity of TV sets produced in Vital Signs.

*3 Suppose that with no international trade, Virtual Reality in problem 1 produces and consumes 10 TV sets a day and Vital Signs produces and consumes 60 TV sets a day. Now suppose that the two countries begin to trade with each other.

a Which country exports TV sets?

b What adjustments are made to the amount of each good produced by each country?

c What adjustments are made to the amount of each good produced by each country?

d What can you say about the terms of trade (the price of a TV set expressed as computers per TV set) under free trade?

4 Suppose that with no international trade, Virtual Reality in problem 1 produces and consumes 50 TV sets a day and Vital Signs produces and consumes 20 TV sets a day. Now suppose that the two countries begin to trade with each other.

a Which country exports TV sets?

b What adjustments are made to the amount of each good produced by each country?

c What adjustments are made to the amount of each good consumed by each country?

d What can you say about the terms of trade (the price of a TV set expressed as computers per TV set) under free trade?

*5 Compare the total quantities of each good produced in problems 1 and 2 with the total quantities of each good produced in problems 3 and 4.

a Does free trade increase or decrease the total quantities of TV sets and computers produced in both cases? Why or why not?

b What happens to the price of a TV set in Virtual Reality in the two cases? Why does it rise in one case and fall in the other?

c What happens to the price of a computer in Vital Signs in the two cases? Why does it rise in one case and fall in the other?

6 Compare the international trade in problem 3 with that in problem 4.

a Why does Virtual Reality export TV sets in one of the cases and import them in the other case?

b Do the TV producers or the computer producers gain in each case?

c Do consumers gain in each case?

*Solutions to odd-numbered problems are available on *Parkin Interactive.*

*7 The figure depicts the international market for soybeans.

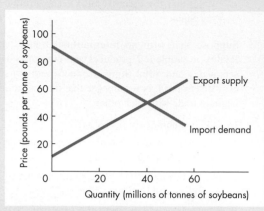

a If the two countries did not engage in international trade, what would be the prices of soybeans in the two countries?

b What is the world price of soybean if there is free trade between these countries?

c What quantities of soybeans are exported and imported?

d What is the balance of trade?

8 If the soybean importing country in problem 7 imposes a tariff of £20 per tonne, what is the world price of soybeans and what quantity of soybeans gets traded internationally? What is the price of soybeans in the importing country? Calculate the tariff revenue.

*9 If the soybean importing country in problem 7 imposes a quota of 30 million tonnes on imports of soybeans,

a What is the price of soybeans in the importing country?

b What is the revenue from the quota?

c Who gets this revenue?

10 If the soybean exporting country in problem 7 imposes a VER of 30 million tonnes on its exports of soybeans,

a What is the world price of soybean now?

b What is the revenue of soybean growers in the exporting country?

c Which country gains from the VER?

Critical Thinking

1 Study *Reading Between the Lines* on pp. 766–767 and then answer the following questions.

a Why is there a gap between the world price of sugar and the EU price of sugar?

b Who are the gainers and who are the losers from a tariff on sugar imports into the European Union?

c According to the report, how much does the European Union export each year and how much of this is eligible for subsidy?

d Who would gain and who would lose from a cut in the sugar quota as the report recommends?

e What arguments are there for a sugar tariff? How valid are these arguments?

f What arguments are there for a sugar export subsidy? How valid are these arguments?

g Oxfam calls for a cut in the quota. What policy would you recommend and why?

h The WTO has recently ruled that EU export subsidies must be removed by 2006. What effect will the elimination of these subsidies have on sugar producers and consumers in the European Union and in the rest of the world?

Web Exercises

Use the links on Parkin Interactive to work the following exercises.

1 Read the EU document on "Facts and Figures" about sugar policy and the Oxfam briefing paper, *Dumping on the World*.

a What are the main differences between the EU facts and figures document and the Oxfam report?

b Do you support or oppose the EU sugar policy? Provide your reasons using the concepts of efficiency and equity.

2 Study the Web *Reading Between the Lines* on steel dumping, and then answer the following questions:

a What is the argument in the news article for limiting steel imports?

b Evaluate the argument. Is it correct or incorrect in your opinion? Why?

c Would you vote to eliminate steel imports? Why or why not?

d Would you vote differently if you lived in another steel-producing country? Why or why not?

Chapter 34

International Finance

After studying this chapter you will be able to:

◆ Explain how international trade is financed, describe a country's balance of payments accounts, and explain what determines the amount of international borrowing and lending

◆ Describe the foreign exchange market and explain how the exchange rate is determined in alternative international monetary systems

◆ Describe the European Monetary Union and explain the benefits and costs of the euro

Make My DEY!

The US dollar ($), the EU euro (€), and the Japanese yen (¥) are the world's three most widely used currencies, followed by the pound (£). These currencies fluctuate in value against each other every day on the foreign exchange market. Why? Why aren't steps taken to stabilize the value of each currency in terms of the others? Why don't we go further and follow the suggestion of Nobel Laureate Robert Mundell and create a global currency – what Mundell called the DEY (dollar + euro + yen)?

Financing International Trade

When Dixons, an electrical goods retail chain, imports Sony CD players, it doesn't pay for them with pounds – it uses Japanese yen. When Harrods imports Armani suits, it pays for them with euros. And when a Japanese restaurant buys a consignment of fine malt whiskey, it uses pounds. Whenever we buy things from another country, we use the currency of that country to make the transaction. It doesn't make any difference what the item being traded is; it might be a consumer good or a capital good, a building, or even a business.

We're going to study the markets in which money – in different types of currencies – is bought and sold. But first we're going to look at the scale of international trading and borrowing and lending, and at the way in which we keep our records of these transactions. Such records are called the balance of payments accounts.

Balance of Payments Accounts

A country's **balance of payments accounts** record its international trading and its borrowing and lending. There are three balance of payments accounts:

1   Current account

2   Capital account

3   Change in reserve assets

The **current account** records the receipts from the sale of goods and services to foreigners, the payments for goods and services bought from foreigners, income and other transfers (such as foreign aid payments) received from and paid to foreigners. By far the largest items in the current account are the receipts from the sale of goods and services to foreigners (the value of exports) and the payments made for goods and services bought from foreigners (the value of imports). Net income is the earnings from foreign financial assets such as bonds and shares, and net earnings of UK workers abroad and foreign workers in the United Kingdom. Net transfers – gifts to foreigners minus gifts from foreigners – are relatively small items.

The **capital account** records all the international borrowing and lending transactions. Whereas the earnings from investments abroad are recorded in the current account, the capital account balance records the actual investments abroad and foreigners' investments in the United Kingdom. It is the difference between the amount that a country lends to and borrows from the rest of the world.

The **change in reserve assets** shows the net increase or decrease in a country's holdings of foreign currency reserves that comes about from the official financing of the difference between the current account and the capital account. In practice, the change in reserve assets is an item in the capital account. It is itemized separately here so that you can see how the financing of the gap between current account and capital account adds to or subtracts from reserve assets.

Table 34.1 shows the UK balance of payments accounts in 2003. Items in the current account and capital account that provide foreign currency to the United Kingdom have a plus sign and items that cost the United Kingdom foreign currency have a minus sign. The table shows that in 2003, UK imports of goods exceeded UK exports of goods and the net trade in goods and services was a deficit of £20.4 billion. How do we pay for imports that exceed the value of our exports? That is, how do we pay for our current account deficit? We pay by borrowing from abroad. The capital account tells us by how much. We borrowed £357 billion but made loans of £339.9 billion, so our net foreign borrowing was £17.1 billion.

Table 34.1

UK Balance of Payments Accounts in 2003

	(billions of pounds)
Current account	
Exports of goods and services	277.5
Imports of goods and services	−310.2
Net income	22.1
Net transfers	−9.8
Current account balance	−20.4
Capital account	
Foreign investment in the United Kingdom	357.0
UK investment abroad	−339.9
Capital account balance	17.1
Balancing Item	1.7
Change in reserves assets	
Increase(+)/Decrease(−) in official UK reserves	−1.6

Source: UK Balance of Payments: The Pink Book, 2004, Office for National Statistics, London.

Some capital and current account transactions do not get recorded. These transactions include unidentified capital flows, illegal international trade such as the import of illegal drugs, and illegal smuggling to evade tariffs or taxes. We call the net total of all these items the *balancing item*, which in 2003 was £1.7 billion.

Net borrowing from abroad minus the current account deficit is the balance that is financed from official UK reserves. Official UK reserves are the government's holdings of foreign currency. In 2003, those reserves decreased by £1.6 billion.

The numbers in Table 34.1 give a snapshot of the balance of payments accounts in 2003. Figure 34.1 puts that snapshot into perspective by showing the balance of payments between 1990 and 2003. Because the economy grows and the price level rises, changes in the balance of payments expressed in pounds do not convey much information. To remove the influences of growth and inflation, Figure 34.1 shows the balance of payments as a percentage of nominal GDP.

As you can see, the current account balance is almost a mirror image of the capital account balance. The change in reserve assets is small compared with the balances on these other two accounts. A large current account deficit (and capital account surplus) occurred in 1990 but declined for most of the 1990s before increasing in 1999 and then decreasing again.

You will perhaps obtain a better understanding of the balance of payments accounts and the way in which they are linked together if you consider the income and expenditure, borrowing and lending, and the bank account of an individual.

Individual Analogy

An individual's current account records the income from supplying the services of factors of production and the expenditure on goods and services. Consider, for example, Joanne. She earned an income in 2003 of £25,000. Joanne has £10,000 worth of investments that earned her an income of £1,000. Joanne's current account shows an income of £26,000. Joanne spent £18,000 buying goods and services for consumption. She also bought a new house, which cost her £60,000. So Joanne's total expenditure was £78,000. The difference between her expenditure and income is £52,000 (£78,000 minus £26,000). This amount is Joanne's current account deficit.

Figure 34.1

The Balance of Payments: 1990–2003

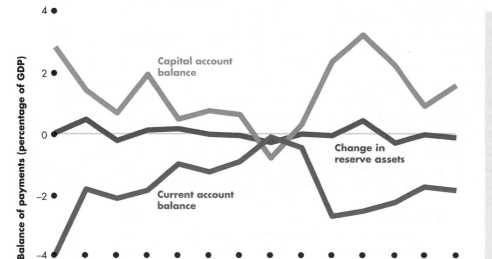

The balance of payments shows a continuous current account deficit from 1990 to 2003. The capital account balance mirrors the current account balance. When the current account balance is negative, the capital account balance is positive – we borrow from the rest of the world. Fluctuations in the change in reserve assets are usually small compared with fluctuations in the current account balance and the capital account balance.

Source: Office for National Statistics.

To pay for expenditure of £52,000 in excess of her income, Joanne has either to use the money that she has in the bank or to take out a loan. In fact Joanne took a mortgage of £50,000 to help buy her house. This mortgage was the only borrowing that Joanne did, so her capital account surplus was £50,000. With a current account deficit of £52,000 and a capital account surplus of £50,000, Joanne was still £2,000 short. She got that £2,000 from her own bank account. Her cash holdings decreased by £2,000.

Joanne's income from her work and investments is analogous to a country's income from its exports. Her purchases of goods and services, including her purchase of a house, are analogous to a country's imports. Joanne's mortgage – borrowing from someone else – is analogous to a country's foreign borrowing. The change in her bank account is analogous to the change in the country's reserve assets.

Borrowers and Lenders, Debtors and Creditors

A country that is borrowing more from the rest of the world than it is lending to it is called a **net borrower**. Similarly, a **net lender** is a country that is lending more to the rest of the world than it is borrowing from it. A net borrower might be going deeper into debt or might simply be reducing its net assets held in the rest of the world. The total stock of foreign investment determines whether a country is a debtor or a creditor.

A **debtor nation** is a country that during its entire history has borrowed more from the rest of the world than it has lent to it. It has a stock of outstanding debt to the rest of the world that exceeds the stock of its own claims on the rest of the world. The United Kingdom is currently a debtor nation, but for a long time it was a creditor. A **creditor nation** is a country that has invested more in the rest of the world than other countries have invested in it. The largest creditor nation today is Japan.

At the heart of the distinction between a net borrower/ net lender and a debtor/creditor nation is the distinction between flows and stocks, which you have encountered many times in your study of macroeconomics. Borrowing and lending are flows – amounts borrowed or lent per unit of time. Debts are stocks – amounts owed at a point in time. The flow of borrowing and lending changes the stock of debt. But the outstanding stock of debt depends mainly on past flows of borrowing and lending, not on the current period's flows. The current period's flows determine the *change* in the stock of debt outstanding.

During the 1960s and the 1970s, the UK current account periodically swung from surplus to deficit. When the current account was a surplus, the capital account was a deficit. On the whole the United Kingdom was a net lender to the rest of the world. It was not until the late 1980s that it became a significant net borrower.

Most countries are net borrowers. But a small number of countries, which includes oil-rich Saudi Arabia and Japan, are huge net lenders.

The United Kingdom today is a small net debtor. There are many countries that are debtor nations. The United States is one. But the largest debtor nations are the capital-hungry developing countries. The international debt of these countries grew from less than one-third to more than one-half of their gross domestic product during the 1980s and created what was called the "Third World debt crisis".

Does it matter if a country is a net borrower rather than a net lender? The answer to this question depends mainly on what the net borrower is doing with the borrowed money. If borrowed money is used to finance investment that in turn is generating economic growth and higher income, borrowing is not a problem. If the borrowed money is being used to finance consumption, then higher interest payments are being incurred and, as a consequence, consumption will eventually have to be reduced. In this case, the more the borrowing and the longer it goes on, the greater is the reduction in consumption that will eventually be necessary. We'll see below whether the United Kingdom has been borrowing for investment or for consumption.

Current Account Balance

What determines the current account balance and the scale of a country's net foreign borrowing or lending? To answer this question, we need to recall and use some of the things that we learned about in the national income accounts. Table 34.2 will refresh your memory and summarize the necessary calculations for you. Part (a) lists the national income variables that are needed, with their symbols. Their values in the United Kingdom in 2003 are also shown.

Part (b) presents two key national income equations. First, equation (1) reminds us that GDP, Y, equals aggregate expenditure, which is the sum of consumption expenditure, C, investment, I, government expenditures on goods and services, G, and net exports (exports, X, minus imports, M). Equation (2) reminds us that aggregate income is used in three different ways. It can be consumed, saved or paid to the government in net taxes

(taxes net of transfer payments). Equation (1) tells us how our expenditure generates our income. Equation (2) tells us how we dispose of that income.

Part (c) of the table takes you into some new territory. It examines surpluses and deficits. We'll look at three surpluses/deficits – those of the current account, the government's budget and the private sector. To get these surpluses and deficits, first subtract equation (2) from equation (1) in Table 34.2. The result is equation (3). By rearranging equation (3), we obtain a relationship for the current account – exports minus imports – that appears as equation (4) in the table.

The current account, in equation (4), is made up of two components. The first is net taxes minus government expenditures and the second is saving minus investment. These items are the surpluses/deficits of the government and private sectors. Net taxes minus government expenditures on goods and services is the budget balance. If that number is positive, the government's budget is a surplus and if the number is negative, it is a deficit.

The **private sector surplus or deficit** is the saving minus investment. If saving exceeds investment, the private sector has a surplus to lend to other sectors. If investment exceeds saving, the private sector has a deficit that has to be financed by borrowing from other sectors. As you can see from our calculations, the current account deficit is equal to the sum of the other two deficits – the government's budget deficit and the private sector deficit. In the United Kingdom in 2003, the private sector had a deficit of £19 billion and the government sector had a deficit of £13 billion. The government sector deficit plus the private sector deficit equals the current account deficit of £32 billion.

Part (d) of Table 34.2 shows you how investment is financed. To increase investment, either private saving, the government surplus, or the current account deficit must increase.

The calculations that we've just performed are really nothing more than bookkeeping. We've manipulated the national income accounts and discovered that the current account deficit is just the sum of the deficits of the government and private sectors. But these calculations do reveal a fundamental fact. Our international balance of payments can change only if either our government budget balance changes or our private sector surplus or deficit changes.

We've seen that our current account deficit is equal to the sum of the government budget balance and the private sector balance. Is the private sector surplus equal to the government's budget deficit so that the current

account deficit is zero? Does an increase in the government budget deficit bring an increase in the current account deficit?

You can see the answer to this question by looking at Figure 34.2 (overleaf). This figure plots the three sector balances – the government sector budget balance $(T - G)$, the private sector balance $(S - I)$, and the foreign sector balance $(M - X)$. To remove the effects of growth and inflation, all three balances are measured as percentages of GDP.

Table 34.2

Sector Balances in 2003

	Symbols and equations	Billions of pounds
(a) Variables		
Gross domestic product (GDP)	Y	1,100
Consumption expenditure	C	721
Investment	I	181
Government expenditures on goods and services	G	230
Exports	X	277
Imports	M	309
Saving	S	162
Net taxes	T	217
(b) Domestic Income and Expenditure		
Aggregate expenditure	(1) $Y = C + I + G + X - M$	
Uses of income	(2) $Y = C + S + T$	
(1) minus (2)	(3) $0 = I - S + G - T + X - M$	
(c) Surpluses and Deficits		
Current account	(4) $X - M = (T - G) + (S - I)$ $= -13 - 19 = -32$	
Government budget	(5) $T - G = 217 - 230 = -13$	
Private sector	(6) $S - I = 162 - 181 = -19$	
(d) Financing Investment		
Investment is financed by the sum of:		
Private saving,	$S = 162$	
Net government saving and	$T - G = -13$	
Net foreign saving	$M - X = 32$	
That is:	(7) $I = S + (T - G) + (M - X)$ $= 181$	

Source: Office for National Statistics.

The private sector balance tends to mirror the government sector balance. The private sector was in surplus (savings greater than investment) during the 1990s and the increasing government sector deficit meant that the current account was in deficit during this period. Between 1999 and 2001, the government sector moved into surplus, but now the private sector was in a strong deficit so the current account remained in deficit. In recent years, the private sector and the government sector have both been in deficit and so the current account has gone further into deficit. The private sector balance is saving minus investment. If saving exceeds investment, a private sector surplus is lent to other sectors. If investment exceeds saving, borrowing from other sectors finances a private sector deficit.

Is the UK Borrowing for Consumption or Investment?

We noted above that whether international borrowing is a problem or not depends on what that borrowed money is used for. Since 1990, the United Kingdom has borrowed nearly £6 billion a year, on average. Over these same years, the government sector has had an average deficit of £8 billion a year and the private sector has had an average surplus (saving minus investment has been positive) of £3 billion a year. So private sector saving has been more than sufficient to pay for investment in plant and equipment. Does the fact that foreign borrowing has financed a government deficit mean that we are borrowing to consume?

Our foreign borrowing probably has been financing public consumption to some degree. But not all government expenditures are for consumption. More than 10 per cent of government expenditures are on investment goods. But there is no sure way to divide government expenditures into a consumption component and an investment component. Some items, such as the expenditure on improved roads and bridges, are clearly investment. But what about expenditure on education and healthcare? Are these expenditures consumption or investment? A case can be made that they are investment – investment in human capital – and that they earn a rate of return at least equal to the interest rate that we pay on our foreign debt.

However, most of the foreign investment in the United Kingdom is in the private sector and is undertaken in the pursuit of the highest available profit. Foreigners diversify their lending to spread their risk. We do the same. Some of our saving is used to finance investment in firms in the United Kingdom, some is lent to the government and some is used to finance investment in other countries.

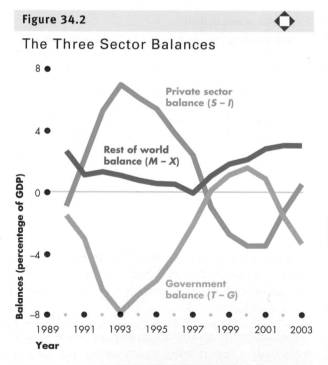

Figure 34.2

The Three Sector Balances

During the 1990s, the private sector was in surplus, the government sector was in deficit and the current account was in deficit. In 1999–2001, the government sector was in surplus but the private sector was in strong deficit as consumer spending boomed. In recent years, the private sector and the government sector were both in deficit and the current account was in a greater deficit.

Source: Office for National Statistics.

Review Quiz

1 When a British wine merchant makes an order for a consignment of wine from a French vineyard, which currency gets used to make the transaction?

2 When a German manufacturer buys semi-manufactured parts from a South Welsh factory, which currency gets used to make the transaction?

3 What types of transactions do we record in the balance of payments accounts?

4 What transactions does the current account record? What transactions does the capital account record? What does the change in reserves record?

5 How are the current account balance, the government sector balance, and the private sector balance related?

The Foreign Exchange Market and the Exchange Rate

When we buy foreign-made goods or invest in another country, we must obtain some of that country's currency to make the transaction. When people in the rest of the world buy UK-made goods or invest in the United Kingdom, they use pounds. We get foreign currency and people in the rest of the world get pounds in the foreign exchange market. The **foreign exchange market** is the market in which the currency of one country is exchanged for the currency of another.

The foreign exchange market is made up of thousands of people: importers and exporters, banks and specialists in the buying and selling of foreign exchange called foreign exchange brokers. The foreign exchange market opens on Monday morning in Hong Kong. As the day advances, markets open in Singapore, Tokyo, Bahrain, Frankfurt, London, New York, Chicago and San Francisco. As the West Coast markets in the United States close, Hong Kong is only an hour away from opening for the next day of business. The sun barely sets on the foreign exchange market. Dealers around the world are continually in contact by telephone and on any given day, billions of dollars, yen, euros and pounds change hands.

The price at which one currency exchanges for another is called a **foreign exchange rate**. For example, on 23 August 2003, one pound bought 1.489 euros, 198.6 Japanese yen, and 1.81 US dollars.

Exchange Rate Fluctuations

Figure 34.3 shows what happened to the exchange rate of the pound in terms of the Japanese yen (red line) and the US dollar (blue line) between January 1979 and July 2004. Over this period, the pound has both depreciated and appreciated.

Currency depreciation is the fall in the value of one currency in terms of another currency. For example, if the pound falls from 200 yen to 180 yen, it depreciates by 10 per cent. Between 1979 and 1985, the pound fell from 560 yen to 223 yen, a depreciation of 60 per cent.

Currency appreciation is the rise in the value of one currency in terms of another currency. For example, if the pound rises from $1.20 to $1.80, it appreciates by 50 per cent. Between 1984 and 1987, the pound did appreciate by 50 per cent.

We've just expressed the pound in terms of the yen and the US dollar. But we can express the value of the

Figure 34.3

Exchange Rates

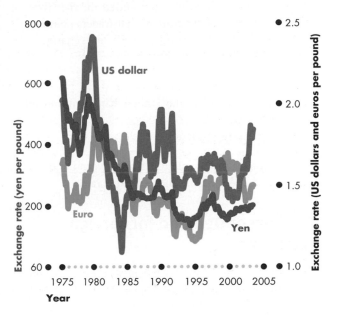

The exchange rate is the price at which two currencies can be traded. The yen–pound exchange rate, expressed as yen per pound, shows that the pound has fallen in value – depreciated – against the yen. The US dollar–pound exchange rate is expressed as US dollars per pound. The pound depreciated against the US dollar between 1980 and 1985 and appreciated against the dollar between 1985 and 1990. Since 2001, the pound has appreciated against the US dollar and the yen.

Source: Bank of England.

pound in terms of any currency. We can also express the exchange rate of the yen in terms of the pound. When the pound depreciates against the yen, the yen appreciates against the pound.

Why does the pound fluctuate so much in value? Why did it depreciate sharply from 1979 to 1985? Why did it appreciate in 1986? To answer questions like these, we need to know what determines the foreign exchange rate.

The exchange rate is a price: the price of one country's money in terms of another country's money. And like all prices, demand and supply determine the exchange rate. So to understand what determines the exchange rate, we need to study demand and supply in the foreign exchange market. We'll begin on the demand side of the market.

Demand in the Foreign Exchange Market

The quantity of pounds demanded in the foreign exchange market is the amount that traders plan to buy during a given time period at a given exchange rate. This quantity depends on three main factors:

1 The exchange rate
2 The interest rate in the United Kingdom and other countries
3 The expected future exchange rate

We first look at the relationship between the quantity of pounds demanded and the exchange rate.

The Law of Demand for Foreign Exchange

People do not buy pounds because they enjoy them. The demand for pounds is a *derived demand*. People demand pounds so that they can buy UK-made goods and services (UK exports). They also demand pounds so that they can buy US assets such as bonds, shares, businesses and property. Nevertheless, the law of demand applies to pounds just as it does to anything else that people value.

Other things remaining the same, the higher the exchange rate, the smaller is the quantity of pounds demanded in the foreign exchange market. For example, if the price of the pound rises from 200 yen to 240 yen and nothing else changes, the quantity of pounds that people plan to buy in the foreign exchange market decreases. Why does the exchange rate influence the quantity of pounds demanded?

There are two separate reasons and they are related to the two sources of the derived demand for pounds:

◆ Exports effect
◆ Expected profit effect

Exports Effect

The larger the value of UK exports, the larger is the quantity of pounds demanded on the foreign exchange market. But the value of UK exports depends on the exchange rate. The lower the exchange rate, with everything else the same, the cheaper are UK-made goods and services, so the more the United Kingdom exports and the greater is the quantity of pounds demanded to pay for these exports.

Expected Profit Effect

The larger the expected profit from holding pounds, the greater is the quantity of pounds demanded in the foreign exchange market. But expected profit depends on the exchange rate. The lower the exchange rate, other things remaining the same, the larger is the expected profit from buying pounds and the greater is the quantity of pounds demanded on the foreign exchange market.

To understand this effect, suppose you think the pound will be worth 220 yen by the end of the month. If today, a pound costs 200 yen, you buy pounds today. But a person who thinks that the pound will be worth 200 yen at the end of the month does not buy pounds today.

But suppose the exchange rate falls to 190 yen per pound. Now, the people who think the pound will be worth 200 yen at the end of the month buy pounds. At the lower exchange rate, more people think they can profit from buying pounds, so the quantity of pounds demanded increases.

For the two reasons we've just reviewed, other things remaining the same, when the foreign exchange rate rises, the quantity of pounds demanded decreases, and when the foreign exchange rate falls, the quantity of pounds demanded increases.

Figure 34.4 shows the demand curve for pounds in the foreign exchange market. When the foreign exchange rate rises, other things remaining the same, the quantity of pounds demanded decreases – there is a movement up along the demand curve as shown by the arrow that points upward.

When the exchange rate falls, other things remaining the same, the quantity of pounds demanded increases – there is a movement down along the demand curve as shown by the arrow that points downward.

Changes in the Demand for Pounds

A change in any influence on the number of pounds that people plan to buy in the foreign exchange market other than the exchange rate brings a change in the demand for pounds. And a change in the demand for pounds brings a shift in the demand curve for pounds as Figure 34.5 illustrates. The forces that change the demand for pounds are:

◆ The interest rate in the United Kingdom and other countries
◆ The expected future exchange rate

Figure 34.4

The Demand for Pounds

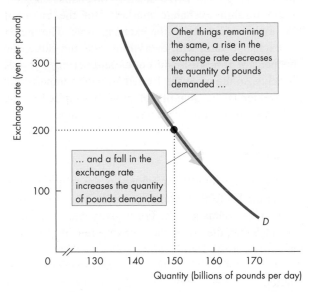

The quantity of pounds that people plan to buy depends on the exchange rate. Other things remaining the same, if the exchange rate rises, the quantity of pounds demanded decreases and there is a movement up along the demand curve for pounds. If the exchange rate falls, the quantity of pounds demanded increases and there is a movement down along the demand curve for pounds.

Figure 34.5

Changes in the Demand for Pounds

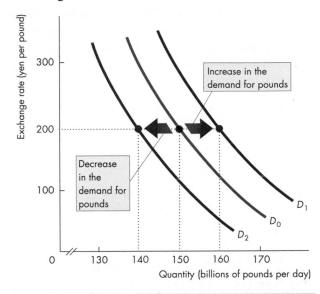

A change in any influence on the quantity of pounds that people plan to buy, other than the exchange rate, brings a change in the demand for pounds. The demand for pounds increases if the UK interest rate differential increases or the expected future exchange rate rises. The demand for pounds decreases if the UK interest rate differential decreases or the expected future exchange rate falls.

The Interest Rate in the United Kingdom and Other Countries

People and businesses buy financial assets to make a return. The higher the interest rate that people can make on UK assets compared with foreign assets, the more UK assets they buy. What matters is not the level of UK interest rates, but the UK interest rate minus the foreign interest rate, a gap that is called the **UK interest rate differential**.

If the UK interest rate rises and the foreign interest rate remains constant, the UK interest rate differential increases. The larger the UK interest rate differential, the greater is the demand for UK assets and the greater is the demand for pounds on the foreign exchange market.

The Expected Future Exchange Rate

Other things remaining the same, the higher the expected future exchange rate, the greater is the demand for pounds. To see why, suppose you are Toyota's finance manager. The exchange rate is 200 yen per pound, and you think that by the end of the month, it

will be 240 yen per pound. You spend 200,000 yen today and buy £1,000. At the end of the month, the pound is 240 yen, as you predicted it would be, and you sell the £1,000. You get 240,000 yen. You've made a profit of 40,000 yen.

The higher the expected future exchange rate, other things remaining the same, the greater is the expected profit and so the greater is the demand for pounds.

Figure 34.5 summarizes the above discussion of the influences on the demand for pounds. A rise in the UK interest rate differential or a rise in the expected future exchange rate increases the demand for pounds and shifts the demand curve rightward from D_0 to D_1. A fall in the UK interest rate differential or a fall in the expected future exchange rate decreases the demand for pounds and shifts the demand curve leftward from D_0 to D_2.

Policy decisions of central banks determine the UK interest rate differential. But a large number of factors influence the expected future exchange rate. We'll review those factors after we've studied the supply side and equilibrium in the foreign exchange market.

The Supply of Pounds in the Foreign Exchange Market

The quantity of pounds supplied in the foreign exchange market is the amount that traders plan to sell during a given time period at a given exchange rate. This quantity depends on the same three main factors that influence the demand for pounds:

1 The exchange rate
2 The interest rate in the United Kingdom and other countries
3 The expected future exchange rate

Let's look first at the relationship between the quantity of pounds supplied in the foreign exchange market and the exchange rate.

The Law of Supply of Foreign Exchange

People in the United Kingdom supply pounds in the foreign exchange market when they buy other currencies. And they buy other currencies so that they can buy foreign-made goods and services (UK imports). They also supply pounds and buy foreign currencies so that they can buy foreign assets such as bonds, shares, businesses and property abroad. The law of supply applies to pounds just as it does to anything else that people plan to sell.

Other things remaining the same, the higher the exchange rate, the greater is the quantity of pounds supplied in the foreign exchange market. For example, if the price of the pound rises from 200 yen to 240 yen and nothing else changes, the quantity of pounds that people plan to sell in the foreign exchange market increases. Why does the exchange rate influence the quantity of pounds supplied?

There are two reasons, and they parallel the two reasons on the demand side of the market:

◆ Imports effect
◆ Expected profit effect

Imports Effect

The imports effect is a mirror image of the exports effect on the demand side of the foreign exchange market. The larger the value of UK imports, the larger is the quantity of foreign currency demanded to pay for

these imports. And when people buy foreign currency, they supply pounds. So the larger the value of UK imports, the greater is the quantity of pounds supplied in the foreign exchange market. But the value of UK imports depends on the exchange rate. The higher the exchange rate, with everything else the same, the cheaper are foreign-made goods and services to UK residents, so the more the United Kingdom imports and the greater is the quantity of pounds supplied in the foreign exchange market to pay for these imports.

Expected Profit Effect

The expected profit effect influences the supply side of the market for foreign exchange for the same reasons as those on the demand side. For a given expected future exchange rate, the higher the exchange rate the greater is the expected loss from holding pounds so the greater is the quantity of pounds supplied in the foreign exchange market.

For the two reasons we've just reviewed, other things remaining the same, when the foreign exchange rate rises, the quantity of pounds supplied increases and when the foreign exchange rate falls, the quantity of pounds supplied decreases.

Figure 34.6 shows the supply curve of pounds in the foreign exchange market. A change in the exchange rate brings a movement along the supply curve as shown by the arrows on supply curve S.

Changes in the Supply of Pounds

A change in any influence on the amount of pounds that people plan to sell in the foreign exchange market other than the exchange rate brings a change in the supply of pounds and a shift in the supply curve of pounds. Supply either increases or decreases. These other influences parallel the other influences on demand but have exactly the opposite effects. These influences are:

◆ The interest rate in the United Kingdom and other countries
◆ The expected future exchange rate

The Interest Rate in the United Kingdom and Other Countries

The larger the UK interest rate differential, the smaller is the demand for foreign assets and the smaller is the supply of pounds on the foreign exchange market.

Figure 34.6

The Supply of Pounds

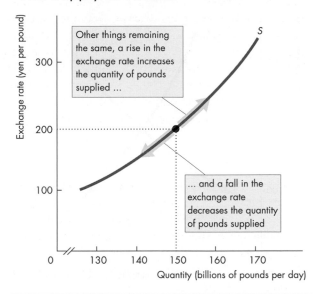

The quantity of pounds that people plan to sell depends on the exchange rate. Other things remaining the same, if the exchange rate rises, the quantity of pounds supplied increases and there is a movement up along the supply curve of pounds. If the exchange rate falls, the quantity of pounds supplied decreases and there is a movement down along the supply curve for pounds.

Figure 34.7

Changes in the Supply of Pounds

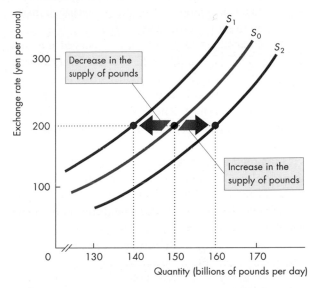

A change in any influence on the quantity of pounds that people plan to sell, other than the exchange rate, brings a change in the supply of pounds. The supply of pounds increases if the UK interest rate differential decreases or the expected future exchange rate falls. The supply of pounds decreases if the UK interest rate differential increases or the expected future exchange rate rises.

The Expected Future Exchange Rate

Other things remaining the same, the higher the expected future exchange rate, the smaller is the supply of pounds. To see why, suppose the pound is trading at 200 yen per pound today and you think that by the end of the month, the pound will be 240 yen per pound. You were planning on selling pounds today, but you decide to hold off and wait until the end of the month. If you supply pounds today, you get only 200 yen per pounds. But at the end of the month, if the rate is 240 yen per pound as you predict, you'll get 240 yen for each pound you supply. You'll make a profit of 20 per cent if you wait.

So the higher the expected future exchange rate, other things remaining the same, the smaller is the expected profit from selling pounds today and the smaller is the supply of pounds today.

Figure 34.7 summarizes the above discussion of the influences on the supply of pounds. A rise in the UK interest rate differential or a rise in the expected future exchange rate decreases the supply of pounds and shifts the supply curve leftward from S_0 to S_1.

A fall in the UK interest rate differential or a fall in the expected future exchange rate increases the supply of pounds and shifts the supply curve rightward from S_0 to S_2.

Market Equilibrium

You've now seen what determines demand and supply in the foreign exchange market and what makes demand and supply change. Our next task is to see how the exchange rate is determined.

Equilibrium in the market for pounds depends on currency traders' demand for pounds and the supply of pounds that we've just examined. It also depends on whether and how the Bank of England intervenes in the foreign exchange market. There are three possible cases to consider:

1   Flexible exchange rate

2   Fixed exchange rate

3   Managed exchange rate

A **flexible exchange rate** is one that is determined by market forces in the absence of central bank intervention. Under a flexible exchange rate, the Bank of England takes no actions in the foreign exchange market (other than to set the UK interest rate).

A **fixed exchange rate** is one that is pegged at a value determined by the central bank. Under a fixed exchange rate, the Bank of England announces that the pound is going to be kept close to a specified price in terms of some other currency. The Bank then buys or sells pounds in the foreign exchange market to maintain the declared value.

A **managed exchange rate** is one that is influenced by the central bank's transactions to smooth out excessive fluctuations.

Between 1945 and 1971, the pound (like most currencies) had a fixed exchange rate. Since the early 1970s, the exchange rate of most currencies has been flexible, with occasional intervention to manage fluctuations in the exchange rate. We'll first see how a flexible exchange rate is determined.

Flexible Exchange Rate Equilibrium

Figure 34.8 shows how demand and supply in the foreign exchange market determine the exchange rate. The demand curve is *D*, and the supply curve is *S*. As in all the other markets you've studied, the price (the exchange rate) acts as a regulator. If the exchange rate is too high, there is a surplus – the quantity supplied exceeds the quantity demanded. In Figure 34.8, if the exchange rate is 300 yen per pound, there is a surplus of pounds. If the exchange rate is too low, there is a shortage – the quantity supplied is less than the quantity demanded. In Figure 34.8, if the exchange rate is 100 yen per pound, there is a shortage of pounds.

At the equilibrium exchange rate, there is neither a shortage nor a surplus. The quantity supplied equals the quantity demanded. In Figure 34.8, the equilibrium exchange rate is 200 yen per pound and the equilibrium quantity is £150 billion a day.

The forces of supply and demand relentlessly pull the foreign exchange market to its equilibrium. Foreign exchange dealers are constantly looking for the best price they can get. If they are selling, they want the highest price available. If they are buying, they want the lowest price available. Information flows from dealer to dealer through the worldwide computer network and the price adjusts second by second to keep buying plans and selling plans in balance. That is, the exchange rate adjusts second by second to keep the market at its equilibrium.

Equilibrium Exchange Rate

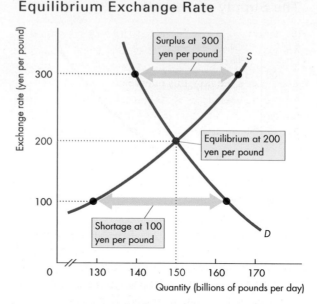

The demand curve for pounds is *D* and the supply curve is *S*. If the exchange rate is 300 yen per pound, there is a surplus of pounds and the exchange rate falls. If the exchange rate is 100 yen per pound, there is a shortage of pounds and the exchange rate rises. If the exchange rate is 200 yen per pound, there is neither a shortage nor a surplus of pounds and the exchange rate remains constant. The market is in equilibrium.

If the demand for pounds increases and the supply of pounds does not change, the exchange rate rises. If the demand for pounds decreases and the supply of pounds does not change, the exchange rate falls. Similarly, if the supply of pounds decreases and the demand for pounds does not change, the exchange rate rises. If the supply of pounds increases and the demand for pounds does not change, the exchange rate falls. These predictions about the effects of changes in demand and supply are exactly the same as those for any other market.

The demand side and supply side of the foreign exchange market have two common influences – the expected future exchange rate and the UK interest rate differential. A change in either of these factors changes *both* demand and supply and in *opposite* directions. So if the pound is expected to appreciate, the demand for pounds increases, the supply of pounds decreases and the pound does appreciate. Similarly, if the pound is expected to depreciate, the demand for pounds decreases, the supply of pounds increases and the pound does depreciate.

Intervention in the Foreign Exchange Market

Fluctuations in the exchange rate that arise from fluctuating expectations are one reason that some economists favour central bank intervention in the foreign exchange market. Let's see how this intervention works.

The Bank of England cannot avoid influencing the exchange rate because it sets the UK interest rate, which influences both demand and supply in the foreign exchange market. A rise in the UK interest rate, other interest rates remaining the same, increases the demand for pounds, decreases the supply of pounds and increases the exchange rate. A fall in the UK interest rate has the opposite effects.

But the Bank of England can intervene directly in the foreign exchange market either to fix the exchange rate or to smooth out exchange rate fluctuations.

Suppose the Bank of England wants the exchange rate to be fixed at 200 yen per pound. If the exchange rate rises above 200 yen, the Bank sells pounds. If the exchange rate falls below 200 yen, the Bank buys pounds. By these actions, the Bank keeps the exchange rate close to its target rate of 200 yen per pound.

Figure 34.9 shows this intervention in the foreign exchange market. The Bank of England wants to fix the pound at 200 yen per pound and takes actions to achieve that outcome.

Suppose that the demand for pounds is D_0 and the supply of pounds is S_0. The equilibrium flexible exchange rate is 180 yen per pound. At 200 yen per pound, £145 billion are demanded and £155 billion are supplied. The Bank of England must take the surplus of £10 billion off the market. The Bank uses its foreign currency reserves to buy £10 billion pounds. The Bank's action prevents the exchange rate from falling and keeps the exchange rate at its target.

Now suppose that the demand for pounds is D_1 and the supply of pounds is S_1. The equilibrium flexible exchange rate is 220 yen per pound. At 200 yen per pound, £155 billion are demanded and £145 billion are supplied. The Bank of England must now provide enough pounds to satisfy the shortage of £10 billion. The Bank sells £10 billion pounds in exchange for yen (or another currency). The Bank's action now prevents the exchange rate from rising above its target.

If the demand fluctuates between D_0 and D_1, the Bank can repeatedly intervene in the foreign exchange market. Sometimes the Bank buys and sometimes it sells, but on average, it neither buys nor sells.

But suppose that demand and supply change permanently to D_0 and S_0. In these circumstances, the Bank

Figure 34.9

Foreign Exchange Market Intervention

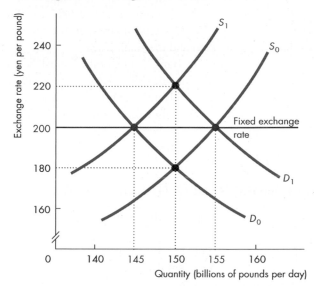

The Bank of England fixes the exchange rate at 200 yen per pound. When the demand for pounds is D_0, the supply of pounds is S_0, and the equilibrium flexible exchange rate is 180 yen per pound. At 200 yen per pound, there is a surplus of pounds, which the Bank must buy by selling foreign currency reserves. When the demand for pounds is D_1, the supply of pounds is S_1, and the equilibrium flexible exchange rate is 220 yen per pound. At 200 yen per pound, there is a shortage of pounds, which the Bank must provide by buying foreign currency.

cannot maintain the exchange rate at 200 yen per pound for long. To do so, the Bank would have to use its foreign currency reserves to buy pounds *every* day. So the Bank's foreign currency reserves fall and eventually it would run out of reserves and have to abandon its attempt to fix the exchange rate.

Knowing that this outcome is inevitable, traders expect the pound to depreciate, so the demand decreases to less than D_0 and the supply increases to more than S_0, making the quantity of reserves that the Bank loses every day even larger.

Alternatively, suppose that demand and supply change permanently to D_1 and S_1. In this situation, the Bank must *sell* pounds *every* day and buy foreign currency to keep the exchange rate at 200 yen per pound.

Now, traders expect the pound to appreciate, so the demand for pounds increases to more than D_1 and supply decreases to less than S_1, making the quantity of reserves that the Bank acquires every day even larger.

While there is no physical limit to the upside change in reserves, holding foreign currency becomes dangerous for the Bank. At some point, the pound does appreciate, which means that the foreign currency held by the Bank depreciates. Traders (speculators) in the foreign exchange market gain and the Bank loses.

In the long run, the Bank's intervention must be to reinforce the equilibrium flexible exchange rate rather than to try to achieve a different long-run outcome.

Reading Between the Lines on pp. 788–789 looks at the challenge faced by the People's Bank of China as it tried to hold the value of its currency fixed in 2004.

Exchange Rate in the Long Run

We've seen that changes in the expected future exchange rate influence the current actual exchange rate. But what determines the expected future exchange rate? The answer is the fundamental forces that determine the value of money. They are:

◆ Purchasing power parity

◆ Interest rate parity

Purchasing Power Parity

Suppose the price of a pair of Levi jeans is £20 in London and $36 in New York. If the exchange rate is $1.80 per pound, the two monies have the same value. You can buy the jeans in London or New York for either £20 or $36 and it costs you the same in both places and monies.

This situation is called **purchasing power parity**, which means *equal value of money*. If purchasing power parity does not prevail, powerful forces go to work. To understand these forces, suppose that Levis cost £30 in London and $36 in New York and the exchange rate is still $1.80 per pound. The US dollar in New York now buys more than the pound in London.

You can spend £20 to buy $36 on the foreign exchange market and then buy a pair of Levis in New York, or you can buy a pair of Levis for £30 in London. If all (or most) prices are higher in pounds in the United Kingdom than in dollars in the United States, then people will sell pounds on the foreign exchange market and the value of the pound will fall.

Expecting the pound to fall, the demand for pounds decreases, the supply of pounds increases and the exchange rate falls. When the exchange rate has fallen to $1.20 per pound, purchasing power parity is restored. A pair of Levis now costs $36 in either London or New York in both pounds and US dollars.

Similarly, if Levis costs £10 in London and $36 in New York with an exchange rate of $1.80 per pound, the pound buys more in London than in New York. People will generally expect that the value of the pound will rise. The demand for pounds will increase, the supply of pounds will decrease and the exchange rate will rise. When the exchange rate has risen to $3.60 per pound, purchasing power parity is restored. Again a pair of Levis costs $36 in either London or New York in both pounds and US dollars.

Ultimately, the value of money is determined by the price level, which in turn is determined by aggregate supply and aggregate demand (see Chapter 22, pp. 488–489). So the deeper forces that influence the exchange rate have tentacles that spread throughout the economy. If prices in the United Kingdom rise faster than those in other countries, the pound depreciates. And if prices rise more slowly in the United Kingdom than in other countries, the pound appreciates.

Interest Rate Parity

Suppose a bank deposit in pounds in London earns 5 per cent a year and a US dollar bank deposit in New York earns 3 per cent a year. In this situation, why does anyone deposit money in New York? Why doesn't all the money flow to London? The answer is because of exchange rate expectations. Suppose people expect the pound to depreciate by 2 per cent a year. This 2 per cent depreciation must be subtracted from the 5 per cent interest to obtain the net return of 3 per cent a year that an American can earn by depositing funds in London. The two returns are equal. This situation is one of **interest rate parity**, which means *equal rates of return*.

Adjusted for risk, interest rate parity always prevails. Funds move to get the highest return available. If for a few seconds a higher return is available in London than in New York, the demand for pounds increases and the pound appreciates until interest rate parity is restored.

Review Quiz

1 How is the exchange rate determined?
2 How can the Bank of England influence the foreign exchange market?
3 How do changes in the expected future exchange rate influence the actual exchange rate in the flexible exchange rate system?
4 What is purchasing power parity and how does it influence exchange rate expectations?

European Monetary Union

On 1 January 1999, 11 countries formed a European Monetary Union (EMU) and irrevocably fixed the values of their currencies against the euro. Greece joined on 1 January 2001. Table 34.3 shows the exchange rates of national currencies for the 12 participating countries. As you know, membership of the EMU is a highly charged and controversial issue. Let's review the benefits and costs of the euro.

The Benefits of the Euro

Four benefits of a single currency in Europe are:

◆ Transparency and competition improve

◆ Transactions costs decrease

◆ Foreign exchange risk eliminated

◆ Real interest rates fall

Transparency and Competition Improve

A single currency provides a single unit of account so that prices are easily compared across the entire Eurozone. A country might gain a competitive advantage by becoming more efficient, but it cannot gain an advantage by artificially lowering the prices of its exports through a depreciation of its currency.

Table 34.3

Euro Conversion Rates

Country	Currency unit	Units per euro
Austria	schilling	13.7603
Belgium	franc	40.3399
Finland	markka	5.94573
France	franc	6.55957
Germany	deutschmark	1.95583
Greece	drachma	340.750
Ireland	pound	0.787564
Italy	lira	1936.27
Luxembourg	franc	40.3399
Netherlands	guilder	2.20371
Portugal	escudo	200.482
Spain	peseta	166.386

Source: ECB

Transactions Costs Decrease

A single currency eliminates foreign exchange transactions costs – the costs of exchanging pesetas for francs at a bank or travel agent, such as commission charges or the margin between the buy and sell exchange rates we see posted in banks and currency exchanges. The removal of these costs benefits the consumer, who knows that a euro in France buys the same as a euro in Germany.

The total benefit from eliminating the transactions costs of currency exchange has been estimated at 0.3 to 0.4 per cent of EU GDP a year.[1] For a country with an advanced banking system as in the United Kingdom, the EU Commission estimates that the benefits would be 0.1 per cent of GDP a year.

Foreign Exchange Risk Eliminated

With a single currency, exporters and importers no longer face foreign exchange risk. For example, Alpine Gardens, an Austrian garden company, has ordered a consignment of garden gnomes to be supplied by Britannia Gnomes Ltd., a Gloucester company, in three months' time. The contract and the price are set today, but payment will take place in three months' time. Alpine Gardens has to pay £50,000 in three months' time. To protect itself against an adverse change in the exchange rate, it pays a premium to insure against an exchange rate change.[2]

The reduction in exchange rate risk improves trade between EU countries. Cacharel, the French clothing designer can source its material from Rome or from Paris. On a strict exchange rate comparison, the Italian product is cheaper. But in the past the exchange rate between the French franc and Italian lira has fluctuated unpredictably. Cacharel doesn't want to be tied into a contract with the Italian supplier if the price in francs fluctuates with the exchange rate. They source the material from the more expensive French supplier because they are guaranteed a price but they have to charge their customers the higher price. A single currency eliminates this exchange rate risk. Cacharel can source its material from Rome, pay a lower price and pass the benefits of the lower price on to their customers. The lower price

---

[1] Commission of the European Communities, 'One Market, One Money: An Evaluation of the Potential Benefits and Costs of Forming an Economic and Monetary Union', 1990, *European Economy*, 44, Brussels.

[2] Alpine Gardens buys pounds in the forward market, paying a commission to the foreign currency operator which ensures the delivery of £50,000 in three months' time at an exchange rate specified today irrespective of what the exchange rate will be in three months' time.

increases the quantity demanded of Cacharel clothing, which in turn increases the orders from Rome.

The removal of exchange risk means that many large companies are able to reduce their administration and financial management costs. They also no longer need to diversify their operations across boundaries and can consolidate them on one location.

Real Interest Rates Fall

You know that the nominal interest rate equals the real interest rate plus the expected inflation rate. In long-term bond markets, the nominal interest rate is the long-term real interest rate plus the expected long-term inflation rate plus a premium for risk. The risk premium arises from uncertainty about default and future inflation.

If the ECB delivers low inflation and develops a reputation for low inflation, its low inflation targets become credible and inflation uncertainty is reduced. A single currency and a common monetary policy governed by the ECB lead to a convergence of inflation rates and interest rates within the Eurozone. With inflation and interest rates in the Eurozone at common low levels, the risk premium and the long-term interest rate will be lower and investment greater.

Let's now look at some of the costs of the euro.

The Economic Costs of the Euro

Two costs of a single currency in Europe are:

◆ Shocks that need national monetary policy
◆ Loss of sovereignty

Shocks that Need National Monetary Policy

Many, perhaps most economic shocks that call for a monetary policy response are country specific shocks or shocks that affect different countries in different ways.

For example, the dismantling of the Berlin Wall had a major impact on the German economy but barely any effect on the economies of Ireland and Portugal. Also, the shock had different effects on the two parts of Germany. East German workers were less productive and earned lower wage rates than their West German counterparts. Productivity and earnings differences induced a massive reallocation and relocation of jobs and people. A common monetary policy might stimulate the economy in the East and bring inflation to the West or keep inflation in check in the West and bring prolonged recession in the East.

An oil price increase is an example of a common shock that has different effects on different economies. In Germany, an oil importer, the price rise imparts a negative aggregate supply shock and creates a current account deficit. In the United Kingdom, an oil exporter, the price rise imparts a positive supply shock and creates a current account surplus. A common monetary policy might stimulate economic activity in Germany and bring inflation to the United Kingdom or hold inflation in check in the United Kingdom and bring stagnation in Germany.

A common monetary policy is inadequate to deal with the results of country specific shocks.

Loss of Sovereignty

In principle, fiscal policy might be used to pursue national economic policy goals. But in the case of the EMU, the Stability and Growth Pact places limits on the use of fiscal policy and replaces national freedom of action with a common regional policy.

Common regional policy enables transfers to be made from Germany and France to Italy and Spain. But a political consensus must be found to sustain such transfers. In effect, a single currency implies a political union. A loss of monetary sovereignty implies a loss of political sovereignty.

The Optimum Currency Area

When there are benefits and costs, they must be weighed against each other and an optimum outcome found. Imagine a world in which the Welsh leek and Scottish thistle exchange for each other and for the English pound at exchange rates that fluctuate every day. The United Kingdom is almost certainly better off using one currency rather than three. Is Europe better off using the euro than 12 national currencies? And why stop at Europe! Would the world be better off with one currency rather than its 200-plus currencies?

To answer these questions, we need the concept of an **optimal currency area**, a geographical area that is better served with a single currency than with several currencies. Robert Mundell, an economics professor at Columbia University in New York City won the Nobel Prize in 1999 for his work on this topic. Mundell claimed that the key factor required for an optimal currency area is free labour mobility either across regions or between jobs.

On this criterion, Scotland, Wales and England are better off with a single currency that they would be with

Box 34.1
The Economic Effects of Currency Unions

Jeffrey Frankel of Harvard University and David Rose, of the University of California, Berkeley have examined the change in international trade and real GDP in 200 countries or territories that have formed or joined currency unions. Their findings are remarkable.

They find that belonging to a currency union *triples* international trade with other members of the currency union. They also find that trade does not get diverted from other areas. Instead, total trade increases. They also find strong evidence that increased international trade brings a large increase in income. Finally, they find that the gains in income come entirely from trade expansion and not from factors such improved central bank credibility or monetary policy.

More speculatively, Frankel and Rose apply their results to hypothetical cases of countries that are currently outside currency unions joining a currency union. Of special interest are their findings about European countries joining the Eurozone. Figure 1 shows the numbers. In the United Kingdom, which falls in the middle of the pack, trade with other Eurozone members would expand by 60 per cent of real GDP and real GDP itself would expand by 20 per cent!

Figure 1

Estimated Effects of Joining the Euro

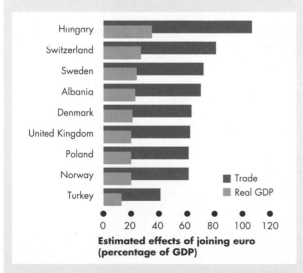

Estimated effects of joining euro (percentage of GDP)

Source: Frankel, Jeffery A and Rose, Andrew, 'An Estimate of the Effect of Common Currencies on Trade and Income', *Quarterly Journal of Economics*, 117 Issue 2, May 2002.

an English pound a Welsh leek and a Scottish thistle. No cultural or language barriers hamper the movement of labour across the Severn bridge. If a factory closes down in Merseyside and another opens in Clwyd, workers from Merseyside can travel to North Wales to seek employment.

Lack of regional mobility is not a problem if there is mobility between jobs. For example, if Volkswagen closes a Polo production plant in Pamplona, Spain and opens a new plant in Wolfsburg, Germany, we would not expect former Spanish car workers to migrate to Germany – although by current EU labour laws there is nothing stopping them from doing just that. If jobless car workers in Pamplona can easily retrain and find a new job in Spain, the absence of regional labour mobility doesn't weaken the case for a single currency.

A second criterion for an optimal currency area is that regions within the area face common economic shocks. It is claimed by some economists that economies with similar industrial structures and extensive trade with each other satisfy this criterion. And it is further claimed that the Eurozone countries have sufficiently similar industrial structures and sufficiently extensive trade links to meet this criterion.

Unlike the country-specific shocks that we've just considered, common shocks can be dealt with by a common monetary policy run by a common central bank. For example, if a rise in the price of oil affected all the countries in a monetary union in the same way, the central bank could react in a way that is appropriate for all the countries in the union.

Even if a country does not share a similar industrial structure and have extensive trade links with its neighbours, some supporters of the Eurozone argue that joining a single currency area will bring convergence to a common industrial structure and stimulate trade flows. For example, each major Canadian city is closer to a major US city than it is to other Canadian cities. But there is significantly more trade among Canadian cities (using one currency) than between the closer Canadian and US cities (using two currencies).

Review Quiz

1   What is the EMU?
2   What are the benefits of a single currency for Europe?
3   What are the costs of a single currency for Europe?
4   What is an optimal currency area?

Reading Between the Lines

Currency Speculation in China?

The Financial Times, 15 April 2004

China's currency reserves swell with hot money

James Kynge

China faces growing pressure from speculators to revalue the renminbi against the U.S. dollar, figures showed yesterday, as premier Wen Jiabao rebuffed a call by U.S. vice-president Dick Cheney to let markets set the exchange rate.

"Hot money", moved into China by speculators and circumventing Beijing's closed capital account, boosted the country's foreign exchange reserves to a record $439.8bn (euro 368bn, £246bn) at the end of March, up $36.5bn since the end of 2003.

The increase in foreign currency reserves which exacerbates domestic inflation by adding to the money supply, came despite a trade deficit of $8.4bn during the first quarter.

The figures show that although the renminbi may not be undervalued from a trade perspective, China's battle now is with speculators who think it will sooner or later have to allow an appreciation.

The currency is virtually pegged at about Rmb8.28 to the U.S. dollar, and although Beijing has said it plans to widen the band within which the currency fluctuates, it has not said when or how.

New figures show setbacks for China's attempts to impose discipline on its banks. Money supply, gauged by the broad M2 measure, was up 19.1 per cent at the end of March and loan growth rose by an annualised 21 per cent – far higher than the contraction of 13 per cent the central bank is aiming for in 2004. Even wholly owned state banks such as the Bank of China showed first-quarter loan growth up nearly 10 per cent, a spokesman said.

But the People's Bank of China remains determined to maintain a stable value for the renminbi in terms of exchange rate and domestic interest rates, officials said.

The Essence of the Story

◆ China has fixed the exchange rate of its currency, the renminbi, at 8.28 renminbi per US dollar.

◆ The People's Bank of China, China's central bank, says it is determined to maintain a stable exchange rate.

◆ China's foreign currency reserves and money supply are increasing rapidly.

◆ China is facing growing pressure from speculators to raise the value of the renminbi.

Economic Analysis

◆ The People's Bank of China pegs the value of the renminbi at 8.28 renminbi per US dollar (or 12 US cents per renminbi).

◆ If the renminbi had a flexible exchange rate, the currency would appreciate. To prevent appreciation, the People's Bank of China intervenes in the foreign exchange market.

◆ Figure 1 shows the market for China's currency. The demand for renminbi is D, the supply is S and with a flexible exchange rate the equilibrium exchange rate would be E, which is greater than 12 US cents per renminbi.

◆ To keep the exchange rate at 12 US cents, the People's Bank of China supplies renminbi and buys US dollars.

◆ The People's Bank is accumulating dollars at a rapid rate – $36.5 billion in three months or about $400 million a *day*!

◆ Rapid growth in China's foreign currency reserves brings rapid growth of the monetary base, which leads to rapid money growth and inflation.

◆ Because China's real GDP grows rapidly, it can permit a rapid money growth rate without inflation. It is the excess money growth rate – money growth minus real GDP growth – that brings inflation.

◆ Figure 2 shows China's money growth rate minus real GDP growth and inflation rate since January 2003. The inflation rate is rising towards around 10 per cent per year.

◆ Speculators are betting the renminbi will appreciate. And this action is increasing the demand for renminbi and making the People's Bank's task even harder.

◆ China's current account surplus is not the cause of the renminbi being undervalued. It is a consequence of the undervaluation. Any current account balance is consistent with a fixed exchange rate provided the capital account and not a change in reserves matches it.

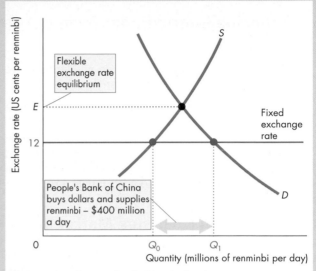

Figure 1 People's Bank of China in foreign exchange market

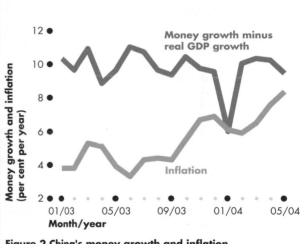

Figure 2 China's money growth and inflation

◆ The People's Bank of China faces a dilemma. Will it maintain the current exchange rate and permit faster inflation or will it allow the renminbi to appreciate?

Summary

Key Points

Financing International Trade
(pp. 772–776)

◆ International trade, borrowing and lending are financed using foreign currency.

◆ A country's balance of payments accounts record its international transactions.

◆ The balance of payments has three accounts: the current account, the capital account, and changes in reserve assets. The sum of the balances in these three accounts is zero.

The Foreign Exchange Market and the Exchange Rate (pp. 777–784)

◆ Foreign currency is obtained in exchange for domestic currency in the foreign exchange market.

◆ The lower the exchange rate, the greater is the quantity of pounds demanded in the foreign exchange market. A change in the exchange rate brings a movement along the demand curve for pounds.

◆ Changes in the expected future exchange rate and the UK interest rate differential change the demand for pounds and shift the demand curve.

◆ The lower the exchange rate, the smaller is the quantity of pounds supplied to the foreign exchange market. A change in the exchange rate brings a movement along the supply curve of pounds.

◆ Changes in the expected future exchange rate and the UK interest rate differential change the supply of pounds and shift the supply curve.

◆ The exchange rate of the pound depends on demand and supply in the foreign exchange market and on whether and how the Bank of England intervenes in the market.

◆ The exchange rate might be fixed or managed by the Bank of England or permitted to be flexible.

◆ Fluctuations in a flexible exchange rate occur because the fluctuations in demand for and supply of pounds are not independent.

◆ To fix the exchange rate, the Bank of England would intervene to remove any excess demand or supply and permit its holdings of foreign exchange reserves to fluctuate.

The European Monetary Union
(pp. 785–787)

◆ The EMU came into being on 1 January 1999 with 11 countries of the European Union joining. Greece joined on 1 January 2001.

◆ The benefits of a single currency are greater competition, lower transactions costs, removal of exchange risk and a lower real interest rate.

◆ The costs of a single currency are the loss of the ability to respond to a national economic shock and the loss of sovereignty.

◆ An optimal currency area is one for which the benefits outweigh the costs.

Key Figures and Table

Key Terms

Problems

*1 Silecon, whose currency is the grain, conducted the following transactions in 2003:

Item	Billions of grains
Imports of goods and services	350
Exports of goods and services	500
Borrowing from the rest of the world	60
Lending to the rest of the world	200
Change in reserve assets	10

a Set out the three balance of payments accounts for Silecon.

b Does the Silecon central bank intervene in the foreign exchange market?

2 Spin, whose currency is the wheel, conducted the following transactions in 2003:

Item	Billions of wheels
Imports of goods and services	100
Exports of goods and services	120
Borrowing from the rest of the would	4
Lending to the rest of the world	24
Change in reserve assets	0

a Set out the three balance of payments accounts for Spin.

b Does the Spin central bank intervene in the foreign exchange market?

*3 The figure below shows the flows of income and expenditure in Dream Land in 2002. The amounts are in millions of euros. GDP in Dream Land is €120 million.

a Calculate Dream Land's net exports.

b Calculate saving in Dream Land.

c How is Dream Land's investment financed?

4 The figure below shows the flows of income and expenditure in Dream Land in 2003. The amounts are in millions of euros. Dream Land's GDP has increased to €130 million but all the other items whose values are provided in the figure remain the same as they were in 2002.

a Calculate Dream Land's net exports in 2003.

b Calculate savings in Dream Land in 2003.

c How is Dream Land's investment financed?

*5 The following tables tell you about Ecflex, whose currency is the band.

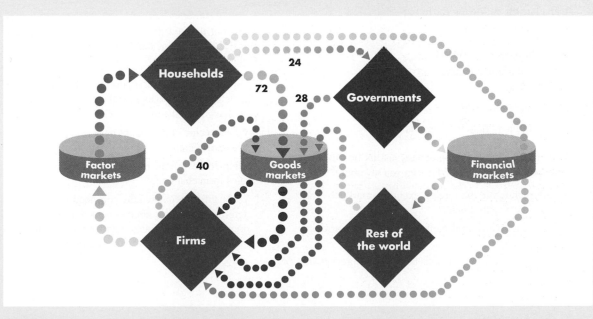

---

*Solutions to odd-numbered problems are available on *Parkin Interactive*.

Item	Billions of bands
GDP	100
Consumption expenditure	60
Government expenditures on goods and services	24
Investment	22
Exports of goods and services	20
Government budget deficit	4

Calculate the following for Ecflex:

a Imports of goods and services

b Current account balance

c Capital account balance

d Net taxes

e Private sector surplus

6 The following table tells you about Ecfix, whose currency is the rock:

Item	Billions of rocks
GDP	200
Consumption expenditure	120
Government expenditures on goods and services	50
Investment	50
Exports of goods and services	40
Saving	45

Calculate the following for Ecfix:

a Imports of goods and services

b Current account balance

c Capital account balance

d Net taxes

e Private sector surplus

f Government deficit or surplus

*7 A country's currency appreciates and its holdings of reserve assets increase. What can you say about:

a Intervention in the foreign exchange market by the country's central bank?

b The possible central bank sources of the currency appreciation?

c The possible private actions behind the appreciation?

8 A country's currency depreciates and its holdings of reserves assets decrease. What can you say about:

a Intervention in the foreign exchange market by the country's central bank?

b The possible sources of the depreciation?

c The possible private actions behind depreciation?

Critical Thinking

1 Study *Reading Between the Lines* on pp. 788–789 and then answer the following questions.

a What is the reason for the increase in speculative flows of foreign currency into China?

b What effect will the increase in speculation have on China's foreign currency reserves?

c If left unchecked, what will be the effect of speculation on the money supply in China?

d What remedial policies can the Peoples Bank of China conduct to offset the effect of speculation that it will increase the value of the renminbi?

Web Exercise

Use the link on *Parkin Interactive* to work the following exercise.

1 Get recent data on the exchange rate of the pound against the US dollar, the Japanese yen and the euro. Then:

a Use the demand and supply model of the foreign exchange market to explain the changes (or absence of changes) in the exchange rates.

b What specific events might have changed exchange rate expectations?

c What forces might have prevented the exchange rates from changing?

d What information would you need to be able to determine whether central bank intervention has prevented each exchange rate from changing by as much as it otherwise would have?

Glossary

Above full-employment equilibrium A macroeconomic equilibrium in which real GDP exceeds potential GDP. (p. 490)

Absolute advantage A person has an absolute advantage if that person can produce more goods with a given amount of resources than another person can; a country has an absolute advantage if its output per unit of inputs of all goods is larger than that of another country. (p. 43)

Adverse selection The tendency for people to enter into agreements in which they can use their private information to their own advantage and to the disadvantage of the less-informed party. (p. 185)

Aggregate demand The relationship between the aggregate quantity of real GDP demanded and the price level. (p. 485)

Aggregate hours The total number of hours worked by all the people employed, both full-time and part-time, during a year. (p. 463)

Aggregate planned expenditure The expenditure that households, firms, governments, and foreigners plan to undertake in given circumstances. It is the sum of planned consumption expenditure, planned investment, planned government expenditures on goods and services, and planned exports minus planned imports. (p. 526)

Aggregate production function The relationship between the quantity of real GDP supplied and the quantities of labour and capital and the state of technology. (pp. 480, 685)

Allocative efficiency A situation in which we cannot produce more of any good without giving up some of another good that we value more highly. (p. 37)

Asymmetric information Valuable information is available to one person but is too costly for anyone else to obtain. (p. 185)

Automatic fiscal policy A change in fiscal policy that is triggered by the state of the economy. (p. 562)

Automatic stabilizers Mechanisms that stabilize real GDP without the need for explicit action by the government. (p. 566)

Autonomous expenditure The sum of those components of aggregate planned expenditure that are not influenced by real GDP. (p. 533)

Autonomous taxes Taxes that do not vary with real GDP. (p. 562)

Autonomous tax multiplier The magnification effect of a change in autonomous taxes on equilibrium expenditure and real GDP. (p. 564)

Average cost pricing rule A rule that sets price equal to average total cost. (pp. 267, 314)

Average fixed cost Total fixed cost per unit of output. (p. 208)

Average product The average product of a factor of production equals total product divided by the quantity of the factor employed. (p. 203)

Average total cost Total cost per unit of output. (p. 208)

Average variable cost Total variable cost per unit of output. (p. 208)

Balance of payments accounts A country's record of its international trading and its borrowing and lending. (p. 772)

Balanced budget A government budget in which revenues and outlays are equal. (p. 557)

Balanced budget multiplier The multiplier that arises from a fiscal policy action that changes *both* government expenditures and taxes by the *same* amount so that the government's budget deficit or surplus remains *unchanged*. (p. 565)

Bank A private firm licensed to take deposits and make loans. In the United Kingdom banks are licensed by the Bank of England under the Banking Act of 1987. (p. 585)

Bank of England The central bank of the United Kingdom. (p. 604)

Barriers to entry Legal or natural constraints that protect a firm from competition from potential new entrants. (p. 252)

Barter The direct exchange of one good or service for other goods and services. (p. 582)

Below full-employment equilibrium A macroeconomic equilibrium in which potential GDP exceeds real GDP. (p. 490)

Big trade-off The conflict between equality and efficiency. (pp. 12, 109)

Bilateral monopoly A situation in which there is a single seller (a monopoly) and a single buyer (a monopsony). (p. 393)

Black market An illegal market in which the price exceeds the legally imposed price ceiling. (p. 120)

Budget An annual statement of projected outlays and revenues during the next year together with the laws and regulations that will support those outlays and revenues. (p. 556)

Budget deficit A government's budget balance that is negative – outlays exceed revenues. (p. 557)

Budget line The limits to a household's consumption choices. (p. 160)

Budget surplus A government's budget balance that is positive – revenues exceed outlays. (p. 557)

Business cycle The periodic but irregular up-and-down movement in economic activity. (p. 420)

Capital The tools, instruments, machines, equipment, buildings and other constructions that businesses now use to produce of goods and services. (p. 5)

Capital account A country's record of its international borrowing and lending transactions. (p. 772)

Capital accumulation The growth of capital resources. (p. 38)

Capture theory A theory of regulation that states that the regulations are the interest of producers. (p. 311)

Cartel A group of firms that has entered into a collusive agreement to restrict output so as to increase prices and profits. (p. 285)

Central bank A public authority that provides banking services to governments and commercial banks, supervises and regulates financial institutions and markets, and conducts monetary policy. (p. 604)

Ceteris paribus Other things being equal – all other relevant things remaining the same. (p. 15)

Chained-volume measure A measure of real GDP calculated by expressing the volume of final goods and services produced each year in pounds that are linked back to the value of the pound in a base year. (p. 446)

Change in demand A change in buying plans that occurs when some influence on those plans other than the price of the good changes. It is illustrated by a shift of the demand curve. (p. 56)

Change in reserve assets The net increase or decrease in a country's holdings of foreign currency reserves that comes about from the official financing of the difference between the current account and the capital account. (p. 772)

Change in supply A change in selling plans that occurs when some influence on those plans other than the price of the good changes. It is illustrated by a shift of the supply curve. (p. 61)

Change in the quantity demanded A change in buying plans that occurs when the price of a good changes but all other influences on buying plans remain unchanged. It is illustrated by a movement along the demand curve. (p. 59)

Change in the quantity supplied A change in selling plans that occurs when the price of a good changes but all other influences on selling plans remain unchanged. It is illustrated by a movement along the supply curve. (p. 62)

Classical A macroeconomist who believes that the economy is self-regulating and that it is always at full employment. (p. 496)

Classical dichotomy At full employment, the forces that determine real variables are independent of those that determine nominal variables. (p. 504)

Classical growth theory A theory of economic growth based on the view that real GDP growth is temporary and when real GDP per person rises above the subsistence level, a population explosion eventually brings real GDP per person back to the subsistence level. (p. 689)

Classical model A model of an economy that determines the real variables – real GDP, employment and unemployment, the real wage rate, consumption, saving, investment, and the real interest rate – at full employment. (p. 504)

Coase theorem The proposition that if property rights exist, if only a small number of parties are involved and if transactions costs are low, then private transactions are efficient. (p. 335)

Collusive agreement An agreement between two (or more) producers to restrict output, raise the price and increase profits. (p. 290)

Command system A method of organizing production that uses a managerial hierarchy. (p. 184)

Common Agricultural Policy A price support programme for farmers in the European Union, which acts as a tariff on non-EU agricultural products. (p. 757)

Common resource A resource that is rival and non-excludable. (p. 348)

Comparative advantage A person or country has a comparative advantage in an activity if that person or country can perform the activity at a lower opportunity cost than anyone else or any other country. (pp. 40, 752)

Competitive market A market that has many buyers and many sellers, so no single buyer or seller can influence the price. (p. 54)

Complement A good that is used in conjunction with another good. (p. 57)

Constant returns to scale Features of a firm's technology that lead to constant long-run average cost as output increases. When constant returns to scale are present, the *LRAC* curve is horizontal. (p. 214)

Consumer equilibrium A situation in which a consumer has allocated his or her available income in the way that maximizes his or her utility. (p. 146)

Consumer Prices Index (CPI) A measure of an average of the prices paid by consumers for a fixed "basket" of goods and services. (p. 470)

Consumer surplus The value of a good minus the price paid for it, summed over the quantity bought. (p. 101)

Consumption expenditure The total payment made by households for consumption goods and services. (p. 439)

Consumption function The relationship between consumption expenditure and disposable income, other things remaining the same. (p. 527)

Contestable market A market in which firms can enter and leave so easily that firms in the market face competition from potential entrants. (p. 298)

Contractionary fiscal policy A decrease in government expenditures on goods and services or an increase in net taxes. (p. 569)

Cooperative equilibrium The outcome of a game in which players agree to collude to make and share monopoly profit. (p. 297)

Copyright A government-sanctioned exclusive right granted to the inventor of a good, service or productive process to produce, use and sell the invention for a given number of years. (p. 341)

Cost-push inflation Inflation that results from an initial increase in costs. (p. 657)

Creditor nation A country that has invested more in the rest of the world than other countries have invested in it. (p. 774)

Cross elasticity of demand The responsiveness of the demand for a good to the price of a substitute or complement, other things remaining the same. It is calculated as the percentage change in the quantity demanded of the good divided by the percentage change in the price of the substitute or complement. (p. 85)

Cross-section graph A graph that shows the values of an economic variable for different groups in a population at a point in time. (p. 20)

Crowding in The tendency for expansionary fiscal policy to increase investment. (p. 631)

Crowding out The tendency for expansionary fiscal policy to decrease investment. (p. 631)

Currency The notes and coins that we use today. (p. 583)

Currency appreciation The rise in the value of one currency in terms of another currency. (p. 777)

Currency depreciation The fall in the value of one currency in terms of another currency. (p. 777)

Currency drain An increase in currency held outside banks. (p. 609)

Current account A record of receipts from the sale of goods and services to foreigners, the payments for goods and services bought from foreigners, income and other transfers received from and paid to foreigners. (pp. 429, 772)

Cyclical surplus or deficit The actual surplus or deficit minus the structural surplus or deficit. (p. 567)

Cyclical unemployment The unemployment arising from the slowdown in the pace of economic expansion. (p. 468)

Deadweight loss A measure of allocative inefficiency. It is equal to the decrease in consumer surplus plus producer surplus that results from producing an inefficient level of production. (p. 106)

Debtor nation A country that during its entire history has borrowed more from the rest of the world than it has lent to it. (p. 774)

Deflation A process in which the price level falls – negative inflation. (p. 427)

Demand The relationship between the quantity of a good that consumers plan to buy and the price of the good, with all other influences on buying plans remaining the same. It is described by a demand schedule and illustrated by a demand curve. (p. 55)

Demand curve A curve that shows the relationship between the quantity demanded of a good and its price, when all other influences on consumers' planned purchases remain the same. (p. 56)

Demand for labour The relationship between the quantity of labour demanded and the real wage rate when all other influences on firms' hiring plans remain the same. (p. 506)

Demand for money The relationship between the quantity of real money demanded and the interest rate when all other influences on the amount of money that people wish to hold remain the same. (p. 592)

Demand-pull inflation Inflation that results from an initial increase in aggregate demand. (p. 655)

Deposit multiplier The amount by which an increase in bank reserves is multiplied to calculate the increase in bank deposits. (p. 588)

Depreciation The decrease in the stock of capital that results from wear and tear and obsolescence. (p. 441)

Deregulation The process of removing previously imposed regulations. (p. 311)

Derived demand The demand for a factor of production, which is derived from the demand for the goods and services produced by the factor. (p. 366)

Desired reserve ratio The ratio of reserves to deposits that banks consider as prudent to hold. (p. 587)

Diminishing marginal rate of substitution The general tendency for the marginal rate of substitution to diminish as a consumer moves along an indifference curve, increasing consumption of the good on the x-axis and decreasing consumption of the good on the y-axis. (p. 164)

Diminishing marginal returns The tendency for the marginal product of an additional unit of a factor of production to be less than the marginal product of the previous unit of the factor. (p. 205)

Diminishing marginal utility The decrease in the marginal utility that a consumer gets from a good as the quantity consumed increases. (p. 144)

Direct relationship A relationship between two variables that move in the same direction. (p. 22)

Discounting The conversion of a future amount of money to its present value. (p. 376)

Discouraged worker A person who does not have a job, is available for work and willing to work but who has given up the effort to find work. (p. 425)

Discretionary fiscal policy A policy action that is initiated by the Chancellor of the Exchequer. (p. 562)

Discretionary policy A policy that responds to the state of the economy in a possibly unique way that uses all the information available, including perceived lessons from past "mistakes". (p. 731)

Diseconomies of scale Features of a firm's technology that lead to rising long-run average cost as output increases. (p. 215)

Disposable income Aggregate income minus taxes plus transfer payments. (pp. 487, 526)

Dominant strategy equilibrium A Nash equilibrium in which the best strategy of each player is to cheat (deny) regardless of the strategy of the other player. (p. 296)

Dumping The sale by a foreign firm of exports at a lower price than its cost of production. (p. 761)

Duopoly A market structure in which two producers of a good or service compete. (p. 284)

Dynamic comparative advantage A comparative advantage that a person or country possesses as a result of having specialized in a particular activity and then, as a result of learning-by-doing, becoming the producer with the lowest opportunity cost. (p. 43)

Economic activity rate The state of the labour market is indicated by this, the employment-to-population ratio and the unemployment rate. (p. 461)

Economic depreciation A change in the market value of capital over a given period. (p. 181)

Economic efficiency A situation that occurs when the firm produces a given output at least cost. (p. 183)

Economic growth The expansion of the economy's production possibilities that results from capital accumulation and technological change. (pp. 38, 419)

Economic model A description of some aspect of the economic world that includes only those features of the world that are needed for the purpose at hand. (p. 14)

Economic profit A firm's total revenue minus its opportunity cost. (p. 181)

Economic rent The income received by the owner of a factor of production over and above of the amount required to induce that owner to offer the factor for use. (p. 384)

Economic theory A generalization that summarizes what we think we understand about the economic choices that people make and the performance of industries and entire economies. (p. 14)

Economic welfare A comprehensive measure of the general state of well-being. (p. 448)

Economics The social science that studies the choices that individuals, governments and entire societies make as they cope with scarcity and the incentives that influence and reconcile those choices. (p. 4)

Economies of scale Features of a firm's technology that lead to a falling long-run average cost as output increases. (pp. 195, 214)

Economies of scope Decreases in average total cost that occur when a firm uses specialized resources to produce a range of goods and services. (p. 195)

Efficiency wage A real wage rate that is set above the full-employment equilibrium wage rate and that balances the costs and benefits of this higher wage rate to maximize the firm's profit. (p. 514)

Elastic demand Demand with a price elasticity greater than 1; other things remaining the same, the percentage change in the quantity demanded exceeds the percentage change in price. (p. 81)

Elasticity of supply The responsiveness of the quantity supplied of a good to a change in its price, other things remaining the same. (p. 88)

Employment rate The percentage of people of working age who have jobs. (p. 462)

Entrepreneurship The human resource that organizes labour, land and capital. (p. 6)

Equation of exchange An equation that states that the quantity of money multiplied by the velocity of circulation equals GDP. (p. 660)

Equilibrium expenditure The level of aggregate expenditure that occurs when aggregate *planned* expenditure equals real GDP. (p. 534)

Equilibrium price The price at which the quantity demanded equals the quantity supplied. (p. 64)

Equilibrium quantity The quantity bought and sold at the equilibrium price. (p. 64)

Equity Economic justice or fairness. Equity is also used to mean ownership of a business. (p. 108)

European Central Bank The central bank that conducts the monetary policy of the Eurozone – the members of the European Monetary Union (EMU) that use the euro. (p. 604)

Excess reserves A bank's actual reserves minus its desired reserves. (p. 587)

Excludable A good or services or a resource is excludable if it is possible to prevent someone from enjoying the benefits of it. (p. 348)

Expansion A business cycle phase between a trough and a peak – the phase in which real GDP increases. (p. 420)

Expansionary fiscal policy An increase in government expenditure on goods and services or a decrease in net taxes. (p. 569)

Exports The goods and services that we sell to people in other countries. (pp. 440, 750)

External benefits Benefits that accrue to people other than the buyer of a good. (p. 244)

External costs Costs that are borne by someone other than the producer of a good or service. (p. 244)

External diseconomies Factors outside the control of a firm that raise its costs as the industry output increases. (p. 241)

External economies Factors beyond the control of an individual firm that lower its costs as the industry output increases. (p. 241)

Externality A cost or a benefit that arises from production of a good or service and falls on someone other than the producer or cost or a benefit that arises from consumption of a good or service and falls on someone other than the consumer. (p. 330)

Factors of production The productive resources which businesses use to produce goods and services. (p. 5)

Feedback-rule policy A rule that specifies how policy actions respond to changes in the state of the economy. (p. 731)

Final good An item that is bought by its final user during the specified time period. (p. 438)

Financial innovation The development of new financial products – new ways of borrowing and lending. (p. 591)

Financial intermediary A firm that takes deposits from households and firms and makes loans to other households and firms. (p. 585)

Firm An economic unit that employs factors of production and that organizes them to produce and sell goods and services. (pp. 44, 180)

Fiscal policy The government's attempt to achieve macroeconomic objectives such as full employment, sustained economic growth and price level stability by setting and changing taxes, making transfer payments and purchasing goods and services. (pp. 431, 487)

Five-firm concentration ratio The percentage of total revenue or value of sales in an industry accounted for by the five firms with the largest value of sales. (p. 190)

Fixed exchange rate An exchange rate that is pegged at a value determined by the central bank. (p. 782)

Fixed-rule policy A rule that specifies an action to be pursued independently of the state of the economy. (p. 731)

Flexible exchange rate An exchange rate that is determined by market forces in the absence of central bank intervention. (p. 782)

Flow A quantity per unit of time. (p. 441)

Foreign exchange market The market in which the currency of one country is exchanged for the currency of another. (p. 777)

Foreign exchange rate The price at which one currency exchanges for another. (p. 777)

Free-rider problem The absence of an incentive for people to pay for what they consume. (p. 348)

Frictional unemployment The unemployment that arises from normal labour turnover. (p. 467)

Full employment A situation which occurs when the unemployment rate equals the natural rate of unemployment – when all unemployment is frictional and structural and there is no cyclical unemployment. (p. 468)

Game theory A tool that economists use to analyze strategic behaviour – behaviour that takes into account the expected behaviour of others and the mutual recognition of independence. (p. 288)

GDP The market value of all final goods and services produced in the economy in a given time period – usually a year. (p. 438)

GDP deflator One measure of the price level, which is the average of current-year prices as a percentage of base-year prices. (p. 446)

General Agreement on Tariffs and Trade An international agreement signed in 1947 to reduce the tariffs on international trade. (p. 757)

Gini coefficient A measure of inequality that equals the area between the line of equality and the Lorenz curve as a percentage of the entire area beneath the line of equality. (p. 399)

Goods and services The objects that people value and produce to satisfy wants. (p. 5)

Government budget deficit The deficit that arises when the government spends more than it collects in taxes. (p. 429)

Government budget surplus The surplus that arises when the government collects more in taxes than it spends. (p. 429)

Government debt The total amount of borrowing by the government. It is the sum of past deficits minus the sum of past surpluses minus the receipts from the sale of assets. (p. 559)

Government expenditures Goods and services bought by the government. (p. 440)

Government expenditures multiplier The amount by which a change in government expenditures on goods and services is multiplied to determine the change in equilibrium expenditure that it generates. (p. 562)

Great Depression A decade (1929–39) of high unemployment and stagnant production throughout the world economy. (p. 418)

Gross domestic product (GDP) The market value of all final goods and services produced in the economy in a given time period – usually a year. (p. 438)

Gross investment The amount spent on purchases of new capital and on replacing depreciated capital. (p. 441)

Growth accounting A method of calculating how much real GDP growth has resulted from growth of labour and capital and how much is attributable to technological change. (p. 685)

Growth rate cycle downturn A pronounced, pervasive and persistent decline in the *growth rate* of aggregate economic activity. (p. 459)

Hotelling Principle The proposition that the price of a resource is expected to rise at a rate equal to the interest rate. (p. 383)

Human capital The knowledge and skill that people obtain from education, on-the-job training and work experience. (p. 5)

Hysteresis The idea that the natural rate of unemployment depends on the path of the actual unemployment rate; so where the unemployment rate ends up depends on where it has been. (p. 513)

Implicit rental rate The firm's opportunity cost of using its own capital. (p. 180)

Imports The goods and services that we buy from people in other countries. (pp. 440, 750)

Incentive A reward that encourages or a penalty that discourages an action. (p. 4)

Incentive system A method of organizing production that uses a market-like system inside the firm. (p. 185)

Income effect The effect of a change in income on consumption, other things remaining the same. (p. 168)

Income elasticity of demand The responsiveness of demand to a change in income, other things remaining the same. It is calculated as the percentage change in the quantity demanded divided by the percentage change in income. (p. 86)

Increasing marginal returns The tendency for the marginal product of an additional unit of a factor of production to exceed the marginal product of the previous unit. (p. 204)

Indifference curve A line that shows combinations of goods among which a consumer is indifferent. (p. 163)

Individual transferable quota (ITQ) A production limit that is assigned to an individual who is free to transfer the quota to someone else. (p. 358)

Induced expenditure The sum of the components of aggregate planned expenditure that vary with real GDP. Induced expenditure equals consumption expenditure minus imports. (p. 533)

Induced taxes Taxes that vary as real GDP varies. (p. 565)

Inelastic demand Where a small percentage change in price results in a proportionately smaller change in the quantity demanded. (p. 81)

Infant-industry argument The proposition that protection is necessary to enable a new industry to grow into a mature industry that can compete in world markets. (p. 761)

Inferior good A good for which demand decreases as income increases. (p. 58)

Inflation A process in which the price level is rising and money is losing value. (pp. 427, 654)

Inflationary gap The amount by which real GDP exceeds potential GDP. (p. 491)

Inflation rate The percentage change in the price level from one year to the next. (p. 472)

Inflation tax A tax on the money that people hold. (p. 672)

Insider–outsider theory A theory of job rationing that says that to be productive, new workers – outsiders – must receive on-the-job training from existing workers – insiders. (p. 514)

Intellectual property rights Property rights for discoveries owned by the creators of knowledge. (p. 341)

Interest The income that capital earns. (p. 6)

Interest rate parity A situation in which the rates of return on assets in different currencies are equal. (p. 784)

Interest-sensitive expenditure curve The relationship between aggregate expenditure plans and the real interest rate when all other influences on expenditure plans remain the same. (p. 615)

Intermediate good An item that is produced by one firm, bought by another firm and used as a component of a final good or service. (p. 438)

International crowding out The tendency for an expansionary fiscal policy to decrease net exports. (p. 631)

Inverse relationship A relationship between variables that move in opposite directions. (p. 23)

Investment The purchase of new plant, equipment and buildings and additions to stocks. (p. 439)

IS **curve** A curve that shows the combinations of real GDP and the interest rate at which aggregate planned expenditure equals real GDP. (p. 648)

Isocost line A line that shows the combinations of labour and capital that can be bought for a given total cost. (p. 223)

Isocost map A series of isocost lines, each one of which represents a different total cost but for given prices of labour and capital. (p. 223)

Isoquant A curve that shows the different combinations of labour and capital required to produce a given quantity of output. (p. 221)

Isoquant map A set of isoquants, one for each different output level. (p. 221)

Job rationing The practice of paying a real wage rate above the market equilibrium level and then rationing jobs by some method. (p. 514)

Job search The activity of people looking for acceptable vacant jobs. (p. 512)

Keynesian A macroeconomist who regards the economy as being inherently unstable and requiring active government intervention to achieve stability. (pp. 496, 636)

Keynesian activist An economist who believes that fluctuations in aggregate demand combined with sticky money wage rates (and/or sticky prices) are the main source of economic fluctuations. (p. 732)

Keynesian model A model of an economy that determines real GDP in the very short run when the price level is fixed. An alternative name is the aggregate expenditure model. (p. 526)

Keynesian theory of the business cycle A theory that regards volatile expectations as the main source of economic fluctuations. (p. 703)

Labour The work time and work effort that people devote to producing goods and services. (p. 5)

Labour productivity Real GDP per hour of labour. (pp. 515, 685)

Land The gifts of nature that we use to produce goods and services. (p. 5)

Law of demand Other things remaining the same, the higher the price of a good, the smaller is the quantity demanded of it. (p. 55)

Law of diminishing marginal rate of substitution The marginal rate of substitution of labour for capital diminishes as the amount of labour increases and the amount of capital decreases. (p. 222)

Law of diminishing returns As a firm uses more of a variable input, with a given quantity of other inputs (fixed inputs), the marginal product of the variable input eventually diminishes. (pp. 205, 506, 686)

Law of supply Other things remaining the same, the higher the price of a good, the greater is the quantity supplied of it. (p. 60)

Learning-by-doing People become more productive in an activity (learn) just by repeatedly producing a particular good or service (doing). (pp. 43, 515)

Least-cost technique The combination of labour and capital that minimizes the total cost of producing a given output. (p. 224)

Legal monopoly A market in which competition and entry are restricted by the granting of a public franchise, a government licence, a patent or a copyright. (p. 252)

Lender of last resort The central bank, which is the source of funds to the banking system when all other sources have been exhausted. (p. 605)

Linear relationship A relationship between two variables that is illustrated by a straight line. (p. 22)

***LM* curve** A curve that shows the combinations of real GDP and the interest rate at which the quantity of real money demanded equals the quantity of real money supplied. (p. 649)

Long run A time frame in which the quantities of all resources can be varied. (p. 202)

Long-run aggregate supply curve The relationship between the quantity of real GDP supplied and the price level when real GDP equals potential GDP. (p. 480)

Long-run average cost curve The relationship between the lowest attainable average total cost and output when both the plant size and labour are varied. (p. 213)

Long-run industry supply curve A curve that shows how the quantity supplied by an industry varies as the market price varies after all the possible adjustments have been made, including changes in plant size and the number of firms in the industry. (p. 241)

Long-run macroeconomic equilibrium A situation that occurs when real GDP equals potential GDP – the economy is on its long-run aggregate supply curve. (p. 489)

Long-run neutrality The proposition that in the long run, a change in the quantity of money changes the price level and leaves all real variables unchanged. (p. 639)

Long-run Phillips curve A curve that shows the relationship between inflation and unemployment when the actual inflation rate equals the expected inflation rate. (p. 668)

Long-term unemployment Unemployment lasting for over one year. (p. 466)

Lorenz curve A curve that plots the cumulative percentage of income against the cumulative percentage of households. (p. 397)

Lucas wedge The accumulated loss of output that results from a slowdown in the growth rate of real GDP per person. (p. 423)

M4 Currency held by the public plus bank deposits and building society deposits. (p. 583)

Macroeconomic long run A time frame that is sufficiently long for real GDP to return to potential GDP so that full employment prevails. (p. 480)

Macroeconomics The study of the performance of the national economy and the global economy. (p. 4)

Macroeconomic short run A period during which during which real GDP has fallen below or risen above potential GDP. (p. 481)

Managed exchange rate An exchange rate that is influenced by the central bank's transactions to smooth out excessive fluctuations. (p. 782)

Margin When a choice is changed by a small amount or by a little at a time, the choice is made at the margin. (p. 13)

Marginal benefit The benefit that a person receives from consuming one more unit of a good or service. It is measured as the maximum amount that a person is willing to pay for one more unit of the good or service. (pp. 13, 36, 98)

Marginal benefit curve A curve that shows the relationship between the marginal benefit of a good and the quantity of that good consumed. (p. 36)

Marginal cost The opportunity cost of producing one more unit of a good or service. It is the best alternative forgone and it is calculated as the increase in total cost divided by the increase in output. (pp. 13, 35, 98, 208)

Marginal cost pricing rule A rule that sets the price of a good or service equal to the marginal cost of producing it. (pp. 266, 313)

Marginal external benefit The benefit from an additional unit of a good or service that people other than the consumer enjoys. (p. 337)

Marginal external cost The cost of producing an additional unit of a good or service that falls on people other than the producer. (p. 333)

Marginal private benefit The benefit from an additional unit of a good or service that the consumer of that good or service receives. (p. 337)

Marginal private cost The cost of producing an additional unit of a good or service that is borne by the producer of that good or service. (p. 333)

Marginal product The change in total product that results from a one-unit increase in the quantity of a factor of production. It is calculated as the change in total product divided by the change in the quantity of the factor of production, when the quantities of all other factors are constant. (p. 203)

Marginal product of labour The additional real GDP produced by an additional hour of labour when all other influences on production remain the same. (p. 506)

Marginal propensity to consume The fraction of a *change* in disposable income that is consumed. It is calculated as the change in consumption expenditure divided by the change in disposable income. (p. 528)

Marginal propensity to import The fraction of the last pound of real GDP spent on imports. (p. 531)

Marginal propensity to save The fraction of a change in disposable income that is saved. It is calculated as the change in saving divided by the change in disposable income. (p. 528)

Marginal rate of substitution The rate at which a person will give up good y (the good measured on the y-axis) to get an additional unit of good x (the good measured on the x-axis) and at the same time remain indifferent (remain on the same indifference curve). (p. 164)

Marginal rate of substitution of labour for capital The increase in labour needed per unit decrease in capital to allow output to remain constant. (p. 221)

Marginal revenue The change in total revenue that results from a one-unit increase in the quantity sold of the good or service. It is calculated as the change in total revenue divided by the change in quantity sold. (p. 228)

Marginal revenue product The change in total revenue that results from employing one more unit of a factor of production (labour) while the quantity of all other factors remains the same. It is calculated as the increase in total revenue divided by the increase in the quantity of the factor (labour). (p. 368)

Marginal social benefit The marginal benefit enjoyed by society – by the consumer of a good or service (marginal private benefit) plus the marginal benefit enjoyed by others (marginal external benefit). (p. 337)

Marginal social cost The marginal cost incurred by the entire society – by the producer and by everyone else on whom the cost falls – and is the sum of marginal private cost and the marginal external cost. (p. 333)

Marginal utility The change in total utility resulting from a one-unit increase in the quantity of a good consumed. (p. 144)

Marginal utility per pound spent The marginal utility obtained from a good divided by the price of the good. (p. 146)

Market Any arrangement that enables buyers and sellers to get information and to do business with each other. (p. 44)

Market demand The relationship between the total quantity demanded of a good or service and its price. It is illustrated by the market demand curve. (p. 142)

Market failure The failure of an unregulated market to achieve an efficient allocation of resources. (p. 308)

Market power The ability to influence the market, and in particular the market price, by influencing the total quantity offered for sale. (p. 252)

Means of payment A method of settling a debt. (p. 582)

Merger The combining of the assets of two or more firms to form a single, new firm. (p. 319)

Microeconomics The study of the choices that individuals and businesses make, the way those choices interact in markets and the influence governments exert on them. (p. 4)

Minimum efficient scale The smallest quantity of output at which long-run average cost reaches its lowest level. (p. 215)

Minimum wage A price floor regulation that prohibits labour services being paid at less than a specified wage rate. (p. 123)

Monetarist A macroeconomist who believes that fluctuations in the quantity of money are the main source of economic fluctuations. (pp. 497, 636, 732)

Monetarist theory of the business cycle A theory that regards fluctuations in the money stock as the main source of economic fluctuations. (p. 704)

Monetary base The sum of the notes and coins held by the public and banks' deposits at the central bank. (p. 605)

Monetary policy The central bank's attempt to achieve macroeconomic objectives by changing the interest rate and changing the quantity of money in the economy. (pp. 431, 487, 604)

Monetary Policy Committee (MPC) The committee at the Bank of England which sets its monetary policy. The committee is made up of the Governor and two Deputy Governors of the Bank together with six other members that include two academic economists. (p. 604)

Money Any commodity or token that is generally acceptable as a means of payment. (p. 582)

Money multiplier The amount by which a change in the monetary base is multiplied to determine the resulting change in the quantity of money. (p. 609)

Money price The number of pounds or euros that must be given up in exchange for a good or service. (p. 54)

Money wage rate The number of pounds that an hour of labour earns. (p. 506)

Monopolistic competition A market structure in which a large number of firms compete with each other by making similar but slightly different products. (pp. 190, 274)

Monopoly A market structure in which there is one firm which produces a good or service that has no close substitute and in which the firm is protected from competition by a barrier preventing the entry of new firms. (pp. 190, 252)

Monopoly control laws Laws that regulate and prohibit monopoly and monopolistic practices. (p. 311)

Monopsony A market structure in which there is just a single buyer. (p. 392)

Moral hazard A situation in which one of the parties to an agreement has an incentive after the agreement is made to act in a manner that brings additional benefits to himself or herself at the expense of the other party. (p. 185)

Multiplier The amount by which a change in autonomous expenditure is magnified or multiplied to determine the change in equilibrium expenditure and real GDP. (p. 536)

Nash equilibrium The outcome of a game that occurs when player A takes the best possible action given the action of player B, and player B takes the best possible action given the action of player A. (p. 289)

National saving The sum of private saving (saving by households and businesses) plus government saving. (p. 441)

Natural monopoly A monopoly that occurs when one firm can supply the entire market at a lower price than two or more firms can. (p. 252)

Natural rate of unemployment The unemployment rate when the economy is at full employment. (pp. 468, 480)

Negative externality An externality that arises from either production or consumption and that imposes an external cost. (p. 330)

Negative relationship A relationship between variables that move in opposite directions. (p. 23)

Neo-classical growth theory A theory of economic growth that proposes that real GDP per person grows because technological change induces a level of saving and investment that makes capital per hour of labour grow. (p. 691)

Net borrower A country that is borrowing more from the rest of the world than it is lending to it. (p. 774)

Net exports The value of exports minus the value of imports. (pp. 440, 750)

Net investment Net increase in the capital stock – gross investment minus depreciation. (p. 441)

Net lender A country that is lending more to the rest of the world than it is borrowing from it. (p. 774)

Net present value The present value of the future flow of marginal revenue product generated by capital minus the cost of the capital. (p. 378)

Net taxes Taxes paid to governments minus transfer payments received from governments. (p. 440)

New classical theory of the business cycle A rational expectations theory of the business cycle that regards unanticipated fluctuations in aggregate demand as the main source of economic fluctuations. (p. 706)

New growth theory A theory of economic growth based on the idea that real GDP per person grows because of the choices that people make in the pursuit of profit and that growth can persist indefinitely. (p. 693)

New Keynesian A macroeconomist who believes that left alone, the economy would rarely operate at full employment and that to achieve and maintain full employment, active help from fiscal policy and monetary policy is required. (p. 496)

New Keynesian theory of the business cycle A rational expectations theory of the business cycle that regards unanticipated fluctuations in aggregate demand as the main source of economic fluctuations. (p. 706)

Nominal GDP The value of the final goods and services produced in a given year valued at the prices that prevail in that same year. It is a more precise name for GDP. (p. 445)

Nominal GDP targeting An attempt to keep the growth rate of nominal GDP steady. (p. 736)

Nominal interest rate The percentage return on an asset such as a bond expressed in terms of money. (p. 614)

Non-excludable A good, service or resource is non-excludable if it is impossible (or extremely costly) to prevent someone from benefiting from it. (p. 348)

Non-renewable natural resources Natural resources that can be used only once and that cannot be replaced once they have been used. (p. 381)

Non-rival A good, service or resource is non-rival if its use by one person does not decrease the quantity available for someone else. (p. 348)

Non-tariff barrier An action other than a tariff that restricts international trade. (p. 757)

Normal good A good for which demand increases as income increases. (p. 58)

Normal profit The expected return for supplying entrepreneurial ability. (p. 181)

Okun gap The gap between real GDP and potential GDP and so is another name for the output gap. (p. 423)

Oligopoly A market structure in which a small number of firms compete. (p. 190)

One-third rule The rule that, with no change in technology, a 1 per cent increase in capital per hour of labour brings, on average, a one-third of 1 per cent increase in real GDP per hour of labour. (p. 686)

Open market operation The purchase or sale of government bonds by the central bank in the open market. (p. 606)

Opportunity cost The highest-valued alternative that we give up to get something. (p. 12)

Optimal currency area A geographical area that is better served with a single currency than with several currencies. (p. 786)

Original income The income that households receive from market activity before government intervention. (p. 396)

Patent A government-sanctioned exclusive right granted to the inventor of a good, service or productive process to produce, use and sell the invention for a given number of years. (p. 341)

Payoff matrix A table that shows the payoffs for every possible action by each player for every possible action by each other player. (p. 288)

Perfect competition A market structure in which there are many firms; each firm sells an identical product; there are many buyers; there are no restrictions on entry into the industry; firms in the industry have no advantage over potential new entrants; and firms and buyers are completely informed about the price of each firm's product. (pp. 190, 228)

Perfectly elastic demand Demand with an infinite price elasticity; the quantity demanded changes by an infinitely large percentage in response to a tiny price change. (p. 81)

Perfectly inelastic demand Demand with a price elasticity of zero; the quantity demanded remains constant when the price changes. (p. 80)

Perfect price discrimination Price discrimination that extracts the entire consumer surplus. (p. 263)

Phillips curve A curve that shows a relationship between inflation and unemployment. (p. 666)

Pigovian taxes Taxes that are used as an incentive for producers to cut back on an activity that creates an external cost. (p. 336)

Planned economy An economic system in which a command system is used to coordinate the entire economy and allocate almost all the economy's resources. (p. 44)

Policy conflict A situation in which the government and the central bank pursue different goals and the actions of one make it harder for the other to achieve its goals. (p. 640)

Policy coordination A situation in which the government and the central bank work together to achieve a common set of goals. (p. 640)

Political equilibrium The outcome that results from the choices of voters, politicians and bureaucrats. (p. 310)

Positive externality An externality that arise from either production or consumption and that provides an external benefit. (p. 330)

Positive relationship A relationship between two variables that move in the same direction. (p. 22)

Potential GDP The value of production when all the economy's labour, capital, land and entrepreneurial ability are fully employed. (p. 419)

Poverty A state in which a household's income is too low for it to be able to buy the quantities of food, shelter and clothing that are deemed necessary. (p. 400)

Preferences A description of a person's likes and dislikes. (p. 36)

Present value The amount of money that, if invested today, will grow to be as large as a given future amount when the interest that it will earn is taken into account. (p. 376)

Price cap regulation A regulation that specifies the highest price that the firm is permitted to set. (p. 315)

Price ceiling A regulation that makes it illegal to charge a price higher than a specified level. (p. 119)

Price discrimination The practice of selling different units of a good or service for different prices or of charging one customer different prices for different quantities bought. (p. 253)

Price effect The effect of a change in the price on the quantity of a good consumed, other things remaining the same. (p. 167)

Price elasticity of demand A units free measure of the responsiveness of the quantity demanded of a good to a change in its price, when all other influences on buyers' plans remain the same. (p. 78)

Price floor A regulation that makes it illegal to trade at a price below a specified level. (p. 123)

Price level The average level of prices as measured by a price index. (pp. 427, 446)

Price support A government guaranteed minimum price of a good. (p. 132)

Price taker A firm that cannot influence the market price of the good or service it produces and sets its own price at the market price. (p. 228)

Principal–agent problem The problem of devising compensation rules that induce an agent to act in the best interest of a principal. (p. 185)

Principle of minimum differentiation The tendency for competitors to make themselves similar as they try to appeal to the maximum number of clients or voters. (p. 351)

Private good A good or service that is both rival and excludable. (p. 348)

Private sector surplus or deficit Saving minus investment. (p. 775)

Privatization The process of selling a government-owned enterprise to private owners. (p. 311)

Problem of the commons The absence of incentives to prevent the overuse and depletion of a resource. (p. 348)

Producer surplus The price of a good minus the opportunity cost of producing it, summed over the quantity sold. (p. 103)

Product differentiation Making a product slightly different from the product of a competing firm. (pp. 190, 274)

Production efficiency A situation in which the economy cannot produce more of one good without producing less of some other good. (p. 33)

Production function The relationship between real GDP and the quantity of labour employed when all other influences on production remain the same. (p. 505)

Production possibilities frontier The boundary between the combinations of goods and services that can be produced and the combinations that cannot. (p. 32)

Production quota An upper limit to the quantity of a good that may be produced in a specified period. (p. 132)

Productivity curve A relationship that shows how real GDP per hour of labour changes as the amount of capital per hour of labour changes with a given state of technology. (p. 685)

Productivity growth slowdown A slowdown in the growth rate of output per person. (p. 419)

Profit The income that an entrepreneur earns. (p. 6)

Progressive income tax A tax on income at an average rate that increases with income. (p. 407)

Property rights Social arrangements that govern the ownership, use and disposal of resources or factors of production, goods and services that are enforceable in the courts. (pp. 45, 334)

Proportional income tax A tax on income at a constant average rate regardless of the level of income. (p. 407)

Public good A good or service that is both non-rival and non-excludable – it can be consumed simultaneously by everyone and from which no one can be excluded. (p. 348)

Public ownership Ownership of a firm or an industry by a government or a government controlled agency. (p. 311)

Public provision The production of a good or service by a public authority that receives its revenue from the government. (p. 339)

Purchasing power parity The equal value of different monies. (p. 784)

Quantity demanded The amount of a good or service that consumers plan to buy during a given time period at a particular price. (p. 55)

Quantity of labour demanded The labour hours hired by the firms in the economy. (p. 506)

Quantity of labour supplied The number of labour hours that all households in the economy plan to work. (p. 508)

Quantity supplied The amount of a good or service that producers plan to sell during a given time period at a particular price. (p. 60)

Quantity theory of money The proposition that in the long run, an increase in the quantity of money brings an equal percentage increase in the price level. (p. 660)

Quota A restriction on the quantity of a good that a firm is permitted to produce or that a country is permitted to import. (p. 760)

Rate of return regulation A regulation that requires a firm to justify its price by showing that its percentage return on its capital is in line with what is normal in competitive industries. (p. 314)

Rational expectation The most accurate forecast possible, a forecast that uses all the available information, including knowledge of the relevant economic forces that influence the variable being forecasted. (pp. 663, 706)

Rational ignorance The decision *not* to acquire information because the cost of doing so exceeds the expected benefit. (p. 352)

Real business cycle theory A theory that regards random fluctuations in productivity that result from technological change as the main source of economic fluctuations. (p. 709)

Real gross domestic product (real GDP) The value of the production of the country's farms, factories, shops and offices, measured in the prices of a single year. It is calculated as the volume of final goods and services produced in a given year, expressed in pounds that are linked back to the pounds in the base year. (pp. 419, 446)

Real income A household's income expressed as a quantity of goods that the household can afford to buy. (p. 161)

Real interest rate The percentage return on an asset expressed in terms of what money will buy. (p. 614)

Real wage rate The wage rate per hour expressed in constant pounds. (pp. 463, 506)

Recession A business cycle phase in which real GDP decreases in two successive quarters. (p. 420)

Recessionary gap The amount by which potential GDP exceeds real GDP. (p. 490)

Reference base period The period in which the RPI is defined to equal 100. (p. 470)

Regressive income tax A tax on income at an average rate that decreases with income. (p. 407)

Regulation Rules administered by a government agency to influence economic activity by determining prices, product standards and types and the conditions under which new firms may enter an industry. (p. 311)

Relative price The ratio of the price of one good or service to the price of another good or service. A relative price is an opportunity cost. (pp. 54, 161)

Renewable natural resources Natural resources that can be used repeatedly without depleting what is available for future use. (p. 381)

Rent The income that land earns. (p. 6)

Rent ceiling A regulation that makes it illegal to charge a rent higher than a specified level. (p. 119)

Rent seeking Any attempt to capture a consumer surplus, a producer surplus, or an economic profit. (pp. 260, 764)

Repo loans The Bank of England's loans to commercial banks under repurchase agreements. (p. 606)

Repo rate The interest rate at which the Bank of England stands ready to make loans to commercial banks. (p. 606)

Required reserve ratio The ratio of reserves to deposits that banks are required, by regulation, to hold. (p. 587)

Reserve ratio The fraction of a bank's total deposits that are held in reserves. (p. 587)

Reserves Cash in a bank's vault plus its deposits at the central bank. (p. 585)

Restrictive practices Agreements between firms on prices, terms and conditions of sale and market share. (p. 319)

Retail Prices Index (RPI) The average of the prices paid by consumers for a fixed basket of goods and services. (p. 470)

Risk A situation in which more than one outcome can occur and the probability (or likelihood) of the outcomes can be estimated. (p. 187)

Rival A good, service or resource is rival if its use by one person decreases the quantity available for someone else. (p. 348)

Saving The amount of income that households have left after they have paid their taxes and bought their consumption goods and services. (p. 440)

Saving function The relationship between saving and disposable income, other things remaining the same. (p. 527)

Scarcity Our inability to satisfy all our wants. (p. 4)

Scatter diagram A diagram that plots the value of one economic variable against the value of another. (p. 21)

Search activity The time spent in looking for someone with whom to do business. (p. 119)

Self-interest The choices that you think are the best for you. (p. 7)

Short run The short run in microeconomics has two meanings. For the firm, it is the time frame in which the quantity of at least one of its inputs is fixed and the quantities of the other inputs can be varied. For the industry, the short run is the period of time in which each firm has a given plant size and the number of firms in the industry is fixed. (p. 202)

Short-run aggregate supply curve A curve that shows the relationship between the quantity of real GDP supplied and the price level in the short run when the money wage rate, other resource prices and potential GDP remain constant. (p. 481)

Short-run industry supply curve A curve that shows how the quantity supplied by the industry varies as the market price varies when the plant size of each firm and the number of firms in the industry remain the same. (p. 235)

Short-run macroeconomic equilibrium A situation that occurs when the quantity of real GDP demanded equals the quantity of real GDP supplied – at the point of intersection of the *AD* curve and the *SAS* curve. (p. 488)

Short-run Phillips curve A curve showing the relationship between inflation and unemployment, when the expected inflation rate and the natural rate of unemployment remain the same. (p. 666)

Shutdown point The output and price at which the firm just covers its total variable cost. In the short run, the firm is indifferent between producing the profit-maximizing output and shutting down temporarily. (p. 234)

Signal An action taken by an informed person (or firm) to send a message to uninformed people. (p. 282)

Single-price monopoly A monopoly that must sell each unit of output for the same price to all its customers. (p. 253)

Slope The change in the value of the variable measured on the *y*-axis divided by the change in the value of the variable measured on the *x*-axis. (p. 26)

Social interest Choices that are best for society as a whole. (p. 7)

Social interest theory A theory that politicians supply the regulation that achieves an efficient allocation of resources. (p. 310)

Stock A quantity measured at a point in time. (p. 441)

Strategies All the possible actions of each player in a game. (p. 288)

Structural surplus or deficit A budget balance that would occur if the economy were at full employment and real GDP were equal to potential GDP. (p. 567)

Structural unemployment The unemployment that arises when changes in technology or international competition destroy jobs that use different skills or are located in different regions from the new jobs that are created. (p. 468)

Subsidy A payment made by the government to a producer. (pp. 131, 340)

Subsistence real wage rate The minimum real wage rate needed to maintain life. (p. 690)

Substitute A good that can be used in place of another good. (p. 57)

Substitution effect The effect of a change in price of one good or service on a consumer's consumption of goods and services when the consumer remains indifferent between the original and the new consumption bundles – that is, the consumer remains on the same indifference curve. (p. 169)

Sunk cost The past cost of buying a plant that has no resale value. (p. 202)

Supply The relationship between the quantity of a good that producers plan to sell and the price of the good when all other influences on selling plans remain the same. It is described by a supply schedule and illustrated by a supply curve. (p. 60)

Supply curve A curve that shows the relationship between the quantity supplied and the price of a good when all other influences on producers' planned sales remain the same. (p. 60)

Supply of labour The relationship between the quantity of labour supplied and the real wage rate when all other influences on work plans remain the same. (p. 508)

Supply of money The relationship between the quantity of real money supplied and the interest rate with all other influences on the amount of money that the banking system creates remaining the same. (p. 594)

Symmetry principle The requirement that people in similar situations should be treated similarly. (p. 110)

Tariff A tax that is imposed by the importing country when an imported good crosses its international boundary. (p. 757)

Tax incidence The division of the burden of the tax between buyers and sellers. (p. 125)

Taylor rule A rule that adjusts the overnight interest rate to equal the neutral real overnight interest rate plus the inflation rate plus one-half the deviation of the inflation rate from its target and one-half of the output gap. (p. 741)

Technological efficiency A situation that occurs when a firm produces a given output by using the least amount of inputs. (p. 183)

Technological change The development of new and better ways of producing goods and services. (p. 38)

Technology Any method of producing goods or services. (p. 182)

Terms of trade The quantity of goods and services that a country exports to pay for its imports of goods and services. (p. 752)

Time-series graph A graph that measures time (for example, months or years) on the *x*-axis and the variable we are interested in on the *y*-axis. (p. 20)

Total cost The cost of all the factors of production a firm uses. (p. 207)

Total fixed cost The cost of the firm's fixed inputs. (p. 207)

Total product The maximum output that a given quantity of inputs can produce. (p. 203)

Total revenue The value of a firm's sales. It is calculated as the price of the good multiplied by the quantity sold. (pp. 82, 228)

Total revenue test A method of estimating the price elasticity of demand by observing the change in total revenue that results from a change in the price, when all other influences on the quantity sold remain the same. (p. 82)

Total surplus The sum of consumer surplus and producer surplus. (p. 313)

Total utility The total benefit or satisfaction that a person gets from the consumption of goods and services. (p. 143)

Total variable cost The cost of the firm's variable inputs. (p. 207)

Trade-off An exchange – giving up one thing to get something else. (p. 11)

Trade union A group of workers organized principally for the purpose of increasing wages and improving conditions. (p. 391)

Transactions costs The costs that arise from finding someone with whom to do business, of reaching an agreement about the price and other aspects of the exchange and of ensuring that the terms of the agreement are fulfilled. The opportunity costs of conducting a transaction. (pp. 194, 335)

Trend A general tendency of a variable to move in one direction. (p. 20)

UK interest rate differential The UK interest rate minus the foreign interest rate. (p. 779)

Unemployment A state in which a person does not have a job but is available for work, willing to work and has made some effort to find work within the previous four weeks. (p. 424)

Unemployment rate The percentage of the people in the workforce who are unemployed. (pp. 425, 461)

Unit elastic demand Demand with a price elasticity of 1; the percentage change in the quantity demanded equals the percentage change in price. (p. 80)

Utilitarianism The principle that states that we should try to achieve the greatest happiness for the greatest number. (p. 108)

Utility The benefit or satisfaction that a person gets from the consumption of a good or service. (p. 143)

Value The maximum amount that a person is willing to pay for a good or service. (p. 100)

Velocity of circulation The average number of times a pound is used annually to buy the goods and services that make up GDP. (p. 660)

Voluntary export restraint An agreement between two governments in which the government of the exporting country agrees to restrain the volume of its own exports. (p. 760)

Voucher A token that the government provides to households, which they can use to buy specified goods and services. (p. 340)

Wages The income that labour earns. (p. 6)

Wealth The value of all the things that people own. (p. 441)

Workforce The sum of the people who are employed and who are unemployed. (pp. 425, 460)

Working-age population The total number of people aged between 16 years and retirement who are not in jail, hospital, or some other form of institutional care. (p. 460)

World Trade Organization An international organization that places greater obligations on its member countries to observe the GATT rules. (p. 757)

Index

Key terms and pages on which they are defined appear in **boldface**.